PHILIP'S

STRE[ET]

Essex

First published in 2003 by

Philip's, a division of
Octopus Publishing Group Ltd
2 Heron Quays, London E14 4JP

First edition 2003
Second impression with revisions 2005

ISBN-10   0-540-08487-5 (pocket)
ISBN-13   978-0-540-08487-6 (pocket)
EAB

© Philip's 2005

Ordnance Survey®

This product includes mapping data licensed from
Ordnance Survey® with the permission of the
Controller of Her Majesty's Stationery Office.
© Crown copyright 2005. All rights reserved.
Licence number 100011710.

Printed and bound in Spain
by Cayfosa-Quebecor

Contents

III   **Key to map symbols**

IV   **Key to map pages**

VI   **Route planning**

X   **Administrative and Postcode boundaries**

1   **Street maps** at 2⅔ inches to 1 mile

384   **Index** of towns and villages

386   **Index** of streets, hospitals, industrial estates, railway
stations, schools, shopping centres and universities
and places of interest

Digital Data

The exceptionally high-quality mapping found in this atlas is available as digital data in TIFF
format, which is easily convertible to other bitmapped (raster) image formats.

The index is also available in digital form as a standard database table. It contains all the details
found in the printed index together with the National Grid reference for the map square in which
each entry is named.

For further information and to discuss your requirements, please contact Philip's on
020 7644 6932 or james.mann@philips-maps.co.uk

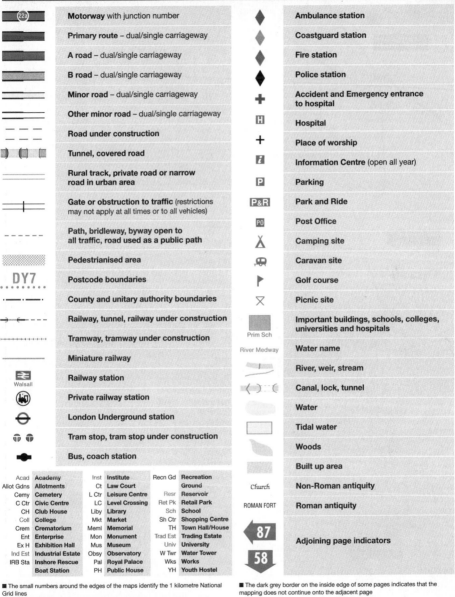

Symbol	Description
Motorway with junction number	(22a)
Primary route – dual/single carriageway	
A road – dual/single carriageway	
B road – dual/single carriageway	
Minor road – dual/single carriageway	
Other minor road – dual/single carriageway	
Road under construction	
Tunnel, covered road	
Rural track, private road or narrow road in urban area	
Gate or obstruction to traffic (restrictions may not apply at all times or to all vehicles)	
Path, bridleway, byway open to all traffic, road used as a public path	
Pedestrianised area	
Postcode boundaries	DY7
County and unitary authority boundaries	
Railway, tunnel, railway under construction	
Tramway, tramway under construction	
Miniature railway	
Railway station	Walsall
Private railway station	
London Underground station	
Tram stop, tram stop under construction	
Bus, coach station	

Symbol	Description
◆	Ambulance station
◇	Coastguard station
◇	Fire station
◆	Police station
✚	Accident and Emergency entrance to hospital
H	Hospital
✚	Place of worship
i	Information Centre (open all year)
P	Parking
P&R	Park and Ride
PO	Post Office
⋏	Camping site
⊕	Caravan site
►	Golf course
✕	Picnic site
Prim Sch	Important buildings, schools, colleges, universities and hospitals
River Medway	Water name
	River, weir, stream
	Canal, lock, tunnel
	Water
	Tidal water
	Woods
	Built up area
Church	Non-Roman antiquity
ROMAN FORT	Roman antiquity
87	Adjoining page indicators
58	

Abbr	Full	Abbr	Full	Abbr	Full
Acad	Academy	Inst	Institute	Recn Gd	Recreation Ground
Allot Gdns	Allotments	Ct	Law Court		
Cemy	Cemetery	L Ctr	Leisure Centre	Resr	Reservoir
C Ctr	Civic Centre	LC	Level Crossing	Ret Pk	Retail Park
CH	Club House	Liby	Library	Sch	School
Coll	College	Mkt	Market	Sh Ctr	Shopping Centre
Crem	Crematorium	Meml	Memorial	TH	Town Hall/House
Ent	Enterprise	Mon	Monument	Trad Est	Trading Estate
Ex H	Exhibition Hall	Mus	Museum	Univ	University
Ind Est	Industrial Estate	Obsy	Observatory	W Twr	Water Tower
IRB Sta	Inshore Rescue Boat Station	Pal	Royal Palace	Wks	Works
		PH	Public House	YH	Youth Hostel

■ The small numbers around the edges of the maps identify the 1 kilometre National Grid lines

■ The dark grey border on the inside edge of some pages indicates that the mapping does not continue onto the adjacent page

The scale of the maps on the pages numbered in blue is 4.2 cm to 1 km • 2⅔ inches to 1 mile • 1: 23810

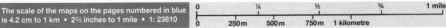

0	¼	½	¾	1 mile
0	250m 500m 750m	1 kilometre		

Cambridgeshire STREET ATLAS

Hertfordshire STREET ATLAS

London STREET ATLAS

West Kent STREET ATLAS

Kent STREET ATLAS

Great Shelford
Sawston
A11
A603
A10
M11
A505
A1307
A143

Cavendish **1**

Hinxton **3** Hadstock **4 5** Shudy Camps **6 7** Haverhill **8 9** Boyton End **10 11** Clare Pentlow
Ickleton Sturmer Stoke by Clare **12 13**
Great Chesterford Ashdon Drapers Green

20 21 Little Walden **22 23** Helions Bumpstead **24 25** Steeple Bumpstead **26 27** Birdbrook Ridgewell **28 29** Belcham Walter **30 31**
Heydon **19** Littlebury Gestingthorpe
Royston Chrishall Elmdon Saffron Walden Hempstead

Nuthampstead Duddenhoe End **40 41** Wendens Ambo **42 43** Radwinter **44 45** **46 47** Cornish Hall End **48 49** Toppesfield **50 51** Audley End **52**
39 Langley Arkesden Newport Elder Street Great Sampford Gainsford End Sible Hedingham
Baldock

Brent Pelham Wicken Bonhunt **64 65** **66 67** Debden **68 69** Little Sampford **70 71** Finchingfield **72 73** Southey Green **74 75** **76**
Buntingford Clavering Widdington Great Bardfield Wethersfield Blackmore End
Quendon Cutlers Green Thaxted Halstead

Stevenage Rickling Green **92 93** Henham **94 95** Richmond's Green **98 99** Shalford Beazley End **102 103** Gosfield
Manuden Broxted **96 97** Bardfield Saling **100 101** High Garrett
Elsenham Duton Hill Lindsell

Stansted Mountfitchet **118 119** Molehill Green **120 121** Great Easton **122 123** Stebbing **124 125** Panfield **126 127** Stisted **128 129**
Birchanger Church End Stebbing Green Rayne Bradwell
Stansted Airport Braintree

Bishop's Stortford **145** Takeley Street **146 147** Takeley **148 149** Great Dunmow **150 151** Felsted **152 153** Great Notley **154 155** Cressing **156**
Great Hallingbury Great Canfield Barnston Willows Green White Notley Silver End

Little Hallingbury **172 173** Taverners Green **174 175** **176 177** Ford End **178 179** Great Leighs **180 181** Church End **182 183**
Ware Sawbridgeworth Hatfield Heath High Easter Pleshey Howe Street Terling Witham
Hertford

Hunsdonbury **197** Gilston **198 199** Sheering **200 201** White Roding **202 203** Leaden Roding **204 205** Great Waltham **206 207** Little Waltham **208 209** **210 211**
Stanstead Abbotts Roydon Matching Green Abbess Roding Mashbury Broomfield Hatfield Peverel
Harlow

Hoddesdon Tye Green **222 223** Tilegate Green **224 225** High Laver **226 227** **228 229** Roxwell **230 231** Boreham **232 233** **234 235**
221 Fyfield Woodham Walter
Lower Nazeing Roydon Hamlet Hastingwood Moreton Willingale Writtle Chelmsford Little Baddow

Cheshunt **243** Bumble's Green **244 245** North Weald Bassett **246 247** Bobbingworth **248 249** **252 253** Great Baddow **254 255** Danbury **256 257**
Cuffley Aimes Green Epping Chipping Ongar Norton Heath **250 251** Loves Green Howe Green Cock Clarks
Potters Bar M25

Waltham Abbey **265** Ivy Chimneys **266 267** Fiddlers Hamlet **268 269** Stanford Rivers **270 271** Blackmore Mill Green **272 273** Margaretting **274 275** **276 277** East Hanningfield **278 279**
Holdbrook Theydon Bois Stapleford Tawney Kelvedon Hatch Doddinghurst Ingatestone West Hanningfield Woodham Ferrers
Enfield

High Beach **287** Abridge **290 291** Navestock Heath **294 295** Mountnessing **296 297** **298 299** South Woodham Ferrers **300 301**
Chingford **288 289** Stapleford Abbotts **292 293** Bentley Pilgrims Hatch Billericay Ramsden Heath Runwell Hullbridge
East Barnet Loughton Shenfield

Southgate Chigwell **310 311** Chigwell Row **312 313** South Weald **314 315** Brentwood **316 317** South Green **318 319** Wickford **320 321** Rawreth
Edmonton Chingford Hatch Woodford Harold Hill Ingrave Dunton Wayletts Nevendon Shotgate **322 323**
Friern Barnet Great Warley Rayleigh
Wood Green

Walthamstow Barkingside **332 333** Romford **334 335** **336 337** West Horndon Laindon **340 341** Basildon **342 343** Thundersley **344 345**
Golders Green Wanstead Goodmayes Upminster **338 339** Langdon Hills Vange Hadleigh
Stoke Newington Ilford

Hackney Becontree **352 353** Elm Park Corbets Tey Bulphan **358 359** **360 361** Winter Gardens **362 363** **364**
Camden Town Islington Barking Dagenham **354 355** North Ockendon Horndon on the Hill Fobbing Canvey Island
Finsbury Shoreditch Bow Rainham **356 357** Stanford-le-Hope
West Ham

City of London Wennington South Ockendon **372 373** Orsett **374 375**
Paddington **369** Aveley Little Thurrock Linford Chadwell St Mary
Westminster Poplar Erith **370 371**
Chelsea Bermondsey Deptford Greenwich

Battersea Woolwich Purfleet Grays **376 377** Tilbury **378 379** East Tilbury **380**
Camberwell Lewisham Swanscombe Northfleet
Clapham Brixton Eltham Crayford Bexley Dartford Gravesend
Streatham Sidcup
Wimbledon Penge Chislehurst Swanley Strood Rochester
Mitcham Bromley

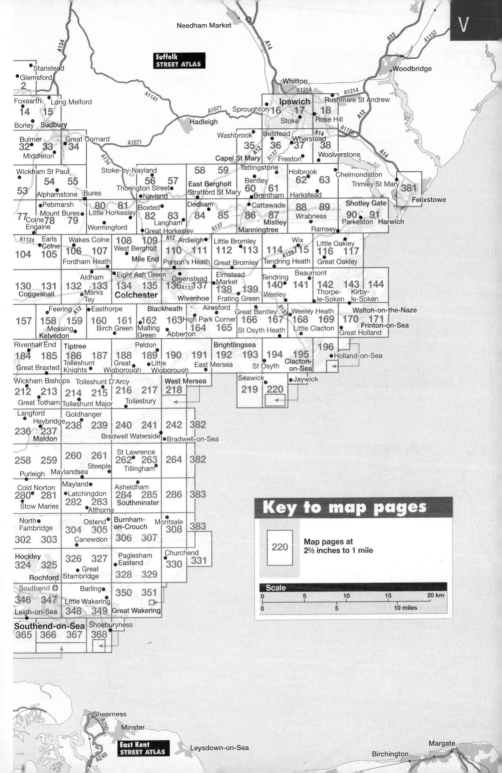

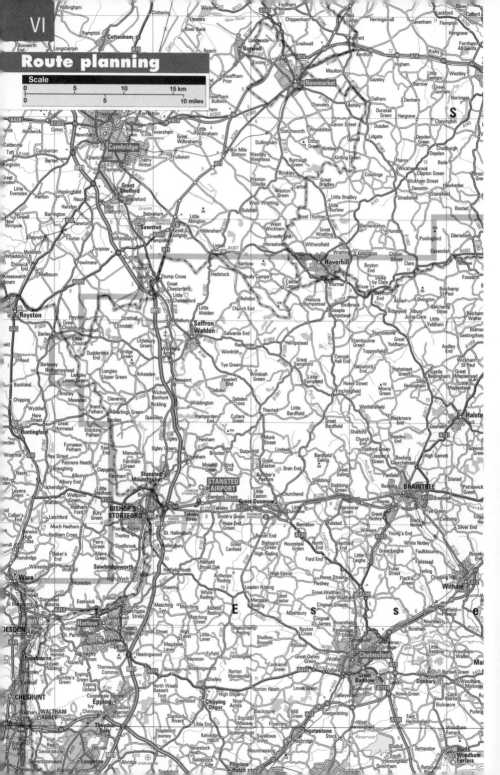

Route planning

Scale

Major administrative and Postcode boundaries

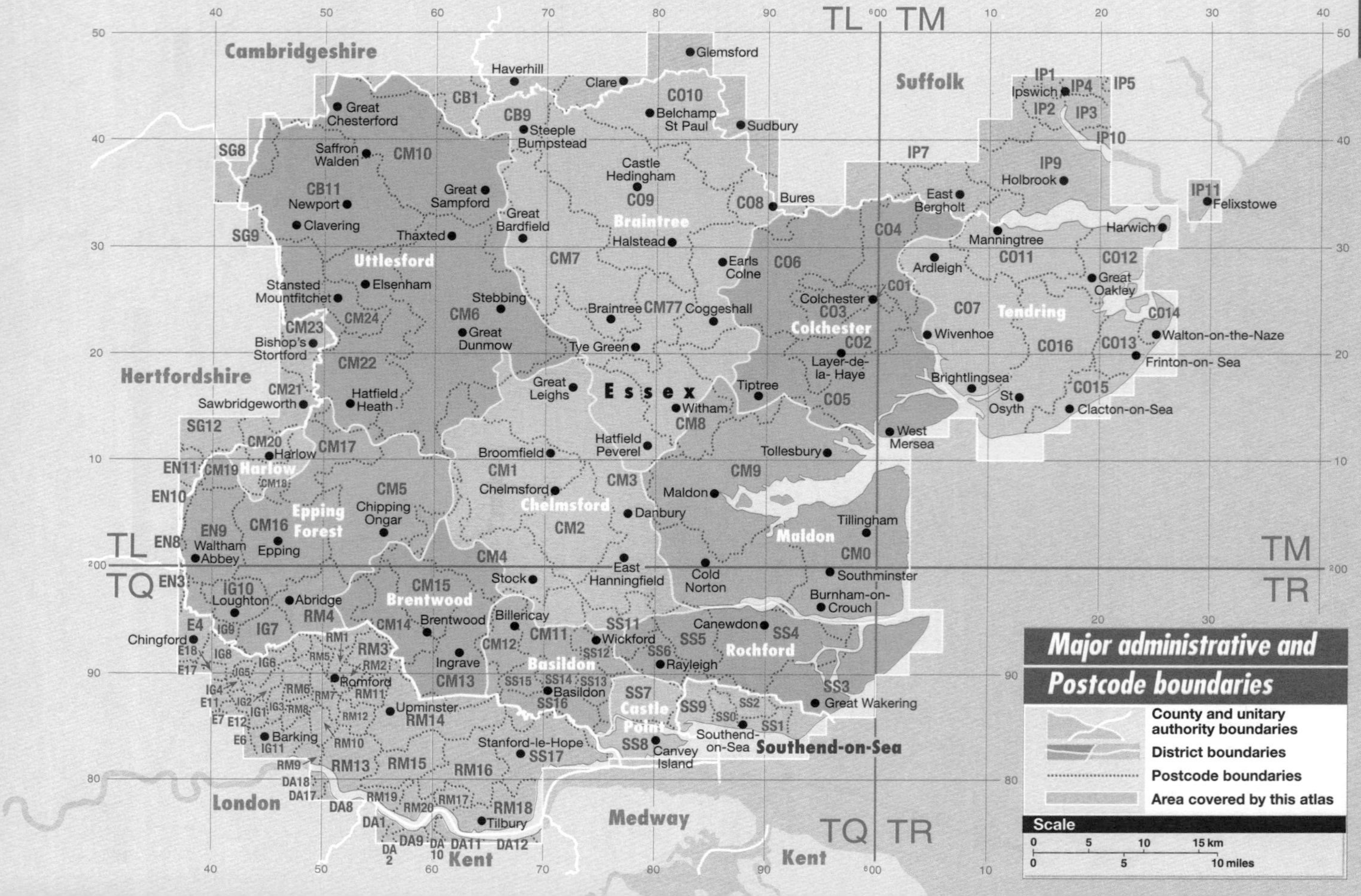

County and unitary authority boundaries
District boundaries
Postcode boundaries
Area covered by this atlas

Scale
0 5 10 15 km
0 5 10 miles

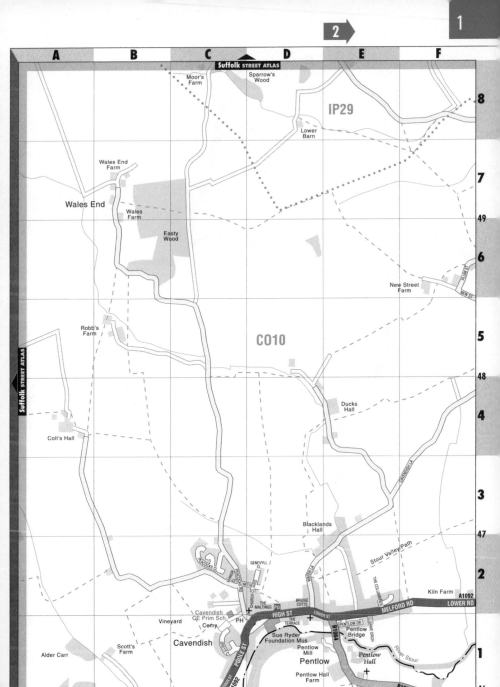

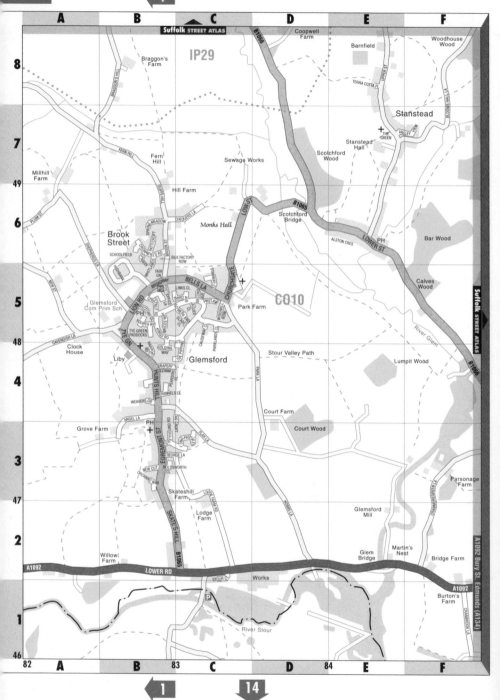

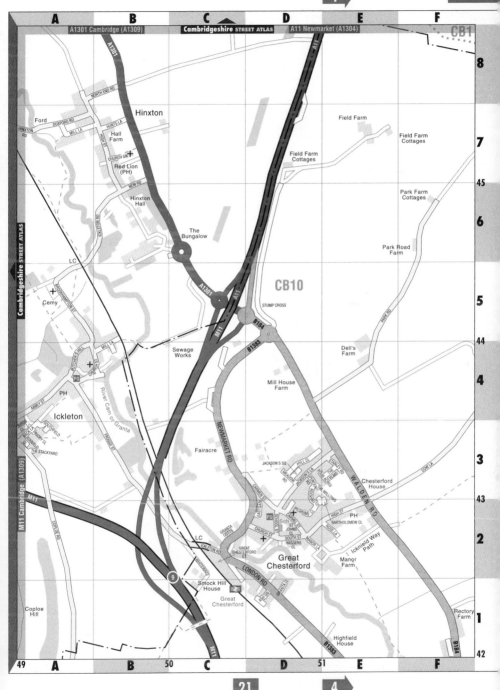

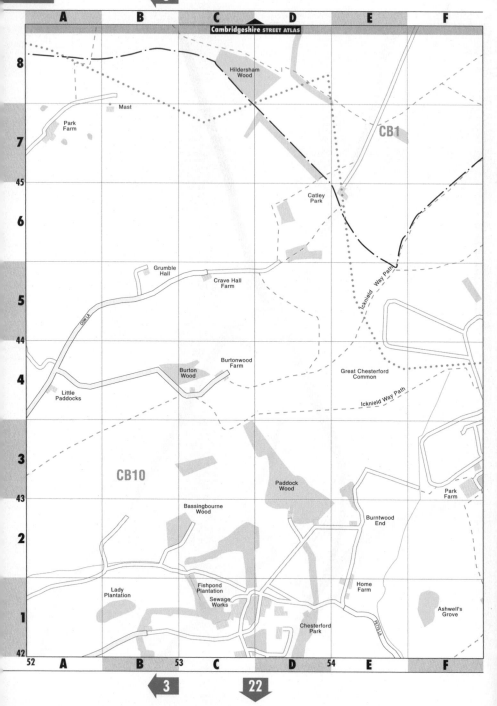

Cambridgeshire STREET ATLAS

A **B** **C** **D** **E** **F**

8

Hildersham Wood

Mast

Park Farm

7

CB1

45

Catley Park

6

Grumble Hall

Crave Hall Farm

5

Icknield Way Path

44

Burtonwood Farm

4

Burton Wood

Great Chesterford Common

Little Paddocks

Icknield Way Path

3

CB10

Paddock Wood

Park Farm

43

Bassingbourne Wood

Burntwood End

2

Lady Plantation

Fishpond Plantation

Home Farm

Ashwell's Grove

1

Sewage Works

Chesterford Park

42

52 **A** **B** 53 **C** **D** 54 **E** **F**

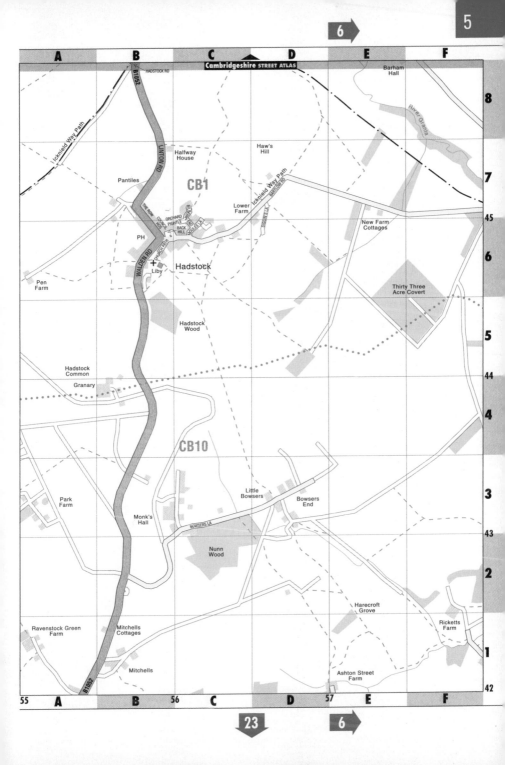

Cambridgeshire STREET ATLAS

A B C D E F

Barham Hall

8

Icknield Way Path

B1052 HADSTOCK RD

LINTON RD

Halfway House

Haw's Hill

CB1

7

Pantiles

THE RINK

ORCHARD PIGHTLE

Lower Farm

Icknield Way Path

BARTLOW RD

New Farm Cottages

45

PH

BACK HILL

Hadstock

Liby

WALDEN RD

CHURCH PATH

Pen Farm

Thirty Three Acre Covert

6

Hadstock Wood

5

Hadstock Common

Granary

44

CB10

4

Park Farm

Monk's Hall

BOWSERS LA

Little Bowsers

Bowsers End

3

43

Nunn Wood

2

Harecroft Grove

Ravenstock Green Farm

Mitchells Cottages

Ricketts Farm

1

Mitchells

Ashton Street Farm

42

55 A B 56 C D 57 E F

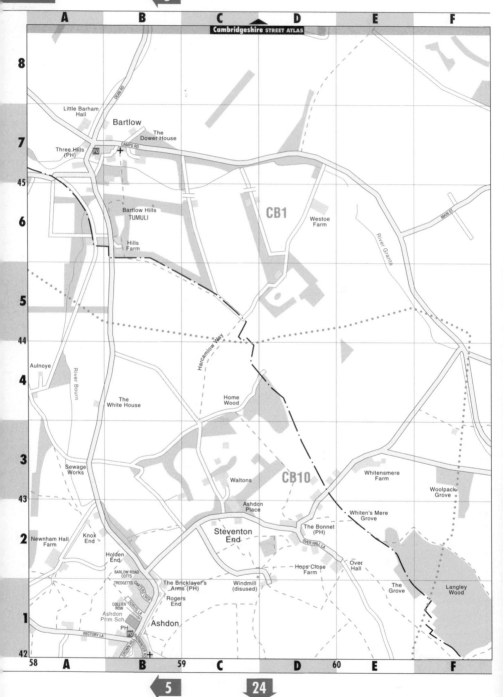

5

Cambridgeshire STREET ATLAS

A   B   C   D   E   F

8

Little Barham
Hall

Bartlow

The
Dower House

Three Hills
(PH)

CAMPS RD

7

45

Bartlow Hills
TUMULI

CB1

Westoe
Farm

Hills
Farm

River Granta

MAIN ST

6

Harcamlow Way

5

44

Aulnoye

River Bourn

The
White House

Home
Wood

4

Sewage
Works

Waltons

CB10

Whitensmere
Farm

Woolpack
Grove

3

43

Ashdon
Place

Whiten's Mere
Grove

Newnham Hall
Farm

Knox
End

Steventon
End

The Bonnet
(PH)

Over
Hall

2

Holden
End

OVER HALL LA

BARLOW ROAD
COTTS

TREDGETTS

CARTER'S CROFT

The Bricklayer's
Arms (PH)

Windmill
(disused)

Hops Close
Farm

The
Grove

Langley
Wood

COLLIER
ROW

Ashdon
Prim Sch

Rogers
End

GOOSE LA

Ashdon

1

RECTORY LA

PH
PO

CROWN HILL

WALDEN RD

42

58   A   B   59   C   D   60   E   F

5

24

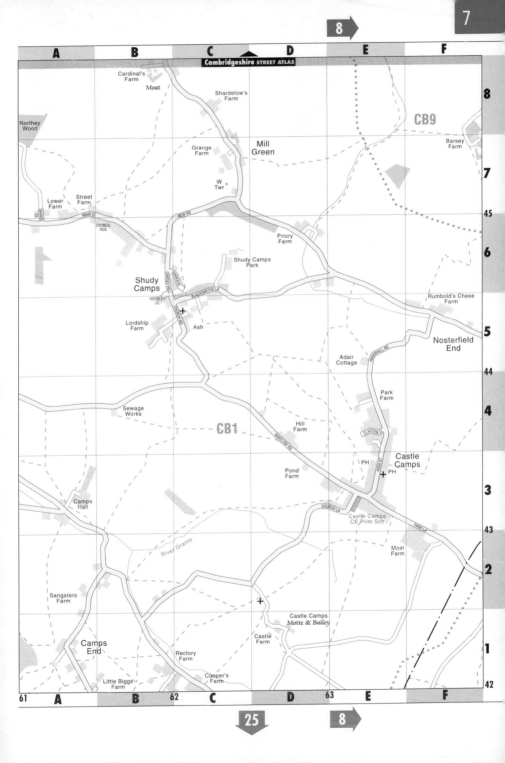

Cambridgeshire STREET ATLAS

CB9

Northey Wood

Cardinal's Farm

Moat

Shardelow's Farm

Mill Green

Grange Farm

Barsey Farm

W Twr

Street Farm

Lower Farm

MAIN ST

NEW RD

COUNCIL HOS

Priory Farm

Shudy Camps Park

Shudy Camps

CARDINAL'S

HOCKLEY CL

BLACKSMITHS LA

Lordship Farm

Ash

Rumbold's Chase Farm

Nosterfield End

Adair Cottage

HIGH HILL RD

Park Farm

Sewage Works

CB1

Hill Farm

CLAYTON CL

HIGH ST

Castle Camps

BARTLOW RD

Pond Farm

PH

PH

Camps Hall

CHURCH LA

Castle Camps CE Prim Sch

PARK LA

River Granta

Moat Farm

Sangsters Farm

Castle Camps Motte & Bailey

Camps End

Castle Farm

Rectory Farm

Cooper's Farm

Little Biggs Farm

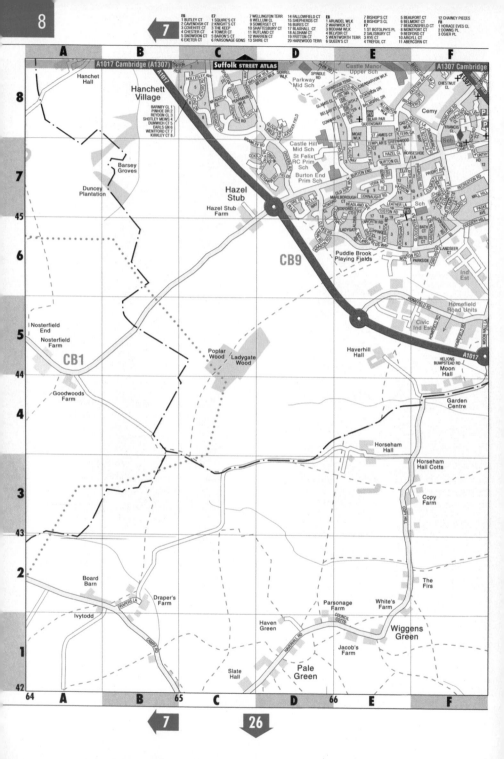

E6
1 BUTLEY CT
2 CAVENDISH CT
3 COVEHITE CT
4 CHESTER CT
5 SNOWDON CT
6 EXETER CT

E7
1 SQUIRE'S CT
2 KNIGHT'S CT
3 THE KEEP
4 TOWER CT
5 BARON'S CT
6 PARSONAGE GDNS

7 WELLINGTON TERR
8 WELLUM CL
9 SOMERSET CT
10 SHAFTESBURY CT
11 RUTLAND CT
12 WARREN CT
13 SHIRE CT

14 FALLOWFIELD CT
15 SHEPHERDS CT
16 BURES CT
17 BLAXHALL CT
18 ALDHAM CT
19 FRITTON CT
20 HAREWOOD TERR

E8
1 ARUNDEL WLK
2 WARWICK CT
3 BODIAM WLK
4 BELVOIR CT
5 WENTWORTH TERR
6 QUEEN'S CT

7 BISHOP'S CT
8 BISHOP'S CL
F7
1 ST ROTOLPH'S PL
2 SALISBURY CT
3 RYE CT
4 TREFOIL CT

5 BEAUFORT CT
6 BELMONT CT
7 BEACONSFIELD CT
8 MONTFORT CT
9 BEDFORD CT
10 ARGYLL CT
11 ABERCORN CT

12 CHAINEY PIECES
F8
1 HORACE EVES CL
2 DOWNS PL
3 OSIER PL

Suffolk STREET ATLAS

A1017 Cambridge (A1307)

A1307 Cambridge

Hanchet Hall

Hanchett Village

BARNBY CL 1
PINHOE DR 2
REYDON CL 3
SHOTLEY MEWS 4
DUNWICH CT 5
EARLS GN 6
WENTFORD CT 7
KIRKLEY CT 8.

Castle Manor Upper Sch

Parkway Mid Sch

Cemy

Barsey Groves

Duncey Plantation

Castle Hill Mid Sch

St Felix RC Prim Sch

Burton End Prim Sch

Hazel Stub

Hazel Stub Farm

CB9

Puddle Brook Playing Fields

Ind Est

Nosterfield End

Nosterfield Farm

CB1

Poplar Wood

Ladygate Wood

Haverhill Hall

Homefield Road Units

Civic Ind Est

Goodwoods Farm

Helions Bumpstead Rd
Moon Hall

Garden Centre

Horseham Hall

Horseham Hall Cotts

Copy Farm

Board Barn

Draper's Farm

Ivytodd

Haven Green

Parsonage Farm

White's Farm

The Firs

Wiggens Green

Jacob's Farm

Slate Hall

Pale Green

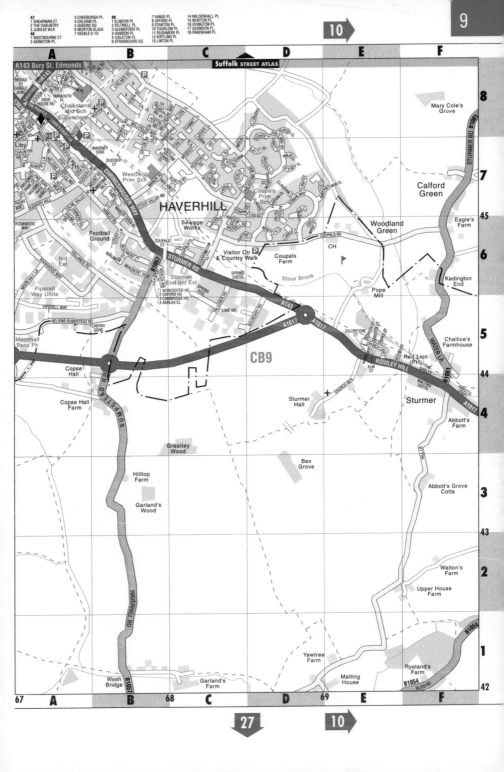

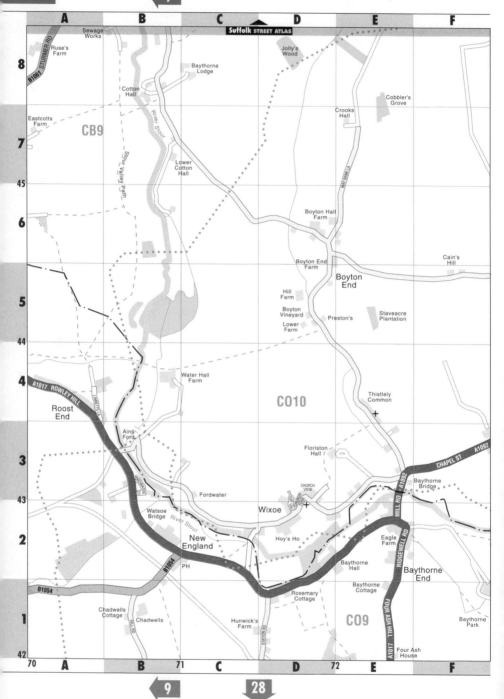

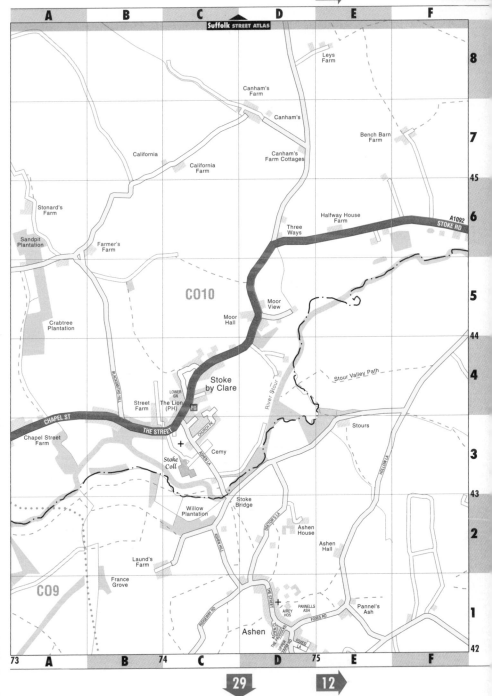

12

Suffolk STREET ATLAS

8

Leys Farm

Canham's Farm

Canham's

7

Bench Barn Farm

California

California Farm

Canham's Farm Cottages

45

Stonard's Farm

Halfway House Farm

A1092
STOKE RD

6

Sandpit Plantation

Farmer's Farm

Three Ways

CO10

Moor View

5

Moor Hall

Crabtree Plantation

44

Stour Valley Path

4

BLACKSMITHS HILL

Stoke by Clare

River Stour

Street Farm

LOWER GN

The Lion (PH)

PO

Chapel Street Farm

CHAPEL ST

THE STREET

CHURCH PK

Stours

Cemy

3

Stoke Coll

ASHEN LA

HALL GRN LA

43

Willow Plantation

Stoke Bridge

Ashen House

2

Ashen Hall

Laund's Farm

DOCTOR'S LA

ASHEN HILL

France Grove

CO9

RIDGEWAY RD

Pannells Ash

Ashen Hall

Pannel's Ash

1

THE STREET

AIREY HOS

FOXES RD

Ashen

THE AIRFIELD

UPPER FERN RD

FOXES LA

42

29   12

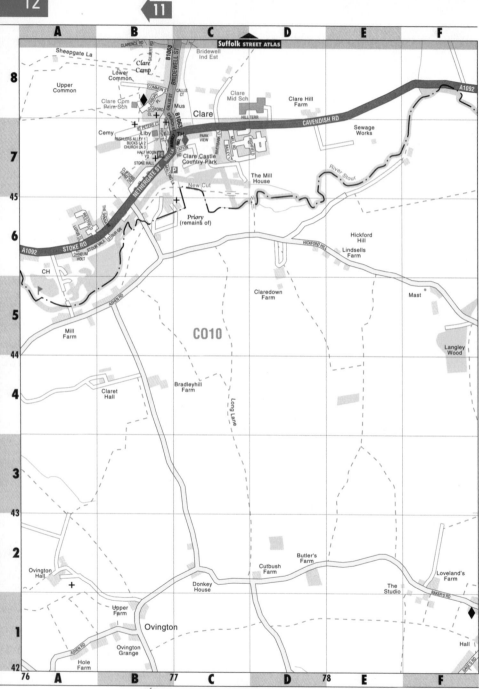

Suffolk STREET ATLAS

8

Sheepgate La

CLARENCE RD

Clare Camp

Upper Common

Lower Common

COMMON ST

Clare Com Prim Sch

Bridewell Ind Est

GILBERT ST

BRIDEWELL ST

B1063

CALLIS CT

Clare Mid Sch

Clare Hill Farm

HILL TERR

PRIORY PL

GOSFORD CL

CALLIS ST

Mus

Clare

CAVENDISH RD

A1092

7

Cemy

ST PETERS CL

Liby

Sewage Works

PASHERS ALLEY 1
BUCKS LA 2
CHURCH LA 3

Park View

MILL RD

RIVERSIDE

BAILEY'S

HALF MOON YD

Clare Castle Country Park

STONE HALL

NETHERGATE ST

STATION

River Stour

45

CLARE HILL

New Cut

The Mill House

Priory (remains of)

6

A1092

STOKE RD

WESTFIELD

THE CHASE

LOWER CT

STOUR VALE

STOUR CM

DANEUM HOLT

HICKFORD HILL

Hickford Hill

Lindsells Farm

CH

ASHEN RD

5

Mill Farm

Claredown Farm

Mast

44

Langley Wood

4

Claret Hall

Bradleyhill Farm

Long Lane

3

43

2

Ovington Hall

Butler's Farm

Cutbush Farm

Loveland's Farm

The Studio

BAKER'S RD

Donkey House

Upper Farm

1

Ovington

Ovington Grange

Hall

42

Hole Farm

ASHEN RD

CADGE S RD

CO10

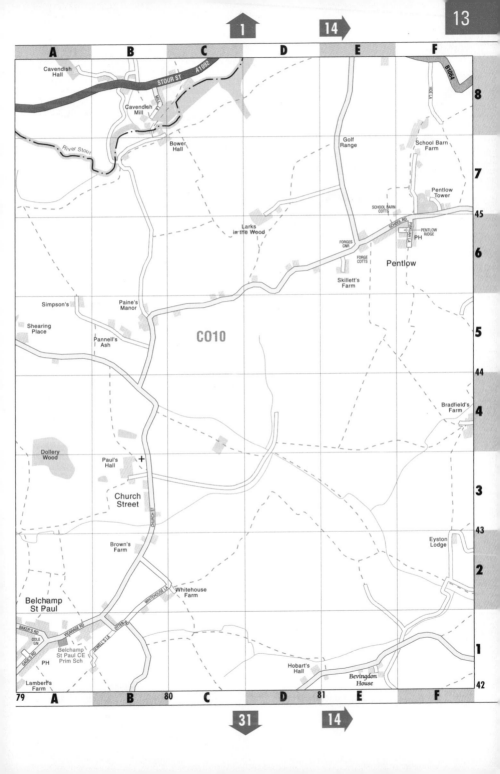

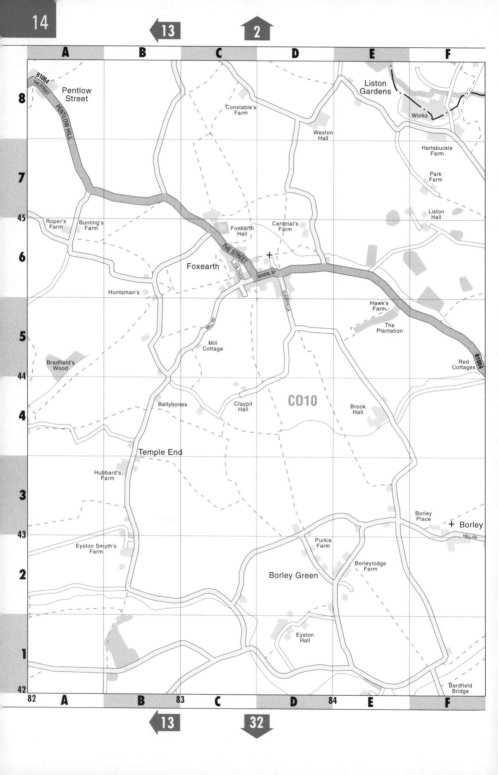

A B C D E F

8

7

45

6

5

44

4

3

43

2

1

42

82 A B 83 C D 84 E F

B1064
THE STREET
PENTLOW HILL

Pentlow
Street

Constable's
Farm

Liston
Gardens

Works

Weston
Hall

Hartsbuckle
Farm

Park
Farm

Roper's
Farm

Bunting's
Farm

Foxearth
Hall

Cardinal's
Farm

Liston
Hall

THE STREET

Foxearth

THE CHASE

SCHOOL ST

Huntsman's

CLAPITT LA

Hawk's
Farm

The
Plantation

MILL RD

Mill
Cottage

B1064

Bradfield's
Wood

Red
Cottages

CO10

Bellybones

Claypit
Hall

Brook
Hall

Temple End

Hubbard's
Farm

Borley
Place

Borley

Eyston Smyth's
Farm

Purkis
Farm

HALL RD

Borleylodge
Farm

Borley Green

Eyston
Hall

Bardfield
Bridge

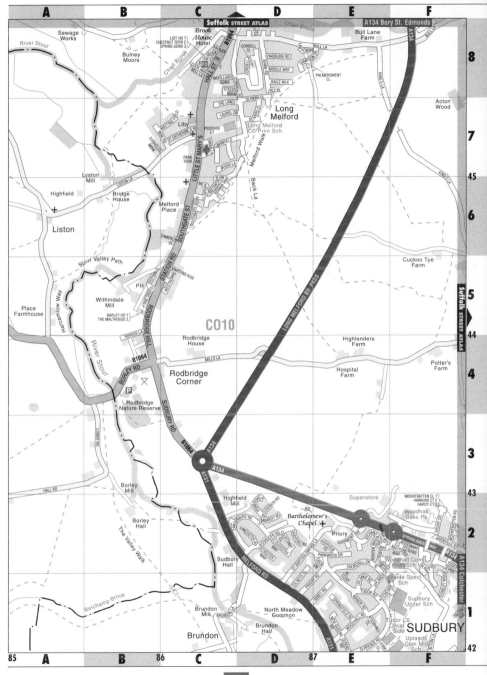

A B C D E F

8
7
45
6
5
44
4
43
3
2
1
42

A134 Bury St. Edmunds

Sewage Works

River Stour

Bulney Moors

Chad Brook

Chad Brook

Brook House Hotel

LIST HO 1
CHESTNUT TERR 2
SPRING GDNS 3

HALL ST

BELLEY

BELL LA

PO

WOOLLARDS GDNS

THE LIMES

MEETING LA

ST CATHERINE'S RD

Liby

PEDDARS CT

PARK TERR

LITTLE ST MARYS

ST MARYS

D'ARCY DR

OLD CT

CORDELL CL

CHADBURN RD

MIDDLE WAY

RAILE WLK

HILL CL

STEEDS MDW

OLIVERS CL

LAUREL DR

CHANFIELD

RENSH LA

Long Melford

Long Melford CE Prim Sch

Melford Way

Back La

Bull Lane Farm

BULL LA

FORTH

SAMPSON

PALMERSWENT CL

BULL LA

KING ST LA

A134

Acton Wood

Lyston Mill

Highfield

Bridge House

LISTON LA

Melford Place

SOUTHGATE GDNS

CAMERON CL

Liston

SOUTHGATE ST

RODBRIDGE RD

Stour Valley Path

Harcamlow Way

Place Farmhouse

River Stour

Withindale Mill

BARLEY HO 1
THE MALTHOUSE 2

STATION RD

ROPERS LA

RODBRIDGE HILL

PH

STEVENS CL

MARTYNS RISE

PH GDNS

WESTGROVE

CO10

Rodbridge House

MILLS LA

Long Melford By-Pass

Cuckoo Tye Farm

Highlanders Farm

Potter's Farm

B1064

BORLEY RD

P

Rodbridge Corner

Rodbridge Nature Reserve

SUDBURY RD

B1064

A134

A134

A131

Hospital Farm

Superstore

Suffolk STREET ATLAS

Borley Mill

Borley Hall

The Valley Walk

HALL RD

LOWER RD

Highfield Mill

CANBURY RD

MIBADUT RD

STEVENSON RD

LANCASTER RD

BRUNDON

St. Bartholomew's Chapel

Priory

CLERMONT RD

CHAUCER RD

GLOUCESTER RD

GREENWAY

ST BARTHOLOMEW'S

BARTHOLOMEW'S RD

COLNES AVE

PARKWOOD DR

HIGH ST LA

DEXTER WAY

CHURCHILL DR

Woodhall Bsns Pk

MOUNTBATTEN CL 1
HAWKINS CT 2
HARDY CT 3

GRENVILLE RD

Woodhall Com Prim Sch

ROSEMARY WAY

SPRINGLANDS WAY

AITE RD

A134

Hillside Specl Sch

Sudbury Upper Sch

Belchamp Brook

Sudbury Hall

MELFORD RD

Brundon Mill

Brundon Hall

Brundon

North Meadow Common

ACRE RD

TUDOR RD

UPLANDS

MELFORD RD

MARTEN RD

NORMAN RD

WOODHALL RD

CLARENCE RD

KING ST LA

Sudbury Upper Sch

Tudor CE Prim Sch

Uplands Com Mid Sch

SUDBURY

A134 Colchester

85 A B 86 C D 87 E F

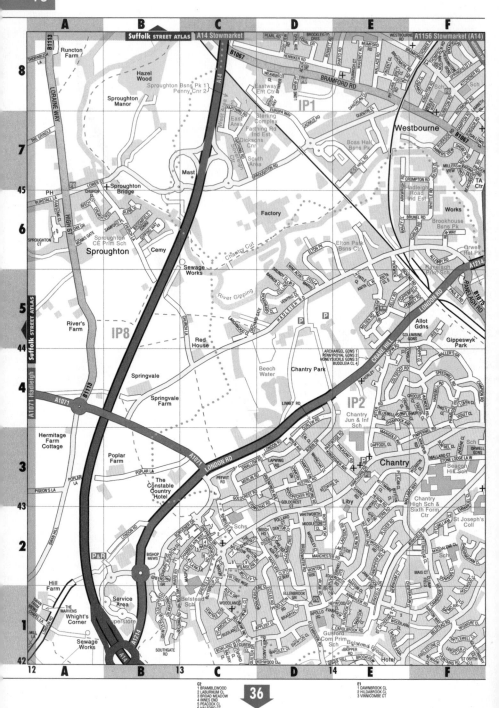

C2
1 BRAMBLEWOOD
2 LABURNUM CL
3 BROAD MEADOW
4 INNES END
5 PEACOCK CL
6 HALFORD CT
7 MERRION CL
8 MATLOCK CL
9 MOTTRAM CL

E1
1 DAWNBROOK CL
2 HILDABROOK CL
3 VINNICOMBE CT

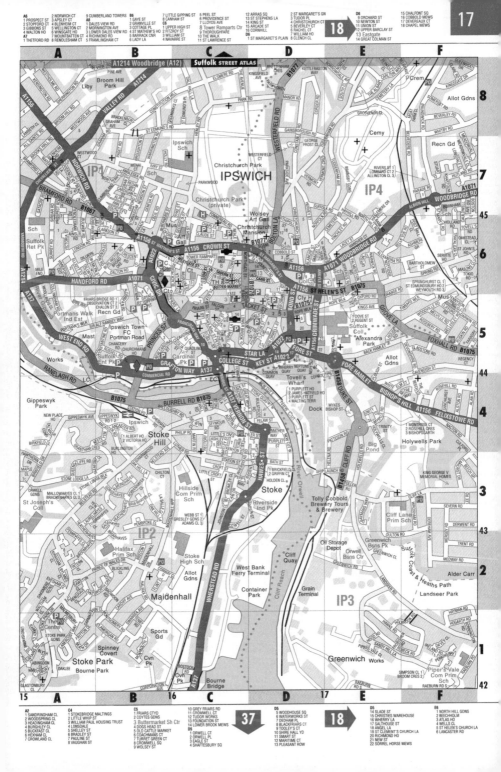

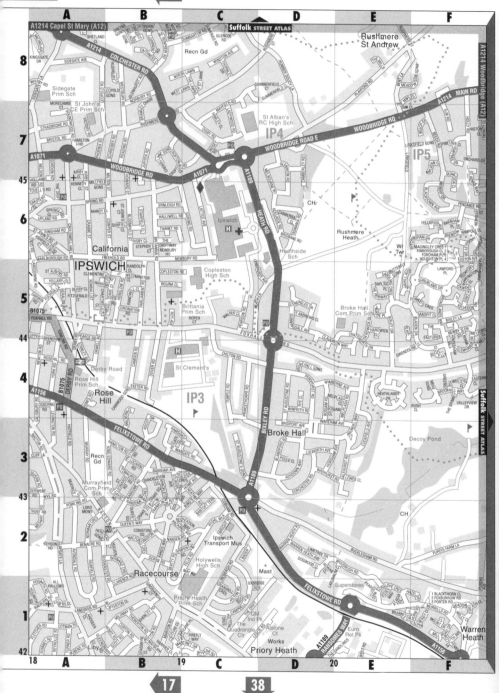

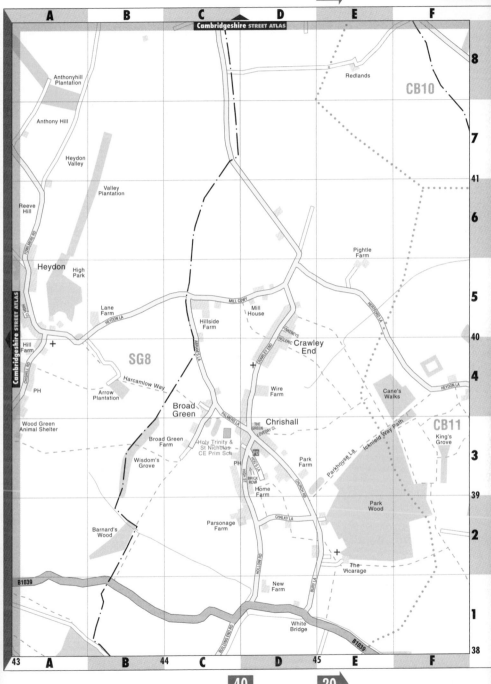

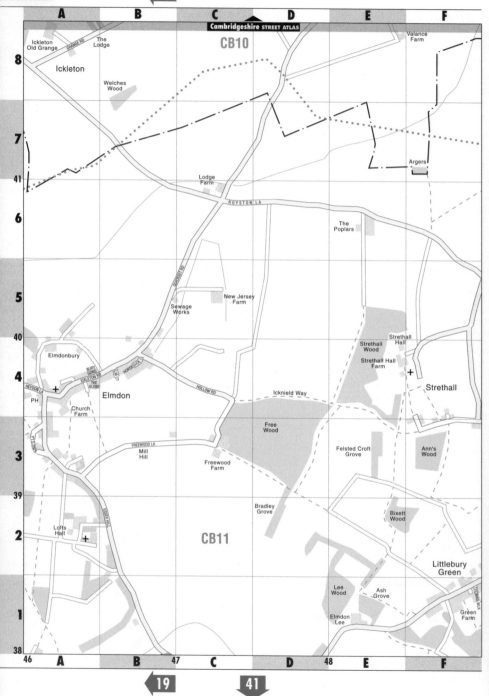

19

Cambridgeshire STREET ATLAS

CB10

A B C D E F

8 Ickleton
Old Grange
GRANGE RD
The Lodge
Ickleton
Welches Wood

Valance Farm

7

41 Lodge Farm

Argers

6 ROYSTON LA

The Poplars

5 QUICKSET RD
New Jersey Farm
Sewage Works

40 Strethall Wood
Strethall Hall
Elmdonbury
BURY GDNS
ICKLETON RD
LEE CT
THE GLEBE
HORNBEAM CL
4 HEYDON LA
PH
Elmdon
HOLLOW RD
Icknield Way
Strethall Hall Farm
Strethall

Church Farm
Free Wood
FREEWOOD LA
Mill Hill
Felsted Croft Grove
Ann's Wood

3 Freewood Farm
Bradley Grove
Bixett Wood

39
Lofts Hall
CB11
Littlebury Green

2

Lee Wood
Ash Grove
Green Farm

1 Elmdon Lee

THOMAS WAY

38
46 A B 47 C D 48 E F

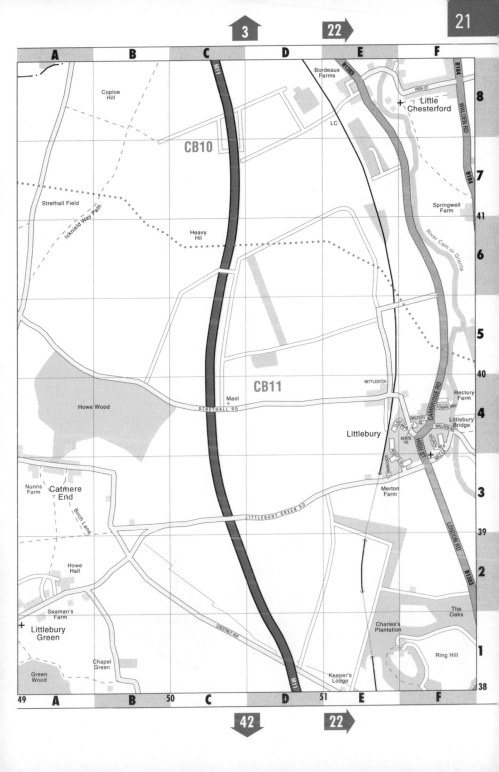

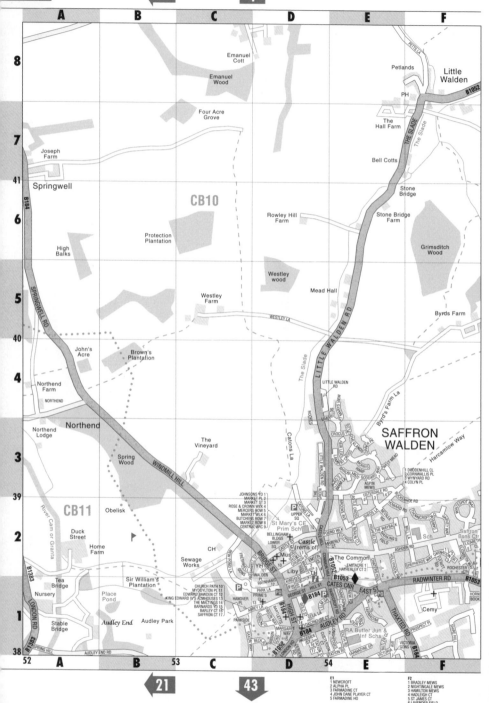

A B C D E F

8

Emanuel Cott

Emanuel Wood

Petlands

Little Walden

PH

B1052

Four Acre Grove

7

The Slade

The Hall Farm

Joseph Farm

Bell Cotts

41

Springwell

CB10

Stone Bridge

B184

Stone Bridge Farm

6

Rowley Hill Farm

Grimsditch Wood

Protection Plantation

High Balks

Westley wood

Mead Hall

5

Westley Farm

Byrds Farm

40

WESTLEY LA

SPRINGWELL RD

John's Acre

Brown's Plantation

The Slade

LITTLE WALDEN RD

Byrd's Farm La

SAFFRON WALDEN

4

Northend Farm

NORTHEND

LITTLE WALDEN RD

Harcamlow Way

Catons La

Northend Lodge

Northend

1 DIDDENHILL CL
2 CORNWALLIS PL
3 WYNYARD RD
4 COLYN PL

3

The Vineyard

Spring Wood

WINDMILL HILL

39

CB11

Obelisk

JOHNSONS YD 1
MARKET PL 2
MARKET ST 3
ROSE & CROWN WLK 4
MERCERS ROW 5
MARKET WLK 6
BUTCHERS ROW 7
MARKET ROW 8
CENTRAL ARC 9

St Mary's CE Prim Sch

Duck Street

Castle (rems of)

River Cam or Granta

Home Farm

BELLINGHAM BLDGS LOWER

CH

The Common

The Waybays

Saffron Bens

Sch

2

B1383

Tea Bridge

Sewage Works

Liby

The Common

B1052

HATHERLEY CT 2

ROCHESTER

RADWINTER RD

B1053

Nursery

Sir William's Plantation

CATES CNR

EAST ST

Cemy

HORN BOOK

1

Stable Bridge

LONDON RD

Place Pond

CHURCH PATH 10
MYDDYLTON PL 11
EDWARD BAWDEN CT 12
KING EDWARD IV'S ALMSHOUSES 13
THE MALTINGS 14
BARNARDS YD 15
BARLEY CT 16
SAFFRON CT 17

HANOVER PL

HIGH ST

B184

AUDLEY RD

RA Butler Jun & Inf Schs

THAXTED RD

B184

Audley End

Audley Park

PARKSIDE

B1052

VICTORIA GDNS

38

52

AUDLEY END RD

SPRING HILL

FARMADINE DR

A B C D E F

53

54

E1
1 NEWCROFT
2 ALPHA PL
3 FARMADINE CT
4 JOHN DANE PLAYER CT
5 FARMADINE HO

F2
1 BRADLEY MEWS
2 NIGHTINGALE MEWS
3 HAMILTON MEWS
4 HADLEIGH CT
5 ST JAMES CT
6 LAVENDER FIELD
7 THE SPIKE
8 CAVENDISH CT

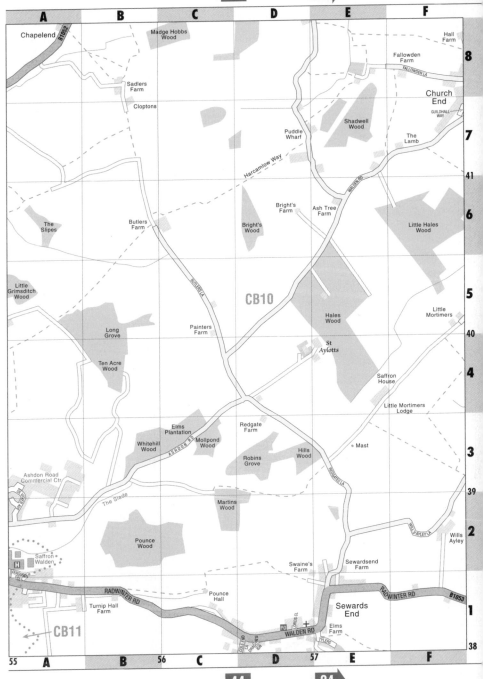

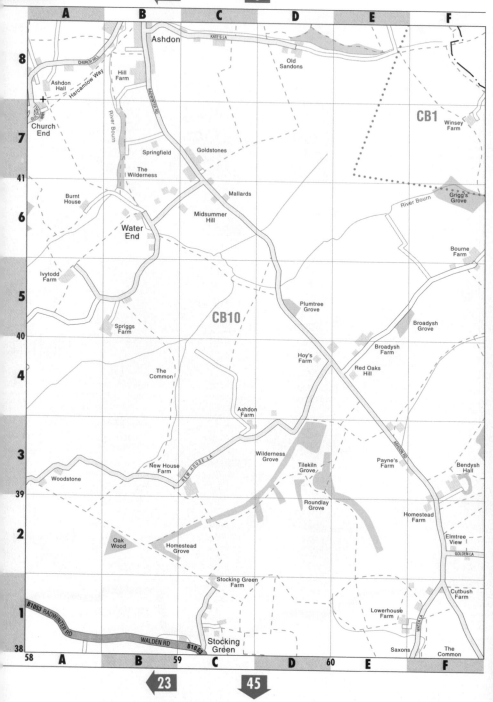

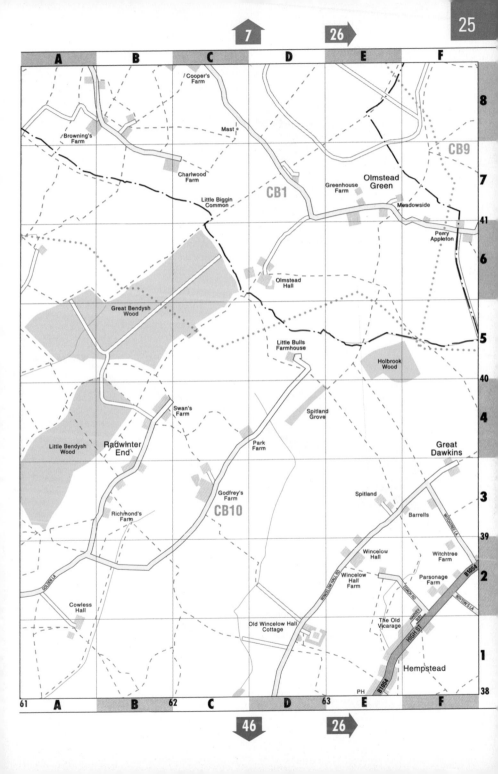

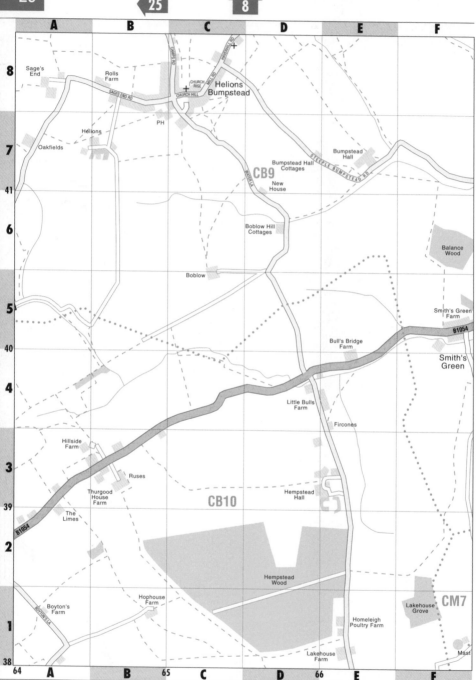

	A	B	C	D	E	F

8

Sage's End

Rolls Farm

CAMPS RD

CHURCH RISE

SAGES END RD

CHURCH HILL

Helions Bumpstead

7

PH

Helions

Oakfields

Bumpstead Hall

Bumpstead Hall Cottages

STEEPLE BUMPSTEAD RD

CB9

41

New House

6

Boblow Hill Cottages

Balance Wood

Boblow

5

Smith's Green Farm

B1054

40

Bull's Bridge Farm

Smith's Green

4

Little Bulls Farm

Fircones

Hillside Farm

3

Ruses

Hempstead Hall

Thurgood House Farm

39

CB10

The Limes

B1054

2

Hempstead Wood

Boyton's Farm

Hophouse Farm

Lakehouse Grove

CM7

BOYTON LA

1

Homeleigh Poultry Farm

Lakehouse Farm

Mast

38

64 | A | B | 65 | C | D | 66 | E | F

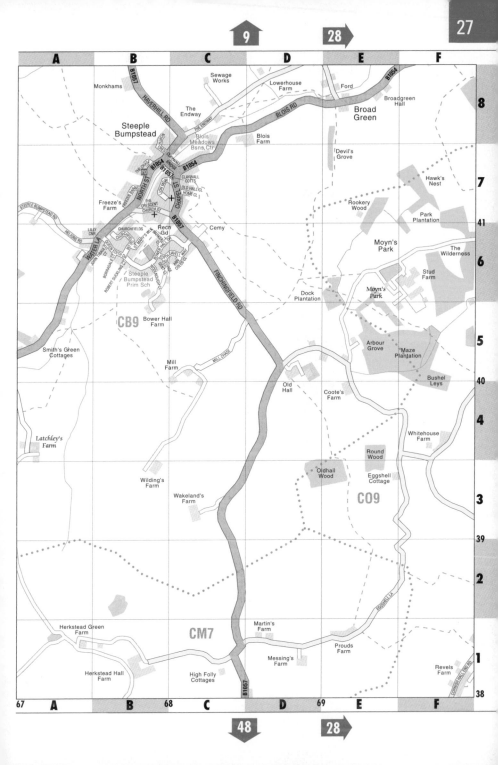

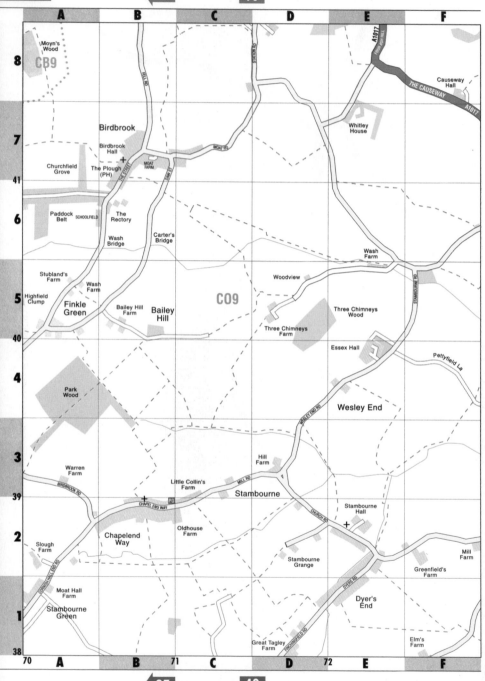

27

10

CB9

Moyn's Wood

Birdbrook

Birdbrook Hall

The Plough (PH)

Churchfield Grove

MOAT FARM

Paddock Belt

SCHOOLFIELD

The Rectory

Wash Bridge

Carter's Bridge

Whitley House

THE CAUSEWAY

Causeway Hall

Wash Farm

Stubland's Farm

Wash Farm

Highfield Clump

Finkle Green

Bailey Hill Farm

Bailey Hill

CO9

Woodview

Three Chimneys Wood

Three Chimneys Farm

Essex Hall

Pettyfield La

Park Wood

Wesley End

Warren Farm

BIRDBROOK RD

Little Collin's Farm

MILL RD

Hill Farm

Stambourne

Stambourne Hall

Chapelend Way

CHAPEL END WAY

Oldhouse Farm

Slough Farm

CORNISH HALL END RD

Stambourne Grange

Greenfield's Farm

Mill Farm

Moat Hall Farm

Stambourne Green

Dyer's End

Great Tagley Farm

Elm's Farm

27

49

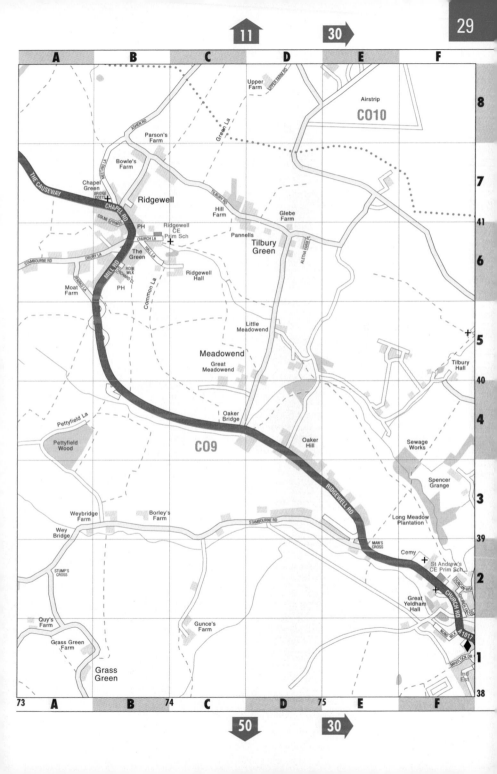

29
12

| | A | B | C | D | E | F |

ASHEN RD

8

Silver
End

Cane's
Cottages

CO10

Knowl
Green

Gage's
House

WAKESHALL LA

Hole
Farm

Cherry Tree
(PH)

Wood Barns
Farm

GAGE'S RD

7

Lodge
Farm

Park
Farm

Wakeshall
Farm

41

Mast

Marshy
Wood

Twelve Acre
Wood

MARSHELL LA

6

Mashay
Farm

Tilbury
Cottage

5

Tilbury
Juxta Clare

BEUCHAMP RD

Red
Barn

Jay's La

MARKET RD

40

Tilbury
Court

Red
House

4

Lodge

Hyde
Wood

CO9

CHURCH
GN

Little
Yeldham

Bendysh
House

The
Hyde

HYDEWOOD RD

SCHOOL RD

3

Brook
Farm

MILL LA

The
Hyde Farm

LITTLE YELDHAM RD

Hall
Green

North
End

NORTH END RD

PH

39

2

ARMSTRONG
WAY

HIGH ST

LITTLE
HYDE
CL

Upper Yeldham
Hall

THE CROFT

LEATHER LA

BUTLERS WAY

Highlands
Farm

1

ROYAL OAK PH

AUNT HIGH ST AUNT

Great
Yeldham

WHITLOCK
DR

POPLAR
CL

Spayne's
Hall

Hunts
Wood

Priestfields
Farm

MARKET
GR

38

| 76 | A | 77 | B | C | 78 | D | E | | F |

29
51

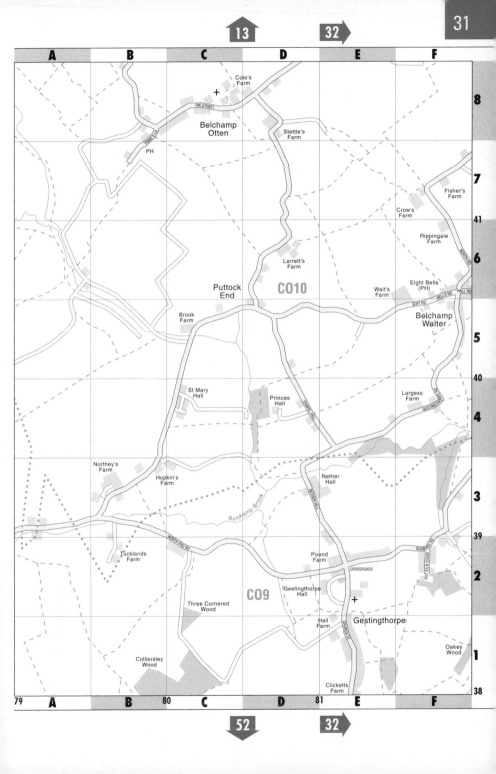

31
14

	A	B	C	D	E	F

8

Newbon

The Rookery

Clark's
Farm

Smeetham
Hall

7

Heaven
Wood

Smeetham
Hall
Cottages

41

6

HALL RD

Belchamp Brook

Belchamp
Hall

SMEETHAM HALL LA

SUDBURY RD

Springgate
Farm

Blackhouse
Farm

5

New
Barns

Goldingham
Hall

CO10

Bulmer

Grigg's
Farm

LEE STREET

ST AGNES'S RISE

SWAINS
CT

CAS ORCH

40

BULMER ST

PO

St Andrew's
CE Prim Sch

SANDY LA

Auberies

4

Lower
Houses

CHURCH RD

SUDBURY RD

Brakey
Hill

3

Upper
Houses

OLD CHURCH LA

Hill
Farm

New
Barn

CO9

Hilltop
Farm

39

Bulmer
Tye

PARK LA

A131

PH

2

Wiggery
Wood

Jenkins
Farm

TYE
CNR

BLACKSMITHS LA

Parsonage
Wood

Wesborough
Hill

Tyecorner
Farm

1

Hole
Farm

A131

38

HEDINGHAM RD

82	A		B	83	C		D	84	E		F

31
53

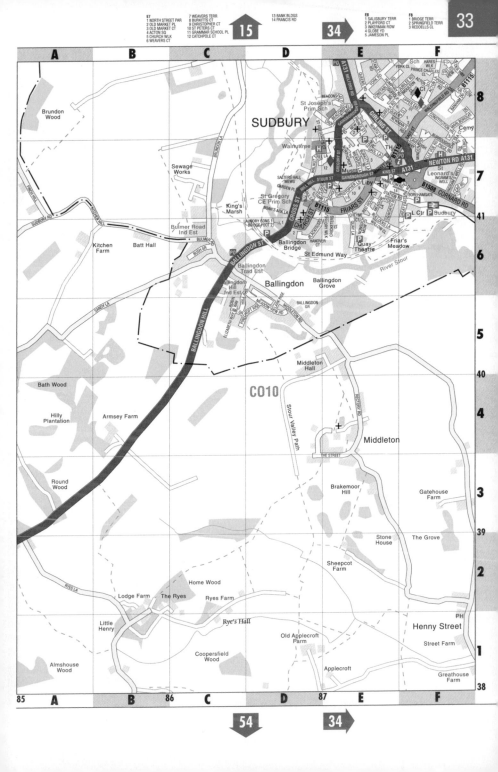

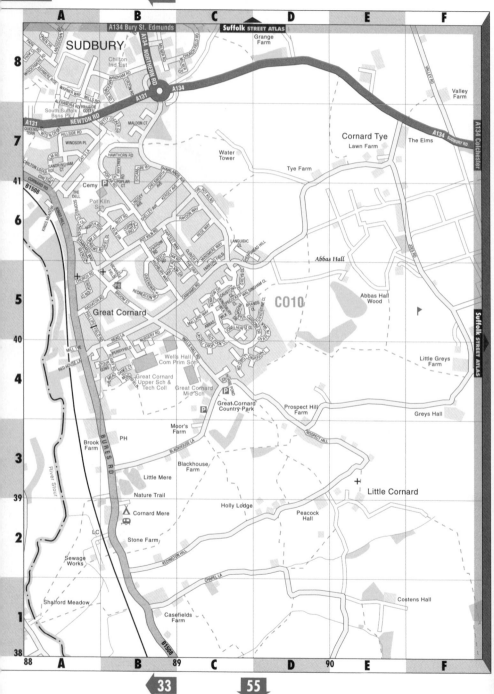

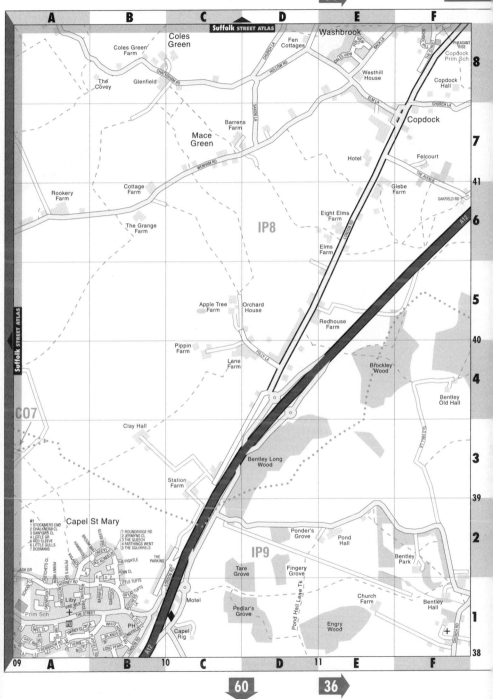

35
16

A B C D E F

8

Copdock
Mill

MILL LA

Belstead Brook

GROVE HILL 1
SPECKLED WOOD CL 2
MONARCH WAY 3
GROVE WLK 4
GREEN OAK GLADE 5

BUTLEY CL

Belstead
Bridge

HOLLY BLUE CL

IP2

Alder
Carr

Ashground
Plantation

Belstead
Rise

CHURCH LA

OAKFIELD RD

A12

7

Belstead
Hall

IP8

CHAPEL LA

HOLLY LA

GROVE HILL

Belstead

Mill Poultry
Farm

Alder
Carr

SWALLOWTAIL CL 6
SKIPPER RD 7
TORTOISESHELL CL 8
FRITILLARY CL 9
GATEKEEPER CL 10
BOATMAN CL 11
MAYFLY CL 12
LACEWING CL 13
SPRINGTAIL RD 14

15 BLACK ARCHES
16 COPPER GR

Spring
Wood

Thorington
Hall

41

6

A12

COCK'S HORNS LA

Blacksmith's
Corner
Street
Farm

THE STREET

A14

Charity
Farm

BENTLEY LA

Spinney
Wood

Wherstead
Wood

Pannington
Hall

Pannington Hall
Cottage

Hill
Covert

5

40

Old Hall
Wood

Clubs
Heath

Bluegate
Farm

4

A137

VALLEY LA

3

Newcome
Wood

Bentley
Manor

Hubbard's Hall
Farm

Tattingstone Trout
Farm

Park
House

39

2

Road
Farm

IP9

Holbrook
Park

1

PH

BRETT'S HORSE HILL

SCHOOL RD

Tattingstone
White Horse

GOSNALL RD

Shrub
Wood

38

A137

LEMONS HILL

12 A 13 B C 13 D 14 E F

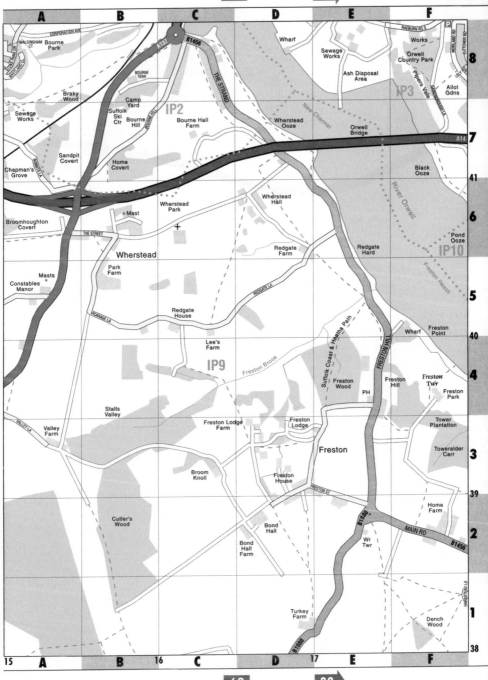

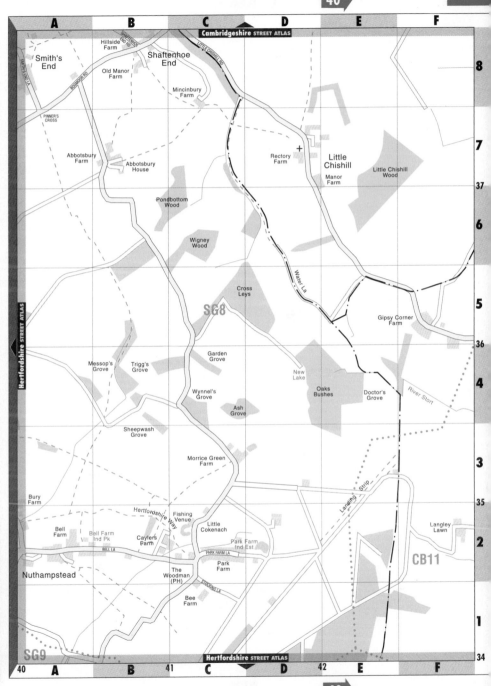

Hertfordshire STREET ATLAS

Smith's End

Hillside Farm

Shaftenhoe End

Old Manor Farm

Mincinbury Farm

PINNER'S CROSS

Abbotsbury Farm

Abbotsbury House

Rectory Farm

Little Chishill

Manor Farm

Little Chishill Wood

Pondbottom Wood

Wigney Wood

Water La

Cross Leys

SG8

Gipsy Corner Farm

Messop's Grove

Trigg's Grove

Garden Grove

New Lake

Oaks Bushes

Doctor's Grove

River Stort

Wynnel's Grove

Ash Grove

Sheepwash Grove

Morrice Green Farm

Landing Strip

Bury Farm

Hertfordshire Way

Fishing Venue

Little Cokenach

Bell Farm

Bell Farm Ind Pk

Caylers Farm

Park Farm Ind Est

Langley Lawn

CB11

BELL LA

PARK FARM LA

Nuthampstead

The Woodman (PH)

Park Farm

STOCKING LA

Bee Farm

SG9

39
19

A **B** **C** **D** **E** **F**

Monkshole Wood

B1039

B1039

8

Lower Pond Street

Building End

Lower Farm

Chiswick Hall

Hope Farm House

Upper Farm

BUILDING END RD

BUILDING END RD

7

SG8

Mead Bushes Wood

Upper Pond Street

COMMON LA

Harcamlow Way

Wicken Water

37

SCHOOL LA

6

Duddenhoe End Farm

Hall

Pickerton Green

High Wood

5

Roughway Wood

Chrishall Common

Oldfield Grove

White Friars Farm

36

Killem's Green

Common La

Lorking's La

4

Grange Farm

Cosh Farm

Hall Grove

Duddenhoe Grange

CB11

The Hall

Harcamlow Way

3

River Stort

Church Farm

Hall

Upper Green

35

THE CAUSEWAY

THE KANGELS

LONG LEY

2

PARK LA

BULL LA

Langley

The Bull (PH)

HIGHFIELDS

Lower Green

Ford

Bury Farm

1

Roper's La

WRETCHING HILL

New Farm

34

43 **A** **B** 44 **C** **D** 45 **E** **F**

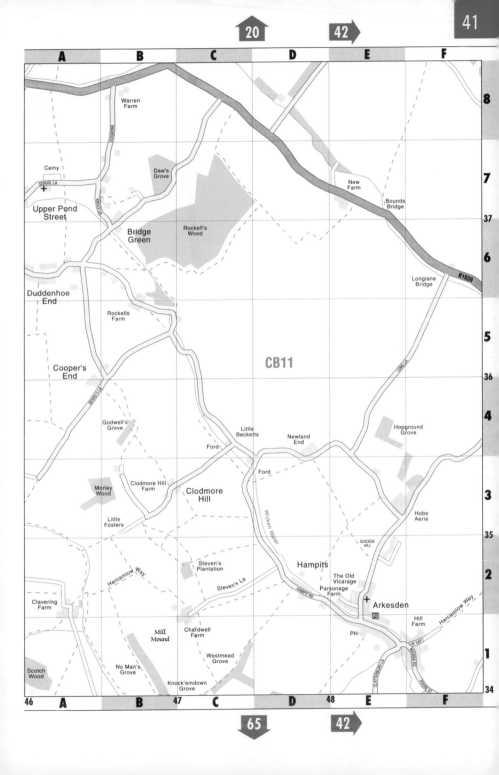

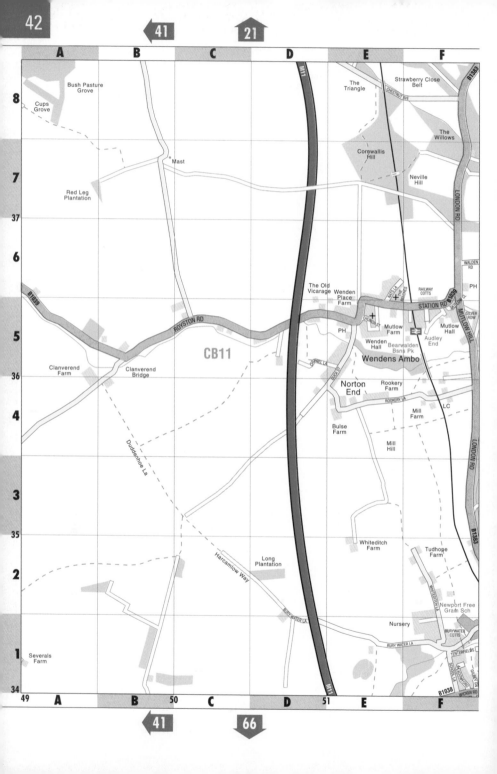

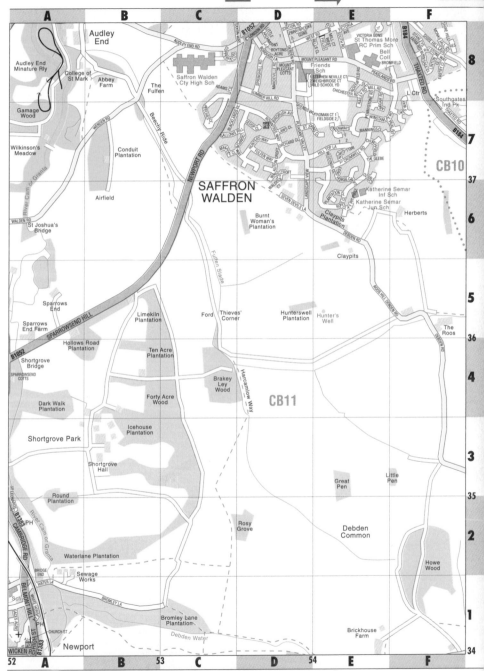

Audley End

Audley End Miniature Rly

College of St Mark

Gamage Wood

Wilkinson's Meadow

Abbey Farm

The Fulfen

Saffron Walden Cty High Sch

B1052

St Thomas More RC Prim Sch

Bell Coll

Southgates Ind Pk

Conduit Plantation

Beechy Ride

Airfield

SAFFRON WALDEN

CB10

St Joshua's Bridge

Burnt Woman's Plantation

Katherine Semar Inf Sch

Katherine Semar Jun Sch

Herberts

Claypits Plantation

Claypits

Fulfen Slade

Sparrows End

Sparrows End Farm

SPARROWSEND HILL

Limekiln Plantation

Ford

Thieves' Corner

Hunterswell Plantation

Hunter's Well

The Roos

Hollows Road Plantation

Shortgrove Bridge

SPARROWSEND COTTS

Ten Acre Plantation

Harcamlow Way

Dark Walk Plantation

Forty Acre Wood

Brakey Ley Wood

CB11

Shortgrove Park

Icehouse Plantation

Shortgrove Hall

Great Pen

Little Pen

Round Plantation

Debden Common

Rosy Grove

River Cam or Granta

Waterlane Plantation

BRIDGE END

WATER LA

Sewage Works

BROMLEY LA

Bromley Lane Plantation

Debden Water

Howe Wood

Brickhouse Farm

BELMONT HILL

Newport

WICKEN RD

	A	B	C	D	E	F

THE DREYS

Sewage Works

The Towers

Shire Hill Farm

Frogsgreen Farm

8

Tiptoft Farm

Bears Hall

Veerman Lodge

7

THAXTED RD

B184

37

Cole End Farm

Brickkiln Leys Farm

Cole End

6

Wr Twr

COLE END LA

Gunters

Thunderley Parsonage

The Old Pig And Whistle (PH)

Six Acre Wood

Harrison's Wood

CB10

5

Thunderley Hall

36

Crowney Wood

THAXTED RD

4

New House Farm

Peverel's Wood

Parsonage Farm

Abbots Manor

Harleyfield Grove

3

Pamphillions

PARSONAGE LA

Purton End

35

Airfield (dis)

WIMBISH WLK

B184

Sewage Works

Carver Barracks

2

Newhouse Farm

CB11

BROAD OAKES CL

AVE

Elder Street

Burnt House

Debden Manor

Freemans

1

Ricketts

WATER LA

34

| 55 | A | B | 56 | C | D | 57 | E | F |

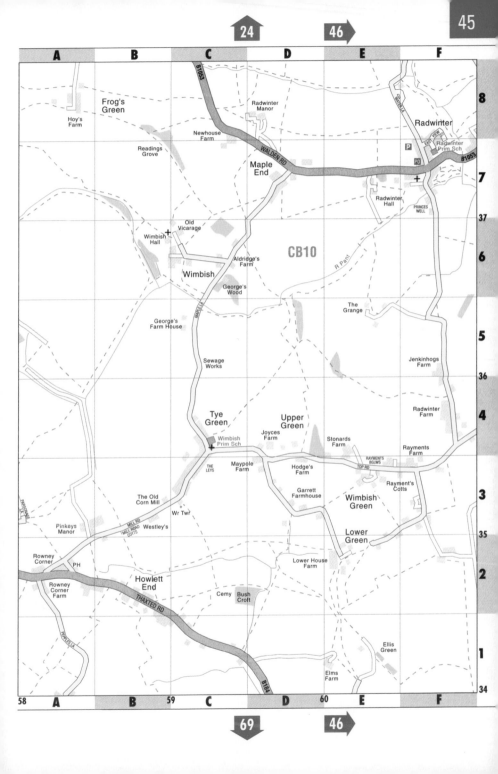

A B C D E F

8

Frog's
Green

Hoy's
Farm

Radwinter
Manor

Radwinter

Newhouse
Farm

Readings
Grove

WALDEN RD

B1053

Maple
End

Radwinter
Prim Sch

EAST VIEW

P
PO

7

Old
Vicarage

Wimbish
Hall

Aldridge's
Farm

CB10

Radwinter
Hall

PRINCES
WELL

37

Wimbish

George's
Wood

R Pant

6

George's
Farm House

The
Grange

MAPLE LA

5

Sewage
Works

Jenkinhogs
Farm

36

Tye
Green

Upper
Green

Radwinter
Farm

4

Wimbish
Prim Sch

Joyces
Farm

Stonards
Farm

Rayments
Farm

THE
LEYS

Maypole
Farm

Hodge's
Farm

RAYMENTS
BGLWS

TOP RD

The Old
Corn Mill

Wr Twr

Garrett
Farmhouse

Rayment's
Cotts

3

MILL RD

Pinkeys
Manor

MILL ROAD
COTTS

Westley's

Wimbish
Green

Rowney
Corner

PH

Lower
Green

35

Rowney
Corner
Farm

Howlett
End

THAXTED RD

Lower House
Farm

2

Cemy

Bush
Croft

FINCHES LA

Ellis
Green

1

Elms
Farm

B184

34

58 A B 59 C D 60 E F

45
25

A **B** **C** **D** **E** **F**

WINCELOW HALL RD

HILL RD

B1054 HIGH ST

Church Farm

CHURCH RD

8

Shelland's Farm

Hill Farm

B1054

LONGCROFT

B1055

+

Equestrian Ctr

Pant Brook House

B1054

PH

B1055

Sharp Crofts Wood

Prentice's Farm

7

Hill Farm

Moss's Farm

37

6

B1053

Anso Corner Farm

B1055

Howses

Anser Gallows Farm

Long Thatch

5

Mortlock's Farm

Clay Wood

River Pant

CB10

36

B1053

4

Little Brockholds Farm

Different Part Grove

Sparrow's Hall

Moor End Farm

Great Brockholds

Goddards Farm

3

Ivytodd's Farm

Barleyfields

Giffords Farm

Byeball's Farm

35

Longmead

TINDON END RD

Broadfields

B1051

2

Collins Cross

The Dovehouse

Bush Cottage

Mill Farm House

Blackhouse Farm

B1051

South Fields

Hole Farm

Grassy Grove

Tindon Manor

Bush Farm

1

Tindon End

Market Farm

Broadcroft Grove

B1051

34

61 **A** **B** **62** **C** **D** **63** **E** **F**

45
70

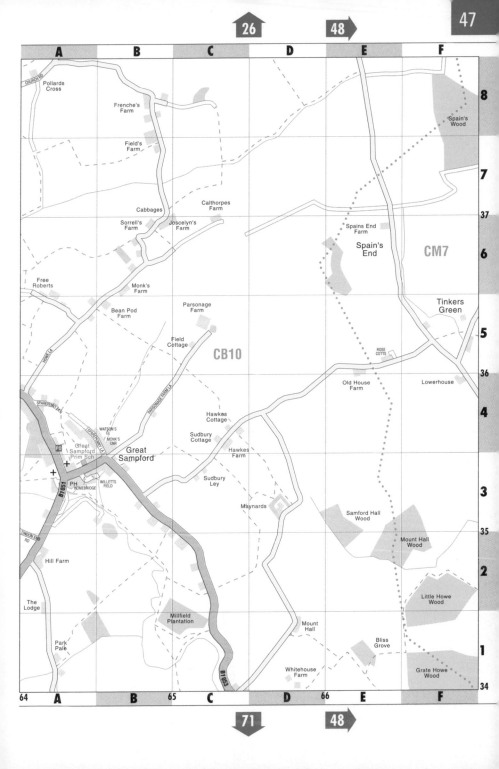

47
27

	A	B	C	D	E	F

8

Little Nortons

Old Robin

Great Nortons

CO9

Bushy Grove

Lopham's Farm

Rockall's Farm

7

Howsey Wood

37

Springlette

Shore Hall

The Grove

White House Farm

Sewage Works

6

Rivett's Farm

MILLERS ROW

FIELDS LA

Briar Cottages

PH

Cornish Hall End

HEARD'S LA

Heard's Farm

Hole Farm

5

CM7

Whitleys

36

Cornish Hall

Jekyll's Farm

4

JEKYLL'S LA

Unwin's Farm

3

New Cover

Little London

Hobtoe's Farm

MILL LA

35

Rook Hall

Yeldhams

2

Howe Farm

Obourne's Farm

1

Spainshall Farm

Bumpstead Lodge

Howe Street

Spain's Hall

Tridgate Ley

34

B1057

67	A	B	68	C	D	69	E	F

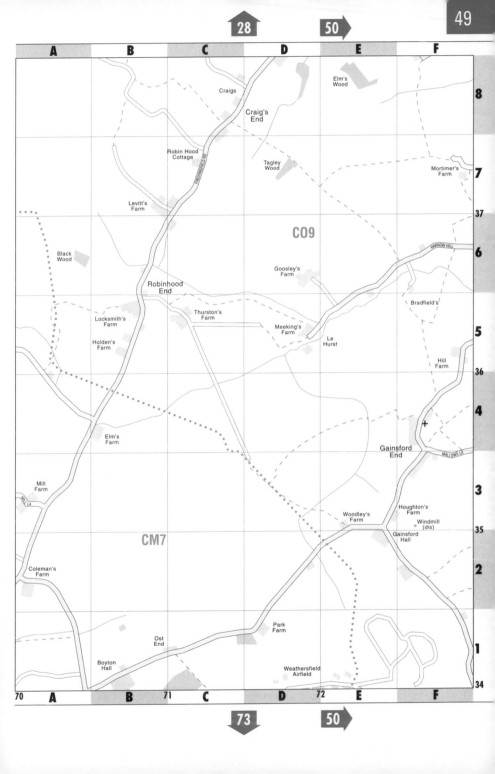

A B C D E F

8

7

37

CO9

6

Craigs

Craig's
End

Elm's
Wood

Mortimer's
Farm

Robin Hood
Cottage

Tagley
Wood

HARROW HILL

Levitt's
Farm

Black
Wood

Goosley's
Farm

Bradfield's

Robinhood
End

5

Locksmith's
Farm

Thurston's
Farm

Meeking's
Farm

Le
Hurst

Hill
Farm

Holden's
Farm

36

Elm's
Farm

4

Gainsford
End

MALLOWS LA

Mill
Farm

MILL LA

3

Houghton's
Farm

Woodley's
Farm

Windmill
(dis)

35

Gainsford
Hall

CM7

Coleman's
Farm

2

Park
Farm

1

Ost
End

Boyton
Hall

Weathersfield
Airfield

34

70 A B 71 C D 72 E F

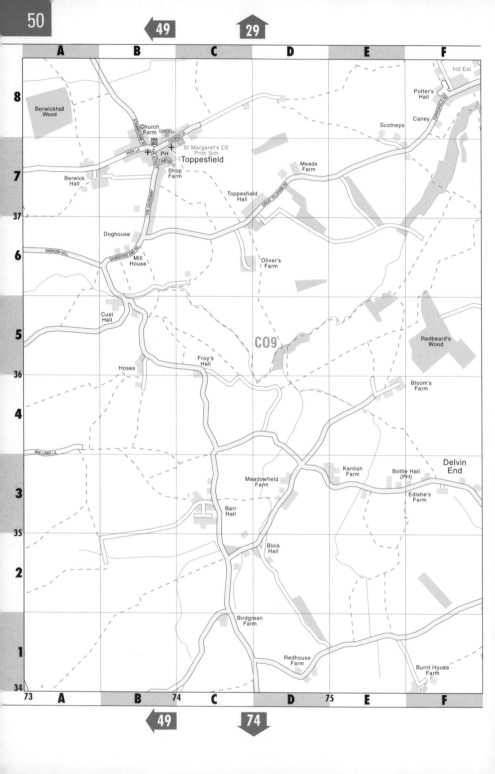

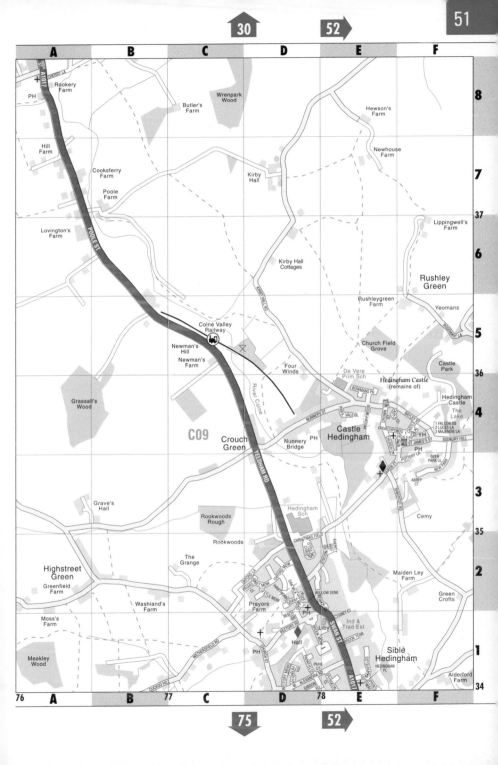

Ridley's Wood

Delvyn's Lane

Delvyn's Farm

CHURCH ST

Audley End

PH

Edeys Farm

Rectory Farm

Parkgate Farm

DELVYN LA

Crouch House

Great Lodge Farm

Branwhite's Grove

The Moat

Lawrence's Farm

C09

Pannells Ash Farm

Odewells

Rosemary Farm

ROSEMARY LA

SUDBURY RD

Pantile Cottage

Little Chelmshoe House

Kendallscroft Grove

ST JAMES'S ST

Byham Hall

Little Lodge Farm

Chelmshoe House Farm

New Barn

Monks Lodge Farm

Monks Lodge

Hosden's Farm

MONKS LODGE RD

St Giles CE Prim Sch

Link Hills

Hopwell's Farm

Great Maplestead

ST GILES CL

STONE COTTS

Lucking Street

Luckinghouse Farm

CHURCH ST

Little Lodge Farm

Purls Cottage

Barrett's Hall

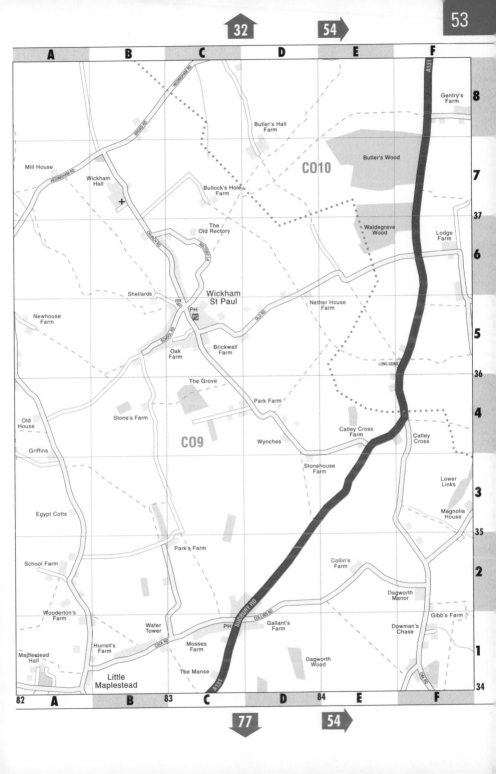

54

53 33

| A | B | C | D | E | F |

8
Old Rectory
Great Henny
Thorncroft Farm
Clay Hill
CHURCH LA
Clay Hill
Rectory
THE STOUR
Dove House Farm
Grove Farm
Stour Valley Path
St Edmund Way
Little Hickbush
Fenn Farm
Hill Place
Tymperly Farm

7
Loshes Meadows
Great Hickbush

37
Loshhouse Farm
Sparrow's Farm

6
Pelham Hall
CHURCH RD
Twinstead
CO10

Twinstead Hall
Hill Farm

Twinstead Green
Furzeground
Lightlands

5
Ansell's Grove
Culverdown

Old Roses Farm
Newhouse Cotts

36
Ansell's Farm

4
Twinsteadhall Wood
HENNY BACK RD
Coppins Farm
MILL LA
LAMARSH RD

Beech Cottage
Cobb's Farm
Alphamstone

Upper Links
LOOKERS LA
Lorkin's Farm
CO8

3
Whitelands Farm
Sycamore Farm

35
Mabbs Corner
CUTLER'S RD

Cripple Corner
Scott's Farm

2
King's Farm
Abbotts
FENN BACK RD

Hawkin's Farm
CO9
Goulds

1
Lower Goulds Farm
STATION RD

Le Mote Hall

34
85 A B 86 C D 87 E F

53 78

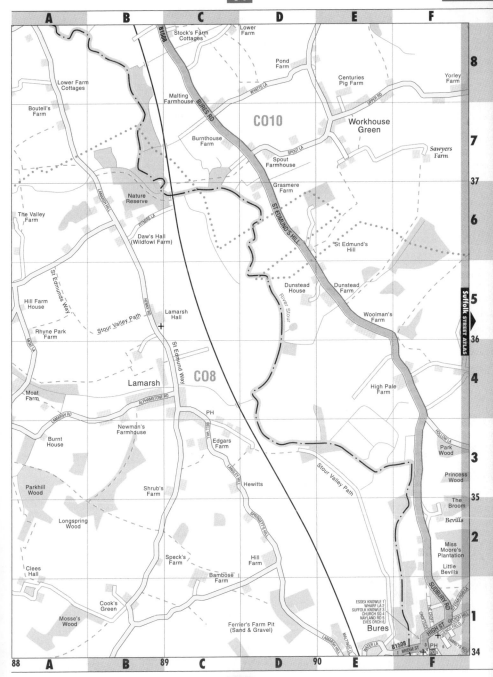

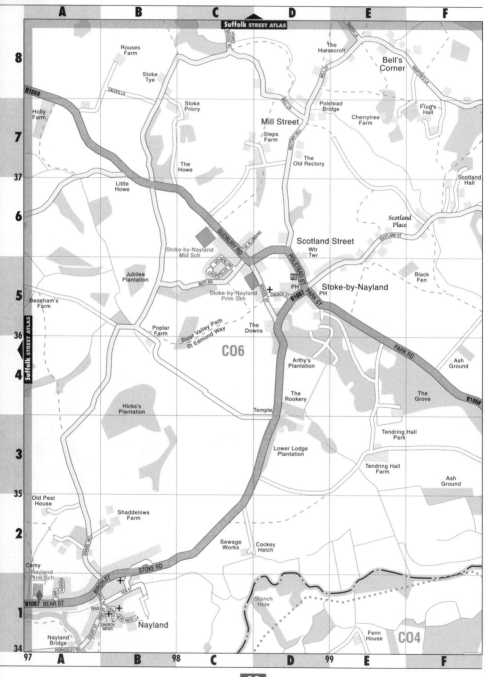

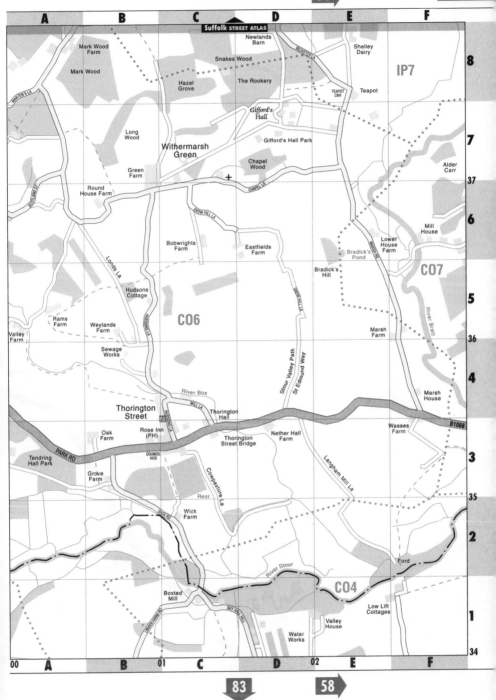

Suffolk STREET ATLAS

A **B** **C** **D** **E** **F**

Mark Wood Farm

Mark Wood

MARTEN'S LA

SCOTLAND ST

Newlands Barn

BECKETT'S LA

Shelley Dairy

IP7

8

Snakes Wood

Hazel Grove

The Rookery

Gifford's Hall

TEAPOT CNR

Teapot

Long Wood

Withermarsh Green

Gifford's Hall Park

7

Chapel Wood

Alder Carr

Green Farm

+

CHAPEL LA

37

Round House Farm

Mill House

BOW HILL LA

Lords La

Bobwrights Farm

Eastfields Farm

Lower House Farm

6

Bradick's Pond

MARSH RD

CO7

Bradick's Hill

River Brett

Hudsons Cottage

CO6

5

Rams Farm

Weylands Farm

HUDSONS LA

Marsh Farm

36

Valley Farm

Sewage Works

BOW HILL LA

Stour Valley Path

St Edmund Way

Marsh House

4

River Box

MILL LA

Thorington Hall

B1068

Thorington Street

Wasses Farm

Rose Inn (PH)

Oak Farm

PARK RD

HOLTONS LA

Thorington Street Bridge

Nether Hall Farm

Langham Mill La

3

Tendring Hall Park

COUNCIL HOS

Grove Farm

Cowpasture La

Resr

35

WICK RD

Wick Farm

2

CO4

Ford

River Stour

Low Lift Cottages

Boxted Mill

SKY HALL HILL

Valley House

1

Water Works

34

A **B** 01 **C** **D** 02 **E** **F**

00

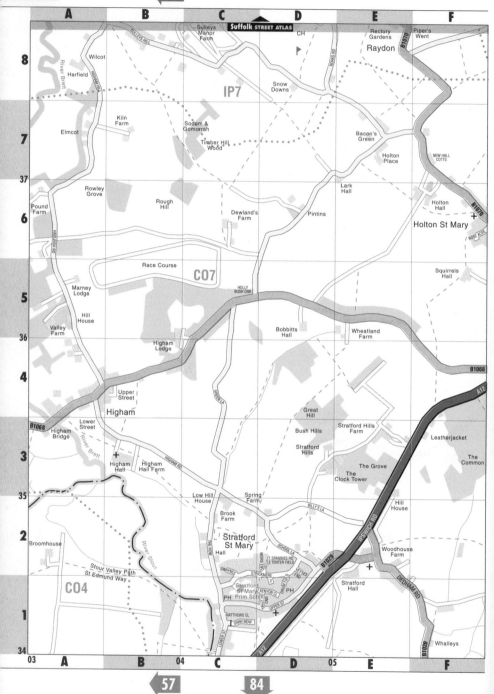

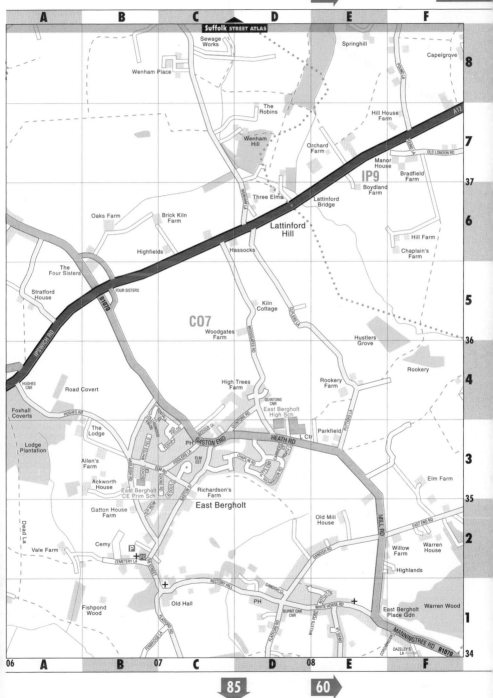

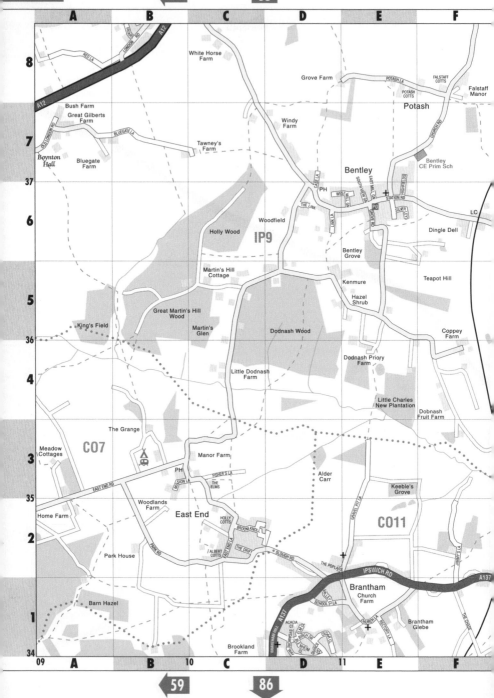

A **B** **C** **D** **E** **F**

8

RED LA
LONDON RD

A12

White Horse
Farm

Grove Farm

POTASH LA

FALSTAFF
COTTS

Falstaff
Manor

POTASH
COTTS

Potash

Bush Farm

Great Gilberts
Farm

7

SUTTON RD

BLUEGATE LA

Tawney's
Farm

Windy
Farm

CHURCH RD

Bentley
CE Prim Sch

Boynton
Hall

Bluegate
Farm

37

EAST MILL GRN

Bentley

SOUTH PETER

EAST MILL GRN

STATION RD

6

PH

WEST
MILL GRN

PH

VY ...

THE LINK

PO

SILVER LES

LC

Holly Wood

Woodfield

IP9

Dingle Dell

Martin's Hill
Cottage

Bentley
Grove

5

Great Martin's Hill
Wood

Kenmure

Hazel
Shrub

Teapot Hill

King's Field

Martin's
Glen

Dodnash Wood

Coppey
Farm

36

Dodnash Priory
Farm

4

Little Dodnash
Farm

Little Charles
New Plantation

Dobnash
Fruit Farm

The Grange

CO7

Manor Farm

3

Meadow
Cottages

PH

Alder
Carr

Keeble's
Grove

EAST END RD

FISHER'S LA

THE
ELMS

MISSION LA

35

Woodlands
Farm

CO11

DANIEL PIT LA

Home Farm

East End

HOLLY
COTTS

BROOM KNOLL

2

Park House

PARK RD

ALBERT
COTTS

BELL LA

THE DRIFT

SLOUGH RD

THE POPLARS

IPSWICH RD

A137

THE CHASE

ST EDMUND

Brantham

Church
Farm

Barn Hazel

1

A137

Brantham
Glebe

ACACIA
CT

SCHOOL CL LA

CHURCH CL

34

Brookland
Farm

09 **A** **B** 10 **C** **D** 11 **E** **F**

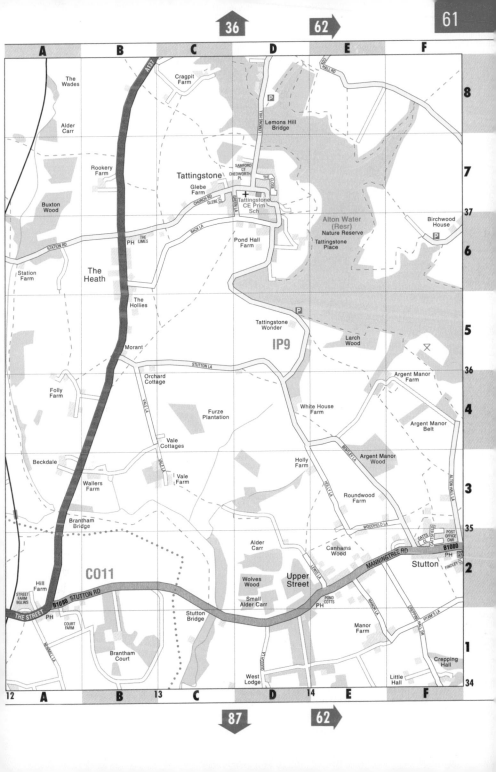

A B C D E F

8

Great Birch Wood

The Dower House

Potash Farm

B1080

The Woodlands

Woodlands Farm

7

Woodley Wood

Little Birch Wood

Hale's Grove

Redhouse Farm

WOODLANDS RD

Freston Grove

CLINCH RD

SAMFORD RD

COUNCIL HOS

37

Halesgrove Cottage

Brown's Farm

Holbrook High Sch

IPSWICH RD

HOLMOEREADE GDNS

6

Brook Farm

BROOMHILL
Holbrook
Prim Sch

Clifton Wood

THE STREET

HEATH RD

LADYMEADE WOOD

COACHMAN'S PADDOCK

Park House

EAST ROW

Crag Hall Covert

Walkgate Cottages

BROOK FARM LA

GIFFORDS

HA PENNY GDNS

Holbrook Gardens

Fish Pond

5

Old Alton Hall Farm

IP9

FIREBRONDS RD

BIRDS VIEW

HEATHFIELD RD

MILL RISE

PO

Holbrook

FIVE ACRES

LITTLE ORCH

CHURCH RD

FISHPOND LA

Alton Hall Cottages

LADY LA

Sewage Works

36

Alton Water
(Rear)
Nature Reserve

BACK HILL

FIR TREE HILL

NEW LA

4

Chestnut Spinney

PRIMROSE HILL

Holbrook Mill

Park Covert

BRICK COTTS

Holbrook Lodge

Wall Farm

HAMPSTEAD RD

Water Sports Ctr

P

P

Visitor Ctr

Lower Holbrook

3

P

+

Royal Hospital Sch

Wall Farm Wharf

P

35

Stutton CE Prim Sch

LANSFIELD RD

HOLBROOK RD

B1080

2

FINDLEY CL
Bay Tree Farm

THE DRIFT

Alton Wharf

The Hermitage

HYAM'S LA

LOWER ST

Suffolk Coast and Heaths Path

STUTTON GN

Stutton House

Markwell's Farm

1

Lower Street

Crowe Hall

CROWE HALL LA

Crowe Hall Farm

34

15 A B 16 C D 17 E F

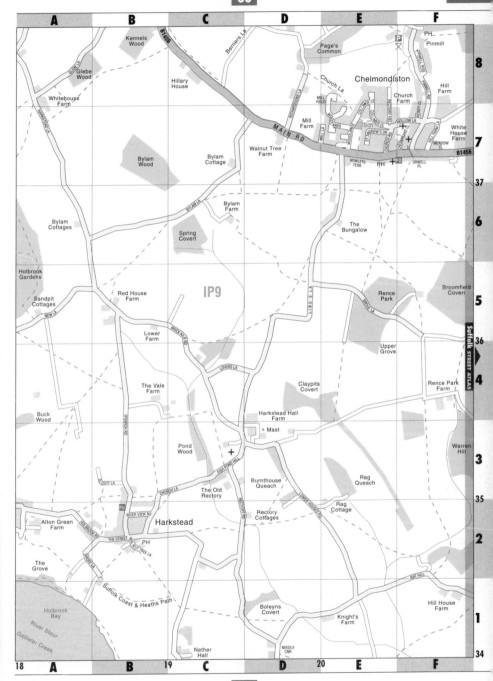

Kennels Wood

Glebe Wood

Whitehouse Farm

Hillary House

Berners La

Page's Common

PH

Pinmill

Chelmondiston

Church La

Hill Farm

Church Farm

White House Farm

Mill Farm

MAIN RD

Bylam Wood

Bylam Cottage

Walnut Tree Farm

Mill Field

Sch

HOWLETS TERR

PH

ORWELL PL

B1456

Bylam Cottages

Bylam Farm

Spring Covert

The Bungalow

IP9

Red House Farm

Rence Park

Broomfield Covert

Holbrook Gardens

Sandpit Cottages

NEW LA

Lower Farm

Upper Grove

Rence Park Farm

The Vale Farm

OVERS LA

Claypits Covert

Warren Hill

Buck Wood

IPSWICH RD

Pond Wood

Harkstead Hall Farm

Mast

Rag Queach

CUSHY LA

CHURCH LA

FISH POND HILL

The Old Rectory

Burnthouse Queach

Rag Cottage

Alton Green Farm

RIVER VIEW RD

RECTORY RD

Rectory Cottages

LOWER HOUSE RD

HOLBROOK RD

THE STREET

PH

Harkstead

The Grove

SANDI LA

NUT TREE LA

Suffolk Coast & Heaths Path

BAT HILL

Hill House Farm

Holbrook Bay

River Stour

Galister Creek

Nether Hall

Boleyns Covert

NEEDLE CNR

Knight's Farm

B1456

Bylam Wood

Suffolk STREET ATLAS

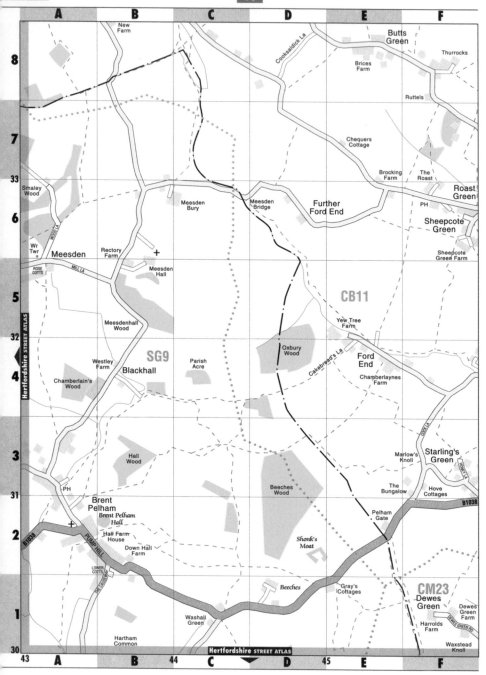

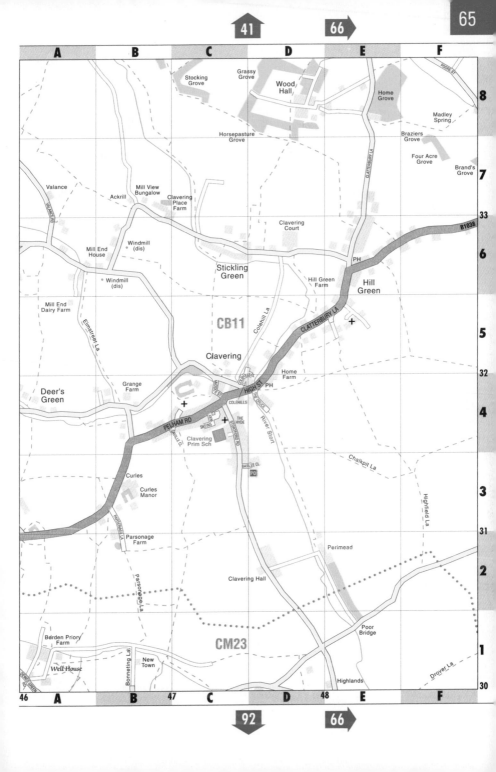

65 42

A B C D E F

8

7

33

6

5

32

4

3

31

2

1

30

49 A B 50 C D 51 E F

65 93

M11

B1038 Cuckingstool End
WICKEN RD
ORCHARD CT
CHERRY GARDEN LA
FRANKLIN LA
BARNARD CL 1
HITCH COMMON RD 2

Newport

Bonhunt Water

Newport Prim Sch

St Helen's Chapel

Bonhunt

Recn Gd

Works

Wicken Hall
PH
Howland Farm
Lower Farm

Wicken Bonhunt

Bonhunt Springs

POOLE ST
Wicken Water
THE MEADS

Brick House

B1038
Howland Farm House

RICKLING RD

Bolsters

Fairwells

CB11

Bushy Lays

Spring Close

Northcroft Spring

Broadfields

Harcamlow Way

Mary Ann's Plantation

Coldhams Farm

Moat Farm

Tinney Springs

Tinney Spinney

Quendon Park

Deer Park

NEWPORT DR

Fireball Hill

Church End Farm

Rickling

Fir Plantation

Sibcopp's Wood

B1383

Codham Wood

Hanginghill

Dark Plantation

Inn

Pond Lay Plantation

Quendon

BRICK KILN LA

Willis's La

CM23

Rickling Hall

Coney Acre

THISTLEY CRES

RICKLING LOWER RD

GREYS HOLLOW

PO

B1383

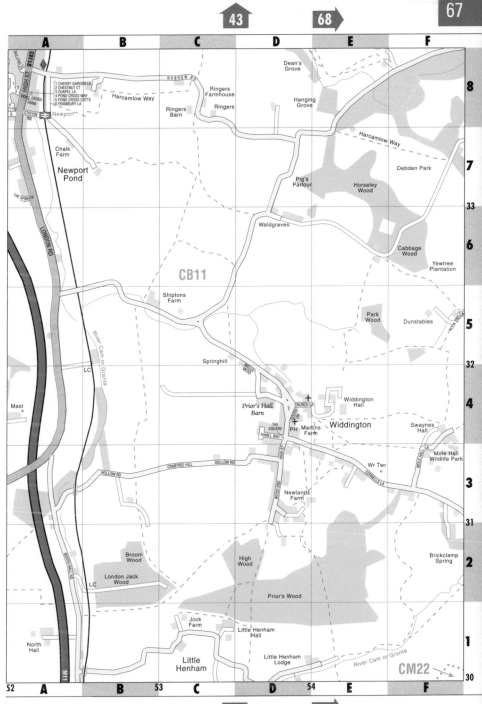

A   **B**   **C**   **D**   **E**   **F**

B1383

HIGH ST

BULLFIELD

1 CHERRY GARDEN LA
2 CHESTNUT CT
3 CHAPEL LA
4 POND CROSS WAY
5 POND CROSS COTTS
6 FRAMBURY LA

POND CROSS FARM

STATION RD

Newport

Harcamlow Way

DEBDEN RD

Ringers Farmhouse

Ringers Barn

Ringers

Dean's Grove

Hanging Grove

8

Chalk Farm

Newport Pond

Harcamlow Way

Pig's Parlour

Horseley Wood

Debden Park

7

THE SPINNEY

LONDON RD

Waldgraves

33

Cabbage Wood

6

CB11

Yewtree Plantation

Shiptons Farm

Park Wood

Dunstables

RUSK END LA

5

River Cam or Granta

LC

Springhill

WELL MEAD

32

Mast

Prior's Hall Barn

SOUTH LA

CHURCH LA

PH

Widdington Hall

Widdington

4

THE SQUARE

HAMEL WAY

Martins Farm

Swaynes Hall

MOLE HALL LA

Mole Hall Wildlife Park

HOLLOW RD

CRABTREE HILL

HOLLOW RD

HIGH ST

WOOD END

Wr Twr

CORNELLS LA

3

NORTH HALL RD

LC

Newlands Farm

31

Broom Wood

London Jack Wood

High Wood

Prior's Wood

Brickclamp Spring

2

M11

North Hall

Jock Farm

Little Henham Hall

Little Henham

Little Henham Lodge

River Cam or Granta

CM22

1

30

52   **A**   **B**   53   **C**   **D**   54   **E**   **F**

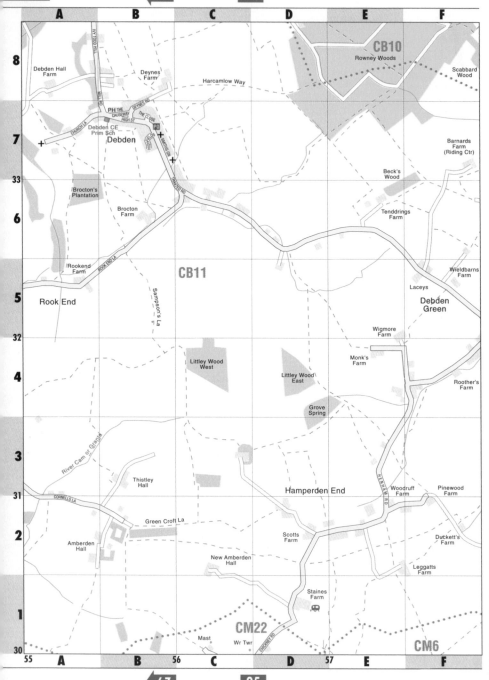

A **B** **C** **D** **E** **F**

CB10

8

Debden Hall
Farm

Rowney Woods

Scabbard
Wood

Deynes
Farm

Harcamlow Way

PH THE
CAUSEWAY

7

+

Debden CE
Prim Sch

Debden

+

+

Barnards
Farm
(Riding Ctr)

Beck's
Wood

33

Brocton's
Plantation

Tenddrings
Farm

Brocton
Farm

6

Wieldbarns
Farm

Rookend
Farm

ROOK END LA

Laceys

5

Rook End

CB11

Sampson's La

Debden
Green

32

Wigmore
Farm

Littley Wood
West

4

Littley Wood
East

Monk's
Farm

Roother's
Farm

Grove
Spring

3

River Cam or Granta

Thistley
Hall

Hamperden End

Woodruff
Farm

Pinewood
Farm

CORNELLS LA

31

Green Croft La

HEMPS RD

2

Amberden
Hall

Scotts
Farm

Duckett's
Farm

New Amberden
Hall

Leggatts
Farm

Staines
Farm

1

CM22

CM6

Mast

Wr Twr

DUCKET RD

30

55

A 56 **B** **C** **D** 57 **E** **F**

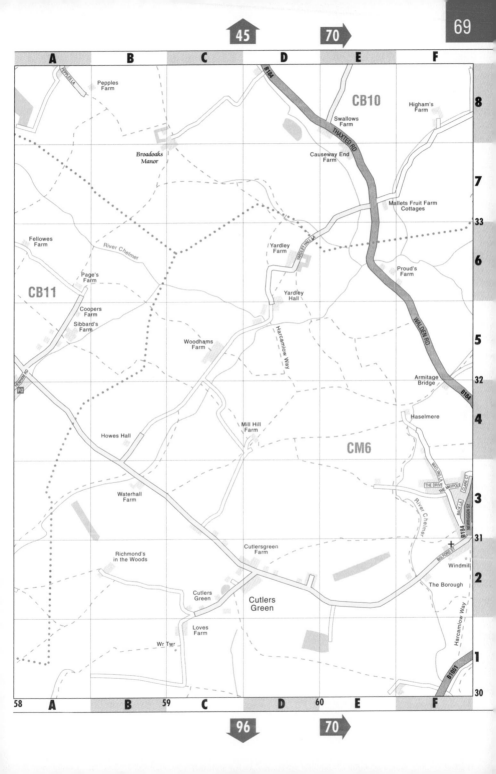

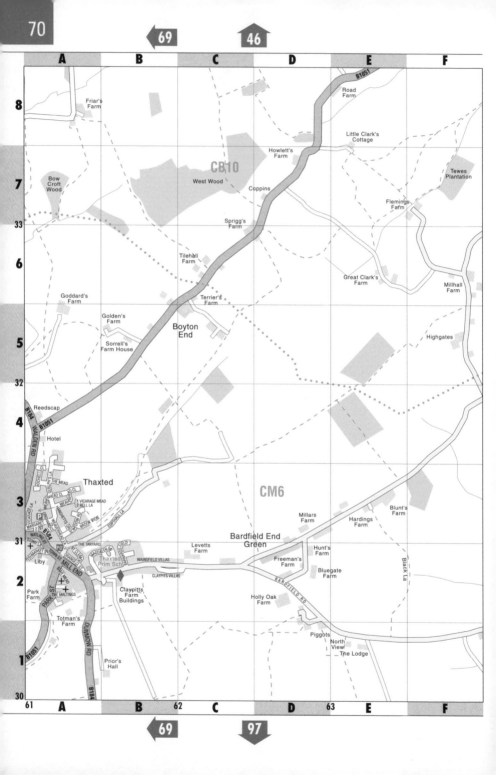

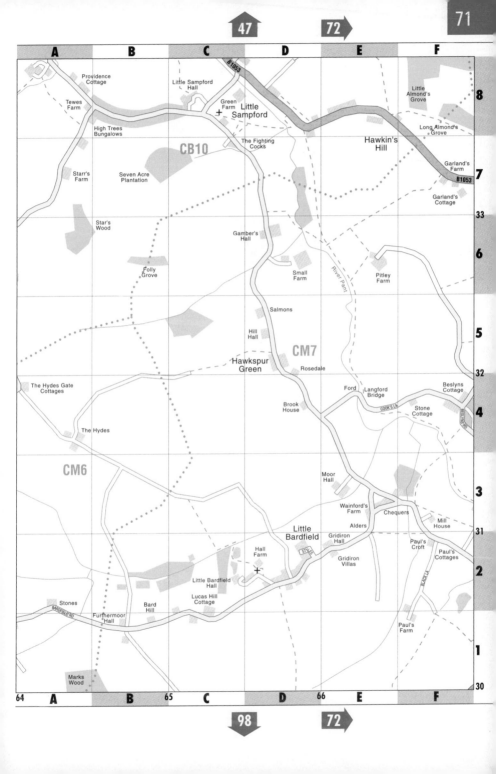

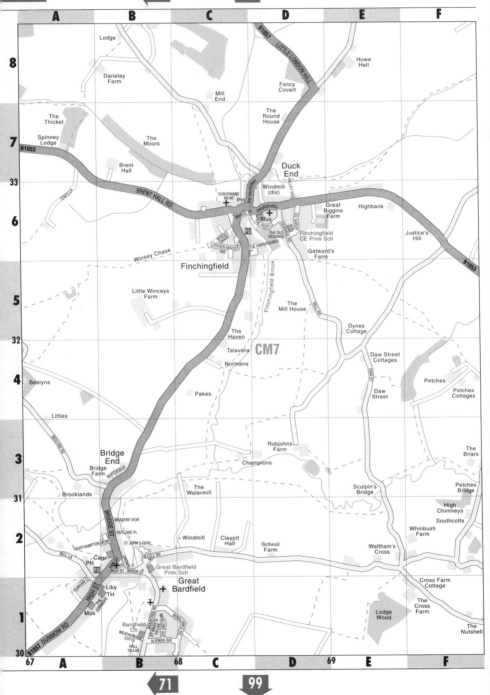

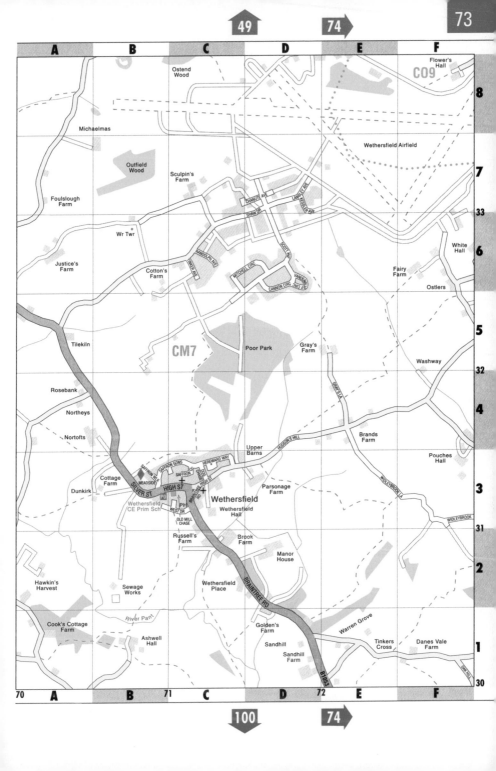

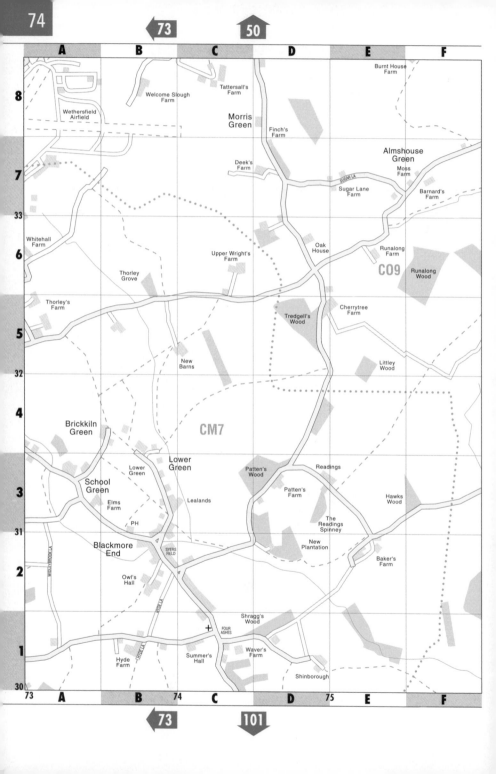

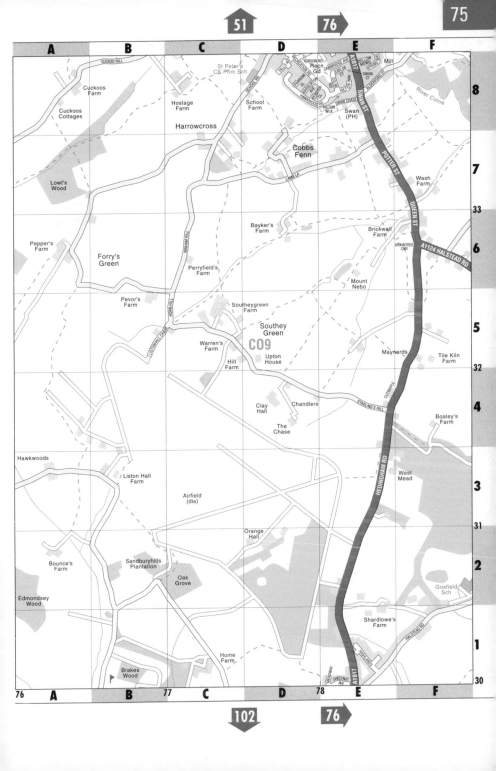

51
76

8
7
33
6
5
32
4
31
2
1
30

A · B · C · D · E · F

76 · 77 · 78

CUCKOO HILL
Cuckoos Farm
Cuckoos Cottages
St Peter's CE Prim Sch
Rec Gd
BIBSON RD
CAMBRIDGE AVE
Mill
River Colne
Hostage Farm
School Farm
SCHOOL RD
HILTON WLK
Swan Chase
Swan (PH)
SWAN ST
Harrowcross
Cobbs Fenn
LAMB LA
POTTER ST
Wash Farm
Lowt's Wood
Bayker's Farm
QUEEN ST
Brickwall Farm
BRAINTREE CNR
A1124 HALSTEAD RD
Pepper's Farm
Forry's Green
DINHAM HILL
Perryfield's Farm
Mount Nebo
Pevor's Farm
HORN HILL
Southeygreen Farm
Southey Green
CO9
Maynards
Tile Kiln Farm
LITTLEDINHAM CHASE
Warren's Farm
Hill Farm
Upton House
CUTMAPLE
Clay Hall
Chandlers
The Chase
STARLING'S HILL
Boaley's Farm
Hawkwoods
Liston Hall Farm
HEDINGHAM RD
West Mead
Airfield (dis)
Orange Hall
Bounce's Farm
Sandburyhills Plantation
Oak Grove
Shardlowe's Farm
HALSTEAD RD
Gosfield Sch
Edmondsey Wood
Home Farm
Brakes Wood
MEADWAY
CHESTNUT AVE
A1017
HIGHLANDS

A B C D E F

8
7
33
6
5
32
4
3
31
2
1
30

Purlshill
Purlshill Plantation
Barretts Hall
Toldishall Cottages
MILL LA
Mill Farm
Hull's Mill Farm
Mill
LANGLEY RD
Dynes Hall
Chestnut Grove
Sewage Works
Wallace's Farm
Dog House Grove
Pearman's Hill
Bennett's Farm
Bennett's Park
A1124
HALSTEAD RD
Foxborough Hills Farm
CO9
Hepworth Hall
Fitz John's Farm
Fitz John's Grove
Foxborough
DOE'S CNR
Brook Street Farm
TOWL CHASE
The Howe
HEDINGHAM RD
BOIS CNR LA
Bradley's House
Broak's Wood
River Colne
Box Mill Plantation
Wash Farm
CHURCHILL AVE
A131
Shardlowe's Wood
Woodcot
Sloe House
BOX MILL LA
COURTAULD HOMES OF REST
Halstead
NORTH MILL CT
H
SUDBURY RD
Sch
Whitehouse Farm
BELLEVUE TERR 1
PAPERMILL COTTS 2
RIVERSIDE CT 3
CAXTON PL 4
TRINITY CT 5
BOIS FIELD TERR
HIGH ST
COLNE RD
Whiteash Green
SLOE HILL
HALSTEAD RD
Gosfield Sch
Crowbridge Farm
SLOUGH FRM RD
STANLEY RD
Trad Est
BAYS DR
CHAPEL
WEAVERS CT
FACTORY
COLCHESTER RD A131
Cemy
VICARAGE CT
Sch
P
P
P
Liby
Sch
Great Spansey Wood
TRINITY ST
ORGANS AVE
DOOLEY RD
ADAMS CT
SWALLOW WLK
KINGFISHER MDWS
Little Spansey Wood
P
FAIRFIELD WAY
RAVENS AVE
ELM DR
The Grange
Russell's Farm
New Wood
Blamsters Farm
A131 MOUNT HILL
RAYMEY RD

A B C D E F
79 80 81

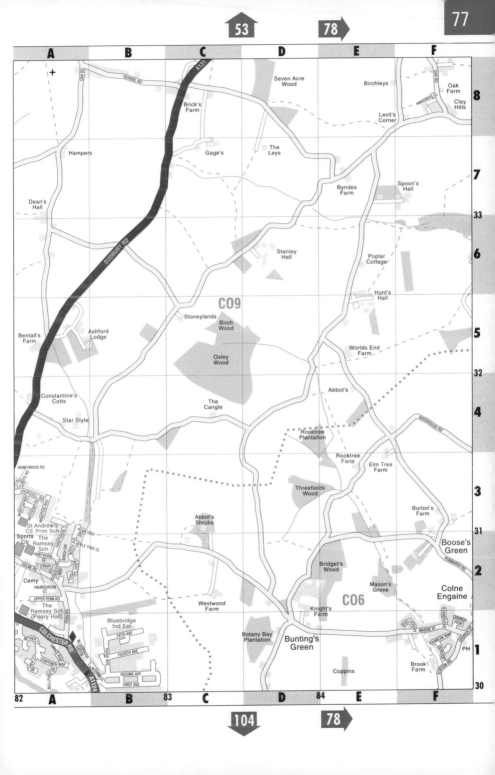

A B C D E F

8

New Barn Farm

PH

Cross End

Le Mote Hall

PEBMARSH RD

St John The Baptist CE Prim Sch

Stapleford's Farm

Montague's Farm

CO9

Pebmarsh

THE STREET

KINGS MEAD

CO8

Peyton Hall

Greathouse Farm

New Wood

Fishpits

7

Hoblets

MILL LA

33

Valiants Farm

Garlands Farm

North Wood

Polstead's Farm

6

Marvel's Garden

Cricks Farm

Lamarsh Park

DAWS CROSS

Hill House

Daws Farm

Preston's Lake

Hungary Hall

Great Wheatley Wood

Poultry Farm

5

Rye Fenn

32

Baggaretts

Peverel's Farm

CO6

The Privet

Manning's Farm

Bramble's Farm

4

Nightingales Farm

Crofts Wood

Brick House Farm

West Grove

Great Catley's Farm

3

Bromptons

Countess Cross

31

OVERHALL HILL

Countesscross Farm

BROOKHOUSE RD

Over Hall

2

Black Bats

THE GREEN

Colne Engaine CE Prim Sch

GREEN WAY

GREEN FARM RD

Chestnut Plantation

Mon

Shrive's Wood

HIGH ST

CHURCH ST

Aldercar

LAMARSH HILL

Home Farm

Colne Park

Instep's Farm

1

Lodge Farm

Millbrook Grove

MILL LA

30

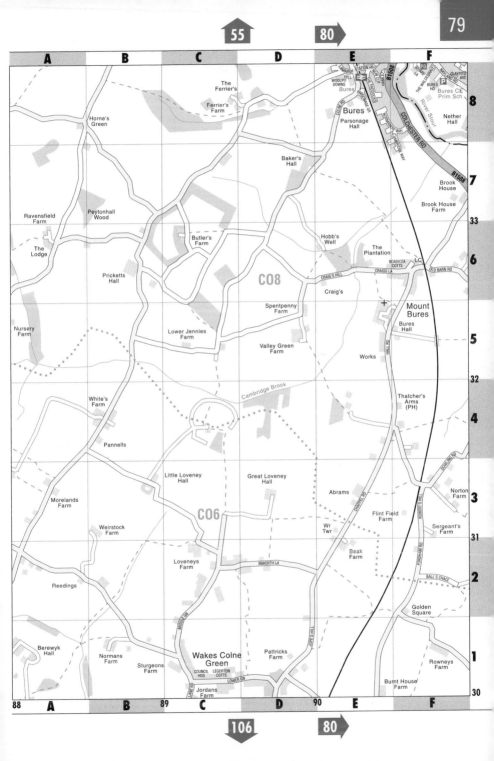

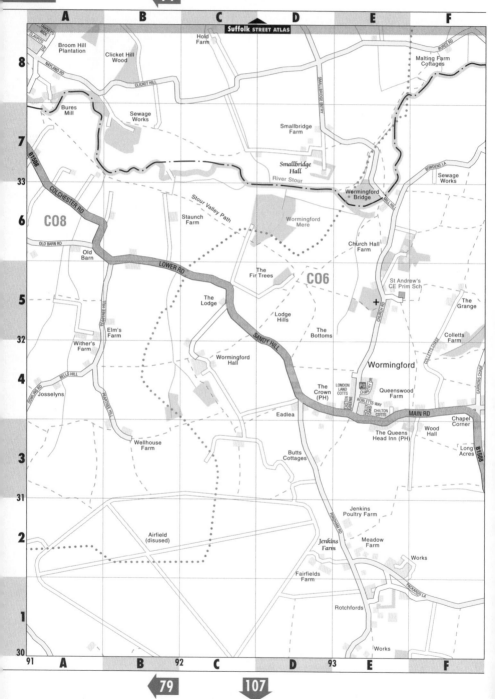

Suffolk STREET ATLAS

A **B** **C** **D** **E** **F**

Broom Hill Plantation
Clicket Hill Wood
Hold Farm
Malting Farm Cottages

8

MAYLAND RD
CLICKET HILL

Bures Mill
Sewage Works

7

Smallbridge Farm

BURES RD

BELL HILL

SMALLBRIDGE ENTRY

Smallbridge Hall

33

River Stour
Wermingford Bridge

BOWDENS LA
Sewage Works

Colchester Rd
B1508

6

CO8

Old Barn Rd
Old Barn

Stour Valley Path
Staunch Farm

Wormingford Mere

Church Hall Farm

LOWER RD

St Andrew's CE Prim Sch
The Grange

5

The Fir Trees

CO6

+

The Lodge
Lodge Hills
The Bottoms

Colletts Farm
COLLETTS CHASE

32

Elm's Farm

Wither's Farm

PEARTREE HILL

Wormingford Hall
SANDY HILL

Wormingford

4

BELLS HILL
DOOLD WOOD RD
Josselyns

The Crown (PH)
LONDON LAND COTTS
ROBLETTS WAY
CHILTON COTTS
Queenswood Farm

CHURCH RD
CARNONS CHASE

Eadiea
MAIN RD
Chapel Corner
Wood Hall
B1508

Wellhouse Farm

The Queens Head Inn (PH)
Long Acres

3

Butts Cottages

31

Jenkins Poultry Farm

2

Airfield (disused)

Jenkins Farm
Meadow Farm

PACKARDS LA

Works

Fairfields Farm

1

Rotchfords

Works

30

91 **A** **B** **92** **C** **D** **93** **E** **F**

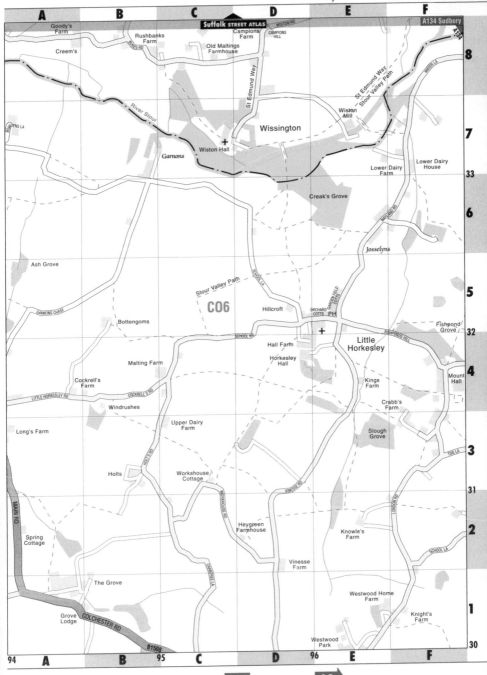

Suffolk STREET ATLAS

A134 Sudbury

Goody's Farm

Creem's

Rushbanks Farm

ROSE'S RD

Old Maltings Farmhouse

Campions Farm

WISTON RD

CAMPIONS HILL

St Edmund Way

St Edmund Way

Stour Valley Path

WATER LA

A133

8

BORDENS LA

River Stour

Wissington

Wiston Mill

7

Garnons

Wiston Hall

Lower Dairy Farm

Lower Dairy House

33

Creak's Grove

6

Ash Grove

Stour Valley Path

Josselyns

HAYLARDS RD

GARNONS CHASE

CO6

Hillcroft

SCHOOL LA

ORCHARD COTTS

GARDEN FIELD COTTS

PH

Fishpond Grove

5

32

Bottengoms

SCHOOL RD

Hall Farm

Horkesley Hall

Little Horkesley

FISHPONDS HILL

Mount Hall

Malting Farm

Kings Farm

Cockrell's Farm

COCKRELL'S RD

Crabb's Farm

4

LITTLE HORKESLEY RD

Windrushes

Slough Grove

TOG LA

Long's Farm

Upper Dairy Farm

3

HOLT'S RD

Holts

Workshouse Cottage

WORKHOUSE RD

VINESSE RD

LONDON RD

31

MAIN RD

Heygreen Farmhouse

Knowle's Farm

SCHOOL LA

2

Spring Cottage

CHARTER LA

Vinesse Farm

The Grove

Westwood Home Farm

Knight's Farm

1

Grove Lodge

COLCHESTER RD

Westwood Park

30

B1508

94

A

B

95

C

D

96

E

F

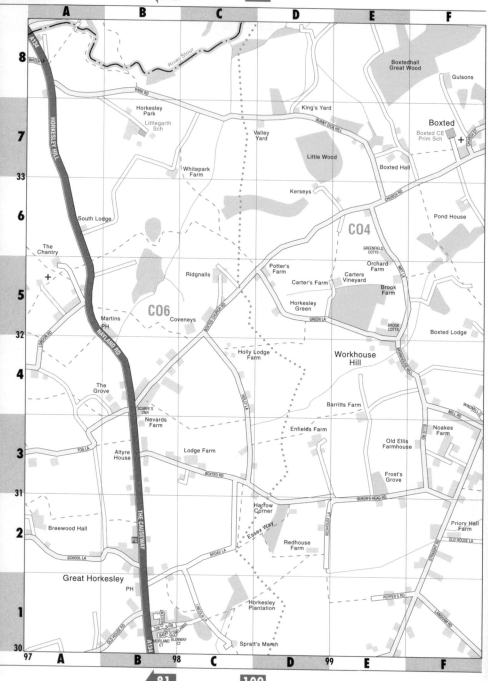

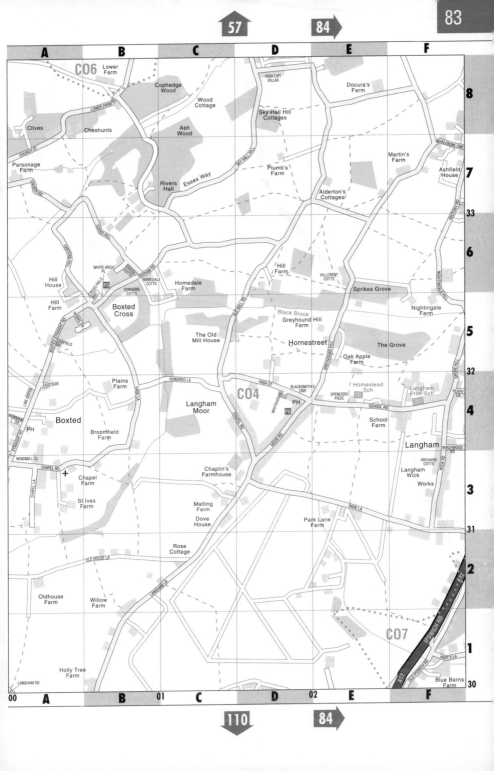

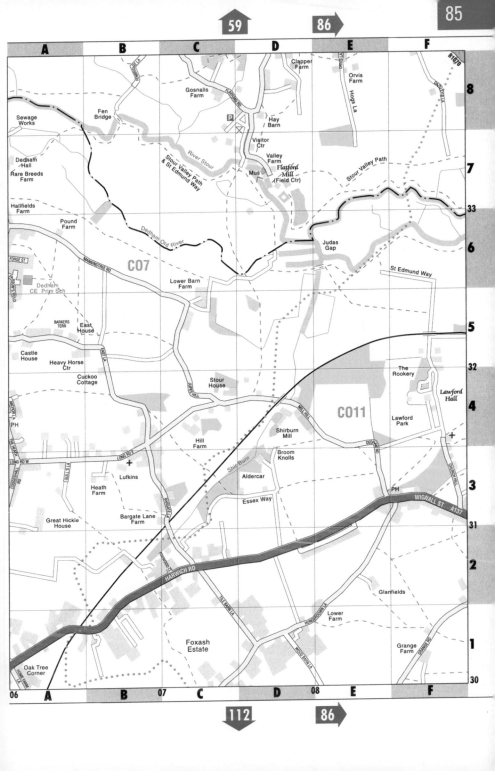

8 Brantham

B1070 Manningtree Rd The Haugh Spooners Wood Braham Wood

7 West Green Cotts Stour Valley Path Brantham Mill Ind Est Bergholt Rd B1070 Wyseman Pl PH New Village Cattawade Brantham Hill Braham Hall Sycamore Way Brooklands Prim Sch Ash Ground Cl Snows Way Welhams Way Sewage Works

33 Riverside Cotts Larman Ct Factory La Works Hardy Pl Truswell Terr Decoy Pond

6 River Stour Marsh Barn Cattawade Bridge Middleheope Creek Cattawade Creek Suffolk Coast & Heaths Path Nature Reserve

Hall Flee

5 Manningtree LC Sewage Works Hopping Bridge Mistley Towers The Stores Mistley

32 St Edmund Way B1352 Causeway Jubilee End Station Rd The Walls Mistley Place Park High St B1352 Mistley

4 Constable Cl Stubbs Cl Cox's Hill Wignall Brook Fitzgerald Dixon Sitwell Ct Dale Hall Essex Way Highfields Prim Sch Riverview High St Stour St Liby Mus New Rd Norman Rd Maltings School Wood

3 Lawford Place Lawford Manningtree High Sch Colchester Rd CO11 Manningtree Park Cotts The Chase Old Hall Kennels Laundry Wood Dairy Wood Furze Hill

A137 Wignall St Parrington Way B1352 Bromley Cnr Claude Oliver Cl Lawford CE Prim Sch Waldegrave Way Long Rd Honeycroft B1035 Acorn Village Community Mistley Hall Dairy House

2 Lawford House Broad Aldhams Farm Dead La Pedler's Cnr Clacton Rd Ford Farm Beech Plantation

1 Lawfordhouse Farm Aldhams Chequers Rd Stacie's Farm Brickkiln Grove B1035

30 09 A B 10 C D 11 E F

← 85   ↓ 113

D4
1 QUAY ST
2 QUAY CTYD
3 BROOKS MALTING
4 ALMA SQ
5 THE CENTRAL MAILTINGS
6 ST MICHAELS CT
7 YORK ST
8 FALKLANDS DR
9 REGENT ST
10 PARSONS YD
11 RAILWAY TERR
12 TRINITY FARM CT
13 BENDALLS CT
14 GASFIELD

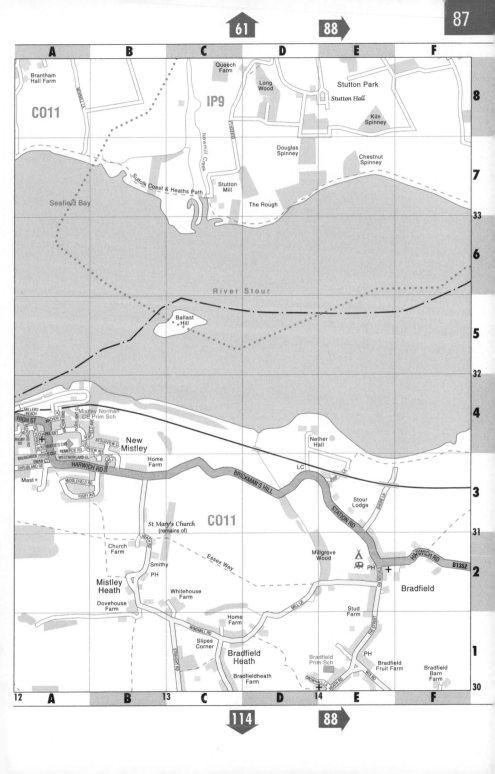

A **B** **C** **D** **E** **F**

Brantham Hall Farm

CO11

Queech Farm

Long Wood

IP9

Stutton Park

Stutton Hall

Kiln Spinney

Douglas Spinney

Chestnut Spinney

Newmill Creek

Suffolk Coast & Heaths Path

Stutton Mill

Seafield Bay

The Rough

River Stour

Ballast Hill

MILLERS REACH

HIGH ST

Mistley Norman CE Prim Sch

New Mistley

Home Farm

Nether Hall

LC

BRUNSWICK RD

SWAN CT

SHRUBLAND RD

HARWICH RD

MIDDLEFIELD RD

RIGBY AVE

Mast

BRICKMAN'S HILL

STATION RD

Stour Lodge

CO11

St Mary's Church (remains of)

Church Farm

Essex Way

Millgrove Wood

PH

HARWICH RD

B1352

Bradfield

Mistley Heath

Smithy

PH

Dovehouse Farm

Whitehouse Farm

Home Farm

MILL LA

Stud Farm

THE STREET

WINDMILL RD

STRAIGHT RD

Slipes Corner

Bradfield Heath

Bradfieldheath Farm

Bradfield Prim Sch

PH

CROWHALL LA

HEATH RD

WIX RD

Bradfield Fruit Farm

Bradfield Barn Farm

A **B** **C** **D** **E** **F**

12 13 14

8 7 33 6 5 32 4 3 31 2 1 30

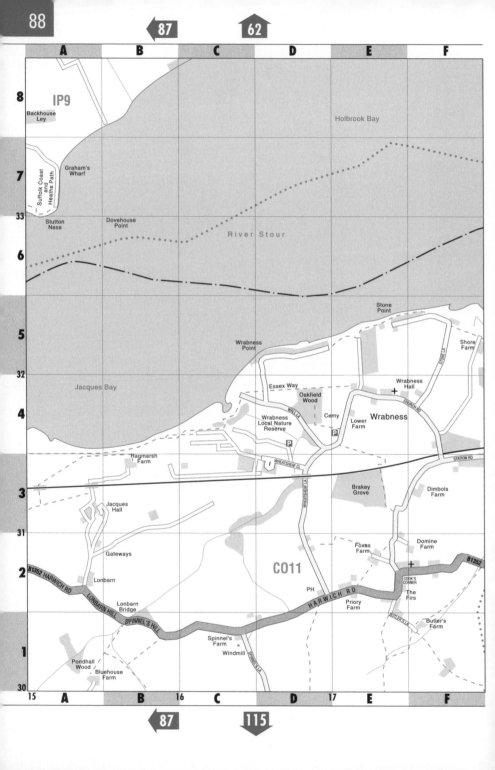

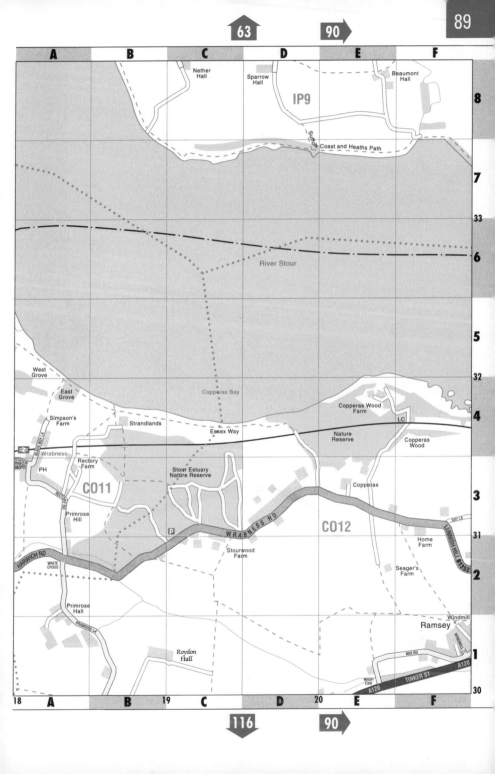

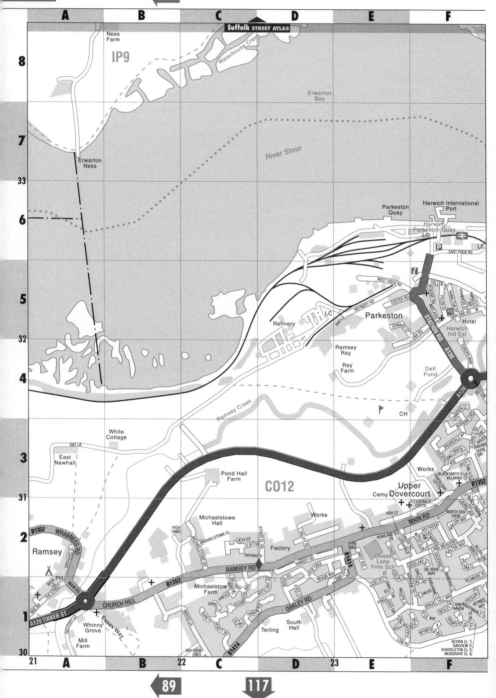

89

Suffolk STREET ATLAS

IP9

Ness Farm

Waterhouse Creek

Erwarton Bay

8

River Stour

7

33

Erwarton Ness

Parkeston Quay

Harwich International Port

6

Harwich Parkeston Quay LC

Parkeston Quay LC

P

EAST DOCK RD LC

WEST DOCK RD

COLLER RD

i

5

Refinery

LC

REFINERY RD

WAY LA

FOSTER RD

Parkeston

STATION RD

Hotel

Harwich Ind Est

A136

32

Ramsey Ray

Ray Farm

Delf Pond

4

Ramsey Creek

CH

A120

White Cottage

RAY LA

3

East Newhall

Pond Hall Farm

CO12

Works

Upper Dovercourt

Cemy

B1352

31

FITZGERALD COTTS

Michaelstowe Hall

Works

ASH CT

MAIN RD

NORTH SEA VIEW

B1352 WRABNESS RD

HIGH OAKS

MICHAELSTOWE CL

DEVY CT

CLAYTON

RAYHAVEN

Factory

RAMSEY RD

2

Ramsey

PH

MAIN RD

B1352

Michaelstow Farm

RAMSEY RD

OAKLEY RD

Chase Lane Prim Sch

B1414

1

A120 TINKER ST

CHURCH HILL

Essex Way

Whinny Grove

Michaelstowe

South Hall

Terling

ACORN CL 1
OAKVIEW 2
SHACKLETON CL 3
MUSGRAVE CL 4

Mill Farm

30

21   A   B   22   C   D   23   E   F

89

117

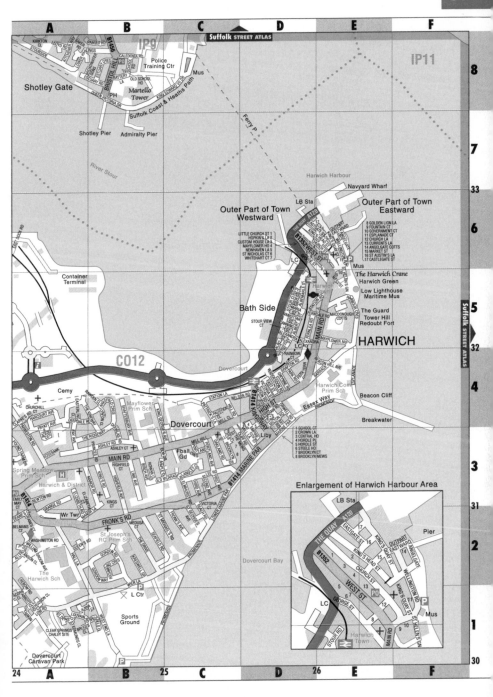

Suffolk STREET ATLAS

IP9

IP11

Shotley Gate

Martello Tower

Police Training Ctr

Mus

Shotley Pier   Admiralty Pier

Suffolk Coast & Heaths Path

River Stour

Ferry P

Harwich Harbour

Navyard Wharf

LB Sta

Outer Part of Town Westward

Outer Part of Town Eastward

8 GOLDEN LION LA
9 FOUNTAIN CT
10 GOVERNMENT CT
11 ESPLANADE CT
12 CHURCH LA
13 CURRENTS LA
14 ANGELGATE COTTS
15 MARKET ST
16 ST AUSTIN'S LA
17 CASTLEGATE ST

LITTLE CHURCH ST 1
HOPKIN LA 2
CUSTOM HOUSE LA 3
MAYFLOWER HO 4
NEWHAVEN LA 5
ST NICHOLAS LA 6
WHITEHART CT 7

Container Terminal

Mus

The Harwich Crane
Harwich Green

Low Lighthouse
Maritime Mus

Bath Side

STOUR VIEW CT

The Guard
Tower Hill
Redoubt Fort

HARWICH

Dovercourt

Cemy

Mayflower Prim Sch

Dovercourt

Harwich Com Prim Sch

Beacon Cliff

Essex Way

Breakwater

Spring Meadow Prim Sch

Harwich & District

Liby

1 SCHOOL LA
2 CROWN LA
3 CENTRAL RD
4 HORDLE PL
5 HORDLE ST
6 STEELE HO
7 BROOKLYN CT
8 BROOKLYN MEWS

Fball Gd

MAIN RD

Wr Twr

FRONK'S RD

St Joseph's RC Prim Sch

Enlargement of Harwich Harbour Area

LB Sta

THE QUAY

EASTGATE ST

Pier

KING'S HEAD ST

OUTPART EASTWARD

ANGELGATE

WELLINGTON RD

KING'S QUAY ST

CHURCH ST

WEST ST

LC

GEORGE ST

STOUR RD

Harwich Town

PO

Mus

MAIN RD

ST HELEN'S LN

The Harwich Sch

Dovercourt Bay

L Ctr

Sports Ground

Dovercourt Caravan Park

CO12

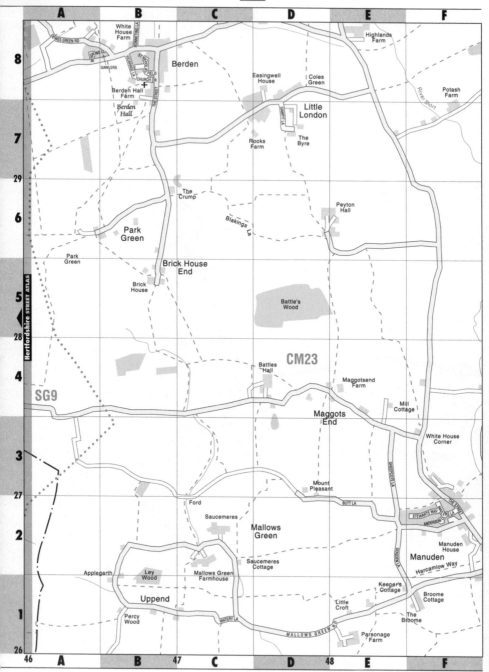

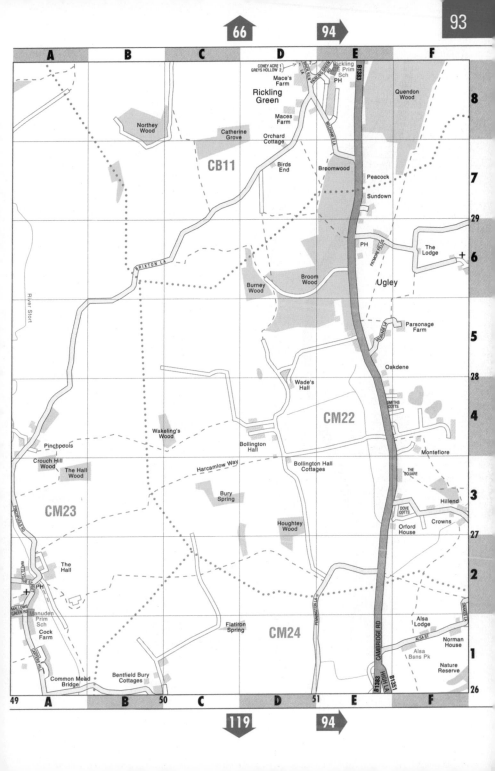

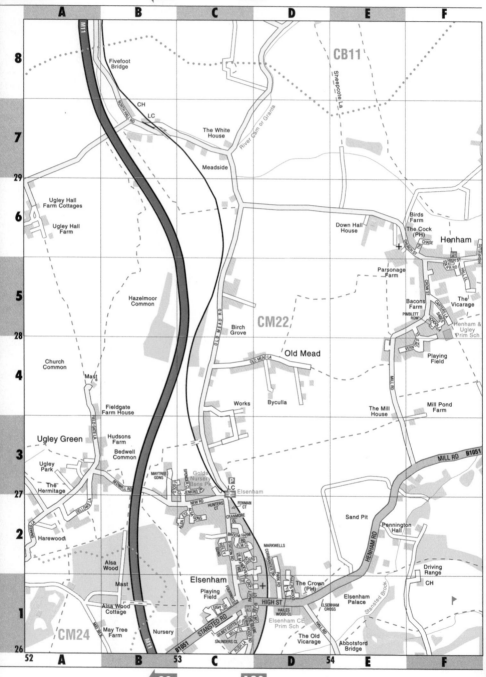

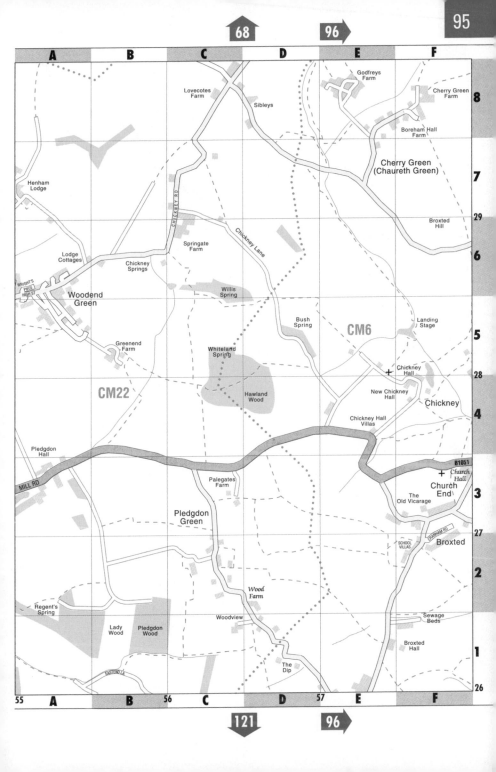

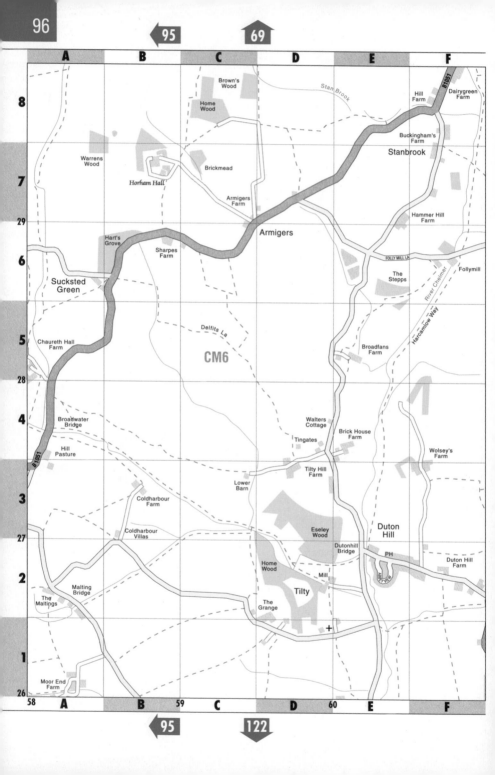

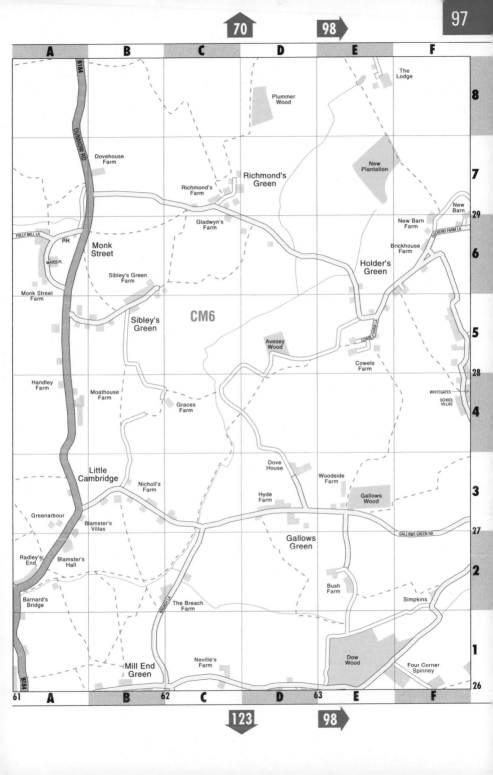

97
71

CM7

B1057
DUNMOW RD

Markswood Farm

Charity Farm

The Grove

Oxen End

Duck End Farm

Bustard Green Lane

Bustard Green

Fann's Farm

Coft Hall

Frenches Farm

Porridge Hall

Daisley Brook

Brazenhead Farm

DAISLEY RD

Templars

CM6

Page's Farm

Tolladay's Farm

Pratt's Farm

LUBBERHEDGES LA

Lindsell

Church End

GALLOWS GREEN RD

LINDSELL LA

Goland's Bridge

Poplar Farm

Carter's Farm

Hill Farm

Stebbing Brook

Holt's Farm

Lashley Hall

Duck End

B1057

Drakeswell

97
124

64 65 66

26 27 28 29
1 2 3 4 5 6 7 8

A B C D E F

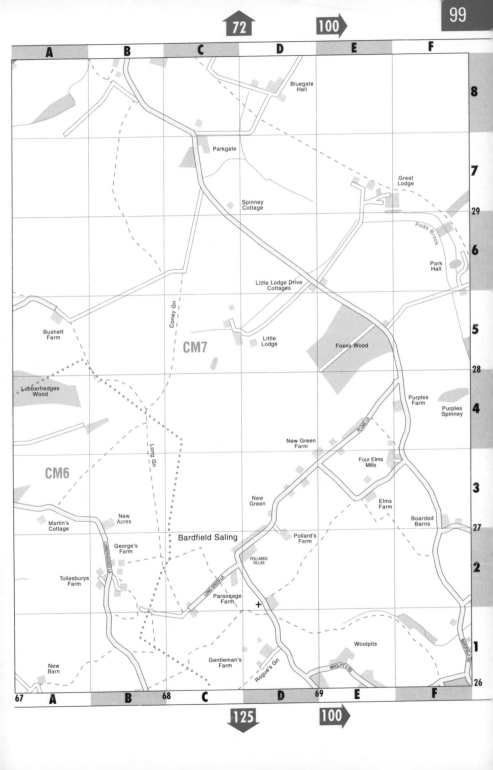

A B C D E F

8

Bluegate
Hall

Parkgate

7

Great
Lodge

Spinney
Cottage

29

Pods Brook

6

Park
Hall

Little Lodge Drive
Cottages

Bushett
Farm

Coney Gn

CM7

Little
Lodge

Foxes Wood

5

28

Lubberhedges
Wood

Purples
Farm

Purples
Spinney

4

New Green
Farm

PLUMS LA

Long Gn

CM6

Four Elms
Mills

3

New
Green

Martin's
Cottage

New
Acres

Elms
Farm

Boarded
Barns

George's
Farm

Bardfield Saling

Pollard's
Farm

27

LUBBERHEDGES LA

POLLARDS
VILLAS

2

Tollesburys
Farm

LONG GREEN LA

Parsonage
Farm

+

Woolpits

BARDFIELD RD

1

New
Barn

Gentleman's
Farm

Rogue's Gn

WOOLPITS RD

26

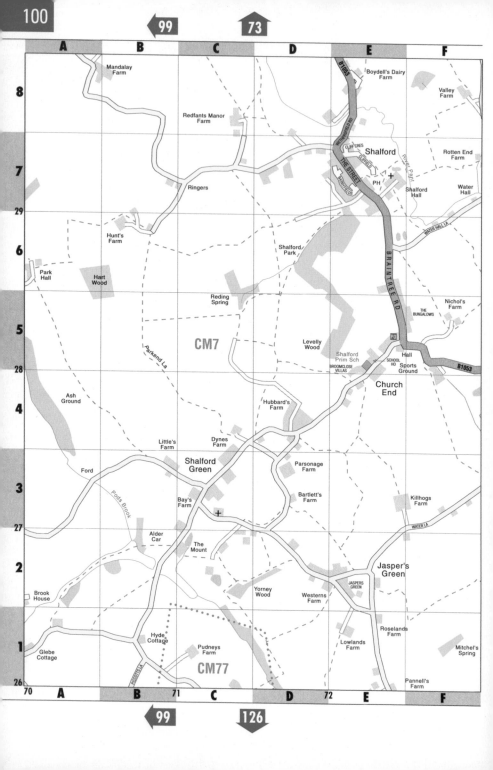

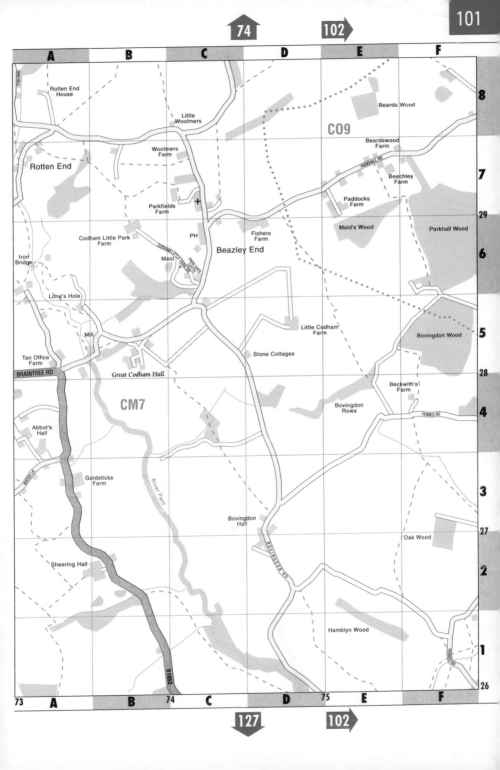

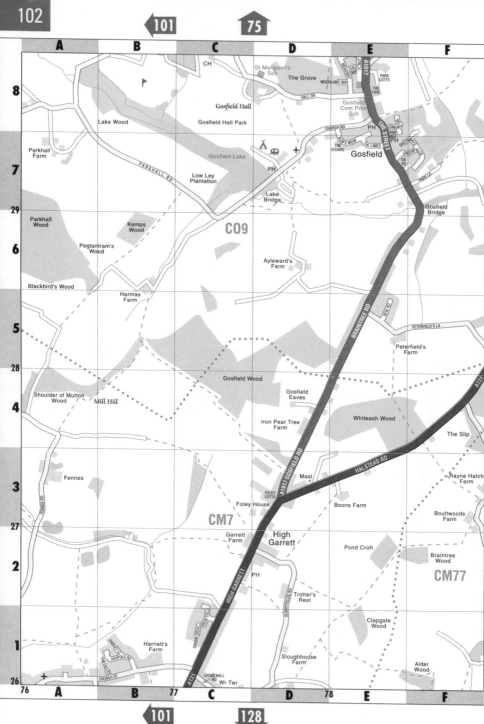

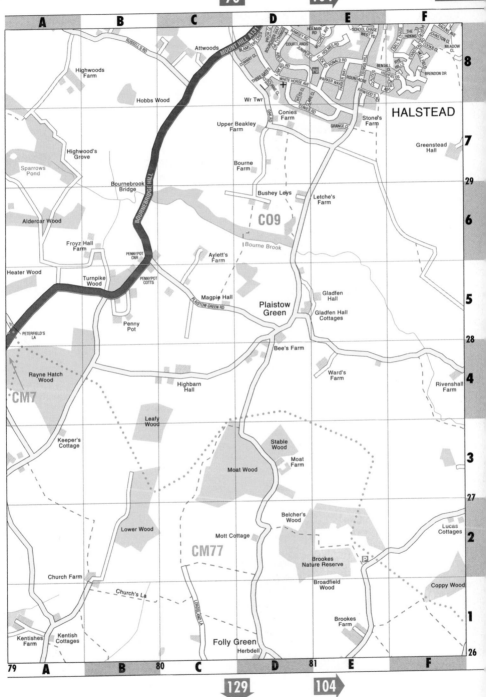

A B C D E F

8

7

29

6

5

28

4

3

27

2

1

26

A B C D E F

79 80 81

HALSTEAD

Attwoods
MOUNT HILL A131
Highwoods Farm
RUSSELL'S RD
Hobbs Wood
White Horse Ave
Wr Twr
Upper Beakley Farm
Conies Farm
Stone's Farm
Greenstead Hall
Highwood's Grove
Sparrows Pond
Bournebrook Bridge
Bourne Farm
Aldercar Wood
Bushey Leys
Letche's Farm
CO9
Bourne Brook
Froyz Hall Farm
PENNYPOT CNR
Aylett's Farm
BOURNEBRIDGE HILL
Heater Wood
Turnpike Wood
PENNYPOT COTTS
Magpie Hall
PLAISTOW GREEN RD
Plaistow Green
Gladfen Hall
Gladfen Hall Cottages
Penny Pot
PETERFIELD'S LA
Bee's Farm
Rayne Hatch Wood
CM7
Highbarn Hall
Ward's Farm
Rivenshall Farm
Leafy Wood
Keeper's Cottage
Stable Wood
Moat Farm
Moat Wood
Belcher's Wood
Lucas Cottages
Lower Wood
Mott Cottage
CM77
LODGE AND LA
Brookes Nature Reserve
Broadfield Wood
Coppy Wood
Church Farm
Church's La
Brookes Farm
Kentishes Farm
Kentish Cottages
Folly Green
Herbdell

129
104

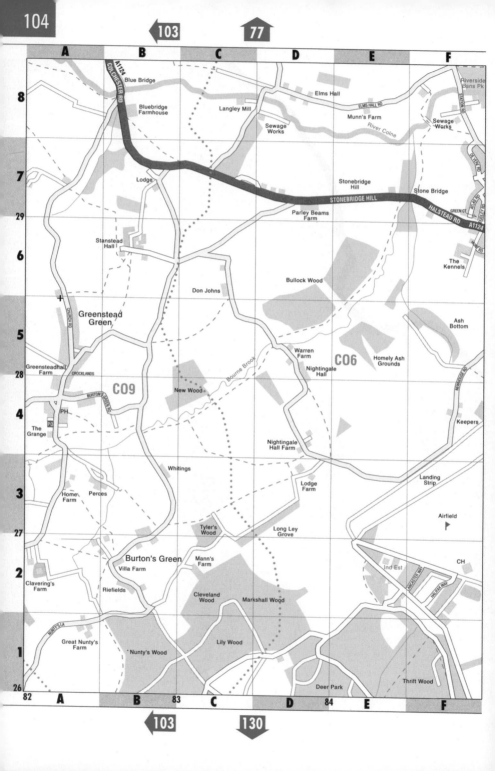

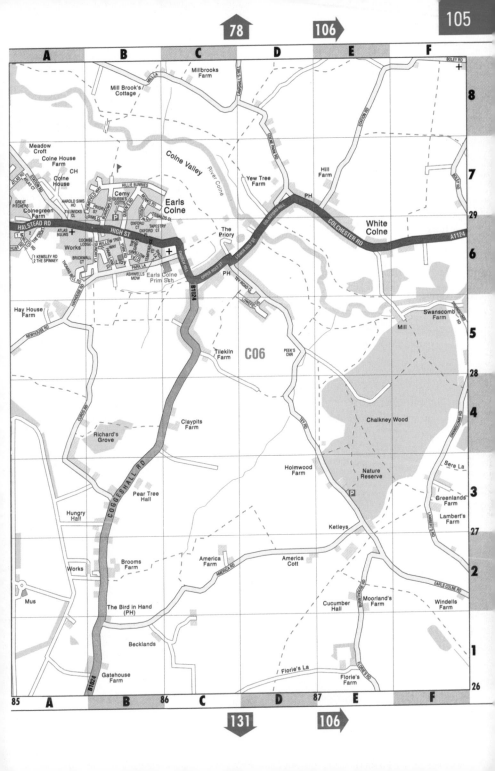

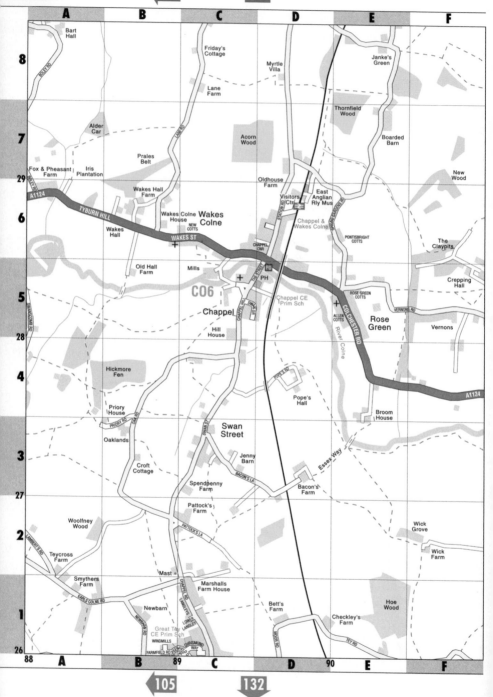

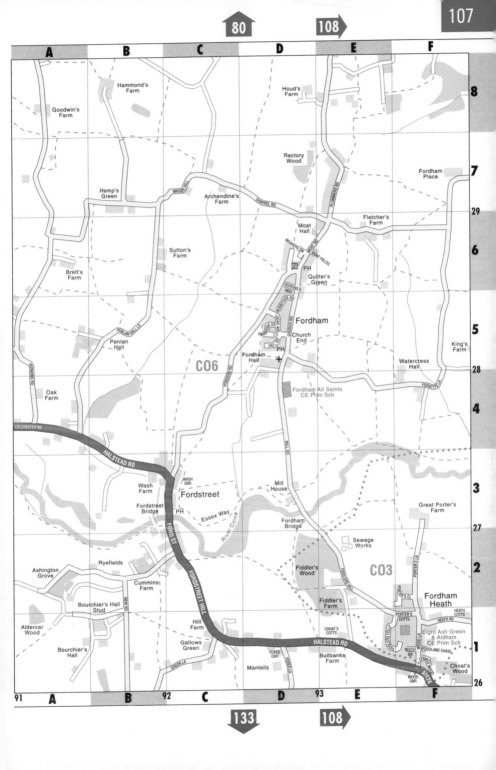

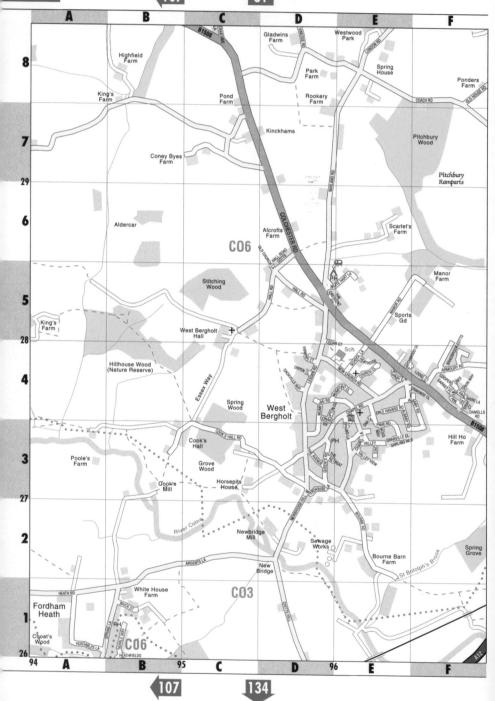

A **B** **C** **D** **E** **F**

B1508

8

Highfield Farm

Gladwins Farm

Westwood Park

Spring House

Ponders Farm

King's Farm

Pond Farm

Park Farm

Rookery Farm

COACH RD

7

Kinckhams

Pitchbury Wood

29

Coney Byes Farm

Pitchbury Ramparts

6

Aldercar

Alcrofts Farm

Scarlet's Farm

CO6

COLCHESTER RD

PH

Manor Farm

5

Stitching Wood

WHITE HART LA

Sports Gd

28

West Bergholt Hall

Sch

CEDAR CT

4

Hillhouse Wood (Nature Reserve)

Spring Wood

West Bergholt

ARMOURY RD

DANIELLS HO

B1508

Essex Way

3

Poole's Farm

Cook's Hall

COOK'S HALL RD

Grove Wood

PH

Hill Ho Farm

27

Cook's Mill

Horsepits House

2

River Colne

Newbridge Mill

Sewage Works

Bourne Barn Farm

St Botolph's Brook

Spring Grove

ARGENTS LA

New Bridge

CO3

HEATH RD

White House Farm

1

Fordham Heath

PH

CO6

A12

Choat's Wood

HUXTABLES LA

HEATHFIELDS

26

94   **A**   **B**   95   **C**   **D**   96   **E**   **F**

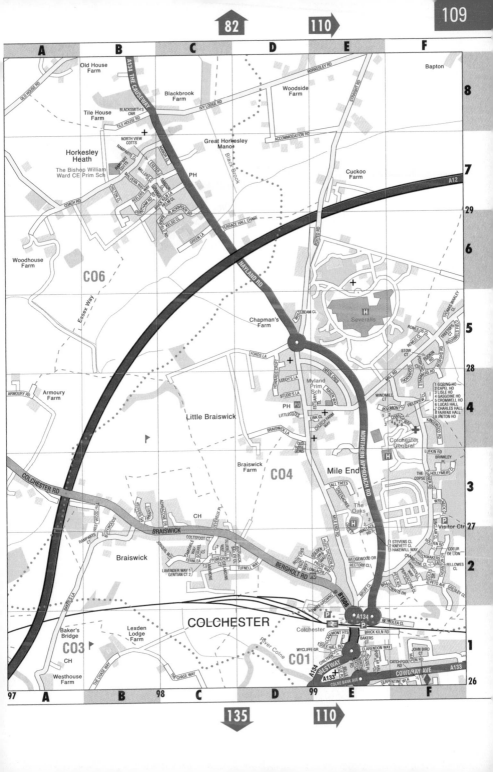

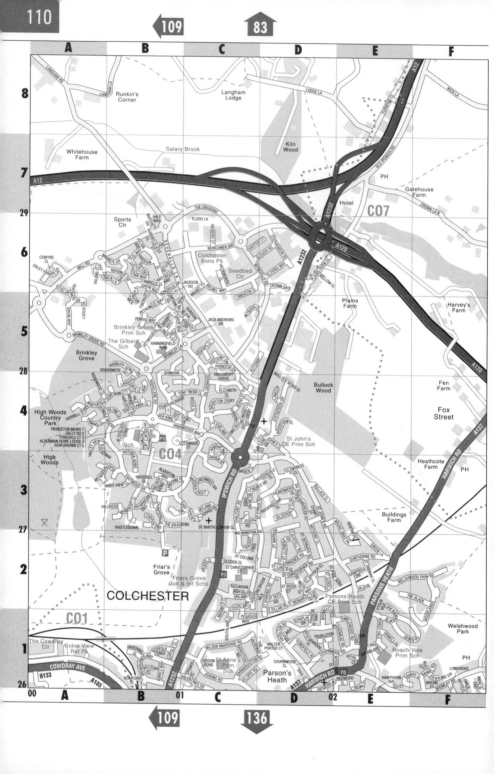

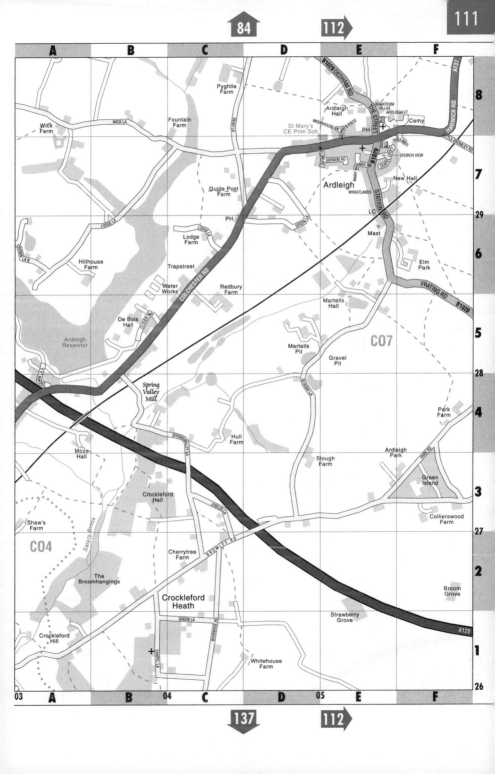

A B C D E F

8

7

29

6

5

28

4

3

27

2

1

26

Home Farm
POND FARM LA
Badliss Hall
FT KNODISHALL
Hungerdowns
Wormseywood Farm
BACK FARM LA
Riddlesdale Farm
GRANGE RD
BARN LA
CO11
Bounds Farm
LITTLE BROMLEY RD
Mast
Badley Hall
Morrow Lane Farm
MORROW LA
Norman's Farm
Jenning's Farm
ARDLEIGH RD
Waterhouse Farm
Old Shields Farm
WATERHOUSE LA
Cattsgreen Farm
Vinces Farm
BACK RD
Chancery Farm
NICHOLS CNR
FRATING RD
B1029
Burnt Heath Cottages
BARN RD
Burnt Heath
MILL LA
BRAZE RD
ARDLEIGH RD
Lilley's Farm
KEYS LA
CARRINGTONS RD
Manning Grove
MERSEA RD
PH
Bromley Cross
BROMLEY CROSS
Carringtons Farm
LITTLE BROMLEY RD
BROXEY RD
COLCHESTER RD
Morants
Pond Farm
CO7
Newhouse
Blue Gate Farm
MOSLEMAN RD
Bromley Brook
Bush Farm
HALL RD
Seven Rivers Cheshire Home
HOCKLEY HILL RD
A120
Elmstead Hall
A120
St George's CE Prim Sch
BROOK ST
B1029
Great Bromley

06 A B 07 C D 08 E F

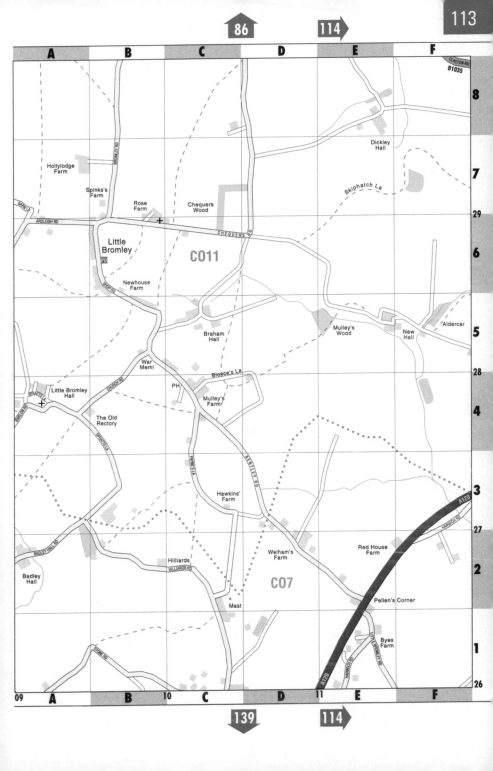

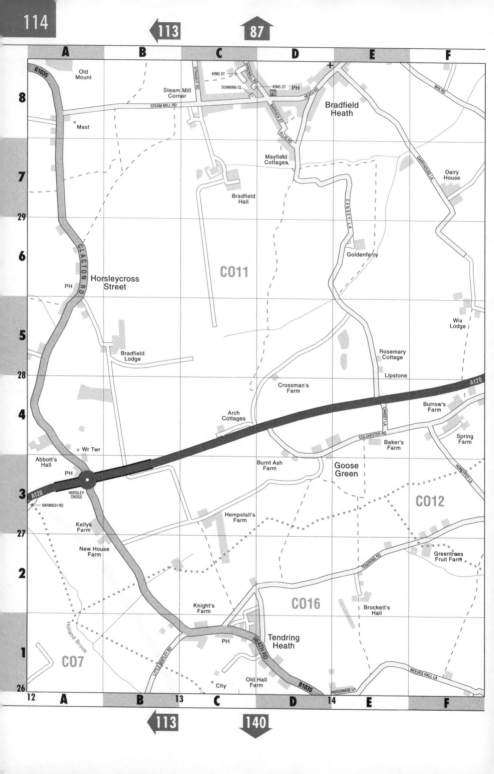

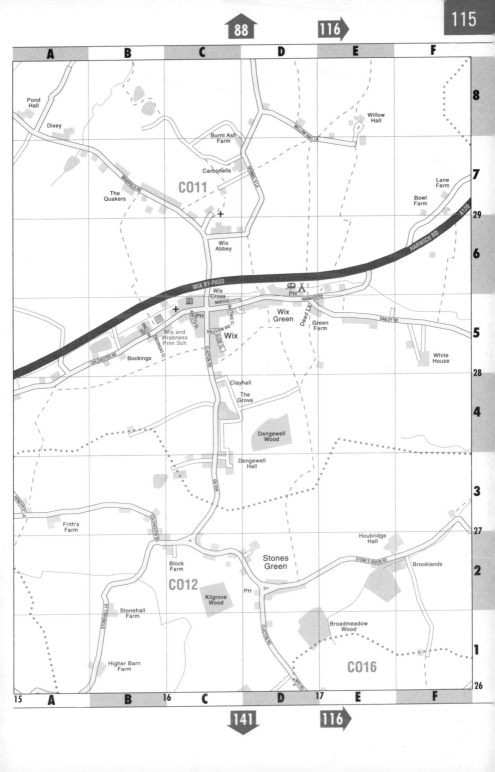

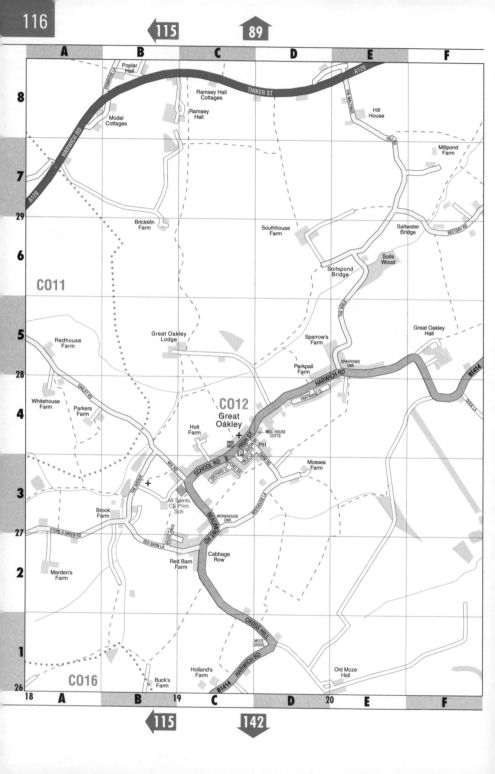

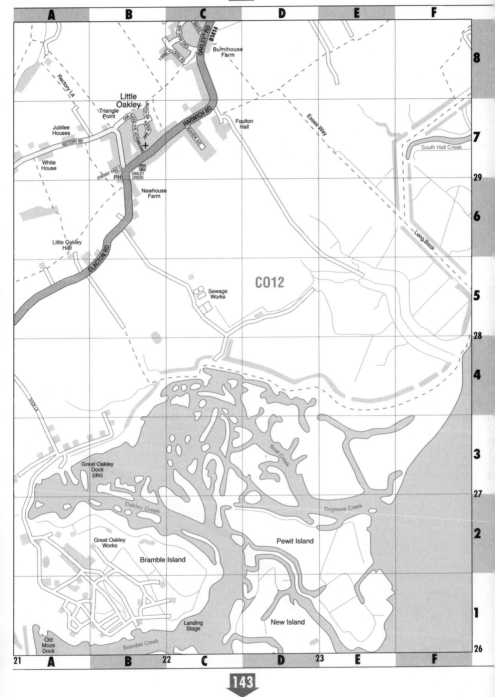

A B C D E F

8
7
29
6
5
28
4
3
27
2
1
26

CO12

Little
Oakley

Triangle
Point

Jubilee
Houses

White
House

Little Oakley
Hall

Factory La

RECTORY RD

CLACTON RD

DOCK LA

Burnthouse
Farm

HARWICH RD

Foulton
Hall

Newhouse
Farm

Essex Way

South Hall Creek

Long Bank

Sewage
Works

Boat Creek

Great Oakley
Dock
(dis)

Oakley Creek

Great Oakley
Works

Bramble Island

Dugmore Creek

Pewit Island

Landing
Stage

New Island

Old
Moze
Dock

Bramble Creek

OAKLEY RD

B1414

BAY VIEW CRES

LONG LODGE LN

RECTOR RD

OAK CLOSE THE HUTHWAITES

CHERRY TREE CL

BEACHEY AVE

PH
PO
OAKLEY
CROSS

21   22   23

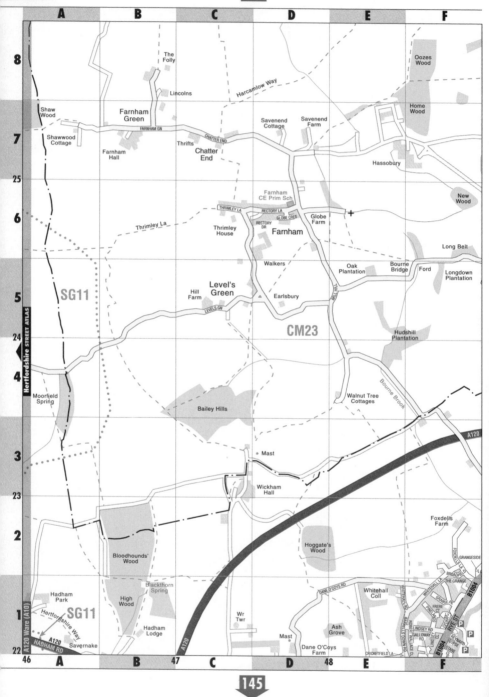

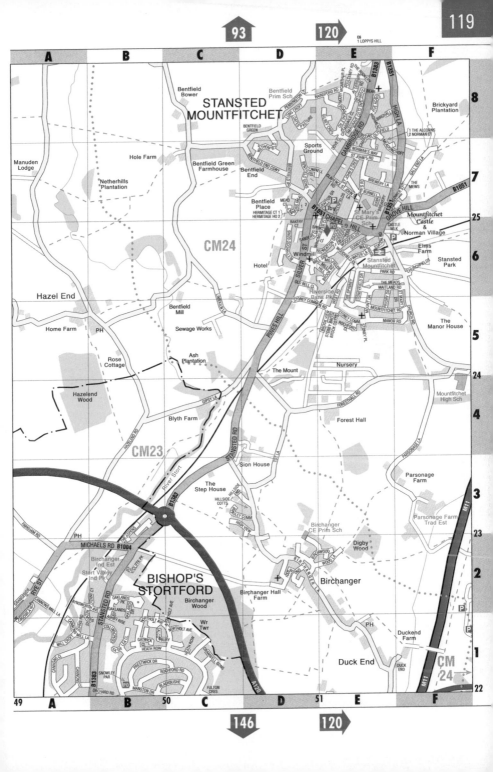

119 94

A B C D E F

8

Old Mill Farm
STANSTED RD B1051
MAIN WLK
M11
The Down Farm
Fuller's End
Elsenham Stud
MILL RD
CHURCH LA
Elsenham Hall
Park Wood

The Bungalow

7

The Lodge
B1051
Stansted House
Mill Wood
Long Plantation
Jubilee Cottage
Gaunt's End

CM22

25

Durrel's Wood
Wilkin's Plantation
Mott's Hall

6

Stansted Park
Tye Green Farm
Tye Green

THE GREEN RD

5

Stansted Hall
The Bourne
Barley Common
ELSENHAM RD
Mast

24

CHURCH RD
Burton Bower
PROCTORS RD

Cvn Pks
Burton Bury
Burton End
Warman's Farm
Highfields Lodge

4

PH
BELMER RD
SOUTH AVE
Control Tower

CM24
Monks Farm

3

Burylodge Cottages
BURY LODGE LA
PINKEY RD
THIRTIETH ST

23

Little Bury Lodge Farm
ELEVENTH AVE
NINTH AVE
EIGHTH AVE
SEVENTH AVE
TENTH AVE
FIFTH AVE
Control Tower
Works
LONG BORDER RD
TAYLORS END RD
BASSINGBOURN RD

2

Bury Lodge
THIRD AVE
SECOND AVE
P
P
P
JOHN LA
London Stansted Airport

1

P
Hotel
ROUND COPPICE RD

22

52 A B 53 C D 54 E F

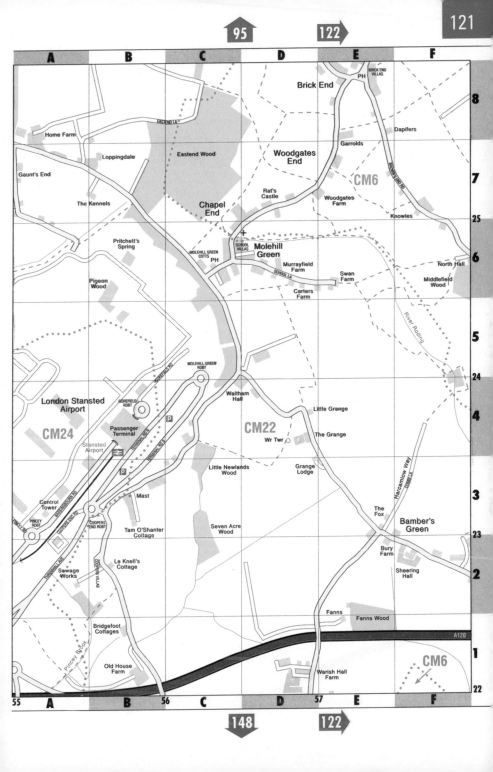

121
96

A **B** **C** **D** **E** **F**

8

Goodfellows

Broadmead

Little Bullen's

Muscombs

REBECCA MEWS

THE ORCHARD

PH

7

Foxholes

Furrows

Great Easton

South
Hill

Croys
Grange

Cox Hill

WATER LA

25

Cherith
House

Sewage
Works

The Grove

King's Farm
House

The Willows

6

BROWN'S END RD

Philipland
Wood

Broxted
Hill

Harcommon Way

CM6

The
Gorse

Perryfields

Easton
Farm

Flemings Hill
Farm

Round
House

The Lays

Middlefield
Wood

Perryfield
Ponds

Little
Easton

5

Brookend

Brookend
Lodge

Broxted Common
Wood

The Old
Laundry

WARWICK
CL

OLD FYE LA

BUTCHERS
PASTURE

24

Easton Lodge

MANOR RD

MAYNARDS
VILLAS

PH

4

Gdns

Easton
Glebe

Great Pond

Little Easton
Farm

Horse Pond

PARK RD

3

River Roding

23

Lower Bamber's Green

CM22

2

The Hoppit

Washlands

White
House

Lodge

A120

1

Frogs Hall
Farm

Frog
Hall

Stone Hall

High Wood

22

A120

58 **A** **B** 59 **C** **D** 60 **E** **F**

121
149

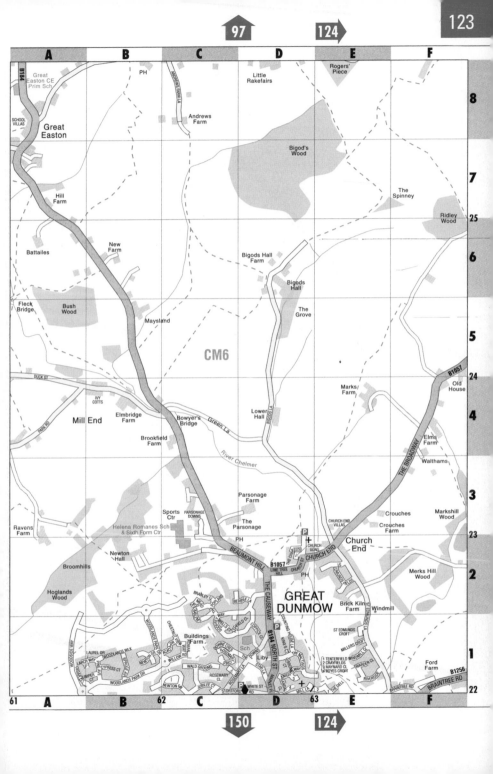

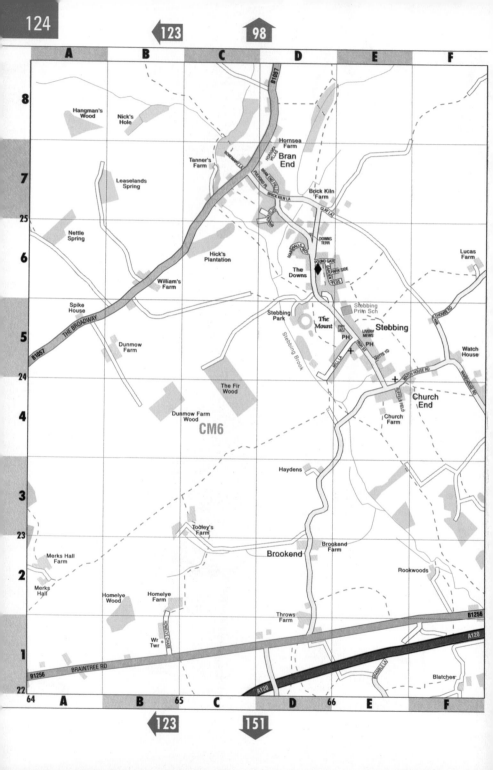

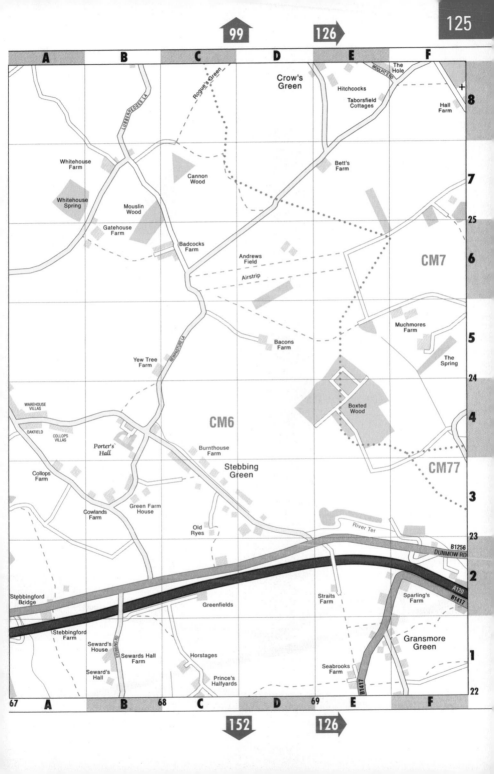

A B C D E F

The Hole
Crow's Green
Hitchcocks
Taborsfield Cottages
Hall Farm
8
WOOLPITS RD

Whitehouse Farm
Cannon Wood
Bett's Farm
7
Whitehouse Spring
Mouslin Wood
25
Gatehouse Farm
Badcocks Farm
Andrews Field
CM7
6
Airstrip

Muchmores Farm
5
Yew Tree Farm
Bacons Farm
The Spring
24
WAREHOUSE VILLAS
Boxted Wood
4
OAKFIELD
COLLOPS VILLAS
CM6
CM77
Porter's Hall
Burnthouse Farm
Stebbing Green
3
Collops Farm
Green Farm House
Cowlands Farm
Old Ryes
River Ter
23
B1256
DUNMOW RD
Stebbingford Bridge
Greenfields
Straits Farm
Sparling's Farm
A120
2
Stebbingford Farm
B1417
Seward's House
Sewards Hall Farm
Horstages
Gransmore Green
1
STEBBING RD
Seward's Hall
Prince's Halfyards
Seabrooks Farm
B1417
22

67 A B 68 C D 69 E F

125
100

A   B   C   D   E   F

8

Saling Hall Gardens
Great Saling
GROVE VILLAS
PO
Chapel Hill
Cold Hall Farm
Ivy Hall
KYNASTON RD

PH
THE MEWS
Piccotts Farm
PICCOTTS LA.
Kynaston's Farm

7

VICARAGE LA.
Saling Grove
CM7
HALL RD

25

Mount's Farm

New Spinney
Lightwaters Farm
Perry Childs Farm

6

CM7
Jubilee Spinney
Park's Farm

Onchor's Farm

5

Golden Grove
Old Hall
Pods Brook

24

Rumley Wood

4

Blackbush Wood
Moor's Farm
Pound Farm
Pound Farmhouse
Gould's Farm

3

Blake House Farm
Craft Ctr
Moor's Spinney
MOORS LA.
CM77
SHALFORD RD
Duckend Green

Rayne Prim Sch
BLYTH'S WAY

23

PH
B1256
Blake End
B1417
DUNMOW RD
ROSS LA.
Rayne
Havering's Farm
BRUNWINS
SMITH'S
PHILIP'S RD
LIPS RD

2

A120
B1417
Broadfield Farm
THE STREET
B1256
HANCE LA.
VAUGHAN
NEW RD
LIGHT NEW ROAD
PHILLIPS
WARNER'S CL
KIDDER RD

1

CM6
Hazelmere Farm
DUNMOW RD
Gatewoods Farm
STATION RD
SYMMONS CL
Little Paddocks
Fairy Hall

22

Graunt Courts
Sorrell's Farm
DRAPERS CHASE
HALL LA.
A120
DRUD

70   A   B   71   C   D   72   E   F

125
153

Oxney Wood

Cow Wood

Great Priory Farm

Little Priory Farm

Choats Farm Stables

River Pant

B1053

Bocking Churchstreet

ST NICHOLAS GDNS 1
CANTERBURY GRANGE 2
HANOVER CT 3
KINGSBRIDGE CL 4

BOVINGDON RD

SPENCER SQ

Schs

PH

Panfield

ST MARY CL

PH

CHURCH END

HALL RD

The Old Deanery

King's Bridge

THE CHASE

COUNCIL BGLWS

Panfield Hall

Panfield Farm

Towerlands L Ctr

CHARTWELL CL

DEANERY HILL

DEAN
ROGERS PL

Cemy

River Blackwater

CHURCH LA

Matthew's Farm

Towerlands Equestrian Ctr

BLENHEIM CL
BLAXILL CL
DOVER CL
ROMNEY CL
WINSTON
HYTHE
DEAL CL
CHURCHILL
STANSTED
WORDSWORTH RD
GAUDEN RD

Polly's Hill
OAST HO
SPINNEY

Park Farm

CM7

Panfield Wood

Mast

Braintree Ent Ctr

Cooper Pk

FLANDERS CL

BRAINTREE

CLAVERING RD
MELLING RD
CAMPS

MAYSENT AVE
BEEDE

DUKES RD

Bocking

EAGLE LA
FAGGOT YD

B1053

TENTER
ARCHS

PILGRIM

SIX BELLS
CT

WOODPACK
LA
FRIARS
WILLIAMS LA

24

Tabor High Sch

CRITTALL DR

Clifford Ct

L Ctr

John Bunyan Jun & Inf Schs

ALEXANDER
LANCASTER WAY
ARNHEM DR
MEADOWSIDE
RX

1 VALENTINE CT
2 DALE HO

DANA
RD

Bocking
PL

Sewage Works

Air Strip

WICKS CL

WARNER DR

Sch

Playing Field

ELM BGLWS

BUNYAN RD

WEAVERS

ST PETER'S
ROSEMARY

ST PETER'S RD

P

Rayne Lodge

SWINBOURNE DR

Springwood Ind Est

BRADBURY DR

Springwood Ct

St Michael's

CONSTABLE RD
GODRIC

H

COGGESHALL RD

B1256

Mus

3

Rayne Hall

CM77

Rayne Hall Farm

CLAP Bridge

BIRCH CL
GILDA TERR

RAYNE RD

THE BRAMBLES
COLLEGE RD

BANK
SCHOOL
PL

MANOR ST

TH Lib

VICTORIA
Ct

23

THE STREET

GORE TERR

Hall

NEW RD

Nursery

Broomhills Ind Est

POD'S BROOK RD

River Brain

Flitch Way

MAPLE
VAUXHALL DR
ACORN

Sch

CLARE RD

William Julien Courtauld

NEW ST

H

THE KENTINGS

ST MICHAEL'S RD
COATES AVE

BODSWORTHY RD

NEWLAND VIEW

BOURNE DL

ONE DL
Mus

Hoppit Bridge

P

2

FAIRY HALL LA

Cemy

WHITETHROATS

MARSHALLS RD

BECK RD

1 COPPER CT
2 GRAYLING CL
3 MEADOW BROWN CT

RIFLE HILL

Marsh Farm

Rifle Hill Works

1

Wenas Farm

Naylinghurst

GLEEMBOROUGH LA

A120

Marshalls Park

P

Bridge Farm

TORTOISESHELL RD
COMMA CL

HOPPIT RD

BUCKWOODS
RD
CHALLIS

22

F1
1 HILLSIDE TERR
2 HILLSIDE HO
3 EDISON CL
4 NEWTON CL
5 DARWIN CL
6 WALL CT
7 FLEMING CL
8 GATEKEEPER CL

F2
1 ST MICHAEL'S LA
2 RUE DE JEUNES
3 THE BRAINTREE FOYER
4 ST MICHAEL'S CT
5 MAZERS CL
6 CHELSEA MEWS
7 COLLINS CL
8 TOM DAVIES HO
9 JAYMAR CT

10 STRUDWICK CL
11 CLAIRMONT CL

F3
1 CHERRY BGLWS
2 WRIGHT CT
3 ST LAWRENCE CT
4 DRURY LA
5 LEATHER LA
6 LITTLE SQ
7 GEORGE YD

8 SANDPIT LA
9 GREAT SQ
10 MARKET ST
11 MARKET PL
12 TOFTS WLK

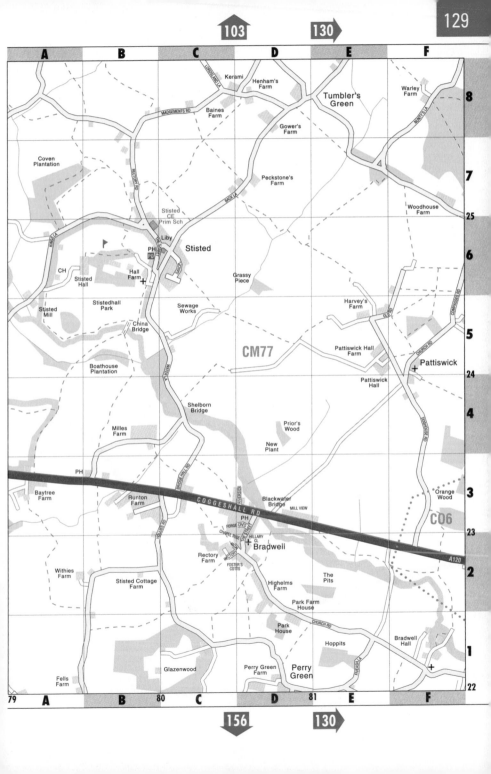

Kerami

Henham's Farm

Tumbler's Green

Warley Farm

MADGEMENTS RD

Baines Farm

Gower's Farm

Coven Plantation

Peckstone's Farm

Woodhouse Farm

BACK LA

Stisted CE Prim Sch

Liby

Stisted

PH PO

CH

Stisted Hall

Hall Farm

Grassy Piece

Harvey's Farm

Pattiswick

Stistedhall Park

Sewage Works

Stisted Mill

China Bridge

CM77

Pattiswick Hall Farm

Pattiswick Hall

Boathouse Plantation

Shelborn Bridge

WATER LA

Milles Farm

Prior's Wood

New Plant

PH

Baytree Farm

Runton Farm

BRIDGE HALL RD

COGGESHALL RD

Blackwater Bridge

MILL VIEW

Orange Wood

CO6

PH

FORGE CRES

Withies Farm

Stisted Cottage Farm

HOLDENS RD

CHAPEL RISE

HILLARY CL

Bradwell

RECTORY RD

FOSTER'S COTTS

Rectory Farm

Highelms Farm

The Pits

Park Farm House

CHURCH RD

A120

Fells Farm

Glazenwood

Perry Green Farm

Park House

Perry Green

Hoppits

Bradwell Hall

THRIFT LA

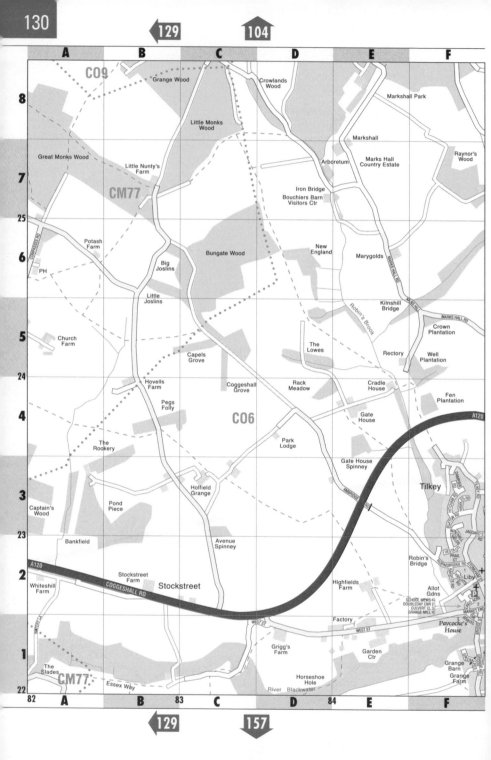

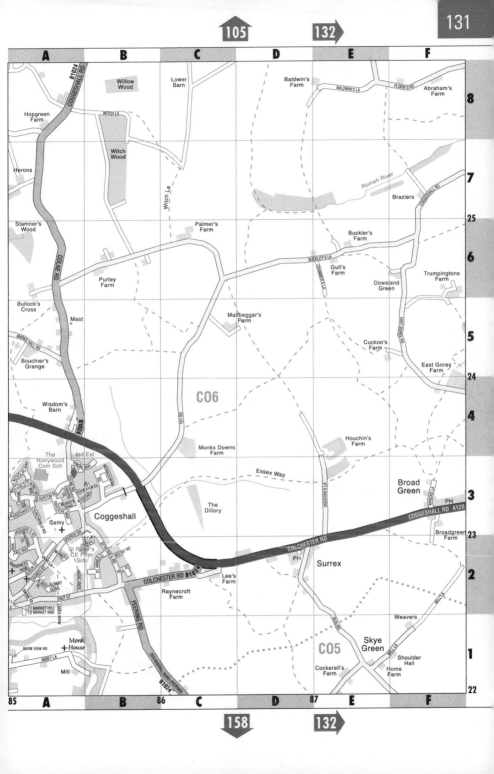

A **B** **C** **D** **E** **F**

FLORIE'S RD
Brookhouse
BROOKHOUSE RD
NEWBARN RD
HARVESTERS WAY
MOOR RD
Moor Farm
TEY RD

Great Tey

Hoe Farm

RECTORY RD

8

WINDMILLS
TAMBOUR CL 2
PH
Warrens Farm
NEW COTTS

Walcott's Farm

Walcott's Hall
Brick Kiln Cottage

COGGESHALL RD

Church House Farm

7

25

Chase Cottage

OLD ROAD

Tey Brook Piggeries

LC

6

Essex Way

Teybrook Farm

Little Tey House

Sparrow Grove

Little Tey House Farm

Stonefield Grove

5

24

East Gores

EAST GORES RD

Upp Hall Farm

Knave's Farm

Little Tey

CO6

GREAT TEY RD

Mott's Farm

Marks Tey

A120

4

Church Farm

Godbolt's Farm

MOTT'S LA

PH

BURY

3

Buxton Cotts

SALMON'S LA

SALMON'S CNR

Elm Farm

Honeylands Farm

COGGESHALL RD

NORMAN CL 1
ROXBOROUGH CL 2

1 KINGSBURY CL
2 STEELE CL

Wks

A120

CHURCH LA

ELM LA

St Andrew's CE Prim Sch

WILSON'S LA

LC

LONDON RD

A12

23

2

ELM LA

Hornigals

CO5

LONDON RD

A12

1

Damyon's Farm

22

A 88 **B** 89 **C** **D** 90 **E** **F**

133 108

| | A | B | C | D | E | F |

8 CO6

A1124

Newlands Farm

Eight Ash Green

PH

HALSTEAD RD

Chitts Hills LC

Chittshill Farm

Seven Arches Farm

River Coline

A12

Bridge Farm

Holmwood House Prep Sch

Maltings Farm House

A12

7 Hotel

Abbots Hall

1 COLUMBINE MEWS
2 SPRING SEDGE CL
3 DAWNFORD CT
4 DAWNFORD CL

COWSLIP CL

HALSTEAD RD

Lexden Springs Sch

A133

LEXDEN MEWS

25 A12

ESSEX YEOMANRY WAY

SWEET BRIAR RD

TOLLGATE

LONDON RD

LEXDEN RD A1124

VICTORIA

Beacon End

BADGERS HOLT

Lexden Prim Sch

SHERIDAN WLK

WORDSWORTH RD

6 Wyvern Farm

TOLLGATE RDBT A112A

B1408

TOLLGATE CT

Liby

BEACON END

MAYFLOWER

NEW

CHARLES

Stanway Prim Sch

COBBLE ROW

DE BURGH RD

1 STIRRUP MEWS
2 SADDLE MEWS

GRYMES DYKE

Home Farm Prim Sch

HUNTERS

5 B1408

LONDON RD

Westside Ctr

CO3

Stanway

NURSERY CL

ELMWOOD

The Heath Sch

St Teresa's RC Prim Sch

MEADOW VIEW

CLAIRMONT RD

HEATH RD

24 Oldhouse Farm

PARTRIDGE WAY

The Stanway Sch

NEW FARM LODGE

WASHINGTON

BARLEY WAY

DALE WAY

4 CHURCH LA

ROBIN

BAILEY DALE

BLACKBERRY RD

JUNIPER CT

Stanway Fiveways Prim Sch

Peartree Bsns Ctr

Jayrest Ctr

DUGARD AVE

MARSDEN

CARSHALTON END

3 Tye Grove

Sand & Gravel Pit

Five Ways

PEARTREE RD

Stanway Green

GRYME S DYKE WAY

JAMES CARTER RD

Mast

THE BRAMBLES

23 Bellhouse Farm

Furze Hill

B1022

Brickwall Farm

SPUR END RD

P

BARBOUR GDNS

2 Sand & Gravel Pit

Sand & Gravel Pit

MALDON RD

Cheshunt Field

1 Hanging Wood

CO6

Warren Plantation

CO2

22 Gol Grove

B1022

Colchester Zoo

Stanway Hall Farm

Butcher's Wood

| 94 | A | | B | 95 | C | | D | 96 | E | | F |

133 161

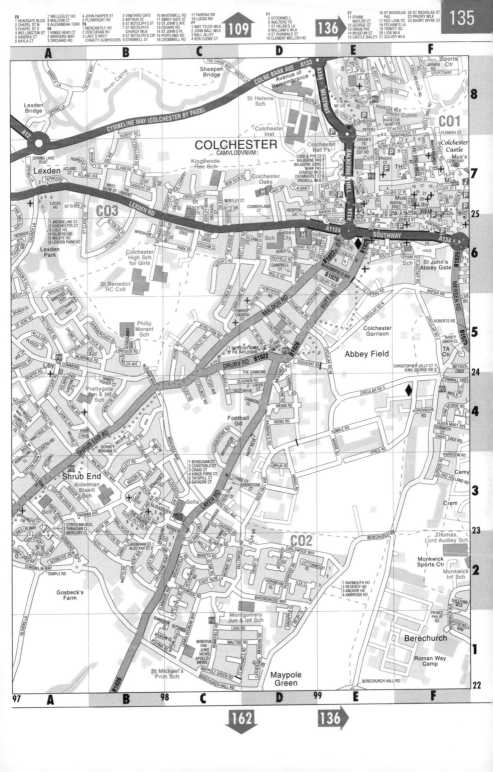

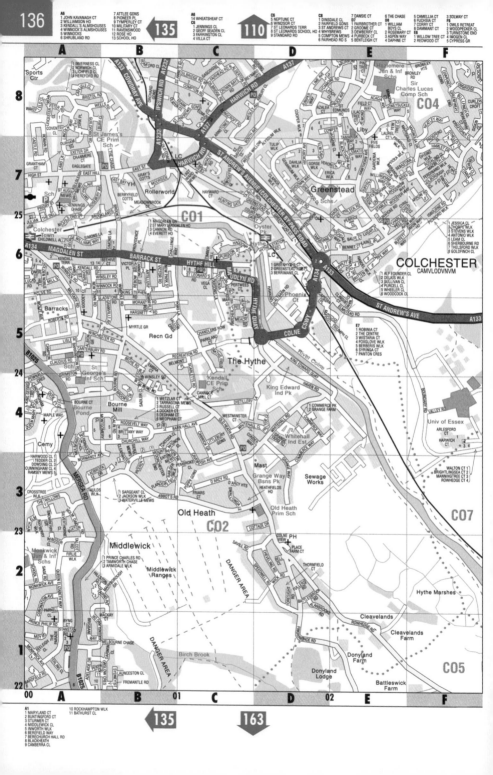

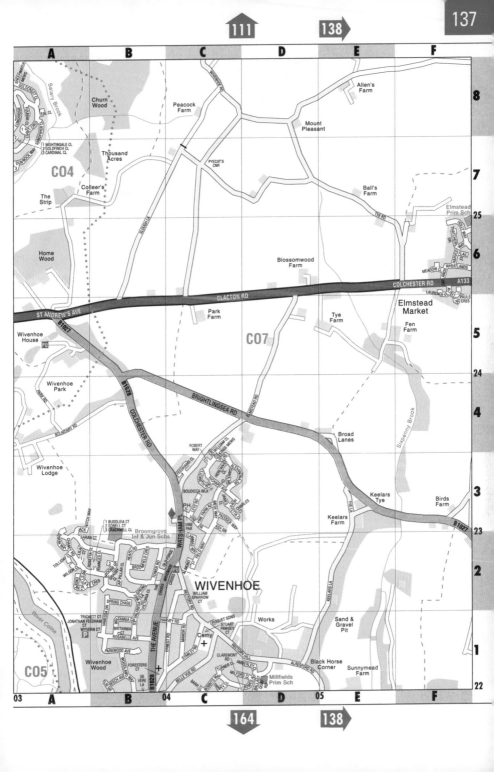

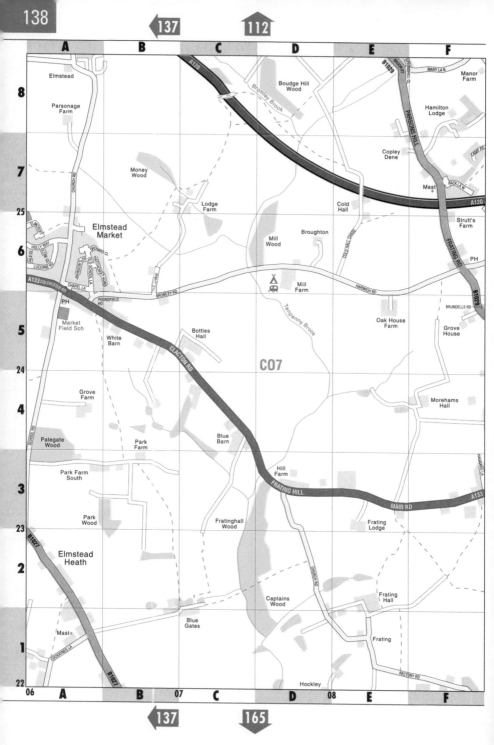

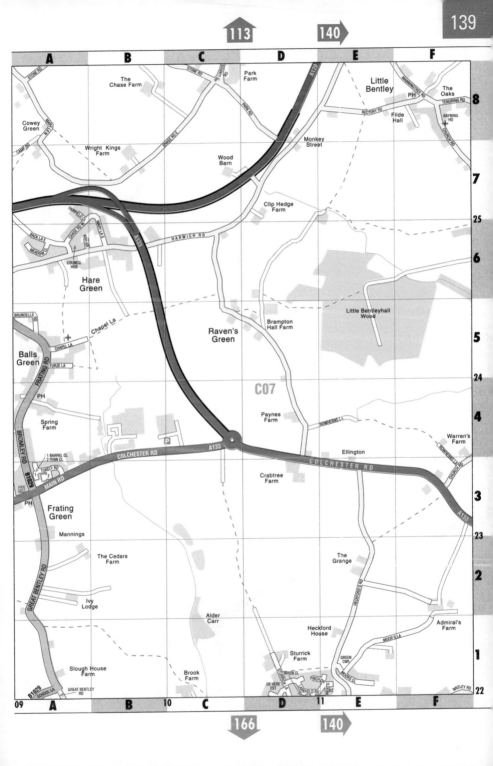

113
140

166
140

A B C D E F

8
25
7
6
5
24
4
3
23
2
1
22

09 10

Little Bentley

The Chase Farm
Park Farm

The Oaks
PH
Filde Hall
BAYNING HO

Cowey Green
Monkey Street

Wright Kings Farm
Wood Barn

Clip Hedge Farm

HARWICH RD

Hare Green

Little Bentleyhall Wood

Chapel La
Brampton Hall Farm

Raven's Green

Balls Green

CHAPEL LA
FURZE LA

C07

FRATING RD

Spring Farm

Paynes Farm
ROWHEDGE LA

Warren's Farm

BROMLEY RD

1 BARREL CL
2 FENN CL

COLCHESTER RD
A133

Ellington

COLCHESTER RD

B1029
MAIN RD

Crabtree Farm

PH

Frating Green

A133

Mannings

The Cedars Farm

The Grange

GREAT BENTLEY RD

Ivy Lodge

Alder Carr

Heckford House

Admiral's Farm

MOOR'S LA

B1029
SCHOOL LA
GREAT BENTLEY RD

Slough House Farm

Brook Farm

Sturrick Farm

GREEN CNR
MOORS CL

DE VERE EST
WREN CL
FINCH CL
OXFIELD RD

WEELEY RD

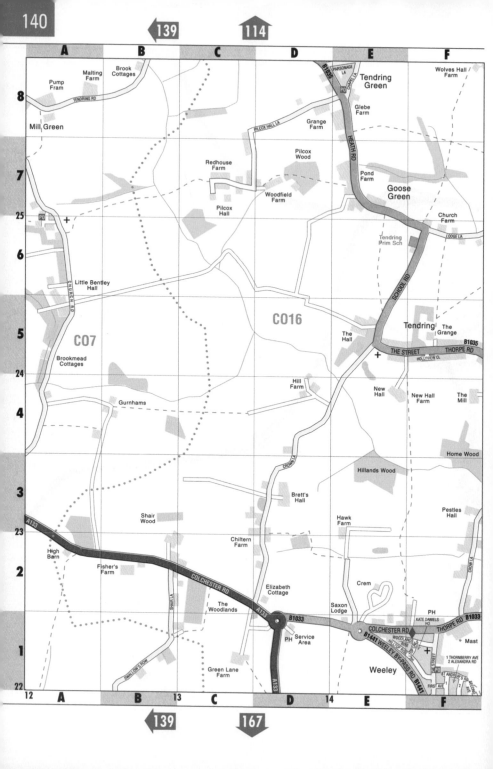

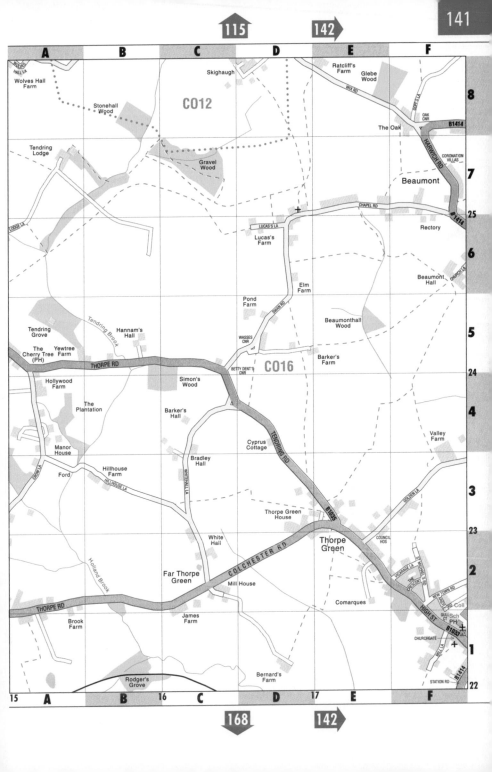

A B C D E F

8

Glebe Farm
Potland
Oldhouse Farm
HARWICH RD
B1414
The Horseshoes
New Moze Hall
CO12
Maze Creek

7

25
Northfield Farm
B1414
HARWICH RD
CHURCH LA

6

Landermere Creek

5
Lower Barn Farm
Quay Farm
Quay (dis)
Beaumont Cut
QUAY LA

24
Beaumont Bridge
Beaumont Quay
CO16
White House
GULL COTTS

4
GOLDEN LA

Landermere Hall
Landermere

3
Thorpe Lodge
New Hall
Kentshill Farm
LANDERMERE RD
WALTON RD

23
CO13

2
PALMERSTON RD
LONSDALE RD
SPRINCE RD
NEW TOWN RD
ARGYLE RD
ROSE RD
1 HILLSIDE COTTS
2 LANDERMERE VIEW
Dale Hill Farm

Thorpe-le-Soken
Tendring Tech Coll
B1414
Elm Farm
OAK CL
ABBEY ST
BYNG HO
The GREEN
Damont's Farm
DAMONT'S MANOR LA
Sneating Hall
SNEATING HALL LA
B1034

1

22
B1414
STOCKTON RD
B1033
FRINTON RD
B1033
Folly Farm
B1034

18 A B 19 C D 20 E F

141 169

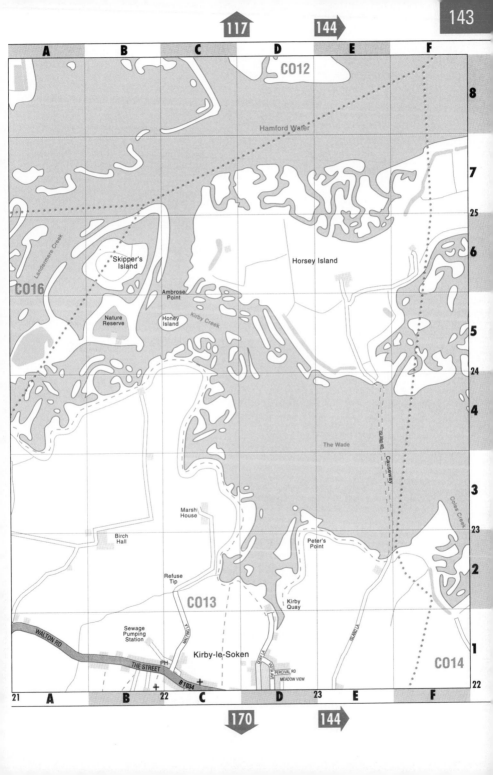

117
144

A B C D E F

CO12

8

Hamford Water

7

25

Landermere Creek

Skipper's
Island

6

CO16

Horsey Island

Ambrose
Point

Nature
Reserve

Honey
Island

Kirby Creek

5

24

4

The Wade

ISLAND RD.

Causeway

3

Colas Creek

Marsh
House

23

Birch
Hall

Peter's
Point

2

Refuse
Tip

CO13

Kirby
Quay

1

Sewage
Pumping
Station

VERNUM

ISLA LA.

WALTON RD

THE STREET

PH

B1034

Kirby-le-Soken

PERCIVAL RD

MEADOW VIEW

VISTA AV.

CO14

21 A B 22 C D 23 E F 22

170
144

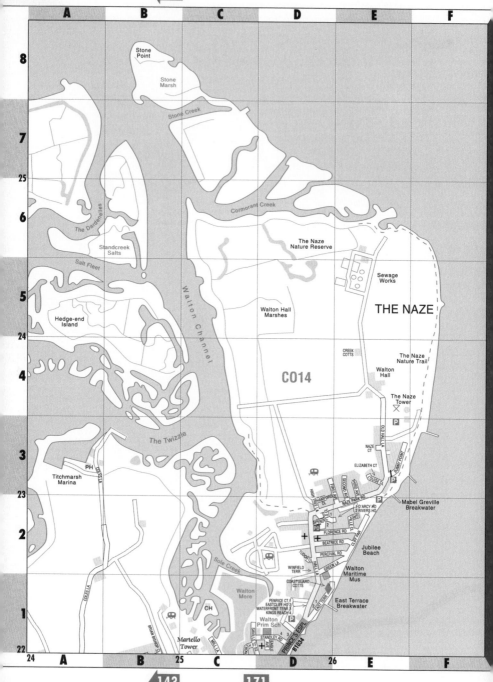

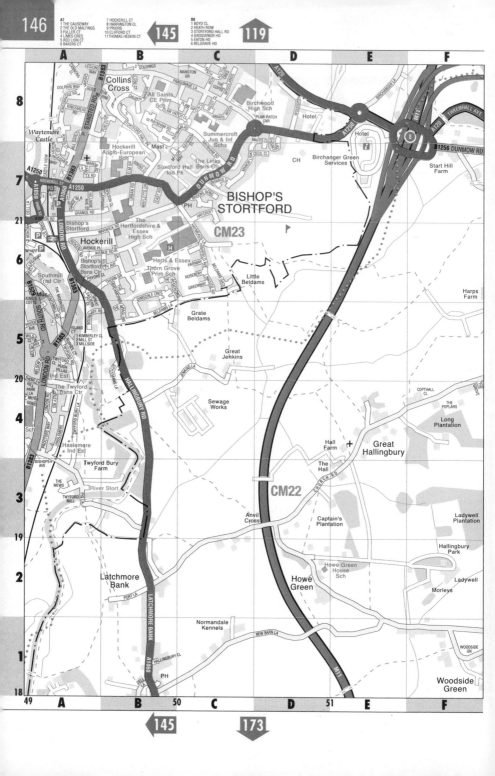

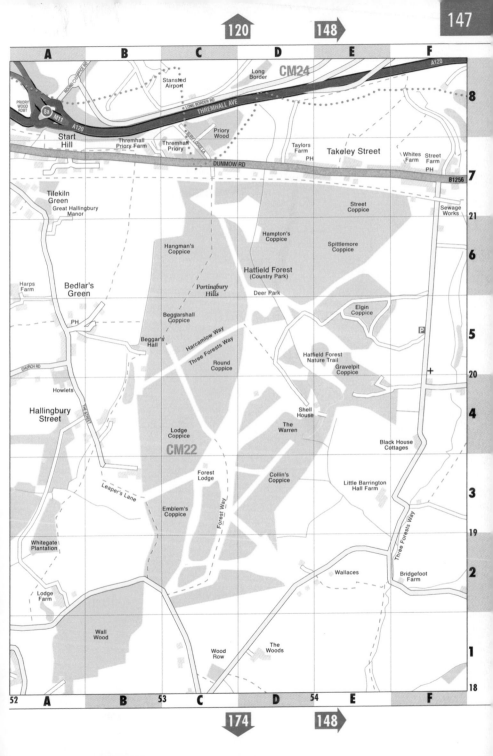

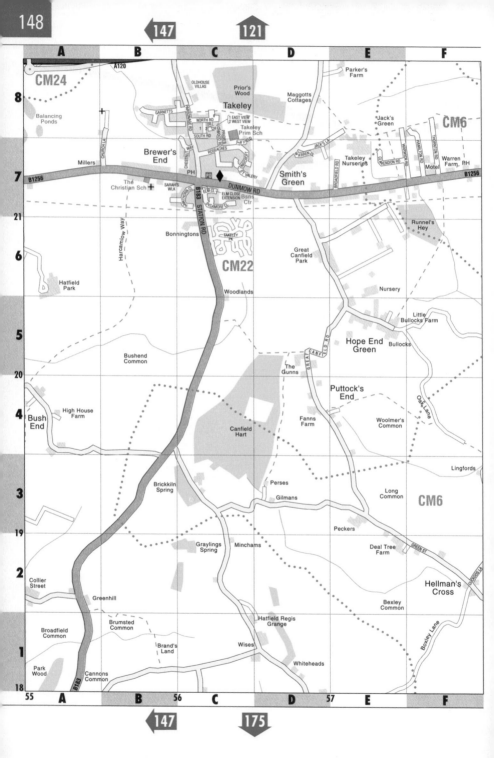

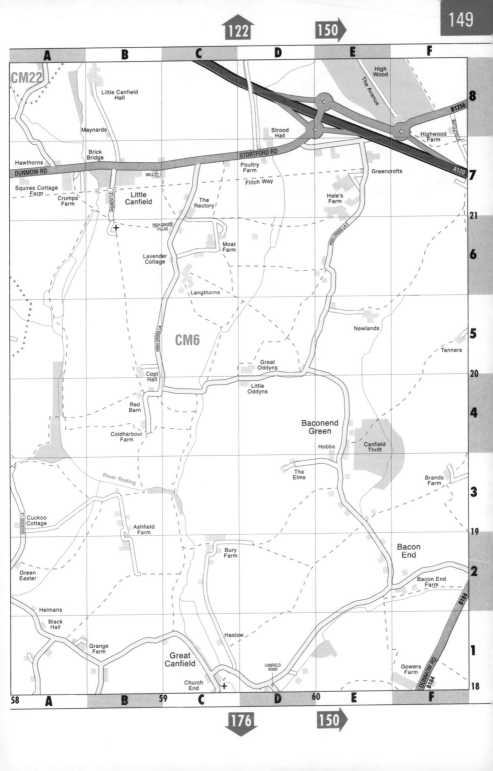

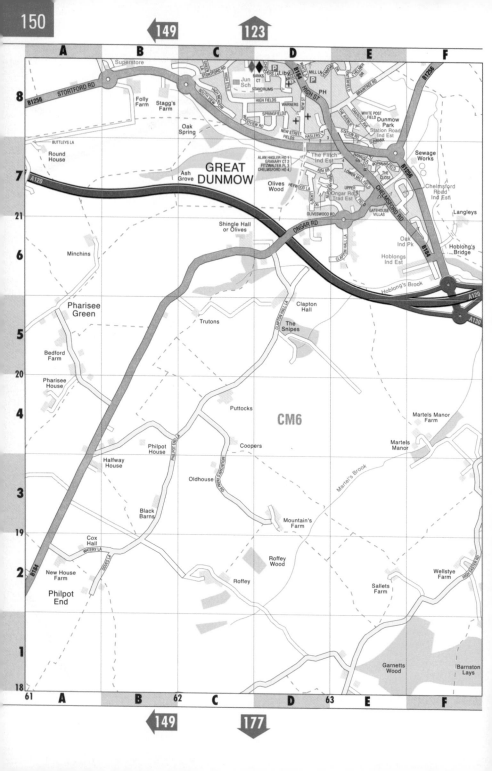

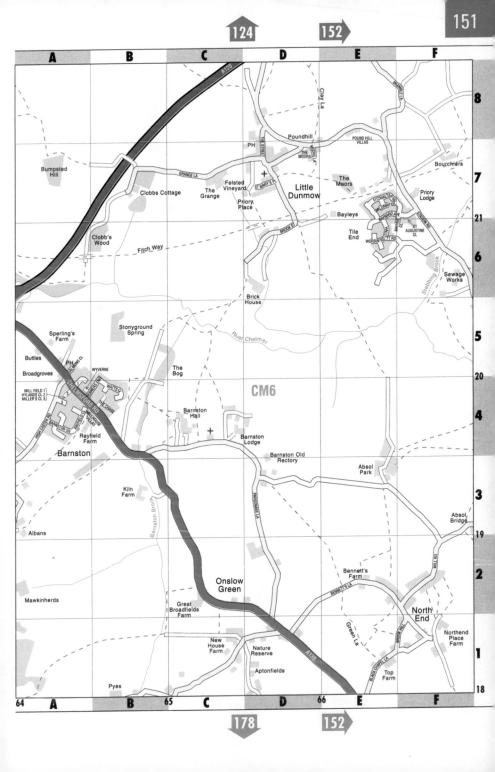

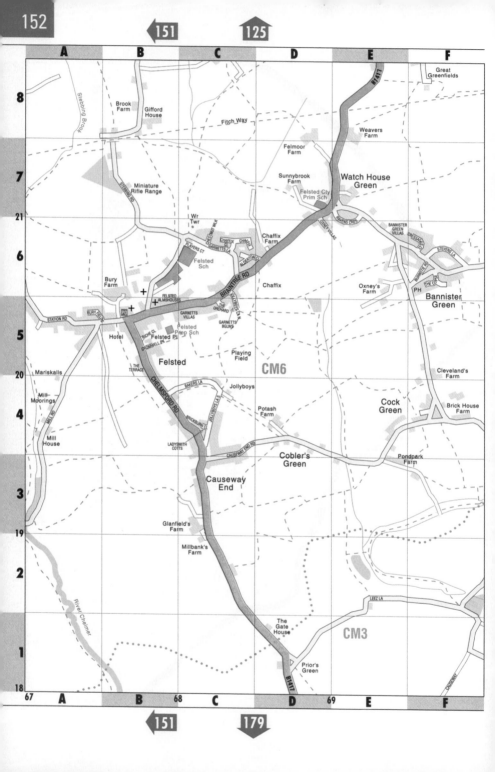

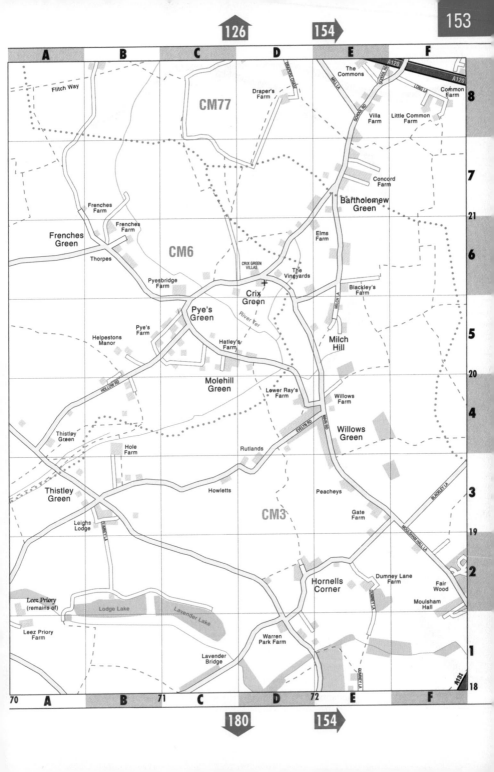

126
154

| A | B | C | D | E | F |

Flitch Way

The Commons

A120
A120

CM77

Draper's Farm

Common Farm

8

Villa Farm

Little Common Farm

Concord Farm

7

Frenches Farm

Bartholomew Green

21

Frenches Farm

Frenches Green

CM6

Elms Farm

6

Thorpes

Pyesbridge Farm

CRIX GREEN VILLAS

The Vineyards

Blackley's Farm

Pye's Green

Crix Green

Pye's Farm

River Ter

Milch Hill

5

Helpestons Manor

Hatley's Farm

Molehill Green

20

HOLLOW RD

Lower Ray's Farm

Willows Farm

4

Thistley Green

Hole Farm

Rutlands

EVELYN RD

MAIN RD

Willows Green

Howletts

Peacheys

3

Thistley Green

Leighs Lodge

CM3

Gate Farm

19

DUNNETT LA

MOULSHAM HALL LA

BLACKLEY LA

Hornells Corner

Dumney Lane Farm

Fair Wood

2

Leez Priory (remains of)

Lodge Lake

Lavender Lake

Moulsham Hall

Leez Priory Farm

DUNNETT LA

Warren Park Farm

1

Lavender Bridge

A131

18

| A | B | C | D | E | F |
70   71   72

180
154

153 127

Lakes Farm
Stanford Farm
Queenborough
N STOCKMAN TERR Tl
QUEENBOROUGH GR 2
A120
A131
A120
B1256
TORTOISESHELL WAY
CLOUDED YELLOW CL
SPECKLED WOOD CL
KEATS RD
LISTER RD
MASEFIELD RD
WORDSWORTH AV
LONGLEAF DR

John Ray Jun & Inf Schs
CM7
The Notley High Sch

THE LAURELS
BRAYMANS
BLICKLING RD
KEXWORTH
CHERRY GDNS
COOPERS CRES
PH
Hill House Farm
Great Notley
Prim Sch
TAILORS CL
BUTTERMERE
SUMMERLEAZE CT
SADDLERS CL
FELBRIGG CL
DANBY
LEDHAM HALL LA
WINDERMERE DR
Hayeswood Farm

21
White Court Prim Sch
1 BURGHLEY CT
2 FRAMLINGHAM WAY
RASMERE DR
CALDBECK WAY
PICKPOCKET LA
Oak Farm
BUCK HILL
CHURCH RD

THORINGTON PINTAIL CRES
BRANCASTER DR
CM77
Row Green
BAKER STA

RICHARD WAY
OTHELLO CL
MEADOW
Card's Farm
Abattoir

WIGEON CL
THE CHASE
GREAT MALLON CL
TEAL CL
AYLESUS

20
Great Slampseys
Friar's Farm

BLACKLEY LA
PH
DAGNETS LA
Lynderswood Farm
Wren Park

Young's End
Lynderswood Court
Dagnets Farm

19
CM8
Hazeltop
GREEN LA

Essex Show Ground
Bushy Wood
Paul's Wood
Hazelton Wood

CM3
Bateman's Farm

BRAINTREE RD
MAIN RD
PANTERS LA
North Whitehouse
Little Walley Hall

A131

Great Notley

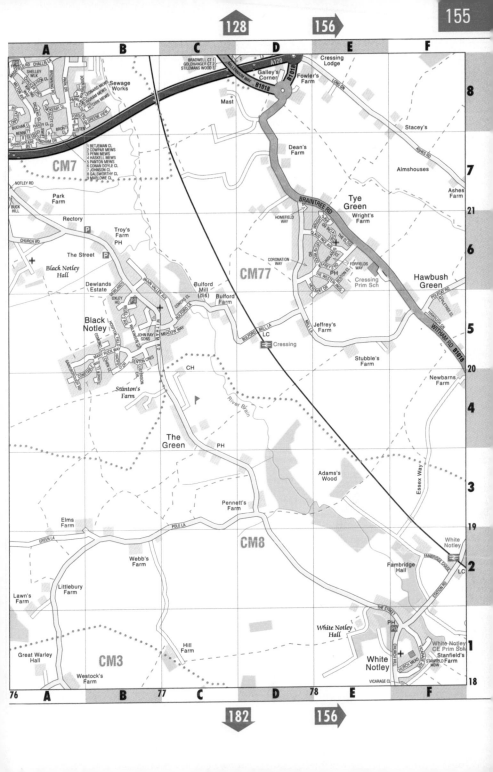

155
129

A B C D E F

8
Lanham
Manor
Farm

Wr
Twr

Lanham
Green

Jubilee
Plantation

Sand & Gravel
Pit

7
Ashes
Farm

PH

Schills
Farm

Link's
Farm

Link's
Wood

Clapdog
Green

Gosling's
Farm

LINK LA

21

Essex Way

6
Cressing

Wright's
Farm

Airfield
(disused)

Mast

Sheepcotes
Farm

POLECAT RD

THE STREET

LANHAM GREEN RD

ASHES RD

Egypts
Farm

Rolph's
Farmhouse

5
CM77

CHURCH RD

SHARPS LA RD

SHEEPCOTES LA

COMFIELD
THE GOSLINGS
WEAVERSFIELD
FRANCIS CL
RUNNACLS
FRANCIS WAY
MANUEL WAY
MANORS

SILVER ST

20

COUNCIL
HOUSES

B1018

Liby
Hotel
THE
SHOPS

Works

Silver
End

Bower
Hall

WESTERN RD

JOSEPH GDNS

4

New
House

WITHAM RD

B1018

3
Sheepcote
Wood

TEMPLE LA

Silver End
Prim Sch

PH

CM8

Park
House

SCHOOL RD

BRISTOL CT

STRETWOLD CT

VALENTINE WAY

MAGDALENE GDNS

19

Rivenhall
Place

2
Cressing
Temple

Cressing
Temple
Barns

Old
Court Room

Essex Way

Hungry
Hall

WITHAM RD

Rivenhall
Thicks

1
Sewage
Works

18
79

A B C 80 D E 81 F

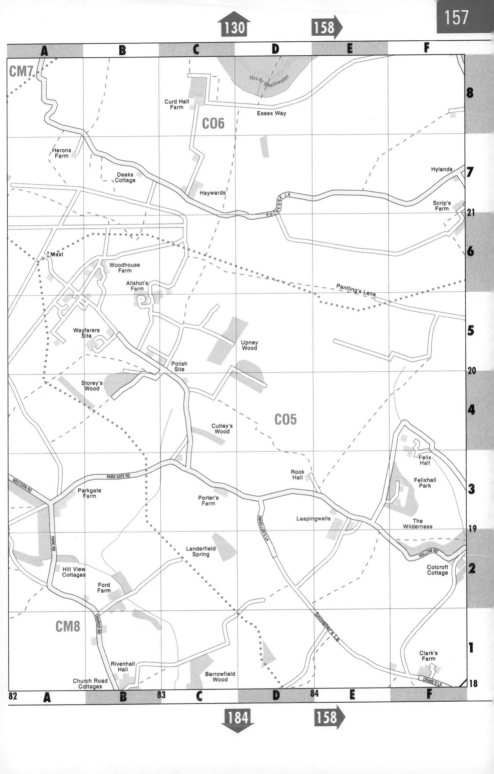

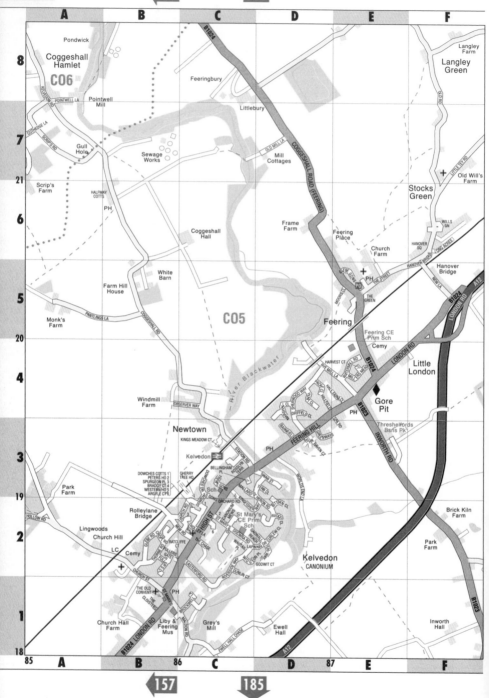

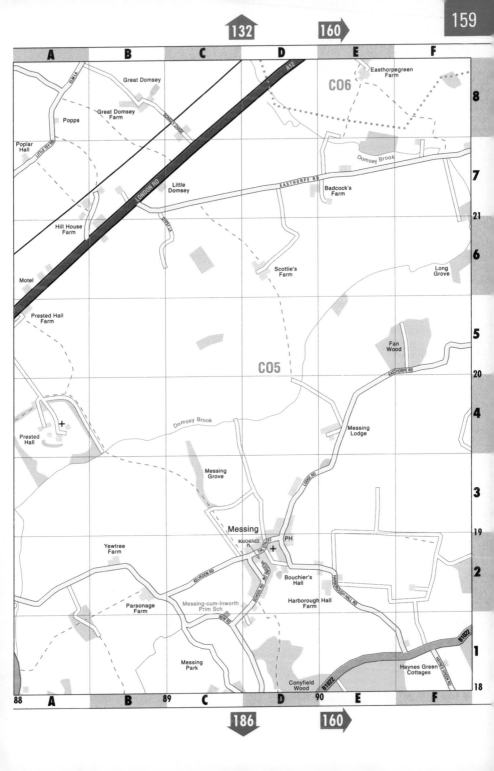

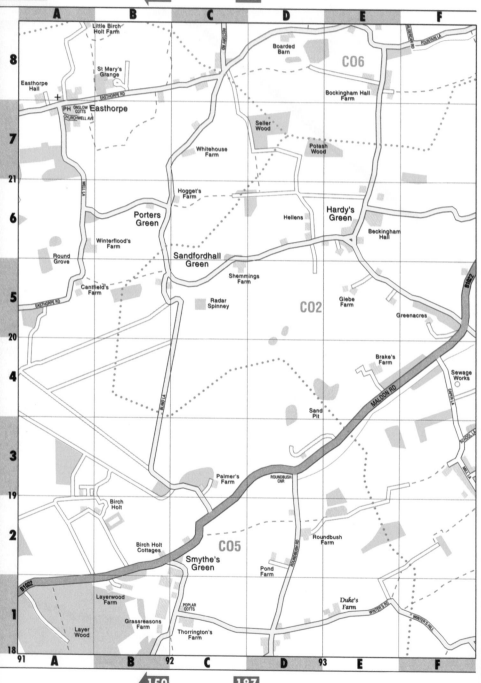

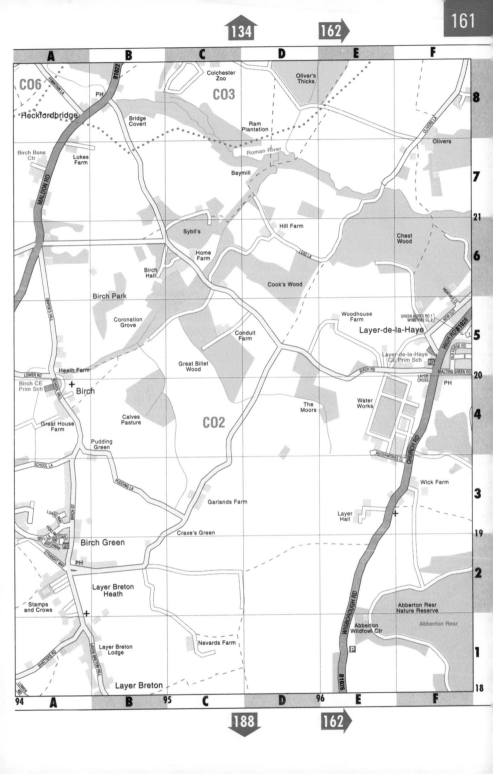

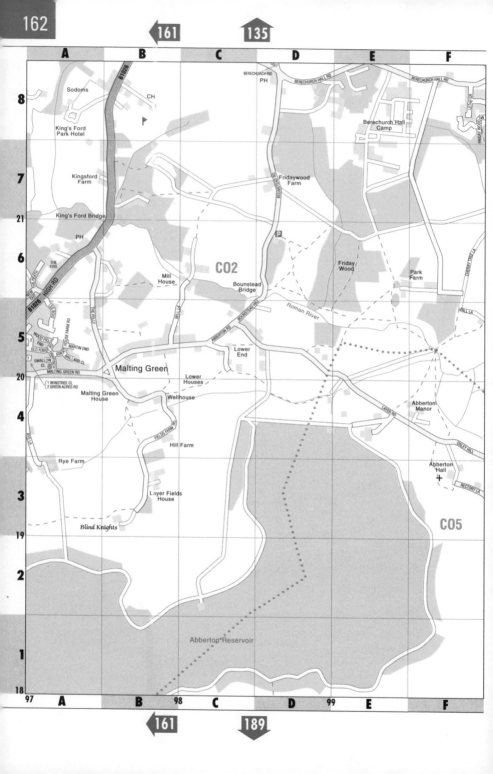

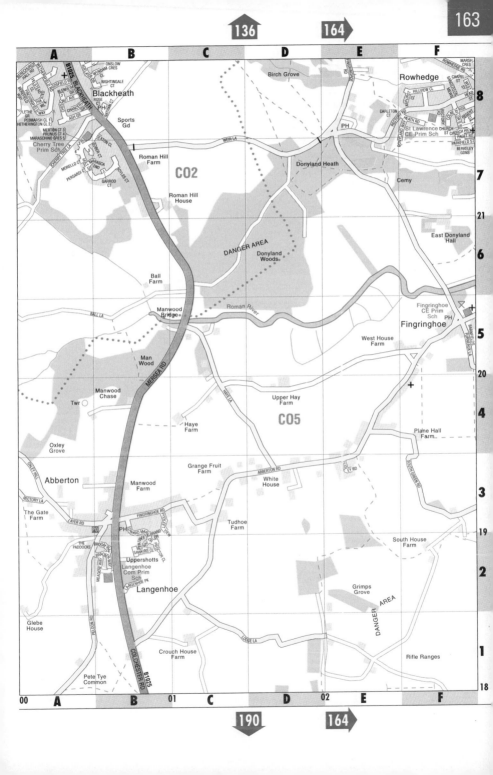

A B C D E F

Birch Grove

Rowhedge

MARSH CRES

ROWHEDGE RD

ST CHAPEL ST

HILLVIEW CL

CARLETON CT

8

BRECKNOCK HALL RD

BEREFIELD LANE WAY

BIRCHFIELD CL

WYNDAM CRES

ONSLOW CRES

NIGHTINGALE CT

HEATH RD

ST CHURCH HILL

St Lawrence Church
CE Prim Sch

PAGET RD

PARKFIELD ST

Blackheath

BLENHEIM

CANT AVE

CHANCEL CT

RUGE AVE

St Lawrence Church

BERKELEY GDNS

FLETHE GR

PEBMARSH CL 1

HETHERINGTON CL 2

ASH GR

Sports
Gd

MERTON CT 3
PRUNUS CT 4
MARASCHINO CRES 5

PH

Cherry Tree
Prim Sch

CHRISTY TREE LA

MORELLO CT

ROOKE LA

PAXSON CL

Roman Hill
Farm

WEIR LA

Donyland Heath

PH

Cemy

7

B1025 BLACKHEATH

PERSARDI CT

MORELLO CT

DAMSON CT

GARROD
CT

BOYLES CT

CO2

Roman Hill
House

Donyland Heath

East Donyland
Hall

21

DANGER AREA

Donyland
Woods

6

Ball
Farm

BALL LA

Manwood
Bridge

Roman River

Fingringhoe
CE Prim
Sch

PH

Fingringhoe

5

Man
Wood

MERSEA RD

West House
Farm

BARWELL CL

FURNEAUX LA

20

Twr

Manwood
Chase

TYE LA

Upper Hay
Farm

4

Haye
Farm

CO5

Plane Hall
Farm

Oxley
Grove

OXLEY HILL

Abberton

RECTORY LA

LAYER RD

Manwood
Farm

FINGRINGHOE RD

Grange Fruit
Farm

ARBERTON RD

White
House

COLT CT RD

SOUTH HOPE LA

3

The Gate
Farm

PO

PH

Tudhoe
Farm

South House
Farm

19

THE
PADDOCKS

BRIDGE RD

BRACKEN WAY

MEADOW WAY

HAWKINS CL

Uppershotts
Langenhoe
Com Prim
Sch

LANGENHOE PK

Langenhoe

Grimps
Grove

DANGER AREA

2

Glebe
House

FINGRINGHOE RD

COLCHESTER RD B1025

Crouch House
Farm

LODGE LA

Rifle Ranges

1

Pete Tye
Common

18

00 A B 01 C D 02 E F

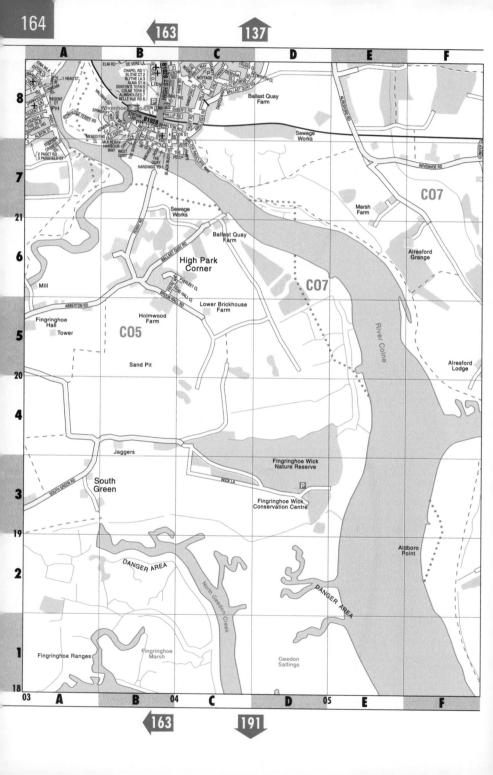

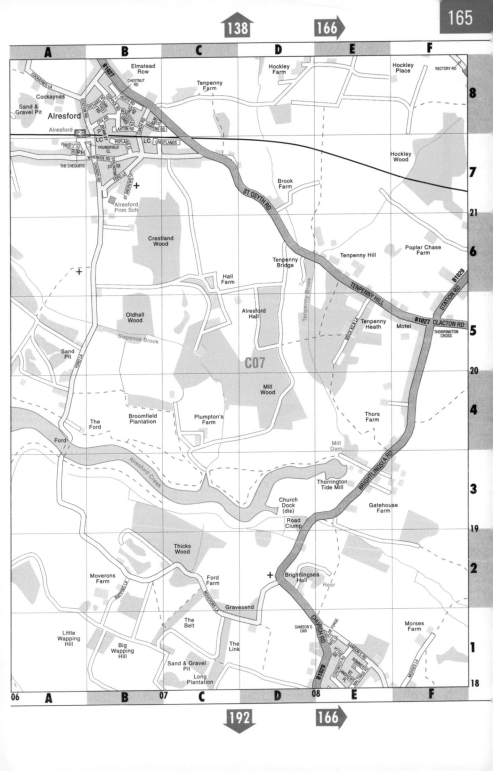

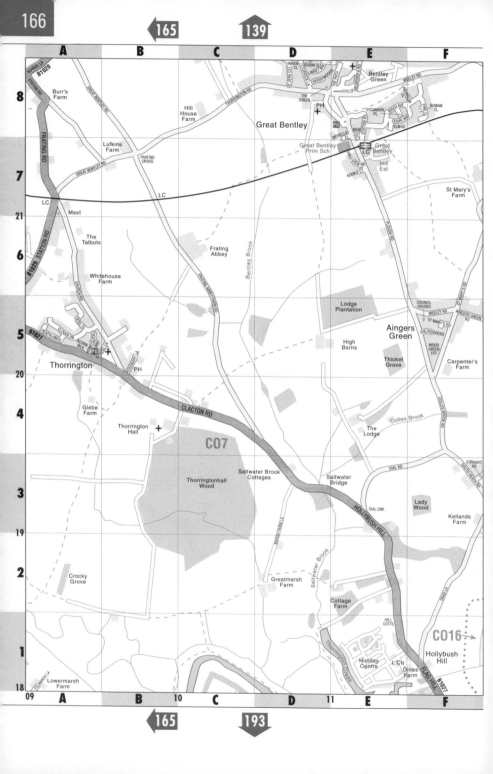

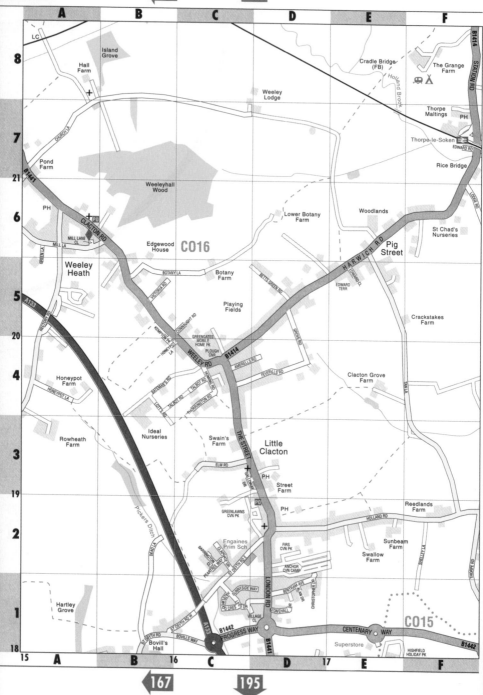

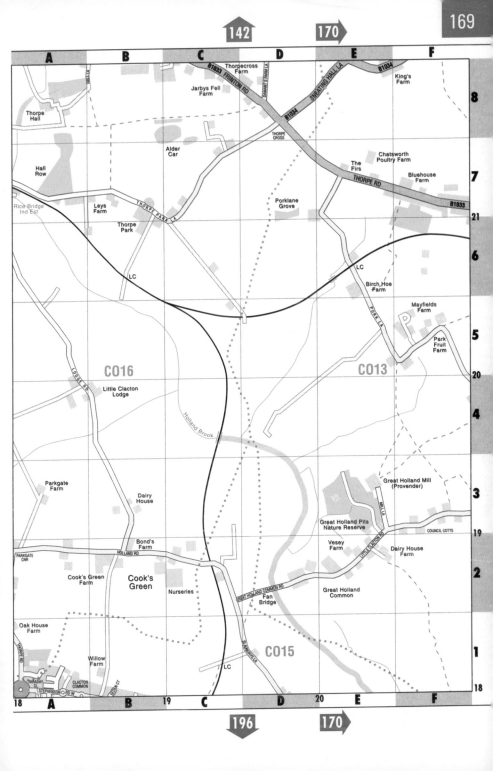

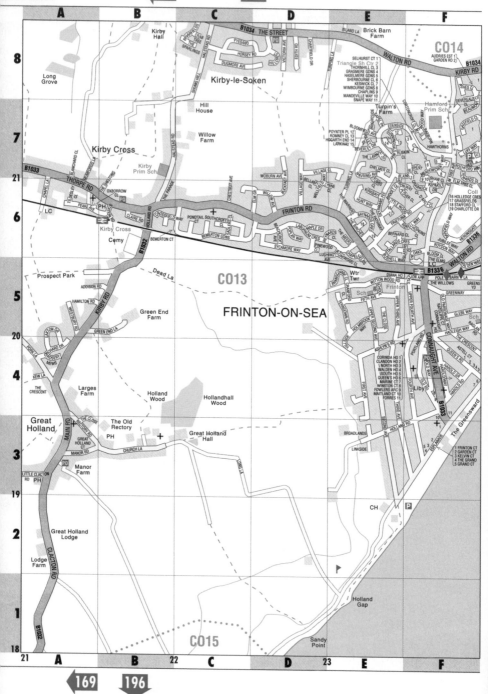

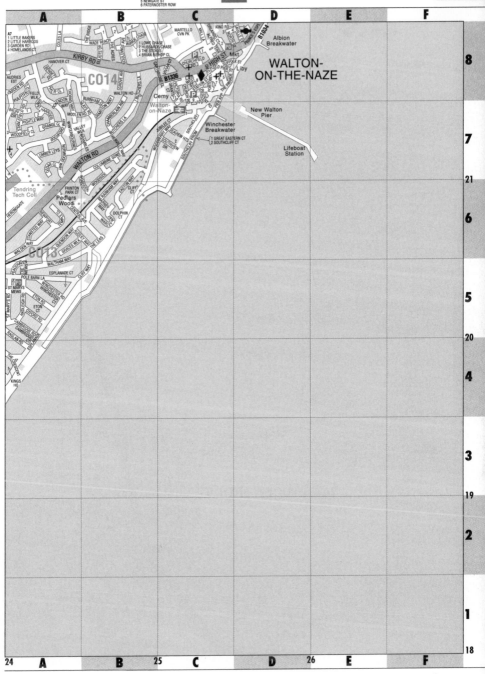

C8
1 MARINA MEWS
2 VICARAGE LA
3 HAVENCROFT CT
4 STRATFORD PL
5 NEWGATE ST
6 PATERNOSTER ROW

7 NEW PIER ST
8 MARTELLO RD
9 AGAR RD
10 AGAR ROAD APP
11 ST BOTOLPH'S TERR

144

A7
1 LITTLE BAKERS
2 LITTLE HARRODS
3 GARDEN RD
4 HOMELANDS CT

WALTON-
ON-THE-NAZE

MARTELLO
CVN PK

Albion
Breakwater

New Walton
Pier

Lifeboat
Station

Winchester
Breakwater

1 GREAT EASTERN CT
2 SOUTHCLIFF CT

Tendring
Tech Coll

Pedlars
Wood

CO14

CO13

KIRBY RD

HANOVER CT

AUDRIES
EST

WALTON RD

HIGH ST

Cemy
Walton-
on-Naze

B1336

B1034

KING RD

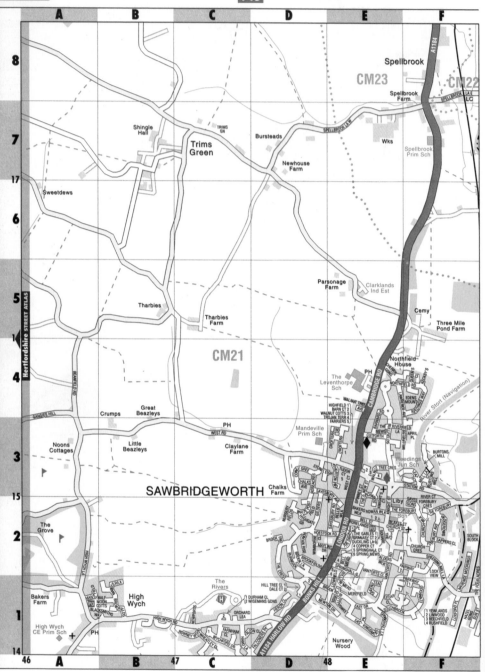

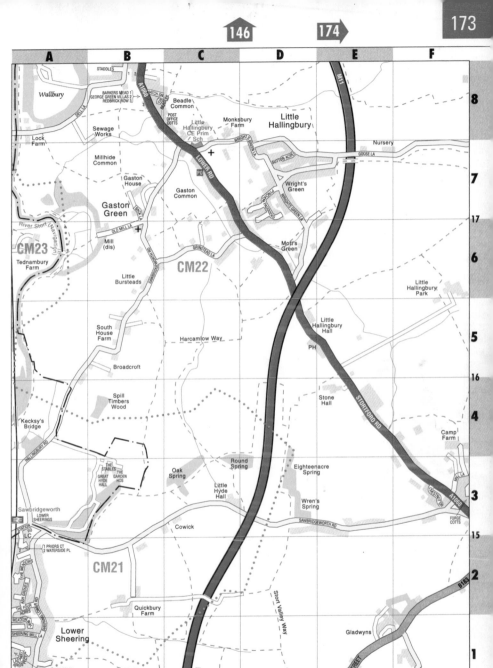

173
147

| | A | B | C | D | E | F |

8
Woodfold
Monk's Wood
Wallis's Spring
Forest Hall
Forest Farm
Footpath Common

7
Harcamlow Way
Child's Common
The Marsh
The Park

17
Ryes Farm
Three Forests Way

6
Forest Way
Copperfields
Lang Bridge
FEATHERS HILL
HIGH ST
PH
PO
DUNMOW RD
B183

Liby
St Mary's CE Prim Sch
BROAD ST

5
The Round Lodge
OLD STREET HILL
CM22
Town Farm
Town Farm
Mus Brook
NEW BURY MDW
Hatfield Broad Oak

16
Corringales
Pincey Brook

4
Town Grove
Lea Green

3
LEA HALL DGLWS
Lea Hall
Ongars
LITTLE HEATH
THE CLOSE
COX LEY
Hatfield Heath CofE Prim Sch
WEST HAYES
THE SHAW
Hatfield Heath
Lancasters

15
STORTFORD RD
PO
PH
CHELMSFORD RD
Stone Bridge

2
B183
Peggerells
BENTLEY VILLAS
Bentley Common
Muchfield Common
Lancaster's Spring
Hill Farm
The Paddocks
CM6

1
Heath Common
Ardley End
Friars
Pooles Cottages
Grange Farm Riding Stables
Hatfield Grange
A1060

14
Sewage Works
Gibsons

| 52 | A | | B | 53 | C | | D | 54 | E | | F |

173
202

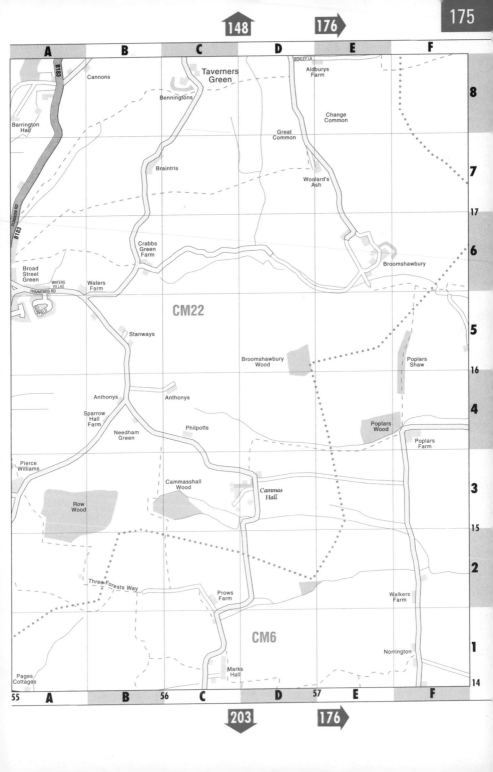

148
176
203
176

A   B   C   D   E   F

8
7
17
6
5
16
4
3
15
2
1
14

55   56   57

Cannons
Taverners Green
BOXLEY LA
Aldburys Farm
Benningtons
Change Common
Barrington Hall
Great Common
B183
Braintris
Woolard's Ash
DUNMOW RD
B183
Crabbs Green Farm
Broomshawbury
Broad Street Green
WATERS VILLAS
Waters Farm
HAMMONDS RD
Waters Farm
CM22
Stanways
Broomshawbury Wood
Poplars Shaw
Anthonys
Anthonys
Poplars Wood
Sparrow Hall Farm
Philpotts
Poplars Farm
Needham Green
Pierce Williams
Cammasshall Wood
Cammas Hall
Row Wood
Three Forests Way
Prows Farm
Walkers Farm
CM6
Norrington
Pages Cottages
Marks Hall

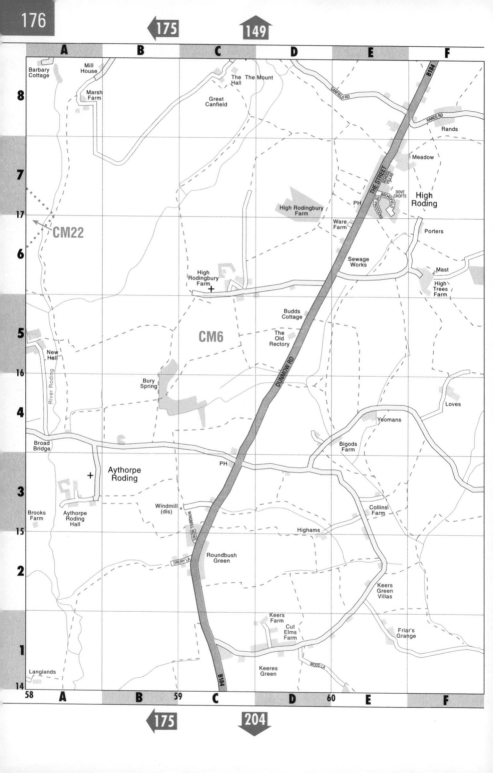

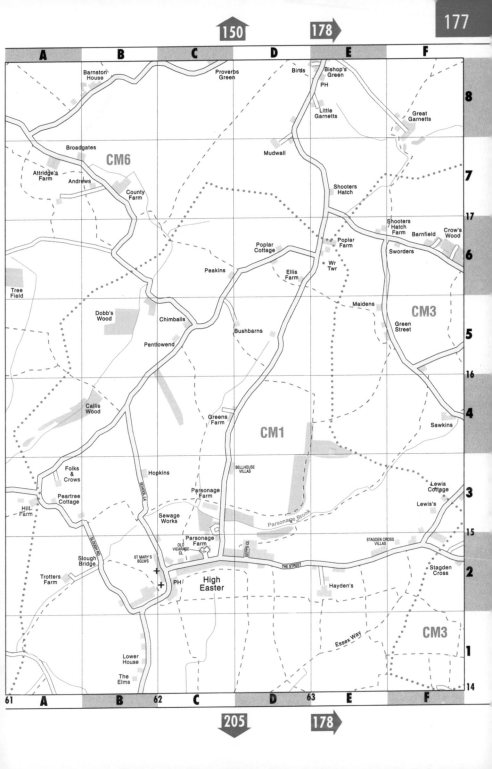

177
151

A B C D E F

8

Pyes Farm

Blackchapel

Parkgate

PH

CM6

King's Farm

7

Quoins

Lawn Hall

17

Houseground

Wall Farm

Coppice Lane

6

Cromps

Smarts

Little Leys

Oldpark Farm

Swallows Farm

The Gorse

5

Yewtree

Lofty Green

Blunts

16

Maggotts

CM3

4

Rolfe's Farm

Upper Harveys

Markhams

Blakes

Park Farm

3

Cut Maple

Essex Way

Post Bridge

Woods Farm

15

Pleshey Grange

GRANGE RD

2

Acreland Green

THE STREET

Acreland

Pleshey

Pleshey Bridge

Poultry Farm

Wheats

PH

1

Raylands

Bury Farm

Essex Way

+

Plesheybury

14

CM1

Jacobs

64 A B 65 C D 66 E F

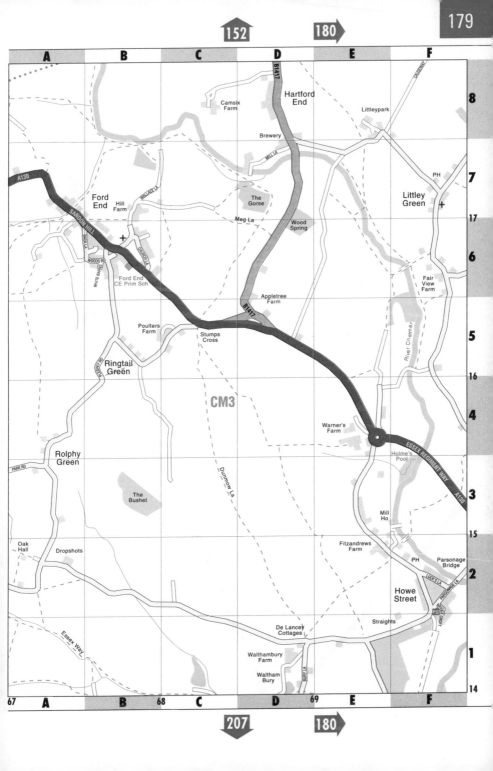

179
153

	A	B	C	D	E	F

8

Court Hill

Breams Farm

Little Warricks

Mattock's Farm

Nurseries

Nurseries

Chadwicks Farm

Great Leighs

Graveleys

7

Nursery Garden

Leighs Hall Farm

Leighs Hall

17

Rochester Farm

6

Mabb's Farm

Old Shaw's Farm

River Ter

Little Leighs

Deres Bridge

PH Sports Gd

BOLINGBROKE CL 1
COOPERS LA 2
HELEN HOW 3
CASTLEFIELDS 4
PEARMAINS 5

WHITES LA

Great Hyde Wood

5

CM3

Essex Way

THE CRESCENT

16

STRAWBROOK FIRE LANE

Lowley's Farm

Osiers

BOCKINGHE LA

4

Liberty Hall

Whitbreads Farm

Straw Brook

WHITBREADS FIELD LA

Well House Farm

Hyde Hall

Hill House

CHATHAM GN

3

Chalk Farm

Bailey's Farm

15

Rectory Farm

RECTORY LA

ESSEX REGIMENT WAY

2

Waltham House

Chathamhill Spring

Little Stonage Farm

Great Stonage Farm

Long's Farm

CHELMER DRIVE LA

Park Farm

River Chelmer

1

BOUNCY HALL LA

Stonage Wood

LONG LA

Alresford

14

70	A	B	71	C	D	72	E	F

A131

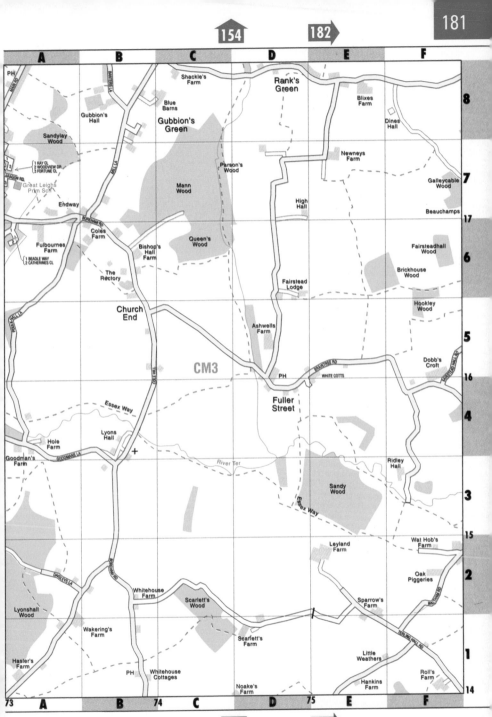

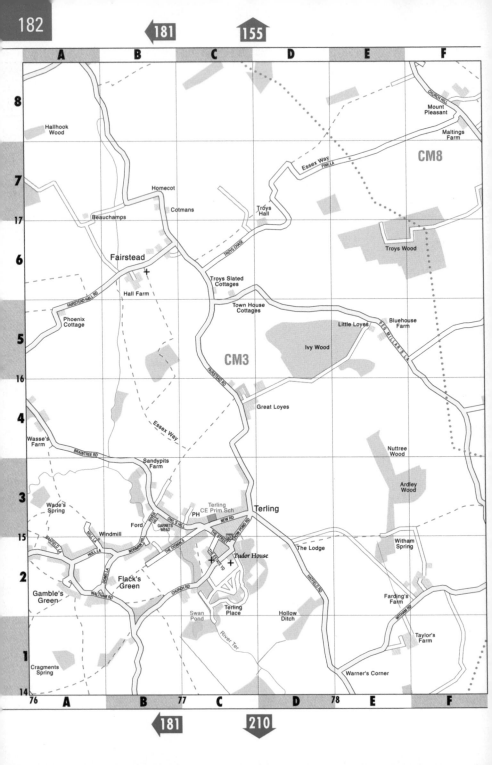

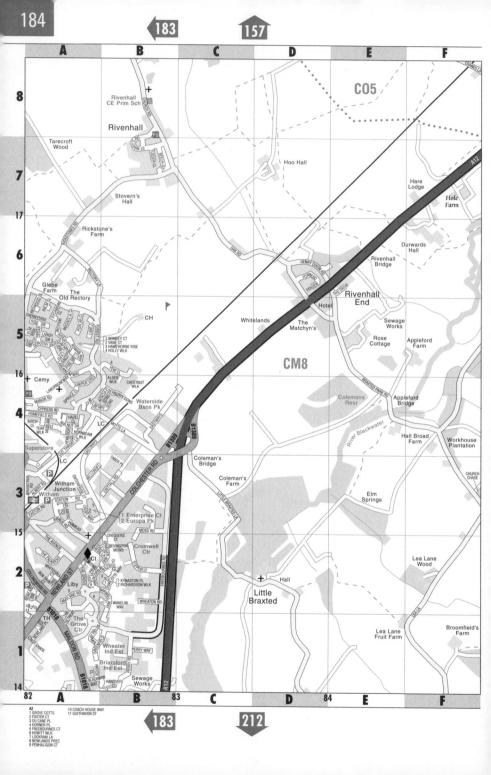

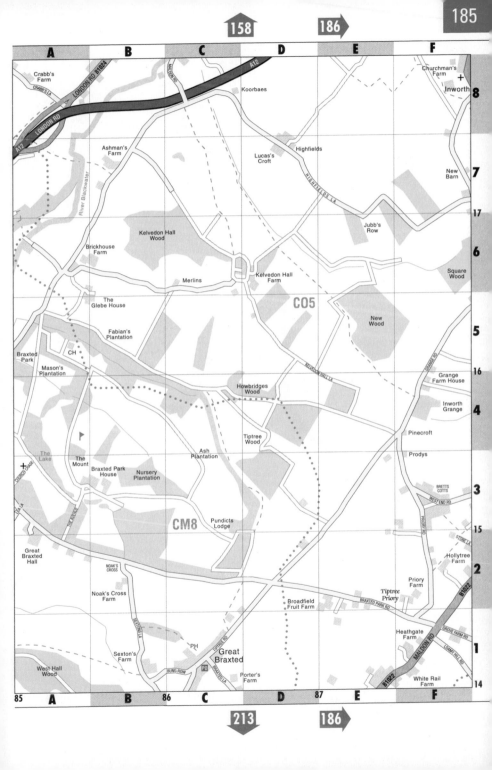

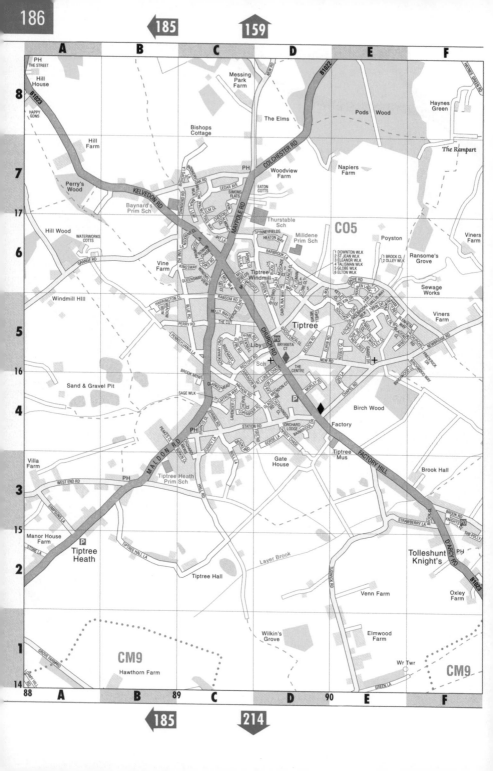

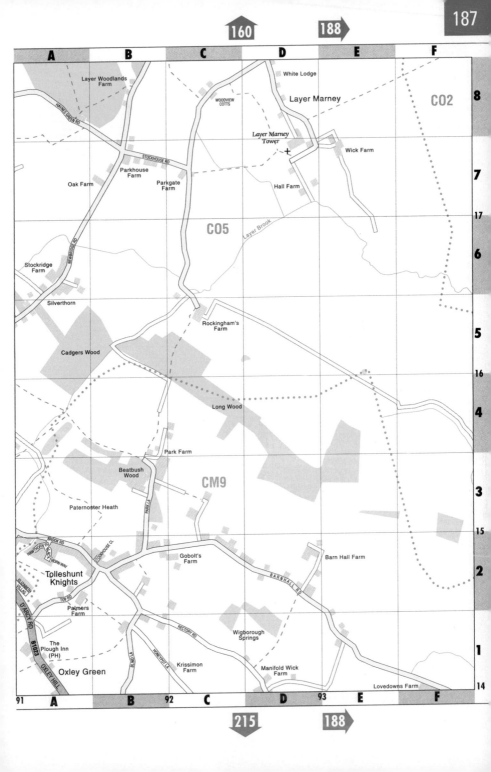

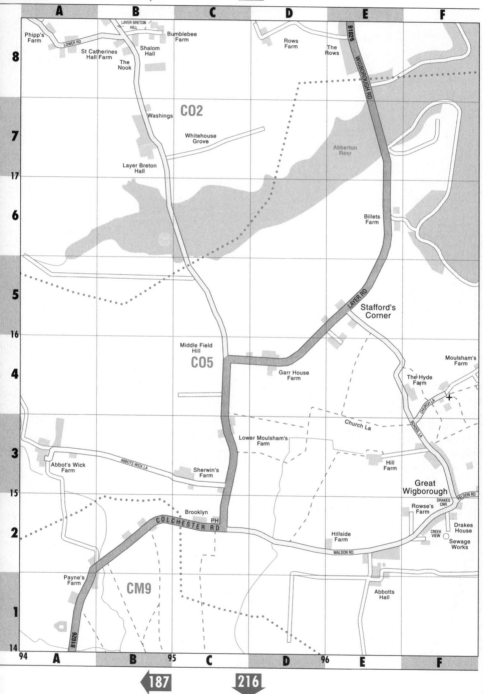

Phipp's Farm
LOWER RD
St Catherines Hall Farm
The Nook
Layer Breton Hill
Shalom Hall
Bumblebee Farm
Rows Farm
The Rows
B1026
WIGBOROUGH RD

CO2
Washings
Whitehouse Grove
Layer Breton Hall

Abberton Resr

Billets Farm

LAYER RD
Stafford's Corner

Middle Field Hill
CO5
Garr House Farm
Moulsham's Farm
The Hyde Farm
CHURCH LA

Church La

Lower Moulsham's Farm

Abbot's Wick Farm
ABBOTS WICK LA
Sherwin's Farm

Hill Farm

Great Wigborough
SCHOOL LA
HELDON RD

Brooklyn
PH
COLCHESTER RD
Rowse's Farm
DRAKES CNR
CREEK VIEW
Drakes House

Hillside Farm
Sewage Works
MALDON RD

Payne's Farm
CM9

Abbotts Hall

B1026

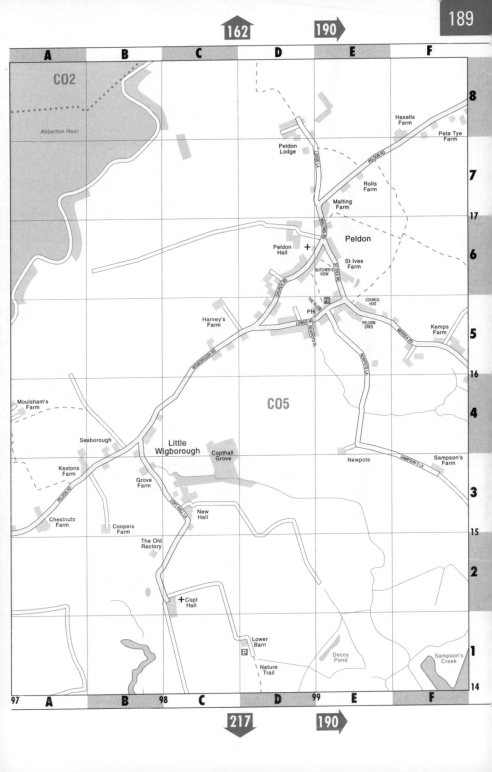

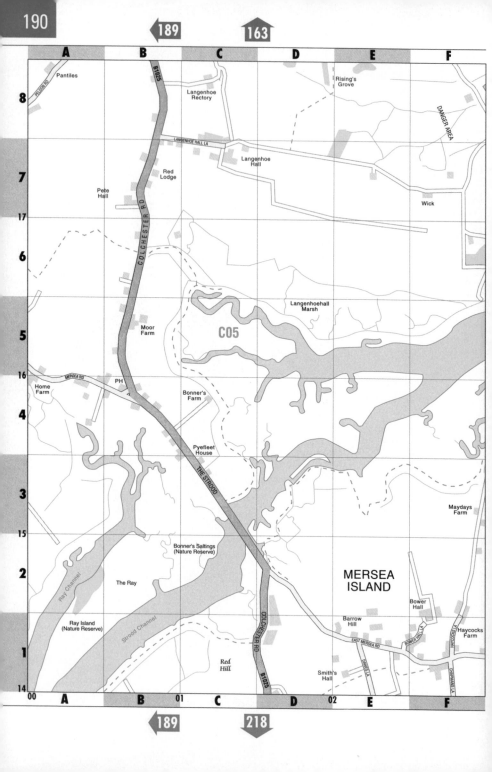

A B C D E F

8

Pantiles

PELDON RD

B1025

Langenhoe
Rectory

Rising's
Grove

DANGER AREA

LANGENHOE HALL LA

Langenhoe
Hall

Red
Lodge

7

Pete
Hall

COLCHESTER RD

Wick

17

6

Langenhoehall
Marsh

Moor
Farm

C05

5

16

Home
Farm

MERSEA RD

PH

Bonner's
Farm

4

Pyefleet
House

THE STROOD

Maydays
Farm

3

15

Bonner's Saltings
(Nature Reserve)

MERSEA
ISLAND

2

Ray Channel

The Ray

COLCHESTER RD

Bower
Hall

Barrow
Hill

Ray Island
(Nature Reserve)

Strood Channel

EAST MERSEA RD

HOWES HALL LA

Haycocks
Farm

CHAPMANS LA

1

Red
Hill

B1025

Smith's
Hall

BARKER LA

14

00 A B 01 C D 02 E F

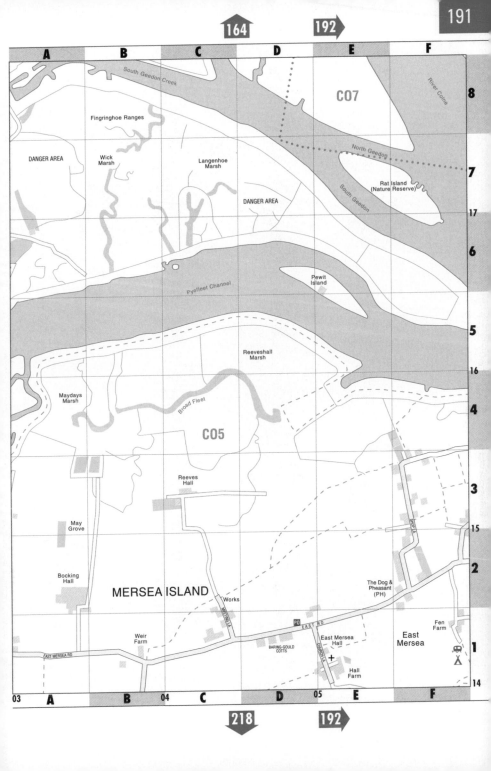

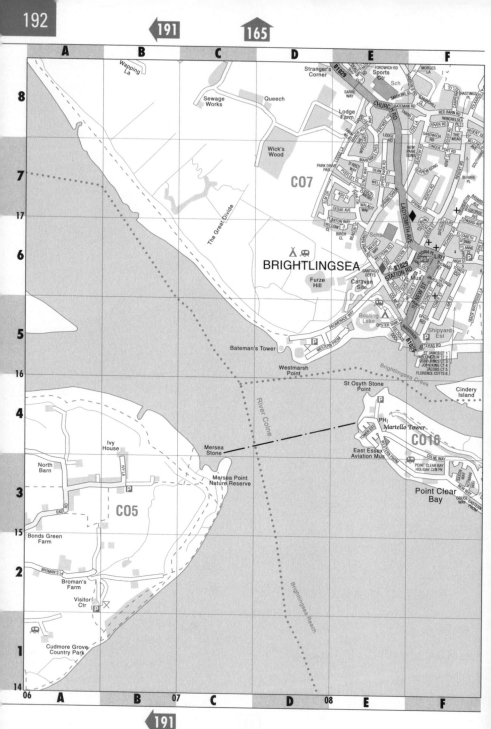

191

165

BRIGHTLINGSEA

CO7

CO5

CO16

Cudmore Grove
Country Park

Point Clear
Bay

Bateman's Tower

Westmarsh
Point

St Osyth Stone
Point

Martello Tower

East Essex
Aviation Mus

Mersea
Stone

Mersea Point
Nature Reserve

Ivy
House

North
Barn

Bonds Green
Farm

Broman's
Farm

Visitor
Ctr

River Colne

Brightlingsea Creek

Brightlingsea Reach

Cindery
Island

Point Clear Bay
Holiday Cvn Park

Colne Way

Furze
Hill

Caravan
Site

Boating
Lake

Oyster Tank Rd

Shipyard
Est

Stranger's
Corner

Sports
Ctr

Lodge
Farm

Wick's
Wood

Queech

Sewage
Works

Wapping
La

The Great Divide

ST JAMES CT 1
WELLINGTON CT 2
JENBOURNE CT 3
JOHN KING CT 4
JACOBS CT 5
FLORENCE COTTS 6

8 17 7 6 5 16 4 15 3 2 1 14

06 A B 07 C D 08 E F

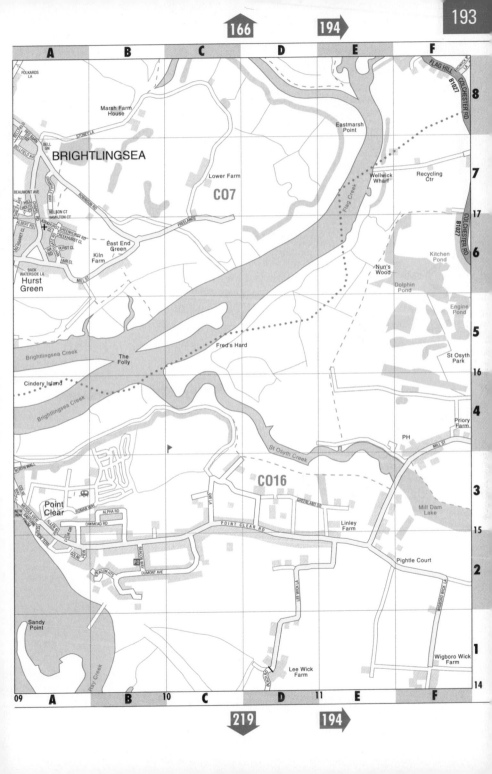

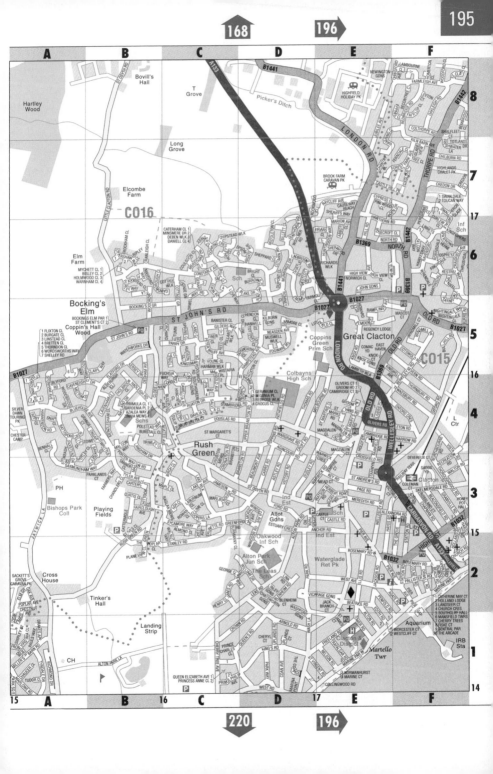

CO13

CLACTON-ON-SEA

Burrsville
Park
Cemy

Cemy

CO15

Treasure Holt
Farm

Sladbury's Old
House

Sladburies

Pond House La

Pond
House

Holland Brook

Smythie's
Farm

Picker's Ditch

FRINTON RD

Holland-on-Sea

Gorse Lane
Ind Est

Valley Farm
Camping Ground

1 CUMBERLAND CT
2 SILVERDALE CT
3 MERRYMOUNT GDNS
4 ST BRELADES CT

Mast

B1027

VALLEY RD

Holland
Park
Prim.
Sch.

Clarendon Pk

Clacton
Cty High Sch

The Windsor
Sch

Sports
Gd

Playing
Field

1 AVONDALE HO
2 HOLLAND HO
3 COTSWOLD CT

1 CONNAUGHT CT
2 CONNAUGHT CL
3 HEYBRIDGE CT
4 WESTMINSTER CT
5 KNIGHTSBRIDGE CT

Colchester
Inst

4 AMBLESIDE CT
5 WINDERMERE CT
6 HADLEIGH CT

7 SURREY CT
8 HAROLD RD
9 HARROLD CT
10 ROSEBANK CT
11 SEAVIEW CT
12 THE TOWERS
13 TURRET HO

1 HOVE CT
2 BOSCOMBE CT
3 THE LODGE
4 SUNDALE CL
5 SOUTHVIEW DR

Queen's Ct

Ascot
Mews

Mansard
Ct

CO13

Holland Haven
Country Park

Nature
Reserve

CO15

Holland
Haven

Holland
Bridge

Mast

Holland Haven

CLACTON RD

FRINTON RD

The Esplanade

Haven Ave

Hertfordshire STREET ATLAS

A B C D E F

Widburyhill Farm
Widbury Wood
Mead Wood
The Dairy Farm
Easneye Wood
The Bournes
Harcamlow Way

8

Easneye
Newgate Wood

Holycross Rd
Easneye Cottage
Ballard's Wood

7

Stansted Hill Stream
Thirsty Spring

13

Sheepcote Farm
LC
SG12
Little Briggens
Newlands
Home Farm Ind Pk
B180

6

Amwell
PH
St Johns La
Capell La
Hill House
Newlands
Hunsdon Rd

5

St John the Baptist CE Prim Sch
Limes Farm
LC
Swing Bridge
Hunsdon Road Cotts

12

Hillside Farm
Marsh La
Meridian Way
LC
Woodham Way
St Margarets
Abbotts Wk
St Andrew's CE Prim Sch
Stanstead Abbotts

4

A1170 Hertford(A10) A1170 Ware
Pepper Hill
B181
St Margarets
Scott Ave
New River Ave
Station Rd
High St
Springwell Ct
The Maltings Ind Est
Horseshoe Ct
Potters Gap
Thele Est
Roydon Rd
Cat's Hill
Coldharbour Wood

A414 Hertford(A10)
Amwell View Sch
Lakes Ct
Marina
Netherfield Ct
Coldharbour Farm

A414
SG13
The Wilderness
Kingfisher Cl
Robin Cl
Piper Cl
Netherfield House
Works
Nursery
Terbets Hill
Stanstead Bury
A414

3

A1170
HODDESDON
The Granary
Lea Valley Wlk
River Lee Navigation
Ryegate Farm
B181

11

St Margaret's Rd
Chelsea Fields
Field Way
New River
EN11
Rye Meads

2

Beechfield
Hailey Ave
Bridle Way (N)
Cranbourne Dri
LC
The John Warner Sch
Cranbourne Ho
Toll House Stream
Toll
CM19

Beyers Prde
Shakespeare Sch
Chaucer Ct
Nursery Rd
Sewage Works

1

A1170 Ware Rd
Bridle Way
Wallers Way
Ditchfield Rd
Mylne Cl
Sch
Murchison Rd
Works
Rye Rd
River Stort
Harcamlow Way

10

37 A B 38 C D 39 E F

B1
1 WESTERN TERR
2 SOUTHERN TERR
3 PARKLAND CL
4 ESTFELD CL
5 CHITTENDEN CL

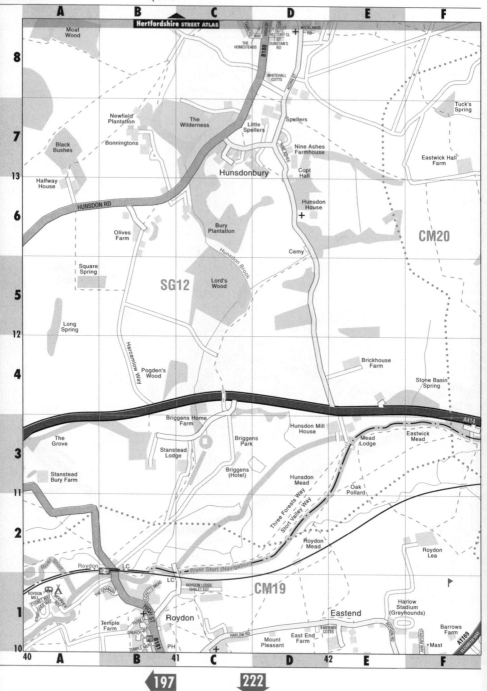

Hertfordshire STREET ATLAS

Moat Wood

Newfield Plantation

The Wilderness

Little Spellers

Spellers

Tuck's Spring

Black Bushes

Bonningtons

Nine Ashes Farmhouse

Eastwick Hall Farm

Halfway House

Hunsdonbury

Copt Hall

HUNSDON RD

Olives Farm

Bury Plantation

Hunsdon House

CM20

Square Spring

Lord's Wood

Cemy

SG12

Hunsdon Brook

Long Spring

Harcamlow Way

Pogden's Wood

Brickhouse Farm

Stone Basin Spring

Briggens Home Farm

A414

The Grove

Stanstead Lodge

Briggens Park

Hunsdon Mill House

Mead Lodge

Eastwick Mead

Stanstead Bury Farm

Briggens (Hotel)

Hunsdon Mead

Three Forests Way

Stort Valley Way

Oak Pollard

Roydon

LC

River Stort (Navigation)

Roydon Mead

Roydon Lea

River Stort

LC

ROYDON LODGE CHALET EST

CM19

Harlow Stadium (Greyhounds)

Roydon Mill

Temple Farm

Roydon

HARLOW RD

Eastend

Barrows Farm

Mount Pleasant

East End Farm

EASTEND COTTS

Mast

Temple Mead

PH

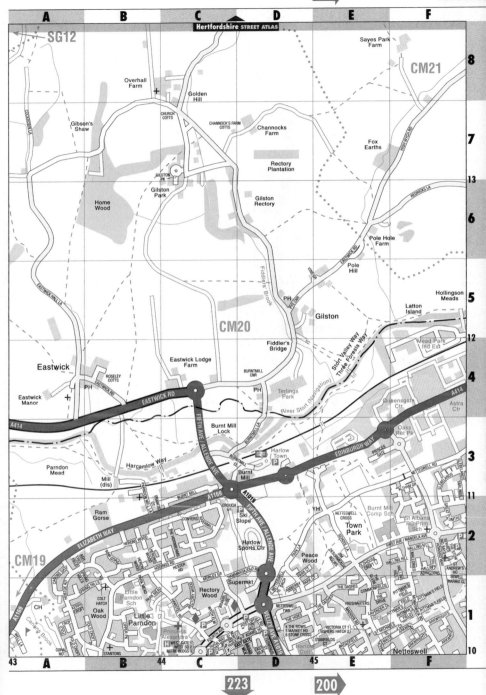

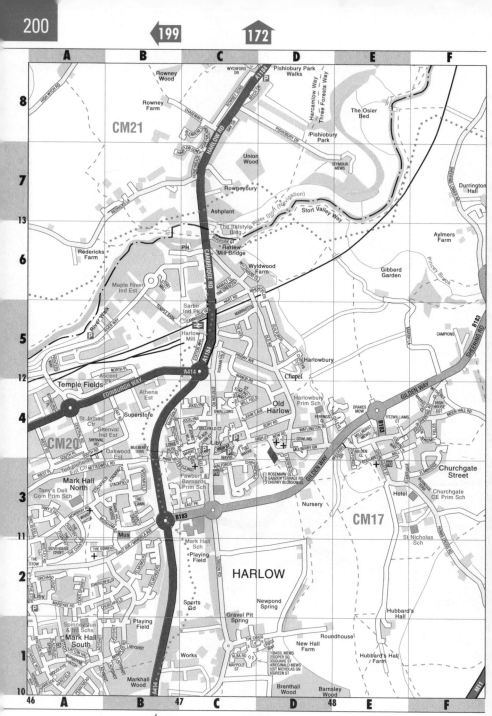

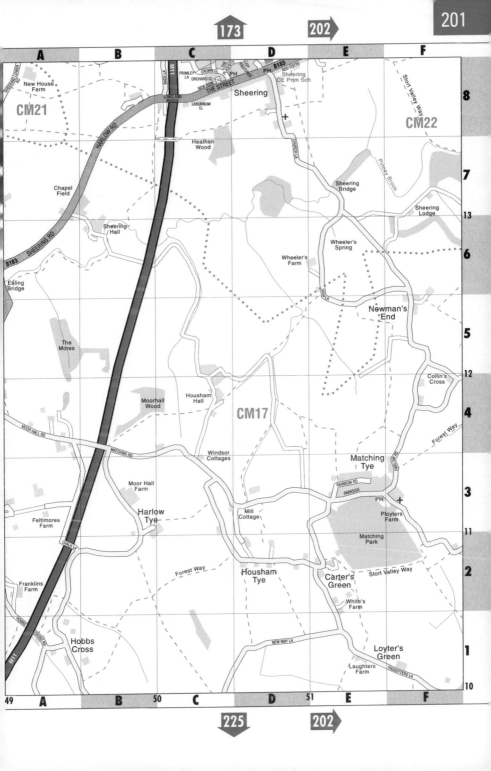

201
174

	A	B	C	D	E	F

A106

8

CM22

CM6

Downhall
Wood

Downhall
Bridge

Thorn
Springs

Parvilles

7

Down Hall
(Hotel)

13

Bob's
Alley

6

The
Gorse

Merry
Meads

Manwood
Green

The Gorse
Wood

Forest Way

Stone Hall
Farm

Kingstons
Farm

5

Stort Valley Way

Matching
Pond

Peartree
Green

Man
Wood

12

Matching

Downhall Rd

4

Matching
Hall

CM17

3

Brick
House

CM5

Airfield
(disused)

Stock
Hall

Putash Rd

Matching
Green

11

More
Spring

PH

2

Newhouse
Farm

Colvers

Perryfield

Matching
Green
CE Prim Sch

Hill Grn

Watersmans
End

Hull
Green

Park
Woods

Little Laver
Hall

Watery La

Little Laver Rd

1

Leather
Bottle

Clarksmead
Spring

Faggotters
Farm

10

52	A	B	53	C	D	54	E	F

201
226

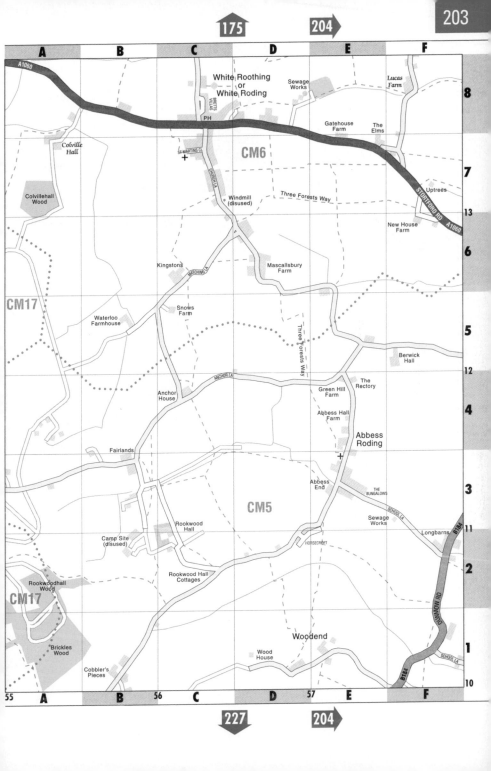

203
176

	A	B	C	D	E	F

8

River Roding

Rodings Prim Sch

B184

DUNMOW RD

Lord's Wood

Leaden Roding

Thatched Cottage

7

Leaden Hall

STORTFORD RD

LAMBTON CL

LEADEN CL

HOLLOWAY CL

BROWNLOWS CL

THE GORSE CL

LORDSWOOD VIEW

Chalks Green

Cloghams Green

Crippings

Skinsley Wood

Chalks Farm

CHALK VILLAS

13

Leaden Roding Bridge

The Old Rectory

B184

Poorhouse Wood

HIGH EASTER RD

Slyces

Chase Wood

6

Meghills

Longstead La

White Hall

CM1

CHELMSFORD RD

5

Hales Farm

CM6

Margaret Roding

Garnish Hall

12

Nether Street

DUNMOW RD

Pig's Spring

Short's Farm

4

Margaret Roding Wood

THE GOSSETTS

3

CM5

Frayes

Highfield Spring

Hockleys

MARKS HALL LA

Four Wantz

A1060

FRAYES CHASE

Marks Hall

Brick House

The Wayside

OSCAR RD

11

2

Waples Mill Farm

Whaypules Mill

1

Beauchamp Roding

BONDS COTTS

SCHOOL LA

Berners Wood

RODEN TERR

Berners Hall

10

58	A	B	59	C	D	60	E	F

203
228

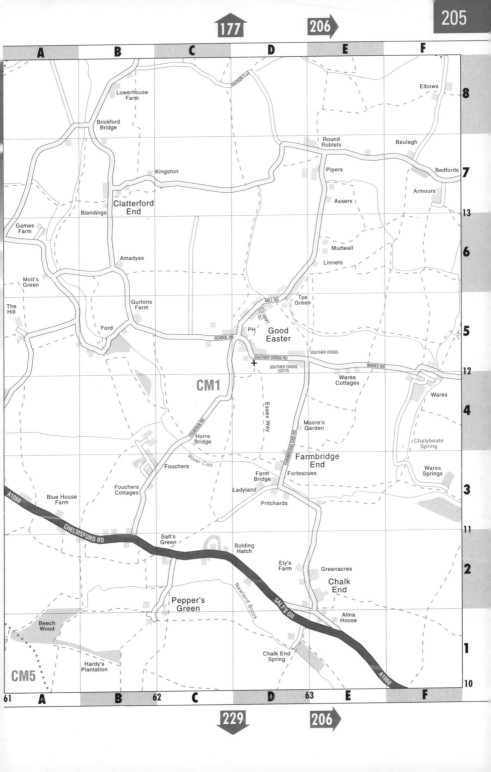

205
178

A **B** **C** **D** **E** **F**

8

Beam Ends

Linsteads

CM3

THE STREET

Baileys

DUCKES LA

Fitzjohn's
Wood

7

Mill
House

Fridays

Wart
Cottages

Bards
Hall

13

MASHBURY RD

Golden Well

6

Mashbury
House

Half
Acre

Smallshoes

BARRACK RD

Gatehouse

5

Winchmore Hill

The
Chase

12

WARES RD

Shop
Cottages

Chignall
Smealy

4

Little
Newarks

Mashbury Hall

The
Bells

Hoddock's
Wood

Mashbury

CM1

3

Great
Newarks

Langleys Farm

11

Howletts
Hall

River Can

2

Nightingale
Wood

Playing
Field

Hall

Chignall Hall Chase
Cottages

1

Little Boyton
Hall

Chignall
Hall

10

64 **A** **B** 65 **C** **D** 66 **E** **F**

205
230

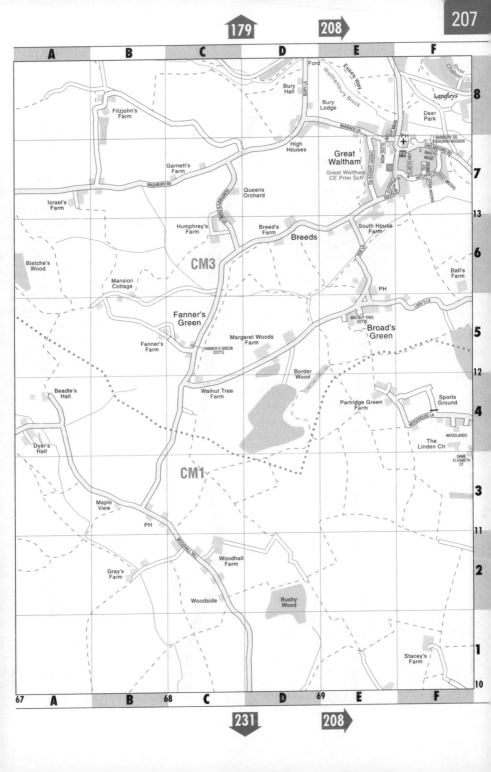

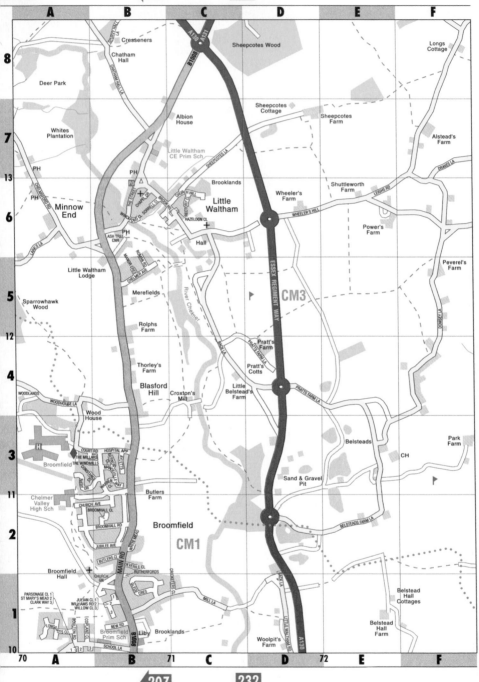

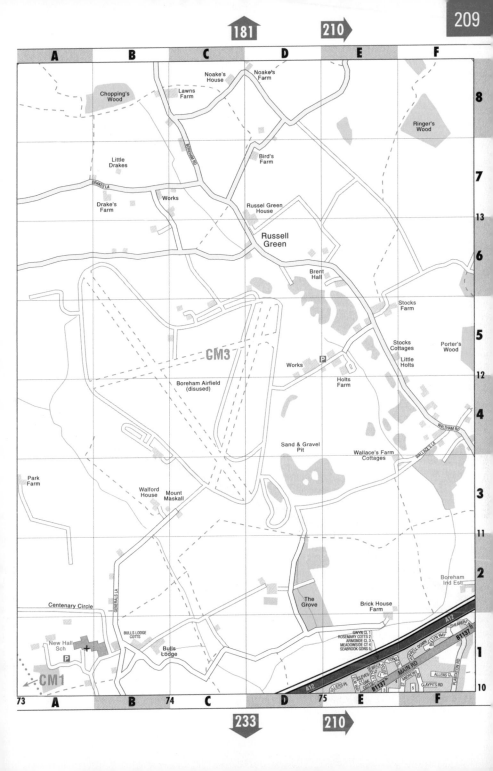

CM8 →

A B C D E F

8

Brockspark Wood

Whitelands

Maddox Hall

Ringer's Farm

Terling Hall Cottages

Terling Hall

Shealy Spring

Termitts Farm

7

TERLING HALL RD

Whitelands Grove

Termitts Chase Cottages

TERMITTS CHASE

13

Porridge Pot

The Rows

Titbeech Wood

Woodside

6

TERLING RD

Lost Wood

CM3

The Grove

Hatfield Peverel

5

STATION TERR

Toppinghoehall Wood

Hatfield Wick

STATION RD

12

Berwick Place

River Ter

SWAN COTTS 1
HAVEN CT 2

A12

4

Toppinghoehall Wood

Berwick Farm

Hatfield Bury Farm

THE STREET

PH

Liby

B1137

Toppinghoe Hall

PH

Hatfield Place

Hatfield Peverel

3

Nursery

Crix

Crabb's Hill Farm

11

Chantry Farm

CHANTRY LA

Crix Farm

Mathcot

Sewage Works

SPORTSMANS LA

2

CHANTRY VILLAS

Hogwells

MAIN RD

Spitman's Gardens

Crabb's Bridge

PORTERS PK I

ORCHARD CLOSE

PH

Roselea

DAMASES LA

Long Wood

Beaumonts

1

Ewers

Mowden

Mowden Hall

Fairfields

Brakeys

MOWDEN HALL LA

10

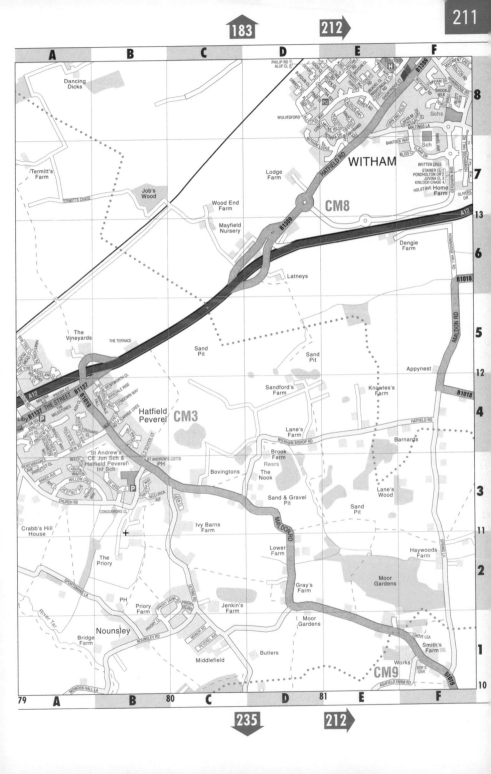

212

Column/Row references
A B C D E F

8 7 13 6 5 12 4 3 11 2 10 1

Place labels

RIVER VIEW
Saul's Bridge
MALDON RD
Sewage Works
A12
BLACKWATER LA
TRIBBLE BRIDGE LA
CUTAWAYS
CONSTANCE CL
LAURENCE AVE
MELTINGS LA
LIFCHILD CL
SCARLETTS
SPARKEY
HALFACRES
Benton Hall
Blue Mills Hill
Blue Mills
Blue Mills Bridge
CH
MALDON RD
Oliver's Farm
Oliver's Farm Nurseries
Glen Acres
SPRAY CHASE
Grove Wood
Glebe Farm Equestrian Ctr
Sparkey Wood
Mope Wood
Sewells Farm
Barn Grove
Hale's Farm
Chantry Wood
West Hall Farm
Threadgold's Farm
Old School House
GREEN MAN LA
PH
CHATLEY LA
WITHAM RD
BIRCH RISE
FINCH'S
HIGH ST
BLYTHE RD
BEECH GN
THE WARRENS
POXEY'S
DUKE CHASE
HANDLEY LA
KELVEDON RD
Wickham Bishops
CHURCH GN
CHURCH COTTS
WILLAND'S
VICAR'S DR
MALLANDS
NACRE DR
SCALEY'S DR
LEIGH DR
CHURCH RD
BLACKSMITHS LA
CHURCH CL
RIVER DR
CROSS RD
BOOTS LA
POOLE ST
ABMOND RD
Liby
PH
GREAT TOTHAM RD
CM8
MAYPOLE RD
MATHEY RD
Grange Farm
Crabb's Farm
Fanners Farm
BACK LA
Wickham Place
River Blackwater
STATION RD
Ballards
GRANGE RD
Hill Place
Wickham Mill Bridge
Whitehouse Farm
St Peter's Church
Garlands
Warren Cottage
WICKHAM HALL LA
Likely Wood
Smallands Hall Farm
CM3
LANGFORD RD
Wickham Hall Cottages
Wickham Hall
Reigate Barn
Whitelands
Wharncliffe
Eastland Wood
Gun Farm
Maypole Wood
Langford Grove
Langford Park
CM9
Matthews Etch
B1018
Great Park
CM9

82 83 84

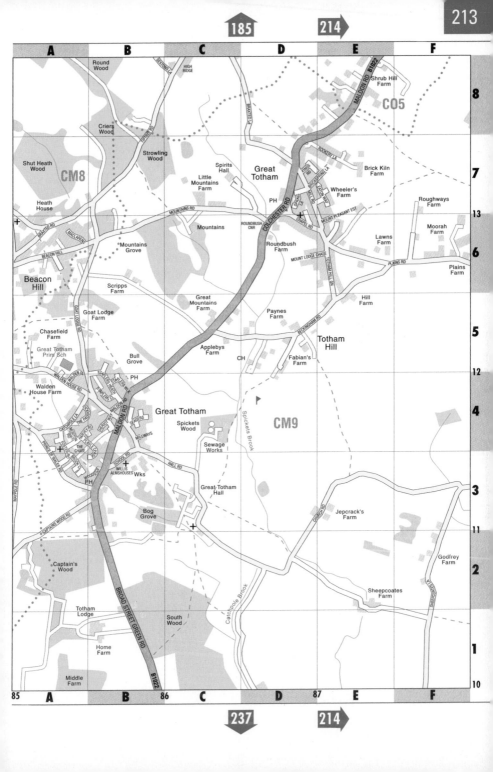

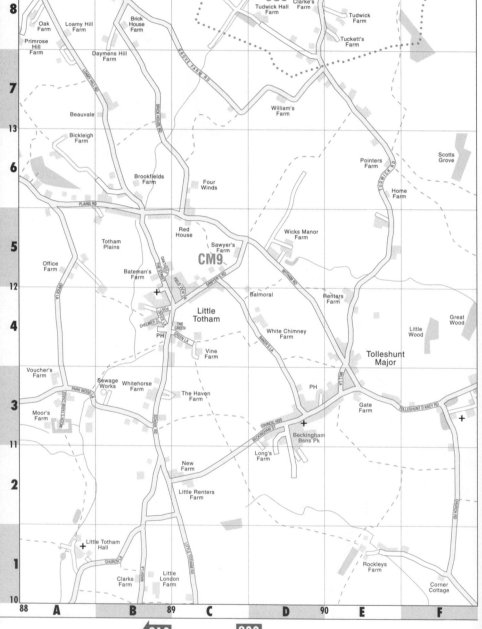

| A | B | C | D | E | F |

8

Oak Farm
Loamy Hill Farm
Grove Farm
Brick House Farm
Primrose Hill Farm
Daymens Hill Farm

Tudwick Hall Farm
Clarke's Farm
Clarke's Barn
Tudwick Farm
Tuckett's Farm

CO5

7

13

Beauvale
Bickleigh Farm

William's Farm

6

Brookfields Farm
Four Winds
Pointers Farm
Scotts Grove
Home Farm

PLAINS RD

5

Office Farm
Totham Plains
Red House
Sawyer's Farm
Wicks Manor Farm

CM9

12

Bateman's Farm
Balmoral
Renters Farm

4

Little Totham
THE GREEN
PH
White Chimney Farm
Little Wood
Great Wood

Tolleshunt Major

3

Voucher's Farm
Sewage Works
Whitehorse Farm
The Haven Farm
PH
Gate Farm

Moor's Farm

11

New Farm
Beckingham Bsns Pk
Long's Farm

2

Little Renters Farm

1

Little Totham Hall
Rockleys Farm

Clarks Farm
Little London Farm
Corner Cottage

10

| 88 | A | B | 89 | C | D | 90 | E | F |

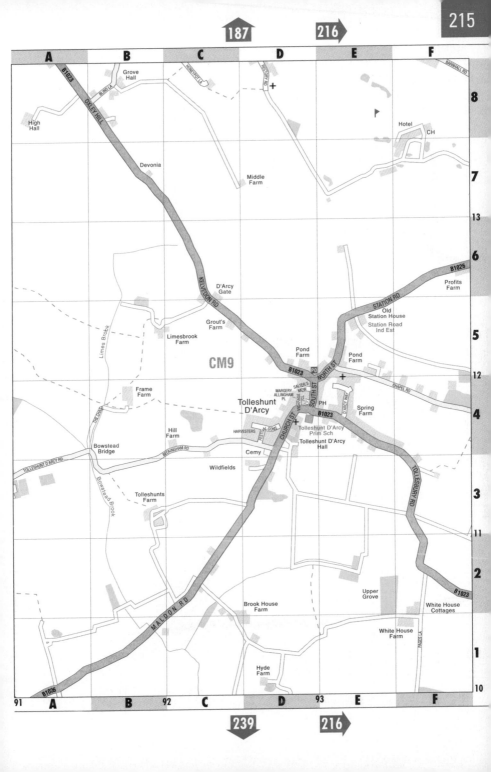

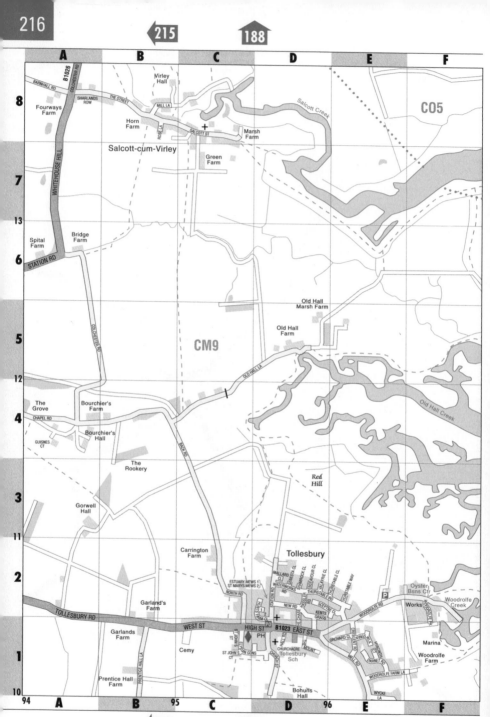

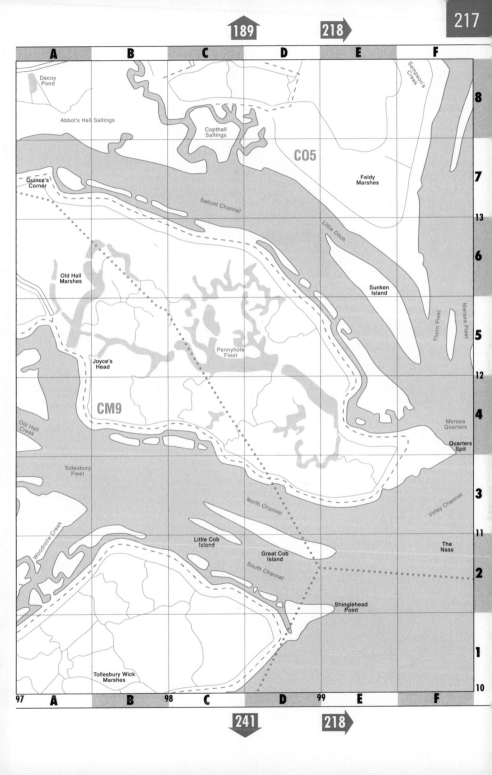

A   B   C   D   E   F

8

Decoy Pond

Abbot's Hall Saltings

Copthall Saltings

Sampson's Creek

CO5

7

Quince's Corner

Salcott Channel

Feldy Marshes

13

Little Ditch

6

Old Hall Marshes

Sunken Island

Thorn Fleet

Mersea Fleet

5

Joyce's Head

Pennyhole Fleet

12

CM9

4

Old Hall Creek

Mersea Quarters

Quarters Spit

Tollesbury Fleet

3

North Channel

Virley Channel

Woodrolfe Creek

Little Cob Island

11

Great Cob Island

The Nass

South Channel

2

Shinglehead Point

1

Tollesbury Wick Marshes

10

A   B   98   C   D   99   E   F

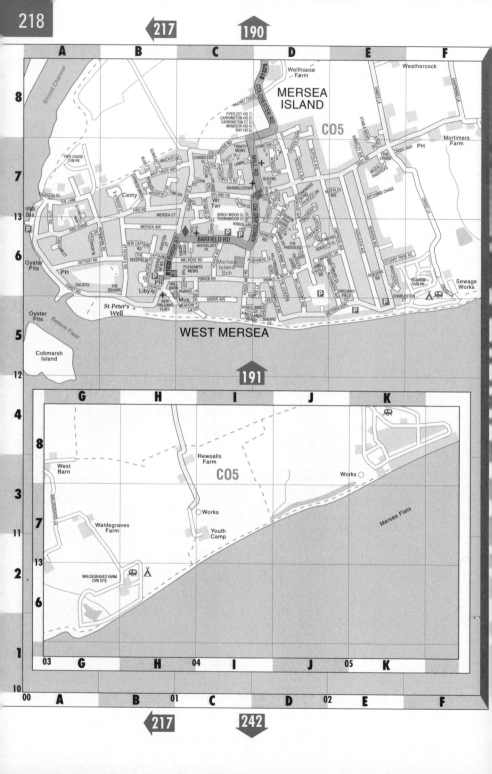

MERSEA
ISLAND

Wellhouse
Farm

Weathercock

CO5

Mortimers
Farm

WEST MERSEA

Cobmarsh
Island

Oyster
Pits

Oyster
Pits

St Peter's
Well

191

West
Barn

Rewsalls
Farm

CO5

Works

Waldegraves
Farm

Works

Youth
Camp

Mersea Flats

WALDEGRAVES FARM
CVN SITE

03   G   H   04   I   J   05   K

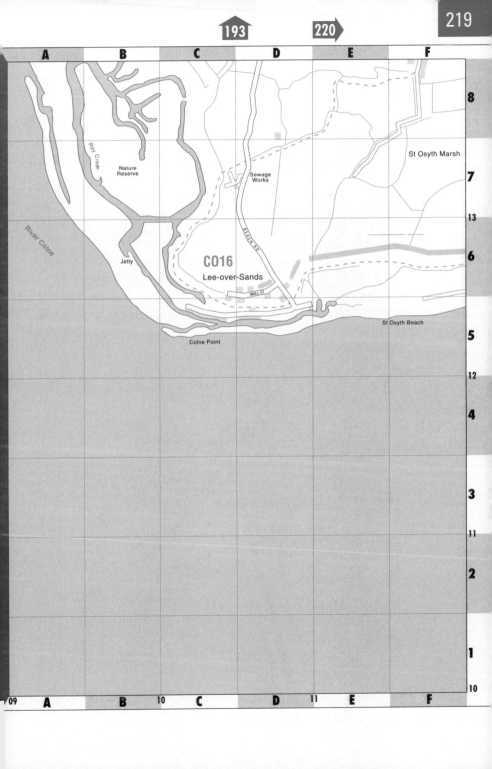

193
220

St Osyth Marsh

Ray Creek

Nature
Reserve

River Colne

Sewage
Works

CO16
Lee-over-Sands

Jetty

BEACH RD

WALL ST

Colne Point

St Osyth Beach

09
10
11

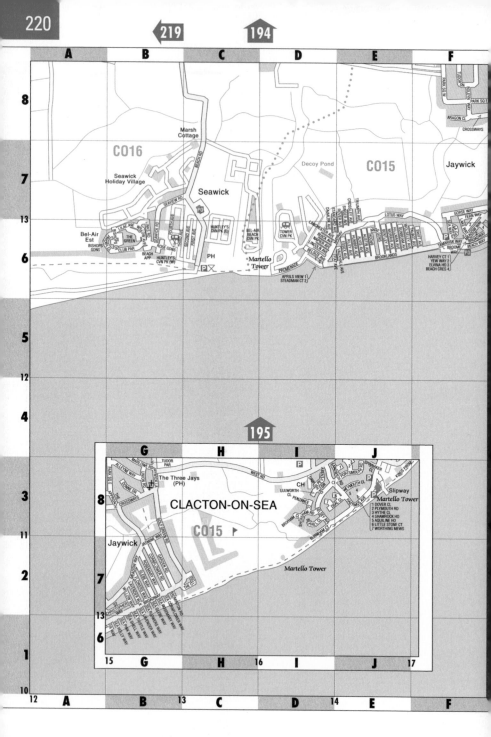

219
194
195

Marsh
Cottage

CO16

Seawick
Holiday Village

Seawick

Decoy Pond

CO15

Jaywick

LOTUS WAY

Bel-Air
Est

BISHOPS
GDNS

THE
GREEN

CLUB PAR

BEACH
APP

ROSE GDNS

HUNTLEY'S
CVN PK (W)

HUNTLEY'S
CVN PK (E)

BEACH RD

SEAVIEW RD

SECOND AVE

FIRST AVE

BEL-AIR
BEACH
CVN PK

TOWER
CVN PK

PH

Martello
Tower

PROMENADE

BROOKLANDS

APRILS VIEW 1
STEADMAN CT 2

GORSE WAY

FERN WAY

TAMARISK WAY

BROOME
WAY

BEACH WAY

HARVEY CT 1
YEW WAY 2
ELVINA HO 3
BEACH CRES 4

PARK SQ W

PARK SQ E

BOLEYN
WAY

TUDOR
WAY

ARAGON CL

CROSSWAYS

CLACTON-ON-SEA

CO15

The Three Jays
(PH)

Jaywick

WEST RD

TUDOR
PAR

PARK SQ E

ALLEYNE WAY

MARLOWE RD

CROSSWAYS

LULWORTH
CL

PENZANCE

PENDINE

BRIXHAM CL

CLACTON RD

CHAPEL RD

BURNHAM CL

CH

PORTSMOUTH

WEYMOUTH CL

SPINNAKER

KINGS PARADE

Slipway
Martello Tower

1 DOVER CL
2 PLYMOUTH RD
3 HYTHE CL
4 SHAMROCK HO
5 AQUILINE HO
6 LITTLE STONE CT
7 WORTHING MEWS

Martello Tower

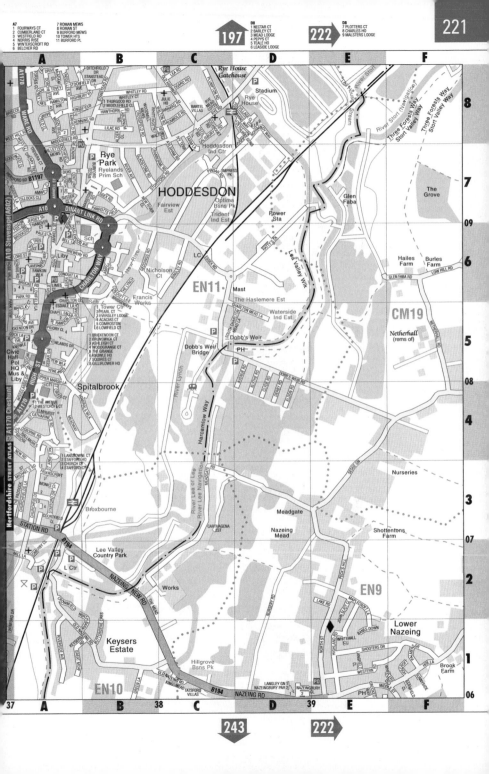

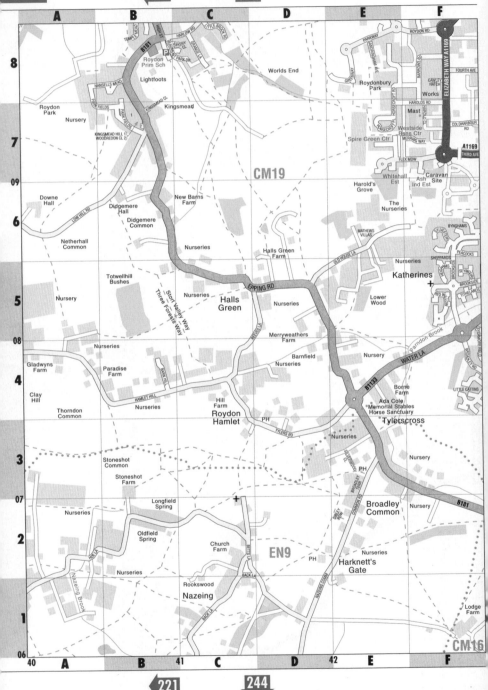

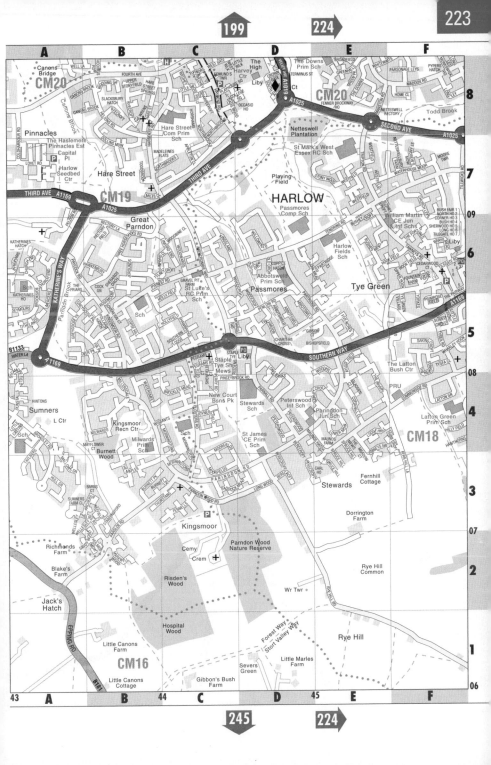

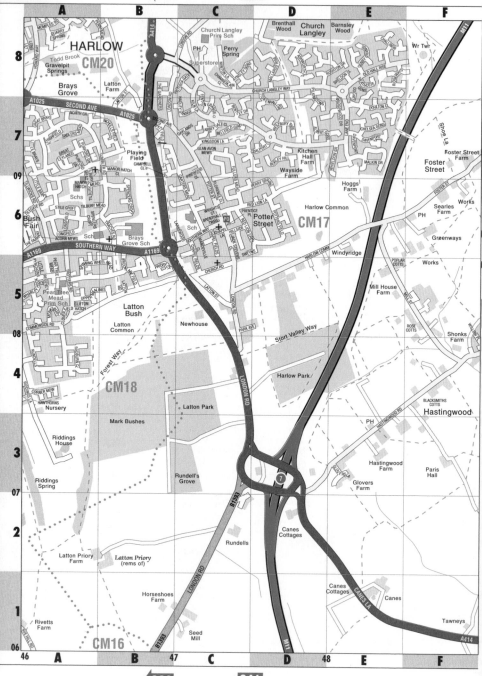

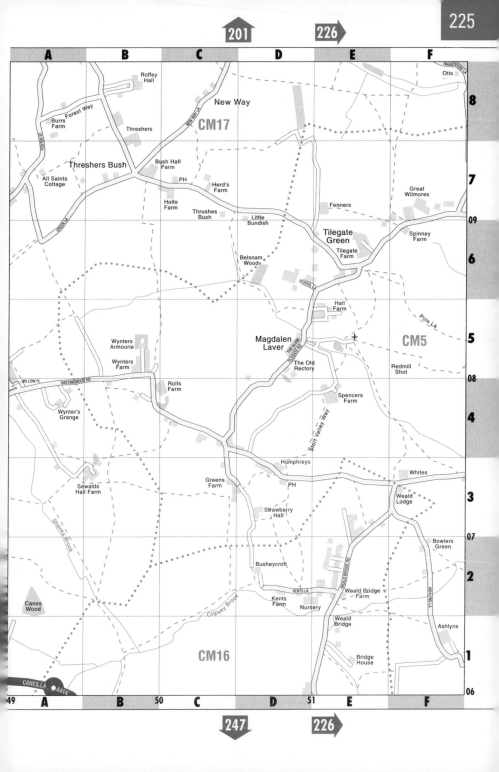

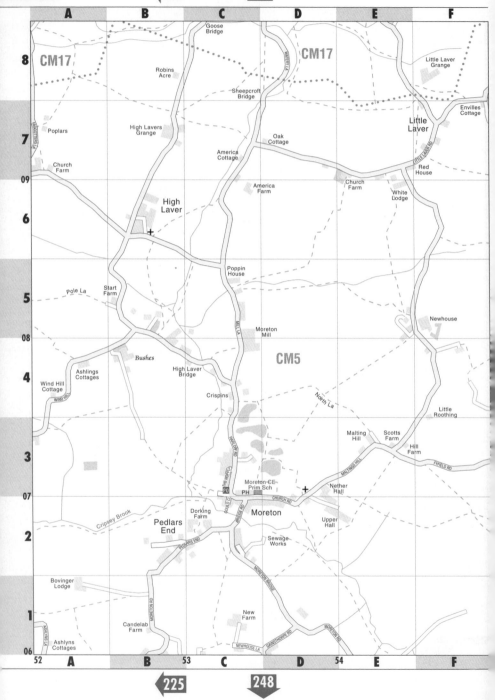

225
202

| | A | B | C | D | E | F |

Goose
Bridge

CM17

Little Laver
Grange

8

Robins
Acre

Sheepcroft
Bridge

CM17

Envilles
Cottage

Poplars

High Lavers
Grange

Little
Laver

7

Oak
Cottage

09

Church
Farm

America
Cottage

America
Farm

Church
Farm

Red
House

High
Laver

White
Lodge

6

Poppin
House

Pole La

Start
Farm

Moreton
Mill

Newhouse

5

08

Bushes

CM5

Ashlings
Cottages

High Laver
Bridge

4

Wind Hill
Cottage

Crispins

North La

Little
Roothing

Malting
Hill

Scotts
Farm

Hill
Farm

3

Moreton CE
Prim Sch

PH

Nether
Hall

07

Cripsey Brook

Dorking
Farm

Moreton

Upper
Hall

Pedlars
End

Sewage
Works

2

Bovinger
Lodge

New
Farm

1

Candelab
Farm

06

Ashlyns
Cottages

Newhouse La

| 52 | A | B | 53 | C | D | 54 | E | F |

225
248

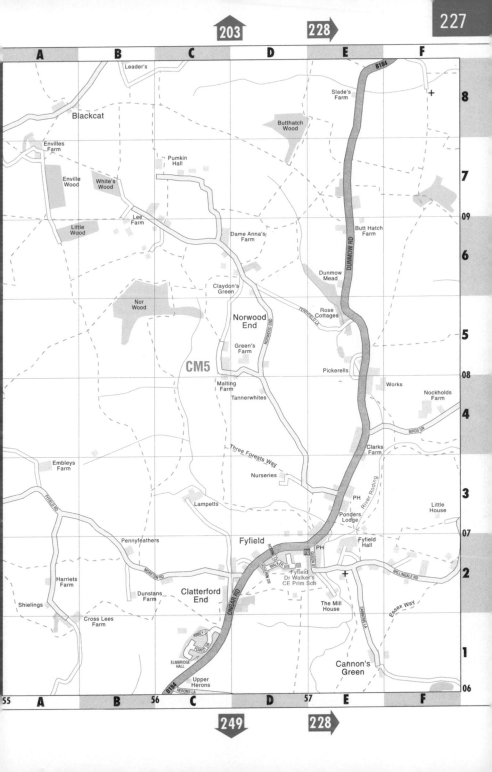

203
228
249
228

A B C D E F

8
7
09
6
5
08
4
3
07
2
1
06

Leader's

Blackcat

Slade's
Farm

B184

Butthatch
Wood

Envilles
Farm

Pumkin
Hall

Enville
Wood

White's
Wood

Lee
Farm

Dame Anna's
Farm

Butt Hatch
Farm

Little
Wood

DUNMOW RD

Claydon's
Green

Dunmow
Mead

Nor
Wood

Norwood
End

PERRYFIELD LA

Rose
Cottages

RINGWOOD RD

CM5

Green's
Farm

Malting
Farm

Pickerells

Works

Nockholds
Farm

Tannerwhites

BIRDS DR

Three Forests Way

Clarks
Farm

Embleys
Farm

Nurseries

River Roding

Lampetts

PH

Little
House

Ponders
Lodge

Pennyfeathers

Fyfield

PH

Fyfield
Hall

LYFIELD RD

Fyfield
Dr Walker's
CE Prim Sch

WILLINGALE RD

MORETON RD

WALKER AVE

QUEEN ST

Harriets
Farm

Dunstans
Farm

Clatterford
End

ONGAR RD

The Mill
House

Essex Way

Shielings

CANONS LA

Cross Lees
Farm

ABBEY CL

FORREST DR

Cannon's
Green

ELMBRIDGE
HALL

Upper
Herons

B184

HERONS LA

55 A B 56 C D 57 E F

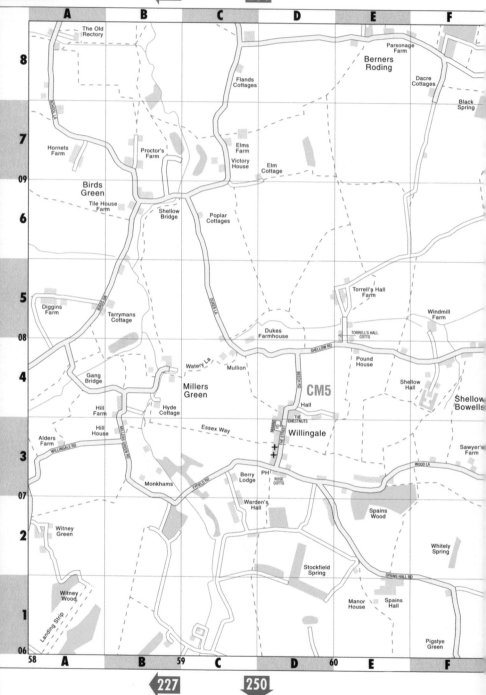

A **B** **C** **D** **E** **F**

The Old Rectory

Parsonage Farm

Berners Roding

Dacre Cottages

Black Spring

8

Flands Cottages

Hornets Farm

Proctor's Farm

Elms Farm

Victory House

Elm Cottage

7

09

Birds Green

Tile House Farm

Shellow Bridge

Poplar Cottages

6

Torrell's Hall Farm

Windmill Farm

5

Diggins Farm

Tarrymans Cottage

Dukes Farmhouse

Torrell's Hall Cotts

08

Shellow Rd

Pound House

Shellow Hall

Shellow Bowells

4

Gang Bridge

Hill Farm

Hyde Cottage

Watery La

Mullion

Millers Green

BEECH RD

CM5

Hall

THE CHESTNUTS

Willingale

3

Alders Farm

Hill House

WILLINGALE RD

MILLERS GREEN RD

Essex Way

THE STREET

MANNS RD

Sawyer's Farm

WOOD LA

07

Monkhams

LYE FIELD RD

Berry Lodge

PH

ROSE COTTS

Warden's Hall

Spains Wood

2

Witney Green

Whitely Spring

Stockfield Spring

SPAINS HALL RD

1

Witney Wood

Landing Strip

Manor House

Spains Hall

Pigstye Green

06

A 58 **B** 59 **C** **D** 60 **E** **F**

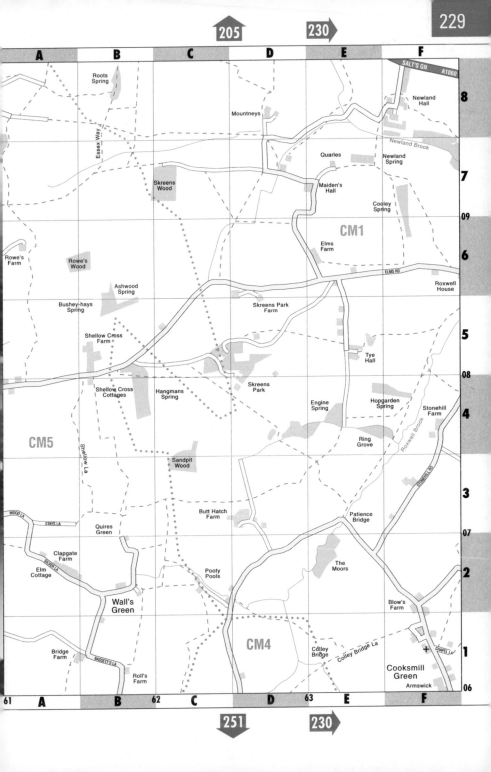

A B C D E F

SALT'S GN A1060

Newland Hall

8

Newland Brook

Roots Spring

Mountneys

Quarles

Newland Spring

7

Essex Way

Skreens Wood

Maiden's Hall

Cooley Spring

CM1

09

Elms Farm

6

Rowe's Farm

Rowe's Wood

ELMS RD

Roxwell House

Ashwood Spring

Skreens Park Farm

Bushey-hays Spring

5

Shellow Cross Farm

Tye Hall

08

Shellow Cross Cottages

Hangmans Spring

Skreens Park

Engine Spring

Hopgarden Spring

Stonehill Farm

4

CM5

Ring Grove

Roxwell Brook

Shellow La

Sandpit Wood

3

STOKELL RD

WOOD LA

STAYS LA

Butt Hatch Farm

Patience Bridge

07

Quires Green

Clapgate Farm

The Moors

2

SILVER LA

Elm Cottage

Pooty Pools

Blow's Farm

Wall's Green

Bridge Farm

BASSETT'S LA

CM4

Colley Bridge

Colley Bridge La

CHAPEL LA

1

Roll's Farm

Cooksmill Green

Armswick

06

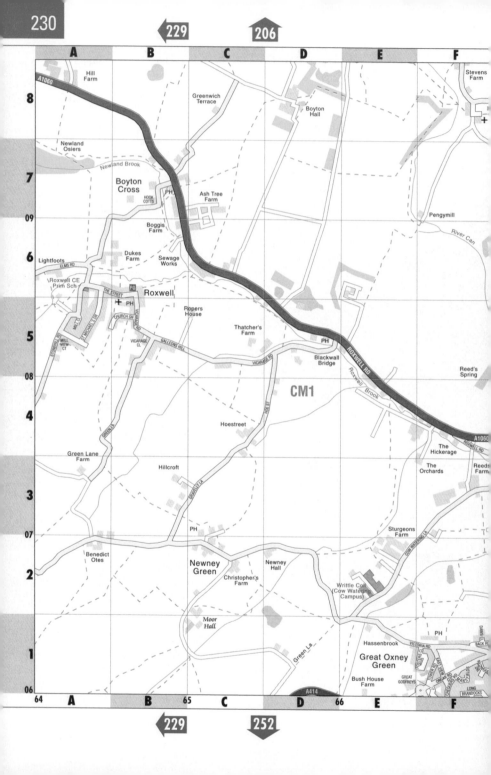

229

206

A1060
Hill Farm
Greenwich Terrace
Boyton Hall
Stevens Farm

8

Newland Osiers
Newland Brook

7
Boyton Cross
HOOK COTTS
PH
Ash Tree Farm
Pengymill

09
Boggis Farm
River Can

6
Lightfoots
ELMS RD
Dukes Farm
Sewage Works

Roxwell CE Prim Sch
THE STREET
Roxwell
Ropers House
Thatcher's Farm
PH
Reed's Spring

5
MILL LA
ST MICHAEL'S DR
CHURCH GN
VICARAGE CL
GALLEONS HILL
VICARAGE RD
Blackwall Bridge
ROXWELL RD

08
MILL VIEW CT
STURGEON RD

CM1
Roxwell Brook

4
GREEN LA
Hoestreet
Roxwell Brook
A1060 ROXWELL RD

Green Lane Farm
Hillcroft
GREEN LA
The Hickerage
The Orchards
Reeds Farm

3

07
PH

2
Benedict Otes
Newney Green
Christopher's Farm
Newney Hall
Sturgeons Farm
COW WATERING LA

Moor Hall
Writtle Coll (Cow Watering Campus)
PH
DAWES

Hassenbrook
VICTORIA RD
GREAT GODFREYS
PH
BACK LA

1
Great Oxney Green
MAN'S
LONG BRANDOCKS

06
Green La
Bush House Farm

64
A

65
B
C

A414
D
66
E

F

229

252

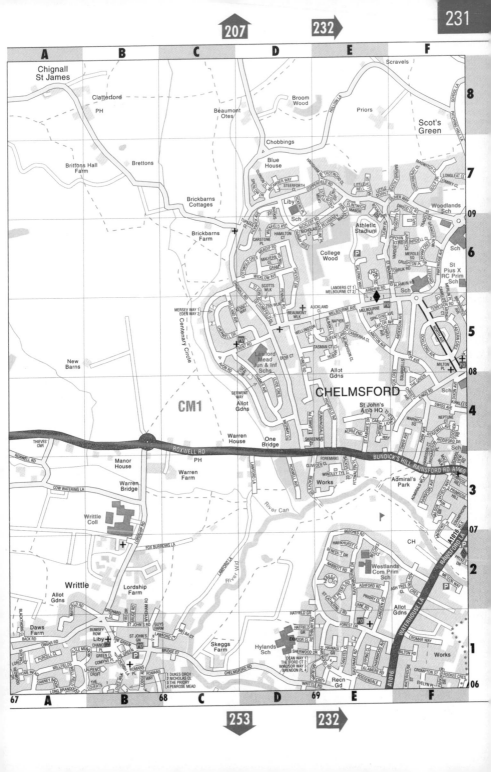

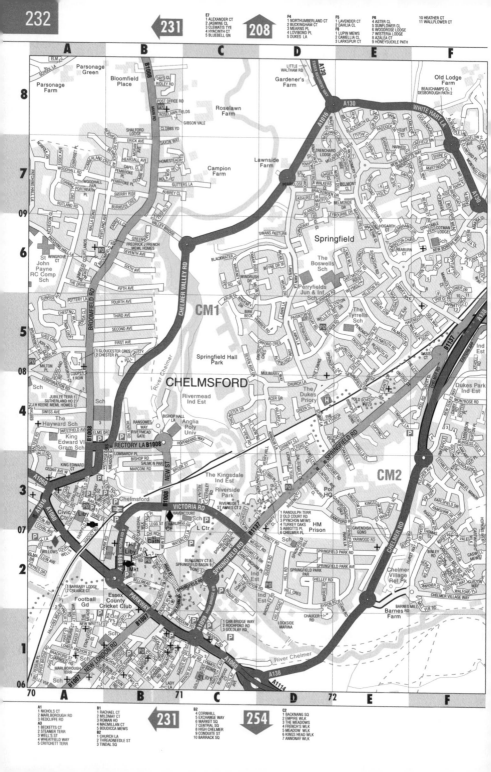

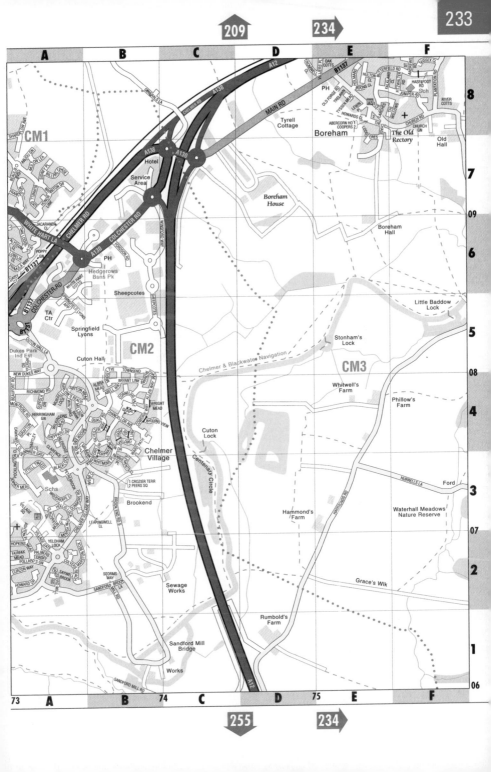

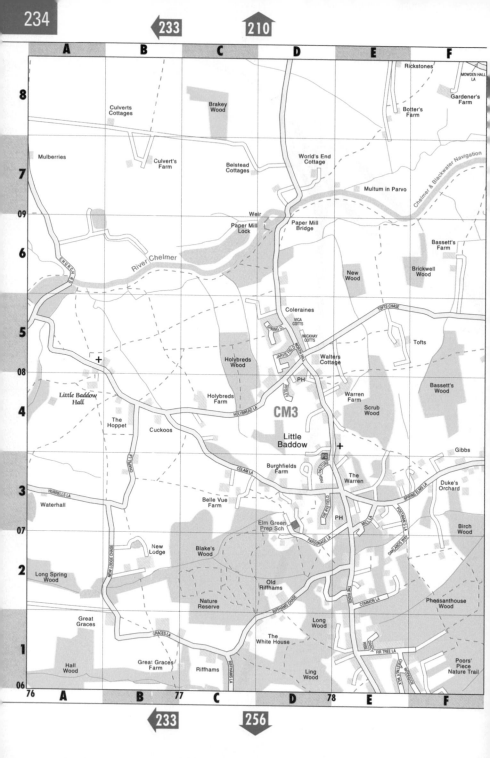

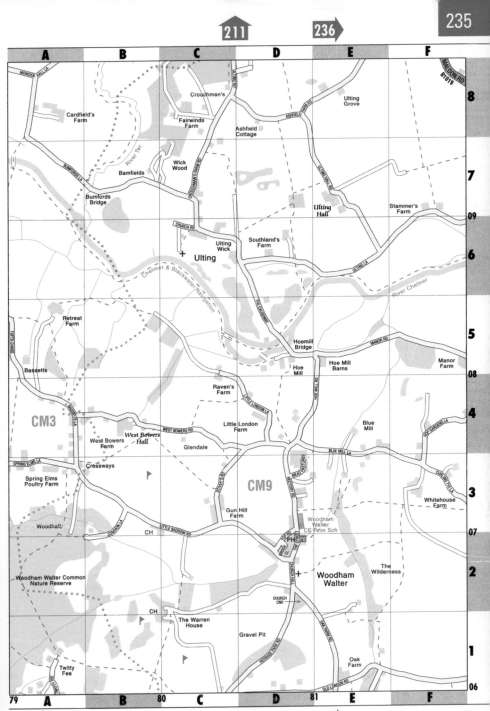

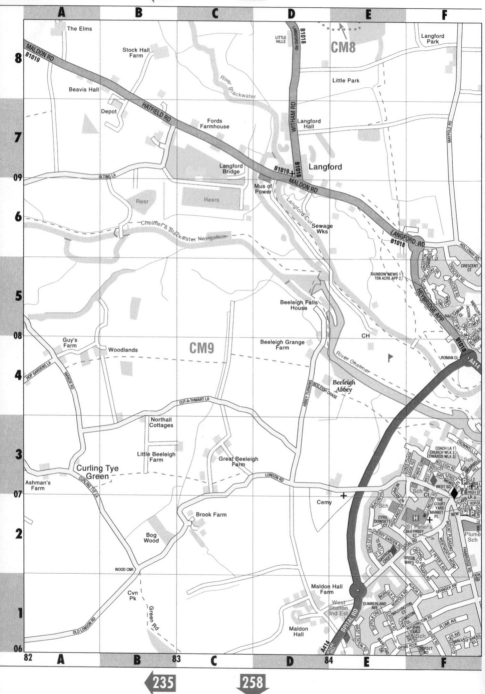

A   B   C   D   E   F

8   MALDON RD
B1019

The Elms

Stock Hall Farm

Little Hills

B1018
LANGFORD RD

CM8

Langford Park

Beavis Hall

River Blackwater

HATFIELD RD

Depot

Fords Farmhouse

WITHAM RD

Little Park

Langford Hall

7

09

ILTING LA

Langford Bridge

B1019
B1018

MALDON RD

Langford

Resr

Resrs

Mus of Power

Langford Cut

Sewage Wks

LANGFORD RD
B1018

6

Chelmer & Blackwater Navigation

HONEYWOOD RD

CRESCENT CT

RAINBOW MEWS 1
TEN ACRE APP 2

HOLBRIDGE APP

5

Beeleigh Falls House

CH

River Chelmer

Guy's Farm

Woodlands

CM9

Beeleigh Grange Farm

ROMAN CL

A414

08

HOP GARDENS LA
MANOR RD

4

Beeleigh Abbey

ABBEY TURNING
BEELEIGH CHASE

CUT-A-THWART LA

Northall Cottages

CROMWELL LA

COACH LA 1
CHURCH LA 2
EDWARDS WLK 3

Sch

3

Curling Tye Green

CURLING TYE LA

Little Beeleigh Farm

Great Beeleigh Farm

LONDON RD

WEST SQ
HIGH ST

THE COURT YARD MARKET

07

Ashman's Farm

Cemy

CYRIL DOWSETT CT

St Peter's

NEW ST

H

GUERNSEY CT

Plume Sch

2

OLD LONDON RD

Brook Farm

Bog Wood

GREEN WAY 3

ST PETER'S AVE

MOUNT PLEASANT

FAMBRIDGE RD

WOOD CNR

1

Cvn Pk

Green Rd

Maldon Hall Farm

West Station Ind Est

CUMBERLAND AVE

WASHINGTON CT

PARK DR

SPITAL RD

Sch

PLUME AVE

DORSET RD

Maldon Hall

A414

06

82   A   B   83   C   D   84   E   F

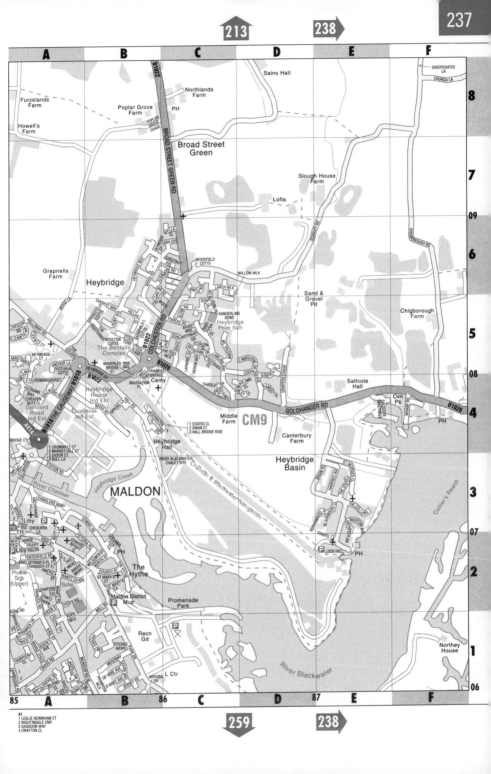

237
214

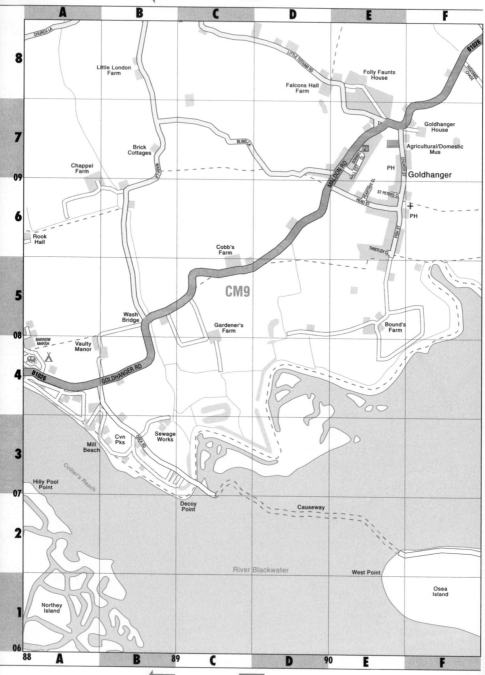

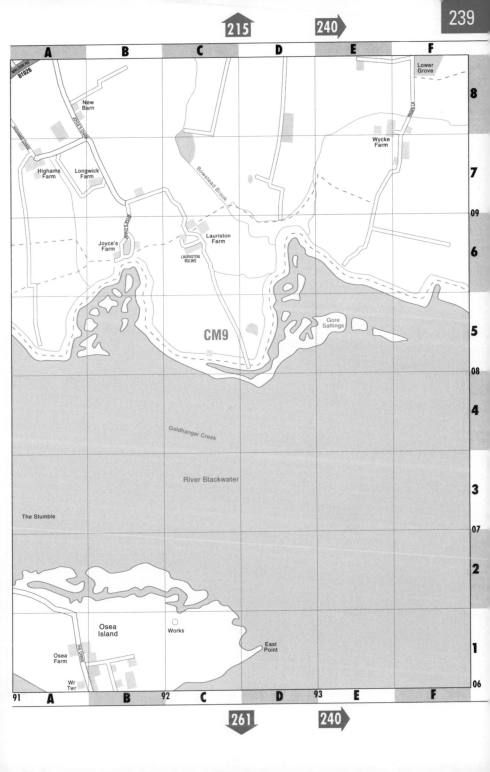

215
240

A B C D E F

8

Lower
Grove

New
Barn

JOYCE'S CHASE

Wycke
Farm

7

Highams
Farm

Longwick
Farm

Bowstead Brook

09

Joyce's
Farm

JOYCE'S CHASE

Lauriston
Farm

6

LAURISTON
BGLWS

Lauriston
Farm

CM9

Gore
Saltings

5

08

4

Goldhanger Creek

River Blackwater

3

07

The Stumble

2

Osea
Island

Works

East
Point

1

Osea
Farm

THE CHASE

Wr
Twr

06

261
240

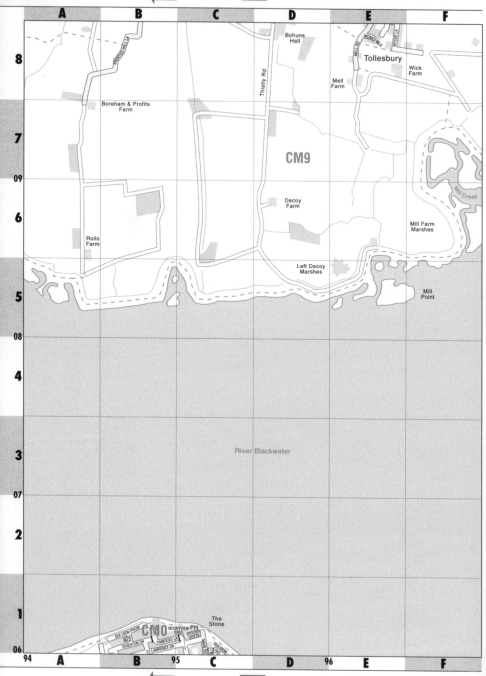

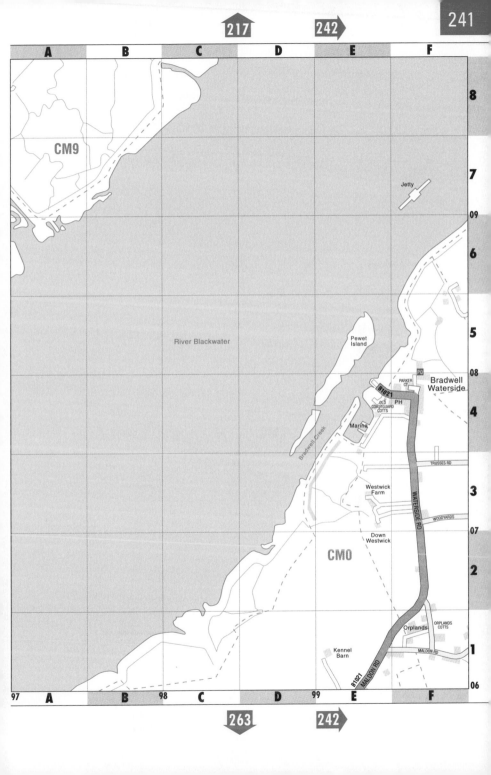

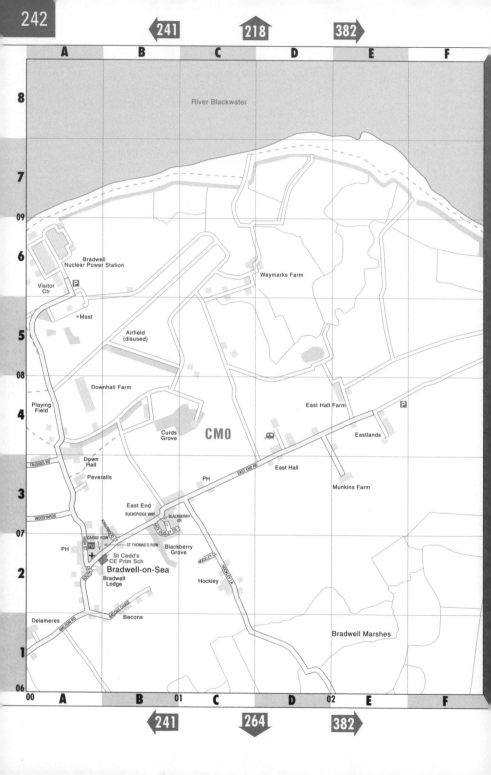

243
222

| A | B | C | D | E | F |

8

Nazeing Park

Nazeingwood Common

BACK LA

Nazeing Brook

+

Curtis Farm

MIDDLE ST

7

CH

Stort Valley Way

Belchers Farm

Nazeing Gate

PH

Epping Green House

NAZEING COMM

BELCHERS LA

Epping Long Green

Sturtsbury Farm

05

Mamelons Farm

Bumble's Green

St Lawrence Farm

Long Green

WALTHAM RD

THE HEIGHTS

BUMBLES GREEN LA

ALTANING CL

THE AVENUE

6

Copy Wood

CM16

The Bungalow

Harold's Park Farm

5

Galleyhill Green

EN9

Nabhill Grove

04

Deerpark Wood

Parvills Farm

Ballhill Wood

4

The Springs

The Manor House

Claverhambury

Three Forests Way

Forest Way

Galley Hill

CLAVERHAMBURY FARM RIGLWS

Sewage Works

Woodyers Farm

Reevesgate Farm

Gills Plantation

3

Brayshill Spring

CLAVERHAMBURY RD

Stocking Grove

Longcroft Grove

Maynards Farm

Cobbinsend Farm

Spratt's Hedgerow Wood

2

Maple Springs

Scatterbushes Wood

Cobbin's Brook

COBBINSEND RD

03

BREACH BARNS CVN PK

Fernhall Farm

LONG ST

Nursery

Fernhall Wood

The Cottages

Rookery Wood

1

Brookmeadow Wood

Willows

FERNHALL LA

02

| 40 | A | B | 41 | C | D | 42 | E | F |

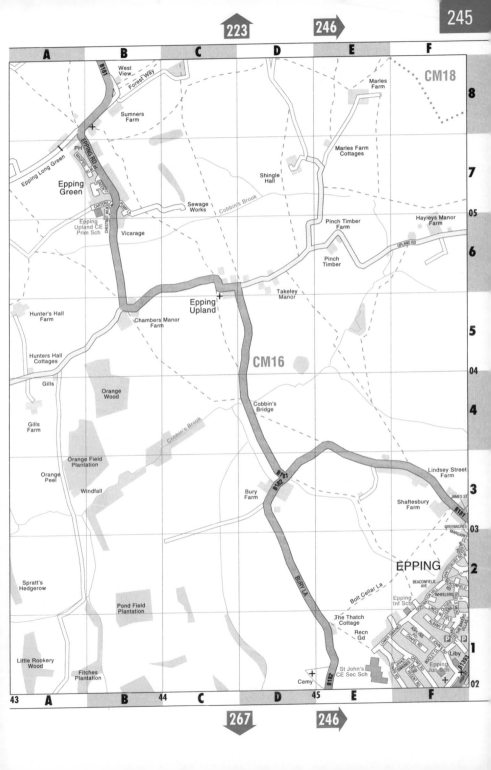

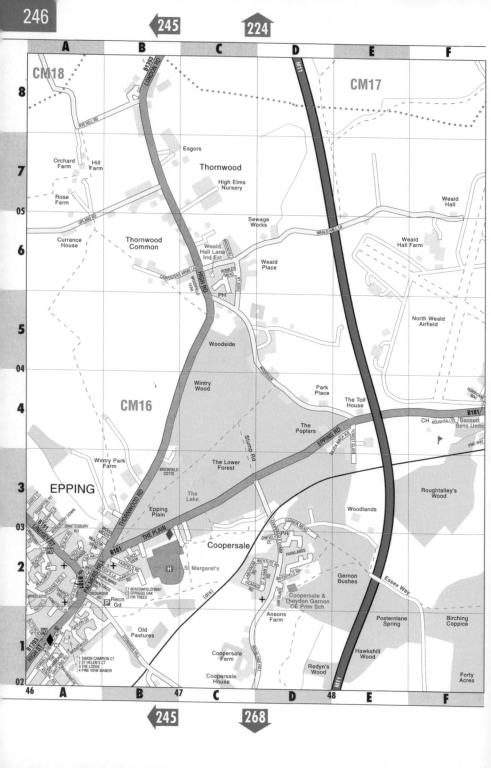

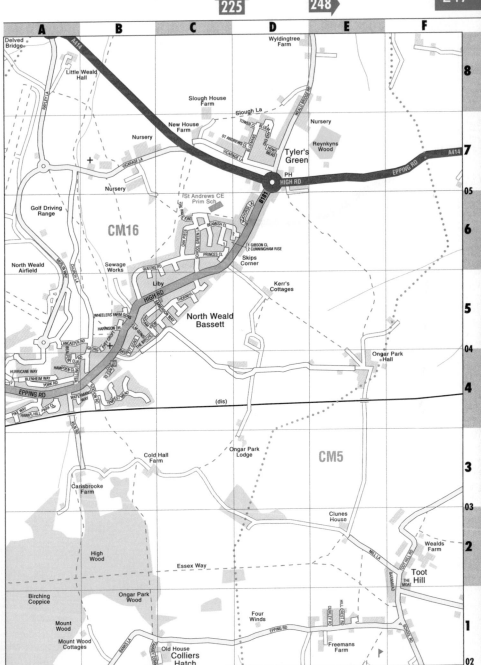

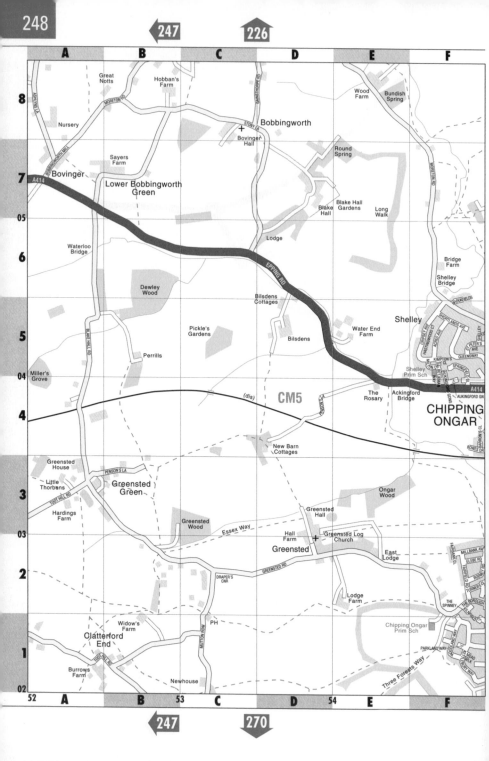

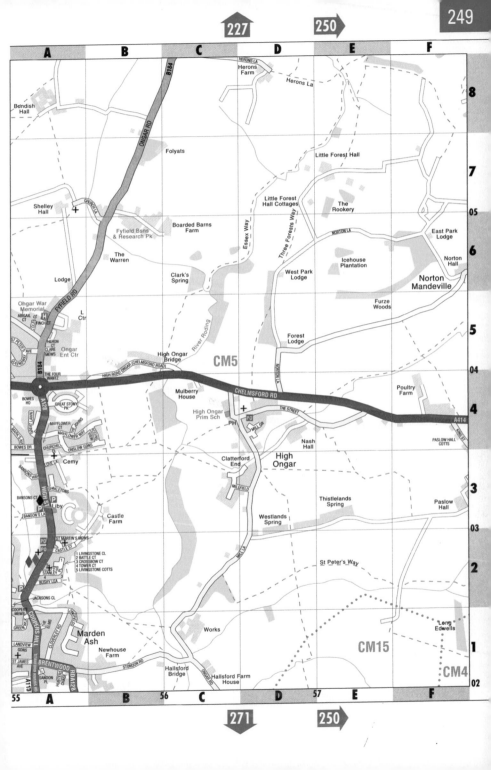

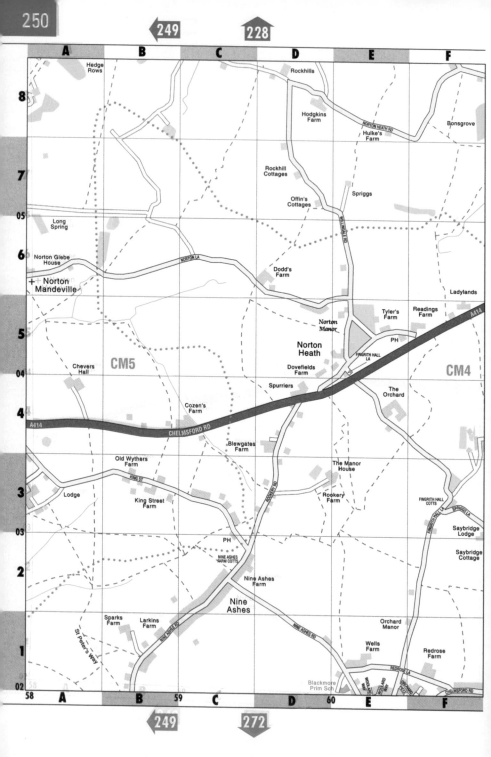

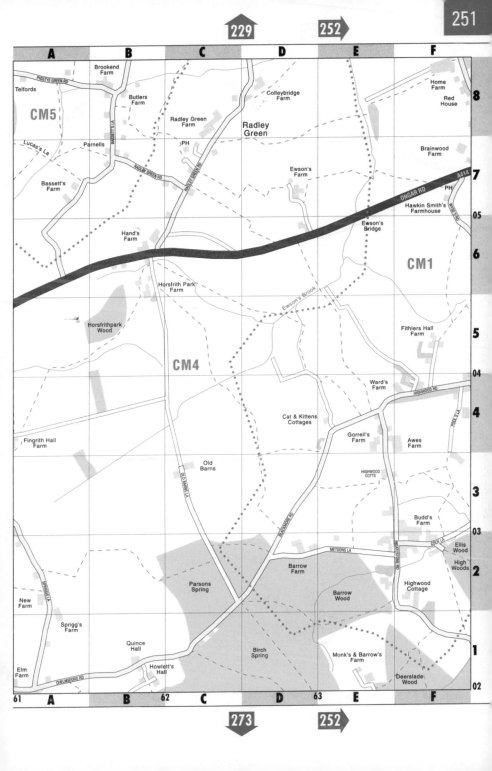

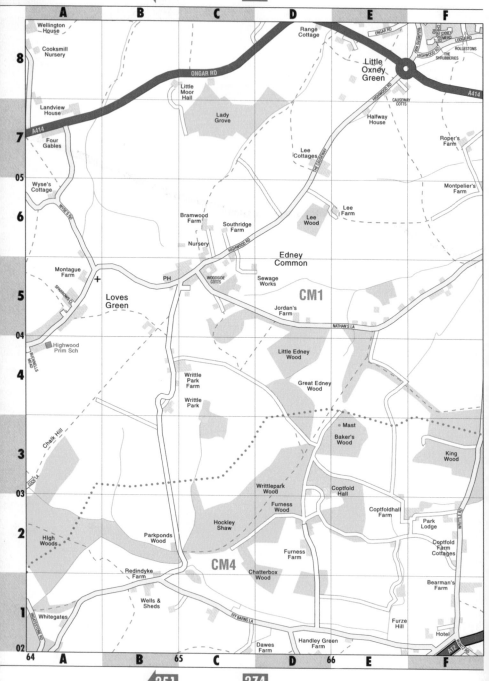

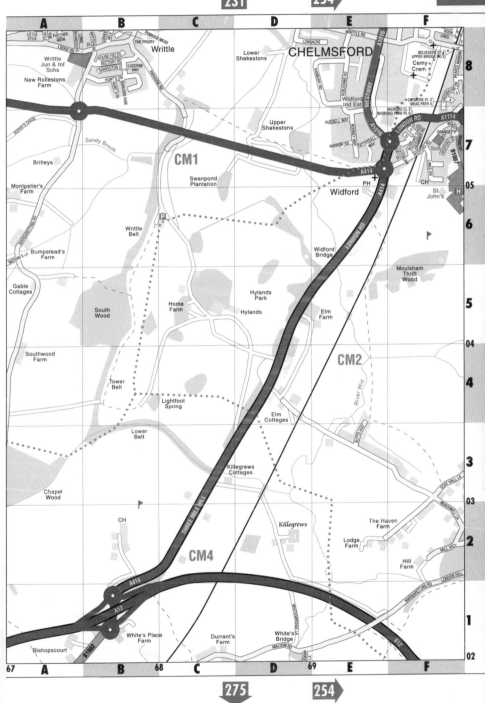

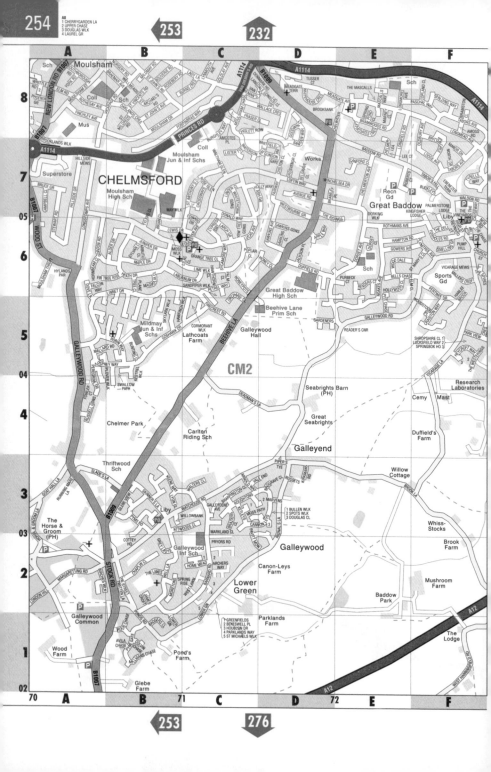

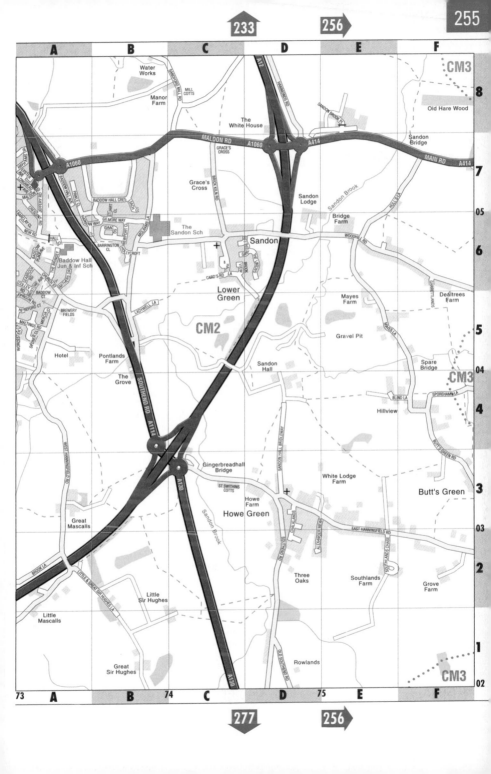

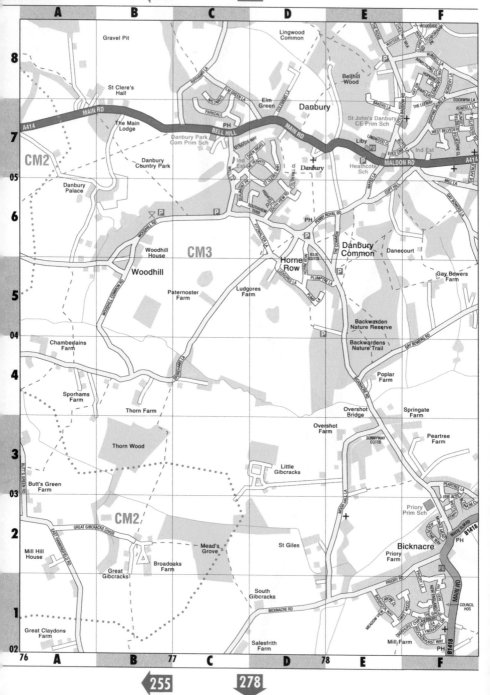

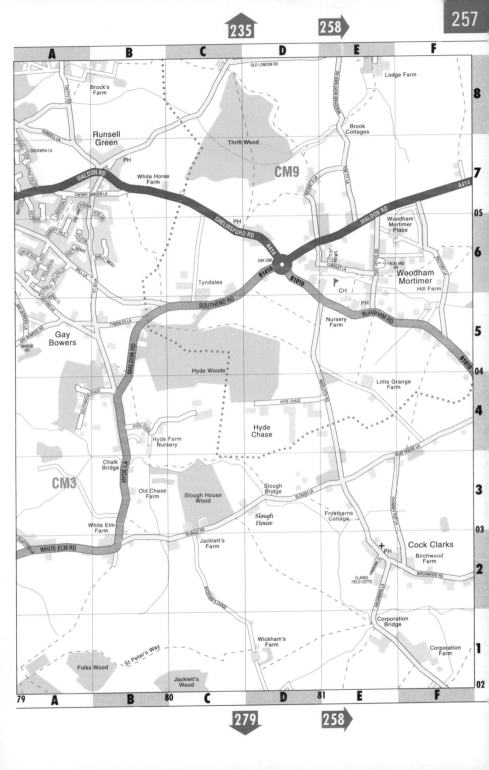

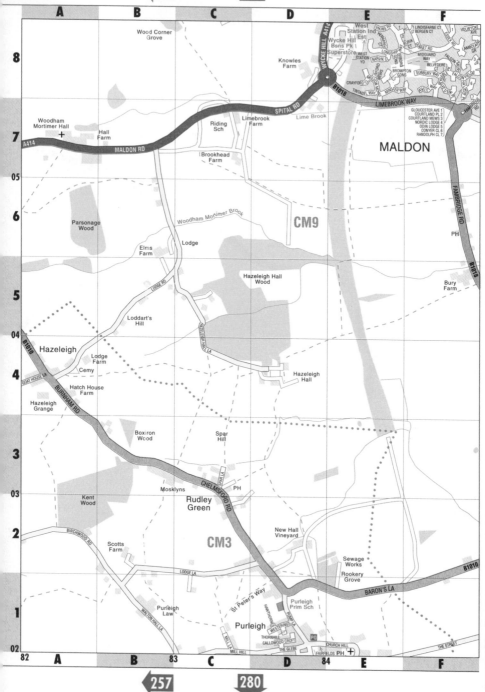

257

236

A **B** **C** **D** **E** **F**

Wood Corner Grove

West Station Ind Est

Wycke Hill Bsns Pk
Superstore

West Station YD

LINDISFARNE CT 1
BERGEN CT 2

VOLURYCKE AVE

Knowles Farm

MIDGUARD WAY

BELVEDERE

BROMPTON GDNS

SUNBURY WAY

FALCON CL

8

Woodham Mortimer Hall

Hall Farm

Riding Sch

Limebrook Farm

Lime Brook

SPITAL RD

LIMEBROOK WAY

GLOUCESTER AVE 1
COURTLAND PL 2
COURTLAND MEWS 3
NORDIC LODGE 4
ODIN LODGE 5
CONYER CL 6
RANDOLPH CL 7

7

A414

MALDON RD

Brookhead Farm

MALDON

FAMBRIDGE RD

05

Parsonage Wood

Woodham Mortimer Brook

CM9

PH

6

Elms Farm

Lodge

B1010

Hazeleigh Hall Wood

Bury Farm

5

Loddart's Hill

LODGE RD

04

Hazeleigh

Lodge Farm

Cemy

SCHLEIGH HALL LA

Hazeleigh Hall

B1010

GOAT HOUSE LA

Hatch House Farm

BURNHAM RD

4

Hazeleigh Grange

Boxiron Wood

Spar Hill

3

03

Kent Wood

Mosklyns

CHELMSFORD RD

TYPES

PH

Rudley Green

New Hall Vineyard

Sewage Works

BIRCHWOOD RD

2

Scotts Farm

CM3

Rookery Grove

B1010

LODGE LA

BARON'S LA

1

WALTON HALL LA

Purleigh Law

St Peter's Way

HAWTHORNS

Purleigh Prim Sch

Purleigh

PO

CHURCH HILL

02

THORNHILL

CALLOWOOD CROFT

WESTERINGS

MILL HILL

THE GLEBE

FAIRFIELDS

PH

THE STREET

A 82 **B** 83 **C** **D** 84 **E** **F**

257

280

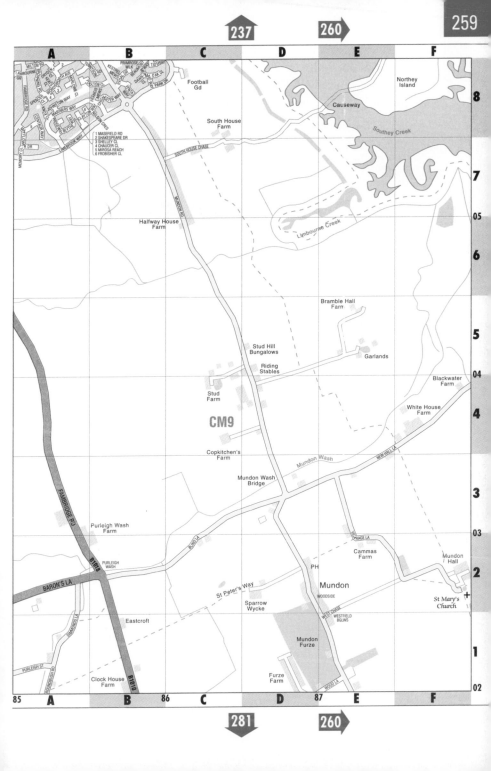

A B C D E F

8

Milton Rd
Lambourne Gr
Browning Cl
Fairbridge Rd
Spencer Gdns
Johnston Way
Century Way
Menhir Dr
Blyth Av
Clark Dr

Primrose Wlk
Kestrel Cl
Tidway
Mariner's Way
Fambridge Way
Dudley Cl
Rothen Way
Park Rd

1 MASEFIELD RD
2 SHAKESPEARE DR
3 SHELLEY CL
4 CHAUCER CL
5 MIROSA REACH
6 FROBISHER CL

Football
Gd

South House
Farm

SOUTH HOUSE CHASE

Northey
Island

Causeway

Southey Creek

05

7

Halfway House
Farm

Limbourne Creek

6

Bramble Hall
Farm

Stud Hill
Bungalows

Riding
Stables

Garlands

Blackwater
Farm

5

04

Stud
Farm

White House
Farm

4

CM9

Copkitchen's
Farm

Mundon Wash

NEW HALL LA

Mundon Wash
Bridge

3

Purleigh Wash
Farm

B1010

CRAGE LA

Cammas
Farm

03

Mundon
Hall

PURLEIGH
WASH

PH

St Mary's
Church

2

BARON'S LA

St Peter's Way

Sparrow
Wycke

Mundon

WOODSIDE

WESTFIELD
BGLWS

WEST CHASE

FAIRBRIDGE RD

B1018

SHACKING LA

Eastcroft

Mundon
Furze

1

PURLEIGH ST

ROCHESTER RD

Clock House
Farm

B1010

Furze
Farm

WOOD LA

02

85 A B 86 C D 87 E F

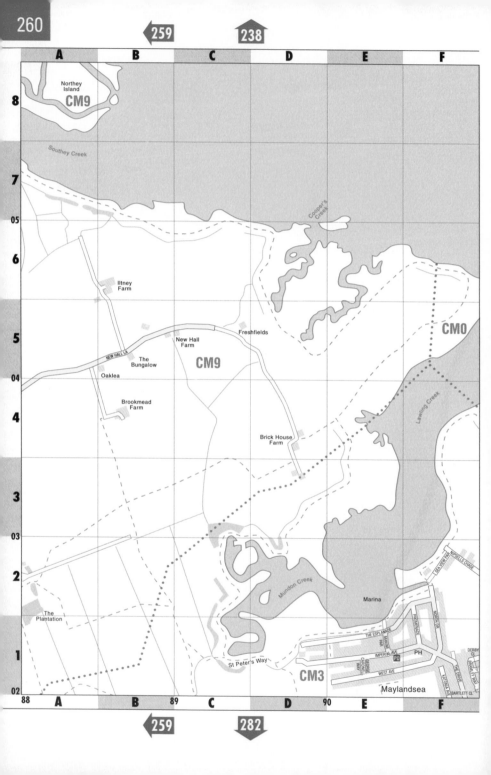

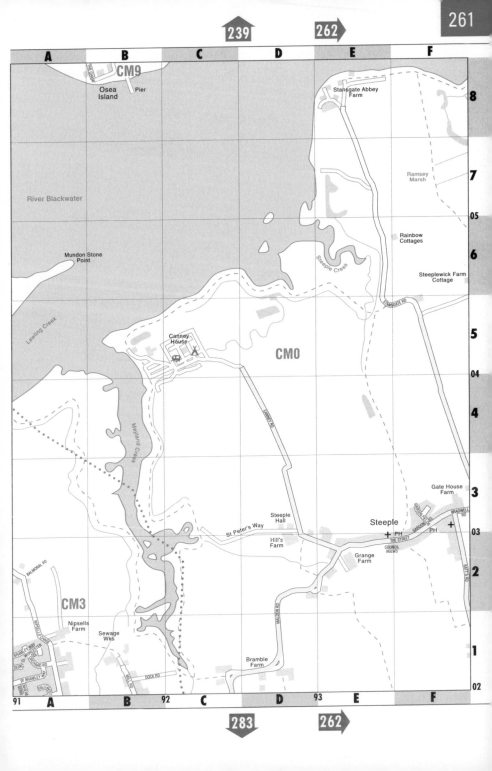

CM9

Osea
Island
Pier

Stansgate Abbey
Farm

Ramsey
Marsh

River Blackwater

05

Rainbow
Cottages

Mundon Stone
Point

Steeplewick Farm
Cottage

Steeple Creek

STANSGATE RD

Lawling Creek

CM0

Canney
House

04

CANNEY RD

Mayland Creek

Gate House
Farm

3

Steeple
Hall

Steeple

BRADWELL
RD

St Peter's Way

PH

03

GARDENERS LA

GARNON'S CH

THE STREET

PH

Hill's
Farm

COUNCIL
BGLWS

CM3

Grange
Farm

BATTS RD

2

Nipsells
Farm

Sewage
Wks

BALMORAL RD

NIPSELLS CHASE

MALDON RD

BRADLEY WAY
WORSTER
DERBY CL
ORCHARD RD

Bramble
Farm

1

ST BRAMLEY JN

HILL RD

DOCK RD

02

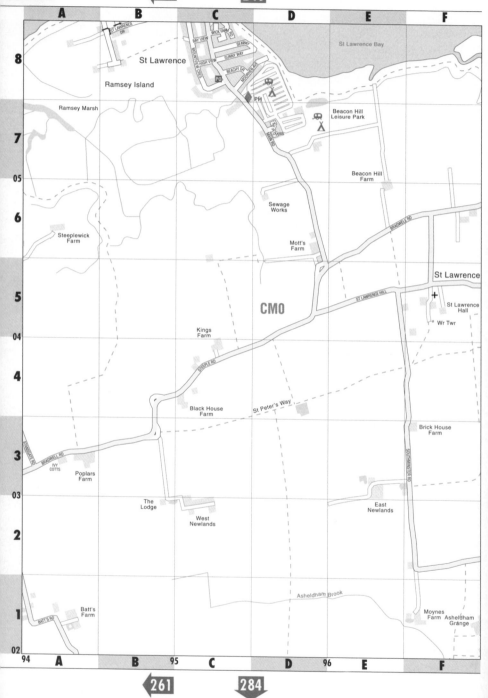

St Lawrence Bay

St Lawrence

Ramsey Island

Ramsey Marsh

WICK FARM

BAY VIEW

HIGH VIEW

SUNNY WAY

BEACHY

MOUNTVIEW CRES

MOORHEN RD

BEACHY DR

PO

PH

WADERS

Beacon Hill
Leisure Park

Beacon Hill
Farm

Steeplewick
Farm

Sewage
Works

Mott's
Farm

St Lawrence

St Lawrence
Hall

Wr Twr

CMO

ST LAWRENCE HILL

Kings
Farm

SHEEPLT RD

BRADWELL RD

Black House
Farm

St Peter's Way

Brick House
Farm

SOUTHMINSTER RD

BRADWELL RD

IVY
COTTS

Poplars
Farm

STANSGATE RD

The
Lodge

West
Newlands

East
Newlands

Asheldham Brook

Batt's
Farm

BATT'S RD

Moynes
Farm

Asheldham
Grange

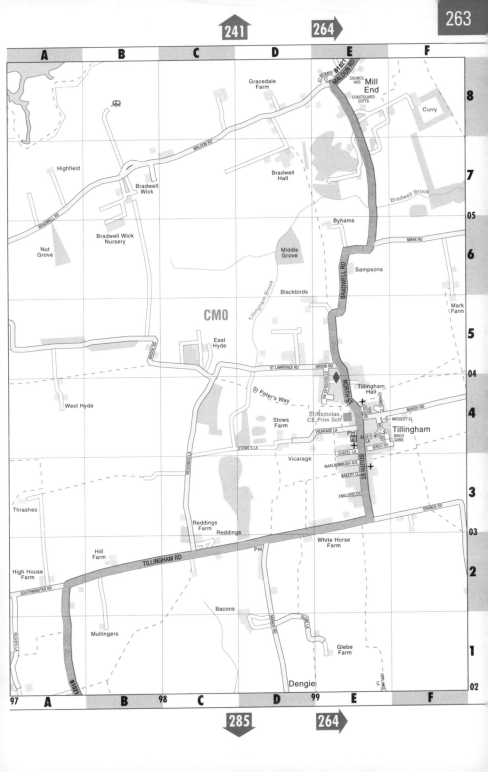

241
264
285
264

263
242
382

A B C D E F

8

Bradwell Marshes

Glebe
Farm

POCKLEY LA

7
Bradwell Brook

St Peter's Way

Sandbeach

Packards
Grove

Weatherwick

05
Packards

MARK RD

6

5
Shingleford

MARSH RD

Dots &
Melons

CM0

Marshhouse
Decoy Pond

04

4
Leggatts

MARSH RD

Marsh
House

3

03
Bridgemans
Farm

Tillingham Marshes

2
Jerry's
Farm

Midlands

Howe
Farm

1
Crosby

ORANGE RD

Howe
Outfall

02
RUSH-BRICK RD

Small Gains

Grange
Farm

00 A B 01 C D 02 E F

263
286
382

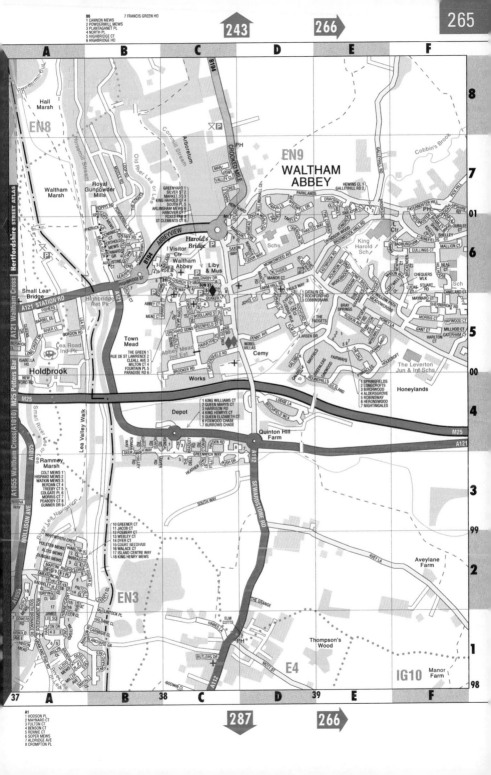

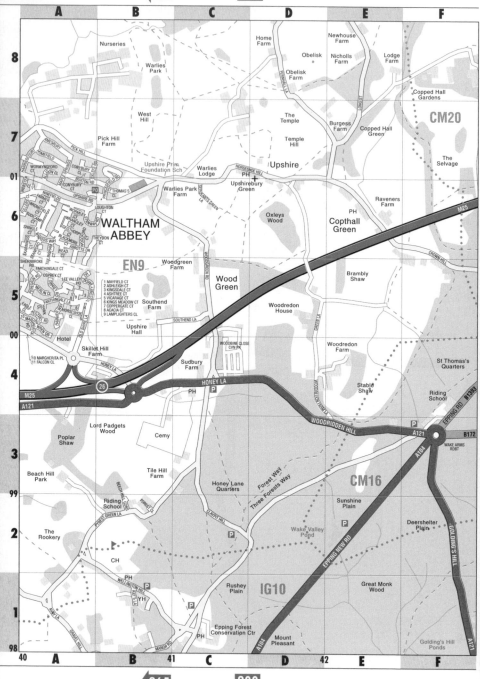

A B C D E F

8

Nurseries

Warlies Park

Home Farm

Newhouse Farm

Obelisk

Nicholls Farm

Lodge Farm

Copped Hall Gardens

CM20

7

West Hill

Pick Hill Farm

The Temple

Obelisk Farm

Burgess Farm

Copped Hall Green

The Selvage

01

Wormyngford CT

Upshire Prim. Foundation Sch

Warlies Lodge

Upshire

Temple Hill

6

WALTHAM ABBEY

EN9

Warlies Park Farm

Upshirebury Green

PH

Copthall Green

PH

Raveners Farm

M25

Woodgreen Farm

Oxleys Wood

5

1 MAYFIELD CT
2 ASHLEIGH CT
3 KINGSDALE CT
4 ASHTREE CT
5 VICARAGE CT
6 KINGS MEADOW CT
7 COPPERGATE CT
8 ACACIA CT
9 LAMPLIGHTERS CL

Southend Farm

Wood Green

Woodredon House

Brambly Shaw

CROWN HILL

Upshire Hall

SOUTHEND LA

Woodredon Farm

St Thomas's Quarters

00

Hotel

10 MARGHERITA PL
11 FALCON CL

Skillet Hill Farm

HONEY LA

Woodbine Close CVN PK

Stable Shaw

Riding School

B1393

4

M25

26

Sudbury Farm

HONEY LA

PH

P

Woodridden Hill

A121

EPPING RD

B172

WAKE ARMS RDBT

A121

A104

3

Poplar Shaw

Lord Padgets Wood

Cemy

Tile Hill Farm

Honey Lane Quarters

Forest Way

Three Forests Way

CM16

Deershelter Plain

GOLDING'S HILL

99

Beach Hill Park

Riding School

Sunshine Plain

Wake Valley Pond

P

2

The Rookery

CH

PH

Rushey Plain

Epping Forest Conservation Ctr

IG10

EPPING NEW RD

Great Monk Wood

Golding's Hill Ponds

A121

1

YH

P

PH

Mount Pleasant

A104

98

40 A B 41 C D 42 E F

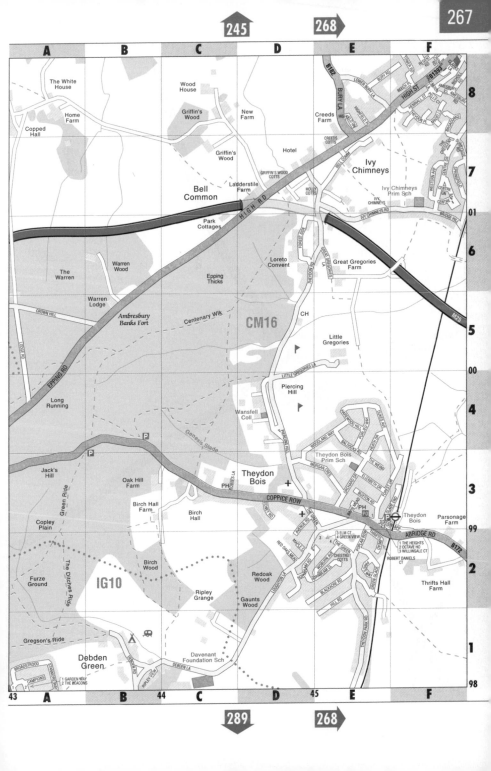

267
246

A B C D E F

8

RAVENSMERE

Stonards
Farm

(dis)

THEYDON
BOWER
1 AMESBURY RD
2 ST GREGORYS HO
3 BYRONS HO
4 TENNYSON HO
5 HARDING HO
6 CONISTON CT
7 HILLCREST WAY

Coopersale
Street

Lodge

Gaynes
Park

Mount
Quarter

Epping

P

BOWER VALE

BOWER
CT

Bower Hill
Ind Est

SUNNYSIDE

CHARLES ST

OAKLEIGH
RISE

7

Fiddlers
Hamlet

Hornes
Farm

Mount
End

01

Steward's
Green

Home
Farm

Masons Bridge
Farm

PH

Little Thorn
Hall

6

CH

CM16

Searles
Hall

Sawkins
Farm

Gardners
Farm

Coopersale
Hall Sch

CH

Sewage
Works

North
House

Tarlins
Farm

North
Lodge

The Rough
Patch

5

M25

00

27

Long
Plantation

6

Peakes
Farmhouse

4

Garnish
Hall

Barber's
Wood

Hill Hall
(rems of)

Fiveponds
Wood

Hobbs
Cross

The
Wilderness

3

Theydon
Priory

Theydon
Garnon

Hobbs Cross
Open Farm

Blunts
Farm

COOPERSALE LA

99

Martins

Bartlemy
Grove

Bush
Grove

2

B172

Hobbscross
Cottages

RM4

CH

ABRIDGE RD

Hydes
Farm

Brook
House

EPPING LA

1

Cemy

Skinners Farm
Cottages

Three Forests
Way

98

M11

B172

A B C D E F

46 47 48

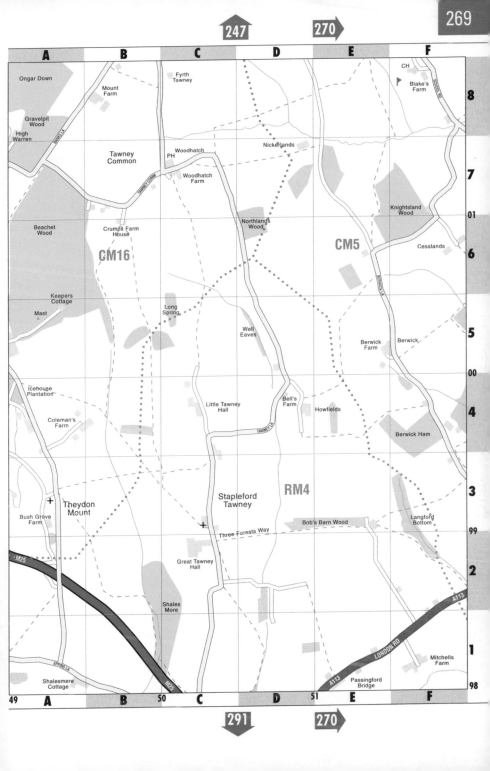

A B C D E F

8

CH

Ongar Down

Mount Farm

Fyrth Tawney

Blake's Farm

SCHOOL RD

Gravelpit Wood

High Warren

BROOK LA

7

Tawney Common

Woodhatch

PH

Nickerlands

Woodhatch Farm

TAWNEY COMMON

01

Beachet Wood

Crumps Farm House

Northlands Wood

Knightsland Wood

CM16

CM5

Cesslands

6

Keepers Cottage

Long Spring

BERWICK LA

Mast

Well Eaves

Berwick Farm

Berwick

5

00

Icehouse Plantation

Little Tawney Hall

Bell's Farm

Howfields

4

Coleman's Farm

TAWNEY LA

Berwick Ham

Stapleford Tawney

RM4

3

Theydon Mount

Bob's Barn Wood

Langford Bottom

Bush Grove Farm

Three Forests Way

99

M25

Great Tawney Hall

2

A113

Shales More

LONDON RD

A113

Mitchells Farm

1

M25

EPPING LA

A113

Passingford Bridge

98

Shalesmere Cottage

49 A B 50 C D 51 E F

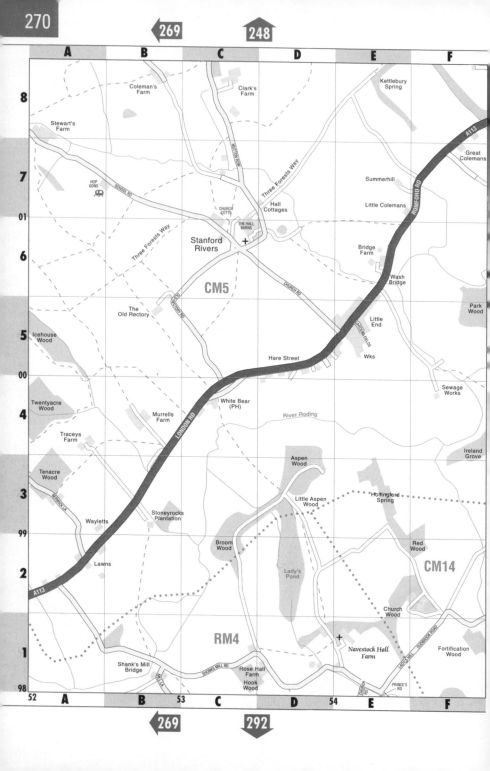

269
248

A B C D E F

8

Coleman's Farm

Clark's Farm

Kettlebury Spring

Stewart's Farm

7

HOP GDNS

SCHOOL RD

MUTTON ROW

Three Forests Way

Summerhill

Little Colemans

Great Colemans

A113

ROMFORD RD

01

CHURCH COTTS

Hall Cottages

THE HALL BARNS

6

Stanford Rivers

Three Forests Way

CM5

CHURCH RD

Bridge Farm

Wash Bridge

Park Wood

The Old Rectory

5

Icehouse Wood

Little End

CROWN FIELDS

Wks

Hare Street

00

White Bear (PH)

Sewage Works

4

Twentyacre Wood

Murrells Farm

LONDON RD

River Roding

Ireland Grove

Traceys Farm

Aspen Wood

3

Tenacre Wood

BEDROCK LA

Wayletts

Stoneyrocks Plantation

Little Aspen Wood

Hollingford Spring

Red Wood

CM14

99

Broom Wood

Lady's Pond

2

A113

Lawns

Church Wood

RM4

Navestock Hall Farm

LANE'S HILL

DUNNINGS ROAD

Fortification Wood

1

Shank's Mill Bridge

MILL LA

SHONKS MILL RD

Rose Hall Farm

Hook Wood

CHURCH RD

PRINCE'S RD

98

52 A B 53 C D 54 E F

269
292

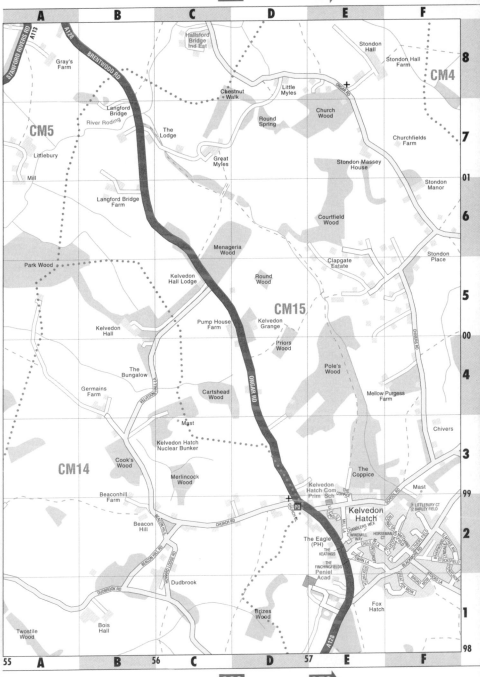

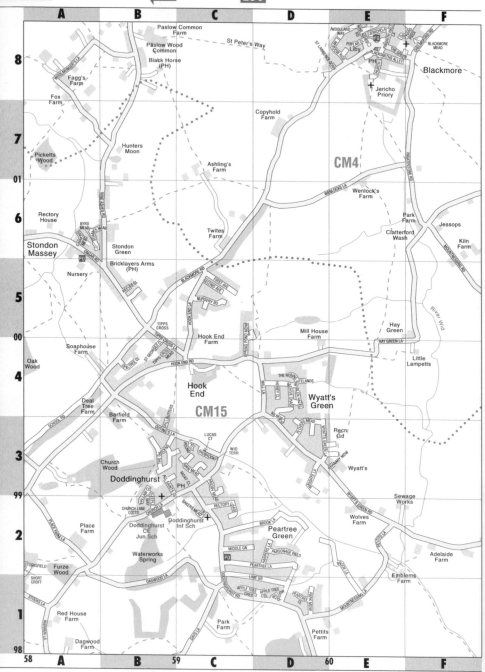

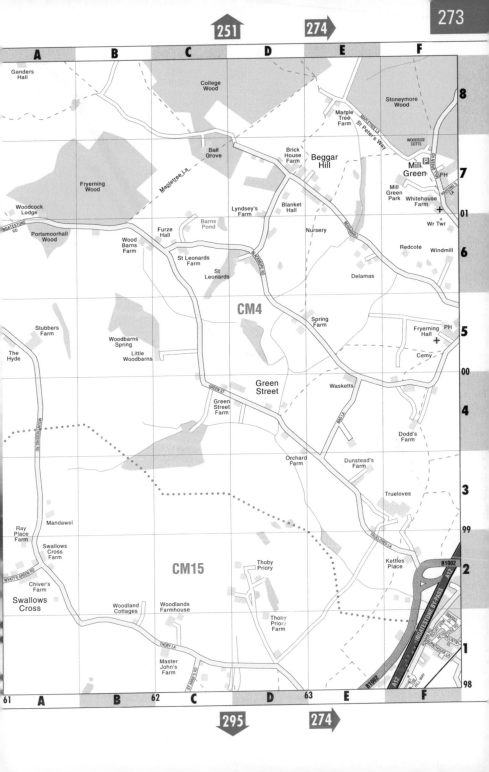

273 252

A B C D E F

8

Millgreen Common
Potter Row Farm
Box Wood
Well Wood
Dawes Farm
Handley Green
Marshalls Farm
Wantfield Cotts
Ewelan Hall
A12
B100

Margaretting CE Prim Sch
Mast
PH
Brookside

7

Harding's Farm
Handley Barnes
Bushey Wood
Osborne's Wood
HARDING'S LA
DOG KENNEL LA
St Peter's Way

01

Millgreen Wood
The Grove
Canterburys

6

MILL LA
BACK LA
MILL GREEN RD
The Grange
Little Hyde Farm
Margaretting Hall
CHURCH LA

Fryerning
Maisonetts
Murcock's Farm
BEGGARHILL

CM4
LC

5

00

Woodfield Cotts
Ingatestone Inf Sch
INGATESTONE BY-PASS
FRYERNING LA
Kingfisher
WILLOW GN
Ray Farm
Anglo-European Sch

4

Ingatestone & Fryerning CE Jun Sch
PARK DR
PINE DR
Rook Wood
Spring Wood
2. THE HOP
1 CLIFTON TERR
2 SPREAD EAGLE PL
3 MILLERS MEWS
Fair Field
CHEQUERS
HIGH ST
Fairacres
Ingatestone
Fairacres
STOCK LA

3

Liby
STONEGATE
Ingatestone
Sewage Works
A12
LC
B1002

99

2

Ingatestone Hall Farm
Buttsbury Hall Farm
ROOKERY
Heybridge
Ingatestone Hall
INGATESTONE RD
White Tyrrells

1

Bacons Farm
MILL LA
BUTTSBURY

98

Tilehurst
Elmbrook Farm

64 A B 65 C D 66 E F

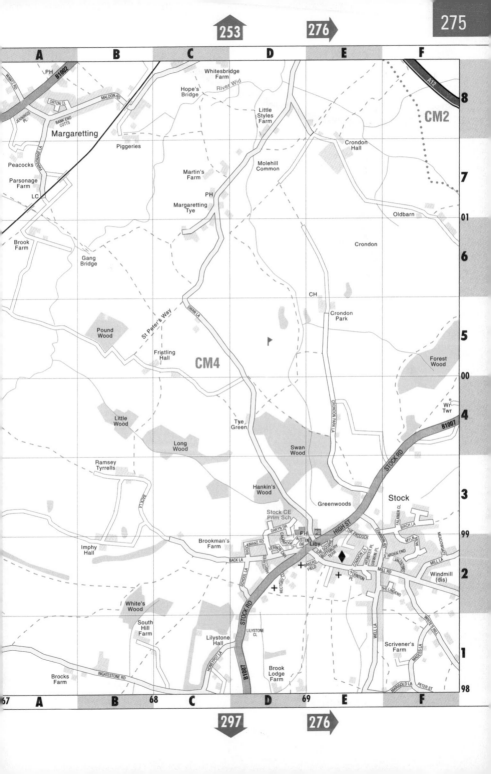

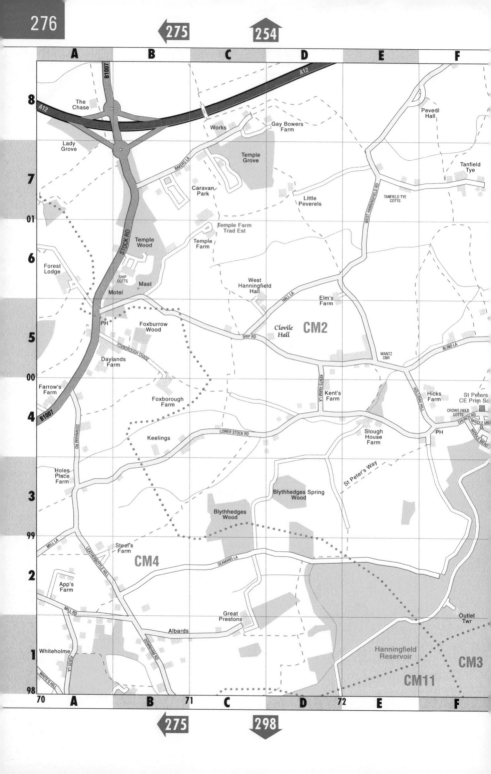

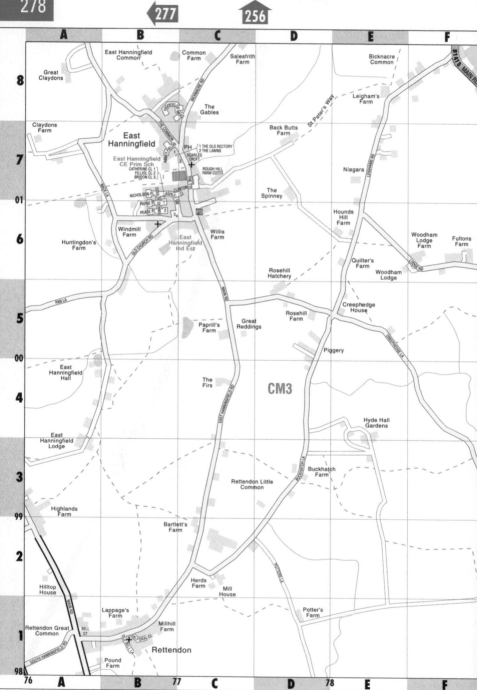

277
256

A **B** **C** **D** **E** **F**

8

Great
Claydons

East Hanningfield
Common

Common
Farm

Salesfrith
Farm

Bicknacre
Common

Leigham's
Farm

The Gables

7

Claydons
Farm

East
Hanningfield

Back Butts
Farm

St Peter's Way

Niagara

East Hanningfield
CE Prim Sch
CATHERINE CL 1
FILLIOL CL 2
BRIDON CL 3

PH 1 THE OLD RECTORY
2 THE LAWNS
SCARLES
CROFT

ROUGH HILL
FARM COTTS

01

NICHOLSON PL
PAYNE PL
PEASE PL

CLINTON
CL

The Spinney

Hounds
Hill
Farm

6

Huntingdon's
Farm

Windmill
Farm

East
Hanningfield
Ind Est

Willis
Farm

Rosehill
Hatchery

Quilter's
Farm

Woodham
Lodge

Woodham
Lodge
Farm

Fultons
Farm

PAN LA

5

Paprill's
Farm

Great
Reddings

Rosehill
Farm

Creephedge
House

00

East
Hanningfield
Hall

Piggery

4

The
Firs

CM3

Hyde Hall
Gardens

3

East
Hanningfield
Lodge

Rettendon Little
Common

Buckhatch
Farm

99

Highlands
Farm

Bartlett's
Farm

2

Hilltop
House

Herds
Farm

Mill
House

Potter's
Farm

1

Rettendon Great
Common

Lappage's
Farm

Millhill
Farm

BELL
CT

ORAL CL

Rettendon

98

SOUTH HANNINGFIELD RD

Pound
Farm

76 **A** **B** 77 **C** **D** 78 **E** **F**

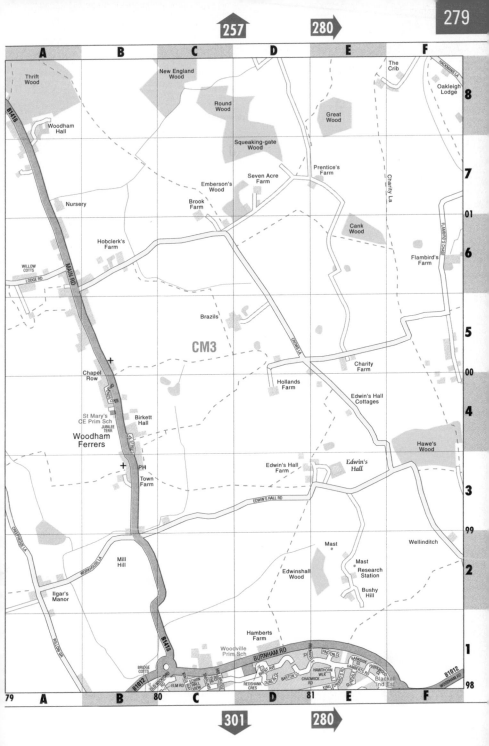

257
280

A   B   C   D   E   F

Thrift
Wood

New England
Wood

Round
Wood

The
Crib

Oakleigh
Lodge

8

B1418

Woodham
Hall

Squeaking-gate
Wood

Great
Wood

Charity La

7

Nursery

Emberson's
Wood

Seven Acre
Farm

Prentice's
Farm

01

Hobclerk's
Farm

Brook
Farm

Cank
Wood

Flambird's
Farm

6

WILLOW
COTTS

MAIN RD

LODGE RD

Brazils

CM3

CROSS LA

Charity
Farm

5

00

Chapel
Row

Hollands
Farm

Edwin's Hall
Cottages

+

St Mary's
CE Prim Sch

Birkett
Hall

Hawe's
Wood

4

JUBILEE
TERR

Woodham
Ferrers

Edwin's Hall
Farm

Edwin's
Hall

PH

3

+

Town
Farm

EDWIN'S HALL RD

Mast

Wellinditch

99

Mill
Hill

Edwinshall
Wood

Mast
Research
Station

2

CHELMSFORD LA

Ilgar's
Manor

Bushy
Hill

WORKHOUSE LA

FILTON DR

Hamberts
Farm

B1418

Woodville
Prim Sch

BURNHAM RD

Blackall
Ind Est

1

BRIDGE
COTTS

B1012

B1012

REDSHANK
CRES

HAWTHORN
WLK

CHADWICK
RD

WOODHAM RD

98

79   A   B   80   C   D   81   E   F

301
280

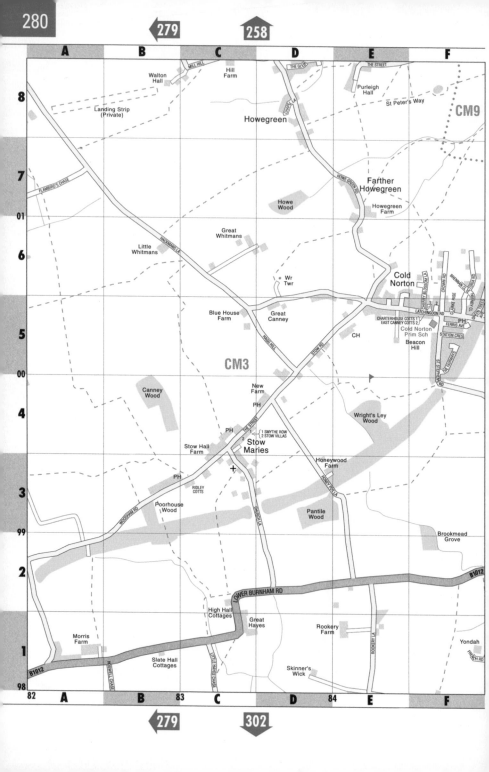

259
282

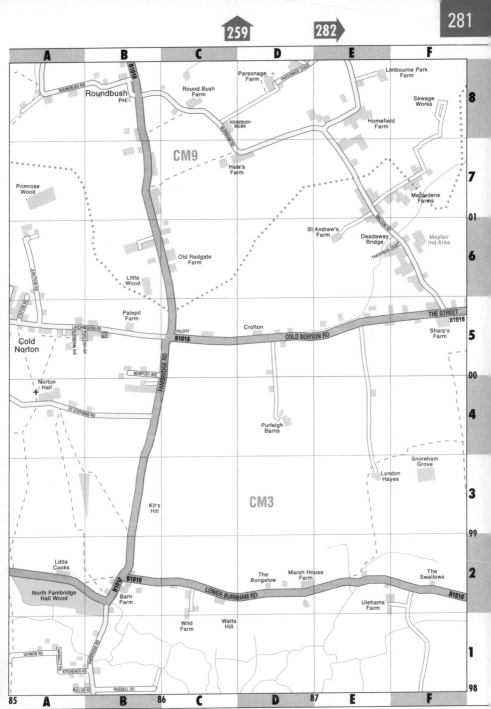

303
282

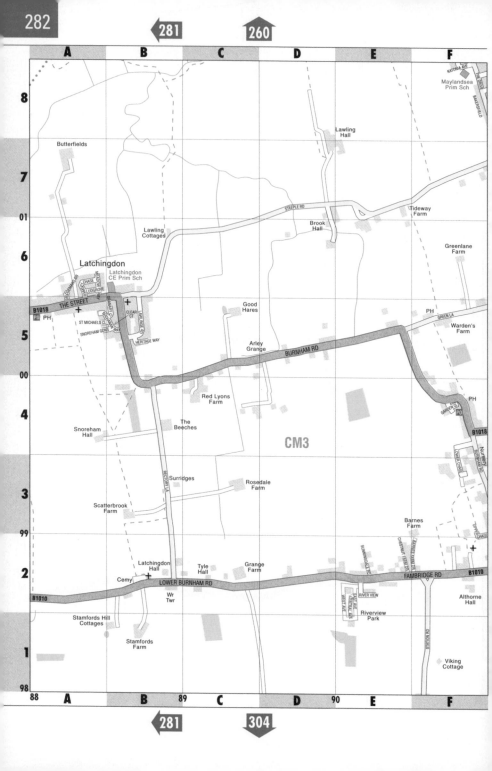

281
260

A **B** **C** **D** **E** **F**

8

Maylandsea
Prim Sch

KATONIA AVE

BAKESFIELD

THE DRIVE

Butterfields

Lawling
Hall

7

01

STEEPLE RD

Tideway
Farm

Lawling
Cottages

Brook
Hall

Greenlane
Farm

6

Latchingdon

Latchingdon
CE Prim Sch

PH

GREEN LA

5

CHASE

LUDGROVE

BR ANGE RD

CLEAR
CT

Warden's
Farm

THE STREET

Good
Hares

B1018

PO PH

ST MICHAELS CL

SNOREHAM GDNS

CHERRY TREE WAY

LWR VALE RD

HERITAGE WAY

Arley
Grange

BURNHAM RD

00

Red Lyons
Farm

PH

GARDEN CT

PO

B1018

4

Snoreham
Hall

The
Beeches

CM3

Nursery

BURNHAM RD

LOWER CHASE

RECTORY LA

Surridges

Rosedale
Farm

3

Scatterbrook
Farm

TUPPER CHASE

99

Barnes
Farm

SUNNINGVALE RD

CHESTNUT FARM DR

ZEBRINE'S FARM CHASE

2

Latchingdon
Hall

Tyle
Hall

Grange
Farm

FAMBRIDGE RD

B1010

Cemy

LOWER BURNHAM RD

VALE AVE

WEST AVE

VALLEY AVE

RIVER VIEW

Althorne
Hall

B1010

Wr
Twr

Riverview
Park

STATION RD

Stamfords Hill
Cottages

1

Stamfords
Farm

Viking
Cottage

98

A 88 **B** 89 **C** **D** 90 **E** **F**

281
304

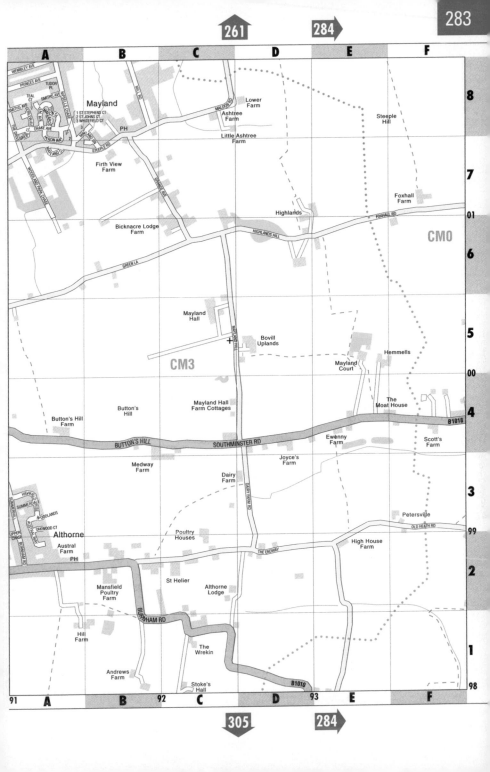

283
262

A B C D E F

8

Rushes Farm

Badnocks Farm

Park Farm

Asheldham Brook

7

Highfields Farm

B1021
SOUTHMINSTER RD

FOXHALL RD

01

THE BRAMBLES

Lunendales

Asheldham Bridge

Colleton Farm

The Grove

6

Sheepcotes

Squeaks House

STEEPLE RD

TILLINGHAM RD

Oldmoor

Theedhams Farm

KNIGHTSWOOD CT

5

CMO

Liby
Spratt's Farm

SHEEPCOTES LA

Northend

CRIPPLEGATE

Newmoor

00

Orchardside Fruit Farm

STEEPLE MEWS

NORTH END

Cripplegate

Witchards

PH

Hillside RD

COMBE RD

SPELLS CL

REGENTS CL

NORTH ST

Southminster

4

B1018

SCOTTS HILL

QUEEN ST

PANTILE HILL

HIGH ST

B1018

STATION RD

Works

Pandole Wood

The Bungalow

ROSE & CROWN MEWS
BREWERS YD
WEST HOLT

THE CHASE

PRIORS CT

MALTINGS

HALL RD

Caidge Farm

PRINCES GATE

STAMMERS CT
THE CHESTNUTS

ABBOT MEWS

Ind Est.

Southminster

Southminster Hall

3

SOUTHFIELD WAY

ROBINSONS CL

DUKES

VICARAGE MDW

THE WELLINGTONS

Schs

Southminster

Hunters Farm

Smyatts Farm House

1 THE BRAMBLES
2 SMYATTS CL

99

FILEY RD

SEAMER RD

SCARBOROUGH RD

SCALBY RD

WHITBY RD

OLD HEATH RD

Kiln Farm

Rose Cottages
PH

BURNHAM RD

Sewage Works

OLD GOLDSANDS RD

2

Lord's Wood

Old Heath Farm

Ratsborough Farm

Rumbolds Cottages

1

SOUTHMINSTER RD
B1021

Goldsand Bridges

98

94 A B 95 C D 96 E F

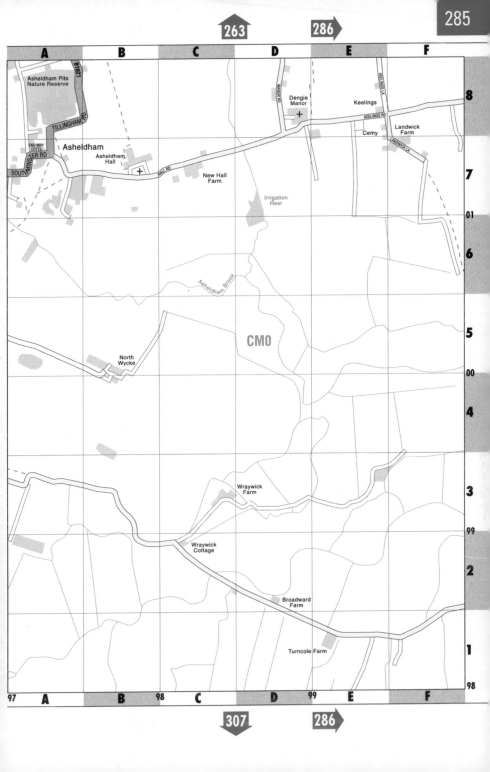

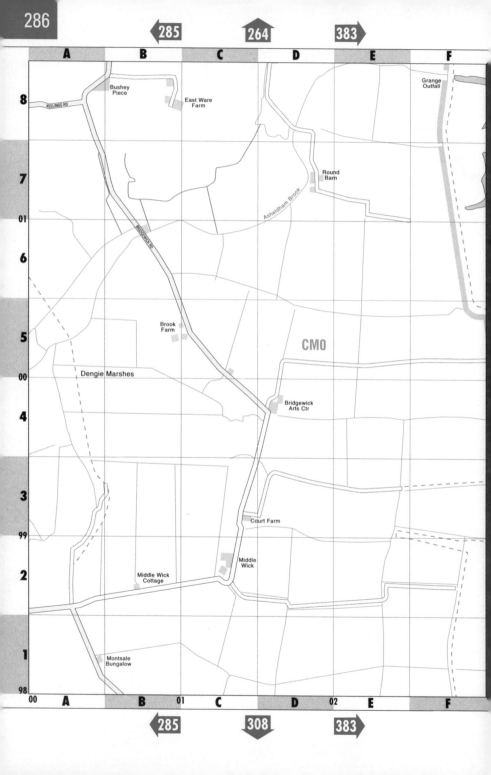

285
264
383

A B C D E F

8

Bushey
Piece
KEELINGS RD
East Ware
Farm

Grange
Outfall

7

Round
Barn

Asheldham Brook

01

6

BRIDGEWICK RD

5

Brook
Farm

CMO

00

Dengie Marshes

4

Bridgewick
Arts Ctr

3

99

Court Farm

2

Middle Wick
Cottage

Middle
Wick

1

Montsale
Bungalow

98

00 A B 01 C D 02 E F

285
308
383

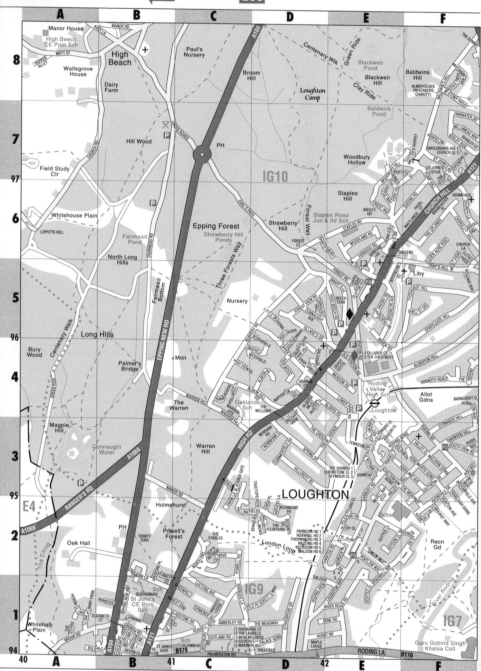

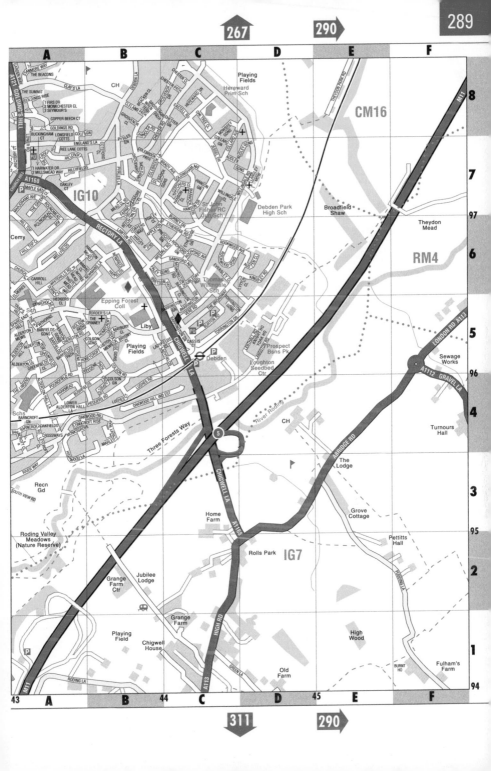

	A	B	C	D	E	F

8

CM16

M11

B172

Theydon Hall

Nurseries

Hill Farm

Sewage Works

River Roding

A113

7

Piggotts Farm

Bloody Mead

ABRIDGE RD

EPPING LA

ONGAR RD

Pryors Farm

Lower Wood

97

Lambourne Place

Turners Ct

Roding Hall

Sawyer's Chase

Ape's Grove

Patch Park

6

GOULDS COTTS 1
AUCTION PL 2
WHITE HALL 3
THE CHESTNUTS 4

PH

PO

THE POPLARS

ORCHID CL

ALDERWOOD

NEW FARM LA

New Farm

Alder Wood

MARKET PL

RIVERS DR

MIDDLE BOY

KNIGHT WK

FIELD VW

ALDERWOODS

LONDON RD

Abridge

A113

Lambourne Prim Sch

RM4

Lambourne Hall

+ Lambourne

Great Wood

5

Great Downs Farm

Soapley's Wood

Three Forests Way

96

HISE LA

Halfmoon Wood

Bishop's Moat

4

A1112

Marchings Farm

Clark's Wood

Bishop's Hall

Dews Hall Farm

MILL LA

3

GRAVEL LA

St John's Farm

PARK SQ

Mast

Gallman's End Farm

TUTTLEBY COTTS

Blackbush Farm

BOURNEBRIDGE LA

HOG LA

95

Taylors Farm

Playing Fields

The Blue House

2

IG7

The Manor House

MANOR RD

Mansfield Outdoor Ctr

Crabtree Hill

1

Brownings Farm

METTLE LA

Willow Park Farm

Billingsbourne

Hop Pole Farm

PH

Lambourne End

P

Harmes Farm

LAMBOURNE SQ

Banks Farm

Three Cornered Plain

Taylor's Plain

Hainault Forest Country Park

Spurgate Plain

94

A1112

	A	B	C	D	E	F

46
47
48

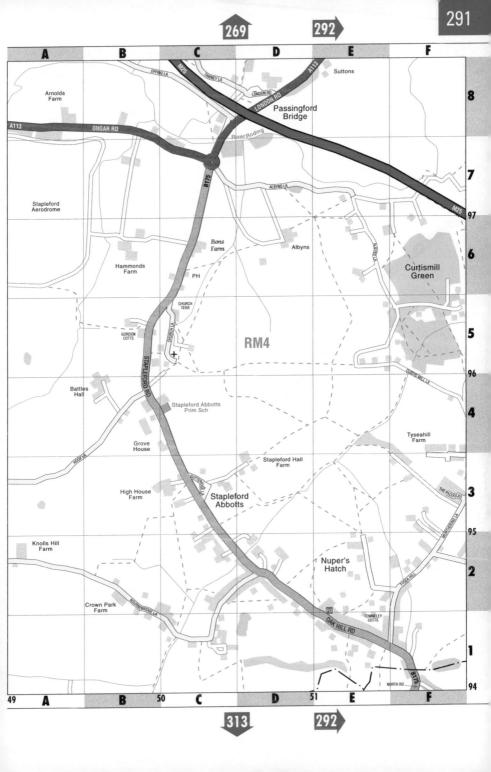

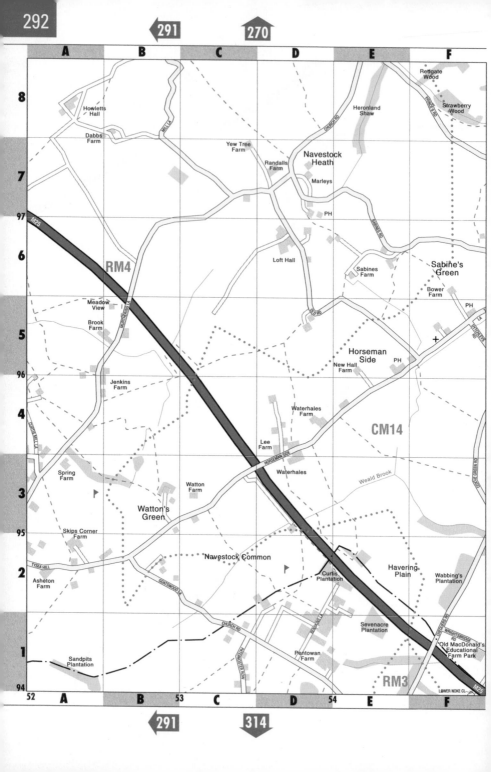

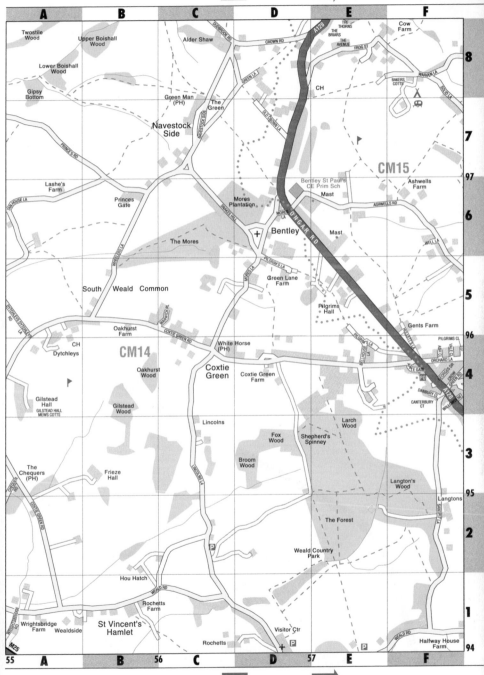

293
272

A B C D E F

8

Cowes Farm

Park Wood

America Farm

7

Wishfields Farm

Heard's Farm

97

Sumner's Farm

Rosecroft

Palmers Farm

Bennett's Farm

6

Howe's Farm

HALL LA

Days Farm

Brickhouse Farm

Crow Green

CM15

5

Brickhouse Wood

Canterbury Tye Hall

DODDINGHURST RD

96

Hatch Rd

A12

Catherine

CROW GREEN LA

THE FIRS

Pilgrims Hatch

HONEYSUCKLE CL
LILAC
TULIP CL
POPPY CL
HEATHER

Bishop's Hall Park

1 PEONY CL
2 ELIZABETH HO
3 MEADOW VIEW
4 WEALDEN HO

Shenfield Hall Farm

4

PRIORY CL

DANES WAY

BALMORAL RD
HAREWOOD RD

The Brentwood Ctr

ALBANY RD
ELIZABETH RD
HIGHGROVE

P

Shenfield Hall Farm

Pilgrims Hatch Prim Sch

3

DOUNSELL CT
DARLINGTON CT

MARLBOROUGH RD
KENSINGTON RD
OSBORNE RD

WINDSOR RD

P

Hall Wood

Shenfield Hall

St Mary's CE Prim Sch

SAWYERS CT

95

High Wood

INGRAVE RD

WARESCOT CL

ST WALDANS RD

KAMPTON AVE

St Helens RC Jun Sch

CHELMSFORD RD A1023

HUTTON RD

2

Calcott Hall Farm

ROBIN HOOD RD

PO

1 DRUMMOND CT
2 GEARY CT

The Hedley Walter High Sch

DODDINGHURST

Convent of Mercy
St Thomas of Canterbury CE Jun & Inf Schs

3 DUKE'S PL
4 INVERMAY CT
5 LAVENHAM CT
6 BURGESS CT
7 HIGHMEAD CT
8 ARGYLL CT
9 RAVENSCOURT

Shenfield

A129

PO

THE COURTYARD

PORTERS CL

COSTEAD MANOR RD
THE RETREAT

MONTBAZON

H

High Wood

SHELTON

ROSE BANK

HIGHLAND AVE

The Essex Nuffield

SHENFIELD RD

1

CM14

CAPON CL
THE RODING

MITFIELD GDNS

VINEWAY
PARK VALE CL

WESTERN RD
HART RD

RULAND RD

PENNYWAYS

HOLLY HO

SHEN PLACE ALMHOUSES

LIMES CT

HOMEHURST HO

Middleton Hall (Brentwood Prep Sch)

Brentwood Com

H

94

58 A 59 B C 60 D E F

WEALD RD
A12
GREEN LA

A128

A1023

293
316

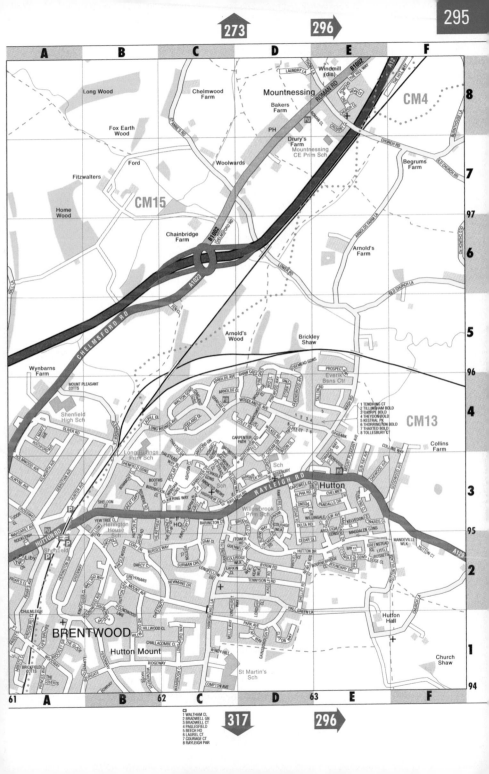

8

7

97

6

5

96

4

3

95

2

1

94

CM4

CM15

CM13

Long Wood

Chelmwood Farm

Mountnessing

Bakers Farm

Windmill (dis)

Fox Earth Wood

PH

Drury's Farm
Mountnessing CE Prim Sch

Begrums Farm

Ford

Woolwards

Fitzwalters

Home Wood

Chainbridge Farm

Arnold's Farm

Wynbarns Farm

Arnold's Wood

Brickley Shaw

Everik Bsns Ctr

PROSPECT

Collins Farm

MOUNT PLEASANT COTTS

Shenfield High Sch

1 TENDRING CT
2 TILLINGHAM BOLD
3 THORPE BOLD
4 THEYDON BOLD
5 KESTRAL PK
6 THORRINGTON BOLD
7 THAXTED BOLD
8 TOLLESBURY CT

Long Ridings Prim Sch

CARPENTER PATH

Hutton

Harrington House Sch

Willowbrook Prim Sch

Shenfield

Liby

BRENTWOOD

Hutton Mount

Hutton Hall

St Martin's Sch

Church Shaw

CHELMSFORD RD

A1023

B1002

ROMAN RD

A12

RAYLEIGH RD

HUTTON RD

A128

CHURCH RD

OLD CHURCH RD

OLD CHURCH LA

C3
1 WALTHAM CL
2 BRADWELL GN
3 BRADWELL CT
4 PAGLESFIELD
5 BEECH HO
6 LAUREL CT
7 COURAGE CT
8 RAYLEIGH PAR

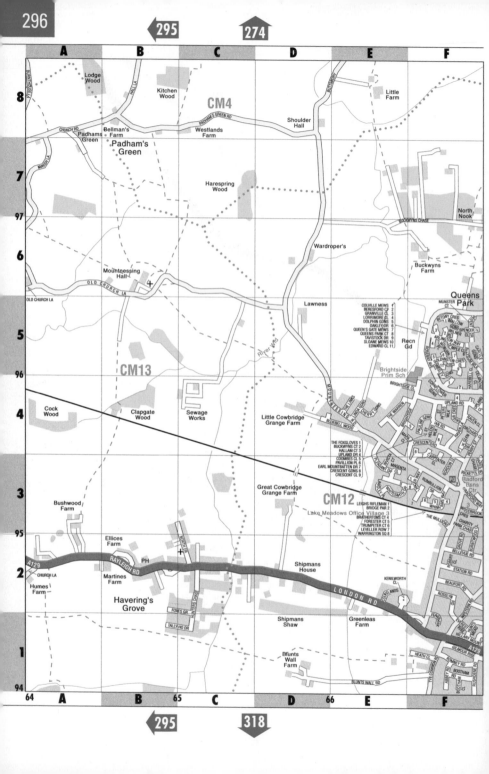

295
274
295
318

CM4

CM13

CM12

Queens Park

Lodge Wood

Kitchen Wood

Little Farm

Shoulder Hall

Bellman's Farm

Westlands Farm

Padhams Green

Padham's Green

Hayespring Wood

North Nook

Wardroper's

Buckwyns Chase

Buckwyns Farm

Mountnessing Hall

Lawness

OLD CHURCH LA

OLD CHURCH LA

Recn Gd

Brightside Prim Sch

COLVILLE MEWS 1
BERESFORD C2 2
GRANVILLE CL 3
LORRIMORE CL 4
DOLPHIN GDNS 5
OAKLEYOR 6
QUEEN'S GATE MEWS 7
QUEENS PARK CT 8
TAVISTOCK DR 9
SLOANE MEWS 10
EDWARD CL 11

Cock Wood

Clapgate Wood

Sewage Works

Little Cowbridge Grange Farm

Bluebell Wood

Brightside CL

THE FOXGLOVES 1
BUCKWYNS CT 2
HALLAM CT 3
UPLAND DR 4
COOMBES CL 5
PAVILLION PL 6
EARL MOUNTBATTEN DR 7
CRESCENT GDNS 8
CRESCENT CL 9

Bushwood Farm

Great Cowbridge Grange Farm

Radford Bans

Ricketts Dr

LEIGHS RIFLEMAN 1
BRIDGE PAR 2
BRATHERTONS CT 4
FORESTER CT 5
TRUMPETER CT 6
LEVELLER ROW 7
WARRINGTON SQ 8

Lake Meadows Office Village 3

Ellices Farm

RAYLEIGH RD

PH

Shipmans House

Martines Farm

CHURCH LA

Humes Farm

Havering's Grove

FONES GR

HUNTAS CHASE

TALLYHO DR

Shipmans Shaw

Greenleas Farm

LONDON RD

KENILWORTH CL

Bfunts Wall Farm

BLUNTS WALL RD

A129

A129

Station Rd

Beaufort Rd

A **B** **C** **D** **E** **F**

WHITE'S HILL

CM3

8

THE CHASEWAY

Bishop's Farm

Kiln Common

Whitelilies Farm

Hanningfield Resr

BRITTONS LA

Great Bishop's Wood

7

Broom Wood

CM4

Fremnells

Downham Rd

Crowsheath Farm

HAWKSWOOD RD

97

Common Farm

Hilltop Nursery

Little Abbott's

6

FOXHEYES LA

Cock Wood

Thrift Wood

Ramsden Back Common

5

Works

Nursery

Downham Rd

PH

TIPLERS BRIDGE

MILL LA

Downham Rd

Windsor Trad Est

Downham

96

PH

Heath Rd

Farrier Sq

Greenacres Farm

4

Hunt's Farm

Ramsden Heath

PH

CM11

Rectory Wood

Chitham's Farm

Downham CE Prim Sch

3

Meepshole Wood

Cox Green

The Orchard Farm

De Beauvoir House

DE BEAUVOIR CHASE

95

PARK LA

CHURCH RD

2

Crays Wood

Kent Hill

Pump Hill

PH

Barrenleys Wood

RAMSDEN PARK RD

Claypitshills Wood

Ramsden Park Farm

1

Ramsden Bellhouse

GLEBE RD

94

A **70** **B** **71** **C** **D** **72** **E** **F**

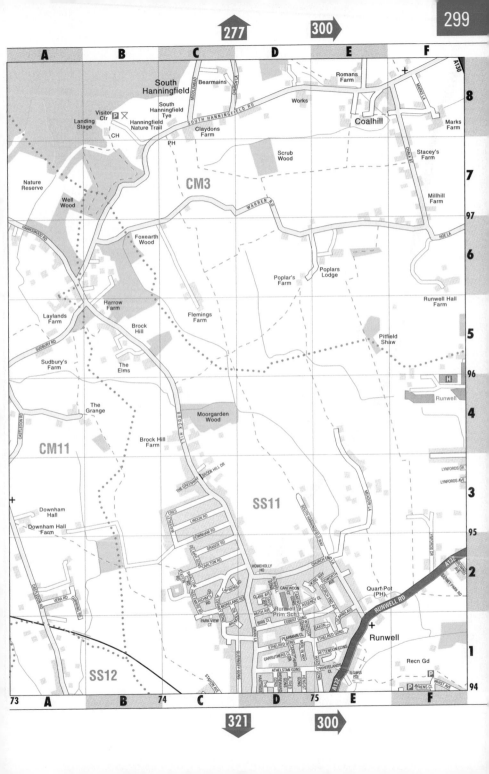

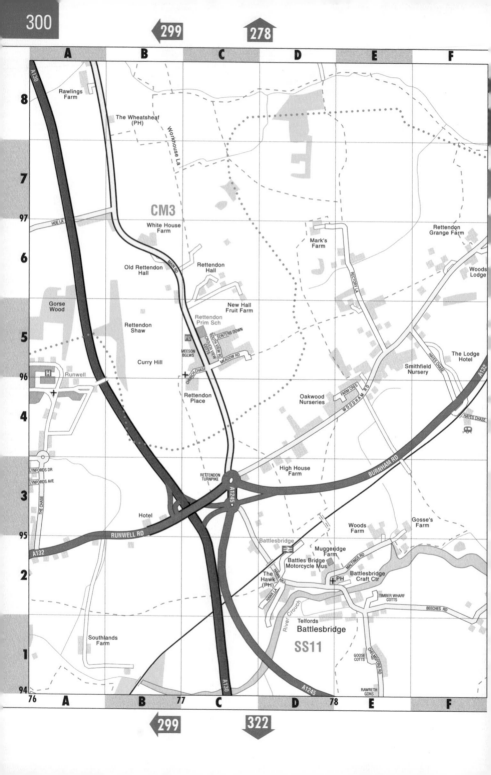

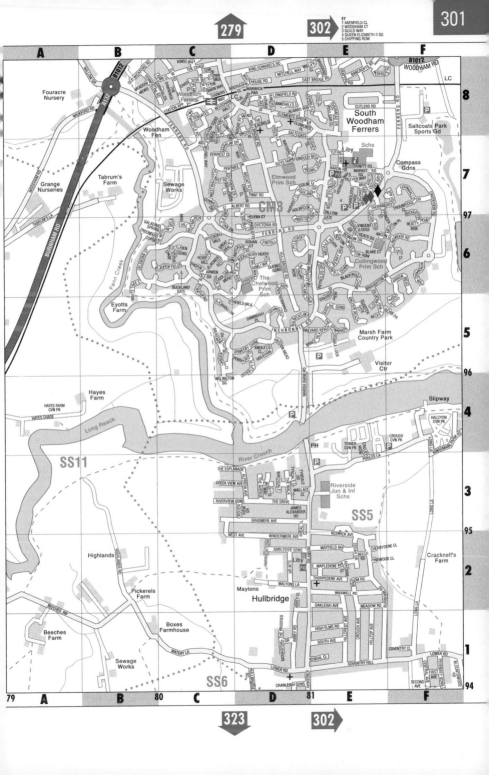

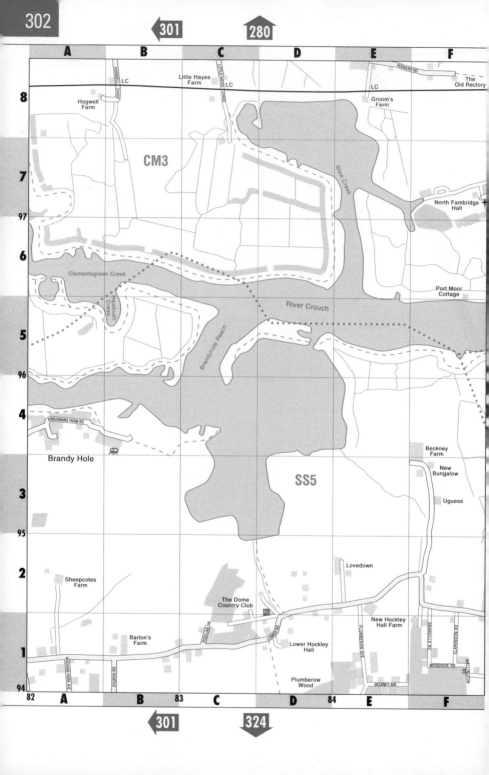

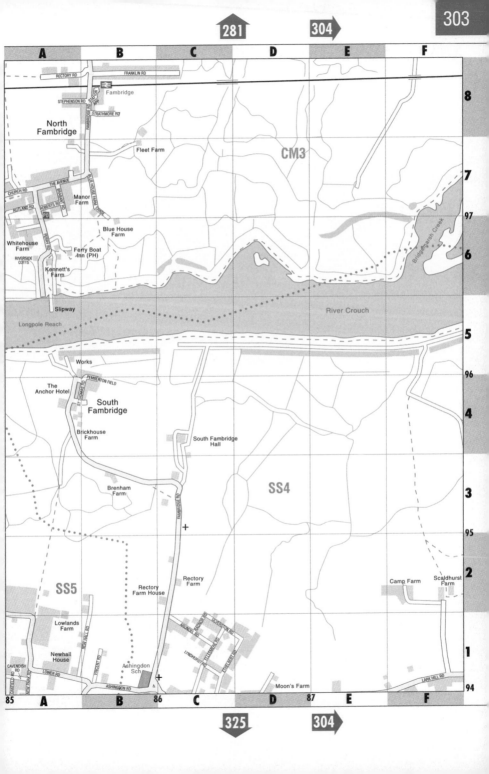

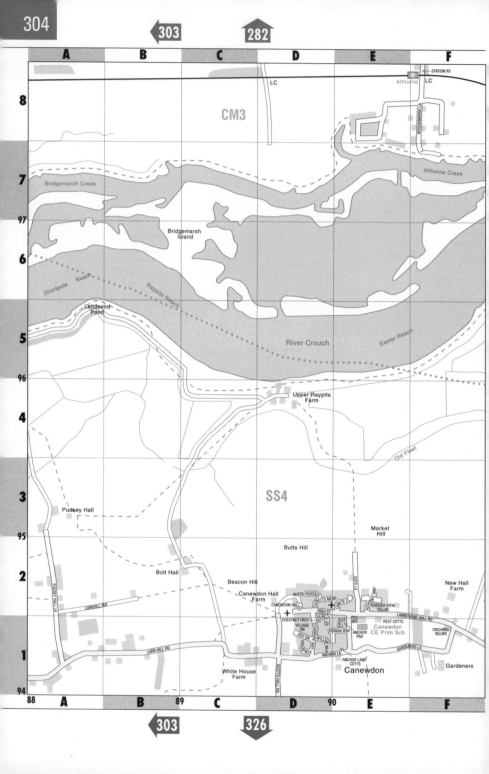

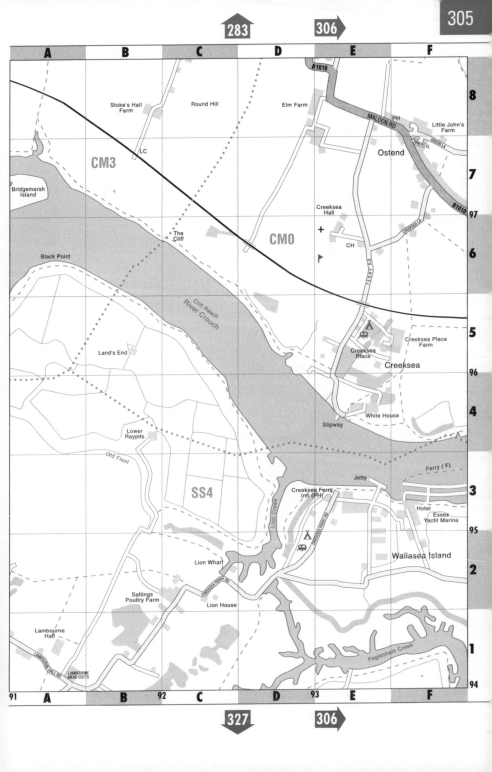

305
284

8

Mangapps Farm Rly Mus

Cemy

Stoneyhills

BUCHAMP'S

BADGERS KEEP

BOUVEL

COBBINS CHASE

STONEY HILLS

Mill Farm

Newman's Farm

Pannel's Brook

7

GREEN LA

MANGAPS DRIVE

MARSHAM WAY

SOUTHMINSTER RD
B1021

ASHWOOD CL

EVES CNR

Pannel's Bridge

Romans Farm

CHASE

Brook Farm Abattoir

97

MEADOW RISE

ST PETERS RD

HAWTHORNS

CHESLYN GDNS

COMPASS GDNS

B1010

MALDON RD

WELLAND RD

St Peter's High Sch & Tech Coll

Hall Farm

St Mary's CE Prim Sch

MARSH RD

DAMMERWICK COTTS

Muscle Bridge

6

HAMBLE WAY

KING CHARLES WAY

WILLOW

MAPLE WAY

PLANE TREE

CHURCH RD
B1010

B1021

THE LEAS

GENERAL RD

MARY'S RD

LEAS CT

Burham Bsns Pk

Springfield Nursery Est

Mayfield Ctr

Springfield Ind Est

Burham-on-Crouch

WOCESTER RD

PRINCES RD

ALEXANDRA RD

BLACKWATER

CMO

BURNHAM-ON-CROUCH

Dammer Wick

5

DORSET WAY

TRENT CL

POPLAR

STATION APP

FOUNDRY LA

LANDS RD

SHEERWATER CL
GALAHAD CL
HERMES DR
Mildmay Ind Est

Country Park

WINSTREE RD

WAYFARER

STATION RD

ALPHA RD

CROUCH

QUEEN S

BOOTH PL

ALLEY

ARCADIA RD

NORMANDY AVE

ARNHEM RD

Superstore

Allot Gdns

Burnham-on-Crouch Prim Sch

96

Caravan Site

Dengie Hundred Sports Ctr

Sports Gd

Liby

MILLFIELD

WESTERN RD

DILLWYN CT

BROCKWALL

MILL RD

Burnham Wick

WICK RD

RAMBLERS WAY

4

P

Marina

Burnham-on-Crouch District Mus

REMEMBRANCE AVE

QUEENS RD

CORONATION RD

REGENT RD

KINGS RD

YORK RD

WITHY CL

RICHARD RD

P

HIGH ST

ARGYLE RD

B1021

Sewage Works

Burnham Wick

3

Gardenness Point

Ferry P

THE PROMENADE

THE BELVEDERE

Slipways

C4
1 CURLEW HO
2 NELSON CT
3 HAMILTON CT
4 GRANVILLE TERR
5 STEBBINGS CT
6 ST MARY'S HO
7 AUGERS
8 HARDINGS-REACH
9 CALMPATCH
10 SUNNYMEAD FLATS

11 BELVEDERE CT
12 THE CROWSNEST
13 THE ANCHORAGE
14 PETTIGROW QUAYS

IRB Sta

PH

River Crouch

Ringwood Bar

95

Overland Point

Grassland Point

Fleet Point

2

Grapnells

GRAPNELLS FARM COTTS

1

WALLASEA ISLAND

SS4

94

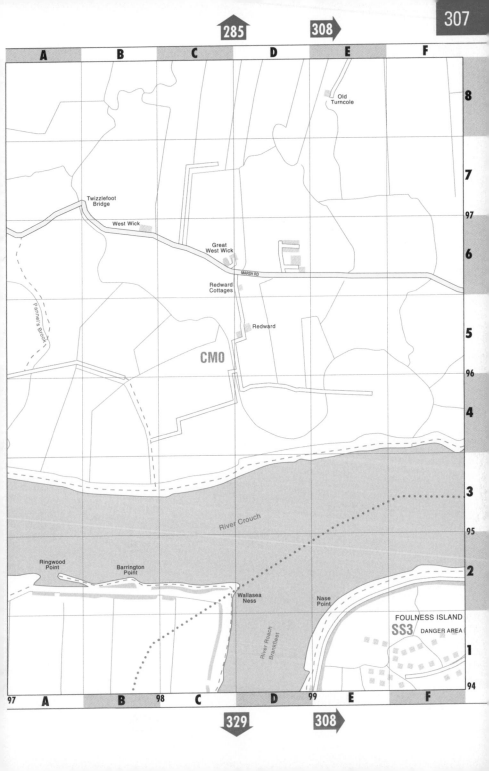

| A | B | C | D | E | F |

8

Old
Turncole

7

97

Twizzlefoot
Bridge

West Wick

Great
West Wick

6

MARSH RD

Redward
Cottages

Pannel's Brook

Redward

5

CMO

96

4

River Crouch

3

95

Ringwood
Point

Barrington
Point

2

Wallasea
Ness

Nase
Point

River Roach
Brankfleet

FOULNESS ISLAND

SS3 DANGER AREA

1

94

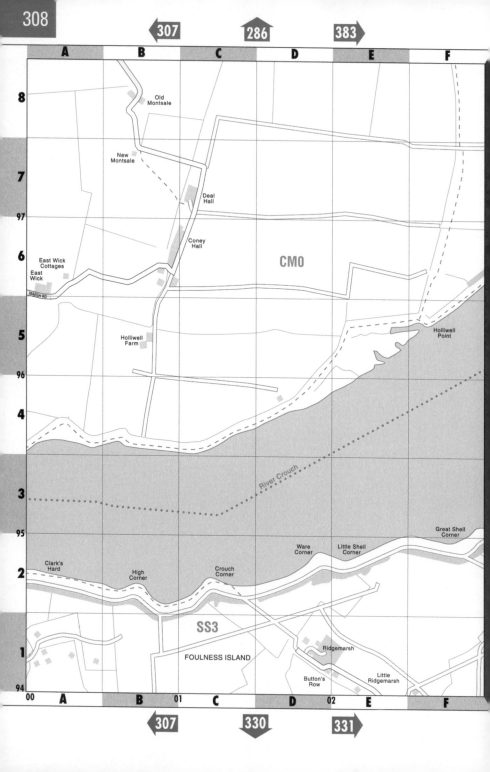

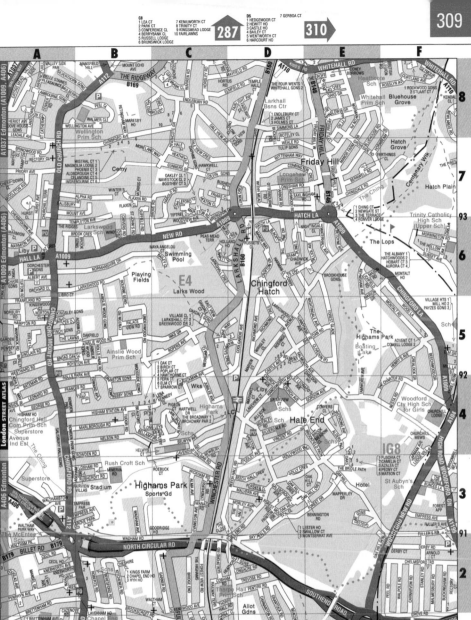

287

310

310

C8
1 LEA CT
2 PARK CT
3 CONFERENCE CL
4 BERRYBANK CL
5 RUSSELL LODGE
6 BRUNSWICK LODGE

7 KENILWORTH CT
8 TRINITY CT
9 KINGSMEAD LODGE
10 FAIRLAWNS

D5
1 HEDGEMOOR CT
2 HEWITT HO
3 CASTLE HO
4 BAILEY CT
5 WENTWORTH CT
6 HARCOURT HO

7 GERBOA CT

F2
1 HILLBORO CT
2 DORCHESTER CT
F1
1 CHATHAM RD
2 WASHINGTON RD
3 CHERRY TREE CT
4 GROSVENOR LODGE
5 TORFELL

309
288

A
B
C
D
E
F
8
7
93
6
5
92
4
3
91
2
1
90
40
41
42
Buckhurst Hill
Buckhurst Hill Com Prim Sch
The Daiglen Sch
The Birkbeck
Holly House
Lord's Bushes
Reeds Forest
Bancroft's Sch
Knighton Wood
Woodford Wells
IG9
New Barns Farm
Chigwell Brook
IG7
Roding Valley
Sewage Works (dis)
LUXBOROUGH
Trinity RC High Sch (Upper)
St Antony's Sch
Wells Sch
Avon House Sch
Trinity RC High Sch (Lower)
West Hatch High Sch
WOODFORD
IG8
River Roding
Woodford
Ray Lodge Prim Sch
Woodford Bridge
Roding Prim Sch
Woodbridge High Sch
Woodford Green
Churchfields Jun Sch
Queen Mary & Westfield Coll (Halls of Residence)
Commerce Est
Superstore
Cemy
Glade Prim Sch
Caterham High Sch
Clayhall
IG5
E18
South Woodford
Woodford Trad Est
SOUTHEND ROAD (NORTH CIRCULAR RD)
A406
A1400 SOUTHEND RD
BROADMEAD RD
A1009
CHIGWELL RD
MANOR RD
B173
B170
RODING LA
M11
A104
A121
A110
A113
A1199
B168
HIGH ROAD WOODFORD GN
EPPING NEW RD
WHITEHALL RD
HIGH RD

A1
1 THE CHILTONS
2 HIGH OAKS LODGE
3 MILLBROOK
4 LANSDOWNE RD
5 WOBURN CT
6 ULLSWATER CT
7 CLEVELAND RD
8 LEIGH CT
9 MARLBOROUGH RD

A2
1 LINDAL CT
2 HOCKLEY CT
3 WOODLEIGH
4 MILNE CT
5 CEDAR CT
6 ELIZABETH CT
7 SILVERMEAD
8 LAUREL MEAD CT
9 MITRE CT
10 PEVENSEY CT
11 LYNDHURST CT
12 RECTORY CT

A3
1 NEW JUBILEE CT
2 CHARTWELL CT
3 GREENWOOD
4 SALWAY LODGE

A4
1 THE TERRACE

309

A4
2 BROOMHILL CT
3 CLIFTON CT
4 FAIRSTEAD LODGE
5 HADLEIGH LODGE
6 BROADMEAD CT
7 WILTON CT
8 FAIRFIELD CT
9 HIGHAM CT

332

B1
1 Station Est
2 STATION APP
3 JAMES CT

C3
1 LISTON WAY
2 ELIZABETH CT
3 COOPERSALE CL
4 SUNSET CT
5 LAMBOURNE CT

C4
1 HOPE CL
2 REX PAR
3 SHALFORD
4 THE RODINGS

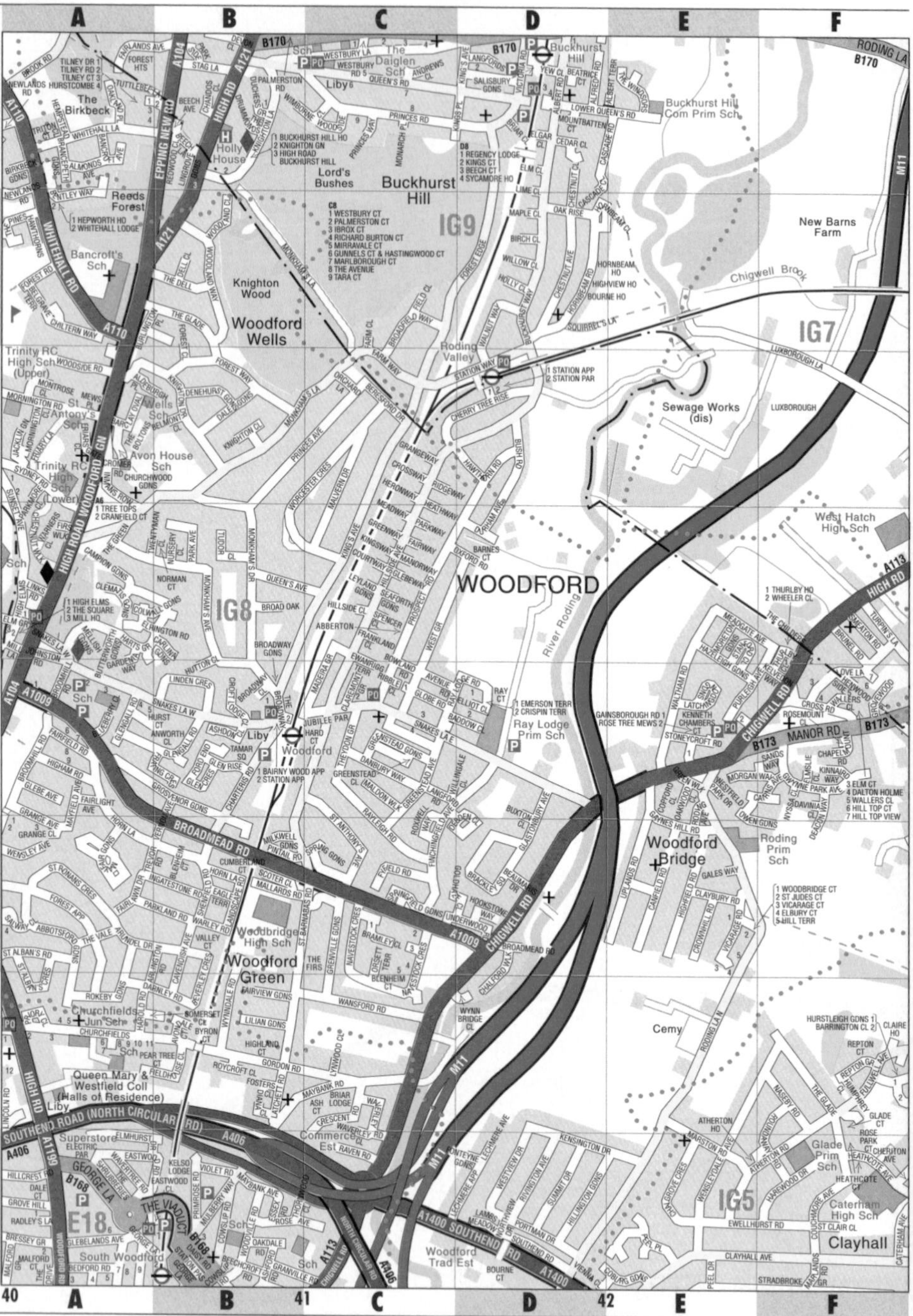

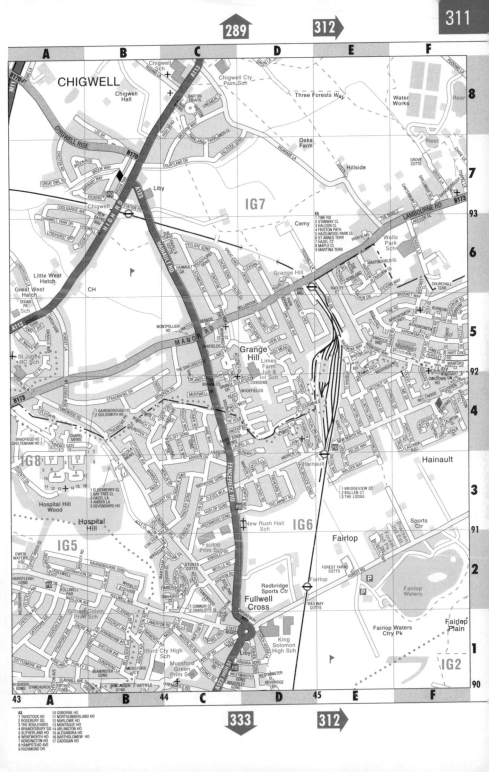

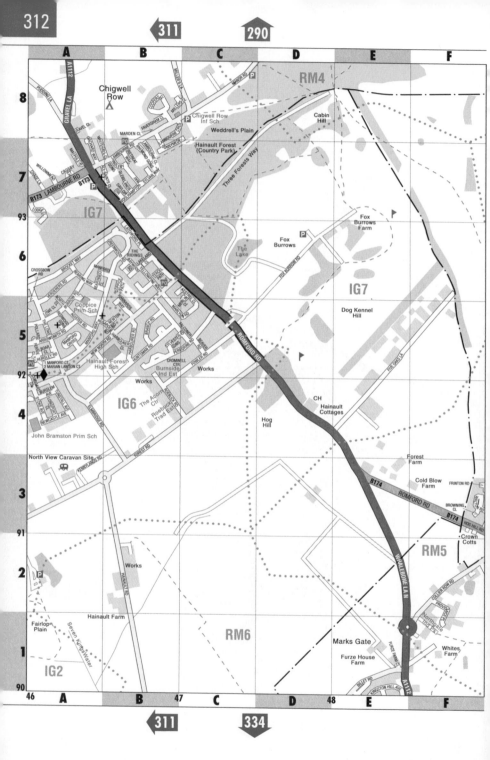

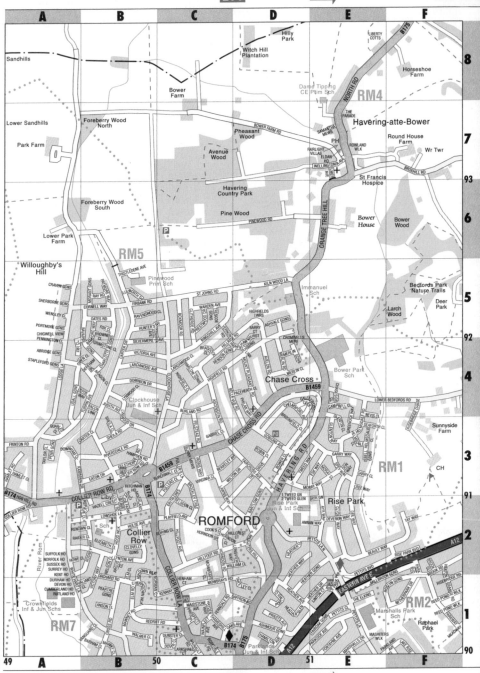

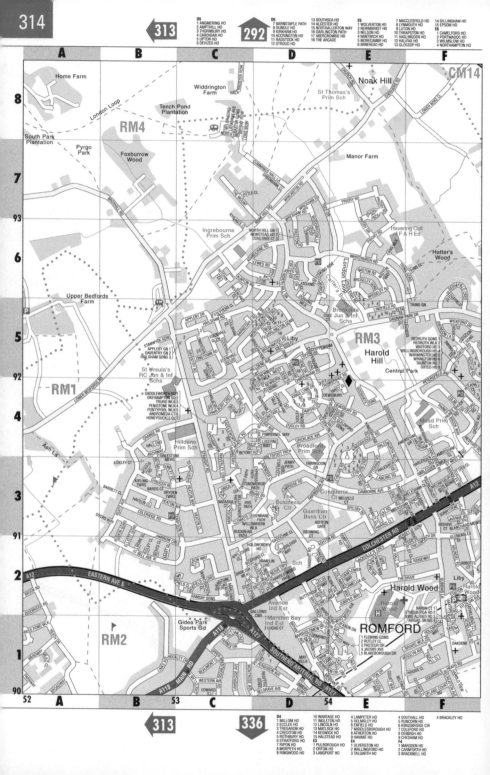

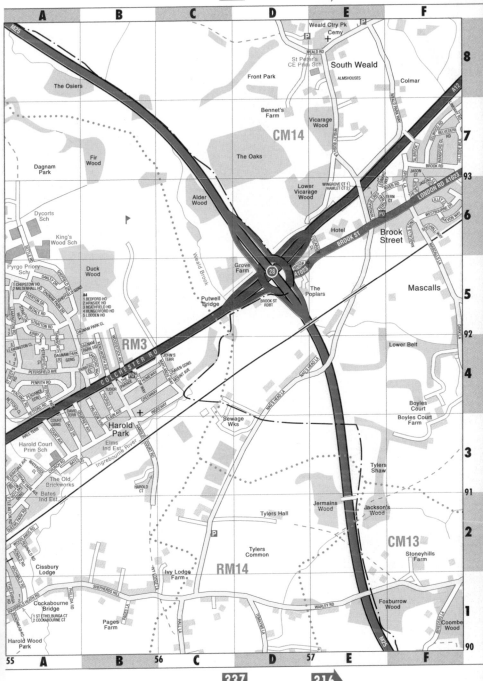

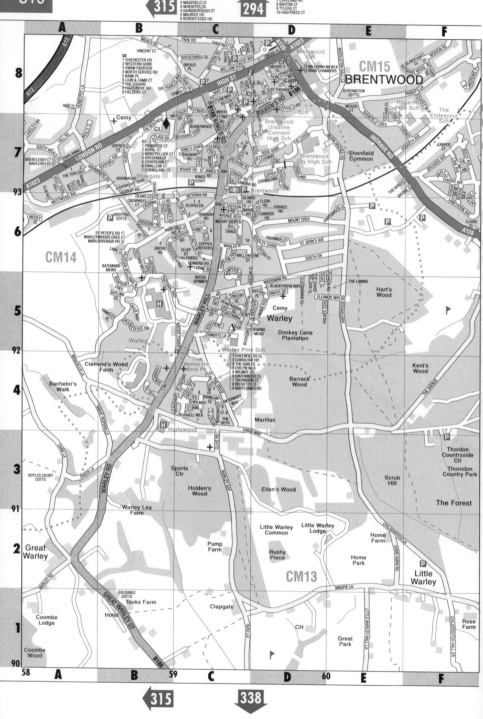

315

294

C6
1 VICTORIA CT
2 MASEFIELD CT
3 WHEATFIELDS
4 GAINSBOROUGH CT
5 MAURICE HO
6 BORDER EDGE HO

C6
7 COPELAND HO
8 BARTON CT
9 TYLERS CT
10 HIGHTREES CT

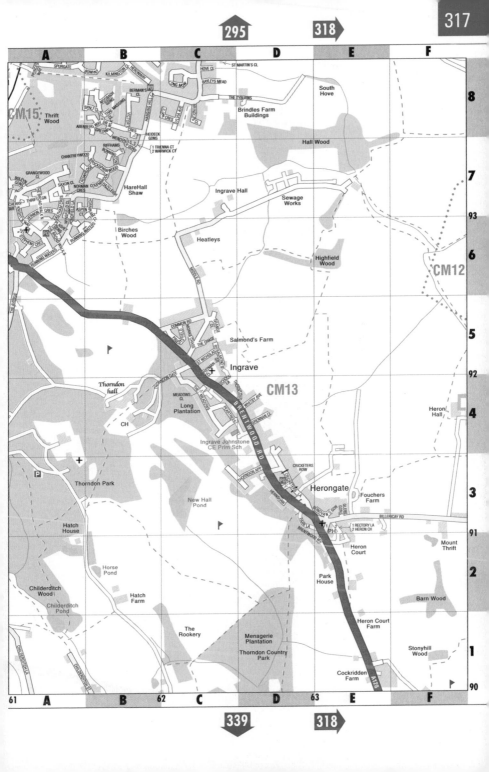

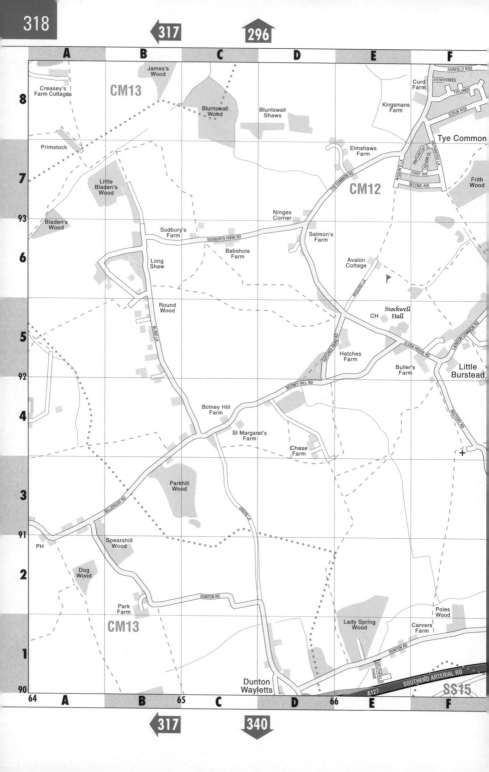

317
296

A **B** **C** **D** **E** **F**

CM13

Creasey's Farm Cottages

James's Wood

8

Curd Farm

FAIRFIELD RISE

CHERRYTREES

TYELANDS

SCRUB RISE

Kingsmans Farm

Bluntswall Wood

Bluntswall Shaws

Tye Common

Primstock

Elmshaws Farm

7

Little Bladen's Wood

TYE COMMON RD

CM12

FIRST AVE

SECOND AVE

Frith Wood

93

Bladen's Wood

Sudbury's Farm

Ninges Corner

SUDBURYS FARM RD

Salmon's Farm

6

Long Shaw

Babshole Farm

Avalon Cottage

WIGGINS LA

Round Wood

BLIND LA

Stockwell Hall

CH

LANGDON COMMON RD

5

HATCHES FARM RD

Hatches Farm

BLOCK HOUSE RD

Buller's Farm

Little Burstead

92

BOTNEY HILL RD

4

Botney Hill Farm

St Margaret's Farm

Chase Farm

BEDFORD RD

Parkhill Wood

BILLERICAY RD

3

GREEN LA

91

PH

Spearshill Wood

Dog Wood

2

Park Farm

DUNTON RD

Poles Wood

CM13

Lady Spring Wood

Carvers Farm

DUNTON RD

1

SOUTHFIELD CHASE

90

Dunton Wayletts

A127

SOUTHEND ARTERIAL RD

SS15

64 **A** **B** 65 **C** **D** 66 **E** **F**

317
340

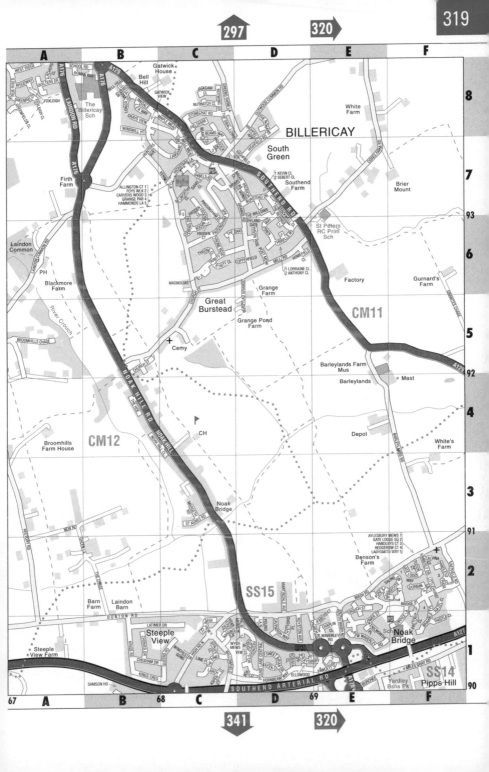

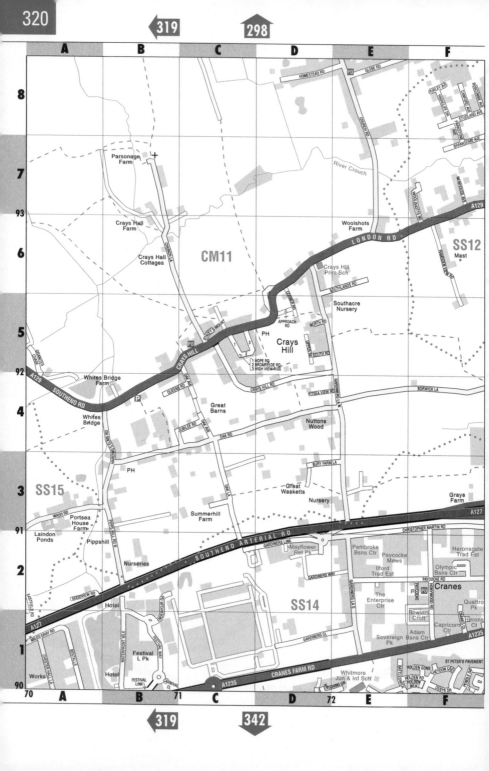

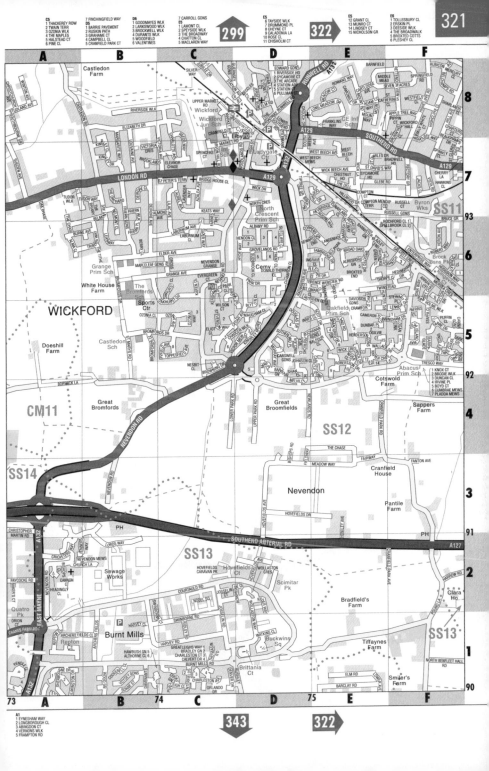

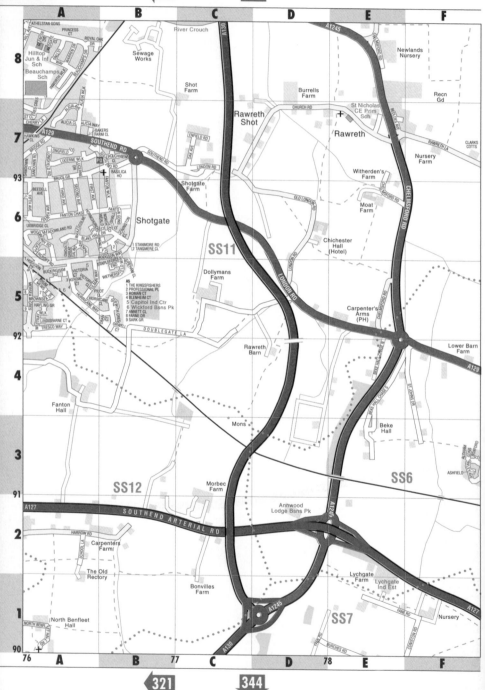

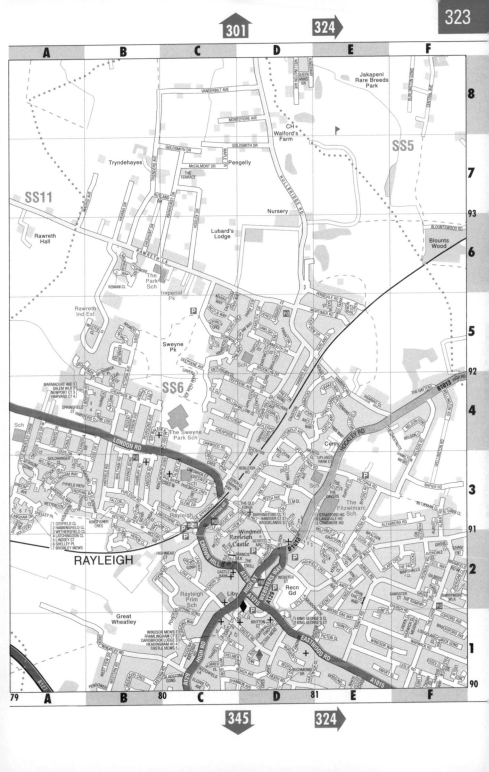

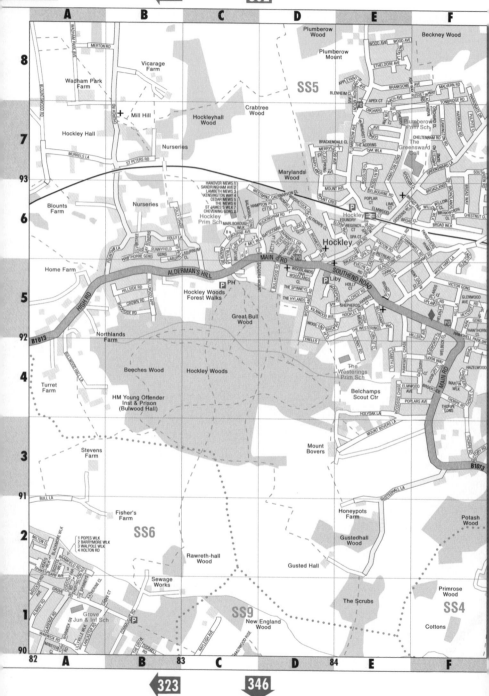

8

Plumberow
Wood
Beckney Wood

Plumberow
Mount

Wadham Park
Farm

Vicarage
Farm

SS5

7

Hockley Hall

Mill Hill

Hockleyhall
Wood

Crabtree
Wood

The
Greensward
Hall

Nurseries

Plumberow
Prim Sch

93

Hockley
Foundry

Blounts
Farm

Nurseries

Marylands
Wood

HANOVER MEWS 1
SANDRINGHAM AVE 2
LAMBETH MEWS 3
KENSINGTON WAY 4
CEDAR MEWS 5
THE MEWS 6
ST JAMES'S WLK 7
CHEVENING GDNS 8

Hockley
Prim Sch

6

Hockley

Home Farm

ALDERMAN'S HILL

Hockley Woods
Forest Walks

Liby

SOUTHEND ROAD

5

Hockley Woods
Forest Walks

PH

Great Bull
Wood

The
Spinneys

The Hylands

HIGH RD

Northlands
Farm

92

B1013

Turret
Farm

Beeches Wood

Hockley Woods

The
Westerings
Prim Sch

4

HM Young Offender
Inst & Prison
(Bulwood Hall)

Belchamps
Scout Ctr

Mount
Bovers

3

Stevens
Farm

Mount
Bovers

B1013

91

BULL LA

Fisher's
Farm

Honeypots
Farm

Potash
Wood

2

SS6

1 POPES WLK
2 BARRYMORE WLK
3 WALPOLE WLK
4 HOLTON RD

Rawreth-hall
Wood

Gustedhall
Wood

Sewage
Works

Gusted Hall

1

Grove
Jun & Inf Sch

SS9

New England
Wood

The Scrubs

Primrose
Wood

SS4

Cottons

90

82   A   B   83   C   D   84   E   F

325
304

A B C D E F

8

7

93

6

5

92

4

2

91

1

90

88 A B 89 C D 90 E F

Scotts Hall Cotts

Scott's Hall

Apton Hall Farm

Old Rectory

Wood Sloppy

Doggetts

Little Stambridge Hall

SS4

Great Stambridge

Stewards Elm Farm

Breade House

Ballards Gore

CH PH

Gore Rd

Gore Farm

PAGLESHAM RD

Moat & Springs

Stambridge Fisheries

Hampton Barns

Ragstone Lodge

Brick House

Bartonhall Creek

Winters

PH

Allott Gdns

Coombes Farm

Stambridge Prim Sch

Great Stambridge Hall

Waldens

Stambridge Mills

Broomhills

River Roach

APTON HALL RD

SCOTTS HALL RD

CHECKSOIL FERRY RD

STEWARDS ELM FARM LA

CAGEFIELD RD

CAGE FIELD COTTS

ASH

DOGGETTS CHASE

LITTLE STAMBRIDGE HALL RD

STAMBRIDGE RD

MILL LA

ROCHEWAY

MOUNTDALE RD

BRICKFIELDS RISE

FEATHERBY WAY

TINKER'S LA

MILLHEAD WAY

RUSHER DR

COOMBES GR

FIELD DR

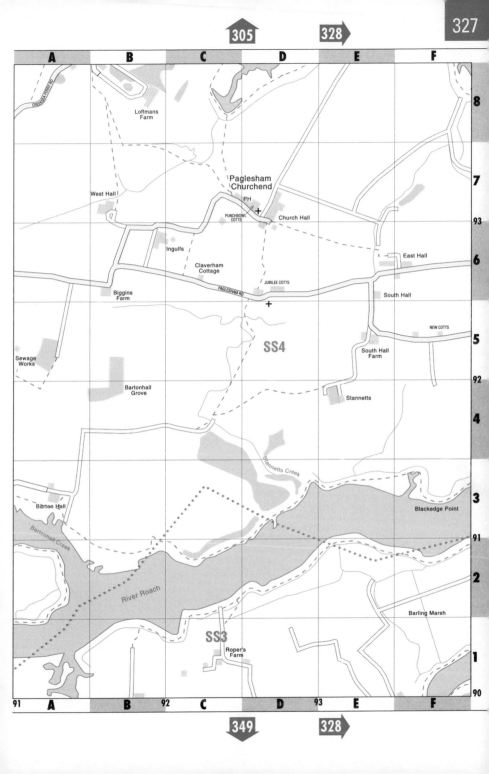

| | A | B | C | D | E | F | |

CHECKLEY FERRY RD

8

Loftmans Farm

West Hall

Paglesham Churchend

PH

7

PUNCHBOWL COTTS

Church Hall

93

Ingulfs

East Hall

6

Claverham Cottage

JUBILEE COTTS

South Hall

Biggins Farm

PAGLESHAM RD

SS4

NEW COTTS

5

Sewage Works

South Hall Farm

92

Bartonhall Grove

Stannetts

4

Stannetts Creek

Barton Hall

Blackedge Point

3

Bartonhall Creek

91

2

River Roach

Barling Marsh

SS3

Roper's Farm

1

90

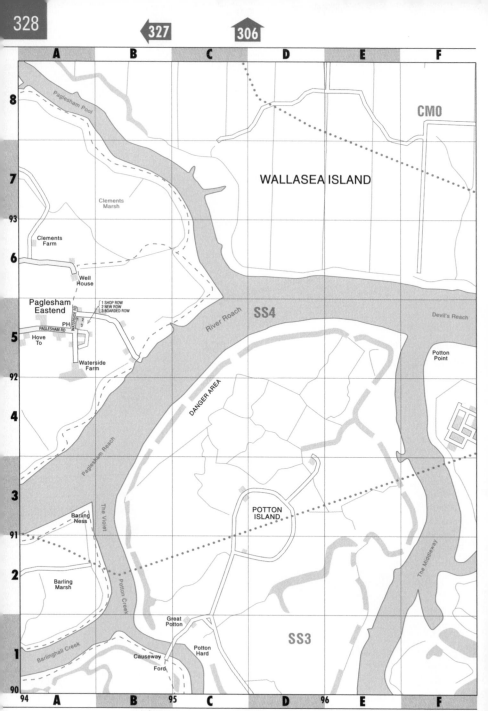

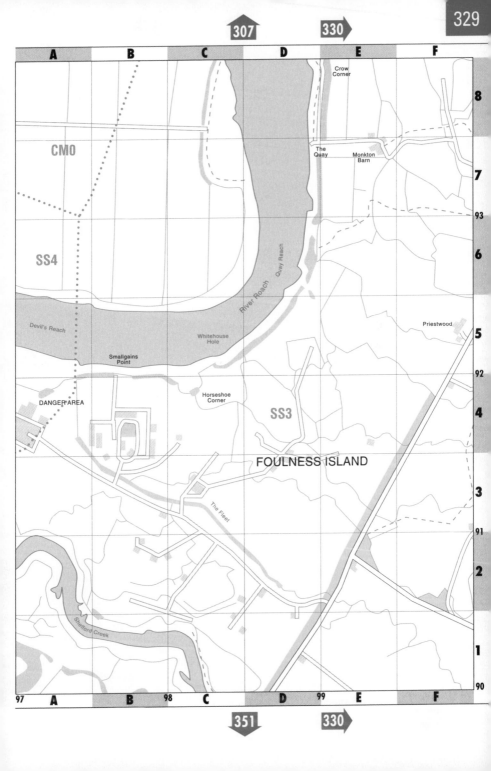

CM0

SS4

Devil's Reach

Smallgains
Point

DANGER AREA

Crow
Corner

The
Quay

Monkton
Barn

River Roach

Quay Reach

Whitehouse
Hole

Horseshoe
Corner

SS3

FOULNESS ISLAND

Priestwood

The Fleet

Shelford Creek

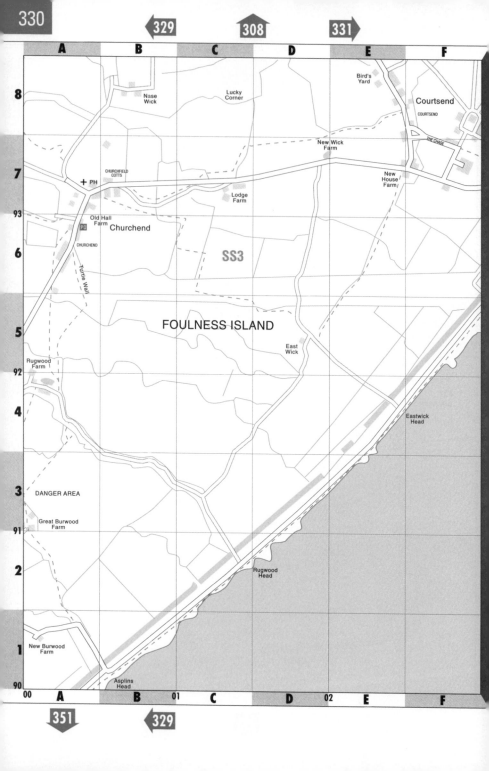

329
308
331

A   B   C   D   E   F

8

Bird's
Yard

Nase
Wick

Lucky
Corner

Courtsend

COURTSEND

New Wick
Farm

THE CHASE

7

CHURCHFIELD
COTTS

+ PH

New
House
Farm

Lodge
Farm

93

Old Hall
Farm

PO   Churchend

SS3

6

CHURCHEND

Turtle Wall

FOULNESS ISLAND

5

East
Wick

Rugwood
Farm

92

4

Eastwick
Head

3

DANGER AREA

Great Burwood
Farm

91

2

Rugwood
Head

1

New Burwood
Farm

90

00   A   B   01   C   D   02   E   F

Asplins
Head

351
329

308

330

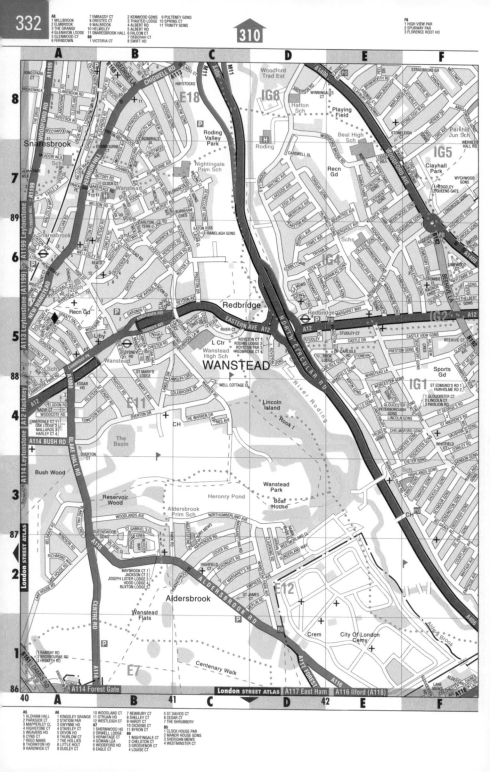

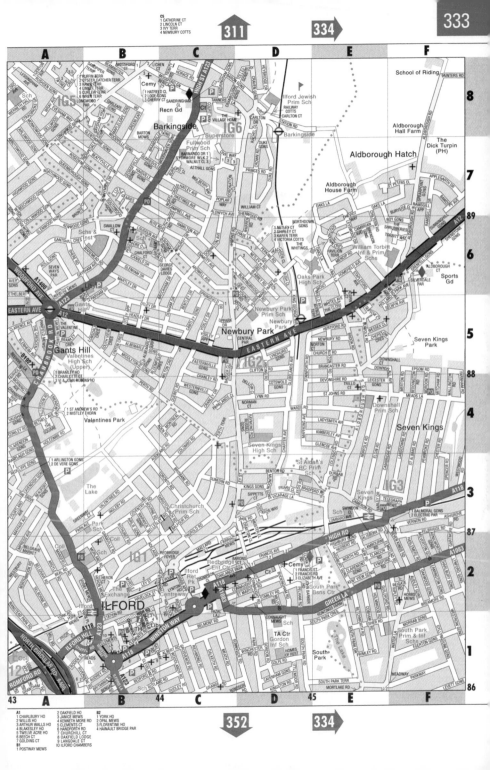

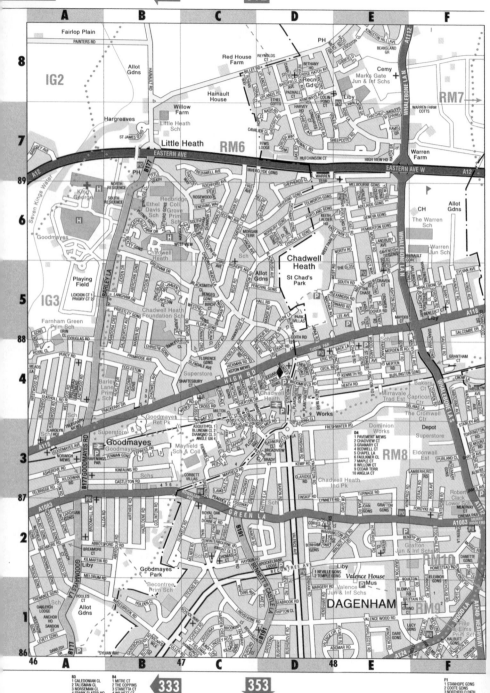

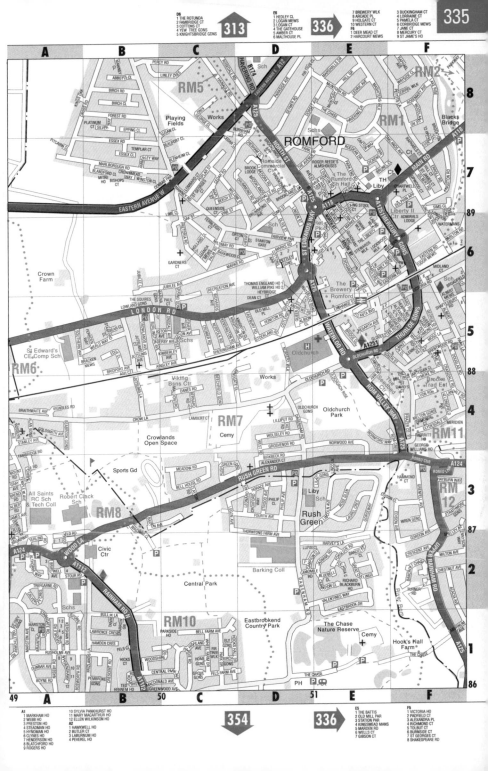

335 314

C7
1 EDINBURGH HO
2 VICTORIA HO
3 ELIZABETH HO
4 MOUNTBATTEN HO
5 SNOWDON CT

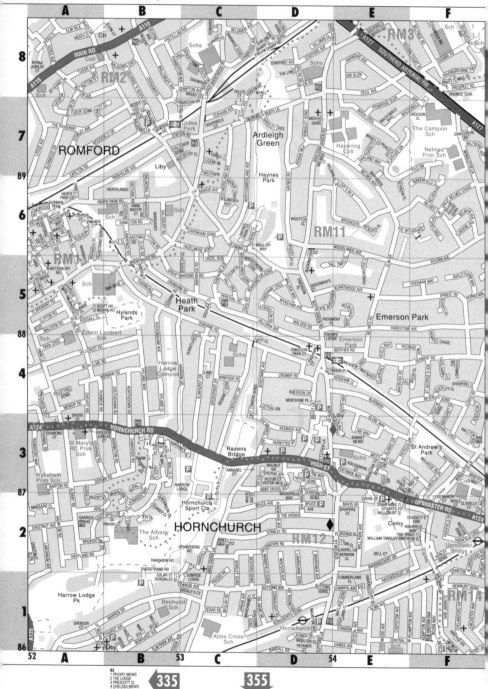

B3
1 PRIORY MEWS
2 THE LODGE
3 PRESCOTT CL
4 CHELSEA MEWS
5 THE CHAPEL

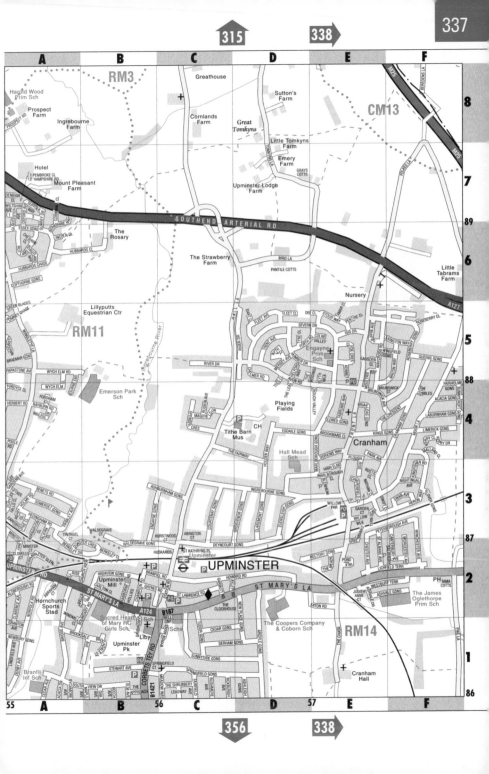

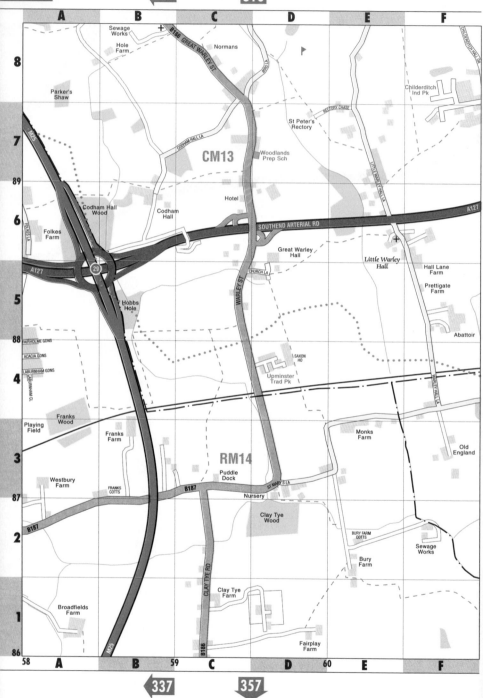

A **B** **C** **D** **E** **F**

8

Sewage
Works
Hole
Farm
B186 GREAT WARLEY ST
Normans

Parker's
Shaw

Childerditch
Ind Pk

RECTORY CHASE

St Peter's
Rectory

7

CODHAM HALL LA

CM13

Woodlands
Prep Sch

A127

89

Codham Hall
Wood
Codham
Hall
Hotel

LITTLE WARLEY HALL LA

6

Folkes
Farm

SOUTHEND ARTERIAL RD

Great Warley
Hall

Little Warley
Hall

Hall Lane
Farm

A127

29

WARLEY ST

CHURCH LA

Prettigate
Farm

5

Hobbs
Hole

WARLEY HALL LA

88

FAIRHOLME GDNS

ACACIA GDNS

LABURNHAM GDNS

LABURNHAM CL

SAXON
HO

Abattoir

4

Upminster
Trad Pk

Playing
Field

Franks
Wood

Franks
Farm

Monks
Farm

Old
England

3

Westbury
Farm

RM14

Puddle
Dock

B187

FRANKS
COTTS

ST MARY'S LA

Nursery

Bury Farm
COTTS

B187

87

Clay Tye
Wood

Sewage
Works

2

CLAY TYE RD

Bury
Farm

Broadfields
Farm

M25

Clay Tye
Farm

1

B186

Fairplay
Farm

86

58 **A** **B** 59 **C** **D** 60 **E** **F**

A B C D E F

The Old Shop

Hill Farm

Old Hall Pond

Octagon Plantation

P

Thorndon Country Park

8

Mill Wood

Jury Hill

Halfway House Motel

Childerditch Hall

Thick Shaw

7

Barrett's Shaw

SOUTHEND ARTERIAL RD

Hollow Bottom Shaw

East Horndon

89

Round Shaw

Nuttys Farm

West Horndon Prim Sch

6

West Horndon

CADOGAN AVE

Old Mill Cottages

STATION RD

5

Horndon Ind Pk

DUNMOW GDNS

PO

1 CHAFFORD GDNS
2 WITHAM GDNS
3 BURNTWOOD CL
4 SAFFRON CL

FRESHWELL GDNS

PO

West Horndon

88

ST MARY'S LA

CM13

Barnards

4

Little Tillingham Hall

BRENTWOOD RD

Blue House Farm

Field House

Middleton Hall

3

Tillingham Hall

87

DUNNINGS LA

2

PEARTREE LA

Slough House

CM14

1

86

A B C D E F

61 62 63

A127
A128
TILBURY RD
CHILDERDITCH HALL DR
CHILDERDITCH LA
THORNDON AVE
CLAPGATE GDNS
BULPHAN BYPASS
A128
CHINA LA

Dunton
Wayletts

CM12

A121

SOUTHEND ARTERIAL RD

A127

Eastlands
Spring

Friern Manor
Wood

Green
Meadows
Nurseries

Brookman's
Farm

Friern Manor
CHASE

MERRYLANDS
CHASE

Automobile
Research Ctr

SS15

Southfields

1 BROADWATER GN
2 WOODSTOCK CRES
3 WOODSTOCK GDNS
4 PRESIDENTS CT
5 HELMORE CT

B148

Friern
Manor

WEST MAYNE

Westmayne
Ind Pk

B1036

Dunton Hills
Farm

CM13

The Old
Rectory

SUMPNERS
LINK

BLACKMORES

MANDEVILLE

B1036

CHURCH RD

WAY

Dunton
Hall

DUNTON PARK
CVN PK

WORCESTER CL 1
SHREWSBURY CL 2
OSWESLEY DR 3
AMERSHAM AVE 4
NAHONIA DR 5
IPSWICH MEWS 6
ALNWICK CL 7
OXFORD CL 8
CAMBRIDGE CL 9
MONMOUTH MEWS 10

Great
Berry

WOODVIEW

Great Berry
Prim Sch

LOWER DUNTON RD

FIRST AVE

HIGH BANK 1
REEVES CL 2

SECOND AVE

CENTRAL AVE

Plotlands
Mus THIRD AVE

Plotlands
Nature Reserve

SS16

Poultry
Farm

Langdon
Conservation
Ctr

FOURTH AVE

Dunton Poultry
Farm

A128

Lower Dunton
Hall

RM14

Balgownie
Farm

BULPHAN BY PASS

BRENTWOOD RD

Motel Garlesters

BRENTWOOD RD

Noke Hall
Farm

DOESGATE LA

Doesgate
Farm

Bentley
Farm

OLD CHURCH HILL

A128

Manor
House

Little
Malgraves

Little
Malgraves
Ind Est

64 A B 65 C D 66 E F

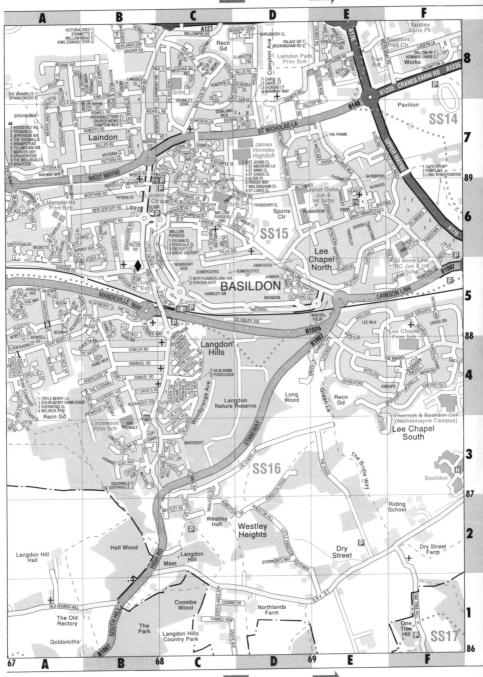

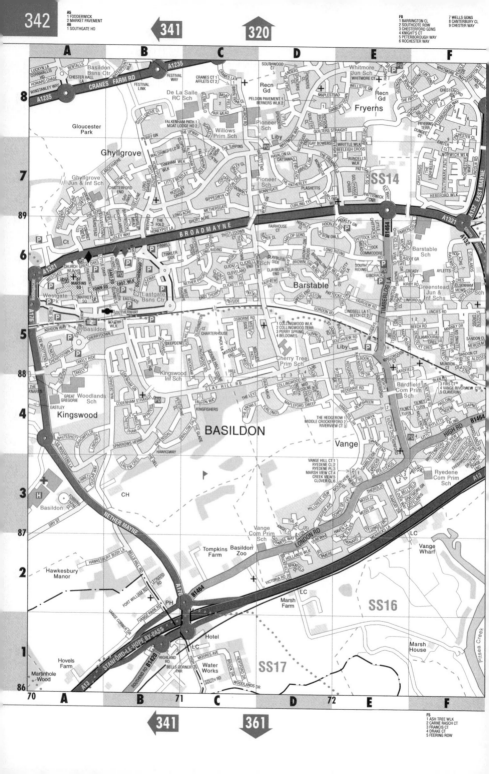

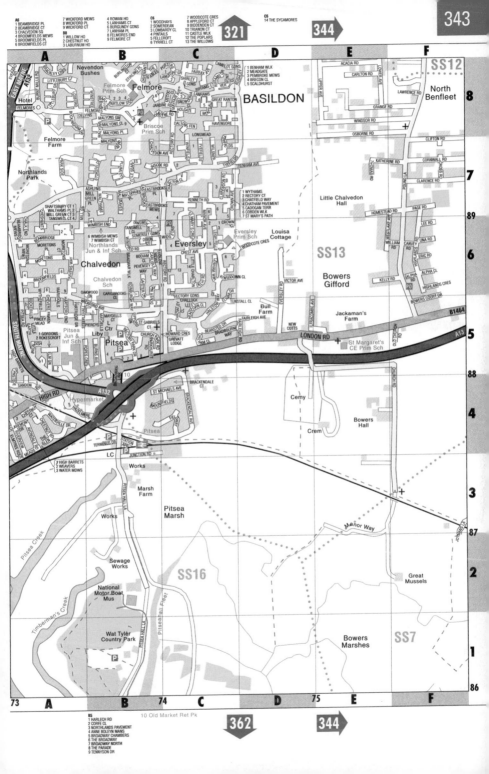

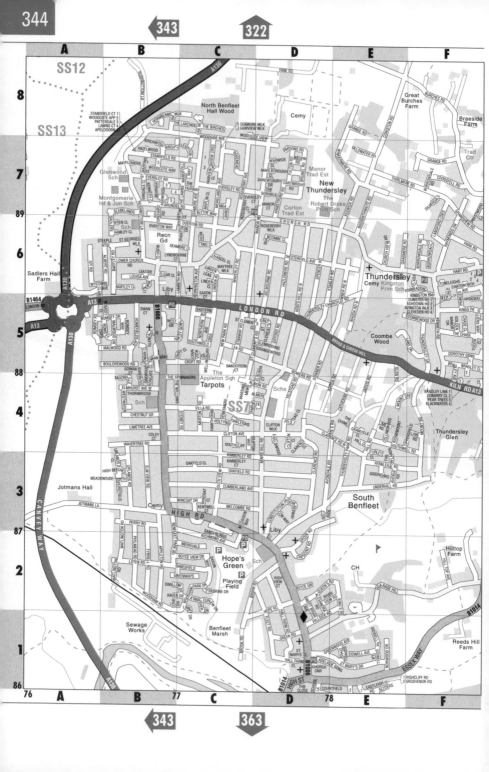

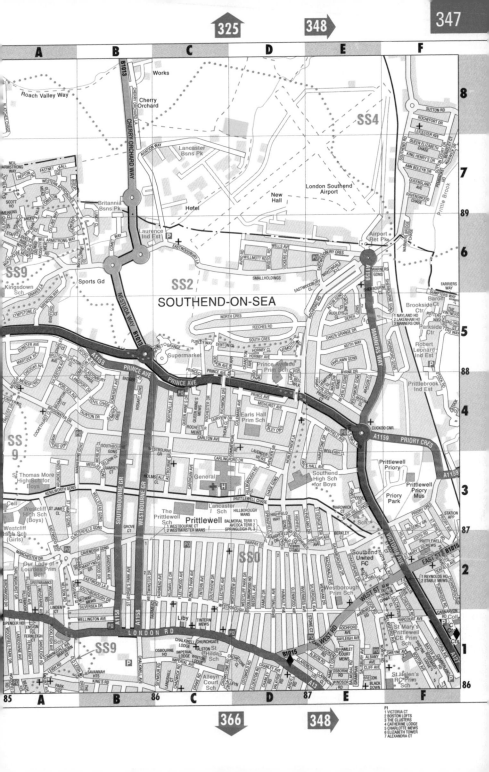

A B C D E F

8

DANGER
AREA

Farm
Cottages

Brimstone
Hill

Fleethead Creek

Swing
Bridge

The Middleway

Narrow Guts

Fleet
Head

POTTON
ISLAND

7

Wakering Creek

89

Rushley
Island

Halfway
House
Farm

Mill Head

6

Rushley
Farm

Little
Wakering
Hall

Millhead
Cottages

Ford

Havengore Creek

5

Oxenham
Farm

Millhead
Villas

Sewage
Works

88

Great
Wakering

SS3

BRIDGE RD

4

HOME FARM CL.
WEDDS WAY

STAITE RD

THE
MALLARDS

HAVENGORE

LINDISEL RD

WHITE HALL RD

Great
Wakering
Common

LANDWICK
COTTS

LITTLE WAKERING HALL LA

THYFORD AVE

MERCERS

NORTH RD

CAPEL

ASHFORD RD

GRES
ORCHARD CL

OLD SCH
HALL CT

MORELAND

RUSHLEY CT

CLAPHAM

Lib

B1017

NEW RD

MORRIN RD

SAMUEL'S
CNR

HIGH ST.

GOODMANS

GLEBE CL.

ALP
CT

BELL
HO

WHITE RD

3

Great
Wakering
Prim Sch

PO

FAIRHEAD

CONWAY AVE

1 LION FIELDS
2 SOUTHGATE MEWS
3 ST JOHN'S CL
4 THE ANCHORAGE
5 RODING CL
6 THE CEDARS

LC

Shoeburyness
New Ranges

ALEXANDRA RD

CROUCHMANS
AVE

SHOPLAND RD

BEAUCHAMPS

MARINERS CT

ELSDORE

MORRIN'S CHASE

MILTON
HALL
CL

87

Crouchmans
Farm

SEAVIEW DR

ESTUARY GDNS

NEW
ENGLAND
CRES

DANGER AREA

BERKELEY AVE

GOLDSWORTHY CL

Crouchmans
Cottage

VICTORIA DR

Morrin's
Point

2

The
Lansdowne

CUPIDS CHASE

CUPID'S
CNR

Black Grounds

POYNTERS LA

SUTTON RD

CHERRYTREE CHASE

WAKERING RD

Poynter's
Point

1

PICKERS WAY

RAPHAEL DR

BRIDGE RD

BUTTS RD

86

94 A B 95 C D 96 E F

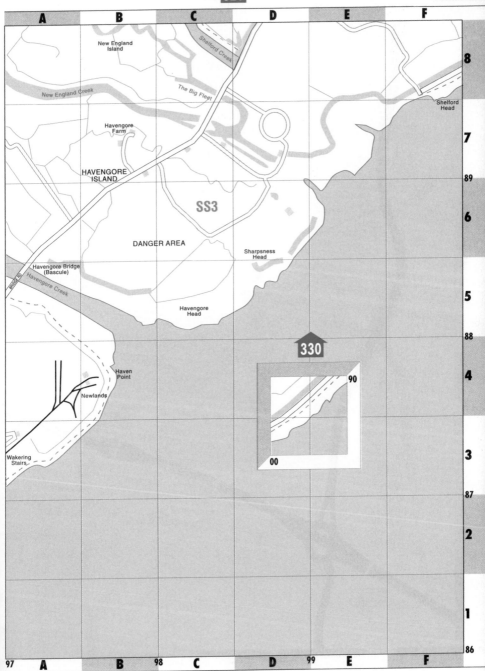

A   B   C   D   E   F

8

New England
Island

Shelford Creek

New England Creek

The Big Fleet

Shelford
Head

7

Havengore
Farm

HAVENGORE
ISLAND

89

SS3

6

DANGER AREA

Sharpsness
Head

Havengore Bridge
(Bascule)

Havengore Creek

5

Havengore
Head

88

330

4

Haven
Point

90

Newlands

Wakering
Stairs

00

3

87

2

1

86

97   A   B   98   C   D   99   E   F

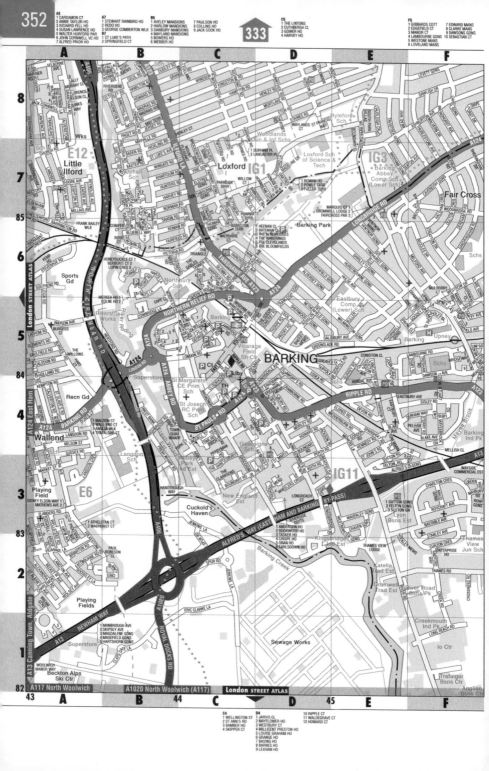

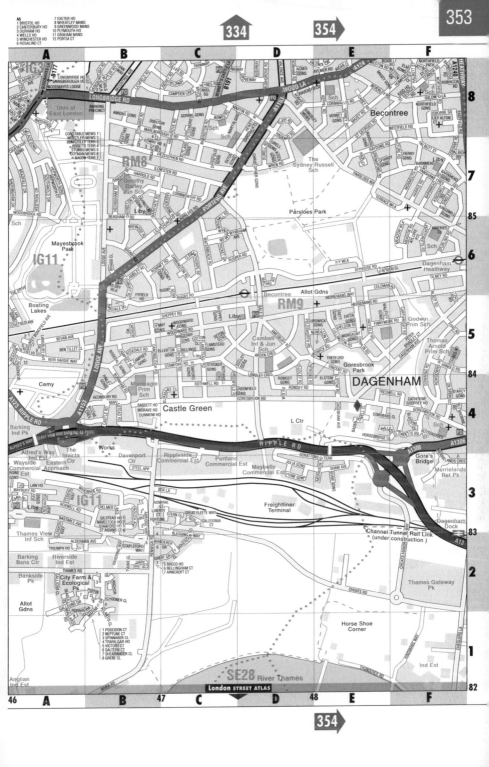

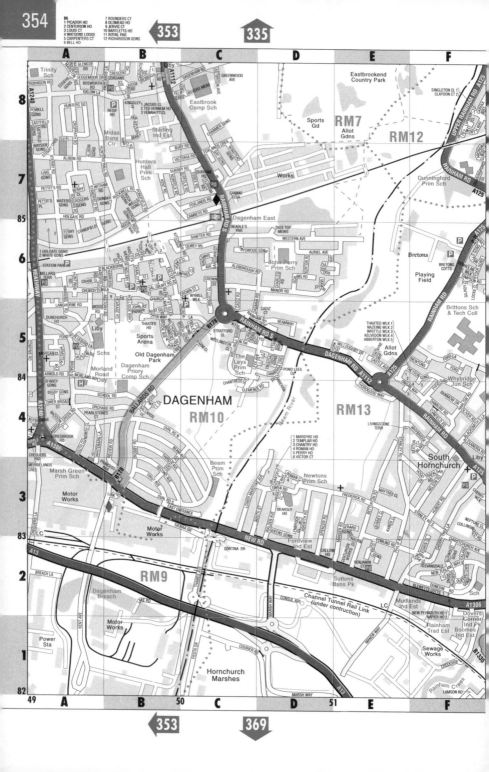

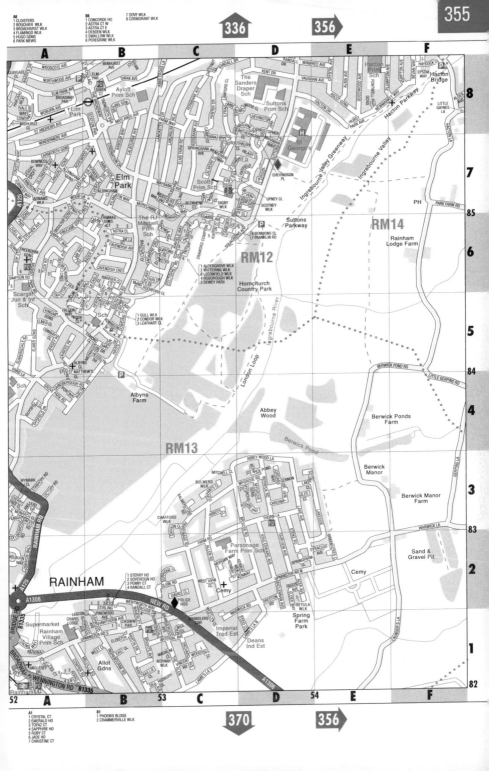

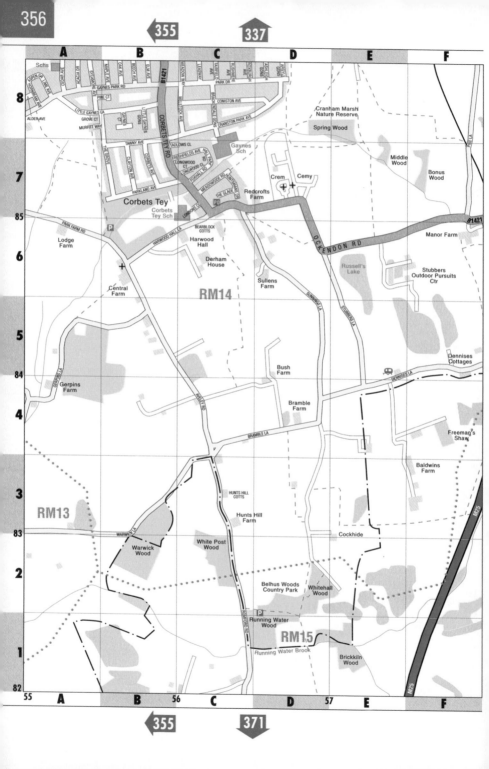

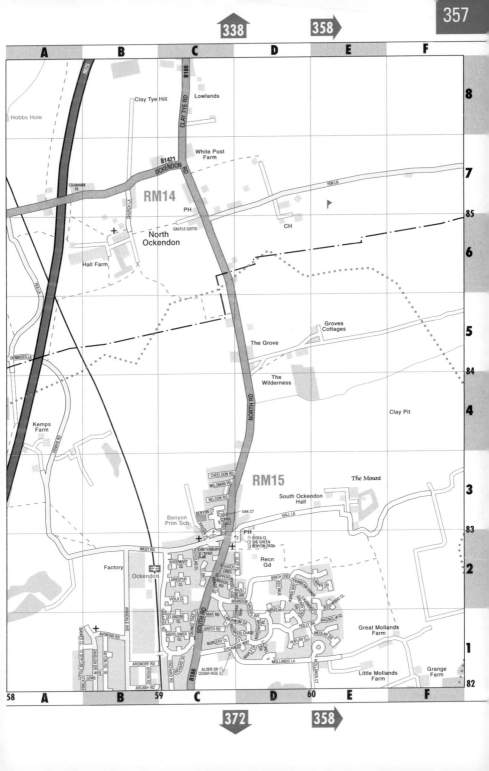

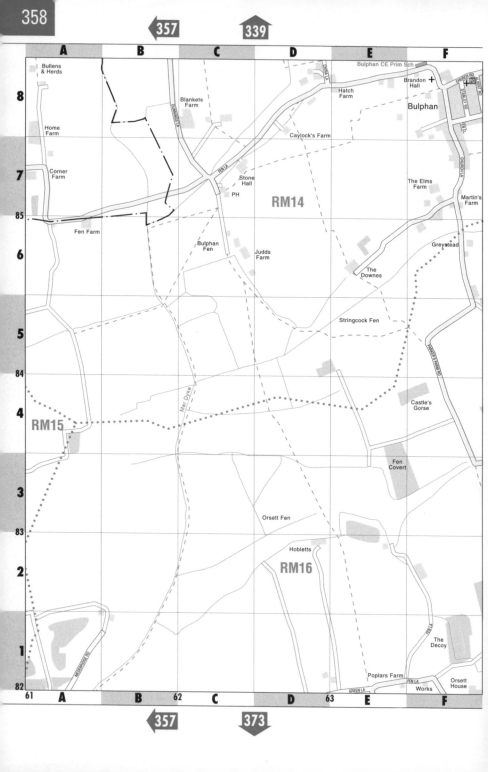

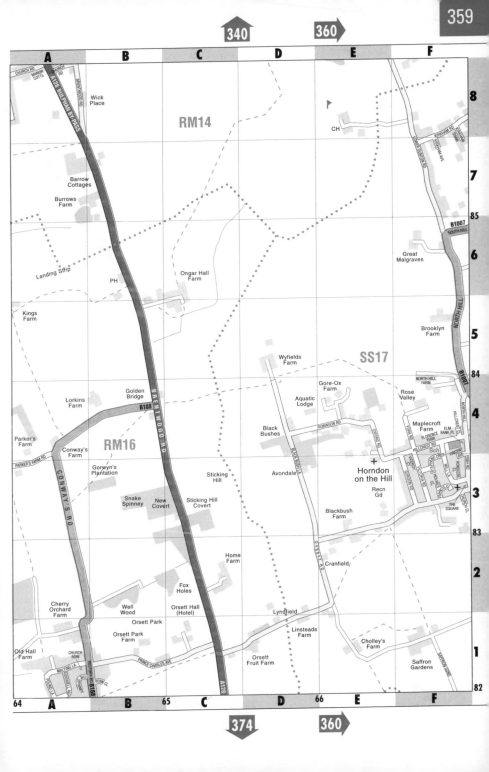

340
360

A B C D E F

8

7

85

6

5

84

4

3

83

2

1

82

RM14

Church Rd
MANOR COTTS
A128 BULPHAN BY PASS
CHURCH RD
BRENTWOOD RD

Wick Place

Barrow Cottages

Burrows Farm

Landing Strip

PH

Kings Farm

Ongar Hall Farm

CH

B1007
SOUTH HILL

Great Malgraves

NORTH HILL

Brooklyn Farm

SS17

Wyfields Farm

Gore-Ox Farm

Aquatic Lodge

Rose Valley

NORTH HILL FARM

B1007

Golden Bridge

B188
BRENTWOOD RD

Lorkins Farm

RM16

Parker's Farm

Conway's Farm

PARKER'S FARM RD

Gorwyn's Plantation

CONWAY'S RD

Snake Spinney

New Covert

Sticking Hill

Sticking Hill Covert

Black Bushes

Avondale

BLACK BUSHES

ROBINSON RD

COLLEGE RD

Maplecroft Farm

FLORENCE TERR
ELM BANK PL.
HILLCREST RD
VINCENT
Sch
HILL CRES

Horndon on the Hill

Recn Gd

THE SQUARE

Blackbush Farm

ORSETT RD

Home Farm

Fox Holes

Cherry Orchard Farm

Well Wood

Orsett Park

Orsett Park Farm

Old Hall Farm

CHURCH ROW

MALTING LA.
POUND LT.
B188
BELL
PEN CL.
BECKWOOD RD

PRINCE CHARLES AVE

Orsett Hall (Hotel)

Cranfield

Lyndfield

Linsteads Farm

Orsett Fruit Farm

Cholley's Farm

Saffron Gardens

SAFFRON GDNS

64 A B 65 C D 66 E F

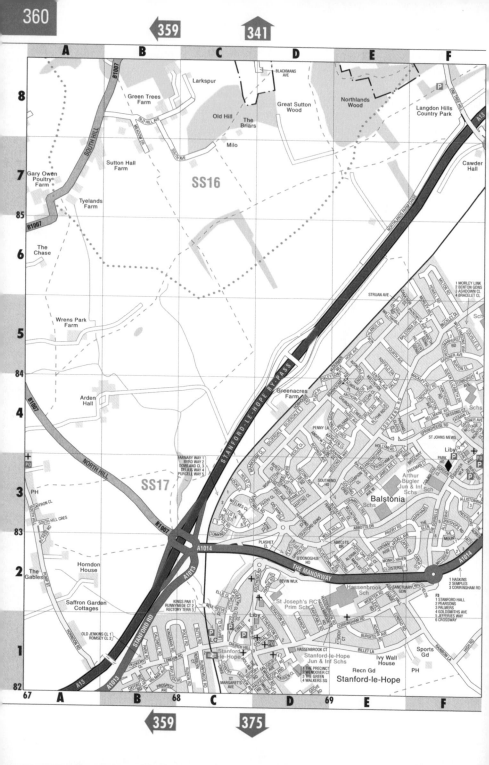

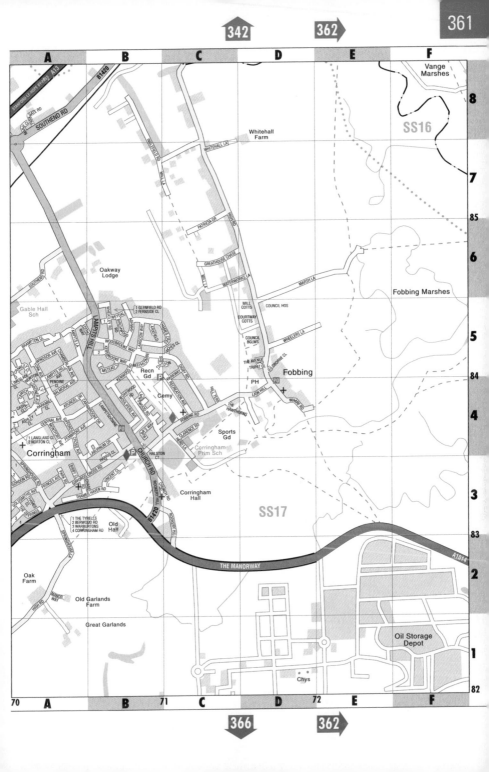

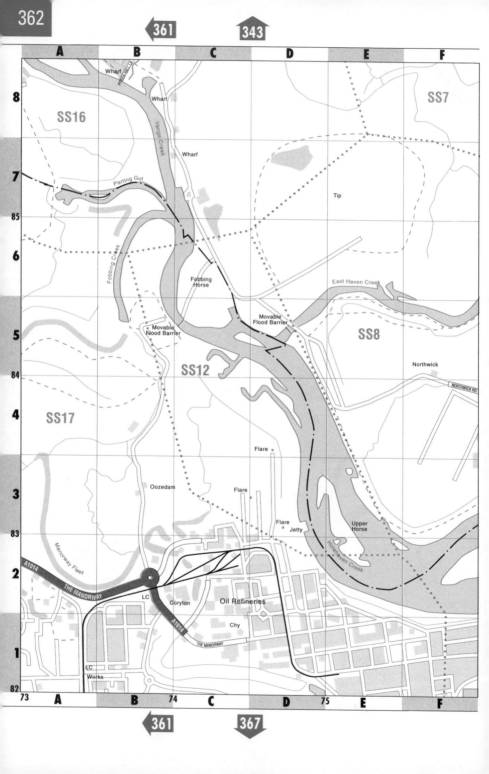

8

SS16

Wharf

PITSEA LA

Wharf

Vange Creek

Wharf

7

Parting Gut

85

Fobbing Creek

6

Fobbing
Horse

Movable
Flood Barrier

Movable
Flood Barrier

East Haven Creek

SS8

5

SS12

84

Northwick

NORTHWICK RD

4

SS17

Flare

3

Oozedam

Flare

Upper
Horse

83

Flare

Flare   Jetty

Holehaven Creek

Manorway Fleet

2

A1014

THE MANORWAY

LC

Coryton

Oil Refineries

A1014

Chy

THE MANORWAY

1

LC

82

Works

SS7

Tip

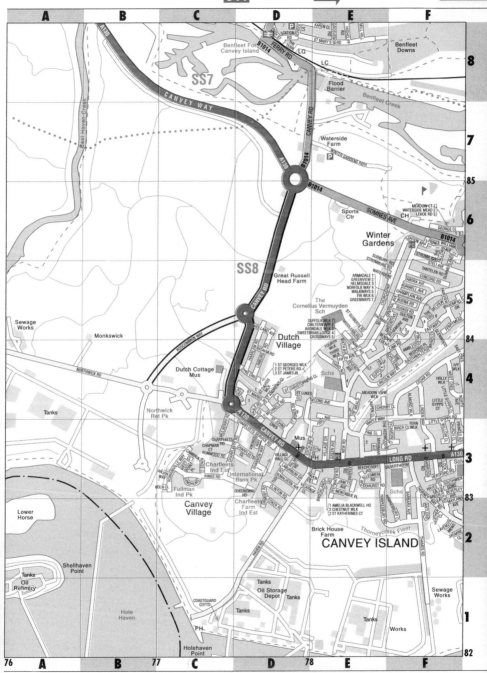

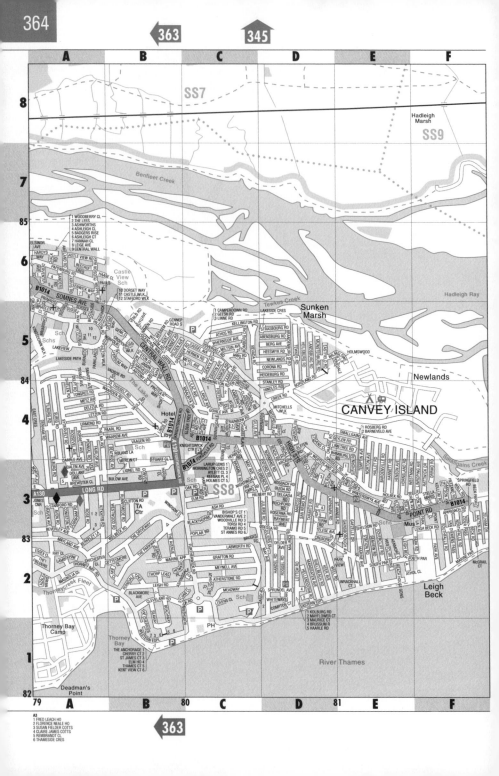

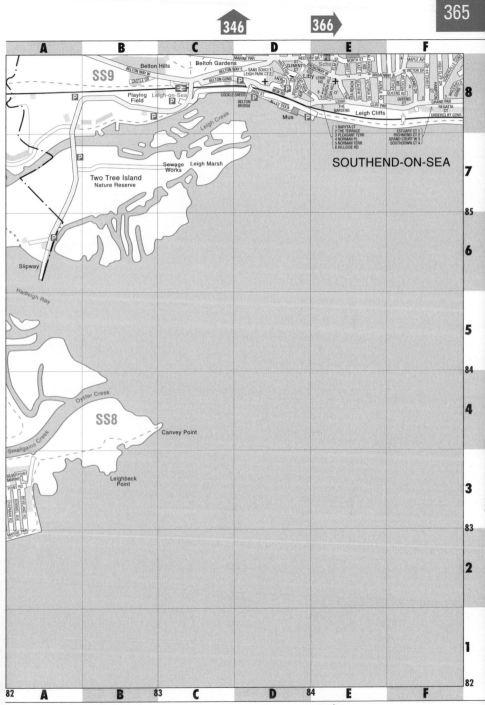

SS9

Belton Hills
Belton Gardens
MARINE PAR
Belton Way W
BELTON WAY W
BELTON WAY E
CASTLE DR
Playing Field
Leigh-on-Sea
BELTON GDNS
SANS SOUCI 1
LEIGH PARK CT 2
ST CLEMENT'S CT
RECTORY GR
Schs
MAPLE AVE
NORTH ST
BROADWAY
VICTOR DR E
Lby
Leigh
COCKLE SHEDS
HIGH ST
NEW RD
LAURA
Leigh
QUEENS RD
GRAND PAR
BELTON BRIDGE
ALLEY DOCK
Mus
Leigh Cliffs
REGATTA CT
UNDERCLIFF GDNS

Leigh Creek

Sewage Works
Leigh Marsh

Two Tree Island
Nature Reserve

SOUTHEND-ON-SEA

1 BARYTA CT
2 THE TERRACE
3 PLEASANT TERR
4 NORMAN PL
5 NORMAN TERR
6 HILLSIDE RD

ESTUARY CT 1
RICHMOND CT 2
GRAND COURT W 3
SOUTHDOWN CT 4

85

Slipway

Hadleigh Ray

6

5

84

Oyster Creek

SS8

Leigh Creek

Canvey Point

Smallgains Creek

SILVERPOINT MARINE
POINT RD
RYELAND RD
RONNIE AVE
CHAPMAN AVE
MARINE PAR

Leighbeck Point

4

3

83

2

1

82

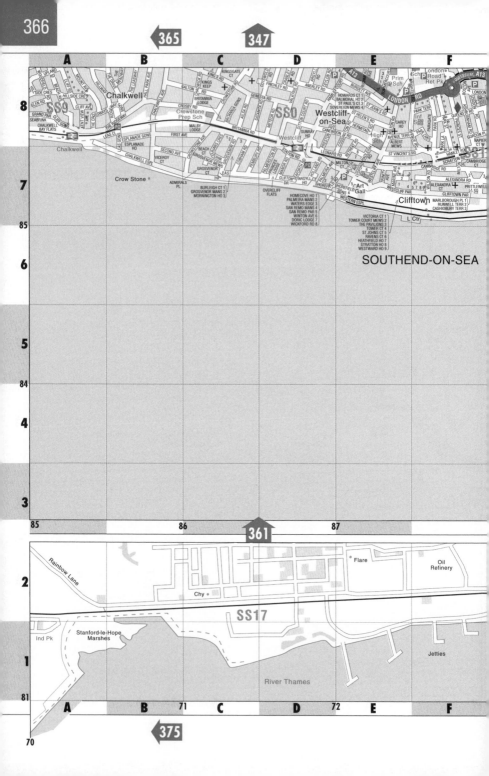

365
347

A **B** **C** **D** **E** **F**

SS9

Chalkwell

8

SS0

Westcliff-
on-Sea

Crowstone
Prep Sch

MALBY
LODGE

Westcliff

Chalkwell

CHALKWELL ESPL

Crow Stone

7

ADMIRALS
PL

BURLEIGH CT 1
GROSVENOR MANS 2
MORNINGTON HO 3

OVERCLIFF
FLATS

HOMECOVE HO 1
PALMEIRA MANS 2
WATERS EDGE 3
SAN REMO MANS 4
SAN REMO PAR 5
WINTON AVE 6
DORIC LODGE 7
WICKFORD RD 8

Art
Gall

Clifftown

MARLBOROUGH PL 1
RUNWELL TERR 2
CASHIOBURY TERR 3

CLIFFTOWN PAR

WESTCLIFF PAR

WESTERN ESPL

L Ctr

85

VICTORIA CT 1
TOWER COURT MEWS 2
THE PAVILIONS 3
TOWER CT 4
ST JOHNS CT 5
RAVENS CT 6
HEATHFIELD HO 7
STRATTON HO 8
WESTWARD HO 9

6

SOUTHEND-ON-SEA

5

84

4

3

85 86 361 87

361

2

Rainbow Lane

Flare

Oil
Refinery

Chy

SS17

Ind Pk

Stanford-le-Hope
Marshes

Jetties

1

River Thames

81

A **B** 71 **C** **D** 72 **E** **F**

375

70

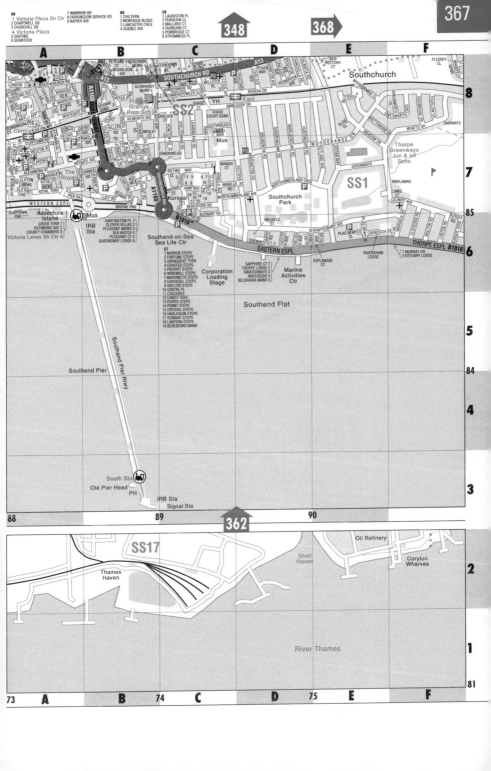

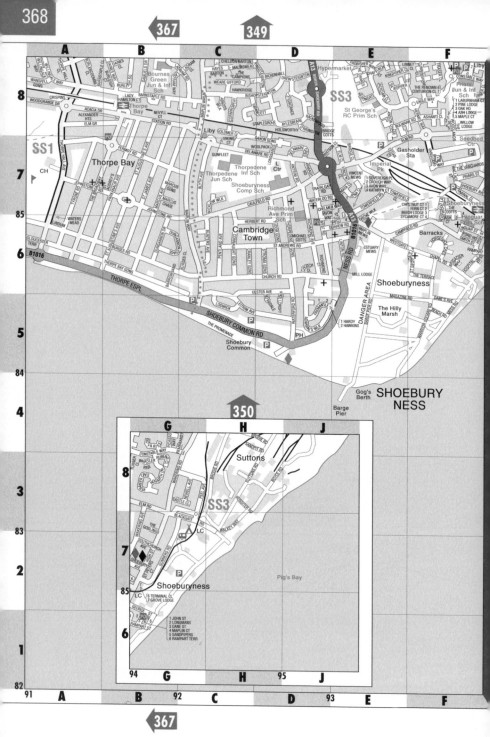

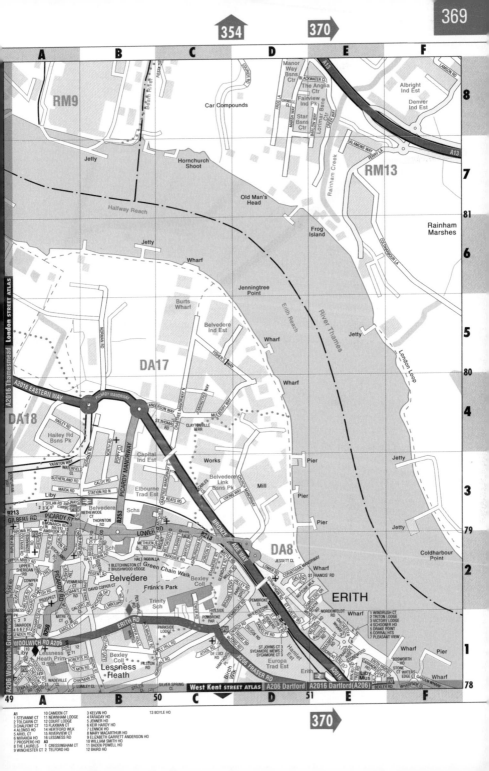

RM9

Car Compounds

Manor Way Bsns Ctr
BLACKWATER CL
The Anglia Ctr
Fairview Ind Pk
Star Bsns Ctr
Albright Ind Est
Denver Ind Est

Jetty

Hornchurch Shoot

Halfway Reach

Old Man's Head

Frog Island

RM13

Rainham Marshes

Jetty

Wharf

Jenningtree Point

Burts Wharf

Belvedere Ind Est

Wharf

Erith Reach

River Thames

Jetty

London Loop

DA17

Wharf

DA18

A2016 EASTERN WAY

PICARDY MANORWAY

Hailey Rd Bsns Pk

Capital Ind Est

Works

Belvedere Link Bsns Pk

Mill

Pier

Pier

Pier

Jetty

Jetty

Jetty

Elbourne Trad Est

Belvedere

Green Chain Walk

1 Bletchington Ct
2 Brushwood Lodge

DA8

JESSETT CL

Wharf
ST FRANCIS RD

Coldharbour Point

GILBERT RD

PICARDY

Belvedere

Frank's Park

Bexley Coll

Trinity Sch

ERITH

Wharf

1 WINDRUSH CT
2 TRITON LODGE
3 VICTORY HO
4 SCHOONER HO
5 DRAKE PORT
6 CORRAL HTS
7 PLEASANT VIEW

ERITH RD

Parkside Lodge

Bexley Coll

Hillside

Pembroke Par

Europa Trad Est

Erith

Wharf

BOSWORTH HO
STONE CT
WATERS EDGE CT

Wharf

Pier

Wharf

WOOLWICH RD A206

Liby

Lessness Heath Prim

Bexley Coll

Lessness Heath

ST JOHNS CT
SYCAMORE MEWS
SYCAMORE CT

Liby
Mus

A1
1 STEVANNE CT
2 TOLCAIRN CT
3 CHALFONT CT
4 ALONSO HO
5 ARIEL CT
6 MIRANDA HO
7 PROSPERO HO
8 THE LAURELS
9 WINCHESTER CT

10 CAMDEN CT
11 NEWNHAM LODGE
12 COURT LODGE
13 FLAXMAN CT
14 HERTFORD WLK
15 RIVERVIEW CT
16 LESSNESS RD
A3
1 CRESSINGHAM CT
2 TELFORD HO

3 KELVIN HO
4 FARADAY HO
5 JENNER HO
6 KEIR HARDY HO
7 LENNOX HO
8 MARY MACARTHUR HO
9 ELIZABETH GARRETT ANDERSON HO
10 WILLIAM SMITH HO
11 BADEN POWELL HO
12 BAIRD HO

13 BOYLE HO

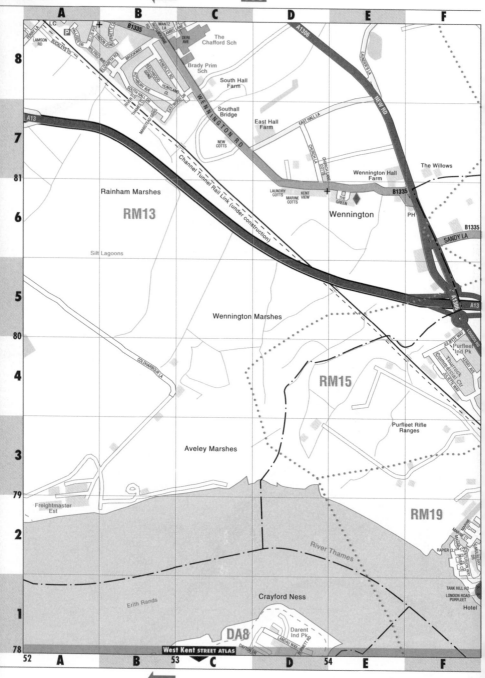

West Kent STREET ATLAS

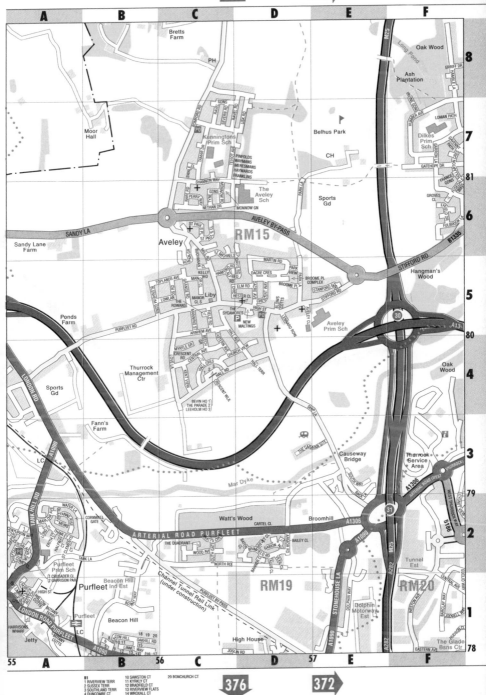

356 372

55 A B 56 C D 57 E F

B1
1 RIVERVIEW TERR
2 SUSSEX TERR
3 SOUTHLAND TERR
4 DUNCOMBE CT
5 HEBERDEN CT
6 WINGROVE DR
7 HOWBURGH CT
8 TRAYFORD CT
9 STORAS CT
10 SAWSTON CT
11 KYRKLY CT
12 BRADFIELD CT
13 RIVERVIEW FLATS
14 WROXALL CT
15 ROOKLEY CT
16 DUNMOSE CT
17 BRANSTONE CT
18 SHORWELL CT
19 BRIGHSTONE CT
20 BONCHURCH CT

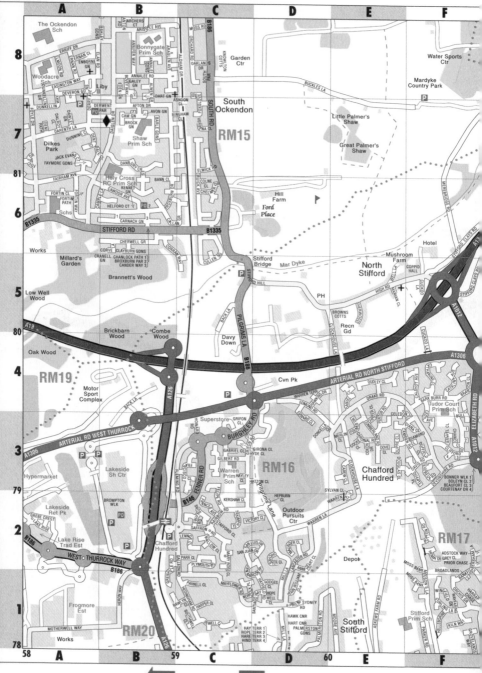

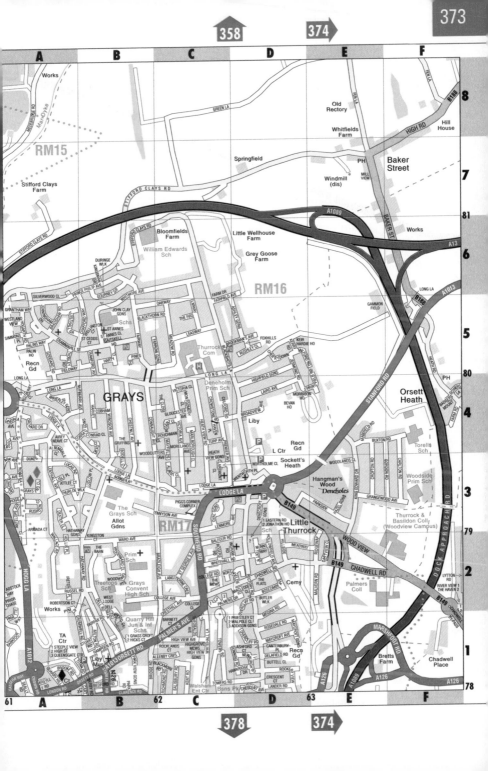

A13
STANFORD RD A1013

CH

St Cleres Hall

Singlewell

St Clere's Comp Sch

WHITWELL CT

Cemy

Wks

8

Mayland

Thames Haven Junction

Sewage Works

The Warren

WHARF RD

7

LC

Mucking

Stanford Marshes

Mucking Creek

81

Bluehouse Farm

BUCKINGHAM HILL RD

MUCKING WHARF RD

WALTON'S HALL RD

Sluice

SS17

6

Golden Cottages

Mucking Marshes

Travelling Crane

Jetty

5

Walton Hall Farm Mus

Walton's Hall

Turner's Farm

80

Sutton's Farm

BUCKINGHAM HILL RD

Linford

HAMPSHIRE GDNS

4

NORTHUMBERLAND RD

ESSEX ROAD

DORSET GDNS

SOMERSET RD

PH

RM18

3

STAFFORD RD

LOWER CRES

EXETER RD

METER

DEVON RD

MEADOW CL

DERBROOK

79

LC

East Tilbury

Sewage Works

MUCKINGFORD RD

HALL DR

FERNING AVE

ALEXANDRA WAY

TORRIDGE

KING GEORGE VI AVE

WEST TILBURY LA

SEVERN

DERBENT

CORONATION AVE

ROMAN RD

ADAMS

STRAIGHTWAY

CLUB

ROACH

WELLAND

CALDER

River Thames

2

BATA AVE

PRINCESS MARGARET RD

THACKERAY AVE

QUEEN ELIZABETH RD

QUEEN MARY AVE

KENSINGTON GDNS

PRINCESS AVE

Lby

CORONATION CT

FRYE

TWEED

ORWELL

WARWICK

AVON

FARM RD

GLOUCESTER RD

Thames Ind Pk

East Tilbury Prim Sch

East Tilbury Marshes

1

East Tilbury

Sand & Gravel Pit

78

67
A
B
68
C
D
69
E
F

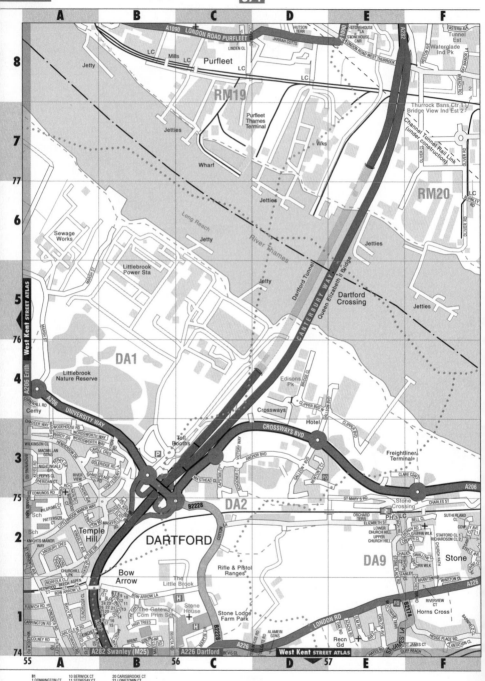

81
1 DONNINGTON CT	10 BERWICK CT	20 CARISBROOKE CT
2 DENNY CT	11 STOKESAY CT	21 LONGTOWN CT
3 BROUGHAM CT	12 CONISBOROUGH CT	22 CLIFTON WLK
4 BEESTON CT	13 PICKERING CT	23 CALSHOT CT
5 ORFORD CT	14 MIDDLEHAM CT	24 DUNSTER CT
6 ALNWICK CT	15 PRUDHOE CT	25 LYDFORD CT
7 BRAMBER CT	16 NORHAM CT	26 PEVERIL CT
8 KENILWORTH CT	17 BOWES CT	27 HARDWICK CRES
9 WARDOUR CT	18 BARNARD CT	28 GRANGE CRES
	19 TATTERSHALL CT	

372
378

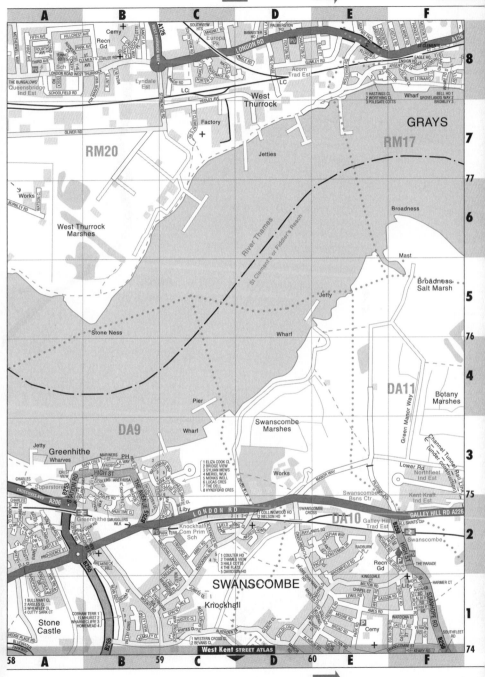

378

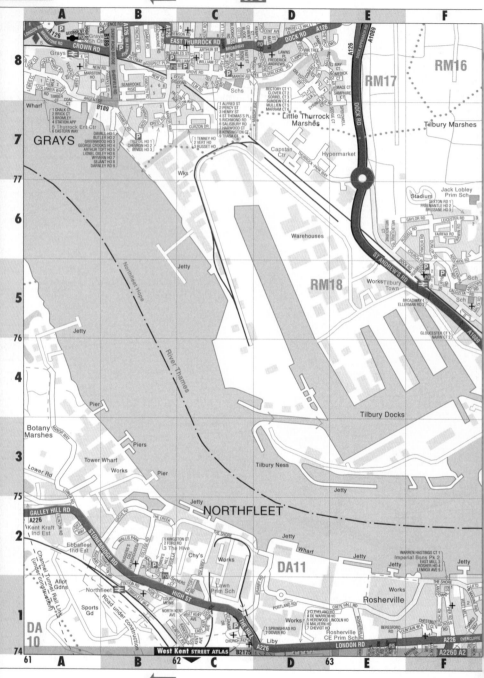

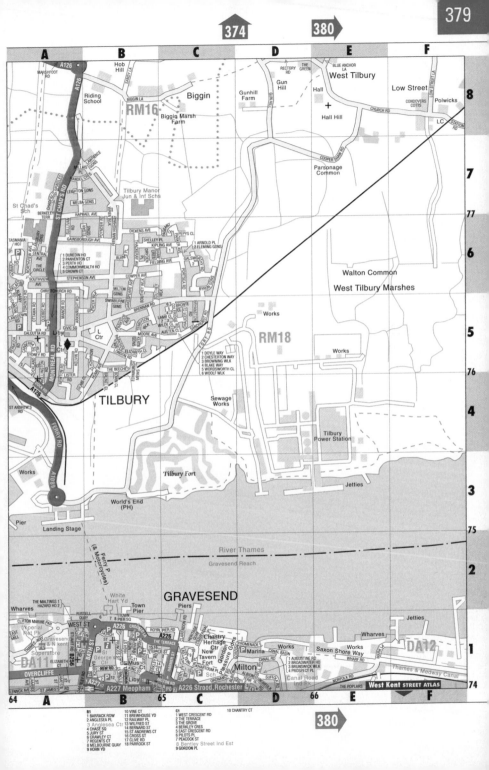

A **B** **C** **D** **E** **F**

8

Redmans
Ind Est

Works

Gravelpit
Farm

LOVE LA

Barvills
Farm

STATION RD

Goshem's
Farm

Coalhouse
Battery
(dismantled)

Buckland

PRINCESS MARGARET RD

7

LINLEY CL

GORDON CL
ESTUARY
COTTS

Bowaters

East
Tilbury

PH

77

Coalhouse
Fort

6

P

RM18

East Tilbury
Marshes

5

Coalhouse
Point

76

West Kent STREET ATLAS

4

River Thames

3

75

2

Saxon Shore Way

Shornmead
Fort

ME3

Shorne
Marshes

National
Sea Training
Coll

Eastcourt
Marshes

Rifle
Range

DA12

1

74

West Kent STREET ATLAS

67 **A** **B** **68** **C** **D** **69** **E** **F**

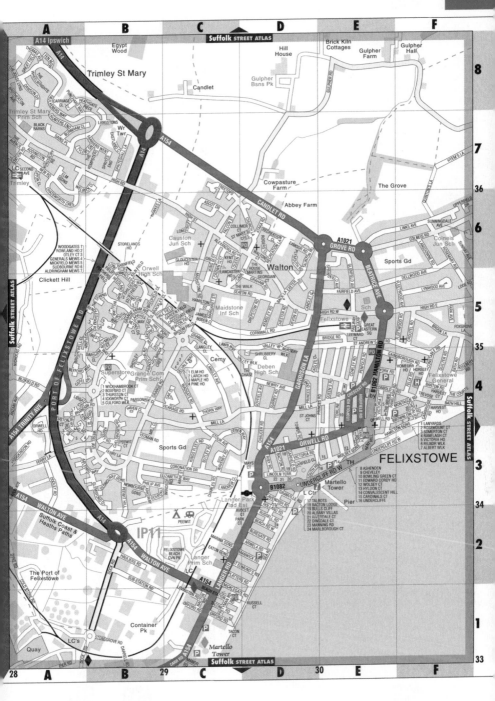

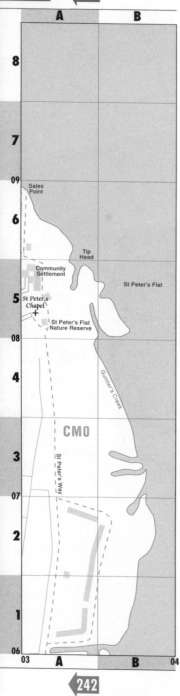

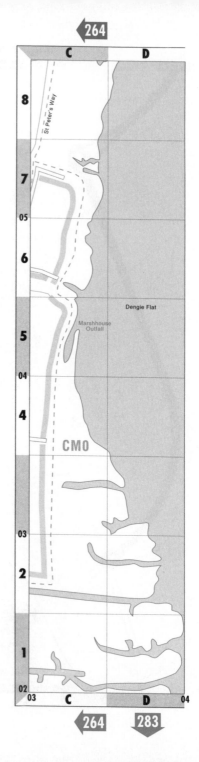

A   B   C   D

8

7

97

6

01

CMO

5

River Crouch

00

CMO

96

Ray Sand

4

3

95

East
Newlands

The Drift
(dis)

99

SS3

2

1

98

94

DANGER AREA

Index

Church Rd **6** Beckenham BR2.......... **53** C6

Place name	Location number	Locality, town or village	Postcode district	Page and grid square
May be abbreviated on the map	Present when a number indicates the place's position in a crowded area of mapping	Shown when more than one place has the same name	District for the indexed place	Page number and grid reference for the standard mapping

Public and commercial buildings are highlighted in magenta. Places of interest are highlighted in blue with a star★

Abbreviations used in the index

Acad	Academy	Comm	Common	Gd	Ground	L	Leisure	Prom	Promenade
App	Approach	Cott	Cottage	Gdn	Garden	La	Lane	Rd	Road
Arc	Arcade	Cres	Crescent	Gn	Green	Liby	Library	Recn	Recreation
Ave	Avenue	Cswy	Causeway	Gr	Grove	Mdw	Meadow	Ret	Retail
Bglw	Bungalow	Ct	Court	H	Hall	Meml	Memorial	Sh	Shopping
Bldg	Building	Ctr	Centre	Ho	House	Mkt	Market	Sq	Square
Bsns, Bus	Business	Ctry	Country	Hospl	Hospital	Mus	Museum	St	Street
Bvd	Boulevard	Cty	County	HQ	Headquarters	Orch	Orchard	Sta	Station
Cath	Cathedral	Dr	Drive	Hts	Heights	Pal	Palace	Terr	Terrace
Cir	Circus	Dro	Drove	Ind	Industrial	Par	Parade	TH	Town Hall
Cl	Close	Ed	Education	Inst	Institute	Pas	Passage	Univ	University
Cnr	Corner	Emb	Embankment	Int	International	Pk	Park	Wk, Wlk	Walk
Coll	College	Est	Estate	Intc	Interchange	Pl	Place	Wr	Water
Com	Community	Ex	Exhibition	Junc	Junction	Prec	Precinct	Yd	Yard

Index of localities, towns and villages

A

Abberton 163 A3
Abbess Roding 203 E4
Abridge 290 A6
Aldham 133 B8
Alphamstone 54 F3
Alresford 165 A8
Althorne 283 A3
Ardleigh 111 E7
Arkesden 41 E2
Ashdon 285 A7
Asheldham 11 D1
Ashen 371 C6
Aveley 371 C6
Aythorpe Roding 176 B3

B

Bardfield Saling 99 C2
Barking 352 D5
Barling 349 E7
Barnston 151 A4
Bartlow 6 B7
Basildon 342 C4
Battlesbridge 300 D1
Beauchamp Roding ..204 A1
Beaumont 141 F7
Beazley End 101 C6
Belchamp St Paul ...13 A2
Belchamp Walter 31 F5
Belstead 36 C7
Belvedere 369 A6
Bentley 60 E7
Berden 92 C8
Bicknacre 256 F2
Billericay 297 B1
Birch 161 A4
Birchanger 119 E2
Birdbrook 28 B7
Bishop's Stortford ..145 D7
Blackheath 163 B8
Blackmore 272 F8
Black Notley 155 B5
Boreham 233 E8
Borley 14 F3
Boxted 82 F7
Bradfield 87 F2
Bradwell 129 D2
Bradwell-on-Sea 242 B2
Bradwell Waterside ..241 F4
Braintree 128 B5
Brantham 60 E1
Brentwood 316 E8
Brightlingsea 192 E6
Broomfield 208 B2
Buckhurst Hill 310 C8
Bulmer 32 E5
Bulmer Tye 32 F2
Bulphan 358 F8
Bures 79 E8
Burnham-on-Crouch .306 D6

C

Canewdon 304 E1
Canvey Island 364 E4
Capel St Mary 35 B2
Castle Camps 7 E3
Castle Hedingham ...51 E4
Cavendish 1 C1
Chadwell St Mary ...374 B1
Chappel 106 C5
Chelmondiston 63 E8
Chelmsford 232 C4
Chigwell 311 B8
Chingford 287 E1
Chipping Ongar 248 F4
Chrishall 19 D3
Clacton-on-Sea 196 B3
Clare 12 C6
Clavering 65 C5
Cock Clarks 257 F2
Coggeshall 131 B3
Colchester 135 D7
Cold Norton 280 E6
Colne Engaine 77 F2
Coopersale 246 C2
Copford 133 D4
Corringham 361 A4
Cressing 156 A6

D

Dagenham 354 C4
Danbury 256 D7

Dartford 376 B2
Debden 68 B7
Dedham 84 F7
Dengie 263 D1
Doddinghurst 272 B3
Downham 298 F4
Duddenhoe End 41 A6

E

Earls Colne 105 C7
East Bergholt 59 C2
East Hanningfield ..278 B7
Easthorpe 160 A7
East Mersea 191 F1
East Tilbury 375 C1
Eastwick 199 A4
Edney Common 252 D5
Eight Ash Green 134 A8
Elder Street 44 E1
Elmdon 20 B4
Elmstead 138 A6
Elsenham 94 C1
Epping 246 A3
Epping Green 245 A7
Erith 369 F2

F

Farnham 118 D6
Feering 158 E5
Felixstowe 381 F3
Felsted 152 B5
Finchingfield 72 C5
Fingringhoe 163 F5
Fobbing 361 D5
Ford End 179 B7
Fordham 107 D5
Fordham Heath 107 F2
Foulness Island 330 C5
Foxearth 14 C6
Frating 139 A3
Frinton-on-Sea 170 D5
Fyfield 227 D2

G

Galleywood 254 D2
Gestingthorpe 31 E1
Gilston 199 E5
Glemsford 2 C4
Goldhanger 238 F7
Gosfield 102 E8
Gravesend 379 C2
Grays 378 A7
Great Baddow 254 E7
Great Bardfield 72 C1
Great Bentley 166 D8
Great Braxted 185 C1
Great Bromley 112 F1
Great Canfield 149 C1
Great Chesterford ..3 D2
Great Cornard 34 B5
Great Dunmow 122 F7
Great Easton 122 F7
Great Hallingbury ..146 E4
Great Henny 54 C8
Great Holland 170 A3
Great Horkesley ...82 B1
Great Leighs 180 F7
Great Maplestead ..52 D2
Great Notley 154 B7
Great Oakley 116 C4
Great Sampford 47 B3
Great Tey 132 C8
Great Totham 213 B4
Great Wakering 350 A4
Great Waltham 207 E7
Great Warley 316 A2
Great Wigborough ..188 F3
Great Yeldham 30 A1
Greenhithe 377 A3
Greenstead Green ..104 A5

H

Hadleigh 345 E3
Hadstock 5 C6
Halstead 76 D2
Harkstead 63 B2
Harlow 200 C2
Harwich 91 E5
Hastingwood 224 F4
Hatfield Broad Oak .174 F5
Hatfield Heath 174 B3

Hatfield Peverel ...211 B4
Haverhill 9 C7
Havering-atte-Bower .313 E2
Hawkwell 325 A4
Helions Bumpstead .26 C8
Hempstead 25 F1
Henham 94 F6
Heybridge 237 B6
Heybridge Basin ...237 D3
Heydon 19 A5
High Beach 288 B8
High Easter 177 C2
High Ongar 249 D3
High Roding 176 F7
High Wych 172 B1
Hinxton 3 B7
Hockley 324 C6
Hoddesdon 221 C7
Holbrook 62 C5
Holdbrook 265 A5
Holland-on-Sea 196 F5
Hook End 272 C4
Hornchurch 336 C2
Horndon-on-the-Hill .359 E3
Howe Green 255 D3
Howe Street 179 F2
Hullbridge 301 D2
Hunsdonbury 198 C7

I

Ickleton 3 A4
Ilford 333 B2
Ingatestone 274 C3
Ingrave 317 D5
Ipswich 17 C7

J

Jaywick 220 F7

K

Kelvedon 158 D2
Kelvedon Hatch 271 E2
Kirby Cross 170 B7
Kirby-le-Soken 170 C8

L

Lamarsh 55 B4
Langford 236 D7
Langham 83 F4
Langley 40 C2
Laindon 282 A6
Lawford 86 B3
Layer-de-la-Haye ..161 F5
Leaden Roding 204 C8
Lindsell 98 A3
Linford 375 A4
Little Baddow 234 D4
Little Bentley 139 E8
Little Bromley 113 B6
Little Burstead 318 F5
Littlebury 21 E4
Little Clacton 168 D3
Little Dunmow 151 D7
Little Easton 122 F5
Little Hallingbury ..173 D8
Little Horkesley ...81 E4
Little Ilford 352 A7
Little Leighs 180 E6
Little Maplestead ..53 B1
Little Oakley 117 B7
Little Totham 214 C4
Little Wakering 349 D6
Little Waltham 208 C6
Little Warley 316 A4
Little Yeldham 30 E4
Long Melford 15 D7
Loughton 288 D3
Lower Nazeing 221 F1

M

Maldon 237 B3
Manningtree 86 E4
Manuden 92 F2
Margaret Roding ...204 D5
Margaretting 275 A8
Marks Tey 132 E4
Mashbury 206 C4
Matching Green 202 D3
Mayland 283 B8

Messing 159 D3
Mistley 86 F4
Moreton 226 D2
Mountnessing 295 D8
Mundon 259 E2

N

Navestock Heath ...292 D7
Navestock Side 293 C7
Nayland 56 B1
New Mistley 87 B4
Newport 43 A1
North Benfleet 321 F8
North End 151 F2
North Fambridge ..303 A8
Northfleet 378 C2
North Ockendon ...357 B6
North Weald Bassett .247 C5
Nuthampstead 39 A2

O

Orsett 374 B8

P

Paglesham Eastend ..328 A5
Panfield 127 B7
Pattiswick 129 F5
Pebmarsh 56 B3
Peldon 189 E6
Pentlow 13 F6
Pilgrims Hatch 294 A4
Pleshey 178 E2
Point Clear Bay ...192 F3
Purfleet 371 B1
Purleigh 258 C1

Q

Quendon 66 F2

R

Radwinter 45 F8
Rainham 355 A2
Ramsden Heath 298 B4
Ramsey 89 F1
Rawreth 322 E7
Rayleigh 323 B2
Rayne 126 E2
Redbridge 332 C5
Rettendon 278 B1
Rickling Green 93 D8
Ridgewell 29 B7
Rivenhall 184 B8
Rochford 325 E1
Romford 335 E7
Rowhedge 163 F8
Roxwell 230 B6
Roydon 198 C1
Rushmere St Andrew .18 E8

S

Saffron Walden 22 E3
St Lawrence 262 B8
St Osyth 194 B4
Salcott-cum-Virley ..216 B8
Sawbridgeworth ...172 C3
Seawick 220 C2
Sewards End 23 E1
Sewardstone 287 C8
Shalford 100 E7
Sheering 201 D8
Shenfield 294 E2
Shotley Gate 91 A8
Shudy Camps 7 B6
Sible Hedingham ...51 E1
Silver End 156 E4
South Benfleet 344 E3
Southend-on-Sea ..366 F6
South Hanningfield .299 C8
Southminster 284 E4
South Ockendon ...372 C2
South Woodham Ferrers .301 E8
Spellbrook 172 E8
Sproughton 16 B6
Stambourne 28 D3
Standford-le-Hope ..360 E1
Stansted 2 F7
Stanstead Abbotts .197 E4

Stansted Mountfitchet .119 C8
Stapleford Abbotts .291 C3
Stapleford Tawney ..269 C3
Stebbing 124 E5
Steeple 261 E3
Steeple Bumpstead .27 B8
Stisted 129 C6
Stock 275 F3
Stoke by Clare 11 C4
Stoke-by-Nayland ..56 E5
Stondon Massey ...272 A6
Stow Maries 280 C4
Stratford St Mary ..58 C2
Sturmer 9 F4
Stutton 61 F2
Sudbury 33 D8
Swanscombe 377 D1

T

Takeley 148 C8
Tattingstone 61 C7
Taverners Green ...175 C8
Tendring 140 F5
Terling 182 C3
Thaxted 70 A3
Theydon Bois 267 D3
Theydon Mount ...269 A3
Thorington Street ..57 B4
Thornwood 246 C7
Thorpe-le-Soken ..142 B1
Thorrington 166 A5
Threshers Bush 225 B7
Thundersley 344 E6
Tilbury 379 B4
Tilgate Green 225 E6
Tillingham 263 F4
Tiptree 186 D5
Tollesbury 216 D2
Tollesbury 240 E8
Tolleshunt D'arcy ..215 D4
Tolleshunt Knights .187 A2
Tolleshunt Major ..214 E4
Toot Hill 247 F2
Toppesfield 50 C7
Trimley St Mary ...381 B8

U

Ugley 93 E6
Ulting 235 C6
Upminster 337 D2

W

Wakes Colne 106 C6
Wallend 352 A4
Waltham Abbey ...265 D7
Walton-on-the-Naze .171 D8
Wanstead 332 C5
Washbrook 35 E8
Weeley 140 E1
Weeley Heath 168 A5
Wendens Ambo 42 E5
Wennington 370 E6
West Bergholt 108 D3
West Hanningfield .277 B4
West Horndon 339 C5
West Mersea 218 C5
West Tilbury 379 E8
Wethersfield 73 C3
Wherstead 37 B6
White Colne 105 E6
White Notley 155 E1
White Roding 203 D8
Wicken Bonhunt ...66 C7
Wickford 321 A5
Wickham Bishops ..212 D5
Wickham St Paul ..53 C5
Widdington 67 E4
Willingale 228 D3
Wimbish 45 C6
Witham 183 E4
Wivenhoe 137 C2
Wix 115 C5
Woodford 310 D5
Woodham Ferrers ..279 B4
Woodham Mortimer .257 F6
Woodham Walter ...235 E2
Woolverstone 38 B1
Wormingford 80 E4
Wrabness 88 E4
Writtle 231 A2
Wyatts Green 272 D4

A

Aalten Ave SS8 ....364 F3
Abacus Prim Sch SS12 .321 F5
Abbas Wlk CO10 ....34 C5
Abberton IG8 ....310 C5
Abberton Rd
  Fingringhoe CO5 ....163 D3
  Layer-de-l-H CO2 ......162 C5
Abberton Resr Nature
  Reserve* CO2 ....161 F2
Abberton Wildfowl Ctr*
  CO2 ....161 E1
Abbess Cl CM1 ....231 E2
Abbey Cl Fyfield CM5 ....227 C7
Abbey Dale Cl CM17 .....224 C7
Abbey Fields CM3 ....278 B7
Abbey Gate St ￼ CO2 ..135 F6
Abbey La Coggeshall CO6 131 A1
  Saffron Walden CB10 ....22 D1
Abbey Mdw CO9 ....51 D2
Abbey Mead Ind Est EN9 265 C5
Abbey Park Ind Est IG11 352 C4
Abbey Rd Barking IG11 ..352 B4
  Barking IG11 ....352 C3
  Billericay CM12 ....296 F1
  Greenhithe DA9 ....377 C2
  Hullbridge SS5 ....301 D1
  Ilford IG2 ....333 D6
  Sudbury CO10 ....15 E1
Abbey St Ickleton CB10 ...3 A4
  Thorpe-le-S CB10 .....142 A1
Abbey Turning CM9 .....236 D4
Abbey View CM6 ....65 C6
Abbey Wood La RM13 ...355 D3
Abbotsbury Cl IP2 ......17 E4

Abbots Cl
  Brentwood CM15 ....295 A1
  Clacton-on-S CO15 ....195 E6
  Rainham RM13 ....355 D3
  Wix CO11 ....115 C5
Abbots Ct SS15 ....341 C4
Abbotsford Gdns IG8 ...310 A3
Abbotsford Rd IG3 .....334 B2
Abbots Gdns CO16 .....194 C4
Abbots Hall Ave & Jun Schs
  SS17 ....223 D6
Abbots La CO6 ....134 A7
Abbotsleigh Rd CM3 ....301 E7
Abbots Manor CM7 .....236 F5
Abbot's Rd CO12 ....91 F2
Abbots Ride CM11 ......297 C2
Abbotsweld CM18 ....223 D5
Abbotsweld Prim Sch
  CM18 ....223 D6
Abbots Wick La CO5 ...188 E3
Abbots Wlk SS3 ....368 C8
Abbotswood SS7 ....345 C5
Abbotswood Gdns
  Ilford IG5 ....333 A8
  Redbridge IG5 ....332 F8
Abbott Rd CO12 ....90 F2
Abbotts Cl Romford RM7 335 B6
  Southend-on-S SS9 ....346 E5
Abbotts Cres E4 ....309 D6
Abbotts Croft CB9 .....9 F4
Abbotts Dr E4 ....310 A6
Abbotts Pl CM2 ....232 D3
Abbotts Rise SG12 .....197 D4
Abbotts Way
  Bishop's Stortford CM23 145 E3
  Stanstead Mnts SG12 .197 D4
  Sturmer CB9 ....9 E5
Abbotts Dr
  Stanford-le-H SS17 ...360 D2
  Waltham Abbey EN9 ...266 A6
Abbotts Hall Chase SS17 368 A7
Abbotts Pl CM2 ....232 D3
Abbotts Rise SG12 .....197 D4
Abbotts Way
  Bishop's Stortford CM23 .145 E3
  Stanstead Mnts SG12 .197 D4
Abbs Cross Gdns RM12 .336 D3
Abbs Cross La RM12 ...336 C2
Abbs Cross Sch RM12 ..336 C1
Abdy Ave CO12 ....90 E2
Abell Way CM13 ....317 B8
Abenberg Way CM13 ...317 B8
Abensburg Rd SS8 .....364 D5
Abercorn Cl CB9 ....8 F7
Abercorn Gdns RM6 ...334 A6
Abercorn Way CM8 .....176 E4
Abercrombie Ho CM7 ..127 E3
Affleck Rd CM7 ....127 E3
Afflets Ct SS14 ....342 C8
Afton Dr RM15 ....372 B7
Agar Rd ￼ CO14 ......171 C8
Agar Road App ￼ CO14 171 C8
Agate Rd CO15 ....195 F2
Agincourt Rd CO15 ....195 D6
Agister Rd IG7 ....312 A5
Agnes Ave Ilford IG1 ...352 B8
  Southend-on-S SS9 ...346 B2
Agnes Gdns RM8 ....353 D8
Agricultural/Domestic Mus*
  CM9 ....212 F4
Aidan Cl RM8 ....353 E8
Ailsa Rd SS0 ....366 C8
Ainger Rd CO12 ....90 E2
Aingers Green Rd CO7 .167 A5
Ainsley Ave RM7 ....335 C5
Ainslie Rd IP1 ....17 A6

Abercrombie Ho ￼ RM3 314 D5
Abercrombie Way CM18,
  CM19 ....219 C2
Aberdeen Gdns IG4 ....332 A4
Aberdour Rd IG3 ......334 B2
Abigail Cl CM5 ....249 A5
Abigail Mews RM3 .....314 F1
Abingdon Cl IP7 ....17 A1
Abingdon Ct SS13 .....321 A1
Abinger Cl Barking IG11 .353 A8
  Clacton-on-S CO15 ....195 C6
Abington Ct RM4 ......337 C3
Abington Pl ￼ CB9 .....9 A8
Abraham Ct RM14 .....357 A2
Abraham Dr CM6 ......106 B4
Abram's La SG8 ....19 C4
Abreys SS7 ....345 A7
Abridge Gdns RM5 ....313 A4
Abridge Rd Chigwell IG7 289 E4
  Theydon Bois CM16 ...268 A1
Abridge Way IG11 .....353 B3

Acacia Ave
  Colchester CO4 ....136 E6
  Hornchurch RM12 ....335 F2
Acacia Cl IP3 ....18 E1
Acacia Ct Brantham CO11 .60 D1
  Waltham Abbey EN9 ...266 A5
Acacia Dr
  Great Dunmow CM6 ...123 C1
  Maldon CM9 ....236 F1
  Southend-on-S SS1 ....368 A8
  Upminster RM14 ......356 A8
Acacia Gdns
  Upminster RM14 ......337 F4
  Witham CM8 ....184 B4
Acacia Rd Basildon SS13 343 E8
  Greenhithe DA9 ....376 E1
Acacias Ct EN11 ......221 A6
Accommodation Rd CO9 107 D7
Accrington Ho ￼ RM3 .314 D5
Acer Ave RM13 ....355 D2
Acer Gr Chelmsford CM1 232 D4
  Ipswich IP8 ....16 C2
Achilles Way CM7 .....128 C5
Achnacone Dr CO4 ....109 C3
Acland Ave CO3 ....135 B7
Acland Ct CO3 ....135 A7
Acle Cl IG6 ....311 B3
Aconbury Rd RM9 .....353 B4
Acorn Ave Braintree CM7 127 E2
  Halstead CO9 ....76 D1
Acorn Cl Chingford E4 ..309 B5
  Colchester CO4 ....110 D4
  Harwich CO12 ....90 F1
  Ipswich IP2 ....16 C2
Acorn Ct IG2 ....333 E6
Acorn La The IG6 .....312 B4
Acorn Mews CM18 ....224 A6
Acorn Pl Basildon SS16 .341 B5
  Maldon CM9 ....236 F5
Acorn St SG12 ....198 D8
Acorns The Chigwell IG7 311 E6
  Hockley SS5 ....324 E7
Acorn Trad Est RM20 .377 D8
Acorn Wlk CO7 ....166 A5
Acre Rd RM8 ....354 B5
Acres Ave CM5 ....248 F5
Acres End CM1 ....231 E4
Acres The SS17 ....360 F3
Acton Cl CO10 ....33 E7
Acton Gn CO10 ....33 E7
Acton La CO10 ....33 F8
Acton Sq ￼ CO10 .....33 E7
Ada Cole Meml Stables Horse
  Sanctuary* CM19 .....222 E4
Adair Rd IP1 ....16 D8
Adalia Cres SS9 ....346 B3
Adalia Way SS9 ......346 B2
Adam Bsns Ctr SS14 ..320 F1
Adams Cl IP2 ....17 C3
Adams Ct Halstead CO9 .76 D2
  Saffron Walden CB11 ..43 C8
Adam's Elm Ho SS9 ...346 E2
Adams Glade SS4 .....325 D6
Adams Rd SS17 ......360 E1
Adam Way SS13 ......321 E8
Adderley Rd CM23 ....145 F7
Addington Rd ￼ RM3 .381 A7
Addison Ct CM16 .....268 A8
Addison Gdns RM17 ..373 C2
Addison Rd
  Great Holland CO13 ..170 B5
  Redbridge IG6 ....311 C2
  Sudbury CO10 ....34 B8
  Wanstead E11 ....332 A5
Adelaide Dr CO2 ......136 A1
Adelaide Gdns
  Dagenham RM6 ....334 E6
  South Benfleet SS7 ...344 D1
Adelaide Rd Ilford IG3 ..333 B2
  Ipswich IP4 ....18 D6
Adelaide St CO12 ......90 F5
Adeliza Cl IG11 ......352 C5
Adelphi Cres RM12 ...336 B2
Adelsburg Rd SS8 ....364 C4
Aden Rd IG1 ....333 C4
Adingtons IP4 ....18 D6
Admiral Cl IG11 ......353 C3
Admiral Rd IP8 ....36 E8
Admirals Cl E18 ......332 B7
Admirals Lodge RM1 ..335 F6
Admirals Pl SS0 ......366 C7
Admirals Wlk
  Chelmsford CM1 ......231 F3
  Greenhithe DA9 ....377 B2
  Hoddesdon EN11 .....221 B4
  Southend-on-S SS3 ...368 D5
  Wivenhoe CO7 ....164 B8
Adnams Wlk RM12 ....355 A7
Adrian Ho RM8 ....354 B4
Adstock Way RM17 ...372 F2
Advent Cl IG8 ....309 F5
Adventure Island* SS1 .367 A7
Advice Ave RM4 ......373 A4
Aetheric Rd CM7 ......127 E3

Ainslie Wood Cres E4 ..309 B5
Ainslie Wood Gdns E4 .309 B5
Ainslie Wood Prim Sch
  E4 ....309 B5
Ainslie Wood Rd E4 ..309 B5
Aintree Cres IG6 ......311 C1
Aintree Gr RM14 ......336 F1
Airborne IP4 ....346 B5
Airborne Ind Est SS9 .346 B5
Aire Dr RM15 ....357 B1
Aire Wlk CM8 ....183 E2
Airey Hos CO10 ....11 D1
Airey Neave Ct RM16 .373 A4
Airfield Way RM12 ....355 C6
Airlie Gdns IG1 ....333 B3
Airport Ret Pk SS2 ...347 F6
Airthrie Rd IG3 ....334 B2
Aisne Rd CO2 ....135 D4
Ajax Cl CM7 ....128 B5
Akenfield Cl ￼ CM3 ...301 E7
Akersloot Pl CO5 .....218 C6
Alamein Gdns DA2 ...376 D1
Alamein Rd
  Burnham-on-C CM0 ..306 C4
  Chelmsford CM1 ......231 F6
  Colchester CO2 ......135 C2
  Swanscombe DA10 ...377 D7
Alanbrooke Rd CO2 ..136 D2
Alan Cl SS9 ....346 E6
Alan Dr CO16 ....168 D1
Alan Gr RM7 ....335 A4
Alan Grs SS9 ....346 E6
Alan Hasler Ho CM6 ..150 D7
Alan Rd Ipswich IP3 ....17 F4
  Witham CM8 ....183 E1
Alan Way CO3 ....134 E7
Albany Ave SS0 ......347 E1
Albany Chase CO15 ..196 D6
Albany Cl Chelmsford CM1 231 E5
  West Bergholt CO6 ...108 E4
Albany Ct Chingford E4 .287 B3
  Epping CM16 ....245 F1
Albany Gdns E CO15 ..196 B3
Albany Gdns W CO15 .196 B3
Albany Rd Dagenham RM6 334 F5
  Pilgrims Hatch CM15 .294 B3
  Rayleigh SS6 ....324 A1
  Tilbury RM18 ....379 A6
  West Bergholt CO6 ...108 E4
  Wickford SS12 ....321 D6
Albany Sch The RM12 .336 B2
Albany The Ipswich IP4 .17 E8
  Woodford IG8 ....309 F6
Albany Villas IP11 ....221 A1
Albany Way CO15 ....196 D6
Alba Rd CM17 ....200 C1
Albemarle App IG1 ...333 B5
Albemarle Gdns
  Braintree CM7 ....128 C5
  Ilford IG2 ....333 A6
Albemarle Link CO12 ..232 F8
Albemarle Prim Sch
  CO12 ....91 D5
Albemarle Rd RM17 ..373 A4
Albemarle St
  Colchester CO4 ......136 C8
  Harwich CO12 ....91 D5
Albert Cl Grays RM16 .373 C3
  Rayleigh SS6 ....323 F3
  Rochford SS4 ....325 C6
Albert Cotts CO7 .....60 C2
Albert Cres E4 ....309 A6
Albert Dr SS13 ....342 C8
Albert Gdns
  Romford RM1 ....335 F5
  Southend-on-S SS0 ..366 E8
Albert Pl CO6 ....131 A2
Albert Rd Braintree CM7 128 A3
  Brightlingsea CO7 ...193 A6
  Buckhurst Hill IG9 ...310 D8
  Bulphan RM14 ....358 F8
  Burnham-on-C CM0 ..306 C4
  Dagenham RM8 ......353 A3
  Ilford IG1 ....333 C1
  Rayleigh SS6 ....323 F3
  Rochford SS4 ....325 C7
  Romford RM1 ....335 F5
  South Benfleet SS7 ...344 B6
  Southend-on-S,Bournes Green
  SS1 ....349 A1
  Southend-on-S SS1 ..367 B7
  South Woodham Ferrers
  CM3 ....259 D7
  Swanscombe DA10 ...377 F1
  Witham CM8 ....184 A3
Albert St Brentwood CM14 316 C5
  Colchester CO1 ......135 E8
  Harwich CO12 ....91 D5
Albert Terr IG9 ....310 E8
Albert Wlk IP11 ......381 E4
Albion Cl RM7 ....335 D5
Albion Ct Billericay CM12 297 A2
  Chelmsford CM2 .....232 B1
Albion Gr CO2 ....136 A5
Albion Hill Ipswich IP4 ..17 F7
  Loughton IG10 ....288 C4
Albion Pl IG10 ....288 D4
Albion Rd
  Gravesend DA12 .....379 D1
  South Benfleet SS7 ..344 D4
  Southend-on-S SS0 ..347 E1
Albion St CO5 ....164 A8
Albion Terr
  Gravesend DA12 .....379 D1
  Sewardstone E4 .....287 B5
Albra Mead CM2 .....233 B4
Albright Ind Est RM13 .369 F8
Albrighton Croft CO4 ..110 C4
Albury Mews E12 .....332 C2

Albyns SS16 ....341 C4
Albyns Cl RM13 ......355 A5
Albyns La RM4 ....291 D7
Alcester Ho ￼ RM3 ...314 D5
Alconbury CM23 ......119 B1
Alcorns The CM24 ....119 E7
Alcotes SS14 ....342 F5
Aldborough Ct
  Chingford E4 ....309 B7
  Ilford IG2 ....333 F6
Aldborough Rd
  Dagenham RM10 .....354 C6
  Ilford IG2 ....333 F8
  Upminster RM14 .....337 B3
Aldborough Rd N IG2 .333 F6
Aldborough Rd S IG3 .333 E4
Aldeburgh Cl
  Clacton-on-S CO16 ..195 B4
  Haverhill CB9 ....8 E8
Aldeburgh Gdns CO4 ..110 B4
Aldeburgh Pl IG8 ....310 A6
Alder Ave RM14 .....355 F8
Aldербury Lea CM3 ..256 F1
Alderbury Rd CM24 ..119 E8
Aldercar Rd CO6 .....108 E4
Alder Cl Basildon SS15 319 D1
  Bishop's Stortford CM23 145 D4
  Hoddesdon EN11 ....221 B8
Alde Rd CB9 ....9 A8
Alder Dr Chelmsford CM2 256 F8
  South Ockendon RM15 357 C1
Aldergrove Wlk RM12 .355 C6
Alderfield IP2 ....36 F8
Alderleys SS7 ....345 D4
Alderman Ave IG11 ..353 A2
Alderman Blaxhill Sch
  CO2 ....135 B3
Alderman Howe Lodge
  CO4 ....110 B8
Alderman Rd IP1 ......17 B5
Alderman's Hill SS5 ..324 C5
Alderman Wlk SS17 ..360 E5
Alderney Gdns SS11 ..299 C2
Alders Ave IG8 ....309 E4
Aldersbrook House Coll of
  Railway Tech E12 ...333 A1
Aldersbrook La E12 ..332 F1
Aldersbrook Prim Sch
  E12 ....332 C2
Aldersbrook Rd E12 ..332 C2
Alders Cl E11 ....332 B2
Aldersey Gdns IG11 ..352 D6
Aldersgrove EN9 ....265 E5
Aldersley Cl CM21 ...172 E2
Alderton Cl Felsted CM6 152 C6
  Loughton IG10 ....289 A5
  Pilgrims Hatch CM15 294 B4
Alderton Hill La IG10 .289 A5
Alderton Hill IG10 ....288 F4
Alderton Jun & Inf Schs The
  IG10 ....289 A4
Alderton Mews IG10 ..289 A4
Alderton Rd
  Colchester CO4 ......136 C8
  Orsett RM16 ....374 E7
Alderton Rise IG10 ...289 A4
Alderton Way IG10 ...288 E4
Alder Way CO10 ......33 B8
Alderton Wlk Ilford IG2 .352 D7
Alford Gdns IG11 ....352 D7
Alhalows St IP3 ......18 A1
Allington Cl IP4 ......17 F7
Allington Ct CM11 ...297 C2
Allington Cl RM8 ....334 C3
Aldis Mews EN3 .....265 A2
Aldon Cl CO12 ....90 C1
Aldona CM21 ....173 B6
Aldrich Way E4 ......309 A8
Aldridge Ave ￼ EN3 .265 A1
Aldridge Ct CM2 .....233 A4
Aldrin Cl SS17 ....360 E2

Alexandra Rd continued
  Harwich CO12 ....91 D5
  Ipswich IP4 ....17 E6
  Rainham RM13 ....354 F4
  Rayleigh SS6 ....323 F3
  Rochford SS4 ....325 C7
  Romford RM1 ....335 F5
  Sible Hedingham CO9 .51 D1
  Southend-on-S,Clifftown
  SS1 ....366 F7
  Southend-on-S,Leigh Cliffs
  SS1 ....365 E8
  Sudbury CO10 ....34 A7
  Tilbury RM18 ....378 F5
  Wallend E6 ....352 A2
  Wanstead E18 ....332 B8
  Weeley CO16 ....140 F1
Alexandra St
  Harwich CO12 ....91 D5
  Southend-on-S SS1 ..367 A7
Alexandra Terr ￼ CO3 135 E6
Alexandra Way RM18 .375 B3
Alexandria Dr SS6 ...323 A4
Alfells Rd CO7 ....137 F6
Alf Eounder Cl CO4 ..136 E6
Alf Lowne Ct RM16 ..374 A3
Alford Rd CO4 ....369 C1
Alfreda Ave SS5 .....301 D3
Alfred Gdns SS11 ....299 D1
Alfred Prior Ho ￼ E12 .352 A8
Alfred Rd Aveley RM15 .371 C5
  Brentwood CM14 ....316 D8
  Buckhurst Hill IG9 ...310 D8
Alfred's Gdns IG11 ..352 E3
Alfred St RM17 ....378 C8
Alfred's Way (East Ham &
  Barking By-Pass) IG11 352 D3
Alfred's Way Ind Est
  IG11 ....353 A4
Alfred Terr CO14 .....171 C8
Alfreg Rd CM8 ....211 D8
Algars Way CM3 .....301 D8
Algers Rd IG10 ......288 D4
Algers Rd IG10 ......288 D4
Alibon Gdns RM10 ...354 A7
Alibon Rd RM10 .....354 A7
Alicia Ave SS11 .....322 A7
Alicia Cl SS11 ....322 A7
Alicia Way SS11 .....322 A7
Alicia Wlk SS11 .....322 A7
Alienor Ave CM7 .....72 B1
Alkerden La DA10 ...377 C1
Allandale SS7 ....345 A7
Allandale Rd RM11 ..335 F4
Allectus Way CM8 ...211 D8
Allenby Cres RM17 ..373 C1
Allenby Dr RM11 ....336 F3
Allenby Rd IP2 ......16 F6
Allen Cotts CO6 .....106 C5
Allendale Dr CO6 ....133 D4
Allen Rd RM13 ......355 F2
Allens Cl CM3 ....209 E1
Allens Rd CM11 .....298 C5
Allensway SS17 ....360 F3
Allen Way
  Chelmsford CM2 .....233 B4
  Point Clear B CO16 ..185 D3
Allerton Cl SS4 ......325 C6
Alley Dock SS9 ......365 D8
Alleyn Court Prep Sch
  SS3 ....349 A3
Alleyn Court Sch SS0 .347 C1
Alleyn Ct CM11 .....233 A6
Alleyne Way CO15 ..220 D8
Alleyn Pl SS0 ....347 C1
Allfields CO12 ....91 A2
All Hallows Ct IP3 ...18 A1
Allington Ct IP4 ......17 F7
Allington Ct CM11 ...297 C2
Allington Cl RM8 ....334 C3
Allison Cl EN9 ......266 A7
Allistonway SS17 ...360 F3
Allmains Cl EN9 ....244 B6
Allnutts Rd CM16 ...268 A6
Alloa Rd IG3 ....334 A2
All Saints Ave CO3 ..135 A4
All Saints CE Prim Sch
  Bishop's Stortford CM23 146 B8
  Great Oakley CO12 ..116 C3
  Harwich CO12 ....90 F3
  Maldon CM9 ....236 F2
All Saints Cl
  Chigwell IG7 ....312 A7
  Doddinghurst CM15 ..272 C2
  Swanscombe DA10 ...377 F2
All Saints RC Sch & Tech Coll
  RM8 ....335 A3
All Saints' Rd IP1 ....17 A8
Allyn Wlk CM23 .....146 A4
Allysum WAY CM23 ..145 D4
Alma Ave Chingford E4 .309 C3
  Hornchurch RM12 ...336 E1
Alma Cl
  South Benfleet SS7 ..346 A2
  Wickford SS12 ......321 A5
Alma Dr CM1 ....232 A2
Alma Link CM1 ......297 A1
Alma Rd
  South Benfleet SS7 ..346 A2
  Swanscombe DA10 ..377 F2
Alma Sq ￼ CO11 ....86 D4
Alma St ￼ IG8 ......164 B8
Almere Rd SS12 ....344 D4
Almond Ave SS12 ...321 C7
Almond Cl
  Clacton-on-S CO15 ..195 C3
  Grays RM16 ....374 A3
  Tiptree CO5 ....186 C6
  Wivenhoe CO7 ......137 C2
Almondhayes IP2 ....17 B3
Almonds Ave IG9 ...310 A8

Almond Way CO4 ....136 E8
Almond Wlk SS8 ....363 F4
Almshouses
  Brentwood CM14 ....315 E8
  Ingatestone CM4 ....274 B3
  Wivenhoe CO7 ....164 B8
Almshouses The IG11 .352 C6
Almshouses (Whitakers
  Charity) IG10 ....288 F3
Alnesbourn Cres IP3 ..38 D7
Al-Noor Muslim Prim Sch
  SS1 ....334 B3
Alnwick Cl SS16 .....340 F5
Alnwick Ct ￼ DA2 ..369 A1
Alonso Ho ￼ DA17 ..369 A1
Alp Ct SS3 ....350 A3
Alpe St IP1 ....17 B7
Alpha Cl Basildon SS13 343 F6
  Braintree CM7 ....128 A2
Alphamstone Rd CO8 ..2 E6
Alpha Pl
  ￼ Bishop's Stortford CM23 145 F8
  ￼ Saffron Walden CB11 .22 E1
Alpha Rd Basildon SS13 .343 F6
  Brentwood CM13 ....295 D3
  Burnham-on-C CM0 ..306 C5
  Chingford E4 ....309 B7
  Point Clear B CO16 ..193 B3
Alport Ave CO2 ......135 C4
Alracks SS15 ....341 G6
Alresford Gn SS12 ..321 E6
Alresford Prim Sch CO7 165 B7
Alresford Rd CO7 ....164 E8
Alresford Sta CO7 ...165 A8
Alfred's Gdns IG11 ..352 E3
Alsa Bsns Pk CM24 ...93 F1
Alsa Gdns CM22 .....94 C2
Alsa Leys CM22 ......94 C2
Alsa St CM24 ....93 F1
Alston Cres CO10 .....2 E6
Alston Ct SS0 ....347 C1
Alstone Ct IP3 ....18 D1
Alston Rd IP3 ....17 F4
Altar Pl SS15 ....341 C7
Altbarn Cl CO4 ......110 C5
Altbarn Rd CO2 .....136 D5
Altham Gr CM20 .....199 C3
Althorne Cl SS13 ...321 B1
Althorne Sta CM3 ...304 F8
Althorne Way
  Canewdon SS4 ......304 E2
  Dagenham RM10 ....335 A2
Althorpe Cl SS5 .....324 D6
Alton Dr CO3 ....135 B6
Alton Gdns SS2 .....347 E5
Alton Hall La IP9 ....61 F3
Alton Park Jun Sch
  CO15 ....195 D2
Alton Park La CO15 .195 B1
Alton Park Rd CO15 .195 D3
Alton Rd CO15 ....195 C4
Alton Water (Resr)*
  IP9 ....62 B3
Alton Water Visitor Ctr*
  IP9 ....62 A4
Aluf Cl CM8 ....211 E8
Aluric Cl RM16 ......374 B2
Alverstoke Rd RM3 ..314 F2
Alverstone Rd E12 ..352 A8
Alverton Cl CM77 ...154 B6
Alverton Way CO4 ...110 B3
Alvis Ave CO15 ......220 E6
Alwen Gr RM15 ......372 B8
Alwyne Ave CM15 ...295 A3
Alyssum Cl CM1 ....233 A6
Alyssum Cl IG7 .....136 D8
Amanda Cl IG7 ......311 D4
Amanda Mews RM7 .335 C6
Amber Ct ￼ RM1 ...335 E6
Amberden SS15 ....341 D5
Amber La IG6 ....311 B3
Amberley Cl CO7 ....137 D1
Amberley Rd IG9 ....288 C1
Amberley Way RM7 .335 B7
Amberry Ct CM20 ...199 D1
Ambleside CM16 ...268 A8
Ambleside Ave RM12 .355 B7
Ambleside Ct CO15 ..196 A3
Ambleside Dr SS1 ...367 D8
Ambleside Gdns
  Hullbridge SS5 ....301 C2
  Redbridge IG4 ....332 F6
Ambleside Wlk SS8 ..363 F6
Ambridge Rd CO10 ..130 B3
Ambrook Rd DA17 ..369 A3
Ambrose Ave CO3 ...134 F4
Ambrose Ct CO6 ....133 D4
Ambros Ho CO10 ....135 D2
Amcotes Pl CM2 ....232 C4
Ameland Rd SS8 ....364 A6
Amelia Blackwell Ho
  SS8 ....363 E3
Amerells Rd CO16 ...168 C4
America Rd CO6 .....105 C2
Amersham Ave SS14 .340 F5
Amersham Dr RM3 ..314 F4
Amersham Rd RM3 ..314 F4
Amersham Wlk RM3 .314 F4
Amery Gdns RM2 ...336 B8
Amesbury Dr E4 ....287 A1
Amesbury Ct CM16 ..267 F8
Amesbury Rd
  Dagenham RM9 .....353 D5
  Epping CM16 ....267 F8
Amid Rd SS8 ....364 C5
Amos Hill CO10 ......54 B8
Amos Rd CO4 ....342 D4
Ampers End SS14 ...342 C6
Ampthill Ho ￼ RM3 .314 D5
Amwell Ct
  Hoddesdon EN11 ....221 A7

Avenue Gate IG10 ....**288** C3
Avenue Ind Est
Chingford E4 ....**309** A4
Romford RM3 ....**334** D2
Avenue Pl CM23 ....**146** A6
Avenue Rd
Bishop's Stortford CM23 ..**146** B6
Brentwood CM14 ....**316** C6
Chelmsford CM2 ....**205** E2
Hoddesdon EN11 ....**221** D5
Ilford RM6 ....**334** C4
Ingatestone CM4 ....**274** B3
Romford RM3 ....**314** F3
South Benfleet SS7 ....**344** E3
Southend-on-S,Clifftown
SS0 ....**366** F8
Southend-on-S,Leigh Cliffs
SS9 ....**365** C8
Theydon Bois CM16 ....**267** D3
Witham CM8 ....**184** A3
Woodford IG8 ....**310** C4
Avenue Terr Ilford IG2 ..**333** C5
Southend-on-S SS0 ....**366** E8
Avenue The
Billericay CM12 ....**297** A2
Braintree CM7 ....**127** F3
Brentwood CM13 ....**316** F4
Canvey Island SS8 ....**364** B2
Chingford E4 ....**309** D5
Clacton-on-S CO15 ....**196** B7
Colchester CO3 ....**135** C6
Danbury CM3 ....**256** F7
Fobbing SS17 ....**361** D5
Great Braxted CM8 ....**185** A3
Great Dunmow CM6 ....**150** E8
Great Oakley CO12 ....**116** B3
Greenhithe DA9 ....**377** B2
Hadleigh SS7 ....**345** E3
Hoddesdon EN11 ....**221** A4
Hornchurch RM12 ....**336** D2
Hullbridge SS5 ....**301** D3
Ipswich IP1 ....**17** C8
Kelvedon Hatch CM15 .....**293** E8
Loughton IG10 ....**288** E3
Lower Nazeing EN9 ....**244** C6
North Fambridge CM3 ......**303** A7
Romford RM1 ....**335** D7
Trimley St M IP11 ....**181** A7
Wanstead E11 ....**332** B6
Washbrook IP8 ....**35** F7
Wendford CO6 ....**108** D3
Witham CM8 ....**184** A2
Wivenhoe CO7 ....**137** B1
Avery Gdns Ilford IG2 ...**333** A6
Redbridge IG2 ....**332** F6
Avey La High Beach IG10 .**288** A8
Waltham Abbey EN9 ....**265** E2
Aviation Way SS2 ....**347** B7
Avignon Cl CO2 ....**136** B4
Avila Chase CM4 ....**254** B1
Avington Wlk SS7 ....**144** D4
Avocet Cl
Frinton-on-S CO13 ....**170** E6
Kelvedon CO5 ....**158** D2
West Mersea CO5 ....**218** D7
Avocet Ct IP11 ....**381** D2
Avocet Way CM9 ....**237** C5
Avon Cl SS4 ....**325** C5
Avondale Cl
Loughton IG10 ....**288** F2
Rayleigh SS6 ....**303** F7
Avondale Cres
Ilford IG4 ....**332** D6
Avondale Ct
Southend-on-S SS9 ....**346** D1
Woodford E18 ....**310** B2
Avondale Dr
Loughton IG10 ....**288** F3
Southend-on-S SS9 ....**346** F4
Avondale Gdns SS17 ....**360** E5
Avondale Ho CO15 ......**196** A3
Avondale Rd
Basildon SS16 ....**343** A4
Clacton-on-S CO15 ....**196** A3
Ipswich IP3 ....**18** A2
Rayleigh SS6 ....**323** F2
South Benfleet SS7 ....**344** D3
Woodford IG8 ....**363** E4
Avondale Wlk SS8 ....**363** E4
Avon Gn RM15 ....**372** B7
Avon House Sch IG8 .....**310** A6
Avon Rd
Canvey Island SS8 ....**364** A3
Chelmsford CM1 ....**231** C5
Upminster RM14 ....**337** D5
Avontar Rd RM15 ....**357** B1
Avon Terr IG10 ....**288** F3
Avon Way Colchester CO4 ...**136** E5
Southend-on-S SS3 ....**368** C7
Wanstead E18 ....**332** A8
Avon Way Ho CO4 ....**136** F6
Avril Wlk CM8 ....**183** E3
Avril Way E4 ....**309** C5
Avro Rd SS2 ....**347** D6
Axe St IG11 ....**352** C4
Aylesbeare SS3 ....**368** D8
Aylesbury Dr
Basildon SS16 ....**340** F5
Great Notley CM77 ....**154** C5
Holland-on-S CO15 ....**196** F6
Aylesbury Mews SS15 ...**319** F2
Aylets Field CM18 ......**223** E5
Aylett Cl SS8 ....**364** C4
Aylett Rd RM9 ....**337** C2
Ayletts Basildon SS14 ...**342** F6
Broomfield CM1 ....**205** B8
Aylmer Rd RM8 ....**334** E1
Ayloffe Rd Colchester CO4 **110** C1
Dagenham RM9 ....**353** F6
Ayloff Prim Sch RM12 ..**355** B8
Ayloffs Cl RM11 ....**336** E6
Ayloffs Wlk RM11 ....**336** E6
Aylsham La RM3 ....**314** D6

Aylsham Rd EN11 ....**221** C8
Aynsley Gdns CM17 .....**224** C8
Aynsworth Ave CM23 ...**119** B2
Ayr Gn RM1 ....**313** E2
Ayron Rd RM15 ....**357** B1
Ayr Way RM1 ....**313** E2
Azalea Ave SS12 ....**321** C7
Azalea Cl IG1 ....**352** B7
Azalea Ct
B Chelmsford CM1 ....**232** F6
Chingford IG8 ....**309** E3
Colchester CO4 ....**136** D8
Azalea Mews SS8 ....**364** A2
Azalea Way CO16 ....**195** C4

B

Baardwyk Ave SS8 ....**364** E3
Babbacombe Gdns IG4 ...**332** E7
Babington Rd
Dagenham RM8 ....**353** C8
Hornchurch RM12 ....**336** B3
Back Hamlet IP3 ....**17** E5
Back Hill Hadstock CB1 ....**5** B6
Holbrook IP9 ....**62** E4
Back La Broomfield CM1 ..**208** D1
Colchester CO3 ....**134** C7
Dagenham RM6 ....**334** E4
East Hanningfield CM3 ....**278** B7
Felixstowe IP11 ....**381** D5
Ford End CM3 ....**179** B6
Grays RM20 ....**372** B4
Great Oakley CO12 ....**116** C4
Ickleton CB10 ....**3** A3
Ingatestone CM4 ....**274** A6
Little Hallingbury CM22 ...**173** B7
Little Waltham CM3 ....**208** A4
Lower Nazeing EN9 ....**222** C1
Pleshey CM3 ....**178** E2
Purfleet RM19 ....**371** E3
Ramsey CO12 ....**90** A1
Rochford SS4 ....**325** F1
Sheering CM22 ....**173** D7
South Ockendon RM16 .....**372** C5
Sisted CM7 ....**129** C7
Stock CM4 ....**275** D2
Tattingstone IP9 ....**61** C6
Thaxted CM6 ....**69** F3
Washbrook IP8 ....**35** E8
Wickham Bishops CM8 .....**212** F4
Back La E CO7 ....**139** A6
Back La W CO7 ....**138** F7
Backnang Sq CM2 ....**232** C2
Back Rd Ardleigh CO7 .....**112** B5
Tollesbury CM9 ....**216** D4
Writtle CM1 ....**231** A1
**Backwarden Nature
Reserve*** CM3 ....**256** E4
Backwardens Nature Trail*
Wivenhoe CO7 ....**137** D1
Bacon Link RM5 ....**313** B4
Bacons Chase CM0 ....**242** B2
Bacon's La CO6 ....**106** C3
Bacton Lodge IP11 ......**381** B3
Bacton Rd IP11 ....**381** D3
Badburgham Ct EN9 .....**265** F6
Baddeley Cl EN3 ....**265** A2
Baddow Cl
Dagenham RM10 ....**354** A4
Woodford IG8 ....**310** D4
Baddow Ct CM2 ....**255** A6
Baddow Hall Ave CM2 ...**255** A7
Baddow Hall Cres CM2 ..**257** B7
Baddow Hall Jun & Inf Sch
CM2 ....**255** A6
Baddow Place Ave CM2 ..**255** A6
Baddow Rd
Chelmsford CM2 ....**232** C1
Great Baddow CM2 ....**254** E7
Baden Powell Cl RM9 ....**353** E4
Baden Powell Dr CO3 ....**135** A4
Baden Powell Ho
DA17 ....**369** A3
Baden Rd IG1 ....**352** B7
Bader Cl IP3 ....**18** C2
Bader Way RM13 ....**355** B6
Badger Cl IG2 ....**333** C4
Badger Gr SS14 ....**128** B3
Badger Hall Ave SS7 ....**345** A4
Badgers Bank IP2 ....**16** E1
Badgers Cl
Galleywood CM2 ....**254** B1
Southend-on-S SS0 ....**347** B4
Badgers Gn CO6 ....**132** E3
Badgers Gr CO6 ....**82** B1
Badgers Holt CO3 ....**134** D6
Badgers Keep CM0 ......**306** B8
Badgers Mount
Chadwell St M RM16 ......**373** F4
Hockley SS5 ....**324** C5
Badgers Rise SS8 ....**364** A6
Badgers Reach CM2 .....**233** D4
Badgers The SS16 ....**341** B4
Badgers Way SS7 ....**345** B4
Badley Hall Rd CO7 .....**128** B3
Badminton Rd CO15 ......**220** F2
Badshah Ave IP3 ....**18** B3
Bag La CM4 ....**273** C4
Bagley's Spring RM6 ....**334** E7
Bagshaw Rd CO12 ....**91** D4
Bailey Bridge Rd CM7 ...**127** E5
Bailey Cl Chingford E4 ....**309** C6
Haverhill CB9 ....**9** D7
Ipswich IP2 ....**16** E6
Purfleet RM19 ....**371** D2
Bailey Ct E4 ....**309** D5
Bailey Dale CO3 ....**134** C4
Bailey La CO10 ....**12** C7
Bailey Rd SS9 ....**346** B2
Bailey The SS9 ....**323** C2
Baillie Cl RM13 ....**355** B1
Bainbridge Dr CO5 ......**186** D4
Bainbridge Rd RM9 .....**353** F8

Baines Cl CO3 ....**135** A5
Baird Cl IP2 ....**16** F7
Baird Ho B DA17 ....**369** A3
Bairny Wood App IG8 ...**310** B4
Baker Ave CM1 ....**211** A3
Baker Mews CM0 ....**237** A2
Baker Rd IP9 ....**91** A8
Bakers Cl CM3 ....**301** D8
Bakers Cotts CM15 ......**293** F8
Bakers Ct
B Bishop's Stortford
CM23 ....**146** A7
Colchester CO1 ....**109** E1
Dagenham RM8 ....**334** F4
Baker's Ct SS14 ....**321** A2
Bakers Farm Cl SS11 ....**322** A7
Bakersfield CM3 ....**282** F8
Bakers Field CM4 ....**275** E2
Epping CM16 ....**245** F1
Felsted CM6 ....**152** C4
Ingatestone CM4 ....**274** B4
West Hanningfield CM2 ....**276** B7
Baker's La Colchester CO4 **109** A2
Great Notley CM7 ....**154** D6
Tollesunt Major CM9 ......**214** D4
Bakers Mdw CM1 ....**207** F7
Bakers Mead CM3 ....**207** F7
Bakers Mews CM4 ....**274** B4
Baker's Rd CO10 ....**12** F2
Baker St Chelmsford CM2 ..**232** A1
Orsett RM16 ....**373** F6
Bakers Villas The CM16 .**245** F1
Bakers Wlk CM21 ......**172** E2
Bakery Cl Roydon CM19 ..**222** C8
Tillingham CM0 ....**263** E3
Bakery Ct CM24 ....**119** E6
Balaclaas Rd CO7 ....**267** E4
Baldry Cl IP8 ....**16** C1
Baldwin's Hill IG10 .....**288** F8
Baldwin's La CO6 ....**131** E8
Bale Cl CO3 ....**134** D4
Balfe Ct CO4 ....**136** F6
Balfour Cl SS12 ....**321** E5
Balfour Rd Grays RM17 ...**373** C2
Ilford IG1 ....**333** C3
Balgonie Rd E4 ....**287** D1
Balgores Cres RM2 ......**336** B8
Bacic Ct RM3 ....**314** B3
Balgores La RM2 ....**336** B7
Balgores Sq RM2 ....**336** B7
Balkerne Gdns CO1 .....**135** E7
Balkerne Hill CO3 ....**135** E7
Balkerne Pas CO1 ....**135** E7
Ball Alley B CO1 ....**135** E7
Ballards Cl RM10 ....**354** B4
Ballards Rd RM10 ....**354** B3
Ballards Wlk SS15 ......**341** E7
Ballast Quay Rd
Fingringhoe CO5 ....**164** B6
Wivenhoe CO7 ....**137** D1
Ballingdon Gr CO10 .....**33** D5
Ballingdon Hill CO10 ....**33** C5
Ballingdon Hill Ind Est
CO10 ....**33** C6
Ballingdon St CO10 .....**33** D6
Ballingdon Trad Est CO10 **33** C6
Balliol Ave E4 ....**309** E6
Ball La Abberton CO2 .....**162** F5
Blackheath CO2 ....**163** B5
Ball's Chace CO8 ....**79** F2
Ball's Green CO7 ....**76** F1
Balmerino Ave SS7 ......**345** C6
Balmoral Ave
Clacton-on-S CO15 ....**195** D3
Corringham SS17 ....**361** A4
Stanford-le-H SS17 ....**360** E3
Balmoral Cl
Billericay CM11 ....**297** E1
Ipswich IP2 ....**16** F1
Balmoral Ct CM2 ....**232** C2
Balmoral Dr CB9 ....**8** E8
Balmoral Gdns
Hockley SS5 ....**324** C6
Ilford IG3 ....**333** F3
Balmoral Ho SS0 ....**366** E8
Balmoral Rd
Hornchurch RM12 ....**336** D1
Mayland CM3 ....**261** A2
Pilgrims Hatch CM15 .....**294** B4
Romford RM2 ....**336** B6
Southend-on-S SS0 ....**347** E1
Balmoral Terr SS0 ......**347** D2
Balstonia Dr SS17 ......**360** F5
Baltic Ave SS1 ....**367** A8
Balton Way CO12 ....**90** F2
Bamber Ho B IG11 ......**352** C4
Bamford Rd IG11 ....**352** C6
Bampton Rd RM3 ....**314** E2
Bancroft Ave IG9 ....**310** A8
Bancroft Chase RM12 ...**335** F2
Bancrofts Rd CM3 ....**301** E8
Bancroft's Sch IG8 ......**310** A7
Bandhills Cl CM3 ....**301** D8
Banes Down EN9 ....**221** E1
Bangs Cl CB1 ....**7** A7
Banham Dr CO10 ....**33** F8
Banister Cl CO16 ....**195** C5
Bankart La CM2 ....**232** F4
Bank Bldgs B CO10 ......**33** E7
Bank Chambers CM15 ...**316** D8
Bank End Cotts CM4 ....**275** A8
Bankfoot RM17 ....**373** A1
Bank Pas CO1 ....**135** E7
Bank Pl B CM14 ....**316** C8
Bank Rd IP4 ....**17** E6
Bank St Braintree CM7 ...**127** F3

Bank St continued
Gravesend DA11,DA12 ....**379** B1
Banks Way E12 ....**352** A8
Banks Cl RM15 ....**372** B6
Bann Cl RM15 ....**372** B6
Banner Cl RM19 ....**371** D2
Bannister Dr CM13 ......**295** C3
Bannister Gn SS12 ......**321** E6
Bannister Green Villas
CM6 ....**152** E6
Bannister Ho RM20 ......**377** D8
Bansons Cft CM5 ....**249** A3
Banson's La CM5 ....**249** A3
Bansons Way CM5 ......**249** A3
Bantel Villas EN11 ......**221** C8
Banters La CM3 ....**154** B1
Bantock Way CM8 ......**211** F7
Bantoft Terr IP3 ....**18** C2
Banyards RM11 ....**336** E7
Banyardway SS4 ....**325** C4
Barbara Ave SS8 ....**363** F7
Barbara Cl SS4 ....**325** E2
Barbary Lodge CM2 .....**232** A2
Barbel Cl CM6 ....**265** A5
Barbel Rd CO4 ....**110** F1
Barberry Cl RM3 ....**314** C3
Barbour Gdns CO2 ......**136** D6
Barbour Gn SS12 ....**321** D5
Barbrook La CO5 ....**186** D6
Barbrook Way CM3 .....**256** E1
Barclay Cl CM2 ....**255** A6
Barclay Ct EN11 ....**221** A5
Barclay Oval IG8 ....**310** A6
Barclay Rd SS13 ....**321** E1
Barclay Way RM20 ......**371** F1
Bardell Cl CM1 ....**231** F6
Bardeville Rd SS8 ......**364** E3
Bardeswell Cl CM14 ....**316** C8
Bardfield Cl RM1 ....**135** E6
Bardfield Ave RM6 ......**334** D8
Bardfield Com Prim Sch
SS16 ....**342** E4
Bardfield Ctr CM7 ......**72** B1
Bardfield Rd
Bardfield Saling CM7 ....**99** F1
Frinton-on-S CO13 ....**170** F6
Rayleigh SS6 ....**323** A3
Bards Ct RM3 ....**314** B3
Barfield Rd CO5 ....**218** C6
Barfields IG10 ....**289** A5
Barfields Gdns IG10 ....**289** A5
Barfields Path IG10 .....**289** A5
Bargate La CO7 ....**85** C3
Barge Pier Rd SS3 ......**368** A5
Barham Cl RM7 ....**313** B1
Baring-Gould Cotts CO5 **191** D1
Barington Ct CM3 ......**295** C3
Barkantine Sh CM1 ....**223** E3
Barker Cl Ipswich IP2 .....**16** D5
Lawford CO11 ....**86** D4
Steeple Bumpstead CB9 ...**27** B6
Barker Rd CO10 ....**15** E2
Barkers Mead CM22 ....**173** E8
Barkers Terr CO7 ....**85** A5
Baron Ct Romford RM1 ..**314** F2
Southend-on-S SS2 ....**347** F5
Baron Gdns IG6 ....**333** C8
Baronia Croft CO4 ......**110** C3
Baron Rd Dagenham RM8 **334** D3
South Woodham Ferrers
CM3 ....**301** E7
Barons Court Inf Sch
SS0 ....**366** F8
Barons Ct SS14 ....**333** D2
Baron's Ct B CB9 ....**8** E7
Barons Bros CM25 ....**145** D5
Barons Way SS16 ....**341** B4
Baronswood Way CO2 ..**135** D2
Barrack Cnr B IP1 ......**17** B6
Barrack Cl
Great Waltham CM3 ....**207** E8
Harwich CO12 ....**91** D4
Ipswich IP1 ....**17** B6
Barrack Rd CM1 ....**206** B5
Barrack Row B DA11 ....**379** B1
Barrack Sq B CM2 ......**232** B2
Barrack St Bradfield CO11 **114** D8
Colchester CO1 ....**136** B6
Barra Glade SS12 ....**321** F5
Barras Ct EN3 ....**265** A2
Barr Cl CO7 ....**137** C1
Barrel Ct CO7 ....**139** A3
Barrells Down Rd CM23 .**118** E1
Barrett Cl RM3 ....**314** B3
Barrett La B CM23 ......**145** F7
Barrie Pavement B
SS12 ....**321** D5

Barnards Ave SS8 ....**364** D4
Barnards Field CM6 .....**70** B2
Barnards Yd CB10 ....**22** D1
Barnby Cl CB9 ....**8** C8
Barncombe Cl SS17 .....**344** D6
Barncroft Cl
Colchester CO4 ....**110** B3
Loughton IG10 ....**289** A4
Barncroft Gn IG10 ......**289** A4
Barncroft Rd IG10 ......**289** A4
Barn Cl CM21 ....**172** E3
Barnes Cl IG8 ....**310** D5
Barnes Farm Dr CM3 ...**282** F2
Barnes Farm Jun & Inf Scls
CM2 ....**233** A3
Barnes Ho B IG1 ....**352** B7
Barnes Mill Rd CM2 .....**232** F2
Barnes Rd IG1 ....**352** C7
Barnet Park Rd SS11 ...**299** F2
Barnett Ct RM17 ....**373** C1
Barneveld Ave SS8 .....**364** E3
Barnfield Capel St M IP9 ..**35** E1
Epping CM16 ....**246** A3
Feering CO5 ....**158** D3
Felixstowe IP11 ....**381** B6
Hatfield Broad Oak CM22 .**175** A5
Manningtree CO11 ....**86** D4
Wickford SS11 ....**321** E8
Barnfield Cl
Greenhithe DA9 ....**376** F1
Hoddesdon EN11 ....**221** A8
Lower Nazeing EN9 ....**221** F1
Barnfield Cotts CM9 ....**237** B5
Barnfield Mews CM1 ....**232** A6
Barnfield Pl CM8 ....**183** F1
Barnfield Rd CO6 ....**109** C6
Barn Fields CO5 ....**163** F5
Barn Folds CO3 ....**134** C6
Barn Gn CM1 ....**204** B8
Barn Hall Ave CO2 ......**136** C4
Barnhall Rd CM9 ....**187** D2
Barnham Pl IP5 ....**18** F6
Barn Hill CM19 ....**222** B4
Barn La CM21 ....**112** F7
Barnmead CM5 ....**247** F2
Barn Mead Braintree CM7 **128** D2
Doddinghurst CM15 ....**272** C3
Harlow CM18 ....**223** E6
Theydon Bois CM16 ......**267** E3
Barnmead Gdns RM9 ...**353** F7
Barnmead Rd RM9 ......**353** F7
Barnmead Way CM0 .....**306** B8
Barns Ct CM19 ....**223** B3
Barnsley Rd RM3 ....**314** F3
Barnstaple Cl SS1 ......**368** A8
Barnstaple Path B RM3 **314** D5
Barnstaple Rd
Romford RM3 ....**314** C5
Southend-on-S SS1 ....**368** B8
Barnston Gn SS16 ......**151** A4
Barnston Way CM13 ....**295** C4
Barn The RM17 ....**373** B2
Barn View Rd CO6 ......**131** A1
Barnwell Dr SS5 ....**324** D6
Barnyard The SS16 .....**341** A4
Baron Ct Romford RM1 ..**314** F2
... (see Baron Ct above)

Barfields CM7 ....**100** E7
Barrymore Wlk SS6 .....**324** A2
Barstable Rd SS17 ......**360** D1
Barstable Sch SS14 .....**342** F6
Bartholomew Cl CB10 ....**3** E2
Bartholomew Dr RM3 ...**314** D1
Bartholomew Ho B IG8 **311** A3
Bartholomew Rd B
CM23 ....**145** F6
Bartholomew St IP4 ....**17** F6
Bartlett Cl CM5 ....**260** F1
Bartletts Rayleigh SS6 ...**346** A8
Saffron Walden CB10 ......**22** D1
Bartletts Ho B RM10 ....**354** B6
Bartley Cl SS7 ....**344** B6
Bartlow End SS17 ....**360** F8
Bartlow Ho SS13 ....**341** B8
Barton Ave RM7 ....**331** C8
Barton Cl Chigwell IG7 ...**311** C8
Ipswich IP4 ....**18** C4
South Woodham F CM3 ....**279** D1
Barton Ct B CM4 ....**316** C6
Barton Friars IG7 ....**311** C8
Barton Mdws IG6 ....**333** C7
Barton Rd Felixstowe IP11 **381** F4
Hornchurch RM12 ....**336** B3
Bartram Ave N CM7 ....**128** C3
Bartram Ave S CM7 ....**128** C3
Barwell Way CM8 ....**184** B2
Baryta Cl SS17 ....**360** C1
Baryta Ct SS9 ....**365** E8
Basbow La B CM23 ......**145** F7
Basedale Rd RM9 ....**353** B5
Basildon Ave IG5 ....**311** A2
Basildon Bsns Ctr SS14 .**342** A8
Basildon Dr SS15 ....**341** C8
Basildon Hospl SS16 ....**342** A4
Basildon Rd SS15 ....**341** E8
Basildon Rise SS15 .....**341** E8
Basildon Sta SS14 ......**342** A5
Basildon Trad Ctr SS14 .**341** F8
Basildon Zoo* SS16 ....**342** C4
Basilica Ho SS11 ....**322** F4
Basil Mews CM7 ....**200** C1
Basing Ho B IG11 ......**352** D4
Basin Rd CM9 ....**237** E3
Bassenthwaite Rd SS7 .**344** E7
Bassett Bsns Units CM16 **246** D8
Bassett Gdns CM16 .....**247** B5
Bassett Ho RM9 ....**353** B4
Bassetts La CM3,CM9 ...**235** A4
Bassetts La CM5 ....**251** B8
Bassingbourn Rd CM24 .**121** A3
Bassingham Cres CO5 ..**186** E5
Bastable Ave IG11 ......**353** A3
Bata Ave RM18 ....**375** B1
Batavia Rd SS8 ....**364** D4
Bate-Dudley Dr CM0 ....**242** B3
Bateman Cl IG11 ....**352** C6
Bateman Rd
Brightlingsea CO7 ....**192** E8
Chingford E4 ....**309** A4
Batemans Mews CM14 ..**316** B8
Batemans Rd CO16 .....**168** B4
Bates Ard RM6 ....**315** A3
Bates Rd Maldon CM9 ....**237** A4
Romford RM3 ....**315** A3
Bath Ct CB9 ....**8** F6
Bath Hill IP11 ....**381** F4
Bath Rd Dagenham RM6 .**334** C5
Felixstowe IP11 ....**381** E3
Bath St Gravesend DA11 .**379** B1
Ipswich IP1 ....**17** D3
Wivenhoe CO7 ....**164** B8
Bathurst Cl B CO2 ......**136** A1
Bathurst Rd IG3 ....**333** F3
Baton Cl RM19 ....**371** D2
Battery La IP9 ....**91** B8
Battisford Dr CO16 .....**195** A4
Battis The B RM1 ....**335** E5
Battle Rd DA17 ....**288** A2
Battle Rd DA17 ....**369** A2
Battlesbridge Craft Ctr*
SS11 ....**300** D2
**Battlesbridge Motorcycle
Mus*** SS11 ....**300** D2
Battlesbridge Sta SS11 .**300** D2
Battlesbrook Rd CO2 ...**136** D2
Battleswick SS14 ....**320** D1
Batt's Rd CM0 ....**284** A8
Bawden Way CM2 ....**254** D8
Bawdsey Ave IG2 ....**333** F7
Bawdsey Cl CO16 ....**195** B3
Bawn Cl CM7 ....**128** A4
Bawtree Way CO3 ....**135** A5
Baxter Ave SS2 ....**347** B7
Baxter Gdns RM3 ....**314** C8
Baxter Rd IG1 ....**352** B7
Baxters CM3 ....**257** A7
Bayard Ave CO7 ....**192** F7
Bay Cl SS8 ....**364** B2
Bayley St CO9 ....**77** A1
Bayly Rd DA1 ....**376** A6
Bay Manor La RM20 ....**376** F8
Baymans Green Rd CM3 **303** B5
Baynard Ave CM6 ....**151** E7
Baynards Cres CO13 ....**170** F8
Baynes Pl B CM19 ......**223** A2
Bay Rd CO10 ....**91** D4
Bays Dr CO9 ....**77** A1
Baytree Cl CO11 ....**115** C5
Bay Tree Cl IG6 ....**311** B3
Baytree Ct CM7 ....**128** F2
Baytree Ho E4 ....**287** B2
Bay View End SS5 ......**324** D2
Bay View Cl
Harwich CO12 ....**90** C1
Little Oakley CO12 ....**117** C8

Baywood Sq IG7 ....312 B6
Beach App CO16 ....220 B6
Beach Ave SS9 ....366 A8
Beach Cres CO15 ....220 F6
Beachcroft Ave CO13 .170 D6
Beach Ct
  Great Wakering SS3 .....350 C3
  Southend-on-S SS0 ....366 C7
Beaches Cl SS1 ....325 A4
Beach House Gdns SS8 .364 E2
Beach Rd
  Canvey Island SS8 ....364 D4
  Clacton-on-S CO15 ....195 F2
  Harwich CO12 ....91 C2
  Point Clear B CO16 ....219 D6
  Southend-on-S, Shoeburyness
    SS1 ....368 F5
  Southend-on-S SS1 ....367 C7
  St Osyth CO16 ....194 B2
  West Mersea CO5 ....218 C5
Beach Rd W IP11 ....381 D2
Beach's Dr CM1 ....231 D3
Beach Station Rd IP11 .381 C1
Beachway SS8 ....364 B2
Beach Way CO15 ....220 F6
Beachy Dr CM0 ....220 C8
Beacon Cl CO7 ....192 E6
Beacon End Ctyd CO3 .134 C6
Beacon Field IP11 ....381 C5
Beaconfield Ave CM16 .246 A2
Beaconfield Rd CM16 ..246 A2
Beaconfield Way CM16 .246 A2
Beacon Hill
  Kelvedon Hatch CM14 ...271 C2
  Maldon CM9 ....236 E2
  Purfleet RM19 ....371 B1
  Wickham Bishops CM8 ...213 A6
Beacon Hill Ave CO12 ...91 E4
Beacon Hill Sch
  RM19 ....371 B1
Beacon Hill Sch IP2 ...16 F3
Beacon Hts CO16 ....193 B2
Beaconsfield Ave CO13 .135 E6
Beaconsfield Cl CO10 ...33 C8
Beaconsfield Ct ⑦ CO8 ...8 F7
Beaconsfield Rd
  Clacton-on-S CO15 ....195 F3
  Ipswich IP1 ....16 E8
  Sudbury CO10 ....33 C8
Beacons The IG10 ....262 A1
Beacontree Ave E17 .....309 D1
Beacon Way
  Colchester CO3 ....134 C6
  Point Clear B CO16 ....193 B2
Beadel Cl CM8 ....211 E8
Beadle's Par RM10 ....354 C6
Beadles The CM2 ....173 B8
Beadle Way CM3 ....181 A6
Beadon Dr CM7 ....128 A1
Beads Hall La CM15 .....294 B4
Beal High Sch IG4 ....332 E7
Beal Rd IG1 ....333 A2
Beam Ave RM10 ....354 A8
Beambridge SS13 ....343 A6
Beambridge Ct ② SS13 .343 A6
Beambridge Mews SS13 .343 A6
Beambridge Pl ① SS13 .343 A6
Beaminster Gdns
  Ilford IG6 ....333 B8
  Redbridge IG6 ....311 B1
Beamish Cl CM16 ....247 C6
Beam Prim Sch RM10 ...354 C2
Beams Cl CM11 ....319 C8
Beams Way CM11 ....319 C8
Beamway RM10 ....354 D5
Beanfield Rd CM21 ....172 A4
Bean Rd DA9 ....377 F2
Beansland Gr RM4 ....334 E8
Bearblock Cotts RM14 .356 C6
Bear Cl RM7 ....335 B5
Beard's La CM1 ....41 A4
Beardsley Dr CM1 ....232 F7
Beardsley Terr RM8 .....353 B7
Beard's Terr CO6 ....131 A3
Bearing Cl IG7 ....312 A6
Bearing Way IG7 ....312 A6
Bear St CO6 ....56 A1
Bearsted Dr SS13 ....343 C5
Bearwalden Bsns Pk CB11 42 F5
Beaton Cl DA7 ....369 F4
Beatrice Ave
  Canvey Island SS8 ....364 B4
  Felixstowe IP11 ....381 E5
Beatrice Cl Hockley SS5 .324 D6
  Ipswich IP3 ....18 A3
Beatrice Ct IG9 ....310 D8
Beatrice Rd
  Clacton-on-S CO15 ....195 E2
  Walton-on-t-N CO14 ...144 E2
Beatty Gdns CM7 ....128 C4
Beatty La SS14 ....342 E6
Beatty Rd IP3 ....18 E2
Beatty Rise CM3 ....301 F6
Beattyville Gdns IG6 ...333 B7
Beauchamps CM0 ....306 B8
Beauchamps Cl CM1 ....232 F8
Beauchamps Dr SS13 ...322 A8
Beauchamps Sch SS13 ..322 A8
Beaufort Cl Chingford E4 .309 B4
  Grays RM16 ....173 B2
  North Weald Bassett CM16 247 A4
  Romford RM7 ....335 C7
Beaufort Gdns
  Braintree CM7 ....128 A4
  Ilford IG3 ....333 A3
Beaufort Rd
  Billericay CM12 ....296 F2
  Ilford IG3 ....333 A4
Beaufort St ⑤ CB9 ...8 F7
Beaulieu Bvd CM1 ....233 A7
Beaulieu Dr EN9 ....265 B6
Beauly Way RM1 ....313 E2

Beaumaris Dr IG8 ....310 D3
Beaumont Ave
  Brightlingsea CO7 ....193 A7
  Clacton-on-S CO15 ....195 D3
Beaumont Cl
  Colchester CO4 ....109 F4
  Romford RM2 ....314 C1
  Walton-on-t-N CO14 ...170 F7
Beaumont Cres RM13 ...355 A6
Beaumont Ct CO9 ....9 B6
Beaumont Gdns CM3 ...295 C3
Beaumont Hill CM6 .....123 D2
Beaumont Park Dr CM19 222 B8
Beaumont Pk CM6 ....256 C6
Beaumont Pl CM7 ....128 E3
Beaumont Rd CM12 .....116 C2
Beaumont Vale CM9 .....9 B6
Beaumont Way CM9 .....259 B8
Beaumont Wlk CM1 .....231 D5
Beaver Cl CO3 ....134 E4
Beaver Rd IG6 ....312 C5
Beaver Twr SS9 ....346 E6
Beazley End SS12 ....321 E6
Bebington Cl CM12 .....297 A3
Beccles Ct SS11 ....321 D8
Beccles Dr IG11 ....352 F6
Beche Rd CO2 ....136 B5
Becker Rd CO3 ....134 E4
Beckers Green Prim Sch
  CM7 ....128 D2
Beckers Green Rd CM7 .128 D2
Beckett Ave E6 ....352 A2
Becket Cl
  Brentwood CM13 ....316 C4
  Rochford SS4 ....325 D5
Beckett Dr SS17 ....360 D4
Becketts Cl SS11 ....341 A6
Becketts Ct
  Brentwood CM13 ....316 C4
  Chelmsford CM1 ....232 A3
Beckett's La IP7 ....57 D8
Becket Way SS1 ....301 E5
Beckford Rd CO11 ....87 A4
Beckingham Bsns Pk
  CM9 ....214 D3
Beckingham Rd
  Great Totham CM9 ....213 D5
  Tolleshunt D'arcy CM9 ..215 C4
Beckingham St CM9 .....214 D3
Beckney Ave SS5 ....302 E1
Beck Rd Canvey Island SS8 364 F3
  Saffron Walden CB11 ...22 D1
Beckton Alps Ski Ctr *
  E6 ....352 A1
Becontree Ave RM8 .....334 D2
Becontree Ct CO15 ....195 F8
Becontree Prim Sch
  RM8 ....334 B1
Becontree Sta RM9 .....353 D6
Bedalls Rd SS4 ....315 A5
Beddington Rd IG3 .....333 F4
Bedells Ave CM7 ....155 B5
Bede Rd RM6 ....334 C5
Bedford Cl Braintree CM7 128 B4
  Rayleigh SS6 ....323 D1
Bedford Cres IG6 ....186 D5
Bedford Ct ⑧ CB9 .....2 C1
  Colchester CO4 ....109 F5
Bedford Ho ① RM14 ..315 A4
Bedford Pl
  Basildon SS13 ....363 F4
  Chingford E17 ....309 A1
  Colchester CO4 ....109 F5
  Grays RM17 ....373 B1
  Holland-on-S CO15 ....196 D5
Bedford Rd
  Ilford IG1 ....333 B1
  Wallend E6 ....352 A3
  Woodford E18 ....310 A1
Bedfords Plc Nature Trails*
  RM4 ....313 F5
Bedford St IP1 ....17 B6
Bedloes Ave SS11 ....322 E7
Bedwell Cl E6 ....334 D4
Bedwell Rd
  Belvedere DA17 ....369 A1
  Ugley CM22 ....94 B3
Beecham Ct SS15 ....341 C8
Beech Ave Braintree CM7 127 F5
  Brentwood CM13 ....316 F7
  Chigwell IG9 ....310 B8
  Halstead CO9 ....77 A2
  Rayleigh SS6 ....323 D3
  Upminster RM14 ....356 B8
  Wivenhoe CO7 ....137 B1
Beech Cl
  Burnham-on-C CM0 .....306 B6
  Hornchurch RM12 ....336 B1
  Loughton IG10 ....289 B6
  Sproughton IP8 ....16 A6
  Takeley CM22 ....148 D8
Beechcombe SS17 ....361 B5
Beechcroft Ave SS17 ...375 A2
Beechcroft Rd
  Canvey Island SS8 ....363 E3
  Woodford E18 ....310 B1
Beech Ct Basildon SS14 .342 E5
  ③ Buckhurst Hill IG9 ..310 D8
  Dartford DA1 ....376 A1
  ⑥ Ilford E12 ....333 A1
Beech Dr CM21 ....200 C8
Beech Gr
  Billericay CM12 ....297 A4
  Ilford IG1 ....333 A2
  Redbridge IG1 ....332 F3
  Southend-on-S SS9 ....346 B7
  Wanstead E11 ....310 A7

Beechfield
  Hoddesdon EN11 ....197 A2
  Sawbridgeworth CM21 ...172 E2
Beechfield Gdns RM7 ...335 C4
Beechfield Wlk EN9 ....265 D4
Beech Gdns RM10 ....354 C5
Beech Gn CM8 ....212 F5
Beech Gr Aveley RM15 ..371 C1
  Fordham Heath CO3 .....107 F1
  Haverhill CO9 ....8 F8
  Ipswich IP3 ....17 F3
  Little Oakley CO12 ....117 B7
  Redbridge IG6 ....311 E4
  Rush Green RM5 ....18 F7
  Sible Hedingham CO9 ....35 C8
Beech Hall Cres E4 .....309 D3
Beech Hall Rd E4 ....309 B3
Beech Hill CO3 ....135 A6
Beech Hill Gdns IG9 ...302 D7
Beech Ho
  ⑤ Brentwood CM13 ....295 C3
  Ipswich IP3 ....16 D2
Beechholm ② IP4 ......17 E6
Beech La IG9 ....310 B8
Beechlands CM23 ....145 F5
Beech Lodge SS3 ....368 F7
Beechmont Gdns SS2 ..347 E4
Beech Pl CM16 ....257 F8
Beech Rd Basildon SS14 .342 F5
  Great Cornard CO10 ....34 B6
  Hadleigh SS7 ....345 E2
  Hadleigh SS5 ....301 E2
  Rivenhall CM8 ....184 B7
  Rushmere St A IP5 ....18 F7
  Willingale CM5 ....228 D4
Beech Rise CM3 ....211 A3
Beech Spinney CM14 ..316 C5
Beech St RM7 ....335 C7
Beech Terr IG10 ....288 E5
Beech Tree Glade E4 ..287 F1
Beechwood Cl CO12 ...173 D2
Beechwood Dr IG8 ....309 F5
Beechwood Gdns
  Ilford IG5 ....333 A7
  Rainham RM13 ....370 B8
  Redbridge IG5 ....332 F6
Beechwood Pk E18 ....332 F6
Beecroft Cres SS8 ....346 B7
Beedell Ave
  Southend-on-S SS0 ....347 D2
  Wickford SS11 ....322 A6
Beehive Chase CM15 ..272 D4
Beehive Cl CO7 ....59 C3
Beehive Ct
  Colchester CO1 ....136 A6
  Hatfield Heath CM22 ..174 A3
  Romford RM3 ....314 F3
Beehive La Basildon SS14 342 B6
  Chelmsford CM2 ....254 C5
  Ilford IG1 ....333 A5
  Redbridge IG1 ....332 E6
Beehive Lane Prim Sch
  CM2 ....254 D5
Beeleigh Ave SS16 ....341 C3
Beeleigh Chase CM9 ...236 D4
Beeleigh Cl
  Colchester CO2 ....136 A1
  Southend-on-S SS2 ....347 E3
Beeleigh Cross SS14 ..342 E7
Beeleigh E SS14 ....342 E8
Beeleigh Link CM2 ....237 D6
Beeleigh Rd CM9 ....236 F3
Beeleigh W SS14 ....342 E7
Beeston Ct ④ DA2 ....376 B1
Beggarhill CM4 ....273 E6
Begonia Cl E6 ....352 F6
Begonia Pl CO16 ....196 C1
Beke Hall Chase N SS6 322 E4
Beke Hall Chase S SS6 322 E4
Bekeswell La CM2 ....253 F2
Bekeswell Pl CM2 ....254 C2
Bel-Air Beach Cvn Pk
  CO15 ....220 C6
Bel-Air Est CO16 ....220 A6
Belcham Rd CM0 ....30 B5
Belchamps Rd SS11 ...321 F8
Belchamp St Paul CE Prim
  Sch CO10 ....12 E3
Belchamps Way SS3 ..324 E5
Belcham's La CO11 ....93 E8
Belcher Rd ④ EN11 ...221 A7
Belchers La EN9 ....244 C7
Beldams Cl CO16 ....142 A1
Beldams Gate CM23 ..146 B6
Beldams La CM23 ....146 B5
Belfairs Cl SS9 ....346 D2
Belfairs Ct SS9 ....346 B6
Belfairs Dr
  Dagenham RM6 ....334 C4
  Southend-on-S SS9 ....346 D2
Belfairs High Sch SS9 346 C2
Belfairs Park Cl SS9 ..346 C5
Belfairs Park Dr SS9 ..346 B5
Belgrave Av RM2 ....314 D1
Belgrave Cl
  Chelmsford CM2 ....254 D7
  Ipswich IP3 ....17 E8
  Rayleigh SS6 ....323 B4
  Southend-on-S SS9 ....346 B7
Belgrave Ho ⑥ CM23 .146 B8
Belgrave Market IG1 ..333 A2
Belgrave Rd
  Billericay CM12 ....297 A4
  Ilford IG1 ....333 A2
  Redbridge IG1 ....332 F3
  Southend-on-S SS9 ....346 B7
  Wanstead E11 ....310 A7
Belgrave Terr IG8 ....310 A7
Belgravia Mans SS1 ...367 D6
Belhus Woods Ctry Pk*
  RM15 ....356 D2
Bellamy Cl E4 ....309 B4
Bellamy Rd E4 ....309 B4
Bell Ave RM3 ....314 B2
Bell Cl Colchester CO2 .136 D2

Bell Cl continued
  Greenhithe DA9 ....388 F2
  Ipswich IP7 ....17 C4
Bell Cnr RM14 ....337 C2
Bell Coll CB11 ....43 E8
Bell Comm CO7 ....267 E7
Belle Cl IP4 ....18 A4
Belle Staines Pleasaunce
  E4 ....309 A8
Belle Vue CM2 ....232 A1
Bellevue Ave SS1 ....367 C8
Bellevue Mews SS1 ...348 C1
Bellevue Pl SS1 ....367 C8
Belle Vue Rd
  Billericay CM12 ....296 F2
  Hornchurch RM11 ....336 F3
  Southend-on-S SS2 ....348 C1
Belle Vue Rd
  Chingford E17 ....309 D1
  Colchester CO1 ....109 E1
  Romford RM5 ....313 C4
  Southend-on-S SS0 ....367 C8
  Sudbury CO10 ....33 F7
  Wivenhoe CO7 ....137 C1
Bell Farm Ave RM10 ..355 C1
Bell Farm Gr CM12 ...319 B8
Bell Farm Ind Pk SG8 .39 B2
Bellfield CO16 ....342 E3
Bellfield Ave CO7 ....193 A8
Bellfield Cl CO7 ....193 A8
Bellfield Gdns CM17 ..224 C7
Bellflower Path CM3 ..314 C3
Bell Gn CO7 ....193 A7
Bell Hill Danbury CM3 256 C7
  Lamarsh CO8 ....54 E8
Bell Hill CM12 ....319 B8
Bell Ho
  ④ Dagenham RM10 ...354 B6
  Great Wakering SS3 ....350 A3
  Southend-on-S SS9 ....346 D5
Bellhouse La
  Pilgrims Hatch CM14 ..293 E4
  Southend-on-S SS9 ....346 D5
Bellhouse Rd SS9 ....346 D5
Bell House Rd RM7 ...335 C4
Bellhouse Villas CM1 .177 D3
Bellingham Bldgs CB10 22 D2
Bellingham Cl CM22 ..133 E5
Bellingham La SS6 ...323 D2
Bellingham Rd CM9 ..236 F4
Bella Great Bardfield CM7 72 A2
Belloc Cl
  Hoddesdon EN11 ....221 A6
  Ipswich IP7 ....17 C4
  Nuthampstead SG8 ....39 B2
  Thaxted CM6 ....127 A7
Bellmaine Ave SS17 ..360 F4
Bellmead CM1 ....232 B2
Bell Mead
  Ingatestone CM4 ....274 B3
  Sawbridgeworth CM21 .172 E2
Bell-Reeves Cl SS17 ..360 F4
Bells Chase CM2 ....254 E6
Bells Cl CB11 ....43 E8
Bells Hill
  Bishop's Stortford CM23 145 E7
  Bures CO8 ....80 A4
Bells Hill Rd SS16 ...342 B2
Bells La CO10 ....31 F6
Bell St Great Baddow CM2 254 F6
  Sawbridgeworth CM21 .172 E2
Bells Wlk CM21 ....172 C2
Bell Wlk SS2 ....347 D4
Belmans Ct CO12 ....91 A2
Belmer Rd CM24 ....120 D4
Belmonde Dr CM1 ....232 E7
Belmont Ave
  Upminster RM14 ....336 F2
  Wickford SS12 ....321 B7
Belmont Cl
  Chelmsford CM1 ....232 E7
  Chingford E4 ....309 D5
  Wickford SS12 ....321 B7
  Woodford E18 ....310 B6
Belmont Cres CO4 ....110 C3
Belmont Ct ⑥ CB9 ...9 E7
Belmont Hill CB11 ....43 A1
Belmont Pk CO1 ....136 C5
Belmont Rd Grays RM17 377 F8
  Hornchurch RM12 ....336 D1
  Ilford IG1 ....333 C1
  Ipswich IP1 ....16 C1
Belsay Ct CB9 ....8 D8
Belsize Ave CO15 ....220 D6
Belstead Ave IP2 ....17 A3
Belstead Rd IP2 ....16 C2
Belsteads Farm La CM3 208 E2
Belstedes SS15 ....341 D6
Beltinge Rd RM3 ....314 B3
Belton Bridge SS9 ...365 D8
Belton Gdns SS9 ....365 C8
Belton Way E SS9 ....365 C8
Belton Way W SS9 ...365 C8
Beltwood Rd CM7 ....369 C2
Belvawney Cl CM1 ...231 E6
Belvedere Ave
  Hockley SS5 ....324 C6
  Redbridge IG5 ....311 B1
Belvedere Cl
  Burnham-on-C CM0 .....306 C3
  Chelmsford CM2 ....253 F8
  Maldon CM9 ....257 B3
Belvedere Ct ④ SS7 ..345 D4
Belvedere Ind Est DA17 .369 C5
Belvedere Jun & Inf Schs
  DA17 ....369 B3
Belvedere Link Bsns Pk
  DA8 ....369 C3
Belvedere Pl CM0 ....258 F8

Belvedere Rd
  Brentwood CM14 ....315 F7
  Burnham-on-C CM0 .....306 C3
  Danbury CM3 ....256 F7
  Ipswich IP1 ....17 F7
Belvedere Sta DA17 ..369 B3
Belvedere The CM0 ...306 C4
Belvoir Cr ④ CB9 ....8 E8
Belvoir The CM4 ....274 A3
Bembridge Cl CO15 ..195 F8
Bemerton Ct CO13 ...170 B6
Bemerton Gdns CO13 .170 C6
Benacre Rd IP3 ....18 A2
Benbow Dr CM3 ....301 E6
Bendalls Ct ⑯ CO11 ..86 D4
Benderloch SS8 ....363 E4
Bendlowes Rd CM7 ...72 C1
Benedict Cl CM6 ....72 F3
Benedict Dr CM1 ....231 E2
Benets Rd RM11 ....337 A3
Benezet St IP1 ....17 B6
Benfield Way CM2 ...128 B2
Benfleet For Canvey Island
  Sta SS7 ....363 D8
Benfleet Park Rd SS7 344 B2
Benfleet Rd SS7 ....345 B2
Bengal Rd IG1 ....333 B1
Bengeo Gdns RM6 ...334 C5
Benhall Cl CO16 ....195 C8
Benham Wlk SS13 ...343 C8
Benhooks Ave CM23 .145 E5
Benhooks Pl ① CM23 145 E5
Benhurst Ave CM12 ...336 B1
Benhurst Prim Sch
  RM12 ....336 B1
Benjamin Cl RM11 ...336 A5
Benjamin Ct RM13 ...354 E2
Benleigh Ho SS6 ....323 C3
Bennet Ct CO4 ....136 E6
Bennett Ct Braintree CM7 155 A8
  Walton-on-t-N CO14 ...171 A8
Bennett Rd
  Dagenham RM6 ....334 E4
  Ipswich IP1 ....16 D8
Bennett's Ave CM3 ...277 F3
Bennett's Castle La RM8 334 D1
Bennett's Cl CM6 ....151 E2
Bennett Way CM3 ....211 A4
Bennington Rd IG8 ...309 E3
Bennions Cl RM12 ...355 D6
Bennison Dr RM3 ....314 E1
Benrek Cl IG6 ....311 C2
Ben Sainty Ct CM8 ...184 A2
Benskins Cl CO13 ....92 A8
Benskins La RM4 ....292 D1
Benson Ct ④ EN3 ...265 A1
Benson Rd RM17 ....378 C8
Bensusan Ct CO2 ....135 B3
Bentall Cl CO9 ....103 F8
Bentalls SS14 ....320 A1
Bentalls Ct SS17 ....348 A4
Bentalls Complex The
  CM9 ....237 B5
Bentfield End Cswy
  CM24 ....119 D7
Bentfield Gdns CM24 .119 D7
Bentfield Green CM24 119 D8
Bentfield Prim Sch
  CM24 ....119 D8
Bentley Cl CM22 ....174 B2
Bent Hill IP11 ....381 E3
Ben Tillet Cl IG11 ....353 A5
Benta La CO7 ....18 E8
Bentleigh Ct ⑧ CO1 ..136 D7
Bentley Ave CO15 ....220 E6
Bentley CE Prim Sch IP9 67 E2
Bentley Cl CM23 ....145 F5
Bentley Ct CO13 ....135 C7
Bentley Dr Harlow CM17 224 C7
  Ilford IG2 ....333 C5
Bentley La Belstead IP8 36 C6
  Stutton IP9 ....61 E3
Bentley Rd
  Little Bromley CO11 ...113 D3
  Weeley Heath CO7,CO16 .167 E6
  Witham CM8 ....183 E4
Bentley St DA12 ....379 C4
Bentleys The SS7 ....347 A7
Bentley's St Paul's CE Prim Sch
  CM15 ....293 D6
Bentley Street Ind Est
  DA12 ....379 C1
Bentley Way IG8 ....310 A7
Benton Cl Cressing CM7 155 E6
  Witham CM8 ....212 A7
Benton Gdns IG1 ....360 F5
Bentons SS14 ....345 C5
Bentry Cl RM8 ....334 E2
Bentry Rd RM8 ....334 F2
Benvenue Ave SS9 ...346 F6
Benyon Rd RM15 ....357 C3
Benyon Prim Sch RM15 357 C2
Berberis Cl SS14 ....340 F4
Berberis Cl IG11 ....352 B6
Berberis Wlk ⑤ CM4 136 E7
Berbice La CM23 ....123 D2
Berdan Ct IG5 ....265 A3
Berberis SS16 ....342 D5
Berechurch Hall Rd CO2 162 D8
Berechurch Rd CO2 ..135 E2
Bere Cl CM9 ....377 C2
Berecroft CM18 ....223 D3
Berefield Way ⑧ CO2 136 A1
Berens Cl SS11 ....299 F1
Berens Ct SS17 ....345 D4
Beresford Ave
  Billericay CM12 ....296 F5
  Hadleigh SS7 ....345 D4
Beresford Ct IG8 ....310 C6
Beresford Gdns

Beresford Gdns continued
  Hadleigh SS7 ....345 D4
Beresford Mans ① SS1 367 C7
Beresford Rd
  Chingford, Chingford Green
    E4 ....287 E1
  Chingford, Highams Park
    E17 ....309 B2
  Gravesend DA11 ....378 E1
  Southend-on-S SS1 ....367 C7
Bergamot Rd E3 ....8 C8
Berg Ave SS8 ....364 D5
Bergen Ct CM9 ....258 E8
Bergholt Ave IG2 ....332 E6
Bergholt Rd
  Branham CO11 ....86 B7
  Colchester CO4 ....109 D2
Berica Cl IG6 ....333 C8
Beridge Rd CO9 ....76 D2
Berifle Pl CO7 ....192 F7
Berkeley Cl
  Hornchurch RM11 ....337 B2
  Ipswich IP4 ....17 E8
Berkeley Cl SS4 ....347 F7
Berkeley Dr
  Billericay CM12 ....297 A5
  Hornchurch RM11 ....337 A2
Berkeley Gdns
  Rowhedge CO5 ....163 F7
  Woodford E18 ....346 A1
Berkeley La SS8 ....364 A3
Berkeley Rd CO15 ....195 F5
Berkeley Terr RM18 ..379 A7
Berkeley Dr CM2 ....232 F2
Berkhampstead Rd
  DA17 ....369 A1
Berkley Cres ④ DA12 379 C1
Berkley Cl SS0 ....347 E2
Berkley Hill SS17 ....360 E4
Berkley Rd DA12 ....379 B1
Berkshire Cl SS9 ....346 C5
Berkshire Way RM11 ..337 A3
Berman's Cl CM23 ...317 B8
Bermuda Rd Ipswich IP3 18 F2
  Tilbury RM18 ....379 A5
Bernard Ct CO13 ....170 E6
Bernard Cres IP3 ....18 F2
Bernard Gr EN9 ....265 B6
Bernard Rd RM7 ....335 C4
Bernards Cl IG6 ....311 D3
Bernard St ⑤ CM2 ..379 B1
Berners End CM6 ....151 B4
Berners St IP1 ....17 B6
Berners Wlk SS14 ....342 D8
Bernice Ct RM13 ....355 C1
Bernside CM7 ....127 F2
Bernwell Rd E4 ....309 E2
Berrimans Cl CO4 ..136 D6
Berrybank Cl E4 ....309 E8
Berry Cl Basildon SS16 .341 B5
  Dagenham RM10 ....354 A7
Berry La SS16 ....18 F1
  Wickford SS12 ....321 B6
Berryfield Cotts CO1 136 B7
Berry La SS16 ....341 A4
Berryman Cl RM8 ...334 C1
Berrymore Wlk SS6 .323 F2
Berrys Arc SS6 ....323 B2
Berry Vale CM3 ....301 E6
Bersham La RM17 ...336 E4
Berther Rd RM11 ...336 E4
Bertholds Mews EN9 265 B6
Berwick Ave CM1 ...168 D1
Berwick Ct RM4 ....232 B7
Berwick Cres SS4 ...345 C5
Berwick Pond Cl RM13 355 D5
Berwick Pond Rd RM13 355 F5
Berwick Rd RM13 ...355 D3
Berwood Rd SS17 ...360 F3
Beryl Rd CO12 ....90 D1
Beslyns Rd CM7 ....72 A3
Betchworth Rd IG3 ..333 E1
Bethany Ho RM6 ....334 D4
Betheli Ave IG1 ....333 A4
Betjeman Cl
  Braintree CM7 ....155 A8
  Rayleigh SS6 ....323 F3
Betjeman Way CM5 .248 F5
Betjeman Mews SS2 .348 A2
Betony Cres CM12 ..296 F5
Betony Wlk CM9 ....314 D4
Betony Wlk CO9 ....77 A8
Betoyne Ave E4 ....309 F6
Betoyne Cl CM1 ....297 D2
Betterton Rd RM13 ..354 E3
Betts Green Rd CO16 168 D5
Betts La SS5 ....222 C2
Betty Cocker Gr CO10 34 B7
Betty Dent's Cnr CO10 141 C5
Betula Wlk RM13 ...355 B5
Beulah Rd Epping CM16 .246 A2
  Hornchurch RM11 ....336 C1
Bevan Ave IG11 ....353 A5
Bevan Ho RM16 ....373 D4
Bevan St SS2 ....377 C1
Bevan Way RM12 ...336 A3
Beveland Rd SS8 ....365 A3
Beverley Ave
  Canvey Island SS8 ....364 A3
  West Mersea CO5 ....218 C2
Beverley Cl
  Hornchurch RM11 ....336 F4
  Orsett RM16 ....374 D7
Beverley Cres IG8 ...310 B3

Beverley Ct [5] IP4 17 D6
Beverley Dr CO13 170 E7
Beverley Gdns
Hornchurch RM11 336 F4
Southend-on-S SS2 347 E4
Beverley Rd Chingford E4 309 D4
Colchester CO3 135 D6
Dagenham RM9 353 E8
Ipswich IP4 17 F8
Beverley Rise CM11 297 C1
Bevil Ct EN11 197 A1
Bevile Ho RM17 378 B7
Bevington Mews CM8 184 B2
Bevin Ho RM15 371 C4
Bevin Wlk SS17 360 D2
Bevis Cl DA2 376 C1
Bewick Ct CO9 51 E2
Bewley Ct SS2 348 E2
Bexhill Cl CO15 220 I8
Bexhill Dr RM17 377 F8
Bexley Ave CO12 90 F1
Bexley Coll DA17 369 C2
Bexley Coll Erith Rd Campus DA17 369 B1
Bexley Gdns RM6 334 B6
Bexley Rd DA8 369 F1
Beyers Gdns EN11 197 A1
Beyers Prospect EN11 197 A1
Beyers Ride EN11 197 A1
Bibb Way IP1 17 A5
Bibby Cl SS17 361 A3
Bickenhall SS3 368 D8
Bickerton Point CM3 301 F6
Bicknacre Rd
Danbury CM3 256 F4
East Hanningfield CM3 278 C8
Biddenden Ct [9] SS13 343 C6
Bideford Cl Romford RM3 314 C2
Southend-on-S SS0 347 A5
Biggin La RM16 379 B8
Bight The CM3 301 F5
Bignells Croft CO4 110 C4
Bigods La CM6 123 D4
Bijou Cl CO5 186 D6
Bilberry End CB1 5 C7
Billericay Rd
Ingrave CM13 317 F3
Little Burstead CM12,CM13 318 B3
Billericay Sch The CM12 319 B8
Billericay Sta CM12 297 A3
Billers Chase CM1 233 A7
Billet La Hornchurch RM11 336 D4
Stanford-le-H SS17 360 E1
Billet Rd Chingford E17 309 A2
Ilford RM6 334 C8
Billings Cl RM9 353 C5
Billy's La CO7 58 D2
Bilsdale Cl CO4 110 C4
Bilton Rd Chelmsford CM1 231 F1
Hadleigh SS7 345 E3
Bingham Cl RM15 372 B7
Bingley Rd EN11 221 C6
Binley Rd CM2 232 F2
Birchalls CM24 119 E8
Bircham Rd SS2 348 A2
Birchanger CE Prim Sch CM23 119 D2
Birchanger Ind Est CM23 119 B2
Birchanger La CM23 119 D2
Birch Ave
Great Bentley CO7 166 E8
Harwich CO12 91 B3
Birch Bsns Ctr CO2 161 A7
Birch CE Prim Sch CO2 161 A4
Birch Cl Braintree CM7 127 C2
Brightlingsea CO7 192 E6
Buckhurst Hill IG9 310 D7
Canewdon SS4 304 E1
Canvey Island SS8 363 F3
Clacton-on-S CO15 195 C3
Rayleigh SS6 323 C3
Romford RM7 335 B8
South Benfleet SS7 344 B7
South Ockendon RM15 357 D1
Witham CM8 184 A4
Birch Cres
Hornchurch RM11 336 E7
South Ockendon RM15 357 D2
Birch Ct Chingford E4 309 B4
Dagenham RM6 334 C5
Birchdale SS5 301 D3
Birchdale Gdns RM6 334 D4
Birch Dr Brantham CO11 60 D1
Halstead CO9 77 A2
Birche Cl SS9 346 E4
Birches The
Brentwood CM13 316 E7
Kirby Cross CO13 170 E6
North Weald Bassett CM16 247 B5
South Benfleet SS7 344 C8
Birches Wlk CM2 254 A2
Birch Gdns
Dagenham RM10 335 C1
Tillingham CM0 263 E4
Birch Gn SS12 321 D7
Birch La CM4 275 F3
Birchmores SS15 341 A7
Birch Pl DA9 376 E1
Birch Rd Layer-de-l-H CO2 161 E5
Romford RM7 335 B8
Tillingham CM0 263 E4
Birch Rise CM8 212 E6
Birch St Birch CO2 161 A3
Nayland CO6 56 A1
Birch View CM16 246 B2
Birchway CO2 161 A2
Birchwood
Birchanger CM23 119 D2
South Benfleet SS7 344 B7
Waltham Abbey EN9 265 E5
Birchwood Cl
Brentwood CM13 316 C4
Birchwood Cl *continued*
Tiptree CO5 186 F5
Birch Wood Cl CO5 218 D6
Birchwood Dr SS9 347 A2
Birchwood High Sch CM23 146 C8
Birchwood Rd
Cock Clarks CM3 257 F2
Corringham SS17 361 B5
Dedham CO7 84 B3
Langham CO4 84 A4
Birchwood Way CO5 186 F5
Birdbrook Cl
Brentwood CM13 295 B3
Dagenham RM10 354 C5
Birdbrook Rd CO9 28 A3
Birdbush Ave CB11 43 D7
Bird La
Great Warley CM13 338 D8
Little Warley CM13 316 C1
Tiptree CO5 186 E4
Upminster RM14 337 D6
Birds Cl Ickleton CB10 3 A3
Ramsden Heath CM11 298 C5
Birds Farm Ave RM5 313 B2
Birds Gn CM5 228 A5
Birk Beck CM1 232 C5
Birkbeck Gdns IG8 310 A8
Birkbeck Rd
Brentwood CM13 295 D3
Ilford IG2 333 D6
Romford RM7 335 D3
Birkdale Ave RM3 315 A3
Birkdale Rise CM3 211 B4
Birkfield Cl IP2 17 A4
Birkfield Dr IP2 16 F2
Birkin Cl CO5 186 C3
Birs Cl SS11 299 D1
Biscay SS2 347 A7
Biscay Cl CB9 9 C7
Bishop Hall La CM1 232 B4
Bishop Mews IP8 16 B2
Bishop Rd
Chelmsford CM1 232 B3
Colchester CO2 135 A3
Bishops Ave
Braintree CM7 128 B3
Dagenham RM6 334 C5
Bishop's Ave CM23 145 F3
Bishops' CE & RC Prim Sch The CM1 232 F6
Bishops Cl SS13 321 A2
Bishop's Cl [8] CB9 8 E8
Bishops Court Gdns CM2 232 E4
Bishops Ct
Greenhithe DA9 376 E2
Romford RM7 335 B7
Bishop's Ct
Canvey Island SS8 364 D3
[7] Haverhill CB9 8 E8
Bishops Dr CO16 220 B6
Bishopsfield CM18 223 E5
Bishopsgarth IP3 17 F4
Bishops Gdns CO16 220 A6
Bishop's Hall Rd CM15 294 B3
Bishop's Hill IP3 17 E4
Bishops La CO5 186 C7
Bishop's La CO9 54 B3
Bishops Park Coll CO16 195 A3
Bishops Park Way CM23 145 B7
Bishops Rd
Stanford-le-H SS17 360 F3
Wickford SS12 321 D3
Bishop's Stortford Bsns Ctr CM23 146 A6
Bishop's Stortford Coll CM23 145 E7
Bishop's Stortford High Sch The CM23 145 F4
Bishop's Stortford Mus* CM23 146 A6
Bishop's Stortford Sta CM23 146 A6
Bishopsteignton SS3 349 D1
Bishops Wlk CM15 316 F8
Bishop William Ward CE Prim Sch The CO6 109 B7
Bisley Cl CO16 195 B6
Bittern Cl Ipswich IP2 16 E3
Kelvedon CO5 158 D2
Bittern Ct E4 287 D2
Bixley Dr IP4 18 E5
Bixley La IP4 18 F5
Bixley Rd IP3 18 D3
Blackacre Rd CM16 267 E2
Black Adder Cotts EN9 243 D8
Blackall Ind Est CM3 279 E1
Black Arches IP8 36 E8
Black Barns IP11 381 A7
Blackberry Gr CM0 242 B3
Blackberry Rd CO3 134 C4
Blackborne Rd RM10 354 B6
Black Boy La CO11 89 A4
Black Bread Cl CM7 128 D3
Blackbrook Rd CO6 109 C7
Black Buoy Hill CO7 164 B7
Blackbush Ave RM6 334 D6
Blackbushe CM23 119 C1
Black Bush La SS17 359 D3
Blackbush Spring CM20 200 A1
Black Chapel La
North End CM6 151 E1
Pleshey CM6 178 E8
Blackdown SS0 347 E1
Blackdown Ave IP5 18 F6
Blackfriars CO10 33 D6
Blackfriars Ct [8] IP4 17 D5
Blackgate Rd SS3 368 G7
Blackheath CO2 163 A8
Blackhorse La CM16 247 D6
Black Horse La IP1 17 C6
Blackhouse La CO10 34 C3
Black La CM7 71 F2
Blacklands Cl CB11 43 C7
Blackley La Braintree CM3 153 F3
Great Notley CM77 154 A4
Black Lion Ct CM17 200 C4
Blacklock CM2 233 A3
Blackman Way CM8 184 A1
Blackmore Ave SS8 364 B2
Blackmore Ct EN9 266 A6
Blackmore Mead CM4 272 F8
Blackmore Prim Sch CM4 250 E1
Blackmore Rd
Blackmore CM1 251 D3
Buckhurst Hill IG9 288 E2
Grays RM17 373 C1
Hook End CM15 272 C5
Ingatestone CM4 273 D6
Kelvedon Hatch CM15 271 F2
Blackmores SS15 340 F6
Blackmore Wlk SS6 324 A2
Blackshots La RM16 373 C5
Blacksmith Cl
Billericay CM12 297 B5
Chelmsford CM1 232 E8
Dagenham RM6 334 C5
Blacksmiths Alley CM4 272 E8
Blacksmiths Cl CM23 145 B5
Black Smiths Cl SG12 197 A7
Blacksmith's Cnr CO6 109 B8
Blacksmith's Cnr CO4 83 D4
Blacksmiths Cotts CM17 224 F4
Blacksmiths Hill CO10 11 B4
Blacksmiths La
Bulmer Tye CO10 32 F2
Shudy Camps CB1 7 C6
Wickham Bishops CM8 212 E5
Blacksmith's La
Harwich CO12 90 F2
Rainham RM13 354 F4
Blacksmiths Way CM21 172 B1
Blackthorn Ave CO4 136 E7
Blackthorn Cl Ipswich IP3 18 E1
Writtle CM1 231 A1
Blackthorn Ct SS16 341 A4
Blackthorne Dr E4 309 D6
Blackthorne Rd SS8 364 C3
Blackthorn Rd
Grays RM16 373 B5
Harwich CO12 90 F2
Hockley SS5 324 F8
Witham CM8 183 E4
Blackthorn Way
Brentwood CM14 316 D5
Tolleshunt Knights CM9 187 A2
Blackwater SS7 344 F4
Blackwater Ave CO4 110 E1
Blackwater Cl
Burnham-on-C CM0 306 C5
Chelmsford CM1 232 C6
Heybridge Basin CM9 237 E3
Rainham RM13 369 E8
Southend-on-S SS3 349 E1
Blackwater Dr CO5 218 A6
Blackwater La CM8 212 B8
Blackwater Way CM7 128 A4
Blackwell Dr CM7 127 C4
Blackwood Chine CM3 301 E6
Bladen Dr IP4 18 F5
Bladon Cl Braintree CM7 127 E7
Tiptree CO5 186 E5
Blaine Dr CO13 170 F7
Blair Cl
Bishop's Stortford CM23 145 C7
Rushmere St A IP4 18 E5
Blair Par CB9 8 E8
Blake Ave IG11 352 F4
Blakeborough Dr RM3 314 E1
Blake Cl Lawford CO11 86 B4
Rainham RM13 354 F4
Blake Ct CM3 301 E6
Blake Dr Braintree CM7 128 C4
Clacton-on-S CO16 195 D6
Blake Hall Cres E11 332 A3
Blake Hall Dr SS11 322 A6
Blake Hall Gdns* CM5 248 D7
Blake Hall Rd
Chipping Ongar CM5 248 A5
Wanstead E11 332 A4
Blake Rd CM8 183 F5
Blakes Ct CM21 172 E2
Blakesley Ho [4] E12 333 A1
Blake Way RM18 379 C5
Blamsters Cres CO9 103 D8
Blanchard Cl CO13 170 A7
Blanchard Gr EN3 265 B1
Blanchard Mews RM3 314 F3
Blanche St IP4 17 D6
Blandford Cl RM7 335 B7
Blandford Cres E4 287 C2
Blandford Rd IP3 18 D3
Blaney Cres E6 352 B2
Blatches Chase
Rayleigh SS2 346 F7
Southend-on-S SS2 347 A8
Blatchford Ho [8] RM10 335 A1
Blaxhall Ct [17] CB9 8 E7
Blenheim Ave IG2 333 A5
Blenheim Chase SS9 346 E3
Blenheim Cl
Bicknacre CM3 256 F2
Braintree CM7 127 E7
Brantham CO11 60 D1
Hockley SS5 324 E8
Romford RM7 335 C7
Sawbridgeworth CM21 200 C8
Upminster RM14 337 E3
Blenheim Cres SS9 346 E2
Blenheim Ct
Bishop's Stortford CM23 145 C7
Clacton-on-S CO15 195 D2
Hornchurch RM12 355 C7
[4] Ipswich IP1 17 A7
[4] Wickford SS11 322 A5
Woodford IG8 310 B3
Woodford IG8 310 C2
Blenheim Dr CO2 163 A8
Blenheim Gdns
Aveley RM15 371 B5
Mayland CM3 261 A1
Blenheim Mews SS9 346 E3
Blenheim Park Cl SS9 346 F4
Blenheim Prim Sch SS9 346 F3
Blenheim Rd
Clacton-on-S CO15 195 D2
Ipswich IP1 17 A7
Pilgrims Hatch CM15 294 A3
Blenheim Way
North Weald Bassett CM16 247 A4
Tiptree CO5 186 F5
Blessing Way IG11 353 C3
Bletchington Ct DA17 369 A2
Blewetts Cotts RM13 354 F2
Blickling Cl IP2 17 B2
Blickling Rd CM77 154 C8
Bligh Rd DA11 379 A1
Blind La Easthorpe CO2 160 B4
Eight Ash G CO6 134 A8
Goldhanger CM9 238 C7
Howe Green CM2 255 F4
Little Burstead CM12 318 B5
Mundon CM9 259 C2
Tolleshunt Knights CM9 187 B1
West Hanningfield CM2 276 F5
Bliss Cl CM8 211 F7
Blithbury Rd RM9 353 B6
Blithe Ct CO7 164 B8
Blockhouse Rd RM17 378 C8
Blofield Rd IP11 381 A4
Blois Meadows Bsns Ctr CB9 27 C8
Blois Rd
Steeple Bumpstead CB9 27 D8
Sturmer CB9 9 F1
Blomville Rd RM8 334 E1
Bloom Cl CO13 170 F6
Bloomfield Ave CO13 170 E7
Bloomfield Cres IG2 333 B5
Bloomfield Ho CM7 128 A3
Bloomfield St IP4 18 B6
Bloomfields The IG11 352 C6
Blooms Hall La CO10 2 F8
Blossom Cl RM9 353 F4
Blott Rise CM8 211 F8
Blountswood Rd
Hockley SS5 324 A8
Hullbridge SS5 323 F6
Blower Cl SS6 323 F3
Blows Cotts RM15 371 D5
Blue Anchor La RM18 374 E1
Bluebell Ave CO16 195 C4
Bluebell Cl Ipswich IP2 16 E4
Romford RM7 335 E2
Witham CM8 183 E3
Bluebell Gn [5] CM1 232 E7
Bluebell Way
Colchester CO4 109 C2
Ilford IG1 352 B6
Bluebell Wood CM12 296 E4
Blueberry Cl IG8 310 A4
Bluebird La RM10 354 A5
Bluebridge Cotts CO9 77 A1
Bluebridge Ind Est CO9 77 B1
Bluegate La IP9 60 B7
Bluegate Pk CM14 316 B7
Bluehouse Ave CO16 195 A4
Blue House Farm Chase CM3 303 B7
Bluehouse Rd E4 309 E7
Bluemans CM16 247 D7
Bluemans End CM16 247 D7
Blue Mill La CM9 235 E4
Blue Mills Hill CM8 212 B7
Blue Rd CO5 186 C5
Bluestem Rd IP3 38 E8
Blunden Cl RM8 334 C3
Blundens The CO6 56 C6
Blunt's Hall Dr CM8 183 D1
Blunts Hall Rd CM8 183 D1
Blunts Wall Rd CM12 296 E1
Blyford Rd CO16 195 A4
Blyford Way IP11 381 A4
Blyth Ave SS3 368 C7
Blyth Cl IP2 17 A1
Blythe La CO7 164 B8
Blythe Rd
Hoddesdon EN11 221 D5
Stanford-le-H SS17 360 E4
Blythe Way Maldon CM9 259 A8
South Benfleet SS7 344 C7
Blyth's Mdw CM7 127 F3
Blyth's Way CM77 126 F2
Blythswood Rd IG3 334 A4
Blyth Wlk RM14 337 E5
Blythwood Gdns CM24 119 D6
Blyton Cl SS12 321 D5
Boadicea Cotts CO8 79 F6
Boadicea Way CO2 135 C4
Boar Cl IG7 312 A5
Boarded Row SS4 328 A5
Boardman Ave E4 287 B4
Boars Tye Rd CM8 156 D6
Boatman Cl IP8 36 E8
Bobbing Cl SS4 325 F2
Bobbingworth Mill CM5 248 A7
Bobbits La IP9 36 F8
Bobbits Way CO7 164 C8
Bober Ct CO2 163 B7
Bocking Church Street Prim Sch CM7 127 F8
Bocking End CM7 127 F3
Bockingham Gn SS13 343 A8
Bocking Pl CM7 127 F3
Bockings Elm Par CO16 195 B5
Bocking's Gr CO16 195 B5
Bodell Cl RM16 373 B3
Bodiam Cl Basildon SS13 343 B6
Ipswich IP3 18 D4
Bodiam Rd IP3 18 D4
Bodiam Wlk [3] CB9 8 E8
Bodle Ave DA10 377 E1
Bodley Cl CM16 245 F1
Bodmin Rd CM1 232 D5
Bogmoor Rd SG8 39 A8
Bohemia Chase SS9 346 D5
Bohun Cl CM3 180 F7
Boiler Ho The SS4 325 E2
Bois Field Terr CO9 76 E2
Bois Hall Gdns CO9 76 F3
Boley Dr CO15 196 A4
Boleyn Cl Billericay CM12 297 A5
Grays RM16 372 F3
Loughton IG10 288 E3
Southend-on-S SS9 346 C7
Boleyn Ct IG9 288 B1
Boleyn Gdns
Brentwood CM13 317 A7
Dagenham RM10 354 C5
Boleyns Ave CM7 127 F6
Boleyn Way Boreham CM3 209 F1
Clacton-on-S CO15 220 F8
Haverhill CB9 8 D7
Redbridge IG6 311 C4
Boley Rd CO6 106 A8
Bolford St CM6 69 F2
Bolingbroke Cl CM3 180 F7
Bolney Dr SS9 346 C7
Bolton La IP4 17 D6
Boltons The IG8 310 A6
Bommel Ave SS8 365 A3
Bonchurch Ave SS9 346 D2
Bonchurch Ct [20] RM19 371 B1
Bonds Cotts CM5 204 A1
Bond St Chelmsford CM2 232 C2
Grays RM17 378 C8
Ipswich IP4 17 D5
Bonet Mews RM11 336 E3
Bonham Cl CO15 196 A5
Bonham Gdns RM8 334 D2
Bonham Rd RM8 334 D1
Bonington Chase CM1 232 E6
Bonington Rd RM12 355 D7
Bonks Hill CM21 172 D1
Bonner Wlk RM16 372 F3
Bonneting La CM23 92 B8
Bonnington Rd IP3 17 F1
Bonningtons CM13 317 B7
Bonnygate SS14 342 D7
Bonnygate Prim Sch RM15 372 B8
Boomes Ind Est RM13 354 F1
Boone Pl CM8 184 A2
Boons Cl CM3 233 E8
Bootham Cl CM12 296 F1
Bootham Rd CM12 296 F1
Booth Ave CO4 136 C8
Boothby Ct E4 309 C7
Booth Pl CM0 306 C5
Booths Ct CM13 295 B3
Borda Cl CM1 232 A5
Border Edge Ho [6] CM14 316 C6
Border's La IG10 289 B5
Boreham Cl SS11 322 B5
Borehamgate CO10 33 F7
Boreham Ind Est CM3 209 F2
Boreham Prim Sch CM3 233 F8
Boreham Rd
Great Leighs CM3 181 B7
Little Waltham CM3 181 B2
Borland Cl DA9 377 A2
Borley Ct RM16 374 D7
Borley Rd CO10 15 B4
Borman Cl SS9 347 A6
Borough La CB11 43 D8
Borough The CM5 248 F2
Borradale Ct CB9 27 B6
Borrett Ave SS8 364 A4
Borrowdale Ave IP4 17 E8
Borrowdale Cl
Redbridge IG4 332 E7
Thundersley SS7 344 F6
Borrowdale Rd
Thundersley SS7 344 F6
Thundersley SS7 344 F7
Borwick La Basildon CM11 320 F4
Wickford CM11,SS12 321 A4
Bosanquet Rd EN11 221 C8
Boscawen Gdns CM7 128 C4
Boscombe Ave
Grays RM17 373 D2
Hornchurch RM11 336 D4
Wickford SS12 320 F8
Boscombe Ct CO15 196 F6
Boscombe Mews SS2 367 B8
Boscombe Rd SS2 348 B1
Bosgrove E4 309 C8
Boss Hall Bsns Pk IP1 16 E7
Boss Hall Rd IP1 16 E7
Bostock Rd IP2 17 C1
Boston Ave Rayleigh SS6 323 B4
Southend-on-S SS2 347 F1
Boston Lofts [2] SS2 347 F1
Boston Rd IP4 17 F7
Boswell Ave SS4 325 D5
Boswells Dr CM2 232 C2
Boswells Sch The CM1 232 D6
Bosworth Cl SS5 324 F4
Bosworth Cres RM3 314 C4
Bosworth Ho DA8 369 E1
Bosworth Rd
Dagenham RM10 335 A1
Southend-on-S SS9 346 C7
Botanical Way CO16 194 A5
Botany Cotts RM19 371 A1
Botany Dr CM7 128 D3
Botany La CO16 168 B5
Botany Terr RM19 371 A1
Botany Way RM19 371 B1
Botelers SS16 341 E4
Boteley Cl E4 309 D8
Botney Hill Rd CM12 318 D4
Boucheries Pl CO5 159 D2
Bouchers Mead CM1 232 F7
Bouchiers Barn Visitors Ctr* CO6 130 D7
Bouchier Wlk [2] RM13 355 A6
Boudicca Mews [5] CM2 232 B1
Boudicca Wlk CO7 137 C3
Bouldrewood Rd SS7 344 B5
Boulevard The
[3] Redbridge IG8 311 A3
Rochford SS4 325 F3
Boulter Gdns RM13 355 A7
Boulton Cotts CM9 237 B5
Boulton Rd RM8 334 F2
Boult Rd SS15 341 C8
Boundary Cl IG3 352 E8
Boundary Dr CM13 295 E2
Boundary Rd
Barking IG11 352 C3
Barking IG11 352 D4
Bishop's Stortford CM23 146 A5
Colchester CO4 136 F4
Romford RM1 336 A5
Southend-on-S SS9 346 B8
Sturmer CB9 9 D5
Upminster RM14 337 B2
Wivenhoe CO7 137 A4
Bounderby Gr CM1 231 E7
Bounstead Hill CO2 162 C5
Bounstead Rd CO2 162 D7
Bourchier Ave CM7 128 D5
Bourchier Way CO9 103 D8
Bourne Ave SS15 341 A8
Bournebridge Cl CM13 295 E2
Bournebridge Hill CO9 103 B6
Bournebridge La RM4 291 B2
Bourne Cl Basildon SS15 341 A8
Halstead CO9 103 D8
Bourne Ct Braintree CM7 128 D1
Colchester CO2 136 A4
Wanstead E11 332 A6
Woodford IG8 310 D1
Bourne End RM11 337 A4
Bourne Gdns E4 309 B6
Bourne Hill IP2 37 B7
Bourne Ho IG9 310 D7
Bourne Mill* CO2 136 B4
Bournemouth Park Prim Sch SS2 348 B2
Bournemouth Park Rd SS2 348 B2
Bournemouth Rd CO15 196 F6
Bourne Rd Colchester CO2 136 B4
Haverhill CB9 9 B8
West Bergholt CO6 108 E2
Bournes Green Chase SS3 349 B1
Bournes Green Jun & Inf Sch SS1 368 B8
Bourne Terr IP2 37 B8
Bourne The CM23 146 A8
Bouvel Dr CM0 306 B8
Bouverie Rd CM2 254 B8
Bovey Way RM15 372 B8
Bovills Way CO16 168 C1
Bovingdon Rd CM7 101 D2
Bovinger Way SS1 348 F1
Bow Arrow La
Dartford DA1 376 A1
Dartford DA2 376 B1
Bowbank Cl SS3 349 F1
Bowden Dr RM11 336 E3
Bowdens La CO6 80 F7
Bower Cl RM5 313 D3
Bower Ct CM16 268 A7
Bower Farm Rd RM4 313 D7
Bower Gdns CM9 236 F3
Bower Hall Dr CB9 27 B6
Bower Hall La CO5 190 F1
Bower Hill CM16 268 A7
Bower Hill Ind Est CM16 268 A7
Bower La SS14 342 E8
Bowerman Rd RM16 374 A2
Bower Park Sch RM1 313 E4
Bowers Cl CM8 156 E3
Bowers Court Dr SS13 343 F5
Bowers Ho [5] IG11 352 B5
Bowers Rd SS7 344 D5
Bower Vale CM16 268 A7
Bowes Ct [17] DA2 376 B1
Bowes Dr CM5 249 A4
Bowes Ho CM5 249 A4
Bowes Rd Dagenham RM8 353 C8
Wivenhoe CO7 137 D1
Bowfell Ct SS16 341 A5
Bowfell Dr SS16 341 A5
Bowhay CM13 317 B8
Bowland Dr IP8 16 C1
Bowland Rd IG8 310 C4
Bowlers Croft SS14 320 F2
Bowling Cl [14] CM23 145 F6
Bowling Green Ct IP11 381 E4
Bowls The IG7 311 F7
Bowman Ave SS9 346 B6
Bowmans Pk CO9 51 E4
Bowmont Cl CM13 295 B3
Bown Cl RM18 379 B5
Bowness Way RM12 355 A7
Bowsers La CB10 5 C3
Bowthorpe Cl IP1 17 B7
Bowyer Ct [4] E4 287 C1
Box Cl SS15 319 D1
Boxford Cl SS6 322 F3
Boxford Ct
Felixstowe IP11 381 A4
Haverhill CB9 8 E7
Boxhouse La CO7 84 C5
Box La IG11 353 C3
Boxley La CM22 175 D8
Box Mill La CO9 76 E3
Boxmoor Rd RM5 313 C5
Boxoll Rd RM9 334 F1
Boxted Ave CO16 195 C4
Boxted CE Prim Sch CO4 82 F7
Boxted Church Rd CO6 82 C5
Boxted Cl IG9 288 E1
Boxted Rd Colchester CO4 109 E6
Great Horkesley CO6 82 C3
Boxted Straight Rd CO4 83 A5
Boyce Gn SS7 344 D2

Boyce Hill Cl SS9 ....346 B5
Boyce Rd
Southend-on-S SS3 ....348 E8
Stanford-le-H SS17 ....360 C3
Boyce View Dr SS7 ....344 C2
Boyd Cl ① CM23 ....146 B8
Boyd Ct SS12 ....321 F5
Boydell's Dairy Farm*
CM7 ....100 E8
Boyden Cl SS2 ....348 F2
Boydin Cl CM8 ....211 E8
Boydlands IP9 ....35 A1
Boyes Cl SS7 ....344 C3
Boyle Ho ⑨ DA17 ....369 A3
Boyles Court Cotts
CM14 ....316 A3
Boyles Ct CO2 ....163 B7
Boyne Dr CM1 ....232 D6
Boyne Rd RM10 ....335 A1
Boyton Cl SS7 ....345 A5
Boyton Rd IP3 ....18 B1
Boytons SS5 ....164 A5
Boytons Acre CB11 ....43 D8
Boyton Vineyard* CO10 ....10 D5
Brabant Rd CM3 ....303 A7
Braber Gdns CM11 ....298 C4
Bracelet Cl SS17 ....360 F5
Brace Wlk CM3 ....301 E5
Brackenbury Cl IP1 ....17 B8
Bracken Cl IG10 ....289 B8
Brackendale CM11 ....297 D2
Brackendale Ave SS13 ....343 C4
Brackendale Cl SS5 ....324 E7
Brackendale Ct SS13 ....343 C4
Bracken Dell SS6 ....323 E3
Brackenden Dr CM1 ....232 D7
Bracken Dr IG7 ....311 C4
Bracken End IG6 ....311 F7
Bracken Mews
Chingford E4 ....287 C1
Romford RM7 ....335 B5
Brackens Dr CM14 ....316 D5
Brackens The CO4 ....110 B3
Bracken Way
Abberton CO5 ....163 B2
Thundersley SS7 ....345 A4
Brackley Cl IP11 ....381 C5
Brackley Cres SS13 ....343 A8
Brackley Ho ④ RM3 ....314 F4
Brackley Sq IG8 ....310 D3
Bracknell Ho ⑤ RM3 ....314 F4
Bracks La CO6 ....131 F3
Bradbourne Rd RM17 ....378 B8
Bradbourne Way SS11 ....343 C5
Bradbrook Cotts CO6 ....108 F4
Bradbury Dr CM7 ....127 D3
Braddick Cl CM15 ....217 C7
Braddock Cl RM5 ....313 C4
Braddy Ct CO5 ....158 C2
Bradfield Cl ⑪ RM18 ....371 B1
Bradfield Dr IG11 ....353 A7
Bradfield Ho IG8 ....311 A4
Bradfield Prim Sch CO11 ....87 E1
Bradford Bury SS9 ....346 C6
Bradford Rd IG1 ....333 E3
Bradford Ct CM7 ....128 A4
Bradford St
Braintree CM7 ....128 A4
Chelmsford CM2 ....232 A1
Brading Ave CO15 ....196 A1
Brading Cres E11 ....332 B2
Bradleigh Ave RM17 ....373 C2
Bradley Ave SS7 ....344 F5
Bradley Cl
Canvey Island SS8 ....364 A5
Great Dunmow CM6 ....123 C2
Thundersley SS7 ....344 F5
Bradley Comm CM7 ....113 C3
Bradley Gn SS13 ....321 C1
Bradley Link SS7 ....344 F5
Bradley Mews ① CB10 ....22 F2
Bradley Rd SS7 ....344 F5
Bradley Way SS4 ....325 F1
Bradshaw Rd RM16 ....373 A5
Bradwall Ave RM10 ....335 A2
Bradwall Ct RM12 ....155 B6
Bradwell Ct
Braintree CM7 ....155 C8
Brentwood CM13 ....295 C3
Bradwell Gn ③ CM13 ....295 C3
Bradwell Ho SS11 ....321 F7
Bradwell Power Sta Visitor
Ctr* CM0 ....242 A6
Bradwell Rd
Buckhurst Hill IG9 ....288 E2
Steeple CM0 ....262 A3
St Lawrence CM0 ....262 E6
Tillingham CM0 ....263 E6
Brady Ave IG10 ....289 C7
Brady Ct RM8 ....334 D3
Brady Prim Sch CO11 ....370 C8
Braemar Ave CM2 ....254 B8
Braemar Cres SS9 ....346 A2
Braemar Rd RM11 ....337 A5
Braemar Wlk SS13 ....343 B6
Braemores SS8 ....363 F5
Braemore Cl CO4 ....110 D3
Braeside Sch
Buckhurst Hill IG9 ....288 B1
Buckhurst Hill IG9 ....310 C8
Braeside
Billericay CM12 ....297 A5
Grays RM16 ....372 F4

Braintree Freepost Sta
CM7 ....128 B1
Braintree Mus & Heritage
Ctr* ⑩ CM7 ....127 F3
Braintree Rd
Cressing CM77 ....155 C7
Dagenham RM10 ....335 A1
Felsted CM6 ....152 C6
Gosfield CO9 ....102 E5
Great Bardfield CM7 ....72 B1
Great Dunmow CM6 ....124 A1
Shalford CM7 ....100 E6
Terling CM3 ....181 E5
Wethersfield CM7 ....73 D2
Witham CM8 ....183 F4
Braintree Sta CM7 ....128 A2
Braintree Town FC CM7 ....128 C2
Brain Valley Ave CM7 ....155 B6
Brairwood CT SS9 ....346 D5
Braiswick CO4 ....109 C4
Braiswick La CO4 ....109 D4
Braiswick Pl SS15 ....341 B8
Braithwaite Ave RM7 ....335 A4
Braithwaite Dr CM6 ....109 F2
Brambar Ct ⑥ DA2 ....376 B1
Bramble Cl SS2 ....346 B7
Bramble Cres SS7 ....346 A5
Bramble Croft DA8 ....369 C2
Brambledown CO5 ....218 C7
Bramble Dr IP3 ....18 E1
Bramble La
Little Dunmow CM6 ....151 F8
Upminster RM14 ....356 D4
Bramble Rd
Canvey Island SS8 ....364 C3
Hadleigh SS7 ....345 F6
Southend-on-S SS9 ....346 B7
Witham CM8 ....183 E4
Bramble Rise CM20 ....199 C1
Brambles CO14 ....171 B7
Brambles The
Basildon SS13 ....341 A8
Bishop's Stortford CM23 ....145 C6
Braintree CM7 ....127 E3
Chigwell IG7 ....311 C4
Colchester CO3 ....134 F3
Southminster CM0 ....284 D3
Steeple CM0 ....284 A7
Bramble Tye SS15 ....319 F1
Bramblewood ① IP8 ....16 C2
Bramblings The CO4 ....109 D6
Bramerton Rd SS6 ....329 D6
Bramfield La CO16 ....324 A2
Bramfield Rd W SS6 ....323 F2
Bramford La IP1 ....16 F8
Bramford Rd IP1 ....16 D1
Bramley Chase CM3 ....18 B7
Bramley Cl Alresford CO7 ....165 B8
Braintree CM7 ....128 A1
⑨ Woodford IG8 ....310 C3
Bramley Cres ⑩ IG2 ....333 A5
Bramley Ct
Hadleigh SS7 ....345 E2
Bramley Gdns IG6 ....333 C8
Bramley Ho IG2 ....333 A5
Bramley Link SS15 ....340 E6
Bramley Way SS15 ....340 E6
Bramley Wlk CM8 ....183 F4
Bramwoods Rd CM2 ....254 C6
Brancaster Dr CM7 ....154 C6
Brancaster Pl IG10 ....288 F6
Brancaster Rd IG2 ....333 E5
Branch Rd Hadleigh SS7 ....345 E2
Redbridge IG6 ....312 B5
Brand Cl CM7 ....127 F7
Brand Dr CO5 ....163 B3
Brandenburg Rd SS8 ....364 D5
Brandesburton Sq ④ IG8 ....311 A3
Brandon Cl
Billericay CM12 ....297 A5
Southend-on-S SS0 ....347 A4
Bramshill Cl IG7 ....311 E5
Brandon Cl
Great Baddow CM2 ....254 F8
Bramston Gn CM8 ....183 F4
Bramston Link SS15 ....340 E6
Bramston Way SS15 ....340 E6
Bramston Wlk CM8 ....183 F4
Brandon Groves Ave
RM15 ....357 D2
Brandon Rd
Braintree CM7 ....127 D2
Felixstowe IP11 ....381 A4
Brandville Gdns IG6 ....333 B8
Bran End Fields CM6 ....124 D7
Branfil Inf & Jun Schs
RM14 ....356 A8
Branfil Rd RM14 ....337 B2
Branksome Ave
Hockley SS5 ....324 E8
Stanford-le-H SS17 ....360 E4
Wickford SS12 ....320 F7
Branksome Cl SS12 ....348 C1
Bransby Gdns IP4 ....18 A5
Branscombe Cl CO13 ....170 C5
Branscombe Gdns SS1 ....349 B1
Branscombe Sq SS1 ....349 B1

Branscombe Wlk SS1 ....349 B1
Branston Ct CO16 ....195 C4
Branstone Ct ⑰ RM7 ....335 B5
Branston Rd CO15 ....195 D3
Brantham Hill Ind Est
CO11 ....86 C8
Brantham Mill Ind Est
CO11 ....86 B7
Branton Rd DA9 ....377 F3
Brasenose Ct CM12 ....322 D7
Brathertons Ct CM12 ....296 F3
Braxted Cl SS4 ....325 C4
Braxted La
Great Braxted CM8 ....185 C1
Great Totham CM8,CM9 ....213 D8
Braxted Park Rd
Rivenhall CM8 ....185 E2
Tiptree CO5 ....185 C2
Braxted Rd CM8 ....213 A6
Brayds ⑩ SS15 ....341 A6
Braybrooke SS14 ....342 B6
Braybrooke Gdns CB11 ....43 D8
Brayburn Ct SS10 ....189 C4
Bray Ct SS3 ....349 E2
Brayes Mews SS4 ....325 F1
Brayfield Ct SS9 ....346 E4
Brays Grove Sch CM18 ....224 B6
Brays La SS4 ....325 E5
Brays Mead CM18 ....224 B6
Brays Springs E19 ....265 C5
Braziers Cl CM2 ....254 C3
Braziers Quay CM23 ....146 A6
Brazier's Wood Rd IP3 ....38 B8
Breach Barns Cvn Pk
EN9 ....244 B1
Breach Barns La EN9 ....243 F1
Breachfield Rd CO2 ....135 C2
Breach La Dagenham RM9 ....354 A2
Great Easton CM6 ....97 B2
Bread & Cheese Hill SS7 ....344 E5
Break Egg Hill CM4 ....297 D3
Breakneck Hill DA9 ....377 B2
Bream Ct CO4 ....110 F1
Bream Gdns E6 ....352 A2
Breamore Ct IG3 ....333 F2
Breamore Rd IG3 ....333 F2
Breams Field SS16 ....341 C4
Breco Ho IG11 ....353 B2
Brecon Cl CO4 ....347 E1
Brecon Cl Basildon SS13 ....343 C8
Brede Ct E6 ....352 A2
Bredfield Cl IP11 ....381 B5
Bree Ave CO6 ....132 E3
Bree Hill CM3 ....301 C6
Brempsons SS14 ....342 A7
Brendans Cl RM11 ....356 D3
Brendon SS15 ....341 D5
Brendon Cl CO5 ....186 D4
Brendon Dr Halstead CO9 ....103 F8
Rushmere St A IP5 ....18 F6
Brendon Gdns IG2 ....333 D6
Brendon Pl CM1 ....231 E1
Brendon Rd SS13 ....343 B8
Brendon Way SS0 ....347 A5
Brennan Cl CM3 ....280 F6
Brennan Rd RM18 ....379 B5
Brent Ave CM3 ....259 D2
Brent Cl Dartford DA2 ....376 B1
Frinton-on-S CO13 ....170 F7
Witham CM8 ....183 E2
Brent Ct RM2 ....336 C8
Brentfield Rd DA1 ....376 A1
Brentford Cl SS13 ....321 C1
Brenthall Twrs CM17 ....224 C6
Brenthleigh Ct CM14 ....316 A7
Brent Way DA2 ....376 B1
Brentwood Cathedral*
CM14 ....316 D8
Brentwood Com Hospl
CM15 ....294 E1
Brentwood Cty High Sch
CM14 ....316 D7
Brentwood Pl CM15 ....294 D1
Brentwood Rd
Bulphan CM14 ....315 A2
Chipping Ongar CM5,CM15 ....271 B8
Grays RM16 ....374 C4
Holland-on-S CO15 ....317 D4
Ingrave CM13 ....317 D4
Orsett RM16,RM14 ....359 B4
Romford RM1,RM2 ....336 B5
West Horndon CM13 ....339 E8
Brentwood Sch CM15 ....316 D8
Brentwood Sta CM14 ....316 D7
Brentwood Ursuline Convent
High Sch CM14 ....316 D8
Bressey Gr E18 ....309 F1
Bressingham Gdns CM1 ....301 C7
Bretons Cl SS15 ....341 B6
Bretons Cotts RM13 ....354 F6
Brett Cl IP1 ....16 E8
Bretten Cl CO16 ....195 A4
Brettenham Ave E17 ....309 A2
Brettenham Cres E17 ....17 D8
Brettenham Dr SS1 ....367 E8
Brettenham Rd E17 ....309 A2
Brett Gdns RM9 ....353 E5
Bretts Cotts RM15 ....185 F3
Bretts Villas CM8 ....203 C8
Brevet Cl RM19 ....371 D2
Brewers Cl CM23 ....145 C7
Brewers Fields CM2 ....284 D4
Brewery Fields CM2 ....255 A5
Brewery La CM24 ....119 E7
Brewery Rd EN11 ....221 B6
Brewery The RM1 ....335 G6
Brewery Wlk ② RM1 ....335 G6
Brewery Yd CM4 ....319 F7
Brewhouse Yd ⑧ DA11 ....389 F3
Brewood Rd RM8 ....353 B6
Brewster Cl CO10 ....34 C4
Breydon Way IP3 ....38 D7

Brian Bishop Cl CO14 ....171 B8
Brian Cl Chelmsford CM2 ....254 B6
Hornchurch RM11 ....355 B8
Brian Rd RM6 ....334 C6
Briar Cl Billericay CM11 ....319 C7
Buckhurst Hill IG9 ....310 D8
Hockley SS5 ....324 F4
Briardale Ave CO2 ....90 F3
Briarfields CO13 ....170 C8
Briarhayes IP2 ....17 B2
Briarhayes Cl IP2 ....17 B3
Briarleas Gdns RM14 ....337 E4
Briar Rd Ardleigh CO7 ....112 A4
Romford RM3 ....314 D5
Briary The Harlow CM18 ....223 E4
Kelvedon Hatch CM15 ....293 E8
Briars Wlk RM3 ....314 F1
Briarswood
Chelmsford CM3 ....364 A5
Briar View CM11 ....319 D7
Briarview Ct E4 ....309 D4
Briarwood CM5 ....271 F2
Briarwood Ave CO15 ....196 F6
Briarwood Dr SS9 ....346 C6
Briarwood End CO4 ....110 B3
Briary The SS2 ....321 B7
Brices Way CO10 ....2 B5
Briceway SS7 ....360 F4
Brickbarns CM3 ....180 F7
Brickburn Cl CM6 ....152 C4
Brick Cotts SS9 ....62 F4
Brick End CM6 ....265 F6
Brick Kiln Cl CM7 ....378 A8
Brickhouse Cl CO6 ....78 A3
Brick House La CM3 ....209 F1
Brick House Rd CM9 ....214 E7
Brick Kiln La
Great Horkesley CO6 ....109 C7
Rickling Green CB11 ....66 D1
Stebbing CM6 ....124 D7
Thorrington CO7 ....165 E5
Brick Kiln Rd
Chelmsford CM2 ....255 C7
Colchester CO1 ....109 E1
Harkstead IP9 ....63 C5
Brick Kiln Way CM7 ....127 C3
Brickmakers La CO4 ....109 F2
Brickman's Hill CO11 ....87 A8
Brick Row SS8 ....19 D3
Brickspring La CM9 ....213 D7
Brick St CO3 ....108 B1
Brickwall Cl CM0 ....306 C4
Brickwall Ct SS16 ....105 B6
Bridewell Ind Est CO10 ....12 C8
Bridewell St CO10 ....12 C8
Bridgecote La SS15 ....319 F2
Bridge Cotts
Cavendish CO10 ....1 D2
Ridgewell CO9 ....29 B7
Southend-on-S SS3 ....368 D8
South Woodham F CM3 ....279 B1
Bridge Croft CM3 ....179 F2
Bridge Ct Grays RM17 ....378 B8
Maldon CM9 ....237 A3
Bridge End Chingford E17 ....309 C2
Newport CB11 ....43 A2
Bridge End La CM77 ....154 C8
Bridge End St CM77 ....154 C8
Bridgefield Cl CM24 ....136 C7
Bridge Foot CO10 ....33 D6
Bridgeford Ho ⑨ CM23 ....145 F6
Bridge Hall Rd CM7 ....129 C3
Bridge Hill Epping CM16 ....248 A7
Fordham CM6 ....107 C7
Bridge House Ct SS13 ....343 B2
Bridge House La CM23 ....282 A6
Bridgemans Gn CM3 ....242 B8
Bridgemarsh La CM3 ....304 F8
Bridgend Ct CM3 ....301 E8
Bridge Par SS9 ....296 F3
Bridges Dr DA1 ....376 B2
Bridges Ct SS2 ....367 F8
Bridge St Basildon SS15 ....319 F2
Bishop's Stortford CM23 ....145 F7
Bures CO8 ....55 E2
Coggeshall CO6 ....130 F1
Finchingfield CM7 ....72 C6
Great Bardfield CM7 ....72 A5
Great Yeldham CO9 ....30 A8
Halstead CO9 ....76 E2
Ipswich IP1 ....17 C5
Manningtree CO11 ....86 D4
Moreton CM5 ....226 C2
Rayleigh SS6 ....323 C5
Saffron Walden CB10 ....22 D2
Witham CM8 ....183 F1
Writtle CM1 ....231 C1
Bridge Terr ① CO10 ....13 F8

Bridge View DA9 ....377 B3
Bridgeview Cl IG6 ....311 D4
Bridge View Ind Est
RM9 ....376 F8
Bridgeway EN11 ....352 F5
Bridgeways EN11 ....221 B6
Bridgewick Rd CM0 ....286 B6
Bridgewater Cl RM3 ....314 D5
Bridgewater Dr SS0 ....347 A4
Bridgewater Rd Ipswich IP2 ....16 D2
Romford RM3 ....314 D5
Bridgewater Wlk RM3 ....314 D5
Bridle Cl EN11 ....197 A2
Bridle Path The IG8 ....309 E3
Bridlewalk CO13 ....297 D6
Bridle Way SE12 ....197 A6
Bridle Way (N) EN11 ....197 B2
Bridle Way (S) EN11 ....197 A1
Bridon Cl CM23 ....278 B6
Bridport Ave Ipswich IP3 ....335 B5
Bridport Rd RM1 ....232 D5
Bridport Way CM7 ....128 D4
Brierley Ave CO5 ....218 E7
Brierley Cl RM11 ....336 C5
Brierley Paddocks CO5 ....218 E7
Brigadier Way SS3 ....368 H6
Brighstone Ct ③ RM17 ....371 B1
Bright Cl CO10 ....195 D6
Brighten Rd SS1 ....366 F8
Brightlingsea Ct CO7 ....136 F4
Brightlingsea Inf Sch
CO7 ....192 E6
Brightlingsea Jun Sch
CO7 ....192 E6
Brightlingsea Mus CO7 ....192 F6
Brightlingsea Rd
Thorrington CO7 ....165 E3
Wivenhoe CO7 ....137 C4
Brighton Ave E17 ....367 D8
Brighton Rd
Holland-on-S CO15 ....196 H6
Wallend E6 ....352 A2
Brights Ave RM13 ....354 F6
Brightside Billericay CM12 ....296 E4
Kirby Cross CO13 ....170 E7
Brightside Cl CM12 ....296 F4
Brightside Prim Sch
CM12 ....296 F5
Brightwell Ave SS0 ....347 D2
Brightwell Cl IP11 ....381 A4
Brigstock Rd DA17 ....369 B2
Brimfield Rd RM19 ....371 D2
Brimsdown Ave SS15 ....341 B6
Brimstone Ct CM7 ....154 E8
Brimstone Rd IP8 ....36 E8
Brindles
Canvey Island SS8 ....363 F5
Hornchurch RM11 ....336 E7
Brindles Cl
Brentwood CM14 ....317 C8
Linford SS17 ....375 A2
Brindley Rd CO15 ....196 B8
Brindwood Rd E4 ....309 A7
Bringey The CM2 ....255 A6
Brinkley Cres CO4 ....110 D2
Brinkley Green Rd CO4 ....110 A5
Brinkley La CO4 ....110 B5
Brinkley Pl CO4 ....109 F5
Brinkworth Cl SS15 ....324 F6
Brinkworth Rd SS15 ....332 E8
Brinsmead RM3 ....315 A1
Brisbane Ho RM18 ....378 F6
Brisbane Rd Ilford IG1 ....333 C3
Ipswich IP4 ....18 A6
Brisbane Way CO2 ....136 A1
Briscoe Prim Sch SS13 ....343 B8
Briscoe Rd Basildon SS13 ....343 B7
Hoddesdon RM13 ....221 A8
Rainham RM13 ....355 D3
Briscoe Rd CO7 ....137 B1
Brise Cl CM7 ....128 E4
Bristol Cl SS16 ....323 C5
Bristol Ct CM8 ....156 E3
Bristol Hill IP9 ....81 B8
Bristol Ho ② IG11 ....353 A5
Bristol Rd Colchester CO1 ....136 A8
Southend-on-S SS2 ....347 D6
Bristowe Ave CO2 ....255 A6
Bristowe Dr RM16 ....374 D7
Britannia Bsns Pk SS2 ....347 B7
Britannia Cl EN11 ....297 B2
Britannia Cres CO7 ....137 B1
Britannia Ct
Basildon SS13 ....321 C1
Wivenhoe CO7 ....137 B1
Britannia Lodge SS0 ....366 C8
Britannia Pl ② SS2 ....343 C5
Britannia Rd
Brentwood CM14 ....316 C5
Ilford RM1 ....333 B1
Ipswich IP4 ....18 B6
Britannia Way CO7 ....137 B1
Britannia Wlk CM8 ....156 F4
British Legion Rd E4 ....309 F8
Britric Cl CM3 ....151 F6
Brittain Rd RM8 ....334 F1
Brittania Prim Sch IP4 ....18 B5
Britten Cl
Great Baddow CM2 ....254 F6
Witham CM8 ....211 F7
Britten Ct SS3 ....323 D1
Britton Cl CM1 ....205 E8
Brittons Sch & Tech Coll
RM13 ....354 F5
Brixham Cl
Clacton-on-S CO15 ....220 E8
Rayleigh SS6 ....323 D5
Brixham Gdns IG3 ....352 F7

Brixton La CB11,CM23 ....93 B6
Brixton Cl SS15 ....324 E6
Broadclyst Ave SS9 ....346 D5
Broadclyst Cl SS11 ....349 B1
Broadclyst Gdns SS11 ....349 B1
Broadcroft Cres CB9 ....8 F8
Broadcroft
Bishop's Stortford CM23 ....118 F2
Harlow CM20 ....199 C1
High Roding CM6 ....176 E7
Broadfield Cl RM1 ....335 F6
Broadfield Rd CM22 ....148 E7
Broadfields
High Wych CM21 ....172 B1
Wivenhoe CO7 ....137 C3
Broadfields Prim Sch
CM20 ....199 E1
Broadford Way IG9 ....310 C7
Broadgate EN9 ....265 F7
Broadhope Ave SS17 ....375 C8
Broadhurst Ave IG3 ....352 F8
Broadhurst Gdns IG7 ....311 C6
Broadhurst Wlk ③ RM13 ....355 E6
Broad La CO6 ....82 C2
Broadlands
Frinton-on-S CO13 ....170 C3
Grays RM17 ....372 F1
Thundersley SS7 ....345 A6
Broadlands Ave
Hockley SS5 ....324 F6
Rayleigh SS6 ....323 D3
Broadlands Rd SS5 ....324 F6
Broadlands Way
Colchester CO4 ....110 B1
Rushmere St A IP4 ....18 F5
Broadlawn SS9 ....346 C4
Broadleaf Ave CM23 ....145 D4
Broadley Rd CM19 ....222 E3
Broadmayne SS13,SS14,SS2 ....342 C6
Broad Mdw CM15 ....271 F1
Broad Meadow ③ IP8 ....16 C2
Broadmead Rd
Colchester CO4 ....110 E1
Woodford IG8 ....310 B3
Woodford IG8 ....310 C3
Broadmere Cl CO15 ....196 E7
Broadmere Rd IP1 ....16 E8
Broad Oak IG8 ....310 D5
Broad Oak Ct E4 ....309 A5
Broad Oakes Cl CB10 ....44 E2
Broadoaks CM16 ....267 F8
Broad Oaks SS12 ....321 E6
Broadoaks Cres CM7 ....110 C3
Broad Oak Way SS6 ....323 E1
Broad Oke IP1 ....17 B6
Broad Par SS5 ....324 E6
Broad St Braintree CM7 ....128 B7
Swanscombe DA10 ....389 F7
Wickham St P CM22 ....53 B8
Broadstone Rd E4 ....336 A2
Broad Street Green Rd
....237 C7
Broadstrood
Loughton IG10 ....267 A1
St Osyth CO16 ....194 B5
Broadview Ave RM11 ....334 D3
Broadview Ho RM8 ....334 D3
Broadwalk E4 ....332 A8
Broadwalk IG8 ....310 B3
Broadwater Gdns IP9 ....91 A8
Broadwater Gn SS15 ....344 F2
Broadwater Ho DA12 ....379 D1
Broadway Barking IG11 ....352 C4
Clacton-on-S CO15 ....220 C7
Glemsford CO10 ....2 B5
Grays RM17 ....355 A1
Romford RM2 ....314 A1
Silver End CM8 ....156 D4
Tilbury RM18 ....378 F5
Broad Way SS9 ....324 F6
Broadway Ave CO7 ....137 C3
Broadway Chambers ⑧
....343 B5
Broadway Cl IG8 ....310 B4
Broadway Ct CM8 ....156 D5
Broadway Link SS13 ....343 B5
Broadway Mkt SS6 ....311 D1
Broadway N SS13 ....343 B5
Broadway Par
Chingford E4 ....309 C4
Hornchurch RM11 ....355 B8
Broadway The
⑧ Basildon SS13 ....343 B5
Chelmsford E4 ....309 C4
Dagenham RM8 ....335 A1
Great Easton CM6 ....123 F3
Hornchurch RM11 ....355 B8
Loughton IG10 ....289 C5
Wickford SS12 ....321 D8
⑧ Woodford IG8 ....310 B4
Broadway W SS9 ....365 E8
Broad Wk N The CM13 ....317 A6
Broad Wlk Harlow CM20 ....199 C1
Hockley SS5 ....324 F6
Brock Bsns Pk SS11 ....321 F6
Brock Cl Tiptree CO5 ....186 E6
Witham CM8 ....211 E8
Brockdish Ave IG11 ....353 C4
Brockenbank Lodge RM8 ....334 C4

Brockenhurst Dr SS17 ...375 C8
Brockenhurst Gdns IG1 352 C7
Brockenhurst Way CM3 256 F1
Brocket Cl IG7 ...311 F6
Brocket Rd EN11 ...221 A6
Brockett Rd RM16 ...374 B3
Brocket Way IG7 ...311 F5
Brock Gn RM15 ...372 B7
Brockham Cl CO16 ...195 B6
Brockham Dr IG2 ...333 C6
Brock Hill SS11 ...299 C4
Brock Hill Dr SS11 ...299 C3
Brockles Mead CM19 ...223 C4
Brockley Cres Ipswich IP1 16 D8
  Ronford RM5 ...313 C3
Brockley Gr CM13 ...295 A1
Brockley Rd CM2 ...232 D2
Brocksford Ave SS6 ...323 F1
Brocks Mead CM6 ...122 E7
Brocksparkwood CM13 317 B7
Brockton Cl RM1 ...335 F7
Brockwell La CO5 ...158 C1
Brockwell Wlk 5 SS3 321 D6
Brodie Rd Chingford E4 ...349 C6
  Southend-on-S SS3 ...368 H8
Brodie Wlk SS12 ...321 F5
Brograve Cl CM2 ...254 D3
Broke Hall Com Prim Sch
  IP4 ...18 E5
Broke Hall Gdns IP3 ...18 D4
Broman's La CO5 ...192 A2
Bromefield Cl EN9 ...266 A6
Bromfield Rd CM11 ...320 C5
Bromfield CB11 ...43 E8
Bromfords Cl SS12 ...321 B5
Bromfords Dr SS12 ...321 B5
Bromfords Sch The
  SS12 ...321 B6
Bromhall Rd RM8 ...353 B6
Bromley RM17 ...377 F8

Brook La continued
  Galleywood CM2 ...254 E3
  Sawbridgeworth CM21 ...172 D2
Brookland CO5 ...186 C4
Brooklands
  Clacton-on-S CO15 ...220 E6
  Colchester CO1 ...136 B7
  Rayleigh SS6 ...323 D3
  Wickford SS12 ...321 B7
Brooklands App RM1 ...335 D7
Brooklands Ave SS9 ...346 F6
Brooklands Cl RM7 ...335 D7
Brooklands Gdns
  Clacton-on-S CO15 ...220 E6
  Hornchurch RM11 ...336 C5
Brooklands La RM7 ...335 D7
Brooklands Pk SS15 ...340 F6
Brooklands Prim Sch
  CO1 ...86 D8
Brooklands Rd
  Brantham CO11 ...86 D8
  Romford RM7 ...335 D7
Brooklands Rise CO11 ...86 D8
Brooklands Sq SS8 ...363 E3
Brooklands Wlk CM2 ...254 A7
Brooklane Field CM18 ...224 B5
Brook Lodge
  Romford RM7 ...335 D7
  Southend-on-S SS9 ...346 B7
Brooklyn Ave IG10 ...288 E5
Brooklyn Ct Harwich CO12 91 C3
  Loughton IG10 ...288 E5
Brooklyn Dr SS6 ...323 D5
Brooklyn Mews CO12 ...91 C3
Brooklyn Rd CO12 ...91 C3
Brookman's Ave RM16 373 D5
Brookmans Rd CM14 ...337 E4
Brookmans Rd CM ...275 D2
Brook Mdw CO9 ...51 D1
Brook Mdws CO5 ...186 C4
Brook Mead
  Basildon SS15 ...341 B7
  Great Waltham CM3 ...207 E8
Brook Meadow Cl IG8 ...309 E4
Brook Par IG7 ...311 B7
Brook Rd Aldham CO6 ...133 B7
  Brentwood,Brook Street
  CM14 ...315 F7
  Brentwood CM14 ...315 D5
  Buckhurst Hill IG9 ...288 A1
  Epping CM16 ...268 A6
  Great Tey CO6 ...132 C7
  Ilford IG2 ...333 E5
  Loughton IG10 ...288 E4
  Rayleigh SS6 ...345 D8
  Romford RM2 ...313 F2
  Sawbridgeworth CM21 ...172 E1
  South Benfleet SS7 ...344 C2
  Stansted Mountfitchet
  CM24 ...119 C6
  St Lawrence CM0 ...263 E5
  Tillingham CM0 ...263 B5
  Tiptree CO5 ...186 F3
Brook Rise IG7 ...311 A7
Brook Road Ind Est Sch 08 34 D8
Brookscroft Rd E17 ...309 B2
Brook Service Rd CB9 ...9 A7
Brooks Hall Rd IP1 ...17 A7
Brookside Billericay CM11 297 C6
  Canvey Island SS8 ...364 A5
  Harlow CM19 ...223 A5
  Hockley SS5 ...324 F4
  Hoddesdon EN11 ...221 A6
  Hornchurch RM11 ...336 E6
  Margaretting CM4 ...277 F6
  Redbridge IG6 ...311 C4
  Waltham Abbey EN9 ...265 E7
Brookside Ave SS3 ...350 C2
Brookside Cl
  Billericay CM11 ...297 C6
  Colchester CO2 ...136 B4
Brookside Ct SS2 ...347 F5
Brookside Jun & Inf Sch
  RM3 ...314 E5
Brooks Malting 5 CO11 ...40 F6
Brook's Mans 3 IG3 ...334 B3
Brook's Par 5 IG3 ...334 B3
Brook St Belvedere DA17 369 B1
  Brentwood CM14 ...315 E6
  Chelmsford CM1 ...232 B3
  Colchester CO1 ...136 B7
  Colne Engaine CO6 ...77 F1
  Dedham CO7 ...84 F7
  Glemsford CO10 ...2 86
  Great Bardfield CM7 ...72 B2
  Great Bromley CO7 ...112 E1
  Little Dunmow CM6 ...151 D6
  Manningtree CO11 ...86 D4
  Wivenhoe CO7 ...164 C8
Brook St Rdbt CM14 ...315 D5
Brook Terr CO15 ...51 E1
Brook Vale CO16 ...194 B3
Brookview IP2 ...36 E8
Brook View
  Chelmsford CM2 ...255 C6
  Stansted Mountfitchet
  CM24 ...119 E5
Brookway RM13 ...70 A3
Brook Way IG7 ...311 B7
Brook Wlk CM8 ...211 F8
Broomcolse Villas CM7 100 E5
Broom Cres IP3 ...17 F1
Broome Cl CM11 ...297 D5
Broome Gr CO7 ...137 B2
Broomfield SS5 ...371 D5
  Broome Rd CM1 ...297 D5
Broome Farm Way CO15 ...94 C2
Broomfield Hadleigh SS7 345 D4

Broomfield continued
  Harlow CM20 ...200 B3
  Silver End CM8 ...156 C5
Broom Field IP11 ...381 C5
Broomfield Ave
  Loughton IG10 ...288 F3
  Rayleigh SS6 ...323 A3
  Southend-on-S SS9 ...346 F5
Broomfield Cl RM5 ...313 D3
Broomfield Comm IP8 ...16 B6
Broomfield Cres CO7 ...137 B2
Broomfield Gn SS8 ...363 F5
Broomfield Hospl CM1 ...208 A3
Broomfield Prim Sch
  CM1 ...208 B1
Broomfield Rd
  Chelmsford CM1 ...232 A5
  Dagenham RM6 ...334 D4
  Swanscombe DA10 ...377 E2
Broomfields
  Basildon SS13 ...343 A6
  Hatfield Heath CM22 ...174 A3
Broomfields Ct 5 SS13 343 A6
Broomfields Mews 4
  SS13 ...343 A6
Broomfields Pl 3 SS13 343 A6
Broomsgrove Inf & Jun Sch
  CO7 ...137 B2
Broomhall Cl CM1 ...208 B2
Broomhall Rd CM1 ...208 B2
Broomhayes IP7 ...17 A2
Broomhill IP9 ...62 D6
Broomhill Ct 2 IG8 ...310 A4
Broomhill Rd Ilford IG3 334 A2
  Woodford IG8 ...310 A4
Broom Hill Rd IP1 ...17 A8
Broomhills Chase CM12 319 A5
Broomhills Ind Est Cm7 127 D2
Broomhills Rd CO5 ...218 D5
Broomhill Wlk IG8 ...309 F3
Broom Knoll CO7 ...60 C2
Broom Rd SS16 ...301 E2
Broom St CO10 ...34 B5
Broomstick Hall Rd EN9 265 E6
Broom Way Abberton CO5 163 B2
  Capel St M IP9 ...35 B2
Broomways SS3 ...350 C3
Broomwood Gdns CM15 294 A3
Broomwood La CM11 ...298 A8
Broseley Gdns RM3 ...314 E6
Broseley Rd RM3 ...314 E6
Brotherton Ave IP11 ...381 A8
Broton Dr CO9 ...76 E2
Brougham Ct SS3 ...360 A4
Brougham Ct 5 DA2 ...376 B1
Brougham Glades CO3 134 D5
Broughton Cl CO2 ...135 C4
Broughton Rd
  Hadleigh SS7 ...345 F2
  Ipswich IP1 ...17 B7
  South Woodham Ferrers
  CM3 ...301 C6
Browne Cl
  Brentwood CM14 ...294 B1
  Romford RM5 ...313 B5
Browning Ave SS2 ...348 B2
Browning Cl
  Colchester CO3 ...134 F6
  Romford RM5 ...312 F3
Browning Dr SS12 ...321 C5
Browning Rd
  Braintree CM7 ...155 A8
  Brantham CO11 ...86 C7
  Dartford DA1 ...376 A3
  Maldon CM9 ...259 A8
Brownings Ave CM1 ...232 A5
Browning Wlk RM18 ...379 C5
Brownlea Gdns IG3 ...334 A2
Brownlow Bend SS14 ...342 D6
Brownlow Cross SS14 ...342 D6
Brownlow Gn SS14 ...342 D6
Brownlow Rd IP11 ...381 F4
Brownlows Cl CM0 ...237 C3
Browns Ave SS11 ...299 F2
Browns Ceta RM16 ...372 E5
Brownsea Dr SS2 ...322 A5
Brownsea Way CO3 ...135 A4
Brown's End Rd CM6 ...121 F7
Broxbourne Ave E18 ...332 B7
Broxbourne Rd E7 ...332 A1
Broxbourne Sta EN10 ...221 A3
Broxburn Dr RM15 ...372 B6
Broxburn Par RM15 ...372 B6
Broxhill Rd
  Havering-atte-B RM4 ...314 B7
  Romford RM4 ...313 F7
Broxted Cl 5 SS12 ...321 E6
Broxted Dr SS12 ...321 E6
Broxted End SS12 ...321 E6
Broxted Mews CM13 ...295 C3
Bruce Ave RM12 ...336 D2
Bruce Gr Chelmsford CM2 254 A7
  Wickford SS11 ...322 A7
Bruce Rd CM1 ...231 B1
Bruces Wharf Rd RM17 378 A8
Bruff Cl CO4 ...109 E2
Bruff Dr CO14 ...171 A7
Bruges Cl CO12 ...91 A1
Bruges Rd SS8 ...364 C3
Brundells Rd CO7 ...139 A5
Brundish SS13 ...343 A5
Brundon La CO10 ...33 C7
Brunel Cl Romford RM1 335 E7
  Tilbury RM18 ...379 B5
Brunel Ct CO14 ...110 C6
Brunel Rd Braintree CM7 128 A1
  Chigwell IG8 ...310 F5
  Ipswich IP2 ...16 F6
  South Benfleet SS7 ...346 C7
Brunel Way
  Colchester CO4 ...110 C6
  South Woodham Ferrers
  CM3 ...301 C7

Brunswick Ave RM14 ...337 E4
Brunswick Cl
  Hoddesdon EN11 ...221 A6
  Upminster RM14 ...337 E4
Brunswick Gdns IG6 ...311 C3
Brunswick House Cut
  CO11 ...87 A3
Brunswick Lodge 6 E4 309 C8
Brunswick Pl SS6 ...323 B5
Brunswick Rd
  Holdbrook EN3 ...265 A1
  Ipswich IP4 ...17 D6
  Southend-on-S SS1 ...367 D7
Brunwin Rd CM7 ...126 F2
Brunwins Cl SS11 ...321 F8
Brushwood Lodge DA17 369 A2
Brussels Cl CO12 ...91 B1
Brussum Rd SS8 ...364 D2
Bruton Ave SS0 ...347 A5
Bryanita Cl CO5 ...186 D5
Bryan Rd CM23 ...145 F8
Bryanstone Mews CO3 134 E5
Bryanston Rd RM18 ...379 C5
Bryant Ave Romford RM3 314 D1
  Southend-on-S SS1 ...367 E6
Bryant Link CM2 ...232 C8
Bryant Row RM3 ...314 C8
Bryant's La CM9 ...259 D7
Bryce Rd RM8 ...353 C8
Bryn Farm Cl SS14 ...342 C8
Bryon Ave IP11 ...382 A5
Bryzy Cl IG10 ...289 B5
Buchanan Cl RM15 ...371 C5
Buchanan Gdns SS12 321 E5
Buchanan Way CM3 ...282 A5
Buchan Cl CM7 ...155 A8
Buckanan Path RM3 ...314 C2
Buckenhoe Rd CB10 ...22 E3
Buckeridge Way CM0 ...242 B3
Buckerills SS13 ...343 A6
Buckfast Ave CO13 ...170 D6
Buckfast Cl 5 IP2 ...17 A2
Buckhatch La CM3 ...278 D3
Buck Hill CM7 ...154 F6
Buckhurst Hill Com Prim Sch
  IG9 ...310 E8
Buckhurst Hill Ho IG9 310 B8
Buckhurst Hill Sta IG9 310 D8
Buckhurst Way IG9 ...310 E6
Buckingham Cl RM11 ...336 D6
Buckingham Ct
  2 Chelmsford CM2 ...232 F4
  Loughton IG10 ...289 A7
  Southend-on-S SS1 ...335 F6
Buckingham Dr CO4 ...136 E7
Buckingham Hill Rd
  Linford SS17,RM16 ...374 F5
  Stanford-le-H SS17 ...375 A7
Buckingham Rd
  Basildon SS15 ...341 E8
  Haverhill CB9 ...8 C5
  Hockley SS5 ...324 D6
  Ilford IG1 ...333 D2
  Wanstead E11 ...332 C6
  Woodford E18 ...309 F2
Buckingham Sq
  SS11 ...349 C1
Buckland Cl CO2 ...12 B7
Buckland Gate CM5 ...301 D1
Buckleberry Heath CM3 301 D6
Buckleys Chase CM12 ...296 F6
Buckleys Ct CM12 ...254 D2
Buddleia Cl IP2 ...16 E4
Buddleia Ct CO7 ...137 A2
Budna Rd SS8 ...363 A2
Budoch Cl IG3 ...334 A2
Budoch Dr IG3 ...334 A2
Buffett Way CO4 ...136 E6
Buglers Rise CM1 ...253 B8
Buick Ave CO15 ...220 D6
Building End Rd
  Chrishall SG8 ...8 E7
  Duddenhoe End SG8 ...40 B8
Bulbecks Wlk CM3 ...301 D5
Bulford La CM77 ...155 C5
Bulford Mill La CM77 ...155 C6
Bullace Cl CO4 ...110 D3
Bullbanks Rd DA17 ...369 C2
Bull Cl Basildon SS16 ...342 C5
  Grays RM16 ...372 F4
Bullen Cl IG6 ...311 E4
Bullen Wlk CM2 ...254 C3
Buller Rd Barking IG11 ...352 E5
  Basildon SS15 ...341 B7
  North Fambridge CM3 281 A1
Bullfields Newport CB11 ...67 A3
  Sawbridgeworth CM21 ...172 C1
Bullfinch Cl
  Colchester CO4 ...136 F8
  Harwich CO12 ...90 C1
Bullfinch Dr CO9 ...77 A1
Bull Hill Rd CO15 ...195 F5
Bullivant Cl DA9 ...377 C2
Bull La Dagenham RM10 335 B1
  Hockley SS5 ...324 C6
  Langley CB11 ...40 C2
  Long Melford CO10 ...15 E8
  Maldon CM9 ...237 A3
  Rayleigh SS6 ...323 D2
  Tiptree CO5 ...186 C3

Burmanny Cl CO15 ...195 C3
Burnaby Rd
  Gravesend DA11 ...378 E1
Burne Ave SS17 ...321 A6
Burnell Gate CM1 ...233 A7
Burnells Way CM24 ...119 E7
Burnell Rd CM13 ...316 C4
Burnels Ave E6 ...352 A2
Burnet Cl IP6 ...36 D8
Burnet Pk CM19 ...223 B3
Burnett Rd DA8 ...370 D1
Burney Dr IG10 ...289 C6
Burnham Ave CM3 ...281 A5
Burnham Cl Ipswich IP4 ...17 F7
  Primley St M IP11 ...381 A7
  Walton-on-N CO14 ...171 B8
Burnham Cres E11 ...332 C2
Burnham Ct CO15 ...220 I8
Burnham-on-Crouch District
  Mus* CM0 ...306 B4
Burnham-on-Crouch Prim
  Sch CM0 ...306 C5
Burnham Rd
  Althorne CM3 ...283 B1
  Battlesbridge SS11 ...300 E3
  Chelmsford CM2 ...218 D5
  Dagenham RM9 ...353 D8
  Hullbridge SS5 ...301 E2
  Latchingdon CM3 ...282 D5
  Mundon CM9 ...281 C8
  Romford RM2 ...335 D8
  Southend-on-S SS9 ...346 C1
  Southminster CM0 ...280 A4
  Southminster CM0 ...284 D3
  South Woodham F CM3 ...279 D1
  Woodham Mortimer CM3,
  CM3 ...257 E5
Burnley Rd RM20 ...377 A6
Burnsall Cl CM11 ...43 I8
Burns Ave Basildon SS13 343 A5
  Colchester CO3 ...134 F6
  Dagenham RM6 ...334 A5
Burns Cl Billericay CM11 ...297 E3
  Maldon CM9 ...237 A1
Burns Cres CM2 ...254 C8
Burnside
  Canvey Island SS8 ...364 A5
  Dagenham RM8 ...334 C2
  Sawbridgeworth CM21 ...172 D2
Burnside Ave E4 ...309 A4
Burnside Cres CM1 ...232 D2
Burnside Cl IG E6 EN1 335 F5
Burnside Rd RM6 ...334 A5
Burnside Terr CM17 ...200 F3
Burns Pl RM18 ...379 B6
Burnt Dick Hill CO4 ...82 D7
Burnt Ho IG7 ...289 F1
Burnthouse La
  Ingatestone CM4 ...277 E1
  Mountnessing CM4,CM3 296 A8
Burnthouse Rd CO6 ...105 E2
Burnt Mill CM20 ...199 C3
Burnt Mill Comp Sch
  CM20 ...199 C4
Burntmill Cnr CM20 ...199 D4
Burntmill La CM20 ...199 D3
Burnt Mills Rd SS13 ...321 C6
Burnt Oak Lodge SS9 346 A2
Burntwood Ave RM11 316 C7
Burntwood Cl
  Billericay CM12 ...296 F2
  South Woodham S SS13 339 D5
Burnway RM11 ...316 C4
Burr Cl Basildon SS16 ...340 E5
  Harwich CO12 ...90 C1
Burrell Rd IP2 ...17 C4
Burr Hill Chase SS2 ...347 E5
Burroughs Piece Rd CO10 33 F7
Burrow Cl IG7 ...311 F5
Burrow Gn IG7 ...311 F5
Burrows Chase EN9 ...265 D4
Burrows Cl
  Clacton-on-S CO15 ...195 D6
  Lawford CO11 ...105 A7
Burrows Rd CO15 ...105 B7
Burrows Way SS6 ...323 C1
Burrs Rd CO15 ...196 A7
Burry Way SS17 ...361 B4
Burrswood Pl CM9 ...237 E3
Burses Way CM3 ...295 C2
Burslem Ave IG6 ...312 A4
Burstall La IP8 ...16 C6
Burstall Cl CO16 ...195 B4
Burstead Dr CM11 ...297 B5
Burstead Grange CM11 319 D6
Burton Cl
  Corringham SS17 ...360 F5
  Thaxted CM6 ...69 B3
Burton Dr EN3 ...265 A2
Burton End Prim Sch CB11 ...8 D7
Burton Pl CM7 ...232 F4
Burton Rd Loughton IG10 289 C5
  Wanstead E18 ...332 B8
Burton's Green Rd CO9 104 B8
Burtons Mill CM21 ...172 F1
Burts Wharf DA17 ...369 C5
Burwell Ave SS3 ...363 F5
Burwood Cl CM2 ...232 C1
Burwood Gdns RM13 354 E3
Bury Cl Colchester CO1 136 A8
  Marks Tey CO6 ...132 F4
Bury Farm Cotts RM14 337 A1
Bury Farm La CM11 ...320 D3
Bury Fields CM6 ...152 A5

Bury Gdns CB11 ....20 A4
Bury La Chrishall SG8 ....19 D1
  Epping CM16 ....245 D2
  Great Waltham CM3 ....207 D8
  Hatfield Peverel CM3 ....210 F4
Bury Lodge La
  Great Hallingbury CM22 ..147 C7
  Stansted Mountfitchet
  CM24 ....120 A2
Bury Rd Chingford E4 ....287 E4
  Dagenham RM10 ....354 C7
  Epping CM16 ....267 E8
  Harlow CM17 ....200 D4
Buryside CI IG3 ....333 F7
Bury The CO16 ....194 A4
Burywater Cotts CB11 ....42 F1
Bury Water La CB11 ....42 E1
Burywoods CO4 ....109 B3
Bush CI Maldon CM9 ....333 D6
Bushell Way CO13 ....170 E6
Bush Elms Rd RM11 ....378 B8
Bushey CI Capel St M IP9 .....35 A1
  Chingford E4 ....309 C7
  South Woodham Ferrers
  CM3 ....301 E7
Bushey Croft CM18 ....223 E7
Bushey Ct CM1 ....92 B2
Bush Fair CM18 ....223 F6
Bushfields IG10 ....289 A4
Bush Gr CO10 ....33 C6
Bushgrove Rd RM8 ....334 D1
Bush Hall Rd CM12 ....297 C5
Bush Ho CM18 ....223 F6
Bush La CB10 ....46 D2
Bush Rd
  Great Sampford CB10 ......46 E2
  Wanstead E11 ....332 A4
  Woodford IG9 ....310 D6
Bushway RM8 ....334 D1
Bushwood E11 ....332 A3
Bushy Lea CM5 ....249 A2
Bushy Mead SS15 ....341 B8
Business Ctr The RM4 ....314 D3
Busway SS16 ....341 A5
Butchers Hill CB10 ....3 A4
Butchers La Capel St M IP9 ..35 B1
  Walton-on-t-N CO14 ......171 B7
Butchers Pasture CM6 ....122 F5
Butchers Row CB10 ....22 D1
Butchers View CO5 ....189 F6
Bute Ct CB9 ....8 F6
Bute Rd IG6 ....333 B6
Butler CI CB11 ....22 E1
Butler Ct 2 RM8 ....335 A3
Butler Ho RM17 ....378 F8
Butler Rd Dagenham RM8 ...353 B8
  Halstead CO9 ....76 D2
Butlers CI CM1 ....208 B2
Butlers Dr E4 ....265 C1
Butlers Gr SS16 ....341 B3
Butler's Hall La CM23 ....148 E3
Butlers La CO11 ....23 C5
Butler's La CO11 ....88 E1
Butlers Way CO9 ....30 A1
Butler Wlk RM17 ....373 D2
Butley CI IP2 ....36 F8
Butley Rd E11 ....331 C3
Butneys SS14 ....342 B7
Buttell CI RM17 ....373 D1
Butterbur Chase CM3 ....301 C6
Buttercross La CM16 ....246 A1
Buttercup CI
  Billericay CM12 ....297 A4
  Ipswich IP8 ....16 C2
  Romford RM3 ....314 D2
Buttercup Way CM0 ....284 C3
Buttercup Wlk CM8 ....163 E4
Butterfield Rd CM3 ....233 E8
Butterfly Gdns IP4 ....18 E5
Butteridges CI RM9 ....353 F4
Butter Market IP1 ....17 C6

Buttermere CM77 ....154 C7
Butterswest Rise CM21 .....172 E1
Butterworth Gdns IG8 ....310 A5
Butterys SS17 ....367 E8
Buttfield CI RM10 ....354 B6
Butt La Maldon CM9 ....92 E2
  Manuden CM23 ....92 E2
Buttleys La CM6 ....149 F8
Buttondene Cres EN10 ....221 B1
Button Rd RM17 ....372 F2
Button's Hill CM3 ....283 B4
Butt Rd Colchester CO3 ......135 E5
  Great Cornard CO10 ......34 B6
  Stoke-by-N CO6 ....56 C5
Buttsbury CM4 ....274 E1
Buttsbury Inf Sch [The] 297 B5
Buttsbury Jun Sch The
  CM12 ....297 B5
Buttsbury Rd IG1 ....352 C7
Buttsbury Terr CM4 ....275 E2
Butts Green Rd RM11 ....336 D5
Butts Green Rd CM2 ....255 F3
Butts La Danbury CM3 ....258 C7
  Stanford-le-H SS17 ....375 C8
Butts Paddock SS14 ....304 D2
Butts Rd SS17 ....360 C1
Butts Way CM2 ....253 E3
Buxey CI CO5 ....218 B7
Buxton Ave SS9 ....346 A3
Buxton CI
  Southend-on-S SS9 ....346 A3
  Woodford IG8 ....310 D4
Buxton Cotts CO6 ....132 A3
Buxton Link SS15 ....340 E6
Buxton Lodge CI11 ....332 B2
Buxton Rd Chingford E4 .....287 D2
  Coggeshall CO6 ....130 F3
  Colchester CO2 ....136 A3
  Grays RM16 ....373 E4
  Ilford IG2 ....333 E5
  Theydon Bois CM16 ......267 E3

Buxton Rd continued
  Waltham Abbey EN9 ......266 A6
Buxton Sq SS9 ....346 A3
Buyl Ave SS8 ....346 A3
Byfield SS9 ....346 F7
Byfield Rd CM13 ....339 C5
Byfletts SS16 ....342 F4
Byford Rd SS6 ....323 E3
Bylam La IP9 ....63 C6
Byland CI CM2 ....17 A2
Bylands CI CM23 ....145 D6
Byng Cres CO18 ....142 B1
Byng Ct CO2 ....136 A1
Byng Gdns CM7 ....128 C4
Bynghams CM19 ....222 E6
Byng Ho CO16 ....142 B1
Bypass Rd CO16 ....194 B5
By-Pass Rd SS17 ....360 A2
Byrd Cotts SS15 ....341 C8
Byrd Mead CM15 ....272 A6
Byrd's Farm La CB10 ....22 E3
Byrd Way SS17 ....360 C3
Byrne Dr SS2 ....347 E5
Byron Ave Colchester CO3 ..134 F7
  Southend-on-S SS2 ....348 B2
  Wickford SS11 ....309 F1
Byron CI Basildon SS15 .....341 B6
  E1 Wanstead E11 ....332 A7
  Woodford E18 ....310 B2
Byron Dr CM8 ....212 E5
Byron Gdns RM18 ....379 C6
Byron Mans RM14 ....337 C1
Byron Rd
  Brentwood CM13 ....295 D2
  Chelmsford CM2 ....232 D2
  Dartford DA1 ....376 B3
  Byrons Ho CM16 ....268 A8
  Rayleigh SS6 ....323 C3
  Byron Rd RM3 ....314 C2
  Byron Wks SS11 ....321 F7
Byrony CI CM8 ....183 D4
Bysouth CI IG5 ....311 B2
Bywater Rd CM3 ....301 C6

Cabborns Cres SS17 ....375 D8
Cabinet Way SS9 ....346 C6
Cables CI CO8 ....369 C3
Cadenhouse Mews CO3 ....134 E7
Cadiz Ct RM10 ....354 D5
Cadiz Rd RM10 ....354 C6
Cadmore La EN8 ....243 A2
Cadmus Rd IP1 ....16 D7
Cadogan CI E8 ....139 D5
Cadogan Gdns E18 ....332 B8
Cadogan T IG8 ....311 A3
Cadogan Terr SS13 ....343 C7
Caernarvon CI
  Hockley SS5 ....324 D6
  Hornchurch RM11 ....337 A3
Caernarvon Dr IG5 ....311 A2
Caernarvon Wlk CB9 ....8 E8
Cage End CM22 ....174 F5
Cage End CI CM22 ....174 F5
Cage Field Cotts SS4 ....324 E4
Cagefield Rd SS4 ....324 E4
Cage La Boxted CO4 ....83 B4
  Felixstowe IP11 ....381 D5
Caidge Row CM0 ....242 A2
Cairns Ave IG8 ....310 F4
Cairns Rd CO2 ....136 D2
Caister CI SS16 ....343 B6
Caithness CI IP4 ....18 B8
Caladonia La 3 SS12 ....321 E5
Calamint Rd CM0 ....183 D3
Calbourne Ave RM12 ....355 B8
Calcott CI CM14 ....294 B1
Calcroft Ave EN9 ....377 B2
Calcutta Rd RM18 ....378 F5
Caldbeck CM77 ....154 C6
Caldbeck Way CM77 ....154 C6
Caldecott Rd SS17 ....360 B1
Caldewell Rd SS17 ....360 B1
Caldy Rd DA17 ....369 B3
Caledonia CI IG1 ....334 B3
Caledonia CI 3 IG3 ....334 B3
Caledonia Rd IP9 ....91 B8
Caledon Rd E6 ....352 A5
Calford Dr CB9 ....8 C8
California CI CO4 ....110 B4
California Rd CO11 ....87 A4
Callan Gr RM15 ....372 B6
Callis Ct CO10 ....12 C8
Callis CI CO10 ....12 B8
Callow Ho RM13 ....354 D2
Callowood Croft CM5 ....258 D1
Calmore CI RM12 ....355 B8
Calmpatch 9 CM1 ....306 C4
Calne Ave IG5 ....311 B2
Calshot Ave RM16 ....372 F4
Calshot Ct 3 DA2 ....376 B1
Calverley CI CM23 ....146 A8
Calverley Cres RM10 ....335 A2
Calvert CI DA17 ....369 B2
Calvert Dr SS13 ....321 C1
Calverton Rd E6 ....352 A4
Calves La CO6 ....56 B8
Calvina CI SS15 ....319 F2

Cambell Jun & Inf Sch
  CM21 ....297 B5
Camberley Rd IP4 ....18 D7
Camberton Rd CM7 ....127 E6
Cambeys Rd RM10 ....354 C7
Camborne Ave RM3 ....314 B3
Camborne CI CM1 ....232 E5
Camborne Way RM3 ....314 B3
Cambrai Rd CO2 ....135 D4
Cambria CI
  Canvey Island SS8 ....363 C3
  New Mistley CO11 ....87 B3
Cambrian Ave IG2 ....333 E6
Cambridge Ave
  Romford RM2 ....336 C8

Cambridge Ave continued
  Sible Hedingham CO9 .....75 E8
Cambridge CI
  Basildon SS16 ....340 F5
  Stock CM4 ....275 D2
Cambridge Ct
  Clacton-on-S CO15 ....195 E4
  Frinton-on-S CO13 ....171 A5
  Southend-on-S SS1 ....366 F7
Cambridge Dr IP2 ....16 F1
Cambridge Gdns
  Grays RM16 ....374 B2
  Rochford SS4 ....325 C5
Cambridge Ho
  Harlow CM17 ....200 C5
  Haverhill CB9 ....9 B6
Cambridge Park Rd IG11 ...332 A4
Cambridge Pk E11 ....332 A5
Cambridge Rd
  Barking IG11 ....352 C5
  Canvey Island SS8 ....363 F3
  8 Chingford E4 ....287 D1
  Clacton-on-S CO15 ....195 E4
  Colchester CO1 ....135 C5
  Felixstowe IP11 ....381 F4
  Harlow CM17 ....200 C6
  Ilford IG3 ....333 E3
  Littlebury CB11 ....21 F4
  Newport CB11 ....43 A2
  Sawbridgeworth CM21 ...172 E4
  Southend-on-S SS1 ....366 F7
  Stansted Mountfitchet
  CM24 ....119 E8
  Wanstead E11 ....332 A4
Cambridge Way CO8 ....79 F8
Camden CI CM1 ....232 F6
Camden Ct 3 DA17 ....369 A1
Camden Rd Grays RM16 ....372 F3
  Ipswich IP3 ....18 B4
  Wanstead E11 ....332 B5
Camelford Ho 1 RM3 ......314 E6
Camelia CI IG8 ....309 E4
Camellia Ave CO16 ....195 C4
Camellia CI
  2 Chelmsford CM1 ....232 F6
  Romford RM3 ....314 E2
Camellia Cres CO16 ....195 C5
Camellia Ct 3 CO4 ....106 C8
Camelot CI CM1 ....231 F5
Camelot Way SS16 ....343 C8
Cameron CI
  Braintree CM7 ....127 F8
  Brentwood CM14 ....274 B3
  Ingatestone CM4 ....15 C6
  Long Melford CO10 ......346 C2
  Stanford-le-H SS17 ....360 E6
Cameron PI SS12 ....321 E5
Cameron Rd IG3 ....333 F3
Cam Gn RM15 ....372 B7
Camms Terr RM10 ....354 C7
Camoise CI CO16 ....50 B7
Camomile Dr SS11 ....321 E8
Camomile Rd RM7 ....335 D2
Camomile Way CO4 ....109 C2
Campbell Ave IG6 ....333 C7
Campbell Dr
  Chelmsford CM2 ....254 A7
  Harlow CM17 ....224 B7
  Romford RM1 ....313 E4
  2 Wickford SS12 ....321 C5
Campbell CI CO15 ....135 D6
Campbell Dr CO4 ....110 E2
Camper Rd SS1 ....367 D6
Campfield Rd SS3 ....368 E6
Campion CI RM7 ....335 D2
Campion Rd RM17 ....378 D8
Campion Gdns IG8 ....310 A5
Campion Rd
  Colchester CO2 ....136 A5
  Ipswich IP2 ....16 F4
Campions Harlow CM17 ....200 F5
Campions Hill CO6 ....81 D8

Candover Rd RM12 ....336 B3
Candy Terr 17 SS1 ....367 C7
Candytuft Rd CM1 ....232 F6
Cane Hill RM3 ....314 D1
Caneland Ct IP4 ....265 F5
Canes CA CM17 ....224 E1
Canes Mill Ct CM7 ....128 A5
Canewdon CE Prim Sch
  SS4 ....304 E1
Canewdon CI SS11 ....299 D2
Canewdon Gdns SS11 ......299 D2
Canewdon Hall CI SS4 ......304 C1
Canewdon Rd
  Rochford SS4 ....325 D8
  Southend-on-S SS2 ....366 D8
Canewdon View Rd SS4 ....325 D6
Canfield CI IG3 ....145 E8
Canfield Rd
  Great Canfield CM6 ......149 D1
  High Roding CM6 ....149 C5
  Rainham RM13 ....354 F4
  Woodford IG8 ....310 E3
Canford Ave SS12 ....320 F8
Canford CI CM2 ....254 E7
Cangle Junc CB9 ....9 A8
Canhams Rd CO10 ....34 C5
Canns St 11 IP1 ....17 B6
Canna Gdns SS12 ....321 F5
Cann Hall Prim Sch
  E11 ....195 D6
Canning St CO12 ....91 D5
Cannington Rd RM9 ....353 C6
Cannock Mill Ct CO2 ....136 C4
Cannon Circ CM7 ....73 D6
Cannon Leys CM7 ....254 D3
Cannon Mews 11 EN9 .....265 B6
Cannons CI CM3 ....343 B6
Cannons CI
  Bishop's Stortford CM23 ..119 A1
  Colchester CO2 ....135 B6
Cannon St CO1 ....135 A6
Cannons The CO2 ....135 D8
Cannons Villas CM22 ....174 F5
Canon Ave RM6 ....334 C6
Canon CI SS17 ....360 F2
Canonium Mews CO5 ......158 C2
Canon Palmer RC High Sch
  IG3 ....333 B3
Canons Brook CM19 ....218 B8
Canons CI CM3 ....266 C8
Canons Gate CM20 ....199 A2
Canonsleigh Cres SS9 ......346 E1
Canonsleigh Rd RM9 ....353 B5
Cansey La CO11 ....114 E6
Canterbury Ave
  Redbridge IG1 ....332 E4
  Southend-on-S SS2 ....348 A3
  Upminster RM14 ....337 F2
Canterbury CI
  1 Basildon SS14 ....342 F8
  Chigwell IG7 ....311 F7
  Ipswich IP2 ....36 F8
  Rayleigh SS6 ....323 C5
Canterbury Cres SS15 ......340 F6
Canterbury Grange CM7 ...127 F8
Canterbury Par RM15 ......357 C2
Canterbury PI RM17 ....373 C1
Canterbury Rd
  Colchester CO2 ....136 A5
  Holland-on-S CO15 ....196 E5
  Sudbury CO10 ....15 C2
Canterbury Way
  Brentwood CM13 ....316 C4
  Chelmsford CM1 ....231 E4
  Dartford DA2 ....376 D5
Canters The SS7 ....345 B5
Cantley Gdns IG2 ....333 C5
Cant Way CM7 ....128 A4
Canuden Rd CM1 ....231 E2
Canute CI SS4 ....304 E2
Canvey Jun & Inf Schs
  SS8 ....363 F3
Canvey Rd Basildon SS13 ..343 F6
  Canvey Island SS8 ....346 B1
Canvey Way SS7 ....344 A3
Canwick Gr CO2 ....136 C4
Capadocia St SS1 ....367 A6
Cape CI Barking IG11 ....352 B5
  Colchester CO3 ....134 F5
Capel CI Chelmsford CM2 ...232 F6
  Rayne CM77 ....126 F2
Capel Dr SS13 ....352 F8
Capel Ho CO4 ....109 D6
Capel Pk CO13 ....170 E7
Capel Rd Colchester CO3 ...295 D4
  Rayne CM77 ....126 F2
Capel St Mary CE Prim Sch
  IP9 ....35 C6
Capelston Rd SS3 ....341 F6
Capel Terr 5 SS1 ....367 C7
Capels La CO2 ....160 F4
Capital Ind Est DA17 ....369 B3
Capital Ind Pk RM3 ....221 A7
Capon CI CM1 ....232 F6
Capons La CM3 ....257 A5
Cappell La SG12 ....197 B2
Capricorn CM7 ....154 F5
Capricorn Ctr
  Basildon SS14 ....320 F1
Capstan CI CO5 ....218 D7

Capstan CI RM6 ....334 B5
Capstan Dr CM2 ....376 C3
Capstan Rd CO7 ....112 D4
Capstan Rd RM18 ....378 D7
Capstan PI CO4 ....136 D5
Captains Rd CO5 ....218 B6
Captains Wood Rd CM8,
  CM9 ....213 A3
Caracalla Way CO4 ....110 B6
Caravan Site The RM15 ....371 D3
Caravel CI RM16 ....372 F3
Carbis CI E4 ....287 D1
Carbury CI RM12 ....355 C6
Cardamon CI 11 E12 ....332 A8
Cardiff Ave IP2 ....17 B2
Cardigan Ave SS0 ....347 C3
Cardigan Gdns IG3 ....334 A2
Cardigan Ho 3 RM3 ....314 D5
Cardigan St IP1 ....17 B7
Cardinal CI CM2 ....232 F6
Cardinal Dr IG6 ....311 C4
Cardinal Pk IP1 ....17 C5
Cardinal Rd RM16 ....372 E3
Cardinal Way SS13 ....335 C5
Cardinals Ct IP1 ....381 E3
Cardinals Ct IP1 ....17 C5
Carisbrooke Ave
  Clacton-on-S CO15 ....196 A7
Carisbrooke CI
  Basildon SS13 ....343 B6
  Hornchurch RM11 ....337 A3
Carisbrooke Dr 2 DA2 .....376 B1
Carisbrooke Dr
  Corringham SS17 ....361 B4
  South Woodham Ferrers
  CM3 ....301 C7
Carisbrooke Rd
  Pilgrims Hatch CM15 .....294 B3
  Southend-on-S SS0 ....347 E1
Carisbrook Lodge SS6 ......323 C1
Carleton Ct CO5 ....163 E8
Carleton Rd CO8 ....369 D1
Carl Ho CM18 ....223 E3
Carlina Gdns IG8 ....310 B5
Carlingford Dr SS0 ....347 C2
Carlisle CI CO1 ....136 A8
Carlisle Gdns IG1 ....332 E5
Carlisle Ho IG1 ....332 E5
Carlisle Way SS13 ....343 B6
Carlton Ave
  Greenhithe DA9 ....376 E1
  Southend-on-S SS0 ....347 C4
Carlton CI
  Great Veldham CO9 ......30 A2
  Upminster RM14 ....337 B2
Carlton Ct Ilford IG8 ....333 D8
  Southend-on-S SS0 ....348 A1
Carlton Dr Hadleigh SS7 ...345 C4
  Ilford IG6 ....333 D8
Carlton Rd Basildon SS13 ..343 E8
  Clacton-on-S CO15 ....196 B5
  Grays RM16 ....373 F3
  Romford RM2 ....336 A7
Carnation CI SS14 ....342 A8
Carnation St RM16 ....369 A8
Carnation Dr CB10 ....22 F2
Carnegie CI EN3 ....265 B1
Carne Rasch Ct 12 RM8 ...335 A7
Carnforth Gdns RM12 ......355 A7
Carnforth Rd RM13 ....314 F4
Carnival CI SS14 ....320 B1
Carnival Gdns SS9 ....346 D4
Carolbrook Rd IP2 ....16 E1
Carol CI SS15 ....341 D7
Carolina Way CM8 ....186 D5
Caroline's CI CO2 ....347 E5
Carolyn Ho IG3 ....334 A3
Carousel Stps 8 SS1 ....367 C7
Carpenter CI CM2 ....296 F3
Carpenters Dr CM77 ....154 B7
Carpenters The CO5 ....218 D7
Carrack Ho OA8 ....369 E1
Carraways CM8 ....212 B8
Carriage CI IP11 ....381 A8
Carriage Dr CM2 ....232 E7
Carriage Mews IG1 ....333 C2
Carrick Dr IG6 ....311 C2
Carriers CI CO5 ....218 A7
Carriers Ct CO7 ....59 D3
Carrington Ct CO5 ....218 D7
Carrington Ho CO5 ....218 D7

Carrington Rd DA1 ....376 A1
Carringtons Rd CO7 ....112 D4
Carrington Way CM7 ....127 F8
Carroll Gdns 3 SS12 ....321 D6
Carroll Gdns 3 SS12 ....321 D6
Carroll Hill IG10 ....288 F6
Carron Mead CM3 ....301 F6
Carrow Rd RM9 ....353 B5
Carr Rd E17 ....309 A1
Carrs Rd CO15 ....195 D3
Carrs St SN 17 C6
Carruthers CI SS11 ....299 D1
Carruthers Dr SS11 ....299 C1
Carsey CI CM11 ....298 C4
Carsey Hill CB1 ....7 B6
Carshalton End CO4 ....134 F4
Carson Rd CM11 ....297 D5
Carsons Dr CO10 ....34 D5
Carstone PI CM1 ....231 F2
Carswell CI
  Brentwood CM13 ....295 D3
  Redbridge IG4 ....332 D7
Carswell Gdns SS12 ....321 D5
Cartbridge CI CO14 ....171 B8
Cartel CI RM19 ....371 D2
Carte PI SS16 ....341 A5
Carter CI RM5 ....313 B3
Carter Dr RM5 ....313 B4
Carters CI CO16 ....195 B3
Carters Croft CB10 ....6 B1
Cartersfield Rd EN9 ....265 C5
Carters Hill Boxted CO4 ....83 A1
  Manuden CM23 ....93 A1
Carters La
  Epping Green CM16 ......245 B7
  Henham CM22 ....94 F5
  Wickham Bishops CM8 ...222 F2
Carters Leys CM23 ....145 D8
Carters Mead CM17 ....224 C6
Carters Vineyard 4 CM2 ...82 E5
Cartermarsh La CO10 ......221 C3
Carthagena Est EN9 ....221 C3
Cart La Chingford E4 ....287 A1
  Grays RM17 ....373 B1
Cartlodge Ave SS11 ....321 E8
Cartwright Rd
  Dagenham RM9 ....353 F5
  South Benfleet SS7 ....344 D7
Cartwright Wlk CM2 ....232 F7
Carvers Wood CM8 ....212 C8
Cascade CI IG9 ....310 D8
Cascade Rd IG9 ....310 D8
Cascades SS1 ....367 C7
Case La IP9 ....60 D7
Casey La CM0 ....263 E4
Cashiobury Terr SS1 ....366 F7
Cashmere Way SS16 ....342 D2
Caspian Way DA10 ....377 E2
Cassel Ave SS8 ....346 C1
Cassino Rd
  Chelmsford CM2 ....231 E6
  Colchester CO2 ....135 C3
Cassis Ct IG10 ....289 C5
Casslee Rd SS14 ....320 B8
Castell Rd IG10 ....289 B5
Castle Ave Chingford E4 ...309 D5
  Hadleigh SS7 ....345 D1
  Haverhill CB9 ....8 E7
  Rayleigh SS6 ....323 A3
Castlebank CM3 ....354 E5
Castle Bailey 3 CO1 ....135 F7
Castle Cl Dedham CO7 .....84 F4
  Saffron Walden CB10 ....22 D2
Castle Hill Mid Sch CB9 .....8 D7
Castle Hill Prim Sch CO16 ..195 E7
Saffron Walden CB10 ......22 D2
Castle House * CO7 ....85 E4
Castle La
  Castle Hedingham CO9 ...51 F4
  Hadleigh SS7 ....345 D1
Castle Manor Upper Sch
  CB9 ....8 E8
Castle Mews CO6 ....57 E1
Castle Mews SS6 ....323 C1
Castle Point Transport Mus *
  SS8 ....364 E3
Castle Rd
  Clacton-on-S CO15 ....136 A7
  Dagenham RM9 ....353 B4
  Grays RM17 ....373 B1
  Hadleigh SS7 ....345 E2
  Hoddesdon EN11 ....197 C1
  Rayleigh SS6 ....323 D1
  Swanscombe DA10 ......377 F1
Castle St
  Bishop's Stortford CM23 ..145 F6
  Chipping Ongar CM5 ....249 A2
  Greenhithe DA9 ....377 A2
  Saffron Walden CB10 ....22 D2
  Swanscombe DA10 ......377 F1

Castle Terr SS6 ....323 C2
Castleton Rd
  Chingford E17 ....309 D1
  Ilford IG3 ....334 B3
  Southend-on-S SS2 .....348 E1
Castle View CM23 ....146 A7
Castle View Rd SS8 ....364 A6
Castle View Sch SS8 ....364 B6
Castleward Cl CO7 ....164 C8
Castle Way CO16 ....194 A4
Castle Wlk
  11 Basildon SS13 ......343 C6
  Canvey Island SS8 .....364 A5
  Haverhill CB9 ....8 E8
  Stansted Mountfitchet
  CM24 ....119 E6
Caswell Cl SS17 ....361 A4
Caswell Mews CM2 ......232 F2
Catalina Ave RM16 ......372 F4
Catalin Ct EN9 ....265 D6
Catchpole Ct 5 CO10 ...33 E7
Catchpole La CM0 ......213 A4
Catchpool Rd CO1 ......135 F8
Caterham Ave IG5 ......311 A1
Caterham Cl CO16 ......195 C6
Caterham Ct EN9 ....265 F5
Caterham High Sch IG5 .310 F1
Cater Mus The* CM2 ....297 A2
Cater Wood CM12 ....297 B3
Cates Cnr CB10 ....22 E1
Catharine Cl RM16 ......372 F4
Cathedral CE Prim Sch
  CM1 ....232 C3
Cathedral Dr SS15 .....341 C7
Cathedral Wlk CM1 .....232 B3
Catherine Cl
  Clacton-on-S CO15 .....196 A5
  East Hanningfield CM3 ..278 B7
  Pilgrims Hatch CM15 ...294 A4
Catherine Ct 1 IG2 ...333 C5
Catherine Godfrey Ho
  RM9 ....353 F4
Catherine Hunt Way
  CO2 ....135 C2
Catherine Lodge 6 SS2 347 F1
Catherine May Ct CO15 .195 F3
Catherine Rd
  Romford RM2 ....336 B6
  South Benfleet SS7 ....344 E4
Catherines Cl CM3 .....181 A6
Catons La CB10 ....22 D2
Cat's La CO10 ....34 A7
Cattawade End SS14 ...342 D7
Cattawade Link SS14 ...342 D7
Cattawade St CO11 ......86 C7
Cattermole Ct CO16 ....195 B3
Catts Cl IP9 ....61 F2
Cattsfield IP9 ....61 F2
Cauldwell Ave E4 ....17 F7
Cauldwell Hall Rd IP4 ...18 A6
Caulfield Rd
  Southend-on-S SS3 .....368 D7
  Wallend E6 ....352 A5
Causeway CM3 ....152 F1
Causeway Bsns Ctr The 56
  CM23 ....145 F7
Causeway Cl CO10 ....2 C5
Causeway Cotts CM1 ....252 E8
Causeway End CO11 .....86 B5
Causeway End Rd CM6 .152 C3
Causeway Reach CO15 .195 E7
Causeway The
  1 Bishop's Stortford
  CM23 ....146 A7
  Braintree CM7 ....127 F4
  Colchester CO4 ....110 C1
  Edney Common CM1 ....252 D7
  Finchingfield CM7 ....72 D6
  Great Baddow CM2 .....254 F7
  Great Dunmow CM6 ....123 D2
  Great Horkesley CO6 ....82 B2
  Halstead CO9 ....76 E1
  Harkstead SG9 ....64 B1
  Haverhill CB9 ....8 E7
  Henham CB11 ....68 A7
  Langley CB11 ....40 C3
  Maldon CM9 ....237 A4
  Ridgewell CO9 ....28 F8
  Toppesfield CO9 ....50 B7
  Ugley CM11 ....235 D5
Causton Jun Sch IP11 ..381 C6
Causton Rd CO1 ....135 E8
Caustons Cl CO10 ....34 C5
Causton Sq RM10 ....354 A5
Causton Way SS6 ....323 D4
Cautherly La SG12 .....197 A5
Cavalier Cl RM4 ....334 D7
Cavell Cres Dartford DA1 .376 B3
  Romford RM3 ....314 E1
Cavell Rd CM11 ....297 C1
Cavendish Ave
  Colchester CO2 ....136 C3
  Hornchurch RM12 ......355 B6
  Woodford IG8 ....310 B3
Cavendish CE Prim Sch
  CO10 ....1 C2
Cavendish Cres RM12 ...355 B6
Cavendish Ct
  Chingford E4 ....287 E2
  2 Haverhill CB9 ....8 E6
  5 Saffron Walden CB10 ...22 F2
Cavendish Dr
  Clacton-on-S CO15 .....195 A4
  Lawford CO11 ....86 B6
Cavendish Gdns
  Barking IG11 ....352 F7
  Braintree CM7 ....128 C5
  Chelmsford CM2 ......232 E3
  Dagenham RM6 ....334 E6
  Ilford IG1 ....333 A3
  Southend-on-S SS0 .....347 B2

Cavendish La CO10 ....1 F3
Cavendish Rd
  Chingford E4 ....309 C4
  Clare CO10 ....12 D7
  Felixstowe IP11 ....381 D3
  Hockley SS5 ....303 A1
  Rochford SS5 ....303 A1
Cavendish St IP3 ....17 F5
Cavendish Way
  Basildon SS15 ....319 D1
  Sudbury CO10 ....33 F7
Cavenham Gdns
  Hornchurch RM11 ......336 C6
  Ilford IG1 ....333 A1
Caversham Ave SS3 ...349 E2
Caversham Park Ave
  SS6 ....323 C4
Cawdor Ave RM15 ......372 B6
Cawdor Ho CM14 ......316 D6
Cawkell Cl CM24 ....119 D7
Cawkwell Cl CM2 ....233 A4
Cawley Hatch CM19 ....222 F8
Caxton Cl CO5 ....186 D4
Caxton Pl CO9 ....76 E2
Caxton Rd EN11 ....197 B2
Caxton Way RM1 ......355 E7
Cazenove Rd E17 ....309 A2
Cecil Ave Barking IG11 ...352 D5
  Grays RM16 ....372 F4
  Hornchurch RM11 ......336 E8
Cecil Cl CM23 ....146 D7
Cecil Ct Harlow CM18 ...223 C5
  Southend-on-S SS2 .....347 G3
Cecil Ho E17 ....309 A2
Cecilia St IP7 ....17 C5
Cecil Jones High Sch
  SS2 ....348 D3
Cecil Jones High Sch (Lower
  Sch) SS2 ....348 B3
Cecil Rd Chingford E17 ..309 A2
  Dagenham RM6 ....334 D4
  Hoddesdon EN11 ......221 C8
  Ilford IG1 ....352 B8
  Ipswich IP1 ....17 B7
Cecil Way SS6 ....323 F2
Cedar Ave
  Brightlingsea CO7 ......192 E7
  Chelmsford CM1 ......232 A3
  Dagenham RM6 ....334 E6
  Tiptree CO5 ....186 C7
  Upminster RM14 ......356 A8
  Wickford SS12 ....321 D5
Cedar Ave W CM1 ......232 A3
Cedar Chase CM9 ......237 C5
Cedar Cl Brantham CO11 ...60 D1
  Brentwood CM13 ......295 D2
  Buckhurst Hill IG9 .....310 D8
  Great Dunmow CM6 ....123 A1
  Rayleigh SS6 ....323 F1
  Romford RM7 ....335 C7
  Sawbridgeworth CM21 ..172 E1
  Southend-on-S SS2 .....348 A2
  Walton-on-t-N CO14 ...171 A7
Cedar Cres CM21 ....86 C3
Cedar Ct
  Bishop's Stortford CM23 ..118 F1
  Epping CM16 ....268 A8
  Southend-on-S SS3 .....368 E7
  5 Wanstead E11 ......332 B6
  West Bergholt CO6 ....108 D5
  5 Woodford E18 ....310 A2
Cedar Dr Hullbridge SS5 .301 E2
  Loughton IG10 ....209 B7
  Witham CM8 ....184 A5
Cedar Gdns RM14 ......337 C1
Cedar Gn EN11 ....221 A5
Cedar Gr CM0 ....306 B6
Cedar Hall Gdns SS7 ..345 A6
Cedar Hall Sch SS7 ....345 B6
Cedar Mews SS5 ......324 C6
Cedar Park Cl SS7 .....345 A6
Cedar Park Gdns RM6 ..334 D4
Cedar Pk
  Bishop's Stortford CM23 ..145 D4
  Havering IG7 ....311 A5
Cedar Rd
  Brentwood CM13 ......295 D3
  Canvey Island SS8 .....363 F4
  Grays RM16 ....374 B3
  Hornchurch RM12 ......336 C1
  Romford RM7 ....335 C7
  Thundersley SS7 ......345 A6
Cedar Rise RM15 ......357 D1
Cedars SS17 ....360 E2
Cedars Rd 6 CO2 ......135 F6
Cedars The
  Buckhurst Hill IG9 .....288 A1
  Gosfield CO9 ....102 E7
  Great Wakering SS3 ...350 B4
  South Woodham Ferrers
  CM3 ....301 D8
Cedar Terr 8 RM8 ......334 D4
Cedar Way CO7 ....166 E8
Cedar Wlk Canewdon SS4 304 D1
  Waltham Abbey EN9 ...265 D5
Cedarwood Ct CM18 ...223 F6
Cedric Ave RM1 ....335 E8
Celandine Ct
  Billericay CM12 ....296 F4
  South Ockendon RM15 .357 C1
Celandine Ct
  Chingford E4 ....309 B7
  Colchester CO4 ....109 C2
Celeborn St CM3 ......301 B6
Celedon Cl RM16 ......372 E4
Cement Block Cotts
  RM17 ....378 C8
Cemetery La
  East Bergholt CO7 ......59 B2
  Ipswich IP4 ....17 E8
Cemetery Rd
  Bishop's Stortford CM23 ..145 F6
  Ipswich IP4 ....17 E6
Centaur Way CM9 .....259 A8
Centaury Ct CO3 ......134 C7

Centenary Way CO15,
  CO16 ....168 E1
Central Arc CB10 ....22 D1
Central Ave Althorne CM3 282 E2
  Aveley RM15 ....371 C4
  Basildon SS16 ....340 E4
  Billericay CM12 ....297 C6
  Canvey Island SS8 .....363 F5
  Corringham SS17 ......361 A4
  Frinton-on-S CO13 ....171 A6
  Grays RM20 ....371 F1
  Hadleigh SS7 ....345 E5
  Hullbridge SS5 ....301 F1
  Ipswich IP3 ....38 E8
  Rochford SS4 ....325 D5
  Southend-on-S SS2 .....348 C1
  Stanford-le-H SS17 ....360 E4
  Tilbury RM18 ....379 A6
Central Cl SS7 ....345 E4
Central Dr RM12 ....336 E1
Central Ho CO12 ....91 D4
Central Maltings The 8
  CO11 ....86 C4
Central Par
  Clacton-on-S CO15 .....195 F2
  Ilford IG2 ....333 D5
Central Park Ave RM10 335 C1
Central Rd Harlow CM20 200 A4
  Stanford-le-h SS17 ....360 D1
Central Sq 7 CM1 ......232 B2
Central Wall SS8 ......364 A6
Central Wall Cotts SS8 364 A5
Central Wall Rd SS8 ...364 B5
Centre Ave CM16 ......267 F7
Centre Dr CM16 ....267 F7
Centre Pl SS11 ....367 C7
Centre Rd
  Dagenham RM10 ......354 B3
  Wanstead E11 ....332 A2
Centre Reach SS2 .....348 A1
Centre The
  2 Colchester CO4 ......136 E7
  Halstead CO9 ....76 E2
  Ipswich IP2 ....17 A1
  Tiptree CO5 ....186 D5
Centreway IG1 ....333 C2
Centurion Ho 2 CO2 ...135 F6
Centurion Way DA18 ..369 A3
Centurion Cl SS3 ......368 F8
Centurion Ho 2 RM10 .354 B6
Centurion Way
  Colchester CO2 ....135 A3
  Purfleet RM19 ....370 F2
  Centurion Works RM13 354 E2
Century Rd EN11 ......221 A7
Ceylon Rd SS0 ....366 D8
Chadacre Ave
  Redbridge IG5 ....332 F8
  Woodford IG5 ....310 F1
Chadacre Rd SS1 ......349 B1
Chadburn Rd SS10 ....15 D8
Chadfields RM18 ....379 A7
Chadview Ct 2 RM6 ...334 D4
Chadville Gdns RM6 ...334 D6
Chadway RM8 ....334 C3
Chadwell Ave RM6 ....334 B4
Chadwell By-Pass RM16 374 A1
Chadwell Heath RM6 ...334 D4
Chadwell Heath Foundation
  Sch RM6 ....334 B5
Chadwell Heath Hospl
  RM6 ....334 B6
Chadwell Heath La RM6 334 C5
Chadwell Heath Sta
  RM6 ....334 D4
Chadwell Hill RM16 ....374 B1
Chadwell Prim Sch RM6 334 C4
Chadwell Rd RM16,RM17 373 D2
Chadwell St Mary Prim Sch
  RM16 ....374 B2
Chadwick Ave E4 ......309 D6
Chadwick Dr RM3 ......314 D1
Chadwick Rd Ilford IG1 ...333 B1
  Southend-on-S SS0 ....366 C8
  South Woodham F CM3 ..279 E1
Chaffinch Cl SS3 ......368 E8
Chaffinch Dr CO12 ....90 E1
Chaffinch Gdns CO4 ...136 F8
Chaffinch Way CO9 .....77 A1
Chaffix CM6 ....152 C6
Chaffix Cl CM6 ....152 C6
Chafford Gdns CM13 ...339 D5
Chafford Hundred Sta
  RM16 ....374 B6
Chafford Sch The RM16 374 C8
Chafford Way
  Grays RM16 ....373 B5
  Ilford RM6 ....334 A6
Chafford Wlk RM13 ...355 C3
Chainey Pieces 15 CB9 ...8 F7
Chaingate Ave SS2 ...348 E2
Chale Ct SS17 ....375 C8
Chalfont Cl SS9 ....346 D4
Chalfont Ct 18 DA17 ...369 A1
Chalfont Rd CO4 ......110 C3
Chalfont Sq 18 IP4 .....17 D6
Chalford Ct IG2 ....333 B6
Chalfords Gdns RM2 ...336 B7
Chalford Wlk IG8 ......310 D3
Chalgrove Cres IG5 ...310 E1
Chalice Cl SS14 ....342 E6
Chalice Way DA9 ....376 F2
Chalk Cl CM7 ....127 D3
Chalk End SS13 ....343 A7
Chalk La CM7 ....201 A2
Chalklands
  Howe Green CM2 ....255 D3
  Saffron Walden CB10 ....22 E3
Chalkners Cl 1 IP9 .....35 A1
Chalk Rd SS8 ....364 A6
Chalks Ave CM21 .....172 D3
Chalks Rd CM8 ....183 F4

Chalk St CM3 ....299 F7
Chalkstone Mid Sch CB9 ...9 A8
Chalkstone Way CB9 .....9 D7
Chalk Villas CM6 ......204 C7
Chalkwell Ave SS0 ....366 B8
Chalkwell Bay Flats SS0 366 A8
Chalkwell Espl SS0 ...366 B7
Chalkwell Hall Jun & Inf
  Sch SS0 ....347 A1
Chalkwell Lodge SS0 ..347 C1
Chalkwell Park Dr SS9 .346 F1
Chalkwell Sta SS9 .....366 A8
Chalky La SG8 ....19 D2
Challacombe SS1 ......347 C5
Challacombe Cl CM13 ..295 C1
Challenge Way CO1 ...136 B6
Challinor CM17 ....224 E8
Challis La CM7 ....155 A8
Challock Lees SS13 ...343 C5
Chalon St IP1 ....17 B5
Chalvedon Ave SS13 ..343 B7
Chalvedon Sch SS13 ..343 B6
Chalvedon Sq 8 SS13 .343 A6
Chamberlain Ave
  Canvey Island SS8 .....364 C4
  Corringham SS17 ......361 A5
  Walton-on-t-N CO14 ...171 B7
Chamberlain Cl CM17 ..224 C8
Chamberlains Ride CM6 301 D6
Chambers Cl DA9 ......377 A2
Chamley Ct CO15 ......196 D5
Champion Cl
  Stanford-le-H SS17 ....360 E3
  Wickford SS12 ....321 D6
Champion Rd RM14 ...337 B2
Champions Gn EN11 ..197 A1
Champions Way
  Hoddesdon EN11 ......197 A1
  South Woodham Ferrers
  CM3 ....301 C8
Champlain Ave SS8 ...363 F5
Champness Rd IG11 ...352 F5
Chance Cl RM16 ....372 F3
Chancel Cl Basildon SS15 341 C7
  South Benfleet SS7 ....344 C6
Chancel Mews
  Chigwell IG8 ....311 A4
  18 Ipswich IP4 ....17 D6
Chancellor Ave CM2 ..232 A4
Chancellor Rd SS1 ....367 B7
Chancery Gr CO2 ......163 A8
Chancery Pl CM1 ......231 B1
Chancery Rd IP1 ....17 B5
Chandler Rd IG10 ......289 B8
Chandlers Chase CM2 ..217 D4
Chandlers Cl
  Bishop's Stortford CM23 145 C4
  Clacton-on-S CO16 ....195 B3
  West Mersea CO5 .....218 C7
Chandlers Cnr RM13 ..355 C1
Chandlers Dr DA8 .....369 E2
Chandlers Quay CM9 ..237 A3
Chandlers Row CO1 ...136 C5
Chandlers Way
  Romford RM1 ....335 E6
  Southend-on-S SS2 ....348 A5
  South Woodham Ferrers
  CM3 ....301 D8
Chandlers Wlk CM15 ..271 E2
Chandos Ave E17 .....309 A1
Chandos Cl IG9 ....310 B8
Chandos Par SS7 ......346 A3
Chaney Rd CO7 ....137 A2
Chanlock Path RM16 ..372 B6
Channing Cl RM11 .....336 F4
Channock's Farm Cotts
  CM20 ....199 C7
Chanterelle CO4 ....110 D3
Chanterelle CO4 ....110 B3
Chanton Cl SS9 ....346 D7
Chantress Cl RM10 ....354 C4
Chantry Cl
  Bishop's Stortford CM23 ..145 E8
  Clacton-on-S CO16 .....195 E7
Chantry Cres SS17 ....360 C1
Chantry Ct 10 DA12 ...379 C1
Chantry Dr
  Ingatestone CM4 ......274 B3
  Wormingford CO6 ......80 E4
Chantry Gn IP2 ....16 C3
Chantry Heritage Ctr*
  DA12 ....379 C1
Chantry High Sch & Sixth
  Form Ctr IP2 ....16 F3
Chantry Ho RM13 .....354 D3
Chantry Jun & Inf Sch
  IP2 ....16 E3
Chantry La Basildon SS15 341 C7
  Boreham CM3 ....210 A3
  Brentwood CM14 ......316 A8
  Chantry Prim Sch DA12 379 C1
Chantry Rd CM23 .....145 E8
Chantry The
  6 Bishop's Stortford CM23 145 F8
  3 Chingford E4 ....287 C1
  Colchester CO3 ....135 C7
  Harlow CM20 ....200 A2
Chantry View CM6 ....124 B8
Chantry Villas CM4 ...210 A2
Chantry Way
  Billericay CM12 ....297 B2
  Rainham RM13 ....354 D3
  Chanute Ave CM7 ......73 D7
Chapel Cl Capel St M IP9 ...35 A1
  Grays RM20 ....377 B8
Chapel Croft
  Ardleigh CO7 ....111 E7
  Ingatestone CM4 ......274 B8
Chapel Ct Billericay CM12 ...297 B2
  Swanscombe DA10 ....377 E1
Chapel Cut CO11 ....87 A4
Chapel Dr CM3 ....208 B6
Chapel End EN11 .....221 A5
Chapel End Ho E17 ...309 B2

Chapel End Inf Sch
  Chingford E17 ....309 B1
  Chingford E17 ....309 B2
Chapel End Jun Sch E17 309 B2
Chapel End Way CO9 ...28 B2
Chapelfields
  Kirby Cross CO13 ......170 E6
  Stanstead Abbotts SG12 ..197 D4
Chapel Fields CM7 ....224 C6
Chapel High CM14 ....316 C8
Chapel Hill
  Belchamp Walter CO10 ...31 D4
  Braintree CM7 ....128 B2
  Halstead CO9 ....76 D2
  Stansted Mountfitchet
  CM24 ....119 E6
Chapel Hill Bsns & Ret Pk
  CM7 ....128 C1
Chapel La Belstead IP8 ...36 C7
  Boxted CO4 ....83 A3
  Chigwell IG7 ....311 F7
  Colchester CO7 ....111 B1
  5 Dagenham RM6 ....334 D4
  Elmstead CO7 ....138 A6
  Great Bromley CO7 ....139 A5
  Great Cornard CO10 ....34 C2
  Great Wakering SS3 ...350 B4
  Hadleigh SS7 ....345 C3
  Harlow CM17 ....224 C6
  Heybridge Basin CM9 ..237 E2
  Kirby Cross CO13 ......170 E6
  Little Baddow CM3 ....234 B3
  Newport CB11 ....67 A8
  Purleigh CM3 ....280 D8
  Roxwell CM1 ....229 F1
  St Osyth CO16 ....194 A4
  Tendring CO16 ....140 E8
  Thorington Street CO6 ...57 D6
  Thorrington CO7 ......166 B5
  Tillingham CM0 ....263 E4
  Washbrook IP8 ....16 A1
  West Bergholt CO6 ....108 E3
Chapel Lodge RM13 ...355 A1
Chapel Mews
  Chigwell IG8 ....311 A4
  18 Ipswich IP4 ....17 D6
Chapel Rd
  Beaumont CO16 ....141 E7
  Boxted CO4 ....83 A3
  Brightlingsea CO7 ......193 A7
  Burnham-on-C CM0 ...306 C4
  Colchester CO3 ....134 C6
  Epping CM16 ....245 F1
  Great Totham CM9 ....213 D6
  Ilford IG1 ....333 B1
  Langham CO4 ....83 D4
  Ridgewell CO9 ....29 B7
  Southend-on-S SS3 ....368 F6
  Tiptree CO5 ....186 E4
  Tollesbunt D'arcy CM9 .215 F4
  West Bergholt CO6 ....108 E4
  Wivenhoe CO7 ....164 B8
Chapel Rise CM7 .....129 D2
Chapel Row 8 CM23 ..145 F6
Chapel St Billericay CM12 297 A2
  Halstead CO9 ....76 E2
  Rowhedge CO5 ....164 A8
  Steeple Bumpstead CB9 ...27 C7
  Stoke by Clare CO10 ....11 A3
  1 Colchester CO2 ......135 E6
  Colchester CO2 ....135 E6
  Tiptree CO5 ....186 E4
Chapel The 8 RM1 ....336 B3
Chaplaincy Gdns RM11 336 E3
Chaplemount Rd IG8 ..310 F4
Chaplin Cl Basildon SS15 319 E1
  Galleywood CM2 ......254 B2
Chaplin Dr CO4 ....110 D1
Chaplin Rd
  Dagenham RM9 ....353 E5
  East Bergholt CO7 ......59 D3
Chaplins CO13 ....170 F7
Chaplin Wlk CO10 ......34 D5
Chapman Ct SS8 ......363 C3
Chapman Rd
  Belvedere DA17 ....369 B1
  Canvey Island SS8 .....365 A3
  Clacton-on-S CO15 .....195 F3
Chapmans Cl SS5 .....301 E8
Chapmans La CO5 .....218 F8
Chapmans Wlk SS9 ...346 B1
Chappel CE Prim Sch
  CO6 ....106 D5
Chappel Cnr CO6 ......106 D6
Chappel Hill CO6 .....106 D6
Chappel Rd Burrs CO6, CO8 278 F3
  Fordham CO6 ....107 D7
  Great Tey CO6 ....106 C1
Chappel & Wakes Colne Sta
  CO6 ....106 D5
Charfinch Cres CM1 ...297 C1
Charfleets Cl SS8 .....363 D3
Charfleets Farm Ind Est
  SS8 ....363 D3
Charfleets Ho SS8 ....363 D3
Charfleets Ind Est SS8 363 C3
Charfleets Rd SS8 ....363 D3
Charfleets Service Rd
  SS8 ....363 D3
Charity Farm Chase
  CM2 ....296 F3
Charlbury Cl RM3 .....314 C4
Charlbury Cres RM3 ..314 C4
Charlbury Gdns IG3 ...333 F2
Charlbury Ho 8 E12 ...333 A1
Charlecote Rd
  Dagenham RM8 ....334 E1
  Great Notley CM7 .....154 C7
Charlemont Rd E6 .....352 A2
Charles Cl SS0 ....347 A5
Charles Ct Colchester CO3 134 D6
  Wivenhoe CO7 ....137 C3
Charles Cvn Pk CO16 ..167 E8

Charles Hall CO4 ......109 F4
Charles Ho 8 EN11 ....221 D8
Charles Pell Rd CO4 ...136 E7
Charles Rd
  Brightlingsea CO7 ......192 F6
  Dagenham RM10 ......354 D6
  Felixstowe IP11 ....381 C3
  Ilford RM6 ....334 D5
Charles St Colchester CO1 136 A6
  Epping CM16 ....268 A7
  Grays RM17 ....378 C8
  Greenhithe DA9 ....377 A3
  Greenhithe, Stone DA9 .376 F2
  Ipswich IP1 ....17 C6
Charleston Ave SS13 ..321 C1
Charleston Ct
  Basildon SS13 ....321 C1
  West Mersea CO5 .....216 E6
Charlotte Ave SS12 ...321 C2
Charlotte Ct Ilford IG2 ..333 A5
  South Woodham Ferrers
  CM3 ....301 D6
Charlotte Dr CO13 .....170 E6
Charlotte Gdns RM5 ..313 A4
Charlotte Mews 5 SS2 347 E6
Charlotte Pl RM20 ....377 B8
Charlotte Rd RM11 ...336 B6
Charlotte Way CM8 ...184 B2
Charlton Cl Basildon SS13 321 C1
  Hoddesdon EN11 ......221 A5
Charlton Cres IG11 ...352 F3
Charlton Mead La EN11 221 B5
Charlton St RM20 ......377 D8
Charlton Way EN11 ...221 B6
Charnock Cl CO13 .....170 E6
Charnwood Ave CM1 ..231 E1
Charnwood Cl IP27 ....17 A4
Charnwood Dr E18 ...332 B7
Charrington Cl CB9 .....9 C6
Charter Ave IG2 ....333 C6
Charter Ct CO4 ....110 C6
Charter Ho CO4 ....109 F4
Charterhouse SS16 ...342 C5
Charterhouse Cotts CM3 289 F5
Charteris Rd IG8 ......310 B4
Charter Rd The IG8 ...309 F1
Charters Cross CM18 .223 D5
Charters Ct SS11 .....321 F8
Charters The CM6 ....123 D2
Charter Way
  Braintree CM7 ....128 C1
  Colchester CO4 ....109 F4
Chartfield Dr CO13 ...170 D8
Chartwell Cl
  Braintree CM7 ....127 E7
  Harlow CM17 ....18 A5
  Waltham Abbey EN9 ...265 E6
Chartwell Ct 2 IG8 ...310 A3
Chartwell Pl RM1 .....335 F7
Chartwell Sq 2 SS1 ...367 A8
Chase Cl SS7 ....344 F5
Chase Court Gdns SS1 367 C8
Chase Cross Rd RM5 ..313 D3
Chase Dr CO5 ....164 C8
Chase End Basildon SS16 342 F3
  Rayleigh SS6 ....323 F2
Chase Gdns Chingford E4 309 A6
  Southend-on-S SS0 ....347 D3
Chase House Gdns RM11 336 F4
Chase La Chigwell IG7 ..312 A7
  Harwich CO12 ....90 E2
  Ilford IG6 ....333 D6
Chase Lane Prim Sch
  CO12 ....90 E2
Chase Nature Reserve The*
  RM7 ....335 C1
Chase Rd
  Brentwood CM14 ......316 C7
  Corringham SS17 ......361 A3
  Southend-on-S SS1 ....367 C8
Chase Rd W CO7 ......139 A6
Chaseside SS4 ....345 E8
Chaseside Cl RM1 .....313 E4
Chase Sq 4 DA11 .....379 B1
Chase The Aldham CO6 ..133 B8
  Barnston CM6 ....151 B4
  Basildon,Langdon Hills SS16 341 E3
  Basildon, Steeple View
  SS15,CM12 ....319 B2
  Billericay CM11 ....297 C2
  Bishop's Stortford CM23 ..145 F6
  Boreham CM3 ....233 E8
  Braintree CM7 ....128 A7
  Brantham CO11 ....60 D1
  Brentwood CM14 ......316 D5
  Brentwood, Warley CM14 316 B6
  Chigwell IG7 ....311 C6
  Colchester CO1 ....136 B7
  2 Colchester,Greenstead
  CO1 ....136 D7
  Dagenham RM7,RM12 ..335 E1
  Elmstead CO7 ....138 B6
  Felixstowe IP11 ....381 D4
  Foulness Island SS3 ...159 D4
  Foxearth CO10 ....14 C6
  Goldhanger CM9 ......239 A1
  Grays RM20 ....377 B8
  Great Bardfield CM7 ...96 F2
  Great Baddow CM2 ...218 E6
  Great Notley CM7 .....154 C5
  Great Tey CO6 ....132 C8
  Great Totham CM9 ....213 A4
  Harlow CM17 ....18 A5
  Henham CM22 ....94 F6
  Holland-on-S CO15 ....196 E5
  Ingrave CM13 ....317 C5
  Kelvedon CO5 ....158 C2
  Loughton IG10 ....288 D2

Chase The continued
Manningtree CO11 ....86 D3
Rayleigh SS6 ....323 F1
Rochford SS4 ....325 C8
Romford RM1 ....335 E8
Southminster CM0 .....284 D4
South Woodham Ferrers
CM3 ....301 C8
Steeple Bumpstead CB9 .27 B7
Thundersley SS7 ......345 A5
Tollesbury CM9 ....216 D2
Tolleshunt D'arcy CM9 .215 B4
Upminster RM14 ......337 E1
West Mersea CO5 ......218 C6
Wickford, Nevendon SS12 .321 A4
Wickford, Runwell SS12 .321 A6
Wickford SS11 ....300 A3
Dagenham RM6 ....334 E5
Chaseway Basildon SS16 .342 F4
Witham CM8 ....183 F5
Chaseways CM21 ......200 C8
Chaseway The
Braintree CM7 ....128 C2
Ramsden Heath CM4 ..298 A8
Chase Way The
Colchester CO13 ......109 C1
Colchester,Lexden CO3 .109 B1
Chaters Hill CO10 .....22 E2
Chatfield Way SS13 ...343 C7
Chatham Hall La CM3 ..208 B8
Chatham Pavement
SS13 ....343 C7
Chatham Rd ■ E16 ....309 F1
Chatham Way CM14 ...316 C8
Chatley Rd CM3 ....180 F7
Chatsworth SS7 ....344 F6
Chatsworth Ave CM7 ..154 B7
Chatsworth Cl CM23 ..145 C7
Chatsworth Cres
Ipswich IP2 ....17 B2
Trimley St M IP11 .....381 A6
Chatsworth Dr CM 118 C6
Chatsworth Gdns
Clacton-on-S CO15 ...195 D2
Hockley SS5 ....324 D6
Chatsworth Rd CO5 ...118 C2
Chatter End CM23 .....118 C7
Chatterford End SS14 .342 B7
Chattesworth Ave RM3 .314 D4
Chattisham Rd IP9 .....35 C8
Chatton Cl ■ SS12 ....321 E5
Chaucer Cl Jaywick CO15 .195 A1
Maldon CM9 ....259 A8
Tilbury RM18 ....379 C5
Chaucer Cres CM7 ....155 A8
Chaucer Ct EN11 ......118 A7
Chaucer Rd
Chelmsford CM2 ......232 D1
Chingford E17 ....309 C1
Felixstowe IP11 ....381 D3
Romford RM3 ....314 B3
Sudbury CO10 ....15 D2
Wanstead E11 ....332 A5
Chaucer Way
Colchester CO3 ....134 F6
Dartford DA1 ....376 A3
Harlow CM20 ....197 A2
Chaucer Wlk SS12 ....321 D5
Chauntry Rd CO 8 F7
Chauntry The ■ CB9 ..9 A7
Cheapside E SS6 .....323 C4
Cheapside W SS6 .....323 B4
Chedburgh Pl ■ CB9 ..9 A8
Cheddar Ave SS0 .....347 A5
Chedington SS3 ......349 C1
Chedworth Pl IP9 .....61 D7
Cheelson Rd RM15 ...357 C3
Cheelson Barton SS1 ..368 C8
Chelmer Ave
Little Waltham CM3 ...208 B5
Rayleigh SS6 ....323 C1
Chelmer Cl
Kirby Cross CO13 .....170 E7
Little Totham CM9 ....214 B4
Chelmer Cres SS11 ..353 B3
Chelmer Dr
Brentwood CM13 .....295 E3
Great Dunmow CM6 ..150 E8
South Ockendon RM15 .372 C6
Chelmer Ho RM11 ....374 A1
Chelmer Lea CM2 .....254 E7
Chelmer Pl CM2 ......232 D3
Chelmer Rd
Braintree CM7 ....128 D1
Chelmsford CM2 .....232 E2
Grays RM16 ....374 A1
Haverhill CB9 ....9 B8
Upminster RM14 .....337 D5
Witham CM8 ....183 F2
Chelmer Terr CM7 ....254 E7
Chelmer Valley High Sch
CM1 ....208 A2
Chelmer Valley Rd CM1 .232 B5
Chelmer Valley Ret Pk
CM2 ....232 E2
Chelmer Village Way
CM2 ....233 A3
Chelmer Way
Burnham-on-C CM0 ...306 A6
Southend-on-S SS3 ...368 D7
Chelmondiston CE Prim Sch
IP9 ....63 E7
Chelmsford Ave
Romford RM5 ....313 D4
Southend-on-S SS2 ..347 F1
Chelmsford Coll
Chelmsford CM1 .....254 A8
Chelmsford CM2 .....254 C7
Chelmsford Cty High Sch for
Girls CM1 ....232 A4
Chelmsford Dr RM14 .336 F1
Chelmsford & Essex Regiment
Mus* CM2 ....254 A8

Chelmsford Gdns IG1 ..332 F4
Chelmsford Ho CM6 ...150 E7
Chelmsford Rd
Barnston CM6 ....151 A4
Battlesbridge SS11 ...300 E1
Brentwood CM15 ....295 B5
Felsted CM6 ....152 B4
Great Dunmow CM6 ..150 E7
Great Waltham CM3 ..208 A6
Hatfield Heath CM22 .174 C3
High Ongar CM5,CM4 .249 D4
Holland-on-S CO15 ...196 D6
Margaret Roding CM6,CM5 .204 E4
Mountnessing CM15 ..295 C6
Ongar CM5 ....258 C3
Rawreth SS13 ....322 E6
Shenfield CM15 ......294 F3
Woodford E18 ....309 F2
Wormald Mortimer CM9 .257 C6
Writtle CM1 ....231 C1
Chelmsford Road Inf Sch
E18 ....150 E7
Chelmsford Sta CM1 ..232 B3
Chelsea Ave SS1 .....367 D6
Chelsea Cl
G ■ Chingford E4 .....287 C1
Rochford SS4 ....325 E2
Southend-on-S SS1 ...367 C8
Sudbury CO10 ....14 C7
Chelsea Fields EN11 .197 B2
Chelsea Mews CM7 ..224 E7
Chelsea Mews
G ■ Braintree CM7 ...127 F2
G ■ Hornchurch RM11 .336 B3
Chelsea Rd CO10 .....33 F7
Chelston Cl E 132 B6
Chelston Rd IG10 ....289 A5
Chertsey Cl SS3 .....349 D1
Chertsey Rd SS1 .....357 C8
Chelvil Cl CO5 ....186 C4
Cherwell Dr CM1 .....231 C5
Cherwell Gr RM15 ...372 B6
Cheryl Ct CO15 ......195 D1
Chesapeake Cl IP9 ...63 F7
Chesapeake Rd IP3 ..38 A8
Chesfield Cl CM23 ...145 F5
Chesham Cl RM7 .....335 D7
Chesham Dr SS15 ....319 B1
Chesham Ho ■ RM3 .314 E4
Chesham Rd IP7 .....17 C7
Cheshire Cl Chingford E17 .309 B2
Hornchurch RM11 ....337 A6
Cheshunt Dr SS6 .....323 B6
Chelwood Cl E4 ......287 B3
Chenies Dr SS15 .....319 B1
Chenies Gn CM23 ....145 C6
Chepstow Ave RM12 ..336 E1
Chepstow Cl CM11 ...297 D5
Chepstow Cres IG3 ..333 E5
Chepstow Ho RM3 ...315 A5
Chepstow Rd CM23 ..145 C8
Chequers
Bishop's Stortford CM23 .145 C8
Buckhurst Hill IG9 ...288 B1
Ingatestone CM4 .....274 B4
Chequers Ct CM8 ....184 B2
Chequers La
Dagenham RM9 ......354 A2
Glemsford CO10 .....2 C6
Great Dunmow CM6 ..150 D8
Maldon CM9 ....237 A2
Chequers Par RM9 ...354 A4
Chequers Rd
Brentwood CM14,RM3 .292 F7
Little Bromley CO11 ..113 C6
Loughton IG10 ....289 B4
Writtle CM1 ....230 F1
Chequers The CO7 ...165 A7
Chequers Wlk CM9 ...265 F6
Cheriton Ave IG5 ....311 A1
Cheriton Rd CM7 ....128 C1
Cherries The SS8 ....364 B1
Cherry Ave CM13 ....316 F7
Cherry Bglws ■ CM7 ..127 F3
Cherry Blossom Cl
Harlow CM17 ....200 C4
Ipswich IP8 ....16 B2
Cherry Blossom La CM3 .280 F6
Cherry Chase CO5 ...186 D4
Cherry Cl
Canvey Island SS8 ...363 F4
Hockley SS5 ....324 F7
Cherry Ct
Canvey Island SS8 ...364 B1
Ilford IG6 ....111 B8
Cherrydown Grays RM16 .373 C6
Cherrydown Ave E4 ..309 A7
Cherrydown E SS15 ..340 A5
Cherrydown W SS15 .342 A5
Cherrydown Wlk RM7 .313 B1
Cherrygarden La ■ CM2 .254 E7
Cherry Garden La
Danbury CM3 ....257 B7
Newport CB11 ....66 F8
Cherry Garden Rd
Great Waltham CM3 ..207 E2
Maldon CM9 ....236 E2
Cherry Gdns
Billericay CM12 ......296 E4
Bishop's Stortford CM23 .146 A8
Dagenham RM9 ......353 F7
Great Notley CM77 ...154 D8
Haverhill CB9 ....9 B8
Sawbridgeworth CM21 .172 E4
Cherry Orch
Chelmsford CM2 .....232 F4
Cherry Orchard La SS4 .347 B8

Cherry Orchard Way
Rochford SS4 ....325 B1
Southend-on-S SS2,SS4 .347 B8
Cherry Row CO3 .....134 F5
Cherry St RM7 ......335 D6
Cherry Tree Ave CO15 .195 C1
Cherrytree Chase SS3 .350 C1
Cherry Tree Cl
Grays RM17 ....378 D8
Halstead CO9 ....77 A2
Little Oakley CO12 ...117 B7
Rainham RM13 ......355 A3
Cherrytree Ct CO3 ...134 F5
Cherry Tree Cl E E18 .309 F1
Cherry Tree Dr RM15 .357 D1
Cherry Tree Ho CO5 ..158 C3
Cherry Tree La
Abberton CO7 ....162 F6
Blackheath CO2 .....163 A7
Rainham RM13 ......354 F2
Cherry Tree Prim Sch
Basildon SS16 ....342 D5
Blackheath CO2 .....163 A8
Cherrytree Rd CO10 ..34 B7
Cherry Tree Rd EN11 .221 A7
Cherrytree Rise CM8 .184 A5
Cherry Tree Rise IG9 .310 D6
Cherrytrees CO15 ....318 F8
Cherry Trees CO15 ...195 F2
Cherry Wlk Grays RM16 .374 A3
Rainham RM13 ......355 A3
Cherrywood Dr CO3 ..134 F5
Cherrywoods CO7 ...166 D8
Chevers Pawen SS13 .343 A5
Chevington Pl RM12 .355 D7
Chevington Way RM12 .355 D8
Cheviot Dr CM1 ......231 C6
Cheviot Ho DA11 ....378 D1
Cheviot Rd RM11 ....336 A4
Cheviot Way IG2 .....333 E7
Chevron Ho RM17 ...378 B7
Chevy Ct CO2 ....90 C2
Cheyne Ct Sudbury CO10 .33 E7
E ■ Wickford SS12 ...321 E5
Chichester Cl
Aveley RM15 ....371 C5
Basildon SS14 ....342 F8
Canvey Island SS8 ...362 A2
Grays RM16 ....373 C2
Chichester Ct CO3 ...135 A7
Chichester Dr 232 C4
Chichester Gdns IG1 .332 F4
Chichester Ho ■ CM14 .316 C8
Chichester Rd
Greenhithe DA9 .....376 F1
Saffron Walden CB11 .43 E8
Southend-on-S SS1 ..367 A8
Chichester Way CM9 .148 C7
Chichester Wharf DA8 .369 E1
Chickney Rd CM22 ...95 C7
Chieftan Dr RM19 ...371 A2
Chigborough Rd CM9 .237 F6
Chignal Rd CM1 .....231 A5
Chignall The ■ SS15 .341 A6
Chigwell Cty Prim Sch
IG7 ....311 B1
Chigwell La IG10 ....289 C5
Chigwell Park Dr IG7 .311 A6
Chigwell Pk IG7 .....311 B6
Chigwell Rd
Wanstead E18 ....310 D3
Woodford E18 ....310 D3
Chigwell Rise IG7 ...311 A7
Chigwell Row Inf Sch
IG7 ....312 B8
Chigwell Sch IG7 ....311 C8
Chigwell St5z IG7 ...311 B7
Chigwell View RM5 ..313 A1
Chilburn Rd CO15 ...196 A7
Childerditch Hall Dr
CM13 ....339 A7
Childerditch Ind Pk
CM13 ....338 F8
Childerditch La
Little Warley CM13 ..338 A4
West Horndon CM13 .339 B5
Childerditch St CM13 .339 B8
Childers Field IP11 ..381 A6
Childers Rd IG10 ....289 B7
Childs Cl RM11 ......336 C5
Childs Ct RM11 .....336 D5
Childwall Alley CO1 .134 F7
Chilford Ct CM7 .....127 D3
Chiltern Ci SS13 ....343 C5
Chilham Ct SS11 ....353 B4
Chiltern App SS8 ....363 E4
Chiltern Cl
Colchester CO4 ......109 E1
Rayleigh SS6 ....323 D3
Chiltern Gdns RM12 .355 B8
Chiltern Rd IG2 .....333 E6
Chilterns The SS8 ...363 E4
Chiltern Way CM0 ...310 A7
Chilton Cl
Chelmsford CM2 .....205 E2
Great Horkesley CO6 .109 B7
Chilton Cotts CO6 ...80 E4
Chilton Ind Est CO10 .34 A6
Chilton Lodge Rd CO10 .34 A6
Chilton Rd Gt Grays RM16 .374 A3
Ipswich IP3 ....18 C4
Chiltons The ■ E18 ..309 F2
Chime The SS7 ......344 E4
Chimney Pot La CM9 .273 A3
Chimswell Way CM9 ..8 C8
Chinchilla Rd SS1 ...368 D8
Chindits La CM14 ....316 C5
Chinery Cl E4 ....309 E7
Chingdale Rd E4 ....310 A7
Chingford Ave
Chingford E4 ....309 B8

Chingford Ave continued
Clacton-on-S CO15 ...195 F8
Chingford CE Inf Sch E4 .287 D1
Chingford CE Jun Sch
E4 ....287 D1
Chingford Foundation Sch
E4 ....287 B1
Chingford Hall Com Prim Sch
E4 ....309 A4
Chingford La IG8 ....288 A4
Chingford Mount Rd E4 .309 A5
Chingford Rd
Chingford E17 ....309 B1
Chingford, Highams Park
E4 ....309 A3
Chingford Sta E4 ....287 E2
Chinnel La CM13 ....42 D5
Chinnery Hill CM23 .145 F5
Chinook CO4 ....110 D4
Chippenham Cl RM3 .314 D5
Chippenham Gdns RM3 .314 D5
Chippenham Rd RM3 .314 D5
Chippenham Wlk RM3 .314 D4
Chipperfield Cl RM14 .337 E3
Chippetts La CO3 ...133 E7
Chippingdell CM8 ...183 F4
Chippingfield CM17 .200 C3
Chipping Hill
E Halstead CO9 .....76 F2
Witham CM8 ....183 F3
Chipping Hill Inf Sch
CM8 ....183 F3
Chipping Ongar Prim Sch
CM5 ....248 F1
Chipping Row E CM3 .301 E7
Chipstead Wlk CO16 .355 C8
Chishill Rd SS0 ......19 A4
Chisholm Ct E SS12 .321 E5
Chislett Row CM2 ...254 C8
Chittenden Cl E SS11 .197 B1
Chittock Gate SS14 .342 E6
Chittock Mead SS14 .342 E6
Chitts Hill CO3 ......108 D1
Chitty's La RM8 .....334 D2
Chivers Rd Chingford E4 .309 B6
Haverhill CB9 ....8 D7
Stondon Massey CM15 .271 F4
Choat's Cotts CO6 ..107 E1
Choats Manor Way RM9 .353 F2
Choats Rd IG11 .....353 E2
Choats Wood CO7 ...107 F1
Chorley Cl SS16 .....340 F5
Chrismund Way CO6 .106 C1
Christchurch Ave
Rainham RM13 ......354 F2
Wickford SS12 ....321 A8
Christchurch Ct ■ IP4 .17 D6
Christ Church Ct CO3 .135 D5
Christchurch Mansion
(Mus)* IP4 ....17 D6
Christchurch Park Hospl
(private) IP1 ....17 C7
Christchurch Prim Sch
IP1 ....333 C3
Christchurch Rd
Ilford IG2 ....333 D3
Southend-on-S SS2 ..348 C1
Tilbury RM18 ....379 A6
Christchurch St IP4 .17 D6
Christie Gdns RM3 ..334 B4
Christie Rd EN9 .....265 B4
Christies Warehouse E
IP4 ....17 D5
Christina Rd CM8 ...211 E8
Christine Chase CO3 .134 F5
Christmas Field CO10 .51 D2
Christopher Cl RM11 .323 D8
Christopher Dr CO16 .168 C2
Christopher Jolly Ct CO2 .135 F4
Christopher La CO10 .33 E7
Christopher Martin Rd
SS14 ....320 F3
Christy Ave CM1 ....204 E1
Christy Cl SS15 .....340 E7
Christy Ct SS15 .....340 E7
Christy Way SS15 ...340 E7
Chudleigh Cres IG3 .352 E8
Chudleigh Rd RM3 ..314 E6
Chulmleigh Cl CM15 .295 A1
Churce Cl ■ RM3 ...355 A1
Church App SS8 .....363 E4
Church Ave
Broomfield CM1 .....208 A2
Chingford E4 ....309 D4
Church Chase
Great Bentwd CM8 ..185 A3
Rettendon CM3 .....300 C5
Church Cl
Canvey Island SS8 ...363 E4
Cavendish CO10 .....1 D1
Kelvedon Hatch CM14 .271 D2
Loughton IG10 ......288 F7
Mountnessing CM15 .295 C6
Southend-on-S SS3 ..368 D6
Sproughton IP8 .....16 A6
West Bergholt CO6 ..108 E4
Wickham Bishops CM8 .212 D5

Church Cres continued
Sproughton IP8 .....16 A6
Church Ct EN10 .....221 A3
Church Dr CM23 ....92 B8
Church Elm La RM10 .354 A6
Churchend SS3 ......330 A6
Church End
Great Dunmow CM6 ..123 C7
Harlow CM19 ....223 A6
Panfield CM7 ....127 B2
Church End Ave SS11 .299 E2
Church End La SS11 .299 E2
Church End Villas CM6 .123 C3
Church Farm CO4 ..109 D4
Church Farm Way CM4 .200 B2
Church Field
Epping CM16 ....246 A2
Saffron Walden CB11 .43 E7
Churchfield Cotts SS3 .330 B7
Churchfield Rd
Coggeshall CO6 .....131 A3
Walton-on-t-N CO14 .171 C8
Church Field Rd CO10 .34 C8
Churchfields
Hoddesdon EN10 ...221 A3
Loughton IG10 ......288 E5
Southend-on-S SS3 ..349 E2
Churchfields Ave
CM24 ....119 F6
Steeple Bumpstead CB9 .27 B6
West Mersea CO5 ...218 B6
Woodford IG8 ....310 A2
Churchfields Dr CB9 .27 B6
Churchfields Inf Sch
E18 ....310 A2
Churchfields Jun Sch
E18 ....310 A2
Churchfields La CO10 .221 A3
Churchgate Glemsford CO10 .2 C5
Thorpe-le-S CO16 ...347 C1
Churchgate CE Prim Sch
CM17 ....200 C3
Churchgate St CM17 .200 D4
Church Gdns CM9 ...123 D2
Church Gn Boreham CM3 .233 F8
Broomfield CM1 .....208 B1
Canewdon SS4 ......304 D2
Coggeshall CO6 .....131 A3
Hinxton CB10 ....3 B7
Little Yeldham CO9 ..30 D4
Roxwell CM1 ....230 B5
Wickham Bishops CM8 .212 D5
Church Gr Cl 118 A4
Church Hill Abb Roding CB10 .24 A8
Basildon SS15 ....341 D8
Earls Colne CO6 .....105 C6
Epping CM16 ....72 D6
Finchingfield CM7 ..72 D6
Grantham DA9 ......376 E2
Harwich CO12 ....90 B1
Helions Bumpstead CB9 .45 F3
Lawford CO11 ....86 F4
Little Waltham CM3 .208 C6
Loughton IG10 ....288 F6
Purleigh CM3 ....258 C1
Rowhedge CO5 .....163 F8
Southend-on-S SS9 .360 C5
Stanford-le-H SS17 .360 C1
White Notley CM8 ...182 F8
Woodham Walter CM9 .235 E2
Church Hollow RM19 .371 C1
Church Housen CM3 .207 F7
Churchill Ave
Halstead CO9 ....77 A3
Ipswich IP4 ....18 B5
Churchill Cl
Brightlingsea CO7 ...192 F8
Chipping Ongar CM5 .249 A4
Churchill Cres SS17 ..64 A7
E Ilford IG2 ....333 B1
Churchill Ct Harwich CO12 .91 A4
E Ilford IG2 ....333 B1
Churchill Dr CO10 ...15 D2
Churchill Lodge SS8 .309 D4
Churchill Mews RM8 .333 F7
Churchill Pk DA1 ....376 A2
Churchill Rd
Braintree CM7 ......127 E7
Grays RM17 ....378 D8
Tiptree CO5 ....186 F5
Churchill Rise SS4 ..127 F4
Churchill Sq E SS1 ..367 A6
Churchill Terr
Braintree CM7 ......127 E6
Chingford E4 ....309 A7
Churchill Way CO2 ..136 A4
Church La Abbdge RM4 .290 E6
Basildon, Burnt Mills SS13 .321 A2
Basildon, Crays Hill CM11 .320 B6
Beaumont CO16 .....142 A6
Belchamp St Paul CO10 .16 A7
Bishop's Stortford CM23 .145 D3
Braintree CM7 ....127 F2
Brantham CO11 ......60 E1
Brentwood CM13 ...295 F2
Bulphan RM14 ......358 E4
Castle Camps CB1 ..7 E3
Castle Hedingham CO9 .51 E4
E Chelmsford, Moulsham
CM1 ....232 B2
Chelmsford, Springfield
CM1 ....232 D4
Chipping Ongar CM5 .249 B7
Clacton-on-S CO15 ..195 C7
Clare CO10 ....12 B7
Colchester CO1 .....136 A7
Colchester,Stanway CO3 .134 C3
Dagenham RM10 ....354 C4
Debden CB11 ....68 A7
Doddinghurst CM15 .272 B2
East Mersea CO5 ...191 E1

Church La *continued*
Elsenham CM22 ....120 E8
Felixstowe IP11 ....381 D6
Ford End CM3 ....179 B6
Great Henny CO10 ....54 D8
Great Holland CO13 ....170 B3
Great Leighs CM3 ....180 D7
Great Tey CO6 ....132 C4
Great Warley CM13 ....338 D5
Great Wigborough CO5 ....188 F4
Harkstead IP9 ....63 B3
Harwich CO12 ....91 E6
Heybridge CM9 ....238 A8
Little Totham CM9 ....214 B1
Loughton IG10 ....288 F6
Margaretting CM4 ....274 E6
Marks Tey CO6 ....133 A4
Mistley CO11 ....86 E4
Nayland CO6 ....56 B1
North Ockendon RM14 ....357 B7
North Weald Bassett CM16 247 A6
Purfleet RM19 ....371 A1
Ridgewell CO9 ....29 B6
Romford RM1 ....335 E7
Sheering CM22 ....201 D7
South Hanningfield CM3 ....299 C8
Sproughton IP8 ....16 B6
Stapleford Abbotts RM4 ....291 C5
Stow Maries CM3 ....280 D3
Takeley,Brewer's End
CM22 ....148 B7
Takeley,Little Canfield CM6 149 B7
Toppesfield CO9 ....50 B7
Washbrook,Copdock IP8 ....35 F7
Washbrook IP8 ....35 D8
Weeley Heath CO16 ....168 A7
Wennington RM13 ....370 D7
West Hanningfield CM2 ....277 A4
White Roding CM6 ....203 C7
Widdington CB11 ....67 D4
Writtle CM1 ....231 B1
Church Lane Cotts
Doddinghurst CM15 ....272 B2
Rainham RM13 ....370 D7
Church Langley Com Prim Sch
CM17 ....224 C8
Church Langley Way
CM17 ....224 D8
Church Leys CM18 ....223 F7
Church Manor CM23 ....146 B8
Church Manorway DA8 .369 D3
Churchmans Ho IP1 ....17 B5
Church Mdws CM7 ....127 F6
Church Mead
Roydon CM19 ....198 B1
White Notley CM8 ....155 F1
Church Mews
Basildon SS15 ....341 B7
Nayland CO6 ....56 B1
Church Par SS8 ....363 E5
Church Park Rd SS13 ....343 B5
Church Path
Greenhithe DA9 ....376 F1
Hadstock CB1 ....5 B6
Northfleet DA11 ....378 C1
Saffron Walden CB10 ....22 D2
Wanstead E11 ....332 A6
Church Pk CO10 ....11 C3
Churchponds CO9 ....51 E4
Church Rd
Alphamstone CO10 ....54 C6
Alresford CO7 ....165 B7
Barking E12 ....352 C6
Barling SS3 ....349 E8
Basildon,Barstable SS14,
SS16 ....342 C6
Basildon,Bowers Gifford
SS13 ....343 F6
Basildon,Great Berry RM14 340 D5
Basildon, Noak Bridge SS15 319 E1
Basildon,Pipps Hill SS15 ....341 E8
Bentley IP9 ....60 F7
Black Notley CM77 ....155 A6
Boxted CO4 ....82 E6
Bradwell CM7 ....129 E1
Brightlingsea CO7 ....192 E8
Buckhurst Hill IG9 ....288 B1
Bulmer CO10 ....32 F4
Bulphan RM14 ....358 F8
Burnham-on-C CM0 ....306 B6
Capel St M IP9 ....35 F1
Chipping Ongar CM5 ....270 D6
Chrishall SG8 ....19 D3
Clacton-on-S CO15 ....196 A3
Copford CO6 ....133 E2
Corringham SS17 ....361 B3
Cressing CM77 ....156 A5
Elmstead CO7 ....138 A7
Erith DA8 ....369 D1
Fordham CO6 ....107 D5
Frating CO7 ....138 D2
Gosfield CO9 ....102 E8
Great Cornard CO10 ....34 A5
Great Hallingbury CM22 ....146 D3
Great Notley CM77 ....154 F6
Great Totham CM9 ....213 E3
Great Yeldham CO9 ....29 F2
Greenhithe DA9 ....376 F2
Greenstead Green CO9 ....104 A5
Hadleigh SS7 ....345 F2
Harlow CM17 ....224 C5
Hatfield Peverel CM3 ....211 A3
Hempstead CB10 ....46 F8
High Beach IG10 ....288 A7
Hockley SS5 ....324 B7
Holbrook IP9 ....62 D5
Ilford IG2 ....333 E5
Kelvedon CO5 ....158 C2
Kelvedon Hatch CM14 ....271 C2
Layer-de-l-H CO2 ....161 F4
Little Baddow CM3 ....234 A6
Little Bentley CO7 ....140 A5
Church Rd *continued*
Little Bromley CO11 ....113 B4
Little Ilford E12 ....352 A7
Moreton CM5 ....226 D2
Mountnessing CM15 ....295 F7
Navestock Heath RM4 ....292 D8
North Fambridge CM3 ....303 A7
Pattiswick CM7 ....129 F5
Peldon CO5 ....189 D6
Ramsden Heath CM11,
SS14,SS16,SS13 ....298 D2
Rawreth SS11 ....322 D7
Rayleigh SS6 ....323 F2
Rivenhall CM8 ....157 B1
Rochford SS4 ....325 C7
Romford,Harold Park RM3 315 A3
Romford RM4 ....292 C1
Shudy Camps CB1 ....7 C5
South Benfleet, New Thundersley
SS7 ....344 D6
Southend-on-S, Cambridge Town
SS3 ....368 D6
Southend-on-S SS1 ....367 A7
Stambourne CO9 ....28 D2
Stansted Mountfitchet
CM24 ....119 F5
Stutton IP9 ....62 A2
Swanscombe DA10 ....377 F1
Tattingstone IP9 ....61 C7
Terling CM3 ....182 B2
Thorrington CO7 ....166 A6
Tilbury RM18 ....378 F6
Tiptree CO5 ....186 D5
Tolleshunt Major CM9 ....214 F2
Ulting CM9 ....235 C6
Walton-on-t-N CO14 ....171 C8
West Hanningfield CM2 ....277 A4
West Mersea CO5 ....218 B6
West Tilbury RM18 ....379 E8
Wickham Bishops CM8 ....212 E5
Wickham St P CO9 ....53 B6
Wormingford CO6 ....80 E5
Wrabness CO11 ....88 F4
Church Rise CB9 ....26 C8
Church Row RM16 ....359 A1
Church Sq Bures CO8 ....55 F1
St Osyth CO16 ....194 A4
Church St
Belchamp St P CO10 ....13 B3
Billericay CM11 ....319 C6
Bishop's Stortford CM23 ....145 F7
Blackmore CM4 ....272 E8
Boxted CO4 ....82 F7
Braintree CM7 ....102 B1
Chelmondiston IP9 ....63 E7
Chelmsford CM1 ....232 B2
Clare CO10 ....12 B7
Coggeshall CO6 ....131 A2
Colchester CO1 ....135 E7
Colne Engaine CO6 ....78 A1
Dagenham RM10 ....354 B6
Gestingthorpe CO9 ....31 E1
Goldhanger CM9 ....238 E7
Gravesend DA11 ....379 B1
Grays RM17 ....378 C8
Great Baddow CM2 ....255 A6
Great Chesterford CB10 ....3 D2
Great Dunmow CM6 ....123 D2
Great Maplestead CO9 ....52 D1
Harwich CO12 ....91 E6
Henham CM22 ....94 F6
Ickleton CB10 ....3 B4
Kelvedon CO5 ....158 B2
Maldon CM9 ....237 B2
Newport CB11 ....43 A1
Rayleigh SS6 ....323 D2
Rowhedge CO5 ....164 A8
Saffron Walden CB10 ....22 D2
Sawbridgeworth CM21 ....172 E2
Sible Hedingham CO9 ....51 D1
Steeple Bumpstead CB9 ....27 B7
Stoke-by-N CO6 ....56 D5
Sudbury CO10 ....33 D6
Tollesbury CM9 ....216 D1
Tolleshunt D'Arcy CM9 ....215 D4
Waltham Abbey EN9 ....265 C6
Wendens Ambo CB11 ....42 E5
Witham CM8 ....183 F4
Church Terr
Stapleford Abbotts RM4 ....291 C5
Stoke by C CO10 ....10 D2
Church View
Ardleigh CO7 ....111 E7
Aveley RM15 ....371 D4
Colne Engaine CO6 ....77 F1
Stoke by C CO10 ....10 D3
Upminster RM14 ....337 B2
Church View Rd SS7 ....344 E6
Churchway SS7 ....345 F2
Churchwell Ave CO5 ....160 A7
Church Wlk
Basildon SS14 ....342 A6
Brentwood CM15 ....294 B2
Colchester CO1 ....135 F7
Littlebury CB11 ....21 F4
Maldon CM9 ....236 F3
Sawbridgeworth CM21 ....172 F2
Sturmer CB9 ....9 E4
5 Sudbury CO10 ....33 E7
Churchwood Gdns IG8 ....310 A6
Churnwood Cl CO4 ....110 D1
Churnwood Rd CO4 ....110 D1
Chuzzlewit Dr CM1 ....231 E7
Cillocks Cl EN11 ....221 A7
Cimarron Cl CM3 ....301 D7
Cinema Par RM8 ....334 F2
Cinnabar Cl IP8 ....36 E8
Cinque Port Rd CO7 ....192 F7
Circle The RM18 ....379 A6
Circular Rd E CO2 ....135 F5
Circular Rd N CO2 ....135 E5
Circular Rd S CO2 ....135 E4
Circular Rd W CO2 ....135 E5
City Rd CO5 ....218 A6
Civic Dr IP1 ....17 B6
Civic Ind Est CB9 ....8 F5
Civic Sq RM18 ....379 A5
Civic Way IG6 ....333 C7
Clachar Cl CM2 ....233 A3
Clacton Common CO15 ....169 A1
Clacton Cty High Sch
CO15 ....196 A4
Clacton & District Hospl
CO15 ....195 E1
Clacton Rd
Bradfield CO11 ....114 A6
Elmstead CO7 ....138 C5
Great Holland CO13 ....170 A2
Holland-on-S CO15 ....196 F7
Little Oakley CO12 ....117 B5
Mistley CO11 ....86 E2
St Osyth CO16 ....194 B4
Thorrington CO7 ....166 C4
Weeley Heath CO16 ....168 A6
Wivenhoe CO7 ....137 C5
Wix CO11 ....115 C5
Wix,Stones Green CO12 ....115 D1
Clacton Sta CO15 ....195 F3
Claire Cl CM13 ....316 F6
Claire Ct CO5 ....218 C7
Claire Ho IG5 ....310 F2
Claire Rd CO13 ....170 B6
Clairmont Cl 11 CM7 ....127 F2
Clairmont Rd CO3 ....134 E5
Clairvale RM11 ....336 E4
Clandon Ho CO13 ....170 F4
Clandon Rd IG3 ....333 E2
Clapgate Dr CO16 ....168 C2
Clapgate La IP3 ....18 A2
Claps Gate La E6 ....352 B1
Clapton Hall La
Great Dunmow CM6 ....150 D5
Great Dunmow CM6 ....150 E6
Clara Reeve Cl CO3 ....134 F4
Clare Ancient House Mus*
CO10 ....12 C7
Clare Ave SS11 ....299 D2
Clare Castle Ctry Pk*
CO10 ....12 C7
Clare Cl CO9 ....103 D7
Clare Com Prim Sch
CO10 ....12 B8
Clare Cswy DA2 ....376 F3
Clare Ct CM6 ....69 F3
Clare Gdns IG11 ....353 A5
Clare James Cotts 4
SS8 ....364 A3
Clare Mews CM5 ....249 A5
Clare Mid Sch CO10 ....12 C8
Claremont Cl Grays RM16 373 C3
Southend-on-S SS0 ....347 E1
Claremont Dr SS16 ....343 A4
Claremont Gdns
Ilford IG3 ....333 E2
Upminster RM14 ....337 D3
Claremont Gr IG8 ....310 C4
Claremont Hts CO1 ....109 E1
Claremont Rd
Basildon SS15 ....341 C8
Hornchurch RM11 ....336 A5
Southend-on-S SS0 ....347 D1
Wivenhoe CO7 ....164 C8
Clarence Ave Ilford IG2 ....333 A5
Redbridge IG1 ....332 F5
Upminster RM14 ....337 A2
Clarence Cl
Chelmsford CM2 ....233 A4
South Benfleet SS7 ....344 D4
Clarence Gate IG8 ....311 A4
Clarence Rd
Basildon SS13 ....343 F7
Clare CO10 ....12 B8
Corringham SS17 ....361 C4
Grays RM17 ....373 B1
Ipswich IP3 ....18 B1
Pilgrims Hatch CM15 ....294 B3
Rayleigh SS6 ....324 A1
South Benfleet SS7 ....344 D3
Southend-on-S SS1 ....367 A7
Stansted Mountfitchet
CM24 ....119 E7
Sudbury CO10 ....15 E1
Clarence Rd N SS7 ....344 E4
Clarence St SS1 ....367 A7
Clarendon Gdns
Ilford IG1 ....333 A4
Redbridge IG1 ....332 F4
Clarendon Pk CO15 ....196 B5
Clarendon Rd
Basildon SS13 ....343 C7
Canvey Island SS8 ....364 C4
Gravesend DA12 ....379 C1
Haverhill CB9 ....8 F6
Hockley SS5 ....302 F1
Takeley CM6 ....148 E7
Wanstead E18 ....332 A8
Clarendon Way CO1 ....109 E1
Clare Rd Braintree CM7 ....127 E2
Ipswich IP4 ....17 F8
South Benfleet SS7 ....344 A6
Clare Way CO16 ....195 B5
Claridge Rd RM8 ....334 D3
Clarissa Rd RM6 ....334 D4
Clarkbourne Dr RM17 ....378 D8
Clarke Mans 8 IG11 ....352 F5
Clarke Rise CM3 ....280 F5
Clarkesmead CO5 ....186 C4
Clarke's Rd CO12 ....90 F3
Clarkia Wlk CO4 ....110 E2
Clarklands Ind Est CM21 172 E5
Clarks Cotts SS11 ....322 F7
Clarks Farm Rd CM3 ....256 F8
Clarks Field Cotts CM3 ....257 E2
Clarkson La CM16 ....267 F8
Clarkson St IP1 ....17 B6
Clarksons The IG11 ....352 C3
Clark's Rd IG1 ....333 D2
Clarks Wood Dr CM7 ....128 D3
Clark Way CM1 ....208 A1
Claters Cl SS2 ....348 F2
Clatterbury La
Arkesden CB11 ....41 E1
Clavering CB11 ....65 D5
Clatterfield Gdns SS0 ....347 B3
Claude Oliver Cl CO11 ....86 A2
Claude St IP1 ....17 C6
Claudian Cl CB9 ....9 D7
Claudian Way RM16 ....374 B3
Claud Ince Ave CM77 ....155 E6
Claudius Rd CO2 ....136 A5
Claudius Way CM8 ....211 E8
Claughton Way CM13 ....295 D3
Claverhambury Farm Bglws
EN9 ....244 A3
Claverhambury Rd EN9 ....244 A3
Clavering SS16 ....342 F4
Clavering Ct SS6 ....323 B3
Clavering Gdns CM13 ....339 D5
Clavering Prim Sch CB11 ....65 C4
Clavering Rd
Braintree CM7 ....127 F6
Wanstead E12 ....332 D2
Clavering Way CM13 ....295 C3
Claverton Way IP4 ....18 E4
Claybrick Ave SS5 ....324 D5
Clayburn Circ SS14 ....342 D6
Clayburn End SS14 ....342 D6
Clayburn Gdns RM15 ....372 B6
Clayburn Side SS14 ....342 D6
Claybury Broadway IG5 ....332 E8
Claybury Rd IG8 ....310 E3
Claydon Cl CB1 ....7 E4
Claydon Cres SS14 ....342 C7
Claydon Ct RM12 ....354 F8
Claydons La SS6 ....345 C7
Claygate Cl RM12 ....355 A8
Clayhall Ave
Redbridge IG5 ....311 A1
Woodford IG5 ....310 E1
Clayhall Rd CO15 ....196 A5
Clay Hill CO10 ....54 C8
Clay Hill Rd SS16 ....342 C4
Clayhive Dr CB9 ....8 F7
Clay La Stebbing CM6 ....124 D7
St Osyth CO16 ....194 C7
Clay Lane Gr CO4 ....110 D4
Claypit Hill
Elsenham CM22 ....120 E5
Loughton EN9 ....266 C2
Clay Pit Piece CB11 ....43 E6
Clay Pits CM7 ....128 D3
Claypits Ave CO8 ....80 A8
Claypits La CO10 ....14 D5
Claypits Rd CM3 ....209 F1
Claypits Villas CM6 ....70 B2
Clay Pits Way CM7 ....128 D3
Claypons CM23 ....146 B7
Clayshotts Dr CM8 ....212 B8
Clayside IG7 ....311 C5
Clay's La IG10 ....289 A8
Clays Mdw CB11 ....21 F4
Clayspring Cl SS5 ....324 D7
Clays Rd CO14 ....171 B7
Clayton Ave RM14 ....356 B7
Clayton Hill Ctry Pk*
EN9 ....243 D8
Clayton Rd Harwich CO12 ....90 C2
Romford RM7 ....335 C3
Claytonville Terr DA17 ....369 C4
Clayton Way CM9 ....259 A8
Clay Tye Rd
North Ockendon RM14 ....357 C8
Upminster RM14 ....338 C1
Claywall Bridge CB9 ....27 C7
Claywall Cotts CB9 ....27 C7
Cleall Ave EN9 ....265 C5
Clear Ct CM3 ....282 B5
Clearing Cl IP8 ....36 E8
Clear Springs Chalet Site
CO12 ....91 A1
Clearwater CO2 ....136 B3
Cleland Path IG10 ....289 B8
Clematis Cl RM3 ....314 C3
Clematis Gdns IG8 ....310 A5
Clematis Tye 3 CM1 ....232 F7
Clematis Way CO4 ....136 E7
Clemence Rd RM10 ....354 C4
Clementhorpe Rd RM9 ....353 C6
Clementine Gdns IP4 ....18 B5
Clement Mellish Ho 10
CO1 ....135 F7
Clements Cl
Chelmsford CM2 ....233 B3
Haverhill CB9 ....8 F7
Clements Ct 5 IG1 ....333 B1
Clements Dr CB9 ....8 F7
Clements Gdns SS5 ....325 A5
Clements Green La CM3 301 D8
Clements Hall La SS5 ....325 A5
Clements Hall Sports Ctr
SS5 ....325 A4
Clements Hall Way SS5 .325 A4
Clements La IG1 ....333 B1
Clement's La CB9 ....8 F7
Clements Pl CM3 ....301 D8
Clements Prim Sch CB9 ....8 F7
Clements Rd Ilford IG1 ....333 B1
Wallend E6 ....352 A5
Clement Way RM14 ....336 F1
Clench Cl 8 IP4 ....17 D6
Clench Rd IP9 ....62 D7
Clerks Piece IG10 ....288 F6
Clermont Ave CO10 ....15 E2
Cleveden Ho SS7 ....344 F6
Clevedon Cl CM77 ....154 C7
Cleveland Cl CO4 ....110 C4
Cleveland Dr SS0 ....347 E3
Cleveland Ho DA11 ....378 D1
Cleveland Prim Sch IG1 .333 B1
Cleveland Rd
Basildon SS14 ....342 C6
Canvey Island SS8 ....364 B2
Ilford IG1 ....333 B1
Wanstead E18 ....332 A8
7 Woodford E18 ....310 A1
Clevelands The IG11 ....352 C6
Cleves Ave CM14 ....294 B1
Cleves Cl IG10 ....288 E3
Cleves Ct CM3 ....209 E1
Cleves Rd CB9 ....8 D6
Cleves Wlk IG6 ....311 C3
Clevis Dr CM3 ....301 E5
Clicket Hill CO8 ....80 B8
Clickett End SS14 ....342 C6
Clickett Hill SS14 ....342 C6
Clickett Side SS14 ....342 C6
Clieveden Rd SS1 ....367 F6
Cliff Ave
Southend-on-S,Chalkwell
SS9 ....366 A8
Southend-on-S SS0 ....347 E1
Cliff Cres CM7 ....100 E7
Cliff Ct CO13 ....171 B6
Cliff Gdns SS9 ....366 A8
Cliffield CM7 ....100 E7
Cliff La IP3 ....17 F3
Cliff Lane Prim Sch IP3 ....17 E3
Clifford Ave IG5 ....311 B1
Clifford Cl SS15 ....341 D5
Clifford Ct 10 CM23 ....146 A7
Clifford Rd Chingford E17 309 C1
Grays RM16 ....372 F3
Ipswich IP4 ....17 F5
Clifford Road Prim Sch
IP4 ....17 F5
Cliff Par
Southend-on-S SS9 ....365 E8
Walton-on-t-N CO14 ....144 E2
Cliff Pl RM15 ....357 D2
Cliff Rd Harwich CO12 ....91 D3
Holland-on-S CO15 ....196 E5
Ipswich IP3 ....17 E3
Southend-on-S SS9 ....366 A8
Cliffsea Gr SS9 ....346 F1
Clifftown Par SS1 ....366 F7
Clifftown Rd SS1 ....367 A7
Cliff Way CO13 ....171 B5
Clifton Ave SS7 ....344 C4
Clifton Cl SS7 ....344 D4
Clifton Ct 3 IG8 ....310 A4
Clifton Dr SS0 ....366 D7
Clifton Hatch CM18 ....224 A5
Clifton Marine Par DA11 378 F1
Clifton Mews SS1 ....367 A7
Clifton Rd Basildon SS13 ....343 F7
Canvey Island SS8 ....364 B3
Gravesend DA11 ....379 A1
Hornchurch RM11 ....336 A5
Ilford IG2 ....333 D5
Loughton IG10 ....288 E5
Rochford SS4 ....325 C7
Cliftons Farm Dr CO10 ....12 B7
Clifton Terr
Ingatestone CM4 ....274 C4
Southend-on-S SS1 ....367 A7
Wivenhoe CO7 ....164 B8
Clifton Way
Brentwood CM13 ....295 D1
Ipswich IP2 ....16 D2
South Benfleet SS7 ....344 C4
Clifton Wlk
22 Dartford DA2 ....376 B1
South Benfleet SS7 ....344 D4
Clifton Wood IP9 ....62 D6
Climmen Rd SS8 ....364 B5
Clingoe Ct CO4 ....136 E5
Clinton Cl CM3 ....278 B7
Clinton Cres IG6 ....311 E4
Clinton Rd SS8 ....363 D3
Clipped Hedge CM22 ....174 B3
Clipper Bvd DA2 ....376 E3
Clipper Bvd W DA2 ....376 D4
Clitheroe Rd RM5 ....313 C5
Cliveden Cl
Chelmsford CM1 ....231 E3
Shenfield CM15 ....294 F2
Clivedon Rd E4 ....309 E5
Clive Rd Belvedere DA17 ....369 A2
Brentwood CM13 ....316 C3
Colchester CO1,CO2 ....136 A6
17 Gravesend DA11 ....379 B1
Romford RM2 ....336 B6
Clobbs Yd CM1 ....232 B8
Clock Ct E11 ....332 B7
Clock Ho SS15 ....341 B6
Clockhouse Ave IG11 ....352 C4
Clockhouse Jun & Inf Sch
RM5 ....313 B4
Clockhouse La
Grays RM16 ....372 E3
Romford RM5 ....313 C4
South Ockendon RM16 ....372 E5
Clock House Par 1 E11 332 B5
Clock House Rd CM12 ....318 F5
Clockhouse The RM14 ....337 C2
Clockhouse Way CM7 ....128 C2
Cloes La CO16 ....195 B4
Cloister Cl RM13 ....355 B1
Cloisters
1 Hornchurch RM13 ....355 A6
Stanford-le-H SS17 ....360 E2
Cloisters The
Basildon SS15 ....341 C6
Braintree CM7 ....128 A5
Kelvedon CO5 ....158 B1
Cloncurry Gdns IP11 ....381 B3
Clopton Dr CO10 ....15 C6
Clopton Gn SS14 ....342 B7
Clore Tikva Sch IG6 ....311 C1
Close The
Brentwood CM14 ....316 D7
Chingford E4 ....309 C3
Clacton-on-S CO15 ....220 H7
Cressing CM77 ....155 E6
Dagenham RM6 ....334 E5
Debden CB11 ....68 B7
Frinton-on-S CO13 ....170 E5
Grays RM16 ....373 C4
Great Dunmow CM6 ....150 E7
Great Holland CO13 ....170 A3
Close The *continued*
Harwich CO12 ....91 A3
Hatfield Heath CM22 ....174 A3
Ilford IG2 ....333 E5
South Benfleet, Hope's Green
SS7 ....344 D1
Sudbury CO10 ....33 F8
Tattingstone IP9 ....61 D7
Thundersley SS7 ....345 B8
Cloudberry Rd RM3 ....314 D4
Clouded Yellow Cl CM7 .154 E8
Clough Rd CO4 ....110 D6
Clova Rd SS9 ....346 F2
Clovelly Cl IP4 ....18 F4
Clovelly Ct
Hornchurch RM11 ....336 F2
Upminster RM14 ....337 A2
Clovelly Gdns RM7 ....313 B2
Clover Ave CM23 ....145 B6
Clover Cl Basildon SS16 ....342 E3
Ipswich IP2 ....16 F4
Clover Ct Colchester CO3 .134 D5
Grays RM17 ....378 D8
Great Cornard CO10 ....34 C6
Clover Dr CO7 ....166 A5
Clover Field Harlow CM18 224 A5
Haverhill CB9 ....8 D8
Cloverlands CO4 ....110 C2
Clover Leas CM16 ....245 F2
Cloverley Rd CM5 ....249 A1
Cloverleys IG10 ....288 D4
Clovers 5 CO9 ....76 D1
Clover Villas SS1 ....367 B7
Clover Way Ardleigh CO7 .111 B5
Basildon SS16 ....342 E3
Cluanie Orch CO10 ....1 E1
Club Par CO16 ....220 B6
Cluff Ct CM14 ....316 C6
Clump Field IP2 ....16 F2
Clunas Gdns RM2 ....336 D8
Clunford Pl CM1 ....232 F7
Cluny Sq SS2 ....348 C3
Clusters The 3 SS2 ....347 F1
Clyde RM18 ....375 C2
Clyde Cres
Chelmsford CM1 ....231 D4
Rayleigh SS6 ....345 D8
Upminster RM14 ....337 E5
Clyde Rd EN11 ....221 D5
Clydesdale Rd
Braintree CM7 ....127 E2
Romford RM11 ....335 F4
Clyde Way RM1 ....313 E2
Clynes Ho 6 RM10 ....335 A1
Coach House Way 10
CM8 ....184 A2
Coach La CM9 ....236 F3
Coachmans Ct 6 IP4 ....17 C5
Coachmans Mead CM7 ....72 C6
Coachman's Paddock IP9 62 D6
Coach Mews CM11 ....297 D5
Coach Rd Alresford CO7 ....165 B8
Great Horkesley CO6 ....109 A7
Hempstead CB10 ....25 F2
Coal Ct RM17 ....378 A8
Coalhouse Fort* RM18 ....380 E6
Coalport Cl CM17 ....224 D7
Coan Ave CO15 ....195 D1
Coaster Stps 4 SS1 ....367 C7
Coastguard Cotts
Bradwell-on-S CM0 ....263 E8
Canvey Island SS8 ....363 C1
Walton-on-t-N CO14 ....144 D1
Coast Rd CO5 ....218 A6
Coates Cl CM9 ....237 B4
Coates Quay CM2 ....232 C2
Coats Hutton Rd CO2 ....135 B3
Cobbetts Ave IG4 ....332 D6
Cobbinsbank EN9 ....265 D6
Cobbins Chase CM0 ....306 B8
Cobbins Cl CM0 ....306 B8
Cobbinsend Rd EN9 ....244 D2
Cobbins Gr CM0 ....306 B8
Cobbins The
Burnham-on-C CM0 ....306 B8
Waltham Abbey EN9 ....265 E6
Cobbins Way CM17 ....200 E4
Cobble Row CO3 ....134 E6
Cobbles The
Brentwood CM15 ....316 E8
Upminster RM14 ....337 F4
Cobbold Mews 16 IP4 ....17 D6
Cobbold Rd IP11 ....381 E4
Cobbold St IP4 ....17 D6
Cobbs La CM22 ....121 F3
Cobbs Pl CM1 ....232 D3
Cobden Pl IP4 ....17 D6
Cobdens IG7 ....311 D4
Cobden Wlk SS13 ....343 C7
Cobham RM16 ....373 B4
Cobham Cl DA9 ....377 B1
Cobham Ho IG11 ....352 C4
Cobham Rd Chingford E17 309 C2
Ilford IG3 ....333 E1
Ipswich IP3 ....18 C2
Southend-on-S SS0 ....366 C7
Cobham Terr DA9 ....377 B1
Cobill Cl RM11 ....336 C7
Coburg Gdns IG5 ....310 E1
Coburg La SS16 ....340 F4
Coburg Pl CM3 ....301 D6
Cockabourne Ct RM3 ....315 A1
Cock and Bell La CO10 ....15 C8
Cockaynes La CO7 ....138 A1
Cockerell Cl SS13 ....321 B1
Cockethurst Cl SS0 ....347 A4
Cockett Wick La CO16 ....194 C1
Cock Gn CM19 ....223 B6
Cock La Blackmore CM1 ....251 F2
Clavering CB11 ....64 F3
Edney Common CM1 ....252 A3
Hoddesdon EN11 ....221 A5
Cockle Sheds SS9 ....365 D8
Cock & Pye Ct CO1 ....135 E7
Cock Rd CO9 ....53 B1

Cockrell's Rd C06 .....81 B4
Cockrobin La CM20 .....199 A7
Codenham Gn SS16 .....342 B5
Codenham Straight
SS16 .....342 A4
Codham Hall La CM13 .....338 C7
Codham Little Park Dr
CM7 .....101 C6
Cody Rd IP3 .....18 C1
Coeur De Lion CM9 .....109 F2
Coggeshall Rd
Ardleigh C07 .....84 F2
Braintree CM7 .....128 C3
Coggeshall C06 .....131 F7
Coggeshall,Marks Tey C06 131 F3
Earls Colne C06 .....105 B3
Great Tey C06 .....132 B7
Kelvedon C05 .....158 B5
Marks Tey C06 .....132 C3
Coggeshall Rd (Feering)
C06 .....158 D7
Coggeshall Way C09 .....77 A2
Cogmore CB11 .....4 D5
Cohen Cl CM7 .....155 B5
Cohort Dr C02 .....127 C3
Cokefield Ave SS2 .....348 D3
Coker Rd SS8 .....363 D2
Cokers Cl CM77 .....155 C5
Coke St C012 .....91 D5
Colam La CM3 .....101 C6
Colbayns High Sch C015 195 D4
Colbert Ave SS1 .....367 F7
Colbourne Cl SS17 .....360 F3
Colchester Ave E12 .....332 F1
Colchester Boys High Sch
C05 .....135 E6
Colchester Bsns Pk C04 110 C6
Colchester Castle*
C01 .....135 F7
Colchester Castle Mus*
C01 .....135 F7
Colchester Cl SS2 .....347 F2
Colchester General Hospl
C04 .....109 E5
Colchester High Sch for Girls
C03 .....135 B6
Colchester Inst C015 .....196 A2
Colchester Institute C03 135 D6
Colchester Natural History
Mus* C03 .....135 F7
Colchester Oaks Hospl
C03 .....135 D7
Colchester Rd
Abberton C05 .....163 B1
Ardleigh C07 .....111 C6
Bures C08 .....79 F8
Chappel C06 .....106 E5
Chelmsford CM2 .....233 A6
Coggeshall C06 .....131 D2
Dedham C07 .....84 E6
Elmstead C07 .....137 F6
Frating C07 .....139 E3
Great Bentley C07,C016 .193 F8
Great Bromley C07 .....142 A7
Great Totham CM9 .....213 D7
C05 .....188 C2
Halstead C09 .....170 F5
Heybridge CM9 .....237 A5
Holland-on-S C015 .....196 D6
Ipswich IP4 .....18 D8
Lawford IP11 .....86 C3
Little Horkesley C06 .....81 A1
Peldon C05 .....190 B6
Romford RM3 .....114 C2
Salcott-cum-virley CM9 216 A5
Southend-on-S SS2 .....347 F2
St Osyth C016 .....194 A5
Thorpe-le-S C016 .....141 D2
Tiptree C05 .....186 D7
Weeley C016 .....140 C2
West Bergholt C06 .....108 D6
West Mersea C05 .....218 C7
White Colne C06 .....105 E6
Witham CM8 .....184 B3
Wivenhoe C07 .....137 B4
Wix C012 .....115 B3
Wix,Goose Green C011 .....114 E4
Worminford C06 .....80 A6
Colchester Ret Pk C01 .....135 E7
Colchester Royal Gram Sch
C03 .....135 D6
Colchester Sta C01 .....109 E1
Colchester Town Sta
C01 .....135 E6
Colchester Zoo* C03 .....134 C1
Cold Hall Chase C07 .....138 E6
Coldharbour La RM13 .....370 B4
Coldharbour Rd CM19 .....223 A7
Coldnailhurst Ave CM7 127 F5
Cold Norton Prim Sch
CM3 .....280 F5
Cold Norton Rd CM3 .....181 A1
Cold Store Rd IP11 .....13 C6
Cole Ave RM16 .....314 C2
Colebroke Dr E11 .....332 C4
Colebrook Gdns IG10 289 B7
Colebrook La IG10 .....289 B7
Colebrook Path IG10 289 B7
Cole Ct IM3 .....314 D5
Cole End La CB10 .....44 D5
Coleford Rd [7] RM3 .....314 E4
Cole Gn C012 .....13 A1
Cole Hill CM5 .....181 B5
Colehills Cl CB11 .....65 C4
Colehills Ct CB11 .....65 C4
Coleman Ct C015 .....195 F3
Coleman Rd
Belvedere DA17 .....369 A2
Dagenham RM9 .....353 E6
Colemans Ave SS8 .....347 D4
Colemans La CM3 .....256 D7
Coleman's La EN9 .....243 E5

Coleman St SS2 .....348 A1
Cole Ness Rd IP3 .....38 A8
Colenso Rd IG2 .....333 E4
Coleridge Rd
Dartford DA1 .....376 B3
Maldon CM9 .....237 A1
Romford RM3 .....314 B3
Tilbury RM18 .....379 C5
Coleridge Wlk CM13 .....295 D2
Coles Cl CM5 .....249 A5
Coles Gn IG10 .....289 A8
Coles La C014 .....144 A1
Coles Oak La C07 .....84 C6
Colet Rd CO13 .....295 D4
Coley Ct SS7 .....344 B4
Colgate Pl EN3 .....265 A2
Colin Cl DA2 .....376 B1
Colin Pond Ct RM5 .....134 D8
Colinton Rd IG3 .....334 B2
Collard Ave IG10 .....289 C7
Collard Gn IG10 .....289 C7
College Ave RM17 .....373 C2
College Cl
Bishop's Stortford CM23 145 D7
Grays RM17 .....373 C2
College Ct C011 .....86 C4
College Gdns
Chingford E4 .....287 B2
Redbridge IG4 .....332 E6
College Ho CM7 .....127 E2
College Pl IP4 .....377 C3
College Rd Braintree CM7 127 E2
Clacton-on-S C015 .....196 A3
Grays RM17 .....373 C2
Northfleet DA11 .....370 B8
College Sq CM20 .....17 C5
College Sta E4 .....367 A8
Coller Rd C012 .....90 F5
Colles Brook Rd C07 166 F4
Colletts Chase C06 .....80 F4
Colley Rd CM2 .....255 A6
Collier Row C010 .....6 B1
Collier Row La RM5 .....313 C1
Collier Row Rd
Dagenham RM6 .....312 F2
Romford RM5 .....313 B3
Colliers The CM7 .....237 E3
Collimer Cl IP11 .....63 E7
Collimer Ct IP11 .....381 C6
Collindale Cl SS8 .....364 D4
Collindale Gdns C016 196 C5
Collingwood SS7 .....344 E4
Collingwood Ave IP3 .....18 B3
Collingwood Ho CM7 128 C5
Collingwood Fields C07 59 B4
Collingwood Ho
Brentwood CM13 .....377 D2
Southend-on-S SS0 347 D2
Collingwood Prim Sch
CM3 .....301 E6
Collingwood Rd
Basildon SS16 .....342 D4
Clacton-on-S C015 .....195 D1
Colchester C03 .....134 E6
Rainham RM13 .....355 A3
South Woodham Ferrers
CM3 .....301 F6
Witham CM8 .....184 A2
Collingwood Terr SS16 342 D5
Collingwood Way SS3 349 E1
Collingwood Wlk CM13 342 D5
Collins Cl
[7] Braintree CM7 .....127 F2
Stanford-le-H SS17 .....360 E2
Collins Cross CM23 .....119 B1
Collins Ho [8] IP11 .....352 B5
Collins Mdw CM19 .....223 B7
Collins Rd C09 .....53 D1
Collinson's IP2 .....16 D5
Collins Way
Brentwood CM13 .....295 F4
Southend-on-S SS9 .....347 A6
Collinwood Gdns
Ilford IG5 .....333 A7
Redbridge IG5 .....332 A8
Collops Villas CM4 .....125 A4
Colman Cl SS17 .....360 D3
Colne RM18 .....375 C3
Colne Bank Ave C03 .....135 D8
Colne Chase CM8 .....183 E2
Colne Cl
South Ockendon RM15 .....372 C6
South Woodham Ferrers
CM3 .....301 E7
Colne Com Sch & Colne Coll
The C07 .....192 E8
Colne Cswy C02 .....136 C8
Colne Ct Braintree CM7 128 C1
East Tilbury RM18 .....375 C2
Colne Dr Romford RM3 314 F4
Southend-on-S SS3 .....349 E1
Colne Engaine CE Prim Sch
C06 .....78 A2
Colneford Hill C06 .....105 D7
Colne Gn IG11 .....352 B6
Colneis Jun Sch IP11 381 F6
Colneis Rd IP11 .....381 F6
Colne Park Rd C06 .....105 D7
Colne Pl SS16 .....342 C5
Colne Rd
Brightlingsea C07 .....192 E6
Bures C08 .....79 E8
Clacton-on-S C015 .....195 F2
Coggeshall C06 .....131 A6
Halstead C09 .....170 D4
Sible Hedingham C09 .....75 E8
Colne Rise C05 .....163 F8
Colne Springs C09 .....29 B6
Colne Terr C02 .....164 B8
Colne Valley CM14 .....337 C5
Colne Valley Cl C09 .....76 D2
Colne Valley Railway*
C09 .....51 C5
Colne Valley Rd CB9 .....9 A7

Colne View
Colchester C02 .....136 D2
Point Clear B C016 .....193 A2
Colne View Ret Pk C01 110 A1
Colne Way C014 .....192 F4
Colne Wlk CM7 .....128 D1
Coln y Rd IG1 .....376 A1
Colneys Cl C010 .....15 D1
Colombo Rd IG1 .....333 C4
Colson Gdns IG10 .....289 B6
Colson Gn IG10 .....289 B6
Colson Rd IG10 .....289 A5
Colson Way IG10 .....289 B5
Colt Hatch CM20 .....199 B1
Colthorpe Rd C015 .....195 F8
Colthurst Gdns IG11 .....221 D8
Coltishall Cl SS11 .....322 B6
Coltishall Rd RM12 .....355 C6
Colt Mews EN3 .....265 A2
Coltsfield CM24 .....119 E8
Coltsfoot Ct
Colchester C04 .....109 C2
Great Hill CB9 .....8 E7
Coltsfoot Path
Romford RM3 .....314 C3
Romford RM3 .....314 D4
Coltsfoot Rd IP2 .....16 E4
Colts The CM23 .....145 E4
Columbia Wharf Rd
RM17 .....378 A8
Columbine Gdns
Ipswich IP2 .....16 E5
Walton-on-t-N C014 .....171 B7
Columbine Mews C014 .134 C7
Columbines The C010 .....1 E2
Columbine Way C014 314 E2
Colvers CM7 .....202 C2
Colville Cl
Corringham SS17 .....360 F5
Great Notley CM77 .....154 D6
Colville Mews CM12 296 F5
Colvin Chase CM7 .....254 B1
Colvin Cl C013 .....134 F7
Colvin Rd Chingford E4 369 C7
Redbridge IG6 .....311 C3
Wanstead E11 .....332 B7
Colwall Gdns IG8 .....310 A5
Colworth Cl SS7 .....345 D4
Colyers Reach CM2 .....233 A2
Colyn Pl C010 .....22 E3
Comac Yd C015 .....195 C5
Combes Rd RM9 .....353 F5
Comet Cl RM19 .....371 A2
Comet Way SS2 .....347 B6
Comfrey Ct RM17 .....378 D8
Comma Cl CM7 .....128 A2
Commerce Est E18 .....310 C1
Commerce Pk C02 .....136 D4
Commerce Way
Colchester C02 .....136 D4
Lawford C011 .....86 B4
Commercial Pl DA12 379 C1
Commercial Rd
Ipswich IP1 .....17 D8
Southend-on-S SS0 347 D4
Commercial Way SS14 342 E6
Commodore Ho IP1 .....342 E6
Common App SS7 .....345 A7
Commonfields CM20 .....199 C1
Commonhall La SS7 .....345 A7
Common Hill CB10 .....22 D2
Common La
Duddenhoe End SG8 .....40 B7
Little Baddow CM3 .....234 E2
Stock CM4 .....275 E2
Thundersley SS7 .....345 B7
Woodham Walter CM9 235 B3
Common Quay IP2 .....17 C5
Common Rd
Great Wakering SS3 .....350 B4
Harlow CM17 .....222 E2
Ingrave CM13 .....317 C5
Stock CM4 .....275 E3
Commonside Rd CM18 223 F4
Common St C010 .....12 B8
Commons The C03 .....135 A5
Common The
Danbury CM3 .....256 E6
East Hanningfield CM3 278 B7
Thundersley SS7 .....345 A7
Commonwealth Ho
RM18 .....379 A5
Como St RM7 .....335 D7
Compasses Rd CM7 .....129 F5
Compass Gdns
Burnham-on-C CM0 .....306 A6
Compass Gdns* CM3 301 F7
Compton Ave
Brentwood CM13 .....295 C1
Romford RM2 .....136 C8
Compton Ct
Canvey Island SS8 .....364 D2
Southend-on-S SS8 .....346 B1
Wickford SS11 .....321 E7
Compton Mews [5] C04 136 C8
Compton Rd C04 .....136 C8
Compton Terr SS11 .....321 E7
Compton Wlk SS11 .....221 A6
Comreston EN11 .....110 A6
Comyns Cl C04 .....110 A6
Comyns Pl CM1 .....231 B1
Comyns Rd RM9 .....354 A5
Conan Doyle Cl CM7 155 A8
Concorde Ho [6] RM12 335 B6
Concord Rd SS8 .....363 F5
Conder Way C02 .....136 D4
Condor Wlk RM12 .....355 B5
Condovers Cotts RM18 379 F8
Conduit La
Hoddesdon EN11 .....221 A6
Woodham Mortimer CM9 257 E6
Conduit La E EN11 .....221 B6
Coney Acre CB11 .....93 D8
Coney Burrows E4 .....309 E8
Coney Gree CM21 .....172 D3

Conference Cl [3] E4 .....309 E3
Congreve Rd EN9 .....265 E6
Conies Rd C09 .....103 D7
Conifer Ave RM5 .....313 B5
Conifer Cl Aresford C07 164 F7
Colchester C04 .....136 E8
Conifer Ct
[7] Bishop's Stortford CM23 145 F8
Ilford IG1 .....316 D5
Conifer Dr CM14 .....309 D5
Conifers SS7 .....345 E3
Coningsby Gdns E4 .....309 B4
Conisborough Ct [12] DA2 376 B1
Coniston SS2 .....347 A7
Coniston Ave
Barking IG11 .....352 E5
Upminster RM14 .....356 C8
Coniston Cl Barking IG11 352 E5
Great Notley CM7 .....154 D6
Rayleigh SS6 .....323 E2
Coniston Cl CM16 .....268 A8
Coniston Gdns IG4 .....332 E7
Coniston Rd
Canvey Island SS8 .....364 A3
Ipswich IP3 .....18 B2
South Benfleet SS7 .....344 E8
Coniston Sq IP3 .....18 B2
Coniston Way IP2 .....355 A7
Connaught Ave
Chingford E4 .....287 D2
Frinton-on-S C013 .....170 F4
Grays RM16 .....373 C3
Loughton IG10 .....288 D5
Connaught Ct C015 .....196 B3
Connaught Dr CM3 .....301 C7
Connaught Gdns
Braintree CM7 .....128 B4
Southend-on-S SS3 .....368 C6
Connaught Gdns E C015 196 B4
Connaught Gdns W
C015 .....196 B3
Connaught Ho
Clacton-on-S C015 .....196 B4
Frinton-on-S C013 .....170 F5
Connaught La IG1 .....333 D2
Connaught Mews [1] C013 333 D2
Connaught Rd
Chingford E4 .....287 E1
Haverhill CB9 .....8 E7
Hornchurch RM12 .....336 D1
Ilford IG1 .....333 D2
Little Clacton C016 .....168 D6
Rayleigh SS6 .....346 A8
Connaught Way C015 297 A5
Connaught Wlk SS6 .....346 A8
Connington Cres E4 .....309 D7
Connor Cl IG6 .....311 C2
Connor Rd RM9 .....353 F8
Conquerer Ct RM2 .....314 D3
Conquerors Ct CM3 211 B3
Conrad Cl RM16 .....373 B4
Conrad Gdns RM16 .....373 B4
Conrad Rd
Stanford-le-H SS17 .....360 E1
Witham CM8 .....183 F5
Consort Cl CM14 .....316 C5
Constable Ave C015 .....195 C6
Constable Cl CM7 .....325 D6
Constable Ho CM7 .....127 E3
Constable Mews RM8 353 B8
Constable Rd
Felixstowe IP11 .....381 F4
Ipswich IP4 .....17 D8
Sudbury C010 .....33 E8
Constable View CM1 232 F6
Constable Way
Black Notley CM7 .....155 B5
Southend-on-S SS3 .....368 G8
Constance Cl
Broomfield CM1 .....208 A3
Witham CM8 .....212 B8
Constantine Rd
Colchester C03 .....135 D5
Ipswich IP1 .....17 B5
Witham CM8 .....211 E8
Constitution Hill
Ipswich IP1 .....17 B8
South Benfleet SS7 .....344 D3
Sudbury C010 .....33 F8
Consul Ave RM13 .....355 F5
Convalescent Hill IP11 381 E3
Convent Cl SS15 .....341 C6
Convent Hill IP11 .....128 A5
Convent La CM7 .....128 A5
Convent Rd SS8 .....344 D3
Con Way SS7 .....344 D3
Conway Ave SS3 .....350 B3
Conway Cl Halstead C09 103 D8
Haverhill CB9 .....8 E7
Conway Rd IP2 .....16 E5
Conyers Cl IG8 .....309 E4
Conyers Gn SS3 .....309 D4
Conyers Way IG10 .....289 B6
Cook Cl C012 .....90 F1
Cook Cres C04 .....136 C7
Cooke Ct CM11 .....372 C6
Cookham Ct SS3 .....349 E2
Cook 's Cl C09 .....103 F8
Cook 's Cl RM5 .....195 D1
Cook's Corner C011 .....88 E2

Cooks Gn SS13 .....321 C1
Cooks Hill C04 .....83 B6
Cook's La Colchester C03 134 F7
Colchester,West Bergholt
C03 .....71 E4
Cooks Bishops Green CM20 200 A2
Coolgardie Ave
Chigwell IG7 .....311 A7
Chingford E4 .....309 D5
Coolyne Way C015 .....196 B7
Coombe Dr SS16 .....341 C1
Coombe Lodge C06 .....105 B6
Coombe Rd Romford RM3 336 E1
Southminster CM0 .....284 D5
Coombe Rise
Chelmsford CM1 .....232 B7
Shenfield CM15 .....294 F1
Stanford-le-H SS17 .....360 E2
Coombes CM12 .....296 F4
Coombes Gr SS4 .....326 B3
Coombes Rd RM9 .....353 F6
Coombewood Dr
Dagenham RM6 .....334 F5
Thundersley SS7 .....344 F5
Cooper Cl DA9 .....379 C6
Cooper Dr CM7 .....127 D4
Cooper Pk CM7 .....127 D4
Coopers CM3 .....233 E8
Coopersale Cl [2] IG8 310 C3
Coopersale Comm CM16 263 D3
Coopersale Hall Sch
CM16 .....268 B5
Coopersale La CM16 268 A3
Coopersales SS15 .....341 A6
Coopersale St CM16 .....268 D7
Coopersale & Theydon
Garnon CE Prim Sch
CM16 .....268 D2
Coopers Ave CM9 .....237 D5
Coopers Cl
Bishop's Stortford CM23 145 D4
Chigwell IG7 .....312 B8
Dagenham RM10 .....354 B6
Coopers Company & Coborn
Sch The RM14 .....337 D2
Coopers Cres
Great Notley CM77 .....154 C8
West Bergholt C06 .....108 F4
Coopers Dr CM11 .....319 C6
Coopers End Rd CM24 121 A3
Coopers End Rdbt CM24 121 B3
Cooper Shaw Rd RM18 379 E7
Coopers Hill CM5 .....249 A1
Coopers La
Clacton-on-S C015 .....195 C3
Great Leighs CM3 .....180 F7
Cooper's La C07 .....84 F5
Coopers Mews CM5 .....249 A2
Cooper's Row CM1 .....232 A5
Coopers Villas CM22 121 B2
Coopers Way SS2 .....348 A5
Coopers Wlk C04 .....136 D8
Coote Gdns RM8 .....334 F1
Copdock Prim Sch IP8 .....35 F8
Copdock SS14 .....342 C7
Copeland Ho [7] CM14 316 C6
Copelands SS4 .....325 D6
Copeman Rd CM13 .....295 D2
Copford Ave SS6 .....323 F1
Copford CE Prim Sch
C06 .....133 D2
Copford Cl
Billericay CM11 .....297 C2
Woodford IG8 .....310 C4
Copford Ct C06 .....133 C4
Copford Rd CM1 .....297 C2
Copland Cl
Broomfield CM1 .....208 A1
Great Baddow CM2 .....254 F8
Copland Rd SS17 .....360 D1
Copleston High Sch IP4 18 C5
Copleston Rd IP4 .....18 B5
Coplow Ho CB10 .....3 A2
Coppen Rd RM8 .....334 F4
Coppens Gn SS12 .....321 C6
Copperas Rd C07 .....192 C5
Copper Beech C16 .....311 A2
Copper Beech St C10 289 A8
Copper Beeches
Brentwood CM14 .....316 C6
Colchester C03 .....345 B7
Thundersley SS7 .....345 B7
Copper Beech Rd RM15 357 C2
Copper Ct Braintree CM7 127 C1
Sawbridgeworth CM21 .....172 E2
Copperfield
Billericay CM12 .....319 D6
Chigwell IG7 .....311 D4
Copperfield Gdns CM14 294 C1
Copperfield Rd
Chelmsford CM1 .....231 E7
Ipswich IP2 .....16 E5
Copperfields
Basildon SS15 .....341 C7
Saffron Walden CB11 .....43 C8
Copperfields Way CM14 314 D2
Coppergate St IP4 .....17 C4
Copper Gr IP8 .....36 E8
Copperhead Ct CM6 .....123 D1
Coppice Cl C010 .....110 B3
Coppice Hatch CM18 223 D6
Coppice La Basildon SS15 319 F1
Pleshey CM6 .....178 E8
Coppice Path IG7 .....312 A5
Coppice Rd C017 .....312 A5
Coppice Rd C017 .....165 B8
Coppice The
Clacton-on-S C015 .....195 D1
Kelvedon Hatch CM15 271 E2
Coppid Hall RM16 .....374 D7
Coppingford End C06 133 D5

Coppings The EN11 .....197 A1
Coppins Cl CM7 .....232 E4
Coppins Green Prim Sch
C015 .....195 E5
Coppins Rd C015 .....195 D4
Coppins The [2] RM6 334 B4
Coprolite St IP3 .....17 E5
Copse Hill IP10 .....223 B5
Copse The Billericay CM12 297 B4
Bishop's Stortford CM23 145 F8
Chingford E4 .....287 F1
Felsted CM6 .....152 F6
Copshall Cl CM18 .....223 E4
Coptfold Cl SS1 .....348 F1
Coptfold Rd CM14 .....316 D6
Coptfold Cl CM22 .....146 F4
Coptfold La CM6 .....70 B3
Copt Hall La C05 .....189 C3
Copt Hill CM3 .....256 E6
Copthorne Ave IG6 .....311 B4
Copthorne Gdns RM11 334 A6
Copy Hill CB9 .....8 E3
Coral Cl Ilford RM6 .....334 D8
South Woodham Ferrers
CM3 .....301 C8
Coral Dr IP1 .....16 D8
Cora Ho CM20 .....199 A1
Coralin Wlk C015 .....134 C6
Coram Gn CM3 .....295 D4
Corasway SS7 .....345 C5
Corbets Ave RM14 .....356 B7
Corbets Tey RM14 .....356 B8
Corbets Tey Sch RM14 356 C7
Corbett Rd E11 .....332 C5
Corbett Villas RM8 .....334 C3
Corbridge Mews [6] RM1 335 F6
Corcorans CM5 .....294 C3
Cordelia Cres SS5 .....323 C3
Cordell Cl C010 .....15 D8
Cordell Pl C010 .....15 D8
Cordell Rd C010 .....15 D8
Corder Rd IP4 .....17 D8
Cordwainers The SS2 348 A5
Cordwinders C07 .....59 F1
Coriander Rd C05 .....186 C4
Cories Cl RM8 .....334 D2
Corinda Ho C013 .....170 F4
Corinthian Manorway
DA8 .....369 D2
Corinthian Rd DA8 369 D2
Coriolanus Cl C02 .....135 A3
Cormorant Wlk
Chelmsford CM2 .....254 C5
[8] Hornchurch RM12 .....355 B6
Cornard Rd C010 .....33 F7
Cornec Ave SS9 .....346 B6
Cornec Chase SS9 .....346 C6
Cornel Cl CM8 .....183 D4
Cornelius Vale CM2 .....233 B4
Cornelius Vermuyden Sch The
SS3 .....363 F5
Cornells La CB11 .....67 E3
Cornell Way RM5 .....313 B5
Corner Ho CM18 .....223 F6
Corner Mdw CM18 .....224 A4
Corner Pk CM3 .....22 E3
Corner Rd CM21 .....320 D6
Cornerth Cres C010 .....34 B6
Cornfields SS14 .....301 C8
Cornflower Cl
Colchester C013 .....134 C7
Ipswich IP2 .....16 E4
Cornflower Dr CM1 .....232 F6
Cornflower Gdns CM12 296 F4
Cornflower Way RM3 334 E2
Cornford Way C011 .....86 B4
Cornhill
[4] Chelmsford CM1 .....232 B2
[8] Ipswich IP1 .....17 C6
Cornhill Ave SS5 .....324 E7
Cornhouse Bldgs SS6 345 C8
Corniche The CM7 .....72 A1
Cornish Gr CM3 .....301 E6
Cornish Hall End Rd
Stambourne C09 .....28 E8
Steeple Bumpstead C09 48 E8
Cornmill End C06 .....133 C1
Corn Mill Ct CM21 .....43 E8
Cornshaw Rd RM8 .....334 D3
Cornsland CM14 .....316 C7
Cornwall Cl Barking IG11 352 F1
Harold Wood RM3 .....337 A7
Lawford C011 .....86 B3
Cornwall Cres CM1 .....232 A7
Cornwall Gate RM19 371 A2
Cornwall Gdns
Braintree CM7 .....128 B4
Rochford SS4 .....325 C5
Cornwallis Dr
Marks Tey C06 .....134 A4
South Woodham Ferrers
CM3 .....301 F7
Cornwallis Ho SS14 .....342 A8
Cornwallis Pl CB10 .....22 E3
Cornwallis Rd
Dagenham RM9 .....353 E8
Haverhill CB9 .....8 F6
Cornwall Rd
Basildon SS13 .....343 F7
Dartford DA1 .....316 D8
Felixstowe IP11 .....381 D5
Pilgrims Hatch CM15 294 B4
Cornwell Cres SS17 .....360 E3
Cornworthy SS3 .....368 C8
Corona Rd Basildon SS16 342 A8
Canvey Island SS8 .....364 D5

Coronation Ave
Braintree CM7 ....127 F2
Colchester CO2 ....136 A2
East Tilbury RM18 ....375 C2
Coronation Cl
Great Wakering SS3 ....349 F4
Ilford IG6 ....333 C7
Coronation Cotts CM15 ....316 E8
Coronation Ct RM18 ....375 C2
Coronation Dr
Felixstowe IP11 ....381 C3
Hornchurch RM12 ....355 B7
Coronation Hill CM16 ....245 F2
Coronation Rd
Bishop's Stortford CM23 ....145 E5
Burnham-on-C CM0 ....306 B4
Clacton-on-S CO15 ....195 C3
Ipswich IP4 ....18 E5
Coronation Villas CO16 ....141 F7
Coronation Way CM7 ....155 D5
Corporation Ave IP2 ....37 A8
Corporation Rd CM1 ....232 A4
Corral Hts Da8 ....369 E1
Corran Way RM15 ....372 B6
Corriander Dr CM2 ....94 D2
Corringham Prim Sch
SS17 ....361 C4
Corringham Rd
Stanford-le-H, Balstonia
SS17 ....360 F2
Stanford-le-H SS17 ....360 E1
Corringham SS17 ....361 A3
Corry Ct 7 CO4 ....136 D8
Corsel Rd SS8 ....364 E3
Cortina Dr RM13 ....154 C3
Cortoncroft Cl CO13 ....170 F7
Corton Rd IP3 ....18 B1
Corton Trad Est SS7 ....344 D7
Corve La RM15 ....372 B6
Cory Dr CM13 ....295 B2
Cosgrove Ave SS0 ....346 B3
Cossington Rd SS0 ....366 E8
Costead Manor Rd CM14 294 B1
Coteford Cl IG10 ....289 B7
Cotelands SS16 ....342 F3
Cotesmore Gdns RM8 ....353 C8
Cotleigh Rd RM7 ....135 C5
Cotman Ave CO11 ....86 B4
Cotman Lodge CM1 ....232 F6
Cotman Mews RM8 ....353 B7
Cotman Rd
Clacton-on-S CO16 ....195 D6
Colchester CO3 ....135 A5
Ipswich IP3 ....18 A1
Cotswold Ave SS6 ....323 D4
Cotswold Cres CM1 ....231 D6
Cotswold Cl
Clacton-on-S CO15 ....196 A3
Highwoods CO4 ....110 C4
Cotswold Dr CO10 ....15 C6
Cotswold Gdns
Brentwood CM13 ....295 E2
Ilford IG2 ....333 D4
Cotswold Rd
Clacton-on-S CO15 ....195 F5
Romford RM3 ....114 F1
Southend-on-S SS0 ....347 D1
Cottage Dr CO2 ....136 D3
Cottage Gn CO16 ....195 C6
Cottage Gr CO16 ....195 C6
Cottage Pl
Chelmsford CM1 ....232 B3
8 Ipswich IP1 ....17 B6
Cottages The SS3 ....368 F7
Cottage Wlk CO16 ....195 C6
Cottesmore Ave IG5 ....311 A1
Cottesmore Ct SS8 ....364 B2
Cottesmore Gdns SS9 ....346 A2
Cottey Ho CM2 ....254 B2
Cottingham Rd IP8 ....16 B1
Cottis Cl SS16 ....341 A3
Cotton Cl RM9 ....353 C5
Cotton La DA2 ....376 C2
Cottons App RM7 ....335 D6
Cottons Ct 8 RM7 ....335 D6
Cottonwood Cl CO2 ....135 D2
Couchmore Ave SS9 ....310 F1
Coulde Dennis CM3 ....278 B7
Coulsdon Cl CO16 ....195 C6
Coulson Ct RM8 ....334 C3
Coulter Ho DA7 ....377 C2
Coulter Mews CM11 ....297 B3
Council Ave SS2 ....186 C2
Council Bglws
Braintree CM7 ....127 F7
Fobbing SS17 ....361 D5
Steeple CM0 ....261 E2
Council Cotts
Great Holland CO13 ....169 F3
Helions Bumpstead CO9 ....8 E1
Council Hos
Bicknacre CM3 ....256 F1
Bradwell-on-S CM0 ....263 E8
Carringham SS17 ....361 D5
Great Bromley CO7 ....139 A6
Hadstock CB1 ....1 A2
Holbrook IP9 ....62 D6
Peldon CO5 ....189 E5
Shudy Camps CB1 ....2 B6
Thorington Street IG6 ....57 B3
Thorpe-le-S CO16 ....141 E2
Tolleshunt Major CM9 ....234 D3
Wakes Colne CO6 ....79 C1
Council Houses
Cressing CM77 ....156 A4
Great Bentley CO7 ....166 F5
Counting House La CM6 123 D1
County Chambers SS1 ....367 A7
County Pl CM2 ....232 B1
Coupals Cl CB9 ....9 C6
Coupals Rd CB9 ....9 C6

Coupals Prim Sch CB9 ....9 D7
Coupals Rd CB9 ....9 E6
Courage Cl CM11 ....336 C5
Courage Ct 7 CM13 ....295 C3
Courage Wlk CM13 ....295 D3
Courtauld Ct CO9 ....76 F1
Courtauld Homes of Rest
CO9 ....76 E3
Courtauld Rd
Basildon SS13 ....321 C2
Braintree CM7 ....128 A4
Court Ave RM3 ....315 A3
Court Cl CM23 ....145 E5
Court Eight CM8 ....183 F5
Court Eighteen CM8 ....183 F5
Court Eleven CM8 ....183 F5
Courtenay Cl CO10 ....15 D2
Courtenay Dr RM16 ....372 F3
Courtenay Gdns RM14 ....337 C3
Court Farm CO11 ....61 A1
Courtfield SS7 ....344 D1
Courtfield Cl EN10 ....221 A3
Court Fifteen CM8 ....183 F5
Court Five CM8 ....183 F5
Court Four CM8 ....183 F5
Court Fourteen CM8 ....183 F5
Court Gdns RM3 ....315 A3
Court Ind Est CM2 ....232 C2
Courtland Ave
Chingford E4 ....309 F8
Ilford IG1 ....333 A3
Redbridge IG1 ....332 F2
Courtland Dr IG7 ....311 C7
Courtland Mews CM9 ....258 F8
Courtland Pl CM9 ....258 F8
Courtlands
Billericay CM12 ....296 E2
Chelmsford CM1 ....232 A6
Halstead CO9 ....103 D8
Southend-on-S SS9 ....346 F7
Court Lodge 11 DA17 ....369 A1
Court Mews DA11 ....378 B1
Court Needham EN3 ....265 A2
Courtney Park Rd SS16 ....341 B5
Courtney Rd RM16 ....374 C4
Court Nine CM8 ....183 F5
Court Nineteen CM8 ....183 F5
Court One CM8 ....183 F5
Court Rd CM1 ....208 A3
Court Seven CM8 ....330 F8
Court Seventeen CM8 ....183 F5
Court Six CM8 ....183 F5
Court Sixteen CM8 ....183 F5
Courts The
Felixstowe IP11 ....381 F4
Rayleigh SS6 ....323 E3
Court Ten CM8 ....183 F5
Court Three CM8 ....183 F5
Court Twenty CM8 ....183 F5
Court Two CM8 ....183 F5
Court View CM4 ....273 F1
Courtway IG8 ....310 C5
Court Way Ilford IG6 ....333 C8
Romford RM3 ....114 E1
Courtway Gdns SS17 ....361 D5
Courtyard The
Braintree CM7 ....128 A4
Brentwood CM15 ....294 B2
Maldon CM9 ....236 F2
Coval Ave CM1 ....232 A6
Coval La CM1 ....232 A2
Coval Wells CM1 ....232 A2
Covehithe Cl 8 CB9 ....8 F6
Covenbrook CM13 ....317 B7
Coventry Cl
Colchester CO1 ....136 A8
Hullbridge SS5 ....301 F1
Coventry Hill SS1 ....301 E1
Coventry Rd IG1 ....333 B3
Coverdale CM8 ....183 E4
Coverdales The IG11 ....352 D3
Coverts CO13 ....316 C4
Covert Rd IG6 ....311 F4
Coverts The
Brentwood CM13 ....295 A1
West Mersea CO5 ....201 C7
Cowbridge La IG11 ....352 B5
Cowdray Ave CO1 ....109 F1
Cowdray Cres CO1 ....135 F7
Cowdray Ctr The CO1 ....110 A2
Cowdray Way RM12 ....155 A8
Cowdrey Mead SS14 ....342 B6
Cowell Ave CM2 ....233 B4
Cowell Gn CO16 ....195 C6
Cowell Lodge IG8 ....309 F5
Cowel St IP2 ....17 C3
Cowels Farm La CM6 ....97 E5
Cow La
Great Chesterford CB10 ....4 A5
Point Clear B CO16 ....193 C3
Cowley Dr DA9 ....377 A2
Cowley Rd
Felixstowe IP11 ....381 E4
Ilford IG2 ....333 A3
Redbridge IG1 ....332 F4
Romford RM3 ....314 B3
Wanstead E11 ....332 B6
Cowlins CM17 ....200 D4
Cowpar Mews CM7 ....155 A8
Cowper Ave RM18 ....379 B8
Cowper Rd
Belvedere DA17 ....369 A2
Rainham RM13 ....355 A1
Cowper St IP4 ....18 B6
Cowslip Cl IP2 ....16 E4
Cowslip Cl CO16 ....195 C6
Cowslip Mead SS14 ....342 B6
Cow Watering La CM1 ....230 E2
Coxbridge Ct CM12 ....297 A2
Coxes Cl SS17 ....360 D3

Coxes Farm Rd CM11 ....319 E7
Coxhall Rd IP9 ....36 E1
Cox La IP4 ....17 D5
Cox Ley CM22 ....174 A3
Coxon Dr RM16 ....372 E3
Cox Rd CO7 ....165 B8
Coxs Cl Haverhill CB9 ....8 D7
South Woodham Ferrers
CM3 ....301 E8
Coxtie Green Rd
Pilgrims Hatch CM14 ....293 C5
South Weald CM14 ....293 A2
Coytes Gdns 8 IP1 ....17 C5
Crabbe St IP4 ....18 A6
Crabb's Hill CM3 ....210 F2
Crabbs Croft CM7 ....128 B3
Crabtree CO13 ....170 C8
Crabtree Ave RM6 ....334 D7
Crabs Croft CM7 ....128 B3
Crabtree CO13 ....170 C8
Crabtree Hill CB11 ....67 C3
Crabtree La CO6 ....81 C1
Crabtree Manorway N
DA17 ....369 C5
Crabtree Manorway S
DA17 ....369 C5
Cracknell Cl CO7 ....137 B2
Crafton Gn CM24 ....119 E7
Craftsmans Sq SS2 ....348 A5
Craig Ct CO2 ....135 B4
Craigdale Rd RM11 ....335 F4
Craigfield Ave CO15 ....196 A6
Craig Gdns E18 ....309 F1
Craig Ho CM7 ....128 A3
Craig's Hill CO8 ....79 E6
Craigs La CO8 ....79 E6
Craiston Way CM2 ....254 F5
Crammavill St RM16 ....373 A5
Cramswell Cl CM8 ....8 E6
Cramphorn Wlk CM1 ....231 F3
Cranberry Cl CO4 ....109 F2
Cranborne RD CM14 ....337 B2
Cranborne Rd
Barking IG11 ....352 D4
Hoddesdon EN11 ....221 C7
Cranbourne Ave E11 ....332 B7
Cranbourne Dr EN11 ....197 C2
Cranbourne Gdns IG6 ....333 C8
Cranbourne Rd EN11 ....197 C2
Cranbourne Prim Sch The
EN11 ....197 B2
Cranbrook Ave RM7 ....345 C4
Cranbrook Coll (Boys)
IG1 ....333 A2
Cranbrook Dr RM2 ....336 C7
Cranbrook La 8 CO10 ....2 F1
Cranbrook Rd IG1,IG2 ....333 A5
Cranbrook Rise
Ilford IG1 ....333 A4
Redbridge IG1 ....332 F5
Cranbrook Rd CO4 ....134 B4
Crane Cl RM10 ....154 A6
Crane Hill IP7 ....16 E4
Cranell Gn RM15 ....372 B5
Cranes Cl SS14 ....320 F1
Cranes Ct SS14 ....342 C8
Cranes Farm Rd SS14 ....320 D1
Cranes La SS14 ....342 C8
Crane's La CO5 ....157 F1
Cranfield Ct
Wickford SS12 ....321 C8
8 Woodford IG8 ....310 A6
Cranfield Park Ave SS12 ....321 F2
Cranfield Park Ct 8
SS12 ....321 D5
Cranford Ct CO13 ....170 E5
Cranham Gdns RM14 ....337 A7
Cranham Pl RM14 ....337 A7
Cranham Rd Henham CM6 ....95 F3
Hornchurch RM11 ....336 B5
Cranleigh Cl CO16 ....195 B6
Cranleigh Dr SS9 ....346 E1
Cranleigh Gdns
Barking IG11 ....352 D6
Hullbridge SS5 ....301 D1
Loughton IG10 ....288 F3
Cranley Ave SS0 ....347 D1
Cranley Dr IG2 ....333 C4
Cranley Gdns SS6 ....323 C6
Cranley Rd IG2 ....333 C4
Southend-on-S SS0 ....347 D1
Cranmer Cl CM12 ....297 B6
Cranmere Ct CO1 ....136 A7
Cranmer Gdns RM10 ....354 C8
Cranmer Ho CM7 ....253 F7
Cranmer's La CO6 ....131 E6
Cranmore Cl CM22 ....94 C2
Cranmoregreen La CO10 ....2 F3
Cranston Ave SS0 ....347 D5
Cranston Gdns E4 ....309 B4
Cranston Park Ave
RM14 ....356 C8
Cranwell Cres SS13 ....18 C1
Cranwell Gdns CM23 ....119 C1
Cranworth Cres 7 E4 ....287 D1
Craven Ave SS8 ....364 A3
Craven Cl SS4 ....325 D6
Craven Ct RM6 ....334 C5
Craven Dr CO4 ....110 C3
Craven Gdns
Barking IG11 ....352 E3
Ilford IG6 ....333 D8
Redbridge IG6 ....333 D8
Romford,Harold Park RM3 315 C4
Romford, Willoughby's Hill
RM5 ....313 A5
Crawford Ave RM16 ....373 B5
Crawford Chase SS12 ....321 C5
Crawford Cl CM2 ....297 C5
Crawley Cl SS7 ....361 A5
Crawley 8 DA11 ....379 B1
Crawley End SG8 ....19 D4

Craword Compton Cl
RM12 ....355 C6
Crayfields CM0 ....284 E5
Crayford Cl CM9 ....258 E8
Crayford Rd CO10 ....15 D2
Craylands SS14 ....342 F7
Craylands Sq DA10 ....377 D2
Craylands Sq DA10 ....377 D2
Grays Hill CM11 ....320 C5
Grays Hill Prim Sch
CM11 ....320 D6
Grays Hill Rd CM11 ....320 D4
Grays View CM12 ....319 B8
Crealock Gr IG8 ....309 F5
Creance Ct CM2 ....232 A2
Creasen Butt Cl CM9 ....237 A4
Creasey Cl RM11 ....336 B2
Creasy Ct SS14 ....342 E6
Crediton Ho 8 RM3 ....314 D4
Credon Cl CO15 ....195 F7
Credon Ct CO15 ....195 F7
Credo Way RM20 ....377 B8
Creeds Cotts CM16 ....267 E7
Creek Cotts CO14 ....144 E4
Creekhurst Cl CO7 ....193 A6
Creekmouth Ind Pk IG11 352 F1
Creek Rd Barking IG11 ....352 F2
Canvey Island SS8 ....364 D4
Creeksea Ferry Rd SS4 ....305 C2
Creekside CO5 ....305 F6
Creekside RM13 ....354 D4
Creek The CM3 ....378 B2
Creek View Basildon SS16 342 E3
Great Wigborough CO5 ....188 F2
Creek View Ave SS5 ....301 D3
Creekview Rd CM3 ....301 F7
Creek Way RM13 ....369 E8
Creephedge La CM3 ....278 E5
Cree Way RM1 ....313 E3
Creffield Rd CO3 ....135 D6
Crepping Hall Dr IP9 ....61 F1
Crescent Ave
Grays RM17 ....378 D8
Hornchurch RM12 ....335 F2
Crescent Cl CM12 ....296 F4
Crescent Ct
Billericay CM12 ....297 A2
Grays RM17 ....373 D1
Heybridge CM9 ....236 F5
Crescent Dr CM15 ....294 E1
Crescent Gdns CM12 ....296 F4
Crescent Rd Aveley RM15 ....373 C4
Basildon SS14 ....342 D8
Bishop's Stortford CM23 ....146 A6
Brentwood CM14 ....316 B6
Canvey Island SS8 ....364 D2
Chingford E4 ....287 E2
Dagenham RM6 ....335 B1
Felixstowe IP11 ....381 E4
Great Baddow CM2 ....255 A7
Heybridge CM9 ....236 F5
Hornchurch RM11 ....336 D4
Ipswich IP1 ....16 F6
Romford RM7 ....335 C5
South Benfleet SS7 ....346 B1
Tollesbury CM9 ....216 E1
Walton-on-t-N CO14 ....171 C8
Woodford IG8 ....310 A6
Crescent The
Clacton-on-S CO15 ....196 B7
Colchester CO4 ....110 C7
Epping CM16 ....267 F7
Frinton-on-S CO13 ....170 E4
Great Holland CO13 ....170 A4
Great Horkesley CO6 ....82 E6
Great Leighs CM3 ....180 E5
Greenhithe DA9 ....377 C2
Hadleigh SS7 ....345 F3
Harlow CM17 ....200 C6
Ilford IG2 ....333 A5
Loughton IG10 ....288 D3
Marks Tey CO6 ....133 A3
Steeple Bumpstead CB9 ....27 B7
Thorpe-le-S CO16 ....141 F6
Upminster RM14 ....337 F4
West Bergholt CO6 ....108 D5
Cromwell Hill CM9 ....236 F3
Cromwell Ho CO4 ....109 F4
Cromwell Ctr The RM8 ....334 B8
Cromwell Lodge IG11 ....352 E2
Cromwell Pk CM6 ....152 B5
Cromwell Rd
Brentwood CM14 ....316 B6
15 Colchester CO2 ....135 F6
Grays RM17 ....373 A1
Hockley SS5 ....324 E6
Saffron Walden CB11 ....43 F7
Cromwell Sq 7 IP1 ....17 C5
Cromwell Trad Est IG11 ....352 E2
Cromwell Way CM8 ....183 F2
Crondon Park La CM4 ....275 E4
Crooked La DA11,DA12 ....379 B2
Crooked Mile EN9 ....265 C7
Crooked Way EN9 ....221 E1
Cropenburg Wlk SS8 ....364 B5
Croppath Rd RM10 ....354 A8
Cropper Gdns CO2 ....137 C1
Crosby Ct IG7 ....312 A7
Crosby Rd
Dagenham RM10 ....354 B4
Southend-on-S SS0 ....366 C8
Crossbow Ct CM9 ....321 C6
Crossbow Rd IG7 ....311 B7
Crosby Cl CM1 ....204 A5
Crosby Rd Witham CM8 ....195 E8
Cold Norton CM3 ....280 F6
Grays RM17 ....373 D3
Hockley SS5 ....324 E5
Ilford IG3 ....333 D7
Saffron Walden CM14 ....293 D8

Cripplegate CM0 ....284 E5
Crispe Ave CM5 ....248 F5
Crispe Ho IG11 ....352 D3
Crispin Cl CB9 ....8 D7
Crispins SS1 ....368 A8
Crispin Terr IG8 ....310 D4
Critchett Terr 8 CM1 ....232 A3
Crittall Cl CM8 ....156 E4
Crittall Dr CM7 ....155 A5
Crittall Rd CM8 ....184 B3
Crix Green Villas CM6 ....153 D6
Croasdaile Cl CM24 ....119 E8
Croasdaile Ct CM24 ....119 E8
Crockleford Rd CM24 ....119 E8
Crocklands CO4 ....104 A5
Crocus Cl
Clacton-on-S CO16 ....195 C4
Ipswich IP2 ....16 E4
Crocus Fields CB10 ....22 E3
Crocus Way CM1 ....232 E7
Croft Cl Braintree CM7 ....128 A3
South Benfleet SS7 ....344 C5
Southend-on-S SS9 ....346 E4
Croft Ct CM1 ....232 E8
Crofters CM21 ....172 E1
Crofters End CM21 ....172 E1
Crofters Wlk CM77 ....154 D8
Croft Gn CO6 ....76 F2
Croft La Haverhill CO9 ....9 B6
Croft Lodge Cl IG8 ....310 B4
Crofton Ave SS17 ....360 F4
Crofton Cl SS7 ....344 C5
Crofton Gr E4 ....309 D6
Crofton Rd Grays RM16 ....373 E3
Ipswich IP4 ....18 B7
Croft Rd
Clacton-on-S CO15 ....195 D4
Kelvedon CO5 ....158 B2
South Benfleet SS7 ....344 C5
Sudbury CO10 ....33 E8
Croftside CO5 ....158 B2
Croft St IP2 ....17 C3
Crofts The SS3 ....349 E4
Croft The Bures CO8 ....55 F1
Chingford E4 ....309 E8
Earls Colne CO6 ....105 A6
Elsenham CM22 ....94 C1
Glemsford CO10 ....12 A5
Great Yeldham CO9 ....30 A2
Loughton IG10 ....289 A7
Rayleigh SS6 ....345 F8
Croft Way CM8 ....184 A3
Cromarty Rd IP4 ....18 D6
Cromar Way CM1 ....231 F1
Crombie Cl IG4 ....332 F6
Crome Cl CO3 ....135 A5
Cromer Ave CO15 ....341 D6
Cromer Cl SS15 ....341 B8
Crome Rd CO16 ....195 D5
Cromer Rd
Brentwood CM14 ....316 B6
8 Ipswich IP1 ....17 C5
Romford RM7 ....335 C5
Southend-on-S SS7 ....367 B8
Woodford IG8 ....310 A6
Cromhurst Ct CO3 ....135 E7
Crompton Cl SS14 ....321 A6
Crompton Pl 8 EN3 ....265 A1
Crompton Rd IP2 ....16 F7
Crompton St CM1 ....231 F1
Cromwell Ave CM7 ....154 B7
Cromwell Cl
Bishop's Stortford CM23 ....145 B7
Boreham CM3 ....233 D8

Crossgate Field IP11 ....381 C5
Cross Gn SS16 ....341 F5
Cross Hill CO12 ....116 D1
Crossing Rd CM16 ....268 A6
Cross La CO5 ....218 F7
Crossley Ave CO15 ....218 F7
Crossness Rd IG11 ....352 F2
Cross Rd Basildon SS13 ....343 F7
Chingford E4 ....287 E1
Dagenham RM6 ....334 E4
Gravesend DA11 ....378 F1
Hadleigh SS7 ....345 B4
Maldon CM9 ....237 A1
Romford RM7 ....335 B8
Witham CM8 ....183 F5
Woodford IG8 ....310 A4
Crossroads CO9 ....31 E2
Cross St Felixstowe IP11 ....381 C6
8 Gravesend DA11 ....379 B1
Saffron Walden CB10 ....22 D1
Sudbury CO10 ....33 D7
Cross The
West Mersea CO5 ....218 E7
Wivenhoe CO7 ....137 B2
Crossway Dagenham RM8 ....353 E3
8 Stanford-le-H SS17 ....160 F1
Woodford IG8 ....310 A6
Cross Way Harlow CM17 ....200 D1
West Mersea CO5 ....218 E7
Crossways
Canvey Island SS8 ....363 E4
Chelmsford CM2 ....254 C7
Clacton-on-S CO15 ....220 G8
Colne Engaine CO6 ....77 F1
Loughton IG10 ....289 A4
Romford RM7 ....336 B8
Shenfield CM15 ....295 A3
Crossways Bvd DA2 ....376 C3
Crossways The SS0 ....366 A8
Crossway The CM11 ....297 D3
Croucher's Farm Rd
CM9 ....235 C7
Crouch Mdw SS15 ....341 E6
Crouch Rd
Burnham-on-C CM0 ....306 C5
Grays RM16 ....374 A1
Crouch St Basildon SS15 ....319 E2
Colchester CO3 ....135 D6
Crouch Valley RM14 ....337 E4
Crouchview Cl SS11 ....322 B7
Crouch View Cotts CM0 ....283 E8
Crouch View Gr SS5 ....301 A1
Crouch View Villas CM0 ....344 E2
Crouch Way SS3 ....368 F2
Croutel Rd IP11 ....381 F5
Crowborough Rd SS2 ....348 A2
Crowe Hall La IP9 ....62 A1
Crow Gn Cl SS15 ....294 A5
Crow Green La SS15 ....294 A5
Crow Green Rd CM15 ....294 A5
Crowhall La CO11 ....87 E1
Crowhurst Rd CO3 ....155 D8
Crow La Romford RM7 ....335 B8
Great Dunmow CM6 ....123 A3
Crowland Cl 7 IP4 ....17 A2
Crowland Rd CO9 ....8 F8
Crowlands Ave RM7 ....335 C5
Crowlands Jun & Inf Schs
RM7 ....335 C5
Crown Ave SS3 ....344 E2
Crown Bays Rd CO4 ....136 C8
Crown Bldgs 8 E4 ....287 D1
Crown Cl Basildon SS13 ....343 C6
Sheering CM22 ....271 D8
Crown Ct RM18 ....379 A5
Crownfield Ave IG2 ....333 E6
Crownfield Rd E15 ....321 B8
Crownfields CM24 ....119 D7
Crownfields Jun & Inf Schs
....313 A1

Crown Gate
Colchester CO4 ....110 D6
Harlow CM20 ....223 D8
Crown Gdns SS4 ....323 C2
Crown Hill Ashdon CB10 ....24 B1
Loughton IG10 ....267 A5
Rayleigh SS6 ....322 F2
Waltham Abbey EN9,CM0 ....266 A6
Crown La N CO7 ....140 D1
Crown La S CO7 ....111 A4
Crown Mdw CM7 ....128 C6
Crown Par RM13 ....355 B1
Crown Rd Billericay CM12 ....297 D3
Grays RM17 ....378 C8
Hockley SS5 ....324 E5
Ilford IG3 ....333 D7
Crown St
Brentwood CM14 ....316 C8
Castle Hedingham CO9 ....51 E4
Dagenham RM10 ....354 C6
Dedham CO7 ....84 D6
Felixstowe IP11 ....381 C6
Great Bardfield CM7 ....72 B2

Crown St *continued*
Ipswich IP1 .....17 C6
Crown Terr CM23 ....146 A7
Crown Way CM0 ....284 C4
Crow Pond Rd CM3 ....182 C3
Crows Field Cotts CM2 ..276 F4
Crows La CM3 .....279 D5
Crownest The CM0 ....306 C3
Crows Rd Barking IG11 ..352 B6
Epping CM16 .....245 F1
Crow St CM22 .....94 F5
Crowstone Ave SS0 ....366 C8
Crowstone Cl SS0 ....347 D1
Crowstone Prep Sch
  Rochford SS4 ....348 B8
  Southend-on-S SS0 ....366 C8
Crowstone Rd
  Grays RM16 ....373 C4
  Southend-on-S SS0 ....366 C8
Croxall Cl CM8 ....183 F2
Croxford Way RM7 ....335 C3
Croxon Way CM0 ....306 B7
Crozier Ave CM23 ....145 C8
Crozier Terr CM2 ....145 C8
Cruce Way CO15 ....192 F3
Crucible Cl IM6 ....334 B5
Cruick Ave RM15 ....372 C6
Crummock Cl CM77 ....154 C6
Crunch Croft 9 E5
Crusader Cl RM7 ....371 A2
Crusader Way CM7 ....128 C2
Crushes Cl CM13 ....295 E3
Crushton Pl CM1 ....231 F6
Crusoe Rd DA8 ....369 D1
Crystal Ave RM12 ....336 E1
Crystal Cl E11 ....355 A1
Crystal Stps ◨ SS1 ....367 C7
Crystal Way RM8 ....354 B3
Cuckfield Ave IP3 ....18 E3
Cuckoo Cnr SS2 ....347 E4
Cuckoo Hill Bures CO8 ....15 B7
Sible Hedingham CO9 ....75 B8
Cuckoo La RM16 ....372 F5
Cuckoos La
  Great Canfield CM6 ....149 A3
  Takeley CM6 ....148 F2
Cuckoo Way CM7 ....127 E6
Cudmore Grove Ctry Pk*
  CO5 ....192 A1
Culford Pl IP3 ....17 F4
Culford Rd RM16 ....373 C4
Culford Wlk IP11 ....381 A3
Cullen Sq RM15 ....372 B1
Cullingham Rd IP1 ....17 A5
Cullings Ct IP9 ....265 F6
Culpepper Cl CM23 ....311 B4
Culverden SS14 ....342 A6
Culver Rise CM3 ....301 E6
Culver St CO1 ....135 F7
Culver St W CO1 ....135 F7
Culvert Cl CO6 ....130 F2
Culver Wlk ◨ CO1 ....135 F7
Cumberland Ave
  Hornchurch RM12 ....336 E1
  Maldon CM9 ....210 C4
  South Benfleet SS7 ....344 C3
  Southend-on-S SS0 ....348 D2
Cumberland Cl
  Braintree CM7 ....128 B4
  Hornchurch RM12 ....336 E1
  Redbridge IG6 ....311 C2
Cumberland Cres CM1 ..232 A7
Cumberland Ho
  Romford RM7 ....313 A1
  Southend-on-S SS2 ....347 H6
Cumberland Rd RM13 ..372 E3
Cumberland St IP1 ....17 B7
Cumberland Towers IP1 .17 A2
Cumbrae Mews SS2 ....321 F5
Cumley Rd CM22 ....247 E1
Cumming Rd CM11 ....299 A2
Cummings Hall La RM3 .314 D7
Cunningham Cl
  Colchester CO2 ....136 A4
  Ilford RM6 ....334 C6
  Southend-on-S SS9 ....368 F8
Cunningham Dr SS2 ....321 F5
Cunningham Rise CM16 .242 D6
Cunnington Rd CM7 ....128 C3
Cunobelin Way CM2 ....216 B2
Cupids Chase SS3 ....350 C2
Cupid's Cnr SS3 ....350 C2
Cuppers Cl CM8 ....105 A4
Cards Rd CO6 ....283 A8
Curlew Ave CO5 ....163 A7
Curlew Cl
  Clacton-on-S CO15 ....195 F6
  Heybridge CM9 ....237 C5
  Colchester CO2 ....158 D2
Curlew Cres SS16 ....342 A3
Curlew Croft CO4 ....136 F8
Curlew Dr SS7 ....344 C2
Curlew Ho CM0 ....306 C4
Curlew Rd RM7 ....335 A8
Curlew Terr IG5 ....333 A8
Curling La RM17 ....372 F1
Curling Tye SS14 ....342 C2
Curling Tye La
  Maldon CM9 ....236 A3
  Woodham Walter CM9 ....208 D7
Curling Wlk SS14 ....342 D7
Currants Farm Rd CM7 .127 E3
Currents La CO12 ....91 E6
Curriers' La IP1 ....17 A5
Curteys CM17 ....200 D5
Curtis Cl
  Clacton-on-S CO15 ....195 B3
  Ipswich IP8 ....16 C1

Curtis Mill La RM4 ....291 F4
Curtis Rd RM11 ....336 F4
Curtis Way SS3 ....323 E4
Curzon Cres IG11 ....352 F2
Curzon Rd IP7 ....378 C7
Curzon Rd CO10 ....34 B8
Curzon Way CM2 ....233 A2
Cusak Rd CM2 ....233 C6
Custerson Ct CB11 ....22 D1
Custerson Dr CM77 ....155 B5
Custom House La CM2 ..91 D6
Cut-A-Thwart La CM9 ..236 C4
Cutforth Rd CM21 ....172 E3
Cuthberga Cl ◨ RM12 ..352 C5
Cut Hedge CM77 ....154 C6
Cuthedge La CO7 ....157 D7
Cutlers Cl CM23 ....145 D5
Cutlers La CO7 ....59 D5
Cutlers Rd CM3 ....301 E8
Cutler St IP1 ....17 C5
Cutmaple CO9 ....75 E4
Cutmore Pl CM2 ....253 F8
Cuton Hall La CM2 ....233 A5
Cut The CO5 ....184 A4
Cut Throat La CM8 ....184 A4
Cutting Dr CO9 ....76 E1
Cutty Sark Ct DA9 ....377 A2
Cygnet Ct
  Bishop's Stortford CM23 145 F6
  Sible Hedingham CO9 ....321 D8
Cypress View CM20 ....371 F2
Cygnet Way CM9 ....198 A1
Cygnet Wlk CO3 ....134 C4
Cymbeline Way (Colchester
  By Pass) CO3 ....135 B8
Cyns Ct ◨ E11 ....332 A5
Cypress Cl
  Clacton-on-S CO15 ....195 E7
  Waltham Abbey EN9 ....265 D5
Cypress Ct CM2 ....123 B1
Cypress Dr CM2 ....254 C6
Cypress Gr
  ◨ Colchester CO4 ....136 F8
  Redbridge IG6 ....311 E4
Cypress Mews CO5 ....218 B2
Cypress Path RM3 ....314 B3
Cypress Rd CM8 ....184 A4
Cyril Child Cl CO4 ....136 E7
Cyril Dowsett Ct CM7 ..236 E2
Czarina Rise SS15 ....341 E8

D

Daarle Ave SS8 ....364 A4
Dacre Ave Aveley RM15 .371 D5
  Redbridge IG5 ....311 A1
Dacre Cl IG7 ....311 C6
Dacre Gdns RM17 ....311 C6
Dacre Gdns IG7 ....311 C6
Dads Wood CM20 ....223 C8
Daen Ingas CM3 ....256 D7
Daffodil Ave CM1 ....294 B4
Daffodil Cl IP2 ....16 E4
Daffodil Gdns IG1 ....352 B7
Daffodil Way CM1 ....232 E7
Dagenham Ave RM9 ....353 E4
Dagenham Dock Sta
  RM9 ....353 F3
Dagenham East Sta
  RM9 ....354 C7
Dagenham Heathway Sta
  RM9 ....354 B4
Dagenham Priory Comp Sch
  RM10 ....354 B4
Dagenham Rd
  Bishop's Stortford CM23 .335 D2
  Rainham RM13 ....354 E5
Dagmar Rd RM10 ....354 C5
Dagnam Park Cl RM3 ..315 A5
Dagnam Park Dr RM3 ..314 F5
Dagnam Park Gdns RM3 315 A4
Dagnam Park Sq RM3 ..315 B4
Dagnets La CM77 ....154 D3
Dagwood La CM15 ....272 B1
Dahlia Cl
  ◨ Chelmsford CM1 ....232 F5
  Clacton-on-S CO16 ....195 C4
Dahlia Gdns IG1 ....352 B7
Dahlia Wlk CO4 ....136 D7
Daiglen Dr RM15 ....372 B7
Daiglen Sch The IG9 ..310 C8
Daimler Ave CM7 ....128 D8
Daines Cl Little Ilford E12 332 F1
  Southend-on-S SS1 ....368 B8
  South Ockendon RM15 ..357 A1
Daines Rd CM11 ....297 C2
Daines Way SS1 ....368 B8
Dains Pl IP11 ....221 C6
Dairy Farm Rd CM3 ....283 D3
Dairyhouse La CO11 ..114 F7
Dairy Rd CM2 ....232 F4
Daisleys La CM3 ....181 A2
Daisy Ct CM1 ....233 A6
Daisy Green Rd CO3 ..133 E8
Daisyley Rd CM6 ....98 B4
Daisy Rd E18 ....310 B1
Dakyn Dr RM15 ....275 D3
Dale Cl Colchester CO3 .134 B7
  Elmstead CO7 ....138 A6
  South Ockendon RM15 ..372 A7
Dale Ct
  Sawbridgeworth CM21 ..172 D1
  Woodford E18 ....310 A1
Dalefield IG9 ....288 D1
Dale Gdns IG8 ....310 B6
Dale Hall La IP1 ....17 C8
Dale Ho CM7 ....127 F2
Dale Rd CM9 ....210 A1
Dale St CM2 ....232 A1
Daleside Gdns IG7 ..311 C7
Dales The Harwich CO12 90 C1
  Rochford SS4 ....325 D4
Dalestone Mews RM3 ..314 B4
Dales View IP8 ....35 E8

Dales View Rd ◨ IP1 ....17 A8
Dale The Thundersley SS7 345 A4
  Wivenhoe CO7 ....164 C8
Daleview Ave CO11 ....115 C5
Dale View Ave E4 ....309 C8
Dale View Cres E4 ....309 C7
Dale View Gdns E4 ....309 D7
Dalewood Cl RM11 ....336 E4
Dalham Pl ◨ CB9 ....9 B7
Dalkeith Rd IG1 ....333 C1
Dallwood Way CM7 ....128 B1
Dalmatia Rd SS1 ....367 D8
Dalmeney SS16 ....341 B4
Dalroy Cl RM15 ....372 A1
Dalrymple Cl CM1 ....232 D3
Daltes La CO16 ....194 C3
Dalton Gdns CM23 ....145 E5
Dalton Holme IG8 ....310 F4
Dalton Rd IP1 ....17 B6
Daltons Fen SS13 ....343 C8
Dalwood SS3 ....349 D1
Dalwood Gdns SS7 ....345 E4
Damases La CM3 ....210 C1
Damant's Farm La CM3 142 D1
Damask Ct SS1 ....367 D6
Damask Mews CM7 ....128 A2
Damask Rd CO3 ....134 C7
Dame Elizabeth Ct CM1 172 E4
Dame Johane Bradbury's Sch
  CB10 ....22 F2
Dames Rd E7 ....332 A1
Dame Tipping CE Prim Sch
  RM4 ....313 E7
Dammant Ct CB9 ....9 C6
Dammerwick Cotts CM0 306 D6
Dampier Rd CO6 ....130 F3
Damselfly Rd IP3 ....38 C8
Danacre SS15 ....341 C7
Danbury Ilford RM6 ....333 D1
  Marks Tey CO6 ....132 F3
  Pilgrims Hatch CM15 ....293 F4
  Southend-on-S SS9 ....346 B4
Danbury Cres RM15 ..372 B7
Danbury Down SS14 ..342 E8
Danbury Mans ◨ SS1 ..352 B5
Danbury Park Com Prim Sch
  CM3 ....256 C2
Danbury Rd
  Loughton IG10 ....288 E3
  Rainham RM13 ....354 F4
  Rayleigh SS6 ....323 B3
Danbury Vale CM3 ....256 C3
Danbury Way IG8 ....310 C4
Dancing Dicks La CM8 .183 A2
Dandalan Cl IP1 ....16 E8
Dandelion Cl RM7 ....335 E2
Dandies Chase SS7 ....346 E7
Dandies Dr SS7 ....346 E7
Dane Acres CM23 ....145 D8
Dane House CM23 ....145 D8
Danehurst Gdns IG4 ..332 F6
Danemead SS11 ....197 A1
Dane O'Coys Rd CM23 .118 E1
Dane Pk CM23 ....145 D8
Danescroft Cl SS9 ....346 D4
Danescroft Dr SS9 ....346 D4
Danes Ct CO10 ....34 A8
Danesfield CO7 ....344 C2
Danesleigh Gdns SS9 ..346 D4
Dane St RM9 ....335 C4
Danes The
  Bishop's Stortford CM23 .368 G6
  Southend-on-S SS3 ....294 A4
Danes Way SS15 ....294 A4
Danette Gdns RM8 ....12 A6
Daneum Holt CO10 ....332 A5
Dangan Rd E11 ....332 A5

Daniel C
Grays, Orsett Heath RM16 374 B3
Daniel Cole Rd CO2 ....135 F4
Daniel Cotts CM11 ....195 C6
Daniell Dr CO2 ....352 B6
Daniells Ho CO6 ....108 F4
Daniel Way CM8 ....154 C8
Dansie Ct CM1 ....136 C8
Danyon Cl RM13 ....355 C3
Daphne Cl CM7 ....128 A2
Daphne Ct ◨ CO4 ....136 D7
Daphne Gdns E4 ....309 C7
Dapier Dr CM7 ....265 C6
D'arcy Ave CM9 ....237 B1
D'arcy Cl CM13 ....295 F7
D'arcy C
Burnham-on-C CM0 ....306 C6
  Kirby Cross CO13 ....170 F6
D'arcy Gdns RM9 ....353 F4
D'Arcy Ho CO14 ....144 D2
D'arcy Rd Colchester CO2 136 C3
  St Osyth CO16 ....186 F2
D'arcy Rise CM3 ....234 E7

D'arcy Way
  Brightlingsea CO7 ....192 E7
  Tollesbunt D'arcy CM9 ..215 E4
Dare Gdns RM8 ....334 E1
Darell Way CM1 ....232 A6
Darenth La SS15 ....341 D2
Darenth Rd SS9 ....346 B1
Darenth Rd Colchester CO1 .91 A2
Darina Ct CO12 ....91 A2
Darkhouse La CO5 ....196 C5
Dark La Brentwood CM14 315 F5
  Great Warley CM14 ....316 A3
  Thundersley SS7 ....345 A6
Darlinghurst Gr ◨ SS9 ..347 A2

Darlinghurst Prim Sch
  SS9 ....346 F2
Darlington Ct CM1 ....232 A6
Darlington Gdns RM3 ..314 D5
Darlington Path ◨ RM3 314 D5
Darnay Rise CM1 ....231 D6
Darnel Way CO3 ....134 C5
Darnel Way CM3 ....216 E1
Darnley Rd
  Gravesend DA11 ....379 B1
  Grays RM17 ....373 B2
  Woodford IG8 ....310 B2
Darrell Cl CM1 ....232 A6
Darrell Rd IP11 ....381 B1
Darsham Ct IP11 ....381 B1
Dart Cl Upminster RM14 .337 D5
  Witham CM8 ....183 D2
Dartfields RM3 ....314 D8
Dartford Gdns RM6 ....334 B6
Dartford Rd CM1 ....372 B7
Dartmouth Cl SS6 ....323 D5
Dartmouth Rd CM1 ....232 E6
Darvell Cres CM17 ....232 E6
Darwell Cl E6 ....352 A3
Darwin Cl
  ◨ Braintree CM7 ....127 F1
  Colchester CO2 ....135 F4
Darwin Rd Ipswich IP4 ..17 F5
  Tilbury RM18 ....378 F6
Dashes The CM20 ....199 E1
Dashwood Cl IP8 ....16 D1
Datchet Dr SS3 ....349 E2
Datchet Ho CO3 ....134 F7
Datchet Way CO3 ....134 F7
Daundy Cl IP2 ....16 C4
Davall Cl CO12 ....90 C1
Davall Ho CM7 ....378 B8
Davenant Foundation Sch
  IG10 ....267 C1
Davenants SS13 ....343 B8
Davenport CM17 ....224 E7
Davenport Ctr IG1 ....353 B3
Daventry Gdns RM3 ..314 C5
Daventry Gn RM3 ....314 C5
Daventry Rd RM3 ....314 C5
Davey Cl Colchester CO1 .136 D6
  Ipswich IP3 ....17 F1
David Ave SS11 ....299 D2
David Coffer Ct DA17 ..369 B2
David Dr RM3 ....315 A3
David Rd RM8 ....334 D2
Davidson Cl CO10 ....34 A8
Davidson Gdns SS12 ..321 E5
Davidson Ho DA9 ....377 C2
Davies Wlk CM1 ....297 C2
David Terr RM3 ....315 A3
Davis Cl SS6 ....323 B6
Davington Gdns RM8 ..353 B7
Davington Rd RM8 ....353 B7
Davinia Cl IG8 ....311 B5
Davis Rd Aveley RM15 ..371 D5
  Grays RM16 ....372 F3
Davy Rd CO15 ....196 C8
Dawber Cl CM3 ....301 D5
Dawes Ave CM2 ....336 E1
Dawes La SS6 ....323 B6
Dawes La CO5 ....376 F2
Dawlish Cres IG3 ....162 A4
Dawlish Dr Ilford IG3 ..332 F7
  Southend-on-S SS6 ....323 D5
Dawlish Rd CO15 ....220 B8
Dawlish Wlk RM3 ....314 C2
Dawnbrook Cl ◨ IP2 ..16 E2
Dawn Cl CM1 ....259 B8
Dawn Cl CO3 ....134 C7
Dawn Ct CO3 ....134 C7
Dawnings The CM1 ....294 B6
Daws Ct CM1 ....230 F1
Daws Cross CM3 ....281 B4
Daw's Hall (Wildfowl Farm)*
  CO8 ....55 B6
Dawson Ave
  Barking IG11 ....352 A8
  Wickford SS11 ....299 B3
Dawson Cl IG11 ....352 A8
Dawson Mews CM1 ....297 B3
Dawson Rd CM1 ....232 F6
Daws St Birdbrook CO9 ..17 D8
Days Cl CM1 ....232 A4
Days La
  Doddinghurst CM15 ....272 C1
  Pilgrims Hatch CM15 ..294 B7
Dayton Dr DA8 ....370 D1
Dazeley's La CM7 ....125 E8
Deacon Rd SS3 ....341 C7
Deacon Way IG8 ....310 F4
Dead La Ardleigh CO7 ..111 C8
  Great Bentley CO7 ....166 F2
  Little Clacton CO16 ....168 B2
Deadman's La CM2 ....254 C4
Deal Cl Braintree CM7 ..127 A8
  Clacton-on-S CO15 ....220 B8
Dealtree Cl CM1 ....272 E4
Dean Cl SS7 ....344 D8
Dean Cl RM7 ....335 D5
Deanery Gdns CM7 ....127 F7
Deanery Hill CM7 ....127 E7
Deane's Cl CO12 ....91 A2
Deanes Ct CO12 ....91 A2
Deanery Ho CO12 ....91 A2
Dean Rd CB1 ....6 B8
Dean Rogers Pl CM7 ..127 E8
Deans Ct CM14 ....316 B6

Deans Ind Est RM13 ..355 D1
Deans Cl CM14 ....316 B6
Dean St CO7 ....192 E7
Dean Way CM1 ....231 E1
Dearsly Ho RM13 ....354 D3
Debden CE Prim Sch
  CB11 ....68 B7
Debden Cl IG8 ....310 D3
Debden Dr CB10 ....44 E2
Debden Gn SS16 ....341 C4
Debden La IG10 ....267 C1
Debden Park High Sch
  IG10 ....289 D7
Debden Rd Loughton IG10 267 B1
  Newport CB11 ....67 A8
Debden Sta IG10 ....289 C5
Debden Way ◨ RM12 ..352 C5
Debden Wlk CM0 ....306 A6
Debden Wlk ◨ RM12 ..355 B6
De Beauvoir Chase
  CM1 ....298 C3
Deben Cl CM7 ....128 D1
Deben Ct CM7 ....183 E2
Deben Dr CO10 ....34 A8
Deben High Sch IP1 ..381 C8
Deben Rd Colchester CO4 110 F1
  Haverhill CB9 ....9 B8
Deben Way IP11 ....381 C3
Deben Wlk CO16 ....195 C6
De Bohun Ct CB10 ....332 B8
De Burgh Rd CO3 ....134 E6
Dedham Ave CO16 ....195 B5
Dedham CE Prim Sch
  CO7 ....85 A6
Dedham Cl CM11 ....297 C2
Dedham Ct CO2 ....136 B4
Dedham Meade CO7 ....84 F3
Dedham Pl ◨ CO7 ....17 D5
Dedham Rd Ardleigh CO7 84 D1
  Billericay CM11 ....297 C2
  Boxted CO4 ....83 C4
  Lawford CO11 ....85 E4
  Stratford St M CO7 ....58 E1
Dee Cl RM14 ....337 E5
Dennies La RM14 ....336 D3
Deepdale SS7 ....344 F6
Deepdale Rd CO12 ....91 A4
Deepdene Ave SS6 ....323 D4
Deepdene Cl E11 ....332 A7
Deepdene Path IG10 ..289 B5
Deepdene Rd IG10 ....289 B5
Deeping Wlk CO16 ....194 B5
Deepwater Rd SS8 ....363 E3
Deerbank Rd CM11 ....297 C3
Deere Ave RM13 ....355 A6
Deerhurst SS7 ....345 E7
Deerhurst Chase CM3 ..256 F1
Deerhurst Cl SS7 ....345 E7
Deerleap Gr E4 ....287 B4
Deerleap Way CM7 ....128 D4
Deer Mead Ct ◨ RM2 ..335 F6
Deer Park Cl CM9 ....211 C3
Deer Park Way EN9 ....265 B4
Deer Pk CM19 ....223 B5
Deeside Wlk ◨ SS12 ..342 B3
Dee Way RM1 ....313 C2
Defoe Cres CO4 ....110 B4
Defoe Par RM10 ....374 B3
Defoe Way RM5 ....313 B4
Deford Rd CM8 ....211 D8
De Greys Cl CO10 ....34 C5
Deidre Chapman Ho
  DA10 ....377 E1
Deirdre Ave SS12 ....321 B7
Deirdre Cl SS12 ....321 B7
Delafield Rd RM17 ....373 D1
Delamere Rd
  Chelmsford CM1 ....231 E1
  Colchester CO4 ....110 B4
Delargy Cl RM16 ....374 A3
De La Salle RC Sch SS14 342 C8
Delaware Cres SS3 ....368 D7
Delaware Rd SS3 ....368 D7
Delder Ave SS8 ....364 D2
Delft Rd SS8 ....364 A4
Delfzul Rd SS8 ....364 A4
Delgada Rd SS8 ....364 A4
Delhi Rd SS13 ....343 C6
Delimands SS13 ....341 F6
Delius Way SS17 ....160 C6
Delius Wlk CO4 ....136 C6
Dell Cl IG8 ....310 B7
Dell Grays RM17 ....373 B2
  Hornchurch RM12 ....200 C4
Dellfield Ct CM17 ....200 C4
Della
  Bishop's Stortford, Hockerill
    CM23 ....146 A7
  Bishop's Stortford, Latchmore Bank
    CM22 ....146 B1
  Spellbrook CM23 ....173 A8
Dellow Cl IG2 ....333 D4
Dellows La CM17 ....223 E2
Dell Rd RM17 ....373 B2
Dells Cl E4 ....287 B7
Dells The CM12 ....203 A1
Dellwood Ave IP11 ....381 F5
Dellwood Gdns IG5 ....333 A8
Delmar Gdns CM9 ....299 C2

Delmores SS16 ....341 C3
Delta Rd CM13 ....295 D3
De Luci Rd DA8 ....369 C4
Delvers Mead RM10 ..354 C1
Delview SS8 ....363 F5
Delvins SS13 ....343 B8
Delvyn's La CO9 ....52 C6
De Mandeville Rd CM21 .94 C2
De-Marci Ct CM7 ....128 D3
Demoiselle Cres IP3 ....38 C8
Denbar Par RM7 ....335 C7
Denbigh Cl RM11 ....337 A7
Denbigh Rd RM3 ....314 A3
Denbigh Rd SS15 ....341 B5
Denby Grange CM17 ..224 E8
Dencourt Cres SS14 ..342 F5
Dene Cl SS6 ....323 D4
Denecroft Gdns RM17 .373 D3
Dene Ct CM1 ....231 D5
Dene Gdns SS3 ....323 D5
Deneholm Prim Sch
  RM16 ....373 C4
Denehurst Gdns
  Basildon SS16 ....340 E4
  Woodford IG8 ....310 B6
Dene Path RM15 ....372 A7
Dene Rd IG9 ....288 E1
Denesmere SS16 ....344 C4
Deneway SS16 ....342 D2
Dengayne SS14 ....342 D6
Dengie Cl CM8 ....211 F8
Dengie Hundred Sports Ctr
  CM0 ....306 B4
Denham Dr CO7 ....164 C8
Denham Dr IG2 ....333 D5
Denham Rd SS8 ....364 A4
Denham Vale SS6 ....323 A3
Denham Way IG11 ....352 F4
Denholm Ct CM8 ....211 B8
Denholme Wlk RM13 ..354 F6
Denmark Gdns IP9 ....62 D6
Denmark Ho CM2 ....232 A2
Denmark Rd E4 ....309 A8
Dennis Ct E17 ....309 D1
Dennises La RM14 ....356 D3
Denny Ave EN9 ....265 D5
Denny Ct
  Bishop's Stortford CM23 .119 B2
  ◨ Dartford DA2 ....376 B1
Danbury Green RM9 ..353 B5
Dent Cl RM15 ....372 A7
Denton App SS0 ....347 C5
Denton Ave SS0 ....347 C5
Denton Cres CM77 ....145 C5
Denton's Terr CO7 ....164 B8
Denton's Terr CO7 ....164 B8
Denver Dr SS13 ....321 F2
Denver La Set RM13 ..369 F8
Depot Cotts IG10 ....288 E4
Derby Ave Romford RM7 .335 C1
  Upminster RM14 ....337 A1
Derby Cl Basildon SS16 ..340 F4
  Billericay CM11 ....297 D5
  Ipswich IP4 ....18 A5
  Mayland CM3 ....261 A1
Derby Ct E18 ....309 F2
Derby Rd Grays RM17 ..373 B1
  Hoddesdon EN11 ....221 D5
  Ipswich IP3 ....18 A4
  Woodford E18 ....309 F2
Derby Road Bridge
  RM17 ....378 B8
Dereham Ave IP3 ....17 F3
Dereham Cl CO2 ....135 C3
Dereham Rd RM5 ....313 B4
Dereham Rd IG11 ....352 F3
Derek Gdns SS2 ....321 F1
Derham Gdns RM14 ..337 C1
Deri Ave RM13 ....355 B1
Dering Cres SS9 ....346 D7
Dering Rd RM14 ....352 A8
Dersingham Ave E12 ..332 A2
Derwent Ave SS8 ....364 A6
Derwent Cl CM2 ....323 E2
Derwent Gdns
  Holland-on-S CO15 ....196 C6
  Redbridge IG4 ....332 E7
Derwent Par RM15 ....372 A7
Derwent Rd
  Highwoods CM4 ....110 C4
  Ipswich IP3 ....17 F3
Derwent Way
  Chelmsford CM1 ....231 D4
  Great Notley CM7 ....154 C7
  Hornchurch RM12 ....355 B7
Desborough Path CM2 .232 F8
Dessons Ct SS17 ....160 F4
De Staunton Ct CO7 ..165 B7
Detmold Cl CM7 ....127 F6
Deveraux Cl CO4 ....170 F8
Devereaux Cl RM14 ..337 C4
Devereaux Pl CO4 ....109 C3
De Vere Ave SS0 ....347 H3
De Vere Cl
  Hatfield Peverel CM3 ..211 B3
  Wivenhoe CO7 ....164 B8
De Vere Ct SS9 ....346 C6
De Vere Est SS9 ....346 C6
De Vere Rd Colchester CO3 133 D6
De Vere La CO7 ....164 D8
De Vere Prim Sch CO9 ..51 E4
De Vere Rd
  Colchester CO3 ....135 A5
  Earls Colne CM6 ....160 C7
De Veres Rd ◨ CO9 ....76 D1

Devereux Ct CO15 ....195 F3
Devereux PI CO4 ....109 C3
Devereux Rd Grays RM16 372 F3
Southend-on-S SS1 ....367 A7
Devereux Way CO12 ....90 F2
Deverill CI CM1 ....208 B2
Deveron Gdns RM15 ....372 A8
Deveron Way RM1 ....313 E2
De Vigier Ave CB10 ....23 A2
Devizes Ho ⑩ RM3 ....314 C6
Devlin Rd IP8 ....16 B1
Devoils La ⑥ CM23 ....145 F7
Devon CI IG9 ....310 B8
Devon Gdns SS4 ....325 C5
Devon Ho Romford RM7 ....313 A1
⑤ Wanstead E11 ....332 A6
Devonport Gdns IG1 ....332 F5
Devon Rd Barking IG11 ....352 E4
Colchester CO2 ....135 B3
Felixstowe IP11 ....381 D5
Devonshire Ct ⑫ SS15 ....341 A8
Devonshire Gdns
Braintree CM7 ....128 B4
Linford SS17 ....375 A3
Devonshire Ho IG6 ....311 B3
Devonshire Rd
Basildon SS15 ....341 A7
Burnham-on-C CM0 ....306 C5
Grays RM16 ....372 F3
Hornchurch RM12 ....336 D2
Ilford IG2 ....333 E4
Southminster CM0 ....284 C4
Devon Way
Canvey Island SS8 ....364 B5
Harwich CO12 ....90 D2
Holland-on-S CO15 ....196 E7
De Warren Ho DA11 ....378 D1
Dewberry CI ⑧ CO4 ....136 D7
Dewes Green Rd
Berden CM23 ....92 A8
Clavering CM23 ....64 F1
Dewey Path RM12 ....355 C6
Dewey Rd RM10 ....354 C6
Dewlands Basildon SS14 ....342 A7
Black Notley CM77 ....155 B6
Dewsbury CI RM3 ....314 E4
Dewsbury Gdns RM3 ....314 E4
Dewsbury Rd RM3 ....314 E4
Dewspreen SS1 ....342 E4
Dewyk Rd SS8 ....364 C5
Dexter CI RM17 ....373 A3
Deyncourt Gdns RM14 ....337 C2
Deynecourt Gdns E11 ....332 C7
Deynes Rd CM1 ....68 B7
Dhobi PI IP1 ....16 F7
Dial CI DA9 ....377 D2
Dial Cnr CO7 ....166 E3
Dial La IP1 ....17 C6
Dial Rd CO7 ....166 E3
Diamond CI
Dagenham RM8 ....334 C3
Grays RM16 ....372 F3
Diamond Ct RM11 ....336 A3
Diana CI Grays RM16 ....372 F3
Woodford E18 ....310 B2
Diana Ho CO11 ....170 E5
Diana Way CO15 ....195 C2
Diban Ave RM12 ....355 B8
Diben Ct RM12 ....355 B8
Dickens Ave Dartford DA1 376 A3
Tilbury RM18 ....379 B6
Dickens CI Braintree CM7 155 A8
Southend-on-S SS2 ....348 B2
⑩ Wanstead E11 ....332 A7
Dickens Dr SS15 ....341 D7
Dickens PI CM1 ....231 D7
Dickens Rd IP2 ....16 F5
Dickens Rise IG7 ....311 B7
Dickens Way RM1 ....335 E7
Dicksons Cnr IP1 ....16 C7
Dicky Moors CM3 ....207 F7
Didsbury CI IP2 ....16 E2
Digby Gdns RM10 ....354 A4
Digby Mews CO5 ....218 C6
Digby Rd Barking IG11 ....352 F5
Corringham SS17 ....361 C5
Ipswich IP4 ....18 C7
Digby Wlk RM12 ....355 C7
Diggens CI IG10 ....288 E6
Dilbridge Rd E CO4 ....136 C8
Dilbridge Rd W CO4 ....136 C8
Dilkes Prim Sch RM15 ....371 F7
Dillestone Ct CB9 ....9 F5
Dilliway Ct CM0 ....306 B4
Dillwyn St IP1 ....17 A6
Dillwyn St W IP1 ....17 A6
Dilston CM3 ....257 A6
Dimsdale Cres CM23 ....146 B6
Dinant Ave SS8 ....363 E4
Dinant Link Rd EN11 ....221 B7
Dinants Cres CO4 ....132 E3
Dinsdale CI ⑪ CO4 ....136 C8
Dinsdale Ct IP11 ....381 D3
Dismals The CM3 ....182 B2
Disney Ct CM4 ....274 B4
Disraeli Rd SS6,SS9 ....346 B8
Distillery La CO2 ....136 A4
Ditchfield Rd EN11 ....197 A1
Ditchingham Gr IP5 ....18 F6
Ditton Court Rd SS0 ....366 D8
Dixon Ave
Chelmsford CM1 ....231 F4
Clacton-on-S CO16 ....195 C6
Dixon CI CO11 ....86 B4
Dixon Ct SS13 ....343 B6
Dixon Way CO7 ....137 A2
Dobbies La CO6 ....132 E3
Dobb's Weir Rd EN11 ....221 D5
Dobsons CI SS6 ....323 E1

Dock Approach Rd
RM16,RM17 ....373 E2
Docker Ct CO2 ....136 B4
Dockfield Ave CO22 ....90 F3
Dock La CO12 ....117 A4
Docklands Rd CM4 ....274 C4
Dock Rd Felixstowe IP11 .381 B2
Grays RM17,RM18 ....378 E7
Dock St IP2 ....17 C4
Dockwra La CM3 ....257 A7
Doctor's La CO10 ....11 D2
Docwra Rd CO5 ....158 C2
Doddenhill CI CO10 ....11 D3
Doddinghurst CE Jun Sch
CM15 ....272 B2
Doddinghurst Rd CM15 294 C2
Doddinghurst Inf Sch
CM15 ....272 B2
Doddinghurst Rd
Brentwood CM15 ....294 D1
Doddinghurst CM15 ....272 C1
Dodmans ⑦ IP7 ....35 A1
Doe's Cnr Halstead CO9 ....76 D5
Hatfield Peverel CM9 ....215 D1
Doesgate La RM14 ....340 C2
Doeshill Dr SS12 ....321 E7
Dog Chase CM7 ....73 C3
Dogden La CM23 ....92 E2
Doggetts Chase SS4 ....326 A4
Doggett's Cnr RM11 ....336 F2
Doggetts La CO6 ....132 F2
Doggetts RM/Hatfd CM15 294 C2
Doghouse Rd CM7 ....129 F4
Dog Kennel La CM4 ....274 C5
Dogs Head St ⑧ IP4 ....17 C5
Dogwood CI IP3 ....18 D2
Dolby Rise CM2 ....232 F2
Dollant Ave SS8 ....364 A3
Dolphin Ave RM1 ....335 F7
Dolphin Ct CO13 ....171 B6
Dolphin Gdns CM12 ....296 F5
Dolphin Motorway Ind Est
RM19 ....371 E1
Dolphins SS0 ....347 D4
Dolphin Way
Bishop's Stortford CM23 .146 A8
Purfleet RM19 ....371 E1
Dombey CI CM1 ....231 F7
Dombey Rd IP2 ....16 F1
Dominic CI EN9 ....265 B6
Dominion Dr RM3 ....313 B4
Dominion Wks RM8 ....334 E3
Domitian CI CO4 ....110 B6
Domsey Bank CO6 ....132 E3
Domsey Chase CO5 ....159 C8
Domsey La CM3 ....208 F5
Dona La CM3 ....182 B2
Donald Dr RM6 ....152 E5
Donald Thorn Ct SS12 .321 D6
Donald Way CM2 ....254 C7
Donard Dr CO6 ....108 D4
Doncaster Ave RM14 .336 F1
Doncella CI RM16 ....372 D3
Don Ct CM8 ....183 A2
Donington Ave IG6 ....333 C6
Donne Dr CO15 ....203 D8
Donne Rd RM8 ....334 C2
Donnington CI ⑪ DA2 376 B1
Donovan's Gdn CM3 ....317 F3
Don Way RM1 ....313 E3
Donyland Way CO5 ....163 F8
Dooley Rd
Felixstowe IP11 ....381 A3
Halstead CO9 ....76 D1
Dorchester Ave EN11 ....221 A8
Dorchester Ct ⑫ E18 .309 F2
Dorchester Gdns E4 ....309 A6
Dorchester Rd
Billericay CM12 ....297 A5
Ipswich IP3 ....18 C3
Dordell Ct CO9 ....50 B8
Dordells SS15 ....341 E6
Dore Ave E12 ....352 A7
Dorian Rd RM12 ....336 A3
Doric Ave SS4 ....325 D5
Doric Lodge SS0 ....366 E7
Dorking Cres CO16 ....195 C6
Dorking Rd RM3 ....314 D6
Dorking Rise RM3 ....314 D6
Dorking Wlk
Great Baddow CM2 ....254 E7
Romford RM3 ....314 D5
Dorkins Way RM14 ....337 B8
Dorothy Barley Jun Sch
RM8 ....353 B7
Dorothy Curtice Ct CO6 .133 D3
Dorothy Farm Rd SS6 .324 A1
Dorothy Gdns
Dagenham RM8 ....353 B8
Thundersley SS7 ....344 F5
Dorothy Sayers Dr CM8 .184 A5
Dorrington Gdns RM12 .336 B4
Dorset Ave
Great Baddow CM2 ....254 E6
Romford RM1 ....335 D8
Dorset CI
Great Baddow CM2 ....254 E6
Halstead CO9 ....76 D1
Holland-on-S CO15 ....196 E6
Dorset Gdns Linford SS17 375 A4
Dorset Rd SS4 ....325 C5
Dorset Ho ⑤ CM21 ....145 C7
Dorset Rd
Burnham-on-C CM0 ....306 C4
Maldon CM9 ....258 F8
Dorset Way
Billericay CM12 ....297 A5
Canvey Island SS8 ....364 A5
Dorvis La CB10 ....6 B1

Doubleday Cnr CO6 ....130 F2
Doubleday Dr CM9 ....236 F5
Doubleday Gdns CM7 ....128 B5
Doubleday Rd IG10 ....289 C6
Doublegate La SS11 ....322 B5
Doublet Mews CM1 ....297 D5
Doucecroft Sch CO5 ....158 C3
Douglas Ave
Chingford E17 ....309 A2
Romford RM3 ....314 E1
Douglas CI
Galleywood CM2 ....254 D3
Grays RM16 ....372 E3
Douglas Dr SS12 ....321 D5
Douglas Gr CM8 ....183 D2
Douglas Rd Chingford E4 .287 F1
Clacton-on-S CO15 ....195 C4
Hadleigh SS7 ....345 F3
Harwich CO12 ....91 B3
Ilford IG3 ....334 A5
Romford RM11 ....335 F5
Douglas Wlk ⑥ CM2 .254 D8
Doug Siddons Ct RM17 .378 C8
Doulton CI CM17 ....224 E7
Doulton Way SS4 ....325 C6
Dounsell Ct CM15 ....294 A3
Dove CI
Bishop's Stortford CM23 .145 E3
Grays RM16 ....372 E3
Stansted Mountfitchet
CM24 ....119 E8
Dovecote SS3 ....349 E1
Dove Cotts CM22 ....93 F3
Dove Cres CO12 ....90 D2
Dove Crofts CM6 ....176 E7
Dovedale
Canvey Island SS8 ....364 E5
Frinton-on-S IP11 ....381 B3
Dovedale Ave IG5 ....311 A1
Dovedale CI
Basildon SS16 ....341 A4
Ramsden Heath CM11 .298 C4
Dovedale Gdns CO15 .196 C6
Dove Dr SS7 ....344 E2
Dovehouse Croft CM20 .200 A2
Dove House Gdns E4 ....309 A8
Dovehouse Mead IG11 .352 D3
Dovehouse Rd SS9 ....346 D8
Dove La CM2 ....254 A6
Dover CI Braintree CM7 .128 C4
Clacton-on-S CO15 ....220 C8
Romford RM5 ....313 C1
Dovercliff Rd SS8 ....364 C5
Dovercourt Caravan Pk
CO12 ....91 A1
Dovercourt Sta CO12 ....91 D4
Dover Rd
Brightlingsea CO7 ....192 F8
Dagenham RM6 ....334 E5
Ipswich IP3 ....18 B4
Northfleet DA11 ....378 D1
Wanstead E12 ....332 A8
Dovers Corner Ind Pk
RM13 ....354 F1
Dovervelt Rd SS8 ....364 C5
Dove Way SS13 ....343 B6
Dovesgate SS7 ....344 E5
Doves La CM6 ....150 B2
Doves Mews SS15 ....319 D1
Dove St IP4 ....17 E5
Dovetree Ct RM3 ....314 D6
Dove Tree Ct CO3 ....134 C5
Dove Wlk ⑭ RM12 ....155 B8
Dowches Cotts CO5 ....158 C2
Dowches Gdns CO5 ....158 C3
Dow Ct CM0 ....284 C4
Dowling CI
Colchester CO2 ....136 A4
Hornchurch RM12 ....355 B5
Dowland CI SS17 ....360 C3
Dowland Wlk SS15 ....341 C7
Dowling Rd SS8 ....79 F3
Downer Rd SS7 ....344 C5
Downer Rd N SS7 ....344 E6
Downesway SS7 ....344 D3
Downey CI SS14 ....342 C7
Downhall CI SS6 ....323 D4
Downhall Park Way SS6 323 D5
Down Hall Prim Sch
SS6 ....323 D5
Down Hall Rd SS6 ....323 D4
Downham Bvd IP9 ....38 C8
Downham CE Prim Sch
CM11 ....298 C4
Downham CI RM5 ....313 A3
Downham Rd
Canvey Island SS8 ....364 A3
Ramsden Heath CM11 .298 D5
Ramsden Heath CM4,CM11 298 D7
Stock CM4 ....276 B1
Wickford SS11 ....299 C3
Downing CI IP2 ....16 F2
Downing Path SS15 ....319 D1
Downing Rd RM9 ....353 F5
Downland Inf Sch IG6 ....265 E5
Downleaze CM3 ....301 E8
Downs Cres
Great Dunmow CM6 ....123 C1
Haverhill CB9 ....8 F8
Downs Gr SS16 ....342 E3
Downshall Ave IG3 ....333 F5
Downshall Prim Sch IG3 333 E4
Downside CI SS7 ....344 D4
Downsland Dr CM14 ....316 C2
Downs PI ⑭ CB9 ....8 F8
Downs Rd
Felixstowe IP11 ....381 B5
Great Dunmow CM6 ....123 D1

Downs The continued
Harlow CM20 ....223 E8
Downsway CM1 ....232 D6
Downs Dr CB9 ....8 E8
Downton Wlk CO5 ....186 D6
Dowsetts La CM11 ....298 C6
Doyle Way RM18 ....379 C5
Dragon CI CM0 ....306 A5
Dragon's Gn CB10 ....23 D1
Drake Ave Ipswich IP3 ....18 B2
Mayland CM3 ....283 A8
Drake CI Brentwood CM14 316 D5
Hadleigh SS7 ....345 C5
Drake Ct ⑤ SS14 ....342 F5
Drake Gdns CM7 ....128 C4
Drake Mews CM12 ....355 B4
Drake Point DA8 ....369 E1
Drake Rd Basildon SS15 .341 D6
Grays RM16 ....372 E4
Southend-on-S SS0 ....347 C1
Drakes App CO15 ....195 A1
Drakes Cnr CO5 ....188 F4
Drakes La Boreham CM3 .209 B7
Little Waltham CM3 ....208 F7
Drakes Mdw CM17 ....200 E4
Drake Sq N IP3 ....18 B2
Drake Sq S IP3 ....18 B2
Drakes The SS3 ....368 E4
Drakes Way SS6 ....323 E4
Drapers Chase
Heybridge CM9 ....237 D4
Rayne CM7 ....153 D8
Draper's Cnr CM5 ....248 C2
Drapers Ct RM12 ....336 E2
Drapers La CB9 ....8 E2
Drapers Rd CM3 ....301 E8
Draycot Rd E11 ....332 B4
Dray Ct CO6 ....109 F4
Drayman's CI CM23 ....145 B5
Draymans Gr CM77 ....154 C8
Draymans Way IP3 ....17 E3
Drayson CI EN9 ....265 E7
Drays The CO10 ....15 B5
Drayton Ave IG10 ....288 F3
Drayton CI Ilford IG1 ....333 D3
⑭ Maldon CM9 ....237 A1
Drewsteignton SS3 ....368 D8
Dreys The CM7 ....204 D8
Driberg Way CM7 ....128 C4
Driffield CI CO5 ....158 D4
Drift The East Bergholt CO7 60 C2
Great Cornard CO10 ....34 C5
Ipswich,Priory Heath IP3 .18 C1
Ipswich,Rose Hill IP4 ....18 A6
Stutton IP9 ....62 C5
Driftway SS16 ....342 F4
Driftway The IP4 ....18 C6
Drive The Barking IG11 ....352 F5
Brentwood CM13 ....316 C4
Buckhurst Hill IG9 ....288 C2
Chelmsford CM1 ....231 F8
Chingford E4 ....287 D2
Clacton-on-S CO15 ....196 B7
Harlow CM20 ....199 E1
Hoddesdon EN11 ....221 B4
Hullbridge SS5 ....301 D3
Ilford IG1 ....333 A3
Loughton IG10 ....288 B8
Mayland CM3 ....282 F8
Rayleigh SS6 ....346 B8
Redbridge E18 ....332 F4
Rivenhall CM8 ....184 F6
Rochford SS4 ....325 F3
Romford, Collier Row RM5 313 D3
Romford, Harold wood RM3 314 F2
Sawbridgeworth CM21 ....172 E2
Southend-on-S SS0 ....366 B6
Thaxted CM6 ....69 F3
Wanstead E18 ....332 A8
Barking IG11 ....353 A6
Driveway The SS8 ....364 B3
Droitwich Ave SS2 ....348 D1
Dronfield Gdns RM8 ....353 C7
Drood CI CM1 ....231 F7
Drovers Mead CM14 ....316 B6
Drovers Way CM23 ....145 C5
Droveway IG10 ....289 B7
Druce The CM11 ....255 D4
Drum Field CO7 ....138 B7
Drummond Ave RM7 ....335 D7
Drummond Ct CM1 ....294 C2
Drummond PI ⑦ SS12 .321 E5
Drummond Rd
Buckhurst Hill IG9 ....110 B8
Epping CM16 ....246 A1
Drury La
Aythorpe Roding CM6 ....176 C2
⑪ Felixstowe IP11 ....381 D5
Ridgewell CO9 ....29 F5
Drury Rd CO2 ....135 C5
Dryden Ave SS2 ....348 B2
Dryden CI Maldon CM9 ....237 B5
Redbridge IG6 ....311 F4
Dryden PI RM18 ....379 B6
Dryden Twrs RM3 ....313 C4
Dry Dock CM7 ....164 B8
Drysdale Ave E4 ....287 B7
Dry St SS16 ....341 E1
Drywoods CM3 ....301 D5
Duarte PI RM16 ....372 F3
Dubarry CI SS7 ....344 E6
Du Cane PI ⑧ CM8 ....184 A2
Duchess CI CM23 ....145 D7
Duchess Gr IG9 ....310 B8
Duck End CM23 ....119 F1
Ducker's La CM1 ....206 C2
Ducketts Mead
Canewdon SS4 ....304 D2

Ducketts Mead continued
Roydon CM19 ....198 B1
Ducketts Wharf ⑩ CM23 145 F6
Ducking Stool Ct RM1 .335 E7
Duck La CM16 ....246 C6
Duckling La CM21 ....172 E2
Duck St Little Easton CM6 122 B2
Wendens Ambo CB11 ....42 E5
Dudbrook Rd CM14 ....271 B1
Duddery CI CB9 ....9 B7
Duddery Hill CB9 ....9 A7
Duddery Rd CB9 ....9 B7
Dudley CI Boreham CM3 .209 E1
Chelmsford CM2 ....136 A4
Grays RM16 ....372 E4
Dudley Ct ⑪ E11 ....332 A6
Dudley Gdns RM3 ....314 D4
Dudley Rd Chingford E17 309 A1
Clacton-on-S CO15 ....195 D3
Earls Colne CO6 ....104 F7
Fingringhoe CO5 ....163 E3
Ilford IG1 ....352 B8
Southend-on-S SS0 ....347 C1
Duffield CI RM10 ....372 F3
Duffield Dr CO4 ....136 E7
Duffield Rd CM2 ....254 D6
Duffries CI CM3 ....207 E7
Dugard Ave CO3 ....134 D5
Duggers La CM7 ....128 A1
Dugmore Ave CO13 ....170 C8
Duke Gdns IG6 ....333 D7
Duke PI SS15 ....341 E8
Duke St IG6 ....333 D7
Dukes Ave Grays RM17 .373 A4
Southend-on-S SS0 ....284 D3
Theydon Bois CM16 ....267 E4
Dukes CI CM6 ....123 D1
Dukes Ct E6 ....352 A4
Dukes Farm CI CM2 ....254 A7
Dukes Farm Rd CM2 ....297 B5
Dukes La
⑭ Chelmsford CM2 ....232 F4
Willingale CM5 ....228 C5
Dukes Orch
Hatfield Broad Oak CM22 .174 F6
Writtle CM1 ....231 B1
Dukes Park Ind Est CM2 .232 F4
Dukes PI CM1 ....294 C1
Dukes Priory Hospl The
CM1 ....232 D2
Dukes Rd Billericay CM11 297 C4
Chelmsford CM1 ....127 F5
Wallend E6 ....352 A4
Dukes Ride CM23 ....145 C7
Duke St Brightlingsea CO7 192 E6
Chelmsford CM1 ....232 B2
Hoddesdon EN11 ....221 A7
Ipswich IP3 ....17 E4
Dulverton Ave SS0 ....347 A5
Dulverton CI SS0 ....347 A5
Dulverton Cotts CO3 ....134 C4
Dulverton Rd RM3 ....314 D4
Dulwich Ct CO15 ....196 D5
Dulwich Rd CO15 ....196 D5
Dumbarton Rd IP4 ....18 C8
Dumfries Rd IP4 ....18 C8
Dumney La
Braintree, Hornells Corner
CM3 ....153 E2
Braintree, Thistley Green
CM6 ....153 B3
Great Leighs CM3 ....180 E8
Dumont Ave CO16 ....142 C3
Dunbar Ave RM10 ....335 A1
Dunbar Gdns RM10 ....354 B7
Dunbar PI SS12 ....321 E5
Duncan CI SS12 ....321 F5
Duncan Rd CO2 ....135 B4
Duncan Rise CO9 ....29 F7
Dunchurch Ho RM10 ....354 A5
Duncombe Ct ⑪ RM19 371 B1
Dundas Mews EN3 ....265 A2
Dundee Ave SS9 ....346 B2
Dundee CI SS9 ....346 C2
Dundee Ct SS14 ....342 F8
Dundonald Dr SS9 ....346 F1
Dunedin Ho RM18 ....379 A5
Dunedin Rd Ilford IG1 ....333 F4
Rainham RM13 ....354 F2
Dunfane CM1 ....297 C5
Dungannon Chase SS3 368 B6
Dungannon Dr SS3 ....368 B6
Dunkeld Ct CM3 ....334 C2
Dunkellin Gr RM15 ....372 A7
Dunkellin Way RM15 ....372 A7
Dunkirk Rd DA1 ....376 A6
Dunkirk Rd CM0 ....306 C5
Dunlin South Woodham Ferrers
SS8 ....279 D1
Dunlin CI SS12 ....282 G2
Dunlin Rd IP2 ....16 E2
Dunmore Rd CM2 ....233 A3
Dunmow CI Ilford RM6 332 C6
Loughton IG10 ....288 E3
Dunmow Gdns CM13 ....339 D5
Dunmow Ho RM9 ....353 D8
Dunmow Rd
Bishop's Stortford CM23 .146 C7
Felsted CM6 ....125 F2
Fyfield CM5 ....227 D1
Great Bardfield CM7 ....98 B8
Great Easton CM6 ....97 A1
Great Hallingbury CM22 .147 C7
Hatfield Broad Oak CM22 .174 D5
High Roding CM6 ....176 D5
Leaden Roding CM6 ....176 D5
Rayne CM7 ....128 A2
Takeley CM22 ....148 C7
Thaxted CM6 ....97 A7
Dunning CI
Bradfield CO11 ....114 C8

Dunning CI continued
South Ockendon RM15 ....372 A7
Dunningford CI RM12 ....354 F7
Dunningford Prim Sch
RM12 ....354 F7
Dunnings La CM13 ....339 B2
Dunnock Way CO4 ....137 A2
Dunnose Ct ⑬ RM19 ....371 B1
Dunoon CI CM7 ....128 D4
Dunoon Ct RM3 ....314 B6
Dunspring La IG5 ....311 B1
Dunstable CI RM3 ....314 D4
Dunstable Rd
Romford RM3 ....314 D4
Stanford-le-H SS17 ....360 D3
Dunstalls CM19 ....223 A4
Dunster Ave SS0 ....347 A5
Dunster Cres RM3 ....313 C1
Dunster CI ⑱ DA2 ....376 B1
Dunster Ct SS0 ....8 E8
Dunster Ho SS7 ....344 F6
Dunthorne Rd CO4 ....110 E2
Dunthorpe Rd CO16 ....195 D6
Dunton Park Cvn Pk
CM13 ....340 E5
Dunton Rd
Basildon CM12,SS15 ....319 B1
Romford RM1 ....335 E7
Duntons Almshouses CO7 84 F6
Dunwich Ct
Colchester CO2 ....135 F4
Haverhill CB9 ....8 C8
Ipswich IP1 ....16 E8
Dupont CI CO16 ....195 D6
Durants Wlk ⑬ SS2 ....321 D6
Durban Gdns RM10 ....354 C5
Durban La SS15 ....319 F2
Durban Rd IG2,IG3 ....333 E3
Durdans The SS16 ....341 B4
Durell Gdns RM9 ....353 D7
Durell Rd RM9 ....353 D7
Durham Ave
Romford RM2 ....336 C7
Woodford IG8 ....310 D5
Durham CI
Great Bardfield CM7 ....72 A1
Sawbridgeworth CM21 .172 C1
Stansted Abbotts SG12 .197 B5
Durham Ho
⑧ Barking IG11 ....353 A5
⑧ Grays RM17 ....378 C8
Durham PI IG1 ....352 B8
Durham Rd Basildon SS16 340 E6
Dagenham RM10 ....354 C7
Rochford SS4 ....325 B6
Durham Sq SS2 ....348 D2
Durham Way SS6 ....323 D5
Duringe Wlk RM16 ....373 B6
Durley Ave SS12 ....320 F8
Durley CI SS7 ....344 E4
Durnell Way IG10 ....289 A6
Durrants CI RM13 ....355 C3
Durrington CI SS16 ....342 C5
Dury Falls CI RM11 ....337 A3
Dutch Cottage Mus*
SS8 ....363 C4
Duxford SS11 ....322 A6
Duxford Ct RM12 ....355 C6
Duxford CB10 ....3 A7
Dycorts Sch RM3 ....315 A6
Dyehouse Mdw CO10 ....15 B7
Dyer Ct EN3 ....265 A2
Dyers Ct CM23 ....145 C5
Dyers Hall CO9 ....50 B7
Dyer's Rd Colchester CO3 .134 C3
Maldon CM9 ....237 A2
Dyers Way RM3 ....314 B3
Dyke Cres SS8 ....363 A4
Dyke Rd IP13 ....381 A2
Dykes Chase CM9 ....236 F3
Dyke St IP1 ....17 C7
Dylan Rd DA17 ....369 A3
Dymchurch CI IG5 ....311 A1
Dymokes Way IG1 ....197 A1
Dyne's Hall Rd CO9 ....76 C8
Dynevor Gdns SS9 ....346 B1
Dytchleys La CM14 ....293 A5
Dytchleys Rd CM14 ....292 F5

E

Eagle Ave Dagenham RM6 334 E5
Walton-on-t-N CO14 ....144 D1
Eagle CI Hornchurch RM12 355 B6
Waltham Abbey EN9 ....266 A5
Eagle Ct ⑩ E11 ....332 A7
Eagle Ho RM17 ....377 F8
Eagle La Braintree CM7 .127 F6
Eagle Rd Harlech CM15 ....271 F2
Wanstead E11 ....332 A6
Eagles CI IP1 ....381 D4
Eagles Rd RM3 ....377 B2
Eagle St ⑧ IP4 ....17 D5
Eagle Terr IG8 ....310 B3
Eagle Way
Bishop's Stortford CM23 .146 C7
Felsted CM6 ....125 F2
Great Warley CM13 ....339 A8
Harlow CM19 ....377 A2
Earl Mountbatten Dr
CM12 ....296 F4
Earls CI CM23 ....145 D6
Earls Colne Prim Sch
CO6 ....105 C6
Earlsdown Ho IG11 ....352 D3
Earlsfield Dr CM2 ....232 E3
Earls Gn IG9 ....8 C8
Earls Hall Ave SS2 ....347 B4
Earls Hall Dr CO16 ....194 E5

Earls Hall Par SS2 ... 347 E4
Earls Hall Prim Sch SS0 ... 347 D4
Earlsmead CM8 ... 183 F3
Earl's Path IG10 ... 288 C6
Earls Wlk RM8 ... 353 B8
Earlswood SS7 ... 344 D4
Earlswood Gdns IG5 ... 333 A8
Earlswood Way CO2 ... 135 D2
Easebourne Rd RM8 ... 353 C7
Easedale Dr RM12 ... 355 B7
Easington Way RM15 ... 372 A8
Eastacre CB10 ... 22 E2
East Anglian Rly Mus* CO6 ... 106 D6
East Area IP1 ... 16 C7
East Ave CM3 ... 282 E2
East Bay CO1 ... 136 B7
East Bergholt CE Prim Sch CO7 ... 59 B3
East Bergholt High Sch CO7 ... 59 D3
East Bergholt Place Gdn* CO7 ... 59 F1
Eastbourne Gr SS0 ... 347 C3
Eastbourne Rd E6 ... 352 A2
East Bridge Rd CM3 ... 301 E8
Eastbrook Ave RM10 ... 354 C8
Eastbrook Comp Sch RM10 ... 354 C8
Eastbrook Dr RM7 ... 335 E2
Eastbrookend Ctry Pk* RM7 ... 335 D1
Eastbrook Rd EN9 ... 265 E6
Eastbrooks SS13 ... 343 B7
Eastbrooks Mews SS13 ... 343 B7
Eastbrooks Pl SS13 ... 343 B7
Eastbury Ave
Barking IG11 ... 352 E4
Rochford SS4 ... 325 D4
Eastbury Comp (Lower) Sch IG11 ... 352 D5
Eastbury Comp Sch IG11 ... 352 F5
Eastbury Ct IG11 ... 352 E4
Eastbury Inf Sch IG11 ... 352 F5
Eastbury Rd
Romford RM7 ... 335 D5
Wallend E6 ... 352 A1
Eastbury Sq IG11 ... 352 F4
Eastby Cl CB11 ... 43 F8
East Cheaney Cotts CM3 ... 280 F5
Eastcheap SS6 ... 323 C4
East Cl RM13 ... 355 B1
Eastcliff Ave CO15 ... 196 B4
Eastcliff Ho CO14 ... 144 D1
Eastcote Gr SS2 ... 348 D3
East Court Ho CO1 ... 136 C7
Eastcourt Ind Sch IG3 ... 334 A3
East Cres SS8 ... 363 F4
East Crescent Rd 5 DA12 ... 379 C1
East Dene Dr RM3 ... 314 D5
East Dock Rd CO12 ... 90 F6
East Dr CM21 ... 172 E1
Eastend Cotts CM19 ... 198 D1
Eastend La CM6,CM22 ... 121 C8
East End La CO7 ... 60 C2
East End Rd
Bradwell-on-S CM0 ... 242 C3
East Bergholt CO7 ... 60 A3
Easten Greene CO6 ... 80 E4
East Entrance RM10 ... 354 B3
Easterford Rd CO5 ... 158 C2
Easterling Cl CO12 ... 91 A4
Eastern App Barking IG11 ... 353 A3
Chelmsford CM2 ... 232 F5
Eastern Ave Aveley RM15 ... 371 C4
Grays RM20 ... 376 F8
Haverhill CB9 ... 8 F8
Ilford IG2 ... 333 D5
South Benfleet SS7 ... 344 C5
Southend-on-S SS2 ... 348 B3
Wanstead E11 ... 332 C5
Eastern Ave E RM1,RM2, RM3 ... 313 E1
Eastern Avenue W RM7 ... 335 B7
Eastern Cl
Rushmere St A IP4 ... 18 F4
Southend-on-S SS2 ... 348 A3
Eastern Cres CM1 ... 231 F5
Eastern Espl
Canvey Island SS8 ... 364 D2
Southend-on-S SS1 ... 367 D6
Eastern Prom CO16 ... 192 F3
Eastern Rd
Brightlingsea CO7 ... 192 E6
Burnham-on-C CM0 ... 306 C5
Grays RM17 ... 373 D2
Rayleigh SS6 ... 323 B1
Romford RM1 ... 335 F6
Easternville Gdns IG2 ... 333 C5
Eastern Way
Belvedere DA18 ... 369 A4
Grays RM17 ... 373 A1
East Essex Aviation Mus* CO16 ... 192 E4
Eastfield Gdns RM10 ... 354 A8
Eastfield Rd
Basildon SS15 ... 319 F2
Brentwood CM14 ... 316 D8
Canvey Island SS8 ... 364 D5
Dagenham RM9,RM10 ... 354 A8
Eastgate
Great Chesterford CB10 ... 3 D2
13 Ipswich IP4 ... 17 D6
Basildon SS14 ... 342 B5
East Gate CM20 ... 199 D1
Eastgate Bsns Ctr SS14 ... 342 B6
Eastgate St CO12 ... 91 D6
East Gores Rd CO6 ... 131 F5
East Hall La RM13 ... 370 D7
Eastham Cres CM13 ... 317 A7
East Hanningfield CE Prim Sch CM3 ... 278 B7
East Hanningfield Ind Est CM3 ... 278 C6
East Hanningfield Rd
Howe Green CM2 ... 255 E2
Rettendon CM3 ... 278 C4
East Haven CO15 ... 195 E5
East Hill CO1 ... 136 A7
Easthorpe Rd
Feering CO5 ... 159 D7
Messing CO5 ... 159 F5
East Kent Ave DA11 ... 378 C1
East La CO7 ... 85 B5
Eastland Ct IP11 ... 381 B7
East Lawn IP4 ... 18 C8
Eastleigh Rd SS7 ... 344 E1
Eastley SS16 ... 341 F4
East Mayne SS13 ... 321 A2
Eastmead IG3 ... 334 A4
East Mersea Rd CO5 ... 190 E1
East Mill Gravesend DA11 ... 379 A1
Halstead CO9 ... 76 F2
East Mill Gn IP9 ... 60 E6
Easton End SS15 ... 341 A6
Easton Rd CM8 ... 184 A3
Easton Way CO13 ... 171 B6
East Park Cl RM6 ... 334 E6
East Pk Harlow CM17 ... 200 C3
Sawbridgeworth CM21 ... 172 E1
East Rd
Bishop's Stortford CM23 ... 146 B7
Dagenham, Chadwell Heath RM6 ... 334 E6
East Mersea CO5 ... 191 D1
Harlow CM20 ... 200 B4
Romford RM7 ... 335 D4
West Mersea CO5 ... 218 E7
East Row Holbrook IP9 ... 62 D6
Wanstead E11 ... 332 A5
East Side CO4 ... 83 A4
East Sq SS14 ... 342 B6
East St Barking IG11 ... 352 C5
Braintree CM7 ... 128 A3
Coggeshall CO6 ... 131 A2
Colchester CO1 ... 136 B7
Grays RM17 ... 378 C8
Grays, West Thurrock RM20 ... 377 E8
Harwich CO12 ... 91 D4
Rochford SS4 ... 325 F2
Saffron Walden CB10 ... 22 E1
Southend-on-S,Leigh Cliffs SS9 ... 365 E8
Southend-on-S SS2 ... 347 F2
Sudbury CO10 ... 33 F8
Tollesbury CM9 ... 216 D1
Wivenhoe CO7 ... 164 B7
East Stockwell St CO1 ... 135 F7
East Terr Gravesend DA12 ... 379 C1
Walton-on-t-N CO14 ... 144 D1
East Thorpe SS14 ... 342 C6
East Thurrock Rd RM17 ... 378 C8
East Tilbury Prim Sch RM18 ... 375 C1
East Tilbury Rd SS17 ... 375 A4
East Tilbury Sta RM18 ... 375 B2
East View Chingford E4 ... 309 C5
Takeley CM22 ... 148 C8
Writtle CM1 ... 230 F1
East View Cl CB10 ... 45 F8
Eastview Dr SS6 ... 323 E5
East Ward Mews CO1 ... 136 C7
Eastway E11 ... 332 B6
Eastway Ent Ctr IP1 ... 16 D8
Eastways
Canvey Island SS8 ... 363 F5
Witham CM8 ... 184 A4
Eastwick Hall La CM20 ... 199 A5
Eastwick Rd
Eastwick CM20 ... 199 B4
Gilston CM20 ... 199 E6
East Wlk Basildon SS14 ... 342 B6
Harlow CM20 ... 199 D1
Eastwoodbury Cl SS2 ... 347 E6
Eastwoodbury Cres SS2 ... 347 E6
Eastwoodbury La SS2 ... 347 C6
Eastwood Bvd SS0 ... 347 A2
Eastwood Cl E18 ... 310 A1
Eastwood Dr
Highwoods CO4 ... 110 B3
Rainham RM13 ... 370 B7
Eastwood Ind Est SS9 ... 346 C6
Eastwood Jun & Inf Schs SS9 ... 346 F6
Eastwood La S SS0 ... 347 B2
Eastwood Old Rd SS9 ... 346 B6
Eastwood Park Cl SS9 ... 346 E6
Eastwood Park Dr SS9 ... 346 E7
Eastwood Rd Ilford IG3 ... 334 A4
Rayleigh SS6 ... 323 E1
Southend-on-S SS9 ... 346 D3
Woodford E18 ... 310 A1
Eastwood Rd N SS9 ... 346 D4
Eastwood Rise
Rayleigh SS9 ... 324 C1
Southend-on-S SS9 ... 346 C8
Eastwood Sch The SS9 ... 346 F5
Eaton Cl Billericay CM12 ... 297 A5
Trimley St M IP11 ... 381 A7
Eaton Cotts CO5 ... 186 D7
Eaton Dr RM5 ... 313 B3
Eaton Gdns
Dagenham RM9 ... 353 E5
Felixstowe IP11 ... 381 C2
Eaton Ho 5 CM23 ... 146 B8
Eaton Mews CO2 ... 136 B3
Eaton Rd
Southend-on-S SS9 ... 346 C2
Upminster RM14 ... 337 E2
Eaton Rise E11 ... 332 C6
Eatons Mead E4 ... 309 A8
Eaton Way CM9 ... 213 E7
Ebbsfleet Ind Est DA11 ... 378 A2
Ebbsfleet Wlk DA11 ... 378 B1
Ebenezer Cl CM8 ... 183 E5
Ebenezer Terr CM2 ... 254 F7
Ebony Cl CO2 ... 135 D2
Eccles Ho 2 RM3 ... 314 D4
Eccles Rd IP2 ... 16 D1
Eccleston Cres RM6 ... 334 B4
Eccleston Gdns CM12 ... 297 A5
Echo Hts E4 ... 287 B1
Eckersley Rd CM1 ... 232 C3
Eddy Cl RM7 ... 335 B5
Eden Cl Holdbrook EN3 ... 265 A1
Witham CM8 ... 183 E3
Eden Gn RM15 ... 372 B8
Edenhall Cl RM3 ... 314 C5
Edenhall Glen RM3 ... 314 C5
Edenhall Rd RM3 ... 314 C5
Eden Rd Haverhill CB9 ... 9 A7
Ipswich IP4 ... 18 B5
Edens Cl CM23 ... 146 B7
Edenside CO13 ... 170 E7
Edens Mount CM21 ... 172 F4
Eden Way CM1 ... 231 C5
Edgar Ho E11 ... 332 A4
Edgar Rd RM6 ... 334 D4
Edgecotts SS16 ... 341 E4
Edgefield Ave
Barking IG11 ... 352 F5
Lawford CO11 ... 86 B3
Edgefield Ct 2 IG11 ... 352 F5
Edgehill Gdns RM10 ... 354 A8
Edgeworth Rd IP2 ... 16 E2
Edgware Rd CO16 ... 195 D5
Edgworth Rd CO10 ... 33 E7
Edinburgh Ave
Corringham SS17 ... 360 F4
Southend-on-S SS9 ... 346 B2
Edinburgh Cl
Rayleigh SS6 ... 323 B5
Witham CM8 ... 212 A8
Edinburgh Gdns
Bishop's Stortford CM23 ... 145 E6
Braintree CM7 ... 128 C4
Edinburgh Ho 1 RM2 ... 336 C7
Edinburgh Mews RM18 ... 379 B5
Edinburgh Pl CM20 ... 200 A4
Edinburgh Way
Basildon SS13 ... 343 B6
Harlow CM20 ... 199 E3
Edison Ave RM12 ... 335 F3
Edison Cl
3 Braintree CM7 ... 127 F1
Hornchurch RM12 ... 335 F3
Edison Gdns CO4 ... 110 C1
Edison Rd CO15 ... 196 F6
Edisons Pk DA2 ... 376 D4
Edith Borthwick Sch The CM7 ... 127 F8
Edith Cavell Way CB9 ... 27 C6
Edith Cl SS8 ... 363 E3
Edith Rd
Canvey Island SS8 ... 363 D3
Clacton-on-S CO15 ... 195 E2
Dagenham RM6 ... 334 D4
Kirby-le-S CO13 ... 170 D8
Southend-on-S SS2 ... 347 F2
Edith Way SS17 ... 361 A5
Edmund Cl CB9 ... 8 F8
Edmund Gn CO9 ... 102 E8
Edmund Rd Grays RM16 ... 372 D4
Rainham RM13 ... 354 E2
Witham CM8 ... 211 E8
Edmund's Twr CM19 ... 223 C8
Edridge Cl RM12 ... 355 D7
Edward Ave
Brightlingsea CO7 ... 192 F7
Chingford E4 ... 309 B4
Edward Bowden Ct CB10 ... 22 D1
Edward Bright Cl CM9 ... 237 A2
Edward Cl Billericay CM12 ... 296 F5
Grays RM16 ... 372 D3
Ipswich IP1 ... 16 F8
Little Clacton CO16 ... 168 E5
Rochford SS4 ... 325 C6
Romford RM2 ... 336 C8
Edward Cordy Ho IP11 ... 381 E3
Edward Ct EN9 ... 265 F6
Edward Dr CM2 ... 254 C7
Edward Francis Jun Sch SS6 ... 323 E3
Edward Gdns SS11 ... 321 D8
Edward Mans 7 IG11 ... 352 F5
Edward Marke Dr CO5 ... 163 B3
Edward Rd
Dagenham RM6 ... 334 E5
Thorpe-le-S CO16 ... 168 F7
Edwards Cl CM13 ... 295 E3
Edwards Hall Jun & Inf Schs SS9 ... 346 C7
Edwards Rd DA17 ... 369 A2
Edward St CO12 ... 90 E5
Edwards Way CM13 ... 295 E4
Edwards Wlk CM9 ... 236 F3
Edward Terr CO16 ... 168 E5
Edwina Gdns IG4 ... 332 E6
Edwin Ave E6 ... 352 A3
Edwin Cl RM13 ... 354 F2
Edwin Hall View CM3 ... 279 C1
Edwin Lambert Sch RM11 ... 336 A4
Edwin's Hall Rd CM3 ... 279 D3
Edwin St DA12 ... 379 B1
Egbert Gdns SS11 ... 299 D1
Egerton Dr SS16 ... 340 E5
Egerton Gdns IG3 ... 333 F1
Egerton Green Rd CO2 ... 135 A3
Egg Hall CM16 ... 246 A2
Egglestone Cl IP2 ... 16 F1
Eggshell La CM7 ... 27 E2
Eglington Rd E4 ... 287 D2
Eglinton Dr CM2 ... 233 B4
Eglinton Rd DA10 ... 377 F1
Egremont St CO10 ... 2 B3
Egremont Way CO3 ... 134 C4
Egret Cres CO4 ... 137 A8
Ehringshausen Way CB9 ... 9 B7
Eight Acre La CO2 ... 135 C2
Eight Ash Green & Aldham CE Prim Sch CO3 ... 107 F1
Eisenhower Rd SS15 ... 341 A6
Elan Rd RM15 ... 372 A8
Elbourne Trad Est DA17 ... 369 B3
Elbury Ct IG8 ... 310 E3
Eldan Ho RM4 ... 313 E7
Elbert Cl SS2 ... 348 E2
Eldeland SS15 ... 341 E7
Elder Ave SS12 ... 321 C6
Elderberry Cl
Basildon SS16 ... 341 B5
Redbridge IG6 ... 311 B3
Elderberry Gdns CM8 ... 184 B4
Elderfield CM17 ... 200 D3
Elder Field CM77 ... 154 B5
Elderfield Wlk E11 ... 332 B6
Elderstep Ave SS8 ... 364 E3
Elderton Rd SS0 ... 347 D1
Elder Tree Rd SS8 ... 364 C4
Elder Way Rainham RM13 ... 355 D2
Wickford SS12 ... 321 C6
Eld La CO1 ... 135 F7
Eldon Cl CO4 ... 110 E1
Eldon Rd EN11 ... 221 D4
Eldonwall Est RM8 ... 334 F3
Eldon Way SS5 ... 324 E6
Eldred Ave CO2 ... 135 B3
Eldred Dr CO10 ... 34 C4
Eldred Gdns RM14 ... 337 E4
Eldred Rd IG11 ... 352 E4
Eleanor Chase SS12 ... 321 C7
Eleanor Cl CO5 ... 186 D6
Eleanor Gdns RM8 ... 334 F2
Eleanor Way CM14 ... 316 E5
Eleanor Wlk CO5 ... 186 D6
Electric Ave SS0 ... 347 C2
Electric Par Ilford IG3 ... 333 F3
Woodford E18 ... 310 A1
Eleven Acre Rise IG10 ... 288 F6
Eleventh Ave CM24 ... 120 B2
Elgar Cl Basildon SS15 ... 341 D8
Buckhurst Hill IG9 ... 310 D8
South Benfleet SS7 ... 344 B6
Elgar Dr CM8 ... 211 F7
Elgar Gdns RM18 ... 379 B6
Elgin Ave Chelmsford CM1 ... 232 A2
Romford RM3 ... 315 B4
Elgin Ho CM14 ... 316 D6
Elgin Rd IG3 ... 333 E4
Elham Dr SS13 ... 343 C6
Elianore Rd CO3 ... 135 B7
Eliot Cl SS12 ... 321 C5
Eliot Mews SS2 ... 348 A2
Eliot Rd Dagenham RM9 ... 353 D8
Dartford DA1 ... 376 B2
Eliot Way CM9 ... 237 A1
Elizabeth Ave Ilford IG1 ... 333 D2
Rayleigh SS6 ... 323 C1
Witham CM8 ... 212 A8
Elizabeth Cl
Highwoods CO4 ... 110 C4
Hockley SS5 ... 324 E4
Lower Nazeing EN9 ... 243 D8
Romford RM7 ... 313 B2
Saffron Walden CB10 ... 22 F2
Tilbury RM18 ... 379 B5
Elizabeth Ct
Buckhurst Hill IG9 ... 288 B1
Gravesend DA11 ... 379 A1
Walton-on-t-N CO14 ... 144 E3
6 Woodford, South Woodford E18 ... 310 A2
2 Woodford, Woodford Green IG8 ... 310 C3
Elizabeth Dr
Theydon Bois CM16 ... 267 E3
Wickford SS12 ... 321 B8
Elizabeth Garrett Anderson Ho 9 DA17 ... 369 A3
Elizabeth Ho
Pilgrims Hatch CM15 ... 294 B3
3 Romford RM2 ... 336 C7
Southend-on-S SS9 ... 346 D7
Elizabeth Rd
Bishop's Stortford CM23 ... 145 E5
Grays RM16 ... 372 F4
Harwich CO12 ... 91 A3
Pilgrims Hatch CM15 ... 294 B3
Rainham RM13 ... 370 B8
Southend-on-S SS1 ... 367 D6
Elizabeth St DA9 ... 376 E2
Elizabeth Twr 6 SS2 ... 347 F1
Elizabeth Villas CO5 ... 187 A2
Elizabeth Way
Basildon SS15 ... 341 D5
Brightlingsea CO7 ... 192 F6
Felixstowe IP11 ... 381 C3
Hadleigh SS7 ... 345 C4
Halstead CO9 ... 76 E2
Harlow CM20 ... 199 B2
Hatfield Peverel CM3 ... 211 A4
Heybridge CM9 ... 237 A5
Saffron Walden CB10 ... 22 F2
Sudbury CO10 ... 33 C5
Wivenhoe CO7 ... 137 C3
Eliza Cook Cl DA9 ... 377 B3
Elkins The RM1 ... 313 E1
Ellenborough Cl CM23 ... 145 D5
Ellenbrook Cl SS9 ... 346 E3
Ellenbrook Gn IP2 ... 16 D1
Ellenbrook Rd IP2 ... 16 D1
Ellen Ct 5 E4 ... 287 C1
Ellen Friend Ho CM23 ... 146 B6
Ellen Way CM77 ... 154 D7
Ellen Wilkinson Ho 12 RM10 ... 335 A1
Ellerman Rd RM18 ... 378 F5
Ellerton Gdns RM9 ... 353 C5
Ellerton Rd RM9 ... 353 C5
Ellesmere Gdns IG4 ... 332 E5
Ellesmere Rd
Canvey Island SS8 ... 363 E3
Rochford SS4 ... 303 C1
Ellie Cl SS17 ... 360 C2
Elliot Cl
South Woodham Ferrers CM3 ... 301 F6
Woodford IG8 ... 310 D4
Elliot Pl CM7 ... 128 C3
Elliots Dr CO14 ... 171 B8
Elliott Gdns RM3 ... 314 B3
Elliott St IP1 ... 17 A6
Ellis Ave RM13 ... 370 A8
Ellis Cl RM16 ... 374 E7
Ellis Rd Boxted CO4 ... 82 F3
Bradfield CO11 ... 114 D8
Clacton-on-S CO15 ... 195 E2
Ellmore Cl RM3 ... 314 B2
Ellswood SS15 ... 319 D1
Elm Ave Heybridge CM9 ... 237 C5
Upminster RM14 ... 356 B8
Elm Bank Pl SS17 ... 359 F4
Elm Bglws CM7 ... 127 D4
Elmbourne Dr DA17 ... 369 B2
Elmbridge CM17 ... 200 F3
Elmbridge Hall CM5 ... 227 C1
Elmbridge Rd IG6 ... 312 A4
Elmbrook 2 E18 ... 332 A8
Elmbrook Dr CM23 ... 145 E3
Elm Cl Alresford CO7 ... 165 B8
Brantham CO11 ... 60 D1
Buckhurst Hill IG9 ... 310 D8
Chelmsford CM1 ... 232 A8
Elsenham CM22 ... 94 C2
Epping Green CM16 ... 245 B7
Great Baddow CM2 ... 254 F6
Great Bentley CO7 ... 166 E8
Haverhill CB9 ... 8 F8
Rayleigh SS6 ... 323 D3
Romford RM7 ... 313 B1
Sible Hedingham CO9 ... 51 D2
Southend-on-S SS3 ... 368 E7
Takeley CM22 ... 148 C7
Tiptree CO5 ... 186 C7
Waltham Abbey EN9 ... 265 D5
Wanstead E11 ... 332 B5
Elm Close Extension CM22 ... 148 C7
Elm Cotts
Southend-on-S SS2 ... 347 F2
Waltham Abbey EN9 ... 265 D1
Elm Cres CO4 ... 136 D7
Elmcroft CO7 ... 138 A6
Elmcroft Ave E11 ... 332 B7
Elmcroft Cl E11 ... 332 B7
Elm Ct Chingford E4 ... 309 C4
Elmdon CB11 ... 20 B4
Sturmer CB9 ... 9 E5
Theydon Bois CM16 ... 267 E2
Woodford IG8 ... 310 F4
Elmdale Dr CO11 ... 86 D3
Elmden Ct CO15 ... 195 E5
Elmdene Ave RM11 ... 336 F6
Elmdon Pl 1 CB9 ... 9 B8
Elmdon Rd RM15 ... 372 A8
Elm Dr Brightlingsea CO7 ... 192 D7
Halstead CO9 ... 76 F1
Harwich CO12 ... 91 B3
Rayleigh SS6 ... 323 D3
Elmer App SS1 ... 367 A8
Elmer Ave Romford RM4 ... 313 E7
Southend-on-S SS1 ... 367 A8
Elmer Cl RM13 ... 355 A5
Elmer Gdns RM13 ... 355 A5
Elm Est CO7 ... 59 C3
Elmfield Cl CO15 ... 196 E7
Elmfield Rd E4 ... 309 D8
Elm Gdns
North Weald Bassett CM16 ... 247 B5
Trimley St M IP11 ... 381 A7
Elm Gn Basildon SS13 ... 343 A5
Billericay CM11 ... 297 E2
Elm Gr
Bishop's Stortford CM23 ... 146 B7
Clacton-on-S CO15 ... 195 F6
Hornchurch RM11 ... 336 E5
Hullbridge SS5 ... 301 D2
Jaywick CO16 ... 195 A2
Kirby Cross CO13 ... 170 D6
Saffron Walden CB10 ... 22 D1
Southend-on-S SS1 ... 368 A8
Wivenhoe CO7 ... 137 B1
Woodford IG8 ... 309 F5
Elm Green La CM3 ... 256 C8
Elm Green Prep Sch CM3 ... 234 D3
Elm Hall Gdns E11 ... 332 B5
Elm Ho Canvey Island SS8 ... 364 B1
Felixstowe IP11 ... 381 C4
Elmhurst Greenhithe DA9 ... 377 B1
Hoddesdon EN10 ... 221 A4
Elmhurst Ave SS7 ... 344 B4
Elmhurst Cl CB9 ... 9 B7
Elmhurst Dr
Hornchurch RM11 ... 336 C4
Ipswich IP3 ... 17 F3
Woodford E18 ... 310 A1
Elmhurst Rd CO12 ... 91 C3
Elmhurst Way IG10 ... 288 F2
Elm La Capel St M IP9 ... 35 A1
Marks Tey CO5,CO6 ... 132 B2
Washbrook IP8 ... 35 E8
Elmores IG10 ... 289 A6
Elm Par RM12 ... 355 B8
Elm Park Ave
Hornchurch RM12 ... 355 A8
Rainham RM12 ... 354 F8
Elm Park Sta RM12 ... 355 A8
Elm Rd Aveley RM15 ... 371 D5
Basildon SS13 ... 321 E1
Bishop's Stortford CM23 ... 145 F8
Canvey Island SS8 ... 364 C3
Chelmsford CM2 ... 254 A8
East Bergholt CO7 ... 59 C3
Grays RM17 ... 378 C8
Greenhithe DA9 ... 376 E1
Hadleigh SS7 ... 345 D2
Little Clacton CO16 ... 168 C3
Romford RM7 ... 313 B1
Elm Rd *continued*
Rushmere St A IP5 ... 18 F7
Southend-on-s, Leigh-on-S SS9 ... 346 E1
Southend-on-s, Shoeburyness SS3 ... 368 E8
South Woodham Ferrers CM3 ... 301 C8
Sudbury CO10 ... 34 A7
Wickford SS11 ... 321 D8
Elm Rise CM8 ... 184 A5
Elms Dr CM1 ... 232 A4
Elms Farm Rd RM12 ... 355 C7
Elms Gdns RM9 ... 353 F8
Elms Hall Rd CO6 ... 104 E8
Elms Ind Est RM3 ... 315 B3
Elmsleigh Dr SS9 ... 346 E3
Elmslie Cl IG8 ... 310 F4
Elms Rd CM1 ... 229 F6
Elm St IP1 ... 17 C6
Elmstead Cl SS17 ... 361 B5
Elmstead Prim Sch CO7 ... 137 F6
Elmstead Rd
Colchester CO4 ... 136 E5
Ilford IG3 ... 333 F2
Wivenhoe CO7 ... 137 D4
Elms The
Chipping Ongar CM5 ... 249 A1
East Bergholt CO7 ... 60 C3
Frinton-on-S CO13 ... 170 F6
Great Chesterford CB10 ... 3 E3
Elm Terr RM20 ... 377 B8
Elmtree Ave CM15 ... 271 F2
Elm Tree Ave CO13 ... 170 F7
Elm Tree Cl CO13 ... 170 F7
Elmtree Rd SS16 ... 343 A4
Elm View Rd SS7 ... 344 B3
Elmway RM16 ... 373 C5
Elm Way Boreham CM3 ... 209 E1
Brentwood CM14 ... 316 A6
Elm Wlk Rayne CM77 ... 126 F2
Romford RM2 ... 336 A8
Elmwood Colchester CO3 ... 134 D6
Sawbridgeworth CM21 ... 172 F1
Elmwood Ave
Colchester CO2 ... 135 B2
Hockley SS5 ... 324 F4
Elmwood Ct SS5 ... 324 E6
Elmwood Dr CO5 ... 218 D7
Elmwood Prim Sch CM3 ... 301 D7
Elounda Ct SS7 ... 344 D4
Elrington Rd IG8 ... 310 A5
Elronds Rest CM3 ... 301 C6
Elsden Chase CM0 ... 284 D4
Elsenham CE Prim Sch CM22 ... 94 D1
Elsenham Cres SS14 ... 342 F6
Elsenham Cross CM22 ... 94 D1
Elsenham Ct SS6 ... 323 B3
Elsenham Mews SS14 ... 342 F6
Elsenham Rd E12 ... 352 A7
Elsenham Sta CM22 ... 94 C3
Elsham Dr CM77 ... 154 B6
Elsinor Ave SS8 ... 364 A6
Elsmere Rd IP1 ... 17 C8
Elstow Gdns RM9 ... 353 E4
Elstow Rd RM9 ... 353 E4
Elstree Gdns IG1 ... 352 C7
Elthorne Pk CO16 ... 195 D4
Eltisley Rd IG1 ... 352 B8
Elton Park Bsns Ctr IP2 ... 16 E6
Elton Pk IP2 ... 16 D6
Elton Wlk CO5 ... 186 D6
Elverston Cl SS15 ... 341 D8
Elvet Ave RM2 ... 336 C7
Elvina Ho CO15 ... 220 F6
Elvin Ct RM2 ... 336 B8
Elwes Cl CO4 ... 110 D1
Elwick Rd RM15 ... 372 C7
Elwin Rd CO5 ... 186 D5
Elwood CM17 ... 224 E8
Ely Cl Rayleigh SS6 ... 323 C4
Southminster CM0 ... 284 D4
Ely Gdns Dagenham RM10 ... 335 C1
Redbridge IG1 ... 332 E4
Ely Pl IG8 ... 311 A5
Ely Rd SS2 ... 348 C2
Elysian Gdns CM9 ... 216 C1
Emanuel Rd SS16 ... 341 B4
Embassy Ct Maldon CM9 ... 237 A2
7 Wanstead E18 ... 332 A8
Emberson Ct CM2 ... 232 F4
Emberson Way CM16 ... 247 C5
Ember Way CM0 ... 306 A6
Emblems CM6 ... 123 C1
Embra Ct CO2 ... 136 B5
Emerald Gdns RM8 ... 335 A3
Emerald Ho 2 RM13 ... 355 A1
Emerson Dr RM11 ... 336 D4
Emerson Park Ct RM11 ... 336 D4
Emerson Park Sch RM11 ... 337 B4
Emerson Park Sta RM11 ... 336 E4
Emerson Pl RM11 ... 336 D5
Emerson Rd IG1 ... 333 A4
Emerson Terr IG8 ... 310 D4
Emily May Ct CO12 ... 91 A3
Emily White Ct SS11 ... 321 F8
Emlen St IP1 ... 17 A6
Emmanuel Cl IP2 ... 16 F3
Emma's Cres SG12 ... 197 B4
Emmaus Way IG7 ... 311 A5
Emmott Ave IG6 ... 333 C6
Emperor Circ IP3 ... 38 C8
Empire Ct CO15 ... 195 E3
Empire Rd CO12 ... 91 D3
Empire Wlk 2 CM2 ... 232 C2
Empress Ave
Chingford E4 ... 309 B3
Ilford IG1 ... 333 A2
Redbridge IG1 ... 332 F2
Wanstead E12 ... 332 D2
West Mersea CO5 ... 218 E6

Empress Ave *continued*
Woodford IG8 ....309 F3
Empress Dr CO5 ....218 D6
Empress Par E4 ....309 A3
Emson Cl CB10 ....22 D2
Emsworth Rd IG6 ....311 B1
Enborne Gn RM15 ....372 A8
Endean Ct CO7 ....137 A2
Endeavour Cl CM9 ....216 D2
Endeavour Dr SS14 ....320 B1
Endeavour Sch The CM15 ....316 F7
Endeavour Way IG11 ....353 A3
Endlebury Ct E4 ....309 D8
Endlebury Rd E4 ....309 C8
Endsleigh Ct CO3 ....135 C7
Endsleigh Gdns IG1 ....332 F3
Endway SS7 ....345 E2
End Way Cotts CM0 ....285 A7
Endways Ct CM15 ....294 C1
Endway The
Great Easton CM6 ....122 F7
Mayland CM3 ....283 D2
Steeple Bumpstead CB9 ....27 C8
Enfield Ho 6 RM3 ....314 E3
Enfield Rd SS11 ....322 C7
Engaines Prim Sch CO16 ....168 C2
Engayne Gdns RM14 ....337 B3
Engayne Prim Sch RM14 ....337 E5
England's La IG10 ....289 B7
Englefield Cl SS5 ....325 A4
Englefields CM0 ....263 E3
Engleric SG8 ....19 D5
Enid Way CO4 ....109 D2
Ennerdale Ave
Great Notley CM77 ....154 C6
Hornchurch RM12 ....355 A7
Ennerdale Ct E11 ....332 A4
Ennismore Gdns SS2 ....348 A3
Ensign Cl SS9 ....347 A1
Ensign Ho RM17 ....377 F8
Enterprise Ct
Braintree CM7 ....128 B2
Witham CM8 ....184 A3
Enterprise Ctr The SS14 ....320 E2
Enterprise Ho
Barking IG11 ....352 F2
Chingford E4 ....287 C2
Enterprise Way SS11 ....321 F6
Enville Way CO4 ....110 B4
Epping Cl Chelmsford CM1 ....231 E1
Clacton-on-S CO15 ....195 F8
Romford RM7 ....335 B8
Southend-on-S SS9 ....346 E7
Epping Forest Coll IG10 ....289 B5
Epping Forest Conservation Ctr* IG10 ....266 C1
Epping Forest District Mus* EN9 ....265 C6
Epping Forest YH* IG10 ....266 B1
Epping Glade E4 ....287 C3
Epping Inf Sch CM16 ....245 F1
Epping Jun Sch CM16 ....245 F1
Epping La
Chipping Ongar RM4 ....269 A1
Stapleford Abbotts RM4 ....291 B8
Theydon Bois RM4 ....268 D1
Epping New Rd
Buckhurst Hill IG9,IG10 ....288 B4
Loughton IG10,CM16 ....266 E2
Epping Rd
Chipping Ongar CM5 ....248 D6
Coopersale CM16 ....246 D4
Epping Green CM16 ....223 A1
Loughton CM16 ....267 A4
Roydon CM19 ....222 D5
Toot Hill CM5 ....247 D1
Epping Sta CM16 ....268 A8
Epping Upland CE Prim Sch CM16 ....245 B7
Epping Way Chingford E4 ....287 B3
Witham CM8 ....183 E1
Epsom Cl Billericay CM11 ....297 D5
Clacton-on-S CO16 ....195 D6
Epsom Ho 18 RM3 ....314 E5
Epsom Mews CM0 ....284 E4
Epsom Rd IG3 ....333 F5
Epsom Way RM12 ....355 F8
Erbury Pl CO10 ....12 B8
Erica Wlk CO4 ....136 D7
Eric Clarke La IG11 ....352 C2
Erick Ave CM1 ....232 B7
Eric Rd Basildon SS13 ....343 F6
Dagenham RM6 ....334 D4
Eridge Cl CM1 ....232 D7
Erin Cl IG3 ....334 A5
Eriswell Rd CB9 ....9 B8
Erith Cres RM5 ....313 C2
Erith Ct RM19 ....371 A2
Erith High St DA8 ....369 E1
Erith Mus* DA8 ....369 E1
Erith Rd DA17 ....369 B1
Erith Sta DA8 ....369 E1
Erle Havard Rd CO6 ....108 E4
Ernalds Cl CO6 ....105 B7
Ernan Cl RM15 ....372 A8
Ernan Rd RM15 ....372 A8
Ernest Rd
Hornchurch RM11 ....336 F5
Wivenhoe CO7 ....137 C1
Ernleigh Rd IP4 ....18 B6
Erriff Dr RM15 ....372 A8
Errington Cl RM16 ....374 B3
Errington Rd CO3 ....135 D5
Erroll Rd RM1 ....335 F7
Erskine Pl 2 SS12 ....321 E6
Erskine Rd CO11 ....86 D4
Esdaile Gdns RM14 ....337 D4
Esdaile La EN11 ....221 A5
Esher Ave RM7 ....335 C5
Esher Rd IG3 ....333 E1
Eskley Gdns
South Ockendon RM15 ....357 B1
South Ockendon RM15 ....372 B8
Esk Way RM1 ....313 E3
Esmond Cl RM13 ....355 B5
Esplanade
Frinton-on-S CO13 ....170 F3
Harwich CO12 ....91 E4
Esplanade Ct
Frinton-on-S CO13 ....171 A5
Harwich CO12 ....91 E6
Southend-on-S SS1 ....367 E6
Esplanade Gdns SS0 ....366 B8
Esplanade Ho SS0 ....366 B8
Esplanade The
Holland-on-S CO15 ....196 G6
Hullbridge SS5 ....301 D3
Mayland CM3 ....260 E1
Essenden Rd DA17 ....369 A1
Essex Ave
Chelmsford CM1 ....232 A7
Clacton-on-S CO15 ....220 E6
Sudbury CO10 ....15 F2
Essex Cl Basildon SS15 ....341 B6
Canvey Island SS8 ....364 A2
Rayleigh SS6 ....323 F2
Romford RM7 ....335 B7
Essex County Cricket Club* CM2 ....232 B2
Essex Cty Hospl CO3 ....135 D6
Essex Gdns
Hornchurch RM11 ....337 A6
Linford SS17 ....375 A4
Southend-on-S SS9 ....346 E4
Essex Hall Rd CO1 ....109 E1
Essex Hill CB11 ....20 B2
Essex Knowle CO8 ....55 F1
Essex Nuffield Hospl The CM15 ....294 E1
Essex Rd Barking IG11 ....352 D5
Braintree CM7 ....128 B4
Burnham-on-C CM0 ....306 C5
Canvey Island SS8 ....364 C4
Chingford E4 ....287 E1
Dagenham, Goodmayes RM6 ....334 C4
Dagenham RM10 ....354 C7
Grays RM20 ....377 A8
Hoddesdon EN11 ....221 C6
Maldon CM9 ....236 F1
Romford RM7 ....335 B7
Woodford E18 ....310 B1
Essex Regiment Way CM3 ....208 D5
Essex Show Ground CM3 ....154 A2
Essex St SS1 ....367 A8
Essex Way
Brentwood CM13 ....316 C4
Ipswich IP3 ....18 E1
South Benfleet SS7 ....344 F1
Essex Yeomanry Way CO3 ....134 B7
Estate Rd SS7 ....345 F3
Estate Yd The CM3 ....182 C2
Estella Mead CM1 ....231 E7
Estfeld Cl 4 EN11 ....197 B1
Estuary Cl Barking IG11 ....353 B2
Colchester CO4 ....109 E4
Estuary Cotts RM18 ....380 D7
Estuary Cres
Clacton-on-S CO15 ....195 D3
Shotley Gate IP9 ....91 B8
Estuary Ct SS9 ....365 F8
Estuary Gdns SS3 ....350 C2
Estuary Lodge SS1 ....367 F6
Estuary Mews
Southend-on-S SS3 ....368 E6
Tollesbury CM9 ....216 D2
Estuary Park Rd CO5 ....218 E6
Estuary Rd IP9 ....91 B8
Ethelbert Gdns IG2 ....333 A6
Ethelbert Rd SS4 ....303 C1
Ethelburga Rd RM3 ....314 F2
Ethel Cotts RM6 ....334 D8
Ethel Davis Sch RM6 ....334 B6
Etheldore Ave SS5 ....324 E8
Ethel Rd SS6 ....346 B8
Ethelred Gdns SS11 ....299 E1
Etheridge Gn IG10 ....289 C6
Etheridge Rd IG10 ....289 C6
Eton Cl SS8 ....364 B5
Eton Ct CO13 ....171 A5
Eton Rd Clacton-on-S CO15 ....195 F4
Frinton-on-S CO13 ....171 A5
Ilford IG1 ....352 D8
Eton Wlk SS3 ....349 E2
Etton Cl RM12 ....336 E2
Euclid Way RM20 ....371 F1
Eudo Rd CO2 ....135 C4
Eugene Cl RM2 ....336 C7
Europa Pk Grays RM20 ....377 C8
Witham CM8 ....184 A3
Europa Trad Est DA8 ....369 D1
Europa Way Harwich CO12 ....90 F4
Ipswich IP3 ....16 D7
Euro Ret Pk IP3 ....18 E1
Eustace Rd
Dagenham RM6 ....334 D4
Ipswich IP1 ....16 E8
Euston Ave IP4 ....18 F6
Euston Ct IP11 ....381 A4
Evabrook Cl IP2 ....16 E1
Evans Cl DA9 ....377 A2
Evansdale RM13 ....354 F2
Evanston Ave E4 ....309 C3
Evanston Gdns IG4 ....332 E5
Eva Rd RM6 ....334 D4
Evelyn Pl CM1 ....231 F1
Evelyn Rd Braintree CM3 ....153 D4
Hockley SS5 ....324 E6
Evelyn Sharp Cl RM2 ....336 D8
Evelyn Sharp Ho RM2 ....336 D8
Evelyn Wlk CM13 ....316 C4
Evelyn Wood Rd CM77 ....155 E6
Everard Rd SS14 ....343 A8
Everest SS6 ....323 D5
Everest Gdns CM23 ....145 E6
Everest Rise CM12 ....296 F1
Everest Way CM9 ....237 B5
Everett Ho CO1 ....136 B6
Everglades The SS7 ....345 F2
Evergreen Ct SS12 ....321 C6
Evergreen Dr CO4 ....110 D4
Evergreens The SS3 ....349 E6
Everik Bsns Ctr CM13 ....295 E4
Everitt Rd CB10 ....22 F2
Everitt Way CO9 ....51 E2
Eversleigh Gdns RM14 ....337 D3
Eversley Cl IG10 ....289 C6
Eversley Ct SS7 ....344 C7
Eversley Lodge EN11 ....221 A6
Eversley Prim Sch SS13 ....343 C6
Eversley Rd
Basildon SS13 ....343 D6
South Benfleet SS7 ....344 C7
Eves Cnr
Burnham-on-C CM0 ....306 B7
Danbury CM3 ....256 E7
Eves Cres CM1 ....232 A5
Eves Ct CO12 ....90 D1
Evesham Ave E17 ....309 A1
Evesham Cl IP2 ....17 A2
Evesham Way IG5 ....333 A8
Eves Orch CO8 ....55 F1
Ewan Cl Colchester CO3 ....134 C6
Southend-on-S SS9 ....346 A3
Ewan Rd RM3 ....314 D1
Ewanrigg Terr IG8 ....310 C5
Ewan Way Colchester CO3 ....134 C7
Southend-on-S SS9 ....346 A3
Ewell Hall Chase CO5 ....158 C1
Ewellhurst Rd IG5 ....310 E1
Ewer Ct CO1 ....136 A6
Exchange St
Romford RM1 ....335 E5
Romford RM1 ....335 E6
Exchange The IG1 ....333 B2
Exchange Way 5 CM1 ....232 B2
Exeter Cl Basildon SS14 ....342 F7
Braintree CM7 ....128 B5
Great Horkesley CO6 ....109 C7
Southend-on-S SS3 ....349 F1
Exeter Ct 6 CB9 ....8 E6
Exeter Dr CO1 ....136 A7
Exeter Gdns IG1 ....332 F3
Exeter Ho
7 Barking IG11 ....353 A5
Southend-on-S SS3 ....349 F1
Exeter Rd Chelmsford CM1 ....232 E5
Dagenham RM10 ....354 B6
Felixstowe IP11 ....381 D5
Ipswich IP3 ....18 B4
Exford Ave SS0 ....347 B5
Exhibition La SS3 ....349 F4
Exley Cl CM4 ....274 B4
Exmoor Cl
Chelmsford CM1 ....231 D1
Redbridge IG6 ....311 C2
Exmoor Rd IP11 ....381 D6
Exmouth Dr SS6 ....323 D5
Exmouth Rd RM17 ....378 B8
Express Dr IG3 ....334 B3
Exton Gdns RM8 ....353 C7
Eyhurst Ave RM12 ....336 B1
Eynesham Way 1 SS13 ....321 A1
Eynsford Rd
Greenhithe DA9 ....377 C2
Ilford IG3 ....333 E2
Eyre Cl RM2 ....336 B7

F

Faber Rd CM8 ....211 E8
Fabians Cl CO6 ....131 A3
Factory Hill CO5 ....186 E3
Factory La CO11 ....86 C3
Factory La E CO9 ....76 E1
Factory La W CO9 ....76 E1
Factory Rd DA11 ....378 C1
Factory Terr CO9 ....76 E2
Faggotters La CM17 ....201 F1
Faggot Yd CM7 ....127 F5
Fagus Ave RM13 ....355 D2
Fairbank Cl CM5 ....248 F2
Fairbrother Ct 1 CO4 ....136 D7
Fairburn Cl 2 SS1 ....367 C8
Fairburn Ct 4 SS1 ....367 C8
Fair Cl CO7 ....193 A6
Fairclough Ave CO16 ....195 B3
Faircross Ave
Barking IG11 ....352 C6
Romford RM5 ....313 D3
Faircross Par IG11 ....352 E7
Fairfax Ave SS13 ....343 C8
Fairfax Dr SS0 ....347 D2
Fairfax Hall CO4 ....109 F4
Fairfax Mead CM2 ....233 A2
Fairfax Rd
17 Colchester CO2 ....135 F6
Grays RM17 ....373 B1
Tilbury RM18 ....378 F6
Fairfield
Great Wakering SS3 ....350 A3
Ingatestone CM4 ....274 C4
Fairfield Ave
Felixstowe IP11 ....381 E5
Grays RM16 ....373 C6
Upminster RM14 ....337 C1
Fairfield Cl
Great Bromley CO7 ....139 A7
Hornchurch RM12 ....336 A2
Fairfield Cres SS9 ....346 F6
Fairfield Ct 8 IG8 ....310 A4
Fairfield Gdns
2 Colchester CO4 ....136 C8
Southend-on-S SS9 ....346 F7
Fairfield Inf Sch IP11 ....381 E5
Fairfield Rd
Braintree CM7 ....127 F2
Brentwood CM14 ....316 C7
Chelmsford CM1 ....232 A3
Chipping Ongar CM5 ....248 F2
Clacton-on-S CO15 ....195 E4
Epping CM16 ....246 B2
Hoddesdon EN11 ....221 A8
Ilford IG1 ....352 B6
Ipswich IP3 ....18 A2
Southend-on-S SS9 ....346 E7
Woodford IG8 ....310 A4
Fairfield Rise CM12 ....318 F8
Fairfields CM3 ....258 D1
Fairfield Way CO9 ....76 F1
Fairford Cl RM3 ....315 B4
Fairford Way RM3 ....315 B4
Fair Gn CO10 ....2 B5
Fairham Ave RM15 ....372 A6
Fairhaven Ave CO5 ....218 E6
Fairhead Rd N CO4 ....136 C8
Fairhead Rd S 6 CO4 ....136 C8
Fairholme Ave RM2 ....336 B7
Fairholme Gdns RM14 ....337 F4
Fairholme Rd Ilford IG1 ....333 A4
Redbridge IG1 ....332 F4
Fairhouse Com Jun & Inf Sch SS14 ....342 D6
Fairhouse Ct SS14 ....342 D6
Fairkytes Ave RM11 ....336 D3
Fairland Cl SS6 ....323 E5
Fairlands Ave IG9 ....310 A8
Fairlawn Dr IG8 ....310 A3
Fairlawn Gdns SS2 ....347 E5
Fairlawns
Brentwood CM14 ....316 A7
10 Chingford E4 ....309 C8
Epping CM16 ....246 B2
Southend-on-S SS1 ....367 F7
Fairlawns Cl RM11 ....336 F4
Fairleads CM3 ....256 F8
Fair Leas CB10 ....22 E3
Fairleigh Ave SS13 ....343 D5
Fairleigh Ct SS9 ....346 D1
Fairleigh Dr SS9 ....346 D1
Fairleigh Rd SS13 ....343 D5
Fairlight Ave
Chingford E4 ....309 D8
Woodford IG8 ....310 A4
Fairlight Cl E4 ....309 D8
Fairlight Rd SS7 ....345 C3
Fairlight Villas RM4 ....313 E7
Fairlop Ave SS8 ....364 A4
Fairlop Cl
Clacton-on-S CO15 ....195 F8
Hornchurch RM12 ....355 B6
Fairlop Gdns
Basildon SS14 ....342 D6
Redbridge IG6 ....311 C3
Fairlop Prim Sch IG6 ....311 C2
Fairlop Rd IG6 ....311 C1
Fairlop Sta IG6 ....311 D2
Fairlop Waters Ctry Pk* IG6 ....311 E1
Fairmead SS6 ....323 B4
Fair Mead SS14 ....342 C8
Fairmead Ave
Hadleigh SS7 ....345 E6
Southend-on-S SS0 ....347 C2
Fairmead Ct E4 ....287 E2
Fairmead Gdns IG4 ....332 E6
Fairmead Ho SS0 ....347 C2
Fairmead Rd IG10 ....288 B6
Fairmeads IG10 ....289 B7
Fairmeadside IG10 ....288 C4
Fairoak Gdns RM1 ....313 E1
Fair Oak Pl IG6 ....311 C1
Fairstead SS14 ....342 A6
Fairstead Hall Rd CM3 ....182 A5
Fairstead Lodge 4 IG8 ....310 A4
Fairstead Rd CM3 ....182 C5
Fairview Billericay CM12 ....297 A1
Canvey Island SS8 ....363 F5
Fairview Ave
Brentwood CM13 ....295 E3
Rainham RM13 ....355 D2
Stanford-le-H SS17 ....360 C1
Fairview Chase SS17 ....375 C8
Fairview Cl Chigwell IG7 ....311 E6
South Benfleet SS7 ....344 C7
Fairview Cres SS7 ....344 C7
Fairview Dr Chigwell IG7 ....311 E5
Southend-on-S SS0 ....347 C4
Fairview Est EN11 ....221 C7
Fairview Gdns
Southend-on-S SS9 ....346 C2
Woodford IG8 ....310 B2
Fairview Ind Pk RM13 ....369 D8
Fair View Lodge SS9 ....346 C2
Fairview Par RM7 ....335 D6
Fairview Rd
Basildon SS14 ....342 F5
Chigwell IG7 ....311 E6
Fairview Villas E4 ....309 B3
Fairview Wlk SS7 ....344 C7
Fairway
Bishop's Stortford CM23 ....146 C6
Chelmsford CM2 ....254 D7
Grays RM16 ....373 B5
Sawbridgeworth CM21 ....172 F2
Wickford SS12 ....321 E3
Woodford IG8 ....310 C5
Fairway Dr CM0 ....306 B5
Fairway Gardens Cl SS9 ....346 C5
Fairway Gdns Ilford IG1 ....352 C7
Southend-on-S SS9 ....346 C5
Fairways Colchester CO4 ....109 B3
Southend-on-S SS1 ....367 F8
Waltham Abbey EN9 ....265 E5
Fairways Prim Sch SS9 ....346 C4
Fairways The
Cold Norton CM3 ....280 F5
Rushmere St A IP4 ....18 E5
Fairway The
Harlow CM18 ....224 A6
Fairway The *continued*
South Benfleet SS7 ....344 C7
Southend-on-S SS9 ....346 C5
Upminster RM14 ....337 D4
Fairycroft Rd CB10 ....22 E1
Fairy Hall La CM77 ....127 A1
Falbro Cres SS7 ....345 D4
Falcon Ave RM17 ....378 C8
Falcon Cl Haverhill CB9 ....9 C8
Rayleigh SS6 ....323 B3
Sawbridgeworth CM21 ....172 C1
Southend-on-S SS9 ....346 F5
Waltham Abbey EN9 ....266 A5
Falcon Cres CO1 ....136 B5
Falcon Ct 6 E18 ....332 B8
Falconer Rd Haverhill CB9 ....9 C5
Redbridge IG6 ....312 C5
Falconers Pk CM21 ....172 D1
Falconer St CM23 ....145 C5
Falcon Fields CM9 ....258 F8
Falcon Mews CM9 ....258 F8
Falcon Pk SS14 ....341 F8
Falcon Rd CM0 ....284 C4
Falcons Mead CM2 ....232 A1
Falcon Sq CO9 ....51 F4
Falcon St Felixstowe IP11 ....381 C6
Ipswich IP1 ....17 C5
Falcon Way
Basildon SS16 ....342 C4
Chelmsford CM2 ....254 A6
Clacton-on-S CO15 ....195 F6
Rainham RM13 ....355 A5
Southend-on-S SS3 ....349 E1
Wanstead E11 ....332 A7
Fal Dr CM8 ....183 E2
Falkenham End SS14 ....342 C7
Falkenham Path SS14 ....342 C7
Falkenham Rise SS14 ....342 C7
Falkenham Row SS14 ....342 C7
Falkirk Cl RM11 ....337 A3
Falkland Cl CM3 ....233 E8
Falkland Ct CM7 ....128 B4
Falkland Gn CM9 ....257 E6
Falklands Dr 8 CO11 ....86 D4
Falklands Rd CM0 ....306 B5
Falkner Cl CM4 ....275 F3
Fallaize Ave IG1 ....352 B8
Fallow Cl IG7 ....311 F5
Fallowden La CB10 ....23 F8
Fallowfield SS3 ....349 D1
Fallowfield Cl CO12 ....90 F3
Fallowfield Ct 14 CB9 ....8 E7
Fallowfield Rd CO2 ....135 C2
Fallow Fields IG10 ....288 C2
Fallows The SS8 ....363 F6
Falmouth Ave E4 ....309 E5
Falmouth Gdns IG4 ....332 E6
Falmouth Rd CM1 ....232 E5
Falstaff Cotts IP9 ....60 F8
Falstaff Pl SS16 ....341 A5
Falstones SS15 ....341 E5
Fambridge Chase CM8 ....155 F2
Fambridge Cl CM9 ....237 A1
Fambridge Ct 2 RM7 ....335 D6
Fambridge Dr SS12 ....321 E6
Fambridge Rd
Althorne CM3 ....282 F2
Cold Norton CM9,CM3 ....281 C5
Dagenham RM8 ....335 A3
Maldon CM9 ....236 F2
Rochford SS4, CM3 ....303 C3
Fambridge Sta CM3 ....303 B8
Fane Rd SS7 ....344 D8
Fanner's Green Cotts CM3 ....207 C5
Fanns Rise RM19 ....371 A2
Fanny's La CO16 ....167 D2
Fanshawe Ave IG11 ....352 C6
Fanshawe Cres
Dagenham RM9 ....353 F7
Hornchurch RM11 ....336 D5
Fanshawe Rd RM16 ....374 A3
Fanton Ave SS12 ....321 F3
Fanton Chase SS11 ....322 A6
Fanton Gdns SS11 ....322 B6
Fanton Wlk SS11 ....322 B6
Faraday Cl Braintree CM7 ....127 F1
Clacton-on-S CO15 ....169 A1
Faraday Ho 4 DA17 ....369 A3
Faraday Rd Ipswich IP4 ....17 F5
Southend-on-S SS9 ....346 C6
Farford Field CO10 ....34 C5
Farina Cl IP1 ....16 F7
Faringdon Ave RM3 ....314 D3
Faringdon Gr RM3 ....314 D3
Farley Dr IG3 ....333 E3
Farmadine CB11 ....22 E1
Farmadine Ct 3 CB11 ....22 E1
Farmadine Gr CB11 ....22 E1
Farmadine Ho 5 CB11 ....22 E1
Farmbridge End Rd CM1 ....205 D4
Farm Cl Brentwood CM13 ....295 C2
Buckhurst Hill IG9 ....310 C7
Dagenham RM10 ....354 C5
Roydon CM19 ....198 B1
Farm Cres SS11 ....300 E4
Farm Dr RM16 ....373 C6
Farm End E4 ....287 E4
Farmer Ct EN9 ....266 A6
Farmers Way CO16 ....195 B3
Farmfield Rd CO6 ....106 B1
Farm Hill Rd EN9 ....265 D6
Farm La EN11 ....221 C8
Farmleigh Ave CO15 ....195 F8
Farm Rd
Canvey Island SS8 ....364 B5
Chadwell St M RM16 ....373 F4
East Tilbury RM18 ....375 C2
Great Oakley CO12 ....116 D3
Rainham RM13 ....355 C2
Farm View SS6 ....323 D5
Farmway RM8 ....334 C1
Farm Way
Buckhurst Hill IG9 ....310 C6
Hornchurch RM12 ....355 C8
Farm Way *continued*
Thundersley SS7 ....345 B6
Farm Wlk CO7 ....192 E8
Farnaby Way SS17 ....360 C3
Farnan Ave E17 ....309 B1
Farne Dr SS12 ....321 F5
Farnes Ave SS12 ....321 C7
Farnes Dr RM2 ....314 C1
Farnham CE Prim Sch CM23 ....118 D6
Farnham Cl CM21 ....172 C1
Farnham Gn CM23 ....118 B7
Farnham Green Prim Sch IG3 ....334 A5
Farnham Rd Ilford IG3 ....333 F4
Romford RM3 ....314 D5
Farnley Rd E4 ....287 E2
Farnol Rd DA1 ....376 A3
Farrance Rd RM6 ....334 E4
Farr Ave IG11 ....353 A3
Farriers
Great Amwell SG12 ....197 A4
Sawbridgeworth CM21 ....172 E3
Farriers Chase CO5 ....218 D6
Farriers Dr CM12 ....297 B5
Farriers End CO3 ....134 D5
Farrier Sq CM11 ....298 C4
Farriers Way
Great Notley CM77 ....154 B7
Southend-on-S SS2 ....347 F5
Farriers Went IP11 ....381 B7
Farringdon Service Rd 8 SS1 ....367 A8
Farrington Cl 3 CO1 ....136 C6
Farrow Gdns RM16 ....373 C5
Farrow Ho CM15 ....294 C1
Farrow Rd CM1 ....253 E7
Farthingale Ct EN9 ....266 A5
Farthingale La EN9 ....266 A5
Farthing Cl CM7 ....128 D4
Farthing Rd IP1 ....16 C7
Farthing Road Ind Est IP1 ....16 C7
Farthings Chase CO5 ....218 E7
Farthings Cl E4 ....309 E7
Farthings Went IP9 ....35 B2
Fastnet SS2 ....347 A7
Fastnet Cl CB9 ....9 D8
Faulds Wlk CO2 ....136 A3
Faulkbourne Rd CM8 ....183 D4
Faulkeners Way IP11 ....381 A8
Faulkner Cl 6 RM8 ....334 D4
Fauna Cl RM6 ....334 C5
Fauners SS16 ....342 A5
Faversham Ave E4 ....287 F1
Faversham Cl IG7 ....312 B8
Faversham Lodge SS1 ....367 E6
Fawbert & Barnards Prim Sch CM17 ....200 C3
Fawbert & Bernard Inf Sch CM21 ....172 E2
Fawcett Dr SS15 ....319 E1
Fawkner Cl CM2 ....232 F2
Fawkon Wlk EN11 ....221 A6
Fawley Cl IP4 ....18 C7
Fawn Rd IG7 ....311 F5
Fawters Cl CM13 ....295 D3
Faymore Gdns RM15 ....372 A7
Fazal Laj IG1 ....333 C2
Fearns Mead CM14 ....316 D5
Featherby Way SS4 ....326 A1
Feathers Field IP11 ....381 B5
Feathers Hill CM22 ....174 E6
Feeches Rd SS2 ....347 D5
Feedhams Cl CO7 ....137 C3
Feenan Highway RM18 ....379 B6
Feering CE Prim Sch CO5 ....158 E4
Feering Dr SS14 ....342 F5
Feering Gn SS14 ....342 F5
Feering Hill CO5 ....158 D3
Feering Mus* CO5 ....158 B1
Feering Rd
Billericay CM11 ....297 C2
Coggeshall CO6 ....131 B1
Feering Row 5 SS14 ....342 F5
Felaw St IP2 ....17 D4
Felbrigg Cl CM77 ....154 B7
Felbrigge Rd IG3 ....333 F3
Felhurst Cres RM10 ....354 C8
Felicia Way RM16 ....374 B2
Felipe Rd RM16 ....372 C3
Felix Rd Felixstowe IP11 ....381 F4
Ipswich IP3 ....18 C2
Felixstowe Beach Cvn Pk IP11 ....381 C2
Felixstowe Cl CO16 ....195 A4
Felixstowe General Hospl IP11 ....381 F4
Felixstowe Rd IP3 ....18 B3
Felixstowe Sta IP11 ....381 E5
Fellbrigg Ave IP5 ....18 F6
Fell Christy CM1 ....232 B5
Fellcroft 5 SS13 ....343 C6
Fellowes Cl CO4 ....109 F2
Fell Rd CO9 ....28 B8
Felmongers CM20 ....200 B2
Felmore Ct 9 SS13 ....343 B8
Felmore Prim Sch SS13 ....343 B8
Felmores SS13 ....343 B8
Felmores End 8 SS13 ....343 B8
Felnor Wlk IP11 ....381 E4
Fels Cl RM10 ....335 B1
Fels Farm Ave RM10 ....335 C1
Felstead Ave IG5 ....311 A2
Felstead Cl
Blackheath CO2 ....163 A8
Brentwood CM13 ....295 C3
South Benfleet SS7 ....344 D4
Felstead Rd
Loughton IG10 ....288 E2
Romford RM5 ....313 C3
South Benfleet SS7 ....344 D4
Wanstead E11 ....332 A4

Felsted Almshouses CM6 .... 152 B6
Felsted Prep Sch CM6 .... 152 D7
Felsted Prim Sch CM6 .... 152 D7
Felsted Rd CM11 .... 297 C2
Felsted Sch CM6 .... 152 C6
Felsted Vineyard* CM6 .... 151 C7
Felton Gdns IG11 .... 352 E3
Felton Rd IG11 .... 352 E3
Feltwell Pl 2 CB9 .... 9 B8
Fenbridge La CO7 .... 59 B1
Fencepiece Rd IG7 .... 311 C3
Fen Cl Brentwood CM15 .... 295 C5
 Bulphan RM14 .... 358 F8
Fengates CM3 .... 301 C8
Fen La Ardleigh CO7 .... 84 D1
 Bulphan RM14 .... 358 C7
 Orsett RM16 .... 357 E7
Fenman Ct CM22 .... 94 C2
Fenman Gdns IG3 .... 334 B3
Fen Mdw IP11 .... 381 A8
Fen Cl Frating CO7 .... 139 A3
 South Woodham Ferrers CM3 .... 301 C8
Fennell Cl CO5 .... 186 C5
Fennells CM19 .... 223 C3
Fennels Cl CB9 .... 9 A7
Fenner Brockway Ho CM20 .... 223 E8
Fenner Rd RM16 .... 372 C3
Fenners Way IG11 .... 321 A2
Fennes Rd CM7 .... 102 A3
Northbank Alderney Rd CM3 .... 301 B8
Fennings Chase CO1 .... 136 A7
Fenno Cl CO3 .... 134 F4
Fen Rd CO9 .... 77 A1
Fen St CO6 .... 56 B1
Fentiman Way RM11 .... 336 E3
Fenton Grange CM17 .... 224 C7
Fenton Rd Grays RM16 .... 372 E3
 Haverhill CB9 .... 9 B8
Fenton Way IP8 .... 35 E8
Fenwick Way SS6 .... 364 A6
Ferdinand Wlk CO4 .... 336 F7
Ferguson Ave RM2 .... 314 D1
Ferguson Cl CB11 .... 23 A2
Ferguson St RM1 .... 314 D1
Fermoy Rd SS1 .... 368 B7
Fernbank Billericay CM12 .... 776 F1
 Buckhurst Hill IG9 .... 288 B1
Fernbank Ave RM12 .... 355 C8
Fernbrook Ave SS1 .... 367 D8
Fern Cl CM12 .... 297 B4
Fern Ct Chingford E4 .... 309 C4
 Southend-on-S SS3 .... 368 F7
 Stanford-le-H SS17 .... 360 D3
Ferndale Cl CO15 .... 341 B6
 Clacton-on-S CO15 .... 195 C2
Ferndale Cres SS8 .... 364 B2
Ferndale Rd Harwich CO12 .... 92 F6
 Rayleigh SS6 .... 323 E5
 Romford RM5 .... 313 C1
 Southend-on-S SS2 .... 348 F1
Ferndate Way RM7 .... 335 B5
Ferndown
 Hornchurch RM11 .... 336 F5
 1 Wanstead E18 .... 332 A8
Ferndown Cl SS7 .... 344 E5
Ferndown Rd CO13 .... 170 E5
Ferndown Way CM3 .... 211 B4
Fern Gr CB9 .... 8 E8
Fernhall La CM0 .... 332 D6
Fernhall La EN9 .... 266 D8
Fernhayes Cl IP7 .... 17 A2
Fern Hill Basildon SS16 .... 341 C4
 Glemsford CO10 .... 2 B7
Fernhill Ct E17 .... 309 D1
Fern Hill La CM18 .... 222 C7
Fernie Cl IG7 .... 312 A5
Fernie Rd CM7 .... 127 D2
Fernlea CO4 .... 109 C2
Fernlea Rd
 Burnham-on-C CM0 .... 306 B5
 Harwich CO12 .... 93 C1
 South Benfleet SS7 .... 344 E3
Fernleigh Ct
 Romford RM7 .... 335 C6
 Southend-on-S SS0 .... 347 A1
Fernleigh Dr SS9 .... 347 A2
Fernside IG9 .... 288 B1
Fernside CO SS17 .... 361 B5
Fern Way CO15 .... 220 F7
Fernways IG1 .... 352 B8
Fern Wlk Basildon SS16 .... 340 E4
 Canvey Island SS8 .... 368 C3
Fernwood SS7 .... 345 E4
Fernwood Ave CO15 .... 196 F5
Ferrers Rd CM3 .... 301 D6
Ferris Ave CM3 .... 280 F5
Ferris Stps 15 SS16 .... 355 A1
Ferro Rd RM13 .... 355 A1
Ferry La Felixstowe IP11 .... 381 A3
 Rainham RM13 .... 369 E7
Ferry Rd
 Burnham-on-C CM0 .... 305 E6
 Fingringhoe CO5 .... 164 B6
 Hullbridge SS5 .... 301 D2
 North Fambridge CM3 .... 363 D8
 South Benfleet SS7 .... 363 D8
 Tilbury RM18 .... 379 A4
Feryby Rd RM16 .... 374 B3
Feryngs Cl CM17 .... 200 D4
Fesants Croft CM20 .... 215 D4
Festival Gdns CM9 .... 215 D4
Festival Link SS14 .... 342 B8
Festival Way SS14 .... 320 B1
Fetherston Rd SS17 .... 360 D1
Feveril Rd CO16 .... 168 D4
Fews Lodge RM6 .... 334 D2
Fiat Ave CO15 .... 220 D6
Fiddlers Cl DA9 .... 377 B3

Fiddlers Folly CO3 .... 107 E1
Fiddlers Hill CO3 .... 107 E2
Fiddlers La CO7 .... 59 C3
Field Cl Abridge RM4 .... 290 B6
 Buckhurst Hill IG9 .... 310 C7
 Chingford E4 .... 309 B4
Field Ct CO4 .... 136 E8
Fielders Ct 9 CM14 .... 316 C8
Fielders The SS8 .... 364 A2
Fieldfare CM11 .... 319 C8
Fieldgate Dock CO7 .... 192 E5
Field Gate La CM7 .... 94 A3
Fieldhouse Cl E18 .... 310 B2
Fielding Ave RM18 .... 379 C6
Fielding Way CM13 .... 295 C3
Field Rd RM15 .... 175 C5
Fields Cl CO16 .... 167 F6
Fields Farm Rd CO2 .... 162 B4
Fieldside CB11 .... 43 E7
Fields Park Cres RM6 .... 334 D6
Fields View CO10 .... 33 F8
Field View RM16 .... 374 A3
Fieldview Cl CO4 .... 109 F4
Field View Dr CM9 .... 214 C4
Fieldway Basildon SS13 .... 343 C4
 Dagenham RM8 .... 353 C8
 Grays RM16 .... 373 A5
 Stanstead Abbotts SG12 .... 197 B4
 Wickford SS12 .... 321 D3
Field Way
 Hoddesdon EN11 .... 197 C2
 Wivenhoe CO7 .... 137 C2
Field Wlk CO14 .... 171 A8
Fiennes Cl CM8 .... 334 C3
Fiesta Dr RM9,RM13 .... 354 C1
Fifth Ave
 Canvey Island SS8 .... 363 E4
 Chelmsford CM1 .... 232 B6
 Frinton-on-S CO13 .... 170 E5
 Grays RM20 .... 377 A8
 Halstead CO9 .... 77 B1
 Stanstead Mountfitchet CM24 .... 120 B2
 Wickford SS11 .... 322 A6
Fifth Ave / Allende Ave CM20 .... 199 C3
Filey Rd CM0 .... 284 A3
Fillebrook Ave SS9 .... 347 A2
Fillebrook Ct SS9 .... 347 A2
Fillioll Cl CM3 .... 278 B6
Filston Rd DA8 .... 369 C1
Finbars Wlk IP4 .... 17 F5
Finborough Cl IP14 .... 18 F6
Finch Cl CM5 .... 249 A5
Finchdale CO15 .... 195 F6
Finch Dr Braintree CM7 .... 127 D4
 Great Bentley CO7 .... 139 D1
Finches Cl SS17 .... 361 C5
Finches The SS7 .... 345 A7
Finchfield SS6 .... 323 D1
Finch Gdns E4 .... 309 A5
Finch Hill CO10 .... 33 A7
Finchingfield Ave IG8 .... 310 C2
Finchingfield CE Prim Sch CM7 .... 72 D6
Finchingfield Guildhall Mus* CM7 .... 72 D6
Finchingfield Rd
 Stambourne CO9 .... 49 C7
 Steeple Bumpstead CM7 .... 27 C6
Finchingfields The CM15 .... 271 E2
Finchingfield Way
 Blackheath CO2 .... 163 A8
 7 Wickford SS12 .... 321 C5
Finchland View CM0 .... 301 D6
Finchley Cl CM2 .... 254 A8
Finchley Cl DA1 .... 376 A1
Finchley Rd Grays RM17 .... 378 B8
 Ipswich IP4 .... 17 E6
Finchmoor CM18 .... 223 D5
Finch's CM8 .... 212 F6
Findley Cl IP9 .... 61 F2
Findon Gdns RM13 .... 370 B8
Finer Cl CO16 .... 195 D5
Fingringhoe CE Prim Sch CO5 .... 163 F5
Fingringhoe Rd
 Abberton CO5 .... 163 B3
 Colchester CO2,CO5 .... 136 D1
Fingringhoe Wick Conservation Ctr* CO5 .... 164 D3
Fingringhoe Wick Nature Reserve & Visitor Ctr* CO5 .... 164 D3
Fingrith Hall Cotts CM4 .... 250 F3
Fingrith Hall La CM4 .... 250 F3
Finham Cl CO4 .... 136 F7
Finnymore Rd RM9 .... 353 E5
Finsbury Pl CO5 .... 76 F2
Finucane Gdns RM13 .... 355 A6
Firbank Rd RM5 .... 313 B5
Firebronds Rd IP9 .... 62 D5
Firecrest Rd CM2 .... 254 C5
Firefly Way IP3 .... 38 B8
Firfield Rd SS7 .... 345 C6
Firham Park Ave RM3 .... 315 A3
Firlands CM23 .... 145 E6
Firlands Ho CM23 .... 145 E6
Firle The SS16 .... 341 C3
Firlie Wlk CO2 .... 136 A2
Firmans SS16 .... 341 B3
Fir Pk CM10 .... 223 B5
Firs Chase CO5 .... 218 A6
Firs Chase Cvn Pk CO5 .... 218 A7
Firs Ct SS16 .... 342 F4
Firs Cvn Pk CO16 .... 168 D2
Firs Dr Loughton IG10 .... 288 A3
 Wickford SS12 .... 321 B1
Firsgrove Cres CM14 .... 316 B6
Firsgrove Rd CM14 .... 316 C6
Firs Hamlet CO5 .... 218 A6

Firs Jun & Mid Sch The CM23 .... 145 E6
Firs Rd Tiptree CO5 .... 186 D4
 West Mersea CO5 .... 218 B7
First Ave
 Basildon RM14,SS16 .... 340 E4
 Billericay CM12 .... 318 F7
 Canvey Island SS8 .... 363 E4
 Chelmsford CM1 .... 232 B5
 Clacton-on-S CO15 .... 196 B4
 Dagenham RM10 .... 354 B3
 Frinton-on-S CO13 .... 170 E4
 Glemsford CO10 .... 2 B5
 Grays RM20 .... 377 A8
 Halstead CO9 .... 77 B1
 Harwich CO12 .... 91 C3
 Hook End CM15 .... 272 C5
 Hullbridge SS5 .... 301 F1
 Ilford RM6 .... 334 C6
 Seawick CO16 .... 220 E6
 Southend-on-S SS9 .... 366 B8
 Stanford-le-H SS17 .... 360 D3
 Stansted Mountfitchet CM24 .... 120 B2
 Walton-on-t-N CO14 .... 144 E3
 Weeley CO16 .... 140 F1
 Wickford SS11 .... 322 A6
First Ave / Mandela Ave CM20 .... 199 F2
Firs The Canvey Island SS8 .... 363 F5
 Gosfield CO9 .... 102 E8
 Grays RM16 .... 373 C5
 Layer-de-l-H CO2 .... 162 A6
 Pilgrims Hatch CM15 .... 294 A3
 Woodford IG8 .... 310 C3
Firstore Dr CO3 .... 134 E7
Firs Wlk IG8 .... 310 A5
Fir Tree Cl Grays RM17 .... 378 D8
 Highwoods CO4 .... 110 B4
 Romford RM1 .... 335 D8
Fir Tree Hill IP9 .... 62 E4
Fir Tree La CM3 .... 234 E1
Fir Tree Rise
 Chelmsford CM2 .... 254 B6
 Ipswich IP8 .... 16 C2
Fir Trees Abridge RM4 .... 290 B6
 Epping CM16 .... 246 B2
Fir Tree Wlk
 Dagenham RM10 .... 353 C8
 Heybridge CM9 .... 209 C7
Fir Way CO15 .... 220 C6
Fir Wlk SS8 .... 363 F5
Firwood's Rd CO9 .... 103 E8
Fishbane Cl IP3 .... 38 B8
Fisher Cl Haverhill CB9 .... 9 D8
 Hoildbrook EN5 .... 265 B2
Fishermans Way CM11 .... 221 D8
Fishermen's Hill DA11 .... 378 B8
Fishers Cl EN8 .... 265 A5
Fishers Hatch CM20 .... 199 E1
Fisher's La CO7 .... 62 C3
Fisher's Way DA17 .... 369 C5
Fisher Way CM7 .... 128 C4
Fishmarket St CM6 .... 70 A2
Fish Pond Hill IP9 .... 63 C3
Fishponds Hill CO6 .... 81 F4
Fishponds La IP9 .... 62 E5
Fish St CM1 .... 238 E6
Fisher Dr CO15 .... 134 E3
Fisk St Barking IG11 .... 352 D3
Fitches Cres CM9 .... 237 A5
Fitches Croft CO6 .... 133 C8
Fitches Mews CM9 .... 237 B1
Fitzgerald Cl CO11 .... 86 B4
Fitzgerald Way CM1 .... 90 F2
Fitzgerald Rd IP14 .... 18 A5
Fitzgerald Rd E11 .... 332 A6
Fitzgilbert Rd CO2 .... 135 E4
Fitzilian Ave RM3 .... 314 F2
Fitzmaurice Rd IP3 .... 18 B3
Fitzpiers CB10 .... 22 E2
Fitzroy Cl CM21 .... 297 A4
Fitzroy St 2 IP1 .... 17 C6
Fitzstephen Rd RM8 .... 353 C7
Fitzwalter La CM3 .... 256 D6
Fitzwalter Pl
 Chelmsford CM1 .... 231 E3
 Great Dunmow CM6 .... 150 D8
Fitzwalter Rd
 Boreham CM3 .... 233 F8
 Colchester CO3 .... 135 B6
 Little Dunmow CM6 .... 151 E7
Fitzwarren SS9 .... 349 D1
Fitzwilliam Cl IP2 .... 16 F2
Fitzwilliam Rd
 Colchester CO3 .... 135 B7
 Hadleigh SS7 .... 345 C2
Fitzwilliams Ct CM17 .... 200 E4
Fitzwarmac Sch The SS6 .... 323 E3
Five Acres Bicknacre CM3 .... 256 F3
 Five Elms Rd RM8 .... 334 F1
 Five Elms Rd RM9 .... 334 F1
 Five Fields CO4 .... 136 E7
 Five Oaks SS7 .... 335 B4
 Five Oaks La IG7 .... 312 E5
 Five Ways CO3 .... 134 D4
 Flag Hill CO7 .... 193 F8
Flagstaff Gr IP9 .... 265 B6
Flagstaff Rd
 Colchester CO2 .... 135 F6
 Waltham Abbey EN9 .... 265 B6
Flail Cl CO7 .... 137 C6
Flambird's Chase
 Purleigh CM3 .... 280 A7
 Stow Maries CM3 .... 279 F6
Flamborough Cl SS9 .... 346 D6
Flamboro Wlk SS9 .... 346 D6
Flamingo Wlk 4 RM13 .... 355 A6

Flamstead Gdns RM9 .... 353 C5
Flamstead Rd RM9 .... 353 C5
Flanders Cl CM7 .... 127 E5
Flanders Field CO2 .... 136 B3
Flanders Rd IG 352 A3
Flatford Dr CO16 .... 195 B5
Flatford Mill (Field Ctr)* CO7 .... 85 D7
Flatford Rd
 East Bergholt CO7 .... 85 C8
 Haverhill CB9 .... 8 C8
Flats The Grays RM17 .... 373 D2
 Greenhithe DA9 .... 377 C2
Flavian Cl CB9 .... 9 D7
Flaxen Cl CO4 .... 309 A7
Flaxen Rd E4 .... 309 A7
Fax La CO10 .... 2 C3
Flaxman Ct 15 DA17 .... 369 A1
Fleet Ave SS4 .... 337 D5
Fleet Cl RM14 .... 337 D5
Fleet Hall Cotts SS4 .... 348 B8
Fleethall Gr RM16 .... 373 A5
Fleethall Rd SS4 .... 348 A8
Fleet Rd SS7 .... 344 D1
Fleetwood Ave
 Felixstowe IP11 .... 381 F5
 Holland-on-S CO15 .... 196 F7
 Southend-on-S SS0 .... 347 C2
Fleetwood Cl CO15 .... 196 F7
Fleetwood Rd IP11 .... 381 F5
Fleming 1 CM7 .... 127 F1
Fleming Gdns
 Romford RM8 .... 314 D1
 Tilbury RM18 .... 379 C6
Fleming Rd RM16 .... 372 C3
Flemings CM13 .... 316 C4
Flemings Farm Rd SS9 .... 346 D8
Flemish Cotts The CO7 .... 84 F6
Flemish Ct CO1 .... 135 F8
Flemming Ave SS9 .... 346 D3
Flemming Cres SS9 .... 346 D4
Fletcher Ct CM11 .... 297 D2
Fletcher Dr SS12 .... 321 E6
Fletcher Rd Chigwell IG7 .... 315 F5
Fletchers CM16 .... 267 E3
Fletchers Sq SS12 .... 348 A5
Flex Mdw CM19 .... 222 F7
Flint Cl Basildon SS16 .... 340 F5
 Ipswich IP2 .... 17 B2
Flint St RM20 .... 377 B8
Flintwich Manor CM1 .... 231 E7
Flitch Ind Est The CM6 .... 150 D7
Flitch La CM6 .... 150 E7
Flixton Cl CO16 .... 195 A5
Flood La CO4 .... 110 C6
Flora Gdns RM6 .... 334 C5
Flora Rd CM8 .... 183 D4
Florence Cl Grays RM20 .... 377 E8
 Hadleigh SS7 .... 345 D3
 Harlow CM12 .... 224 D2
 Hornchurch RM12 .... 336 E2
Florence Cotts CO7 .... 192 F6
Florence Elson Cl 2 .... 352 A8
Florence Gdns
 Dagenham RM8 .... 334 C4
 Hadleigh SS7 .... 345 D3
Florence Neale Ho 2 SS8 .... 364 A3
Florence Rd
 Canvey Island SS8 .... 364 D3
 Walton-on-t-N CO14 .... 144 E2
Florence Root Ho 3 IG4 .... 332 F6
Florence Terr SS17 .... 359 F4
Florence Way SS16 .... 340 B3
Florence Wlk 5 CM23 .... 145 F8
Florentine Ho 11 IG3 .... 334 C6
Florie's Rd CO6 .... 131 F8
Flowers Way CO15 .... 220 G7
Fobbing Farm Cl SS6 .... 342 A3
Fobbing Rd SS17 .... 361 C4
Fodderwick 11 SS14 .... 342 A5
Fogerty Cl SS3 .... 265 B2
Fokville Rd SS8 .... 364 C4
Fold Croft CM20 .... 199 A1
Fold The SS14 .... 342 B6
Foley Cotts CM7 .... 102 D2
Folkards La CO7 .... 192 F8
Folkes Ln RM14,CM13 .... 337 F7
Folkestone Rd E6 .... 352 A2
Folley The CO3 .... 134 D5
Folly Chase SS6 .... 324 B6
Folly La Capel St M IP8 .... 35 D4
Folly Mill La CM6 .... 96 G6
Folly The
 Layer-de-l-H CO2 .... 162 A5
 Tiptree CO5 .... 186 F2
 Wivenhoe CO7 .... 164 C7
 Writtle SS12 .... 197 B4
Fonnereau Rd IP1 .... 17 C6
Fontayne Ave
 Chigwell IG7 .... 311 C6
 Rainham RM13 .... 354 E5
 Romford RM1 .... 313 E1
Fonteyn Ct SS15 .... 341 C8
Fonteyne Gdns IG8 .... 310 D1
Fontwell Park Gdns RM12 .... 355 E8
Forbes Cl RM11 .... 336 F3
Ford Cl Basildon SS15 .... 341 A6
 Rainham RM13 .... 354 F5
Ford End Cl CM7 .... 158 A1
Ford End CE Prim Sch CM3 .... 179 B6
Fordham All Saints CE Prim Sch CO6 .... 107 D4
Fordham Cl RM11 .... 337 A4
Fordham Pl IP4 .... 18 F5
Fordham Rd
 Bures CO6,CO8 .... 79 F2
 Wormingford CO6 .... 106 E8
Fordhams Row RM16 .... 374 B8

Foster Rd continued
 Great Totham CM9 .... 213 A4
 Harwich CO12 .... 90 E5
Fosters Cl Woodford E18 .... 310 B2
 Writtle CM1 .... 230 F1
Foster's Cotts CM7 .... 129 D2
Foster St CM17 .... 225 A7
Foulgar Cl CM3 .... 245 A4
Foundation St 13 IP4 .... 17 C5
Founders Rd EN11 .... 197 B1
Foundry SS5 .... 324 C6
Foundry La
 Burnham-on-C CM0 .... 306 B5
 Copford CO6 .... 133 D5
 Earls Colne CO6 .... 105 B6
 Ipswich IP2 .... 17 C5
Fournes Dr RM16 .... 372 E3
Fountain Ct Harwich CO12 .... 91 C3
 West Mersea CO5 .... 218 D7
Fountain Farm CM18 .... 223 F6
Fountain La Copford CO6 .... 134 A1
 Eastthorpe CO6 .... 160 F8
 Hockley SS5 .... 324 B6
Fountain Pl EN9 .... 265 C5
Fountain Rd CM1 .... 205 D4
Fountains Rd IP2 .... 16 F1
Fountains The IG10 .... 288 D2
Fountain Wlk DA11 .... 378 F1
Four Acres
 Great Chesterford CB10 .... 3 E3
 Saffron Walden CB11 .... 22 E1
Four Ashes The CM21 .... 173 A2
Four Ashes CM7 .... 74 C1
Four Ash Hill CO9 .... 10 E1
Four Sisters CO7 .... 59 B5
Four Sisters Cl SS9 .... 346 F5
Four Sisters Way SS9 .... 346 F5
Fourth Ave Basildon SS16 .... 340 E3
 Chelmsford CM1 .... 232 B5
 Clacton-on-S CO15 .... 196 C4
 Frinton-on-S CO13 .... 170 F4
 Glemsford CO10 .... 2 B5
 Grays RM20 .... 377 A8
 Halstead CO9 .... 77 B1
 Harlow CM19 .... 223 B8
 Wickford SS11 .... 322 A6
 Stanford-le-H SS17 .... 360 C5
 Stansted Mountfitchet CM24 .... 120 B2
Fourth Wlk SS8 .... 363 E4
Four Wantz The CM6 .... 249 A4
Fourways CM22 .... 94 C1
Fourways 11 EN11 .... 221 A7
Four Wents The E4 .... 309 D8
Fowe's La CO10 .... 31 B8
Fowey Ave IG4 .... 332 D6
Fowler Cl SS1 .... 367 C8
Fowler Rd IG6 .... 312 C5
Fowlers Arc CO13 .... 170 F4
Fowlmere Rd SS6 .... 19 A6
Foxborough Chase CM4 .... 276 B5
Foxburrow Rd IP3 .... 18 F1
Fox Burrow Rd IG7 .... 312 D6
Fox Burrows La CM1 .... 231 B2
Fox Cl Romford RM5 .... 313 B5
 Thundersley SS7 .... 344 F6
Fox Cres CM1 .... 231 F4
Foxdells La CM23 .... 118 F2
Foxden CM6 .... 184 D6
Foxendale Folly CO3 .... 134 C7
Foxes Com CO6 .... 107 D1
Foxes Grn RM16 .... 374 A4
Foxes Gr CM13 .... 296 C2
Foxes La Aldham CO3,CO6 .... 133 D8
 Ashen CO10 .... 11 D1
Foxes Par EN9 .... 265 C6
Foxes Rd CO10 .... 11 E1
Foxfield Cl SS5 .... 325 A6
Foxfield Dr SS17 .... 360 E5
Foxglove Cl
 Bishop's Stortford CM23 .... 145 C6
 Clacton-on-S CO15 .... 195 F7
 Hoddesdon EN11 .... 197 C1
 Witham CM8 .... 183 D3
Foxglove Cres IP3 .... 18 E1
Foxglove Gdns 1 CM7 .... 332 C7
Foxglove Rd
 Romford RM7 .... 335 E2
 South Ockendon RM15 .... 372 C7
Foxgloves The CM12 .... 296 F4
Foxglove Way 4 CO4 .... 136 F7
Foxgrove La IP11 .... 381 F5
Foxhall Cl CO7 .... 59 C4
Foxhall Fields CO7 .... 59 C3
Foxhall Rd Ipswich IP3,IP4 .... 18 D5
 Mayland CM0 .... 283 E7
 Steeple CM0 .... 284 B7
 Upminster RM14 .... 337 E7
Foxhatch SS12 .... 321 E4
Fox Hatch CM15 .... 271 E1
Foxhills Rd RM16 .... 374 B6
Foxholes Rd CM2 .... 254 F6
Fox House Rd DA17 .... 369 B1
Foxhunter Wlk CM11 .... 297 D6
Foxlands Cres RM10 .... 354 C7
Foxlands Rd RM10 .... 334 C2
Foxleigh CM23 .... 319 A8
Foxleigh Cl CO12 .... 91 A8
Foxley Dr IG3 .... 146 B8
Fox Manor Way RM20 .... 377 B8
Foxmead CM0 .... 184 D6
Foxmeadows SS7 .... 344 C6
Foxmeads IP3 .... 38 E8
Foxton Rd Grays RM20 .... 377 E8
 Hoddesdon EN11 .... 221 A6
Foxwood Chase EN9 .... 265 C4
Foxwood Cl CO11 .... 85 C2

Foxwood Cres IP4 18 F5
Foxwood Ct SS9 346 D2
Foxwood Pl SS9 346 D2
Fox Yd CO9 53 C5
Foyle Dr RM15 372 A7
Foys Wlk CM11 319 C7
Frambury La CB11 66 F8
Frame The SS15 341 E7
Framlingham Ct
5 Ipswich IP1 17 A8
Rayleigh SS6 323 C1
Framlingham Way CM77 154 C7
Frampton Rd
5 Basildon SS13 321 A1
Epping CM16 246 A3
Ipswich IP3 38 A8
Frances Ave RM16 372 C2
Frances Bardsley Lower Sch RM2 336 B6
Frances Bardsley Upper Sch RM1 336 A5
Frances Cl CO7 137 B2
Frances Cottee Lodge SS6 346 A8
Frances Gdns RM15 371 F7
Frances Gn CM1 233 A7
Frances Rd E4 309 A4
Francis Ave IG1 333 D2
Franciscan Way IP1 17 C5
Francis Cl Haverhill CB9 8 F8
Horndon-on-t-H SS17 359 F3
Tiptree CO5 186 C4
Francisco Cl RM16 372 C3
Francis Ct Harlow CM20 199 B2
Silver End CM8 156 C5
3 Basildon SS14 342 F5
Francis Green Ho 7 EN9 265 B6
Francis Mews CM9 259 B8
Francis Rd Braintree CM7 127 D2
Ilford IG1 333 D2
14 Sudbury CO10 33 E7
Francis St
Brightlingsea CO7 192 F5
Ilford IG1 333 D2
Francis Way
Colchester CO4 110 D1
Silver End CM8 156 C4
Francis Wks EN11 221 B6
Francis Wlk SS6 323 D2
Francombe Gdns RM1 336 A5
Frank Bailey Wlk E12 352 A6
Frank Clater Cl CO4 136 C8
Frankland Cl IG8 310 C5
Frankland Rd E4 309 A5
Franklin Rd
Hornchurch RM12 355 C6
Ipswich IP3 18 B2
North Fambridge CM3 303 B8
Franklins RM15 371 D7
Franklins Way SS11 321 E8
Franklyn Gdns IG6 311 D4
Frank Naylor Ct 11 CO1 135 F7
Franks Cotts RM14 338 B3
Frank Slater Ho 4 IG3 334 B3
Franmil Rd RM12 336 A3
Fraser Cl Basildon SS15 340 F6
Chelmsford CM2 254 C8
Southend-on-S SS3 368 F8
Fraser Rd Erith DA8 369 D1
Ipswich IP1 16 F7
Frating Abbey Farm Rd CO7 166 C6
Frating Cres IG8 310 B4
Frating Cross CO7 166 B7
Frating Ct CM7 128 D1
Frating Hill CO7 138 D3
Frating Rd Ardleigh CO7 111 F6
Great Bromley CO7 138 F6
Thorrington CO7 166 A7
Frayes Chase CM5 204 A3
Frazer Cl RM1 335 F4
Frederica Rd E4 287 D2
Frederick Andrews Ct RM17 378 D8
Frederick Dr CO5 186 F5
Frederick Rd RM13 354 E3
Fred Leach Ho 1 SS8 364 A3
Fredrick J French Meml Homes CM1 232 B6
Fredricks Cl CO11 115 B5
Freeborne Gdns RM13 355 A6
Freebournes Ct 5 CM8 184 A2
Freebournes Rd CM8 184 B2
Freehold Rd IP4 18 B6
Freeland Rd CO15 195 E1
Freelands CO7 193 C6
Freeman Ct SS17 360 F3
Freemantle Ho RM18 378 F6
Freeman Way RM11 336 F5
Freeport Designer Outlet CM77 128 C1
Freewood La CB11 20 B3
Freezes Barns CB9 27 B7
Freightmaster Est RM13 370 A2
Fremantle SS3 368 D5
Fremantle Cl CM3 279 D1
Fremantle Rd
Belvedere DA17 369 A2
Colchester CO2 136 B1
Redbridge IG6 311 C1
Fremnells The SS14 342 D7
French Rd CM3 280 F1
French's Cl SG12 197 B4
French's Wlk 4 CM2 232 C2
Frensham Cl CO3 134 D7
Frere Ct CM23 118 F1
Frere Way CO5 164 B6
Frerichs Cl SS12 321 D5
Freshfields CO12 90 F1
Freshfields Ave RM14 356 C7
Freshwater Cres CM9 237 B4
Freshwater Dr SS16 342 F4
Freshwater La CO15 195 F7
Freshwater Rd RM8 334 E3
Freshwaters CM20 199 E1
Freshwell Ave RM6 334 C7
Freshwell Gdns
Saffron Walden CB10 22 C2
West Horndon CM13 339 D5
Freshwell St CB10 22 D2
Fresh Wharf Est IG11 352 B4
Fresh Wharf Rd IG11 352 B3
Fresian Cl CM7 127 D2
Freston Hill IP9 37 E4
Freston Rd IP3 38 C8
Freston St IP9 37 E3
Frettons SS14 342 E6
Friars IP9 60 B8
Friar's Ave CM15 295 A2
Friars Bridge Rd IP1 17 B5
Friars Cl Basildon SS15 341 C6
Chingford E4 309 C7
Clacton-on-S CO15 195 E6
Colchester CO4 110 C2
Ilford IG1 333 D3
Sible Hedingham CO9 51 D2
Wivenhoe CO7 164 C8
Friar's Cl CM15 295 A2
Friarscroft EN10 221 A3
Friars Ct CO2 136 C3
Friars Ctyd 1 IP1 17 C5
Friars Gate Cl IG8 310 A6
Friars Grove Jun & Inf Schs CO4 110 C2
Friars Jun & Inf Sch SS3 368 F8
Friars La Braintree CM7 127 F4
Hatfield Heath CM22 174 C1
Maldon CM9 236 F2
Friars St Ipswich IP1 17 C5
Southend-on-S SS3 368 F7
Sudbury CO10 33 E7
Friars The Chigwell IG7 311 E6
Harlow CM19 223 A6
Friars Wlk CM2 232 B1
Friars Wood CM23 146 C8
Friary Fields CM9 237 A2
Friary La IG8 310 A6
Friday Hill E4 309 E7
Friday Hill E E4 309 E7
Friday Hill W E4 309 E8
Friday Rd DA8 369 D1
Friday Wood Gn CO2 162 F8
Friedberg Ave CM23 145 D4
Friends Field CO8 55 F1
Friends Sch CB11 43 D8
Friends Wlk CB11 43 D7
Friern Gdns SS12 321 B7
Friern Pl SS12 321 B6
Friern Wlk SS12 321 B7
Frietuna Rd CO13 170 E6
Frimley Ave RM11 337 A3
Frimley Rd IG3 333 E1
Frinton Ct CO13 170 F3
Frinton Dr IG8 309 D3
Frinton Mews IG2 333 A5
Frinton-on-Sea Prim Sch CO13 170 E5
Frinton Park Ct CO14 171 A6
Frinton Rd
Holland-on-S CO15 196 E6
Kirby Cross CO13 170 D6
Romford RM5 313 A3
Thorpe-le-S CO16 142 B1
Frinton Sta CO13 170 F5
Friston Path 4 IG6 311 E5
Frithwood Cl CM12 318 F7
Frithwood La CM12 318 F7
Fritillary Cl IP8 36 E8
Fritton Cl IP2 17 A1
Fritton Ct 19 CB9 8 E7
Frizlands La RM10 335 B1
Frobisher Cl
Basildon SS15 341 D6
Maldon CM9 259 A8
Frobisher Dr CO15 194 F1
Frobisher Prim Sch CO15 194 F1
Frobisher Rd Harwich CO12 90 F1
Ipswich IP3 17 E1
Frobisher Way
Braintree CM7 128 C4
Greenhithe DA9 377 B3
Southend-on-S SS3 349 E1
Froden Brook CM11 319 C7
Froden Cl CM11 319 C7
Froden Ct CM11 319 C6
Frogge St CB10 3 B3
Frog Hall Cl CO5 164 B6
Froghall La IG7 311 D6
Frog La RM13 369 D8
Frog Mdw CO7 84 F7
Frogmore Est RM20 372 A1
Frog St CM15 293 E8
Frome RM18 375 C2
Fronk's Ave CO12 91 C2
Fronk's Rd CO12 91 B2
Front La RM14 337 E4
Front Rd IP3 38 D8
Frowick La CO16 167 B2
Fryatt Ave CO12 91 A4
Fry Cl RM5 313 A4
Fryerning La CM4 274 B4
Fryerns Terr SS14 342 F8
Fryth The SS14 342 E8
Fuchsia Cl RM7 335 E2
Fuchsia Ct 6 CO4 136 D8
Fuchsia La IP4 18 A5
Fuchsia Way CO16 195 C5
Fulbourne Rd E17 309 C1
Fulbrook La RM15 371 F6
Fulcher Ave CM2 232 F3
Fulfen Way CB11 43 D7
Fulford Dr SS9 347 A6
Fullarton Cres RM15 371 F7
Fullbridge CM9 237 A3
Fuller Ct 3 CM23 146 A7
Fuller Rd RM8 353 C8
Fuller's Ave IG8 309 F3
Fullers Cl Romford RM5 313 C3
Waltham Abbey EN9 266 A6
Fuller's Cl CO5 158 B2
Fullers Gate CO5 158 B2
Fuller's La RM5 313 C3
Fullers Mead CM17 224 C7
Fullers Rd CO2 136 D2
Fuller's Rd E18 309 F3
Fullers Terr IG1 352 D7
Fullman Ind Pk SS8 363 C3
Fullwell Ave IG5 311 B2
Fullwell Ct IG5 311 A2
Fullwell Par IG5 311 A2
Fullwood Prim Sch IG6 333 C7
Fulmar Cl CO4 137 A8
Fulmar Rd RM12 355 B6
Fulmar Way SS11 322 A5
Fulton Cres CM23 146 C8
Fulton Ct 3 EN3 265 A1
Fulton Rd SS7 344 D7
Fulwich Rd DA1 376 A1
Furlongs SS16 342 D4
Furlongs The CM4 274 B3
Furlong Way SG12 197 A7
Furneaux La CO5 163 F5
Furness Cl Grays RM16 374 B1
Ipswich IP2 36 F8
Furness Way RM12 355 A7
Furriers Cl CM23 145 C5
Furrow Cl CO3 134 E5
Furrowfelde SS16 342 A4
Further Mdw CM1 253 A8
Furtherwick Park Sch SS8 364 C3
Furtherwick Rd SS8 364 C2
Furze Cres CO7 165 A7
Furze Farm Cl RM6 312 E1
Furze Glade SS16 341 B4
Furze Inf Sch RM6 334 E5
Furze La
Great Bromley CO7 139 A5
Stock CM4 276 A1
Fuschia Ct IG8 309 E4
Fusedale Way RM15 371 F6
Fyefields SS13 343 C7
Fyfield Ave SS12 321 C5
Fyfield Bsns & Research Pk CM5 249 B6
Fyfield Cl CM13 339 D5
Fyfield Dr RM15 371 F6
Fyfield Dr Walker's CE Prim Sch CM5 227 D2
Fyfield Ho RM9 353 B5
Fyfield Path SS6 323 A3
Fyfield Rd
Chipping Ongar CM5 249 A5
Moreton CM5 226 F3
Rainham RM13 354 F4
Willingale CM5 228 C3
Woodford IG8 310 C3

G

Gabion Ave RM19 371 D2
Gablefields CM2 255 D6
Gable Hall Sch SS17 361 A5
Gables The Barking IG11 352 C6
Basildon SS13 343 B8
Haverhill CB9 9 F4
Sawbridgeworth CM21 172 E2
Southend-on-S, Eastwood SS9 346 B6
Southend-on-S SS9 346 D1
Brentwood CM13 316 C4
Gabriel Cl Grays RM16 372 C3
Romford RM5 313 C3
Gaces Acre CB11 43 A1
Gadsden Cl RM14 337 E5
Gadwall Reach CO5 158 D2
Gafzelle Dr SS8 364 E3
Gager Dr CO5 186 E5
Gage's Rd
Belchamp St P CO10 13 A1
Little Yeldham C10 30 F8
Gaiger Cl CM1 232 D7
Gainsborough Ave
Canvey Island SS8 364 E3
Little Ilford E12 352 A7
Tilbury RM18 379 B6
Gainsborough Cl
Billericay CM11 297 B1
Clacton-on-S CO16 195 B6
West Mersea CO5 218 D6
Gainsborough Cres CM2 232 E3
Gainsborough Ct 4 CM14 316 C6
Gainsborough Dr
Lawford CO11 86 C4
Southend-on-S SS0 347 E2
Gainsborough Ho
Barking RM8 353 B8
Redbridge IG8 311 B4
Gainsborough La IP3 37 F7
Gainsborough Pl
Brentwood CM13 295 D1
Chigwell IG7 311 F7
Gainsborough Rd
Black Notley CM77 155 A4
Colchester CO3 135 B5
Dagenham RM8 334 B1
Felixstowe IP11 381 F4
Ipswich IP4 17 D8
Rainham RM13 355 A4
Sudbury CO10 33 E8
Woodford IG8 310 E4
Gainsborough's House Mus* CO10 33 E7
Gainsborough St CO10 33 E7
Gains Cl SS8 364 D4
Gainsford Ave CO15 196 B4
Gainsford End Rd CO9 50 B6
Gainsthorpe Rd CM5 248 D8
Gaitskell Ho RM16 373 B5
Galadriel Spring CM3 301 C6
Galahad Cl CM0 306 B5
Galeborough Ave IG8 309 D3
Gale St RM9 353 D5
Gales Way IG8 310 E3
Galey Gn RM15 372 B8
Galiots CO5 218 A6
Gall End La CM24 119 F7
Galleon Bvd DA2 376 D3
Galleon Cl DA8 369 D2
Galleon Rd RM16 372 C2
Galleons Dr IG11 353 A2
Galleons Hill CM1 230 B5
Galleydene SS7 345 C3
Galleydene Ave CM2 254 C3
Galley Gn SG13 197 A2
Galleyhill Rd EN9 265 E7
Galley Hill Rd
Northfleet DA11 378 A2
Swanscombe DA10 377 F2
Galley Hill Trad Est DA10 377 E2
Galleywood Cres RM5 313 D4
Galleywood Inf Sch CM2 254 C2
Galleywood Rd
Chelmsford CM2 254 A5
Great Baddow CM2 254 E5
Galliford Rd CM9 237 A4
Galliford Road Ind Est CM9 237 A4
Gallions Cl IG11 353 A2
Gallops The SS16 341 B5
Galloway Cl 1 CM23 145 F8
Galloway Dr CO16 168 D3
Galloway Rd CM23 118 F1
Gallows Cnr RM3 314 C2
Gallows Green Rd CM6 97 F2
Gallows Hill CB11 43 C7
Galsworthy Ave RM6 334 B5
Galsworthy Cl CM7 155 A7
Galsworthy Rd RM18 379 C6
Galton Rd SS0 366 C8
Gambleside SS16 342 E3
Gammon Field RM16 373 E5
Gandalf's Ride CM3 301 D6
Gandish Cl CO7 59 D1
Gandish Rd CO7 59 E2
Ganels Cl CM11 319 C7
Ganels Rd CM11 319 C7
Ganges Rd IP9 91 B8
Gangies Hill CM21 172 A4
Ganley Cl 6 CM11 297 B2
Gannet Cl CB9 9 C8
Gannet Rd IP2 16 E3
Gant Ct EN9 265 F5
Gantshill Cres IG2 333 A6
Gants Hill Sta IG2 333 A5
Gaol La CO10 33 E7
Gap The Arkesden CB11 41 F1
Holland-on-S CO15 196 G6
Garbutt Rd RM14 337 C2
Garden Cl Althorne CM3 282 F4
Chingford E4 309 A5
Steeple CM0 261 F3
Garden Ct
Frinton-on-S CO13 170 F3
Upminster RM14 337 E3
Garden Dr CO3 134 E6
Garden End CM4 275 F2
Gardeners CM2 254 D5
Gardeners La SS4 304 F1
Gardeners Rd CO9 76 F1
Gardeners Row CO6 131 A2
Garden Farm CO5 218 D7
Garden Field
Felixstowe IP11 381 C5
Hatfield Peverel CM3 210 F4
Garden Field Cotts CO6 81 E5
Garden Fields
Great Tey CO6 132 C8
Stebbing CM6 124 D6
Steeple CM0 261 E3
Garden Hos The CM21 173 B3
Gardenia Pl CO16 195 B4
Gardenia Way IG8 310 A5
Gardenia Wlk CO4 136 E7
Garden Pl CO10 33 D7
Garden Rd
Clacton-on-S CO15 220 G7
Walton-on-t-N CO14 171 A7
Gardens Fields CM5 270 E5
Gardens The
Doddinghurst CM15 272 B3
Southend-on-S SS9 365 E8
Garden Terr CO9 76 F2
Garden Terrace Rd CM17 200 C4
Garden Way IG10 267 A1
Garden Wharf DA8 369 F1
Gardiner Cl RM8 353 D8
Gardiners Cl SS14 320 D1
Gardiners La N CM11 320 E4
Gardiners La S SS14 320 E2
Gardiners Link SS14 320 D2
Gardiners The CM17 224 B8
Gardiners Way SS14 320 D2
Gardner Ave SS17 361 A4
Gardner Cl E11 332 B5
Gardners Ct RM7 335 C6
Garenne Ct 8 E4 287 C1
Garfield Cl IP11 381 D3
Garfield Rd Chingford E4 287 D1
Felixstowe IP11 381 D3
Garland Rd CO12 90 F5
Garland Way RM11 336 E7
Garling Wlk CO6 108 E3
Garner Cl RM8 334 D3
Garner Rd E17 309 C2
Garners The SS4 325 F2
Garnets Mead CM3 182 B3
Garnetts CM22 148 B8
Garnetts Bglws CM6 152 C5
Garnetts La CM6 152 C6
Garnetts Villas CM6 152 C5
Garnon Mead CM16 246 D3
Garnons Chase CO6 81 A5
Garret Pl CO6 108 F4
Garrettlands CM2 255 F6
Garrick Ho RM12 336 A2
Garrick St DA11 379 B1
Garrison La IP11 381 D4
Garrison Par RM19 371 A2
Garrod Ct CO2 163 B7
Garrods IP9 35 B1
Garron La RM15 371 F7
Garry Cl RM1 313 E3
Garry Way RM1 313 E3
Garth Rd RM15 357 C1
Garthwood Cl CO6 108 E4
Gartmore Rd IG3 333 F2
Gascoigne Gdns IG8 309 E3
Gascoigne Prim Sch IG11 352 C4
Gascoigne Rd
Barking IG11 352 C3
Colchester CO4 136 C8
Gascoigne Way CM11 297 D2
Gascoyne Cl RM3 314 D2
Gasfield 14 CO11 86 D4
Gasgoine Ho CO4 109 F4
Gasson Rd DA10 377 E1
Gaston End CO7 59 C3
Gaston St CO7 59 C3
Gatacre Ct CO2 135 B3
Gatacre Rd IP1 17 A7
Gatefield Cl CO14 170 F7
Gatehope Dr RM15 371 F7
Gatehouse Mews CM4 274 B3
Gatehouse The 4 RM1 335 E6
Gatekeeper Cl
8 Braintree CM7 127 F1
Ipswich IP8 36 E8
Gate Lodge Sq SS15 319 F2
Gate Lodge Way SS15 319 F2
Gate St CM9 236 F3
Gate Street Mews CM9 236 F3
Gateway SS14 342 B6
Gateway Com Prim Sch The DA1 376 B1
Gatscombe Cl SS5 324 D6
Gattens The SS6 323 F4
Gatwick Cl CM23 119 B1
Gatwick View CM12 319 B8
Gatwick Way RM12 336 F1
Gauden Rd CM7 127 F7
Gavenny Path RM15 371 F7
Gavin Way
Colchester,Brinkley Gr CO4 110 A5
Colchester CO4 110 B5
Gawlers CM23 92 B8
Gay Bowers
Basildon SS14 342 D7
Hockley SS5 324 B6
Gay Bowers La CM3 256 F6
Gay Bowers Rd CM3 256 F4
Gay Bowers Way CM8 212 A7
Gaye St 1 IP1 17 B6
Gayfere Rd IG5 332 F8
Gay Gdns RM10 354 C7
Gayleighs SS6 323 D4
Gay Links SS14 342 B7
Gaylor Rd RM18 378 F6
Gaynes Ct RM14 356 B8
Gaynesford SS16 341 E4
Gaynes Hill Rd IG8 310 E3
Gaynes Park Rd RM14 356 B8
Gaynes Rd RM14 337 B2
Gaynes Sch RM14 356 C7
Gaysham Ave IG2 333 B6
Gaysham Hall IG5 333 B8
Gays La SS4 304 E2
Gayton Rd SS2 348 A2
Gaywood SS15 341 A7
Gazelle Ct CO4 110 C4
Gearies Inf Sch IG2 333 B6
Gearies Jun Sch IG2 333 B6
Geariesville Gdns IG6 333 B7
Geary Ct CM14 294 C1
Geary Dr CM14 294 C1
Geddings Rd EN11 221 B6
Geddy Ct RM2 336 B7
Geerings The SS17 361 A3
Geesh Rd SS8 364 C5
Geisthorp Ct EN9 266 A6
Gelsthorpe Rd RM5 313 B3
General Hospl SS0 347 C3
Generals La CM3 209 B2
Generals Mews IP11 381 B5
Genesta Cl CM9 216 D2
Genesta Rd SS0 366 D8
Geneva Gdns RM6 334 E6
Geneva Rd IP1 17 B7
Genever Cl E4 309 A5
Genevyll Cl CO10 1 D2
Genk Cl SS8 364 B5
Gennep Rd SS8 364 B5
Gennep Rd S SS8 364 B5
Gentian Ct CO4 109 C2
Gentry Cl SS17 360 C2
Geoffrey Ave RM3 315 B3
Geoff Seaden Cl 2 CO1 136 C6
George Ave CO7 192 F7
George Avey Croft CM16 247 B5
George Cardnell Way CM3 260 E1
George Cl
Canvey Island SS8 363 F6
Clacton-on-S CO15 195 C2
George Comberton Wlk 3 E12 352 A7
George Crooks Ho RM17 378 B8
George Ct CM2 232 B1
George Cut CO7 192 F6
George Davies Lodge IG6 333 C6
George Frost Cl IP4 17 D7
George Gent Cl CB9 27 B6
George Green Villas CM22 173 B8
George La Glemsford CO10 2 B3
George La *continued*
Wanstead E18 332 B8
Woodford E18 310 A1
George Lovell Dr EN3 265 A2
George Rd Braintree CM7 127 D2
Chingford E4 309 A4
Georges Dr CM15 293 F4
George St Barking IG11 352 C5
Chelmsford CM2 232 B1
12 Colchester CO1 135 F7
Grays RM17 378 A8
Harwich CO12 91 D6
Romford RM1 335 F5
Saffron Walden CB10 22 D1
Southend-on-S SS3 368 G6
George Tilbury Ho RM16 374 B4
Georgeville Gdns IG6 333 B7
George Williams Ho RM7 335 F4
George Williams Way CO1 136 A6
George Yd 7 CM7 127 F3
Georgian Ct IP11 381 D5
Gepp Pl CM2 233 B4
Gepps Cl CM1 177 D2
Gerald Rd RM8 334 F3
Geralds Ave IP4 18 A5
Geranium Cl CO16 195 C4
Geranium Wlk CO4 136 D7
Gerard Ave CM23 145 E4
Gerard Gdns RM13 354 E3
Gerard Rd CO16 195 C6
Gerboa Ct 7 E4 309 D5
Gernon Cl Broomfield CM1 208 B3
Rainham RM13 355 D3
Gernon Rd CO7 111 E7
Gernons SS16 341 F4
Gerpins La RM14 356 A4
Gerrard Cres CM14 316 C7
Gershwin Bvd CM8 211 F7
Gertrude Rd DA17 369 A2
Gestingthorpe Rd CO10 31 F4
Geylen Rd SS8 364 E4
Ghyllgrove SS14 342 B7
Ghyllgrove Cl SS14 342 B8
Ghyllgrove Jun & Inf Sch SS14 342 A7
Gibbards Cott 1 IG11 352 F5
Gibb Croft CM18 223 F4
Gibbfield Cl RM6 334 E8
Gibbons Ct CM6 123 D1
Gibbons St 3 IP1 17 A6
Gibbs Field CM23 145 D5
Gibcracks SS14 342 E6
Gibraltar Cl CM13 316 C4
Gibraltar Ho CM13 316 C4
Gibson Cl
North Weald Bassett CM16 247 C6
Saffron Walden CB10 22 D1
Gibson Ct Harlow CM18 223 E5
7 Romford RM1 335 E5
Gibson Gdns CB10 22 D1
Gibson Rd
Dagenham RM8 334 C3
Sible Hedingham CO9 51 D1
Gibson Vale CM1 232 B8
Gibson Way CB10 22 D1
Gidea Ave RM2 336 A8
Gidea Cl Romford RM2 336 A8
South Ockendon RM15 357 C2
Gidea Park Coll RM2 336 A8
Gidea Park Prim Sch RM2 336 A8
Gidea Park Sta RM2 336 B7
Gideon Cl DA17 369 B2
Gideons Way SS17 360 E3
Giffards Jun & Inf Schs SS17 360 F4
Giffins Cl CM7 127 F1
Gifford Cl IP9 62 D5
Gifford Gn SS13 343 B5
Gifford Pl CM14 316 D5
Gifford Rd SS7 344 D5
Giffords Cross Ave SS17 361 A4
Giffords Cross Rd SS17 361 B3
Giffordside RM16 374 B1
Giffords Pl IP4 18 F6
Gifhorn Rd SS8 364 E3
Gilberd Ct CO4 110 C6
Gilberd Ho CO3 135 A7
Gilberd Rd CO2 136 B4
Gilberd Sch The CO4 110 B5
Gilbert Calvin Prim Sch IG5 311 A1
Gilbert Cl Rayleigh SS6 323 F2
Swanscombe DA10 377 D1
Gilbert Dr SS16 341 A5
Gilbert Rd
Belvedere DA17 369 A3
Clare CO10 12 B8
Grays RM16 372 C3
Romford RM1 335 F7
Gilbert Way CM7 128 C5
Gilbey Ave CM23 146 B6
Gilbey Cotts CM22 94 C1
Gilbey Cres CM24 119 E8
Gilbey Gn CB11 42 F1
Gilchrist Way CM7 127 E4
Gilda Terr CM77 127 B2
Gildborne Cl SS17 361 D5
Gilden Cl CM17 200 E4
Gilden Way CM17 200 D3
Gilderdale Cl CO4 110 D3
Gilders CM21 172 D2
Gilders Way CO16 195 C5
Giles Cl RM13 355 D3
Gillam Way RM13 355 A6
Gill Cl CM9 236 F6
Gillian Cres RM2 314 C1
Gilliflower Ho EN11 221 A5
Gillingham Ho 14 RM3 314 E5
Gills Ave SS8 364 C4
Gill The SS7 345 D5
Gillwell La E4 287 D5
Gilmore Way CM2 255 B6

Gilmour Rise CM12 ....296 F1
Gilpin's Gallop SG12 ....197 B4
Gilpin Way CM7 ....154 C7
Gilroy Cl RM13 ....354 F6
Gilsland IP9 ....26 E4
Gilson Cl CM2 ....232 F2
Gilstead Hall Mews Cotts CM14 ....293 A4
Gilstead Ho IG11 ......353 B3
Gilston Pk CM20 ....199 C7
Gilwell Cl E4 ....287 B5
Gilwell Park Cl CO13 ..135 A4
Gimli Watch CM3 ......301 D6
Gimson Cl CM8 ....183 F2
Gippeswyk SS14 ....17 B4
Gippeswyk Ave IP2 .....17 A4
Gippeswyk Rd IP2 .....17 B4
Gipping Cl CB9 ....8 E6
Gipping Way IP8 ....16 B6
Gipping Way SS9 ......346 D6
Gipsy La
  Bishop's Stortford CM23, CM24 ....121 A4
  Grays RM17 ....378 C8
Girling St CO10 ......33 E8
Girona Cl RM16 ....372 C3
Girton Rd CB9 ....9 B7
Girton Way IP7 ....16 F1
Gisborne Gdns RM13 ..354 F2
Gladden Ct CM8 ......223 E4
Gladden Fields CM3 ..301 C6
Glade Bsns Ctr The RM20 ....371 F1
Glade Cl IG5 ....310 F2
Glade Prim Sch IG5 ..310 F2
Gladeswood Rd DA17 ..369 B2
Glade The Basildon SS16 ...342 C4
  Brentwood CM13 ....295 A1
  Colchester CO4 ....110 F2
  Upminster RM14 ....356 C7
  Woodford, Clayhall IG5 ..310 F2
  Woodford, Woodford Fells IG8 ....310 B7
Gladeview CO15 ......195 F7
Gladeway The EN9 ....265 F6
Gladiator Way CO2 ...135 A2
Gladstone Cl CM2 ....232 B1
Gladstone Gdns SS4 ..323 C1
Gladstone Rd
  Buckhurst Hill IG9 ..288 C1
  Colchester CO1 ....136 B5
  Hockley SS5 ....346 A6
  Hoddesdon EN11 ....221 B7
  Ipswich IP3 ....17 F5
  Tiptree CO5 ....186 D4
Gladwin Rd CO2 .....135 D4
Gladwyns SS15 ......341 E7
Glamis Cl CB9 ......9 B8
Glamis Dr RM11 .....336 E3
Glamis Ho CM14 .....316 C6
Glamorgan Rd IP2 ...17 B1
Glan Avon Mews CM17 ..224 C7
Glanmead CM15 ......294 E1
Glanmire CM11 ......297 D2
Glanthams Cl CM15 ..316 F8
Glanthams Rd CM15 ..316 F8
Glanville Dr RM11 ..336 F3
Glasseys La SS6 ....345 C8
Glastonbury Ave IG8 ..310 D4
Glastonbury Chase SS0 ..347 B5
Glastonbury Cl IP2 ..16 F1
Glebe Ave Braintree CM7 ..127 F6
  Woodford IG8 ......310 A3
Glebe Cl Elmstead CO7 ..138 A3
  Great Wakering SS3 ..350 D3
  Rayleigh SS6 ......323 C3
  Southend-on-S SS1 ..367 E8
  Sproughton IP8 ....16 A1
  Tattingstone IP9 ..61 C7
  Wix CO11 ....115 C5
Glebe Cres
  Broomfield CM1 ....208 B1
  Witham CM8 ....183 E4
Glebe Ct CM23 ......146 B8
Glebe Dr SS6 ......323 C3
Glebe End Capel St M IP9 ..35 B2
  Elsenham CM22 ....94 D1
Glebe Field SS14 ..141 C8
Glebefield Rd CM3 ..211 B4
Glebe Gdns Feering CO5 ..158 E5
  Ingrave CM13 ......316 F1
Glebe Jun & Inf Sch SS6 ..323 C3
Glebe La Chelmondiston IP9 ..63 A8
  Dengie CM0 ....263 D1
  Little Easton CM6 ..122 F5
  Woolverstone IP9 ..38 B1
Glebelands Chigwell IG7 ..212 B7
  Great Horkesley CO6 ..82 B4
  Harlow CM20 ....199 F3
  South Benfleet SS7 ..346 B7
Glebelands Ave
  Ilford IG2 ....333 D5
  Woodford IG8 ......310 A1
Glebe Mdw CM1 ......207 E7
Glebe Rd Chelmsford CM1 ..232 B3
  Chipping Ongar CM5 ..248 F2
  Colchester CO2 ....135 C2
  Dagenham RM10 ....54 F1
  Heybridge CM9 ....237 C5
  Kelvedon CO5 .....158 B2
  Rainham RM13 .....355 C2
  Tiptree CO5 ....186 C4
  Wickford, Ramsden Bellhouse CM11 ..298 F1
  Wickford SS11 ....321 E7
Glebe The Elmdon CB11 ..20 A4
  Elsenham CM22 ....94 C1
  Harlow CM20 ....199 E1
  Peldon CO5 ....159 B8
  Purleigh CM3 ......236 D2
  Saffron Walden CB11 ..43 E7
  Tilgate Green CM5 ..225 D5
Glebe View CM2 .....254 B3
Glebeway IG8 ......310 C5

Glebe Way
  Burnham-on-C CM0 ..306 C6
  Clacton-on-S CO15 ..220 G7
  Frinton-on-S CO13 ..170 F5
  Hadleigh SS7 ......345 F3
  Hornchurch RM11 ..336 E3
Glemham Dr IP4 ....18 F4
Glemsford Cl IP11 ..381 B3
Glemsford Com Prim Sch CO10 ....2 B5
Glenbervie Dr SS9 ..346 F2
Glencoe Dr
  Dagenham RM10 ...354 A8
  Wickford SS11 ....322 A8
Glencoe Rd IP4 ....18 C8
Glencree CM1 ......210 B4
Glen Cres IG8 .....310 B4
Glencrofts SS5 ....324 F6
Glen Ct SS7 ......345 B4
Glendale CM3 .....279 E1
Glendale Ave RM6 ..334 C4
Glendale Cl CM15 ..294 E1
Glendale Gdns SS9 ..346 D1
Glendale Gr CO4 ..110 C3
Glendale Ho CM15 ..294 E2
Glendale Rd
  Burnham-on-C CM0 ..306 C6
  Erith DA8 ....369 C2
Glendower Rd E4 ..287 D1
Gleneagles SS7 ...344 B5
Gleneagles Cl RM3 ..314 F3
Gleneagles Dr IP4 ..18 D5
Gleneagles Way SS9 ..346 C5
Gleneagles Way CM9 ..211 B4
Glenester Cl CM11 ..197 A1
Glen Faba Rd IP9 ..221 F6
Glenfield Ave IP11 ..381 E5
Glenfield Rd SS17 ..361 B5
Glengall Rd IG8 ..310 B4
Glenham Dr IG2 ...333 B6
Glen Hazel CM5 ..272 D4
Glenhurst Ave IP4 ..18 B8
Glenhurst Mans SS1 ..367 B8
Glenhurst Rd SS2 ..348 A2
Glenmead IG9 .....288 C1
Glenmere SS16 ....342 D2
Glenmere Park Ave SS7 ..345 B4
Glenmore SS7 ....325 F2
Glenmore SS2 ....348 D1
Glenmore Way IG11 ..353 A3
Glenny Rd IG11 ..352 C6
Glen Rd Basildon SS16 ..342 F5
  South Benfleet SS7 ..344 E5
  Southend-on-S SS9 ..366 A8
Glenridding SS7 ..344 B5
Glen Rise IG8 ....310 B4
Glenside Billericay CM11 ..297 D2
  Chigwell IG7 ......311 B4
  Great Cornard CO10 ..34 A6
Glen The Basildon SS16 ..343 A4
  Rainham RM13 .....355 C1
  Rayleigh SS6 ......345 E8
  Stanford-le-H SS17 ..360 F3
Glenthorne Gdns IG6 ..333 B7
Glenton Cl RM1 ...313 E3
Glenton Way RM1 ..313 E3
Glentress Cl CO4 ..110 D3
Glenway Ct CO6 ..82 B1
Glenwood SS8 ....363 F5
Glenwood Ave
  Hockley SS5 ......324 F5
  Rainham RM13 ....355 B1
  Southend-on-S, Eastwood SS9 ....346 B2
  Southend-on-S, Prittlewell SS0 ....347 D2
Glenwood Ct E18 ..332 A8
Glenwood Gdns IP4 ..18 F4
Glenwood Gdns E4 ..326 A7
Glenwood Gdns
  Basildon SS16 ....340 E4
  Ilford IG2 ....333 A6
Glenwood Sch SS7 ..344 B7
Gleten Rd SS8 ....364 D4
Glisson Sq CO2 ..135 B4
Globe Cl CO5 .....186 D6
Globe Cres CM23 ..118 D6
Globe Rd
  Hornchurch RM11 ..336 A5
  Woodford IG8 .....310 C5
Globe Yd E10 ....33 E8
Glossop Ho ⬛ RM8 ..314 E5
Gloucester Ave
  Chelmsford CM2 ...254 C6
  Colchester CO2 ...154 C3
  East Tilbury RM18 ..375 C1
Glory Rd RM17 ...373 C4
Gloucester Ho IP11 ..381 C6
  Maldon CM9 ....236 F1
  Rayleigh SS6 .....346 A8
Gloucester Cres CM1 ..232 A5
Gloucester Ct RM18 ..378 F5
Gloucester Gdns
  Braintree CM7 ....128 B4
  Redbridge IG1 ....332 E4
Gloucester Ho IP11 ..381 C6
  Ipswich IP3 ....18 B2
  Little Ilford E12 ..332 F1
  Pilgrims Hatch CM15 ..294 B4
  Romford RM1 ......313 C6
  Wanstead E11 .....332 C6
Gloucester Terr SS1 ..368 A6
Gloucester Way CO10 ..15 D2
Glovers CM3 ......180 F7
Glovers Field CM15 ..271 F2
Glovers La CM17 ..224 E3

Glyders SS7 ......344 E1
Glynde Way SS2 ..348 F1
Glynn Rd CM0 ....306 B5
Goat Hall La
  Chelmsford CM2 ..253 F3
  Galleywood CM2 ..254 A3
Goat House La CM3 ..257 F4
Goat Lodge Rd CM8,CM9 ..223 E4
Goatsmoor La
  Billericay CM4,CM11 ..297 F6
  Stock CM4 ....288 A4
Goatswood La RM4 ..292 B2
Gobions SS16 ....342 A4
Gobions Ave RM5 ..313 D3
Goda Cl CM8 .....211 D2
Goddard Rd RM16 ..373 A5
Goddards Way SS11 ..333 D1
Goddard Way
  Chelmsford CM2 ..232 F2
  Saffron Walden CB10 ..22 E3
Godfreys Mews CM2 ..232 B1
Godfrey's Yd CM6 ..123 C1
Godings Way CM7 ..127 E2
Godman Rd RM16 ..374 B3
Godmans La CO6 ..132 E3
Godric Pl CM7 ...127 F3
Godric Rd CM8 ...211 E8
Godsafe CM17 ....200 E4
Godwin Cl Halstead CO9 ..76 D1
  Sewardstone E4 ..265 B1
Godwin Prim Sch RM9 ..353 E5
Godwit Ct CO5 ...158 D2
Goff's La CO5 ...141 F8
Goings La CO5 ...218 D6
Goirle Ave SS8 ..364 C4
Goldace RM17 ....377 F8
Goldberry Mead CM3 ..301 C6
Gold Cl CM22 ....94 B3
Goldcrest Cl CO4 ..137 A8
Goldcrest Cl IP2 ..16 D3
Goldcrest Dr CM11 ..297 C1
Goldcrest Rd IP2 ..16 D3
Goldenacres CM11 ..232 F8
Golden Cross SS4 ..325 D4
Golden Cross Mews SS4 ..325 D5
Golden Cross Par SS4 ..325 D5
Golden Cross Rd SS4 ..325 D6
Golden Dawn Way CO4 ..109 E2
Golden Jubilee Ct RM12 ..336 A4
Golden La Radwinter CB10 ..25 A2
  Thorpe-le-S CO16 ..141 F3
Golden Lion La CO12 ..91 E6
Goldenlond CO5 ..142 D8
Golden Manor Dr SS7 ..344 F5
Golden Noble Hill CO1 ..136 A6
Goldfinch Cl CO4 ..136 F7
Goldfinch La SS7 ..345 A8
Goldhanger Cl SS6 ..323 B2
Goldhanger Cross SS14 ..342 F2
Goldhanger Ct CM7 ..128 D1
Goldhanger Rd CM9 ..237 D4
Goldhaze Cl IG8 ..310 D3
Golding Cres SS17 ..360 E3
Golding Ct 🔢 IG1 ..403 A1
Goldingham Ave IG10 ..289 C7
Goldingham Dr CM7 ..155 A7
Goldings CM23 ...146 B8
Goldings Cotts CM13 ..316 B1
Goldings Cres SS16 ..342 E3
Golding's Hill IG10,CM16 ..289 A8
Goldings Rd IG10 ..289 A8
Goldings Rise IG10 ..289 A8
Golding Thoroughfare CM2 ....232 F3
Goldington Cres CM12 ..296 F5
Golding Way
  Glemsford CO10 ..2 B4
  St Osyth CO16 ....194 A5
Goldlay Ave CM2 ..254 B6
Goldlay Gdns CM2 ..232 C1
Goldlay Rd CM2 ..232 C1
Goldmer Cl SS8 ..368 C8
Goldsands Rd CM0 ..284 E2
Goldsborough Cres E4 ..309 C8
Goldsmith Ave RM18 ..377 F6
Goldsmith Cl RM13 ..353 A4
Goldsmith Dr SS16 ..156 C5
Goldsmith Ho IG8 ..311 B4
Goldsmiths Ave
  Corringham SS17 ..361 A3
  Stanford-le-H SS17 ..360 F3
Golds Nursery Bsns Pk CM22 ....94 C3
Gold St CB10 ....22 D1
Goldsworthy Dr SS3 ..350 C2
Golfe Rd IG1 ....333 D1
Golf Green Rd CO15 ..220 G8
Golf Ride CM17 ..344 D3
Goodchild Way CO9 ..30 A2
Gooderham Rd RM16 ..374 B4
Goodey Cl CO1 ...136 A6
Goodey Rd IG11 ..352 F5
Goodier Rd CM1 ..231 F4
Goodlake Cl CO12 ..90 F2
Goodliffe Pk CM21 ..119 B2
Goodmans SS3 ...350 B3
Goodmans La CM3 ..180 F4
Goodmayes Ave IG3 ..334 A3
Goodmayes Hospl IG3 ..334 A1
Goodmayes La IG3 ..334 A1
Goodmayes Lodge RM8 ..333 F4
Goodmayes Prim Sch IG3 ....334 B3
Goodmans Rd CM6 ..333 B3
Goodmayes Ret Pk IG3 ..334 A3
Goodmayes Ret Pk IG3 ..334 A3
Goodmayes Wlk 🔢 SS12 ..321 D6
Goodridge Ho F17 ..309 C3
Goodwives Rd SS14 ..320 A2
Goodwin Cl CM2 ..232 D8
Goodwins Cl CB11 ..21 E3
Goodwin Stile CM23 ..145 D5
Goodwood Ave
  Brentwood CM13 ..295 F3

Goodwood Ave continued
  Hornchurch RM12 ..355 E8
Goodwood Cl
  Hoddesdon EN11 ..221 A7
  Thundersley SS7 ..345 B7
Goojerat Rd CO2 ..135 D5
Goose Cotts SS11 ..300 E1
Goose La CM22 ...173 E7
Gooseley La E6 ..352 A2
Gordian Wlk CO4 ..110 B5
Gooshays Dr RM3 ..314 E6
Gooshays Gdns RM3 ..314 E4
Gordian Wlk CO4 ..110 B5
Gordon Ave Chingford E4 ..309 E4
  Hornchurch RM12 ..335 F2
Gordon Cl Billericay CM12 ..296 F3
  East Tilbury RM18 ..380 D7
Gordon Cotts RM4 ..291 B5
Gordon Dr CO4 ...110 C5
Gordon Inf Sch IG1 ..333 D1
Gordon Pl
  🔢 Gravesend DA12 ..379 C1
  Southend-on-S SS1 ..366 F8
Gordon Promenade E DA12 ....379 D1
Gordon Rd Barking IG11 ..352 E4
  Basildon SS14 ....369 C2
  Belvedere DA17 ...369 D7
  Chelmsford CM2 ...254 A6
  Chingford E4 .....287 E2
  Corringham SS17 ..360 F3
  Grays RM16 ....373 F3
  Harwich CO12 .....91 B2
  Holdbrook EN9 ....265 A5
  Horndon-on-t-H SS17 ..359 F3
  Ilford IG1 ....333 D1
  Ipswich IP4 ....18 A7
  Southend-on-S SS9 ..346 B2
  Southend-on-S,Westcliff-on-S SS1 ....366 F8
  Wanstead E11 .....310 B2
  Woodford E18 .....310 B2
Gordon Way CO12 ..91 B2
Gorefield Rd RM13 ..354 D6
Gorefield Rdbt CM24 ..121 B4
Gore La CM77 ....127 A2
Gore Rd Rayne CM77 ..127 A2
Gore Terr CM7 ...127 A2
Gore The SS14 ...342 A7
Goring Cl RM5 ...313 D2
Goring Gdns RM8 ..353 C8
Goring Ho IP4 ...109 C4
Goring Rd Colchester CO4 ..110 C1
  Dagenham RM10 ...354 D6
  Ipswich IP4 ......18 C6
Gorsehayes IP2 ..17 B3
Gorse La
  Clacton-on-S CO15 ..196 A8
  Tiptree CO5 ......186 D4
Gorse Lane Ind Est CO15 ..196 A8
Gorse Rd IP3 ....18 B2
Gorseway RM7 ...335 E3
Gorse Way
  Clacton-on-S CO15 ..220 F7
  Colchester CO3 ...134 C4
Gorse Wlk CO4 ..136 F7
Gosbecks Prim Sch CO2 ..135 A3
Gosbecks Rd CO2 ..135 A1
Gosbecks View CO2 ..135 A2
Gosfield Cl SS6 ..323 A3
Gosfield Com Prim Sch CO9 ....102 C8
Gosfield Hall* CO9 ..102 C8
Gosfield Rd
  Blackheath CO2 ..163 A8
  Braintree CM7 ....102 D3
  Dagenham RM8 ....335 A3
Gosfield Sch CO9 ..75 F2
Gosford Cl CO10 ..16 C8
Gosford Gdns IG4 ..332 F6
Goshawk Dr CM2 ..254 B5
Goslings The
  Silver End CM8 ..156 C5
  Southend-on-S SS3 ..368 G7
Gosport Dr RM12 ..355 D6
Gossetts The CM6 ..204 E4
Gould Cl CM6 ....226 C2
Gouldings Ave CO14 ..171 B8
Goulds Cotts RM4 ..290 B6
Goulds End CO10 ..21 E3
Gould Rd CO5 ....54 F2
Goulton Rd CA1 ..208 A1
Gourney Gr RM16 ..373 B6
Government Ct CO12 ..91 E5
Government Row EN3 ..265 A2
Gowan Brae SS7 ..344 D5
Gowan Cl SS7 ...344 B5
Gowan Ho IG1 ...333 F7
Gowan Lea 🔢 E18 ..332 A7
Gower Ho 🔢 IG11 ..352 C5
Gowers Ave SS16 ..254 E6
Gowers End CO10 ..2 B5
Gowers La CO5 ..143 A6
Gower St IP2 ....17 C4
Gowers The CM20 ..200 B2
Goya Rise SS8 ...368 G8
Goyfield Ave IP11 ..381 D4
Grace Cl IG6 .....311 F4
Grace Gdns CM7 ..128 D3
Grace's Cl CM8 ..212 A7
Grace's Cross CO7 ..255 C7
Graces La CM3 ...234 B1
Graces Wlk CO13 ..171 A6
Grafton Gdns RM8 ..333 F5
Grafton Ind Est RM8 ..334 C8
Grafton Jun Sch RM8 ..334 F7
Grafton Pl
  Canvey Island SS8 ..364 C2
  Dagenham RM8 ...334 F8

Grafton Rd continued
  Harwich CO12 .....91 D4
Graham Ave IP11 ..17 C5
Graham Way IP1 ..17 B8
Graham Cl
  Billericay CM12 ..297 C5
  Brentwood CM13 ..299 C4
  Hockley SS5 ......324 E7
  Stanford-le-H SS17 ..360 E4
Grahame Cl 🔢 SS12 ..321 D5
Grahame Ho SS2 ..348 C3
Graham James Prim Sch SS17 ....360 F3
Graham Mans 🔢 IG11 ..353 A5
Graham Rd
  Felixstowe IP11 ..381 D5
  Ipswich IP1 ......17 B7
Grahams Ct IG6 ...145 D8
Grailands CM23 ..145 D8
Grainger Cl SS2 ..348 A1
Grainger Rd SS2 ..348 A1
Grainger Road Ind Est SS2 ....348 A1
Grammar School Pl 🔢 CO10 ....33 E7
Grampian SS0 ....347 E1
Grampian Gr CM1 ..231 D6
Grampian The EN9 ..265 F7
Granary Barn Mus The* CO7 ....85 D7
Granary Cl CM3 ..282 B5
Granary Ct
  Dagenham RM6 ...334 D4
  Great Dunmow CM6 ..150 D7
  Sawbridgeworth CM21 ..172 E2
Granary Mdw CM15 ..272 E3
Granary The Clare CO10 ..12 B6
  Roydon CM19 .....198 B1
  Stansted Abbotts SG12 ..197 C3
Granby Rd DA11 ..378 D1
Grand Court W SS9 ..365 F8
Grand Ct Dagenham RM8 ..334 E1
  Frinton-on-S CO13 ..170 F3
Grand Dr SS9 ....365 F8
Grand Par SS9 ...365 F8
Grand The CO13 ..170 F3
Grandview Rd SS7 ..344 F7
Grange Ave Mayland CM3 ..283 C7
  South Benfleet SS7 ..346 A5
  Wickford SS12 ...121 C6
  Woodford IG8 ....310 A3
Grange Cl Felixstowe IP11 ..381 C5
  Halstead CO9 ....103 E7
  Ingrave CM13 ....317 C5
  Southend-on-S SS9 ..346 E3
  Walton-on-t-N CO14 ..171 A7
  Woodford IG8 ....310 A3
Grange Com Prim Sch IP11 ....381 B4
Grange Cres Chigwell IG7 ..311 D5
  🔢 Dartford DA2 ..376 B1
Grange Ct
  Chelmsford CM2 ..253 F7
  Clacton-on-S CO16 ..195 A4
  Loughton IG10 ...288 D4
  Waltham Abbey EN9 ..265 C5
Grange Farm Ave IP11 ..381 B5
Grange Farm Rd CO2 ..136 D4
Grange Gdns
  Rayleigh SS6 ....323 B3
  Southend-on-S SS1 ..368 A6
Grange Hill CO6 ..130 F1
Grange Hill Sta IG7 ..311 D6
Grange Ho IG11 ..352 D4
Grange La
  Little Dunmow CM6 ..151 C7
  Roydon CM19 ....130 F2
Grange Par CM11 ..319 C7
Grange Park Dr SS9 ..346 F2
Grange Pk CO5 ..118 F1
Grange Prim Sch SS12 ..321 B6
Granger Ave CM9 ..236 D4
Granger Row RM1 ..231 F6
Granger Way RM1 ..336 A5
Grange Rd Aveley RM15 ..371 C5
  Basildon SS13 ...343 E8
  Billericay CM11 ..319 D7
  Bishop's Stortford CM23 ..118 F1
  Hoddesdon EN11 ..221 A5
  Waltham Abbey EN9 ..265 D2
  🔢 Wanstead E18 ..332 A8
Grange The
  Bishop's Stortford CM23 ..118 F1
  Felixstowe IP11 ..381 B4
  Grays RM17 ....373 B8
  Great Horkesley CO6 ..109 F7
  Harwich CO12 ....91 A3
  Ickleton CB10 ...20 A8
  Ilford IG1 ....352 C8
  Ipswich IP4 ......85 F1
  Little Bromley CO11 ..112 E7
  Pleshey CM3 .....178 E2
  Romford RM3 .....314 B4
  Southend-on-S SS9 ..346 D1
  Thundersley SS7 ..344 F7
  Tillingham CM0 ..264 A1
  Tiptree CO5 ......186 A6
  Wickford SS11 ...299 C2
  Wickham Bishops CM8 ..212 E4
Grangeway
  Thundersley SS7 ..345 A6
  Woodford IG8 ....310 C6
Grange Way CO2 ..136 D3
Grangeway Gdns IG4 ..332 E6
Grange Wlk CM23 ..146 A7
Grangewood SS7 ..344 D5
Grangewood Ave
  Grays RM16 ......373 B6
  Rainham RM13 ...355 C1
Grangewood Cl CM13 ..317 A7

Granites Chase CM11 ..319 F5
Granta Cl CB10 ..3 D1
Granta Cotts CB10 ..3 C2
Grant Cl 🔢 SS12 ..321 E5
Grant Ct 🔢 E4 ..287 C1
Grantham Ave CM77 ..154 B7
Grantham Cres IP2 ..17 A2
Grantham Ct
  Colchester CO1 ...136 A7
  Dagenham RM6 ...334 F4
Grantham Gdns RM6 ..334 F4
Grantham Lodge SS9 ..346 D1
Grantham Rd
  Great Horkesley CO6 ..109 B7
  Ilford IG1 ....333 A1
  Little Ilford E12 ..352 A8
Grantham Way RM16 ..373 A5
Grantley Cl CO6 ..133 C5
Grantock Rd E17 ..309 D2
Grantown Rd RM4 ..336 F2
Grants Ct CO14 ..171 C8
Granville Cl
  Billericay CM12 ..296 F5
  South Benfleet SS7 ..344 E4
  West Bergholt CO6 ..108 E3
Granville Gdns EN11 ..197 A2
Granville Rd
  Clacton-on-S CO15 ..195 F3
  Colchester CO1 ...136 B5
  Epping CM16 .....246 B2
  Felixstowe IP11 ..381 D3
  Hockley SS5 ......302 F1
  Ilford IG1 ....333 B2
  Woodford E18 ....310 B1
Granville St 🔢 IP11 ..17 B6
Granville Terr 🔢 CM0 ..306 C4
Granville Way CO7 ..193 A7
Grapnells SS16 ..342 F4
Grapnells Farm Cotts SS4 ....306 A2
Grasby Cl CO7 ...137 B2
Grasmead Ave SS9 ..346 F2
Grasmere Ave SS5 ..301 D3
Grasmere Cl
  Great Notley CM77 ..154 C6
  Ipswich IP3 ......18 B1
  Loughton IG10 ...288 F7
Grasmere Gdns
  Kirby Cross CO13 ..170 F7
  Redbridge IG4 ...332 F6
  Romford RM3 .....323 D2
Grasmere Rd
  Canvey Island SS8 ..363 E3
  Thundersley SS7 ..344 E6
Grass Croft RM17 ..373 B1
Grassfields CO13 ..170 C6
Grasmere CO4 ...110 B5
Grassmere Rd RM11 ..336 F3
Gratmore Gn SS14 ..342 F3
Gravel Cl IG7 ...312 A8
Gravel Hill Loughton IG10 ..266 A1
  Nayland CO6 .....56 A2
Gravel Hill Way CO12 ..90 F1
Gravel La IG7 ...290 A3
Gravelly La CM3 ..230 C3
Gravel Pit Farm CM19 ..223 C6
Gravel Pit La CO11 ..60 E2
Gravel Rd SS9 ...346 C4
Gravel The CO6 ..130 F2
Gravesend & North Kent Hospl DA11 ......379 A1
Gravesham Sta DA11 ..379 B1
Gravesham Mus* DA11 ..379 B3
Gray Ave RM8 ...334 F3
Gray Gdns RM13 ..355 A6
Graylands RM17 ..377 E8
Grayling Cl CM7 ..127 E1
Grayling Dr CO4 ..110 F1
Grayling Rd IP8 ..36 C8
Gray Rd CO3 ....135 D6
Grays Ave SS16 ..341 C1
Grays Cl CO5 ....218 D6
Grays Convent High Sch RM17 ....373 B2
Grays Cotts RM14 ..337 D7
Grays Cotts CO1 ..136 B7
Grays Ct CM23 ...145 E8
Grays End Cl RM17 ..373 A3
Grays La CM7 ...73 E4
Grays Mead CO7 ..51 D2
Grayshott Rd SS16 ..323 E2
Grays Sch The RM17 ..373 B3
Grays Sch Ctr RM17 ..378 A8
Grays Sta RM17 ..378 A8
Grays Wlk CM13 ..295 D2
Great Baddow High Sch CM2 ....254 D6
Great Bardfield Cage* CM7 ....72 B2
Great Bardfield Cottage Mus* CM7 .....72 A1
Great Bardfield Prim Sch CM7 ....72 C1
Great Bentley Prim Sch CO7 ....166 E7
Great Bentley Rd CO7 ..166 E8
Great Bentley Sta CO7 ..166 F8
Great Berry Farm Chase SS16 ....341 A6
Great Berry La SS16 ..341 A5
Great Berry Prim Sch SS16 ....340 F4
Great Bradfords Jun & Inf Sch CM7 ....128 B4
Great Brays CM18 ..224 A7
Great Burches Rd SS7 ..345 B7
Great Canfield Rd CM22 ..148 D5
Great Chesterford CE Prim Sch CB10 ....3 D2
Great Chesterford Sta CB10 ..3 C1

Great Chesterford Sta
CB10 ....3 C1
Great Cob CM1 ....232 E5
Great Colman St 4 IP4 17 D6
Great Cornard City Pk*
CO10 ....C4 C4
Great Cornard Mid Sch
CO10 ....C4 C4
Great Cornard Upper Sch &
Tech Coll CO10 ....34 B4
Great Cullings RM7 ....335 E2
Great Dunmow CE Jun Sch
CM6 ....150 C8
Great Dunmow Inf Sch
CM6 ....123 D1
Great Eastern Ave 2 SS2 348 A1
Great Eastern CI CM23 .146 A6
Great Eastern Ct CO14 .171 C7
Great Eastern Rd
Brentwood CM14 ......316 C6
Hockley SS5 ....324 E6
Sudbury CO10 ....33 F7
Great Eastern Sq IP11 .381 E5
Great Easton CE Prim Sch
CM6 ....123 A8
Greate House Farm Rd
CO2 ....162 A5
Great Field IP11 ....381 A8
Greatfields Rd IG11 ...352 D2
Great Fleete Way SS11 .353 C3
Great Fox Mdw CM15 ...271 F1
Great Galley CI IG11 ...353 C2
Great Gardens Rd RM11 336 C5
Great Gibcracks Chase
CM2 ....256 A2
Great Gipping St IP1 ...17 B5
Great Godfreys CM1 ....230 F1
Great Gregorie SS16 ...341 F5
Great Gregories La
CM16 ....267 E6
Great Hadham Rd CM23 145 C5
Great Harrods CO14 ...171 A7
Great Hays SS9 ....346 C5
Great Holland Common Rd
CO13 ....169 D2
Great Holland Ct CO13 .172 C3
Greathouse Chase SS17 361 C6
Great Hyde Hall CM21 .173 B3
Great Knightleys SS15 .341 E6
Great Lawn CM5 ....249 A4
Great Leighs Prim Sch
CM3 ....181 A7
Great Leighs Way SS21 .321 C1
Great Leylands CM8 ...224 A7
Great Mdw CM10 ....221 A1
Great Mead SS13 ....349 E1
Great Mistley SS16 .....342 C5
Great Notley Ave CM77 154 C5
Great Oak Ct CO9 ....30 A1
Great Oaks Basildon SS14 342 A6
Brentwood CM13 ....295 B3
Chigwell IG7 ....311 C6
Great Owl Rd IG7 ....311 A7
Great Oxcroft SS15 .....341 B6
Great Pitchers CO6 ....105 A7
Great Plumtree CM20 ..199 F2
Great Ranton SS13 .....343 C8
Great Ropers La CM13 .316 B4
Great Sailing SS11 .....322 A6
Great Sampford Prim Sch
CB10 ....47 A3
Great Smials CM3 ....301 C6
Great Spenders SS14 ...342 D8
Great Sq 8 CM7 ....127 F3
Great Stony Pk CM5 ....249 A4
Great Tey CE Prim Sch
CO6 ....106 C1
Great Tey Rd CO6 ......132 C4
Great Totham Prim Sch
CM 213 A5
Great Totham Rd CM8 .212 F5
Great Tufts IP9 ....35 B1
Great Wakering Prim Sch
SS3 ....350 A3
Great Waltham CE Prim Sch
CM3 ....207 E7
Great Warley St CM13 .316 B1
Great Wheatley Rd SS6 323 B1
Great Whip St IP2 ....17 C4
Great Yeldham Rd CO9 .30 D7
Greaves Ct IG11 ....352 E5
Grebe CI Barking IG11 .353 A1
Ipswich IP2 ....16 E2
Mayland CM3 ....283 A8
Grebe Crest RM20 ......372 A2
Greding WN CM13 ......311 A8
Greenacre La CM4 ......297 E8
Greenacre Mews SS9 ..346 E2
Greenacres
Clacton-on-S CO15 ....196 A5
Coggeshall CO6 ....130 F1
Colchester CO4 ....109 E3
Epping CM16 ....245 F3
Hadleigh SS7 ....345 E3
Greenacres CI RM13 ...355 E2
Green Acres Rd CO2 ...162 A5
Green Ave SS8 ....363 B3
Greenbank CI
Chingford E4 ....309 C8
Romford RM3 ....314 D7
Greenbanks
Southend-on-S SS9 ....347 A2
Saffron Walden CB11 .43 F7
Green CI Chelmsford CM1 232 D4
Epping Green CM16 ...245 B7
Hatfield Peverel CM3 .211 C3
Writtle CM1 ....231 B1
Green Cnr CO7 ....139 E1
Green Ct CO6 ....104 F7
Greendyke SS9 ....363 F5

Greensward Coll The
SS5 ....324 F7
Greensward La SS5 .....324 F7
Greens Yd CO13 ....170 F5
Greens Yd CO1 ....135 E7
Green The
Bishop's Stortford CM23 145 F4
Blackmore CM4 ....272 E8
Chelmsford CM1 ....231 F4
Chingford E4 ....287 D1
Chrishall SG8 ....19 D2
Clacton-on-S CO16 ....195 B2
Colne Engaine CO6 ....78 A2
Feering CO5 ....158 E5
Great Bentley CO7 .....166 D8
Little Totham CM9 .....214 C4
Mistley CO11 ....86 F4
Orsett RM16 ....374 A8
Saffron Walden CB10 .22 D3
Seawick CO16 ....220 B6
Southend-on-S SS9 ....346 E7
Stanford-le-H SS17 ....360 D1
Stansted CO10 ....8 F7
Theydon Bois CM16 ...267 D3
Theydon Bois CM16 ...267 E2
Waltham Abbey EN9 ...265 C5
Wanstead E11 ....332 B5
Wennington RM13 .....376 E6
West Tilbury RM18 .....379 D8
Woodford IG8 ....310 A5
Writtle CM1 ....231 B1
Buckhurst Hill IG9 .....288 B1
South Ockendon RM15 357 D2
Green Trees CM14 ......271 A6
Green Trees Ave CM8 .280 F5
Greenview SS8 ....363 F5
Green View CM16 ......267 E2
Greenway Billericay CM11 297 D2
Bishop's Stortford CM23 146 C6
Brentwood CM13 ....295 A2
Dagenham RM8 ....334 C3
Frinton-on-S CO13 .....170 F5
Harlow CM19 ....222 E8
Romford RM3 ....315 B8
Woodford IG8 ....310 C5
Green Way CO5 ....78 A2
Greenway CI IG1 ....11 F8
Greenway CI SS11 .....333 B3
Greenway Gdns CM7 ...154 D7
Greenways
Canvey Island SS8 .....363 F5
Chelmsford CM1 ....232 B6
Feering CO5 ....158 D3
Gosfield CO9 ....102 F7
Maldon CM9 ....226 A7
Rochford SS4 ....325 F2
Saffron Walden CB11 .43 E7
7 South Benfleet SS7 .344 C2
Southend-on-S SS1 ....367 E7
Greenways CI IP11 ....17 B8
Greenways CI RM11 ...336 D5
Greenways The CO6 ...131 A3
Greenway The
Clacton-on-S CO15 ....196 B7
Wickford SS11 ....299 C3
Greenwich Bsns Pk IP3 17 E2
Greenwich CI IP3 ....17 E2
Greenwich Rd IP3 ......17 E2
Greenwich Way CM0 ..265 C3
Green Wlk
Chipping Ongar CM5 ...249 A1
Loughton IG10 ....288 A2
Woodford IG8 ....310 E4
Green Wlk The E4 ......287 D1
Greenwood 3 IG8 .....310 A3
Greenwood Ave
Dagenham RM10 ....354 B8
South Benfleet SS7 ....344 E1
Greenwood CI CB9 .....8 E7
Greenwood Dr E4 ......309 D5
Greenwood Gdns CO6 .311 C3
Greenwood Gr CO4 ....110 C3
Grove Ctr CM8 ....184 A1
Grove End RM11 ....378 B8
Greenwood Mans 2
IG11 ....353 A5
Greenwood Rd IG2 ....312 B6
Greenyard EN9 ....265 C6
Gregory CI SS5 ....324 F4
Gregory Mews EN9 ....265 B7
Gregory Rd RM6 ....334 D7
Gregorys St CO10 ......33 E7
Grenadier Rd CB9 ......8 C8
Grendel Way CO15 .....196 F6
Grenfell Ave
Holland-on-S CO15 ....196 E6
Hornchurch RM12 .....335 F3
Grenfell Ct CO4 ....110 C1
Grenfell Gdns IG2 ......333 F6
Grennan CI CM13 ....317 D4
Grenville Gdns IG8 ....310 C3
Grenville Rd
Braintree CM7 ....127 E2
Grays RM16 ....372 B1
Sudbury CO10 ....15 F2
Gresham CI CM14 ......316 C7
Gresham Ct 4 CM14 ...316 C7
Gresham Dr RM6 ....334 B5
Gresham Rd CM14 .....316 C7
Gresley CI CO4 ....109 F2
Gresley Dr CM7 ....128 A2
Gresley Gdns IP2 ....17 C3
Gretsed Ct SS5 ....325 F2
Gretna Gdns IP4 ....17 C8
Gretwell Cl CM14 ......316 A5
Greville CI CO13 ....144 E2
Greyfriars CM13 ....295 B2
Grey Friars Rd 10 IP1 .17 C5
Greygoose Pk CM19 ...223 A5
Greyhound Hill CO4 ..138 C1
Greyhound La RM16 ...374 A4
Greyhound Pk SS22 ...348 A1
Greyhound Rd CO10 ...2 B3
Grey Lady Pl CM11 .....297 B3

Grey Ladys CM2 ....254 B2
Greys CI CO10 ....1 C1
Greys Hollow CB11 .....93 D8
Greystone Gdns IG6 ...311 C1
Greystones CI CO3 .....135 A3
Grey Towers Ave RM11 336 D3
Grey Towers Gdns RM11 336 C3
Gridiron Pl RM14 ....337 B2
Grieves Ct CO3 ....134 C4
Griffin Ave
Canvey Island SS8 .....364 C5
Upminster RM14 ....337 E5
Griffin Ct IP2 ....17 D3
Griffins The RM16 ......373 B4
Griffin's Wood Cotts
CM16 ....267 D7
Griffin Wlk CM8 ....376 F2
Griffith CI RM8 ....334 C3
Griffith CI RM16 ....372 C3
Grifon Rd RM16 ....372 C3
Griggs App IG1 ....333 C2
Griggs Gdns RM12 .....355 C7
Grimshaw Way RM1 ...335 F6
Grimstone CI RM5 ......313 A4
Grimston Rd
Basildon SS14 ....342 FB
Colchester CO2 ....134 A4
Grimstone Way CO14 .171 B7
Grimwade CI CO1J 86 D7
Grimwade St IP4 ....17 D5
Grindle The IP8 ....16 A7
Grinstead La CM22 ....173 C6
Groome Ct 2 CO4 ....136 D7
Groom Ho CO15 ....195 E4
Groom Pk CO15 ....195 E4
Groomside CM7 ....128 A2
Grooms La CM8 ....184 A1
Grosvenor CI
Bishop's Stortford CM23 145 D4
Chelmsford CM2 ....254 D7
Ipswich IP4 ....17 E8
Loughton IG10 ....289 B8
Tiptree CO5 ....186 D5
Grosvenor Ct Ipswich IP3 .18 B3
Romford RM3 ....314 E4
Southend-on-S SS2 ....348 A1
Guildhall Way IG10 ....24 A7
Guild Way 3 CM2 ......301 E7
Guilfords CM17 ....200 D5
Guelph's La CM6 ....70 A3
Guernsey CI CM9 ....236 E7
Guernsey Gdns SS11 ..299 D1
Guernsey Way CM7 ....127 D2
Guildford Ct CO3 ....348 A1
Guildford Gdns RM3 ..314 E4
Guildford Rd
Clingford E17 ....309 C2
Colchester CO1 ....136 A8
Ilford IG3 ....333 E2
Romford RM3 ....314 E4
Southend-on-S SS2 ....348 A1
Guithavon Rd CM8 .....183 F2
Guithavon St CM8 ......183 F2
Guithavon Valley CM8 .183 F2
Guithavon St CM8 ......183 F2
Gull Cotts CO16 ....142 D4
Gull Ct CO16 ....141 F1
Gulls Croft CM7 ....128 D3
Gull's La CO7 ....85 A3
Gulph Wlk 1 RM12 ....355 B5
Gulpher Bsns Pk IP11 .381 D8
Gulpher Rd IP11 ....381 E8
Gumley Rd RM20 ......377 F8
Gunfleet St CO14 ....145 C1
Gunfleet Ct CO15 ......196 C4
Gun Hill Dedham CO7 .84 C7
West Tilbury RM18 .....379 D8
Gun Hill Pl SS16 ....342 C5
Gunnels Ct & Hastingwood Ct
6 IG9 ....310 C8
Gunner Dr EN3 ....265 A2
Gunners Gr E4 ....309 C7
Gunners Rd SS3 ....368 F2
Gunning Rd RM17 .....373 D1
Gunn Rd DA10 ....377 E1
Gunson Gate CM2 .....254 D7
Gurdon Rd CO2 ....135 F3
Gurney Benham CI CO2 135 B4
Gurney Cl IG11 ....352 D6
Guru Gobind Singh Khalsa
Coll IG7 ....288 F1
Gusford Com Prim Sch
IP2 ....16 D1
Gustenhall La SS5 ......324 E3
Gutteridge Hall La CO16 142 F7
Gutteridge La RM4 ....291 C3
Gutters La CM1 ....232 C7
Guy Cook CI CO10 .....34 C4
Guys Farm CM1 ....231 B1
Guysfield CI RM13 .....355 A4
Guysfield Dr RM13 .....355 A4
Guy's Retreat IG9 ......288 C2
Gwendalen Ave SS8 ...364 D4
Gwendoline CI IP4 .....18 B3
Gwyn CI CM1 ....209 E1
Gwynne Ho 1 E3 ......332 A6
Gwynne Park Ave IG8 .310 F4
Gwynne Rd CO12 ......91 C4
Gyllyngdune Gdns IG3 .333 F1
Gymnasium St IP1 .....17 B7
Gypsy La CO5 ....159 C6

Grove End continued
Stanford-le-H SS17 ....375 D8
Tiptree CO5 ....186 E6
Woodford E18 ....309 F1
Grover Wlk SS17 ....360 F3
Groves CI RM15 ....357 A1
Groveside Rd E4 ....309 C7
Grove Terr SS1 ....367 A7
Grove The Bicknacre CM3 256 F1
Billericay CM11 ....297 C4
Brentwood CM14 ....315 F6
Clacton-on-S CO15 ....195 F2
Earls Colne CO6 ....105 B6
8 Gravesend DA12 .....379 C1
Great Hallingbury CM22 .146 F4
Southend-on-S SS2 ....348 C2
Stanford-le-H SS17 ....375 D8
Swanscombe DA10 ....377 F2
Upminster RM14 ....356 B7
Witham CM8 ....184 A2
Grove Villas CM7 ....126 A8
Groveway RM8 ....353 D8
Grove Wlk Ipswich IP8 .36 D8
Southend-on-S SS3 ....368 E7
CO 366 E7
Stratford St M CO7 .....30 D5
Hadleigh Road Ind Est
IP2 ....16 D6
Hadleigh Way CO13 ...170 F5
Hadleigh WR CM13 ...102 B1
Hadley Grange CM17 .287 A8
Hadrian Cl Colchester CO4 110 B6
Haverhill CB9 ....9 D7
Hadrians Cl CM8 ....211 E8
Hadrians Way CM9 ....237 A4
Hadstock Rd CB1 ....5 B8
Haggars La CO7 ....138 F3
Haggers CI CB10 ....3 D2
Hagg Hill CM3 ....280 D5
Haglemere Dr IP4 ......17 F7
Haig Ct CM2 ....232 A1
Haig Rd RM16 ....374 A3
Haigville Gdns IG6 .....333 B7
Hailes Wood CM22 ....94 D1
Hailes Wood CI CM22 ..94 D1
Hailey Ave EN11 ....197 A2
Hailey Croft CM8 ....154 D3
Hailey La SG13 ....197 A2
Hailey Rd DA18 ....369 A4
Hailey Rd Bsns Pk DA18 369 A4
Hailsham CI RM3 ....314 C5
Hailsham Gdns RM3 ...314 C5
Hailsham Rd RM3 ......314 C5
Hainault Ave
Rochford SS4 ....325 D4
Southend-on-S SS0 ....347 D2
Hainault Bridge Par 6
IG1 ....333 B2
Hainault CI SS7 ....345 E4
Hainault Forest Ctry Pk*
IG7 ....312 C7
Hainault Forest High Sch
IG6 ....312 B5
Hainault Gore RM6 ....334 E4
Hainault Gr
Chelmsford CM1 ....231 E1
Chigwell IG7 ....311 C6
Hainault Rd Chigwell IG7 311 C6
Dagenham RM6 ....334 C6
Ilford RM6 ....334 D6
North Fambridge CM3 281 A1
Redbridge RM6 ....312 B2
Romford RM5 ....335 C8
Hainault Sta IG6 ....311 F3
Hakewill Way CO4 .....109 E3
Halbutt Gdns RM9 .....334 F1
Halbutt St RM9 ....334 F1
Halcyon Cvn Pk SS5 ..301 F4
Halcyon Way RM11 ....336 F3
Haldane CI EN3 ....265 B1
Haldan Rd E4 ....309 C4
Haldon CI 8 IG7 ....311 A1
Hale CI Chingford E4 ..309 C7
Ipswich IP2 ....16 E2
Hale Cotts DA9 ....377 C2
Hale End RM3 ....314 B4
Hale End Rd E17 ....309 D2
Hales CI CO3 ....135 A5
Haleswen CI IP2 ....36 F8
Halesworth CI RM3 ....314 E4
Halesworth Rd RM3 ...314 E4
Hale The E4 ....309 D3
Hale Way CO4 ....110 B6
Halfacres CM8 ....212 A7
Half Acres CM23 ....145 F8
Halfhides
Brentwood CM16 ......316 C6
Waltham Abbey EN9 ..265 D6
Half Moon Cotts CM21 172 E1
Half Moon La CM16 ...267 F8
Half Moon Yd CO10 ...12 E7
Halford CI 8 IP8 ....16 C6
Halfway Cotts CO5 ....158 D3
Halfway Ct RM17 ....371 A2
Halidon Rise RM3 .....315 B4
Halifax Ho RM3 ....315 B4
Halifax Prim Sch IP2 ..16 D1
Halifax Rd IP2 ....17 A2
Halifax Way CO4 ....104 F2
Hallam CI CM15 ....272 B3
Hallam Ct CM12 ....296 F4
Hall Ave RM15 ....355 C3
Hall Barn CO5 ....158 D5
Hall Barns The CM5 ...270 C6
Hall Bridge Rise CM7 .153 C4
Hall Chase Marks Tey CO6 133 B8
Pleshey CM6 ....178 D8
Hall Cl Great Baddow CM2 255 A6
Henham CM22 ....94 F5
Stanford-le-H SS17 ....360 E4
Hall Cres Aveley RM15 .371 A7
Tilbury RM18 ....379 E8
Hall Dr CO9 ....102 D8

Hadham Ct CM23 ....145 E8
Hadham Gr CM23 ......145 C8
Hadham Rd CM23 ......145 D8
Hadleigh Castle* SS7 .345 D1
Hadleigh Castle Ctry Pk*
SS7 ....345 B1
Hadleigh Ct
Brentwood CM14 ......316 A7
Chingford E4 ....287 E2
Clacton-on-S CO15 ....196 A3
4 Saffron Walden CB10 ..22 F2
Hadleigh Hall Ct SS9 ..346 C1
Hadleigh Inf Sch SS7 ..345 C1
Hadleigh Jun Sch SS7 .345 E3
Hadleigh Lodge 5 IG8 310 A4
Hadleigh Park Ave SS7 345 C3
Hadleigh Rd
Clacton-on-S CO15 ....195 B4
East Bergholt CO7 .....59 B3
Frinton-on-S CO13 .....171 A5
Ipswich IP2 ....16 D5
Southend-on-S SS9 ....346 C1
Southend-on-S,Westcliff-on-S
SS0 ....366 E7

H

Haarlem Rd SS8 ....363 D4
Haarle Rd SS8 ....364 D2
Haase CI SS8 ....364 A6
Habgood Rd IG10 ......288 E6
Hackamore SS7 ....345 B5
Hackmans La
Cock Clarks CM3 ....257 E2
Cold Norton CM3 ......280 B6
Hacton La RM14 ....355 E8
Hacton Par RM12 ......336 A2
Hacton Prim Sch RM12 355 E8
Haddon CI CO16 ....136 C6
Haddon Mead SS13 ...343 A4
Haddow CI CO10 ....1 F5
Hadfelda Sq CM3 ......211 A4
Hadfield Dr CO3 ....135 B4
Hadfield Rd SS17 ......360 D1

Hall Est CM9 238 E7
Hallet Rd SS8 364 E3
Hallett Rd CM6 151 E6
Halley Rd EN9 265 B3
Hall Farm Cl Feering CO5 158 E4
South Benfleet SS7 344 D1
Hall Farm Rd SS7 344 D1
Hall Field IP11 381 C5
Hall Green La CM13 295 D2
Hallingbury Cl CM22 146 B1
Hallingbury Rd
Bishop's Stortford CM22, CM23 146 B4
Sawbridgeworth CM21 173 A4
Halling Hill CM20 199 F2
Halliwell Rd IP4 18 B6
Hall La Brentwood CM15 295 A6
Chelmsford CM2 255 C6
Chingford E4 309 A6
Harwich CO12 91 A2
Ingatestone CM4 274 C1
Ridgewell CO9 29 B6
Romford RM14 315 C1
Shenfield CM15 294 F4
Shenfield CM15 294 F6
South Ockendon RM15 357 D3
Thorpe-le-S CO16 169 B8
Upminster RM14 337 D5
Walton-on-t-N CO14 144 D2
West Hanningfield CM2 276 D6
Hall Mead Sch RM14 337 D3
Hallmores EN10 221 A4
Hallowell Down CM3 301 E6
Hall Park Ave SS0 366 B8
Hall Park Rd RM14 356 C7
Hall Pond Way IP11 381 C5
Hall Rd Asheldham CM0 285 C7
Aveley RM15 371 C4
Belchamp Walter CO10 32 A6
Borley CO10 15 A3
Bures CO8 79 E5
Copford CO6 133 E4
Elsenham CM22 94 D1
Fordham CO6 107 D5
Great Bromley CO7 112 C2
Great Totham CM9 213 C3
Hockley SS5 325 A2
Ilford RM6 334 D5
Maldon CM9 237 B4
Panfield CM7 127 A6
Rochford SS4 325 D1
Romford RM2 336 B8
Southminster CM0 284 E4
Tiptree CO5 186 C3
Tollesbury CM9 216 D1
West Bergholt CO6 108 D5
Hall Rise Sudbury CO10 33 C6
Witham CM8 211 F8
Hall Road Cotts CO6 108 D6
Hallsford Bridge Ind Est CM5 271 C8
Hall St Chelmsford CM2 232 B1
Long Melford CO10 15 C8
Hall Terr Aveley RM15 371 D4
Romford RM3 315 A3
Hall View Rd CO7 166 E7
Hall Villas CM7 72 B1
Hallwood Cres CM15 294 E2
Halsham Cres IG11 352 F7
Halstead Ct 5 SS12 321 C5
Halstead Ho 15 RM3 314 D4
Halstead Hospl CO9 76 E3
Halstead Rd
Braintree CM7 102 E3
Colchester CO3 134 D7
Earls Colne CO6 104 F7
Eight Ash G CO6 134 A8
Fordham CO6 107 B3
Fordham Heath CO6 107 E1
Gosfield CO9 75 F1
Kirby Cross CO13 170 B7
Kirby-le-S CO13 170 C8
Sible Hedingham CO9 76 B6
Wanstead E11 332 B6
Halstead Way CM13 295 C3
Halston Ct SS17 361 B4
Halston Pl CM9 258 F8
Halstow Way SS13 343 C5
Halt Dr SS17 375 B2
Halton Cres IP3 18 C1
Halton Rd RM16 374 C3
Halt Robin La DA17 369 B2
Halt Robin Rd DA17 369 B2
Haltwhistle Rd CM3 301 C8
Halyard Reach CM3 301 E5
Hamberts Rd CM3 279 E1
Hamble Cl CM8 183 E2
Hamble La RM15 371 F8
Hamble Way CM0 306 A6
Hamboro Gdns SS9 346 B1
Hambro Ave SS6 323 D4
Hambro Cl SS6 323 E4
Hambro Hill SS6 323 E4
Hambro Rd CM14 316 D8
Hamden Cres RM10 335 B1
Hamel Way CB11 67 D4
Hamerton Rd DA11 378 B2
Hameway E6 352 A1
Hamford Cl CO14 144 D2
Hamford Dr CO12 116 C3
Hamford Prim Sch CO13 170 F7
Hamilton Ave
Hoddesdon EN11 221 A8
Ilford IG6 333 C6
Romford RM1 313 D1
Hamilton Cl SS9 346 A2
Hamilton Cres CM14 316 C6
Hamilton Ct
Brightlingsea CO7 193 A7
3 Burnham-on-C CM0 306 C4
Chelmsford CM1 231 D6
Clacton-on-S CO15 196 E6
Hamilton Dr RM3 314 E1
Hamilton Gdns
Felixstowe IP11 381 F3
Hamilton Gdns *continued*
Hockley SS5 324 E7
Hamilton Ho IP4 18 A7
Hamilton Mews
Rayleigh SS6 323 F3
3 Saffron Walden CB10 22 F2
Hamilton Prim Sch CO3 135 D5
Hamilton Rd
Colchester CO3 135 D5
Felixstowe IP11 381 E4
Great Holland CO13 170 A5
Ilford IG1 352 B8
Ipswich IP3 18 B3
Romford RM2 336 B6
Sudbury CO10 33 E7
Takeley CM6 148 F7
Wivenhoe CO7 164 B8
Hamilton St
Felixstowe IP11 381 C5
Harwich CO12 90 F5
Hamlet Cl RM5 313 A3
Hamlet Court Mews SS0 347 E1
Hamlet Court Rd SS0 366 E8
Hamlet Ct
Brentwood CM14 315 E6
Bures CO8 79 E8
Hamlet Dr CO4 136 F7
Hamlet Est DA8 369 D1
Hamlet Hill CM19 222 B4
Hamlet Rd
Chelmsford CM2 232 B1
Haverhill CB9 9 B7
Romford RM5 313 A3
Southend-on-S SS1 366 F7
Hamley Cl SS7 344 B6
Hammarskjold Rd CM20 199 D2
Hammond Ct RM12 335 F3
Hammonds Cl RM8 334 C1
Hammonds La
Billericay CM11 319 C7
Brentwood CM13 316 B4
Hammonds Rd
Hatfield Broad Oak CM22 175 A6
Little Baddow CM3 233 E3
Hampden Cl CM16 247 A4
Hampden Cres CM14 316 C5
Hampden Rd Grays RM17 373 B1
Romford RM5 313 B3
Hampit Rd CB11 41 D2
Hampshire Gdns SS17 375 A4
Hampshire Rd RM11 337 A7
Hampshire Villas SS2 367 B8
Hampstead Ave
Clacton-on-S CO16 195 D5
8 Redbridge IG8 311 A3
Hampstead Gdns SS5 324 F7
Hampton Cl SS2 347 E4
Hampton Ct Hockley SS5 324 D6
Southend-on-S,Chalkwell SS9 365 F8
Southend-on-S SS9 346 E1
Hampton Gdns
Sawbridgeworth CM21 200 C7
Southend-on-S SS2 347 E4
Hampton Mead IG10 289 B6
Hampton Rd Chingford E4 309 A5
Great Baddow CM2 254 E6
Ilford IG1 352 C8
Ipswich IP1 16 F7
Hamstel Mews SS2 348 D1
Hamstel Prim Sch SS2 348 D2
Hamstel Rd Harlow CM20 199 C1
Southend-on-S SS2 348 D2
Hamsters Cl CO9 77 F8
Hanbury Gdns CO4 110 B5
Hanbury Rd CM1 253 E8
Hance La CM77 126 F2
Hanchetts Orch CM6 70 A3
Handel Cres RM18 379 B7
Handel Rd SS8 364 D2
Handel Wlk CO4 136 E6
Handford Cut IP1 17 A6
Handford Hall Prim Sch IP1 17 A6
Handford Rd IP1 17 A6
Handforth Rd 6 IG1 333 B1
Hand La CM21 172 C1
Handley Gn SS15 341 C5
Handleys Chase SS15 319 F2
Handleys Ct SS15 319 F2
Handley's La CM8 212 F5
Handsworth Ave E4 309 D4
Handsworth Prim Sch E4 309 D4
Handtrough Way IG11 352 B3
Handy Fisher Ct CO3 135 B4
Hanford Rd RM15 371 C5
Hanging Hill CM13 295 C2
Hanging Hill La CM13 317 B8
Hankin Ave CO12 90 C1
Hanlee Brook CM2 254 F6
Hannah Cl SS8 364 A6
Hannards Way IG6 312 B5
Hannett Rd SS8 364 E3
Hanningfield Cl SS6 323 A3
Hanningfield Nature Trail* CM3 299 B8
Hanningfield Way CO4 110 B5
Hanover Bridge CO5 158 F5
Hanover Cl SS14 342 E5
Hanover Ct Braintree CM7 127 F8
Hoddesdon EN11 221 A7
Ipswich IP4 17 E6
Rayleigh SS6 323 D3
Sudbury CO10 33 D6
Waltham Abbey EN9 265 C6
Walton-on-t-N CO14 171 A8
Witham CM8 184 B1
Hanover Dr SS14 342 E6
Hanover Gdns IG6 311 C3
Hanover Mews SS5 324 D6
Hanover Pl
Brentwood CM14 316 B5
Saffron Walden CB10 22 C1
Hanover Sq CO5 158 F6
Hansells Mead CM19 222 B8
Hanson Cl IG10 289 C7
Hanson Dr IG10 289 C7
Hanson Gn IG10 289 C7
Hanwell Cl CO16 195 D5
Ha'penny Field IP9 62 D5
Ha'penny Gdns IP9 62 D5
Happy Gdns CO5 186 A8
Harberts Rd CM19 223 B8
Harberts Way SS6 323 C5
Harborough Hall Rd CO5 159 E2
Harbour Cres CO12 91 E5
Harbourer Cl IG6 312 B5
Harbourer Rd IG6 312 B5
Harcourt Ave
Harwich CO12 91 A4
Southend-on-S SS2 347 F1
Harcourt Ho 6 E4 309 D5
Harcourt Mews 2 RM2 335 F6
Hard Ct IG8 310 C4
Hardie Rd
Dagenham RM10 335 C1
Stanford-le-H SS17 360 D2
Harding Ho CM16 268 A8
Harding Rd RM16 374 A3
Hardings Cl CO6 133 B8
Harding's Elms Rd CM11 320 B4
Harding's La CM4 274 A7
Hardings Reach 8 CM0 306 C4
Hardings Yd CO7 164 B7
Hardley Cres RM11 336 D7
Hardwick Cl
Great Notley CM77 154 B7
Rayleigh SS6 323 D1
Rushmere St A IP4 18 E5
Hardwick Cres 27 DA2 376 B1
Hardwick Ct
Southend-on-S SS2 347 E3
9 Wanstead E11 332 A5
Hardwicke St IG11 352 C4
Hardwick Rd CB9 9 B8
Hardy SS3 368 D5
Hardy Cl Braintree CM7 155 A8
Brantham CO11 86 C7
Hardy Ct Sudbury CO10 15 F2
9 Wanstead E11 332 A7
Hardy Gr DA1 376 A3
Hardy Rd SS14 342 E8
Hardys Way SS8 364 A6
Harebell Cl
Billericay CM12 296 F4
Highwoods CO4 110 B3
Harebell Dr CM8 183 E3
Harebell Rd IP2 16 F4
Harebell Way RM3 314 D3
Harefield CM20 200 A1
Hare Hall La RM2 336 B7
Hares Chase CM12 296 F3
Haresfield Rd RM10 354 A6
Haresland Cl SS7 345 F6
Hare St CM19 223 B8
Hare Street Com Prim Sch CM19 223 C8
Hare Street Springs CM19 223 B8
Hares Wlk CO10 33 F8
Hare Terr RM20 372 D1
Harewood Ave SS4 325 D5
Harewood Dr IG5 310 F1
Harewood Hill CM16 267 E4
Harewood Rd
Chelmsford CM1 231 E1
Pilgrims Hatch CM15 294 B3
Harewood Terr 20 CB9 8 E7
Harford Cl E4 287 B2
Harford Rd E4 287 B2
Harfred Ave CM9 237 E3
Hargrave Cl CM24 119 E8
Harkilees Way CM7 127 F5
Harkness Cl RM3 314 F5
Harkstead La
Chelmondiston IP9 63 A7
Woolverstone IP9 38 A1
Harkstead Rd IP9 62 F3
Harlech Rd 1 SS13 343 B5
Harlequin Stps 16 SS1 367 C7
Harlesden Cl RM3 314 F4
Harlesden Rd RM3 314 F4
Harlesden Wlk RM3 314 F3
Harley Ct E11 332 A4
Harley St SS9 346 C1
Harlings Gr CM1 232 C3
Harlowbury Prim Sch CM17 200 D4
Harlow Coll CM20 199 D1
Harlow Comm CM17 224 D6
Harlow Fields Sch CM18 223 E5
Harlow Gdns RM5 313 C4
Harlow Mans 2 IG11 352 B5
Harlow Mill Sta CM20 200 C5
Harlow Rd Moreton CM5 226 C3
Rainham RM13 354 F4
Roydon CM19 198 C1
Sawbridgeworth CM21 200 C8
Sheering CM22,CM17 201 B8
Sheering,Matching Tye CM22 201 F3
Harlow Seedbed Ctr CM19 223 A7
Harlow Stad (Greyhounds) CM19 198 E1
Harlow Town Sta CM20 199 D3
Harlton Ct EN9 265 F5
Harman Ave IG8 309 F4
Harman Cl E4 309 D6
Harman Wlk CO16 195 C5
Harmer Ct DA10 377 F1
Harmer Rd DA10 377 F1
Harmer St DA12 379 C1
Harness Cl CM1 232 E7
Harnham Dr CM77 154 C7
Harold Cl Halstead CO9 76 F1
Harlow CM19 222 F7
Harold Court Prim Sch RM3 315 A3
Harold Court Rd RM3 315 B3
Harold Cres EN9 265 C7
Harold Ct RM3 315 B3
Harold Gdns SS11 299 E1
Harold Gr CO13 170 F4
Harold Rd Braintree CM7 127 E2
Chingford E4 309 C7
Clacton-on-S CO15 195 F3
Frinton-on-S CO13 170 F4
Woodford IG8 310 A2
Harold Rise CM9 236 F5
Harolds Rd CM19 222 F7
Harold View RM3 314 F1
Harold Way CO13 170 F4
Harold Wood Hall RM3 314 D2
Harold Wood Hospl RM3 314 E2
Harold Wood Prim Sch RM3 337 A8
Harold Wood Sta RM3 314 F2
Haron Cl SS8 364 B3
Harp Close Rd CO10 33 F8
Harpenden Rd E12 332 C2
Harper Cl RM16 372 C1
Harpers La CM15 272 D2
Harper Way SS6 323 C3
Harp Mdw La CO2 135 D4
Harpour Rd IG11 352 C6
Harpur's Rd CO10 2 B4
Harrap Chase RM17 372 F1
Harridge Cl SS9 346 E3
Harridge Rd SS9 346 E3
Harrier Ave E11 332 B5
Harrier Cl
Hornchurch RM12 355 B6
Ipswich IP3 18 B1
Southend-on-S SS3 349 E1
Harrier Way EN9 266 A5
Harriescourt EN9 266 A7
Harrington Cl
8 Bishop's Stortford CM23 146 A7
Tiptree CO5 186 B5
Harris Cl Romford RM3 314 E3
Wickford SS12 321 F5
Harris Ct SS5 324 E5
Harris Gn CM6 150 E7
Harrison Cl CM13 295 D4
Harrison Ct CM1 231 F3
Harrison Dr
Braintree CM7 128 A1
North Weald Bassett CM16 247 B5
Harrison Gdns SS5 301 D2
Harrison Rd
Colchester CO2 135 F3
Dagenham RM10 354 B6
Waltham Abbey EN9 265 C4
Harrisons CM23 119 D2
Harrisons Wharf RM19 371 A1
Harris Rd RM9 353 F7
Harrods Ct CM11 297 E2
Harrogate Dr SS5 324 F8
Harrogate Rd SS5 324 F7
Harrold Ct CO15 196 A2
Harrold Rd RM8 353 B7
Harrow Cl Hockley SS5 325 A5
Ipswich IP4 18 B5
Harrow Cres RM3 314 B2
Harrow Dr RM11 336 C4
Harrow Gdns SS5 325 A5
Harrow Hill CO9 49 F6
Harrow Lodge RM11 336 C3
Harrow Lodge Campus RM11 336 B4
Harrow Rd Barking IG11 352 E4
Basildon SS12 322 A2
Canvey Island SS8 364 B5
Clacton-on-S CO15 195 F4
Haverhill CB9 8 E7
Ilford IG1 352 C8
North Benfleet SS12 321 F2
Harrow Way CM2 255 A6
Harsnett Rd CO1 136 B5
Harston Dr EN3 265 A1
Hart Cl SS7 345 A6
Hart Cnr RM20 372 D1
Hart Cres IG7 311 F5
Hart Ct E12 352 A5
Hartest Way CO10 34 B6
Hartford Cl SS6 323 B4
Hartford End SS13 343 A5
Hartington Pl SS1 367 B7
Hartington Rd SS1 367 B7
Hartland Cl SS9 346 D7
Hartland Rd Epping CM16 246 A1
Hornchurch RM12 336 A2
Hartley Cl CM2 233 A4
Hartley St IP2 17 C4
Hart Rd Harlow CM17 200 C6
Thundersley SS7 345 B6
Harts Gr IG8 310 A5
Hartshorn Gdns E6 352 A1
Harts La IG11 352 B6
Hart's La CO7 84 B2
Hart St Brentwood CM14 316 C8
Chelmsford CM2 232 A1
Hartswood Cl CM14 316 E6
Hartswood Hospl CM13 316 B4
Hartswood Rd CM14 316 E5
Hartwell Dr E4 309 C4
Harty Cl RM16 373 B5
Harvard Ct
Colchester CO4 110 B4
Rayleigh SS6 323 B4
Harvard Wlk RM12 355 A8
Harvest Cl Marks Tey CO6 133 B4
South Woodham Ferrers CM3 301 D7
Harvest Ct Feering CO5 158 E4
Felixstowe IP11 381 F4
Harvest End CO3 134 D5
Harvesters CM9 215 D4
Harvesters' Way CO6 132 B8
Harvest Ho IP11 381 F4
Harvest La IG10 288 D2
Harvest Rd SS8 364 B5
Harvest Way
Elmstead CO7 137 F6
Maldon CM9 236 F5
Harvey RM16 373 B4
Harvey Cl Basildon SS13 321 B1
Lawford CO11 86 C4
Harvey Cres CO3 134 C4
Harvey Ct CO15 220 F6
Harvey Ctr CM20 223 D8
Harveyfields EN9 265 C5
Harvey Gdns IG10 289 B6
Harvey Ho
4 Barking IG11 352 C5
Ilford RM6 334 D7
Harvey Rd Basildon SS13 321 C1
Colchester CO2 135 B2
Great Totham CM9 213 A4
Ilford IG1 352 B7
Wivenhoe CO7 137 C1
Harvey's La RM7 335 E2
Harvey St CO9 76 F1
Harvey Way
Hempstead CB10 25 F1
Saffron Walden CB10 22 F2
Harwater Dr IG10 288 F7
Harwell Cl CM7 128 D4
Harwich Com Prim Sch CO12 91 E4
Harwich Crane The* CO12 91 E5
Harwich Ct CO4 136 F4
Harwich & District Hospl CO12 91 A3
Harwich Ind Est CO12 90 F5
Harwich International Port CO12 90 F6
Harwich Parkeston Quay Sta CO12 90 F6
Harwich Rd Ardleigh CO7 111 F8
Beaumont CO16 141 F7
Bradfield CO11 87 F2
Colchester CO7 110 F3
Colchester,Greenstead CO1 136 C7
Dedham CO7 84 F1
Great Bromley CO7 139 C6
Great Oakley CO12 116 D5
Lawford CO11 85 C2
Little Bentley CO7 113 E1
Little Clacton CO16 168 E6
Little Oakley CO12 117 C7
New Mistley CO11 87 B3
Ramsey CO11 89 A2
Wix CO11,CO12 116 A7
Wix,Wix Green CO11 115 D5
Wrabness CO11 88 D2
Harwich Sch The CO12 91 A2
Harwich Town Sta CO12 91 D5
Harwood Ave RM11 336 E8
Harwood Cl CO2 136 A4
Harwood Ct RM17 378 C8
Harwood Hall La RM14 356 B6
Haselfoot Rd CM3 233 F8
Haselmere Gdns CO13 170 F7
Haskard Rd RM9 353 D7
Haskell Mews CM7 155 A8
Haskins SS17 360 F2
Haslars Ct CM4 274 C4
Haslemere CM23 146 A4
Haslemere Dr IP4 17 E6
Haslemere Est The EN11 221 D6
Haslemere Ind Est CM23 146 A4
Haslemere Pinnacles Est The CM19 223 A7
Haslemere Rd Ilford IG3 333 F2
Wickford SS12 299 C2
Hasler Rd CM9 216 D2
Haslers La CM6 150 D8
Haslewood Ave EN11 221 A6
Haslingden Ho 11 RM3 314 E5
Hassell Rd SS8 364 D3
Hassenbrook Ct SS17 360 E1
Hassenbrook Ho SS17 360 D1
Hassenbrook Rd SS17 360 E1
Hassenbrook Sch SS17 360 E2
Hasted Cl DA9 377 C1
Hastings Ave
Clacton-on-S CO15 220 J8
Ilford IG6 333 C7
Hastings Cl RM17 377 E8
Hastings Pl CO7 192 F8
Hastings Rd
Colchester CO3 135 A4
Romford RM2 336 B6
Southend-on-S SS1 367 B8
Hastings The SS11 299 D1
Hastingwood Ct CM5 248 F5
Hastingwood Rd CM17 224 E4
Hatchcroft Gdns CO7 138 A6
Hatcher Cres CO2 136 C5
Hatches Farm Rd CM12 318 D5
Hatchfields CM3 207 F7
Hatch Gn CM22 173 B8
Hatch Gr RM6 334 E7
Hatch La E4 309 E7
Hatch Rd CM15 294 B4
Hatch Side IG7 311 A5
Hatchwoods IG8 309 F6
Hatfield Cl
Brentwood CM13 295 D2
Hornchurch RM12 355 D7
Ilford IG6 333 B8
Redbridge IG6 311 B1
Hatfield Dr CM11 297 D2
Hatfield Forest (Ctry Pk)* CM22 147 D6
Hatfield Forest Nature Trail* CM22 147 E5
Hatfield Gr CM1 231 D1
Hatfield Heath Com Prim Sch CM22 174 A3
Hatfield Ho SS4 325 F2
Hatfield Peverel Sta CM3 210 F5
Hatfield Rd
Dagenham RM9 353 E5
Grays RM16 372 D1
Hatfield Peverel CM8 211 F4
Ipswich IP3 18 A3
Langford CM9 236 B7
Rayleigh SS6 323 B3
Terling CM3 182 D2
Witham CM8 211 E7
Hatfields IG10 289 B6
Hathaway Cres E12 352 A6
Hathaway Gdns
Grays RM17 373 A3
Ilford RM6 334 D6
Hathaway Rd RM17 373 B2
Hatherleigh Way RM3 314 D2
Hatherley Ct CB10 22 E2
Hatherley The SS14 342 D7
Hatley Ave IG6 333 C7
Hatley Gdns SS7 344 C5
Hatterill SS15 341 D5
Hatton Cl RM16 372 C3
Hatton Sch IG8 332 D8
Haubourdin Ct CO9 77 A2
Haughley Dr IP4 18 F6
Hauliers Rd IP11 381 B2
Havalon Cl SS14 342 D7
Havana Cl RM1 335 E6
Havana Dr SS6 323 B7
Havant Ho 9 RM3 314 E3
Havelock St IG1 333 B2
Haven Ave CO15 196 G6
Haven Cl Basildon SS16 342 E3
Canvey Island SS8 363 E3
Felixstowe IP11 381 B4
Havencourt CM1 232 B3
Havencroft Ct 3 CO14 171 C8
Haven Ct CM3 210 F4
Havengore Basildon SS13 343 C8
Chelmsford CM1 232 F5
Havengore Cl SS3 350 C3
Havengore Ho SS9 346 E1
Haven Pl RM16 373 C4
Haven Rd
Canvey Island SS8 363 D2
Colchester CO2 136 D4
Haven Rise CM11 319 D6
Havenside SS3 349 E5
Havens The IP3 38 E7
Haven The
Chadwell St M RM16 373 F2
Harwich CO12 90 F3
Havenwood Cl CM13 316 C4
Havergate Rd IP3 38 D8
Haverhill Rd
Castle Camps CB1 7 E5
Chingford E4 287 C1
Helions Bumpstead CB9 8 D1
Steeple Bumpstead CB9 27 C8
Havering Cl
Clacton-on-S CO15 195 E7
Colchester CO4 110 B1
Great Wakering SS3 350 B4
Havering Coll of F & H Ed
Hornchurch RM11 336 E7
Romford, Harold Hill RM3 314 E6
Havering Ctry Pk* RM4 313 C6
Havering Dr RM1 335 E8
Havering Gdns RM6 334 D6
Havering Rd RM1 313 D3
Havering Sixth Form Coll RM11 336 F3
Havering Way IG11 353 B2
Havers Inf Sch CM23 145 E5
Havers La CM23 145 F5
Havers Par CM23 145 F5
Havisham Way CM1 231 E7
Havis Rd SS17 360 E4
Haward Rd EN11 221 C8
Hawbridge IP9 35 A2
Hawbush Gn
Basildon SS13 321 B1
Cressing CM77 155 F5
Hawes La E4 265 C1
Hawes St IP2 17 D3
Hawfinch Rd CO2 162 A5
Hawfinch Wlk CM2 254 B5
Hawk Cl EN9 266 A5
Hawk Cnr RM20 372 D1
Hawkdene E4 287 C3
Hawkenbury CM19 223 B6
Hawkendon Rd CO16 195 A4
Hawke Rd IP3 17 E1
Hawkesbury Bush La SS16 342 B2
Hawkesbury Cl SS8 363 F2
Hawkesbury Rd SS8 363 E2
Hawkes Cl RM17 378 B8
Hawkes La IP11 381 B6
Hawkes Rd CO6 130 F3
Hawkesway CO15 195 F6
Hawk Hill SS11 300 D2
Hawkhurst Cl CM1 231 E2
Hawkhurst Gdns RM5 313 D4
Hawkinge Way RM12 355 C6
Hawkins SS3 368 D5
Hawkins Cl
Cock Clarks CM3 257 E2
Wickford SS11 321 F7
Hawkins Ct CO10 15 F2
Hawkins Dr RM16 372 D4
Hawkins Rd Alresford CO7 165 B8
Colchester CO2 136 D5
Hawkins Way CM7 128 C4
Hawk La SS11 300 D2
Hawkridge SS3 368 C8
Hawkridge Cl RM6 334 C5
Hawkridge Dr RM17 373 D1
Hawks Cl CM3 257 A6
Hawks Hill CM16 247 A4
Hawks La SS5 324 E5

Hawksmoor Gn CM13 ....295 C4
Hawksmouth E4 ....287 C2
Hawksway SS16 ....342 B4
Hawkswood Rd CM11,
 SS11 ....299 A6
Hawkswood Sch E4 ......287 C4
Hawk Terr IG5 ....333 A8
Hawkwell Chase SS5 ....324 E4
Hawkwell Ct E4 ....309 C7
Hawkwell Ho ▮ RM8 ....335 A2
Hawkwell Park Dr SS5 ..325 A5
Hawkwell Park Rd SS5 ..324 F5
Hawkwell Rd SS5 ......324 F6
Hawkwood Cl CM3 ......279 E1
Hawkwood Cres E4 ......287 B3
Hawkwood Rd CO6 ......75 D8
Hawkmark End CO6 ....132 E3
Hawsted IG9 ....288 B2
Hawthorn Ave
 Brentwood CM13 ......316 F6
 Colchester CO4 ....136 E7
 Rainham RM13 ....355 B1
Hawthorn Cl
 Chelmsford CM2 ......254 C6
 Halstead CO9 ....77 A2
 Hockley SS5 ....324 F5
 Takeley CM22 ....148 C7
Hawthorne Dr IP2 ......16 E3
Hawthorne Ct E4 ......309 B4
Hawthorne Gdns SS12 ..324 B6
Hawthorne Rd SS17 ....360 F4
Hawthorne Rise CM8 ....184 A5
Hawthornes CM3 ....258 D1
Hawthorn Pl DA8 ......369 C1
Hawthorn Rd
 Canvey Island SS8 ......364 C3
 Clacton-on-S CO15 ....195 E6
 Great Cornard CO10 ....34 B7
 Hatfield Peverel CM3 ..211 A1
 Hoddesdon EN11 ......221 B8
 Tolleshunt Knights CM9 ..187 A2
 Woodford IG9 ....310 D6
Hawthorn Rise CM23 ..145 F3
 Kirby Cross CO13 ......170 F7
 Sible Hedingham CO9 ..51 D2
 South Benfleet SS7 ....344 C4
 Southend-on-S SS9 ....346 E4
 Woodford IG8 ....310 A7
Hawthorns The
 Burnham-on-C CM0 ....306 A7
 Corringham SS17 ......361 C4
 Danbury CM3 ....257 A7
 Hadleigh SS7 ....345 E2
 Loughton IG10 ....289 A5
Hawthorn Way SS6 ....323 F1
Hawthorn Wlk CM3 ....273 D7
Hawtree Cl SS1 ....367 C7
Hayburn Way RM12 ....335 F3
Haycocks La CO5 ......190 F1
Haycroft CM23 ....146 C7
Hayden Rd EN9 ....264 C6
Haydens Rd CM20 ......223 C8
Hayden Way RM5 ......313 C1
Haydock Cl RM12 ......355 F8
Haydon Cl RM3 ....314 B3
Haydon Rd RM8 ......334 C2
Haye La CO5 ....163 C4
Hayes Barton SS1 ......368 C8
Hayes Cl Chelmsford CM2 ..232 B1
 Grays RM20 ....377 C8
Hayes Dr RM13 ....355 B5
Hayes Farm Cvn Pk
 SS11 ....301 A4
Hayes Hill Farm* EN9 ..243 C3
Hayes La SS8 ....363 F3
Hayes Rd
 Clacton-on-S CO15 ....195 E3
 Greenhithe DA9 ......376 E1
Hay Gn CM3 ....256 F8
Hay Green La CM15 ....272 E4
Hayhill Rd LW 17 E7
Hayhouse Rd CO6 ......105 A6
Hay La CM7 ....128 C3
Hay La S CM7 ....128 C3
Hayle RM18 ....375 C3
Hayley Bell Gdns CM23 ..145 F3
Hayley Cl RM16 ....372 C3
Hayling Gr SS12 ......322 A5
Hayman Rd IP1 ....17 F1
Haymeads La CM23 ....146 C6
Haynes Green Rd CO5 ..187 A8
Haynes Park Ct RM11 ..336 D6
Haynes Rd RM11 ......336 D6
Hayrick Cl SS16 ....341 A4
Haysoms Cl RM1 ......335 E7
Haystocks E18 ....332 C8
Hay Terr RM20 ....377 D1
Haytor Cl CM7 ....128 C2
Haywain The CO3 ......134 D5
Hayward Ct CO1 ......136 D7
Haywards Cl
 Brentwood CM13 ......295 E3
 Ilford RM6 ....334 C6
Haywards Ct EN9 ......265 F5
Hazard Ho DA11 ......379 A1
Hazelbrouck Gdns IG6 ..311 D3
Hazel Cl Basildon SS15 ..319 F2
 Hadleigh SS7 ....345 F3
 Haverhill CB9 ....8 F7
 Hornchurch RM12 ......336 B1
 Southend-on-S SS9 ....346 C2
 Thorrington CO7 ......166 A5
 Witham CM8 ....184 A4
Hazel Ct ▮ Chigwell IG6 ..311 E5
 Loughton IG10 ....288 F6
Hazeldene Rd IG3 ......334 B2
Hazeldon CM3 ....208 C6

Hazel Dr Ipswich IP3 ....18 F1
 South Ockendon RM15 ..357 D2
Hazeleigh CM3 ....232 F3
Hazeleigh Gdns IG8 ....310 E5
Hazeleigh Hall La CM3 ..258 C4
Hazelend Rd CM23 ....119 B4
Hazel Gdns Grays RM16 ..373 E3
 Sawbridgeworth CM21 ..172 F1
Hazel Gr Braintree CM7 ..127 E1
 Dagenham RM6 ....334 C8
Hazel La IG6 ....311 B3
Hazell Ave CO2 ....135 B2
Hazell Cres RM5 ......313 B2
Hazelmere SS13 ......343 B4
Hazelmere Gdns RM11 ..336 C6
Hazel Mews CO7 ......192 E7
Hazel Rise RM11 ......336 C5
Hazelton Rd CO4 ......110 D1
Hazelville Cl CO12 ......90 E1
Hazelwood Hockley SS5 ..324 F4
 Linford SS17 ....375 A2
 Loughton IG10 ....288 B7
 South Benfleet SS7 ....344 B7
Hazelwood Cres CO16 ..142 C2
Hazelwood Ct CM9 ....237 B6
Hazelwood Gdns CM15 ..294 A3
Hazelwood Gr SS9 ....346 E5
Hazelwood Park Cl ▮
 IG7 ....311 E5
Hazlemere Jun & Inf Schs
 CO4 ....136 E8
Hazlemere Rd
 Holland-on-S CO15 ....196 C4
 South Benfleet SS7 ....344 D6
Headcorn Cl SS13 ....343 C5
Headgate CO1 ....135 E6
Headgate Bldg ▮ CO2 ..135 E6
Headingham Ho IP2 ..17 A7
Headingham Ho SS6 ..323 C1
Headingley Cl IG6 ......311 F4
Headingly Cl SS13 ....321 A2
Head La CO10 ....34 B5
Headland Ave CB9 ....8 F7
Headley App IG2 ......333 C6
Headley Chase CM14 ..316 D6
Headley Dr IG2 ....333 B5
Headley Rd CM11 ......297 C4
Head St Colchester CO1 ..135 E7
 Goldhanger CM9 ......238 C6
 Halstead CO9 ....76 F2
 Rowhedge CO5 ....163 F8
Heards La CM7 ....48 C6
Heard's La
 Finchingfield CM7 ......48 D5
 Shenfield CM15 ......294 F6
Hearn Rd RM1 ....335 F5
Hearsall Ave
 Chelmsford CM1 ......232 B7
 Stanford-le-H SS17 ....360 E2
Heath Cl Billericay CM12 ..296 F1
 East Bergholt CO7 ....59 D3
 Romford RM2 ....336 A8
Heathcote Ave IG5 ....310 F1
Heathcote Cl SS13 ....310 F1
Heathcote Gdns CM17 ..224 E8
Heathcote Gr E4 ......309 C8
Heathcote Sch
 Chingford E4 ....309 E8
 Danbury CM3 ....256 E7
Heath Cotts CO3 ......107 F1
Heathcroft Gdns E17 ..309 D2
Heathdene Dr DA17 ..369 B2
Heath Dr Chelmsford CM2 ..254 B6
 Romford RM2 ....314 A1
 Theydon Bois CM16 ..267 E4
Heather Ave Ipswich IP3 ..18 C3
 Romford RM1 ....313 D1
Heather Bank CM11 ..297 C2
Heather Cl
 Bishop's Stortford CM23 ..145 D6
 Canvey Island SS8 ....363 F2
 Clacton-on-S CO15 ....196 B7
 Pilgrims Hatch CM15 ..294 B4
 Romford RM1 ....313 D2
Heather Ct Chelmsford CM2 ..254 B6
 Romford RM1 ....314 A1
 Theydon Bois CM16 ..267 E4
Heather Dr
 Chelmsford CM1 ......134 C5
 Romford RM1 ....313 E1
 South Benfleet SS7 ....346 A2
Heather Gdns
 Romford RM1 ....313 E2
 Waltham Abbey EN9 ..265 F3
Heather Glen RM1 ....313 E1
Heatherleys IP7 ....17 A3
Heatherley Dr IG5 ....332 F8
Heather Way RM1 ....313 D2
Heatherwood Cl E12 ..332 C2
Heathfield Chingford E4 ..309 C7
 Halstead CO9 ....323 D1
 Thundersley SS7 ......345 C6
Heathfield Ho
 ▮ Romford RM3 ......315 A4
 Southend-on-S SS1 ....366 F7
Heathfield Park Dr RM6 ..334 B6
Heathfield Rd
 Chelmsford CM1 ......232 B7
 Holbrook IP9 ....62 D5
Heathfields CO6 ......134 B8
Heathfields Ho CO2 ..136 A4
Heathgate CM6 ....212 D6
Heathgate Piece IP11 ..381 A8
Heath La ▮ IP4 ....18 B4
Heathlands Romford RM2 ..336 B6
 Thorrington CO7 ......166 A5
Heathlands CE Prim Sch
 CO6 ....108 E4
Heathlands Pk IP4 ....18 B4
Heathleigh Dr SS16 ..341 B4
Heath Park Rd RM2 ..336 B6
Heath Park Rd RM2 ..336 B6
Heath Rd Alresford CO7 ..165 B8
 Billericay CM12 ....297 F4
 Bradfield CO11 ....114 D8

Heath Rd continued
 Chadwell St M RM16 ..373 F5
 Colchester CO3 ....134 F5
 Colchester,Stanway Green
 CO3 ....134 D4
 Dagenham RM8 ......334 E4
 East Bergholt CO7 ......59 D3
 Fordham Heath CO3 ..108 A1
 Grays RM16 ....374 A3
 Ipswich IP4 ....18 D6
 New Mistley CO11 ......87 B2
 Ramsden Heath CM11 ..298 A4
 Rowhedge CO5 ....163 F8
 St Osyth CO16 ....167 E1
 Tendring CO16 ....140 E7
 Wivenhoe CO7 ....137 B2
Heath Row CM23 ......119 B1
Heath Sch The CO3 ..134 D5
Heathside CO6 ....108 E4
Heathside Cl IG2 ......333 D6
Heathside Sch IP4 ....18 D6
Heath Terr RM6 ....334 D4
Heath The Dedham CO7 ..85 A4
 Layer-de-I-H CO2 ......162 A6
Heath View Gdns RM16 ..373 C3
Heath View Rd RM16 ..373 C4
Heathway
 Dagenham RM9,RM10 ..354 A6
 Woodford IG8 ....310 C5
Heatley Way CO4 ......136 F8
Heaton Ave RM3 ......314 B3
Heaton Cl Chingford E4 ..309 C7
 Ipswich IP1 ....17 B8
Heaton Grange Rd RM2 ..313 F1
Heaton Way
 Romford RM3 ....314 C3
 Tiptree CO5 ....186 D6
Heberden Ct ▮ RM19 ..371 E1
Heckfords Rd CO7 ......139 E2
Heckworth Cl CO4 ....110 C6
Hedge Dr CO2 ....135 B3
Hedgehope Ave SS4 ..323 D4
Hedge La SS7 ....345 D4
Hedgelands CO6 ......133 D6
Hedgeley IG4 ....332 F7
Hedgemans Rd RM9 ..353 E5
Hedgemans Way RM9 ..353 E6
Hedgerow Ct ▮ E4 ....309 D5
Hedge Place Rd DA9 ..376 F1
Hedgerow Ct SS15 ....319 F2
Hedgerows
 Colchester CO3 ......134 D6
 Sawbridgeworth CM21 ..172 F2
Hedgerows Bsn Pk
 RM7 ....233 A6
Hedgerows The CM3 ..146 B6
Hedgerows The SS16 ..342 E4
Hedgers Cl IG10 ......289 A6
Hedgewood Gdns IG2,
 IG5 ....333 A6
Hedingham Castle (remains
 of)* CO9 ....51 A4
Hedingham Dr SS12 ..321 F6
Hedingham Pl SS4 ....325 D4
Hedingham Rd
 Bulmer Tye CO10 ......32 C1
 Dagenham RM8 ......353 E2
 Gosfield CO9 ....75 E3
 Grays RM16 ....372 C1
 Halstead CO9 ....76 E3
 Hornchurch RM11 ....337 A3
 Wickham St P CO9 ....53 A7
Hedingham Sch CO9 ..51 D3
Hedingham Pl CO9 ......51 E1
Hedley Ave RM20 ......377 C8
Hedley Cl ▮ RM1 ......335 E6
Hedley Walter High Sch The
 ....S5
Heenan Cl SS13 ......321 A3
Heeswijk Rd SS8 ......364 D5
Heidelburg Rd SS8 ....364 D5
Heideck Gdns CM13 ..317 B8
Heighams CM19 ......222 F5
Heights The
 Danbury CM3 ....256 D7
 Loughton IG10 ....288 F7
 Lower Nazeing EN9 ..244 B6
 Theydon Bois CM16 ..267 E3
Heilsburg Rd SS8 ....364 D5
Helden Ave SS8 ......364 D5
Helena Cl SS13 ......324 F5
Helena Ct RM1 ....301 D6
Helena Rd Ipswich IP1 ..17 E3
 Rayleigh SS6 ....323 E3
Helena Romanes Sch & Sixth
 Form Ctr CM6 ....123 C3
Helen How CM1 ......180 F7
Helen Rd RM11 ......336 D8
Helford Ct
 South Ockendon RM15 ..372 B6
 Witham CM8 ....183 D2
Helford Way RM14 ....337 D5
Helions Bumpstead Rd
 CB9 ....9 A7
Helions Park Ave CB9 ..9 A7
Helions Park Gdns CB9 ..9 A7
Helions Park Gr CB9 ....9 A7
Helions Rd Harlow CM19 ..223 B8
 Steeple Bumpstead CB9 ..27 A6
Helions Service Rd CB9 ..9 A7
Helions Wlk CB9 ......9 A7
Hellebore RM17 ......372 F1
Hellendoorn Rd SS8 ..364 D2
Hell Cl CO6 ....109 C7
Helmons La CM2 ......277 A4
Helmore Cl IG11 ......352 F5
Helmores SS15 ......340 F6
Helmsdale SS6 ......363 F5
Helmsdale Cl RM1 ....313 E3
Helmsdale Rd RM1 ..313 E3
Helmsley ▮ E18 ......332 A8
Helmsley Ho ▮ RM3 ..314 E3
Helpeston SS14 ......342 D6
Helston Rd CM1 ......232 E6
Helston Ct E4 ....309 C4

Hemingway Rd CM8 ..183 F5
Hemley Rd RM16 ......374 D7
Hemlock Cl CM8 ......184 A4
Hemmells SS15 ......341 B8
Hemmens Way SS9 ..258 E8
Hemnall St CM16 ......227 C1
Hempstalls SS15 ......341 F5
Hempstead Cl IG9 ....310 A8
Hempstead Rd E17 ..309 D1
Henbane Path RM3 ..314 D3
Henderson Cl RM11 ..336 D7
Henderson Dr DA1 ..376 A3
Henderson Gdns SS12 ..321 E5
Henderson Ho ▮ RM10 ..335 A1
Hendon Cl
 Clacton-on-S CO16 ....195 D5
 Wickford SS12 ....321 D6
Hendon Gdns RM5 ....313 C4
Hengist Gdns SS11 ..299 D1
Hengrave Cl IP2 ......17 A2
Henham Cl CM11 ......297 D2
Henham Ct RM5 ......313 C1
Henham Rd Debden CB11 ..68 E3
 Elsenham CM22 ......94 E2
Henham & Ugley Prim Sch
 CM22 ....347 D4
Henley Cres SS0 ......347 D4
Henley Ct Colchester CO11 ..134 F6
 Ilford IG1 ....352 B8
 Manningtree CO11 ....87 A2
Henley Gdns RM6 ....334 B5
Henley Ho Ilford IG1 ..352 B8
Henney Cl CM3 ....280 F6
Henniker Gate CM2 ..233 A4
Henniker Rd IP1 ......16 D8
Henny Back Rd CO8 ..54 E4
Henny Rd CO8 ....55 B5
Henrietta Cl CO7 ......137 C3
Henry Cl CO15 ....195 C2
Henry De Grey Cl RM17 ..372 F2
Henry Dixon Rd CM8 ..184 D6
Henry Dr SS9 ....346 A2
Henry Green Prim Sch
 RM8 ....334 D2
Henry Rd Chelmsford CM2 ..232 B4
 Ipswich IP3 ....18 B1
Henry's Ave IG2 ......309 F5
Henry St RM17 ....378 C8
Henry's Wlk IG6 ......311 D3
Henshawe Rd RM8 ..334 D1
Henslow Rd IP4 ......18 B5
Henson Ave SS8 ......364 E3
Henstead Gdns IP3 ..18 E2
Henwood Side IG8 ..310 F4
Hepburn Cl RM11 ....372 D2
Hepworth Cl SS11 ....353 A7
Hepworth Gdns RM11 ..353 A7
Hepworth Ho IP1 ......310 A7
Herald Cl CM22 ......145 D6
Heralds Way CM2 ....301 E7
Herbage Park Rd CM9 ..215 B7
Herbert Gdns RM6 ..334 D4
Herbert Gr SS1 ......367 C8
Herbert Rd
 Canvey Island SS8 ....364 C4
 Clacton-on-S CO15 ....195 E3
 Hornchurch RM11 ....336 A4
 Ilford IG3 ....333 E2
 Southend-on-S SS1 ..368 C6
 Swanscombe DA10 ..377 F1
Herd La SS17 ....361 C4
Hereford Ct
 Clacton-on-S CO15 ....196 B3
 Great Baddow CM2 ..255 A5
Hereford Dr CM7 ......128 D5
Hereford Gdns IG1 ....332 A4
Hereford Rd
 Colchester CO1 ......136 A8
 Holland-on-S CO15 ..196 C6
 Wanstead E11 ....332 B6
Hereford Wlk SS14 ..342 F7
Herent Dr IG5 ....332 F8
Hereward Cl
 Waltham Abbey EN9 ..265 C7
 Wivenhoe CO7 ....137 C3
Hereward Gdns SS11 ..299 D1
Hereward Gn IG10 ..289 C8
Hereward Prim Sch
 E3 ....289 C8
Hereward Way CM7 ..73 A2
Herewood Lincoln Ho
 DA11 ....378 D1
Herga Hyll RM16 ......374 A8
Herington Ave CM13 ..295 A2
Herington House Sch
 CM13 ....295 B8
Heriot Ave E4 ....309 A8
Heriot Way CM14 ....295 A6
Heritage Ctr Mus The*
 SS8 ....364 B8
Heritage Quay DA12 ..379 C1
Heritage Way
 Latchingdon CM3 ......282 B5
 Rochford SS4 ....325 E2
Hermes Dr CM0 ......306 B5
Hermes Way SS3 ......368 F8
Hermitage Ave E4 ....309 C4
Hermitage Cl E18 ....332 A8
Hermitage Ct
 Stansted Mountfitchet
 CM24 ....119 D7
 ▮ Wanstead E18 ......332 A7
Hermitage Dr SS15 ..341 C7
Hermitage Ho CM24 ..119 D7
Hermitage Rd SS0 ....346 F2
Hermitage Wlk E18 ..332 A7
Hermon Hill E11 ......332 A7
Hernen Rd SS8 ......364 C5
Herncliff CM23 ......146 C7
Heron Ave E4 ....310 A4
Heron Chase E4 ......317 C3
Heron Cl

Heron Cl continued
 Sawbridgeworth CM21 ..172 C1
Heron Ct
 Bishop's Stortford CM23 ..146 A7
 Chipping Ongar CM5 ..249 A5
 Ilford IG2 ....333 B2
Heron Dale SS14 ......342 D6
Heron Dr SG12 ....197 C3
Heron Flight Ave RM12 ..355 B5
Herongate
 South Benfleet SS7 ....344 B4
 Woodford IG8 ....368 E8
Herongate Rd E12 ....332 C2
Heron Glade CO15 ....195 F7
Heron Mead EN3 ......265 A1
Heron Mews IG1 ......332 D8
Heron Rd Ipswich IP2 ..16 E3
 Kelvedon CO5 ....158 D2
Herons Cl SS14 ......320 F1
Heronsgate CO13 ......170 F6
Heronsgate Trad Est
 SS14 ....320 F2
Herons La CM5 ......249 D8
Heronswood EN9 ....265 E5
Herons Wood CM20 ..199 B2
Heronway
 Brentwood CM13 ......295 B1
 Woodford IG8 ....310 C6
Heron Way
 Frinton-on-S CO13 ..170 E6
 Grays RM20 ....372 B1
 Heybridge CM9 ......237 C5
 Mayland CM3 ....283 A8
 Upminster RM14 ......337 F3
Herrick Pl CO3 ......135 A6
Herringham Gn CM2 ..233 A4
Herringham Inf Sch
 RM16 ....374 B2
Herring's Way CO6 ..107 D6
Herschell Rd SS9 ....346 C1
Hertford Dr SS17 ....342 C1
Hertford La SG8,CB11 ..69 E3
Hertford Rd Barking IG11 ..352 B5
 Canvey Island SS8 ....363 F3
 Hoddesdon EN11 ......222 A8
 Ilford IG2 ....333 E5
Hertfordshire & Essex High
 Sch The CM23 ....146 B7
Hervey St IP4 ....17 D7
Hervilly Way CO14 ..171 B7
Heseltine Ct CO15 ..196 B3
Hesketh Rd E7 ......332 A1
Hesper Rd CO2 ......136 C5
Hesselyn Dr RM12 ..355 B5
Hester Ho CM20 ......199 C2
Hester Pl CM0 ....306 C5
Hetherington Cl CO2 ..163 A8
Hetzand Rd SS8 ......364 F3
Hever Cl SS5 ....324 D6
Hewes Cl CO4 ....136 F7
Hewett Rd RM8 ......353 D8
Hewins Cl EN9 ....265 E7
Hewitt Ho ▮ E4 ......309 D5
Hewitt Rd CO12 ......90 C1
Hewitt Wlk ▮ CM8 ..184 A2
Hexham Cl ▮ IP2 ....17 A2
Heybridge App CM9 ..236 F5
Heybridge Cl
 Clacton-on-S CO15 ..196 B3
 ▮ Romford RM7 ....335 D5
Heybridge Dr Ilford IG6 ..333 D8
 Redbridge IG6 ....311 D1
 Wickford SS12 ....321 E7
Heybridge House Ind Est
 CM9 ....237 B4
Heybridge Prim Sch
 CM9 ....237 C5
Heybridge St CM9 ....237 B5
Heycroft Dr CM7 ......155 E5
Heycroft Prim Sch SS2 ..346 F7
Heycroft Rd Hockley SS5 ..324 F5
 Southend-on-S SS9 ..346 F6
Heycroft Way
 Great Baddow CM2 ..254 F5
 Tiptree CO5 ....186 D6
Heydon La Chrishall SG8 ..19 B5
 Elmdon CB11 ....19 F4
Heygate Ave SS2 ....367 B7
Heymeads Ct CM9 ..237 A5
Heynes Rd RM8 ......353 C8
Heythrop The
 Chelmsford CM2 ......232 D4
 Ingatestone CM4 ......274 A3
Heywood Cl IP2 ......237 B6
Heywood La CM6 ....152 B8
Heywood Way CM9 ..237 B6
Hibbard Ho CM14 ....316 C6
Hickford Hill CO10 ..32 D2
Hickling Cl SS9 ......346 B6
Hickling Rd IG11 ....352 F8
Hickman Ave E4 ......309 C4
Hickman Rd RM6 ....334 C4
Hickory Ave CO4 ....136 D7
Hicks Ct Dagenham RM10 ..335 B1
 Grays RM17 ....369 A1
Hickstars La CM12 ..319 C7
Hidcote Way CM7 ....154 B7
Hides The CM20 ......199 D2
Higham Cl ▮ IG8 ....310 A8
Higham Hill CO7,IP7 ..58 A8
Higham Pl E17 ......309 A4
Higham Rd
 Stratford St M CO7 ..58 B3
 Woodford IG8 ....310 A4
Higham St E17 ......309 A4
Highams Chase CM9 ..239 A8
Highams Park Sch E4 ..309 D4
Highams Park Sta E4 ..309 D4
Highams Rd SS5 ......324 F6

Higham Station Ave E4 ..309 B4
Highams The E17 ......309 C2
Higham View CM6 ....247 B5
High Ash SS17 ......375 A2
Highbank CO10 ......2 B5
High Bank SS16 ......340 F4
Highbank Cl SS9 ......346 F5
High Barrets SS13 ....343 A5
High Beech CE Prim Sch
 IG10 ....288 A8
High Beeches SS7 ....344 B4
High Beech Rd IG10 ..288 E5
Highbirch Rd CO16 ..167 D3
Highbridge Ct ▮ EN9 ..265 B6
Highbridge Ho ▮ CM1 ..265 B6
Highbridge Rd IG11 ..352 B4
High Bridge Rd CM2 ..232 C2
Highbridge St EN9 ..265 B6
Highbury Ave EN11 ..221 A8
Highbury Gdns IG3 ..333 E2
Highbury Terr ▮ CO9 ..76 F2
Highbury Way CO10 ..34 B5
High Chelmer CM14 ..232 B2
High Cl SS3 ....8 F3
Highclere Rd
 Colchester CO4 ......110 B4
 Great Notley CM77 ..154 B6
Highcliff Cres SS4 ..323 B7
Highcliff Dr SS12 ....320 F8
High Cliff Dr SS9 ....365 F8
Highcliffe Cl SS11 ..321 F8
Highcliffe Way SS11 ..321 F8
Highcliff Rd SS7 ......363 E8
High Cloister CM11 ..297 B2
High Croft CO6 ......78 A2
High Cross La CM6 ..149 B5
High Cross La E CM6 ..149 C6
High Cross Villas CM6 ..149 C6
High Easter Rd
 Barnston CM6 ....150 F2
 Leaden Roding CM6 ..204 E6
High Elms Chigwell IG7 ..311 E6
 Upminster RM14 ......337 E3
 Woodford IG8 ....310 A5
High Elms Rd SS5 ....301 E1
High Cloister Clare CO10 ..12 D7
 Harlow CM18 ....224 A7
 Sawbridgeworth CM21 ..172 E3
Highfield App CM11 ..319 D8
Highfield Ave
 Bishop's Stortford CM23 ..119 D8
 Hadleigh SS7 ....345 C4
 Harwich CO12 ....91 B3
Highfield Cl
 Braintree CM7 ......128 A6
 Danbury CM3 ....256 D6
 Romford RM5 ....313 D4
 Southend-on-S SS0 ..347 D2
Highfield Cloisters SS9 ..346 C1
Highfield Cres
 Hornchurch RM12 ....336 F7
 Rayleigh SS6 ....323 D2
 Southend-on-S SS0 ..347 D2
Highfield Ct
 Billericay CM11 ......319 D7
 Ilford IG1 ....91 B3
Highfield Dr
 Colchester CO3 ......135 C7
 Southend-on-S SS0 ..347 D2
Highfield Gdns
 Grays RM16 ....373 D5
 Southend-on-S SS0 ..347 D3
Highfield Gn CO6 ....267 E8
Highfield Gr SS0 ......347 D3
Highfield Holiday Pk
 Clacton-on-S CO16 ..195 F8
 Little Clacton CO15 ..168 F1
Highfield Link RM5 ..313 D4
Highfield Pl CM16 ....227 C1
Highfield Rd
 Billericay CM11 ......319 D7
 Chelmsford CM1 ......231 E4
 Felixstowe IP11 ......381 E4
 Hornchurch RM12 ....336 F7
 Romford RM5 ....313 C4
 Sudbury CO10 ....34 B8
 Woodford IG8 ....310 E3
Highfield Rise CM3 ..283 A3
Highfields Bentley IP9 ..68 E2
 Debden CB11 ....68 E2
 Great Yeldham CO9 ..30 A2
 Halstead CO9 ....103 F8
 Henham CM22 ....94 E1
 Langley CB11 ....40 D2
 Saffron Walden CB10 ..22 D7
Highfields Mead CM8 ..150 D8
Highfields La CO5 ..185 F7
Highfields Prim Sch CM3 ..278 B8
Highfields Rd CM7 ..128 A6
Highfields Stile Rd CM6 ..128 A6
Highfields Twrs RM5 ..313 D5
Highfield Way
 Hornchurch RM12 ....336 F7
 Southend-on-S SS0 ..347 D3
High Gables SS10 ....348 D6
High Garrett CM7 ....102 C2
Highgate Gr CM21 ..172 A5
Highgrove CM15 ......294 B3
Highgrove Ho ▮ CM14 ..316 C8
Highgrove Mews RM17 ..373 C3
Highgrove Rd SS8 ....363 D8
High House Est CM17 ..200 F4
High House La CM18 ..224 A7
High La
 Bishop's Stortford CM24 ..119 F8
 Sheering CM17 ......201 E6
 Stansted Mountfitchet CM24 ..119 F8
Highland Ave
 Brentwood CM15 ......294 D1
 Dagenham RM10 ......335 C1
 Loughton IG10 ....288 F3

Highland Ct E18 ....310 B2
Highland Gr CM11 .....297 B2
Highland Rd
Basildon SS17 ....342 B1
Bishop's Stortford CM23 ..145 F3
Lower Nazeing EN9 .....221 E1
Highlands CO9 ....75 E1
Highlands Ave SS16 ...342 D4
Highlands Bvd SS9 ....346 A2
Highlands Chalet Pk
CO5 ....195 F7
Highlands Cres SS13 ...343 F6
Highlands Ct SS9 ......346 B2
Highlands Dr CM9 .....236 E2
Highlands Gdns IG1 ...332 F3
Highlands Hill CM3 ....283 D6
Highlands Prim Sch IG1 332 F3
Highlands Rd
Basildon SS13 ....343 F6
Rawreth SS11 ....301 B2
High Lift Villas CO4 .....83 D8
High Mdw Billericay CM11 297 C2
High Mead SS6 ....150 C8
High Mdws IG7 ....311 D5
Highmead Rayleigh SS6 .323 B2
Stansted Mountfitchet
CM24 ....119 E8
High Mead Chigwell IG7 311 C8
Hockley SS5 ....324 E5
Highmead Ct
Brentwood CM15 ....294 D1
Rayleigh SS6 ....323 C2
High Oaks Basildon SS16 341 B3
Harwich CO12 ....90 B2
High Oaks Lodge E18 E18 310 A2
High Ongar Prim Sch
CM5 ....249 C4
High Pasture CM3 .....234 D3
High Pastures CM22 ...201 D8
High Pavement SS14 ...342 A6
High Rd
Basildon,Laindon SS16,
SS15 ....341 B6
Basildon,Pitsea SS16 ..343 A4
Chigwell IG7 ....311 B7
Corringham SS17 ......361 C6
Dagenham RM6,IG3 ....334 C4
Epping CM16 ....267 D7
Hockley SS5 ....324 A5
Hoddesdon EN10 ......221 A4
Horndon-on-t-H SS17 ...359 F3
Ilford IG1 ....333 B2
Ilford,Seven Kings IG1,IG3 333 E2
Layer-de-l-H CO2 ......141 A5
Loughton IG9,IG10 .....288 C3
North Weald Bassett CM16 247 B5
Orsett RM16 ....374 A8
Rayleigh SS6 ....323 C1
South Benfleet SS7 ....344 C3
South Ockendon RM16 ..372 E5
Stanford-le-H SS17 ....360 F1
Thornwood CM16 ......246 C6
Woodford E18 ....310 A2
High Rd E IP11 ....381 F5
High Rd N SS15 ....319 C1
High Rd W IP11 ....381 D5
High Ridge CM8 ....213 C8
High Road Ongar (Chelmsford
Rd) CM5 ....249 B5
High Road Woodford Gn
IG8 ....310 A6
High Silver IG10 ....288 D5
High St Axeley RM15 ..371 D5
Billericay CM12 ....297 A2
Bishop's Stortford CM23 ..145 F7
Bradwell-on-S CM0 ....242 A2
Braintree CM7 ....427 F4
Brentwood CM14 ......316 C8
Brightlingsea CO7 .....192 F6
Bures CO8 ....55 F1
Burnham-on-C CM0 ....306 C4
Canewdon SS4 ....304 D2
Canvey Island SS8 ....364 D4
Castle Camps CB1 .....7 E3
Cavendish CO10 ....1 D2
Chelmsford CM1 ....232 B2
Chipping Ongar CM5 ...249 A3
Chrishall SG8 ....19 D3
Clacton-on-S CO15 ....195 F2
Clare CO10 ....12 B7
Clavering CB11 ....65 D4
Colchester CO1 ....135 F7
Debden CB11 ....68 B7
Dedham CO7 ....84 F7
Earls Colne CO6 ......105 B6
Elsenham CM22 ....94 D1
Epping CM16 ....267 F8
Felixstowe IP11 ....381 C6
Gravesend DA11 ......379 B1
Grays RM17 ....273 B8
Great Baddow CM2 ....254 F6
Great Bardfield CM7 ...72 A1
Great Chesterford CB10 ..3 E2
Great Chesterford,Little
Chesterford CB10 .....21 F8
Great Dunmow CM6 ...150 D8
Great Oakley CO12 ...116 C4
Great Wakering SS3 ...350 A4
Great Yeldham CO9 ...30 A1
Greenhithe DA9 ....377 B3
Hadleigh SS7 ....345 D3
Halstead CO9 ....76 E2
Harlow CM17 ....200 C4
Harwich CO12 ....91 D4
Hatfield Broad Oak CM22 ..174 F6
Haverhill CB9 ....9 A7
Hempstead CB10 ......25 F1
Henham CM22 ....94 F5
Hinton CM23 ....120 A4
Hoddesdon EN11 ......221 A5
Hornchurch RM11,RM12 ..336 D3
Ilford IG6 ....333 C8
Ingatestone CM4 .....274 B3

High St continued
Ipswich IP1 ....17 C6
Kelvedon CO5 ....158 C2
Langham CO4 ....83 D4
Lindsell CM11 ....21 F4
Little Wakering SS3 ....349 F4
Maldon CM9 ....237 A2
Manningtree CO11 .....86 D4
Mistley CO11 ....86 F4
Nayland CO6 ....67 A8
Newport CB11 ....67 A8
Northfleet RM17 ......378 C1
Purfleet RM19 ....371 A1
Rayleigh SS6 ....323 D2
Redbridge IG6 ....311 C1
Romford RM1 ....335 E6
Rowhedge CO5 ....164 A8
Roydon CM19 ....198 B1
Saffron Walden CB10 ..22 D1
South Benfleet SS7 ...344 D1
Southend-on-S,Leigh-on-S
SS9 ....365 D8
Southend-on-S, Shoeburyness
SS3 ....368 G7
Southend-on-S SS1 ...367 A8
Southminster CM0 ....284 D4
Sproughton IP8 ....16 A6
Stanford-le-H SS17 ...360 C1
Stansted Abbotts SG12 197 C4
Stebbing CM6 ....124 E5
Stock CM4 ....275 E3
Swanscombe DA10 ...377 F2
Thorpe-le-S CO16 .....141 F1
Tollesbury CM9 ......216 D1
Walton-on-t-N CO14 ...171 C8
Wanstead E11 ....332 A6
West Mersea CO5 .....218 B6
Wethersfield CM7 .....73 C3
Wickford SS12 ....120 C7
Widdington CB11 .....67 D4
Wivenhoe CO7 ....164 B8
High Stile CM6 ....150 C8
High St N CO5 ....218 C7
Highstone Ave E11 ....332 A5
Highstone Ct E11 E11 ...332 A5
High Tree La CO4 .....144 D2
Hightrees CM4 ....275 D2
High Trees DA2 ....376 B1
Hightrees IG IG 316 C6
High View
Birchanger CM23 .....119 D3
St Lawrence CM0 .....262 C8
Highview Ave SS16 ...340 F5
High View Ave
Clacton-on-S CO15 ...195 E6
Grays RM17 ....373 C1
Highview Cl CO10 ....15 E2
High View Cl
Clacton-on-S CO15 ...195 E6
Loughton IG10 ....288 C4
Highview Cres CM13 ..295 C3
High View Ct SS7 ....344 D2
Highview Gdns RM17 ..337 B2
Highview Ho RM6 ....334 E7
High View Par IG4 ...332 F6
Highview Rd SS7 ....345 A7
High View Rd Ipswich IP1 16 D8
Woodford E18 ....309 F1
High View Rise CM3 ..320 C5
Highwood Cl
Brentwood CM14 .....294 B2
Southend-on-S SS9 ..346 F4
Highwood Gdns
Ilford IG5 ....333 A7
Highwood Gdns CM1 ..251 E3
Highwood La IG10 ....289 A3
Highwood Prim Sch
CM1 ....252 A4
Highwood Rd
Edney Common CM1 ..252 C6
Rayleigh SS6 ....324 B6
High Wood Rd EN11 ..197 A1
Highwoods App CO4 ..110 C4
High Woods Country Park
Visitor Ctr* CO4 .....109 F3
High Woods Ctry Pk*
CO4 ....110 B4
Highwoods Prim Sch
CO4 ....110 B4
Highwoods Sq CO4 ...110 B4
High Wych CE Prim Sch
CM21 ....172 A1
High Wych La CM21 ...172 A2
High Wych Rd
Gilston CM21 ....199 F7
High Wych CM21 ....172 B1
Hilary Cl
Hornchurch RM12 ....355 D7
Rochford SS4 ....325 E5
Hilary Cres SS6 ......323 E2
Hilbery Rd SS8 ....364 D3
Hildabrook Cl 2 IP2 ...16 E1
Hildaville Dr SS0 .....147 C3
Hilary Cl Bradwell CM7 ..129 D2
Chelmsford CM1 ....232 D4
Heybridge CM9 ......237 B5
Hildosheim IP4 ......18 A5
Hill Ave SS11 ....318 E7
Hilliboro Ct E18 ......309 F2
Highwood Mans SS0 ..347 D3
Highwood Rd SS0 ....147 D8
Hill Cl Long Melford CO10 ..15 D8
South Benfleet SS7 ..344 E4
Hill Cotts CO7 ......164 A6
Hill Crest RM11 ......336 F2
Hill Cres Chelmsford CM2 232 D2
Hornchurch RM11 ....336 C5
Hillcrest
Clacton-on-S CO15 ...196 A6
Kirby-le-S CO13 .....170 D8

Hillcrest continued
Mayland CM3 ....261 A1
Hillcrest Ave
Basildon SS16 ....340 E3
Grays RM0 ....377 A8
Hulbridge SS5 ......301 E1
Hillcrest Cl SS17 .....359 F4
Hillcrest Cotts CO4 ...83 E6
Hillcrest Ct Harwich CO12 91 C3
Romford RM5 ....313 C2
Hillcrest Dr DA9 ....377 A2
Hillcrest Rd
Chingford E17 ......309 D1
Hockley SS5 ....324 E5
Hornchurch RM11 ....336 C5
Horndon-on-t-H SS17 .359 F4
Loughton SS10 .....288 D3
Southend-on-S SS1 ..367 B8
Hillcrest View CM16 .342 D3
Hillcrest View CM16 ..268 A8
Hillcroft IG10 ....288 A6
Hill Ct Basildon SS14 ..342 C5
Romford RM1 ....335 F7
Hildene Ave RM3 ....314 D5
Hildene Cl RM3 .....314 D5
Hildene Prim Sch RM3 314 C4
Hill Farm La IP9 .....63 F7
Hillfield CO5 ....158 D4
Hillfoot Ave RM5 ....313 C2
Hillfoot Rd RM5 .....313 C2
Hill Gr RM1 ....335 E8
Hillgrove Bsns Pk EN10 221 C1
Hill Hall* CM16 ......268 F4
Hillhouse EN9 ....265 F6
Hillhouse CE Prim Sch
EN9 ....265 F6
Hillhouse Cl CM12 ..297 B4
Hill House Ct CO7 ...193 A7
Hillhouse Dr CM12 ..297 C4
Hill House Dr RM16 ..374 C1
Hillhouse La CO16 ...141 B3
Hill House Rd
Dartford DA2 ....376 C1
Ipswich IP3 ....17 E1
Hillhouse Rd CO7 ...113 C2
Hillie Bunnies CO6 ...105 B7
Hillington Gdns IG8 .310 D1
Hill La Hockley SS5 ..324 F5
Sturmer CB9 ....9 F4
Hillman Ave CO15 ...220 E6
Hillman Cl RM11 ....336 D8
Hillmead Prim Sch
CM23 ....145 C7
Hill Rd Brentwood CM14 316 A7
Chelmsford CM2 ....232 D2
Clacton-on-S CO15 ..195 D6
Coggeshall CO6 .....131 B2
Harwich CO12 ......91 C4
Hempstead CB10 ...46 D8
Ramsey CO12 ......116 E8
South Benfleet SS7 ..344 E3
Southend-on-S SS2 ..347 F2
Theydon Bois CM16 ..267 E2
Hill Rd S CM2 ....232 D2
Hillridge CO4 ....110 B3
Hill Rise RM14 ......337 A2
Hillrise Rd RM5 .....313 C4
Hill's Chace CM14 ...316 C6
Hills Cl CM7 ....127 F4
Hills Cres CO3 .....135 A5
Hillside Belvedere DA8 369 C2
Frinton-on-S CO13 ..170 E4
Grays RM17 ....373 D2
Harlow CM17 ......224 C6
Hillside Ave
Bishop's Stortford CM23 146 A7
Hockley SS5 ....324 F5
Woodford IG8 ......310 C5
Hillside Cl Billericay CM11 297 B1
Woodford IG8 ......310 C5
Hillside Com Prim Sch
IP2 ....17 C3
Hillside Cotts
Birchanger CM23 ...119 C3
Sudbury CO10 .....34 A7
Thorpe-le-S CO16 ..142 A2
Hillside Cres
Holland-on-S CO15 ..196 C5
Ipswich IP3 ....18 C3
Southend-on-S SS9 ..346 B3
Hillside Gdns SG12 ..197 B4
Hillside End CM15 ...119 C3
Hillside Gdns CM7 ...127 F1
Hillside Gr CM7 ....127 F1
Hillside Ho 2 CM7 ..127 F1
Hillside La SG12 ....197 A5
Hillside Mews CM2 ..254 A7
Hillside Rd
Billericay CM11 .....297 B1
Burnham-on-C CM0 ..306 B5
Hockley SS5 ....324 B5
Rayleigh SS9 ....346 C8
South Benfleet SS7 ..344 D1
Southend-on-S SS9 ..365 B8
Southminster CM0 ...284 C4
Sudbury CO10 .....34 A7
Hillside Specl Sch CM7 127 F1
Hillside Terr 8 CM7 ..127 F1
Hillside Wlk CM14 ...315 F7
Hillsleigh Mews CO1 ..136 A7
Hills Rd IG9 ....288 B1
Hill St CB10 ....22 D1
Hilston Cl CO2 ......136 B2
Hill Terr Clare CO10 ..12 C8
Corringham SS17 ...361 C4
Woodford IG8 ......310 E3
Hill The Harlow CM17 200 D4
Northfleet DA11 ....378 C1
Hill Top IG10 ....289 A6

Hilltop Ave SS5 ......301 E1
Hill Top Ave SS7 ....344 F2
Hill Top Cl Colchester CO1 ..2 D6
Rayleigh SS6 ......323 C1
Hilltop Cres CO16 ...140 F1
Hill Top Ct IG8 ......310 F4
Hilltop Jun & Inf Sch
...322 A8
Hilltop Rd Basildon SS15 341 E7
Hill Top Rise CO16 ...140 E1
Hill Top Rise SS16 ...346 D4
Hill Top View IG8 ...310 F4
Hill Tree Cl CM21 ...172 D1
Hillview CM4 ....256 F1
Hillview Ave RM11 ...336 D5
HillView Cl CO5 .....163 F8
Hill View Cres IG1 ...332 F5
Hillview Ct SS6 .....360 F5
Hillview Rd SS6 .....323 C3
Hill View Rd CM1 ...232 C4
Hillway Billericay CM11 297 D2
Southend-on-S SS0 ..366 A8
Hill Way The
Ingatestone CM4 ...273 F1
Mountnessing CM15 ..295 F8
Hillwood Ct CM13 ...295 B3
Hillwood Gr
Brentwood CM13 ...295 B1
Wickford SS11 .....321 E7
Hillwoodgon Gdns CO5 218 D6
Hilly Field CM18 ....223 F4
Hillyfields IG10 .....289 A7
Hilly Rd SS15 ......341 D7
Hilton Cl CO11 .....86 D4
Hilton Rd
Canvey Island SS8 ..364 A5
Ipswich IP3 ....18 C1
Hilton Way CO9 ....75 E8
Hilton Wlk
Canvey Island SS8 ..364 A5
Sible Hedingham CO9 ..75 C8
Hilversum Way SS8 ..364 B5
Hind Cl IG7 ....311 F5
Hindles Rd SS8 .....364 D4
Hindmans Way RM9 ..353 F1
Hind Terr RM20 ....372 D1
Hines Cl CO6 ....133 B8
Hines Rd IP3 ....18 A2
Hinguar Prim Sch SS3 368 F6
Hinguar St SS3 ....368 F6
Hintesham Cl IP4 ...18 F5
Hintlesham Dr IP11 ..381 B5
Hintons CM19 ......223 A4
Hinxton Rd CB10 ...3 A7
Hipkins CM23 ......145 A5
Hispano Mews EN3 ..265 A2
Histon Cl IP5 ....18 F7
Hitcham Rd CO6 ...130 D1
Hitchcock Pl CO10 ..15 E1
Hitch Common Rd CB11 ..66 F8
Hitchin Cl RM3 .....314 C6
Hitchin Mews CM7 ...155 B8
Hitchman Ho RM1 ...335 E6
Hither Blakers CM0 ..301 D8
Hitherfield Rd RM8 ..334 B1
Hitherwood Cl RM12 ..355 D8
Hitherwood Rd CO2 ..135 C4
Hive Cl CM14 ......316 A8
Hive La LA11 ......378 B2
Hive The DA11 ....378 B1
HMS Ganges Association
Mus* IP9 ....91 C8
Hobart Cl CM1 .....231 E5
Hobart Cl IG8 ......309 F6
Hobart Rd
Dagenham RM9 ....353 D8
Redbridge IG6 .....311 C1
Tilbury RM18 ......379 A6
Hobbs Cross Open Farm*
CM16 ....268 D3
Hobbs Cross Rd
Epping CM16 ......268 C4
Harlow CM17 ......200 F3
Hobbs Dr CO4 .....83 A5
Hobbs La CO10 ....2 C10
Hobbs Mews SG3 ...334 F2
Hoblongue Rd SS17 ..360 D4
Hobleythick La SS0 ..347 D4
Hobtoe Rd CM20 ...117 A3
Hockerill Anglo-European
Sch CM23 ....146 B7
Hockerill Ct 7 CM23 ..146 A7
Hockerill St CM23 ...146 A7
Hockley SS14 ......342 D6
Hockley Bradwell-on-S CM0 ..7 B5
Shudy Camps CB1 ..7 B5
Hockley Cl 8 E18 ...310 A2
Hockley Dr RM2 ....314 C1
Hockley Gn SS14 ...342 E6
Hockley La CM0 ....242 C2
Hockley Prim Sch SS5 324 E6
Hockley Rd Basildon SS14 342 D6
Rayleigh SS6 ......323 E4
Hockley Rise SS5 ...324 E5
Hockley SS5 ......324 E5
Hockley Woods* SS5 ..324 A4
Hockney Gdns IP3 ...38 A8
Hoddesdon Ind Ctr EN11 221 C7
Hoddesdon Rd
Belvedere DA17 ...369 A1
Stanstead Abbotts EN11 ..197 E6
Hodgenson Rd IP11 ..381 A3
Hodgson Ct SS11 ...322 A5
Hodgson Way SS11 ..322 B6
Hodskinson Rd RM20 ..296 F4
Hodson Pl 1 EN2 ...265 A1
Hoecroft EN9 ......221 F1

Hoe Dr CO3 ....135 A5
Hoe La Abridge RM4 ..290 C4
Great Waltham CM3 ..207 E6
Lower Nazeing EN9 ..222 A2
Pentlow CO10 .....13 F8
Rettendon CM3 ...300 A6
Hoe Mill Rd CM9 ...235 E4
Hoe St CM1 ....230 D4
Hoestock Rd CM21 ..172 D2
Hoe The CM12 ....319 B4
Hoffmanns Way CM1 ..232 B4
Hogarth Ave CM15 ..316 F7
Hogarth Cl CO5 ....218 D6
Hogarth Ct CM1 ....232 E6
Hogarth Dr SS3 ....368 G8
Hogarth End CO13 ..170 E7
Hogarth Prim Sch CM15 316 F7
Hogarth Rd
Dagenham RM8 ....353 B7
Grays RM16 ....373 A5
Ipswich IP3 ....18 A1
Hogarth Reach IG10 288 F4
Hogarth Sq IP3 ....18 A1
Hogarth Way SS4 ..325 C6
Hogg La RM16,RM17 ..373 A2
Hog Hill Rd RM5 ....313 A3
Hog's La SG8 ......19 D3
Hogwell Chase
Hullbridge CM3 ....302 B8
South Woodham F CM3 280 B1
Holbeck Rd SS14 ...342 F8
Holbek Rd SS8 .....364 E3
Holbourgh Cl CO4 ..136 F7
Holbrook Cl
Billericay CM12 ....297 D2
Clacton-on-S CO15 ..195 B4
South Woodham Ferrers
CM3 ....301 E7
Holbrook Cres IP11 ..381 B4
Holbrook Wlk CO5 ..186 E5
Holbrook High Sch IP9 62 D6
Holbrook Ho SS7 ...345 E3
Holbrook Prim Sch IP9 62 D6
Holbrook Rd
Harkstead IP9 .....63 A2
Haverhill CB9 ......8 E6
Ipswich IP3 ....17 F1
Stutton IP9 ....62 A2
Holcombe Cres IP2 ..16 D2
Holcombe Rd IG1 ...333 A4
Holdbrook Way RM3 ..314 F1
Holden Braintree CM7 128 A2
Dagenham RM8 ....334 B1
Ipswich IP2 ....17 D3
Holden Gdns
Basildon SS14 .....320 F1
Brentwood CM14 ...316 D5
Holden Rd Basildon SS14 320 F1
Colchester CO4 ....109 F2
Holden Way CM14 ..337 D4
Holden Wlk SS14 ...320 F1
Holdsworth Cl CO10 ..2 B3
Holecroft EN9 ......265 E5
Holford Rd SS17,RM18 374 E4
Holgate SS13 ......343 C8
Holgate Ct 8 RM1 ..335 E6
Holgate Gdns RM10 354 A6
Holgate Rd RM10 ...354 A7
Holkham Ave CM3 ..301 D5
Holkham Cl IP4 .....18 F5
Holland Ave SS8 ...363 D5
Holland Cl RM7 ....335 C6
Holland Haven Ctry Pk
CO15 ....196 B8
Holland Ho Chingford E4 290 C4
Clacton-on-S CO15 ..196 A3
Holland Lodge CO15 ..195 F3
Holland Park Ave CM3 353 F6
Holland Park Cres
CO15 ....196 B5
Holland Pk CO15 ...196 B5
Holland Rd
Clacton-on-S, Holland on S
CO15 ....196 B4
Clacton-on-S, Rush Green
CO15 ....195 F2
Frinton-on-S CO13 ..170 E3
Ipswich IP4 ....17 F6
Kirby Cross CO13 ..170 B6
Little Clacton CO16 ..168 E2
Southend-on-S SS0 ..366 B8
Wallend E6 ....352 A5
Hollands Cl CB9 ....9 A6
Hollands Wlk SS16 .342 D2
Holledge Cres CO13 ..170 E6
Hollesley Ave CB9 ...8 C8
Holley Gdns CM11 ..297 B3
Holliday Hill CM7 ...276 F4
Hollidge Way RM10 ..354 B5
Hollies RM14 ....337 B2
Hollies Rd CM7 ....129 C3
Hollies The
Stanford-le-H SS17 ..360 D1
8 Wanstead E11 ....332 A6
Holliland Croft CO6 ..132 C8
Hollington Gr CO2 ..161 A3
Hollis Lock SS4 .....233 A3
Hollis Pl RM17 ....373 D2
Hollivel Cl CO13 ...134 D6
Holloway Cl CM6 ...294 C7
Holloway Cres CM9 ..204 C8
Holloway Rd RM19 ..371 A1
Hollowfield Ave RM17 338 B5
Hollow La Ashen CO10 ..11 E3
Broomfield CM1 ....231 E8
Bures CO8 ....55 F3
Chelmondiston IP9 ..63 F7
Hollow Rd Braintree CM7 153 B4
Chrishall SG8 .....19 D2
Elmdon CB11 ......20 A4
Kelvedon CO5 ....157 F2

Hollow Rd continued
Washbrook IP8 .....35 D8
Widdington CB11 ...67 C3
Hollow The IG8 ....309 F6
Hollybank Basildon SS16 340 D4
Witham CM8 ......183 F1
Holly Blue Cl IP8 ...36 E8
Hollybush Cl E11 ...332 A6
Holly Bush Cnr CO7 ..58 C5
Hollybush Hill
Great Bentley CO7 ..166 E3
Wanstead E11 .....332 A6
Holly Cl Buckhurst Hill IG9 310 D7
Burnham-on-C CM0 ..306 B6
Colchester CO2 ....135 C2
Ipswich IP3 ....18 F1
Holly Cotts
East Bergholt CO7 ..60 C2
Epping CM16 .....267 D7
Holly Cres IG8 .....309 D3
Hollycroft CM2 .....254 C8
Hollycross Rd SG12 ..197 B7
Holly Ct Billericay CM12 297 A2
Clacton-on-S CO15 ..195 E4
Hockley SS5 ......324 E5
Holly Dr Chingford E4 ..287 B2
South Ockendon RM15 ..357 D1
Holly End CM19 ....223 C5
Hollyford CM11 ....297 C5
Holly Gr SS16 .....340 F5
Holly Hill Rd DA17 ..369 B1
Holly Ho CM15 ....294 D1
Hollyhock Rd CB10 ..252 B8
Holly Hoad IG9 ....310 B8
Holly La Belstead IP8 ..36 C7
Hollymead SS17 ...360 E4
Hollymead Cl CO4 ..109 F3
Holly Oaks CO6 ...80 E4
Holly Rd Colchester CO3 134 C4
Ipswich IP1 ....17 B7
Rushmere St A IP5 ..18 F7
Hollytree Ct CO2 ...135 C3
Holly Trees CM4 ...316 C6
Holly Trees Prim Sch
CM14 ....316 C6
Hollyview Cl CO16 ..140 F5
Holly Way
Chelmsford CM2 ...254 D7
Elmstead CO7 ....138 A6
Tiptree CO5 ......186 C5
Holly Wlk
Canvey Island SS8 ..363 F4
Witham CM8 ......184 B5
Hollywood Cl CM2 ..254 E6
Hollywood Way SS8 ..309 D4
Holman Cres CO3 ..135 A4
Holman Rd CO9 ...103 E8
Holmans CM3 .....233 C8
Holmbrooke Way CO13 ..170 E5
Holme Rd RM11 ...137 A3
Holmes Cl SS17 ...359 F3
Holmes Ct
Canvey Island SS8 ..364 C4
Chingford E4 ......309 D8
Holmes Mdw CM19 ..223 C5
Holmes Rd CO9 ...103 E8
Holme Wlk SS12 ...321 F5
Holmhurst Rd DA17 ..369 A1
Holmoak IP9 ......62 D6
Holm Oak CO2 ....136 A3
Holmsdale Cl SS0 ..347 C3
Holmswood SS8 ...364 E5
Holmswood House Prep Sch
CO3 ....134 D8
Hoimwood Ave CM15 ..295 A3
Hoimwood Cl CO16 ..195 B6
Holmwood House Prep Sch
CO3 ....134 D8
Hoimwood Rd IG3 ...333 E2
Holst Ave Basildon SS15 341 C8
Witham CM8 ......211 F7
Holst Cl SS17 .....360 C3
Holstock Rd IG1 ...333 C2
Holsworthy SS3 ...368 D8
Holsworthy Ho RM3 ..314 D2
Holt Cl IG7 ....311 F5
Holt Dr Blackheath CO2 163 A7
Wickham Bishops CM8 ..212 E5
Holt Farm Jun & Inf Sch
SS4 ....325 D3
Holt Farm Way SS4 ..325 D4
Holton Rd
Canvey Island SS8 ..364 F3
Rayleigh SS6 ......324 A2
Holt Rd RM3 ......314 E3
Holt's Rd CO6 ....81 B3
Holt The IG6 ......311 F6
Holt Way IG6 .....311 F5
Holtynge SS7 .....344 C4
Holybread La CM3 ..234 C4
Holy Cross RC Prim Sch
Harlow CM18 .....224 A6
South Ockendon RM15 ..372 B7
Holy Family RC Prim Sch
South Benfleet SS7 ..344 D5
Holyfield Hall Farm*
EN9 ....243 C4
Holyfield Rd EN9 ...243 D2
Holyoak La SS1 ...324 E4
Holyrood CO12 ....90 F2
Holyrood Cl IP2 ...18 F1
Holyrood Dr SS0 ...347 B2
Holy Trinity CE Prim Sch
CO9 ....76 D2
Holy Trinity & St Nicholas CE
Prim Sch SG8 ....19 C3
Holywells High Sch IP3 ..18 C1
Holywells Prim Sch IP3 ..18 C1

Holywells Rd IP3 .....17 E3
Homebridge CM10 .....47 A3
Homebush Ho E4 .....287 B2
Home CI Harlow CM20 .....223 F8
  Steeple Bumpstead CB9 .....27 C7
Homecove Ho SS0 .....366 D7
Homecroft Gdns IG10 .....289 B5
Homedale Cotts CO4 .....83 B6
Home Farm CI SS3 .....350 B4
Home Farm Ind Pk SG12 197 F5
Home Farm La
  Ardleigh CO7 .....112 A8
  Dedham CO7 .....85 A1
Home Farm Prim Sch
  CO3 .....134 F6
Home Farm Rd CM13 .....316 E2
Homefield Capel St M IP9 .35 B1
  Southminster CM0 .....284 E5
  Waltham Abbey EN9 .....266 A7
Homefield Ave IG2 .....333 E6
Homefield CI
  Billericay CM11 .....319 D6
  Chelmsford CM1 .....231 D5
  Epping CM16 .....246 A1
Homefield Rd
  Colchester CO2 .....135 C1
  Haverhill CB9 .....8 F5
  Witham CM8 .....184 A4
Homefield Road Units SP9 .8 F5
Homefields Ave SS7 .....344 B5
Homefield Way
  Cressing CM77 .....155 D2
  Earls Colne CO6 .....105 B7
Home Gdns RM10 .....195 C1
Homeholly Ho SS11 .....299 D2
Homehurst Ho CM15 .....294 D1
Homelands Ct CO14 .....171 A7
Homelands Gr CM11 .....298 C4
Homelye Chase CM6 .....124 B1
Home Mdws CM12 .....297 A2
Homemead DA9 .....377 B1
Home Mead
  Basildon SS15 .....341 B8
  Galleywood CM2 .....254 C2
  Writtle CM1 .....231 A1
Homeorr Ho IP11 .....381 F4
Homerton CI CO15 .....195 F8
Homesdale CI IU 332 A6
Homes Of Rest IG1 .....333 D1
Homestead CM1 .....232 B7
Homestead CI SS7 .....345 D3
Homestead Ct SS16 .....341 C2
Homestead Dr SS3 .....345 D2
Homestead Rd
  Basildon,Bowers Gifford
  SS13 .....343 E1
  Dagenham RM8 .....334 F2
  Hadleigh SS7 .....345 D2
  Ramsden Heath SS13 .....320 D8
Homestead Sch CO4 .....83 E4
Homesteads The SG12 .198 D8
Homestead Way SS7 .....345 D3
Homeway RM3 .....315 B4
Homey Bridge Rd CO6 .....56 C8
Homing Rd CO16 .....168 C4
Honeybourne CM23 .....145 E4
Honey Brook EN9 .....265 E6
Honey CI Chelmsford CM2 .304 A6
  Dagenham RM8 .....334 B6
Honeycroft Lawford CO11 .86 B3
  Loughton IG10 .....289 B5
Honey La Clavering CB11 .....64 F3
  Waltham Abbey EN9 .....265 E5
Honeymeade CM21 .....200 C7
Honey Pot Hall CO15 .....195 F3
Honeypot La
  Basildon SS14 .....342 B6
  Brentwood CM14 .....316 A8
  Little Clacton CO16 .....168 A4
  Stock CM4 .....271 F2
  Tolleshunt Knights CM9 .187 B1
  Weeley Heath CO16 .....168 B4
  Wix CO11 .....114 F3
Honey Pot La CM3 .....280 D3
Honeypots CM2 .....254 C6
Honeysuckle CI
  Bishop's Stortford CM23 .145 C6
  Pilgrims Hatch CM15 .....294 B4
  Romford RM3 .....314 C4
Honeysuckle CI IG1 .....352 B6
Honeysuckle Gdns IP2 ..16 E4
Honeysuckle Way
  CM1 .....232 F6
Honeysuckle Way
  Colchester CO4 .....136 E8
  Thorrington CO7 .....166 A5
  Witham CM8 .....184 C8
Honeywood Ave CO6 .....131 A3
Honeywood Rd CO9 .....77 A3
Honiley Ave SS12 .....321 E3
Honington CI SS11 .....322 B6
Honiton Rd Romford RM7 335 D5
  Southend-on-S SS1 .....347 C6
Honorius Dr CO4 .....110 B6
Honor Link CM1 .....233 A7
Honywood CI CO6 .....132 E3
Honywood Com Sch The
  CO6 .....131 A3
Honywood Rd
  Basildon SS14 .....320 F2
  Colchester CO3 .....135 D6
Honywood Way CO13 .170 F7
Hood CI SS12 .....321 E6
Hood Gdns CM7 .....128 C4
Hood Lodge E11 .....332 B2
Hood Rd Ipswich IP3 .....17 E1
  Rainham RM13 .....354 F3
Hood Wlk RM7 .....313 B2
Hook Cotts CM1 .....230 B7
Hook End La CM15 .....272 C5
Hook End Rd CM15 .....272 C4

Hook Field CM18 .....223 F6
Hook La RM4 .....291 A3
Hooks Hall Dr RM10 .....335 C1
Hookstone Way IG8 .....310 D3
Hooley Dr SS6 .....323 C6
Hoo The CM12 .....200 C5
Hoover Dr SS15 .....340 F6
Hope Ave SS17 .....360 E5
Hope CI Ilford RM6 .....334 D7
  Mountnessing CM15 .....215 D8
  L Woodford IG8 .....310 C4
Hope Rd Basildon CM11 .320 C5
  Canvey Island SS8 .....364 D3
  South Benfleet SS7 .....344 D2
  Swanscombe DA10 .....377 F1
Hope Terr RM7 .....372 D1
Hopewell CI RM16 .....372 D1
Hop Gardens La CM9 .....235 F4
Hop Gdns CM5 .....270 A7
Hopgrounds The CM7 ...72 D6
Hopkins CI
  Chelmsford CM2 .....233 A3
  Kirby Cross CO13 .....170 F6
  Romford RM2 .....336 C8
Hopkin's La CO12 .....91 D6
Hopkins Mead CM2 .....233 A2
Hopkirk CI CM3 .....256 F8
Hoppet The CM4 .....274 C4
Hoppett Rd E4 .....309 E8
Hopping Jacks La CM3 .256 F7
Hoppit Mead CM7 .....127 F1
Hoppit Rd EN9 .....265 B7
Hoppitt The CM5 .....226 C3
Hopton Rise CP0 .....59 B2
Hop View CO7 .....59 B2
Horace Ave RM7 .....335 D3
Horace Eves CI **1** CB9 ..8 F8
Horace Rd
  Billericay CM11 .....297 C4
  Ilford IG6 .....333 C8
  Southend-on-S SS1 .....367 B7
Hordle CI CO12 .....91 D4
Hordle St IP2 .....91 D4
Horkesley Hill CO6 .....82 A7
Horkesley Rd
  Great Horkesley CM4 .109 E8
  Nayland CO6 .....56 A1
Horkesley Way SS12 .....321 E6
Horksley Gdns CM13 .295 C3
Horley IP7 .....16 F4
Horley CI CO16 .....195 C6
Hornbeam Ave RM14 ..356 A8
Hornbeam Chase RM15 .357 D2
Hornbeam CI
  Barking IG11 .....353 A2
  Brentwood CM13 .....310 D7
  Buckhurst Hill IG9 .....310 D7
  Chelmsford CM2 .....254 A6
  Colchester CO2 .....135 D2
  Ilford IG1 .....352 D7
  Theydon Bois CM16 .....267 E2
Hornbeam Gr E4 .....309 F7
Hornbeam Ho IG9 .....310 D7
Hornbeam La E4 .....287 E4
Hornbeam Rd
  Buckhurst Hill IG9 .....310 D7
  Theydon Bois CM16 .....267 D2
Hornbeams The
  Harlow CM20 .....199 C2
  Little Oakley CO12 .....117 B7
Hornbeam Way SS15 ..319 D1
Hornbeam Wlk CM8 .....184 A4
Horn Book CB10 .....22 F1
Hornby Ave SS0 .....347 D5
Hornby CI SS0 .....347 D5
Hornchurch CV SS11 .....195 C3
Hornchurch Ctry Pk*
  RM12 .....355 D6
Hornchurch Rd RM11 .336 B3
Hornchurch Sports Stad
  RM14 .....337 A2
Hornchurch Sta RM12 .336 D1
Horndon CI RM5 .....313 C2
Horndon Gdn RM5 .....313 C2
Horndon Ind Pk CM13 .339 C5
Horndon on the Hill CE Prim
  Sch SS17 .....359 F4
Horndon Rd
  Horndon-on-t-H SS17 ..360 A1
  Romford RM5 .....313 C2
Horne Row CM3 .....256 D5
Horner PI **4** CM8 .....184 A2
Horner's Cnr SS3 .....349 F4
Hornet Way CM0 .....306 B5
Hornford Way RM7 .....335 C4
Horn Hill CO9 .....75 C5
Horn La IG8 .....310 A3
Hornminster Glen RM11 337 A2
Hornsby La RM14 .....374 A5
Hornsby Sq SS15 .....340 F7
Hornsby Way SS15 .....340 F7
Hornsea Villas CM6 .....124 D7
Hornsland Rd SS8 .....364 E3
Hornck Rd IG2,IG6 .....333 C6
Horn Yd **2** DA11 .....379 B1
Horrocks CI CO2 .....136 A4
Horsebridge CI RM9 .....353 E4
Horsecroft CM5 .....203 D2
Horsecroft PI CM19 .....222 E7
Horsecroft Rd CM19 ..222 E7
Horse & Groom La CM4 254 A3
Horseman Side CM14 ..292 D3
Horse Pond CI CO10 ....34 C4
Horseshoe CI
  Billericay CM11 .....297 A5
  Elmdon CB11 .....20 B4
  Waltham Abbey EN9 .....266 A5
Horseshoe Cres SS3 ..368 F6
Horseshoe Ct SG12 ....197 D4
Horseshoe Hill EN9 .....266 C7
Horsey Rd CO13 .....170 C8
Horsham Ave IP3 .....18 D3

Horshams CM19 .....223 C8
Horsley Cross
  Basildon SS14 .....342 B7
  Bradfield CO11 .....114 A3
Horsley Ho IP11 .....381 F4
Horsley Rd E4 .....309 C8
Hortus Rd E4 .....309 C8
Hospital App CM1 .....208 B3
Hospital Cotts CM14 .316 B6
Hospital Field CM77 .....155 B5
Hospital La CO3 .....135 D6
Hospital Rd
  Colchester CO3 .....135 C6
  Southend-on-S SS3 .....368 F6
Hossack Rd IP3 .....38 A8
Houblon Dr CM2 .....254 C2
Houblons Hill
  Coopersale CM16 .....246 D1
  Epping CM16 .....268 C8
Houchin Dr CM5 .....227 D2
Houchin's La CO6 .....131 E3
Houghton PI IP4 .....18 F5
House Martins The IP11 381 D6
Hove CI Brentwood CM13 317 C8
  Grays RM17 .....378 A8
Hove Ct CO15 .....196 F6
Hovefields Ave SS12 ..321 D3
Hovefields Cvn Pk SS12 321 C2
Hovefields Dr SS12 .....321 D3
Hoveton Way IG6 .....311 B3
Howard Chase SS14 .342 A8
Howard CI Braintree CM7 128 C3
  Haverhill CB9 .....8 D7
  Loughton IG10 .....288 E3
  Waltham Abbey EN9 .....265 D5
Howard Cres SS13 .....343 C5
Howard Ct IG11 .....352 D4
Howard Dr CM2 .....233 A2
Howard Lodge Rd CM14 271 C2
Howard PI SS8 .....364 B2
Howard Rd Barking IG11 352 D4
  Dartford DA1 .....376 A1
  Grays RM16 .....372 C3
  Holland-on-S CO15 .....196 C4
  Ilford IG1 .....352 B8
  Saffron Walden CB10 .....22 E2
  Upminster RM14 .....337 D2
Howards Chase SS0 .347 F2
Howards CI CM3 .....233 E8
Howards Croft CO4 .....109 D5
Howards Ct SS0 .....366 E8
Howard St IP4 .....18 B6
Howard Vyse Ct CO15 ..195 C5
Howard Way CM20 .....199 F2
Howbridge CE Jun Sch
  CM8 .....211 F8
Howbridge Hall Rd
  Witham CM8 .....211 F6
  Witham CM8 .....211 F7
Howbridge Inf Sch The
  CM8 .....211 F8
Howbridge Rd CM8 .....211 F8
Howburgh CI **7** RM9 ..371 B1
Howe Ave CM13 .....18 C3
Howe Chase CO9 .....76 E4
Howe CI Colchester CO4 .136 D7
  Romford RM7 .....313 A2
Howe Green House Sch
  CM22 .....146 D2
Howe Green Rd CM3 ..280 E7
Howe La CB10 .....47 A5
Howell CI RM6 .....334 C6
Howell Rd SS17 .....360 F6
Howerd Ho CM14 .....316 C6
Howfield Gn EN11 .....197 A1
Howlets Terr IP9 .....63 E7
Howse Rd EN9 .....265 B4
Hows Mead CM16 .....247 D7
Hoxter Way CO10 .....15 E2
Hoxton CI CO16 .....195 D5
Hoylake Gdns RM3 .....315 A3
Hoynors CM3 .....257 A7
Hubbards Chase
  Hornchurch RM11 .....337 A6
  Walton-on-t-N CO14 ..171 B8
Hubbards CI RM11 .....337 B6
Hubert Rd
  Brentwood CM14 .....316 B7
  Colchester CO3 .....135 B8
  Rainham RM13 .....354 F3
Hucklesbury Ave CO15 .196 E7
Hucknall CI RM3 .....314 F4
Hudson CI
  Clacton-on-S CO16 .....195 C5
  Grays RM20 .....371 F1
  Harwich CO12 .....91 A1
  Haverhill CB9 .....9 C6
Hudson Cres SS9 .....346 E6
Hudson Ct SS9 .....346 E6
Hudson Rd SS9 .....346 D6
Hudsons CI SS17 .....360 D3
Hudson's Hill CM7 .....73 D4
Hudsons La CO6 .....57 B5
Hudson Way SS8 .....364 A6
Huggens Coll (Almshouses)
  DA11 .....378 B2
Hugh Dickson Rd CO4 .109 E2
Hughes Cnr CO7 .....59 A4
Hughes Rd
  East Bergholt CO7 .....85 A4
  Grays RM16 .....374 A3
Hughes Stanton Way
  CO11 .....86 B4
Hugh Villas CM23 .....146 A5
Hugo Gdns **8** RM13 .355 A6
Hullbridge Rd
  Rayleigh SS6 .....323 D7
  South Woodham Ferrers
  CM3 .....301 D6
Hullett's La CM16 .....293 F4
Hull Gn CM7 .....202 D2
Hull Gr CM19 .....223 A3
Hull La CM3 .....182 A2

Hull's La CM2 .....255 E7
Hulse Ave Barking IG11 .352 E6
  Romford RM7 .....313 B2
Hulton CI CM3 .....233 E8
Hulver Ct IP3 .....18 B2
Humber Ave
  Clacton-on-S CO15 .....220 E6
  South Ockendon RM15 ..371 F7
Humber CI SS4 .....342 C1
  Clacton-on-S CO16 .....195 C4
  Tollesbury CM9 .....216 E1
Humber Doucy La IP4 ..18 D8
Humber Dr RM14 .....337 D5
Humber Rd
  Chelmsford CM1 .....232 C5
  Witham CM8 .....183 D2
Hume Ave RM18 .....379 B5
Hume CI RM18 .....379 A4
Humphrey CI IG5 .....310 F2
Humphrey's Farm La
  CM3 .....242 C7
Humphries CI RM9 .....353 F8
Humphry Rd CO10 .....33 E8
Hundon PI **4** CB9 .....9 B8
Hundred La CO4 .....83 C4
Hungerdown La CO11 ...85 C1
Hungerford Ho **4** RM3 .315 A4
Hunnable Rd CM7 .....127 E2
Hunsdon CI RM9 .....353 E6
Hunsdon Rd SG12 .....197 F8
Hunsdon Road Cotts
  SG12 .....197 E5
Hunt Ave CM9 .....237 B5
Hunt CI CO5 .....158 D4
Hunt Dr CO16 .....195 D6
Hunter Ave CM15 .....295 A3
Hunter Dr Braintree CM7 128 C2
  Hornchurch RM12 .....355 C8
  Lawford CO11 .....86 A3
  Wickford SS12 .....321 E6
Hunter Rd IP3 .....38 C8
Hunters Ave CM21 .....319 B7
Hunters Chase
  Brentwood CM13 .....296 C2
  Chipping Ongar CM5 .....249 A1
Hunter's Chase CO7 .....84 E2
Hunters CI CO15 .....134 F5
Hunters CI CO12 .....114 D3
Hunters End IP11 .....381 A7
Hunter's Gr RM5 .....313 B5
Hunters Hall Prim Sch
  RM10 .....352 E8
Hunters Hall Rd RM10 ..354 A7
Hunters Rd IG1 .....352 B7
Hunters Ridge CO4 .....110 B4
Hunters Sq RM10 .....354 A8
Hunters Way
  Chelmsford CM2 .....232 F7
  Saffron Walden CB11 ...43 D7
Huntingdon Rd SS1 .....367 D7
Huntingdon Way CO15 .195 E6
Hunting Gate CO1 .....136 C7
Huntings Farm IG1 .....333 E2
Huntings Rd RM10 .....354 A6
Huntland CI RM13 .....370 B8
Huntley Ave DA11 .....378 C1
Huntley's Cvn Pk (E)
  CO16 .....220 C6
Huntley's Cvn Pk (W)
  CO16 .....220 B6
Hunt Rd CO6 .....105 A6
Hunt's CI CM1 .....253 B8
Hunt's Dr CM1 .....253 B8
Hunt's Farm CI CM9 ..216 D2
Hunts Hill CO10 .....2 A4
Hunts Hill Cotts RM14 .356 C3
Hunts La CB10 .....3 A6
Huntsman Rd IG6 .....312 B5
Huntsmans Dr RM14 ..356 C7
Hunts Mead CM12 .....297 A1
Hunt Way CO13 .....170 E6
Hurnwicke Rd CO4 .....136 E7
Hurnard Ci CM11 .....297 B2
Hurnard Dr CO3 .....135 A7
Hurrell Down
  Boreham CM3 .....209 F1
  Highwoods CM4 .....110 A4
Hurricane Rd SS14 .....233 F3
Hurricane CI SS11 .....322 B5
Hurricane PI IP3 .....18 C1
Hurricane Way
  North Weald Bassett CM16 247 A4
  Wickford SS11 .....322 A5
Hursley Rd Chigwell IG7 .115 F5
  Redbridge IG2 .....312 A5
Hurst Ave E4 .....309 A7
Hurstbourne Gdns IG11 .352 C8
Hurst CI
  Bishop's Stortford CM23 ..145 D4
  Brightlingsea CO7 .....193 A6
  Chingford E4 .....309 A7
Hurstcombe IG9 .....310 A8
Hurst Ct IG8 .....310 B4
Hurst Ho SS7 .....345 B7
Hurstlands CI RM11 .....336 C5
Hurstleigh Gdns IG5 .311 A2
Hurst Park Ave RM12 ..355 E8
Hurst Rd IG9 .....288 E1
Hurstwood
  Chelmsford CM2 .....232 F2
  Southend-on-S SS9 .....346 F4
Hurstwood Ave
  Pilgrims Hatch CM15 .....294 B2
  Wanstead E18 .....332 B7
Hurstwood Ct RM11 .....337 C2
Huskards RM14 .....337 C2
Hutchins CI RM12 .....336 E1
Hutchinson CI CO5 .....186 D4
Hutchinson Ho RM4 .....334 D7
Hutland Rd IP4 .....17 F7
Hutson Terr RM19 .....376 D8
Hutton All Saints CE Prim Sch
  CM13 .....295 D3
Hutton CI IG8 .....310 B4
Hutton Ct CM13 .....295 F2
Hutton Dr CM13 .....295 D2
Hutton Gate CM13 .....295 B2

Hutton PI CM13 .....295 B3
Hutton Rd
  Brentwood CM15 .....295 A2
  Shenfield CM15 .....294 F2
Hutton Village CM13 ..295 F2
Huxley Dr RM6 .....334 B4
Huxtables La CO3 .....108 C1
Hyacinth CI Barking IG11 352 B6
  Clacton-on-S CO16 .....195 C4
  Tollesbury CM9 .....216 E1
Hyacinth Ct **4** CM2 .....232 E7
Hyams La IP9 .....62 E6
Hyam's La IP9 .....61 F1
Hycliffe Gdns IG7 .....311 C6
Hyde Chase Danbury CM3 257 B4
  Woodham Mortimer CM9 .257 D4
Hyde CI RM16 .....372 C3
Hyde Gn CM3 .....257 B7
Hyde Hall Gdns* CM3 ..278 E4
Hyde La Danbury CM3 ..257 B3
  Danbury CM3 .....257 B6
  Wethersfield CM7 .....74 B2
Hyde Mead Ho EN9 .....243 E8
Hyde Mead Ho EN9 .....243 E8
Hyde Rd CO10 .....33 E7
Hyder Rd RM16 .....374 C3
Hyde The Basildon SS16 341 C4
  Clavering CB11 .....65 C4
Hydeway SS7 .....344 F6
Hyde Way SS12 .....321 D6
Hyde Wood La SS4 .....325 F7
Hydewood Rd CO9 .....30 B3
Hyem's La IP11 .....381 F7
Hyh Ho E17 .....309 B2
Hyland CI RM11 .....336 B4
Hyland Gate CM11 .....319 D6
Hyland House Sch E17 .309 D1
Hylands CI CM6 .....151 A4
Hylands House Sixth Form
  Coll SS9 .....347 A3
Hylands Par CM2 .....254 A6
Hylands Rd E17 .....309 D1
Hylands Sch CM1 .....231 D1
Hylands The SS5 .....324 D5
Hyland Way RM11 .....336 B4
Hyldon Ct IP11 .....381 E3
Hyleford Sch IG3 .....352 D8
Hyll CI CB10 .....3 D3
Hyndford Cres DA9 .....377 C2
Hyndman Ho **5** RM9 ..335 A1
Hyntle CI IP7 .....16 E5
Hynton Rd RM8 .....334 C8
Hythe CI Braintree CM7 .127 E6
  Clacton-on-S CO15 .....220 J8
Hythe CI CO7 .....165 E1
Hythe Hill CO1 .....136 C6
Hythe Quay CO2 .....136 D5
Hythe Sta CO4 .....136 D6
Hythe Station Rd CO2 .136 D6
The CM9 .....237 B2

Ian Rd CM12 .....296 F4
Ibbetson Path IG10 .....289 B6
Ibrox Ct **3** IG9 .....310 C8
Ibscott CI RM10 .....354 C6
I Butts Rd SS3 .....350 C1
Iceni Way CO2 .....135 B3
Ickleton PI **3** CB9 .....9 B8
Ickleton Rd Elmdon CB11 ..20 A4
  Great Chesterford CB10 ..3 C2
  Hinxton CB10 .....3 B6
Icknield CI CB10 .....3 A3
Icknield Dr IG2 .....333 B6
Ickworth CI CM77 .....154 C7
Ickworth Cres IP4 .....18 F5
Ickworth Ct IP11 .....381 A3
Ilchester Rd RM8 .....353 C7
Ilex CI CO2 .....135 D2
Ilford Chambers IG1 .....333 B1
Ilford Cty High Sch IG6 .311 B1
Ilford Hill IG1 .....333 A1
Ilford Jewish Prim Sch
  IG6 .....333 D8
Ilford La IG1 .....352 B7
Ilford Prep Sch IG3 .....344 J3
Ilford Ret Pk IG1 .....333 C2
Ilford Sta IG1 .....333 B2
Ilford Trad Est SS14 .....320 E2
Ilford Ursuline High Sch
  .....333 B2
Ilfracombe Ave
  Basildon SS13 .....343 D5
  Southend-on-S SS0 .....367 D8
Ilfracombe Cres RM12 ..355 C8
Ilfracombe Gdns RM6 .334 B4
Ilfracombe Rd SS2 .....348 C1
Ilgars Rd SS11 .....299 E1
Ilmington Dr SS13 .....321 A1
Immanuel Sch RM5 .....313 D5
Imogen CI **4** CO4 .....136 F8
Imperial Ave
  Mayland CM3 .....260 E1
  Southend-on-S SS0 .....347 C1
Imperial Bsns Pk DA11 .378 F1
Imperial Lodge SS0 .....347 C1
Imperial Pk Rayleigh SS6 .323 C6
  Southend-on-S SS3 .....368 E7
Imperial Ret Pk DA11 ..379 C7
Imperial Trad Est RM13 ..355 C1
Imphal Ct CO2 .....135 C1
Impress Pk EN11 .....221 C7
Inchbonnie Rd CM3 .....301 D5
Ingarfield Rd CO15 .....196 E6
Ingatestone By-Pass
  CM4 .....274 B5
Ingatestone & Fryerning CE
  Jun Sch CM4 .....274 A3
Ingatestone Hall* CM4 .274 C2
Ingatestone Inf Sch CM4 274 B4
Ingatestone Rd
  Blackmore CM4 .....272 F7
  Edney Common CM4 .....252 A1
  Roxwell CM1 .....251 F2

Ingatestone Rd continued
  Stock CM4 .....275 B1
  Wanstead E12 .....332 C3
  Woodford IG8 .....310 B3
Ingatestone Sta CM4 ..274 A3
Ingaway SS16 .....341 F5
Ingelrica Ave CM3 .....211 B3
Ingels Mead CM16 .....245 F2
Ingestre St CO12 .....91 D4
Ingham Rd CB9 .....9 B8
Ingleby Gdns IG7 .....312 B7
Ingleby Rd
  Dagenham RM10 .....354 B6
  Grays RM16 .....374 C3
  Ilford IG1 .....333 B3
Inglefield Rd SS17 .....361 B7
Inglegien RM11 .....337 A4
Inglehurst Gdns IG4 ..332 F6
Inglenook CO15 .....196 B7
Ingleside CR CB11 .....22 D1
Ingleton Ho **1** RM3 ...314 D4
Inglewood CI
  Hornchurch RM12 .....355 D8
  Redbridge IG6 .....311 F4
Inglis Rd CO3 .....135 D6
Ingram Mews CM7 .....155 B8
Ingram Rd RM17 .....373 C2
Ingram's Piece CO7 .....111 E8
Ingram's Well CO10 ....33 F7
Ingram's Well Rd CO10 ..33 F7
Ingrave CI SS12 .....321 E6
Ingrave Ho RM9 .....353 B4
Ingrave Johnstone CE Prim
  Sch CM13 .....317 C4
Ingrave Rd
  Brentwood CM13, CM15 .316 E7
  Romford RM1 .....335 E7
Ingrebourne Ct E4 .....309 D8
Ingrebourne Gdns RM14 337 D3
Ingrebourne Prim Sch
  RM3 .....314 C6
Ingrebourne Rd RM13 ..355 E7
Ingrebourne Valley*
  RM13 .....355 E7
Ingress Gdns DA9 .....377 D2
Ingress Park Ave DA9 ..377 D2
Ingreway RM3 .....315 A4
Inkerman Row **8** CO10 ..33 E8
Inkerpole PI CM2 .....232 F4
Inks Gn E4 .....309 C5
Inmans Row IG8 .....310 A6
Innes CI SS12 .....321 E5
Innes End IP8 .....16 C2
Innham Hill CO9 .....75 C6
Innova Way EN3 .....265 A3
Inskip Dr RM11 .....336 E3
Inskip Rd RM8 .....334 D3
Institute Rd CM16 .....246 D2
Integrated Support Ctr,PRU
  CM18 .....223 F4
International Bsns Pk
  SS8 .....363 D3
Inverclyde Gdns RM6 .334 D7
Invermay Ct CM1 .....294 C1
Inverness Ave SS0 .....347 D2
Inverness CI CO11 .....136 A8
Inverness Dr IG6 .....311 E4
Invicta CI CM12 .....296 E3
Invicta Ctr The IG11 .....353 A4
Invicta Rd DA2 .....376 B1
Inworth La CO6 .....79 D2
Inworth Rd CO5 .....158 E3
Inworth Wlk
  S Colchester CO2 .....136 A1
  Wickford SS11 .....322 A8
Iona Way SS12 .....321 F6
Iona Wlk CO5 .....164 A8
Ipswich High Sch IP9 ...38 C2
Ipswich Hospl IP4 .....18 C6
Ipswich Mews SS11 .....340 F5
Ipswich Mus* IP1 .....17 C6
Ipswich Pre Prep Sch IP1 17 B7
Ipswich Rd Ardleigh CO7 ..83 F8
  Brantham CO11 .....60 E2
  Colchester CO4 .....110 C3
  Dedham CO7 .....84 B6
  Harkstead IP9 .....63 B3
  Holbrook IP9 .....62 E6
  Holland-on-S CO15 .....196 D6
  Ipswich IP10 .....38 F6
  Stratford St M CO7 .....58 E2
Ipswich Sch IP1 .....17 C7
Ipswich Sta IP2 .....17 B4
Ipswich Transport Mus*
  .....17 A3
Ireland Rd IP3 .....17 F1
Ireton Ho CO4 .....109 F4
Ireton PI RM17 .....373 A2
Ireton Rd CO3 .....135 D5
Iris CI Chelmsford CM1 ..232 F5
  Ipswich IP2 .....16 E3
  Pilgrims Hatch CM15 .....294 B4
Iris Path RM3 .....314 C3
Iriam Rd IP2 .....16 D1
Iron Latch La CO3 .....134 C8
Irons Way RM5 .....313 C3
Ironwell La Hockley SS5 .325 A3
  Rochford SS4 .....325 E2
Irvine Gdns RM15 .....371 F7
Irvine PI SS12 .....321 D6
Irvine Rd CO3 .....135 C5
Irving CI
  Bishop's Stortford CM23 ..145 D4
  Hockley SS5 .....324 E5
Irvington CI SS9 .....346 D4
Irvon Hill Rd SS12 .....321 C7
Isaac Sq CM2 .....255 B6
Isabella Ho EN8 .....265 A5
Isbell Gdns RM1 .....313 E3
Isher CI CM14 .....316 D7
Ishams Chase CM8 .....212 C2
Isis Dr RM14 .....337 E5
Island Centre Way EN3 .265 A2

Island Ct CM23 .....146 A5
Island La C013 .....143 E1
Island Rd C014 .....143 E4
Italstyle Bldg The CM20 200 C6
Iver Rd CM15 .....294 B3
Ives C015 .....335 F7
Ivinghoe Rd RM8 .....353 B7
Ivor Brown Ct C04 .....110 B4
Ivry St IP1 .....17 B7
Ivy Barns La
  Ingatestone CM4 .....274 A8
  Margaretting CM4 .....252 C1
Ivy Bower Cl DA9 .....377 B2
Ivybridge EN10 .....221 A4
Ivy Chimneys CM16 .....267 E7
Ivy Chimneys Prim Sch
  CM16 .....267 E7
Ivy Chimneys Rd CM16 267 E7
Ivy Cl DA1 .....376 A1
Ivy Cotts
  Great Dunmow CM6 .....123 B4
  Steeple CM0 .....262 A3
Ivyhouse Rd RM9 .....353 E6
Ivy La C05 .....192 B3
Ivy Lodge La RM3 .....315 B1
Ivy Lodge Rd C06 .....109 C8
Ivy Rd SS7 .....144 A6
Ivy Terr Hoddesdon EN11 221 C8
  ⊠ Ilford IG2 .....333 C5
Ivy Todd Hill CB11 .....68 A8
Ivy Wlk Canvey Island SS8 363 F4
  Dagenham RM9 .....353 E6
Ixworth Rd C09 .....8 E6

J

Jacaranda Cl CM1 .....233 A6
Jack Andrews Dr C04 .....110 A5
Jack Branch Ct C015 .....195 E2
Jack Cook Ho ⑥ IG11 .....352 B5
Jack Cornwell St E12 .....352 A8
Jackdaw Cl
  Billericay CM11 .....319 C8
  Southend-on-S SS3 .....368 E7
Jack Evans Ct RM15 .....372 A7
Jack Hatch Way C07 .....137 A3
Jacklin Gn IG8 .....310 A6
Jack Lobley Prim Sch
  RM18 .....378 F6
Jacks Cl SS11 .....321 F7
Jack's La CM27 .....148 D7
Jackson Cl
  Greenhithe DA9 .....377 A2
  Hornchurch RM11 .....336 F7
Jackson Ct E11 .....332 B3
Jackson Ho C04 .....110 B6
Jackson Pl CM2 .....254 D6
Jackson Rd Barking IG11 352 D4
  Clacton-on-S C015 .....195 E2
Jacksons Cl CM5 .....249 A2
Jacksons La CM11 .....297 C2
Jackson Sq ⑩ CM23 .....145 F7
Jackson's Sq ⑩ CM23 .....3 D3
Jacksons Mews CM1 .....297 C2
Jackson Sq ⑩ CM23 .....145 F7
Jackson's Sq CM23 .....3 D3
Jack Stevens Cl CM17 .....228 C6
Jacob Cl EN1 .....265 A2
Jacobs Ave RM3 .....314 E1
Jacobs Ct C07 .....192 F6
Jacquard Way CM7 .....128 A2
Jacqueline Ct C03 .....134 E5
Jacqueline Gdns CM13 297 B5
Jade Cl RM8 .....334 C3
Jade Ho ⑥ RM13 .....355 A1
Jaffe Rd IG1 .....333 D3
Jaggard's Rd C06 .....131 A3
Jakapeni Rare Breeds Pk *
  SSS 323 E8
James Alexander Ho
  SSS 301 D3
James Ave RM8 .....334 F3
James Boden Cl IP11 .....381 C5
James Carter Rd C03 .....134 C5
James Ct Romford RM2 .....136 A6
  Wivenhoe C07 .....137 C3
James Croft CM2 .....254 B2
James Ct Chingford E4 .....309 D8
  ⊠ Woodford E18 .....310 B1
James Gdns C016 .....194 B5
James Hatfield Ho IP2 .....17 D4
James Hornsby High Sch The
  SS15 .....341 D7
James Lee Sq EN3 .....265 A1
James Oglethorpe Prim Sch
  The RM14 .....337 F2
Jameson Rd ⑥ C010 .....33 D8
Jameson Rd C015 .....195 C3
James Rd CM2 .....195 C2
James Sq CM11 .....297 E2
James St Barking IG11 .....352 C5
  Brightlingsea C07 .....192 F6
  Colchester C01 .....136 A6
  Epping CM16 .....246 A3
Janebrook Rd IP2 .....16 E2
Jane Ct ⑦ RM1 .....335 F6
Janet Duke Inf Sch
  SS15 .....341 D6
Janet Duke Jun Sch
  SS15 .....341 D6
Janette Ave SS8 .....363 E3
Janice Mews ⑬ IG1 .....333 E1
Janmead Brentwood CM13 295 B2
  Witham CM8 .....184 A3
Janus Cl C09 .....9 D6
Japan Rd RM4 .....334 D5
Japonica Ct C010 .....196 C4
Jaques Cl C010 .....2 C5
Jardine Rd SS13 .....343 C8
Jarmin Rd C01 .....135 F8
Jarndyce CM1 .....231 F6
Jarrah Cotts RM19 .....376 D8
Jarrow Rd RM6 .....334 C5
Jarvis Cl ① IG11 .....352 D4

Jarvis Field CM3 .....234 D5
Jarvis Rd
  Canvey Island SS8 .....364 A6
  Harvis Rd SS7 .....344 E4
Jarvis Way CM3 .....314 E1
Jasmin Cl CM23 .....145 C6
Jasmine Cl Basildon SS16 340 F4
  Canvey Island SS8 .....363 F2
  ⊠ Chelmsford CM1 .....232 E7
  Ilford IG1 .....352 B7
  Ipswich IP2 .....16 F3
Jasmine Rd RM7 .....335 E2
Jasmine Way CM15 .....220 G7
Jason Cl
  Canvey Island SS8 .....364 B5
  Orsett RM16 .....374 E7
Jason Ct CM14 .....315 F6
Jasons Cl CM14 .....315 F6
Jaspers Green CM7 .....100 E2
Jay Cl Great Notley CM77 .154 D8
  Haverhill CB9 .....9 C7
Jaymar Ct ② CM7 .....127 F2
Jayrest Cr C03 .....134 E4
Jays La C06 .....132 F3
Jays La C06 .....110 C3
Jaywick La C015,C016 .195 A3
Jaywick Rd C07 .....9 A8
Jct CM20 .....199 F1
Jeans La CM23 .....145 E7
Jeffcut Rd CM2 .....232 E2
Jefferies Rd IP4 .....17 E6
Jefferies Way ⑥ SS17 .360 F3
Jefferson Ave ③ SS15 .341 A6
Jefferson Cl
  Colchester C03 .....134 E5
  Ilford IG2 .....333 B6
Jeffery Rd CM2 .....255 A2
Jeffery Ct C03 .....134 F5
Jeffrey's Rd CM7 .....155 A6
Jekylls La CM7 .....48 D4
Jellicoe Ct E4 .....309 D4
Jellicoe Way CM7 .....128 C4
Jenkins Dr CM22 .....94 C3
Jenkins La
  Bishop's Stortford CM23 .146 C5
  Walthd IG11 .....352 C2
Jenner Cl CM7 .....127 F5
Jenner Ho ⑧ DA17 .....369 A3
Jenner Mead CM7 .....233 A3
Jenningham Dr RM16 .373 A5
Jennings Cl ① C01 .....136 C6
Jennings Pl CM4 .....275 A8
Jenningtree Way DA17 369 C4
Jenny Path RM5 .....314 D3
Jericho Pl CM4 .....272 E8
Jermayns SS15 .....341 E6
Jermyns Cl IP9 .....35 B2
Jerningham Ave IG5 .311 B1
Jerounds CM19 .....223 B6
Jerounds Com & Inf Sch
  CM19 .....223 B5
Jersey Cl EN11 .....221 A7
Jersey Gdns SS11 .....321 D8
Jersey Rd Ilford IG2 .....352 B8
  Maldon CM9 .....210 A2
  Rainham RM13 .....355 A5
Jersey Way CM7 .....127 D2
Jervis Cl IP9 .....62 D5
Jervis Ct ⑨ RM10 .....354 B6
Jervis Rd CM23 .....145 F6
Jesmond Rd
  Canvey Island SS8 .....364 B2
  Rainham DA9 .....373 D5
Jessel Dr IG10 .....289 C7
Jessett Cl DA8 .....369 D2
Jessica Ct C04 .....110 C3
Jessop Cl C015 .....196 A8
Jetty Wlk RM17 .....378 A8
Jim Desormeaux Bglws
  CM20 .....199 E2
Jimmy's La C011 .....60 F2
Joan Gdns RM8 .....334 E2
Jocelyns CM17 .....200 C4
Jodrell Way RM20 .....371 F1
Joes Rd C010 .....34 F6
John Ball Wlk ② C01 .135 F7
John Barker Ho IG1 .....333 D2
John Bird Ct C01 .....109 F1
John Bramston Prim Sch
  IG6 .....312 A4
John Bramston Sch The
  CM8 .....183 F1
John Bunyan Jun & Inf Schs
  CM7 .....127 E4
John Burns Dr IG11 .....352 E5
John Chilos Way SS6 .....322 A4
John Clay Gdns RM16 .373 B5
John Cornwell VC Ho ⑧
  E12 .....352 C5
John Ct EN11 .....197 A1
John Dane Player Ct ④
  C010 .....22 E1
John Eliot Cl EN9 .....221 E2
John English Ave CM7 127 F1
John Harper St ⑤ C01 .135 E8
John Henry Keene Meml
  Homes CM1 .....232 A4
John Kavanagh Ct ①
  IG6 .....312 A4
John Kent Ave C02 .135 B2
John King Ct C07 .....192 F6
John Parker Cl RM10 .354 B5
John Perry Prim Sch
  RM10 .....354 D6
John Raven Ct C05 .....158 D3
John Ray Gdns CM7 .....155 B5
John Ray Jun & Inf Sch
  CM7 .....154 F8
John Ray St CM7 .....128 A3
Johnson Cl Braintree CM7 155 E1
  Ipswich IP2 .....17 C3
  Rochford SS4 .....325 D5

Johnson Cl continued
  Wickford SS12 .....321 D5
Johnson Ct SS4 .....325 F2
Johnson Rd
  Great Baddow CM2 .....255 A5
  St Osyth C016 .....194 B4
Johnson's Dr C07 .....138 A6
Johnsons Way DA9 .....377 C1
Johnsons Yd CB11 .....22 D2
Johns Rd CM23 .....119 A1
John's Rd DA2 .....376 C1
John St Brightlingsea C07 192 F6
  Grays RM17 .....378 C8
  Southend-on-S SS3 .....368 E7
John's Terr RM3 .....315 C4
Johns The CM5 .....249 A4
Johnston Cl Halstead C09 103 F8
  Holland-on-S C015 .....196 E5
Jonas Cl CM14 .....315 F6
Jonas Cl CM14 .....315 F6
Johnston Rd IG8 .....310 A5
Johnston Way CM9 .....259 A8
John Tibauld Ct CB9 .....27 B6
John Warner Sch The
  EN11 .....197 B1
John William Ct RM16 .372 D1
Jollyboys La N CM6 .....152 C6
Jollyboys La S CM6 .....152 C4
Jonathan Feedham Ct
  C07 .....137 B1
Jonathans RM11 .....336 E3
Jonathon Ho RM17 .....373 D2
Jones Cl SS2 .....347 E3
Jones Cnr CM7 .....344 A3
Jonquil Way C04 .....109 C2
Jordans Cl RM10 .....354 B8
Jordans The SS1 .....348 A2
Jordans Way RM13 .....355 D3
Joscelyne's Yd SS14 .....309 D4
Joseph Cohn Ho CM19 .223 A6
Joseph Gdns C06 .....156 E4
Joseph Lister Lodge C11 332 B3
Josling Cl RM17 .....377 F8
Joslin Rd RM19 .....371 D1
Joslyn Cl EN5 .....265 A2
Josselin Cl C010 .....105 B7
Josselin Cl SS13 .....321 C2
Josselin Rd SS13 .....321 C2
Josse Lyns The IP11 .....381 A8
Jotmans Hall Prim Sch
  SS7 .....344 B4
Jotmans La
  South Benfleet SS7 .....343 F2
  South Benfleet SS7 .....344 A3
Journeymans Way SS14 348 A5
Jovian Way C04 .....110 B6
Joyce Cl EN7 .....265 D5
Joyce's Chase CM9 .....239 A8
Joydon Dr RM6 .....334 B5
Joyes Cl RM3 .....314 D6
Joyners Cl RM9 .....353 F8
Joyners Field CM18 .....223 C4
Jubilee Ave
  Broomfield CM1 .....208 B2
  Chingford E4 .....309 C4
  Clacton-on-S C016 .....195 E8
  Romford RM7 .....335 C6
Jubilee Cl Colchester C03 134 D6
  Greenhithe DA9 .....377 C1
  Harwich C012 .....90 E2
  Hockley SS5 .....324 E5
  Romford RM7 .....335 B6
Jubilee Cotts SS4 .....327 D6
Jubilee Ct
  South Benfleet SS7 .....344 A1
  Great Dunmow CM6 .....123 C1
  Sible Hedingham C09 .....75 E8
  Waltham Abbey EN9 .....265 F6
  Walton-on-t-N C014 .....171 C7
Jubilee Dr SS11 .....321 C8
Jubilee End C011 .....86 C5
Jubilee La C07 .....111 C3
Jubilee Par IG8 .....310 C4
Jubilee Rd Basildon CM20 320 C4
  Grays RM20 .....377 B8
  Rayleigh SS6 .....323 E2
Jubilee Rise CM3 .....257 A6
Jubilee Terr
  Chelmsford CM1 .....232 A4
  Woodham Ferrers CM3 .279 B4
Jubilee Way C013 .....171 C6
Jubilee Wlk C89 .....9 A7
Judge Rd CM2 .....233 B4
Judith Anne Ct RM4 .....337 E2
Judith Ave RM5 .....313 B4
Julia Gdns IG11 .....353 D3
Julian Ave C04 .....110 B6
Julian Cl Broomfield CM1 208 B1
  Haverhill CB9 .....9 C7
Julie Ho EN11 .....221 C8
Julien Court Rd CM7 .....128 A4
Juliers Cl SS8 .....364 D3
Juliers Rd SS8 .....364 D3
Juliette Way RM15 .....370 F5
Junction Rd
  Basildon SS13 .....343 B4
  Brentwood CM14 .....316 C6
  Cold Norton CM3 .....281 A4
  Romford RM1 .....335 F6
Junction Rd E RM6 .....334 E4
Junction Rd W RM6 .....334 E4
Juniper Cl Billericay CM11 297 C4
Juniper Ct
  Brentwood CM13 .....316 F7
  Great Dunmow CM6 .....123 B1
  Ilford RM6 .....334 C5
Juniper Dr
  Chelmsford CM2 .....254 B6
  South Ockendon RM15 .357 E2
Juniper Rd Boreham CM3 233 F8
  Colchester C04 .....134 D5
  Ilford IG1 .....352 B8
  Southend-on-S SS9 .....346 F4
Juniper Way
  Colchester C04 .....136 D8

Juniper Way continued
  Romford RM2 .....314 E2
Juno Mews C02 .....135 C1
Jupes Hill C07 .....85 C4
Jupe's Hill C06 .....79 D1
Jupiter Cl C89 .....9 D6
Jupiter Ho IP4 .....18 B7
Jury St ⑧ DA11 .....379 B1
Justinian Cl C84 .....9 D6
Jutsums Ave RM7 .....335 B5
Jutsums Ct RM7 .....335 B5
Jutsums La RM7 .....335 B5
Juvina Cl CM8 .....211 F7

K

Kale Croft C03 .....134 D5
Kale Rd SS7 .....344 E4
Kamerwyk Ave SS8 .....364 C4
Kangels The C811 .....40 D2
Karen Cl Brentwood CM15 294 C2
  Rainham RM13 .....354 E3
  South Benfleet SS7 .....363 E8
  Stanford-le-H SS17 .....160 C6
Karen Cl SS12 .....321 C6
Karen Terr IG2 .....333 D6
Karina Cl IG7 .....311 E5
Kate Daniels Ho C016 .140 F1
Katella Trad Est IG11 .....352 E2
Kate's La C810 .....24 C8
Katherine Cl SS6 .....324 A1
Katherine Gdns SS13 .343 E7
Katherine Semar Inf Sch
  C811 .....43 E6
Katherine Semar Jun Sch
  C811 .....43 E6
Katherines Hatch CM19 .223 A6
Katherines Ho CM19 .....223 A6
Katherines Prim Sch
  CM19 .....223 A6
Katherine's Way CM19 .223 A6
Kathleen Cl SS17 .....360 E4
Kathleen Dr SS9 .....346 A4
Kathleen Ferrier Cres
  SS5 .....341 D8
Kathryn Ct SS3 .....368 E7
Katonia Ave CM4 .....260 F1
Kavanaghs CM14 .....316 B7
Kavanaghs Terr CM14 .316 B7
Kay Cl CM5 .....181 A7
Kayla Ct C015 .....135 C6
Keable Rd C06 .....133 A8
Keary Rd DA10 .....377 F1
Keating Cl C07 .....86 B4
Keatings The CM15 .....172 E2
Keats Ave Braintree CM7 154 F8
  Romford RM3 .....314 B3
Keats Cl Chigwell IG7 .311 C4
  Maldon CM9 .....259 A8
  Wanstead E11 .....332 B6
Keats Ct Belvedere DA17 369 C3
  Colchester C03 .....134 F6
Keats Sq SS3 .....301 E6
Keats Wlk
  Brentwood CM14 .....295 D2
  Rayleigh SS6 .....324 A2
Kebbles C03 .....135 D6
Kecksys C03 .....135 D6
Kecksys CM1 .....172 F4
Kedington Hill C010 .....34 B2
Keable Cl C015 .....166 C7
Keeble Ct C07 .....166 E7
Keeble Pk CM9 .....258 F8
Keeble's Yd ⑦ C89 .....9 A8
Keeble Way C07 .....128 A3
Keefield CM19 .....223 B3
Keegan Pl SS9 .....364 C4
Keelars La C07 .....137 C2
Keel Cl IG11 .....353 C3
Keelers Way C07 .....109 B7
Keelings La CM0 .....285 E8
Keelings Rd CM0 .....285 E8
Keene View SS14 .....254 B3
Keepers Gn C04 .....109 B3
Keep The ⑧ C89 .....8 E7
Keer Ave SS8 .....364 D2
Keighley Mews C09 .....349 D2
Keighley Rd SS14 .....304 A1
Keir Hardie Ho RM14 .373 D5
Keir Hardie Way IG11 .353 A5
Keith Ave SS17 .....299 D2
Keith Cl C015 .....168 D3
Keith Lauder Ho RM6 .334 E6
Keith Rd IG11 .....352 C6
Keith Way
  Hornchurch RM11 .....336 E4
  Southend-on-S SS9 .....347 E5
Kelburn Way RM13 .....354 F2
Kellington Rd SS8 .....364 C4
Kelly Ho RM15 .....371 C5
Kelly Rd Basildon SS13 .343 E7
  Ipswich IP2 .....16 D3
Kelly Way RM6 .....334 E5
Kelsie Way IG6 .....311 E4
Kelso Cl C06 .....109 C6
Kelso Lodge E18 .....310 B1
Kelston Rd IG6 .....311 B8
Kelvedon Cl
  Billericay CM11 .....297 C2
  Brentwood CM13 .....295 E3
  Rayleigh SS6 .....323 A3
Kelvedon Dr IP4 .....18 F5
Kelvedon Gn CM3 .....259 D3
Kelvedon Hall La
  Kelvedon Hatch CM14 271 A4
  Tiptree C05 .....185 E5

Kelvedon Hatch Com Prim
  Sch CM15 .....271 E2
Kelvedon Hatch Nuclear
  Bunker* CM14 .....271 C3
Kelvedon Ho IG9 .....288 E2
Kelvedon Rd
  Billericay CM11 .....297 C2
  Coggeshall C06 .....158 A8
  Messing C05 .....159 C2
  Tiptree C05 .....186 B7
  Tolleshunt D'arcy CM9 .215 C6
  Wickham Bishops CM8 .212 F5
Kelvedon St Mary's CE Prim
  Sch C05 .....158 C2
Kelvedon Way IG8 .....310 F4
Kelvedon Wlk RM13 .....354 F4
Kelvin Ct C013 .....170 F3
Kelvin Rd ③ DA17 .....369 A3
Kelvin Rd M8 .....334 C3
Kelvin Rd
  South Benfleet SS7 .....344 D7
  Tilbury RM18 .....379 A5
Kelvinside SS17 .....360 E4
Kemball St IP4 .....18 A5
Kembles SS6 .....322 E5
Kempe Rd CM7 .....72 D6
Kemp Ho E6 .....352 A6
Kempley Ct RM17 .....378 D8
Kemp Rd RM8 .....334 D3
Kempson Dr C010 .....34 C5
Kempston Hd IP11 .....381 B7
Kempton Ave RM12 .....336 F1
Kempton Cl SS7 .....345 B7
Kempton Pk C016 .....168 B5
Kempton Rd E6 .....352 A4
Kemsley Ct DA9 .....377 B1
Kemsley Rd
  Earls Colne C06 .....105 A6
  Felixstowe IP11 .....381 D5
Ken Cooke Ct ④ C01 .135 F7
Kendal Ave Barking IG11 352 E4
  Epping CM16 .....268 A8
Kendal Cl Hullbridge SS5 .301 E1
  Rayleigh SS6 .....323 E2
  Woodford IG8 .....309 F8
Kendal Croft RM12 .....355 A7
Kendal Ct ⑨ Chingford E4 287 C1
  Wickford SS11 .....322 A5
Kendale RM16 .....374 B3
Kendall CE Prim Sch
  C01 .....136 C4
Kendall Rd C01 .....136 A6
Kempster's Almshouses ③
  Epping CM16 .....268 A8
Kendall Terr 136 A6
Kendal Rd EN9 .....265 C4
Kendal Way SS9 .....346 E2
Kendon Cl E11 .....332 B6
Kenholme SS9 .....346 E4
Kenilworth Ave
  Chingford E17 .....309 A1
  Romford RM3 .....315 B4
Kenilworth Cl CM12 .....296 E2
Kenilworth Ct
  Chingford E4 .....309 C8
  ⊠ Dartford DA2 .....376 B1
Kenilworth Gdns
  Hornchurch RM11 .....336 D1
  Ilford IG3 .....333 F2
  Loughton IG10 .....288 F3
  Rayleigh SS6 .....323 E3
  Southend-on-S SS0,SS9 347 A3
Kenilworth Gr C014 .....142 A2
Kenilworth Pl C015 .....319 E1
Kenilworth Rd C015 .....196 E6
Kenley Cl SS13 .....321 C2
Kenley Gdns RM12 .....336 F2
Kenmar Cl SS6 .....346 A8
Kenmore Cl SS8 .....364 E2
Kennedy Ave SS15 .....340 F7
Kennedy Cl Ipswich IP4 .18 A6
  Rayleigh SS6 .....346 A8
Kennedy Rd IG11 .....352 E4
Kennedy Way C015 .....168 C4
Kennel La CM12,CM11 .319 C7
Kennet Cl RM14 .....337 E5
Kenning Rd EN11 .....221 B8
Kennington Ave SS7 .....344 D6
Kennington Prim Sch
  RM15 .....371 C7
Kennylands Rd IG6 .....312 A3
Kensington Ct RM17 .378 C8
Kensington Dr IG8 .....310 D1
Kensington Gdns
  Billericay CM12 .....297 A4
  East Tilbury RM18 .....375 C2
  Redbridge IG2 .....332 F3
Kensington Ho ⑧ IG8 .311 A3
Kensington Rd
  Ipswich IP1 .....17 A8
  Pilgrims Hatch CM15 .294 A3
  Romford RM7 .....335 C5
Kenstone Cl C015 .....218 B6
Kent Ave
  Canvey Island SS8 .....364 B5
  Dagenham RM6 .....354 A1
  Southend-on-S SS9 .....346 F3
Kent Cl Basildon SS15 .....341 D7
  Brightlingsea C07 .....192 F6
  Ilford IG6 .....311 F4

Kent Dr RM12 .....355 D8
Kent Elms Ct SS9 .....346 F5
Kent Elms Cnr SS9 .....346 F5
Kentford Rd RM11 .....135 E4
Kent Gdns CM7 .....128 B4
Kent Green Cl SS5 .....324 F5
Kent Ho Felixstowe IP11 381 C6
  Romford RM7 .....313 A2
Kentings The CM7 .....127 F2
Kentish Rd DA17 .....369 A2
Kent Kraft Ind Est
  Northfleet DA11 .....378 A2
  Swanscombe DA10 .....377 F2
Kentmere C04 .....110 E2
Kenton Way SS16 .....340 F5
Kent Rd Dagenham RM10 354 B7
  Grays RM17 .....373 C1
Kent's Ave C015 .....196 E6
Kents Farm La CM2 .....276 D4
Kents Grass CM9 .....216 D2
Kents Hill Jun & Inf Sch
  SS7 .....344 D4
Kents Hill Rd SS7 .....344 D4
Kents Hill Rd N SS7 .344 D6
Kents La CM16 .....225 D2
Kents Yd C011 .....127 F4
Kent View Aveley RM15 .371 C4
  Rainham RM13 .....370 D6
Kent View Ave SS9 .....366 A8
Kent View Cr SS8 .....364 B1
Kent View Gdns IG3 .....333 E2
Kent View Rd SS16 .....342 F4
Kent Way SS6 .....346 A8
Kentwell Ct IP14 .....18 F4
Kentwell Cl SS4 .....344 C3
Kenway Rainham RM13 .355 D2
  Romford RM5 .....313 C1
  Southend-on-S SS2 .....348 A2
Kenway Cl RM13 .....355 C2
Kenway Wlk RM13 .....355 D2
Kenwood Gdns Ilford IG2 333 A6
  ⊠ Wanstead E18 .....332 B8
Kenwood Rd SS17 .....361 B5
Kenworthy Rd CM7 .....127 F2
Kenyon Cl C07 .....58 D1
Kenyon St IP9 .....17 C4
Keppel Rd RM9 .....353 E8
Kerby Rise CM2 .....232 F2
Kernow Ct CM11 .....354 E4
Kerridge's Cut C011 .....87 A4
Kerril Croft CM20 .....199 A1
Kerry Ave RM15 .....370 F4
Kerry Cl RM14 .....337 C4
Kerry Ct C011 .....136 C7
Kerry Dr RM14 .....337 B4
Kerry Rd RM13 .....373 D5
Kersbrooke Way SS17 .361 B5
Kersey Ave C010 .....34 B6
Kersey Dr C016 .....135 C3
Kersey Gdns RM18 .....195 B5
Kersey Rd IP11 .....381 B3
Kershaw Cl Grays RM16 .372 C2
  Hornchurch RM11 .....336 E4
Kershaw Rd RM14 .....335 A1
Kershaws Cl SS12 .....321 C6
Kessler Ave CM7 .....373 D7
Kesteven Cl IG6 .....311 F4
Kesteven Rd IP2 .....17 B4
Kestral Pk SS13 .....295 E4
Kestrel Cl
  Hornchurch RM12 .....355 B5
  Redbridge IG6 .....312 C6
Kestrel Gdns CM23 .....145 C6
Kestrel Gr SS6 .....323 B3
Kestrel Ho SS3 .....349 F1
Kestrel Rd Haverhill CB9 .9 C7
  ⊠ Ipswich IP2 .....16 D3
  Waltham Abbey EN9 .....266 A5
Kestrel Way C015 .....195 F6
Kestrel Wlk C015 .....254 B5
Keswick Ave
  Holland-on-S C015 .....196 C6
  Hornchurch RM11 .....336 D3
  Hullbridge SS5 .....301 E2
Keswick Cl
  Kirby Cross C013 .....170 F7
  Rayleigh SS6 .....323 E2
Keswick Gdns IG4 .....332 F7
Keswick Ho ⑭ RM3 .....314 D4
Keswick Rd SS4 .....344 E7
Ketley Cl C015 .....186 E5
Ketleys IP2 .....17 C4
Ketleys View CM7 .....127 A7
Kettering Rd RM13 .....314 E3
Kettlebaston Way IP14 .17 D8
Kettlebury Way CM5 .....248 F1
Kevin Cl CM13 .....319 D7
Kew La C013 .....170 C8
Keyes Cl SS3 .....349 E1
Keyes Rd DA1 .....376 A3
Keyes Way CM7 .....128 C4
Keymer Way C03 .....134 F4
Keynes Way C012 .....90 F1
Keynsham Ave IG8 .....309 D6
Key Rd C015 .....195 E3
Keysers Rd EN10 .....221 B1
Keysland SS7 .....345 B7
Key St IP1 .....17 D5
Keys The CM13 .....316 D1
Khartoum Rd Ilford IG1 .352 B7
  Ipswich IP1 .....17 F7
Khartoum Villas C07 .....111 E8
Kibcaps SS16 .....341 F4
Kidder Rd CM77 .....126 F1
Kidd Ho RM9 .....353 F8
Kidman Cl RM2 .....336 C8
Kielder Cl IG6 .....311 F4
Kielder Ct CM23 .....146 A6
Kilbarry Wlk CM11 .....297 D6

Kilburn Gdns CO16 ....195 D5
Kildermorie Cl CO4 ......110 D3
Kildowan Rd IG3 ....334 A3
Kilmaine Rd CO12 ....90 F2
Kilmarnock Gdns RM8 ..334 C1
Kilmartin Rd IG3 ....334 A2
Kilmartin Way RM12 ....355 B7
Kilmington Cl CM13 ......317 B8
Kiln Barn Ave CO15 ....94 C2
Kiln Cotts Danbury CM3 .256 D6
  Dedham CO7 ....84 F5
Kiln Dr CO10 ....34 B6
Kilnfield
  Chipping Ongar CM5 ....248 F2
  Wyatts Green CM15 ......272 C3
Kiln Field IP11 ....381 B5
Kiln La Harlow CM17 .....224 C7
  Manningtree CO11 ....86 D4
Kiln Rd Hadleigh SS7 ....345 A4
  North Weald Bassett CM16 247 A4
Kiln Shaw SS16 ....341 C4
Kilns Hill CO6 ....130 F5
Kiln Way RM17 ....372 F1
Kilnwood Ave SS5 ....324 D5
Kiln Wood La RM4 ....313 D5
Kilowan Cl SS16 ....340 F4
Kilsby Wlk RM9 ....353 B6
Kiltie Rd CO5 ....186 E5
Kilworth Ave
  Brentwood CM15 ....295 A3
  Southend-on-S SS1 ......367 B8
Kimberley Ave Ilford IG2 333 E4
  Romford RM7 ....224 C5
Kimberley Cl CM23 ....146 A5
Kimberley Cl SS7 ....344 C3
Kimberley Rd
  Chingford E4 ....287 E1
  Colchester CO1 ....136 E5
  Little Wakering SS3 .....349 E6
  South Benfleet SS7 .....344 C3
Kimberley Way E4 ....287 E1
Kimberly Dr SS15 ....319 F2
Kimpton Ave CM15 ....294 C2
Kimpton's Cl SS5 ....248 F5
Kincaid Rd CO16 ....194 A4
Kinfauns Ave RM11 ......336 C5
Kinfauns Rd IG3 ....334 B3
Kingaby Gdns RM13 .....355 A5
King Alfred Rd RM3 .....314 F1
King Charles Rd CO3 ....230 B6
King Coel Rd CO3 ....134 D7
King Edmund Sch The
  SS4 ....325 E5
King Edward Ave
  Burnham-on-C CM0 ....306 B6
  Rainham RM13 ....355 D2
King Edward Dr CM1 .....232 A3
King Edward Dr RM16 ...373 E3
King Edward Ind Pk CO2 136 D5
King Edward IV's Almshouses
  CB11 ....22 D1
King Edward Quay CO2 .136 D6
King Edward Rd
  Basildon SS15 ....341 B8
  Brentwood CM14 ....316 C7
  Greenhithe DA9 ....377 A2
  Ipswich IP3 ....18 B1
  Romford RM1 ....335 F5
King Edward's Rd
  Barking IG11 ....352 D3
  South Woodham Ferrers
  CM3 ....301 D8
  Stanford-le-H SS17 .....375 D8
King Edward Terr SS16 .340 F4
King Edward VI Gram Sch
  CM1 ....232 A3
King Edward VII Dr IP9 .91 C8
King Edward Way CM8 ..211 E8
Kingfisher Ave Ipswich IP2 16 E1
  Wanstead E11 ....332 B5
Kingfisher Cl
  Brentwood CM14 ....295 A2
  Colchester CO4 ....136 F8
  Haverhill CB9 ....9 C8
  Heybridge CM9 ....237 C5
  Southend-on-S SS3 .....368 E8
  Stanstead Abbotts SG12 .197 C3
Kingfisher Cres SS6 .....323 E7
Kingfisher Dr
  Greenhithe DA9 ....377 A1
  Harwich CO12 ....90 E1
  South Benfleet SS7 .....344 C2
Kingfisher Gate CM7 ....128 A5
Kingfisher Lodge CM2 ..254 F7
Kingfisher Mdws CO9 ...76 F1
Kingfisher Rd RM14 .....337 F3
Kingfishers Basildon SS16 342 C4
  Inglestone CM4 ....274 C5
Kingfishers The ■ SS11 322 A5
Kingfisher Way
  Bishop's Stortford CM23 .146 A7
  Kelvedon CO5 ....158 C2
  Roydon CM19 ....200 F1
King George Ave IG2 ....333 D5
King George Cl RM7 ....335 C8
King George Hospl IG3 .334 A6
King George Rd
  Colchester CO2 ....138 C4
  Waltham Abbey EN9 .....265 C5
King George's Ave CO12 .91 B4
King George's Cl SS6 ...323 D1
King George's Ct SS6 ...323 D1
King George's Dr SS11 .321 A7
King George's Pl CM9 ..237 A2
King George's Rd CM5 .294 B3
King George VI Ave
  RM18 ....375 B2
King George V Memorial
  Homes IP11 ....17 F3
King Harold Ct EN9 .....265 C6
King Harold Rd CO3 .....135 A4
King Harold Sch EN9 ...265 E6

King Henrys Ct EN9 .....265 C3
King Henry's Dr SS4 ....347 F7
King Henry's Mews EN3 265 A2
King John Sch The SS7 .345 B3
Kingley Cl SS12 ....321 B7
Kingley Dr SS12 ....321 B7
Kings Acre CO6 ....130 F2
King's Ave
  Clacton-on-S CO15 .....196 D5
  Dagenham RM6 ....334 F5
  Ipswich IP4 ....17 E5
King's Ave
  Buckhurst Hill IG9 ......310 D8
  Woodford IG8 ....310 D8
Kingsbridge Cir ■ RM3 314 E4
Kingsbridge Cl
  Braintree CM7 ....127 F8
  Romford RM14 ....314 E4
Kingsbridge Ind Est
  IG11 ....352 E2
Kingsbridge Rd
  Barking IG11 ....352 D2
  Bishop's Stortford CM23 .146 A8
  Romford RM3 ....314 E4
Kingsbury Cl CO6 ....132 F3
Kingsbury Rd IP11 ......381 A7
Kingsbury Wlk CO10 ....34 A5
Kings Chase CM8 ....184 A1
King's Chase CM14 ......316 C7
Kings Cl
  Canvey Island SS8 .....363 C3
  Lawford CO11 ....86 A4
  Rayleigh SS6 ....323 E2
King's Cl CO16 ....194 A3
King's Cotts CM23 ......146 A6
Kings Cres SS15 ....319 B1
Kingscroft SS2 ....348 B1
Kings Croft CM0 ....284 D4
Kings Ct
  Bishop's Stortford CM23 .146 A8
  ❷ Buckhurst Hill IG9 ...310 D8
  Burnham-on-C CM0 ......306 B4
  Harwich CO12 ....91 B3
  Holland-on-S CO15 .....196 C5
King's Ct CM6 ....123 D1
Kingsdale Cl
  Swanscombe DA10 ......377 E1
  Waltham Abbey EN9 .....266 A5
Kingsdale Ind Est The
  CM1 ....232 C3
Kingsdon La CM17 ......224 C7
Kingsdown Cl SS13 .....343 C6
Kingsdown Rd SS2 .....346 F6
Kingsdown Wlk SS8 ....364 A5
Kings Eight CM14 ......316 C7
Kings Farm Chingford E17 309 B2
  Rayleigh SS6 ....323 E5
Kingsfield EN11 ....221 A8
Kingsfield Ave IP1 ......17 D8
Kings Fleet Rd IP11 ....381 C3
Kings Ford Ct CO2 .....135 B3
Kingsford Dr CM2 ......233 E8
King's Ford Jun & Inf Sch
  CO2 ....135 C3
Kingsgate Cl SS10 .....366 C8
Kingsgate Dr IP4 ....17 F8
Kings Gdns Ilford IG1 ..333 D3
Kingston Cres CM2 .....232 C5
Kingston Ct Grays RM17 373 B3
Northfleet DA11 ....378 B2
Kingston Hill SS16 .....341 D2
Kingston Hill Ave RM6 .334 E8
Kingston Mews CO15 ..195 C3
Kingston Prim Sch SS7 344 E6
Kingston Rd Ilford IG1 ..16 F8
  Ipswich IP1 ....16 F8
  Romford RM7 ....335 F7
Kingston Ridge SS16 ...341 D3
Kingston Way SS7 .....344 F6
King Street Mews ■
  CM3 ....145 F7
Kingsview Cl SS1 ....321 F6
Kingsway Harwich CO12 .91 A4
  Hullbridge SS5 ....323 D8
  Southend-on-S SS0 .....347 A2
  Tiptree CO5 ....186 C6
  Woodford IG8 ....310 C5
Kings Way
  Billericay CM11 ....319 D6
  South Woodham F CM3 .279 C1
  Way IP3 ....18 C2
Kingsway Mews SS0 ....347 B2
Kings Wlk CM9 ....216 E1
Kingswode Hoe Sch
  CO3 ....135 C7
Kingswood Chase SS4 .346 D3
Kingswood Cl CM11 ....297 C2
Kingswood Cres SS3 ...323 B1
Kingswood Ct
  Basildon SS14 ....342 E5
  Bradwell-on-S CM0 .....242 B2
  Chingford E4 ....309 A5
Kingswood Inf Sch SS16 342 B5
Kingswood Lodge SS9 ..346 D3
Kingswood Rd
  Basildon SS14 ....342 C5
  Colchester CO4 ....109 F4
  Ilford IG3 ....334 A5
Kingswood Sch RM3 ...315 A6
Kingswell Ave CO15 ...195 C5
King Williams Ct EN9 ..265 C5
Kinlett Cl CO4 ....110 B4
Kinloch Chase CM8 ....217 C6
Kinnaird Way IG8 ......310 F4
Kino Rd CO14 ....171 D8
Kipling Ave RM18 ......375 A8
Kipling Cl
  Brentwood CM14 ....316 B5
  Chelmsford CM1 ....232 A5
Kipling Mews SS2 ......348 A2
Kipling Rd DA1 ....376 B2
Kipling Twrs RM3 ......314 A3
Kipling Way CM7 ......155 A8
Kirby Cl Ipswich IP4 ....18 A7
  Loughton IG10 ....288 E2
  Redbridge IG6 ....311 E4

Kings Meadow Ct continued
  Waltham Abbey EN9 ....266 A5
Kings Meadow Rd CO1 .135 F8
Kingsmead Rd CM23 ....146 A5
Kingsmere SS7 ....345 C5
Kingsmere Cl CO5 ......218 D7
Kings Mews Chigwell IG7 311 C8
  Wivenhoe CO7 ....137 C4
Kingsmill Gdns RM9 ...353 F7
Kingsmill Rd RM9 ......353 F7
Kingsmoor Jun & Inf Sch
  CM18 ....223 C4
Kingsmoor Rd CM19 ...223 B5
Kings Oak RM7 ....335 A8
King Solomon High Sch
  IG6 ....311 D1
Kings Par
  Holland-on-S CO15 ....196 E5
  Stanford-le-H SS17 ....360 C1
Kingspark Ct E18 ......332 A8
Kings Pk SS7 ....344 F5
Kings Prom
  Buckhurst Hill IG9 ....310 D8
  Loughton IG10 ....288 D2
Kings Prom CO15 ......220 J8
King's Quay St CO12 ...91 E6
Kings Rd Basildon SS15 319 B1
  Braintree CM7 ....127 E6
  Burnham-on-C CM0 .....306 B4
  Canvey Island SS8 ....363 C3
  Chelmsford CM1 ....231 F4
  Glemsford CO10 ....2 B5
  Great Totham CM9 .....213 D7
  Halstead CO9 ....76 E1
  Rayleigh SS6 ....323 E2
  Southminster CM0 .....284 D4
King's Rd Barking IG11 .352 C5
  Brentwood CM14 ....316 C7
  Chingford E4 ....287 D1
  Clacton-on-S CO15 ....195 D1
  Harwich CO12 ....91 B3
  Romford RM1 ....336 A6
  South Benfleet SS7 ...344 E2
  Southend-on-S SS0 ....347 B1
Kings Reach CO14 .....144 D1
Kings Road Prim Sch
  CM1 ....231 F4
King St
  Bishop's Stortford CM23 .145 F7
  Bradfield CO11 ....114 C8
  Castle Hedingham CO9 ..51 F4
  Felixstowe IP11 ....381 C6
  Gravesend DA12 ....379 B1
  High Ongar CM5 ....250 B3
  ❶ Ipswich IP1 ....17 C6
  Maldon CM9 ....237 A1
  Saffron Walden CB10 ...22 D1
  Stanford-le-H SS17 ....360 C1
  Sudbury CO10 ....33 E7
Kingsteignton SS3 .....368 D8
King Stephen Rd CO1 ..136 B6
Kingston Ave
  Chelmsford CM2 ....232 E3
  Southend-on-S SS3 ....349 E2
Kingston Chase CM6 ...236 F5
Kingston Cl CM11 ......319 B1
Kings CL Clacton-on-S CO15 195 D3
  Wickford SS12 ....321 C6
Knox Ct CM9 ....259 A8
Knox Cres Clacton-on-S CO15 195 C5
  Wickford SS12 ....321 F5
Knox Gdns CO15 ....195 E5
Knox Rd CO15 ....195 D5
Knutsford Cl IP8 ....16 C1
Kohima Rd CO2 ....135 B1
Kolburn Cl CO4 ....136 B8
Kolburg Rd SS8 ....364 D2
Kollum Rd SS8 ....364 E3
Koln Cl SS8 ....363 C5
Komberg Cres SS8 .....364 C5
Konnybrook SS7 ......345 A4
Korndyk Ave SS8 .....364 C4
Kreswell Gr CO12 ......91 B2
Kuan Yin Cl CM23 .....145 D3
Kyme Rd RM11 ....335 F5
Kynance Cl RM3 ....314 C6
Kynaston Pl CM8 ......184 B2
Kynaston Rd CM7 .....127 A7
Kynaston Cl SS17 .....360 E1
Kyrkly Ct ■ RM19 .....371 B1

Kirby Cl continued
  Romford RM3 ....315 A5
Kirby Cross Sta CO13 ..170 B6
Kirby Hall Rd CO5 ......51 D5
Kirby Prim Sch CO13 ...170 B7
Kirby Rd Basildon SS14 .342 F6
  Great Holland CO13 ...170 B8
  Walton-on-t-N CO14 ...171 B8
Kirby St IP4 ....18 A6
Kirkbare CO13 ....170 E6
Kirkham Ave SS16 .....359 F7
Kirkham Cl IP2 ....17 A2
Kirkham Ho ❶ RM3 ....314 D5
Kirkham Rd SS17 ......359 F8
Kirkham Shaw SS17 ...359 F8
Kirkhurst Cl CO7 ....193 A6
Kirkland Ave SS5 ......311 A1
Kirklees CM1 ....231 F4
Kirklees Rd RM8 ......353 C7
Kirkley Ct CB9 ....8 C8
Kirkmans Rd CM2 .....254 D3
Kirk Pl CM2 ....232 F3
Kirkton Cl IP9 ....91 A8
Kirtling Pl ■ CB9 .....9 B8
Kirton Cl RM12 ....355 C6
Kitchener Rd
  Chingford E17 ....309 B2
  Dagenham RM10 ....354 B6
  Ipswich IP1 ....16 C4
  North Fambridge CM3 ..281 A1
Kitchener Way IP9 .....91 A8
Kitchen Field CM7 .....128 D3
Kitchen Hill CO10 ......33 B6
Kittatts Rd SS8 ....364 A1
Kittiwake Cl CM3 ......199 C1
Kittiwake Cl IP2 ....16 E3
Kittiwake Dr CM0 .....237 C5
Knebworth Ave E17 ...309 A2
Knebworth Cl CM23 ...146 A5
Knebworth Ho E17 ....309 A2
Knevett Cl CM4 ....274 C8
Knightbridge Wlk CM12 297 A4
Knight Cl ❶ E4 ....287 F8
Knight Ho IG10 ....289 D5
Knighton Cl Romford RM7 335 D5
  Woodford IG8 ....310 B6
Knighton Dr IG8 ....310 B8
Knighton La IG9 ....310 B8
Knighton La IG9 ....310 B8
Knighton Rd
  Romford RM7 ....335 C5
  Wanstead E7 ....332 A1
Knights SS15 ....341 D7
Knightsbridge Cl CO2 .135 C3
Knightsbridge Ct CO15 196 B3
Knightsbridge Gdns ❺
  RM7 ....335 D6
Knights Cl
  Bishop's Stortford CM23 .145 C8
  Kelvedon CO5 ....86 C4
  Tiptree CO5 ....186 F3
Knight's Ct
  ❹ Basildon SS14 ....342 F8
  ❷ Haverhill CB9 ....8 E7
  Sawbridgeworth CM21 ..172 E2
Knights Manor Way CM1 376 A2
Knightsmead Sch RM15 372 A6
Knights Rd Braintree CM7 128 D1
  Coggeshall CO6 ....130 E2
Knight St
  Sawbridgeworth CM21 ..172 E2
  South Woodham Ferrers
  CM3 ....301 E7
Knights Way
  Great Dunmow CM6 ....123 D1
  Redbridge IG6 ....311 C4
Knight's Way CM1 ......17 B7
Knightswick Ctr SS8 ...364 C4
Knightswick Rd SS8 ...364 B4
Knightwood Rd RM14 .290 B6
Knightwood Rd RM13 .355 E3
Knivet Cl SS16 ....323 C1
Knockhall Chase DA9 ..377 C2
Knockhall Cty Prim Sch
  DA9 ....377 C2
Knockhall Rd DA9 .....377 D2
Knole Cl CM3 ....301 D5
Knole La CM11 ....321 A7
Knollcroft SS3 ....368 D6
Knoll The Billericay CM12 297 B4
  Rayleigh SS6 ....323 D2
Knowle Ho EN11 ......221 A5
Knowles Cl CO9 ....76 E1
Knowle The
  Basildon SS16 ....342 C4
  Hoddesdon EN11 ......221 A5
Knowlton Cotts RM15 .372 C8

Laburnum Cl RM14 .....338 A4
Laburnum Cl SS13 .....368 F8
Laburnum Gdns RM14 .337 F4
Laburnum Ave
  Hornchurch RM12 .....336 A2
  Wickford SS12 ....321 C6
Laburnum Cl
  Clacton-on-S CO15 ....195 C3
  Great Bentley CO7 .....166 F8
  Hockley SS5 ....324 C6
Laburnum Ave SS16 ....359 F7
Laburnum Cl IP2 ....16 C2
  Ipswich,Warren Heath IP18 .16 C2
  Steering CM22 ....201 C8
  Wickford SS12 ....321 C6
Laburnum Cres SS15 ..170 D6
Laburnum Dr
  Chelmsford CM2 ....254 C6
  Corringham SS17 ......361 B4
Laburnum Gr
  Basildon SS14 ....342 F5
  Chigwell IG7 ....312 B7
Lamborne Cres
  Basildon SS14 ....342 F5
  Chigwell IG7 ....312 B8
Lambourne Ct ❶ IG8 ..310 D2
Lambourne Dr CM13 ...295 C3
Lambourne Gdns
  ❷ Barking IG11 ....352 F5
  Chingford E4 ....309 A8
  Hornchurch RM12 .....336 A2
Lambourne Gr CM9 ....258 F8
Lambourne Hall Rd SS4 304 A2
Lamborne Mead Cotts
  SS4 ....305 A1
Lamborne Prim Sch
  RM4 ....290 B5
Lamborne Rd
  Barking IG11 ....352 F5
  Chigwell IG7 ....311 F7
  Ilford IG3 ....333 E2
Lambourne Sq RM4 ...290 C1
Lambourni Cl SS3 .....349 E2
Lamb's La RM13 ....355 D2
Lamb's La N RM13 ....355 C2
Lamb's La RM13 ....355 D2
Lambs Mdw IG8 ......310 D1
Lamerton Rd IG6 .....311 B1
Lammas Dr CM7 ......128 D3
Lammas Way CO7 ....137 C2
Lamont Cl ■ SS12 ....321 E5
Lamport Cl ❶ E17 ....309 C2
Lampern Cl CM12 .....297 C6
Lampern Cres CM12 ..297 C6
Lampern Mews CM12 .297 C6
Lampeter Ho ❹ RM3 .314 E3
Lampetsdowne SS17 ..361 B4
Lampits IN11 ....221 B6
Lampits Hill SS17 .....361 B5
Lampits Hill Ave SS17 361 A5
Lampits La SS17 ......361 A5
Lamplighters Cl EN9 ..266 A5
Lamson Rd RM13 .....354 F1
Lancaster Ave
  Barking IG11 ....352 E4
  Wanstead E18 ....332 B7
Lancaster Bsns Pk SS2 .347 C7
Lancaster Cl CM15 ....294 A4
Lancaster Ct ❷ SS1 ..367 B8
Lancaster Dr
  Basildon SS16 ....340 F5
  Hornchurch RM12 .....355 C8
  Loughton IG10 ....288 E3
Lancaster Gdns
  Rayleigh SS6 ....346 A8
  Southend-on-S SS1 ...367 B8
Lancaster Gdns E CO15 196 A3
Lancaster Gdns W CO15 196 A3
Lancaster Ho IP11 ....381 C5
Lancaster Pl IG1 ......352 C8
Lancaster Rd Grays RM16 372 D2
  ❶ Ipswich IP4 ....17 E6
  North Weald Bassett CM16 247 A5
  Rayleigh SS6 ....324 A1
  Sudbury CO10 ....15 D2
  Southend-on-S SS0 ...347 C3
Lancaster Way
  Bishop's Stortford CM23 .145 C8
  Braintree CM7 ....127 E4
  Earls Colne CO6 ......104 F2
Lancelot Rd IG6 ......311 E3
Lancer Way CM12 .....297 A4
Lanchester Ave CO15 .220 D6
Lancing Ave IP4 ......18 A8
Lancing Rd Ilford IG2 .333 D5
  Romford RM3 ....314 E3
Landau Way DA8 .....370 D1
Land Cl CO16 ....195 C5
Landermere SS14 ....342 E7
Landermere Rd CO16 .142 A2
Landere View CO16 ..142 A2
Lander Rd RM17 ....373 D1
Landisdale Cl CM23 ..231 E5
Landseer Cl
  Clacton-on-S CO15 ...195 C2
  Haverhill CB9 ....8 F6
Landseer Ct
  Colchester CO3 ......135 B5
  Ipswich IP3 ....17 E2
Landshill Ct SS0 .....347 C1
Landview Gdns CM5 ..249 A1
Landwick Cotts SS3 ..350 D4
Laneburst IG8 ....310 E1
Lane Ave DA9 ....377 C1
Lane End CM17 ....224 E7
Lane Mews E12 ....332 F1
Lanercost Way IP2 ....17 A1
Lane Rd CO6 ....106 B7
Laneside Ave RM8 ...334 F4
Lane The Mistley CO11 .86 F4

Laburnum Cl RM14 .....338 A4
Lambert Ct RM7 ....335 C4
Lambert's Rd CO6 .....105 F3
Lambeth Cl IP1 ....16 F8
Lambeth Mews SS5 ...324 C6
Lambeth Rd
  South Benfleet SS7 ...344 C6
  Southend-on-S SS9 ...346 E6
Lambeth Wlk CO15 ...195 E5
Lamb La CO9 ....75 D7
Lambley Rd RM9 .....353 B6
Lambourne
  Canvey Island SS8 ....364 A2
  East Tilbury RM18 ....375 C2
Lambourne Cl
  Chigwell IG7 ....312 B7
  Clacton-on-S CO15 ...195 F8
  Colchester CO3 ....134 C4

L

Laars Ave SS8 ....364 C5

Lane The *continued*
West Mersea CO5 218 A7
Langdale CM77 154 C7
Langdale Cl RM8 334 C3
Langdale Ct 9 IG1 333 B1
Langdale Dr CO4 110 B4
Langdale Gdns
Chelmsford CM2 254 D8
Hornchurch RM12 355 A7
Langdale Ho SS6 323 D2
Langdon Conservation Ctr*
SS16 340 E3
Langdon Cres E6 352 A3
Langdon Hills Ctry Pk*
SS17 360 F8
Langdon Mews CM11 297 B3
Langdon Nature Reserve*
SS16 341 D4
Langdon Rd Rayleigh SS6 323 B3
Wallend E6 352 A4
Langdon Sch E6 352 B4
Langdon Way SS17 361 B5
Langemore Way CM11 297 B1
Langenhoe SS12 321 E6
Langenhoe Com Prim Sch
CO5 163 B2
Langenhoe Hall La CO5 190 C7
Langenhoe Pk CO5 163 B2
Langer Park Ind Est
IP11 381 D3
Langer Prim Sch IP11 381 C2
Langer Rd IP11 381 C2
Langfield Cl EN9 221 E1
Langford Cres SS7 344 F6
Langford Gn CM13 295 C4
Langford Gr SS13 343 C8
Langford Rd
Heybridge CM9 236 F6
Langford CM9 236 D8
Wickham Bishops CM8,
CM9 212 C2
Woodford IG8 310 C4
Langfords IG9 310 D8
Langham Cres CM12 319 C7
Langham Ct RM11 336 D4
Langham Dr
Clacton-on-S CO16 195 B4
Ilford RM6 334 B5
Rayleigh SS6 323 A3
Langham La CO4 83 B2
Langham Prim Sch CO4 83 F4
Langham Rd CO4 82 F1
Langhorne Rd RM10 354 A5
Langland Cl SS17 361 A4
Langley Ave
Felixstowe IP11 381 C4
Wethersfield CM7 73 D7
Langley Cl
Felixstowe IP11 381 C5
Harwich CO12 91 C3
Romford RM3 314 D3
Southend-on-S SS9 346 B7
Langley Cres
Dagenham RM9 353 D5
Wanstead E11 332 C4
Langley Dr
Brentwood CM14 316 A7
Wanstead E11 332 B4
Langley Gdns RM9 353 D5
Langley Gn EN9 221 D1
Langley Hill CO8 55 C3
Langley Mdw IG10 289 D7
Langley Pl CM12 296 E3
Langleys Basildon SS16 342 B4
Great Tey CO6 106 C1
Langport Dr SS0 347 B4
Langport Ho 3 RM3 314 E3
Langside Cl SS15 341 B8
Langston Rd IG10 289 D5
Langstons IP11 381 B7
Langthorne Cres RM17 373 C2
Langthornes 1 CM11 297 B2
Langton Ave
Chelmsford CM1 231 E5
Wallend E6 352 A2
Langtons Jun & Inf Sch
RM11 336 E3
Langton Way RM16 374 C2
Languidic Cl CO10 34 C6
Langwood CO5 218 C7
Lanham Green Rd CM77 156 A7
Lanham Pl 7 SS13 343 B8
Lanhams SS13 343 C8
Lanhams Ct 5 SS13 343 B8
Lansbury Ave
Barking IG11 353 A5
Dagenham RM6 334 E6
Lansbury Cres DA1 376 A2
Lansbury Gdns RM18 379 A6
Lansdown Ave SS7 345 F6
Lansdowne Ave SS9 347 A1
Lansdowne Cl CO5 186 C6
Lansdowne Ct EN10 221 A3
Lansdowne Dr SS6 323 C3
Lansdowne Prim Sch
RM18 378 F5
Lansdowne Rd
Chingford E4 309 A8
Felixstowe IP11 381 F6
Ilford IG3 333 F4
Ipswich IP4 18 A5
Wanstead E18 332 A8
Lansdowne Sq DA11 378 F1
Lansdown Rd RM18 379 A5
Lantern Stps 18 SS1 367 C7
Lanvalley Rd CO3 134 E6
Lanyards IP11 381 F4
La Plata Gr CM14 316 B7
Lappmark Rd SS8 364 D3
Lapwater Cl SS9 346 C2
Lapwater Ct SS9 346 C2
Lapwing Dr
Heybridge CM9 237 C5
Kelvedon CO5 158 D2
Lapwing Rd Ipswich IP2 16 D3
Lapwing Rd *continued*
Wickford SS11 299 C2
Larch Cl Basildon SS15 319 C1
Colchester CO4 136 D8
Larches The
Boreham CM3 233 E8
South Benfleet SS7 344 C8
Larch Gr Chelmsford CM2 254 C6
Witham CM8 184 A5
Larch Ho IP11 381 C4
Larch Way CM6 123 B1
Larch Wlk CM9 237 C6
Larchwood CM23 145 D5
Larchwood Ave RM5 313 B4
Larchwood Cl Ipswich IP2 16 C5
Romford RM5 313 C4
Southend-on-S SS9 346 B6
Larchwood Gdns CM15 294 A3
Lark Cl CM14 316 B6
Larke Rise SS2 347 D5
Larkfield SS17 361 B5
Larkfield Cl SS4 325 D4
Larkfield Rd CO7 139 D1
Larkhill Ave SS4 304 A2
Lark Hill Rd SS4 304 B1
Larkhill Rise IP4 18 E5
Larkhill Way IP11 381 B5
Larkin Cl CM13 295 C2
Lark Rise CO10 33 D5
Larkrise Prim Sch CM2 254 E6
Larks Cl CB9 9 C7
Larksfield Cres CO12 91 B4
Larksfield Rd IP9 62 A2
Larkshall Bsns Ctr E4 309 D8
Larkshall Cres E4 309 C6
Larkshall Ct Chingford E4 309 C5
Romford RM7 313 C1
Larkshall Rd E4 309 D6
Lark's La Broomfield CM3 208 A6
Great Waltham CM3 207 F5
Larkspur Cl
Bishop's Stortford CM23 145 D6
South Ockendon RM15 357 C2
Witham CM8 183 E4
Larkspur Ct 3 CM1 232 F6
Larkspur Rd IP2 16 F3
Larks Rise CO9 77 A1
Larksway
Bishop's Stortford CM23 145 C6
Felixstowe IP11 381 B3
Larkswood CM17 224 C6
Larkswood Ct E4 309 D5
Larkswood Jun & Inf Sch
E4 309 B6
Larkswood Rd
Chingford E4 309 B6
Corringham SS17 361 B4
Larkswood Wlk 2 SS12 321 D6
Larkway CO13 170 E7
Larman Ct CO11 86 C7
Larneys The CO13 170 E7
Larsen Dr EN9 265 D5
Larup Ave SS8 364 C4
Larup Gdns SS8 364 C4
La Salette RC Prim Sch
RM13 354 F2
La Salle Cl IP2 17 B3
Lascelles Cl CM15 294 A4
Lascelles Gdns SS4 325 D6
Latchett Rd E18 310 B2
Latchetts Shaw SS16 342 B4
Latchford Pl IG7 312 B6
Latching Cl RM3 314 D6
Latchingdon CE Prim Sch
CM3 282 B6
Latchingdon Cl SS6 323 A3
Latchingdon Gdns IG8 310 E4
Latchingdon Rd CM3 281 B5
Latchmore Bank
Bishop's Stortford CM22 146 B2
Little Hallingbury CM22 173 B8
Lathcoates Cres CM2 254 E8
Lathom Rd E6 352 A5
Latimer Dr Basildon SS15 319 B1
Hornchurch RM12 336 D1
Lattice Ave IP4 18 C6
Latton Bush Ctr The
CM18 223 F5
Latton Gn CM18 223 F4
Latton Green Prim Sch
CM18 223 F4
Latton Hall Cl CM20 200 A1
Latton Ho CM18 224 B5
Latton St
Harlow, Brays Grove CM20 224 B7
Harlow, Potter Street
CM17 224 C5
Launceston Cl
Colchester CO2 136 B1
Romford RM3 314 C2
Launder's La RM13 355 F1
Laundry Cotts RM13 370 D6
Laundry Gdns CO10 33 D6
Laundry La
Lower Nazeing EN9 243 E6
Mountnessing CM15 295 D8
Laura Cl E11 332 C6
Laurel Ave Harwich CO12 90 F2
Wickford SS12 321 C7
Laurel Cl Brentwood CM13 295 B4
Clacton-on-S CO15 196 B7
Redbridge IG6 311 D4
Southend-on-S SS9 365 D8
Laurel Cres RM7 335 E3
Laurel Ct
6 Brentwood CM13 295 C3
Colchester CO4 136 E8
Laurel Dr
Great Dunmow CM6 123 B1
Long Melford CO10 15 C7
South Ockendon RM15 357 D1
Laurel Gdns E4 287 B2
Laurel Gr 4 CM2 254 A8
Laurelhayes IP2 17 A3
Laurel La RM12 336 E2
Laurel Mead Ct 8 E18 310 A2
Laurels The
Braintree CM7 128 A3
Great Notley CM77 154 C8
Rayleigh SS6 345 F8
South Woodham Ferrers
CM3 301 D8
8 Belvedere DA17 369 A1
Buckhurst Hill IG9 288 C1
Laurence Ave CM8 212 A8
Laurence Cl CO7 137 F6
Laurence Croft CM1 231 B1
Laurence Ind Est SS2 347 B6
Laurie Wlk RM1 335 E6
Lauriston Bglws CM9 239 C6
Lauriston Pl 1 SS1 367 C8
Lavehham Ho E17 309 B2
Lavender Ave CM15 294 B3
Lavender Cl
Bishop's Stortford CM23 145 D6
Harlow CM20 199 E1
Romford RM3 314 D3
South Ockendon RM15 357 E1
Tiptree CO5 186 C4
Witham CM8 183 E4
Lavender Ct 1 CM1 232 F5
Lavender Dr CM0 284 C3
Lavender Field
Haverhill CB9 8 D8
6 Saffron Walden CB10 22 F2
Lavender Gr SS0 347 D3
Lavender Hill IP2 16 F4
Lavender Mews
Canvey Island SS8 363 F2
Southend-on-S SS0 347 D3
Lavender Pl IG1 352 B7
Lavender Way
Colchester CO4 109 C2
Wickford SS12 321 C7
Lavender Wlk CO15 220 G7
Lavenham Cl CO16 195 B4
Lavenham Ct
Brentwood CM15 294 D1
Colchester CO2 135 C2
Lavenham Rd IP2 16 E5
Lavers The SS6 323 E3
Lawford CE Prim Sch
CO11 86 B2
Lawford Cl RM12 355 C8
Lawford La
Chelmsford CM1 231 D3
Writtle CM1 231 C1
Lawford Mead Inf Sch
CM1 231 D5
Lawford Mead Jun Sch
CM1 231 D5
Lawford Pl IP4 18 F5
Law Ho IG11 353 A3
Lawling Ave CM9 237 C5
Lawlinge Rd CM3 282 B5
Lawn Ave SS2 348 B2
Lawn Chase CM8 183 F1
Lawn Farm Gr RM6 334 E7
Lawn La CM1 232 D6
Lawn Prim Sch DA11 378 C1
Lawn Rd DA11 378 C2
Lawns Cl CO5 218 C7
Lawns Cres RM17 378 D8
Lawns Ct SS7 344 B7
Lawns Pl RM17 378 D8
Lawns The
Chelmsford CM1 232 D5
Chingford E4 309 A5
East Hanningfield CM3 278 C7
Ipswich IP4 18 C8
South Benfleet SS7 344 C7
Brentwood CM14 316 E5
Lawns Way RM5 313 C3
Lawn The CM20 200 B3
Lawn Way IP11 381 C5
Lawrence Ave
Little Ilford E12 352 A8
Sawbridgeworth CM21 172 E4
Stanstead Abbotts SG12 197 C4
Lawrence Cres RM10 335 B1
Lawrence Gdns RM18 379 B7
Lawrence Hill E4 309 A8
Lawrence Moorings
CM21 172 F2
Lawrence Rd
Basildon SS13 343 F8
Romford RM2 336 B6
Laws Cl CB11 43 D7
Lawshall's Hill CO6 78 D1
Lawton Rd IG10 289 B6
Laxton Ct CO3 135 A4
Laxton Gr CO13 170 A5
Laxton Rd CO7 165 B8
Laxtons SS17 360 D3
Laxtons The SS4 325 D5
Layborne Ave RM3 314 C8
Layer Breton Hill CO2 161 B1
Layer Cross CO2 161 F5
Layer Ct CO2 135 D4
Layer-de-la-Haye CE Prim
Sch CO2 161 F5
Layer Marney Tower*
CO5 187 D8
Layer Rd Abberton CO5 162 E4
Abberton CO5 163 A3
Colchester CO2 135 C3
Great Wigborough CO5 188 E5
Haverhill CB9 8 E7
Layzell Croft CO10 34 C4
Leach Cl CM2 255 B7
Lea Cl
Bishop's Stortford CM23 119 B1
Braintree CM7 128 D1
Lea Ct 1 E4 309 C8
Leadale Ave E4 309 A8
Leaden Cl CM6 204 D8
Leader Ave E12 352 A7
Leafy Way CM13 295 D1
Lea Gr CM23 119 B1
Lea Hall Bglws CM22 174 B3
Lea La CM8 184 F2
Leam Cl CO4 136 F7
Leamington Cl RM3 315 A4
Leamington Gdns IG3 333 F2
Leamington Rd
Hockley SS5 324 F7
Romford RM3 315 A5
Southend-on-S SS1 367 C8
Leapingwell Cl CM2 233 A3
Lea Rd Grays RM16 374 A1
Hoddesdon EN11 221 C8
Holdbrook EN9 265 A5
South Benfleet SS7 344 C5
Lea Road Ind Pk EN9 265 A5
Leas Cl SS0 366 B8
Leas Ct CM0 306 C6
Leas Gdns SS0 366 B8
Leaside SS7 344 B6
Lea Side CO5 218 D6
Leaside Bsns Ctr EN3 287 A7
Leaside Lodge 6 EN11 221 D8
Leas La CO2 161 D6
Leas Rd
Clacton-on-S CO15 195 D2
Colchester CO2 135 C1
Leas Sch The CO15 195 D2
Leas The
Burnham-on-C CM0 306 C6
Frinton-on-S CO13 171 B6
Ingatestone CM4 274 A2
Southend-on-S SS0 366 C7
Upminster RM14 337 D4
Leasway Brentwood CM14 316 D7
Grays RM16 373 C5
Rayleigh SS6 323 C2
Upminster RM14 356 C8
Wickford SS12 321 B6
Leasway The SS0 366 B8
Leat Cl CM21 172 F3
Leathart Cl RM12 355 B5
Leatherbottle Hill CM4 276 A2
Leather La
5 Braintree CM7 127 F3
Great Yeldham CO9 30 A1
Haverhill CB9 8 E7
Hornchurch RM11 336 D3
Southend-on-S SS1 367 A8
Lea Valley Rd E4 287 A3
Leaview EN9 265 B6
Leaview Ct E4 287 C1
Lea Way CM12 319 B8
Le Cateau Rd CO2 135 E6
Lechmere App IG8 310 D1
Lechmere Ave
Chigwell IG7 311 C6
Woodford IG8 310 D1
Leconfield Wlk RM12 355 C6
Lede Rd SS8 364 B4
Lee Ave RM6 334 E5
Lee Chapel La SS16 341 D3
Lee Chapel Prim Sch
SS16 341 F4
Leech's La CO4 109 D4
Lee Cl SG12 197 C4
Leecon Way SS4 325 E3
Lee Ct CM2 254 E7
Leeds Rd IG1 333 D3
Leeford CM1 231 F6
Lee Gardens Ave RM11 337 A3
Lee Gr IG7 311 B8
Leeholm Ho RM15 371 C4
Lee Lotts SS3 350 A4
Lee Rd Basildon SS13 343 F6
Harwich CO12 91 C3
Ipswich IP3 17 F3
Lees Manor Ct RM11 336 F2
Lees The SS8 364 A6
Lee Valley Ctry Pk*
EN10 221 B2
Lee Valley Ho EN9 266 A5
Lee Valley Park* EN3 287 A8
Lee Valley Park Vst Ctr*
EN9 265 C6
Leeward Ct IP11 381 E5
Leeward Rd CM3 301 E5
Leeway The CM3 256 F7
Lee Wick La CO16 193 D2
Lee Wlk SS16 341 E5
Lee Woottens La SS16 342 A4
Leez La CM3 152 E2
Leez Priory* CM3 153 A2
Legerton Cotts CO6 79 C1
Legg St CM1 232 B3
Legions Way CM23 146 A8
Legon Ave RM7 335 C3
Legra Ave EN11 221 A6
Leicester Ave SS4 347 F8
Leicester Cl
Colchester CO1 136 A8
Ipswich IP2 16 F1
Jaywick CO15 194 F1
Leicester Ct CM8 156 D3
Leicester Gdns IG3 333 E4
Leicester Rd Tilbury RM18 378 F6
Wanstead E11 332 B6
Leige Ave SS8 364 D4
Leigham Court Dr SS9 346 F1
Leighams Rd CM3 278 E7
Leigh Ave IG4 332 D7
Leigh Beck Jun & Inf Schs
SS8 364 E3
Leigh Beck La SS8 364 E2
Leigh Beck Rd SS8 364 F3
Leighcliff Rd SS9 365 F8
Leighcroft Gdns SS9 346 D4
Leigh Ct 8 E18 310 A1
Leigh Dr Elsenham CM22 94 C1
Romford RM3 314 D6
Wickham Bishops CM8 212 D5
Leigh Fells SS13 343 C6
Leighfields SS7 345 B6
Leighfields Ave SS9 346 D6
Leighfields Rd SS9 346 D6
Leigh Gdns SS9 346 C1
Leigh Hall Rd SS9 346 E1
Leigh Heath Ct SS9 346 A2
Leigh Heritage Ctr*
SS9 365 D8
Leigh Hill SS9 365 E8
Leigh Hill Cl SS9 365 E8
Leigh Ho SS9 365 E8
Leigh Hts SS7 345 F3
Leigh Jun & Inf Schs
SS9 346 E1
Leighlands Rd CM3 301 E7
Leigh-on-Sea Sta SS9 365 C8
Leigh Park Cl SS9 346 C1
Leigh Park Ct SS9 365 D8
Leigh Park Rd SS9 365 D8
Leigh Rd
Canvey Island SS8 364 B2
Southend-on-S SS9 346 F1
Wallend E6 352 A6
Leighs Rd CM3 208 E6
Leighs Rifleman CM12 296 F3
Leighton Ave
Little Ilford E12 352 A7
Southend-on-S SS9 346 F1
Leighton Gdns RM18 379 B7
Leighton Rd Ipswich IP3 38 A8
South Benfleet SS7 344 C7
Leighton Sq IP3 38 A8
Leigh View Dr SS9 346 F4
Leighville Gr SS9 346 D1
Leighwood Ave SS9 346 E5
Leinster Rd SS15 341 D6
Leiston Rd CB9 8 E7
Leitrim Ave SS3 368 C5
Lekoe Rd SS8 363 F6
Lely Rd IP3 37 F8
Lemons Hill IP9 61 D8
Lena Kennedy Cl E4 309 C4
Lenham Way SS13 343 C6
Lenmore Ave RM17 373 C3
Lennard Row RM15 371 D5
Lennox Ave DA11 379 A1
Lennox Cl Grays RM16 372 C2
Romford RM1 335 F5
Lennox Dr SS12 321 F5
Lennox Gdns IG1 332 F3
Lennox Ho 7 DA17 369 A3
Lennox Rd DA11 378 F1
Lenthall Ave RM17 373 A3
Lenthall Rd IG10 289 D5
Leonard Ave RM7 335 D3
Leonard Dr SS6 323 A4
Leonard Mews CM7 155 B8
Leonard Rd Basildon SS16 342 B2
Chingford E4 309 A4
Southend-on-S SS0 366 D7
Leonard Way CM14 315 E6
Leon Dr SS16 342 D3
Leopold Gdns IP4 18 B8
Leopold Rd
Felixstowe IP11 381 E4
Ipswich IP4 18 A8
Les Bois CO2 162 A5
Leslie Cl SS9 346 D6
Leslie Dr SS9 346 D6
Leslie Gdns SS6 323 F1
Leslie Newnham Ct 1
CM9 237 A1
Leslie Pk CM0 306 C4
Leslie Rd Ipswich IP3 18 D1
Rayleigh SS6 323 F1
Lesney Gdns SS4 325 D3
Lessingham Ave IG5 333 A8
Lessington Ave RM7 335 C5
Lessness Heath Prim Sch
DA17 369 A1
Lessness Pk DA17 369 A1
Lessness Rd
Belvedere DA17 369 A1
15 Erith DA17 369 A1
Lester Ho IG8 311 A3
Lethe Gr Blackheath CO2 163 A8
Colchester CO2 162 F8
Letton Cl IP9 35 A1
Lettons Chase CM3 301 E6
Letzen Rd SS8 364 A4
Leveller Row CM12 296 F3
Levels Gn CM23 118 C5
Levens Way CM77 154 C6
Leventhorpe Sch The
CM21 172 E4
Lever La SS4 325 F1
Lever Sq RM16 374 A2
Leverton Jun & Inf Schs The
EN9 265 F5
Leverton Way EN9 265 C6
Leveson Rd RM16 374 B3
Levett Gdns IG3 352 F8
Levett Rd Barking IG11 352 E6
Stanford-le-H SS17 360 E2
Levine Gdns IG11 353 D3
Levington Rd
Felixstowe IP11 381 C1
Ipswich IP3 18 A3
Lewes Cl Grays RM17 378 A8
Ipswich IP3 18 E3
Lewes Rd Romford RM3 314 D6
Southend-on-S SS2 348 C3
Lewes Way SS7 345 B7
Lewin Pl CM3 233 E8
Lewis Ave E17 309 A2
Lewis Cl CM15 294 F2
Lewis Dr CM2 254 B6
Lewis La IP9 61 E2
Lewis Rd
Hornchurch RM11 336 C5
Swanscombe DA10 377 E1
Lewis Way RM10 354 B6
Lexden Ct CO3 135 C7
Lexden Dr RM6 334 B5
Lexden Gr CO3 134 F7
Lexden Mews CO3 134 F7
Lexden Park Ho CO3 135 A7
Lexden Pl CO3 134 E7
Lexden Prim Sch CO3 134 E6
Lexden Rd Colchester CO3 135 B7
Lexden Rd *continued*
West Bergholt CO6 108 D4
Lexden Springs Sch CO3 134 E7
Lexham Ho 9 IG11 352 D4
Lexington Way RM14 337 F5
Leybourne Dr CM1 232 E7
Leyburn Cres RM3 314 E3
Leyburn Rd RM3 314 E3
Leycroft Cl IG10 289 A4
Ley Field Marks Tey CO6 132 E3
Takeley CM22 148 C7
Leyfields CM77 126 F1
Leyland Ct SS1 367 B8
Leyland Gdns IG8 310 C5
Leys Ave RM10 354 C5
Leys Cl RM10 354 D5
Leys Dr CO16 168 C1
Leyside CM77 126 F2
Leysings SS16 341 E4
Leys Prim Sch The
RM10 354 C5
Leys Rd CO7 137 C3
Ley St IG1,IG2 333 D3
Leys The Basildon SS16 342 C4
Chelmsford CM2 232 F5
Wimbish CB10 45 C3
Leyswood Dr IG2 333 E6
Ley The CM7 128 D1
Leyton Ct CO15 195 F8
Leywood Cl CM7 128 D2
Liberty Cotts RM4 313 E8
Liberty Ct IG11 353 C3
Liberty II Ctr RM1 335 F7
Liberty The RM1 335 E6
Library Hill CM14 316 D8
Libro Ct E4 309 A6
Lichen Ct IG6 333 B8
Lichfield Cl
Chelmsford CM1 231 E4
Colchester CO1 136 A8
Lichfield Rd
Dagenham RM8 334 C1
Woodford IG8 309 E6
Lichfields The SS14 342 F7
Lichfield Terr RM14 337 F2
Lidgate Ct IP11 381 A4
Lidius Dr CO4 110 A5
Lie Field Cl CM7 128 D3
Lifchild Cl CM8 212 A7
Lifstan Way SS1 367 E7
Lilac Ave
Canvey Island SS8 364 C4
Seawick CO16 220 B6
Wickford SS12 321 C7
Lilac Cl Chelmsford CM2 254 C6
Pilgrims Hatch CM15 294 B4
Lilac Ct CO7 137 A2
Lilac Gdns RM7 335 E3
Lilac Rd EN11 221 B8
Lilac Tree Ct CO4 136 E8
Lilford Rd CM11 297 C4
Lilian Cres CM13 317 C8
Lilian Gdns IG8 310 B2
Lilian Impey Dr CO4 110 B5
Lilian Pl SS6 346 A8
Lilian Rd CM0 306 C5
Lillechurch Rd RM8 353 C6
Lilley Cl CM14 315 F6
Lilley's La CO7 112 D4
Lilliard Cl EN11 197 B2
Lillies The CM7 102 B1
Lilliput Rd RM7 335 D4
Lilly Cnr CB9 27 B6
Lillyputts Equestrian Ctr
RM11 337 A5
Lillyville Wlk SS6 324 A1
Lily Alton Ct RM9 353 F8
Lily Cl CM1 232 F6
Lilystone Cl CM4 275 D1
Limberg Rd SS8 363 D4
Limbourne Ave RM8 334 F4
Limbourne Dr CM9 237 D5
Limburg Rd SS8 363 D4
Lime Ave Brentwood CM13 316 F7
Colchester CO4 136 D8
Harwich CO12 91 B3
Southend-on-S SS9 346 C2
Upminster RM14 356 A8
Limebrook Way CM9 258 E7
Lime Cl Buckhurst Hill IG9 310 D8
Clacton-on-S CO15 195 C3
Romford RM7 335 C7
South Ockendon RM15 357 C2
Witham CM8 184 A5
Lime Ct Hockley SS5 324 E6
Hornchurch RM11 336 C4
Limefields CB10 22 D4
Lime Gr
Doddinghurst CM15 272 D1
Haverhill CB9 9 C5
Redbridge IG6 311 F4
Sudbury CO10 33 C5
Limekiln La CM24 119 C5
Lime Lodge SS9 346 C2
Lime Pl SS15 319 C1
Lime Rd SS7 344 E4
Limerick Gdns RM14 337 F4
Limes Ave Chigwell IG7 311 C4
Wanstead E11 332 B7
Limes Cres 4 CM23 146 A7
Limes Ct Brentwood CM15 294 D1
Hoddesdon EN11 221 A6
Limes Farm Jun & Inf Sch
IG7 311 D5
Limeslade Cl SS17 361 A4
Lime St CO7 192 F5
Limes The Ardleigh CO7 111 F7
Brentwood CM13 316 F7
Clacton-on-S CO15 196 A3
Galleywood CM2 254 B2
Gosfield CO9 102 E7
Ingatestone CM4 274 C4

Limes The *continued*
Long Melford CO10 . . . . .15 C7
Purfleet RM19 . . . . .371 A1
Rayleigh SS6 . . . . .323 F1
Romford RM11 . . . . .336 D8
Tattingstone IP9 . . . . .61 B6
Limetree Ave SS7 . . . . .344 B4
Limetree Dr IP3 . . . . .18 D2
Lime Tree Hill CM6 . . . . . . .123 D2
Limetree Rd SS8 . . . . .364 E4
Lime Way CM0 . . . . .306 A5
Lime Wlk CM0 . . . . .254 C6
Lincewood Prim Sch
Basildon SS16 . . . . .341 B3
Basildon SS16 . . . . .341 C4
Lincoln Ave
Clacton-on-S CO15 . . . . .220 D6
Romford RM7 . . . . .335 E3
Lincoln Chase SS2 . . . . .348 E3
Lincoln Cl
Bishop's Stortford CM23 . . . .145 D5
Hornchurch RM11 . . . . .337 A6
Lincoln Ct ■ Ilford IG2 . . .133 C5
Redbridge IG1 . . . . .132 F4
Lincoln Gdns IG6 . . . . .132 E4
Lincoln Ho ■ RM3 . . . . . . .314 D4
Lincoln La CO6 . . . . .82 C1
Lincoln Rd Basildon SS14 .342 F7
Rochford SS4 . . . . .325 C5
Woodford E18 . . . . .310 A2
Lincolns Field CM16 . . . . . . .245 F1
Lincolns La CM4 . . . . .293 C3
Lincoln Terr IP11 . . . . .381 D3
Lincoln Way
Canvey Island SS8 . . . . .363 E4
Colchester CO1 . . . . .136 A8
Linda Gdns CM12 . . . . .296 E4
Lindal Ct ■ E18 . . . . .310 A2
Lindbergh Rd IP3 . . . . .18 C2
Linden Cl Chelmsford CM2 . .205 F7
Colchester CO4 . . . . .110 E1
Lawford CO11 . . . . .86 B3
Purfleet RM19 . . . . .376 C8
Rayleigh SS6 . . . . .323 F1
South Benfleet SS7 . . . . .344 C6
Linden Cres IG8 . . . . .344 C6
Linden Ct SS9 . . . . .347 A2
Linden Dr CO15 . . . . .195 E7
Linden Leas SS7 . . . . .344 C6
Linden Rd SS7 . . . . .344 C6
Linden Rise CM12 . . . . .316 D5
Linden St RM7 . . . . .335 D6
Lindens The
Basildon SS16 . . . . .341 A5
Bishop's Stortford CM23 . . . .145 F6
Braintree CM7 . . . . .128 A1
Colchester CO3 . . . . .135 B7
Halstead CO9 . . . . .103 F8
Loughton IG10 . . . . .288 F4
Stock CM4 . . . . .275 F2
Linden Way SS8 . . . . .363 F4
Linde Rd SS8 . . . . .364 B4
Lindfield Rd RM3 . . . . .314 C6
Lindhurst Dr CM11 . . . . .298 C4
Lindisfarne Ave SS9 . . . . . .347 A2
Lindisfarne Cl IP2 . . . . .17 A1
Lindisfarne Ct
Basildon SS12 . . . . .322 A5
Maldon CM9 . . . . .258 E8
Lindisfarne Rd RM8 . . . . . . .334 C1
Lindon Rd SS11 . . . . .299 C3
Lindsell Gn SS14 . . . . .342 E5
Lindsell La Basildon SS14 .342 E5
Lindsell CM6 . . . . .98 B2
Lindsell Pk CM6 . . . . .10 . . .34 B6
Lindsey Cl
Bishop's Stortford CM23 . . . .118 F1
Brentwood CM14 . . . . .316 A6
Lindsey Ct Rayleigh SS6 . . . .323 A3
■ Wickford SS12 . . . . .321 E5
Lindsey Rd
Bishop's Stortford CM23 . . . .118 F1
Dagenham RM8 . . . . .334 C1
Great Wakering SS3 . . . . .350 B4
Ipswich IP4 . . . . .18 C7
Lindsey St CM16 . . . . .246 A2
Lindsey Way RM11 . . . . .336 C8
Lindum SS1 . . . . .368 A6
Line Cotts CO4 . . . . .83 A4
Linfold Cl CM7 . . . . .128 D4
Linford Cl CM19 . . . . .223 C6
Linford Cres CM9 . . . . .200 E7
Linford End CM19 . . . . .223 C6
Linford Mews CM9 . . . . .258 E8
Linford Rd RM16 . . . . .374 C1
Lingcroft SS16 . . . . .342 A4
Lingfield Ave RM14 . . . . . . .337 A1
Lingfield Dr SS4 . . . . .326 A3
Lingmere Cl IG7 . . . . .311 C8
Lingrove Gdns IG9 . . . . .310 B8
Ling's La IP9 . . . . .63 D5
Lingwood Cl CM3 . . . . .256 E7
Link Cl CO4 . . . . .109 E4
Linkdale CM12 . . . . .319 B8
Link La IP9 . . . . .60 D6
Link Rd
Bishop's Stortford CM23 . . . .145 F8
Brightlingsea CO7 . . . . .193 A6
Canvey Island SS8 . . . . .363 F4
Capel St M IP9 . . . . .35 A1
Clacton-on-S CO15 . . . . .195 D2
Dagenham RM9 . . . . .354 B3
Halstead CO9 . . . . .103 D8
Rayleigh SS6 . . . . .323 D3
Stanford-le-H SS17 . . . . .360 D3
Links Ave Felixstowe IP11 .381 F6
Romford RM2 . . . . .314 B1
Links Bsns Ctr The
CM23 . . . . .146 C7
Links Cl CO10 . . . . .2 C5
Links Ct SS1 . . . . .367 F7

Links Dr CM2 . . . . .253 F7
Linksfield IP5 . . . . .18 F7
Linksfield Gdns IP5 . . . . .18 F7
Linkside Chigwell IG7 . . . . . .311 C5
Friston-on-S CO13 . . . . .170 E3
Linkside Rd CM23 . . . . .146 C6
Links Rd Cressing CM7 . . . . .156 C7
Seawick CO16 . . . . .220 B6
Woodford IG8 . . . . .310 A5
Links The CM12 . . . . .296 E4
Linksway SS9 . . . . .346 C4
Links Way SS7 . . . . .345 F3
Link The IP9 . . . . .60 D6
Linkway Basildon SS14 . . . .342 B6
Dagenham RM8 . . . . .353 C8
Link Way
Bishop's Stortford CM23 . . . .145 E6
Hornchurch RM11 . . . . .336 E3
Linkway Rd CM14 . . . . .315 F7
Linley Ct RM18 . . . . .380 D7
Linley Cres RM7 . . . . .335 C8
Linley Gdns CO15 . . . . .195 D2
Linne Rd SS8 . . . . .364 C5
Linnet Cl SS3 . . . . .368 E8
Linnet Dr Chelmsford CM2 .254 B6
South Benfleet SS7 . . . . .344 C2
Linnet Rd IP2 . . . . .16 D4
Linnets Basildon SS14 . . . . .342 A3
Clacton-on-S CO15 . . . . .195 F6
Linnett Cl E4 . . . . .309 C6
Linnet Terr IG5 . . . . .333 A8
Linnetts La CB9 . . . . .10 A4
Linnet Way
Great Bentley CO7 . . . . .166 D8
Purfleet RM19 . . . . .371 B1
Linroping Ave SS8 . . . . .364 F3
Linsdell Rd IG11 . . . . .352 C4
Linstead Cl CO16 . . . . .195 A4
Linton Cl CB11 . . . . .43 FB
Linton Ct RM1 . . . . .313 E1
Linton Rd Barking IG11 . . . .352 C5
Hadstock CB1 . . . . .29 B8
Southend-on-S SS3 . . . . .368 E6
Lintons The
■ Barking IG11 . . . . .352 C5
Chelmsford CM2 . . . . .255 D6
Linwood CM21 . . . . .172 E2
Lionel Hurst Ct CO10 . . . . . .34 C5
Lionel Oxley Ho RM17 . . . . .378 B8
Lionel Rd SS8 . . . . .364 B3
Lion Fields SS3 . . . . .350 B3
Lionfield Terr CM1 . . . . .232 D3
Lion Hill SS17 . . . . .361 D4
Lion La CM12 . . . . .297 A2
Lion & Lamb Ct ■ CM14 .316 C8
Lion Mdw CM9 . . . . .27 B7
Lion Rd CO10 . . . . .2 B5
Lion St IP1 . . . . .17 C6
Lion Wlk ■ CO1 . . . . .135 F7
Liphook Cl RM12 . . . . .354 FB
Lippitts Hill SS16 . . . . .341 C3
Lippitts Hill IG10 . . . . .287 F7
Lisa Cl CM2 . . . . .297 D8
Lisle Ho
Colchester,Lexden CO3 . . . . .135 A7
Colchester,Mile End CO4 . . . .109 E4
Lisle Pl RM17 . . . . .373 A3
Lisle Rd CO2 . . . . .136 A5
Lister Ave RM3 . . . . .314 E1
Lister Rd Braintree CM7 . . . .154 FB
Tilbury RM18 . . . . .379 A5
Lister Tye CM2 . . . . .254 C7
Lister Ho CO10 . . . . .15 B8
Liston Cl CO16 . . . . .15 B6
Liston La CO10 . . . . .15 B6
Liston Way ■ IG8 . . . . .310 C3
Listowel Rd RM10 . . . . .335 A1
Litchborough Pk CM3 . . . . . .256 FB
Litchfield CO12 . . . . .90 F4
Litchfield Cl CO15 . . . . .195 E5
Littell Tweed CM2 . . . . .213 A3
Little Aston Rd RM3 . . . . . . .315 A3
Little Baddow Rd
Danbury CM3 . . . . .207 E4
Woodham Walter CM9 . . . . . .235 C3
Little Bakers CO14 . . . . .171 A7
Little Belhus Ct RM15 . . . . .357 A1
Little Bentley SS14 . . . . .342 B7
Little Bentley Rd CO16 . . . .114 B1
Little Berry La SS16 . . . . . . .341 A4
Little Bradfords CM7 . . . . . .128 A4
Little Braxted La CM8 . . . . .184 C3
Little Brays CM18 . . . . .224 A6
Little Bromley Rd
Ardleigh CO7 . . . . .112 B7
Great Bromley CO7 . . . . .112 F3
Little Bentley CO7 . . . . .113 E1
Little Brook Hospl The
DA2 .376 C1
Littlebrook Manor Way
DA1 .376 A2
Little Brook Rd CO19 . . . . . .222 C8
Littlebury Ct
Basildon SS13 . . . . .343 A8
Kelvedon Hatch CM15 . . . . . .271 F2
Littlebury Gdns CO2 . . . . . . .136 C4
Littlebury Gn SS13 . . . . .343 A8
Littlebury Green Rd CB11 .21 D3
Little Cattins CM19 . . . . . . .222 E4
Little Charlton SS13 . . . . . . .343 A8
Little Chishill Rd SG8 . . . . . .39 C8
Little Chittock SS14 . . . . . . .342 E6
Little Church St CO12 . . . . . .91 D6
Little Clacton Rd
Clacton-on-S CO16 . . . . .195 B7
Great Holland CO13 . . . . .169 E2
Littlecotes CO4 . . . . .109 D4
Littlecroft CM3 . . . . .301 D6
Little Croft St IP2 . . . . .17 C3
Little Dodden SS16 . . . . .341 F4
Little Dorrit CM1 . . . . .231 E7
Little Dragons CO10 . . . . . . .288 D5
Littlefield Rd CO2 . . . . .135 C2
Little Fields CM7 . . . . .255 A7

Little Fretches SS9 . . . . .346 E4
Little Friday Rd E4 . . . . .309 E8
Little Garth SS13 . . . . .343 A5
Littlegarth Sch CO6 . . . . .82 B7
Little Gaynes Gdns
RM14 . . . . .356 B8
Little Gaynes La RM14 . . . .356 B8
Little Gearies IG6 . . . . .333 B7
Little Gipping St ■ IP1 . . .17 B6
Little Gr ■ IP9 . . . . .35 A1
Little & Great Sir Hughes La
CM2 .255 B2
Little Gregories La
CM16 . . . . .267 D5
Little Grove Field CM9 .223 C8
Little Gulls ■ IP9 . . . . .35 A1
Little Gypps Cl SS8 . . . . . . .363 F4
Little Gypps Ct SS8 . . . . . . .363 F4
Little Gypps Rd SS8 . . . . . . .363 F3
Little Hallingbury CE Prim Sch
CM22 . . . . .173 C7
Little Harrods CO14 . . . . . . .171 A7
Little Hayes Chase
Hullbridge CM3 . . . . .302 C8
South Woodham F CM3 . . . . .280 C1
Little Hays SS9 . . . . .346 B6
Little Heath
Hatfield Heath CM22 . . . . . . .174 A3
Ilford RM6 . . . . .334 B7
Little Heath Sch RM6 . . . . . . .334 B7
Little Hills CM9 . . . . .236 D8
Little Holt ■ E11 . . . . .332 A6
Little Horkesley Rd CO6 . . .81 A4
Littlehurst La SS15 . . . . .319 F2
Little Hyde Cl CO9 . . . . .30 A2
Little Hyde La CM4 . . . . . . .274 B6
Little Hyde Rd CO9 . . . . .30 A2
Little Kingston SS16 . . . . . .341 D2
Little Lancaster CM1 . . . . . .43 D8
Little Laver Rd CM5 . . . . . . .226 F7
Little London Hill CM7 . . . . .72 D8
Little London La CM9 . . . . . .235 D4
Little Lullaway SS15 . . . . . . .341 F7
Little Malgraves Ind Est
RM14 . . . . .340 F1
Little Mdw CM1 . . . . .231 A1
Little Mdws CM9 . . . . .257 E6
Littlemoor Rd IG1 . . . . .333 D1
Little Nell CM1 . . . . .231 E7
Little Norsey Rd CM1 . . . . .297 C4
Little Oaks SS14 . . . . .342 A6
Little Orch IP9 . . . . .62 D5
Little Oxcroft SS15 . . . . .341 B6
Little Paddocks CM7 . . . . . .126 F1
Little Parndon Sch CM20 199 B1
Little Pluckett's Way
IG9 . . . . .288 D1
Little Pound CM15 . . . . .272 C3
Little Pynchons CM18 . . . . .224 A5
Little Russets CM15 . . . . . . .295 E2
Little's Cres IP2 . . . . .17 C4
Little Searles SS13 . . . . .343 B7
Little Spenders SS14 . . . . . .342 D8
Little Sq ■ CM7 . . . . .127 F3
Little St EP9 . . . . .265 C3
Little Stambridge Hall Rd
SS4 . . . . .326 B3
Little Stile CM1 . . . . .253 A8
Little St Mary's CO10 . . . . . .15 D7
Little Stone Ct CO15 . . . . . . .220 J8
Little Tey Rd CO5 . . . . .158 F7
Littlethorpe SS16 . . . . .342 F4
Little Thorpe SS1 . . . . .349 B1
Little Thurrock Prim Sch
RM17 . . . . .373 D3
Littleton Ave E4 . . . . .287 F1
Little Totham Rd CM9 . . . . .238 D8
Little Tufts IP9 . . . . .35 B1
Little Wakering Hall La
SS3 . . . . .350 A4
Little Wakering Rd SS3 . . . .349 E6
Little Walden Rd CB10 . . . . .22 E5
Little Waltham CE Prim Sch
CM3 .208 B7
Little Waltham Rd CM3 . . . .208 D1
Little Warley Hall La
CM13,RM14 . . . . .338 E6
Little Wheatley Chase
SS6 . . . . .323 A4
Little Whip St ■ IP2 . . . . . . .17 C4
Little Wlk CM20 . . . . .223 D8
Little Wood CO13 . . . . .170 F6
Little Yeldham Rd CO9 . . . . .30 C3
Livery Mews CM5 . . . . .124 E5
Livingstone Cl CM5 . . . . . . .249 A2
Livingstone Cotts CM5 . . . .249 A2
Livingstone Terr RM13 . . . .354 F4
Llewellyn Cl CM1 . . . . .232 D3
Lloyd Mews EN1 . . . . .265 A1
Lloyd Rd Dagenham RM9 . . .353 F5
Shotley Gate IP9 . . . . .91 A8
Lloyds Ave ■ IP1 . . . . .17 C6
Lloyd Wise Cl SS2 . . . . .348 D3
Loamy Hill Rd
Little Totham CM9 . . . . .214 A7
Tiptree CO5 . . . . .185 F1
Loates Pasture CM24 . . . . . .119 D8
Lobelia Cl CM1 . . . . .233 A6
Locarno Ave SS11 . . . . .299 F2
Locarno Rd IP3 . . . . .18 B3
Locke Cl Rainham RM13 . . . .354 F6
Stanford-le-H SS17 . . . . .360 C3
Lockhart Ave CO3 . . . . .135 C7
Lockhart Lodge E4 . . . . .287 E2
Lock Hill CM9 . . . . .237 E2
Lockram La Witham CM8 .183 F2
■ Witham CM8 . . . . .184 A2
Lock Rd IG11 . . . . .352 C7
Locks Hill SS4 . . . . .325 F1
Lockside Marina CM2 . . . . .232 E6
Locksley Cl SS2 . . . . .348 F2
Lock View CM7 . . . . .172 F2
Lockwood Wlk RM1 . . . . . . .335 E6
Lockyer Rd RM19 . . . . .376 C8
Lodden Ho ■ RM3 . . . . .315 A4

Lodge Ave
Dagenham RM8 . . . . .353 B6
Great Baddow CM2 . . . . .254 F7
Romford RM2 . . . . .336 A7
Lodge Cl Brentwood CM13 295 E2
Chigwell IG7 . . . . .312 A7
Clacton-on-S CO15 . . . . .195 E4
Little Oakley CO12 . . . . .117 C8
Rayleigh SS6 . . . . .323 E1
Thundersley SS7 . . . . .345 A5
Lodge Cres CM3 . . . . .233 E7
Lodge Ct
Hornchurch RM12 . . . . .336 E2
West Bergholt CO6 . . . . .108 F4
Lodge Farm Cl SS9 . . . . . . .346 D5
Lodge Farm La CM13 . . . . . .194 D4
Lodge Farm Rd CO10 . . . . . . .2 C3
Lodge Hall CM18 . . . . .223 E4
Lodge Hill IG4 . . . . .332 E7
Lodge La Abberton CO5 . . . .163 D1
Ardleigh CO7 . . . . .111 B6
Ardleigh CO7 . . . . .111 C6
Brightlingsea CO7 . . . . .192 E7
Grays RM16,RM17 . . . . .373 B3
Langham CO4 . . . . .110 D8
Peldon CO5 . . . . .189 E7
Purleigh CM3 . . . . .258 C2
Romford RM5 . . . . .313 A4
Tendring CO16 . . . . .140 F6
Waltham Abbey EN9 . . . . . . .265 D4
Lodgelands Cl SS6 . . . . .323 F1
Lodge Rd Braintree CM7 . . .127 F1
Brightlingsea CO7 . . . . .192 E8
Little Clacton CO16 . . . . .169 A5
Little Oakley CO12 . . . . .117 C8
Loughton CM16 . . . . .267 A5
Maldon CM9 . . . . .236 F3
Messing CO5 . . . . .159 D3
Thorpe-le-S CO16 . . . . .168 F6
Tiptree CO5 . . . . .184 B5
Woodham Mortimer CM3,
CM9 .258 B5
Writtle CM1 . . . . .253 A8
Lodge The Epping CM16 . . .246 A1
Holland-on-S CO15 . . . . .196 F6
■ Hornchurch RM11 . . . . . . .336 B3
Redbridge IG6 . . . . .311 E3
Lodge Villas IG8 . . . . .309 F4
Lodwick SS3 . . . . .368 C5
Loewen Rd RM16 . . . . .374 A3
Loftin Way CM2 . . . . .254 D7
Logan Ct ■ RM1 . . . . .335 E6
Logan Link SS12 . . . . .321 F5
Logan Mews ■ RM1 . . . . . .335 E6
Loman Path RM15 . . . . .301 D8
Lombard Ave IG3 . . . . .333 E3
Lombard Ct Ipswich IP4 . . . .17 F7
Romford RM7 . . . . .335 C7
Lombards Chase CM13 . . . . .339 D5
Lombards The RM11 . . . . . . .336 E8
Lombardy Cl ■ SS13 . . . . . .343 C6
Lombardy Pl CM1 . . . . .232 B3
Lombardy Rd CO10 . . . . .15 D2
Lombarn Hill CO11 . . . . .88 A2
London Hill
Chelmsford CM2 . . . . .253 F2
Galleywood CM2 . . . . .254 A2
Rayleigh SS6 . . . . .323 D3
London Land Cotts CO6 . . . .80 E4
London Rd Abridge RM4 . . . .290 A6
Aveley RM15 . . . . .371 A4
Barking IG11 . . . . .352 A4
Basildon,Vange SS16 . . . . . . .342 D3
Basildon,Xylonite SS14 . . . . .341 E5
Billericay CM12 . . . . .296 D4
Bishop's Stortford CM23 . . . .146 A1
Braintree CM7 . . . . .127 E1
Brentwood CM14 . . . . .316 A7
Capel St M IP9 . . . . .35 B1
Chigwell Chigwell CM5 . . . . .270 C4
Clacton-on-S CO15 . . . . .195 E7
Colchester CO3 . . . . .134 D6
Copford CO3,CO6 . . . . .133 D4
Feering CO5 . . . . .158 F6
Grays RM17,RM20 . . . . .377 D8
Great Chesterford CB10 . . . . . .3 D2
Great Horkesley CO6 . . . . .81 F2
Great Notley CM77 . . . . .155 B2
Greenhithe DA9,DA2 . . . . . . .377 C2
Hadleigh SS7 . . . . .345 D3
Harlow CM17 . . . . .200 C2
Harlow, Latton Bush CM17 224 C4
Ipswich,Chantry IP2 . . . . .16 C3
Ipswich,Chantry IP2 . . . . .16 F5
Ipswich IP1 . . . . .17 A6
Loughton IG10 . . . . .288 B6
Maldon CM9 . . . . .236 D3
Marks Tey CO6 . . . . .133 A5
Newport CB11 . . . . .67 A6
Northfleet RM17 . . . . .378 E1
Romford RM7 . . . . .335 B5
Saffron Walden CB11 . . . . .43 D8
Sawbridgeworth CM21 . . . . .170 C1
South Benfleet SS7 . . . . .344 D5
Southend-on-S SS9 . . . . .346 D4
Southend-on-S,Westcliff-on-S
SS1 .366 F8
Stanford-le-H SS17 . . . . .360 B1
Stapleford Tawney RM4 . . . . .291 D8
Tilbury RM18 . . . . .379 B5
Washbrook IP8 . . . . .35 E6
Waltham Abbey EN9 . . . . .42 E7
Wendens Ambo,Littlebury
CB11 .42 F7
Wickford SS11,SS12 . . . . . . .322 C5
London Road Purfleet
RM19 . . . . .376 B8
London Road Ret Pk
SS9 . . . . .366 F8
London Road West Thurrock
RM20 . . . . .377 A8
Londons Cl RM14 . . . . .356 C7

London Southend Airport
SS2 . . . . .347 E7
London Stansted Airport
CM24 . . . . .121 A4
Lone Barn Cl IP1 . . . . .16 D8
Longacre Chelmsford CM2 253 E8
Colchester CO4 . . . . .109 E2
Long Acre Basildon SS14 .342 C7
Harlow CM17 . . . . .200 B4
Longacre Rd
Chingford E17 . . . . .309 D2
Cressing CM77 . . . . .155 E6
Longacres CM7 . . . . .128 A1
Long Acres CO5 . . . . .158 F5
Longaford Way CM13 . . . . . .295 C1
Long Banks CM18 . . . . .223 D5
Long Border Rd
Great Hallingbury CM22,
CM24 . . . . .147 C8
Longbow SS2 . . . . .348 E2
Long Brandocks CM1 . . . . . .231 A1
Longbridge Ho RM8 . . . . . . .353 B8
Longbridge Rd
Barking IG11 . . . . .352 E7
Dagenham RM8 . . . . .353 B8
Long Comm CM9 . . . . .236 F5
Longcroft Felixstowe IP11 381 C6
Hempstead CB10 . . . . .46 E8
Takeley CM22 . . . . .148 C7
Long Croft CM24 . . . . .119 D8
Long Croft Dr EN8 . . . . .265 A5
Longcroft Rd CO4 . . . . .136 C8
Longcroft Rise IG10 . . . . . . .289 B4
Longcrofts EN9 . . . . .265 E6
Long Ct RM19 . . . . .371 A2
Long Deacon Rd E4 . . . . . . .287 E1
Longdon Ct RM1 . . . . .335 F6
Longedryve CO2 . . . . .135 C4
Longfellow Dr CM3 . . . . .255 C2
Longfellow Rd CM9 . . . . .237 A1
Longfield Harlow CM18 . . . .224 A6
Loughton IG10 . . . . .288 D4
Longfield Mdw
CM16 . . . . .183 E5
Long Field IP11 . . . . .381 B6
Longfield Ave RM11 . . . . . . .336 C8
Longfield Cl SS11 . . . . .322 A7
Longfield Cotts CO10 . . . . . .289 A7
Longfield Rd
Capel St M IP9 . . . . .35 B2
Great Baddow CM2 . . . . .254 E8
South Woodham Ferrers
CM3 .301 D8
Longfields
Chipping Ongar CM5 . . . . . . .249 A1
St Osyth CO16 . . . . .194 D4
Long Gages SS14 . . . . .342 B7
Long Gdns CO9 . . . . .53 F5
Long Gn Braintree CM7 . . . . .155 E8
Chigwell IG7 . . . . .311 E5
Long Green La CM7 . . . . .99 C2
Longhams Dr CM3 . . . . .301 D8
Longhayes Ave RM6 . . . . . . .334 D7
Longhayes Ct RM6 . . . . .334 D7
Longhedges CB11 . . . . .22 E1
Long Ho CM18 . . . . .223 F6
Long Horse Croft CB11 . . . . .43 E7
Longhouse Rd RM16 . . . . . . .374 B3
Long La Arkesden CB11 . . . . .41 E5
Chadwell St M RM16 . . . . . . .373 F5
Grays RM16 . . . . .373 C5
Great Holland CO13 . . . . .170 C3
Hullbridge SS5 . . . . .302 F8
Rayne CM7 . . . . .153 F8
Longland Bridge CM22 .201 C8
Longleaf Dr CM1 . . . . .155 A8
Longleat Cl CM1 . . . . .231 F7
Long Ley Harlow CM20 . . . . .223 F8
Langley CB11 . . . . .40 D2
Long Leys E4 . . . . .309 C4
Long Lyndeswood SS15 341 F6
Longmans SS3 . . . . .368 G6
Long Mdw
Brentwood CM13 . . . . .317 C8
Romford RM3 . . . . .314 C8
Longmead SS13 . . . . .343 C8
Longmead Ave CM2 . . . . . . .254 F8
Longmead Cl CM15 . . . . .294 E1
Long Meadow
Bishop's Stortford CM23 . . . .145 D6
Great Notley CM77 . . . . .154 B5
Long Meadow Dr SS1 . . . . . .321 E8
Long Meadows CO12 . . . . . . .90 F2
Longmeads CM8 . . . . .212 E5
Longmeads Cl CM1 . . . . .215 E6
Long Melford CE Prim Sch
CO10 .15 C7
Longmore Ave CM2 . . . . . . .254 E8
Long Pastures CO10 . . . . .2 C3
Long Perry IP9 . . . . .35 B1
Longport Cl IG6 . . . . .312 A4
Long Rd
Canvey Island SS8 . . . . .364 A3
Lawford CO11 . . . . .86 C3
Long Rd E CO7 . . . . .187 B3
Long Rd W CO7 . . . . .84 E3
Longsford CM23 . . . . .146 C7
Long Reach Cl IG11 . . . . . . .352 D1
Long Reach Rd IG11 . . . . . . .352 F1
Longridge CO4 . . . . .136 F8
Long Riding SS14 . . . . .342 D6
Long Ridings Ave CM13 295 C4
Long Ridings Prim Sch
CM13 . . . . .295 B4
Longsands SS3 . . . . .368 D7
Longshaw Prim Sch E4 .309 D7
Longshaw Rd E4 . . . . .309 D7
Longship Way CM9 . . . . .258 E8
Longstock Cl SS14 . . . . .342 D5
Longs La CM3 . . . . .180 F1
Long St Ipswich IP3 . . . . .17 E5

Longstomps Ave CM2 . . . . .254 A7
Longstraw Cl CO3 . . . . .134 D6
Longtail CM11 . . . . .297 D5
Longtown Cl RM3 . . . . .314 C5
Longtown Rd RM3 . . . . .376 B1
Longtown Rd RM3 . . . . .314 C5
Longview Way RM5 . . . . . . .313 D2
Longwick SS16 . . . . .341 C4
Long Wlk EN8 . . . . .243 A1
Long Wood CM18 . . . . .223 D3
Longwood Cl RM14 . . . . .356 C7
Longwood Cl RM14 . . . . .356 C7
Longwood Gdns
Ilford IG5,IG6 . . . . .333 A8
Redbridge IG5 . . . . .333 A8
Longwood Par IG6 . . . . .333 B8
Long Wyre St CO1 . . . . .135 F7
Lonsdale ■ IP2 . . . . .17 C4
Lonsdale Ave
Brentwood CM13 . . . . .295 C4
Romford RM7 . . . . .335 C5
Lonsdale Cres IG2 . . . . .333 B5
Lonsdale Cres IG2 . . . . .333 B5
Lonsdale Ct SS2 . . . . .348 D3
Lonsdale Rd
Southend-on-S SS2 . . . . .348 D3
Thorpe-le-S CO16 . . . . .142 A2
Wanstead E11 . . . . .332 A4
Looe Gdns IG6 . . . . .333 B8
Looe Rd IG6 . . . . .381 F5
Loompits Way CB11 . . . . . . .43 D7
Loop Rd EN9 . . . . .265 F5
Loppys Hill ■ CM24 . . . . . .119 E6
Loraine Way IP8 . . . . .16 A8
Lord Ave IG5 . . . . .332 F8
Lord Gdns IG5 . . . . .332 F7
Lord Holland Rd CO2 . . . . . .135 F3
Lord Mews IP3 . . . . .18 A2
Lord Roberts Ave SS9 . . . . .346 A3
Lords Ave CM23 . . . . .145 B7
Lords Cl CB10 . . . . .23 D1
Lord's Croft La CB9 . . . . .9 A8
Lordship Cl CM13 . . . . .295 D2
Lordship Rd CM1 . . . . .231 B3
Lordsland La CM77 . . . . .103 C1
Lord St EN11 . . . . .221 A6
Lords Way SS13 . . . . .321 B2
Lordswood Rd CO2 . . . . .135 C2
Lordswood View CM6 . . . . .204 D7
Lorien Gdns IP3 . . . . .301 C6
Lorimar Bsns Ctr RM13 .369 E8
Lorkin's La CO10 . . . . .54 C4
Lorkin Way CO6 . . . . .108 F4
Lorne Gdns E11 . . . . .332 C7
Lorne Rd CM14 . . . . .316 C6
Lornes Cl SS2 . . . . .348 D3
Lorraine Cl CM11 . . . . .319 D6
Lorraine Ct ■ RM1 . . . . . . .335 E6
Lorrimore Cl CM12 . . . . .296 F5
Lotem Rd SS7 . . . . .344 D2
Lottem Rd SS8 . . . . .364 D2
Lott's Rd CO16 . . . . .168 C8
Lotus Way CO15 . . . . .220 E7
Loudoun Ave IG6 . . . . .333 B6
Loughton Cl EN9 . . . . .266 B6
Loughton La CM16 . . . . .246 D2
Loughton Seedbed Ctr
IG10 .289 D5
Loughton Sta IG10 . . . . .288 E4
Loughton Way IG9 . . . . .288 E3
Louisa Ave SS7 . . . . .344 A6
Louis Cl SS6 . . . . .323 A3
Louis Ct ■ RM10 . . . . .354 B6
Louis Dr E SS6 . . . . .323 A4
Louis Dr SS6 . . . . .323 A4
Louis Dr W SS6 . . . . .323 A4
Louis Cl CO14 . . . . .144 C4
Louise Ct ■ E11 . . . . .332 C8
Louise Gdns RM13 . . . . .354 C4
Louise Graham Ho ■
IG11 .352 D4
Louise Rd SS6 . . . . .323 E2
Louse La CO7 . . . . .84 E4
Louvain Dr CM2 . . . . .232 F7
Louvaine Ave SS12 . . . . .321 B7
Louvain Rd CO12 . . . . .91 A1
Loveday Cl SS8 . . . . .363 D3
Love La Ballingdon CO10 . . . .34 A8
Love La ■ Ashdon ■ RM15 .371 C4
Brightlingsea CO7 . . . . .192 F8
Chigwell IG8 . . . . .310 C3
Chipping Ongar CM5 . . . . . . .249 A2
East Tilbury RM18 . . . . .380 C8
Rayleigh SS6 . . . . .323 C2
Lovelace Ave SS1 . . . . .367 D8
Lovelace Gdns
Barking IG11 . . . . .353 A8
Southend-on-S SS3 . . . . .348 D1
Lovelace Villas SS2 . . . . .348 D1
Lovell Mews ■ SS11 . . . . . .352 F5
Lovell Rise SS9 . . . . .347 A6
Lovell Wlk RM12 . . . . .355 A6
Lovens Cl SS4 . . . . .364 C2
Lovers La IP9 . . . . .63 C4
Lovers La
Great Bentley CO7 . . . . .167 A7
Greenhithe DA9 . . . . .377 D3
Loves Wlk CM1 . . . . .231 E6
Lovet Rd CM19 . . . . .243 A1
Low Way CO16 . . . . .195 C6
Lowbrook Pl ■ CM2 . . . . . .254 F7
Lowbrook Rd IG1 . . . . .352 D3
Low Cl DA9 . . . . .377 A2
Lowe Chase CO14 . . . . .144 C1
Lowe Cl IG7 . . . . .312 A5
Lowefields CO6 . . . . .106 C5
Lowen Rd RM13 . . . . .354 D3
Lower Alderton Hall La
IG10 .289 B4
Lower Anchor St CM2 . . . . .232 A1
Lower Ave SS13 . . . . .343 B4
Lower Bedfords Rd RM1,
RM3 .314 A4
Lower Broad St RM10 . . . . .354 A4
Lower Brook Mews IP1 . . . .17 C5
Lower Brook St IP4 . . . . .17 C5

Lower Burnham Rd CM3 281 C2
Lower Bury La CM16 ....267 E8
Lower Chase CM3 ....282 F4
Lower Church Hill DA9 .376 E2
Lower Church Rd SS7 ...344 B6
Lower Cloister CM11 ....297 B2
Lower Cotts SG9 ....64 A2
Lower Cres SS17 ....375 A3
Lower Dales IP1 ....16 F8
Lower Dales View Rd 3
IP1 ....17 A8
Lower Downs Slade C89 ..9 A8
Lower Dunton Rd SS17,
RM14,CM13 ....340 D4
Lower Farm Rd C04,CO6 .57 B1
Lower Gn
Galleywood CM2 ......254 C2
Stoke by Clare CO10 ...11 C4
Wakes Colne CO6 ....79 C1
Lower Harlings IP9 ......91 A8
Lower Holt St CO6 ......105 D6
Lower Houses Rd IP9 ....63 D2
Lower King CM7 ....128 D1
Lower Lambricks SG6 ...323 D4
Lower Langley CO6 .....106 C1
Lower Mardyke Ave
RM13 ....354 C3
Lower Marine Par CO12 .91 C3
Lower Mdw CM18 ......223 E4
Lower Mill Field CM6 ...150 E7
Lower Noke CL RM3,
CM14 ....314 F8
Lower Orwell St IP4 .....17 D5
Lower Park Cres CM23 .145 F5
Lower Park Rd
Belvedere DA17 ....369 A2
Brightlingsea CO7 ......192 E6
Loughton IG10 ....288 E4
Rochford SS13 ....321 C4
Lower Queen's Rd IG10 .310 D8
Lower Rd Belvedere DA17 369 B3
Birch CO2 ....188 A8
Borley CO10 ....15 B3
Glemsford CO10 ....2 E2
Great Amwell SG12 ....197 A6
Hullbridge SS5 ....301 F1
Little Hallingbury CM22 .173 C7
Loughton IG10 ....289 A8
Mountnessing CM15 ...295 D6
Northfleet DA11 ....378 A3
Peldon CO5 ....189 D5
Rochford SS4 ....302 D2
Tilbury RM18 ....379 A3
Wormingford CO8,CO6 ...80 B5
Lower Sheerings CM21 .173 A3
Lower Southend Rd
SS11 ....321 D8
Lower Sq CB10 ....22 D2
Lower St Basildon SS16 .319 E1
Cavendish CO10 ....1 D1
Sproughton IP8 ....16 A7
Stanstead CO10 ....2 E6
Stutton IP9 ....62 B2
Lower Sunken Rd CM4 ..276 C4
Lower Swaines CM16 ...245 F1
Low Thw IG7 ....312 A5
Lowewood Mus* EN11 ..221 A5
Lowfield CM21 ....172 E1
Lowfield Ct EN11 ....221 A6
Lowfield La EN11 ....221 A6
Low Hall Cl E4 ....287 A2
Lowland Gdns RM7 .....335 B5
Lowlands Rd RM15 .....371 C5
Low Lighthouse Maritime
Mus* CO12 ....91 E5
Low Rd CO12 ....90 E1
Lowry CS13 ....349 F1
Lowry Gdns IP3 ....38 A8
Lowry Rd RM8 ....353 B7
Lowshoe La RM5 ....313 B2
Low St CO10 ....2 C6
Low Street La
East Tilbury RM18 ....379 F8
West Tilbury RM18 .....374 F1
Loxdon Ct RM6 ....334 B5
Loxford SS13 ....343 A8
Loxford La IG1 ....352 D7
Loxford Rd IG11 ....352 A8
Loxford Sch of Science &
Tech IG1 ....352 D7
Loxham Rd E4 ....309 B3
Loxley Ct RM3 ....314 B3
Loyola Prep Sch IG9 ...288 C1
Luard Way Birch CO2 ..161 A3
Witham CM8 ....183 F1
Lubbards Cl SS6 ....302 B5
Lubberhedges La CM6 .125 B8
Lubbins Park Com Prim Sch
SS8 ....364 C2
Lucam Lodge SS4 ......325 F2
Lucas Ave
Chelmsford CM2 ....254 C6
Fordham CO6 ....107 D5
Lucas Cres DA9 ....377 C3
Lucas Ct
Doddinghurst CM15 ...272 C3
Romford RM7 ....314 D1
Waltham Abbey EN9 ...265 F6
Lucas Hall CO4 ....109 F4
Lucas Ho CO3 ....135 A7
Lucas Rd
8 Colchester CO2 ......135 F6
Grays RM17 ....373 A3
Sudbury CO10 ....33 F7
Lucas's La CO16 ....141 D6
Lucerne Dr SS11 ....322 A7
Lucerne Rd CO7 ....138 A6
Lucerne Way
Romford RM3 ....314 D4
Writtle CM1 ....253 B8
Lucerne Wlk SS11 .....322 A7
Luces La CO9 ....51 F4
Lucius Cres CO4 ....110 B6

Lucksfield Way CM2 ...254 F5
Luck's La CM3 ....179 F2
Luckyn La SS14 ....341 F8
Lucton Mews IG10 .....289 B5
Luctons Ave IG9 ....288 C1
Lucy Cl CO3 ....134 C6
Lucy Gdns RM8 ....334 E1
Lucy La N CO3 ....134 B7
Lucy La S CO3 ....134 C2
Lucy Rd SS1 ....367 B7
Ludgores La CM3 ......256 D5
Ludgrove CM3 ....282 A6
Ludham Cl IG6 ....311 C2
Ludham Hall La CM77 ..154 D7
Ludlow Mews SS13 ....343 B6
Ludlow Pl RM17 ....373 B3
Luff Way CO14 ....170 F7
Lufkin Rd CO4 ....109 F3
Lugar Cl CO4 ....136 E6
Lugg App E12 ....333 A1
Luker Rd SS1 ....342 A8
Lukin Cres E4 ....309 D7
Lukin's Dr CM6 ....105 B2
Lukinstone Cl IG10 ....288 E3
Lullington Rd RM9 ....353 E5
Lulworth Ave IG9 ......18 D3
Lulworth Cl
Clacton-on-S CO15 ....220 E8
Stanford-le-H SS17 ....375 B8
Lulworth Dr RM5 ......313 B1
Romford RM5 ....313 B5
Lumber Leys CO14 ....171 A7
Lumley Cl CM2 ....369 A1
Luncies Rd SS14 ....342 F5
Lundy Cl Haverhill CB9 ..9 D7
Southend-on-S SS2 ....347 B7
Lunnish Hill CO12 ....89 F2
Lupin Cl RM7 ....335 D2
Lupin Dr CM1 ....232 F6
Lupin Mews 8 CM1 ...232 F6
Lupin Rd IP2 ....16 E5
Lupin Way CO16 ......195 C4
Lupton Cl SS13 ....295 A1
Lushes Ct IG10 ....289 B4
Lushes Rd IG10 ....289 B4
Lushington Ave CO13 ..191 G4
Lushington Rd CO11 ....86 C4
Lutea Cl SS15 ....319 D1
Luther Dr CO5 ....186 E5
Luther King Cl 1 ....17 C4
Luthers Cl CM15 ......271 E2
Luton Ho 1 RM6 ....314 E5
Lutus Cl CO10 ....12 A6
Luxborough IG7 ....310 F6
Luxborough La IG7 ....310 D3
Luxford Pl CM21 ......172 F1
Lych Gate SS5 ....341 C6
Lychgate Ind Est SS6 ..322 C1
Lydford Ct 23 CM2 ....376 B1
Lydford Rd SS10 ....366 E7
Lydgate Cl CO11 ....86 B4
Lydia Dr CO16 ....193 A2
Lyme Rd SS2 ....348 C1
Lymington Ave
Clacton-on-S CO15 ....196 A8
Southend-on-S SS9 ...346 E1
Lymington Rd RM8 ....334 E3
Lympstone Cl SS9 .....347 A5
Lynbrook Cl RM3 ......314 A6
Lynceley Grange CM16 .246 A2
Lynch The EN11 ....221 B6
Lyndale CM15 ....271 F2
Lyndale Ave SS2 ......348 B3
Lyndale Ct RM20 ....377 B8
Lyndene SS7 ....344 B6
Lyndhurst Ave IP4 ....128 D5
Lyndhurst Ct 1 E18 ...310 A2
Lyndhurst Dr
Bicknacre CM3 ....256 F1
Hornchurch RM11 .....336 C4
Lyndhurst Gdns
Barking IG11 ....352 E6
Ilford IG2 ....333 D5
Lyndhurst Rd
Chingford E4 ....309 C3
Clacton-on-S CO15 ....196 C8
Southend-on-S SS7 ....360 F4
Rochford SS3 ....303 C1
Lyndhurst Rise IG7 ....311 A6
Lyndhurst Way CM13 .295 D2
Lyndon Rd DA17 ....369 A2
Lynford Gdns IG3 .....333 F7
Lynghts Ave SS11 .....300 A3
Lynfords Dr
Wickford, Runwell SS11 .299 F2
Wickford SS11 ....300 A3
Lynmouth Ave CM2 ...232 C1
Lynmouth Gdns CM2 ..232 C1
Lynmouth Ho 3 RM3 .314 E5
Lynne Cl CO13 ....170 E6
Lynnett Rd RM8 ....334 D2
Lynn Rd IG2 ....333 E7
Lynn View Cl SS7 .....344 C5
Lynstede CS14 ....343 A5
Lynton Ave RM7 ......313 B2
Lynton Cres IG2 ....333 B5
Lynton Ct CO14 ....171 A6
Lynton Dr CM1 ....232 C1
Lynton Ho IG1 ....333 C2
Lynton Rd Chingford E4 .309 B6
Hadleigh SS7 ....345 C3
Southend-on-S SS1 ...367 F6
Lynwood Ave IP11 ....381 C5
Lynwood Cl 12 Romford RM5 313 B4
Woodford E18 ....310 A2
Lynwood Dr RM5 ......313 B3
Lynwood Gn SS4 ......303 B1
Lyon Bsns Est IG11 ...352 E3
Lyon Cl Clacton-on-S CO15 196 A4
Galleywood CM2 ......254 B3

Lyon Rd RM1 ....335 F4
Lyons Hall Prim Sch
CM7 ....128 D4
Lyons Hall Rd CM7 ....128 D8
Lysander Rd IP3 ....38 C8
Lyster Ave CM2 ....255 A7
Lytton Cl IG10 ....289 D6
Lytton Rd
Chadwell St M RM16 ..373 F2
Grays RM16 ....374 A2
Romford RM2 ....336 B6
Lyttons Way EN11 .....197 A1

M

Mabbitt Way CM2 ......110 B5
Maberly Ct CB10 ....22 D2
Mabey's Wlk CM21 ....172 B1
McAdam Cl EN11 ......221 A8
Macaulay Rd SS16 ....341 A5
Macbeth Cl CO4 ....136 F7
McCalmont Dr SS6 ....323 C7
Macclesfield Ho 7 RM3 314 E5
McClintock Pl EN3 ....265 B2
McDivitt Wlk SS9 .....347 A6
Macdonald Ave
Dagenham RM10 ......335 B1
Hornchurch RM11 .....336 F7
Southend-on-S SS0 ...347 E2
Macdonald Rd E17 ....309 C1
Macdonald Way RM11 .336 E7
MacDonough Cotts CO12 91 E5
Mace Cl RM17 ....378 E8
McEntee Sch The E17 .309 A2
Mace Wlk CM1 ....231 F3
McGrail Ct SS8 ....364 F2
Macgregor Dr SS12 ...321 E5
McIntosh Cl RM1 ......335 E8
McIntosh Rd RM1 .....335 E8
Macintyres Wlk SS4 ..325 C6
Mackay Ct CO2 ....136 B1
Mackenzie Cl SS12 ...321 E6
McKenzie Rd EN10 ...221 A3
Mackley Dr SS17 ......360 F5
Maclarens Cl SS8 .....213 A6
Maclaren Way 5 SS12 321 E5
Maclennan Ave RM13 .355 D2
Macleod Cl RM17 .....373 D2
Macmillan Cl 4 CM2 ..232 B1
Macmillan Gdns DA1 .376 A3
Macmurdo Cl SS9 .....346 D7
Macmurdo Rd SS9 ....346 D7
Macon Way RM14 .....337 F5
Madden Cl DA18 ......368 C4
Maddocks Cl SS8 ......287 D1
Maddox Rd CM0 ......223 E8
Madeira Ave SS9 ......346 E2
Madeira Gr IG8 ....310 C4
Madeira Rd CO15 .....196 D4
Madeleines Flats CM19 .182 B8
Madeline Gr IG1 ....352 D7
Madeline Pl CM1 ......231 E6
Madells CM16 ....267 F8
Madgements Rd CM7 .129 C8
Madles La CM4 ....275 F1
Madras Ho IG1 ....352 B8
Madras Rd IG1 ....352 B8
Madrid Ave SS6 ....323 B7
Mafeking Ave IG2 ....333 B6
Magazine Farm Way
CO3 ....135 A6
Magazine Rd SS3 .....368 E6
Magdalen Cl CO15 ....195 E4
Magdalen Ct CO15 ...195 E4
Magdalen Cl IP2 ....16 F2
Magdalen Cres CM8 ..156 D3
Magdalene Gdns E6 ..352 A1
Magdalen Gn CM13 ...295 C3
Magdalen Gr
Colchester CO1 ....136 B6
Thaxted CM6 ....70 B2
Magdalen Rd CO15 ...195 E4
Maldon St SS18 ....310 C4
Magenta Cl CM12 .....296 E3
Magingley Cres IP5 ....18 F6
Magna Mead SS3 .....349 D7
Magnaville Rd CM23 ..145 E4
Magnet Rd RM20 ......377 C8
Magnolia Cl
Canvey Island SS8 ....364 A2
Chelmsford CM2 ......254 B6
South Ockendon RM15 .357 E1
Upminster RM14 ......337 F4
Magnolia Ct CM1 ......136 B8
Magnolia Dr CO4 .....136 F8
Magnolia Lodge E4 ...309 B7
Magnolia Pl SS17 .....360 E4
Magnolia Rd CO4 .....135 B5
Magnolias The CM11 ..319 C6
Magnolia Way
Pilgrims Hatch CM15 ..294 B4
Rochford SS4 ....348 A8
Magnum Cl RM13 .....355 C1
Magpie Cl RM14 ....256 B4
Magpie Cl Harwich CO12 .92 F5
Ipswich IP8 ....16 C2
Magpie La CM13 ....316 E2
Magpies CM16 ....245 A7
Magwitch Cl CM1 .....231 F7
Mahonia Dr SS16 .....340 F5
Maida Ave E4 ....287 B2
Maida Way E4 ....287 B2
Maidenburgh St CO1 ..135 F7
Maidenhall Inf Sch IP2 ..17 A2
Maidenhall Gn IP2 .....17 A2
Maidment Cres CM8 ..156 C1
Maidstone Inf Sch IP11 .381 C5
Maidstone Rd
Felixstowe IP11 ....381 C5
Grays RM17 ....378 A8
Mailers La CM23 ......118 F5
Maine Cres SS6 ....323 A6
Main Rd Bicknacre CM3 .279 A6

Main Rd continued
Boreham CM3 ....209 F1
Braintree CM3 ....153 D4
Broomfield CM1 ....208 B2
Chelmondiston IP9 .....63 D7
Chelmsford CM2 ......255 F7
Danbury CM3 ....256 A7
Danbury CM3 ....256 D7
East Hanningfield CM3 .278 C5
Frating CO7 ....138 E3
Great Holland CO13 ...170 A3
Great Leighs CM3 .....180 F7
Harwich, Bath Side CO12 .91 E5
Harwich, Dovercourt CO12 .91 B3
Hawkwell SS5 ....324 F4
Hockley SS5 ....324 D6
Ramsey CO12 ....90 A1
Rettendon CM3,SS11 ..300 B6
Romford RM1 ....336 A8
Rushmere St A IP5 .....18 F8
St Lawrence CM0 ......262 D7
Woolverstone IP9 ......38 B2
Wormingford CO6 ......80 F4
Main St CB1 ....6 F6
Mais Ct IP2 ....16 E1
Maitland Cl CO3 ....170 C4
Maitland Pl SS3 ....349 E1
Maitland Rd E15 ......353 D8
Stansted Mountfitchet
CM24 ....119 C6
Maitlands SG10 ....288 F6
Maizey Ct CM15 ......294 A4
Majendie La CO6 ....51 F4
Makanen Ho IG9 ......288 C1
Makepeace Rd E11 ...332 A7
Makins Rd CO12 ....90 F5
Malan Sq RM12 ......355 B6
Malby Lodge SS0 .....366 D6
Malcolm Way E11 ....332 A7
Maldon Court Sch CM9 236 F3
Maldon C
8 Colchester CO13 ...135 E6
Great Cornard CO10 ...34 B7
Wallend E6 ....352 A4
Maldon Ho IG9 ....288 E2
Maldon Prim Sch CM9 237 A2
Maldon Rd Birch CO2 .160 E4
Bradwell-on-S CM0 ...242 A1
Bradwell-on-S, Mill End
CM0 ....263 C7
Bradwell Waterside CM0 .241 F1
Burnham-on-C CM0 ...305 E8
Colchester, Abbey Field
CO3 ....135 D5
Colchester,Stanway Green
CO3 ....134 D1
Dagenham RM7 ......335 C4
Danbury, Gay Bowers CM3 257 B5
Danbury, Runsell Green
CM3 ....257 B7
Goldhanger CM9 ......238 E7
Great Baddow CM2 ...228 B1
Great Totham CM9 ....212 E6
Great Wigborough CO5 .188 E2
Hatfield Peverel CM3,CM9 210 D3
Kelvedon CO5 ....158 C1
Langford CM9 ....236 D6
Langford CM9 ....236 D6
Latchingdon CM3 .....261 B1
Margaretting CM4 ....227 D4
Mayland CM3 ....261 D1
Southend-on-S SS3 ...349 E1
Tiptree CO5 ....186 B3
Witham CM8 ....212 A6
Woodham Mortimer CM9 257 B2
Maldon Wik CB9 ....10 D8
Maldon Wlk IG8 ....310 C4
Malford Ct E18 ....310 A1
Malford Gr IG8 ....310 A1
Malgraves SS13 ....343 B7
Malgraves Pl SS13 ...343 B7
Malin Cl CM7 ....224 E7
Malkin Dr CM17 ......174 F6
Mallard Cl
Great Notley CM77 ...154 C5
Kelvedon CO5 ....158 C3
Layer-de-I-H CO2 .....162 F6
Tollesbury CM9 ....216 D2
Mallard Ct Chingford E4 .287 A1
Ilford IG2 ....333 C2
8 Southend-on-S SS1 .367 C8
Mallard Rd CM7 ......224 E7
Mallards Mayland CM3 .283 A8
Southend-on-S SS3 ...349 E1
Wanstead E11 ....332 A4
Mallards Rd Barking IG11 .353 A3
Woodford IG8 ....310 A3
Mallards Rise CM17 ..224 D8
Mallards The SS3 .....349 E1
Mallard Way
Brentwood CM13 .....295 B2
Great Cornard CO10 ...34 C5
Ipswich IP2 ....16 F2
Mallinson Cl RM12 ...355 C7
Mallion Cl EN9 ....199 C7
Mallory Rd CM1 ......209 E7
Mallory Way CM7 ....297 A1
Mallow Cl RM17 ......378 F8
Mallow Gdns CM1 ...296 F5
Mallowhayes Cl IP2 ...17 B3
Mallows Field CO9 ....76 E1
Mallow Wlk EN9 ......223 A3
Mallows Green Rd CM23 .92 D1
Mallows La CO9 ....49 F3
Mall The CM1 ....336 B3
Malmesbury IP2 ....309 F2
Malmesbury Rd E18 .309 F2
Malmstead SG8 ....368 C6

Malpas Rd
Dagenham RM9 ....353 D6
Grays RM16 ....374 C3
Maltsters Lodge 9 EN11 221 D8
Malta Rd RM18 ....378 F5
Maltese Rd CM1 ......232 A4
Malthouse Pl 6 RM1 .335 E6
Malthouse Rd CO11 ..86 D4
Malthouse The CO10 ..15 B5
Malting Cotts CB9 .....9 F4
Malting Farm La CO7 .84 D2
Malting Green Rd CO2 .162 A5
Malting La Clare CO10 ..12 B7
Kirby-le-S CO13 ......143 C1
Orsett RM16 ....359 A1
Malting Rd
Colchester CO2 ....135 C1
Peldon CO5 ....189 E6
Maltings Chase CM4 .274 B3
Maltings Cl CO6 ....57 B3
Maltings Ct SS8 ......211 F8
Maltings Dr CM16 ....246 A2
Maltings Hill CM5 ....226 E3
Maltings Ind Est The
SG12 ....197 D4
Maltings La Epping CM16 226 A2
Witham CM8 ....211 F8
Maltings Rd
Battlesbridge SS11 ...300 E2
Brightlingsea CO7 ....165 E1
Great Baddow CM2 ...255 A5
Maltings The
Cavendish CO10 ....1 D2
Gravesend DA11 ....379 A1
Great Dunmow CM6 ..123 D1
Great Easton CM6 .....96 E2
Ramsey CO12 ....116 E8
Rayleigh SS7 ....127 A2
Romford RM1 ....335 F4
Saffron Walden CB10 ..22 D1
Southminster CM0 ....284 E4
Thaxted CM6 ....70 A2
Maltings View CM7 ..128 A3
Malting Wharf CO11 ..86 D4
Malting Terr IP2 ......17 D4
Malting Villas Rd SS4 .325 F2
Malting Yd CO7 ......164 B8
Maltings Park Rd CO6 .108 F4
Malvern SS3 ....348 B1
Malvern Ave
Canvey Island SS8 ....363 D3
Chingford E4 ....309 D3
Malvern Cl
Chelmsford CM1 .....231 D6
Ipswich IP3 ....18 B4
Rayleigh SS6 ....323 D4
Rushmere St A IP5 .....18 F8
Malvern Dr Ilford IG3 .352 F8
Woodford IG8 ....310 D3
Malvern Gdns IG10 ..288 F3
Malvern Ho DA11 ....378 D1
Malvern Ho Grays RM17 373 E2
Hockley SS5 ....324 F8
Hornchurch RM11 ....336 A5
Malvern Way CO6 .....79 F5
Malwood Dr SS7 ......344 B5
Malwood Rd SS7 .....344 B5
Malyon Cl SS13 ......343 B8
Malyon Court Cl SS7 .345 B4
Malyon Rd CM8 ......211 F8
Malyons SS13 ....343 B8
Malyons Cl SS13 .....343 B8
Malyons Gn SS13 ....343 B8
Malyons La SS13 .....301 D2
Malyons Mews SS13 .343 B8
Malyons Pl SS13 .....343 B8
Malyons The SS13 ...343 B8
Manbrough Ave E6 ...352 A2
Manchester Dr SS9 ...346 F2
Manchester Rd
Holland-on-S CO15 ...196 E6
Ipswich IP2 ....16 E2
Manchester Way RM10 354 B8
Mandeville Cl CM17 ..224 C6
Mandeville Prim Sch
CM21 ....172 D3
Mandeville Rd
Saffron Walden CB11 ..43 D8
Mandeville Wlk CM13 .295 C2
Mandy Cl IP4 ....18 A6
Manfield Gdns CO10 ..34 A5
Manford Cl IG7 ....312 B6
Manford Cross IG7 ...312 A5
Manford Way IG7 ....311 F5
Manford Prim Sch IG7 .311 F5
Manford Way
Chigwell IG7 ....311 E5
Hainault IG7 ....312 A5
Mangapp Chase CM0 .306 B8
Mangapps Farm Rly Mus*
CM0 ....306 A8
Manilla Rd SS1 ....367 D5
Mannering Gdns SS3 .347 A3
Manners Cnr SS2 .....347 E5
Manners Way SS2 ....347 E5
Manningfield Rd CM2 .255 C1
Manning Rd CM23 ....146 A4
Mannings IG4 ....18 F5
Mannington Cl IP4 ....18 F5
Mannock Ct CO4 .....136 F4
Manningtree High Sch
CO11 ....86 D4
Manningtree Mus*
CO11 ....86 D4

Manningtree Rd
Brantham CO11 ....86 A8
Dedham CO7 ....85 B6
East Bergholt CO7 .....59 F3
Little Bentley CO7 ....139 F8
Stutton IP9 ....61 F2
Manningtree Sta CO11 .86 A5
Mannin Rd RM6 ......334 B5
Mannock Dr IG10 .....289 C7
Manns Way SS6 ......323 C5
Manor Ave Basildon SS13 343 C7
Hornchurch RM11 ....136 C6
Little Waltham CM3 ...208 B5
Manor Ct 3 Barking IG11 352 F5
Chingford E4 ....287 E1
South Benfleet SS7 ..344 D7
Southend-on-S SS1 ...367 C7
Waltham Abbey EN9 ..265 D6
Manor Dr CM2 ....254 F7
Manor Farm CI CB9 ....9 B7
Manor Farm Dr E4 ...309 E7
Manor Fields Prim Sch
CM3 ....145 D5
Manor Hatch CO18 ...224 A7
Manor Hatch CM18 ...224 B7
Manor Ho CM0 ....257 A5
Manor House Gdns 2
E11 ....332 B5
Manor House Way CO7 .192 E8
Manor Inf Sch SS12 ..352 F6
Manor Jun Sch IG11 ..352 F6
Manor La
Great Chesterford CB10 ...3 D2
Harwich CO12 ....91 B2
Stutton IP9 ....61 E2
Manor Links CM23 ...146 C7
Manor PI CM7 ....128 A3
Manor Prim Sch The
RM1 ....335 F6
Manor Rd Abridge RM4 .290 E2
Barking IG11 ....352 F6
Basildon SS15 ....341 B7
Bishop's Stortford CM23 .146 A7
Chelmsford CM2 .....255 C1
Chigwell IG7 ....311 C5
Colchester CO3 ......135 F7
Dagenham RM10 .....354 D6
Dengie CM0 ....263 D1
Felixstowe IP11 ......381 C1
Grays,Little Thurrock Marshes
RM17 ....377 C8
Grays,West Thurrock
RM20 ....377 D8
Great Holland CO13 .170 A3
Harlow CM17 ....200 C5
Harwich CO12 ....211 C1
Hatfield Peverel CM3 .211 C1
Haverhill CB9 ....9 B7
High Beach SS10 .....288 B8
Hockley SS5 ....324 C6
Hoddesdon EN11 .....221 A7
Ilford RM6 ....334 B6
Ipswich IP4 ....17 D8
Little Easton CM6 ....122 F5
Loughton IG10 ....288 C3
Maldon CM9 ....236 A4
Romford RM1 ....336 A6
South Benfleet SS7 ..344 D6
Southend-on-S SS2 ..348 E4
South Woodham Ferrers
CM3 ....301 C8
Stanford-le-H SS17 ..360 D8
Stansted Mountfitchet
CM24 ....119 E5
Sudbury CO10 ....15 E1
Swanscombe DA10 ...377 D1
Tilbury RM18 ....379 A5
West Bergholt CO6 ..108 E5
Witham CM8 ....184 A4
Wivenhoe CO7 ....137 C1
Woodham Walter CM9 .235 E5
Manors CM8 ....156 D4
Manor Sq RM8 ....334 C2
Manor St CM7 ....128 A3
Manors Way CM8 .....156 C4
Manor Trad Est SS7 ..344 D7
Manorway IG8 ....310 C5
Manor Way
Brentwood CM14 .....316 A7
Corringham SS17 ....309 D6
Corringham SS17 ....361 A2
Grays RM17 ....378 C2
Holland-on-S CO15 ..196 G6
Northfleet RM17 .....378 A3
Rainham RM13 ....354 E1
Swanscombe DA10 ...377 E3
Manor Way Bsns Ctr
RM13 ....369 D8
Manorway The
Corringham SS17 ....361 D2
Stanford-le-H SS17 ..360 D2
Mansard Cl RM12 ....336 A2
Mansard Ct CO15 ....196 C5
Mansbrook Bvd IP3 ...38 D7
Man's Cross CM9 .....29 E2
Manse Chase CM9 ...237 A1
Mansel Cl SS6 ....323 C6
Mansel Gr E17 ....309 A2
Manser Rd RM13 ....354 E3
Mansfield CM21 ......172 A1

Mansfield Gdns RM12 . . . . .336 D2
Mansfield Hill E4 . . . . .287 B1
Mansfield Rd Ilford IG1 . . .333 A2
  Wanstead E11 . . . . .332 B5
Mansfields CM1 . . . . .230 F1
Mansfield Twrs CO15 . . .195 F2
Manstead Gdns
  Dagenham RM6 . . . . .334 C4
  Rainham RM13 . . . . .370 B7
Mansted Gdns SS4 . . . . . .325 D5
Manston Dr CM23 . . . . . .119 B1
Manston Rd CM20 . . . . . .223 E8
Manston Way RM12 . . . . .355 B6
Manton Rd EN3 . . . . .265 A1
Manuden Prim Sch CM23 . .93 A2
Manwick Rd IP11 . . . . . .381 D2

Maple Ave
  Bishop's Stortford CM23 . .145 D8
  Braintree CM7 . . . . .127 D2
  Heybridge CM9 . . . . .237 C6
  Southend-on-S SS9 . . . . . .365 F8
  Upminster RM14 . . . . .356 B8
Maple CI
  Bishop's Stortford CM23 . .145 D8
  Brentwood CM13 . . . . .316 F7
  Buckhurst Hill IG9 . . . . . . .110 D7
  Clacton-on-S CO15 . . . . . .195 C3
  Halstead CO9 . . . . .77 A2
  Harwich CO12 . . . . .91 B3
  Hornchurch RM12 . . . . . . .336 B1
  Ipswich IP2 . . . . .17 A3
  □ Redbridge IG6 . . . . .311 E5
  Theydon Bois CM16 . . . . . .267 D2
Maplecroft La EN9 . . . . .221 E2
Maple Ct
  Clacton-on-S CO15 . . . . . .196 D4
  Southend-on-S SS3 . . . . . .368 F8
Maple Gdns SS13 . . . . . .342 D4
Maple Gr CM23 . . . . .145 DB
Maple Ho IP11 . . . . .381 C4
Maple La CB10 . . . . .45 C5
Maple Leaf CO5 . . . . .186 C7
Mapleleafe Gdns IG6 . . .333 B8
Maple Lodge IG9 . . . . . . .288 D1
Maple Mead CM12 . . . . . .119 C8
Maple Rd Grays RM17 . . .378 C8
  Great Cornard CO10 . . . . . .34 B5
Maple River Ind Est
  CM20 . . . . .200 B6
Maples SS17 . . . . .360 E2
Maplesfield SS7 . . . . .345 D4
Maple Springs CM23 . . . .145 DB
Maple Springs EN9 . . . . . .265 F4
Maple Sq SS2 . . . . .348 B2
Maplestead E4 . . . . .342 D8
Maplestead Rd RM9 . . . . .353 B4
Maples The Harlow CM19 .223 B3
  Rushmere St A IP4 . . . . . . .18 E8
  □ Wickford SS11 . . . . . . .321 C5
Mapleton Rd E4 . . . . .287 A7
Mapleton La CM4 . . . . . .273 E8
Maple Tree La SS16 . . . . .347 B5
Maple Way
  Burnham-on-C CM0 . . . . . .306 A6
  Canvey Island SS8 . . . . . . .363 E3
  Colchester CO2 . . . . .136 A4
Maplin CI SS7 . . . . .344 C7
Maplin Ct
  Clacton-on-S CO15 . . . . . .196 D4
  Southend-on-S SS3 . . . . . .368 A5
Maplin Gdns SS13 . . . . . .342 E5
Maplin Mews SS13 . . . . . .368 A6
Maplin Way SS1 . . . . .368 C6
Maplin Way SS1 . . . . .349 C1
Mapperley CI □ E11 . . . .332 A1
Mapperley Dr IG8 . . . . . .309 E3
Marasca End CO2 . . . . . . .163 A7
Maraschino Cres CO2 . . . .163 A7
Marbled White Dr IP8 . . . .36 E8
Marchmant CI RM12 . . . . .336 A2
Marconi Gdns CM15 . . . . .294 C4
Marconi Rd CM1 . . . . .232 B3
Marcos Rd SS8 . . . . .364 D3
Marcus Ave SS1 . . . . .368 B7
Marcus Chase SS1 . . . . . .368 B7
Marcus CI Colchester CO4 .110 B6
  Haverhill CB9 . . . . .9 D7
Marcus Gdns SS1 . . . . . . .368 B7
Marden Ash □ SS15 . . . . .341 A6
Marden Ash IG7 . . . . .312 B8
Marden Rd □ RM1 . . . . . .335 E5
Mardyke Ho RM13 . . . . . .354 D3
Mardyke Rd CM20 . . . . . .200 A2
Marennes Cres CO7 . . . . .192 F2
Maresby Ho E4 . . . . .309 B8
Mareth Rd CO2 . . . . .135 C2
Margaret Ave
  Brentwood CM15 . . . . .295 A3
  Chingford E4 . . . . .287 B3
Margaret Bondfield Ave
  IG11 . . . . .353 A5
Margaret CI
  Brightlingsea CO7 . . . . . . .193 A6
  Epping CM16 . . . . .245 F2
  Romford RM2 . . . . .336 B6
  Waltham Abbey EN9 . . . . . .265 D6
Margaret Rd
  Colchester CO1 . . . . .135 F8
  Epping CM16 . . . . .246 A2
  Romford RM2 . . . . .336 B6

Margaret St
  Felixstowe IP11 . . . . .381 C5
  Thaxted CM6 . . . . .70 A3
Margaretting CE Prim Sch
  CM4 . . . . .274 F8
Margaretting Rd
  Chelmsford CM2 . . . . .253 F1
  Galleywood CM2 . . . . .254 A2
  Wanstead E12 . . . . .332 C3
  Writtle CM1 . . . . .253 A6
Margaret Way
  Redbridge IG4 . . . . .332 E5
  Saffron Walden CB10 . . . . . .22 D2
Margarite Way SS12 . . . .321 B7
Margate Rd IP3 . . . . .18 C6
Margery Allingham PI
  CM9 . . . . .215 D4
Margery Rd RM8 . . . . .334 D1
Margeth Rd CM12 . . . . . .319 C3
Margherita Pl EN9 . . . . . .266 A5
Margherita Rd EN9 . . . . . .266 A5
Margraten Ave SS8 . . . . .364 D6
Margrave Gdns □ CM23 .145 E5
Marguerite Dr SS9 . . . . . .346 F1
Marguerite Way CM23 . . .145 C6
Maria Ct CO2 . . . . .136 C5
Mariam Gdns CM12 . . . . .336 F2
Marian CI RM16 . . . . .372 E5
Maria Ave SS6 . . . . .323 C3
Maria St CO12 . . . . .91 D5
Marie CI SS17 . . . . .361 A8
Marie Ct E4 . . . . .309 D5
Marigold Ave
  Clacton-on-S CO16 . . . . . .195 C4
  Ipswich IP2 . . . . .16 E3
Marigold Ct
  Chelmsford CM1 . . . . .232 F6
  Colchester CO4 . . . . .136 EB
Marigold La CM4 . . . . . . .275 F1
Marigold Pl CM17 . . . . . .200 B4
Marina Ave SS6 . . . . .323 C3
Marina CI SS2 . . . . .347 E4
Marine CI SS17 . . . . .361 A8
Marine Ct E4 . . . . .309 D5
Marina Gdns
  Clacton-on-S CO15 . . . . . .196 C5
  Woodford IG5 . . . . .310 F1
  Romford RM7 . . . . .335 C6
Marina Mews □ CO14 . . .171 C8
Marina Point CO15 . . . . . .195 D1
Marina Rd CM3 . . . . .211 A4
Marina Ave SS6 . . . . .323 C3
Marina CI SS2 . . . . .347 E4
Marine CI SS9 . . . . .346 A1
Marine Ct SS17 . . . . .361 A8
Marine Par
  Canvey Island SS8 . . . . . . .364 F2
  Harwich CO12 . . . . .91 D3
  Mayland CM3 . . . . .260 E1
  Southend-on-S, Leigh-on-S
  SS0 . . . . .366 E7
  Southend-on-S SS9 . . . . . .367 B7
Marine Par E CO15 . . . . . .196 B3
Marine CI SS9 . . . . .346 A1
Marine Par W CO15 . . . . .195 E1
Mariner Rd E12 . . . . .332 A8
Mariners Ct
  Great Wakering SS3 . . . . . .350 C3
  Greenhithe DA9 . . . . .377 B3
Mariners Way CM9 . . . . . .259 A8
Marion Ct CO15 . . . . .195 E6
Marion CI IG6 . . . . .311 D3
Marionette Stps □ SS7 . .367 C7
Marion Gr IG8 . . . . .309 A5
Marisco Cl RM16 . . . . . . .374 B2
Mariskals SS13 . . . . .343 A6
Maritime Ave CM9 . . . . . .237 E3
Maritime CI □ RM4 . . . . .377 B2
Maritime Ct □ IP4 . . . . . . .17 D5
Marjorams Ave IG10 . . . .289 A7
Mark Ave E4 . . . . .287 B3
Market Ave SS12 . . . . . . .321 C8
Market End CO1 . . . . .135 EB
Market Field Sch CO7 . . .138 A5
Market Gr CO9 . . . . .30 A1
Market Hill Clare CO10 . . .12 B7
  Coggeshall CO6 . . . . .131 A2
  Halstead CO9 . . . . .76 E2
  Maldon CM9 . . . . .9 A8
  Maldon CM9 . . . . .237 A3
  Saffron Walden CB10 . . . . . .22 D2
  Sudbury CO10 . . . . .33 E7
Market Hill La CM6 . . . . .237 A3
Market Pl Abridge RM4 . .290 B6
  □ Braintree CM7 . . . . . . .127 F3
  Great Dunmow CM6 . . . . . .123 D1
  Ingatestone CM4 . . . . .274 B4
  Maldon CM9 . . . . .236 F7
  Romford RM1 . . . . .335 E6
  Saffron Walden CB10 . . . . . .22 D2
  Southend-on-S SS1 . . . . . .367 A7
Market Rd
  Chelmsford CM1 . . . . .232 B2
  Wickford SS12 . . . . .321 C7
Market Row CB10 . . . . .22 D1
Market Sq Basildon SS14 .342 A5
  □ Bishop's Stortford CM23 .145 F7
  □ Chelmsford CM1 . . . . . .232 B2
  Rochford SS4 . . . . .325 F2
  South Woodham Ferrers
  CM3 . . . . .301 E7
  Waltham Abbey EN9 . . . . . .265 C6

Market St
  □ Bishop's Stortford CM23 .145 F7
  □ Braintree CM7 . . . . . . .127 F3
  Harlow CM17 . . . . .200 C4
  Harwich CO12 . . . . .91 E6
  Saffron Walden CB10 . . . . . .22 D2
Market Wlk CB10 . . . . . . .22 D1
Market Yd □ CO1 . . . . . . .287 B2
Mark Hall Cycle Mus &
  Gdns* CM20 . . . . .200 B3
Mark Hall Moors CM20 . .200 B3
Mark Hall Sch CM7 . . . . . .200 C3
Markham Ho RM10 . . . . . .335 A1
Markhams SS17 . . . . .360 F3
Markhams Chase SS15 . . .341 D7
Marking's Field CB10 . . . .22 E2
Mark La DA13 . . . . .379 F1
Markland CI CM2 . . . . . . .254 C3
Markland Dr CM0 . . . . . . .236 E1
Marklay Dr CM3 . . . . .301 C7
Mark Rd CM3 . . . . .263 F6
Mark's Ave CM5 . . . . .249 A4
Marks CI Billericay CM12 .296 F4
  Ingatestone CM4 . . . . .273 F1
Marks Ct SS1 . . . . .367 C7
Marks Gate Inf Sch RM6 .334 B8
Marks Gate Jun Sch
  RM6 . . . . .334 B8
Marks Gdns CM7 . . . . . . .128 C3
Marks Hall Cty Est*
  CO6 . . . . .130 E7
Marks Hall La CM6 . . . . . .204 E3
Marks Hall Rd CO6 . . . . . .130 E6
Marks La CM3 . . . . .299 F8
Marks Rd RM7 . . . . .335 D6
Marks Tey Rdbt CO6 . . . . .133 A4
Marks Tey Sta CO6 . . . . . .133 B4
Mark Wade CI E12 . . . . . .332 D2
Markwell Wood CM19 . . .223 B2
Markyate Rd RM8 . . . . . . .353 B7
Marlands Rd
  Redbridge IG5 . . . . .332 EB
  Woodford IG5 . . . . .310 F1
Marlborough Ave CM0 . . .263 E3
Marlborough Ct
  Bishop's Stortford CM23 . .145 F5
  Clacton-on-S CO15 . . . . . .195 C3
  Grays RM16 . . . . .373 C4
  South Benfleet SS7 . . . . . .344 D7
  Wanstead E4 . . . . .337 D3
Marlborough Dr
  Redbridge IG5 . . . . .332 EB
  Sudbury CO10 . . . . .33 FB
Marlborough Gdns
  RM14 . . . . .337 E4
Marlborough Ho CM14 . . .316 B6
Marlborough Pl SS1 . . . . .366 F7
Marlborough Rd
  Braintree CM7 . . . . .128 A4
  □ Chelmsford CM2 . . . . . .232 A1
  Chingford E4 . . . . .309 B4
  Dagenham RM8 . . . . .353 CB
  Ipswich IP4 . . . . .18 A6
  Pilgrims Hatch CM15 . . . . .294 A3
  Romford RM7 . . . . .335 B7
  Southend-on-S SS3 . . . . . .367 DB
  □ Woodford E18 . . . . . . .310 A1
Marlborough Terr CM2 . . .232 A1
Marlborough Way CM7 . . .297 A5
Marlborough Wlk SS5 . . . .324 C6
Marle Gdns EN9 . . . . .265 C7
Marlescroft Way IG10 . . .289 A4
Marlin CI SS7 . . . . .345 E6
Marlow Ave RM19 . . . . . . .371 A2
Marlowe CI
  Billericay CM12 . . . . .297 B5
  Braintree CM7 . . . . .155 A8
  Maldon CM9 . . . . .259 A8
  Redbridge IG6 . . . . .311 C2
Marlowe Rd
  Clacton-on-S CO15 . . . . . .220 GB
  Jaywick CO15 . . . . .195 A1
  Marlow Gdns CO2 . . . . . . .134 F6
  Marlow Gdns SS12 . . . . . .321 F8
Marlpits Rd CM5,CM9 . . . .257 E4
Marlyon Rd IG6 . . . . .312 B5
Marmara Ave E4 . . . . .309 A6
Marmion App E4 . . . . .309 A6
Marmion Ave E4 . . . . .309 A6
Marmion Rd SS6 . . . . .323 B4
Marmaduke Ave SS6 . . . .323 B4
Marne Rd CO2 . . . . .135 E4
Marney CI CM2 . . . . .254 EB
Marney Way CO13 . . . . . .171 B6
Marquis CI CM23 . . . . . . .145 B7
Marquis Ct SS12 . . . . .352 E7
Marram Ct CO3 . . . . .134 B6
Marram CI RM15 . . . . .378 E8
Mar Rd RM15 . . . . .357 C1
Marriotts CM17 . . . . .200 C5
Marsden Ho □ RM3 . . . . .314 F4
Marsden Rd □ RM3 . . . . .314 F4
Marshall CI Feering CO5 . .158 D4
  Southend-on-S SS9 . . . . . .346 A3
Marshalls SS4 . . . . .325 D4
Marshalls CI SS3 . . . . .349 F4
Marshalls Park Sch RM1 .313 E1
Marshalls Piece CM6 . . . .124 D6
Marshalls Rd
  Braintree CM7 . . . . .127 E1
  Romford RM7 . . . . .335 D7
Marshams CM23 . . . . .145 CB
Marsh Cres CO5 . . . . .184 C3
Marsh Farm Country Pk*
  CM3 . . . . .301 E5

Marsh Farm La CO7 . . . . .166 D3
Marsh Farm Rd CM3 . . . .301 D4
Marshfoot Rd RM16,
  RM17 . . . . .373 F1
Marsh Green Prim Sch
  RM10 . . . . .354 A3
Marsh Green Rd RM10 . . .354 A4
Marsh Hill EN9 . . . . .243 E4
Marsh La Fobbing SS17 . . .361 D6
  Harlow CM17 . . . . .200 EB
  Mountnessing SS12 . . . . . .296 A7
  Stanstead Abbotts SG12 . .197 D4
Marsh Rd
  Burnham-on-C CM0 . . . . . .307 B7
  Thorington Street CO6,CO7 .57 E6
  Tillingham CM0 . . . . .264 B4
Marsh St Dartford DA1 . . .376 A3
  Dartford DA1 . . . . .376 A5
  South View CO SS16 . . . . .342 E3
Marsh Way
  Brightlingsea CO7 . . . . . . .192 E6
  Rainham RM13 . . . . .369 DB
Marshy La CO9, CO10 . . . . .30 C7
Marston Bay Ind Est
  RM2 . . . . .314 D1
Marston Beck CM2 . . . . . .206 A2
Marston CI RM10 . . . . . . .335 A1
Marston Ho RM17 . . . . . . .378 AB
Marston Rd CM7 . . . . .127 CB
Martello Cvn Pk CO14 . . .171 CB
Martello Rd □ CO14 . . . . .171 CB
Marten Rd E17 . . . . .309 A1
Martham CI CO6 . . . . .56 FB
Martens Mdw CM7 . . . . . .128 C3
Martham CI CO6 . . . . .311 B2
Martina Terr □ IG6 . . . . . .311 F5
Martin CI CM11 . . . . .297 B1
Martindale Ave SS15 . . . .319 D2
Martin Dr Dartford DA2 . . .376 C7
  Rainham RM13 . . . . .355 B1
Martin End CO2 . . . . .162 A5
Martinet Gn IP3 . . . . .18 C1
Martingale CI RM7 . . . . . .345 B5
Martingale CI CM1 . . . . . .232 F7
Martingale Dr CM1 . . . . . .232 F7
Martingale Rd CM11 . . . . .297 D6
Martin Gdns RM8 . . . . . . .353 DB
Martini Dr EN3 . . . . .265 A2
Martin Rd Aveley RM15 . . .371 D5
  Dagenham RM8 . . . . .353 DB
  Ipswich IP2 . . . . .17 A1
Martins CI SS17 . . . . .360 D3
Martin's Ct SS2 . . . . .348 A1
Martinsdale CO15 . . . . . . .195 F6
Martinsfield CI IG7 . . . . . .311 E6
Martin's Rd CO9 . . . . .76 E1
Martin Wlk SS9 . . . . .346 D3
Martlesham CI RM12 . . . . .355 C7
Martley Dr IG2 . . . . .333 B6
Martock Ave SS0 . . . . .347 A6
Martyns Gr SS0 . . . . .347 B2
Martyns Rise CO10 . . . . . . .15 C5
Marvens CM2 . . . . .254 D3
Marvens The IP8 . . . . .16 A1
Marwell CI RM1 . . . . .336 A6
Maryborough Gr CO2 . . . .136 D2
Mary La N CO7 . . . . .137 A8
Maryland CI □ CO2 . . . . .136 A1
Marylands Ave SS5 . . . . . .324 D7
Mary La S CO7 . . . . .139 B6
Mary Macarthur Ho
  □ Belvedere DA17 . . . . . .369 A6
  Dagenham RM10 . . . . .335 A1
Mary McArthur PI CM24 .119 EB
Maryon Rd IP3 . . . . .18 B1
Mary Park Gdns CM23 . . .145 F4
Mary Rose CI CM16 . . . . .372 C2
Mary Ruck Way CM7 . . . . .155 B5
Mary Warner Rd CO7 . . . .137 A4
Mascalls La
  Brentwood CM14 . . . . .315 F6
  Great Warley CM14 . . . . . .316 A4
Mascalls The CM2 . . . . . . .254 EB
Mascalls Way CM2 . . . . . .254 EB
Mascot CI CO4 . . . . .136 D5
Mascot Sq CO4 . . . . .136 D5
Masefield Ave EN9 . . . . . .265 D5
Masefield Cres RM3 . . . . .314 C2
Masefield Ct □ CM14 . . . .316 C6
Masefield Dr
  Colchester CO3 . . . . .134 F6
  Upminster RM14 . . . . .337 C4
Masefield Gdns CO7 . . . . .352 A1
Masefield Rd
  Braintree CM7 . . . . .155 A8
  Dartford DA1 . . . . .376 B2
  Grays RM16 . . . . .373 A3
  Maldon CM9 . . . . .259 AB
Mashay Rd CO9 . . . . .30 D5
Mashbury Rd CM1 . . . . . .206 B6
Mashiters Hill RM1 . . . . . .313 DB
Mashiters Wlk RM1 . . . . . .313 D6
Mason CI CO2 . . . . .135 B3
Mason Ct □ CO7 . . . . . . .193 A6
Mason Rd
  Clacton-on-S CO16 . . . . . .195 B3
  Colchester CO1 . . . . .109 F1
  Woodford IG8 . . . . .309 E6
Masons CI IP4 . . . . .18 F4
Masons Ct □ CM23 . . . . .145 E7
Masterman Wharf □
  CM23 . . . . .145 F7
Matchett Dr CO4 . . . . .110 B6
Matching Field CM5 . . . . .271 F2
Matching Gn SS14 . . . . . .320 D1
Matching Green CE Prim Sch
  CM17 . . . . .202 D2

Matching La
  Bishop's Stortford CM23 . .145 DB
  White Roding CM6 . . . . . . .203 C6
Matching Rd
  Harlow,Harlow Tye CM17 .201 B4
  Harlow, Matching CM22 . . .202 BB
  Hatfield Heath CM22 . . . . .174 B2
Matfield CI CM1 . . . . .232 D3
Mathams Dr CM23 . . . . . .145 D5
Mathart Ct E4 . . . . .309 D4
Mather Way IP2 . . . . .17 D4
Mathews Ave E6 . . . . .352 A3
Mathews Ct E6 . . . . .77 A3
Mathews Villas CM19 . . . .222 E6
Mathieson Ho E4 . . . . .287 E2
Matlock CI □ IP2 . . . . . . .16 C2
Matlock Gdns RM12 . . . . .336 E1
Matlock Ho □ RM3 . . . . . .314 D4
Matlock Rd SS8 . . . . .363 F3
Matson CI IG8 . . . . .309 E3
Matson Rd IP11 . . . . .16 FB
Matthews CI
  Romford RM3 . . . . .314 F2
  Stratford St M CO7 . . . . . . .58 C1
Maud Gdns IG11 . . . . .352 F3
Maudlyn Rd CO1,CO4 . . . .136 C6
Maugham CI SS12 . . . . . .321 D5
Maunder CI CM16 . . . . . . .372 D2
Maunds Farm CM18 . . . . .223 E4
Maunds Hatch CM18 . . . .223 E4
Maurice Ho □ CM4 . . . . .316 C6
Maurice Rd SS8 . . . . .364 D3
Mavis Gr RM12 . . . . .336 E2
Mawney CI RM7 . . . . .313 B1
Mawney Prim Sch RM7 . . .335 D6
Mawney Rd RM7 . . . . .335 C6
Maxey Gdns RM9 . . . . . . .353 EB
Maxey Rd RM9 . . . . .353 EB
Maximfeldt Rd DA8 . . . . . .369 E1
Maxim Rd DA8 . . . . .369 D2
Maya Angelou Ct E4 . . . . .309 C6
Maya CI SS3 . . . . .368 E7
Mayall Ct EN3 . . . . .265 A1
May Ave
  Canvey Island SS8 . . . . . . .364 C3
  Canvey Island SS8 . . . . . . .364 D2
Maybank Ave
  Hornchurch RM12 . . . . . . .355 C7
  Woodford E18 . . . . .310 B1
Maybank Rd E18 . . . . .310 C2
Maybells Commercial Est
  IG11 . . . . .353 DB
Mayberry Wlk CO2 . . . . . .136 A3
Maybrick Rd RM11 . . . . . .336 C5
Maybrook Ct E11 . . . . . . .332 B3
Maybury CI
  Loughton IG10 . . . . .289 B5
  Marks Tey CO6 . . . . .132 F3
Maybury Rd Barking IG11 .353 A3
  Ipswich IP4 . . . . .18 B1
Maybush Rd RM11 . . . . . .336 E4
Maycroft Ave RM17 . . . . . .373 D1
Maycroft Gdns RM17 . . . .373 D1
May Ct RM17 . . . . .378 EB
Mayda Ct CO9 . . . . .76 D1
Maydeb Ct RM6 . . . . .334 F5
Maydells SS13 . . . . .343 B5
Maydells SS13 . . . . .343 B5
Maydene CM3 . . . . .301 D7
Mayer Rd EN9 . . . . .265 B3
Mayesbrook Rd
  Barking IG11 . . . . .352 F4
  Dagenham IG3,RM8 . . . . . .334 B1
Mayes CI CM23 . . . . .146 DB
Mayesford Rd RM6 . . . . . .334 CB
Mayes La Chelmsford CM2 .255 F5
  Danbury CM3 . . . . .256 E6
  Harwich CO12 . . . . .90 C1
Mayespark Prim Sch
  IG3 . . . . .334 A1
Mayes Pl CM16 . . . . .97 A6
Mayfair Ave
  Basildon SS13 . . . . .343 CB
  Dagenham RM6 . . . . .334 D5
  Ilford IG1 . . . . .333 A3
Mayfair Gdns IG8 . . . . . . .310 A3
Mayfair Ind Area CM8 . . .281 F6
Mayfield
  Swanscombe DA10 . . . . . .377 E1
  Waltham Abbey EN9 . . . . . .265 D5
Mayfield Ave
  Hullbridge SS5 . . . . .301 E2
  Southend-on-S SS2 . . . . . .347 E4
  Woodford IG8 . . . . .310 A4
Mayfield CI
  Colchester CO4 . . . . .110 C2
  Harlow CM17 . . . . .200 F4
  Mayfield Ct EN9 . . . . .266 A6
Mayfield CO CM16 . . . . . .306 A5
Mayfield Gdns CM14 . . . .294 C1
Mayfield Pk CM23 . . . . . . .145 D3
Mayfield Rd
  Belvedere DA17 . . . . .369 C2
  Chingford E4 . . . . .309 DB
  Dagenham RM8 . . . . .334 C3
  Ipswich IP4 . . . . .18 C7
  Writtle CM1 . . . . .231 A2
Mayfields RM16 . . . . .373 C4
Mayfield Sch & Coll
  RM8 . . . . .334 C3
Mayflower Ave
  Billericay CM11 . . . . .297 C2
Mayflower CI
  Colchester CO3 . . . . .134 D6
  Lower Nazeing EN9 . . . . . .243 DB
  Southend-on-S SS2 . . . . . .347 B6
  South Ockendon RM15 . . . .357 C1
Mayflower Ct
  Canvey Island SS8 . . . . . . .364 D2
  Chipping Ongar CM5 . . . . .249 A4
  Harlow CM19 . . . . .223 B4
Mayflower Dr CM9 . . . . . .259 A7
Mayflower Gdns CM23 . . .145 B6

Mayflower High Sch
  CM12 . . . . .297 C5
Mayflower Ho
  □ Barking IG11 . . . . .352 D4
  Brentwood CM13 . . . . .316 C4
  Harwich CO12 . . . . .91 D6
Mayflower Prim Sch
  CO12 . . . . .91 B4
Mayflower Rd
  □ Billericay CM11 . . . . . . .297 B2
  Grays RM16 . . . . .372 C1
Mayflower Ret Pk SS14 . . .320 D2
Mayflowers SS7 . . . . .344 B7
Mayflower Way
  Chipping Ongar CM5 . . . . .249 A4
  Sudbury CO10 . . . . .15 C2
Mayfly CI IP8 . . . . .36 EB
Mayford Way CO16 . . . . . .195 B6
Maygreen Cres RM11 . . . .336 A4
Mayhew Cl E4 . . . . .309 A7
Mayland Ave SS8 . . . . . . .364 A2
Mayland CI
  Heybridge CM9 . . . . .237 D3
  Mayland CM3 . . . . .283 A7
Mayland Gn CM3 . . . . . . .283 A7
Mayland Hill CM3 . . . . . . .283 C5
Mayland Mans □ IG11 . . .352 B5
Mayland Rd DA8 . . . . .184 A2
Maylands Ave RM12 . . . . .355 A4
Maylands Dr CM7 . . . . . . .154 DB
Maylands Green Prim Sch
  CM3 . . . . .282 FB
Maylands Way RM3 . . . . . .315 C4
Maylins Dr CM21 . . . . . . .172 D2
Maynard CI CM6 . . . . .123 D1
Maynard Ct
  □ Holdbrook EN3 . . . . . . .265 A1
  Waltham Abbey EN9 . . . . . .265 F5
Maynards RM11 . . . . .336 F4
Maynards Villas CM6 . . . .122 F5
Mayne Crest CM1 . . . . . . .232 E6
Maypole CI CM11 . . . . .43 C7
Maypole Ct □ CM16 . . . . .246 F6
Maypole Dr Chigwell IG7 .312 A2
  St Osyth CO16 . . . . .194 B4
Maypole Green Rd CO2 . . .135 C1
Maypole Rd Maldon CM9 .236 F7
  Tiptree CO5 . . . . .186 C6
  Wickham Bishops CM8,CM9 .212 F2
Maypole St CM17 . . . . . . .200 C1
Maypole Way CM9 . . . . . . .69 F3
May Rd Chingford E4 . . . . .309 A4
  Ipswich IP3 . . . . .18 C2
Mays CI IP11 . . . . .381 D3
Maysent Ave CM7 . . . . . . .127 F5
May's La CO7 . . . . .44 A6
Mayswood Gdns RM10 . . .354 C6
May Terr IG1 . . . . .352 EB
May Terre CM22 . . . . .190 A3
Maytree WIk SS7 . . . . .344 D6
May Villa RM2 . . . . .314 D1
Mayville Rd IG1 . . . . .352 B7
Maywin Dr RM11 . . . . .336 F3
May Wlk Chelmsford CM2 .254 C7
  □ Wanstead E11 . . . . . . .332 A1
Maze Green Rd CM23 . . . . .94 A1
Maze Green Rd CM23 . . . .145 C7
Mazers Ct □ CM7 . . . . . . .127 F2
Maze The SS9 . . . . .346 D7
Mazoe CI CM23 . . . . .145 F5
Mazoe Rd CM23 . . . . .145 F5
Meachen Rd CO2 . . . . . . .136 A1
Mead CI Grays RM16 . . . . .373 B4
  Loughton IG10 . . . . .289 B7
  Romford RM2 . . . . .314 A1
Mead Cres E4 . . . . .309 C6
Mead Ct
  Clacton-on-S CO15 . . . . . .195 E3
  Stansted Mountfitchet
  CM24 . . . . .119 D7
  Waltham Abbey EN9 . . . . . .265 B5
Meade CI CM11 . . . . .297 D5
Meade Rd CM11 . . . . .297 D5
Meadgate SS13 . . . . .343 CB
Meadgate Ave
  Great Baddow CM2 . . . . . .254 DB
  Woodford IG8 . . . . .310 E5
Meadgate Prim Sch
  CM2 . . . . .254 EB
Meadgate Rd EN9 . . . . . . .221 C3
Meadgate Terr CM2 . . . . . .254 DB
Mead Gr RM6 . . . . .334 DB
Mead Lodge □ E4 . . . . . .287 C1
Meadowbrook Ct CO1 . . .136 B7
Meadow Brown Ct CM7 . .127 E1
Meadow CI
  Billericay CM11 . . . . .297 C2
  Canvey Island SS8 . . . . . . .363 F6
  Harlow CM18 . . . . .223 EB
  Wickford SS11 . . . . .321 EB
Meadow Dr Basildon SS16 .360 BB
  Southend-on-S SS3 . . . . . .367 B7
  South Ockendon RM15 . . . .357 C1
Meadowgate CM7 . . . . . . .154 CB
Meadow Grass CI CO3 . . .134 B6
Meadow La Sudbury CO10 .33 E7
  West Mersea CO5 . . . . . . .218 C5
  Wickford SS11 . . . . .321 EB
Meadowland Rd SS11 . . . .322 A6

Meadowlands
Bishop's Stortford CM23 ....119 A2
Hornchurch RM11 ....336 C4
Meadow Mews CM3 ....301 B8
Meadow Rd Barking IG11 353 A5
Colchester CO2 ....155 D1
Dagenham RM9 ....353 F6
Epping CM16 ....245 C7
Grays RM16 ....373 C5
Great Chesterford CB10 ....3 D3
Hadleigh SS7 ....345 E2
Hullbridge SS5 ....301 E2
Loughton IG10 ....288 A2
Rettendon CM3 ....300 C5
Romford RM7 ....335 C3
Meadow Rise
Billericay CM11 ....297 C2
Blackmore CM4 ....272 E8
Meadows Cl CM13 ....317 C4
Meadows The
Bishop's Stortford CM23 ...145 E5
Chelmsford CM2 ....232 C2
Ingrave CM13 ....317 C4
Sawbridgeworth CM21 .....173 A2
Meadowsweet Cl CM23 145 C6
Meadowvale Cl IP4 ....17 F7
Meadow View
Basildon SS16 ....340 E4
Bicknacre CM3 ....256 E1
Epping CM16 ....246 A2
Great Bardfield CM7 ....72 B2
Kirby-le-S CO13 ....144 C3
Pilgrims Hatch CM15 ......294 C3
St Osyth CO16 ....194 B4
Tiptree CO5 ....186 B5
Meadow View Cl CO3 ...134 E5
Meadow View Rd CO10 ...33 D5
Meadow View Wlk SS8 363 E4
Meadow Way
Abberton CO5 ....163 B2
Black Notley CM77 ....115 B1
Burnham-on-C CM0 ....306 C4
Chigwell IG7 ....311 C8
Clacton-on-S CO15 ....220 C7
Hockley SS5 ....324 E6
Latchingdon CM3 ....282 A6
Sawbridgeworth CM21 .....173 A1
Upminster RM14 ....337 C1
Wickford SS12 ....321 E3
Meadow Way The CM11 297 C2
Meadow Wlk
[5] Chelmsford CM2 ....9 C5
Dagenham RM9 ....353 F6
Wanstead E18 ....332 A7
Mead Park Ind Est CM20 109 F4
Mead Pastures CM9 ......235 D3
Mead Path CM2 ....253 F8
Mead Prim Sch RM3 .....314 F4
Meads Cl CM4 ....274 B4
Meads Ct CM15 ....316 E8
Meadside CM7 ....73 B3
Meads La IG3 ....333 F4
Meads The Basildon SS16 343 A4
Chelmsford CM2 ....232 A1
Ingatestone CM4 ....274 B4
Stansted Mountfitchet
 ....119 F6
Upminster RM14 ....337 E2
Wicken Bonhunt CB11 .....66 A7
Meadsway CM13 ....316 C4
Mead The Basildon SS15 341 B8
Brightlingsea CO7 ....192 F0
Great Cornard CO10 ......34 B4
Great Dunmow CM6 ....123 C2
Hoddesdon EN10 ....221 B2
Thaxted CM6 ....70 A3
Meadway
Canvey Island SS8 ....364 C2
Gosfield CO9 ....102 E8
Grays RM17 ....373 D2
Hoddesdon EN11 ....221 A4
Lawford CO11 ....86 B3
Maldon CM9 ....237 B1
Rayleigh SS6 ....323 E1
Romford RM2 ....314 A1
South Benfleet SS7 ....344 C7
Woodford IG8 ....330 C5
Mead Way IG3 ....352 E8
Meadway Ct RM8 ....334 F2
Meadway The
Buckhurst Hill IG9 ....288 D1
Loughton IG10 ....288 F3
Southend-on-S SS0 ......366 B8
Mead Wlk CM5 ....248 F1
Meakins Cl SS9 ....347 A7
Mearns Pl [9] CM2 ......232 F4
Mearth Rd IG1 ....333 C1
Medebridge Rd
Grays RM15,RM16 ....373 A8
South Ockendon RM16 ....358 A1
Medick Cl CM17 ....378 E8
Medina Rd RM17 ....373 D2
Medlar Cl CM8 ....184 A4
Medlar Ct RM15 ....357 E1
Medlar Rd CM7 ....73 D7
Medlars Mead CM22 ....174 F5
Medley Rd CM77 ....126 F2
Medoc Cl SS13 ....343 C8
Medora Rd RM7 ....333 A3
Medusa Ct Harwich CO12 ..91 B2
Holland-on-S CO15 ....196 C5
Medway CM0 ....306 A6
Medway Ave CM77 ....183 D2
Medway Cl
Chelmsford CM1 ....231 D4

Medway Cl continued
Ilford IG1 ....352 C7
Medway Cres SS9 ....346 B1
Medway Rd IP3 ....17 F2
Meekings Rd CO10 ....34 B8
Meers The CO13 ....170 E6
Meeson Bghws CM3 .....300 C5
Meeson Mdws CM9 ......258 E8
Meeson's La RM17 ....372 F1
Meesons Mead SS4 .....325 E3
Meeting Field CM10 .....15 C7
Meeting La
East Mersea CO5 ....191 C1
Ridgewell CO9 ....29 B7
Meeting Wlk CB9 ....9 B7
Meggison Way SS7 ......344 C3
Meggy Tye CM2 ....233 B5
Megs Way CM7 ....128 B2
Meister Cl IG1 ....333 D3
Melanie Ct SS4 ....325 D6
Melba Ct CM3 ....231 C1
Melba Gdns IP18 ....379 B7
Melbourne Ave CM1 .....231 E5
Melbourne Chase CO2 ..136 B1
Melbourne Ct
Chelmsford CM1 ....231 E5
Tilbury RM18 ....378 E6
Melbourne Gdns RM6 ...335 C4
Melbourne Par CM1 .....231 E5
Melbourne Park Prim Sch
CM1 ....231 F6
Melbourne Quay [9]
DA11 ....379 B1
Melbourne Rd
Clacton-on-S CO15 ......195 E4
Ilford IG1 ....333 B3
Ipswich IP4 ....18 D7
Tilbury RM18 ....378 E6
Melcombe Rd SS7 ....344 C3
Meldrum Rd IG3 ....334 A2
Melford Ave IG11 ....352 F6
Melford Ct IP18 ....18 F5
Melford Gr CM7 ....154 B7
Melford Pl CM14 ....294 C1
Melford Rd Cavendish CO10 1 E2
Ilford IG1 ....333 D2
Sudbury CO10 ....15 D2
Melford Way IP11 ....381 A3
Melksham Cl CM3 ....314 F3
Melksham Dr RM3 ....314 F3
Melksham Gdns RM3 ....314 F3
Melksham Grn RM3 .....314 F3
Melis Cl IP11 ....381 B5
Mellish Cl IG11 ....352 F4
Mellish Gdns IG8 ....310 A5
Mellish Way RM11 ......336 C6
Mellor Chase CO3 ....134 E7
Mellow Mead SS15 .....341 B8
Mellow Purgess CO5 ....341 C6
Mellow Purgess Cl SS15 341 C6
Mellow Purgess End
SS15 ....341 C6
Mellows Rd IG5 ....332 F8
Mel Rd Tollesbury CM9 216 E1
Tollesbury CM9 ....240 E8
Melplash Cl IP3 ....18 E4
Melrose Gdns
Clacton-on-S CO15 ......196 C5
Ipswich IP4 ....18 B8
Melrose Rd CO5 ....218 C6
Melstock Ave RM14 .....356 C8
Melton Cl CO16 ....195 A4
Melton Gdns RM1 ....335 C6
Melville Ct Romford RM3 314 E1
Southend-on-S SS1 ......367 D6
Melville Dr SS12 ....321 D4
Melville Heath CM1 .....301 E6
Melville Rd Ipswich IP4 ..17 F5
Rainham RM13 ....351 B5
Memory Cl CM9 ....259 A7
Menai Ct IP1 ....17 B7
Mendip Cl Rayleigh SS6 .323 D4
Wickford SS11 ....321 E7
Mendip Cres SS0 ....347 A4
Mendip Dr IP5 ....18 F6
Mendip Rd
Chelmsford CM1 ....231 D6
Hornchurch RM11 ....336 A4
Ilford IG2 ....333 E7
Southend-on-S SS0 ......347 A4
Mendips The CO10 ......34 B7
Mendoza Cl RM11 ....336 E6
Menish Way CM2 ....233 A3
Menthone Pl RM11 ......336 D6
Mentmore SS16 ....341 B4
Menzies Ave SS15 ......340 F6
Meon Cl CM1 ....232 C6
Meopham Ct CO2 ....136 B4
Mercantile Ho [1] CO1 135 F6
Mercer Ave SS3 ....350 A4
Mercer Rd CM7 ....297 D5
Mercers Ave CM19 .....223 A5
Mercers Ave CM23 .....146 B4
Mercers Way CO10 .....135 E8
Merchant St CM3 ....301 E7
Mercia Cl CM7 ....255 A5
Mercury Cl
Colchester CO2 ....135 A3
Wickford SS11 ....321 F8
Mercury Ct [8] RM1 ....335 F6
Mercury Gdns RM1 .....335 F6
Mercury Pl CM9 ....226 B5
Merdle Sq CM3 ....231 F6
Merebridge Rd RM16 ..373 C2
Meredene SS14 ....342 F5
Meredith Rd
Clacton-on-S CO15 ......195 E3
Grays RM16 ....374 A2

Merediths Cl CO7 ....164 B8
Merefield CM21 ....172 E1
Mere Gdns IP4 ....18 F4
Meres Cl CM8 ....183 F1
Meresman RM15 ....371 D7
Mereworth Rd CM14 ....301 C5
Meriadoc Dr CM3 ....301 D6
Meriden Cl IG1 ....311 C2
Meriden Ct CO15 ....196 A5
Meridian Way SG12 .....197 B5
Meridien RM1 ....333 F6
Meriel Wlk DA9 ....377 B3
Merilies Cl SS0 ....347 B3
Merilies Gdns SS0 ......347 B3
Merino Cl E11 ....332 C7
Merivale Cl CO11 ....86 C3
Merivale Rd CO11 ....86 B3
Merlin Cl Grays RM16 ...372 E3
Redbridge IG6 ....312 C6
Romford RM5 ....313 D4
Waltham Abbey EN9 .....266 A5
Merlin Ct SS8 ....364 B3
Merlin End CO4 ....110 F1
Merlin Gdns RM5 ....313 D4
Merlin Gr IG6 ....311 C3
Merlin Pl CM1 ....231 F5
Merlin Mead CO5 ....276 F4
Merlin Rd CO1 ....135 F8
Merlin Rd Ingrave CM13 .141 C6
Merlins Keep [9] CM23 146 C2
Merrimans Rd CM2 .....332 D2
Merlin Way
North Weald Bassett CM16 247 A6
Wickford SS11 ....299 D1
Mermagen Dr RM13 ....355 B5
Mermaid Way CM9 .....259 B8
Merriam Cl Brantham CO11 86 D8
Chingford E4 ....309 C5
Merricks La SS16 ....342 E3
Merrielands Cres RM9 ..353 F3
Merrielands Ret Pk RM9 353 F3
Merrill Pl [9] CM23 ....145 E5
Merring Way CM19 .....222 F7
Merrion Pl [7] IP2 ....16 C2
Merritt Ho RM3 ....314 E1
Merrivale SS7 ....344 C2
Merrivale Ave IG4 ....332 D7
Merry Fiddlers RM8 .....334 F2
Merryfield App SS9 .....346 E4
Merryfields Ave SS5 ....324 D7
Merryhill Cl E4 ....287 B2
Merrylands SS15 ....341 A7
Merrylands Chase CM13 341 D7
Merrylands Prim Sch
SS15 ....341 A6
Merrymead Chase CM15 294 D1
Merrymount Gdns CO15 196 B5
Mersea Ave CO5 ....218 C7
Mersea Cres SS12 ......321 F6
Mersea Ct CO5 ....218 B7
Mersea Fleet Way CM7 128 C1
Mersea Ho IG11 ....352 E6
Mersea Island Sch CO5 218 C6
Mersea Island Sch CO5 218 B6
Mersea Point Nature
 Reserve* CO5 ....192 C3
Mersea Rd
Abberton CO2,CO5 ......163 B5
Colchester CO2 ....136 C6
Peldon CO5 ....189 F5
Mersea View CO16 .....193 A3
Mersey Ave RM14 ......337 D5
Mersey Rd Ipswich IP3 .17 F2
Witham CM8 ....183 E2
Mersey Way CM1 ....221 C6
Merstham Dr CO16 .....195 C6
Merton Ct CO2 ....163 A7
Merton Pl Grays RM16 .374 A2
South Woodham Ferrers
CM3 ....301 F6
Merton Rd Barking IG11 352 F5
Hockley SS5 ....324 A8
Ilford IG3 ....333 F4
South Benfleet SS7 .....344 C4
Messant Cl RM3 ....314 D1
Messines Rd CO2 ....163 C2
Messing~cum~Inworth Prim
 Sch CO5 ....159 C2
Messing Gdns CO5 .....159 D2
Mess Rd SS3 ....368 F5
Meteor Rd SS0 ....366 D8
Meteor Way CM1 ....231 F2
Metford Cres CO3 ......265 A1
Methersgate SS14 ......342 C7
Methuen Rd DA17 ......369 B2
Metsons La CM7 ....251 E2
Metz Ave SS8 ....364 A4
Mews Ct CM2 ....232 B1
Mews Pl IG8 ....310 A6
Mews The
Bishop's Stortford CM22 146 A3
Felixstowe IP11 ....381 E4
Frinton-on-S CO13 ......171 A5
Grays RM17 ....373 C2
Harlow CM18 ....223 E4
Harwich CO12 ....91 C3
Hockley SS5 ....324 C6
Panfield CM7 ....126 A7
Rayleigh IG6 ....312 B6
Romford RM1 ....335 E7
Sawbridgeworth CM21 ..172 E3
Stansted Mountfitchet
CM24 ....119 F7
Meyel Ave SS8 ....364 C5
Meynell Ave SS8 ....364 C5
Meynell Rd RM3 ....314 B3
Meyrick Cres CO2 .....135 F5
Mey Wlk SS5 ....324 C6
Micawber Way CM1 ....231 D7
Michael Gdns CM2 .....233 C6
Michaels Cl SS3 ....368 D6
Michaels Rd CM23 .....145 A2
Michaelstowe Cl CO12 .90 C2
Michaelstowe Dr CO12 .90 C2
Mickfield Mews IP11 ...381 B5

Micklegate Rd IP11 .....381 C1
Midas Bsns Ctr RM10 ..354 B8
Mid Colne SS16 ....342 D4
Middleborough CO1 ....135 E8
Middle Boy RM4 ....135 C6
Middle Cloister [3] CM2 297 B2
Middle Gn
Doddinghurst CM15 ....272 C2
Wakes Colne CO6 ......107 D6
Middleham Ct [4] DA2 ..376 B1
Middle King CM7 ....128 D1
Middlemead
South Hanningfield CM3 299 C8
West Hanningfield CM2 277 C3
Middle Mead
Rochford SS4 ....325 F2
Wickford SS11 ....321 E8
Middle Mead Cl CM2 ...276 F4
Middle Rd CO1 ....135 F8
Middle Rd Ingrave CM13 141 C6
Wickford SS11 ....321 E8
Middle Row [5] CM23 ..145 E7
Middlesborough Ho [7]
RM3 ....314 D1
Middlesburg SS8 ....363 E5
Middlesex Ave SS9 ....346 C4
Middle St Clavering CB11 .65 C4
Lower Nazeing EN9 .....244 A8
Middleton Ave E4 ......309 A7
Middleton Cl
Ipswich IP2 ....16 D2
Middleton Gdns IG2 ....333 B5
Middleton Hall (Brentwood
 Prep Sch) IM5 ....294 E1
Middleton Hall La CM15 294 D1
Middleton Rd
Shenfield CM15 ....294 F1
Sudbury CO10 ....33 D5
Middleton Row CM3 ....15 D8
Middle Way Colchester CO4 110 A5
Ilford IG6 ....311 C3
Middlewick Cl [2] CO2 136 A1
Midguard Way CM9 ....210 B5
Midhurst Ave SS0 ......347 D4
Midhurst Cl RM12 ......355 A8
Midland Ct CO2 ....135 C4
Midland Ct RM1 ....335 F6
Midsummer Mdw SS3 ..349 C1
Midway CO15 ....220 E6
Midway Rd CO2 ....135 C2
Mighell Ave IG4 ....332 C6
Milbank CM7 ....233 B4
Milbanke Cl SS3 ....349 E1
Milbanke St SS3 ....349 E1
Milburn Cres CM1 .....231 D1
Milch La CM3 ....153 E6
Mildenhall Ho RM3 ....315 A5
Mildenhall Pl [4] CB9 ..9 B8
Milden Rd IP2 ....16 E5
Mildmay Cl CM6 ....151 F7
Mildmay Ct [8] CM2 ..232 B1
Mildmay Ind Est CM2 ..306 B5
Mildmay Jun & Inf Schs
CM2 ....254 C5
Mildmay Rd
Burnham-on-C CM0 ....306 C5
Chelmsford CM2 ....232 B1
Ilford IG1 ....333 B1
Romford RM7 ....335 C6
Midmays CM3 ....256 C7
Mildred Cl DA1 ....376 A1
Mildred Ho RM3 ....315 A5
Mile Cl EN9 ....265 C6
Mile End IP9 ....17 A6
Mile End Rd CO4 ......109 E3
Miles Cl Colchester CO3 134 C6
Harlow CM19 ....223 B7
Miles Gray Rd SS14 ...319 F1
Milestone Rd CA7 .....339 F6
Milestones The CM3 ...211 A4
Milford Cl CO7 ....137 D1
Milford Rd RM16 ......373 D6
Military Ct [6] CM1 ....136 A6
Military Rd CO1 ....136 A6
Military Way CO2 ......90 C1
Milkwell Gdns IG8 .....310 A3
Milkwell La IG8 ....310 A3
Millais Ave CO12 ......352 A7
Millais Pl RM18 ....379 B7
Millard Terr RM10 .....354 B8
Millars The CM1 ....208 A3
Millars Cl SS15 ....248 F2
Millbridge Rd CM8 .....183 F7
Millbrook Chigwell IG7 311 C8
[1] Wanstead E18 ......332 A8
[3] Woodford E18 ......310 A1
Millbrook Gdns
Romford IG4 ....332 B6
Romford RM1 ....335 E7
Sawbridgeworth CM21 172 E3
Steeple Bumpstead CB9 27 C5
Millbrook Rd CM8 .....183 F7
Mill Chase Halstead CO9 77 A3
Mill Cl Elsenham CM22 94 C1
Harwich CO12 ....90 C1
Roxwell CM1 ....204 C6
Tillingham CM0 ....263 E4
Tiptree CO5 ....179 C6
Mill Cotts
Corringham SS17 ......361 D5
Great Baddow CM2 ....217 B8
Mill Croft CB9 ....8 A7
Mill Croft CM3 ....119 A1
Mill Cswy SS8 ....258 C1
Mill Ct Braintree CM7 .128 B2

Mill Ct continued
Takeley CM6 ....149 B7
Milldene Prim Sch CO5 186 D6
Mill End CM6 ....75 F8
Millennium Way CM7 ..155 D8
Millennium Wlk CM14 .316 D8
Miller Ave EN3 ....265 A1
Miller's Barn Rd CO15 .195 A1
Millers Cl
Bishop's Stortford CM23 145 C5
Braintree CM7 ....128 A8
Chigwell IG7 ....312 B8
Colchester CO3 ....134 C6
Great Horkesley CO6 ..109 B7
Miller's Cl CM6 ....151 A4
Millers Croft
Great Baddow CM2 ....254 F6
Great Dunmow CM6 ...123 E1
Millersdale CM19 ......223 B4
Millers Dr CM77 ....154 C7
Millers Green Rd CM5 228 B3
Millers La Colchester CO3 134 D6
Stansted Abbots SG12 197 C4
Miller's La IG7 ....290 B1
Millers Mead CO5 .....158 E4
Millers Mews CM4 .....274 C4
Millers Reach CO11 ...87 A4
Millers Row CM7 ......48 C6
Millers View IP11 .....16 F7
Millfield
Burnham-on-C CM0 ...306 B4
High Ongar CM5 ......249 D3
Mill Field Barnston CM6 151 A4
Chelmondiston IP9 ....63 E8
Harlow CM17 ....200 C4
Millfield Cl CO5 ....323 E3
Millfield Gdns IP4 .....18 A6
Millfields Danbury CM3 257 A6
Sawbridgeworth CM21 172 F3
Stansted Mountfitchet
CM24 ....119 E6
Writtle CM1 ....231 A1
Millfields CO5 ....186 C6
Millfields Prim Sch CO7 137 D1
Millfields Way CM9 ....210 B4
Mill Gn Basildon SS13 343 A7
Colchester CO2 ....136 A4
Mill Gr CM5 ....249 D4
Mill Grange CM0 ......306 B7
Mill Green Cl SS13 ....343 B7
Mill Green Pl SS13 ....343 B7
Mill Green Rd CM4 ....273 F7
Millhaven Cl RM6 .....334 B5
Millhead Way SS4 .....326 B1
Mill Hill Braintree CM7 ..128 B2
Chelmsford CM2 ......232 C3
Farnham CM23 ....118 E5
Harwich CO12 ....91 C3
Haverhill CB9 ....9 A7
Lawford CO11 ....85 D4
Manningtree CO11 ....86 C4
Purleigh CM3 ....258 C1
Shenfield CM15 ......294 F2
South Benfleet SS7 ...363 E8
Mill La
Arkesden CB11 ....42 E7
Birch CO2 ....161 A3
Bradwell CO11 ....87 D2
Broomfield CM1 ......204 B1
Cavendish CO10 .....1 B8
Chelmondiston IP9 ...63 E7
Cogeshall CO6 ....131 F1
Colne Engaine CO6 ..105 B8
Corringham SS17 ....361 C6
Cressing CM77 ......155 B6
Dagenham RM8 .....334 E5
Dedham CO7 ....84 F7
Felixstowe IP11 .....381 C4
Finchingfield CM7 ...48 F3
Fobbing SS17 ....361 D7
Ford End CM3 ......179 D7
Grays RM16 ....372 D1
Great Easton CM6 ..123 D1
Great Leighs CM3 ..181 B7
Great Maplestead CO9 76 E8
Harkstead SG9 .....64 A2
Harlow CM17 ....200 C4
Hatfield Heath CM22 173 F3
High Ongar CM5 ....249 D2
Hinxton CB10 ....3 B2
Hoddesdon EN11 ...221 A2
Horndon-on-t-H SS17 359 F3
Ickleton CB10 ......3 B4
Ingatestone CM4 ...274 A6
Kelvedon Hatch CM15 248 F6
Lindsell CM6 ....121 B5
Little Baddow CM3 ..234 E3
Little Yeldham CO9 ..30 A3
Maldon CM9 ....237 A3
Manningtree CO11 ..86 B4
Moreton CM5 ....226 E6
Navestock Heath RM4 292 B8
Pebmarsh CO9 .....78 A7
Purleigh CM3 ......258 C1
Ramsden Heath CM11 298 B5

Mill La continued
Rayne CM7 ....153 E8
Rochford SS4 ....326 B2
Saffron Walden CB10 ..22 F2
Salcott-cum-virley CM9 216 B8
Sawbridgeworth CM21 ..174 E4
Seaxredstone E4 ......287 A6
Stebbing CM6 ....124 E5
Stock CM4 ....275 F2
Stoke-by-N CO6 ......56 D7
Sudbury CO10 ....33 D7
Terling CM3 ....182 A4
Thaxted CM6 ....70 F5
Thornington Street CO6 57 C4
Thorpe-le-S CO16 ....141 F1
Tolleshunt Major CM9 ..214 E3
Toot Hill CM5 ....247 E2
Walton-on-t-N CO14 ..171 C8
Washbrook IP8 ....161 A6
Weeley Heath CO16 ...168 A6
Witham CM8 ....183 F1
Woodford IG8 ....309 F5
Wyatts Green CM15 ..272 D4
Mill Lane Cl CO16 .....168 A6
Mill Lodge SS3 ....368 G6
Millom Ho RM3 ....314 D4
Mill Park Ave RM12 ..336 E2
Mill Park Dr CM7 .....128 B1
Mill Race CM2 ....197 D4
Mill Rd Aveley RM15 ..371 C6
Billericay CM11 ....319 D6
Boreham CO10 ......10 E2
Boxted CO4 ....82 F4
Burnham-on-C CM0 ...306 C7
Clare CO10 ....12 C7
Colchester CO4 ......109 F4
Debden CB11 ....68 B8
East Bergholt CO7 ...59 E2
Elder Street CB10 ...45 B3
Felsted CM6 ....152 A4
Finchingfield CM7 ...72 D5
Foxearth CO10 ......2 C6
Foxearth CO10 ......14 C5
Great Bardfield CM7 .72 B2
Great Totham CM9 ..213 D7
Haverhill CB9 ....9 A7
Helions Bumpstead CB9 26 C8
Heybridge CM9 ......94 C4
Ilford IG1 ....333 A1
Maldon CM9 ....237 B2
Margaret Roding CM6 205 D5
Marks Tey CO6 ......133 C4
Mayland CM3 ....283 B8
North End CM6 ......151 F2
Ridgewell CO9 ......29 B6
Stanbourne CO9 ....28 C3
Stock CM4 ....275 C7
Tillingham CM0 .....263 E4
West Mersea CO5 ...218 D7
Mill Rise IP9 ....62 D5
Mill Road Cotts CB10 45 B3
Millside CM21 ....146 A5
Mill Side CM24 ......119 E6
Millsmead Way IG10 .288 F7
Millson Bank CM2 ....233 A4
Mills Rd CO10 ....34 A8
Mill St
Bishop's Stortford CM23 146 A5
Brightlingsea CO7 ....193 A6
Colchester CO1 ......136 A6
Harlow CM17 ....224 F5
Nayland CO6 ....56 B1
St Osyth CO16 .....193 F4
Mills The IP4 ....18 E8
Milrow IP2 ....16 C2
Milton Ave Basildon SS16 340 F4
Braintree CM7 ....155 A8
Hornchurch RM12 ...335 F7
Rayleigh SS6 ....323 B8
Southend-on-S SS2 ..348 A1
Milton Cl
Chipping Ongar CM5 ..248 F5
Colchester CO4 .....110 B7
Holland-on-S CO15 ..196 E6
Waltham Abbey EN9 .265 C5
Milton Ct
Dagenham RM8 .....334 D4
Milton Gdns RM17 ...193 F8
Milton Hall Cl SS3 ...350 A3
Milton Hall Prim Sch
SS0 ....366 E8
Milton Pl Chelmsford CM1 205 A3
Gravesend DA12 ....379 C1
Southend-on-S SS1 ..367 B6
Milton Rd Belvedere DA17 369 A2
Brentwood CM14 ....316 E2
Corringham SS17 ....360 F6
Gravesend DA12 ....379 B1
Grays RM17 ....373 B1
Harwich CO12 ......91 D4
Lawford CO11 ......86 B2

Milton Rd *continued*
Maldon CM9 259 A8
Romford RM1 336 A5
Southend-on-S SS0 366 E8
Swanscombe DA10 377 E1
Witham CM8 183 F5
Milton St Ipswich IP4 18 B6
Southend-on-S SS2 348 A1
Swanscombe DA10 377 D1
Waltham Abbey EN9 265 C5
Miltsin Ave SS8 364 C5
Milverton Gdns IG3 333 F2
Milwards CM19 223 B4
Milwards Prim Sch CM19 223 B4
Mimosa Cl Basildon SS16 340 F4
Chelmsford CM1 232 F6
Pilgrims Hatch CM15 294 B4
Romford RM3 314 C3
Mimosa Ct CO4 136 E8
Minchen Rd CM20 200 A1
Minden Rd CO10 33 F7
Minehead Ho 6 RM3 314 E5
Minerva Cl Harwich CO12 90 F1
Haverhill CB9 9 D6
Minerva End CO2 135 C1
Minerva Rd E4 309 B3
Minos Way IP1 16 D8
Minsmere Dr CO16 195 C6
Minsmere Rd IP3 38 D8
Minsmere Way CO10 34 C6
Minster Cl SS6 324 A1
Minster Ct RM11 337 A3
Minster Rd SS15 341 C6
Minster Way
Hornchurch RM11 337 A3
Maldon CM9 258 E8
Minters Cotts CO11 115 C5
Minton Hts SS4 325 C6
Minton La CM17 224 C8
Miramar Ave SS8 363 E3
Miramar Way RM12 355 D7
Miranda Ho 6 DA17 369 A1
Miranda Wlk CO4 136 E7
Mirosa Dr CM9 237 B1
Mirosa Reach CM9 259 A8
Mirravale Ct 5 IG9 310 C8
Mirravale Trad Est RM6 334 E4
Mirror Stps 1 SS1 367 C7
Mission La CO7 60 B3
Mistley End SS16 342 C5
Mistley Norman CE Prim Sch CO11 87 A4
Mistley Path SS16 342 C5
Mistley Place Park* CO11 86 E4
Mistley Rd CM20 200 A2
Mistley Side SS16 342 C5
Mistley Sta CO11 86 F4
Mistley Thorn IG1 333 A4
Mistley Towers* CO11 86 F4
Mistral Ct E4 309 B7
Mitcham Rd IG3 333 F4
Mitchell Ave CO9 76 E1
Mitchell Circ CM7 73 C6
Mitchell Cl Erith DA17 369 C3
Rainham RM13 355 C3
Mitchells Ave SS8 364 D4
Mitchells Wlk SS8 364 D4
Mitchel Way CM3 301 D8
Mitre Bldgs CM20 199 C1
Mitre Ct Belvedere DA17 369 A2
1 Dagenham RM6 334 B4
9 Woodford E18 310 A2
Mitre Gdns CM23 146 A4
Mitre Ho RM7 335 B7
Mitre Way IP3 17 F4
Mitton Vale CM2 232 F2
Moat Cl
Doddinghurst CM15 272 C3
Ramsden Heath CM11 298 C3
Moat Edge Gdns CM12 297 A4
Moat End SS1 349 B1
Moat Farm CO9 28 B7
Moat Farm Chase CM8 183 F3
Moat Farm Cl IP4 17 F8
Moat Field SS14 342 C8
Moat Fields CO6 107 D6
Moat La CO8 55 A4
Moat Lodge Ho SS14 342 C7
Moat Rd Birdbrook CO9 28 C7
Fordham CO6 107 D6
Moat Rise SS6 323 D1
Moat The CM5 247 F2
Moat Wlk CB9 8 E8
Moblin Lodge IG9 288 C1
Modlen Rd CO14 171 B7
Moffat Ave IP4 18 B8
Mole Hall La CB11 67 F3
Mole Hall Wildlife Pk* CB11 67 F3
Molehill Green Cotts CM22 121 C6
Molehill Green Rdbt CM22 121 C5
Molesworth EN11 197 A2
Mollands SS16 342 F4
Mollands Ct RM15 357 E1
Mollands La RM15 357 D1
Mollison Ave EN3 265 A3
Molrams La CM2 255 B6
Momples Rd CM20 200 B1
Monarch Cl Haverhill CB9 8 C8
Rainham RM13 355 A3
Tilbury RM18 379 B5
Monarch Pl IG9 310 C8
Monarch Rd DA17 369 A3
Monarch Way IP8 36 D8
Monastery Rd SS15 341 C6
Monkchester Cl IG10 289 A8
Monkdowns Rd CO6 131 B3
Monkham's Ave IG8 310 B5
Monkham's Dr IG8 310 B5
Monkhams Hall EN9 243 C2
Monkham's La IG8 310 B6
Monklands Ct 2 CO9 76 D1
Monksbury CM18 224 A5
Monks Chase CM13 317 C5
Monks Cl EN10 221 A3
Monk's Cnr CB10 47 B4
Monks Ct CM8 183 E3
Monksford Dr SS5 301 D1
Monks Gate IP8 16 A6
Monksgrove IG10 289 A4
Monks Haven SS17 360 E2
Monks Hill CB11 43 F8
Monkside SS14 342 D7
Monk's La CO7 84 D4
Monks Lodge Rd CO9 52 D2
Monks Mead CM3 256 F2
Monks Rd CO6 105 B7
Monks Well DA9 377 C3
Monkswick Rd CM20 199 F1
Monks Wlk CM9 240 E8
Monkswood Ave EN9 265 D6
Monkswood Dr CM23 145 D6
Monkswood Gdns IG5 333 A8
Monkwick Ave CO2 135 F1
Monkwick Jun & Inf Schs CO2 136 A2
Monkwood Cl RM1 336 A6
Monmouth Ave E18 332 B8
Monmouth Cl IP2 17 B1
Monmouth Mews SS16 340 F5
Monmouth Rd RM9 353 F7
Monnow Gn RM15 371 C6
Monnow Rd RM15 371 C6
Monoux Cl CM11 297 D1
Monoux Gr E17 309 A2
Mons Ave CM11 297 D2
Mons Rd CO2 135 D4
Montague Ave SS9 346 B2
Montague Bldgs 2 SS1 367 B8
Montague Ho 13 IG8 311 A3
Montague Pl SS8 363 E3
Montague Rd IP11 381 F4
Montague Way CM12 297 A4
Montagu Gdns CM1 232 F7
Montalt Ho IG8 309 F6
Montalt Rd IG8 309 F5
Montbazon Ct CM14 294 B1
Montbretia Cl CO3 134 D6
Montbretia Ct CO16 195 C4
Monteagle Ave IG11 352 C6
Monteagle Prim Sch RM9 353 B4
Montefiore Ave SS6 323 D8
Montfort Ave SS17 361 A4
Montfort Ct 8 CB9 8 F7
Montfort Gdns IG6 311 C4
Montgomerie Inf & Jun Sch SS7 344 B7
Montgomery Cl
Chelmsford CM1 232 E7
Colchester CO2 136 B4
Grays RM16 373 C4
Montgomery Cres RM3 314 D5
Montgomery Ct SS3 349 E1
Montgomery Jun & Inf Sch CO2 135 D2
Montgomery Rd IP2 17 B1
Monton Rise IP2 16 D2
Montpelier Cl CM12 297 A5
Montpelier Gdns RM6 334 C4
Montpellier Ct 3 CM14 316 C7
Montpellier Ho IG7 311 C5
Montreal Rd Ilford IG1 333 C4
Tilbury RM18 379 A5
Montrose Ave RM2 314 C1
Montrose Cl IG8 310 A6
Montrose Ct IP3 17 F4
Montrose Rd CM2 233 A4
Montsale SS13 343 C8
Montserrat Ave IG8 309 D3
Moonhall Bsns Pk CB9 9 A5
Moon Hall La CB9 9 A6
Moons Cl SS4 325 D7
Moorcroft SS4 325 D6
Moorcroft Ave SS7 345 E6
Moore Ave Grays RM20 372 E1
Tilbury RM18 379 B5
Moore Cl CM11 297 D5
Moore Cres RM9 353 B4
Moore Ho RM11 336 A5
Moore Rd DA10 377 E1
Moores Ave SS17 342 C1
Moorescroft CM15 271 E2
Moore's Pl CM14 316 D8
Moore Twr CM18 223 F7
Moorfield Ct CM8 183 F1
Moorfields CM18 223 C4
Moor Hall La
Bishop's Stortford CM23 145 C3
Bishop's Stortford,Thorley CM23 145 B3
Danbury CM3 256 E2
Moor Hall Rd CM17 201 A4
Moorhen Ave CM0 262 C8
Moorhen Way CM19 198 A1
Moorhouse Gn CO7 111 E8
Moorings The CM23 146 A5
Moor La RM14 337 F4
Moorland Cl RM5 313 B2
Moorlands Reach CM21 173 A1
Moor Park Cl SS9 346 C5
Moor Park Gdns SS9 346 C5
Moor Rd Great Tey CO6 132 C8
Langham CO4 83 D4
Moors Cl Feering CO5 158 E5
Great Bentley CO7 139 E1
Moors Croft CM7 128 D3
Moor's Farm Chase CM9 214 A3
Moorsfield CO10 34 B4
Moorside CO1 136 B7
Moors La
Little Dunmow CM6 151 D7
Rayne CM77 126 D3
Moor's La CO7 139 E1
Moors The CM6 151 D7
Mope La CM8 212 D6
Mopsies Rd SS14 342 E6
Moran Ave CM1 232 B7
Morant Gdns RM5 313 B5
Morant Rd Colchester CO1 136 B5
Grays RM16 374 B3
Moray Cl RM1 313 E3
Moray Way RM1 313 E3
Mordaunt Gdns RM9 353 E5
Morden Rd RM6 334 E4
Mordon Rd IG3 333 F4
Morebarn Rd CO7 112 E2
Morecambe Cl RM12 355 B7
Morecambe Ct IP4 18 A7
Morecambe Ho 5 RM3 314 E5
Moreland Ave SS7 344 C7
Moreland Cl
Great Wakering SS3 350 A4
South Benfleet SS7 344 C6
Moreland Rd SS11 299 C2
Morelands Ave RM16 373 C4
Moreland Way E4 309 C7
Morella Cl CO7 166 E8
Morello Ct CO2 163 A7
Moremead EN9 265 D6
Mores La CM14 293 D5
Moreton Bridge CM5 226 D1
Moreton CE Prim Sch CM5 226 C3
Moreton Gdns IG8 310 E5
Moreton Rd
Chipping Ongar CM5 248 F7
Fyfield CM5 227 B2
Moreton CM5 248 B8
Moretons Basildon SS13 343 A6
Galleywood CM2 254 B2
Moretons Ct SS13 343 A6
Moretons Mews SS13 343 A6
Moretons Pl SS13 343 A6
Morgan Cl RM10 354 A5
Morgan Cres CM16 267 E3
Morgan Terr RM6 334 C6
Morgan Way
Rainham RM13 355 C2
Woodford IG8 310 E4
Morland Ct CO6 82 B1
Morland Prim Sch IP3 38 A8
Morland Rd
Dagenham RM10 354 A5
Ilford IG1 333 B2
Ipswich IP3 37 F8
Morland Road Day Hospl RM10 354 A4
Morley Ave E4 309 D3
Morley Gr CM20 199 C2
Morley Hill SS17 360 F5
Morley Link SS17 360 F5
Morley Rd Barking IG11 352 D4
Dagenham RM6 334 E6
Halstead CO9 76 F2
Tiptree CO5 186 D4
Morley Sq RM16 374 A2
Morleys Rd CO6 105 A6
Mornington Ave
Ilford IG1 333 A4
2 Ipswich IP1 17 A8
Rochford SS4 326 A2
Mornington Cl IG8 310 A6
Mornington Cres
Canvey Island SS8 364 C4
Hadleigh SS7 345 F3
Mornington Ho SS0 366 C8
Mornington Rd
Canvey Island SS8 364 C4
Chingford E4 287 D2
Loughton IG10 289 C6
Woodford IG8 309 F6
Morningtons CM19 223 C4
Morpeth Ho 8 RM3 314 D4
Morrab Gdns IG3 333 F1
Morrells SS16 341 F4
Morrin's Chase SS3 350 D3
Morrins Cl SS3 350 D3
Morris Ave
Billericay CM11 297 D1
Clacton-on-S CO15 220 E6
Morris Ct Basildon SS15 341 B7
Chingford E4 309 B7
Holdbrook EN3 265 A2
Waltham Abbey EN9 265 F5
Morris Gdns DA1 376 A2
Morris Harp CB10 22 E3
Morris Ho CM18 223 C5
Morrison Ho RM16 373 D4
Morrison Rd IG11 353 E3
Morris Rd
Chelmsford CM2 232 D2
Dagenham RM8 334 F2
Romford RM3 314 B3
Morrow La CO7 112 A6
Mors End CO7 58 D2
Morses La CO7 165 F1
Morten Rd CO1 135 E8
Mortimer Rd
Hatfield Peverel CM3 211 A4
Rayleigh SS6 323 E5
Mortlake Rd IG1 352 D8
Morton Rd CM9 213 A4
Morton Way CO9 77 A3
Mosbach Gdns CM13 317 B8
Moseley St SS2 348 D1
Moss Bank RM17 372 F2
Moss Cl SS16 342 E3
Mossdown Cl DA17 369 A2
Moss Dr SS16 342 E3
Mossfield Cl CO3 135 C6
Mossford Ct Ilford IG6 333 B8
Redbridge IG6 311 B1
Mossford Gn IG6 333 C8
Mossford Green Prim Sch IG6 311 C1
Mossford La IG6 311 C1
Moss La Hornchurch RM11 336 A5
Moss La *continued*
Romford RM1 335 F5
Moss Path CM2 254 C3
Moss Rd Colchester CO3 134 E4
Dagenham RM10 354 A5
South Ockendon RM15 372 C8
Witham CM8 184 B3
Moss Way CO6 108 E3
Moss Wlk CM2 254 B6
Motehill SS16 341 C4
Motherwell Way RM20 372 A1
Mottram Cl 9 IP2 16 C2
Motts Cl CM7 127 E4
Motts La CM8 184 B4
Mott's La CO6 132 D4
Mott St High Beach IG10 288 A8
Sewardstone IG10 287 E8
Motts Yd CM6 124 E5
Moules La CB1 5 C6
Moulsham Chase CM2 254 C8
Moulsham Dr CM2 254 B8
Moulsham Hall La
Braintree CM3 153 F2
Great Leighs CM3 154 A1
Moulsham High Sch CM2 254 B7
Moulsham Jun & Inf Schs CM2 254 B7
Moulsham St
Chelmsford CM1 232 B2
Chelmsford CM2 232 B1
Moulsham Thrift CM2 254 A6
Moulton Cl CO10 33 F8
Moultrie Way RM14 337 E5
Mountain Ash Ave SS9 346 B6
Mountain Ash Cl
Colchester CO4 110 C2
Southend-on-S SS9 346 B6
Mountain's Farm Rd CM6 150 C3
Mountains Rd CM8,CM9 213 C7
Mount Ave
Brentwood CM13 295 B2
Chingford E4 309 B7
Hockley SS5 324 F7
Rayleigh SS6 323 C3
Romford RM3 315 C4
Southend-on-S SS0 366 A8
Mountbatten Cl CO10 15 F2
Mountbatten Ct
Buckhurst Hill IG9 310 D8
7 Ipswich IP1 17 A7
Mountbatten Dr
Colchester CO2 136 B4
Southend-on-S SS3 349 E1
Mountbatten Ho 4 RM2 336 C7
Mountbatten Rd
Braintree CM7 128 C4
Sudbury CO10 15 F2
Mountbatten Way CM1 232 E7
Mount Bovers La SS5 324 E3
Mount Cl Rayleigh SS6 323 C2
Wickford SS11 321 E8
Mount Cres
Brentwood CM14 316 D6
Hockley SS5 324 D6
South Benfleet SS7 344 E4
Mountdale Gdns SS9 346 F4
Mount Dr Ipswich IP3 18 F1
Stansted Mountfitchet CM24 119 E5
Mount Echo Ave E4 287 B1
Mount Echo Dr E4 287 B1
Mountfield Cl SS17 360 E3
Mountfield Rd E6 352 A2
Mountfields SS13 343 C4
Mountfitchet Castle & Norman Village* CM24 119 F6
Mountfitchet High Sch CM24 119 F4
Mountfitchet Rd CM24 119 E5
Mount Hill CO9 76 D1
Mounthill Ave CM2 232 D3
Mount Lodge Chase CM9 213 E6
Mountnessing SS7 345 D2
Mountnessing CE Prim Sch CM15 295 E7
Mountnessing La CM15 272 E1
Mountnessing Rd
Billericay CM12 296 E4
Blackmore CM4 272 F6
Mountnessing CM15,CM4 273 A4
Mountney Cl CM4 273 F1
Mount Pleasant
Halstead CO9 76 E1
Ilford IG1 352 C7
Maldon CM9 236 F2
Mount Pleasant Ave CM13 295 E4
Mount Pleasant Cotts
Brentwood CM15 295 A4
Saffron Walden CB11 43 D8
Mount Pleasant Est CM9 213 E6
Mount Pleasant Rd
Chigwell IG7 311 D6
Romford RM5 313 D4
Saffron Walden CB11 43 E8
South Woodham Ferrers CM3 301 D7
Mount Rd Braintree CM7 128 A3
Coggeshall CO6 131 B2
Dagenham RM8 334 F3
Epping CM16 268 E6
Haverhill CB9 9 B7
South Benfleet SS7 344 F4
Wickford SS11 321 E8
Mount Rise 4 CO9 76 D1
Mounts Rd DA9 377 B1
Mount The
Billericay CM11 297 E3
Brentwood CM14 316 C7
Colchester CO3 134 F6
Romford RM3 314 C7
Mount The *continued*
Stanford-le-H SS17 360 F3
Tollesbury CM9 216 D1
Mount View
Billericay CM11 297 E2
Brentwood CM14 316 C6
Mountview Cl SS16 342 E3
Mountview Cres CM0 262 C8
Mountview Rd CO15 196 A5
Mount View Rd E4 287 D2
Mount Way SS11 321 E8
Moverons La CO7 165 C2
Movers La IG11 352 E4
Mowbray Rd CM20 200 A3
Mowbrays Cl RM5 313 C1
Mowbrays Rd RM5 313 C1
Mowbrey Gdns IG10 289 C8
Mowden Hall La
Hatfield Peverel CM3 210 D1
Ulting CM3 235 A8
Mowlands IP9 35 B1
Moy Rd CO2 136 A1
Moze Cross CO12 116 D1
Muckingford Rd RM18, SS17 374 E2
Mucking Hall Cotts SS3 349 B8
Mucking Hall Rd SS3 349 C8
Mucking Wharf Rd SS17 375 C7
Mudlands Ind Est RM13 354 F2
Muggeridge Rd RM10 354 B8
Muir Pl SS12 321 D5
Muirway SS7 344 B7
Mulberries The CM7 128 A2
Mulberry Ave CO2 136 A4
Mulberry Cl Chingford E4 309 A8
Romford RM2 336 C7
Mulberry Ct Barking IG11 352 F5
Bishop's Stortford CM23 146 A5
Mulberry Dr RM19 370 F2
Mulberry Gdns CM8 184 A4
Mulberry Gn CM17 200 D4
Mulberry Harbour Way CO7 164 B8
Mulberry Hill CM15 294 F2
Mulberry Rd SS8 363 C3
Mulberrys The SS2 348 A3
Mulberry Terr CM17 200 B4
Mulberry Way
Belvedere DA17 369 C4
Chelmsford CM1 232 D4
Ilford IG6 333 C7
Woodford E18 310 B1
Mullberry Gdns SS16 341 B5
Mullein Ct RM17 378 E8
Mullins Rd CM7 127 F6
Mullions The CM12 296 F3
Multon Lea CM1 233 A7
Mumford Cl CO6 108 E4
Mumford Rd Ipswich IP1 16 E8
West Bergholt CO6 108 D4
Mumfords La CO13 170 A7
Mundon Ct SS14 342 F5
Mundon Gdns IG1 333 D3
Mundon Rd
Braintree CM7 128 D1
Maldon CM9 259 C7
Mungo Park Rd RM13 355 A6
Munnings Cl IP3 38 B8
Munnings Dr CO16 195 D6
Munnings Rd CO3 135 A5
Munnings Way CO11 86 B5
Munro Ct 18 SS12 321 E5
Munro Rd CM8 183 F5
Munsons Alley CM0 284 D4
Munsterburg Rd SS8 364 D5
Munster Ct CM12 296 F5
Murchison Cl CM1 231 E5
Murchison Rd EN11 197 B1
Murfitt Way RM14 356 A8
Murray Cl CM7 127 F6
Murrayfield Com Prim Sch IP3 18 A2
Murray Ho SS1 367 F6
Murray Rd IP3 18 A3
Murray Way SS12 321 D5
Murrell Lock CM2 233 A4
Murrels La SS5 324 A7
Murrills Rd IP3 18 F1
Murthering La
Navestock Heath RM4 292 B5
Stapleford Abbotts RM4 291 F3
Murton Slade 6 CB9 9 A8
Murtwell Dr IG7 311 C4
Muscade Cl CO5 186 D6
Museum St
14 Colchester CO1 135 F7
Ipswich IP1 17 C6
Saffron Walden CB10 22 D2
Musgrove Cl CO12 90 F1
Musk Cl CO3 134 D7
Musket Gr SS9 346 B7
Muskham Rd CM20 200 B3
Mus of Power* CM9 236 D6
Muswell Wlk CO16 195 D5
Mutlow Cl CB11 42 F5
Mutlow Hill CB11 42 F5
Mutton Row CM5 270 C7
Mychett Cl CO16 195 B6
Myddylton Pl CB10 22 D2
Mygrove Cl RM13 355 D3
Mygrove Gdns RM13 355 D3
Mygrove Rd RM13 355 D3
Myland Hall Chase CO4 110 C3
Myland Prim Sch CO4 109 E4
Mylne Ct EN11 197 A1
Myln Mdw CM4 275 F2
Mynards Way CM3 256 C7
Mynchens SS15 341 E6
Myneer Pk CO6 131 B2
Myrtle Gr Aveley RM15 371 C4
Colchester CO2 136 B5
Myrtle Rd
Brentwood CM14 316 C6
Ilford IG1 333 B2
Ipswich IP3 17 E4
Myrtle Rd *continued*
Romford RM3 314 C4
Myson Way CM23 146 B7

N

Nabbott Rd CM1 231 E2
Nacton Cres IP3 18 B2
Nacton Rd
Felixstowe IP11 381 C1
Ipswich,Racecourse IP3 18 B2
Ipswich,Rose Hill IP3 18 A3
Nadir Ct E11 332 A4
Naffenton Rise IG10 288 D4
Nagle Cl E17 309 D1
Nag's Head La CM14 315 D4
Nails La 18 CM23 145 F7
Nairn Ct RM18 378 F5
Nairn Ho CM14 316 C6
Nalla Gdns CM1 232 A6
Namur Rd SS8 364 C5
Nancy Smith Cl CO2 135 F5
Nansen Ave SS4 325 D6
Nansen Rd
Holland-on-S CO15 196 D6
Ipswich IP3 18 B2
Nantwich Ho 4 RM3 314 E5
Napier Ave
Clacton-on-S CO15 220 D6
9 Southend-on-S SS1 367 A8
Napier Cl Basildon SS14 342 D6
Hornchurch RM11 336 B3
Napier Cres SS12 321 E5
Napier Ct CM1 231 E5
Napier Ct W SS1 366 F8
Napier Gdns SS7 345 C6
Napier Ho RM13 354 F2
Napier Rd Colchester CO2 135 F6
Rayleigh SS6 323 F3
Wallend E6 352 A3
Narboro Ct RM1 336 A5
Nare Rd RM15 371 C6
Narvik Cl CM9 258 E8
Naseby Rd
Dagenham RM10 335 A1
Woodford IG5 310 F2
Nash Cl Colchester CO3 135 B5
Lawford CO11 86 B5
Nash Dr CM1 208 A3
Nash Gdns IP3 38 B8
Nash Rd RM6 334 D7
Nassau Rd CO16 194 B4
Natal Rd IG1 352 B8
Natasha Ct RM3 314 C3
Nathan Cl RM14 337 E3
Nathan Ct CO2 163 B8
Nathan's La CM1 252 E5
National Motor Boat Mus* SS16 343 B2
National Sea Training Coll DA12 380 A1
Nation Way E4 287 C1
Nats La CB11 42 E6
Naunton Way RM12 336 D1
Navarre Gdns RM5 313 B5
Navarre St 4 IP1 17 C6
Navestock Cl
Chingford E4 309 C7
Rayleigh SS6 323 A3
Navestock Cres IG8 310 C2
Navestock Gdns SS1 348 F1
Navestock Ho IG11 353 B3
Navestock Side CM14 293 C7
Navigation Pl CM9 237 B4
Navigation Rd CM2 232 C2
Nayland Cl SS12 321 E7
Nayland Dr CO16 195 B4
Nayland Ho SS2 347 E5
Nayland Prim Sch CO6 56 A1
Nayland Rd Bures CO8 79 F8
Colchester CO6 109 D6
Felixstowe IP11 381 A4
Great Horkesley CO6 82 B4
Haverhill CB9 8 E6
Little Horkesley CO6 81 F6
West Bergholt CO6 108 D7
Nayling Rd CM7 127 C2
Naze Ct CO14 144 E3
Nazeingbury Cl EN9 221 D1
Nazeingbury Par EN9 221 D1
Nazeing Comm EN9 244 D8
Nazeing Ho IG9 288 E2
Nazeing New Rd EN10 221 B2
Nazeing Prim Sch EN9 243 E8
Nazeing Rd EN9 221 D1
Nazeing The SS14 342 E6
Nazeing Wlk RM13 354 E5
Naze Nature Reserve The* CO14 144 D6
Naze Nature Trail The* CO14 144 E4
Naze Park Rd CO14 144 E2
Neal Ct EN9 265 F6
Neale Ct RM11 336 F2
Neale Rd CO9 76 E1
Neale St IP1 17 C6
Neasden Ave CO16 195 D5
Neasham Rd RM8 353 B7
Neath Dr IP2 17 A1
Neave Cres RM3 314 D2
Nectar Ct 1 EN11 221 D8
Needham Cl CM11 297 B3
Needle Cnr IP9 63 D1
Neil Armstrong Way SS9 347 A6
Nelmes Cl RM11 336 F6
Nelmes Cres RM11 336 F6
Nelmes Ct RM11 336 D7
Nelmes Prim Sch RM11 336 F7
Nelmes Rd RM11 336 E5
Nelmes Way RM11 336 E7
Nelson Cl
Brentwood CM14 316 D5
Rayleigh SS6 323 F4
Romford RM7 313 B2

Nelson Cres CM9 . . . .**259** B8
Nelson Ct
Brightlingsea CO7 . . . . . . **193** A7
2 Burnham-on-C CM0 . . **306** C1
Nelson Dr SS9 . . . .**346** F1
Nelson Gdns
Braintree CM7 . . . .**128** C4
Rayleigh SS6 . . . .**323** F4
Nelson Gr CM1 . . . .**231** F3
Nelson Ho
Greenhithe DA9 . . . .**377** D2
3 Romford RM3 . . . .**314** E5
Nelson Mews SS1 . . . . .**367** A7
Nelson Pl CM3 . . . .**301** E6
Nelson Prim Sch E6 . . . .**352** A3
Nelson Rd Basildon SS14 .**342** E6
Bishop's Stortford CM23 .**146** A5
Chingford E4 . . . .**309** B4
Clacton-on-S CO15 . . . . .**195** E1
Colchester CO3 . . . .**134** E6
Harwich CO12 . . . .**91** D4
Ipswich IP4 . . . .**18** A6
Orsett RM16 . . . .**374** D7
Rainham RM13 . . . .**354** F3
Rayleigh SS6 . . . .**323** F4
Rochford SS4 . . . .**325** D6
Southend-on-S SS9 . . . . .**347** A2
Wanstead E11 . . . .**332** B7
Nelson St
Brightlingsea CO7 . . . . . .**192** F6
Southend-on-S SS1 . . . . .**367** A7
Wallend E6 . . . .**352** A4
Nelson Way RM11 . . . . .**336** F6
Neptune Ct RM13 . . . . . .**354** F3
Neptune Ct Barking IG11 .**353** B2
Chelmsford CM1 . . . .**231** F4
5 Colchester CO1 . . . . .**136** C6
Neptune Quay IP4 . . . . . .**17** D5
Neptune Wlk CM8 . . . . . .**183** D2
Neptune Wlk DA8 . . . . . .**369** D2
Nesbit Cl SS12 . . . .**321** C5
Neptune Sq IP4 . . . .**17** D5
Ness Rd SS3 . . . .**368** E6
Ness Wlk CM8 . . . .**183** D2
Nesta Rd IG8 . . . .**309** F4
Nestuda Way SS2 . . . . . .**347** B5
Nethan Dr RM15 . . . .**371** C6
Nether Ct CO9 . . . .**77** A1
Netherfield SS7 . . . .**345** A4
Netherfield Ct SG12 . . . .**197** D3
Netherfield La SG12 . . . .**352** D5
Netherfield La SG12 . . . .**197** E3
Nethergate St CO10 . . . .**12** B7
Netherhall Rd CM19 . . . .**221** F5
Nether Hill CO9,CO10 . . . .**31** D3
Nether Mayne SS16 . . . .**342** B3
Netherpark Dr RM2 . . . .**313** F1
Nether Priors SS14 . . . . .**342** C6
Nether Rd CO10 . . . .**1** D2
Nethewode Ct DA17 . . . .**369** B3
Netley Cl IP2 . . . .**36** FB
Netley Ct SG12 . . . .**333** D6
Netley Rd IG12 . . . .**333** D6
Netteswellbury Farm
CM18 . . . .**223** F7
Netteswell Cross CM20 .**199** E2
Netteswell Orch CM20 . .**199** D1
Netteswell Rectory
CM20 . . . .**223** E8
Netteswell Twr CM20 . . .**199** D1
Nettleditch CB11 . . . .**21** E4
Nevada Rd SS8 . . . .**364** C5
Nevell Rd RM16 . . . .**374** B3
Nevendon Grange SS12 .**321** C6
Nevendon Mews SS13 . .**321** B2
Nevendon Rd
Basildon SS13 . . . .**321** A2
Wickford SS12 . . . .**321** B4
Nevern Cl SS6 . . . .**345** E8
Nevern Rd SS6 . . . .**334** D1
Neville Gdns RM8 . . . . . .**334** D1
Neville Rd
Dagenham RM8 . . . .**334** D1
Redbridge IG6 . . . .**311** C2
Neville Shaw SS14 . . . . .**342** B6
Nevill Way IG10 . . . .**288** E3
Nevin Dr E4 . . . .**287** B1
Nevis Cl RM1 . . . .**313** E4
Nevyll Ct SS1 . . . .**368** B8
Newark Cl IP2 . . . .**16** F1
New Ave SS16 . . . .**341** A4
New Barn La CM22 . . . . .**146** D1
Newbarn Rd CO6 . . . .**106** B1
New Barns Way IG7 . . . . .**311** B7
Newbery Side SS15 . . . . .**341** C5
Newbiggen St CM6 . . . . . .**69** F3
Newbourne Gdns IP11 . .**381** B3
New Bowers Way CM1 . .**232** F6
Newbridge Hill CO6 . . . .**108** D2
Newbridge Rd Birch CO5 .**187** A6
Tiptree CO5 . . . .**186** F5
Newbridge Rd RM17 . . . .**373** D1
Newbury Cl
Bishop's Stortford CM23 .**145** E8
Romford RM3 . . . .**314** D4
Newbury Cotts E4 . . . . .**312** C3
Newbury Ct E4 . . . .**332** A7
Newbury Gdns
Romford RM3 . . . .**314** D4
Upminster RM14 . . . .**336** F1
Newbury Ho IP4 . . . .**18** B6
New Bury Mdw CM22 . . .**174** F5
Newbury Park Prim Sch
IG2 . . . .**333** D8
Newbury Park Sta IG2 . .**333** D8
Ilford IG2 . . . .**333** E5
Ipswich IP4 . . . .**18** B6
Newbury Rd RM3 . . . . . .**314** D4
Newbury Wlk RM3 . . . . .**314** D5
Newby Dr IP4 . . . .**18** B8
New Captains Rd CO5 . .**218** B6
New Cardinal St IP1 . . . .**17** B5

Newcastle Ave
Colchester CO3 . . . .**134** F4
Redbridge IG6 . . . .**312** A4
New Century Rd SS13 . . .**341** B6
New Church Rd CO6 . . . .**108** E4
Newcomen Way CM0 . . .**110** C6
New City Rd E13 . . . .**144** C3
New Cotts Basildon SS13 .**343** D5
Great Tey CO6 . . . .**132** C8
Rainham RM13 . . . .**370** C7
Rochford SS4 . . . .**327** F5
Wakes Colne CO6 . . . . . .**106** C6
New Court Bsns Pk
CM18 . . . .**223** C4
Newcourt Rd CM2 . . . . . .**232** D3
Newcroft E1 CB10 . . . .**22** E1
New Cut Bures CO8 . . . . . .**79** E8
Glemsford CO10 . . . .**2** E3
Great Bentley CO7 . . . . . .**166** E8
Layer-de-H CO2 . . . .**161** F5
New Cut E IP2,IP3 . . . . . .**17** D4
New Cut W IP7 . . . .**17** D4
New Dukes Way CM7 . . .**127** E4
Newell Ave SS3 . . . .**368** G8
New England Cl CM0 . . .**256** F1
New England Cres SS3 . .**350** C2
New Farm Dr RM4 . . . . . .**290** C6
New Farm La CO7 . . . . . .**165** A6
New Farm Rd CO3 . . . . . .**134** D6
New Ford Rd EN8 . . . . . .**265** A4
New Forest La IG7 . . . . . .**311** A4
Newgate St Chingford E4 .**309** E7
3 Walton-on-N CO14 . . .**171** C8
Newhall SS4 . . . .**325** D6
New Hall Cotts CO7 . . . . . .**58** F7
Newhall Ct EN9 . . . .**265** F6
New Hall Dr RM3 . . . .**314** E2
New Hall La CM9 . . . .**259** F4
New Hall Rd SS4 . . . .**303** B1
New Hall Sch CM3 . . . . . .**205** A1
New Hall Vineyard
CM3 . . . .**258** D2
Newham Ho IG10 . . . . . .**288** D3
Newham Way E6 . . . .**352** A1
Newhaven La CO12 . . . . . .**91** D6
Newhouse Ave
Ilford RM6 . . . .**334** D8
Wickford SS12 . . . .**320** F7
Newhouse La CO6 . . . . . .**226** C1
New House La CB10 . . . . .**24** C3
Newhouse Rd CO6 . . . . .**104** F5
Newhythe CO3 . . . .**134** E7
Newington Ave SS2 . . . . .**348** E2
Newington Cl SS2 . . . . . .**348** F2
Newington Gdns
Clacton-on-S CO15 . . . . .**195** FB
Southend-on-S SS2 . . . . .**348** E2
New Jubilee Ct **4** IG8 . .**310** A3
New Kiln Rd CO3 . . . .**135** C7
New La Feering CO5 . . . . .**158** F5
Holbrook IP9 . . . .**63** A5
Newland Ave CM7 . . . . . .**72** B1
Newland Pl CM8 . . . .**184** A1
Newlands Cl
Billericay CM12 . . . .**297** B4
Brentwood CM13 . . . .**295** D2
Newlands Dr CM4 . . . . . .**184** A2
Newlands Gn SS15 . . . . .**341** B8
Newlands La CO6 . . . .**56** B1
Newlands Prec **8** CM8 .**184** A2
Newlands Rd
Billericay CM12 . . . .**297** B4
Canvey Island SS8 . . . . . .**364** D5
Wickford SS12 . . . .**321** D4
Woodford IG8 . . . .**309** F3
Newlands Spring Prim Sch
CM1 . . . .**231** D7
Newland St CM8 . . . .**184** A2
New Lodge Chase CM4 . .**184** A2
New London Rd CM2 . . . .**322** C1
New Maltings RM15 . . . .**371** D5
Newman Cl RM11 . . . . . .**336** E6
Newman Dr CO4 . . . .**83** A4
Newmans Cl IG10 . . . . . .**289** B6
Newmans Dr CM13 . . . . .**295** C2
Newmans La IG10 . . . . . .**289** B6
Newman's Rd CO10 . . . . .**33** F8
Newmarket Ho **2** RM3 . .**314** E5
Newmarket Rd CO10 . . . . .**3** C3
Newmarket Way RM12 . .**355** E8
Newmill La Brantham CO11 .**61** A1
Stutton CO11 . . . .**57** A8
New Moor Cl CM0 . . . . . .**284** E4
New Moor Cres CM0 . . . .**284** E4
New Nabbotts Way CM1 .**232** E7
Newnham Cl
Braintree CM7 . . . .**127** E2
Loughton IG10 . . . .**288** D3
Newnham Dr CM7 . . . . . .**236** E3
Newnham Gn CM9 . . . . . .**236** E3
Newnham Lodge **10**
DA17 . . . .**369** A2
New North Rd IG6 . . . . . .**311** D4
New Orleans Flats CO5 . .**218** B5
New Park CO9 . . . .**51** F3
New Park Gdns CO7 . . . .**192** F7
New Park Rd
Rochford SS5 . . . .**303** A1
South Benfleet SS7 . . . . .**344** C5
New Park St CO1 . . . .**136** B6
Newpasture La CM6 . . . .**125** C5
Newpiece IG10 . . . .**289** A6
New Pier St CO14 . . . . . .**171** C8
New Place Gdns RM14 . .**337** D2
New Place Ho IP2 . . . .**17** C4
New Plymouth Ho RM13 .**354** F2
New Pond La CB10 . . . . . .**22** C2
Newport Ave CM3 . . . . . .**281** B5
Newport Ct
Great Baddow CM2 . . . . .**255** B8
Harwich CO12 . . . .**91** A1
Newport Cres SS4 . . . . . .**323** B4
Newport Dr
Clacton-on-S CO15 . . . . .**196** A7

Newport Dr continued
Rickling Green CB11 . . . . . .**66** F4
Newport Free Gram Sch
CB11 . . . .**42** F1
Newport Prim Sch CB11 . . .**66** F7
Newport Rd CB11 . . . .**43** C7
Newports CM21 . . . .**172** C1
Newport Sta CB11 . . . .**67** A8
Newport Way CO13 . . . . .**171** A6
Newports SS6 . . . .**189** C5
Newpots La CO5 . . . .**189** C5
Newquay Cl IP5 . . . .**18** F6
New Queens Rd CO **15** E1
New Rd Abridge RM4 . . . .**290** D3
Aldham CO6 . . . .**107** B2
Basildon CM12 . . . .**319** A3
Brentwood CM14 . . . . . .**316** D8
Broomfield CM1 . . . .**208** B1
Broomfield CM0 . . . .**306** C5
Canvey Island SS8 . . . . . .**363** E3
Chingford E4 . . . .**309** C6
Clacton-on-S CO15 . . . . .**134** D6
Dagenham RM9,RM10,
RM13 . . . .**354** C2
Elsenham CM22 . . . .**94** C2
Gosfield CO9 . . . .**102** E5
Gravesend DA11 . . . .**379** B1
Grays RM17 . . . .**378** B8
Great Baddow CM2 . . . . .**255** A6
Great Wakering SS3 . . . . .**350** C3
Hadleigh SS7 . . . .**345** D3
Harlow CM17 . . . .**200** D4
Hatfield Peverel CM3 . . . .**221** A4
Hinxton CB10 . . . .**3** B6
Hoddesdon EN10 . . . . . .**221** A4
Ilford IG3 . . . .**333** E2
Ingatestone CM4 . . . . . .**274** C4
Kelvedon CO5 . . . .**158** C2
Long Melford CO10 . . . . . .**15** E7
Messing CO5 . . . .**159** C1
Mistley CO11 . . . .**86** E4
Rainham RM13 . . . .**355** B2
Rayne CM77 . . . .**127** A1
Saffron Walden CB10 . . . .**22** E1
Shudy Camps CB1 . . . .**7** C7
Southend-on-S SS9 . . . . .**365** D8
Terling CM3 . . . .**182** C3
Tiptree CO5 . . . .**186** D5
Tollesbury CM9 . . . .**216** D2
Trimley St M IP11 . . . . . .**381** A4
New River Ave SG12 . . . .**197** B4
New River Cl EN11 . . . . .**221** B7
New Road Terr CM77 . . . .**126** F1
New Row
Pagelsham Eastend SS4 . .**328** A5
Sheering CM22 . . . .**201** C8
New Rush Hall Sch IG6 . .**311** C3
Newry Ave IP11 . . . .**381** D4
Newson St IP1 . . . .**17** B7
New St Braintree CM7 . . . .**127** F2
Brightlingsea CO7 . . . . . .**192** F6
Chelmsford CM1 . . . .**322** E2
Glemsford CO10 . . . .**2** A5
Great Dunmow CM6 . . . . .**150** D8
Halstead CO9 . . . .**76** E1
21 Ipswich IP4 . . . .**17** D5
Maldon CM9 . . . .**236** F2
Sawbridgeworth CM21 . .**172** E3
Sudbury CO10 . . . .**33** E8
Newstead Ho RM3 . . . . . .**314** D6
Newstead Rd SS3 . . . . . .**350** B4
New Street Fields CM6 . .**150** D8
Newsum Gdns SS6 . . . . .**323** A3
New Swan Yd DA11 . . . . .**379** B1
New Thorpe Ave CO16 . .**142** A2
New Town Cl
Colchester CO1 . . . .**136** A6
Thorpe-le-S CO16 . . . . . .**141** F2
New Town Rd
6 Colchester CO1 . . . . .**136** A6
Thorpe-le-S CO16 . . . . . .**141** F2
New Village CO11 . . . . . .**86** C7
New Wanstead E11 . . . . .**332** A5
New Waverley Rd SS15 . .**319** E1
New Way La CM17 . . . . . .**201** D1
New Writtle St CM2 . . . .**232** B1
New Zealand Way **1** RM13 **354** F2
Nexus The CO1 . . . .**135** E8
Nicholas Cl
South Ockendon RM15 . . .**357** C2
Writtle CM1 . . . .**204** B1
Nicholas Ct
Chelmsford, Scot's Green
CM1 . . . .**231** D6
Witham CM8 . . . .**183** F2
Nicholas Rd
Dagenham RM8 . . . .**334** F1
Felixstowe IP11 . . . .**381** A4
Nicholl Rd Basildon SS14 .**341** C7
Epping CM16 . . . .**211** B8

Nicholls Field CM18 . . . .**224** B7
Nichols Cl CO3 . . . .**86** B3
Nichols Cnr CO7 . . . .**112** A5
Nichols Cl **5** CM2 . . . . . .**232** A1
Nichols Gr CM7 . . . .**128** A3
Nicholson Cres SS2 . . . .**345** C3
Nicholson Ct EN11 . . . . .**221** B6
Nicholson Ho SS1 . . . . . .**367** B8
Nicholson Rd IG3 . . . . . .**278** B7
Nicholson Rd SS7 . . . . . .**345** B3
Nickleby Rd CM1 . . . .**205** F7
Nickolsons Gr CO1 . . . . .**136** A6
Nicola Mews IG6 . . . . . .**311** B4
Nicolas Wlk RM16 . . . . .**374** B4
Nien-Oord CO16 . . . .**195** C4
Nigel Mews IG1 . . . .**352** B8
Nightingale Ave
Chingford E4 . . . .**309** E5
Clacton-on-S CO15 . . . . .**195** E1
Colchester CO4 . . . .**137** A8
Harwich CO12 . . . .**90** F1
Rayleigh SS6 . . . .**323** B3
Southend-on-S SS2 . . . . .**347** E6
Witham CM8 . . . .**211** F8
Nightingale Cnr **2** CM9 .**237** A1
Nightingale Cl
Blackheath CO2 . . . .**163** A8
1 Wanstead E11 . . . . .**332** B6
Nightingale Dr RM1 . . . .**376** A3
Nightingale Hill CO4 . . . .**83** F6
Nightingale La E11 . . . . .**332** B6
Nightingale Mews **2**
CB10 . . . .**22** F2
Nightingale Prim Sch
E18 . . . .**332** C7
Nightingale Rd
Canvey Island SS8 . . . . . .**364** C3
Ipswich IP3 . . . .**38** A8
Nightingales
Basildon SS16 . . . .**340** F5
Waltham Abbey EN9 . . . .**265** E5
Saffron Walden CB10 . . . .**22** E2
Nightingale Way CO15 . .**195** F5
Nineacres CM7 . . . .**128** A1
Nine Ashes Farm Cotts
CM4 . . . .**250** C2
Nine Ashes Rd
Blackmore CM4 . . . .**250** D1
Stondon Massey CM15 . .**272** B6
Ninefields EN9 . . . .**265** F6
Ninth Ave CM24 . . . .**120** B2
Nipsells Chase CM3 . . . .**261** A1
Niton Ct SS17 . . . .**375** C8
Niven Cl SS12 . . . .**321** E5
Noak's Ark La CO10 . . . . .**33** D7
Noak Bridge Prim Sch
SS15 . . . .**319** F1
Noakes Ave CM2 . . . .**254** E6
Noak Hill CM12 . . . .**319** C4
Noak Hill Cl CM12 . . . . . .**319** B4
Noak Hill Rd
Basildon CM12 . . . .**319** B4
Romford RM3 . . . .**315** A7
Noak's Cross CM9 . . . . .**185** B2
Noaks Rd IP7 . . . .**58** D8
Nobel Sq SS13 . . . .**321** C2
Nobel Villas EN9 . . . .**265** D5
Nobles Green Cl SS9 . . . .**346** E7
Nobles Green Rd SS9 . . . .**346** E7
Nobles The CM23 . . . . . .**145** D6
Noel Sq RM8 . . . .**353** C8
Nonsuch Cl IG6 . . . .**311** B4
Nonsuch Mdw CO10 . . . .**33** E8
Nook The
Stansted Abbotts SG12 . .**197** B4
Wivenhoe CO7 . . . .**164** C8
Norbury Cl CO6 . . . .**132** F3
Norbury Gdns RM6 . . . . .**334** D6
Norbury Rd Chingford E4 .**309** A5
Ipswich IP4 . . . .**18** B8
Nordenfeldt Rd DA8 . . . .**369** D1
Northcroft CO10 . . . .**2** B6
North Cross Rd IG6 . . . . .**311** C3
North Dell CM1 . . . .**232** E7
Northdene Ave CO12 . . . .**90** F1
Northenden Gdns CO12 . .**333** E6
North Dr Basildon SS14 . .**341** C6
North Benfleet SS12 . . . .**321** F1
North Hill CM12 . . . .**319** A4
Northbank Rd E17 . . . . . .**309** C1
North Barn EN10 . . . .**221** B1
North Circular Rd
Chingford E17 . . . .**309** B2
Ilford IG1,E12 . . . .**333** A1
Wanstead IG1 . . . .**332** D5
Woodford E18 . . . .**310** C1
North Cl Dagenham RM10 .**354** A6
Ongar CM5 . . . .**17** E8
Redbridge IG7 . . . .**312** A5
North Colne CO16 . . . . . .**342** D4
North Cres
Southend-on-S SS2 . . . . .**347** D5
Steeple Bumpstead CB9 . .**27** B7
Wickford SS12 . . . .**321** D7
North Crescent Prim Sch
SS12 . . . .**321** D7
North Crockerford SS16 .**342** E4
Northcroft CO10 . . . .**2** B6
North Cross Rd IG6 . . . . .**311** D5
North Dell CM1 . . . .**232** D7
Northdene CO13 . . . .**311** D5
North Dr Brentwood CM13 .**296** C2
Great Baddow CM2 . . . . .**254** F7
Hornchurch RM11 . . . . . .**136** D4
Lower Nazeing EN9 . . . . .**221** E1
Maldon CM9 . . . .**86** D4
Manningtree CO11 . . . . . .**86** D4
Rochford SS4 . . . .**325** F2
Romford RM1 . . . .**335** D7
Southend-on-S SS9 . . . . .**365** E8
Southminster CM0 . . . . .**284** D4
Sudbury CO10 . . . .**33** E8
Tillingham CM0 . . . .**263** E4
Tolleshunt D'arcy CM9 . . .**215** E5
Walton-on-N CO14 . . . . .**171** C8
North Station Rd CO1 . . .**135** E8
North Street Par **7** CO10 .**33** F7
North Terr CM23 . . . .**145** F8
Northumberland Ave
Basildon SS15 . . . .**341** C5
Hornchurch RM11 . . . . . .**336** C6
Southend-on-S SS1 . . . . .**367** D7
Wanstead E12 . . . .**332** C2
Northumberland Cl
Brentwood CM14 . . . . . .**316** C5
Saffron Walden CB11 . . . .**22** A4
Northumberland Cres
SS1 . . . .**347** D4
Northumberland Ct **1**
IG8 . . . .**232** F4
Northumberland Ho **11**
IG8 . . . .**311** A3
Northumberland Rd
SS17 . . . .**375** A4
Northview Ave E11 . . . . .**166** C2
North View Caravan Site **
E16 . . . .**312** A3
North View Cotts CO16 . .**109** B7
Northview Dr
Southend-on-S SS0 . . . . .**347** D2
Woodford IG8 . . . .**347** C4
North W SS0 CO14 . . . . .**193** A3
North Wall CO16 . . . .**322** B6
Northwick Park Jun & Inf
Schs SS8 . . . .**363** E4
Northwood Rd CM14 . . .**374** F8
Northwold Rise SS8 . . . .**363** B4
Northwood Ho CO16 . . . .**374** B4
Northwood Gdns IG5 . . .**333** A7
Norton Ave SS0 . . . .**364** E3
Norton Cl Chingford E4 . .**309** A5
Corringham SS17 . . . . . .**361** A4

Norman Cl continued
Waltham Abbey EN9 . . . .**265** D6
Norman Cres
Brentwood CM13 . . . . . .**317** A7
Ipswich IP3 . . . .**18** A2
Rayleigh SS6 . . . .**323** E5
Norman Ct Ilford IG1 . . . .**333** D4
Stansted Mountfitchet
CM24 . . . .**119** E7
Woodford IG8 . . . .**310** B5
Normandie Way CO8 . . . .**79** E8
Normandy Ave
Burnham-on-C CM0 . . . . .**306** C5
Colchester CO2 . . . .**136** A3
Normandy Way EN11 . . .**221** D8
Norman Hill CM3 . . . . . .**182** B2
Normanhurst
Brentwood CM13 . . . . . .**295** C3
Clacton-on-S CO15 . . . . .**195** E1
Harwich CO12 . . . .**287** D2
Norman Pl SS9 . . . .**365** E8
Norman Rd
Belvedere DA17 . . . .**369** B3
Clacton-on-S CO15 . . . . .**196** E6
Hornchurch RM11 . . . . . .**336** B4
Ilford IG1 . . . .**352** B7
Rayleigh SS6 . . . .**323** E5
Wanstead E11 . . . .**86** D4
Normansfield CM6 . . . . .**150** E7
Normanshire Dr E4 . . . . .**309** B6
Normans Rd SS8 . . . .**364** D4
Norman Terr SS9 . . . . . .**365** E8
Norman Pk E4 . . . .**309** E8
Norman Way
Colchester, Lexton CO3 . .**135** B6
Colchester, Shrub End CO3 .**135** B4
Point Clear B CO16 . . . . .**192** F3
Norris Cl
Bishop's Stortford CM23 .**146** C7
Braintree CM7 . . . .**128** C5
Norris La EN11 . . . .**221** A7
Norris Rd EN11 . . . .**221** A6
Norris Rise **3** EN11 . . . .**221** A1
Norseman Cl **3** IG3 . . . .**334** A3
Norsey Cl CM11 . . . .**297** B3
Norsey Dr CM11 . . . .**297** D3
Norsey Rd CM11 . . . .**297** C4
Norsey View Dr CM12 . . .**297** B6
*Norsey Wood Nature
Reserve* **1** CM11 . . . . .**297** D4
Northallerton Way **19**
RM3 . . . .**314** D5
Northampton Cl CM7 . . .**128** D5
Northampton Gr SS16 . . .**340** F4
Northampton Ho 4 RM3 .**314** E6
Northampton Mdw CM7 . .**72** B2
North Ave
Canvey Island SS8 . . . . . .**364** A3
Chelmsford CM1 . . . .**231** F5
Haverhill CB9 . . . .**8** E8
Southend-on-S SS0 . . . . .**347** E1
Northbank Rd E17 . . . . . .**309** C1
North Barn EN10 . . . .**221** B1
North Benfleet Hall Rd
Basildon SS12 . . . .**322** A1
North Benfleet SS12 . . . .**321** F1
North Hill CM12 . . . .**319** A4
Northbank Rd E17 . . . . . .**309** C1
Northbrook Rd IG3 . . . . .**333** A2
Northbrooks CM19 . . . . .**223** C7
Northbury Jun & Inf Schs
IG11 . . . .**352** C6
North Cl Dagenham RM10 .**354** A6
Ongar CM5 . . . .**17** E8
Redbridge IG7 . . . .**312** A5
North Colne CO16 . . . . . .**342** D4
North Cres
Southend-on-S SS2 . . . . .**347** D5
Steeple Bumpstead CB9 . .**27** B7
Wickford SS12 . . . .**321** D7
North Crescent Prim Sch
SS12 . . . .**321** D7
North Crockerford SS16 .**342** E4
Northcroft CO10 . . . .**2** B6
North Cross Rd IG6 . . . . .**311** D5
North Dell CM1 . . . .**232** D7
Northdene CO13 . . . .**311** D5
North Dr Brentwood CM13 .**296** C2

Northfield Rd continued
Sawbridgeworth CM21 . .**172** E4
Northfields RM17 . . . . . .**373** D2
Northfleet Ind Est DA11 .**377** F3
Northfleet Sta DA11 . . . .**378** B1
North Gate CM20 . . . . . .**199** C1
Northgate Dr CM23 . . . .**145** F8
Northgate Ind Pk RM5 . .**312** F3
Northgate Prim Sch
CM23 . . . .**145** E8
Northgate St
Colchester CO1 . . . .**135** F8
Ipswich IP1 . . . .**17** C6
North Gr CM18 . . . .**224** A7
North Hall Colchester CO1 .**135** E7
North Hall Rd CB11 . . . . . .**67** A2
North Hill Colchester CO1 .**135** E7
Horndon-on-t-H SS17 . . .**361** A4
Little Baddow CM3 . . . . .**234** D5
North Hill Dr RM3 . . . . . .**314** D6
North Hill Farm SS17 . . .**359** F4
North Hill Gdns **1** RM3 . .**17** E6
North Hill Gn RM3 . . . . . .**314** D6
North Hill Rd IP4 . . . .**17** E6
North Ho
Frinton-on-S CO13 . . . . .**170** F4
Harlow CM18 . . . .**223** F6
North Kent Ave DA11 . . . .**378** C1
Northlands App SS16 . . .**341** C1
Northlands Cl SS17 . . . . .**360** E5
Northlands Farm Chase
SS17 . . . .**360** E7
Northlands Jun & Inf Sch
SS17 . . . .**343** B6
Northlands Pavement **3**
SS13 . . . .**343** B5
North Lawn IP4 . . . .**18** C8
North Mill Pl CO9 . . . .**76** E3
Northolme C3 RM16 . . . .**373** C3
Northolt Ave CM23 . . . . .**119** B1
Northolt Way RM12 . . . .**355** C7
4 Waltham Abbey EN9 . .**265** B6
North Prim Sch CO1 . . . .**135** E8
North Rd Basildon CM11 .**320** D5
Belchamp Walter CO10 . . .**31** F6
Belvedere DA17 . . . .**369** B4
Brightlingsea CO7 . . . . . .**192** F7
Clacton-on-S CO15 . . . . .**195** F6
Dagenham RM6 . . . .**334** C6
Great Yeldham CO9 . . . . .**30** A2
Havering-atte-B RM4 . . . .**291** F1
Hoddesdon EN11 . . . . . .**221** A7
Ilford IG3 . . . .**333** E2
Purfleet RM19 . . . .**371** C2
Romford RM4 . . . .**313** F2
Southend-on-S SS0 . . . . .**347** E1
South Ockendon RM15 . . .**357** D4
Takeley CM22 . . . .**148** C8
Tollesbury CM9 . . . .**216** C2
North Residence IG3 . . . .**334** B6
North Rise CO10 . . . .**34** A6
North Road Ave CM14 . . .**316** C8
North Sea View CO12 . . . .**90** F2
North Service Rd 4
CM14 . . . .**316** C8
North Shoebury Rd SS3 .**349** D1
North St Barking IG11 . . .**145** C8
8 Bishop's Stortford CM23 .**145** F7
Great Dunmow CM6 . . . .**123** D1
Great Wakering SS3 . . . . .**350** B4
Hornchurch RM11 . . . . . .**136** D4
Lower Nazeing EN9 . . . . .**221** E1
Maldon CM9 . . . .**86** D4
Manningtree CO11 . . . . . .**86** D4
Rochford SS4 . . . .**325** F2
Romford RM1 . . . .**335** D7
Southend-on-S SS9 . . . . .**365** E8
Southminster CM0 . . . . .**284** D4
Sudbury CO10 . . . .**33** E8
Tillingham CM0 . . . .**263** E4
Tolleshunt D'arcy CM9 . . .**215** E5
Walton-on-N CO14 . . . . .**171** C8
North Station Rd CO1 . . .**135** E8
North Street Par **7** CO10 .**33** F7
North Terr CM23 . . . .**145** F8
Northumberland Ave
Basildon SS15 . . . .**341** C5
Hornchurch RM11 . . . . . .**336** C6
Southend-on-S SS1 . . . . .**367** D7
Wanstead E12 . . . .**332** C2
Northumberland Cl
Brentwood CM14 . . . . . .**316** C5
Saffron Walden CB11 . . . .**22** A4
Northumberland Cres
SS1 . . . .**347** D4
Northumberland Ct **1**
IG8 . . . .**232** F4
Northumberland Ho **11**
IG8 . . . .**311** A3
Northumberland Rd
SS17 . . . .**375** A4
Northview Ave E11 . . . . .**166** C2
North View Caravan Site **
E16 . . . .**312** A3
North View Cotts CO16 . .**109** B7
Northview Dr
Southend-on-S SS0 . . . . .**347** D2
Woodford IG8 . . . .**347** C4
North Weald Cl SS11 . . . .**322** B6
Northwick Park Jun & Inf
Schs SS8 . . . .**363** E4
Northwood Rd CM14 . . .**374** F8
Northwold Ret Pk SS8 . .**363** B4
Northwood Ho CO16 . . . .**374** B4
Northwood Gdns IG5 . . .**333** A7
Norton Ave SS0 . . . .**364** E3
Norton Cl Chingford E4 . .**309** A5
Corringham SS17 . . . . . .**361** A4

Norton Ct IG2 . . . . **333** D5
Norton Heath Rd CM5 . . . **250** E8
Norton La
High Ongar CM5 . . . . **249** D5
High Ongar, Norton Mandeville
CM4,CM5 . . . . **250** C6
Norton Rd
Chelmsford CM1 . . . . **232** A3
Dagenham RM10 . . . . **354** D6
Haverhill CB9 . . . . **8** E6
Ingatestone CM4 . . . . **274** B4
Norway Cres CO12 . . . . **90** F3
Norway Wlk RM13 . . . . **355** C1
Norwich Ave SS2 . . . . **348** C2
Norwich Cl
Clacton-on-S CO16 . . . . . . **195** E6
Colchester CO1 . . . . **136** A8
Southend-on-S SS4 . . . . . . **348** C2
Norwich Cres SS6 . . . . **323** C5
Norwich Ct ⬛ IP1 . . . . **17** A7
Norwich Ho SS4 . . . . **325** D5
Norwich Mews IG3 . . . . . . **334** A3
Norwich Rd IP1 . . . . **17** A7
Norwich Wlk SS14 . . . . . . **342** F7
Norwood Ave
Clacton-on-S CO15 . . . . . . **196** B5
Romford RM7 . . . . **335** E4
Norwood Cl DA1 . . . . **376** A3
Norwood Dr SS7 . . . . **344** E1
Norwood End
Basildon SS14 . . . . **342** D7
Fyfield CM5 . . . . **227** D5
Norwood Way CO14 . . . . **171** A7
Notcutts CO7 . . . . **59** E1
Notley Gn CM7 . . . . **154** B6
Notley Green Prim Sch
CM7 . . . . **154** C8
Notley High Sch The
CM7 . . . . **154** F8
Notley Rd CM7 . . . . **154** F8
Nottage Cl
Corringham SS17 . . . . **360** F4
Wivenhoe CO7 . . . . **164** C8
Nottidge Rd IP4 . . . . **17** E6
Nottingham Rd CO15 . . **196** E6
Nottingham Way SS16 . . **340** F5
Nounsley Rd CM3 . . . . **211** B1
Nuneaton Rd RM9 . . . . **353** E5
Nunnery St CO9 . . . . **51** D4
Nunns Cl CO6 . . . . **131** A2
Nunn's Rd CO1 . . . . **135** E7
Nunns Mdw CO9 . . . . **102** E7
Nuns Wlk CO9 . . . . **29** C1
Nunty's La
Greenstead Green CO9 . . . **104** A1
Pattiswick CM7 . . . . **129** F8
Nursery Cl
Bishop's Stortford CM23 . . **145** F6
Colchester CO3 . . . . **134** C5
Ilford RM6 . . . . **334** D5
Rayleigh SS6 . . . . **323** D1
South Ockendon RM15 . . . **357** C1
Woodford IG8 . . . . **365** A3
Nursery Dr CM7 . . . . **128** A5
Nursery Fields CM21 . . . . **172** D2
Nursery Gdns SS15 . . . . . . **341** D8
Nursery La CM4 . . . . **256** F8
Nursery Rd
Bishop's Stortford CM23 . . **145** F6
Chelmsford CM2 . . . . **254** B8
Great Cornard CO10 . . . . **34** B5
Hoddesdon EN11 . . . . **197** B1
Hook End CM15 . . . . **272** C5
Loughton IG10 . . . . **288** C5
Lower Nazeing EN9 . . . . **221** D2
Stanford-le-H SS17 . . . . **360** E3
Nursery Rise CM6 . . . . **150** D7
Nursery Wlk
Felixstowe IP11 . . . . **381** D5
Romford RM7 . . . . **335** D5
Nutberry Ave RM11 . . . . . **373** A4
Nutberry Cl RM16 . . . . **373** A4
Nutbrowne Rd RM9 . . . . . **354** A4
Nutcombe Cres SS4 . . . . . **325** D4
Nutfield Gdns IG3 . . . . **334** A2
Nuthatch Cl CA11 . . . . **319** C8
Nutter La F11 . . . . **332** C6
Nuxley Rd DA17 . . . . **369** A1
Nyall Ct RM2 . . . . **336** D8
Nyssa Cl IG8 . . . . **310** A4
Nyth Cl RM14 . . . . **337** D5

O

Oakapple Cl CO2 . . . . **135** D1
Oak Ave Basildon CM11 . . **320** C4
Jaywick CO16 . . . . **195** A2
Upminster RM14 . . . . **356** B8
Wickford SS11 . . . . **322** C7
Oakbank CM13 . . . . **295** E4
Oak Bglws CM7 . . . . **127** E3
Oak Chase SS12 . . . . **321** A7
Oak Cl Felixstowe IP11 . . **381** C4
Maldon CM9 . . . . **259** B8
Rushmere St A IP4 . . . . **18** E7
Thorpe-le-S CO16 . . . . **142** A1
Waltham Abbey EN9 . . . . . **265** D5
West Bergholt CO6 . . . . **108** E4
Oak Cnr Beaumont CO16 . . **141** F8
Woodham Mortimer CM9 . . **257** D6
Oak Cotts CM3 . . . . **233** E8
Oak Ct Chingford E4 . . . . . **309** B4
Hadleigh SS7 . . . . **345** E2
South Ockendon RM15 . . . **357** C3
Oakdale Cl E4 . . . . **309** C5
Oakdale Gdns E4 . . . . **309** C5
Oakdale Inf Sch E18 . . . . . **310** B1
Oakdale Jun Sch E18 . . . . **310** B1
Oakdale Rd E18 . . . . **310** B1
Oakdene RM3 . . . . **314** F1
Oak Dene Cl RM11 . . . . **336** B5

Oakdene Rd SS13 . . . . **343** C8
Oakdene Way IG7 . . . . **311** F5
Oak Dr CM21 . . . . **200** C8
Oak Eggar Chase IP8 . . . . . **36** D8
Oak End CM18 . . . . **223** F6
Oaken Grange Dr SS2 . . . **347** E5
Oak Fall CM8 . . . . **184** A5
Oak Farm Rd CM9 . . . . **235** E1
Oakfield Chingford E4 . . . . **309** B5
Stebbing CM6 . . . . **123** E1
Oakfield Cl SS7 . . . . **344** C3
Oakfield Dr CO4 . . . . **110** A3
Oakfield Ho ⬛ IG1 . . . . **333** B1
Oakfield La CM1 . . . . **204** F3
Oakfield Lodge ⬛ IG1 . . . **333** B1
Oakfield Prim Sch SS12 . **322** E5
Oakfield Rd Belstead IP8 . . **36** A7
Ilford IG1 . . . . **333** B1
Rochford SS4 . . . . **303** A1
South Benfleet SS7 . . . . **344** C3
Washbrook IP8 . . . . **35** F6
Oakfields Chigwell IG7 . . . **310** C6
Loughton IG10 . . . . **289** A4
Oakfield Wood* CO11 . . . **88** D4
Oak Glade CM6 . . . . **246** D2
Oak Glen RM11 . . . . **336** E8
Oak Gn CM11 . . . . **297** D1
Oak Gr IP8 . . . . **16** A6
Oak Hall CM23 . . . . **145** E8
Oakhall Ct E11 . . . . **332** B5
Oak Hall Rd E11 . . . . **332** B5
Oakham Cl SS16 . . . . **340** F5
Oakham Ct SS9 . . . . **346** E2
Oak Haven CO12 . . . . **90** F1
Oak Hill Beazley End CM7 **101** A8
Chingford IG8 . . . . **309** E3
Wethersfield CM7 . . . . **73** F1
Oak Hill Cl IG8 . . . . **309** D3
Oak Hill Cres IG8 . . . . **309** E3
Oak Hill Ct IG8 . . . . **309** E3
Oak Hill Gdns IG8 . . . . **309** F2
Oak Hill La IP2 . . . . **17** B3
Oakhill Prim Sch IG8 . . . . **309** E4
Oak Hill Rd RM4 . . . . **291** E1
Oak Ho Ipswich IP2 . . . . **16** D2
Southend-on-S SS9 . . . . **368** F8
Oakland Farm Ind Est
CM4 . . . . **297** F6
Oakland Gdns CM13 . . . . **295** C4
Oakland Pl IG9 . . . . **310** A8
Oakland Rd CO12 . . . . **91** C3
Oaklands Ave
Colchester CO3 . . . . **134** C5
Romford RM1 . . . . **335** F7
Oaklands Cl
Bishop's Stortford CM23 . . **119** B2
Great Notley CM77 . . . . **154** D8
Oaklands Cres CM2 . . . . . **254** B8
Oaklands Dr
Bishop's Stortford CM23 . . **119** B2
Harlow CM17 . . . . **224** C7
South Ockendon RM15 . . . **372** C8
Oaklands Inf Sch CM2 . . . **254** B8
Oaklands Mews SS4 . . . . **325** C4
Oaklands Park Ave IG1 . **333** C2
Oaklands Pk CM23 . . . . . . **119** B2
Oaklands Sch SS10 . . . . . . **288** D4
Oaklands Way CM3 . . . . . **234** C2
Oaklea Ave CM2 . . . . **232** E3
Oakleafe Gdns IG6 . . . . . . **333** B8
Oaklee IP2 . . . . **17** A1
Oakleigh Ave
Hullbridge SS5 . . . . **301** E2
Southend-on-S SS1 . . . . **367** D8
Oakleigh Ct CM23 . . . . **145** D6
Oakleigh Lodge IG3 . . . . . **334** A1
Oakleigh Park Dr SS9 . . . **346** E1
Oakleigh Rd CO15 . . . . **195** F8
Oakleigh Rise CM16 . . . . . **268** A7
Oakleighs SS7 . . . . **344** C4
Oakley Ave Barking IG11 . **332** F5
Rayleigh SS6 . . . . **322** F3
Oakley Cl Chingford E4 . . . **309** C7
Grays RM20 . . . . **377** C8
Oakley Cross CO12 . . . . . . **117** B7
Oakley Ct SS10 . . . . **289** A7
Oakley Dr Billericay CM12 **296** F5
Romford RM3 . . . . **315** A3
Oakley Rd Braintree CM7 . **127** F7
Harwich CO12 . . . . **90** D1
Wix CO11 . . . . **115** E5
Oak Lodge CI1 . . . . **332** A4
Oak Lodge Ave IG7 . . . . . . **311** D5
Oak Lodge Tye CM7 . . . . . **233** A6
Oakmead Rd CO16 . . . . **193** B3
Oakmoor Way IG7 . . . . . . **311** E5
Oakmead Rd CO10 . . . . **15** A8
Oak Rd Basildon CM11 . . . **320** C4
Canvey Island SS8 . . . . **364** C3
Chappel CO6 . . . . **106** B3
Epping CM16 . . . . **245** F1
Grays RM17 . . . . **378** C8
Great Cornard CO10 . . . . **34** B6
Greenhithe DA9 . . . . **376** E1
Halstead CO9 . . . . **103** D7
Heybridge CM9 . . . . **237** B6
Little Maplestead CO9 . . . . . . **77** A8
Pebmarsh CO9 . . . . **78** A5
Ramsden Heath CM11 . . . . **298** D5
Rivenhall CM8 . . . . **184** C6
Rochford SS4 . . . . **325** E2
Rochford RM3 . . . . **314** F2
Tiptree CO5 . . . . **186** C7
Oak Rd N SS7 . . . . **345** E2

Oak Rd S SS7 . . . . **345** E2
Oak Ridge CO12 . . . . **117** B7
Oak Rise CO12 . . . . **310** D7
Oakroyd Ave CM6 . . . . **150** E8
Oaks Ave RM5 . . . . **313** C1
Oaks Dr CO3 . . . . **135** D7
Oaks Gr E4 . . . . **309** E8
Oaks Hospl The CO4 . . . . . **109** E3
Oaks La IG2 . . . . **333** E7
Oaksmere Gdns IP21 . . . . . **17** A2
Oaks Park High Sch IG2 . **333** E6
Oaks Pl CO4 . . . . **109** E2
Oaks Ret Pk RM20 . . . . **199** F3
Oak St
Bishop's Stortford CM23 . . **145** F6
Romford RM7 . . . . **335** C6
Oakstead Cl IP4 . . . . **18** A6
Oaks The Billericay CM12 **319** C6
Chingford IG8 . . . . **309** E3
Dartford DA2 . . . . **376** B1
Frinton-on-S CO13 . . . . **170** F6
Oaktree Cl
⬛ Bishop's Stortford CM23 **145** F7
Brentwood CM13 . . . . **316** F7
Oak Tree Cl IG10 . . . . **289** C8
Oak Tree Cotts CO6 . . . . . **133** B8
Oaktree Gr IG1 . . . . **352** D7
Oak Tree Rd CO7 . . . . **165** B4
Oaktrees CM9 . . . . **214** B5
Oakview CO12 . . . . **90** F1
Oakway RM16 . . . . **373** C5
Oak Wlk Hockley SS5 . . . . **324** E7
Sible Hedingham CO9 . . . . . . **51** D2
South Benfleet SS7 . . . . **344** B8
Southend-on-S SS9 . . . . **346** D4
Oakwood Ave
Brentwood CM13 . . . . **295** E3
Clacton-on-S CO15 . . . . . . **196** F7
Southend-on-S SS9 . . . . **346** E5
West Mersea CO5 . . . . **218** D7
Oakwood Chase RM11 . . **336** F4
Oakwood Cl
Kirby Cross CO13 . . . . **170** E6
South Benfleet SS7 . . . . **344** B5
Woodford IG8 . . . . **310** E4
Oakwood Ct
Althorne CM3 . . . . **283** A3
Chingford E4 . . . . **287** E2
Romford RM2 . . . . **336** C8
Southend-on-S SS9 . . . . **346** E5
Oakwood Dr
Billericay CM12 . . . . **297** C5
West Mersea CO5 . . . . **218** D7
Oakwood Est RM20 . . . . **200** B4
Oakwood Gdns Ilford IG3 **333** F2
Southend-on-S SS9 . . . . **218** D7
Oakwood Gr SS13 . . . . **343** B6
Oakwood Hill IG10 . . . . . . **289** B4
Oakwood Hill Ind Est
IG10 . . . . **289** B4
Oakwood Inf Sch CO15 . . **195** D2
Oakwood Rd
Corringham SS17 . . . . **361** B4
Rayleigh SS6 . . . . **323** C4
Southend-on-S SS9 . . . . **346** E5
Oak Yd CO9 . . . . **76** E2
Oasis Ct CM1 . . . . **232** F5
Oasthouse Ct CB10 . . . . **22** D2
Oast House Spinney
CM7 . . . . **127** F6
Oat Way SS4 . . . . **325** F2
Oates Rd RM5 . . . . **313** B5
Oatfield Cl CO3 . . . . **134** D6
Oatlands CO7 . . . . **137** F6
Oban Ct SS11 . . . . **322** B5
Oban Ho IG11 . . . . **352** D3
Oban Rd SS2 . . . . **348** C1
Oban St IP1 . . . . **17** B7
Oberon Cl CO4 . . . . **82** F6
Obrey Way CM23 . . . . **145** E3
Observation Ct IP1 . . . . **17** B5
Observer Way CO5 . . . . . . **158** C4
Occasio Ho CM20 . . . . **223** C8
Ockelford Ave CM1 . . . . . . **231** F5
Ockendon Sch The
RM15 . . . . **372** A8
Ockendon Sta RM15 . . . . **357** B2
Ockendon Way CO14 . . . . **171** A8
Octave Ho CM16 . . . . **267** F3
Octavia Dr CM8 . . . . **211** F7
Oddcroft CO6 . . . . **77** F1
Odell Cl IG11 . . . . **352** F5
Odeon The IG11 . . . . **352** D5
Odessa Rd SS8 . . . . **364** D3
Odin Lodge CM9 . . . . **258** F8
O'Donoghue Ho SS17 . . . **360** F2
Office La CM9 . . . . **214** A4
Ogard Rd EN11 . . . . **221** C8
Ogilvie Ct SS12 . . . . **321** E5
Oglethorpe Rd RM10 . . . **335** A4
Okehampton Rd RM3 . . . **314** C4
Okehampton Sq RM3 . . . **314** C4
Old Barn La CM2 . . . . **277** F2
Old Barn Rd CO8 . . . . **80** A6
Old Barns La CM4 . . . . **251** C3
Old Bell Ct CM24 . . . . **119** D6
Old Bell La CM4 . . . . **278** B1
Old Brickworks The
RM3 . . . . **315** A3
Oldbury Ave CM2 . . . . **254** F8
Oldbury Cotts SS3 . . . . **349** D3
Old Burylodge La CM24 **120** A4
Old Cattle Market ⬛ IP4 . . **17** C5
Oldchurch Gdns RM7 . . . **335** D4
Old Church Hill SS16 . . . **341** A1
Oldchurch Hospl RM7 . . . **335** D5
Old Church La
Bulmer CO10 . . . . **32** F3
Bulmer Tye CO10 . . . . **32** F2
Mountnessing CM13 . . . . . **296** B6
West Bergholt CO6 . . . . **108** D5
Oldchurch Rd RM7 . . . . **335** E4

Old Church Rd
Basildon SS13 . . . . **343** F5
Chingford E4 . . . . **309** A7
East Hanningfield CM3 . . . **278** B6
Oldchurch Rise RM7 . . . . **335** E4
Old Clements La CB9 . . . . . . **8** F7
Old Coach Rd CO1 . . . . **136** B7
Old Coastguard Cotts
CM0 . . . . **241** E4
Old Convent The CO5 . . . **158** B1
Old Court Rd CM2 . . . . **232** D3
Old Croft CM1 . . . . **205** D5
Old Crown La CM14 . . . . . **293** D7
Old Ct Chelmsford CM2 . . **232** D3
Long Melford CO10 . . . . **15** D8
Olde Forge CO7 . . . . **165** E1
Old Ferry La CM12 . . . . **297** A4
Old Ferry Rd CO7 . . . . **164** B8
Oldfield Rd IP8 . . . . **16** B1
Oldfields CM14 . . . . **316** C6
Old Forge CO7 . . . . **137** C2
Old Forge Rd
Boreham CM3 . . . . **233** E8
Layer-de-l-H CO2 . . . . **163** A5
Old Forge The SS6 . . . . . . **323** C3
Old Foundry Rd IP4 . . . . . . **17** D6
Old Hall Cl CM9 . . . . **235** E1
Old Hall Ct SS3 . . . . **350** A4
Old Hall La Capel St M IP9 **35** F3
Tollesbury CM9 . . . . **216** C5
Walton-on-t-N CO14 . . . . . **171** B8
Old Hall Rise CM17 . . . . . **224** E8
Old Heath Prim Sch
CO2 . . . . **136** D3
Old Heath Rd
Colchester CO1,CO2 . . . . . . **136** C4
Southminster CM3,CM0 . . **284** A2
Old Highway EN11 . . . . **221** C8
Old Hill Ave SS16 . . . . **360** B8
Oldhouse Croft CM20 . . . **199** E2
Old House La Boxted CO4 . **83** E2
Lower Nazeing EN9 . . . . **243** F8
Roydon CM19 . . . . **222** C6
Old House Rd CO6 . . . . **109** A8
Oldhouse Villas CM7 . . . . **148** C8
Old Ipswich Rd CO7 . . . . . **110** E7
Old Jenkins Cl SS12 . . . . . **360** F1
Old Leigh Rd SS9 . . . . **347** A1
Old London Rd
Capel St M IP9 . . . . **35** F7
Woodham Walter CM9 . . . **235** E1
Old Macdonald's Educational
Farm Pk* CM14 . . . . **292** F1
Old Maltings The ⬛
CM23 . . . . **146** A7
Old Market Ct ⬛ CO10 . . . . **33** E7
Old Market Pl CO10 . . . . . . **33** E7
Old Market Ret Pk ⬛
SS13 . . . . **343** B5
Old Mead SS2 . . . . **347** A7
Oldmead Ho ⬛ RM10 . . . . **354** B6
Old Mead Rd CM22 . . . . **94** C5
Old Mill Chase CM7 . . . . . **173** C4
Old Mill Ct E18 . . . . **332** C8
Old Mill La
Coggeshall CO5 . . . . **158** D7
Great Wakering SS3 . . . . . . **350** B6
Hatfield Peverel CM3 . . . . . **211** A4
Haverhill CB9 . . . . **8** F7
Hockley SS5 . . . . **324** F7
Old Mill Rd Langham CO4 . **83** D5
Saffron Walden CB11 . . . . . . **22** D1
Old Oaks EN9 . . . . **265** E7
Old Orch CM18 . . . . **224** B6
Old Parsonage Ct CO13 . **170** F5
Old Parsonage Way
CO13 . . . . **170** F5
Old Pier St CO14 . . . . **171** C8
Old Rd Clacton-on-S CO15 **195** E4
Frinton-on-S CO13 . . . . **170** F4
Harlow CM17 . . . . **224** C3
Navestock Heath RM4 . . . . **292** D5
Pattiswick CM7 . . . . **129** F5
Wickham St P CO9 . . . . **53** D5
Old Rectory Ct SS2 . . . . . . **348** E1
Old Rectory Rd CM5 . . . . **270** B5
Old Rectory The CM3 . . . . **278** B7
Old River La CM23 . . . . **145** F7
Old Rope Wlk CB9 . . . . **8** E7
Old Rose Gdns CO4 . . . . . . **109** D4
Old School Cl CO16 . . . . . . **194** A4
Old School Ct CM3 . . . . **211** B3
Old School Field CM1 . . . **232** E4
Old School Ho CM9 . . . . **91** B8
Old School Ho The CO5 . **164** A8
Old School La CO7 . . . . **138** A6
Old School Mdw SS2 . . . . **349** E4
Old School Yd CB11 . . . . . . **43** D8
Old Ship La SS4 . . . . **325** F2
Old Shire La EN9 . . . . **266** A5
Old Southend Rd
Southend-on-S SS1 . . . . **367** B7
West Hanningfield CM2 . . . **277** B8
Old Station Rd IG10 . . . . . **288** E4
Old Street Hill CM22 . . . . **174** D5
Old St The IP9 . . . . **35** B1
Old Vicarage Cl CM7 . . . . **177** C2
Old Vicarage Rd CO12 . . . **91** C3
Old Vicarage The CM7 . . **152** E6
Old Way CO13 . . . . **170** F4
Old Wickford Rd CM3 . . . **180** B8
Oldwyk SS14 . . . . **342** E4
Olive Ave SS9 . . . . **346** A2
Olive Gr CO2 . . . . **135** D2
Oliver Cl CM8 . . . . **184** B2
Oliver Pl RM6 . . . . **334** B5
Olivers Cl
Clacton-on-S CO15 . . . . . . **195** E4

Olivers Cl continued
Great Melford CO10 . . . . **15** D7
Olivers Cres SS12 . . . . **350** B4
Olivers Ct CO15 . . . . **195** E4
Olivers Dr CM8 . . . . **212** A7
Olivers La CO2 . . . . **135** A1
Olivers Rd CO15 . . . . **195** E4
Oliver Way CM1 . . . . **231** F7
Olive St RM7 . . . . **335** D6
Oliveswood Rd CM6 . . . . **150** D7
Olivia Dr SS9 . . . . **346** F2
Ollards Ct IG10 . . . . **288** C4
Ollard's Gr IG10 . . . . **288** D5
Olley Wlk CO5 . . . . **158** C3
Olympic Bsns Ctr SS14 . . **320** F2
Omnibus Way E17 . . . . **309** A1
One Tree Hill SS16,SS17 . **341** F1
Ongar Cl
Clacton-on-S CO16 . . . . . . **195** B4
Ilford RM6 . . . . **334** C6
Ongar Ent Ctr CM5 . . . . . . **249** A5
Ongar Pl CM14 . . . . **316** D8
Ongar Rd Abridge RM4 . . . **290** C7
Brentwood CM5 . . . . **294** B2
Fyfield CM5 . . . . **227** C2
Great Dunmow CM6 . . . . . . **150** D6
Kelvedon Hatch CM15 . . . . **271** D4
Margaret Roding CM6 . . . . **204** D3
Pilgrims Hatch CM15 . . . . . **294** A3
Stondon Massey CM15 . . . **271** E8
Writtle CM1 . . . . **230** F1
Ongar Road   Trad Est
CM6 . . . . **150** D7
Ongar War Meml Hospl
CM5 . . . . **249** A5
Ongar Way RM13 . . . . **354** E4
Onslow Cl E4 . . . . **309** D8
Onslow Cotts CO5 . . . . **160** A7
Onslow Cres CO2 . . . . **136** B1
Onslow Gdns
Chipping Ongar CM5 . . . . . **249** A4
Wanstead E18 . . . . **332** C8
Opal Ave IP1 . . . . **16** D8
Opal Mews ⬛ IG1 . . . . **333** B2
Ophir Rd CO7 . . . . **192** F5
Optima Bsns Pk EN11 . . . **221** C2
Orange Gr IG2 . . . . **311** C4
Orange St CM6 . . . . **364** D4
Orange Tree Cl CM2 . . . . . **254** C6
Orange Tree Hill RM4 . . . **313** E6
Orchard Ave
Billericay CM12 . . . . **297** C5
Brentwood CM13 . . . . **316** F7
Downham CM11 . . . . **298** E2
Halstead CO9 . . . . **76** D2
Hockley SS5 . . . . **324** E7
Maldon CM9 . . . . **236** F2
Newport CB11 . . . . **66** F8
Ramsey CO12 . . . . **90** A2
Ridgewell CO9 . . . . **29** B6
Saffron Walden CB11 . . . . . . **43** D7
Sheering CM22 . . . . **201** C8
Southminster CM0 . . . . **284** D4
Stansted Mountfitchet CM24 **120** B6
Thaxted CM6 . . . . **70** A3
Tollesbury CM9 . . . . **216** E1
Wanstead E11 . . . . **332** B7
Writtle CM1 . . . . **231** B1
Orchard Cotts
Boreham CM3 . . . . **210** A2
Langham CO4 . . . . **83** F3
Little Horkesley CO6 . . . . **81** E5
Orchard Croft CM20 . . . . **200** A2
Orchard Ct CO3 . . . . **135** C7
Orchard Dr Braintree CM7 **128** A1
Grays RM17 . . . . **373** A4
Thorpe-le-S CO16 . . . . **141** D3
Theydon Bois CM16 . . . . . . **267** E3
Orchard End CO5 . . . . **218** E6
Orchard Gate IP2 . . . . **16** C5
Orchard Gdns
Colchester CO4 . . . . **136** B8
Waltham Abbey EN9 . . . . . **265** C5
Orchard Gr
Rushmere St A IP5 . . . . **18** F7
Southend-on-S SS9 . . . . **346** F6
Orchard La
Pilgrims Hatch CM15 . . . . . **293** F4
Woodford IG8 . . . . **310** C6
Orchard Lea CO15 . . . . **172** C1
Orchard Mead SS9 . . . . . . **346** E5
Orchard Mews CO5 . . . . . **186** D4
Orchard Piece CM4 . . . . . . **272** F8
Orchard Pightle CB11 . . . . . **5** C6
Orchard Rd Alresford CO7 **165** B8
Belvedere DA17 . . . . **369** A2
Blackmore CM4 . . . . **272** F8
⬛ Colchester CO4 . . . . **136** A6
Dagenham RM10 . . . . **354** A4
Kelvedon CO5 . . . . **158** C3
Maldon CM9 . . . . **236** F2
Mayland CM3 . . . . **261** A4
Romford RM7 . . . . **313** B1
South Benfleet SS7 . . . . **344** B7
Southminster CM0 . . . . **284** E4

Orchard Rd continued
Swanscombe DA10 . . . . **377** E2
Orchards CM8 . . . . **183** F1
Orchard Side SS9 . . . . **346** F6
Orchard St
Chelmsford CM2 . . . . **232** B1
⬛ Ipswich IP1 . . . . **17** D6
Orchards The
Epping CM16 . . . . **268** A7
Sawbridgeworth CM21 . . . **172** E3
Orchard Terr CM7 . . . . **127** F2
Orchard The Felsted CM6 **152** C5
Wickford SS12 . . . . **321** B7
Orchard Way
Chigwell IG7 . . . . **312** A7
Glemsford CO10 . . . . **2** D3
Orchid Ave CM8 . . . . **183** E4
Orchid Cl Abridge RM4 . . . **290** B6
Ipswich IP7 . . . . **16** E4
Orchid Pl CM3 . . . . **301** D8
Orchis Gr RM17 . . . . **372** F1
Orchis Way RM1 . . . . **314** F4
Ordnance Rd DA12 . . . . . . **379** C1
Orestes Ct ⬛ E18 . . . . **332** A8
Oreston Rd RM13 . . . . **355** D2
Orford Cres CM1 . . . . **232** D5
Orford Ct ⬛ DA2 . . . . **376** A3
Orford Rd Felixstowe IP11 **381** C1
Haverhill CB9 . . . . **8** F6
Wanstead E18 . . . . **332** B8
Orford St IP1 . . . . **17** B7
Oriel Cl CO10 . . . . **34** B6
Oriel Gdns IG5 . . . . **332** F8
Oriole Way CM23 . . . . **145** C6
Orion Cl SS14 . . . . **321** A1
Orion War CM7 . . . . **128** B4
Orkney Cl SS9 . . . . **9** D7
Orkney Gdns SS12 . . . . . . **321** F5
Orlando Cl CO4 . . . . **110** C8
Orlando Dr SS13 . . . . **321** C1
Ormesby Chine CM3 . . . . **301** D5
Ormond Cl RM3 . . . . **314** D1
Ormonde Ave
Rochford SS4 . . . . **325** E3
South Benfleet SS7 . . . . **346** C4
Ormonde Cl CO6 . . . . **108** C4
Ormonde Cr RM1 . . . . **335** F4
Ormonde Gdns SS6 . . . . . **346** A2
Ormonde Rise IG9 . . . . **288** F1
Ormonds Cres CM3 . . . . . **279** B4
Ormsby St SS8 . . . . **363** D3
Orpen Cl CO6 . . . . **108** D4
Orpen's Hill CO2 . . . . **161** A5
Orplands Cotts CM0 . . . . **241** F1
Orrmo Rd SS8 . . . . **364** F3
Orsett Ct SS9 . . . . **346** C5
Orsett CE Prim Sch
RM16 . . . . **374** B4
Orsett End SS14 . . . . **342** D7
Orsett Heath Cres RM16 **374** A8
Orsett Hospl RM16 . . . . . . **374** A8
Orsett Rd Pk RM16 . . . . . . **374** A8
Orsett St Grays RM17 . . . **373** B1
Horndon-on-t-H SS17 . . . . **359** D2
Orsett Terr IG8 . . . . **310** C2
Orsino Wlk CO4 . . . . **136** F7
Orton Cl CM4 . . . . **275** A8
Orton Rd CM7 . . . . **335** D6
Orton Ho ⬛ RM13 . . . . **314** E3
Orvis La CO7 . . . . **59** E1
Orwell Ret Pk IP2 . . . . **16** C1
Orwell Ct CM23 . . . . **375** C2
Orwell Bsns Ctr IP3 . . . . . **17** E2
Orwell Cl Colchester CO4 **110** E1
Rainham RM13 . . . . **369** D8
Orwell Country Pk*
IP10 . . . . **38** B6
Orwell Ct ⬛ Ipswich IP4 . . **17** D5
Orwell Gdns IP2 . . . . **17** A3
Orwell High Sch IP11 . . . . **381** C5
Orwell Ho IP11 . . . . **381** A4
Orwell Hts IP2 . . . . **16** C1
Orwell Lodge ⬛ E18 . . . . **332** A7
Orwell Way
Burnham-on-C CM0 . . . . . . **306** A4
Clacton-on-S CO15 . . . . . . **195** C6
Orwell Wlk CM8 . . . . **183** E8
Osbert Rd CM8 . . . . **211** E8
Osborne Cl
Clacton-on-S CO15 . . . . . . **196** A2
Hornchurch RM11 . . . . **336** B5
Osborne Ho ⬛ IG8 . . . . . . **314** A4
Southend-on-S SS4 . . . . . . **316** B6
Osborne Rd
Basildon,Barstable East
SS13 . . . . **342** C5
Buckhurst Hill IG9 . . . . **288** F1
Dagenham RM9 . . . . **353** F7
Hoddesdon EN10 . . . . **221** A8
Hornchurch RM11 . . . . **336** C5
Ipswich IP3 . . . . **18** A4
Pilgrims Hatch CM15 . . . . . **294** B3
Southend-on-S SS5 . . . . . . **324** D5
West Mersea CO5 . . . . **218** F5
Osborne Sq RM9 . . . . **353** F8
Osborne St CO2 . . . . **135** F6
Osborne Ave SS5 . . . . **324** C6
Osborne Gdns ⬛ CM23 **145** E5
Osborne Ho Pl SS2 . . . . . . **347** G1
Osborne Rd DA17 . . . . **369** A1
Osea Rd CM9 . . . . **238** B3
Osea Way CM1 . . . . **232** D7

Osier Pl [3] CB9 ....8 F8
Osmond Cl CM7 .....155 B5
Osprey Cl
  Southend-on-S SS3 ...349 E1
  Wanstead E11 ....332 A7
Osprey Cl
  Brentwood CM14 .....316 B7
  Waltham Abbey EN9 ..266 A5
Osprey Rd Haverhill CB9 ..9 C7
  Waltham Abbey EN9 ..266 A5
Ospreys CO15 ....195 F6
Ospreys The SS9 ......346 F1
Osprey Way CM2 ......254 A5
Ostell Cres EN3 ....265 A1
Osterley Dr SS16 ......340 F5
Osterley Pl CM3 ....301 D5
Ostler Cl CM23 ....145 C4
Othello Cl CO4 ....136 F8
Otho Dr CO4 ....110 A6
Otley App IG2 ....333 B5
Otley Ct IP11 ....381 B5
Otley Dr IG2 ....333 B5
Ottawa Gdns RM10 ....354 D5
Ottawa Rd IM18 ....379 A5
Otten Rd CO10 ....13 B1
Otterbourne Rd E4 ....309 D7
Ottershaw Way CO16 ..195 B6
Ouida Rd SS8 ....364 D3
Oulton Ave SS8 ....363 F5
Oulton Cl CO12 ....90 F3
Oulton Cres IP3 ....352 F7
Oulton Rd IP3 ....17 E2
Oundle Ho [8] RM3 ....314 D5
Our Lady Immaculate RC Prim
  Sch CM2 ....232 A1
Our Lady of Lourdes Prim Sch
  SS9 ....347 A2
Our Lady of Lourdes RC Prim
  Sch E11 ....332 A5
Our Lady of Lourdes RC Prim
  Sch SS9 ....323 A4
Ouse Chase CM8 ....183 D2
Outing Cl SS1 ....367 C7
Outing's La CM15 .....272 B3
Outlook Rd CM15 .....272 B3
Outpart Eastward CO1 ..91 E6
Outwood Common Rd
  CM11 ....297 E3
Outwood Farm Cl CM11 297 E1
Outwood Farm Rd CM11 297 E1
Oval Gdns RM17 ....373 C3
Oval Rd N RM10 ....354 B3
Oval Rd S RM10 ....354 B3
Overchurch Cl CF89 ....8 F7
Overcliffe DA11 ....379 A1
Overcliff Flats SS0 ....366 D7
Overcliff Rd RM17 .....373 C3
Overhall Ho CO8 ....78 C2
Over Hall La CB10 ......6 G2
Overmead Dr CM3 .....301 E8
Overstone Ct CO10 ....135 A2
Overstrand Ho RM12 ..336 B2
Overton Cl SS7 ....344 C6
Overton Ct E11 ....332 A4
Overton Dr
  Dagenham RM6 ......334 C4
  South Benfleet SS7 ...344 C6
Overton Rd SS7 ....344 B6
Ovington Gdns CM2 ...297 A5
Ovington Pl [10] CB9 ...90 F8
Owen Cl RM5 ....313 B4
Owen Gdns IG8 ....310 E4
Owen Ward Cl CO2 ....135 A3
Owen Waters Ho IG5 ..311 A2
Owlets Hall CM7 ......336 F8
Owl's Hill CM3 ....202 F3
Owls Retreat [1] CO4 ..136 F8
Oxborrow Cl CO13 .....170 A6
Oxcroft CM23 ....145 E7
Oxcroft Ct SS15 ......341 B6
Oxendon Dr EN11 .....221 A5
Oxenford CI CO1 ....90 F1
Oxford Ave Grays RM16 374 A2
  Hornchurch RM11 ....337 A7
Oxford Ct Basildon SS16 340 F5
  Great Cornard CO10 ..34 A6
Oxford Cres CO15 .....195 F4
Oxford Ct
  Brentwood CM14 .....316 D6
  Chelmsford CM2 .....232 E4
  Colchester CO3 ......135 E6
  Earls Colne CO6 .....105 B6
Oxford Ho CO9 ....9 B6
Oxford La CO9 ....51 D2
Oxford Mdw CO9 ....51 C2
Oxford Pl CO6 ....105 B6
Oxford Rd
  Canvey Island SS8 ...364 D3
  Clacton-on-S CO15 ...195 F4
  Colchester CO3 .....135 D6
  Frinton-on-S CO13 ...171 A5
  Halstead CO9 ....77 A1
  Horndon-on-t-H SS17 .359 F4
  Ilford IG1 ....352 C7
  Ipswich IP4 ....17 D4
  Manningtree CO11 ....86 D4
  Rochford SS4 ....325 E4
  Stanford-le-H SS17 ...360 B1
  Woodford IG8 ......310 E4
Oxley Cl RM2 ....314 C1
Oxley Gdns SS17 ......360 D1
Oxley Hill Abberton CO5 163 A3
  Tolleshunt Knights CM9 .175 A8
Oxley Ho CM7 ....155 B5
Oxley Parker Dr CO4 ..110 A6
Oxleys Rd EN9 ....266 A7
Oxleys The CM7 ......207 E6
Oxlip Rd CM8 ....177 A4
Oxlow La RM10 ....354 A8
Oxney Mead CM2 .....254 B2
Oxney Villas CM6 .....152 D6
Oxted Ho RM3 ....314 F5

Oxton Cl CO5 ....164 A8
Oxwich Cl SS17 ....361 A4
Ox Yd CO9 ....102 E7
Oyster Bsns Ctr CM9 ..210 E2
Oyster Catcher Terr IG5 333 A8
Oyster Cl CO5 ....218 C7
Oyster Cotts CM0 .....240 C1
Oyster Pk CO1 ....136 D6
Oyster Pl CM2 ....232 F4
Oyster Tank Rd CO7 ..192 E5
Oziers CM23 ....43 E7
Oziers CM22 ....94 C2
Ozonia Ave SS12 .....321 C5
Ozonia Cl SS12 ....321 B5
Ozonia CI SS12 ....321 B5
Ozonia Way SS12 .....321 C5
Ozonia Wlk [3] SS12 ..321 C5

P

Paarl Rd SS8 ....364 B4
Pacehealth Cl RM5 ...313 D4
Pacific Cl DA10 ....377 E2
Packard Ave IP3 ......18 B2
Packards La CO6 ......80 F1
Packe Cl CO5 ....158 D4
Paddock Cl
  Billericay CM11 ......319 C7
  Harwich CO12 ....91 C4
  Orsett RM16 ....374 B8
  Southend-on-S SS9 ..346 E7
Paddock Dr CM1 ......232 E8
Paddock Mead CM18 ..223 C3
Paddocks The
  Abberton CO5 ......163 A2
  Ashen CO10 ....11 D1
  Bures CO8 ....79 E8
  Great Bentley CO7 ..166 F5
  Great Totham CM9 ..213 A4
  High Roding CM6 ....176 F2
  Inglestone CM4 .....274 B3
  Orsett RM16 ....374 B8
  Rayleigh SS6 ....323 F2
  Stapleford Abbotts RM4 291 F3
  West Mersea CO5 ...218 D6
  Witham CM8 ....184 A2
Paddock The
  Bishop's Stortford CM23 145 D3
  Hoddesdon EN10 .....221 A3
  Stock CM4 ....275 E3
Paddock Way CO7 ....137 E7
Padfield Cl [3] RM1 ...335 F5
Padgets The EN9 .....265 E5
Padgetts Way SS5 ....301 D3
Padham's Green Rd CM4 296 C8
Padnall Cl RM6 ....334 D8
Padnall Rd RM6 ......334 C8
Paeony Chase CO5 ...218 C8
Pageant Cl RM18 .....379 C6
Page Cl Dagenham RM9 353 E7
  Witham CM8 ....211 D8
Page Rd Basildon SS13 343 F7
  Tolleshunt D'Arcy CM9 215 F1
Pages Cl CM23 ....145 D5
Pages La Romford RM3 315 B1
  Tollesbury CM9 .....239 F8
Paget Cl CM22 ....94 C1
Paget Rd Ilford IG1 ...352 B8
  Ipswich IP1 ....17 B7
  Rowhedge CO5 .....163 F8
  Wivenhoe CO7 .....164 C8
Pagette Way RM17 ...373 A2
Paglesfield [3] CM11 ..295 C3
Paglesham Eastend SS4 328 A5
  Rochford SS4 ....327 C6
Paignton Ave CM1 ...232 D5
Paignton Cl SS6 .....323 A7
Paines Brook Rd RM3 314 F4
Paines Brook Way RM3 314 F4
Painswick Ave SS7 ...360 F5
Painters Rd IG2,RM6 ..334 A8
Pakenham Pl [18] CO9 ..9 B8
Pakes Way CM16 .....267 E2
Palace Gdns
  Bishop's Stortford CM23 145 E5
  Buckhurst Hill IG9 ..288 D1
Palace Gr SS15 ....341 E8
Palace View Rd E4 ...309 B5
Palatine Ps SS15 ......340 F6
Palepit CM3 ....281 C5
Paley Gdns IG10 .....289 B6
Palfrey Hts CO11 ......86 D8
Palin Ho RM10 ....373 A5
Palins Way RM10 ....373 A5
Palister Dr RM13 .....370 B8
Palliser Rd CO15 .....195 F2
Pall Mall SS9 ....346 E1
Palm Cl Chelmsford CM2 254 C6
  Witham CM8 ....184 A5
Palmeira Ave SS0 ....366 D7
Palmeira Mans SS0 ..366 D7
Palmer Cl SS15 ......341 D6
Palmer Ct RM1 ......336 A4
Palmer Rd CM8 ......184 D3
Palmers [5] SS17 ....360 F3
Palmers Coll RM17 ...373 E2
Palmers Croft CM2 ...233 A2
Palmers Dr RM17 ....373 C2
Palmers La EN9 ......221 F1
Palmers La
  [6] Bishop's Stortford CM23 145 F7
  Chrishall SG8 ....19 C2
Palmerston Cl [2] CO1 310 C8
Palmerston Rd
  Canvey Island SS8 ...363 D3
  Rainham RM13 ......355 C3
  Harwich, Parkeston CO12 90 F4
  Harwich, Upper Dovercourt
    ....91 A4

Palmerston Rd continued
  Ipswich IP4 ....17 E6
  Southend-on-S SS0 ..366 D7
Palmerswick Way IG5 333 A8
Palmerswent Cl CO10 ..15 D8
Palm Mews SS15 .....319 D1
Palm Rd RM7 ....335 C6
Pamela Ct [8] RM1 ...335 F6
Pamela Gdns CM23 ..145 F3
Panadown SS15 ......341 F6
Pamplins SS15 ....341 E6
Panadown SS15 ......341 F6
Pancroft RM4 ....290 B6
Panfield La CM7 ......127 C5
Panfield Mews IG2 ...333 D5
Panfields SS15 ....341 A6
Pan La CM5 ....277 F5
Pannells Ash CO10 ...11 D1
Pannells Cl CO10 ......2 B4
Pantile Ave SS1 .....348 C3
Pantile Cl CM8 ......212 A7
Pantile Cotts RM14 ..337 D6
Pantile Ct CM0 ......284 C4
Pantile Mead CM0 ...284 C4
Pantiles The CM2 ....297 A4
Pantlings La CO5 ....158 A5
Panton Cres [7] CO4 ..136 E7
Panton Mews IG2 ....333 D5
Panventon CE RM18 ..379 A5
Pan Wlk CM1 ....231 D5
Papenburg Rd SS4 ..371 D5
Papermill Cotts CM7 ..207 F4
Papillon Rd CO3 .....135 E7
Paprills SS16 ....341 E5
Parade Ct CO12 ......90 C1
Parade IP4 ....17 F7
Parade The
  [5] Basildon SS13 ....343 B5
  Brentwood CM14 ....316 C7
  Colchester CO2 .....136 A1
  Kirby Cross CO13 ...170 B6
  Romford RM4 ....313 E7
  Swanscombe DA10 ..377 E3
  Walton-on-t-N CO14 ..171 C8
  Wickford SS11 ......321 E5
  Romford RM5 ....315 B4
Paradise Rd
  Waltham Abbey EN9 ..265 C5
  Writtle CM1 ....253 B8
Paradise Pk IP4 ......18 E5
Pargat Dr SS9 ......346 C7
Pargetters Hyam SS5 324 F6
Parham Dr IG2 ......333 A5
Paringdon Jun Sch
  CM18 ....223 D4
Paringdon Rd CM18,
  CM19 ....223 C3
Parish Cl RM11 ......336 B2
Parish Way SS15 ....341 C7
Parkanaur Ave SS1 ..348 C3
Park Ave Barking IG11 .352 C3
  Brentwood CM13 ....295 D1
  Canvey Island SS8 ..364 F2
  Chelmsford CM1 ....205 F4
  Felixstowe IP11 ....381 F5
  Grays RM20 ....277 B8
  Harlow CM17 ....224 A2
  Ilford IG1 ....333 A3
  Southend-on-S SS9 ..346 D1
  Upminster RM14 ....337 E4
  Wallend E6 ....352 A3
  Woodford IG8 ......310 B5
Park Bvd
  Clacton-on-S CO15 ..196 D8
  Romford RM2 ....313 F2
Park Chase Hadleigh SS7 345 C4
  St Osyth CO16 ......194 C5
Park Cl
  North Weald Bassett CO16 247 A4
  Sudbury CO10 ......15 C2
  Wickford SS12 .....321 F3
Park Cotts Gosfield CO9 102 E8
  Manningtree CO11 ...86 D5
  St Osyth CO16 ......194 A5
Park Cres
  Hornchurch RM11 ...336 A4
  Southend-on-S SS0 ..366 F8
Park Ct [2] Chingford E4 309 B5
  Felixstowe IP11 ....381 D2
  Harlow CM20 ....199 D2
  Sible Hedingham CO9 ..51 E5
Parkdale CM9 ....256 C7
Park Dr Braintree CM7 ..155 A4
  Brightlingsea CO7 ..192 E7
  Clacton-on-S CO15 ..195 D2
  Coggeshall CO6 ....131 A3
  Halstead CO9 ....76 E1
  Hatfield Heath CM22 174 B2
  Ingatestone CM4 ...274 B3
  Maldon CM9 ....237 B1
  Romford RM1 ......336 A3
  Wickford SS12 .....321 E6
Park End Rd RM1 ....335 E7
Parker Ave CM18 ....211 D7
Parker Ct RM1 ......241 F4
Parker Rd
  Chelmsford CM2 ...232 D3
  Grays RM17 ....377 F8
Parker's Farm Rd RM6 358 F5
Parker's Way CO6 ...106 A4
Parker Way CO9 .....103 E6
Parkes Rd IG7 ......311 E6
Parkeston Rd
  Felixstowe IP11 ....381 B4
  Harwich, Parkeston CO12 .90 F4
Park Farm Ind Est SS8 39 C2
Park Farm La SG8 ....39 C2
Park Farm Rd
  Hornchurch RM14 ..356 A4
  Upminster RM14 ...356 A4
Parkfields Hadleigh SS7 345 C4

Parkfields continued
  Sible Hedingham CO9 ..51 D1
Park Fields CM19 ....222 B7
Parkfield St CO5 .....185 C4
Parkgate SS0 ....366 F8
Parkgate Cnr CO16 ..169 A2
Park Gate Cotts CM7 ..101 C6
Park Gate Rd
  Corringham SS17 ...361 A8
  Silver End CM8 .....157 B3
Park Gdns Erith DA8 ..369 D2
  Hockley SS5 ....324 F5
Park Grange IG7 .....311 D5
Parkhall Rd
  Beazley End CM7 ...101 E7
  Gosfield CO9 ....102 B7
Park Hill Harlow CM17 200 B4
  Loughton IG10 .....288 D4
Parkhill Cl RM12 ....336 C2
Parkhill Jun Sch
  Ilford IG5 ....333 A8
  Redbridge IG5 .....332 F8
Parkhill Rd E4 ......287 C2
Park Ho SS17 ....360 F3
Parkhurst Dr SS6 ....323 C7
Parkhurst Rd
  Basildon SS13 ......343 B5
  Little Ilford IG2 ....352 A8
  Parkeston CO12 ....90 F4
Parkinson Dr CM1 ...231 F1
Parkins The IP9 ......35 C2
Park La Aveley RM15 ..371 D5
  Aveley RM15 ....371 D5
  Clacton-on-S CO15 ..195 D2
  St Southend-on-S SS0 366 F8
  Stoke-by-N CO6 ....56 D5
  Thaxted CM6 ....70 A2
Parkland Ave
  Romford RM1 ....313 F1
  Upminster RM14 ...337 E4
Parkland Cl Chigwell IG7 311 C7
  [3] Hoddesdon EN11 197 B1
Parkland Ct CO11 ...310 B3
Parklands Billericay CM11 ..319 D8
  Braintree CM7 .....155 A8
  Canvey Island SS8 ..364 A5
  Chigwell IG7 ....311 C7
  Coopersale CM16 ...246 D2
  Rochford SS4 ......325 D3
  Waltham Abbey EN9 ..266 A7
Parklands Ave SS6 ..323 E2
Parklands Cl
  Glemsford CO10 ......2 C5
  Ilford IG2 ....333 C4
Parklands Dr CM1 ...232 D3
Parklands Jun & Inf Sch
  RM1 ....336 A3
Parklands Jun Sch RM1 335 D8
Parkland Way CM5 ...248 F1
Park Lane CO15 ......195 D2
Park Mdw CM15 .....272 D1
Parkmead IG10 .....288 D1
Park Mead CM20 ....199 B1
Park Mews [8] RM13 355 A6
Parkmill Cl SS17 ....361 A4
Parkmore Cl IG8 ....310 A6
Park North IP7 ....17 D8
Park Rd Ardleigh CO7 ..111 B8
  Brentwood CM14 ...316 B8
  Canvey Island SS8 ..306 B5
  Chelmsford CM1 ...232 B2
  Clacton-on-S CO15 ..195 D2
  East Bergholt CO7 ...60 B2
  Elsenham CM22 .....94 E5
  Ford End CM3 ......179 A3
  Great Chesterford CB10 ..3 E5
  Harwich CO12 ......91 A5
  Hoddesdon EN11 ...221 D1
  Ilford IG1 ....333 D1
  Ipswich IP1 ....17 B7
  Little Bentley CO7 ..139 D8
  Little Easton CM6 ..122 F3
  Little Horkesley CO6 ..82 B8
  Maldon CM9 ....237 A2
  Pleshey CM3 ....178 F4
  Riverhall CM3 ......179 F1
  Southend-on-S,Clifftown
    ....366 F8
  Southend-on-S,
    Prittlewell SS2 ...347 F4
  Stanford-le-H SS17 ..360 B1
  Stansted Mountfitchet
    CM24 ....119 E7

Park Rd continued
  Wivenhoe, Wivenhoe Park
    ....137 A4
Park Sch for Girls IG1 ..333 B3
Park Sch The SS6 ....323 B6
Parkside Grays RM16 ..373 E3
  Haverhill CB9 ....8 F6
  Saffron Walden CB10 ..22 C1
Parkside CI
  Corringham SS17 ...361 A8
  Southend-on-S SS9 ..346 C4
Park Side Basildon SS13 343 A7
  Billericay CM11 ....297 C2
  Southend-on-S SS9 ..347 A1
  Stebbing CM6 ......124 D6
Parkside Ave Ipswich IP4 17 D7
  Romford RM1 ......335 D8
  Tilbury RM18 ......375 B1
Parkside Ct [2] E11 ..332 A5
Parkside Ctr SS2 ....347 F7
Parkside Ho RM10 ...335 C1
Parkside Quarter CO1 135 E8
Parkside Rd DA17 ...369 C2
Parkside Terr IG1 ...352 C7
Park Sq RM4 ....290 E3
Park Sq W
  Clacton-on-S CO15 ..220 G8
  Jaywick CO15 ......195 A1
Park Sth Southend-on-S SS0 366 F8
  Stoke-by-N CO6 ....56 D5
Park St Southend-on-S SS0 366 F8
  Thaxted CM6 ....70 A2
Parkstone Ave
  Hadleigh SS7 ....345 B4
  Hornchurch RM11 ..336 E5
  Southend-on-S SS2 ..320 F8
Parkstone Dr SS2 ...347 E4
Park Terr Greenhithe DA9 377 B8
  Harwich CO12 ......91 D4
  Long Melford CO10 ..91 D4
  Romford RM11 .....336 A4
  Tiptree CO5 ....179 F8
Park The CO11 ....86 D3
Park Vale CO9 ....51 E4
Park View Aveley RM15 371 D5
  Canvey Island SS8 ..364 E2
  Clare CO10 ....12 C7
  Hoddesdon EN11 ...221 A5
Park View Cres CM2 ..254 F5
Park View Ct
  Southend-on-S SS9 ..346 C4
  Wickford SS11 .....299 C1
  Woodford IG8 ......310 B5
Park View Gdns
  Grays RM17 ....373 B1
  Redbridge IG4 .....332 E7
Park View Ho RM10 ..336 F2
Park View Rd IP1 ....17 B8
Parkview Rise SS6 ...334 D5
Parkway
  Chelmsford CM1,CM2 232 C5
  Corringham SS17 ...361 C5
  Harlow CM20 ......222 E8
  Ilford IG3 ....333 F1
  Orsett RM16 ....374 A8
  Rayleigh SS6 ....345 B8
  Romford RM2 ......313 F1
  Sawbridgeworth CM21 172 F1
  Shudy Camps CB1 ....7 C6
  Woodford IG8 ......310 C5
Park Way
  Clacton-on-S CO15 ..195 D1
  Shenfield CM15 ....294 F1
Parkway Cl SS9 .....346 F7
Parkway Mdw SG8 ...22 B2
Parkway Thes SS8 ...364 B2
Parkwood IP11 ......17 C7
Parkwood Ave CO7 ..137 B1
Park Wood La CM9 ..214 A3
Parliament Rd E4 ...309 B8
Parmenter Dr CO10 ..34 C5
Parnall Rd CM18 ....223 D4
Parndon Ho IG10 ....289 D3
Parndon Mill La CM20 199 B3
Parndon Nature
  Reserve* CM19 ....223 D2
Parndon Wood Rd CM18,
  CM19 ....223 D2
Parnell Cl Colchester CO2 136 A2
  Grays RM16 ....372 C1
Parnham Pl IP4 ......18 B5
Parnham Rd SS7 ....369 A3
Parr Cl Braintree CM7 128 D4
  Grays RM16 ....372 C2
Parr Dr CO3 ....134 E4
Parrington Way CO11 ..86 A3
Parrotts Field CM11 221 B7
Parr Rd IG3 ....333 D3
Parry Cl SS17 ....360 D3
Parry Dr CO16 ......195 D7
Parslae Rd IP9 ......15 F7
Parsloes Ave RM9 ...353 E7
Parsloes Prim Sch RM9 353 D8
Parsonage Chase CM9 281 D8
Parsonage Cl
  Broomfield CM1 ....208 A1
  Felixstowe IP11 ...381 D3
  Pleshey CM3 ....178 E4
  Rivenhall CM8 .....123 C3
Parsonage Farm La SS16 47 B4
Parsonage Farm Prim Sch
  RM13 ....355 E4
Parsonage Farm Trad Est
  ....355 E4
Parsonage Field CM23 ..22 E7
Parsonage Gdns [3] CM7 127 F3
Parsonage Gr CO8 ...79 C2
Parsonage La
  Barnston CM6 ......151 D3
  Basildon SS15 .....341 D3
  Bishop's Stortford CM23 146 C8

Parsonage La continued
  Clavering CB11 ......65 B3
  Elder Street CB10 ....44 F3
  Howe Street CM3 ...179 F2
  Little Baddow CM3 ..234 D2
  Margaretting CM4 ...275 A7
  Stansted Mountfitchet
    CM24 ....119 E7
  Tending CO16 ......140 E8
Parsonage Leys CM20 .223 F8
Parsonage Rd
  Grays RM20 ....377 C8
  Rainham RM13 .....355 C2
  Takeley CM22 ......148 C8
Parsonage St CO9 ....76 F1
Parsons Cnr SS3 .....349 D2
Parsonside CO7 ......85 A6
Parson's Field CO7 ...85 A6
Parson's Heath CO4 ..110 E2
Parson's Heath CE Prim Sch
  CO4 ....110 E2
Parsons Hill CO3 ....138 F8
Parsons Hill CO3 ....136 C6
Parsons La CO1 .....136 C6
Parsons Lawn SS3 ...349 D1
Parsons Rd SS7 .....344 D7
Parsons Yd [10] CO11 ..86 D4
Partridge Ave CM1 ..231 F1
Partridge Cl CO12 ...116 D4
Partridge Cl CM18 ..223 E6
Partridge Dr CO6 ...106 D5
Partridge Gn SS13 ..343 A5
Partridge Rd
  Harlow CM18 ......223 D5
  Ipswich IP2 ....16 E3
Partridge Way SS13 ..134 C4
Parvills EN9 ....265 D2
Paschal Way CM2 ...254 F8
Pasfield E9 ....265 D2
Pashlers Alley CO10 ..12 B7
Paske Ave CO9 ....42 F3
Paslowes SS16 ......342 F4
Paslow Hall Cotts CM5 249 F4
Passingham Ave CM11 319 C6
Passingham CM13 ...294 D2
Passmores Comp Sch
  CM18 ....223 D6
Pasteur Dr RM3 .....314 D1
Paston Cl CM3 ......279 E1
Pastoral Way CM14 ..316 B5
Pasture Rd RM9 ....353 F7
Pastures The IP4 ....18 F7
Patching Hall La CM1 205 F3
Paternoster Cl EN9 ..266 E7
Paternoster Hill EN9 266 F7
Paternoster Row
  [4] Walton-on-t-N CO14 171 C8
Pathfields Rd CO15 ..195 D4
Pathways SS15 ......342 E5
Patman The CO7 ....137 A4
Patmore Cl CM21 ...145 C8
Patmore Fields CM22 ..93 A3
Patmore Rd
  Colchester CO4 .....110 D1
  Waltham Abbey EN9 265 E5
Patmore Way RM5 ..313 B5
Patricia Dr
  Corringham SS17 ...361 C6
  Hornchurch RM11 ...336 E3
Patricia Gdns
  Billericay CM11 ....319 D7
  Bishop's Stortford CM23 145 E5
Patrick Gr CO5 ......163 B6
Patten Cl CO6 ....132 F3
Patterson Cl DA1 ...376 A2
Pattison Rd IP3 ......17 E4
Pattison CI CO6 ....2 B6
Pattiswick Cnr SS14 ..342 E7
Pattiswick Sq SS14 ..342 E7
Pattocks SS14 ......342 E7
Pauinard CI CM3 ....205 B4
Patrick's La CO12 ....91 C4
Paul Ct RM7 ....335 C5
Pauline Gl CO15 ....196 B6
Pauline Gdns CM22 ..296 F4
Paul Spr IP2 ....17 C4
Paul Robeson Cl E6 ..352 B8
Pauls Cres CO7 ......137 F6
Pauls La EN11 ......221 A6
Paulson Ho [7] IG11 ..352 B5
Paul Spendlove Cl CO4 341 C8
Pauls Way CO15 ....195 A1
Pavement Mews [1] RM6 334 D4
Pavet Cl CM3 ....258 B3
Pavilion Cl CM12 ...296 F4
Pavilion Pl CM2 ....296 F4
Pavitt Mdw CM2 ....254 C2
Pawle CI CM2 ....233 B4
Paxfords CM23 ......145 A3
Paxton Rd CO15 ....196 B8
Paycock CI SS14 ....320 F2
Paycoke Mews SS14 320 F2
Paycoke Rd SS14 ...320 F2
Paycocke's House*
  CO6 ....130 E1
Paycocke Way CO6 ..131 A3

Paycock Rd CM19 .....223 A6
Payne Cl IG11 .....352 F5
Payne Pl CM3 .....278 B6
Paynes La EN9 .....243 C7
Payne's La CO11 .....113 C3
Paynters Mead SS16 .....342 E3
Payzes Gdns IG8 .....309 F5
Peabody Ct EN3 .....265 A2
Peacehaven CO13 .....171 A5
Peace Rd CO3 .....134 D7
Peach Ave SS5 .....324 E8
Peacock Cl Braintree CM7 127 F1
Dagenham RM8 .....334 C2
Hornchurch RM11 .....336 E7
5 Ipswich IP8 .....16 C2
Peacocks CM19 .....222 F6
Peacocks Cl CO10 .....1 C2
Peacocks Rd CO10 .....1 C2
Peacock St 7 DA12 .....379 C1
Peake Ave CO13 .....170 A6
Peakes Cl CO5 .....186 B4
Peaketon Ave IG4 .....332 D6
Pea La RM14 .....357 A6
Peal Rd CB11 .....43 F7
Pearce Manor CM2 .....253 F8
Pearce Rd IP3 .....18 A5
Pearcy Cl RM3 .....314 E3
Pearl Ct EN11 .....221 A6
Pearl Dr CM7 .....128 C3
Pearl Rd IP1 .....16 D8
Pearlstones Ct RM10 .....354 A4
Pearmain Cl SS11 .....299 D1
Pearmains CM3 .....180 F7
Pearmain Way CO3 .....134 C4
Pearmain Wlk CB9 .....8 C8
Pearse Way IP3 .....18 E1
Pearson Rd IP3 .....18 C5
Pearsons 2 SS17 .....360 F3
Pearsons Ave SS6 .....323 B4
Pearsons Cl CO10 .....2 B4
Peartree Bsns Ctr CO3 .....134 E4
Peartree Cl
Braintree CM7 .....128 A1
Doddinghurst CM15 .....272 D1
Goldhanger CM9 .....238 E6
Southend-on-S SS2 .....348 C3
South Ockendon RM15 .....357 C3
Pear Tree Cl
Basildon SS15 .....319 C1
Halstead CO9 .....77 A3
Pear Tree Ct E18 .....310 B2
Peartree Gdns
Dagenham RM8 .....353 B8
Romford RM7 .....313 B1
Peartree Hill CO8 .....80 A5
Peartree La
Bicknacre CM3 .....256 F3
Bulphan CM14 .....339 F1
Doddinghurst CM15 .....272 D2
Pear Tree Mead CM18 .....224 A5
Pear Tree Mead Prim Sch
CM18 .....224 A5
Peartree Rd CO3 .....134 E4
Peartrees CM13 .....317 C4
Pear Trees SS7 .....344 F4
Peartree Way CO16 .....168 C2
Peartree Wlk CM12 .....297 A4
Pease Cl RM12 .....355 B5
Pease Pl CM3 .....278 B6
Peaslands Rd CB11 .....43 E8
Peas Mead Terr E4 .....309 C6
Pebmarsh Cl CO2 .....163 A8
Pebmarsh Dr SS12 .....321 E6
Pebmarsh Rd
Alphamstone CO8 .....54 E2
Colne Engaine CO6 .....77 F2
Peck's Hill EN9 .....221 E2
Pecockes Cl CO10 .....34 C5
Peddars Ct CO10 .....15 C7
Pedder's Cl CO3 .....134 F3
Pedlars Cl CM3 .....257 A6
Pedlars End CM5 .....226 C2
Pedlars Path CM3 .....257 A6
Pedler's Cnr CO11 .....86 D2
Pedley Rd RM8 .....334 C3
Peek's Cnr CO6 .....105 D5
Peel Ave SS3 .....368 G8
Peel Cl E4 .....309 B8
Peel Cres CM7 .....127 E3
Peel Dr IG5 .....310 E1
Peel Pl IG5 .....310 E1
Peel Rd Chelmsford CM2 .....232 F4
Woodford E18 .....309 F2
Peel St 5 IP1 .....17 C6
Peel Way RM3 .....314 F1
Peerage Way RM11 .....336 F4
Peers Sq CM2 .....233 A4
Peerswood Rd CO2 .....135 D2
Peewit Ct IP11 .....381 B3
Peewit Cvn Pk IP11 .....381 C2
Peewit Hill IP11 .....381 B3
Peewit Rd IP2 .....16 C3
Pegasus Way
Braintree CM7 .....127 E5
Colchester CO4 .....110 C1
Pegelm Gdns RM11 .....336 F4
Peggotty Cl CM1 .....231 F6
Peggy's Wlk CB11 .....21 E3
Peg Millar's La CM3 .....182 E5
Pegrams Ct CM18 .....223 C5
Pegrams Rd CM18 .....223 C5
Peldon Cres CO5 .....189 E5
Peldon Pavement SS14 .....342 D8
Peldon Rd Abberton CO5 .....189 B4
Great Wigborough CO5 .....189 A3
Harlow CM19 .....223 A6
Pelham Ave IG11 .....352 F4
Pelham Cl CO12 .....90 F2
Pelham Pl SS17 .....360 E4
Pelham Rd Clavering CB11 .....65 C4
Ilford IG1 .....333 D2
Southend-on-S SS2 .....348 E1
Pelham Rd *continued*
Wanstead E18 .....332 B8
Pelham's La 18 CO1 .....135 F7
Pelican Cl IP2 .....16 E3
Pelly Ave CM8 .....212 A8
Pelly Ct CM16 .....267 F8
Pemberton Ave
Ingatestone CM4 .....274 B4
Romford RM2 .....336 B8
Pemberton Ct CM4 .....274 B4
Pemberton Field SS4 .....303 B4
Pemberton Gdns RM6 .....334 E6
Pembrey Way RM12 .....355 D6
Pembridge Ct 5 SS1 .....367 C8
Pembroke Ave
Corringham SS17 .....361 A4
Maldon CM9 .....236 F1
Pembroke Bsns Ctr
SS14 .....320 E2
Pembroke Cl
Billericay CM12 .....297 B5
Colchester CO2 .....136 C3
Erith DA8 .....369 D2
Hornchurch RM11 .....337 A7
Ipswich IP2 .....17 B3
Pembroke Gdns
Clacton-on-S CO15 .....196 E6
Dagenham RM10 .....335 B1
Pembroke Ho SS4 .....347 F7
Pembroke Mews SS13 .....343 C8
Pembroke Par DA8 .....369 C1
Pembroke Pl
Chelmsford CM1 .....232 B7
Sudbury CO10 .....15 D2
Pembroke Rd Erith DA8 .....369 D2
Ilford IG3 .....333 F4
Pembury Rd SS0 .....366 C7
Pendine Cl SS17 .....361 A4
Pendle Cl SS14 .....321 A1
Pendle Dr SS14 .....320 F1
Pendlestone SS7 .....345 C4
Pendleton Rd IP2 .....16 D1
Pendower SS6 .....323 B1
Penerley Rd RM13 .....370 B8
Penfold Rd
Clacton-on-S CO15 .....195 E2
Felixstowe IP11 .....381 E4
Penhaligon Ct 9 CM8 .....184 A2
Penhurst Ave SS2 .....347 F2
Penhurst Rd IG6 .....311 B3
Peniel Acad CM15 .....271 E1
Penistone Wlk RM3 .....314 C4
Penlan Hall La CO6 .....107 B5
Penlow Rd CM18 .....223 D5
Penn Cl Capel St M IP9 .....35 B2
Orsett RM16 .....359 B1
Penn Gdns RM5 .....313 A3
Pennial Rd SS8 .....364 A4
Pennine Rd CM1 .....231 D5
Pennington Cl RM5 .....313 A4
Pennington La CM22,CM24 93 D2
Penningtons CM23 .....145 C5
Penn Mews CM7 .....155 A8
Pennsylvania La CO5 .....186 C5
Penny Cl RM13 .....355 B2
Penny Cnr IP1 .....16 C8
Penny Ct RM13 .....355 B2
Penny Fields CM14 .....316 C6
Penny La Ipswich IP3 .....18 F1
Stanford-le-H SS17 .....360 E4
Penny Mdw IP9 .....35 A1
Pennymead CM20 .....200 A1
Pennypot Cnr CO9 .....103 B6
Pennypot Cotts CO9 .....103 B5
Pennyroyal Cres CM8 .....183 E4
Pennyroyal Gdns IP2 .....16 E4
Penny Royal Rd CM3 .....256 D6
Penny's La CM4 .....274 F8
Pennystone Rd CB11 .....43 E8
Penny Stps 14 SS1 .....367 C7
Penrhyn Ave E17 .....309 A2
Penrhyn Cres E17 .....309 A2
Penrhyn Gr E17 .....309 A2
Penrice Cl CO4 .....136 E6
Penrice Ct CO14 .....144 D1
Penrith Cres RM13 .....355 A7
Penrith Rd Redbridge IG6 311 F4
Romford RM3 .....315 A4
Penrose Mead CM1 .....253 B8
Penshurst CM17 .....200 C3
Penshurst Dr CM3 .....301 D5
Penshurst Pl CM77 .....154 B6
Penshurst Rd IP3 .....18 D4
Penson's La
Chipping Ongar CM5 .....248 D4
Toot Hill CM5 .....248 B3
Penstemon Dr DA10 .....377 E2
Penticton Rd CM7 .....127 D2
Pentire Cl RM14 .....337 E5
Pentire Rd E17 .....309 D2
Pentland Ave
Chelmsford CM1 .....232 A6
Southend-on-S SS3 .....368 C6
Pentlow Dr CO10 .....1 E1
Pentlow Hawke Cl CB9 .....9 B7
Pentlow Hill CO10 .....14 A8
Pentlow Ridge CO10 .....13 F6
Pentlow Way IG9 .....288 E2
Pentney Rd 5 E4 .....287 D1
Penwood Cl CM11 .....297 D6
Penzance Cl
Chelmsford CM1 .....232 E5
Clacton-on-S CO15 .....220 I8
Penzance Gdns RM3 .....315 A4
Penzance Rd
Romford RM3 .....315 A4
Rushmere St A IP5 .....18 F6
Peony Cl CM15 .....294 B3
Peony Ct IG8 .....309 E3
Pepper Alley IG10 .....288 A8
Peppercorn Cl CO4 .....109 F2
Peppercorn Way IP2 .....17 D3
Pepper Hill SG12 .....197 A4
Pepper's Rd CO4 .....82 E1
Pepples La Debden CB10 .....69 A8
Pepples La *continued*
Elder Street CB10 .....45 A1
Pepys Cl Dartford DA1 .....376 A3
Tilbury RM18 .....379 C6
Pepys Ct 4 EN11 .....221 D8
Pepys St CO12 .....91 D5
Percival Gdns RM6 .....334 D5
Percival Rd
Hornchurch RM11 .....336 C5
Kirby-le-S CO13 .....143 D1
Walton-on-t-N CO14 .....144 D2
Percy Cottis Rd SS4 .....325 E3
Percy Rd Ilford IG3 .....334 A4
Romford RM7 .....335 C8
Southend-on-S SS9 .....346 D1
Percy St RM17 .....378 C8
Peregrine Cl
Basildon SS16 .....342 B4
Bishop's Stortford CM23 .....145 D6
Clacton-on-S CO15 .....195 F7
Southend-on-S SS3 .....349 E1
Peregrine Ct CO4 .....136 F8
Peregrine Dr
Chelmsford CM2 .....254 A4
South Benfleet SS7 .....344 C2
Peregrine Gdns SS6 .....323 B3
Peregrine Rd IG6 .....312 C5
Peregrine Wlk 6 RM12 .....355 B6
Peregrin Rd EN9 .....266 A5
Perkins Cl DA9 .....376 F2
Perkins Rd IG2 .....333 D6
Perkins Way IP3 .....17 F1
Perriclose CM1 .....232 D7
Perrin Pl CM2 .....232 A1
Perry Cl RM13 .....354 D3
Perryfield
Great Cornard CO10 .....34 B4
Matching Green CM17 .....202 C2
Perryfield La CM5 .....227 E5
Perryfields Jun & Inf Sch
CM1 .....232 D6
Perry Gn SS14 .....342 B8
Perry Gr DA1 .....376 A3
Perry Hill Chelmsford CM1 232 D3
Lower Nazeing EN9 .....243 F8
Perry Ho RM13 .....354 D3
Perry La CO4 .....84 A4
Perryman Ho IG11 .....352 C4
Perrymans Farm Rd IG2 333 D6
Perry Rd Harlow CM18 .....223 C4
South Benfleet SS7 .....344 B3
Tiptree CO5 .....186 C5
Witham CM8 .....184 B1
Perry Spring
Basildon SS16 .....342 D5
Harlow CM17 .....224 D6
Perry St CM12 .....297 B5
Perry Way Aveley RM15 .....371 C6
Witham CM8 .....184 B1
Persardi Ct CO2 .....163 A7
Pershore Cl IG2 .....333 B6
Pershore End CO3 .....134 E5
Perth Cl CO2 .....136 A1
Perth Ho RM18 .....379 A5
Perth Rd Barking IG11 .....352 D4
Ilford IG1,IG2 .....333 B4
Perth Terr IG2 .....333 C4
Pertwee Cl CO7 .....192 E8
Pertwee Dr
Great Baddow CM2 .....254 F6
South Woodham Ferrers
CM3 .....301 D7
Pertwees Ct CO1 .....136 C6
Pertwee Way CO5 .....163 B2
Pesthouse La CO12 .....116 D3
Petands Ct RM12 .....336 D1
Peterborough Ave RM14 337 F3
Peterborough Gdns IG1 332 E4
Peterborough Way 5
SS14 .....342 F8
Peter Bradley Ct RM9 .....353 F5
Peter Bruff Ave CO16 .....195 C5
Peterfield's La CO9 .....102 F5
Peterhouse Cl IP2 .....16 F2
Peters Cl RM8 .....334 D3
Peters Ct SS15 .....341 B6
Petersfield CM1 .....232 B7
Petersfield Ave RM3 .....314 F5
Petersfield Cl RM3 .....315 A4
Peter's Gr IP9 .....35 A1
Peters Ho CO5 .....158 C2
Peter St CM4 .....297 F8
Peterswood CM18 .....223 D4
Peterswood Inf Sch
CM18 .....223 D4
Peto Ave CO4 .....109 F2
Petrebrook CM2 .....233 A3
Petre Cl Ingatestone CM4 274 A2
West Horndon CM13 .....339 C5
Petrel Way CM2 .....254 C6
Petresfield Way CM13 .....339 C5
Petrolea Cl CO4 .....109 F1
Petronius Way CO4 .....110 B5
Pett Cl RM11 .....336 B2
Petticrow Quays CM0 .....306 C3
Pettit La CM77 .....156 A4
Pettits Bvd RM1 .....313 E2
Pettits Cl RM1 .....313 E1
Pettits La
Doddinghurst CM15 .....272 E2
Romford RM1 .....335 F8
Pettits La N RM1 .....313 E2
Pettit's Pl RM10 .....354 A7
Pettit's Rd RM10 .....354 A7
Pettley Gdns RM7 .....335 D6
Petts La CB10 .....4 E1
Petunia Cres CM1 .....232 F6
Petworth Cl
Great Notley CM77 .....154 B7
Wivenhoe CO7 .....164 C8
Petworth Gdns SS2 .....348 F2
Petworth Way RM12 .....354 F8
Pevensey Ct 10 E18 .....310 A2
Pevensey Dr CO15 .....220 I8
Pevensey Gdns SS5 .....301 F1
Pevensey Way SS13 .....343 B6
Peverel Ave CM3 .....211 C1
Peverel Ho 4 RM10 .....335 A2
Peverells Rd CB10 .....44 D1
Peveril Ct 26 DA2 .....376 B1
Pewsey Cl E4 .....309 A5
Pewterers Ave CM23 .....145 C4
Pharos La CO5 .....218 C6
Pheasant Rd IP2 .....16 E3
Pheasant Rise IP8 .....35 F8
Phelips Rd CM19 .....223 B3
Philan Way RM5 .....313 D4
Philbrick Cres E SS6 .....323 C3
Philbrick Cres W SS6 .....323 C3
Philip Ave
Felixstowe IP11 .....381 B3
Romford RM7 .....335 D3
Philip Cl
Pilgrims Hatch CM15 .....294 C3
Romford RM7 .....335 D3
Walton-on-t-N CO14 .....171 A8
Philip Morant Sch CO3 .....135 B5
Philippa Way RM16 .....374 B2
Philip Rd Ipswich IP2 .....17 C4
Rainham RM13 .....354 E2
Witham CM8 .....211 E8
Philips Cl CM77 .....126 F2
Philips Rd CM77 .....126 F2
Philip Sydney Rd RM20 .....372 D1
Phillida Rd RM3 .....315 A1
Phillip Rd CO7 .....164 B8
Phillips Chase CM7 .....128 A5
Phillips Field Rd CO10 .....34 A5
Phillips Ho RM16 .....374 A8
Philmead Rd SS7 .....344 B2
Philpot End La CM6 .....150 B4
Philpott Ave SS2 .....348 E2
Phoenix Bldgs 1 RM13 .....355 B1
Phoenix Ct Chingford E4 .....309 B7
Colchester CO2 .....136 D5
Phoenix Gr CM2 .....254 A8
Phoenix Prim Sch SS15 .....341 C6
Phoenix Rd IP4 .....18 A7
Phoenix Way SS7 .....345 C7
Picador Ho 1 RM10 .....354 B6
Picardy Manorway DA17 369 B4
Picardy Rd DA17 .....369 A2
Picardy St DA17 .....369 A3
Picasso Way SS3 .....350 A1
Piccotts La CM7 .....126 B8
Pickering Ave E6 .....352 A2
Pickering Ct 13 DA2 .....376 B1
Pickers Way CO15 .....196 E7
Picketts SS8 .....363 D4
Picketts Ave SS9 .....346 E4
Picketts Cl SS9 .....346 E4
Pickford Wlk CO4 .....136 F7
Pick Hill EN9 .....266 A7
Pickpocket La CM77 .....154 D6
Pickwick Ave CM1 .....231 D6
Pickwick Cl SS15 .....341 D7
Pickwick Rd IP2 .....16 E5
Picton Cl SS6 .....323 E1
Picton Gdns SS6 .....323 E1
Pier App CO14 .....171 C8
Pier Ave CO15 .....195 E2
Pierce Glade CO5 .....186 C5
Piercing Hill CM16 .....267 D4
Piercys SS13 .....343 B5
Pier Gap CO15 .....195 F2
Pier Hill SS1 .....367 A7
Pier Rd Felixstowe IP11 .....381 A1
Gravesend DA11 .....378 F1
Greenhithe DA9 .....377 B3
Pierrefitte Way CM7 .....127 E3
Pierrot Stps 5 SS1 .....367 C7
Pigeon Ct E4 .....309 C4
Pigeon's La IP8 .....16 A3
Piggs Corner Complex
RM17 .....373 C3
Pightle The Capel St M IP9 35 B2
Finchingfield CM7 .....72 D6
Haverhill CB9 .....9 A8
Pightle Way CO14 .....171 A7
Pig La CM22 .....146 A3
Pigotts Way CM23 .....145 E5
Pigstye Green Rd CM5 .....251 A8
Pike Way CM16 .....247 A4
Pilborough Way CO3 .....134 E3
Pilcox Hall La CO16 .....140 D8
Pilgrim Cl CM7 .....127 F5
Pilgrims Cl
Billericay CM11 .....297 B2
Great Chesterford CB10 .....3 D2
Pilgrims Hatch CM15 .....293 F4
Southend-on-S SS2 .....348 E1
Pilgrims Ct DA1 .....376 A2
Pilgrims Hatch Prim Sch
CM15 .....294 A3
Pilgrims La RM16 .....372 C5
Pilgrim's La
Pilgrims Hatch, Bentley
CM14 .....293 D5
Pilgrims Hatch CM14 .....293 E4
Pilgrims' Rd DA10 .....377 E3
Pilgrims View DA9 .....377 C1
Pilgrims Way SS7 .....345 F3
Pilgrims Wlk 4 CM11 .....297 B2
Pilgrim Way SS15 .....341 C6
Pilkingtons CM17 .....224 D8
Pilot Cl SS11 .....322 A5
Pilots Pl 6 DA12 .....379 C1
Pimblett Row CM22 .....94 F5
Pimpernel Rd IP2 .....16 F3
Pimpernel Way RM3 .....314 D4
Pinceybrook Rd CM18 .....223 C4
Pincey Mead SS13 .....343 A5
Pincey Rd CM24 .....120 F3
Pincey Rdbt CM24 .....121 A3
Pinchpools Rd CM23 .....93 A3
Pindar Rd EN11 .....221 C7
Pine Ave
Great Dunmow CM6 .....123 B1
Ipswich IP1 .....17 B8
Pine Cl Brantham CO11 .....86 D8
Pine Cl *continued*
Canvey Island SS8 .....363 E3
Great Bentley CO7 .....166 F8
Ingatestone CM4 .....274 C4
Southend-on-S SS9 .....346 B5
7 Wickford SS12 .....321 C5
Pine Cres CM13 .....295 D5
Pinecroft
Brentwood CM13 .....295 B2
Romford RM2 .....336 C7
Pinecroft Gdns CO4 .....110 B3
Pinecroft Rise CO10 .....33 D5
Pine Ct RM14 .....356 B8
Pine Dr CM4 .....274 C4
Pine Gr
Bishop's Stortford CM23 .....146 B6
West Mersea CO5 .....218 B7
Witham CM8 .....184 A5
Pine Ho IP11 .....381 C4
Pinelands CM23 .....118 F1
Pine Lodge SS3 .....368 F8
Pine Rd SS7 .....345 D2
Pines Hill CM24 .....119 D5
Pines Rd CM1 .....231 D5
Pines The Basildon SS15 .....319 C1
Grays RM16 .....373 B5
Hatfield Peverel CM3 .....211 A5
Woodford IG8 .....310 A7
Pinetree Cl IP5 .....18 F7
Pine Tree Ct CO4 .....136 E8
Pine Tree Pl SS4 .....325 E2
Pinetrees SS7 .....345 C3
Pineview Ct E4 .....287 C1
Pine View Manor CM16 .....246 A1
Pine View Rd IP1 .....17 A8
Pinewood SS17 .....375 B3
Pinewood Ave
Rainham RM13 .....355 B1
Southend-on-S SS9 .....346 D5
Pinewood Cl
Clacton-on-S CO15 .....195 E7
Harlow CM17 .....224 C7
Hullbridge SS5 .....301 E2
Kirby Cross CO13 .....170 D6
Pinewood Prim Sch
RM5 .....313 B5
Pinewood Rd RM4 .....313 D6
Pinewood Way CM13 .....295 D4
Pinfolds RM15 .....371 D7
Pinhoe Dr CB9 .....8 C8
Pinkeneys SG8 .....19 D5
Pinkham Dr CM8 .....211 F8
Pink La CM3 .....182 D7
Pinkney Cl CB10 .....44 E2
Pinkuah La CO10 .....13 F6
Pinley Gdns RM9 .....353 B4
Pinmill SS14 .....342 B6
Pin Mill Cl IP2 .....16 C1
Pinmill Rd IP9 .....63 F8
Pinnacles EN9 .....265 E5
Pinners Cl CM0 .....305 F7
Pinner's Cross SG8 .....39 A7
Pintail Cl IP2 .....16 E3
Pintail Cres CM77 .....154 C6
Pintail Rd IG8 .....310 B3
Pintails 4 SS13 .....343 C6
Pintolls CM3 .....301 D6
Pioneer Pl 8 CO1 .....136 A6
Pioneer Sch
Basildon SS14 .....342 C7
Basildon SS14 .....342 C8
Pipchin Rd CM1 .....231 F6
Piperell Way CB9 .....9 A5
Piperell Way Units CB9 .....9 A5
Piper Rd CO3 .....135 B7
Pipers Cl CB9 .....9 C6
Piper's Tye CM2 .....254 D3
Pipers Vale Cl IP3 .....17 E1
Piper's Vale Com Prim Sch
IP3 .....17 F1
Pippin Ct SS11 .....321 F8
Pippins Rd CM0 .....306 C6
Pippins The Glemsford CO10 2 C4
Halstead CO9 .....76 D2
Pipps Hill Rd N CM11 .....320 B3
Pirie Rd CO6 .....108 E3
Pishiobury Dr CM21 .....200 D8
Pitcairn Cl RM7 .....335 A7
Pitcairn Rd IP1 .....16 E8
Pit La CO5 .....186 C6
Pitmans Cl SS1 .....367 A8
Pitmire La CO8 .....55 B6
Pitsea Hall La SS16 .....343 B3
Pitsea Jun & Inf Sch
SS13 .....343 A5
Pitsea Rd SS14 .....343 A5
Pitsea Sta SS13 .....343 B4
Pitsea View Rd CM11 .....320 D4
Pitseaville Gr SS16 .....342 E5
Pitt Ave CM8 .....212 A8
Pitt Chase CM2 .....254 E5
Pittfields SS16 .....341 B5
Pitt Gn CM8 .....212 A8
Pittman Cl CM13 .....317 C5
Pittman Gdns IG1 .....352 C7
Pittman's Field CM20 .....199 F1
Pitts End CO7 .....59 D3
Place Farm Ct CO2 .....136 D2
Place Farm La CM15 .....272 A2
Place Farm Prim Sch CB9 .....8 F8
Pladda Mews SS12 .....321 F5
Plains Farm Cl CO7 .....110 D6
Plains Field CM7 .....128 D1
Plains Rd
Great Totham CM9 .....213 F6
Little Totham CM9 .....214 A6
Plains The E4 .....287 E2
Plain The CM16 .....246 B3
Plaistow Cl SS17 .....360 D2
Plaistow Green Rd CO9 .....103 C5
Plaiters Way CM7 .....128 D3
Plane Tree Cl
Burnham-on-C CM0 .....306 B6
Chelmsford CM2 .....254 B6
Plane View Cl CO16 .....195 B2
Plantaganet Pl 3 EN9 .....265 B6
Plantagenet Gdns RM6 .....334 D4
Plantagenet Pl RM6 .....334 D4
Plantation Cl
Greenhithe DA9 .....376 F1
Saffron Walden CB11 .....43 E6
Plantation Rd CM3 .....209 F1
Planton Way CO7 .....192 E6
Plashet Cl SS17 .....360 D2
Plashet Gdns CM13 .....317 A6
Plashets CM22 .....173 D1
Plashetts SS14 .....342 D7
Plas Newydd SS1 .....367 E6
Plas Newydd Cl SS1 .....367 E6
Platford Gn RM11 .....336 E7
Platinum Ct RM7 .....335 B8
Platters Cl IP3 .....38 B7
Platters Rd IP11 .....381 C2
Plaw Hatch Cl CM23 .....146 B8
Plaw Hatch Cnr CM23 .....146 D8
Players Ct CM6 .....152 C6
Playfield Ave RM5 .....313 C2
Playfield Rd IP9 .....35 B1
Playford Ct 2 CO10 .....33 E8
Playford Rd IP4 .....18 E8
Playhouse Sq CM20 .....223 C8
Playle Chase CM9 .....213 B4
Plaza Way SS1 .....367 D8
Pleasant Ct SS1 .....367 B7
Pleasant Dr CM12 .....296 E3
Pleasant Mews SS1 .....367 B7
Pleasant Rd
Bishop's Stortford CM23 .....145 E8
Southend-on-S SS1 .....367 B7
Pleasant Row 13 IP4 .....17 D5
Pleasants Mews CO5 .....218 C6
Pleasant Terr SS9 .....365 E8
Pleasant Valley CB11 .....43 D7
Pleasant View DA8 .....369 E1
Pleshey Cl
Southend-on-S SS1 .....367 F8
6 Wickford SS12 .....321 E6
Pleshey Rd CM3 .....179 B5
Plotlands Mus* SS16 .....340 E3
Plotlands Nature Reserve*
SS16 .....340 E3
Plotters Ct 7 EN11 .....221 D8
Plough Cnr CO16 .....168 C4
Plough Dr CO3 .....135 A5
Plough La CO10 .....33 D7
Ploughmans Cl CM23 .....145 C5
Ploughmans Headland
CO3 .....134 E5
Ploughmans La CM77 .....154 C8
Plough Rd CO7 .....166 E6
Plough Rise RM14 .....337 E4
Plough St IP3 .....17 E4
Plover Cl CO13 .....170 E6
Plover Gdns RM14 .....337 F3
Plover Rd IP2 .....16 E2
Plovers Mead CM15 .....272 D3
Plovers The CM0 .....262 D7
Plover Wlk CM2 .....254 B5
Plowmans SS6 .....323 E4
Plowman Way RM8 .....334 C3
Plowright Ho 5 CO1 .....135 E8
Ployters Rd CM18 .....223 C4
Plumberow SS15 .....341 E6
Plumberow Ave SS5 .....324 E7
Plumberow Mount Ave
SS5 .....324 E8
Plumberow Prim Sch
SS5 .....324 E7
Plume Ave
Colchester CO3 .....135 A4
Maldon CM9 .....236 F1
Plume Sch (Lower) CM9 237 A2
Plume Sch (Upper) CM9 236 F2
Plumleys SS13 .....343 B7
Plummers Rd CO6 .....107 E7
Plumpton Ave RM12 .....336 F1
Plumpton Rd EN11 .....221 C8
Plumptre La CM3 .....256 D5
Plums La CM7 .....99 E4
Plum St CO10 .....2 A6
Plumtree Ave CM2 .....254 F6
Plumtree Cl RM10 .....354 C6
Plumtree Mead IG10 .....289 A6
Plymouth Ho 10 IG11 .....353 A5
Plymouth Rd
Chelmsford CM1 .....232 E5
Clacton-on-S CO15 .....220 J8
Felixstowe IP11 .....381 D6
Grays RM16 .....372 C2
Plymtree SS1 .....349 C1
Pochard Way CM77 .....154 C5
Pocklington Cl CM2 .....233 A3
Pod's Brook Rd CM7 .....127 D2
Pods La CM77 .....126 D2
Point Cl SS8 .....364 F3
Point Clear Bay Holiday Cvn
Pk CO16 .....192 F3
Point Clear Rd CO16 .....193 D3
Point Rd SS8 .....364 F3
Pointwell La CO6 .....158 A8
Pole Barn La CO13 .....170 F5
Polecat Rd CM77 .....155 F5
Polegate Cotts RM17 .....377 E8
Pole Hill Rd E4 .....287 C2
Pole La CM8 .....155 C3
Polesworth Rd RM9 .....353 D5
Poley Rd SS17 .....360 C1
Police Hos RM13 .....355 C2
Pollard Cl IG7 .....312 A5
Pollard Ct IP2 .....16 D2
Pollard Hatch CM19 .....223 B5
Pollards Cl Loughton IG10 288 C4
Rochford SS4 .....325 F2
Pollards Ct SS4 .....325 E2
Pollard's Gn CM2 .....232 F2
Pollards Villas CM7 .....99 D2
Pollard Wlk CO16 .....195 C5
Polley Cl CO13 .....170 E7
Polstead Cl SS6 .....323 A3
Polsteads SS16 .....342 E3

Q

Queen's Gate Mews
CM12 . . . . .296 F5
Queens Gdns
Rainham RM13 . . . . .354 D3
Upminster RM14 . . . . .337 F5
Queen's Gdns CM7 . . . . . .127 B7
Queen's Grove Rd E4 . . . .287 D1
Queen's Head Rd CO4 . . . .82 E3
Queen's Ho CO13 . . . . . . .170 F4
Queensland Ave SS4 . . . .347 F7
Queensland Cres CM1 . . .231 E5
Queensland Dr CO2 . . . . .136 A1
Queens Lodge SS7 . . . . . .345 C3
Queensmere SS7 . . . . . . .345 B5
Queens Mews CO5 . . . . . .218 B6
Queens Park Ave CM2 . . .297 B5
Queen's Park Ct CM12 . . .296 F5
Queens Pk
Basildon, Crays Hill CM11 . .320 B4
Basildon, Steeple View
SS15 . . . . .319 C1
Braintree CM7 . . . . .127 F5
Loughton IG10 . . . . .288 F6
North Weald Bassett CM16 .247 B6
Rayleigh SS6 . . . . .323 E2
Southend-on-S,Chalkwell
SS9 . . . . .365 F8
Southend-on-S,Clifftown
SS1 . . . . .366 F8
Sudbury CO10 . . . . .33 E8
Queen's Rd Barking IG11 .352 C6
Brentwood CM14 . . . . .316 D8
Buckhurst Hill IG9 . . . . .310 C8
Burnham-on-C CM0 . . . . . .306 C3
Chelmsford CM2 . . . . .232 D2
Clacton-on-S CO15 . . . . . . .195 D1
Colchester CO3 . . . . .135 C6
Earls Colne CO6 . . . . .105 B7
Felixstowe IP11 . . . . .381 E4
Frinton-on-S CO13 . . . . . . .170 F4
Harwich CO12 . . . . .91 A2
South Benfleet SS7 . . . . . . .344 D2
West Bergholt CO6 . . . . . . .108 D3
Wivenhoe CO7 . . . . .164 C8
Queens Sq CB9 . . . . .9 A8
Queen's Sq IP3 . . . . .18 B2
Queen St
Brentwood CM14 . . . . .316 C5
Brightlingsea CO7 . . . . .192 F6
Castle Hedingham CO9 . . . . .51 E3
Chelmsford CM2 . . . . .232 A3
Coggeshall CO6 . . . . .131 A2
Colchester CO1 . . . . .135 F7
Felixstowe IP11 . . . . .381 C6
Fyfield CM5 . . . . .227 E2
Gravesend DA12 . . . . .379 B1
Great Oakley CO12 . . . . . . .116 C4
Haverhill CB9 . . . . .9 A8
Ipswich IP1 . . . . .17 C5
Maldon CM9 . . . . .237 A2
Romford RM7 . . . . .335 D5
Sible Hedingham CO9 . . . . . .75 F6
Southminster CM0 . . . . . . .284 C4
Queens Terr CO10 . . . . . . .34 A7
Queenstown Gdns RM13 .354 F2
Queensway
Chipping Ongar CM5 . . . . . .248 F5
Clacton-on-S CO15 . . . . . . .196 D5
Great Cornard CO10 . . . . . . .34 B5
Haverhill CB9 . . . . .8 E8
Lawford CO11 . . . . .86 C4
Southend-on-S SS1 . . . . . . .367 B8
Tiptree CO5 . . . . .186 C6
Queen's Way IP3 . . . . .18 B3
Queens Way SS8 . . . . . . .363 D3
Queensway Lodge SS7 . . .367 B7
Queens Wlk E4 . . . . .287 D1
Queenswood Ave
Brentwood CM13 . . . . .295 D4
Chingford E17 . . . . .309 C7
Queenswood Gdns E11 . . .332 B2
Queen Victoria Dr IP9 . . . .91 B8
Quendon Dr EN9 . . . . . . .265 D6
Quendon Pl 17 CB9 . . . . . . .9 B8
Quendon Rd SS14 . . . . . .342 E8
Quendon Way CO13 . . . . .171 A6
Quennell Way CM12 . . . . .295 D2
Quentin Cl IP1 . . . . .16 E8
Quickset Rd CB11 . . . . . . .20 C5
Quickside Hill CM11 . . . . . .41 E2
Quilp Dr CM1 . . . . .231 F7
Quilter Dr IP8 . . . . .16 C3
Quilter Rd IP11 . . . . .381 F4
Quilters Cl Basildon SS14 .342 D8
Holland-on-S CO15 . . . . . . .196 F6
Quilters Dr CM12 . . . . . . .319 A8
Quilters Inf & Jun Schs
CM12 . . . . .297 A1
Quilters Straight SS14 . . .342 E8
Quince Cl CO11 . . . . .60 D1
Quince Tree Cl RM15 . . . .357 C1
Quinion Cl CM1 . . . . .231 D7
Quintons Cnr CO7 . . . . . .137 D5
Quintons La IP11 . . . . .381 F7
Quintons Rd CO7 . . . . .59 D4
Quorn Gdns SS9 . . . . .346 A1
Quorn The CM4 . . . . .274 A3

R

R A Butler Jun & Inf Schs
CB11 . . . . .22 E1
Rachael Clarke Cl SS4 . . . .360 E4
Rachael Ct CM2 . . . . .232 B1
Rachel Cl IG6 . . . . .156 F4
Rachel Cl IG6 . . . . .333 D8
Rachel Ct 11 IP4 . . . . .17 D6
Rackenford SS3 . . . . .368 D8

Radbourne Cres E17 . . . . .309 D1
Radburn Cl CM18 . . . . . . .224 A4
Radburn Pl DA10 . . . . . . .377 E2
Radcliffe Dr IP2 . . . . .16 D2
Radford Bsns Ctr CM12 . . .296 F3
Radford Cres CM12 . . . . . .297 A3
Radford Cres CM12 . . . . . .297 A3
Radford Ho CM12 . . . . . . .297 B3
Radford Way
Barking IG11 . . . . .352 F2
Billericay CM12 . . . . .297 A3
Radiator Rd CO10 . . . . . . .34 A5
Radley Ave IG3 . . . . .353 F4
Radley Cl IG7 . . . . .311 E6
Radley Green Rd CM4,
CM5 . . . . .251 C7
Radley's La E18 . . . . .310 A1
Radleys Mead RM10 . . . . .354 B6
Radnor Cres IG4 . . . . .332 A6
Radnor Rd SS4 . . . . .303 C1
Radstock Ho 11 RM3 . . . . .314 D5
Radstocks CM12 . . . . .297 B3
Radwinter Ave SS12 . . . . .321 D6
Radwinter Prim Sch CB10 .45 F7
Radwinter Rd Ashdon CB10 .24 B7
Saffron Walden CB10 . . . . . .23 B1
Sewards End CB10 . . . . .23 F1
Raeburn Cl CO13 . . . . . . .170 F7
Raeburn Rd IP3 . . . . .18 A1
Raeburn Rd S CM23 . . . . . .17 F1
Raglan Mews CO15 . . . . . .195 C3
Raglan Rd CO13 . . . . .171 A5
Ragley Cl CM7 . . . . .154 B6
Rahn Rd CM16 . . . . .268 A8
Raider Cl RM7 . . . . .313 B2
Raile Wlk CO10 . . . . .15 D8
Railey Rd CB11 . . . . .43 E8
Railway App
Basildon SS15 . . . . .341 A6
Felixstowe IP11 . . . . .381 C6
Railway Cotts Ilford IG6 . .333 D8
Redbridge IG6 . . . . .311 D2
Railway Pl
Belvedere DA17 . . . . .369 A3
13 Gravesend DA11 . . . . . .379 B1
Railway Sq
Brentwood CM14 . . . . .316 C7
Chelmsford CM1 . . . . .232 A3
Railway St Braintree CM7 .128 A3
Chelmsford CM1 . . . . .232 A3
Dagenham RM9 . . . . .334 C4
Manningtree CO11 . . . . .86 D4
Northfleet DA11 . . . . .378 A2
Railway Terr
Chingford E17 . . . . .309 C2
Clacton-on-S CO15 . . . . . . .195 F3
11 Manningtree CO11 . . . . .86 D4
Southend-on-S SS2 . . . . . . .348 A3
Rainbow Ave SS8 . . . . . . .364 C4
Rainbow Ct CO12 . . . . .91 D4
Rainbow La SS17 . . . . . . .360 F1
Rainbow Mead SS4 . . . . . .211 A5
Rainbow Mews CM9 . . . . .236 F5
Rainbow Rd
Canvey Island SS8 . . . . . . .364 C4
Grays RM16 . . . . .372 C2
Sheering CM17 . . . . .201 E3
West Mersea CO5 . . . . .218 D6
Rainbow Way CO6 . . . . . . .77 F1
Raine Ave E4 . . . . .8 D8
Rainham Rd RM13 . . . . . . .354 F3
Rainham Rd N RM10 . . . . .335 B2
Rainham Rd S RM10 . . . . .336 C2
Rainham Sta RM13 . . . . . .355 A1
Rainham Village Prim Sch
RM13 . . . . .355 A1
Rainham Way CO13 . . . . . .171 B6
Rainsborowe Rd CO2 . . . .135 C4
Rainsford Ave CM1 . . . . . .231 F7
Rainsford La CM1 . . . . . . .231 F7
Rainsford Rd
Chelmsford CM1 . . . . .231 F7
Stansted Mountfitchet
CM24 . . . . .119 E8
Rainsford Way RM12 . . . . .336 A3
Raleigh Dr SS15 . . . . .341 D5
Rambler Cl CO3 . . . . .134 D6
Ramblers Way CM0 . . . . . .306 D4
Ram Gorse CM20 . . . . . . .199 F2
Rampart Cotts CO6 . . . . . .109 B7
Rampart Cl CO6 . . . . .109 B7
Rampart St SS3 . . . . .368 G6
Ramparts The SS6 . . . . . .323 F2
Rampart Terr SS3 . . . . . . .368 G6
Ramplings Ave CO15 . . . . .195 E5
Rampton Cl E4 . . . . .309 A7
Ramsay Dr SS16 . . . . .342 E3
Ramsay Gdns RM3 . . . . . .314 C2
Ramsay Rd E7 . . . . .332 A1
Ramsden Cl CO15 . . . . . . .196 A5
Ramsden Dr RM5 . . . . . . .313 A3
Ramsden Park Rd CM11 .298 D1
Ramsden View Rd SS12 . . .320 F6

Rana Dr CM7 . . . . .127 F4
Randall Cl CM6 . . . . .123 D1
Randall Cl RM13 . . . . .355 B2
Randall Dr RM12 . . . . .355 D8
Randalls Dr CM13 . . . . . . .295 E3
Randolph Ave CM7 . . . . . . .73 C6
Randolph Cl Ipswich IP4 .148 C5
Maldon CM9 . . . . .258 F8
Southend-on-S SS9 . . . . . . .346 E3
Randolph Gr RM6 . . . . . . .334 C6
Rands Rd DM6 . . . . .176 F8
Rands Way IP3 . . . . .38 B6
Randolph Terr CM1 . . . . . .232 D3
Randway SS6 . . . . .323 D1
Randwell Cl IP4 . . . . .18 B5
Ranelagh Ct IP11 . . . . .381 E4
Ranelagh Gdns Ilford IG1 .333 A3
Redbridge IG1 . . . . .332 F3
Wanstead E11 . . . . .332 C6
Ranelagh Prim Sch IG1 . . .333 A2
Ranelagh Rd
Felixstowe IP11 . . . . .381 E4
Ipswich IP2 . . . . .17 A5
Wallend E6 . . . . .352 A3
Ranger's Rd
Buckhurst Hill E4,IG9,IG10 .288 A2
Chingford E4 . . . . .287 F2
Ranger Wlk CO2 . . . . .136 B3
Rangoon Cl CO2 . . . . .135 B1
Ransome Cl IP8 . . . . .16 A6
Ransome Cres IP3 . . . . . . .18 B2
Ransome Rd IP3 . . . . .18 B2
Ransomes Europark IP3 .284 E8
Ransomes Way
Chelmsford CM1 . . . . .232 B4
Ipswich IP3 . . . . .38 D8
Ransom Rd CO5 . . . . .186 C5
Rantree Fold SS16 . . . . . . .341 F4
Ranulf Cl CM17 . . . . .200 C6
Ranulph Way CM3 . . . . . . .211 B3
Ranworth Ave EN11 . . . . . .197 B2
Raphael Ave
Romford RM1 . . . . .335 F8
Tilbury RM18 . . . . .379 B7
Raphael Dr
Chelmsford CM1 . . . . .232 F7
Southend-on-S SS3 . . . . . . .368 A5
Raphael Ind Sch RM11 . . .336 A5
Raphaels SS14 . . . . .341 E6
Raphaels Ct RM1 . . . . . . .335 F7
Rapier Cl RM19 . . . . .371 A2
Rapier St IP2 . . . . .17 C3
Ratcliffe Cl
Frinton-on-S CO13 . . . . . . .170 F5
Kelvedon CO5 . . . . .158 B2
Ratcliffe Rd CO3 . . . . .134 E6
Rat Hill IP9 . . . . .63 F2
Rat La SS6 . . . . .345 C8
Ratsborough Chase CM0 .284 C2
Ratt's La IG10 . . . . .266 B1
Rattwick Dr SS8 . . . . .364 F3
Ratty's La EN11 . . . . .221 D6
Ravel Ave CM5 . . . . .288 A7
Ravel Gdns RM15 . . . . . . .371 C7
Ravel Rd RM15 . . . . .371 D7
Raven Cl CM12 . . . . .296 F4
Raven Cres CM12 . . . . . . .296 F4
Ravencroft RM16 . . . . . . .374 B4
Ravendale Way SS3 . . . . . .349 D1
Raven Dr SS7 . . . . .344 C2
Ravenings Par IG3 . . . . . . .334 A3
Raven La CM12 . . . . .296 F4
Ravenoak Way IG7 . . . . . .311 E5
Raven Rd E18 . . . . .310 C1
Ravens Ave CO5 . . . . .76 F1
Ravensbourne Cres RM3 .336 E8
Ravensbourne Dr CM0 . . .231 E2
Ravensbourne Gdns IG5 .311 B2
Ravensbourne Sch RM3 .314 D2
Ravenscourt Cl RM12 . . . .294 D1
Ravenscourt Cl RM12 . . . .336 E1
Ravenscourt Dr
Basildon SS16 . . . . .342 E5
Hornchurch RM12 . . . . .336 E1
Ravenscourt Gr RM12 . . . .336 E2
Ravens Cres CM6 . . . . . . .152 E6
Ravenscroft Prim Sch
CO16 . . . . .195 B4
Ravens Ct SS1 . . . . .366 F7
Ravensdale Basildon SS16 .342 B4
Clacton-on-S CO15 . . . . . . .195 F6
Ravensfield Basildon SS16 .342 F6
Dagenham RM9 . . . . .353 D8
Ravensmere CM16 . . . . . . .246 A1
Ravenswood 11 CO1 . . . . .136 A6
Ravenswood Ave IP3 . . . . .38 C8
Ravenswood Chase SS4 . . .347 F7
Ravenswood Cres RM5 . . .313 B5
Ravenswood Com Prim Sch
IP3 .38 C8
Ravenswood Way IP3 . . . . .38 B8
Raven Way CO4 . . . . .109 E4
Rawden Cl CO12 . . . . .91 B4
Rawdon Dr RM11 . . . . .221 A5
Rawlings Cres CO4 . . . . . .110 B5
Rawlyn Cl RM16 . . . . .372 C1
Rawreth Gdns SS11 . . . . . .300 E1
Rawreth La SS11 . . . . .323 B6
Rawstron Rd CO3 . . . . . . .135 C7
Ray Ave CO12 . . . . .91 A3
Rayburne Ct IG9 . . . . .288 C1
Rayburn Rd RM11 . . . . . . .337 A4
Ray Cl Canvey Island SS8 .364 A2
Clacton-on-S SS9 . . . . .346 B1
Raycliff Ave CO15 . . . . . . .195 E7
Ray Ct IG8 . . . . .310 D4
Raydons Gdns RM9 . . . . . .353 E7
Raydons Rd RM9 . . . . .353 E7
Raydon Way CO10 . . . . . . .34 C6
Rayfield CM16 . . . . .246 A2
Ray Gdns IG11 . . . . .353 A3
Rayhaven CO12 . . . . .90 D2
Ray Ho CO5 . . . . .218 D7

Ray La Harwich CO12 . . . . .90 E5
Ramsey CO12 . . . . .90 A3
Rayleigh Ave
Rayleigh SS9 . . . . .346 B8
Southend-on-S SS0 . . . . . . .347 E1
Rayleigh Cl
Braintree CM7 . . . . .128 C4
Brentwood CM13 . . . . .295 C3
Colchester CO4 . . . . .110 B1
Rayleigh Downs Rd SS6 .346 B7
Rayleigh Dr SS9 . . . . .346 D3
Rayleigh Ho SS6 . . . . .323 C1
Rayleigh Mans CO2 . . . . . .135 C5
Rayleigh Par 8 CM3 . . . . .295 C3
Rayleigh Prim Sch SS6 . . .323 C2
Rayleigh Rd
Brentwood CM13 . . . . .295 D3
Hutton CM13 . . . . .295 C3
Stanford-le-H SS17 . . . . . . .360 B1
Thundersley SS7 . . . . .345 C6
Woodford IG8 . . . . .310 B5
Rayleigh Sta SS6 . . . . .323 C3
Rayleighs The CO2 . . . . . .135 C5
Rayleys La CM16 . . . . .247 A8
Ray Lodge Prim Sch
IG8 . . . . .310 D4
Ray Lodge Rd IG8 . . . . . . .310 D4
Ray Mead CM3 . . . . .207 F7
Rayment Ave SS8 . . . . . . .364 D3
Rayments Bglws CB10 . . . .45 E3
Raymond Ave E18 . . . . . . .309 F1
Raymond Gdns IG7 . . . . . .312 B7
Raymond Rd CM3 . . . . . . .301 C7
Raymonds Dr SS7 . . . . . . .344 F6
Raymouth Ho CO2 . . . . . . .135 D2
Rayne Prim Sch CM7 . . . .126 F2
Rayne Rd CM7 . . . . .127 D3
Rayner Rd CO2 . . . . .135 E4
Rayners Cl DA11 . . . . .378 B1
Rayner Way CO9 . . . . .76 E1
Raynes Ave E11 . . . . .332 C4
Raynham Cl CM23 . . . . . . .146 C7
Raynham Rd CM23 . . . . . .146 B8
Raynhams CB10 . . . . .22 D1
Ray Rd RM5 . . . . .313 B5
Rayside SS14 . . . . .342 C5
Ray The CM1 . . . . .232 E5
Ray Wlk SS9 . . . . .346 B1
Reaburn Cl CM12 . . . . . . .232 E6
Read Cl SS5 . . . . .325 A4
Read Ct EN9 . . . . .266 A6
Reader's Cnr CM2 . . . . . . .62 D5
Readers Ct CM2 . . . . .232 A3
Reading Cl SS16 . . . . .340 F5
Reading Rd IP4 . . . . .18 B7
Readings The CM18 . . . . . .223 F5
Reads Cl IG1 . . . . .333 B3
Reaper Rd CO3 . . . . .135 A5
Rebecca Gdns CM8 . . . . . .156 E4
Rebecca Meade CM6 . . . .122 F8
Rebels La SS3 . . . . .348 F3
Rebow Rd Harwich CO12 . .91 A2
Wivenhoe CO7 . . . . .164 B8
Rebow St CO1 . . . . .136 B6
Recketts Cl CO15 . . . . .196 B4
Recreation Ave
Corringham SS17 . . . . .361 C4
Romford, Harold Wood
RM3 . . . . .314 F1
Romford RM7 . . . . .335 C6
Southend-on-S SS9 . . . . . . .346 C7
Recreation Cl IP11 . . . . . . .381 D6
Recreation Cl SS9 . . . . . . .346 F2
Recreation Ground
CM16 . . . . .119 E6
Recreation La IP11 . . . . . . .341 D6
Recreation Rd
Clacton-on-S CO15 . . . . . . .195 D3
Colchester CO1 . . . . .136 C5
Sible Hedingham CO9 . . . . . .8 F7
Recreation Way
Brightlingsea CO7 . . . . .192 F7
Ipswich IP3 . . . . .18 B2
Recreation Wlk
Great Cornard CO10 . . . . . . .34 B5
Ramsden Heath CM11 . . . . .298 C5
Rectory Ave SS4 . . . . .325 C6
Rectory Chase
Doddinghurst CM15 . . . . . .272 C2
Little Warley CM13 . . . . . . .338 C7
Southend-on-S SS2 . . . . . . .348 E1
Rectory Cl
Bishop's Stortford CM23 . .146 D3
Chingford E4 . . . . .309 A7
Colchester CO4 . . . . .109 E2
Glemsford CO10 . . . . .2 B8
Hadleigh SS7 . . . . .345 E3
Hunsdonbury SG12 . . . . . . .197 B8
Ingatestone CM4 . . . . .274 B4
Littlebury JB11 . . . . .21 F4
Little Waltham CM3 . . . . . .208 C6
Stock CM4 . . . . .273 C2
Rectory Cres E11 . . . . .332 C5
Rectory Ct Basildon SS15 .340 C7
Grays RM17 . . . . .178 C8
Loughton IG10 . . . . .289 A7
Woodford E18 . . . . .309 F2
Rectory Dr CM23 . . . . .118 D6
Rectory Field
Chelmondiston IP9 . . . . .63 E7
Harlow CM19 . . . . .200 C1
Rectory Garth SS6 . . . . . . .323 D2
Rectory Gdns
Basildon SS15 . . . . .343 C6
Upminster RM14 . . . . .337 D2
Rectory Gr
Southend-on-S SS9 . . . . . . .346 E3
Wickford SS11 . . . . .321 F7
Rectory Hill
East Bergholt CO7 . . . . .59 C1
Stoke-by-N CO6 . . . . .57 A4
Wivenhoe CO7 . . . . .137 C1

Rectory La Abberton CO5 .163 A3
Ashdon CB10 . . . . .6 A1
Brantham CO11 . . . . .60 E1
Chelmsford CM1 . . . . .232 B4
Farnham CM23 . . . . .118 C6
Great Leighs CM3 . . . . .180 D7
Harlow CM19 . . . . .200 A2
Ingrave CM13 . . . . .317 E3
Latchingdon CM3 . . . . .282 B3
Loughton IG10 . . . . .289 B6
Ramsey CO12 . . . . .90 A1
Rettendon SS11 . . . . .300 E6
Sible Hedingham CO9 . . . . . .51 D1
Stanford-le-H SS17 . . . . . . .184 A6
Woodham Mortimer CM9 . . .257 F6
Rectory Mdw CM7 . . . . . . .129 C2
Rectory Mdws CO9 . . . . . . .51 D1
Rectory Park Dr SS13 . . . .343 B5
Rectory Rd Aldham CO6 . .132 F7
Basildon SS13 . . . . .343 C6
Copford CO6 . . . . .133 C1
Dagenham RM10 . . . . .354 B5
Frating CO7 . . . . .138 F1
Grays RM17 . . . . .373 D2
Great Henny CO10 . . . . .33 E4
Great Holland CO13 . . . . . .170 A3
Hadleigh SS7 . . . . .345 E3
Harkstead IP9 . . . . .63 C2
Hockley SS5 . . . . .325 B4
Ipswich IP2 . . . . .17 C4
Langham CO4 . . . . .83 F7
Little Bentley CO7 . . . . .139 E8
Little Burstead CM12 . . . . . .319 A2
Little Ilford E12 . . . . .352 A7
Little Oakley CO12 . . . . .117 A7
North Fambridge CM3 . . . . .303 A8
Orsett RM16 . . . . .374 B8
Rowhedge CO5 . . . . .163 E8
Sible Hedingham CO9 . . . . . .51 D1
Stanford-le-H SS17 . . . . . . .360 C1
Stisted CM7 . . . . .129 E7
Tiptree CO5 . . . . .186 C5
Tollesbury CM9 . . . . .201 F7
Tolleshunt Knights CM9 . . .187 C1
Weeley Heath CO16 . . . . . .167 F3
West Tilbury RM18 . . . . . . .379 D8
Wivenhoe CO7 . . . . .137 C2
Woodham Walter CM9 . . . . .235 D3
Wrabness CO11 . . . . .89 A3
Writtle CM1 . . . . .253 B8
Rectory Terr Hockley SS5 .325 B4
Stanford-le-H SS17 . . . . . . .360 C1
Rectory Wood CM20 . . . . .199 C1
Red Barn La CO12 . . . . . . .116 B2
Red Barn Rd CO7 . . . . . . .192 F8
Redbrick Row CM23 . . . . . .173 B8
Redbridge Coll RM6 . . . . . .334 B6
Redbridge Ct IG4 . . . . .332 D5
Redbridge Ent Ctr IG1 . . . .333 C2
Redbridge Foyer IG1 . . . . .333 C2
Redbridge Inf Sch IG4 . . . .332 E6
Redbridge Jun Sch IG4 . . .332 E6
Redbridge La E IG4 . . . . . .332 C5
Redbridge La W E11 . . . . . .332 C5
Redbridge Rd IG3 . . . . .7 C6
Redbridge Sports Ctr
IG6 . . . . .311 D2
Redbridge Sta IG4 . . . . . . .332 D5
Redbrook Ct SS7 . . . . .375 A3
Redbury Cl RM13 . . . . .355 C3
Redcar Rd RM3 . . . . .314 F5
Redcliff Dr SS0 . . . . .365 F8
Redcliffe Gdns CM24 . . . . .119 E6
Redcliffe Rd 14 CM2 . . . . . .232 B1
Redcliff Rd CO15 . . . . .195 D6
Red Cotts CM22 . . . . .201 D8
Reddells Cl 3 CO16 . . . . . . .33 F8
Redden Court Comp Sch
RM3 . . . . .336 F8
Redden Court Rd RM3 . . . .336 F8
Reddings Cl CB11 . . . . .43 D7
Reddings Ct SS11 . . . . . . .300 E8
Rede Way CO10 . . . . .34 C6
Redesdale Gdns RM12 . . . .314 D1
Redfern Gdns RM2 . . . . . . .314 D1
Redgate La CB10 . . . . .37 D5
Redgates Cl SS2 . . . . .322 A8
Redgates Pl CM2 . . . . .232 D4
Redgrave Rd SS16 . . . . . . .342 E4
Redgrove Ho CM16 . . . . . .246 A2
Redhills Rd CM3 . . . . .301 E8
Redhouse La CO4 . . . . .82 D2
Red House Ct
Great Cornard CO10 . . . . . . .34 A4
Sudbury CO10 . . . . .33 E7
Redif Ho RM10 . . . . .354 B8
Redinge The CM11 . . . . . . .319 D7
Red La IP9 . . . . .60 E8
Red Lion Cl SS17 . . . . .360 D4
Red Lion Cres CM7 . . . . . .224 C6
Red Lion La CM7 . . . . .123 A2
Red Lion La CM17 . . . . . . .201 C1
Red Lion Yd 17 CO1 . . . . . .135 F7
Redman Ind Est RM18 .380 A8
Redmayne Dr CM2 . . . . . . .253 F8
Redmill CO3 . . . . .134 D4
Red Oaks Mead CM16 . . . .267 D2
Redoubt Ct CO14 . . . . .171 B8
Redo Ho 2 E12 . . . . .352 A7
Red Rd CM14 . . . . .316 B6
Redricks La CM20 . . . . . . .199 E5
Redriff Rd RM7 . . . . .313 B1
Redrose La CM4 . . . . .252 A1
Redrose Wlk CO16 . . . . . .195 C4
Redruth Cl CM1 . . . . .205 D6
Redruth Ho CO4 . . . . .110 D2
Redruth Rd RM3 . . . . .314 F5
Redruth Wlk CM1 . . . . . . .205 D6
Redshank Cl CB9 . . . . .9 C7
Redshank Cres CM3 . . . . .279 D1
Redshank Dr CM9 . . . . . . .237 C5
Red Sleeve 58 IP9 . . . . .35 A1
Redstock Rd SS2 . . . . .348 A2
Redvers Cl CM23 . . . . .119 A2
Redwing Cl IP2 . . . . .16 D3
Redwing Ct RM3 . . . . .314 D3
Redwing Dr CM11 . . . . . . .319 C8
Redwood Chase RM15 . . . .357 D1
Redwood Cl
Colchester CO4 . . . . .110 E1
Witham CM8 . . . . .184 A5
Woodford IG9 . . . . .310 B8
Redwood Ct
2 Colchester CO4 . . . . . . .136 E8
Dartford DL1 . . . . .376 A1
Redwood Dr
Basildon SS15 . . . . .319 D1
Writtle CM1 . . . . .230 F1
Redwood Gdns
Chingford E4 . . . . .287 B3
Redbridge IG7 . . . . .312 A5
Redwoods The SS8 . . . . . .342 C1
Reed Cl CO16 . . . . .195 C5
Reede Gdns RM10 . . . . . . .354 B7
Reede Rd RM10 . . . . .354 B6
Reede Way RM10 . . . . .354 B6
Reed Hall Ave CO2 . . . . . .135 E3
Reedings Jun Sch CM21 .172 E3
Reedland Way IP11 . . . . . . .381 B5
Reed Mans 7 E11 . . . . .332 A5
Reed Pond Wlk
Basildon SS16 . . . . .341 B4
Romford RM2 . . . . .313 F1
Reeds La CB9 . . . . .9 A8
Reeds Way SS12 . . . . .321 C8
Ree Lane Cotts IG10 . . . . .289 A7
Reesland Ct E12 . . . . .352 A6
Reeves Cl Basildon SS14 .340 F4
Stondon Massey CM15 . . . .272 B5
Reeves La CM19 . . . . .222 D5
Reeves Way CM3 . . . . .301 E7
Refinery Rd CO12 . . . . .90 E5
Regal Cl CM2 . . . . .254 D8
Regan Cl SS17 . . . . .360 E4
Regarder Rd IG7 . . . . .312 B5
Regarth Ave RM1 . . . . .335 E5
Regatta Ct SS9 . . . . .365 F8
Regency Cl
Bishop's Stortford CM23 . . .145 E7
Chelmsford CM2 . . . . .232 D3
Chigwell IG2 . . . . .311 C5
Rochford SS4 . . . . .325 E2
Wickford SS11 . . . . .299 D2
Regency Ct 4
Brentwood CM14 . . . . .316 C8
Harlow CM18 . . . . .224 A5
Heybridge CM9 . . . . .237 A5
Hockley SS5 . . . . .324 E6
Ipswich IP3 . . . . .17 F5
Regency Gdns RM11 . . . . .336 C4
Regency Gn
Colchester CO2 . . . . .135 A4
Southend-on-S SS2 . . . . . . .347 F3
Regency Lodge
1 Buckhurst Hill IG9 . . . . .310 D8
Clacton-on-S CO15 . . . . . . .195 E5
Regent Cl
Brightlingsea CO7 . . . . .192 F8
Grays RM16 . . . . .373 C4
Rayleigh SS6 . . . . .323 B4
Regent Ct Basildon SS15 .341 E8
Romford RM2 . . . . .336 B8
Rowhedge CO5 . . . . .164 F8
Regent Dr CM12 . . . . .296 F5
Regent Gdns IG3 . . . . .334 A5
Regent Rd
Brightlingsea CO7 . . . . .192 F7
Epping CM16 . . . . .245 F1
Regents Cl
Highwoods CO4 . . . . .110 C5
Southminster CM0 . . . . . . .284 D4
Regents Ct
Burnham-on-C CM0 . . . . . .306 B4
7 Gravesend DA11 . . . . . . .379 B2
Regents Pk IG8 . . . . .311 A3
Regents Pl IG8 . . . . .288 D2
Regent Sq DA17 . . . . .369 B2
Regent St Ipswich IP4 . . . .17 E6
11 Manningtree CO11 . . . . .86 D4
Rowhedge CO5 . . . . .164 C8
Regina Cl IP4 . . . . .18 B5
Regimental Way CO2 . . . . .216 E8
Regina Rd CM1 . . . . .205 D6
Regis Ave CO16 . . . . .195 D6
Reigate Cl IP3 . . . . .18 B3
Reigate Rd IG3 . . . . .333 E3
Rembrandt Cl
3 Canvey Island SS8 . . . . .364 A3
Southend-on-S SS3 . . . . . . .368 G8
Rembrandt Gr CM1 . . . . . .232 B6
Rembrandt Way CO3 . . . . .135 B5
Rembrow Rd IP9 . . . . .35 A1
Remembrance Ave
Hatfield Peverel CM3 . . . . . .211 A3
Southminster CM0 . . . . . . .306 B4
Remercie Rd CO11 . . . . . . .87 A4
Remus Cl CO4 . . . . .109 F5
Renacres SS14 . . . . .342 F4
Rendlesham Cl 8 IP11 . . . .17 A7
Rendlesham Rd
Felixstowe IP11 . . . . .381 B5
Ipswich IP1 . . . . .17 A4
Renfrew Rd IP4 . . . . .18 C7
Rennie Ct 5 EN3 . . . . .265 A1
Rennie Pl CM1 . . . . .232 F7
Renoir Pl CM1 . . . . .232 F7
Renown St SS3 . . . . .368 H8
Renown The SS3 . . . . .368 F8
Renwick Rd IG11 . . . . .352 D4
Repton Ave RM2 . . . . .336 A8
Repton Cl SS13 . . . . .321 A1
Repton Ct Basildon SS13 .321 A1
Woodford IG5 . . . . .310 F2
Repton Dr RM2 . . . . .336 A8

Repton Gr
Southend-on-S SS2 347 A7
Woodford IG5 310 F2
Repulse Cl RM5 313 B2
Reservoir Cl DA9 377 C1
Rest Cotts SS4 304 E1
Retford Cl RM3 315 A4
Retford Path RM3 315 A4
Retford Rd RM3 315 A4
Retingham Way E4 309 B8
Retreat Rd Hockley SS5 324 E6
Southend-on-S SS0 366 E7
Retreat The
Brentwood CM14 294 B1
Grays RM17 378 B8
Shenfield CM13 295 B3
West Bergholt CO6 108 D3
Witham CM8 184 A1
Retreat Way IG7 312 B7
Rettendon Cl SS6 323 A3
Rettendon Gdns SS11 299 E1
Rettendon Prim Sch
CM3 300 C5
Rettendon Turnpike
SS11 300 C3
Rettendon View SS11 321 F8
Reubens Rd CM13 295 B3
Reverdy Ho CO2 135 E2
Review Rd RM10 354 B4
Rex Par 2 IG8 310 C4
Reydon Ave E11 332 C5
Reydon Cl CB9 8 C8
Reydon Ho IP3 18 A2
Reymead Cl CO5 218 C6
Reynard Copse CM23 118 F1
Reynard Ct CM2 254 F6
Reynard Hts CO4 136 C8
Reynards Cl CO13 170 D6
Reynards Copse CO4 110 A3
Reynolds Ave
Colchester CO3 135 B5
Dagenham RM6 334 C4
Ipswich IP3 38 A8
Little Ilford E12 352 A7
Reynolds Ct
Felixstowe IP11 381 B5
Ilford RM6 334 D8
Reynolds Gate CM3 301 E6
Reynolds Ho SS2 347 F2
Reynolds Rd IP3 18 A1
Rhapsody Cres CM14 316 B5
Rhoda Rd SS7 344 E4
Rhoda Rd N SS7 344 E5
Rhodes Ave CM23 145 F5
Rhum Mews SS12 322 A5
Ribble Cl IG8 310 C4
Riby Rd IP11 381 D3
Rice Bridge Ind Est
CO16 169 A7
Richard Alibon Prim Sch
RM10 354 A7
Richard Ave
Brightlingsea CO7 192 F6
Wivenhoe CO7 137 C3
Richard Blackburn Ho
RM7 335 E2
Richard Burn Way CO10 15 E2
Richard Burton Ct 4
IG9 310 C8
Richard de Clare Com Prim
Sch CO9 76 F1
Richard Fell Ho 3 E12 352 A8
Richards Ave RM7 335 C5
Richardson Cl DA9 376 F2
Richardson Gdns 12
RM10 354 B6
Richardson Pl CM1 231 F4
Richardson Rd CO7 59 D3
Richardsons La IP9 63 D8
Richardson Wlk
Colchester CO3 134 F5
Witham CM8 184 B2
Richards Wlk CO15 195 E6
Richard Whittington Prim Sch
The CM23 145 E4
Rich Cl CM3 180 F7
Riche Cl CM6 152 B5
Riches Rd IG1 333 C2
Richmond Ave
Chingford E4 309 D5
South Benfleet SS7 344 C2
Southend-on-S, Cambridge Town
SS3 368 D6
Southend-on-S SS1 367 A7
Southend-on-S,Westcliff-on-S
SS0 366 E8
Richmond Ave Prim Sch
SS3 368 D6
Richmond Cl CM23 145 C7
Richmond Cres
Chingford E4 309 D5
Harwich CO12 91 B2
Richmond Ct
4 Romford RM1 335 F5
Southend-on-S,Chalkwell
SS9 365 F8
Southend-on-S SS3 368 D6
Richmond Dr
Jaywick CO15 195 A1
Rayleigh SS6 345 D8
9 Redbridge IG8 311 A3
Southend-on-S SS0 347 C4
Richmond Ho 20 IP4 17 D5
Richmond Pk IG10 288 D2
Richmond Rd
Chelmsford CM2 233 A4
Chingford E4 287 D1
Grays RM17 373 C1
Ilford IG1 333 C1
Ipswich IP1 16 F8
Romford RM1 335 F5
West Mersea CO5 218 D6
Wickford SS11 299 C2
Richmond St SS2 348 D1
Richmond Way E11 332 A2
Ricketts Dr CM12 296 F3
Rickling SS16 342 F4
Rickling CE Prim Sch
CB11 93 E8
Rickling Green Rd
Quendon CB11 66 E1
Rickling Green CB11 93 E8
Rickling Rd CB11 66 B6
Rickstones Rd CM8 184 A6
Rickstones Sch The CM8 183 F6
Riddiford Dr CM1 231 F4
Riddings La CM18 224 A4
Riddles Dr CO4 109 F2
Ridgemount SS7 344 E4
Ridges The E4 309 A6
Ridge The Braintree CM7 128 B6
Little Baddow CM3 234 E2
Walton-on-t-N CO14 171 B8
Ridgeway Billericay CM12 319 A8
Brentwood CM13 295 B1
Colchester CO4 110 A4
Grays RM17 373 E2
Ingatestone CM4 274 A2
Maldon CM9 259 A8
Rayleigh SS6 323 C1
Woodford IG8 310 C6
Ridgeway Gdns
Redbridge IG4 332 E6
Southend-on-S SS0 366 B8
Ridgeways CM17 224 E8
Ridgeway The
Braintree CM7 128 A1
Chingford E4 287 C1
Harwich CO12 91 B3
Romford, Harold Wood
RM3 314 F2
Romford RM2 336 A7
Southend-on-S SS0 366 B8
Ridgewell Ave CM1 231 F4
Ridgewell CE Prim Sch
CO9 29 B6
Ridgewell Cl RM10 354 B4
Ridgewell Rd
Birdbrook CO9 10 E2
Great Yeldham CO9 29 E3
Ridgewell Way CO2 135 F1
Ridgmont Pl RM11 336 D5
Ridgwell Ave RM16 359 A1
Ridings Ave CM77 154 B7
Ridings The
Bishop's Stortford CM23 145 D4
Canvey Island SS8 364 A5
Great Baddow CM2 254 D7
Rochford SS4 325 F1
Redbridge IG7 312 B6
Ridlands Cl CM77 155 E6
Ridley Cl Barking IG11 352 F5
Romford RM3 314 B2
Ridley Cotts CM3 280 C3
Ridley Gdns CM22 94 C2
Ridley Rd Basildon SS13 321 C1
Chelmsford CM1 232 B8
Riffams Ct SS13 343 C8
Riffams Dr SS13 343 C8
Riffhams CM13 317 B7
Riffhams Chase CM3 234 D2
Riffhams Dr CM2 255 A7
Riffhams La Danbury CM3 256 C8
Little Baddow CM3 234 C1
Rifle Hill CM7 127 F1
Rifle Hill Works CM7 127 F1
Rigby Ave CO11 87 A3
Rigby Gdns RM16 374 B2
Rigby Mews IG1 333 A2
Rigby Pl EN3 265 A2
Rigby Rd CO11 87 A4
Rignal's La CM2 254 D3
Riley Ave CO15 220 E6
Rimini Cl CO2 135 C3
Ringham Rd IP4 18 A6
Ringwood Ave RM12 336 D2
Ringwood Dr SS9 346 C7
Ringwood Ho 9 RM3 314 D4
Ripley Cl CO16 195 B6
Ripley Rd Belvedere DA17 369 A2
Ilford IG3 333 F2
Ripley View IG10 267 B1
Ripon Gdns IG1 332 E4
Ripon Ho 7 RM3 314 D4
Ripple Ct 10 IG11 352 D4
Ripple Jun Sch IG11 352 E4
Ripple Prim Sch IG11 352 E5
Ripple Rd Barking IG11 352 C5
Barking IG11 352 E4
Dagenham IG11 353 D4
Rippleside SS14 342 F6
Rippleside Commercial Est
IG11 353 C4
Ripple Way CO4 110 B1
Risby Cl
Clacton-on-S CO16 195 A4
Ipswich IP4 18 B6
Risdens CM18 223 D5
Risebridge Chase RM1 313 F3
Risebridge Rd RM2 314 A2
Rise Park Bvd RM1 313 F2
Rise Park Jun & Inf Sch
RM1 313 D2
Rise Park Par RM1 313 E1
Rise Pk SS15 341 F6
Rise The
Buckhurst Hill IG9 288 D1
Chingford E4 287 E1
Eight Ash G CO6 134 A8
Wanstead E11 332 A6
Riseway CM15 316 E7
Risings Terr RM11 336 F8
Rising The CM11 297 D1
Ritabrook Rd IP2 16 E1
Rivendell Vale CM3 301 C6
Rivenhall Thundersley SS7 345 B8
Wickford SS11 322 A6
Rivenhall CE Prim Sch
CM8 184 B8
River Ave EN11 221 B7
Riverbank Cl CO10 12 C7
River Blackwater Chalet Site
CM9 237 C3
River Cl Halstead CO9 76 F1
Holdbrook EN8 265 A5
Rainham RM13 370 B8
Wanstead E11 332 C5
River Cotts CM3 233 F8
River Ct Purfleet RM19 370 F2
Sawbridgeworth CM21 172 F3
Wanstead E11 332 C5
Riverdale SS9 346 D7
Riverdale Ct IP11 381 D3
Riverdale Rd DA8 369 C1
Riverdene Rd IG1 333 B1
River Dr RM14 337 D5
Riverfield La CM21 172 E3
River Hill CM3 182 B3
River Lee Ctry Pk*
EN9 243 B1
River Mead CM7 128 A4
Rivermead Gate CM1 232 B4
Rivermead Ind Est CM1 232 B4
River Meads SG12 197 C4
Rivermill CM20 199 C2
River Rd Barking IG11 352 E2
Barking IG11 353 B1
Brentwood CM14 315 F6
Buckhurst Hill IG9 288 E1
River Road Bsns Pk IG11 352 F2
Riversdale Rd RM5 313 B3
Rivers Ho CO14 144 D2
Rivers Hospl The CM21 172 C1
Riverside
Bishop's Stortford CM23 145 F7
Bradwell CM7 129 D3
Chelmsford CM1 232 C3
Great Dunmow CM6 123 E1
Riverside Ave EN10 221 A1
Riverside Ave E CO11 86 C5
Riverside Ave W CO11 86 C5
Riverside Bsns Pk
Earls Colne CO6 104 F8
Stansted Mountfitchet
CM24 119 E6
Riverside Cotts
Barking IG11 352 D3
Brantham CO11 86 C7
North Fambridge CM3 303 A6
Stanstead Abbotts SG12 197 C4
Riverside Ct Chingford E4 287 B3
Halstead CO9 76 E2
Harlow CM20 200 C6
Riverside Ho SS12 321 D8
Riverside Ind Est
Barking IG11 353 A2
Rochford SS4 325 F1
Riverside Ind Pk IP2 17 D3
Riverside Jun & Inf Schs
SS5 301 E3
Riverside Pk CM1 232 C3
Riverside Rd
Burnham-on-C CM0 306 C4
Ipswich IP1 16 F7
Riverside Way CO5 158 C2
Riverside Wlk
16 Bishop's Stortford CM23 145 F7
Colchester CO1 135 E8
Wickford SS12 321 B8
Riverside Works IG11 352 B5
Riversmead EN11 221 A5
Rivers St IP4 17 F7
Riverton Dr CM0 240 B1
Rivertons SS16 342 F4
Riverview SS16 343 A4
River View Althorne CM3 282 E2
Braintree CM7 127 F1
Dartford DA1 376 A3
Grays RM16 374 A1
Holbrook IP9 62 D5
Manningtree CO11 86 C4
Witham CM8 212 A8
River View Cl SS15 319 C1
Riverview Ct
Basildon SS16 342 E4
14 Belvedere DA17 369 A1
Greenhithe DA9 376 F1
Riverview Flats 13 RM19 371 B1
Riverview Gdns SS5 301 C3
Riverview Rd DA9 377 A2
River View Rd
Harkstead IP9 63 B2
South Benfleet SS7 344 E2
Riverview Terr 1 RM19 371 B1
River Way Harlow CM20 200 B5
Loughton IG10 289 A3
Riviera Dr SS1 367 D8
Rivington Ave IG8 310 D1
Rivish La CO10 15 C7
RJ Mitchell Prim Sch The
RM12 355 B6
Roach RM18 375 C2
Roach Ave SS6 323 D1
Roach Vale
Colchester CO4 110 E1
Southend-on-S SS9 346 F7
Roach Vale Prim Sch
CO4 110 E1
Robeck Rd IP3 17 F1
Robert Cl Billericay CM12 296 F2
Chelmsford CM2 232 F4
Chigwell IG7 311 F5
Robert Clack Lower Sch
RM8 334 F2
Robert Clack Sch RM8 335 A3
Robert Daniels Ct CM16 267 E2
Robert Drake Prim Sch The
SS7 344 D7
Robert Leonard Ind Est
SS2 347 F5
Roberts Cl RM3 314 B2
Roberts Ct CM2 254 E7
Robert's Hill CO8 79 F3
Robertson Ct RM17 373 B2
Robertson Dr SS12 321 E5
Roberts Rd Basildon SS15 341 B7
Belvedere DA17 369 A1
Chingford E17 309 B2
Colchester CO1,CO2 136 A5
North Fambridge CM3 303 A7
Robert Suckling Ct CB9 27 B6
Robert Wallace Cl CM23 118 F1
Robert Way
Wickford SS11 321 F6
Wivenhoe CO7 137 C3
Robin Cl Billericay CM12 297 C6
Great Bentley CO7 166 D8
Haverhill CB9 9 C7
Romford RM5 313 D3
Stanstead Abbotts SG12 197 C3
Robin Cres CO3 134 B4
Robin Dr IP2 16 D3
Robin Hood Rd
Brentwood CM15 294 C2
Elsenham CM22 94 C1
Robinia Cl Basildon SS15 319 D1
Redbridge IG6 311 E4
Robinia Ct 1 CO4 136 E7
Robinsbridge Rd CO6 130 F2
Robinsdale CO15 195 F6
Robin's La CM16 267 C3
Robinson Cl
Bishop's Stortford CM23 145 F5
Hornchurch RM12 355 B5
Robinson Rd
Brightlingsea CO7 193 A7
Dagenham RM10 354 A8
Horndon-on-t-H SS17 359 E4
Robinsons Cl CM0 284 D3
Robins The CM15 272 D4
Robinsway EN9 265 E5
Robin Way
Chelmsford CM2 254 B5
Sudbury CO10 33 C5
Robjohns Rd CM1 253 E8
Robletts Way CO6 80 E4
Roborough Wlk RM12 355 C6
Rochdale Way CO4 136 E6
Roche Ave SS4 325 E2
Rochefort Dr SS4 347 F8
Rochehall Way SS4 348 B8
Rochelle Cl CM6 70 A3
Rochester Cl CM7 128 D4
Rochester Ct CB10 22 F2
Rochester Dr SS0 347 C4
Rochester Gdns IG1 332 F4
Rochester Mews SS0 347 C4
Rochester Way
Basildon SS14 342 F7
Sudbury CO10 15 D2
6 Basildon SS14 342 F8
Rocheway SS4 326 A2
Rochford Ave
Brentwood CM15 295 A4
Ilford RM6 334 C6
Loughton IG10 289 C6
Southend-on-S SS0 347 E1
Waltham Abbey EN9 265 D5
Rochford Cl
Hornchurch RM12 355 B6
Stansted Mountfitchet
CM24 119 E5
Wickford SS11 321 F6
Rochford Cty Prim Sch
SS4 325 E2
Rochford Garden Way
SS4 325 E3
Rochford Gn IG10 289 C6
Rochford Hall Cl SS4 325 F1
Rochford Hall Cotts SS4 325 D1
Rochford Ho EN9 265 D6
Rochford Rd
Bishop's Stortford CM23 119 C1
Canvey Island SS8 364 D3
Chelmsford CM2 232 C1
Southend-on-S SS2 347 E5
St Osyth CO16 194 B4
Rochford Sta SS4 325 E1
Rochford Way
Frinton-on-S CO13 170 F7
Walton-on-t-N CO14 171 A7
Rockall SS2 347 A7
Rockall Cl CB9 9 D7
Rockchase Gdns RM11 336 E5
Rock Gdns RM10 354 B7
Rockhampton Wlk 10
CO2 136 A1
Rockingham Ave RM11 336 B4
Rockingham Cl CO4 110 D3
Rocklands Ct RM17 373 C1
Rockleigh Ave SS9 347 A1
Rockleigh Ct CM15 295 A2
Rockwell Rd RM10 354 B7
Rockwood Gdns IG10 289 C6
Rodbridge Dr SS1 367 F8
Rodbridge Hill CO10 15 B5
Rodbridge Nature Reserve*
CO10 15 B4
Roddam Cl CO3 135 C6
Roden Cl CM17 200 F4
Roden St IG1 333 A1
Roden Terr CM5 204 A1
Roding Ave IG8 310 E4
Roding Cl Fyfield CM5 227 D2
Great Wakering SS3 350 B4
Roding Ct CM7 128 D1
Roding Dr CM15 271 F2
Roding Gdns IG10 288 E3
Roding Hall RM4 290 B6
Roding Hospl IG4 332 D8
Roding La
Buckhurst Hill IG9,IG7 288 E1
Chigwell IG7 289 A1
Roding La N IG8 310 E2
Roding La S IG4 332 D7
Roding Leigh CM3 301 E7
Roding Lodge IG1 332 D5
Roding Prim Sch
Barking RM8 353 C7
Woodford IG8 310 E3
Roding Rd IG10 288 F3
Rodings Ave SS17 360 D4
Rodings Ct E4 309 D5
Rodings Prim Sch CM6 204 C8
Rodings The
Southend-on-S SS9 346 D7
Upminster RM14 337 D5
4 Woodford IG8 310 C4
Roding The CM14 294 B1
Roding Valley High Sch
IG10 288 E4
Roding Valley Meadows
(Nature Reserve)*
IG10 289 A2
Roding Valley Sta IG9 310 D6
Roding View
Buckhurst Hill IG9 288 D1
Chipping Ongar CM5 249 B4
Roding Way
Rainham RM13 355 D3
Wickford SS12 321 E7
Rodney Cres EN11 221 A8
Rodney Gdns CM7 128 C4
Rodney Rd
Chipping Ongar CM5 248 F2
Wanstead E11 332 B7
Rodney Way
Chelmsford CM1 253 E7
Romford RM7 313 B2
Rodwells SS3 349 E4
Roebuck Ct E4 309 C3
Roebuck La IG9 288 C1
Roebuck Rd IG6 312 B4
Roebuck Trad Est IG6 312 B4
Roedean Cl SS2 348 F1
Roedean Dr RM1 335 E7
Roedean Gdns SS2 348 F2
Rogation Cl CO3 134 D6
Roger Reede's Almshouses
RM1 335 E7
Rogers Cl IP11 381 D6
Rogers Gdns RM10 354 A7
Rogers Ho 9 RM10 335 A1
Rogers Rd
Dagenham RM10 354 A7
Grays RM17 373 C2
Roggel Rd SS8 364 D2
Rohan Ct SS6 301 D6
Rokeby Gdns IG8 310 A2
Rokells SS14 342 A7
Rokell Way CO13 170 F6
Rokescroft SS13 343 A5
Roland La SS8 364 B4
Rolands Cl CM1 232 B7
Roles Gr RM6 334 E7
Rollerworld* CO1 136 B7
Rollestons CM1 252 F8
Rolley La CO5 158 C2
Roll Gdns IG2 333 A6
Rolls Park Ave E4 309 B5
Rolls Park Rd E4 309 B5
Rolph CE Prim Sch CO16 141 F1
Rolph Cl CO16 142 A2
Romagne Cl SS17 359 F3
Romainville Way SS8 363 C3
Roman RM18 375 C2
Roman Cl Maldon CM9 236 F4
Mountnessing CM15 295 E8
Rainham RM13 354 D3
Roman Ct Braintree CM7 128 C1
Saffron Walden CB11 43 E7
3 Wickford SS11 322 A5
Roman Ho
8 Chelmsford CM2 232 B1
Rainham RM13 354 D3
Roman La CM24 120 B2
Roman Mews 7 EN11 221 A7
Roman Rd Colchester CO1 136 A7
Ilford IG1 352 B6
Ingatestone CM4 273 F1
Little Waltham CM3 208 B5
Mountnessing CM15 295 E8
Roman Rise CM21 172 D2
Romans Farm Chase
CM0 306 C7
Romanshurst CM9 237 A4
Romans Pl CM1 231 B1
Roman St 8 EN11 221 A7
Romans Way CM1 231 B1
Roman Vale CM17 200 C5
Roman Way
Billericay CM12 319 A8
Burnham-on-C CM0 306 B8
Great Dunmow CM6 123 C1
Haverhill CB9 9 B8
Littlebury CB11 21 F4
Long Melford CO10 15 C6
Point Clear B CO16 193 A3
Waltham Abbey EN9 265 B4
Romany Stps 17 SS1 367 C7
Rom Cres RM7 335 F4
Romeland EN9 265 C6
Romford Cl CO4 136 B8
Romford Rd Aveley RM15 371 C7
Chipping Ongar CM5 270 F7
Ilford E12 333 A1
Redbridge IG6 312 C5
Upminster RM15 356 C1
Romford Sta RM1 335 E5
Romney Chase RM11 337 A5
Romney Cl Braintree CM7 127 E6
Brightlingsea CO7 165 E1
Clacton-on-S CO16 195 D5
Kirby Cross CO13 170 E7
Romney Ho SS4 325 F2
Romney Rd
Billericay CM12 296 F1
Ipswich IP3 38 A8
Romsey Cl Hockley SS5 324 D6
South Benfleet SS7 344 B5
Stanford-le-H SS17 360 B1
Romsey Cres SS7 344 B5
Romsey Dr SS7 344 B5
Romsey Gdns RM9 353 D4
Romsey Rd
Dagenham RM9 353 D4
South Benfleet SS7 344 A5
Romsey Way SS7 344 B5
Romside Commercial Ctr
RM7 335 D7
Romulus Cl CO4 109 F5
Rom Valley Way RM7 335 E4
Ronald Dr SS6 323 A4
Ronald Hill Gr SS9 346 D1
Ronald Park Ave SS0 347 C2
Ronald Rd Halstead CO9 103 E8
Romford RM3 315 A2
Roneo Cnr RM12 335 F3
Roneo Link RM12 335 F3
Ronnie La E12 352 A8
Ronver Lodge E4 309 E7
Roodegate SS14 342 A6
Rook Cl RM13 355 A5
Rook End La CB11 68 B5
Rookeries The CO6 133 B4
Rookery Chase CO7 84 E2
Rookery Cl
Great Chesterford CB10 3 D3
Hatfield Peverel CM3 211 A5
Rayleigh SS6 323 C2
Stanford-le-H SS17 360 B1
Rookery Cres RM10 354 B5
Rookery Ct RM20 377 A8
Rookery Hill SS17 361 C3
Rookery La
Great Totham CM9 213 E7
North Fambridge CM3 280 E1
Tiptree CO5 186 C7
Wendens Ambo CB11 42 E4
Rookery Mead CM3 301 D8
Rookery Rd CM4 250 D3
Rookery The Grays RM20 377 A8
Lawford CO11 86 C4
Stansted Mountfitchet
CM24 119 E8
Rookery View RM17 373 D1
Rookes CB10 22 D3
Rookes Cres CM1 231 F1
Rookley Ct 15 RM19 371 B1
Rook Lodge IG1 332 D5
Rookwood Ave IG10 289 C6
Rookwood Cl
Clacton-on-S CO15 195 D7
Grays RM17 373 B2
Rookwood Gdns E4 309 F8
Rookwood Ho IG11 352 D3
Rookwood Way CB9 9 A6
Rookyards SS16 342 E5
Roosevel Ave SS8 364 A4
Roosevelt Rd 1 SS15 341 A6
Roosevelt Way
Colchester CO2 136 B4
Dagenham RM10 354 D6
Roos Hill Debden Rd
CB11 43 E5
Roothings The CM9 237 B5
Roots Hall Ave SS2 347 F2
Roots Hall Dr SS2 347 E2
Roots La CM8 212 E5
Roper Ct IP4 18 C5
Ropers Ave E4 309 C5
Roper's Chase CM1 253 A7
Ropers La CO10 15 B5
Rope Wlk Ipswich IP4 17 E5
Maldon CM9 237 A1
Rosabelle Ave CO7 137 B1
Rosalind Cl CO4 136 F7
Rosalind Ct 6 IG11 353 A5
Rosary Gdns SS0 347 B4
Rosbach Rd SS8 364 D3
Rosberg Rd SS8 364 E3
Roscommon Way SS8 363 C4
Rose Acre Basildon SS14 342 F6
Stratford St M CO7 58 F6
Roseacre Cl RM11 336 F4
Roseacres
Sawbridgeworth CM21 172 D3
Takeley CM22 148 C7
Rose Ave Colchester CO3 134 C4
Woodford E18 310 B1
Rosebank Harwich CO12 91 A3
Waltham Abbey EN9 265 E6
Rose Bank CM14 316 D7
Rosebank Ave RM12 355 C7
Rosebank Ct CO15 196 A2
Rosebank Rd CO5 218 B6
Rosebay Ave CM12 296 F5
Rosebay Cl CM8 183 D3
Roseberry Ave
Basildon SS16 341 B4
South Benfleet SS7 344 C7
Roseberry Cl RM14 337 F5
Roseberry Ct SS7 344 C7
Roseberry Gdns RM14 337 F5
Roseberry Wlk SS7 344 C7
Rosebery CM23 146 C6
Rosebery Ave CO1 136 A7
Rosebery Rd
Chelmsford CM2 254 B8
Felixstowe IP11 381 F4
Grays RM17 377 E8
Ipswich IP4 17 F5
Rosebury Ct CM13 295 D3
Rosebury Sq 2 IG8 311 A3
Rose Cl 10 SS12 321 E5
Rose Cotts
Great Sampford CM7 47 E5
Harkstead SG9 64 A5
Harlow CM17 224 F5
Willingale CM5 228 D3
Rose Cres CO4 109 D2
Rosecroft Cl
Basildon SS16 341 A4
Clacton-on-S CO15 195 E6
Rose & Crown Mews
CM0 284 D4

Rose & Crown Wlk CB10 . . .22 D2
Rose Ct Blackheath CO2 . . .163 B8
Ilford IG1 . . . . .352 B6
Rosedale Cotts CO3 . . . . . .133 F5
Rosedale Gdns RM9 . . . . . .353 B5
Rosedale Rd
Dagenham RM9 . . . . .353 B5
Grays RM17 . . . . .373 D1
Romford RM1 . . . . .335 C8
Rosedene Gdns IG2 . . . . . .333 A7
Rose Dr CM0 . . . . .284 D3
Rosefinch Cl CB9 . . . . .9 C7
Rose Gdns Braintree CM7 128 A2
Seawick CO16 . . . . .220 B6
Rose Glen
Chelmsford CM2 . . . . .254 C7
Romford RM7 . . . . .335 E3
Rose Green Cotts CO6 . . . .106 E5
Rose Hatch Ave RM6 . . . . .334 D8
Rose Hill CM7 . . . . .128 A2
Rosehill Cres IP3 . . . . .17 F4
Rose Hill Prim Sch IP3 . . . .18 A4
Rosehill Rd IP3 . . . . .17 F4
Rose Ho **15** CO1 . . . . .136 A6
Rose La Billericay CM12 . . .297 A2
Dagenham RM8 . . . . .334 E7
Great Chesterford CB10 . . . . .3 E2
Ipswich IP1,IP4 . . . . .17 C5
Salcott-cum-virley CM9 . . .216 B8
Wivenhoe CO7 . . . . .164 B7
Roselaine SS14 . . . . .342 B7
Roselands Ave EN11 . . . . .197 A1
Roselawn Fields CM1 . . . . .232 B8
Roseleigh Cotts CM20 . . . .199 B4
Rosemary Ave
Braintree CM7 . . . . .127 F4
Felixstowe IP11 . . . . .381 F6
Romford RM1 . . . . .335 F8
Rosemary Cl
Great Dunmow CM6 . . . . .123 C1
Harlow CM17 . . . . .200 C4
South Ockendon RM15 . . .357 C2
Tiptree CO5 . . . . .186 C5
Rosemary Cotts CM3 . . . . .258 C8
Rosemary Cres
Clacton-on-S CO15 . . . . . .195 F2
Great Dunmow CM6 . . . . .123 C1
Tiptree CO5 . . . . .186 C5
Rosemary Dr **1** CO4 . . .136 D8
Rosemary Dr IG4 . . . . .332 D6
Rosemary Gdns
Dagenham RM8 . . . . .334 F3
Sudbury CO10 . . . . .15 F2
Rosemary La
Castle Hedingham CO9 . . . .52 A5
Great Dunmow CM6 . . . . .123 C1
Halstead CO9 . . . . .76 E2
Stebbing CM6 . . . . .124 C7
Thorrington CO7 . . . . .166 B5
Rosemary Lodge SS2 . . . .347 F1
Rosemary Rd CO15 . . . . . .195 F2
Rosemary Rd W CO15 . . . .195 E2
Rosemead 344 C7
Rosemead Gdns CM13 . . .295 D5
Rosemount CM19 . . . . . . .223 A5
Rosemount Cl IG8 . . . . . . .310 F4
Rosemount Ct IP11 . . . . . .381 F4
Rose Park Ct IG5 . . . . .310 F1
Rose Rd SS8 . . . . .364 A3
Roserna Rd SS8 . . . . .364 D3
Rosery Mews CO13 . . . . . .170 A4
Rose St DA11 . . . . .378 B1
Roses The IG8 . . . . .309 F3
Rose Tree Mews IG8 . . . . .310 E4
Rosetta Cl CO7 . . . . .137 B2
Rosetti Terr RM8 . . . . .353 B8
Rose Vale EN11 . . . . .221 A6
Rose Valley CM14 . . . . . . .316 D7
Rose Valley Cres SS17 . . . .360 E4
Rose Way SS4 . . . . .348 A8
Rose Wlk CO9 . . . . .29 B6
Rosewood Ave RM12 . . . . .355 A7
Rosewood Cl
Highwoods CO4 . . . . .110 A4
South Ockendon RM15 . . .357 C2
Rosewood Ct RM6 . . . . . . .334 C6
Rosewood La SS3 . . . . .368 F7
Rosherville Ct Prim Sch
DA11 . . . . .378 E1
Rosherville Way DA11 . . . .378 E1
Rosilian Dr SS5 . . . . .302 C1
Roslings Cl CM1 . . . . .231 D5
Roslyn Gdns RM2 . . . . . . .313 F1
Rossall Cl RM11 . . . . .336 A5
Ross Ave RM8 . . . . .334 F3
Ross Cl Haverhill CB9 . . . . . .9 D7
Saffron Walden CB11 . . . . .43 E6
Rossdene Gdns CM6 . . . . .204 D7
Rossendale CM23 . . . . .118 E1
Rossendale Cl CO4 . . . . . . .110 D3
Rosshill Ind Pk SS2 . . . . . .348 A4
Rossiter Rd SS3 . . . . .368 H8
Rossland Ct CO15 . . . . . . .195 F3
Rosslyn Ave Chingford E4 309 F8
Dagenham RM8 . . . . .334 E7
Romford RM3 . . . . .314 F1
Rosslyn Cl SS5 . . . . .324 E7
Rosslyn Ct SS17 . . . . .360 C1
Rosslyn Rd Barking IG11 . .352 D5
Billericay CM12 . . . . .296 F5
Hockley SS5 . . . . .324 E7
Rosslyn Terr CO5 . . . . .158 C3
Ross Way SS16 . . . . .341 B3
Rothbury Ave RM13 . . . . . .370 B8
Rothbury Ho **5** RM3 . . .314 D4
Rothbury Rd CM1 . . . . . . .231 C6
Roth Dr CM13 . . . . .317 B8
Rothesay Ave CM2 . . . . . . .254 A8
Rothmans Ave E4 . . . . .309 E8
Rothwell Cl SS9 . . . . .346 C6
Rothwell Gdns RM9 . . . . . .353 C4

Rothwell Rd RM9 . . . . .353 C4
Rotunda The **7** RM7 . . .335 D6
Rough Hill Farm Cotts
CM3 . . . . .278 C7
Roughtalls CM16 . . . . .246 F4
Roughtons CM2 . . . . .254 C3
Roundacre Basildon SS14 342 A6
Halstead CO9 . . . . .103 E8
Roundaway Rd IG5 . . . . . . .310 F1
Roundbush Bglws CM9 . . .281 C8
Roundbush Cnr
Birch CO5 . . . . .160 D3
Great Totham CM9 . . . . . .213 D6
Roundbush Rd Birch CO5 160 D2
Mundon CM9 . . . . .281 A8
Round Cl CO3 . . . . .135 B7
Round Coppice Rd
Great Hallingbury CM24 . .147 A8
Stansted Mountfitchet
CM24 . . . . .120 B1
Rounders Ct **7** RM10 . . .354 B6
Round Hill Rd SS7 . . . . . . .348 A2
Roundhills EN9 . . . . .265 E4
Roundmead Ave IG10 . . . .289 A7
Roundmead Cl IG10 . . . . . .289 A7
Roundridge Rd IP9 . . . . . . .35 B2
Roundwood Ave CM13 . . .295 B2
Roundwood Cl CM23 . . . . .119 B2
Roundwood Lake CM13 . . .295 B2
Roundwood Rd IP4 . . . . . . .18 A7
Rounton Rd EN9 . . . . .265 E6
Rous Chase CM2 . . . . .254 B1
Rous Rd IG9 . . . . .288 E1
Rourth Ave IP3 . . . . .18 F1
Rover Ave
Clacton-on-S CO15 . . . . . .220 E6
Redbridge IG6 . . . . .311 F4
Rowallan Cl CO3 . . . . .135 A3
Rowallen Par RM8 . . . . . . .334 C3
Rowan Cl Clacton-on-S
CO15 . . . . .186 C6
Rowan Cl
Clacton-on-S CO15 . . . . . .195 C3
Great Bentley CO7 . . . . . . .166 F8
Harwich CO12 . . . . .91 B3
Ilford IG1 . . . . .352 D7
Ipswich IP3 . . . . .18 D2
Rayleigh SS6 . . . . .323 B6
Rowan Dr CM9 . . . . .237 C5
Rowan Gr RM15 . . . . .371 C6
Rowan Green E CM13 . . . .316 F7
Rowan Green W CM13 . . . .316 F7
Rowanhayes Cl IP2 . . . . . . .17 B3
Rowan Ho
Basildon SS13 . . . . .343 B8
Ilford IG1 . . . . .352 D7
Rowan Pl CO1 . . . . .109 E1
Rowans The Aveley RM15 371 C5
Hadleigh SS7 . . . . .324 D4
Rowdowns Rd RM9 . . . . . .353 F5
Rowedge CM13 . . . . .317 B7
Rowedge Cl SS13 . . . . . . .321 D2
Rowedge Ct CO7 . . . . .136 F4
Rowedge Ferry Rd CO7 . . .164 A6
Rowedge Rd CO2,CO5 . . .136 E1
Rowherns La CO7 . . . . . . .139 F4
Rowland Cres IG7 . . . . . . .311 E6
Rowland Ho IP11 . . . . .381 B5
Rowlands Rd RM8 . . . . . . .334 F2
Rowlands The SS7 . . . . . . .344 E3
Rowland's Yd CO12 . . . . . . .90 E2
Rowland Wlk RM4 . . . . . . .313 E7
Rowley Cl CO11 . . . . .86 D8
Rowley Hill CB9 . . . . .9 E5
Rowley Mead CM16 . . . . . .246 C6
Rowley Rd RM16 . . . . .374 A8
Rowney Ave Rowe CB10 . . .44 E2
Rowney Gdns
Dagenham RM9 . . . . .353 C6
Sawbridgeworth CM21 . . .200 C8
Rowney Rd RM9 . . . . .353 B6
Rowney Wood CM21 . . . . .172 C1
Rowventre Way CB11 . . . . .43 D7
Rowsham Rd IG11 . . . . . . .199 D1
Row The Hadstock CB1 . . . .5 B7
Stratford St M CO7 . . . . . . .58 C2
Roxborough Cl CO6 . . . . . .132 E3
Roxburgh Ave RM14 . . . . .337 C1
Roxburgh Rd CO16 . . . . . .167 F6
Roxwell Ave CM1 . . . . .231 D3
Roxwell CE Prim Sch
CM1 . . . . .230 A6
Roxwell Gdns CM13 . . . . .295 C4
Roxwell Ho CO16 . . . . .188 C2
Roxwell Rd Barking IG11 . .353 A3
Chelmsford CM1 . . . . .230 E5
Writtle CM1 . . . . .231 A4
Roxy Ave RM6 . . . . .334 C4
Royal Artillery Way SS2 . .348 F7
Royal Cl Ilford IG3 . . . . . . .334 A4
Rochford SS4 . . . . .325 D5
Royal Ct Basildon SS15 . . .341 B7
Brentwood CM14 . . . . .316 C5
Colchester CO4 . . . . .110 E1

Royal Ct continued
Maldon CM9 . . . . .237 A1
Royal Docks Rd E6 . . . . . . .352 B1
Royal Gunpowder Mills*
EN9 . . . . .265 B7
Royal Hospl Sch The IP9 . .62 D3
Royal Jubilee Ct RM2 . . . .336 A8
Royal Liberty Sch The
RM2 . . . . .336 C8
Royal Mews SS1 . . . . .367 A7
Royal Oak Chase SS15 . . .341 C8
Royal Oak Ct IP8 . . . . .334 C2
Royal Oak Dr SS11 . . . . . .322 A8
Royal Oak Gdns **6** CM23 145 F6
Royal Par **11** RM10 . . . .354 B6
Royal Pier Rd DA12 . . . . . .379 C1
Royal Sq CO7 . . . . .84 F7
Royals The SS1 . . . . .367 A7
Royal Terr SS1 . . . . .367 A7
Roy Ave IP3 . . . . .18 B5
Roycraft Ave SS11 . . . . . . .352 F3
Roycroft Cl C18 . . . . .310 B2
Roydon Bridge SS14 . . . . .342 D8
Roydon Cl IG10 . . . . .288 E2
Roydon Lodge Chalet Est
CM19 . . . . .198 C1
Roydon Mill CM19 . . . . . . .198 A1
Roydon Prim Sch CM19 . .222 B8
Roydon Rd Harlow CM20 198 E1
Stanstead Abbotts SG12 . .197 E4
Roydon Sta CM19 . . . . . . .198 B2
Roydon Way CO13 . . . . . . .170 F6
Rudlands IP6 . . . . .17 E3
Royer Cl SS5 . . . . .325 A4
Royns IG2 . . . . .333 F6
Royle Cl RM2 . . . . .336 B6
Royston Ave
Basildon SS15 . . . . .319 D1
Chingford E4 . . . . .309 B5
Southend-on-S SS2 . . . . . .348 B3
Royston Dr IP2 . . . . .16 D2
Royston Gdns IG1 . . . . . . .332 D5
Royston La CO5 . . . . .20 C6
Royston Par IG1 . . . . .332 D5
Royston Rd Romford RM3 315 A3
Southend-on-S SS2 . . . . . .348 B3
Ruaton Dr CO16 . . . . .195 C4
Rubens Cl SS3 . . . . .368 G8
Rubens Gate CM1 . . . . . . .232 F7
Rubens Rd IP3 . . . . .18 A1
Rubicon Ave SS11 . . . . . . .322 A8
Rubin Pl IP3 . . . . .265 A2
Ruby Ct **5** Rainham RM13 355 A1
Southend-on-S SS9 . . . . . .346 E5
Rudd Ct CO4 . . . . .110 F1
Rudkin Rd CO4 . . . . .109 F5
Rudlands IP6 . . . . .17 E3
Rudsdale Way CO3 . . . . . . .134 D5
Rue de Jeunes **2** CM7 .127 F2
Rue De St Lawrence
EN9 . . . . .265 C5
Ruffels Field CM6 . . . . . . .124 E4
Ruffles Cl SS6 . . . . .323 D3
Ruffles Rd CB9 . . . . .9 C7
Rugby Gdns RM9 . . . . .353 C6
Rugby Rd Dagenham RM9 353 C6
Great Cornard CO10 . . . . . .34 B4
Rugosa Cl CO3 . . . . .134 D5
Rumbolt Terr SS4 . . . . . . .325 C5
Rumbald Rd CM11 . . . . . . .221 C8
Rumballion Dr CM12 . . . . .296 F3
Rumford Sh Hall The
RM1 . . . . .335 E7
Rumsey Fields CM3 . . . . . .218 A7
Rumsey Row CM1 . . . . . . .231 B1
Runcorn Ho **8** RM3 . . . .314 E4
Rundells CM18 . . . . .224 A4
Rundells Wlk CM18 . . . . . .342 E7
Rundels The SS7 . . . . .345 A6
Runnacles St CM8 . . . . . . .156 C5
Runnacles Way IP11 . . . . .381 B5
Running Mare La CM2 . . . .254 A3
Running Waters CM13 . . . .317 A6
Runnymede Chase SS7 . . .345 A5
Runnymede Ct SS17 . . . . .360 C1
Runnymede Rd
Canvey Island SS8 . . . . . . .364 B3
Stanford-le-H SS17 . . . . . .360 C1
Rushell Cl CM18 . . . . .256 F7
Russell La CM3 . . . . .256 F8
Russell View CM3 . . . . . . .257 A7
Russell Gdns SS11 . . . . . . .299 D2
Runwell Hospl SS11 . . . . . .300 A5
Runwell Terr SS11 . . . . . . .299 D2
Runwell Rd SS11 . . . . .300 B3
Runwell Terr SS1 . . . . .367 A6
Rupert Rd CM0 . . . . .284 C4
Rural Cl RM11 . . . . .336 B3
Rural Vale DA11 . . . . .378 E1
Rurik Ct CM9 . . . . .258 F8
Rush Cl Rushmere St A IP4 .18 F4
South Benfleet SS7 . . . . . .344 B6
Rushbury Cl IP4 . . . . .18 B8
Rush Cl Rushmere St A IP4 18 F4
South Benfleet SS7 . . . . . .344 B6
Rushcroft Rd E4 . . . . .309 B3
Rush Croft Sch E4 . . . . . . .309 B3
Rushdene Rd
Billericay CM12 . . . . .296 F1
Brentwood CM15 . . . . .294 C2
Rushden Gdns Ilford IG5 333 A8
Redbridge IG5 . . . . .311 A1
Rushenden Cl Grays RM17 373 E4
Romford RM1 . . . . .336 A6
Rush Dr EN9 . . . . .265 C3
Rushes Ct CM23 . . . . .146 A5
Rushes La CM23 . . . . .146 A5
Rushes Mead CM18 . . . . . .223 D6
Rushfield CM21 . . . . .200 F3
Rush Green Gdns RM7 . . .335 D3
Rush Green Inf Sch RM7 335 D3
Rush Green Rd
Clacton-on-S CO16 . . . . . .195 B2

Rush Green Rd continued
Romford RM7 . . . . .335 D3
Rush La CM22 . . . . .94 C1
Rushleigh Gn CM23 . . . . . .145 C4
Rushley SS13 . . . . .321 D1
Rushley Cl Grays RM16 . . .373 D5
Great Wakering SS3 . . . . . .371 C8
Rushleydale CM1 . . . . .232 E5
Rushmere Ave RM14 . . . . .337 C1
Rushmere Cl CO5 . . . . .218 D6
Rushmere Pl **11** CB9 . . . .9 B8
Rushmere Rd IP4 . . . . .18 F5
Rushmere St
Ipswich IP4,IP5 . . . . .18 E8
Rushmere St A IP5 . . . . . . .18 E8
Rushmoor Dr CM7 . . . . . . .128 B1
Rusholme Ave RM10 . . . . .335 A1
Rushton Cn RM1 . . . . .336 A6
Rushton Gr CM7 . . . . .128 A1
Rushton Rd CM7 . . . . .224 E8
Ruskin Ave
Southend-on-S SS2 . . . . . .348 B2
Upminster RM14 . . . . .337 C4
Ruskin Cl CO13 . . . . .170 F6
Ruskin Dene CM12 . . . . . .297 A3
Ruskin Gdns RM8 . . . . . . .314 B3
Ruskin Gr DA1 . . . . .376 A2
Ruskin Path **5** SS12 . . .321 D5
Ruskin Rd
Belvedere DA17 . . . . .369 A2
Chelmsford CM2 . . . . .232 E2
Grays RM16 . . . . .374 A2
Ipswich IP4 . . . . .17 F5
Stanford-le-H SS17 . . . . . .360 C1
Ruskins The CM7 . . . . .126 F1
Ruskoi Rd SS8 . . . . .363 F5
Rusper Rd RM9 . . . . .353 C6
Russell Cl Basildon SS15 341 B6
Colchester CO15 . . . . .196 A3
Russell Ct Colchester CO2 136 B4
Felixstowe IP11 . . . . .381 D2
Wickford SS11 . . . . .321 F7
Russell Gdns
Chelmsford CM2 . . . . .254 A4
Ilford IG1 . . . . .333 D4
Wickford SS11 . . . . .321 F7
Russell Gr SS4 . . . . .326 A2
Russell Lodge **6** E4 . . . .309 A8
Russell Quay DA11 . . . . . . .379 A1
Russell Rd
Buckhurst Hill IG9 . . . . . . .288 C3
Colchester CO15 . . . . .196 A3
Enfield EN1 . . . . .177 B2
Felixstowe IP11 . . . . .381 D2
Gravesend DA12 . . . . .379 D1
Ipswich IP1 . . . . .17 B6
North Fambridge CM3 . . . .281 B1
Tilbury RM18 . . . . .378 F5
Tilbury RM18 . . . . .379 A5
Russell's Rd Gosfield CO9 .76 A1
Halstead CO9 . . . . .103 B8
Russell Way CM1 . . . . .253 E7
Russel Rd RM17 . . . . .373 C2
Russell Ct Braintree CM7 .128 A1
Stanford-le-H SS17 . . . . . .360 D3
Russet Cl CO5 . . . . .184 B6
Russets Galleywood CM2 .254 D3
Hornchurch RM11 . . . . . . .336 E7
Russets Ct E4 . . . . .309 D6
Russets The SS4 . . . . .325 D5
Russett Cl CB9 . . . . .8 D8
Russetts SS16 . . . . .341 A5
Russet Way
Burnham-on-C CM0 . . . . .306 C6
Hockley SS5 . . . . .324 F8
Rustic Cl Braintree CM7 . .128 C3
Upminster RM14 . . . . .337 E3
Rutherford Cl
Billericay CM11 . . . . .297 A5
Southend-on-S SS9 . . . . . .346 C6
Rutherfords CM1 . . . . .208 B1
Rutherford Cl SS13 . . . . . .321 D6
Rutland App RM11 . . . . . . .337 A6
Rutland Ave
Colchester CO2 . . . . .135 B3
Southend-on-S SS1 . . . . . .367 E7
Rutland Ct SS15 . . . . .341 A6
Rutland Dr
Hornchurch RM11 . . . . . . .337 A6
Rayleigh SS6 . . . . .323 C7
Rutland Gdns
Braintree CM7 . . . . .128 A4
Dagenham RM8 . . . . .353 C7
Rochford SS4 . . . . .325 C5
Rutland Ho RM7 . . . . .313 A1
Rutland Pl CM7 . . . . .72 B2
Rutland Rd
Chelmsford CM1 . . . . .232 A7
Ilford IG1 . . . . .333 B1
North Fambridge CM3 . . . .303 A7
Wanstead E11 . . . . .332 B6
Rydal Cl CM9 . . . . .259 B8
Rydal Way RM7 . . . . .154 C6
Rydal Wlk IP3 . . . . .18 C2
Ryde Ave CO15 . . . . .196 A3
Ryde Cl SS9 . . . . .346 B4
Ryde Dr SS17 . . . . .375 C8
Ryder Gdns RM13 . . . . . . .354 F6
Ryder Way SS13 . . . . .321 D2
Ryde The SS9 . . . . .346 B5
Rye Cl Brightlingsea CO7 . .165 E3
Colchester CO3 . . . . .134 C6
Hatfield Peverel CM3 . . . . .211 A3
Hornchurch RM12 . . . . . . .378 D7
Ipswich IP3 . . . . .18 D4
Ryecroft CM19 . . . . .223 B8
Ryecroft Ave IG5 . . . . .311 A1
Ryecroft Rd SS5 . . . . .8 F7
Ryedene SS16 . . . . .342 F3
Ryedene Cl SS16 . . . . .342 F3

Ryedene Com Prim Sch
SS16 . . . . .342 F3
Ryedene Pl SS16 . . . . .342 F3
Ryefeld Cl EN11 . . . . .197 B2
Rye Field The CM3 . . . . . . .234 D3
Rye Grass Way CM7 . . . . . .128 B1
Rye Hill Rd CM18 . . . . .223 E2
Rye Hills CO9 . . . . .103 FB
Rye House Sta EN11 . . . . .221 C8
Rye La CO2 . . . . .162 A4
Ryelands Prim Sch EN11 .221 B7
Rye Mead SS16 . . . . .341 C4
Rye Mead Cotts EN11 . . . .221 C8
Rye Mill La CO5 . . . . .158 D4
Rye Rd EN11 . . . . .221 D8
Ryes La Bumer CO10 . . . . . .33 A2
Hatfield Heath CM22 . . . . .174 B7
Rye St CM23 . . . . .118 F1
Rye Wlk CM4 . . . . .274 A2
Rygate Rd CO1 . . . . .135 F7
Rykhill RM16 . . . . .374 B3
Rylands IP9 . . . . .35 A2
Rylands Rd SS2 . . . . .348 D2
Ryle The CM1 . . . . .253 A8
Rylstone Way CB11 . . . . . . .43 F8
Rysley CM3 . . . . .234 D4

S

Sabina Rd RM16 . . . . .374 C2
Sabines Rd RM4 . . . . .292 E6
Sable Way SS15 . . . . .340 F7
Sackett's Grove Caravan Pk
CO16 . . . . .195 A2
Sacketts Grove Cvn Pk
CO15 . . . . .194 F2
Sackville Cl CM1 . . . . .231 E3
Sackville Cres RM3 . . . . . .314 D2
Sackville Gdns IG1 . . . . . . .332 F3
Sackville Rd SS2 . . . . .348 E1
Sackville Way CO6 . . . . . . .108 D4
Sacred Heart of Mary RC Girls
SS1 . . . . .367 C8
Sacred Heart RC Sch
SS1 . . . . .367 D8
Saddle Mews CO3 . . . . . . .134 E6
Saddle Rise CM1 . . . . .232 E8
Saddlers Cl
Bishop's Stortford CM23 . .145 C4
Great Notley CM7 . . . . . . .154 B7
Saddleworth Rd RM3 . . . . .314 C4
Saddleworth Sq RM3 . . . . .314 C4
Sadds Yd CO15 . . . . .195 F3
Sadler Cl CO2 . . . . .136 B4
Sadlers SS7 . . . . .344 B6
Sadlers Cl Billericay CM11 297 D5
Kirby Cross CO13 . . . . . . .170 C6
Sadlers Mead CM18 . . . . . .224 A7
Saffory Cl SS9 . . . . .346 C7
Saffron Bsns Ctr CB10 . . . .22 F2
Saffron Cl
Horndon-on-t-H SS17 . . . .360 A3
West Horndon CM13 . . . . .339 D5
Wethersfield CM7 . . . . .73 C3
Saffron Croft CM9 . . . . . . .236 E2
Saffron Ct Basildon SS15 .340 F6
Saffron Rd Grays RM16 . . .372 C2
Romford RM5 . . . . .313 D1
Saffron Walden Cty High Sch
CB11 . . . . .43 C8
Saffron Walden Mus*
CB10 . . . . .22 D2
Saffron Walden YH*
CB11 . . . . .23 A2
Saffron Walden Hospl
CB11 . . . . .43 A2
Saffron Wlk
Billericay CM11 . . . . .297 B2
Brentwood CM15 . . . . .73 B3
Sadgefield CM7 . . . . .24 E2
Sage Ct SS7 . . . . .346 A2
Sages CM22 . . . . .94 F5
Sages End Rd CB9 . . . . .26 B8
Sage Wlk CO5 . . . . .186 C4
St Agnes Dr SS8 . . . . .364 D6
St Agnes Rd CM12 . . . . . . .319 C3
St Agnes Way IP5 . . . . .18 F6
St Aidans Ct IG11 . . . . .353 B3
St Aidan's RC Prim Sch
IG1 . . . . .333 D3
St Alban's Rd E6 . . . . .352 A2
St Alban's Cres IG8 . . . . . .310 A2
St Alban's RC High Sch
IP4 .18 C7
St Alban's RC Prim Sch
RM12 . . . . .355 B5
St Albans Rd IG3 . . . . .333 F4
St Alban's Rd
Clacton-on-S CO15 . . . . . .196 A3
Colchester CO3 . . . . .135 D7
Coopersale CM16 . . . . . . .246 F2
Woodford IG8 . . . . .310 A3
St Andrews Ave
Hornchurch RM12 . . . . . . .355 A8
Rainham RM12 . . . . .354 F7
St Andrew's Ave CO4 . . . . .137 A5
St Andrew's Ave (Colchester
By-Pass Rd) CO4 . . . . . . .136 D7
St Andrew's CE Jun Sch &
Hatfield Peverel Inf Sch
CM3 . . . . .211 B3
St Andrew's CE Prim Sch
Bulmer CO10 . . . . .32 E4

St Andrew's CE Prim Sch
continued
Great Yeldham CO9 . . . . . . .29 F2
Halstead CO9 . . . . .77 A3
Marks Tey CO6 . . . . .132 E3
St Andrew's Gdns SG12 . .197 D4
Weeley CO16 . . . . .167 F8
Wormingford CO6 . . . . .80 E5
St Andrews Cl
Alresford CO7 . . . . .165 B7
Clacton-on-S CO15 . . . . . .186 A4
Ipswich IP4 . . . . .18 D5
North Weald Bassett CM16 247 D7
St Andrew's Cotts CM3 . . .211 B3
St Andrews Ct
3 Colchester CO4 . . . . .136 C8
1 Gravesend DA11 . . . .379 B1
St Andrews Dr CM17 . . . . .201 D2
St Andrew's Dr IP9 . . . . . . .63 E7
St Andrews Gdns CO4 . . . .110 E1
St Andrew's Ho CM0 . . . . .284 C4
St Andrew's Jun & Inf Schs
CM0 . . . . .136 D7
St Andrew's La SS15 . . . . .341 C7
St Andrew's Mdw CM18 . .223 E7
St Andrews Pl
Brentwood CM15 . . . . .316 F8
Brightlingsea CO7 . . . . . . .165 E1
St Andrew's Rd
Boreham CM3 . . . . .209 F1
Great Cornard CO10 . . . . . .34 A6
Halstead CO9 . . . . .76 F1
Romford RM7 . . . . .335 D5
Southend-on-S SS3 . . . . . .368 D6
St Andrew's Rd
Clacton-on-S CO15 . . . . . .195 E3
Felixstowe IP11 . . . . .381 E5
Hatfield Peverel CM3 . . . . .211 A4
Redbridge IG1 . . . . .332 F4
Rochford SS4 . . . . .325 E2
Tilbury RM18 . . . . .378 E5
Weeley CO16 . . . . .140 F1
St Andrew's Rise CO10 . . . .34 C5
St Anne Line RC Jun & Inf
Schs SS15 . . . . .341 C6
St Annes RM16 . . . . .373 B5
St Annes Cl
Coggeshall CO6 . . . . .131 B2
Grays RM16 . . . . .373 B5
St Annes Ct CM4 . . . . .273 A8
St Anne's Pk EN10 . . . . . . .221 A4
St Anne's Prim Sch CO4 110 C1
St Annes Rd SS8 . . . . .364 E3
St Anne's Rd
Colchester CO4 . . . . .136 C8
Mountnessing CM15 . . . . .295 C8
St Annes Terr **8** IG6 . . .311 E5
St Ann's Hill EN10 . . . . . . .221 A4
St Anns Cl SS11 . . . . .352 C4
St Anns Rd CO15 . . . . .195 E4
St Ann's Rd
2 Barking IG11 . . . . . . .352 C4
Southend-on-S SS2 . . . . . .348 A1
St Anselm's RC Prim Sch
DA1 . . . . .376 A2
St Anthony's Ave IG8 . . . . .310 A6
St Anthony's Dr CM2 . . . . .254 C7
St Antony's RC Prim Sch
IG8 . . . . .310 A6
St Aubins Ct CO15 . . . . . . .196 B4
St Aubyns Rd IP4 . . . . .18 A5
St Aubyn's Sch IG8 . . . . . .309 F3
St Audrey's Cl SS6 . . . . . . .323 C7
St Augustine Mews CO1 . .136 E7
St Augustine Rd
Grays RM16 . . . . .374 B2
Ipswich IP3 . . . . .18 B3
St Augustine's Ave SS6 . . .368 B7
Hoddesdon EN11 . . . . .221 B6
Ilford IG2 . . . . .333 E8
St Austell Rd CO4 . . . . . . .110 D2
St Austin's La CO12 . . . . . . .91 E6
St Awdry's Rd IG11 . . . . . .352 D5
St Barbara's Rd CO2 . . . . .135 D4
St Barnabas Rd IG8 . . . . . .310 C3
St Bartholomew Cl CO4 . .110 C3
St Bartholomews La
. . . . .15 D2
St Bede's RC Prim Sch
RM6 . . . . .334 C6
St Benedict RC Coll CO3 136 B6
St Benet's Rd SS2 . . . . . . .347 F3
St Bernard Rd CO4 . . . . . .110 D2
St Bernard's High Sch
SS0 . . . . .366 E8
St Botolph's Church Wlk **7**
CO2 . . . . .135 F6
St Botolph's Cir **8** CO2 135 F6
St Botolph's Pl **11** CB9 . . .8 F7
St Botolph's Prim Sch
CO13 . . . . .171 C8
St Botolph's Way **7** IP2 . .16 E1
St Brelades Ct CO15 . . . . .196 B5
St Bride Ct CO4 . . . . .110 D2
St Brides Ct **8** EN10 . . .221 A4
St Catherines Cl
Colchester CO2 . . . . .135 D1
Wickford SS11 . . . . .321 F8
St Catherines Ct CM23 . . .145 E7
St Catherine's Ct **1** IP2 .16 E1
St Catherine's Hoddesdon C E
Prim Sch EN11 . . . . .221 B6
St Catherines Rd E4 . . . . .309 A8
St Catherine's Rd
Chelmsford CM1 . . . . .231 E2
Long Melford CO10 . . . . . .15 C7
St Cecilia Rd RM16 . . . . . .374 B2
St Cedd's CE Prim Sch
CM0 . . . . .242 B2
St Cedds Ct RM16 . . . . . . .373 B5

St Cedd's Sch CM1 ....232 A4
St Chads CI SS15 ....341 C7
St Chad's Gdns RM6 ....334 E4
St Chad's Rd
 Dagenham RM6 ....334 E4
 Tilbury RM16,RM18 ....379 A7
St Chad's Sch RM18 ....379 A6
St Charles Dr SS11 ....321 E7
St Charles Rd CM14 ....294 B1
St Christopher Dr C04 ....110 D2
St Christopher Rd C04 ....110 D2
St Christopher Sch The
 SS9 ....346 F4
St Christophers CI SS8 ......363 D4
St Christophers Way
 C015 ....220 G7
St Clair
 Clacton-on-S C015 ....195 F8
 Woodford SG3 ....310 F1
St Clair's Dr C016 ....194 B5
St Clair's Rd C016 ....194 B5
St Clare Dr C03 ....135 A7
St Clare Mdw SS4 ....325 F3
St Clare Rd C03 ....135 A6
St Clare's RC Prim Sch
 C016 ....195 B4
St Clement Rd C04 ....110 D2
St Clements Ave
 Grays RM20 ....377 B8
 Southend-on-S SS9 ....70 A2
St Clement's Church La
 1P4 ....17 D5
St Clements CI SS5 ....324 C5
St Clements CI SS7 ....344 D5
St Clements Cres SS7 ....344 D5
St Clements Ct
 Grays RM1 ....377 F8
 Purfleet RM19 ....371 A2
 Waltham Abbey EN9 ....265 C6
St Clements Dr
 Clacton-on-S C015 ....195 B5
 Southend-on-S SS9 ....346 E3
St Clement's Dr SS9 ....346 E3
St Clement's Hospl IP1 .....18 B4
St Clements Rd
 Grays RM20 ....377 C7
 South Benfleet SS7 ....344 D5
St Clere's Comp Sch
 SS17 ....375 C8
St Cleres Cres SS11 ....321 F7
St Cleres Hall La C016 .....194 B3
St Cleres Way CM1 ....256 D7
St Columb Ct C04 ....110 C2
St Cross Ct EN11 ....221 A4
St Cross RC Prim Sch
 EN11 ....221 A4
St Cuthberts Rd EN11 ......197 C1
St Cyrus Rd C04 ....110 D3
St Davids CI E11 ....332 B6
St David's Ct RM1 ....335 A6
St Davids Dr SS9 ....346 A3
St David's Rd
 Basildon SS16 ....341 B4
 Ipswich IP3 ....18 B3
St David's Terr SS11 ....346 A3
St David's Way SS17 ....321 E7
St Davids Wlk SS8 ....363 D4
St Denis Ct C012 ....91 A1
St Dominic Rd C04 ....110 D2
St Dunstan's Rd SG12 .....198 D8
St Edith's CI CM12 ....297 A1
St Ediths La CM12 ....297 A1
St Edmundsbury Ho IP4 ....17 E6
St Edmunds CI C012 ....91 A1
St Edmunds Ct CM4 ....110 C2
St Edmund's Cl C04 ....136 C8
St Edmunds Croft CM6 .....123 E1
St Edmunds Fields CM6 ....123 E1
St Edmund's Hill C08,
 C010 ....55 D6
St Edmunds Ho C04 ....136 C8
St Edmunds La Bures CO8 ..51 E4
 Great Dunmow CM6 ....123 E1
St Edmund's PI IP1 ....17 C8
St Edmund's Rd DA1 ....376 A3
St Edmund's Sch
 Felixstowe IP11 ....381 D2
 Ipswich IP1 ....17 B8
 Redbridge IG2 ....332 F5
St Edmund's Way CM7 .....200 C4
St Edward's CE Comp Sch
 RM7 ....335 A5
St Edward's CE Prim Sch
 RM1 ....335 A6
St Edwards Way RM1,
 RM7 ....335 D6
St Egberts Way E4 ....287 C1
St Erkenwald Mews
 IG11 ....352 D4
St Erkenwald Rd IG11 ......352 D4
St Ethelburga CE RM3 .....315 A1
St Fabian's Dr CM1 ....231 E4
St Faith Rd C04 ....110 D2
St Felix RC Prim Sch C8,P7 ..8 D7
St Fidelis' Rd DA8 ....369 D1
St Fillan Rd C04 ....110 D2
St Francis Ct SS2 ....148 C1
St Francis RC Prim Sch
 Braintree CM7 ....127 E4
 Maldon CM9 ....236 F3
St Francis' Rd DA8 ....369 D2
St Francis Way
 Grays RM16 ....374 C3
 Ilford IG2 ....352 D8
St Gabriel's CI E11 ....332 B3
St Gabriels Ct SS13 ....343 B5
St George's Ave
 Grays RM17 ....373 C2
 Harwich C012 ....91 C2
 Hornchurch RM11 ....335 F4
St George's CE Prim Sch
 C07 ....112 E1

Heybridge Basin CM9 ......237 E3
Hook End CM15 ....272 B4
St George's CI C07 ....112 E1
St Georges Ct
 Romford RM1 ....335 F5
 Romford RM7 ....335 C7
St George's Ct CM14 ......294 B2
St George's Ctr DA11 ......379 B1
St George's Dr SS0 ....347 E3
St George's Hospl RM12 ...355 D7
St George's Inf Sch C02 ...136 A4
St George's Jun Sch
 ....136 A5
St George's La SS3 ....368 F6
St George's Park Ave
 SS0 ....347 B2
St George's Rd RM9 ....353 E8
St George's Rd IG1 ....332 F4
St George's St IP1 ....17 C6
St Georges Wlk IP1
 Canvey Island SS8 ....363 D4
 South Benfleet SS7 ....344 B6
St Giles Ave RM10 ....354 B5
St Giles CE Prim Sch SS9 ..52 D2
St Giles CI
 Dagenham RM10 ....354 B5
 Great Maplestead CO9 ....52 D2
 Maldon CM9 ....236 E2
 Orsett RM16 ....374 A8
St Giles Cres CM9 ....236 E2
St Gregory CE Prim Sch
 C010 ....33 D7
St Gregory's Ct C010 ......33 D8
St Gregorys Ho CM16 .....268 A8
St Guiberts Rd SS8 ....363 E5
St Helena Mews C03 ......135 D5
St Helena Rd C03 ....135 D5
St Helena SS03 ....135 D8
St Helens Ave C015 ....196 A8
St Helen's Church La
 1P4 ....17 E6
St Helens Ct RM13 ....355 A1
St Helen's La CM16 ....246 A1
St Helens Gn C012 ....91 E5
St Helen's La CM7 ....135 F7
St Helen's Prim Sch IP4 ...17 E6
St Helen's RC Inf Sch
 CM14 ....316 D8
St Helen's Rd
 Redbridge IG1 ....332 F5
 Southend-on-S SS0 ....366 E8
St Helen's St IP4 ....17 D6
St Helens Wlk CM14 ......296 F4
St Helier Ct C015 ....196 B4
St Hildas Sch SS0 ....347 C1
St Ives CI
 Clacton-on-S C015 ....195 B3
 Romford RM3 ....314 F3
St Ives Rd C05 ....189 C6
St Ivians Dr RM2 ....336 A8
St James Ave SS13 ....368 B7
St James' Ave CM5 ....249 A1
St James Ave E C017 .....360 E3
St James Ave W SS2 .....349 C6
St James CE Prim Sch
 CM18 ....223 D4
St James' CE Prim Sch
 C01 ....136 B7
St James CI
 Canvey Island SS8 ....363 D4
 Southend-on-S SS0 ....347 A3
St James Ct
 Castle Hedingham CO9 ....51 F4
 Gravesend DA11 ....379 A1
St James's Wlk C017 ......324 C6
St James Way CM3 ....145 C3
St Jean Wlk CO5 ....186 D6
St John Fisher RC Jun Sch
 ....
St John Gdns C05 ....195 G6
St John Payne RC Comp Sch
 CM1 ....231 F6
St Johns Ave CM7 ....127 F2
St John's Ave
 Brentwood CM14 ....316 D6
 Chelmsford CM2 ....254 B8
 Colchester CO2 ....135 F6
 Harlow CM17 ....200 C4
St Johns CE Prim Sch
 Buckhurst Hill IG9 ....288 B1
 Ipswich IP4 ....18 A7
 Tollesbury CM9 ....216 C1
St Johns CE Sec Sch
 CM16 ....245 E1
St Johns CI Basildon SS15 .341 C7

St Johns CI continued
 Great Chesterford CB10 ....3 D2
 Great Wakering SS3 ....350 B3
 Saffron Walden CB11 ......43 D7
St John's CE Prim Sch
 Colchester CO1 ....110 C4
 Rainham RM13 ....355 A5
St Johns Cres SS8 ....363 D3
St Johns Cres CM14 ......294 B2
St Johns Ct Erith DA8 .....369 D1
 Felixstowe IP11 ....381 D4
 Mayland CM3 ....283 A8
 Southend-on-S SS1 ....366 F7
St John's Ct
 Buckhurst Hill IG9 ....288 B1
 Ipswich IP4 ....18 B6
 Tollesbury CM9 ....216 C1
St John's Danbury CE Prim
 Sch CM3 ....256 C7
St Johns Dr SS6 ....322 F4
St Johns Gn CM1 ....231 B1
St John's Green Prim Sch
 C02 ....135 F6
St John's Hospl CM2 ......231 B1
St Johns La SG12 ....197 A6
St Johns La CM24 ....119 E7
St John's Lodge IG10 .....288 F7
St Johns Mews SS17 .....360 F4
St Johns PI CM1 ....298 B4
St Johns PI ◼ IG8 ....311 A5
St Johns Rd RM16 ....374 B1
 Ilford IG2 ....333 E4
 Newport CB11 ....313 C5
St John's Rd Barking IG11 .352 E4
 Billericay CM11 ....297 B3
 Chelmsford CM2 ....254 B8
 Chingford, Chingford Hatch
 E4 ....309 C6
 Chingford, Highams Park
 E17 ....309 C1
 Clacton-on-S C015 ....195 C5
 Epping CM16 ....245 F1
 Erith DA8 ....369 D1
 Great Wakering SS3 ....350 B3
 Hadleigh SS7 ....345 C3
 Ipswich IP4 ....18 A6
 Loughton IG10 ....288 F7
 Southend-on-S SS0 ....366 E8
 Stanstead Mountfitchet
 CM24 ....119 C7
 Wivenhoe C07 ....164 C7
 Writtle CM1 ....231 B1
St Johns Sch CM12 ....297 B3
St John's St
 Colchester CO1 ....135 F6
 Tollesbury CM9 ....216 C1
St John's Terr CM7 ....72 B2
St John's Way SS17 ......360 F4
St Johns Wlk CM17 ......200 C4
St John The Baptist CE Prim
 Sch
 Great Amwell SG12 ....197 A5
 Pebmarsh C09 ....78 B8
St Joseph Rd C04 ....110 C3
St Joseph's Coll IP12 .....17 A3
St Joseph's Convent Sch
 E11 ....332 A5
St Joseph's Ct E4 ....287 D2
St Joseph's Prim Sch
 C010 ....33 E8
St Josephs RC Prim Sch
 Bishop's Stortford CM23 .145 E4
 Canvey Island SS8 ....364 B4
 Dagenham RM9 ....353 F8
 Harwich C012 ....91 B2
 South Woodham Ferrers
 CM3 ....301 C7
 Stanford-le-H SS17 ....360 D2
 Upminster RM14 ....337 B2
St Joseph The Worker RC
 Prim Sch CM13 ....295 C3
St Jude Gdns C04 ....110 E2
St Judes CI C04 ....110 C3
St Judes Ct IG8 ....310 E3
St Julian Gr C01 ....136 A6
St Katherine's CE Prim Sch
 SS6 ....364 A5
St Katherines Ct SS8 .....363 E3
St Kathryns PI RM14 .....337 C2
St Kilda's Rd C015 ....294 C2
St Lawrence CE Prim Sch
 C02 ....163 F8
St Lawrence Ct
 ◼ Braintree CM7 ....127 F3
 Southend-on-S SS9 ....346 E6
St Lawrence Dr
 Steeple CM0 ....262 B8
 St Lawrence CM0 ....240 B1
St Lawrence Gdns
 Blackmore CM4 ....272 E8
 Southend-on-S SS9 ....346 E6
St Lawrence Hill CM0 .....262 E5
St Lawrence Rd
 Colchester CO4 ....110 D2
 Tillingham CM0 ....263 D5
 Upminster RM14 ....337 C2
St Lawrence St IP1 ....17 C6
St Leonard's Ave E4 ......309 D4
St Leonard's CE Jun Sch
 CM0 ....284 D4
St Leonards CI
 Grays RM17 ....377 F8
 Newport CB11 ....43 A2
St Leonards Gdns IG1 ....352 C7
St Leonards Rd
 Ipswich IP3 ....18 B3
 Lower Nazeing EN9 ....243 D6
St Leonard's Rd
 Colchester CO1 ....136 C6
 Southend-on-S SS1 ....367 B7

St Leonards School Ho ◼
 C01 ....136 C6
St Leonards Terr ◼ C01 ..136 C6
St Leonards Way RM11 ....336 B2
St Luke's Ave IG1 ....352 B7
St Luke's CE Prim Sch
 C05 ....186 D5
St Luke's Chase SS5 ......186 D5
St Lukes CI Basildon SS15 .341 C7
St Lukes La SS8 ....363 D4
St Luke's CI C04 ....110 D2
St Luke's Path ◼ IG1 .....352 B7
St Lukes PI SS4 ....325 E2
St Luke's RC Prim Sch
 CM19 ....223 C6
St Luke's Rd SS2 ....348 C2
St Luke's Sch IG10 ......289 A6
St Margarets IG11 ....352 D4
St Margaret's Ave SS17 ..375 C8
St Margarets CE Prim Sch
 IG11 ....343 E5
St Margaret's Inf Sch
 C02 ....17 D6
Toppesfield C09 ....50 C7
St Margaret's Ct C016 ....195 C4
St Margaret's Gn ◼ IP4 ..176 C7
St Margarets Hospl
 CM16 ....246 B2
St Margaret's Plain ◼
 IP4 ....17 D6
St Margaret's Rd
 Chelmsford CM2 ....232 E3
 Hoddesdon SG12 ....197 B2
 Wanstead E12 ....332 C2
St Margaret's Sch C09 ...102 D8
St Margaret's St SP4 .....17 D6
St Margaret's Sta SG12 ..197 C4
St Mark Dr C04 ....110 E2
St Mark's Ave DA11 .....378 F1
St Mark's Path SS4 ......325 F2
St Marks RC Prim Sch
 IP2 ....16 F3
St Marks Rd
 Canvey Island SS8 ....363 D4
 Clacton-on-S C015 ....195 E4
 Colchester CO1 ....135 A6
St Mark's West Essex RC Sch
 CM18 ....223 E7
St Martin's CI
 Clacton-on-S C015 ....195 E4
 South Benfleet SS7 ....344 B7
 White Roding CM6 ....203 C7
St Martin's CI
 Brentwood CM13 ....317 C8
 Rayleigh SS6 ....342 E5
St Martin's Mews CM5 ...249 A2
St Martin's Sch CM13 ....317 C8
St Martins Sq SS14 ......342 A6
St Mary Magdalen Ho
 ....136 B6
St Mary's RC Prim Sch IG1 352 D4
St Mary's Art Ctr* C01 ...136 A6
St Mary's Ave
 South Benfleet SS7 ....344 D1
 Southend-on-S SS3 ....349 D1
St Mary's Bglws CM1 ....17 D7
St Mary's CE Foundation Prim
 Sch CM24 ....119 E7
St Mary's CE Prim Sch
 Ardleigh C07 ....138 D2
 Burnham-on-C CM0 ......306 C6
 Hatfield Broad Oak CM22 148 B4
 Saffron Walden CB10 .....22 D2
 Shenfield CM15 ....294 F3
 Woodham Ferrers CM3 ...279 B4
St Marys CI
 South Benfleet SS7 ....344 D1
 Southend-on-S SS3 ....349 D1
St Mary's CI Grays RM17 .378 D8
 Great Baddow CM2 ......254 F6
 Panfield CM7 ....127 B7
St Mary's Cres
 Brentwood CM14 ....295 A4
 Wanstead E11 ....332 A8
St Mary's Dr
 South Benfleet SS7 ....344 E1
 Stansted Mountfitchet
 CM24 ....119 F5
St Mary's Hare Jun Sch
 RM2 ....336 C8
St Mary's Ho ◼ CM0 .....306 C4
St Mary's La Maldon CM0 237 E3
 Upminster RM14 ....338 D3
 West Horndon CM13 .....314 A7
St Marys Lodge E11 ......332 B5
St Marys Mead CM1 .....208 A1
St Mary's Mews
 Frinton-on-S C013 ....171 A5
 Tollesbury CM9 ....216 D2
St Mary's Path SS13 .....343 C7
St Mary's Pk E16 ....281 C8
St Mary's Prittlewell CE Prim
 Sch SS2 ....348 A5
St Mary's Rd
 Chingford E4 ....287 D1
 Hornchurch RM12 ....336 A3
 Ipswich IP4 ....17 F7
 Tilbury RM18 ....378 F5
St Marys Rd Ilford IG1 ...333 D2
 Wickford SS12 ....321 B5
St Mary's Rd
 Braintree CM7 ....128 B3
 Burnham-on-C CM0 ......306 C4
 Clacton-on-S C015 ....195 C4
 Frinton-on-S C013 ....171 A5
 Grays RM16 ....374 B2
 Great Bentley C07 ....166 F6
 Greenhithe DA9 ....376 E2

St Mary's Rd
 Kelvedon CO5 ....158 C2
 Rivenhall CM8 ....184 B7
 South Benfleet SS7 ....363 E8
 Southend-on-S SS2 ....347 F2
St Mary's Sch
 Colchester CO3 ....135 C7
 Copford CO3 ....133 F5
St Mary's Sq CO5 ....158 B1
St Marys View CB10 .....22 E4
St Marys Wlk IG7 ....72 B1
St Marys Way IG7 ....311 A5
St Mary's Wlk CB9 ......87 B6
St Mathew's Ho ◼ IP1 ...17 B6
St Matthew's CE Prim Sch
 IP1 ....17 B6
St Matthew's St IP1 ......17 B6
St Matthew's CI RM13 ...355 A5
St Michaels CE Jun Sch C01 343 C4
St Michael's CE Prim Sch
 Bishop's Stortford CM23 .145 F7
 Braintree CM7 ....127 D2
St Michaels CI
 Aveley RM15 ....371 C6
 Harlow CM20 ....199 E1
 Latchingdon CM3 ....282 A5
St Michaels Ct ◼ C01 ....135 A6
St Michael's Ct ◼ CM7 ...127 F2
St Michael's Dr CM1 .....230 A5
St Michael's Hospl CM7 ..127 E3
St Michael's La ◼ CM7 ...127 F2
St Michael's Prep Sch
 SS9 ....346 C1
St Michael's Prim Sch
 Bishop's Stortford CM23 .145 F7
 Colchester CO1 ....135 C1
St Michaels Rd
 Canvey Island SS8 ....363 D4
 Grays RM16 ....374 B1
St Michael's Rd
 Braintree CM7 ....127 F2
 Chelmsford CM2 ....254 B8
 Hadleigh SS7 ....91 B2
 Harwich C012 ....221 A3
 Thorpe-le-S C016 ....141 F2
St Michaels Wlk CM2 ....254 C2
St Mildreds Rd CM2 .....254 B8
St Monance Way C04 ....110 D2
St Nazaire Rd CM1 ......231 E6
St Neots CI C04 ....110 D2
St Neot's Rd RM3 ....314 F4
St Nicholas Ave RM12 ...336 A1
St Nicholas CE Prim Sch
 Rawreth SS11 ....322 E7
 Tillingham CM0 ....263 E4
St Nicholas CI C012 .....91 C6
St Nicholas Field CM23 ..92 B8
St Nicholas Gdns* CM7 ..127 E2
St Nicholas Gdns C011 ..200 D1
St Nicholas La SS13 .....317 C5
St Nicholas La SS15 .....341 D7
St Nicholas Pas IG10 ....289 A5
St Nicholas Rd
 Tillingham CM0 ....263 E4
 Witham CM8 ....183 F6
St Nicholas St
 Southend-on-S SS2 ....348 E2
St Nicholas St
 ◼ Colchester CO1 ....135 F7
 Ipswich IP1 ....17 C5
St Nicholas Way C06 ....131 A3
St Olave's Rd E6 ....352 A4
St Omar St SS12 ....321 E6
St Osyth CE Prim Sch
 CO16 ....194 B4
St Osyth CE Sch C015 ...195 E3
St Osyth CI SS8 ....363 D4
St Osyth Priory* CO16 ...194 A4
St Osyth Rd
 Alresford C07 ....165 D7
 Clacton-on-S C015 ....195 D3
 Little Clacton C016 ......168 B1
 St Osyth Rd E C016 ......168 C2
 St Osyth Rd W C016 .....168 C1
St Patrick's Dr RM16 .....374 C2
St Patrick's RC Prim Sch
 RM7 ....313 B2
St Paul's CI SS0 ....366 E8
St Pauls Gdns CM12 .....297 A4
St Pauls Rd Barking IG11 352 C4
 Canvey Island SS8 ....363 D4
St Paul's Rd
 Clacton-on-S C015 ....196 A3
 Colchester CO1 ....135 E8
St Pauls Way EN9 ....265 D6
SS Peter & Paul's Prim Sch
 IG1 ....333 D1
St Peter's Ave
 Chipping Ongar CM5 .....249 A5
 Maldon CM9 ....236 F2
St Peters CE Prim Sch
 CM2 ....276 F4
St Peter's CE Prim Sch
 Coggeshall CO6 ....131 B2
 Sible Hedingham CO9 ....75 D8
St Peter's Chapel*
 CM0 ....382 A5
St Peters CI
 Goldhanger CM9 ....238 E6
 Ilford IG2 ....333 F7
 St Peter CM7 ....127 F4
St Peters Ct
 Clare C010 ....12 B7
 Colchester CO1 ....135 E8
 Southend-on-S SS3 ....368 G7

St Peter's CI CM0 ....263 E8
St Peters Field CM0 ......306 A7
St Peter's Flat Nature
 Reserve* CM0 ....382 A5
St Peter's High Sch & Tech
 Coll CM0 ....306 B6
St Peter's Hospl CM0 ....236 F2
St Peter's-in-the-Fields
 CM7 ....127 F4
St Peter's Pavement
 SS14 ....320 F1
St Peters RC Prim Sch
 CM11 ....319 E6
St Peter's RC Prim Sch
 Dagenham RM9 ....353 F4
 Romford RM1 ....335 D8
St Peters Rd
 Canvey Island SS8 ....363 D4
 Grays RM16 ....374 B2
 Hockley SS5 ....324 B7
St Peter's Rd
 Braintree CM7 ....127 F4
 Brentwood CM14 ....316 B6
 Chelmsford CM1 ....231 F2
 Coggeshall CO6 ....131 B2
 West Mersea C05 ....201 E8
St Peter's St
 Colchester CO1 ....135 F8
 Ipswich IP1 ....17 C5
St Peters Terr SS12 ......321 C7
St Peters View C09 ......51 C1
St Peter's Wlk CM12 .....296 F4
St Peter's Wlk CM7 ......127 F3
St Philip's Priory Sch
 C03 ....254 A8
St Philomena's Sch
 C013 ....170 C5
St Pius X RC Prim Sch
 ....231 F6
St Ronans Cres CO8 .....310 A3
St Runwald St ◼ C01 ....135 F7
St Saviour CI C04 ....110 D2
St Stephens Cres CM13 ..317 A4
St Stephens Ct CM3 .....283 A8
St Stephens La ◼ IP1 ....17 C6
St Swithins Cotts CM2 ...255 C3
Saint's Wlk RM16 ....374 C2
St Teresa RC Prim Sch
 RM8 ....353 C8
St Teresa's RC Prim Sch
 Basildon SS14 ....342 F6
 Colchester CO3 ....134 E5
 Rochford SS4 ....325 E3
St Teresa Wlk RM16 .....374 B3
St Theresa Ct E4 ....287 D2
St Thomas CI CM14 .....316 D8
St Thomas' Cres CM14 ..316 D8
St Thomas Gdns IG1 .....352 C6
St Thomas More High Sch for
 Boys SS0 ....347 A3
St Thomas More RC Prim Sch
 CB11 ....43 E8
St Thomas More's RC Prim
 Sch C01 ....136 A7
St Thomas of Canterbury CE
 Jun & Inf Schs CM15 ....294 D2
St Thomas of Canterbury RC
 Prim Sch RM7 ....373 B2
St Thomas Rd
 Belvedere DA17 ....369 C4
 Brentwood CM14 ....316 D8
 Rochford SS4 ....303 B4
St Thomas's CI EN9 .....266 B6
St Thomas's Dr RM17 ....378 C8
St Thomas's Rd
 RM4 ....314 E8
St Thomas's Row CM0 ...242 B2
St Ursula's RC Jun & Inf Schs
 RM3 ....314 B4
St Vincent Chase CM7 ...128 B5
St Vincent Rd CO15 .....195 E1
St Vincents Ave DA1 ....376 A2
St Vincent's RC Prim Sch
 RM8 ....334 C2
St Vincents Rd
 Chelmsford CM2 ....254 B8
 Dartford DA1 ....376 A1
St Vincent's Sch SS0 ....366 E7
St Winifred's CI IG7 .....311 C5
Sainty CI C07 ....164 C8
Sairard CI SS9 ....346 D7
Sairard Gdns SS9 ....346 D7
Sakins Croft CM18 ......223 F5
Saladin Dr RM19 ....371 A2
Salamons Way RM13 ....369 E7
Salary CI C04 ....110 F1
Salcombe Dr IG10 ......288 D4
Salcombe Rd SS5 ....334 F5
Salcombe Rd E17 ....309 C1
Salcott Cres CM7 ....128 C1
Salcott Cres SS12 ......321 F6
Salcott St CM0 ....220 C8
Salehurst Rd IP3 ....18 E3
Salem Wlk SS6 ....323 B4
Salerno Cres C02 ....135 C2
Salerno Way CM1 ....231 E6
Salesbury Dr CM11 .....297 D2
Salford CI CM3 ....278 B1
Saling Gn SS11 ....319 F2
Saling Hall Gardens*
 CM7 ....126 A8
Salisbury Ave
 Barking IG11 ....352 E5
 Basildon SS15 ....341 D5
 Colchester CO3 ....135 D6
 Southend-on-S SS0 ....366 E7
 Stanford-le-H SS17 ......360 D1
Salisbury CI
 Bishop's Stortford CM23 .145 F5
 Upminster RM14 ....337 F2

Salisbury Ct
Clacton-on-Sea CO15 ....196 D5
2 Haverhill CB9 ....8 F7
Southend-on-S SS9 ....346 D2
Salisbury Gdns IG9 ......310 D8
Salisbury Hall Gdns E4 .309 A4
Salisbury Rd Chingford E4 309 A7
Clacton-on-S CO15 ....196 D5
Dagenham RM10 ....354 B6
Grays RM17 ....373 C1
Hoddesdon EN11 ....221 C8
Ilford IG3 ....333 E2
Ipswich IP3 ....18 A4
Romford RM2 ....336 B6
Southend-on-S SS9 ....346 D1
Salisbury Terr **1** CO10 ..33 E8
Salix Rd RM17 ....378 E8
Sallows Cl IP1 ....16 F7
Sally Murray Cl E12 ......352 A8
Salmon's Gr CM13 ....317 C5
Salmon Cl CO3 ....134 F4
Salmon Par CM1 ....232 B3
Salmon Rd DA17 ....369 A1
Salmons Cl CM6 ....151 A5
Salmon's Cnr CO6 ....132 A3
Salmon's La CO6 ....132 A4
Saltash Rd IG6 ....311 D3
Saltcoat Dr SS8 ....301 D8
Saltcoats Pk* CM3 ....301 F8
Saltcote Maltings CM9 ..237 E4
Saltern Ct IG11 ....353 B2
Salter Pl CM2 ....232 F2
Salters CM23 ....145 C4
Salters Hall Mews CO10 .33 D7
Salter's Mdw CM9 ....215 D4
Salters Rd RM16 ....369 E1
Salthouse St **17** IP4 .....17 D5
Saltings The SS7 ....345 D3
Salt's Gn CM1 ....205 D2
Salvia Cl CO16 ....195 C4
Salway Cl IG8 ....310 A3
Salway Lodge **4** IG8 .....310 A3
Samantha Mews RM4 ....313 E7
Samford Cl IP9 ....62 D7
Samford Ct IP9 ....61 D7
Samford Pl IP8 ....16 B6
Samian Cl CM9 ....236 F5
Samphire Cl CM8 ....183 D3
Samphire Rd RM17 ....378 E8
Sampson Dr CO10 ....15 D8
Sampson's La CO5 ....189 F3
Samson Ho SS15 ....319 B1
Samsons CO CO7 ....192 E8
Samson's Cnr CO7 ....165 D1
Samson's Rd CO7 ....165 E1
Samuel Ct IP4 ....17 D6
Samuel Manor CM2 ......232 F3
Samuel Rd SS16 ....341 B4
Samuel's Cnr SS7 ....350 D3
Samuels Dr SS1 ....368 B8
Sanctuary Gdn SS17 .....360 E2
Sanctuary Rd SS9 ....346 A3
Sandbanks SS7 ....345 D2
Sandcliff Rd DA8 ....369 D1
Sanderling Gdns CM7 ...237 C5
Sanderlings SS7 ....344 C2
Sanderling Way DA9 .....377 A1
Sanders Cl CM24 ....119 D7
Sanders Draper Sch The ....
RM12 ....355 D8
Sanderson Cl CM13 ......339 C5
Sanderson St SS7 ....344 C5
Sanderson Mews CO5 ...163 F8
Sanders Rd SS8 ....364 A6
Sandford Ave IG10 ....289 C6
Sandford Cl CO7 ....164 C8
Sandford Mill Rd ....
Chelmsford CM2 ....232 F2
Chelmsford CM2 ....233 B2
Great Baddow CM2 ....215 D4
Sandford Rd CM2 ....232 E3
Sandgate Cl RM7 ....335 C4
Sandhill Rd SS9 ....346 C8
Sandhurst SS8 ....363 C3
Sandhurst Ave IP3 ....17 F4
Sandhurst Cl SS9 ....346 F4
Sandhurst Cres SS9 ......346 F4
Sandhurst Dr IG3 ....352 F8
Sandhurst Rd RM18 ......379 C5
Sandleigh Rd SS9 ....347 A1
Sande Rd CM23 ....146 A7
Sandling Cres IP4 ....18 E5
Sandlings The IP3 ....18 D1
Sandmartin Cres CO3 ....134 C4
Sandon Brook Pl CM2 ...255 E8
Sandon Cl Basildon SS14 342 F5
Great Horkesley CO6 ......107 C7
Rochford SS4 ....325 D3
Sandon Cl Basildon SS14 342 F5
Ilford IG3 ....334 A1
Sandon Hall Bridleway ....
CM2 ....255 D4
Sandon Hill CM3 ....179 A6
Sandon Pl CM5 ....249 A1
Sandon Rd SS14 ....342 F5
Sandon Sch The 255 B6
Sandown Ave ....
Dagenham RM10 ....354 C6
Hornchurch RM12 ....336 D2
Southend-on-S SS0 ....347 B2
Sandown Cl ....
Clacton-on-S CO15 ....196 A8
Wickford SS11 ....322 A7
Sandown Ct RM10 ....354 C6
Sandown Rd Orsett RM16 374 C7
Thundersley SS7 ....345 B7
Wickford SS11 ....322 A7
Sandpiper Cl ....
Colchester CO4 ....137 A8
Greenhithe DA9 ....377 A1
Haverhill CB9 ....9 C8

Sandpiper Cl *continued* ....
Heybridge CM9 ....237 C5
Southend-on-S SS3 ....368 E8
Sandpiper Rd IP2 ....16 E2
Sandpipers SS3 ....368 G6
Sandpiper Terr IG5 ....333 B8
Sandpiper Wlk CM2 ......254 C6
Sandpit Cl IP4 ....18 F5
Sandpit La ....
3 Braintree CM7 ....127 F3
Burnham-on-C CM0 ....306 C5
Pilgrims Hatch CM14 ......293 F2
Sandpit Rd SS3 ....368 H8
Sandra Ct **5** CO2 ....135 E6
Sandringham Ave ....
Harlow CM13 ....222 E8
Hockley SS5 ....324 D6
Sandringham Cl ....
Ilford IG6 ....311 B6
Ipswich IP2 ....16 F2
Stanford-le-H SS17 ....360 E3
Sandringham Ct CO10 ....34 A7
Sandringham Dr CO2 ....136 A4
Sandringham Gdns ....
6 Bishop's Stortford CM23 145 E5
Ilford IG6 ....333 C8
Sandringham Pl CM2 ....232 C2
Sandringham Rd ....
Barking IG11 ....352 F6
Basildon SS15 ....341 E8
Pilgrims Hatch CM15 ......294 B3
Sands Way IG8 ....310 F4
Sandwich Cl CM7 ....127 E6
Sandwich Rd ....
Brightlingsea CO7 ....192 F8
Clacton-on-S CO15 ....220 J8
Sandy Hill IG6 ....80 D5
Sandy Hill La IP11 ....100 C7
Sandyhill Rd IG1 ....352 B8
Sandy La Aveley RM15 ...371 A6
Bulmer CO10 ....32 F5
Grays, Chadwell St Mary ....
RM16 ....374 C1
Grays, West Thurrock ....
RM20 ....377 B8
Sudbury CO10 ....33 B5
Sangster Ct SS6 ....323 F2
San Juan Dr RM16 ....372 C2
San Luis Dr RM12 ....372 C2
San Marcos Dr RM16 ....372 C2
San Remo Mans SS0 .....366 E7
San Remo Par SS0 ....366 E7
San Remo Rd SS0 ....364 D3
San Remo SS10 ....318 E5
Sansom Cl IG7 ....79 F5
Santiago Way RM16 ......372 D1
Sapling Pl IP4 ....18 E5
Sappers Cl CM21 ....172 F2
Sapphire Cl RM8 ....334 C3
Sapphire Ct SS1 ....367 B6
Sapphire Ho **8** RM13 ..355 A1
Sara Cres DA9 ....377 B3
Sarah's Wlk CM2 ....148 F7
Saran Ct CO7 ....137 A2
Sarbir Ind Pk CM17 ......200 C5
Sarcel CM7 ....129 C6
Sargeant Ct CO2 ....136 B3
Sark Gr SS12 ....321 F5
Sarre Ave RM12 ....355 C6
Sarre Way CO7 ....192 E8
Sassoon Way **3** CM9 ...237 A1
Satanita Rd SS0 ....366 D8
Saul's Ave CM5 ....252 C8
Sauls Bridge Cl CM8 .....212 A8
Saunders Ave CM7 ....127 E2
Saunders Cl CM23 ....94 C1
Saunton Rd RM12 ....336 A2
Savannah Hts SS9 ....347 A1
Savernake Rd CM1 ....231 E1
Saville Cl CB11 ....65 C4
Saville Rd RM6 ....334 F4
Saville St CO14 ....144 C1
Savill Rd CO2 ....136 C2
Savill Row IG8 ....309 F4
Savoy Cl SS16 ....341 A5
Savoy Wood CM19 ....223 B2
Sawbridgeworth Rd ....
Hatfield Heath CM22 ......173 A6
Little Hallingbury CM22 ...173 B6
Sawbridgeworth Sta ....
CM21 ....173 A3
Sawkins Ave CM2 ....254 D6
Sawkins Cl Abberton CO5 163 B2
Chelmsford CM2 ....254 D6
Sawkins Gdns CM2 ....254 D6
Sawney Brook CM1 ....231 A1
Sawpit La CM23 ....92 D7
Sawston Cl IP2 ....17 F2
Sawston Ct **10** RM19 ....371 B1
Sawyer's Chase RM4 .....290 B6
Sawyers Ct **3** IP9 ....35 A1
Sawyers Ct CM15 ....294 F3
Sawyers Gr CM15 ....294 F3
Sawyer's Hall La CM15 ..294 D1
Sawyer's Rd CM9 ....214 C5
Saxham Rd IG11 ....352 E3
Saxlingham Rd E4 ....309 D7
Saxmundham Way CO16 195 A3
Saxon Bank CM7 ....128 B2
Saxon Cl Brentwood CM13 317 A7
Colchester CO3 ....134 F4
Halstead CO9 ....76 F2
Rayleigh SS6 ....323 E5
Romford RM3 ....314 F1
Wickford SS11 ....299 E1
Saxon Ct Maldon SS9 .....237 A3
South Benfleet SS7 ....344 C5
Saxon Dr CM8 ....183 D3
Saxon Gdns SS3 ....368 D7
Saxon Ho RM14 ....338 D4
Saxon La IP8 ....35 D7
Saxon Pl SS4 ....325 F2
Saxon Rd IG1 ....352 B7
Saxonville SS7 ....344 B4

Saxon Way ....
Chelmsford CM1 ....232 B7
Holland-on-S CO15 ....196 F4
Maldon CM9 ....237 B1
Point Clear B CO16 ....192 F3
Saffron Walden CB11 ....22 C1
South Benfleet SS7 ....344 C2
Waltham Abbey EN9 ....265 C6
Saxstead Dr CO16 ....195 A4
Sayer Cl DA9 ....377 A2
Sayers SS7 ....345 A7
Sayesbury Ave CM21 ....172 E3
Sayesbury Rd CM21 ......172 E2
Sayes Gdns CM21 ....172 F2
Saywell Brook CM7 ......228 A2
Scalby Rd CM0 ....284 A3
Scaldhurst SS13 ....343 C8
Scarborough Rd ....
Southend-on-S SS9 ....346 E2
Southminster CM0 ....284 A3
Scarfe's Cnr CO6 ....82 B4
Scarfe Way CM4 ....136 E6
Scargill Jun & Inf Sch ....
RM13 ....355 A6
Scarles Croft CM3 ....278 C7
Scarletts SS14 ....342 C8
Scarletts Cl CM8 ....212 A7
Scarletts Rd CO1 ....136 C4
Sceptre Cl CM9 ....299 D2
Scholars Ho **6** E4 ....287 D1
Scholars Rd E4 ....287 D1
School Barn Cotts CO10 ..13 F7
School Chase CO9 ....103 E8
School Cl IP9 ....35 A1
School Ct CO12 ....91 D4
Schoolfield Birdbrook CO9 .28 A6
Glemsford CO10 ....2 B5
Schoolfield Rd RM20 ....377 A8
School Green La CM16 ..247 C6
School Hill Birch CO2 ....161 A4
Washbrook IP8 ....35 F8
School Ho ....
10 Colchester CO1 ....136 A6
Shalford CM7 ....100 E5
Schoolhouse Gdns IG10 289 B5
School La ....
Abbess Roding CM5 ....203 F3
Basildon SS12 ....322 A2
Beauchamp Roding CM5 ...228 A7
Birch CO2 ....161 A4
Brantham CO11 ....60 D1
Broomfield CM1 ....208 B1
Chelmsford CM1 ....231 F8
Chigwell IG7 ....311 F6
Dedham CO7 ....85 B4
Duddenhoe End CB11 ......41 A7
East Bergholt CO7 ....59 B3
Great Bentley CO7 ....166 A8
Great Horkesley CO6 ....82 A2
Great Leighs CM3 ....180 F8
Great Wigborough CO5 ....188 B2
Harlow CM20 ....199 E2
Haverhill CB9 ....8 E7
Henham CM22 ....94 F5
High Easter CM1 ....177 B3
Ingrave CM13 ....317 C4
Lawford CO11 ....86 A4
Little Horkesley CO6 ....81 D5
Mistley CO11 ....86 A7
Newport CB11 ....42 F1
Orsett RM16 ....374 A8
South Benfleet SS7 ....363 D8
Stanford Rivers CM5 ....277 C8
Stratford St M CO7 ....58 D2
Takeley CM22 ....121 D6
Tilgate Green CM5 ....225 D6
West Bergholt CO6 ....108 E4
School Mews CO6 ....130 F2
School Rd Billericay CM12 319 A8
Chipping Ongar CM5 ....270 B7
Colchester CO2 ....136 A2
Copford CO6 ....133 D3
Dagenham RM10 ....354 B4
Downham CM11 ....298 F5
Elmstead CO7 ....138 A4
Frinton-on-S CO13 ....170 E5
Great Oakley CO12 ....116 C3
Great Totham CM9 ....213 B3
Kelvedon Hatch CM15 .....271 F2
Langham CO4 ....85 E8
Little Horkesley CO6 ....81 D4
Little Maplestead CO9 ....77 B8
Little Totham CM9 ....214 B3
Little Yeldham CO9 ....30 D3
Margaret Roding CM1 .....205 C5
Messing CO5 ....160 F2
Pentlow CO10 ....13 F6
Rayne CM7 ....153 E8
Shotley Gate IP9 ....91 B8
Sible Hedingham CO9 ....75 D8
Silver End CM8 ....159 E3
Tendring CO16 ....140 E6
Wickham Bishops CM8 ....212 F5
Wickham St P CO9 ....53 C5
School St Foxearth CO10 ..14 D6
Great Chesterford CB10 .....3 D2
Stoke-by-N CO6 ....56 D5
Sudbury CO10 ....33 E7
School View CM7 ....127 E2
School View Rd CM1 .....231 F3
School Villas ....
Great Easton CM6 ....123 A8
Henham CM6 ....95 F2
High Roding CM6 ....176 E7
Lindsell CM6 ....97 F4
Takeley CM22 ....121 C6
School Way ....
Dagenham RM8 ....334 C1
Southend-on-S SS9 ....346 F3
School Wlk CM7 ....127 F3

Scilla Ct RM17 ....378 D8
Scimitar Pk SS13 ....321 D2
Scofield Ct CO10 ....34 A6
Scoter Cl IG8 ....310 B3
Scotland Rd IG9 ....288 C1
Scotland St CO6 ....56 E6
Scotney Wlk RM12 ....355 D7
Scott Ave ....
Stanstead Abbotts SG12 ...197 B4
Wethersfield CM7 ....73 D6
Scott Cl CM7 ....155 A8
Scott Dr Colchester CO3 .134 F6
Wickford SS12 ....321 E5
Scottes La RM8 ....334 D3
Scott Ho Romford RM1 ...336 A5
Southend-on-S SS9 ....347 A7
Scott Rd ....
Bishop's Stortford CM23 ..145 E6
Grays RM16 ....374 A2
Ipswich IP3 ....18 B1
Stansted Mountfitchet ....
CM24 ....120 B2
Sudbury CO10 ....15 F1
Trimley St M IP11 ....381 A7
Walton-on-t-N CO14 ....144 E3
Weeley CO16 ....167 F8
Wickford SS11 ....322 A6
Seddons Wlk SS5 ....324 E6
Seden Ct CO15 ....169 B1
Sedge Ct RM17 ....378 F8
Sedgefield Cl RM3 ....314 F6
Sedgefield Cres RM3 ....314 F6
Sedgefield Way CM7 ....128 B1
Sedge Gn EN9 ....221 E3
Sedgemoor SS3 ....349 D1
Sedgemoor Dr RM10 ....354 A8
Sedley Rise IG10 ....288 F7
Sedop Cl CB11 ....43 D7
Seedbed Ctr ....
Colchester CO4 ....110 C6
Southend-on-S SS3 ....368 F7
Seedbed Ctr The RM7 ...335 E4
Seedfield The CO5 ....218 B6
Seeleys The CM17 ....200 C4
SE Essex Coll ....
Southend-on-S SS1 ....366 F8
Southend-on-S SS2 ....347 F1
Sejant Ho RM17 ....378 B8
Selborne Ave E12 ....352 A8
Selborne Rd IG1 ....333 A2
Selbourne Rd ....
Hockley SS5 ....324 E6
South Benfleet SS7 ....344 D6
Southend-on-S SS2 ....348 C3
Selby Cl CO5 ....135 D1
Selby Dr CS0 ....347 B3
Seldon Rd CO5 ....169 D1
Selhurst Ct CO14 ....170 F7
Selinas La RM8 ....334 F4
Selkirk Rd E4 ....18 B8
Selsdon Cl RM5 ....313 C2
Selsdon Rd E11 ....332 A4
Seltie Cl RM3 ....313 E3
Selvale Way IP11 ....381 C4
Selwood Rd CM14 ....315 F7
Selworthy Cl ....
Billericay CM11 ....319 C7
Wanstead E11 ....332 A6
Selwyn Ave Chingford E4 309 D4
Ilford IG3 ....333 F5
Selwyn Cl IP2 ....17 C4
Selwyn Inf Sch E4 ....309 C4
Selwyn Jun Sch E4 ....309 C4
Semer Rd ....
Southend-on-S SS2 ....348 C2
Tilbury RM18 ....378 F5
Semper Rd RM16 ....374 C4
Semples SS17 ....360 F2
Septimus Dr CO4 ....110 A5
Serena Ct RM12 ....336 A3
Sergeants Green La EN9 266 C6
Serpentine Rd IP3 ....18 C2
Serpentine Wlk CO1 ......199 F7
Service Industry Bays ....
CO4 ....199 F2
Servite Ho IP4 ....17 F6
Seton Gdns RM9 ....353 C5
Settle Rd RM3 ....315 A6
Seven Acres SS11 ....321 F8
Seven Arches Rd CM14 .316 E7
Seven Ash Gn CM1 ....232 C5
Seven Devils La CB11 ....43 D6
Seven Kings High Sch ....
IG1 ....333 D4
Seven Kings Sta IG3 .....333 E3
Seven Kings Way CO4 ...109 E3
Sevenoaks Ct RM3 ....314 C6
Sevenoaks CM3 ....206 C7
Severalls La CO4 ....110 B6
Severalls Hospl CO4 ......109 E5
Severn Rd ....
Clacton-on-S CO15 ....195 F5
Ipswich IP3 ....17 F3
Severns Field CM6 ....246 A2
Sewards End SS12 ....321 E6
Sewardstone Gdns E4 ....287 B6
Sewardstone Rd ....
Chingford E4 ....287 B5
Sewardstone E4 ....309 C4
Sewardstone St EN9 .....265 C5
Sewell Cl RM16 ....372 C1
Sewell Harris Cl CM20 ..199 E1
Sexton Cl Colchester CO2 163 B8
Rainham RM13 ....354 F4
Sexton Rd RM18 ....378 F6
Sextons La CM8 ....185 B1
Seckford Cl IP4 ....18 F5

Seymore Dr CB9 ....8 D7
Seymour Cl ....
Basildon SS15 ....341 D6
Loughton IG10 ....288 C3
Seymour Ct E4 ....309 F8
Seymour Gdns IG1 ....332 F3
Seymour Mews CM21 ...200 C7
Seymour Pl RM11 ....336 D4
Seymour Rd Chingford E4 287 B1
Hadleigh SS7 ....345 F3
Ipswich IP2 ....17 C4
Jaywick CO15 ....194 F1
Southend-on-S SS0 ....347 C1
Tilbury RM18 ....378 F6
Seymours Harlow CM19 ..222 A5
Harlow CM19 ....223 A5
Seymour's IG10 ....289 A8
Seymour St CM2 ....232 A1
Shackleton Cl CO12 ....90 F1
Shackleton Gdns CM23 .145 E6
Shackleton Rd IP3 ....18 B3
Shackleton Sq IP3 ....18 B3
Shaftenhoe End Rd SG8 ..39 B8
Shafter Rd RM10 ....354 C6
Shaftesbury Ave ....
Harwich CO12 ....91 B4
Southend-on-S SS1 ....367 E6
Shaftesbury Ct ....
Dagenham RM6 ....334 C4
10 Haverhill CB9 ....8 E7
Shaftesbury La DA1 ......376 B3
Shaftesbury Rd ....
Chingford E4 ....287 D1
Epping CM16 ....245 F2
Romford RM1 ....335 F6
Shaftesbury Sq **4** IP4 ...17 D5
Shaftesburys The IG11 ..352 C3
Shafts Rd IP1 ....16 E8
Shaftsbury Ct SS13 ....343 B7
Shair La ....
Great Bentley CO7 ....167 B8
Weeley CO16 ....140 B2
Shakespeare Ave ....
Basildon SS16 ....341 A5
Billericay CM11 ....297 C2
Rayleigh SS6 ....324 A2
Southend-on-S SS0 ....347 C2
Tilbury RM18 ....379 B6
Shakespeare Cl CM7 .....155 A7
Shakespeare Ct IG11 ....197 A2
Shakespeare Dr ....
Maldon CM9 ....259 A8
Southend-on-S SS0 ....347 C2
Shakespeare Rd ....
Colchester CO3 ....134 F6
Dartford DA1 ....376 B3
10 Romford RM1 ....335 F5
Shakespeare Sq IG6 .....311 C4
Shakeston Cl CM1 ....253 B8
Shakletons CM5 ....249 A3
Shalfleet Ct CO15 ....195 F8
Shalford Rd IG8 ....310 C4
Shalford Lodge CM7 .....232 B8
Shalford Prim Sch CM7 .100 E5
Shalford Rd ....
Billericay CM11 ....297 D2
Rayne CM7 ....126 E3
Shamrock Ave IP2 ....16 E4
Shamrock Cl CM5 ....216 D2
Shamrock Ho CO15 ....220 J8
Shangani Rd CM23 ....145 F5
Shanklin Ave CM12 ......297 A2
Shanklin Cl CO15 ....196 A8
Shanklin Dr SS0 ....347 B2
Shannon Ave SS3 ....323 D1
Shannon Cl Haverhill CB9 ..9 D7
Southend-on-S SS0 ....346 E4
Shannon Rd IP3 ....388 A8
Shannon Way ....
Aveley RM15 ....371 C6
Canvey Island SS8 ....363 D3
Shardelow Ave CM1 ......233 A8
Sharlands Cl SS11 ....321 F6
Sharland Row CM7 ....216 A8
Sharnbrook SS3 ....349 D2
Sharpecroft CM20 ....223 C8
Sharpington Cl CM2 .....254 D3
Shatters Rd CO2 ....161 A1
Shaw Ave IG11 ....353 E3
Shawbridge CM19 ....223 C5
Shaw Cl Hornchurch RM11 336 B3
Kirby Cross CO13 ....170 F7
Wickford SS12 ....321 D5
Shaw Cres ....
Brentwood CM13 ....295 D5
Tilbury RM18 ....379 C6
Shaw Dr CM7 ....73 D7
Shaw Gdns IG11 ....353 E3
Shawlands Ave CO10 .....34 B7
Shaw Prim Sch RM15 .....372 B7
Shaw Rd ....
Long Melford CO10 ....15 D8
Witham CM8 ....183 F5
Shaw The CM22 ....174 A4
Shearers The CM23 ......145 C4
Shearers Way CM3 ....209 F1
Shearman Ct **8** CB9 ......9 A7
Shears Cres CO5 ....218 D5
Shears Ct CO5 ....218 D5
Shearwater CI IG11 ....353 A2
Sheds La CB10 ....22 E2
Sheene Gr CM7 ....128 D5
Sheepcotes La CM9 ......213 F8
Sheepcote La CM23 ....92 E3
Sheepcotes CM2 ....233 B5
Sheepcotes La ....
Heybridge CM9 ....237 F8
Little Waltham CM8 ....196 C6
Silver End CM8 ....159 E3
Southminster CM0 ....284 D5
Sheepcotes Rd RM6 .....334 C4
Sheepcot Rd CO9 ....141 F2
Sheepen Pl CO3 ....135 E8
Sheepen Rd CO3 ....135 D8

Southlands Chase CM2 .....255 E2
Southlands Rd CM11 ....320 E6
Southland Terr ⓸ RM19 .371 B1
South Mayne SS14 ....343 A5
Southmill Rd CM23 ....146 A5
Southmill Trad Ctr
CM23 ....146 A6
Southminster Cty Inf Sch
CM0 ....284 D4
Southminster Rd
Althorne CM3 ....283 C4
Asheldham CM0 ....285 A7
Burnham-on-C CM0 ....306 B8
St Lawrence CM0 ....262 F3
Southminster Sta CM0 ....284 E4
South Ordnance Rd EN3 265 A2
South Par
Canvey Island SS8 ....364 E2
South Ockendon RM15 ...372 C8
South Park Bsns Ctr IG3 333 E2
South Park Cres IG1 ......333 E1
South Park Dr
Barking IG11 ....352 E8
Ilford IG3 ....333 E2
South Park Inf Sch IG3 ...333 E1
South Park Prim Sch
IG1 ....333 E1
South Park Rd IG1 ....333 D1
South Park Terr IG1 ....333 E1
South Park Villas IG3 ....352 E8
South Primrose Hill CM1 231 F3
South Rd
Basildon, Crays Hill CM11 .320 D5
Basildon,Vange SS17 .....342 C1
Bishop's Stortford CM23 .146 A5
Dagenham RM6 ....334 E5
Harlow CM20 ....200 A4
Ilford RM6 ....334 C6
Saffron Walden CB11 .....22 E1
South Ockendon RM15 ...372 C7
Takeley CM22 ....148 C8
South Residence IG3 .....334 B6
South Ridge CM11 ....297 C2
South Riding SS14 ....342 E6
Southsea Ave SS9 ....346 D1
Southsea Ho ⓯ RM3 .....314 D5
South St
Bishop's Stortford CM23 .145 F6
Bradwell-on-S CM0 ......242 A2
Braintree CM7 ....127 F2
Brentwood CM14 ....316 C8
Colchester CO2 ....135 E6
Great Chesterford CB10 ...3 D2
Great Waltham CM3 ......207 E7
Ipswich IP1 ....17 B7
Manningtree CO11 ....86 D4
Rainham RM13 ....354 D3
Rochford SS4 ....325 F1
Romford RM1 ....335 E6
Romford RM1 ....335 F5
Stanstead Abbotts SG12 .197 C4
Tillingham CM0 ....263 E3
Tolleshunt D'arcy CM9 ...215 D4
South St Commercial Ctr ⓯
CM23 ....145 F6
South Strand CO11 ....86 C5
South Suffolk Bsns Pk
CO10 ....38 A7
South View
Great Dunmow CM6 .....150 C8
Orsett RM16 ....374 B8
Southview Ave RM18 ....379 A6
Southview Cl CM3 ....301 D8
South View Cl SS6 ....345 F8
South View Cres IG2 .....333 B5
Southview Dr
Holland-on-S CO15 ......196 F6
Southend-on-S SS0 ......347 C2
Walton-on-t-N CO14 ......171 C7
Wanstead E18 ....332 B8
South View Dr RM14 .....337 B1
South View Gn IP9 ....60 E6
Southview Hts RM20 .....377 C8
Southview Rd
Basildon SS16 ....342 E5
Danbury CM3 ....256 D6
Hockley SS5 ....324 F7
South View Rd
Grays RM20 ....377 C8
Loughton IG10 ....288 F3
Rettendon CM3 ....300 C5
South Benfleet SS7 .....344 C3
Southview Sch CM8 .....183 F6
Southview Terr CM3 .....256 D6
Southwalters IG8 ....363 F4
Southwark Path SS14 ....342 E7
South Wash Rd SS15 ....319 F1
Southway Basildon SS16 .341 D2
Brightlingsea CO7 ......192 F7
Colchester CO1, CO3 ....135 E6
South Way Purfleet RM19 371 E3
Waltham Abbey EN9 .....265 D6
South Weald Dr EN9 .....265 D6
South Weald Rd CM14 ...316 A7
Southwell CT RM16 ......372 C1
Southwell Rd SS7 ....344 E4
Southwick Gdns SS8 .....363 F3
Southwick Rd SS8 ....363 F3
South Wlk SS14 ....342 E5
Southwold Cres SS7 .....344 C5
Southwold Dr IG11 ......353 A7
Southwold Way CO16 ...195 A5
Southwood Chase CM3 ..257 A4
Southwood Ct SS14 .....342 D8
South Woodford Sta ⓯
E18 ....310 B1
Southwood Gdns
Ilford IG2 ....333 B7
Rayleigh SS9 ....346 B8

Southwood Prim Sch
RM9 ....353 E8
Sovereign Cl
Braintree CM7 ....128 D4
Rochford SS4 ....325 E2
Sovereign Cres CO3 ....135 C6
Sovereign Ct
Brentwood CM14 ......316 C7
Harlow CM19 ....223 B5
Southend-on-S SS9 ....346 E2
Sovereign Ctr IP1 ....16 C7
Sovereign Ho RM13 ....355 B2
Sovereign Mews SS0 ...366 E8
Sovereign Pk SS14 ......320 E1
Sovereign Pl SS3 ....346 E7
Sovereign Rd IG11 .....353 C2
Sowerberry Cl CM1 ....231 F7
Sowrey Ave RM13 ......355 A6
Spa Ct SS5 ....324 F6
Spa Dr CM0 ....241 B1
Spa Dr CM0 ....240 B1
Spains Hall Pl SS16 ....342 C5
Spains Hall Rd CM6 ....228 E2
Spalding Ave CM1 .....231 E5
Spalding Cl CM7 ....127 E4
Spalding Ct CM1 ......232 A3
Spalding Way CM2 ....254 F8
Spalt Cl CM13 ....317 B8
Spanbeek Rd SS8 .....364 B5
Spanbies Rd CO7 .....58 D2
Spansey Ct ⓵ CO9 ...76 D1
Spa Rd Feering CO5 ..158 E4
Hockley SS5 ....324 E6
Witham CM8 ....183 E2
Sparepenny Hill IG10 ..288 F5
Sparepenny La N CB10 ..47 A4
Sparepenny La S CB10 ..47 A4
Sparkey Cl CM8 ....212 A7
Sparks Cl RM8 ....334 D2
Sparks La CO9 ....29 A6
Spar La CM3 ....258 C3
Sparling Cl CO2 ....135 C2
Sparlings The CO13 ...170 C8
Sparrow Cl CO9 ....75 D8
Sparrow Ct E4 ....309 C4
Sparrow Gr RM10 .....335 B1
Sparrow Rd CO10 .....34 B6
Sparrows Cl CM1 .....252 A5
Sparrows Cnr CO2 ...116 E5
Sparrowsend Cotts CB11 43 A4
Sparrowsend Hill CB11 .43 A5
Sparrows Herne
Basildon SS16 ....342 B4
Clacton-on-S CO15 ...195 F6
Sparrow's La
Hatfield Heath CM22 ...174 F1
White Roding CM22 ....202 E6
Sparsholt Rd IG11 .....352 E4
Spartan Cl CB9 ....8 C8
Spearpoint Gdns IG2 ..333 E7
Speckled Wood Cl IP8 ..36 D8
Speckled Wood Ct CM7 .154 E8
Speedwell Cl CM8 .....183 D4
Speedwell Ct RM17 ...378 E7
Speedwell Rd
Colchester CO2 ....136 D2
Ipswich IP2 ....16 F4
Spellbrook Cl CM23 ...321 F6
Spellbrook La E CM22 .172 E8
Spellbrook La W CM23 .172 E7
Spellbrook Prim Sch
CM23 ....172 F7
Spells Cl CM0 ....284 D4
Spencer Ct
Billericay CM12 ....296 F5
Elsenham CM22 ....94 C3
Maldon CM9 ....259 A8
Stansted Mountfitchet
CM24 ....119 C6
Woodford IG8 ....310 C5
Spencer Ct
Hornchurch RM12 .....336 A1
South Woodham Ferrers
CM3 ....301 C7
Spencer Gdns SS4 ....325 E5
Spencer Ho SS0 ....347 A1
Spencer Rd Chingford E17 309 C1
Great Chesterford CB10 ...3 D3
Ilford IG3 ....333 F3
Rainham RM13 ....354 D3
South Benfleet SS7 ....344 D6
Thorpe-le-S CO16 .....142 A2
Spencer St
Harlow CM20 ....233 A5
Springfield Nursery Est
CM0 ....306 A5
Springfield Park Ave
CM2 ....232 E2
Spencers Croft CM18 ..224 B6
Spencers Ct SS12 .....321 C7
Spencers Piece CO4 ...83 E4
Spencer Sq CM7 ......127 F8
Spencer Wlk RM18 ....379 B6
Spenders Cl CO14 ....144 D2
Spenders Cl SS14 .....342 D8
Spenlow Dr CM1 ......231 D7
Spennells The CO16 ..142 A2
Spenser Ave RM14 ....337 C4
Spenser Way CO15 ...194 F1
Speyside Wlk ⓶ SS12 .321 E5
Spey Way RM1 ....313 E3
Spicers La CO10 ....15 C8
Spike The ⓵ CB10 ....22 F2
Spillbutters CM15 ....272 B1
Spilsby Rd RM3 ....314 E3
Spindle Beams CM3 ..325 F1
Spindle Rd CB9 ....8 D8
Spindrift Way CO7 ...164 B8
Spingate Cl HA12 .....353 D7
Spinks La CM8 ....183 F1
Spinnaker Cl
Barking IG11 ....353 B2
Clacton-on-S CO15 ...220 J8
Spinnaker Dr CM9 ....237 E3
Spinnakers The SS7 ...344 B4
Spinnaker The CM3 ...301 E5
Spinnel's Hill CO11 ....88 B1

Spinnel's La Wix CO11 .....115 D7
Wrabness CO11 ....88 C1
Spinner Cl IP1 ....16 D8
Spinney Cl Rainham RM13 354 E3
Wickford SS11 ....321 F7
Spinney Ct CM21 ....172 E2
Spinneyfields CO5 ....186 D6
Spinney Gdns RM9 ......353 E7
Spinney Jun & Inf Schs
CM20 ....200 A1
Spinneys The
Hockley SS5 ....324 D5
Ilford IG4 ....324 A1
Southend-on-S SS9 .....346 F7
Spinney The
Billericay CM12 ....297 B4
Braintree CM7 ....128 C1
Brentwood CM13 ....295 C3
Chipping Ongar CM5 ...248 F1
Earls Colne CO6 ....105 A6
Newport CB11 ....67 A7
Orsett RM16 ....359 A1
Rushmere St A IP4 .....18 F4
Stansted Mountfitchet
CM24 ....119 C6
Loughton IG10 ....289 B5
Spinnywood SS15 .....341 A8
Spinning Wheel Mead
Sales Green Ctr CM19 ..222 E7
Spire Rd SS15 ....341 C7
Spires The
Bishop's Stortford CM23 145 D7
Great Baddow CM2 ...254 F6
Spital La CM14 ....315 F6
Spital Rd Maldon CM9 .256 F2
Maldon CM9 ....258 D7
Spitfire Cl IP3 ....18 B1
Sporehams La
Danbury CM3 ....256 C4
Howe Green CM2,CM3 .255 F4
Sportsman La CM4 ....341 A1
Sportsmans La CM4 ..211 A2
Sportsway CO1 ....135 F8
Spots Wlk CM2 ....254 D3
Spout La CO10 ....55 D7
Spratt Hall Rd E11 ....332 A5
Spratts La CO11 ......113 B4
Spread Eagle Pl CM4 .274 C4
Spriggs La CM4 ....251 A2
Spriggs Oak CM4 ....246 A2
Springbank Ave
Hornchurch RM12 .....355 C7
Lawford CO11 ....86 B3
Springbok Ho CM2 ...254 F5
Spring Chase
Brightlingsea CO7 .....192 E7
Wivenhoe CO7 ....137 B2
Spring Cl
Clacton-on-S CO16 ...195 C5
Colchester CO4 ....110 C3
Dagenham RM8 ......334 D3
Little Baddow CM3 ...234 D5
Spring Cotts CB9 .....9 C6
Spring Ct E18 ....332 B8
Spring Elms La CM3 ..234 F3
Springett's Hill CO8 ...55 D2
Springfarm CM11 ....355 D2
Springfield Epping CM16 267 F7
Hadleigh SS7 ....345 D4

Spring Gdns continued
Long Melford CO10 .....15 C8
Rayleigh SS6 ....323 C2
Romford RM7 ....335 C5
Woodford IG8 ....310 C3
Spring Gr IG10 ....288 D3
Spring Mews CM21 ..272 E2
Springhall La CM21 ..172 E2
Springhall Rd CM21 ..172 E2
Springhead Rd DA11 .378 D1
Spring Hill CM11 .....222 A1
Springhill Cl CO7 .....138 E8
Springhill Rd CB11 ...43 D8
Spring Hills CM20 ....199 B1
Springhouse La SS17 .361 A3
Springhouse Rd SS17 .360 F4
Springhurst Cl CM4 ...17 F6
Spring La Colchester CO3 135 A7
Colchester,Lexden Bridge
CO3 ....135 A8
Eight Ash G CO3 .....108 B1
Great Totham CM9 ...213 D7
Hatfield Peverel CM3,CM9 211 F2
Maldon CM9 ....237 B4
West Bergholt CO6 ...108 E3
Witham CM8 ....212 A7
Wivenhoe CO7 ......137 B2
Springland Cl IP4 ....18 A6
Springlands Way CO10 .2 B6
Spring Lane Rdbt CO3 .135 A7
Springleigh Pl SS0 ...347 D2
Springmead CM7 ....154 D7
Spring Meadow CO10 ..2 B6
Spring Meadow Prim Sch
CO12 ....91 A3
Spring Pond Cl CM2 ..192 F7
Spring Pond Ct CM7 .127 C4
Spring Pond Mdw CM5 272 C4
Springpond Rd RM9 ..353 E7
Spring Rd
Brightlingsea CO7 ....192 F7
Ipswich IP4 ....18 A6
St Osyth CO16 ....194 A3
Tiptree CO5 ....186 C4
Spring Rise
Galleywood CM2 ....254 C2
Haverhill CB9 ....9 D5
Spring Sedge Cl CO3 .134 C7
Springtail Rd IP8 .....36 E7
Spring Vale CM0 .....377 C1
Springvalley La CO7 ..211 C4
Springwater Cl SS9 ..346 C7
Springwater Gr SS9 .346 C7
Springwater Rd SS9 .346 C8
Spring Way CO9 .....51 E1
Springwell Cl SG12 ..197 C3
Springwood CB10,CB11 22 A5
Springwood Ct CM7 .127 C4
Springwood Dr CM7 .127 C4
Springwood Ind Est
CM7 ....127 C4
Springwood Way RM1 .336 A6
Sprites End IP11 ......381 B7
Spriteshall La IP11 ...381 B7
Sprotbrough Rd SS12 322 C2
Sprites La IP9, IP12 ..16 C2
Sproughton Bsns Pk IP1 16 C8
Sproughton CE Prim Sch
IP8 ....16 B6
Sproughton Ct IP8 ...16 A6
Sproughton Rd IP1 ..16 D7
Spruce Ave
Colchester CO4 ......136 E8
Great Dunmow CM6 .123 B1
Spruce Cl Basildon SS15 319 C1
West Mersea CO5 ...218 B7
Witham CM8 ....184 A4
Spruce Hill CM18 ....223 E3
Spruce Hills Rd E17 .309 C1
Sprundel Ave SS8 ...364 D2
Spur Cl RM4 ....290 B6
Spurgate CM13 ......295 E1
Spurgeon Cl CO9 ....51 B1
Spurgeon Pl CO5 ...158 C2
Spurgeon St CO1 ...136 C6
Spurling Rd RM9 ....353 F6
Spur Rd IG11 ....352 C2
Spurway Par ⓶ IG2 .332 F6
Squadrons App RM12 .355 D6
Square St SS17 ......200 C1
Square The
⓻ Brentwood CM14 ...316 C8
Colchester CO2 ......135 B3
Harlow CM20 ....233 A5
Hornbon-on-t-H SS17 .359 F3
Ilford IG3 ....333 A4
Sawbridgeworth CM21 .172 E2
Stansted Mountfitchet CM22 119 A2
Stock CM4 ....275 E2
Tillingham CM0 ......263 E4
West Mersea CO5 ...218 B6
Widdington CB11 ....67 D4
Woodford CB8 ......310 A5
Squires Cl CM23 ....145 C8
Squires Cn EN11 ....221 A5
Squires Ct ⓵ CB9 ..8 E7
Squire St CM1 ....301 E7
Squires The RM7 ....335 B5
Squirrells Ct CM1 ...231 F5
Squirrells SS16 .....341 B3
Squirrels Heath Rd RM3 314 F1
Squirrel's La IG9 ....310 D7
Squirrels The IP9 ...35 A2
Stable Cl Colchester CO3 134 B6
West Mersea CO5 ...218 E7

Stablecroft CM1 ....232 E8
Stablefield Rd CO14 ..171 A7
Stable Mews
Southend-on-S SS2 ..347 F2
West Mersea CO5 ....218 E8
Stables The
Sawbridgeworth CM21 ..173 B3
Buckhurst Hill IG9 ....288 C2
Stacey Ct ⓷ CM23 ..145 F6
Stacey Dr SS16 ......341 C2
Stacey's Mount CM1 .320 C5
Stackfield CM20 .....219 F5
Stackyard The CB10 ..3 A3
Staddles CM22 ......173 B8
Stadium Ind Est SS17 .348 A1
Stadium Trad Est SS7 .345 C7
Stadium Way
Harlow CM19 ....198 F1
Thundersley SS7 .....345 C7
Staffa Cl SS12 ....321 F5
Stafford Ave RM11 ..336 D8
Stafford Cl Grays RM16 372 C2
Greenhithe DA9 ......376 F2
Kirby Cross CO13 ...170 E6
Linford SS17 ....345 A7
Southend-on-S SS9 .347 A6
Stafford Cres CM7 ...124 B8
Stafford Cl EN10 ....221 A3
Stafford Dr EN10 ...221 A3
Stafford Gn SS16 ...340 F4
Stafford Ho
Bishop's Stortford CM23 145 F5
Hoddesdon EN10 ....221 A3
Staffords CM17 .....200 E4
Stafford Wlk CM3 ..364 A5
Stagden Cross SS14 .342 F5
Stagden Cross Villas
CM1 ....177 E2
Staggart Gn IG7 ....311 F4
Stag La IG9 ....310 B8
Stainers CM23 ......145 C5
Staines Rd IG1 ......352 D8
Stainforth Rd IG2 ...333 C3
Stairs Rd SS3 ....350 F4
Stalham Way IG6 ...311 B2
Stalin Rd CO2 ....136 B4
Stallards Cres CO13 .170 E6
Stambourne Rd
Great Yeldham CO9 .29 D3
Ridgewell CO9 ....28 F5
Toppesfield CO9 ....50 B8
Stambridge Prim Sch
SS4 ....326 C2
Stambridge Rd
Clacton-on-S CO15 ..195 C4
Rochford SS4 ....326 C2
Stamford Cl IP2 .....36 F8
Stamford Gdns RM9 .353 C5
Stamford Rd RM9 ...353 C5
Stammers Cl CM0 ...284 D4
Stammers Rd CO4 ..109 F4
Standard Ave CO15 ..220 D6
Standard Rd
Belvedere DA17 ......369 A1
Colchester CO1 ......136 C6
Standen Ave
Hornchurch RM12 ....336 E1
Standen Vale
Great Notley CM77 ...154 B5
Ridgewell CO9 ....28 F5
Toppesfield CO9 .....50 B8
Stanbridge Rd
Clacton-on-S CO15 ...195 C4
Rochford SS4 ....326 C2
Stanfield Gdns RM10 .354 A6
Stanfield Rd RM10 ...354 A7
Standingford CM19 .223 B3
Standley Rd CO14 ...144 D1
Standrums CM6 .....150 D8
Stane Cl CM23 ......118 F1
Stane Field CO6 ....132 E3
Stane Rd CM7 ......127 F6
Stanetta Ct ⓷ RM6 .334 B4
Staneway SS16 .....341 D3
Stanfield Cl CO3 ....134 E3
Stanfield Mdw CM8 .155 F1
Stanfield Rd SS2 ...348 A1
Stanfields Ct CM20 .199 E1
Stanford Cl Romford RM7 335 B5
Woodford IG8 ......310 E5
Stanford Ct EN9 ...266 A6
Stanford Hall ⓵ SS17 360 F3
Stanford Ho IG11 ..353 B3
Stanford-le-Hope By-Pass
Basildon SS16,SS17 ..342 B1
Orsett RM16 ....374 D8
Stanford-le-H SS17 ..360 D4
Stanford-le-Hope Jun & Inf
Schs SS17 ....360 D1
Stanford-le-Hope Sta ⓯
SS17 ....360 C1
Stanier Cl
Southend-on-S SS1 .367 C8
Witham CM8 ....211 F7
Stanley Ave Barking IG11 352 F3
Brightlingsea CO7 ...193 A7
Redbridge IG1 ....332 F3
Stanhope Rd
Dagenham RM8 .....334 F1
Greenhithe DA9 ....376 E2
Ipswich IP3 ....18 A4
Romford RM6 ....334 A7
Stanley Cl Greenhithe DA9 376 E2
Hornchurch RM12 ....336 C2
Stanley Ct CM23 ....146 A6
Stanley Pl CM9 .....249 A2
Stanley Rd Bulphan RM14 358 F8

Stanley Rd continued
Canvey Island SS8 .....364 D4
Chingford E4 ....287 D1
Clacton-on-S CO15 ...195 C2
Felixstowe IP11 ......381 E3
Grays RM17 ....378 B8
Great Chesterford CB10 ...3 E3
Halstead CO9 ....76 D2
Hornchurch RM12 ...336 D2
Ilford IG1 ....333 D2
Rochford SS4 ....325 C7
South Benfleet SS7 ..344 D6
Southend-on-S SS1 ..367 B7
Sudbury CO10 ....33 E8
Swanscombe DA10 ..377 F1
Wivenhoe CO7 ......137 C1
Woodford IG8 ....309 F2
Stanley Rd N RM13 ..354 E4
Stanley Rd S RM13 ..354 F3
Stanley Rise CM2 ...232 F3
Stanleys Farm Rd CM1 143 F8
Stanley Terr CM12 ...297 D6
Stanley Wood Ave CO15 ..15 F1
Stanley Wooster Way
CO4 ....136 E7
Stanmere Cl CO16 ..195 D5
Stanmore Rd
Belvedere DA17 ......369 C2
Wickford SS11 ......322 B6
Stanmore Way
Loughton IG10 ......289 A8
St Osyth CO16 ......194 B4
Stannard Way CO10 ..34 A6
Stannetts SS15 ......341 B8
Stansfield Ct SS7 ...344 B7
Stansfield Rd SS7 ...344 B7
Stansgate Rd
Dagenham RM10 ....335 A1
Steeple CM0 ....261 F5
Stanstead Dr EN11 ..221 B8
Stanstead Rd
Halstead CO9 ....103 F8
Hoddesdon EN11 ...221 A1
Wanstead E11 ......332 B6
Stansted Airport Sta ⓯
CM24 ....121 B4
Stansted Cl
Billericay CM11 .....297 D2
Chelmsford CM1 ...231 E1
Hornchurch RM12 ..355 B6
Stansted Mountfitchet Sta ⓯
CM24 ....119 C6
Stansted Rd
Birchanger CM23 ...119 D3
Bishop's Stortford CM23 119 B2
Colchester CO2 ....136 A1
Elsenham CM22 ....94 C1
Stansted Way CO13 ..171 A6
Stanstreete Field CM77 .154 B5
Stanton PI RM7 .....335 D6
Stanton Pl ⓺ CB9 ..9 B8
Stantons CM20 .....199 B1
Stanway Cl
⓶ Chigwell IG7 ....311 E5
Glemsford CO10 ...2 C5
Stanway Fiveways Prim Sch
CO3 ....134 C6
Stanway Rd
South Benfleet SS7 .344 C5
Stanway Sch The CO3 ..134 D5
Stanwell St CO2 ...135 F6
Stanwyck Dr IG2 ...311 C5
Stanwyck Gdns RM3 314 B5
Stanwyn Ave CO15 .195 E3
Stapleford Abbotts Prim Sch
RM4 ....291 C4
Stapleford Ave IG2 .333 C6
Stapleford Cl
Chelmsford CM2 ...232 A1
Chingford E4 ....309 C7
Stapleford End SS11 314 A4
Stapleford Gdns RM3 313 A4
Stapleford Rd RM4 ..291 B5
Staplegrove SS3 ....368 D8
Staplers Cl CM9 ...213 B4
Staplers Mews CM9 ..213 B4
Staples Rd IG10 ...288 E6
Staples Road Jun & Inf Sch
IG10 ....288 E6
Stapleton Cres RM13 .355 A6
Staple Tye CM18 ....223 C5
Staple Tye Sh Mews
CM18 ....223 C5
Stapley Rd DA17 ...369 A1
Starboard Ave DA9 .377 E1
Starboard View CM3 .301 E6
Star Cl CO15 ....195 C7
Starch House La IG6 311 D1
Starfield Cl CM7 ....127 F3
Star La Epping CM16 .246 A1
Great Dunmow CM6 .123 D1
Great Wakering SS3 349 E3
Ingatestone CM4 ...274 C4
Ipswich IP4 ....17 D5
Starling Cl IG9 .....288 A1
Starling's Hill CO9 .75 E4
Starmans Cl RM9 ..353 E4
Star Mead CM6 ...70 A2
Star Rd CM7 ......94 F6
Start Hill CM22 ....147 A7
State Mans IG6 ....311 C1
Staten Gdns CO15 .195 A1
Station App
Basildon,Laindon SS15 341 C5
Basildon,Pipps Hill SS13 343 B4
Braintree CM7 ......128 A2
Burnham-on-C CM0 .306 B5
Canvey Island SS8 ..363 F6
Clacton-on-S CO15 .170 C5
Grays RM17 ....378 A8
Harlow CM20 ......200 C5

Hockley SS5 ..... 324 E6
North Fambridge CM3 ... 303 B8
Southend-on-S, Prittlewell
  SS2 ..... 347 F2
South Woodham Ferrers
  CM3 ..... 301 C8
Theydon Bois CM16 ... 267 E3
Wanstead E11 ..... 332 A6
Wickford SS11 ..... 321 D8
Woodford IG8 ..... 310 B4
Woodford, South Woodford
  E18 ..... 310 B1
Woodford, Woodford Wells
  IG9 ..... 310 C5
Station Ave Rayleigh SS6 .323 C3
Southend-on-S SS2 ..... 348 A3
Wickford SS11 ..... 321 D8
Station Cotts Cold Norton CM3 .133 D2
Station Cres Cold Norton CM3 ...280 F5
Rayleigh SS6 ..... 323 D3
Station Ct SS12 ..... 321 D8
Station Est 18 ..... 310 B1
Station Gate SS15 ..... 341 C5
Station Hill C08 ..... 79 E8
Station Ind Est CM06 ... 86 D5
Station La Basildon SS13 .343 B5
Harwich CO12 ..... 91 C4
Hornchurch RM12 ... 136 E2
Ingatestone CM4 ..... 274 B3
Station Par Barking IG11 .352 C5
Dagenham RM10 ..... 354 A6
Hornchurch RM11 ..... 355 B8
2 Romford RM1 ..... 335 E5
2 Wanstead E11 ..... 332 A6
Woodford IG9 ..... 310 D6
Station Pas E18 ..... 310 B1
Station Rd Alresford CO7 .165 A8
Althorne CM3 ..... 282 F1
Ardleigh CO7 ..... 111 E7
Belvedere DA17 ..... 369 A3
Bentley IP9 ..... 60 E6
Billericay CM12 ..... 296 F2
Birdbrook CO9 ..... 10 D1
Bishop's Stortford CM23 .146 A7
Bradfield CO11 ..... 87 E3
2 Braintree CM7 ..... 127 F2
Brightlingsea CO7 ..... 192 E6
Burnham-on-C CM0 ... 306 B5
Canvey Island SS8 ..... 364 E2
Chigwell IG7 ..... 311 B7
Clacton-on-S CO15 ..... 195 F3
Clare CO10 ..... 12 C7
Cold Norton CM3 ..... 281 A5
Colne Engaine CO6 ..... 77 F1
Cressing CM8 ..... 156 A3
Earls Colne CO6 ..... 105 E7
East Tilbury RM18 ..... 380 B7
Elsenham CM22 ..... 94 C2
Epping CM16 ..... 268 A8
Felsted CM6 ..... 151 F6
Great Bentley CO7 ..... 166 E8
Great Dunmow CM6 ..... 150 F8
Greenstead Green CO9 .77 A2
Greenhithe DA9 ..... 377 A2
Harlow CM17 ..... 200 C4
Harwich, Bath Side CO12 .91 E5
Harwich, Dovercourt CO12 .91 D4
Harwich, Parkeston CO12 .90 F5
Hatfield Peverel CM3 .210 F5
Haverhill CB9 ..... 9 A8
Hockley SS5 ..... 324 E6
Holbrook IP9 ..... 221 A3
Holdbrook IP9 ..... 265 A5
Ilford, Barkingside IG6 .333 D8
Ilford IG1 ..... 333 B1
Kelvedon CO5 ..... 158 C3
Kirby Cross CO13 ..... 170 B6
Long Melford CO10 ..... 15 C5
Loughton IG10 ..... 288 F6
Maldon CM9 ..... 237 A3
Manningtree CO11 ..... 86 C5
Marks Tey CO6 ..... 133 B4
Newport CB11 ..... 67 A8
Northfleet DA11 ..... 378 B1
North Weald Bassett CM16 247 B4
Rayleigh SS6 ..... 323 C3
Rayne CM77 ..... 126 F1
Romford, Chadwell Heath
  RM6,RM8 ..... 334 D4
Romford, Harold Wood
  RM3 ..... 314 F2
Romford RM2 ..... 336 C7
Saffron Walden CB11 ... 22 D1
Sawbridgeworth CM21 .172 F3
Sible Hedingham CO9 ... 51 E2
South Benfleet SS7 ..... 363 D8
Southend-on-S, Leigh-on-S
  SS9 ..... 346 A1
Southend-on-S, Thorpe Bay
  SS1 ..... 368 B8
Southend-on-S, Westcliff-on-S
  SS0 ..... 366 D7
Southminster CM0 ..... 284 E4
Stanstead Abbotts SG12 .197 C4
Stanstead Mountfitchet
  CM24 ..... 119 E6
Sudbury CO10 ..... 33 E7
Takeley CM22 ..... 148 C7
Thorpe-le-S CO16 ..... 168 F8
Thorrington CO7 ..... 166 A6
Tiptree CO5 ..... 186 C4
Tollesbury CM9 ..... 216 D2
Tolleshunt D'Arcy CM9 .215 E5
Trimley St M IP11 ..... 381 A7
Upminster RM14 ..... 337 C2
Wakes Colne CO6 ..... 106 D6
Wendens Ambo CB11 ..... 42 F5
West Horndon CM13 ..... 339 D5
White Colne CO6 ..... 105 E8

Station Rd continued
White Notley CM8 ..... 155 F2
Wickford SS11 ..... 299 C2
Wickham Bishops CM8 ... 187 E2
Witham CM8 ..... 184 A3
Wivenhoe CO7 ..... 164 B8
Wrabness CO11 ..... 88 F3
Station Road Ind Est
Great Dunmow CM6 ... 150 E7
Tolleshunt D'arcy CM9 .215 E5
Station Sq RM2 ..... 336 B7
Station St Ipswich IP2 ... 17 C3
Saffron Walden CB11 ... 22 D1
Station Terr CM3 ..... 171 C8
2 Thaxted CM6 ..... 210 F5
Station Way
Basildon SS14,SS16 ..... 342 A5
Buckhurst Hill IG9 ..... 310 D6
Colchester CO1 ..... 109 E1
Station Yd IP7 ..... 17 B4
Staveley Cl 4 E11 ..... 332 A6
Staverton Rd RM11 ..... 336 D5
Stays La CM5 ..... 229 A3
Steadman Ct CO15 ..... 220 D6
Steadman Ho 4 RM10 .335 A1
Steamer Terr 5 CM1 .232 A3
Steam Mill Rd CO11 .114 B8
Stebbing Prim Sch CM6 .124 E5
Stebbing Rd CM6 ..... 152 B7
Stebbings SS16 ..... 341 C4
Stebbings Ct 5 CM0 .306 C4
Stebbing Way IG11 ... 353 A3
Steed Cl RM11 ..... 336 B2
Steeds Mdw CO10 ..... 15 C8
Steeds Way IG10 ..... 288 E6
Steel App IG11 ..... 353 B3
Steele Ave DA9 ..... 377 A2
Steele Cl CO6 ..... 132 F3
Steele Ho CO12 ..... 91 C3
Steen Cl CM4 ..... 274 B4
Steeple Bumpstead Prim Sch
  CB9 ..... 27 B6
Steeple Bumpstead Rd
  CB9 ..... 26 E7
Steeple Cl Heybridge CM9 237 D5
Rochford SS4 ..... 325 D3
Steeplefield SS9 ..... 346 E6
Steeplehall SS13 ..... 343 A5
Steeple Mds SS7 ..... 344 B6
Steeple Mdws CM0 ..... 284 B4
Steeple Rd
Latchingdon CM3 ..... 282 D7
Southminster CM0 ..... 262 C4
Steeple CM0 ..... 284 B7
Steeple View
Bishop's Stortford CM23 .145 F8
Grays RM17 ..... 373 A1
Steeple Way CM15 ..... 272 B2
Steerforth Cl CM1 ..... 231 D7
Stell Ave SS8 ..... 363 F5
Stella Maris IP 16 D5
Stella Maris Cl SS8 ..... 364 F3
Sten Cl CM3 ..... 265 A2
Stenning Ave SS17 ..... 375 B2
Stepfield CM8 ..... 184 B2
Stephen Ave RM13 ..... 354 A5
Stephen Cl Haverhill CB9 .8 F8
Long Melford CO10 ..... 15 B5
Stephen Cranfield Cl
  CO5 ..... 164 A7
Stephen Marshall Ave
  CM7 ..... 72 C6
Stephen Neville Ct CB11 .43 D8
Stephens Cl RM3 ..... 314 C5
Stephens Cres SS17 ..... 359 F3
Stephen's Ct IP4 ..... 18 B6
Stephenson Rd
Braintree CM7 ..... 128 A1
Clacton-on-S CO15 ..... 196 B8
Colchester CO4 ..... 110 D6
North Fambridge CM3 .303 A8
Southend-on-S SS9 ..... 346 B5
Stephenson W CO15 .169 A1
Sterling Cl CO3 ..... 134 E5
Sterling Complex IP1 ... 16 D7
Sterling Ind Est RM10 .354 A8
Stern Cl IG11 ..... 353 C3
Sterry Cres RM10 ..... 354 A7
Sterry Ho RM13 ..... 354 A6
Sterry Rd Barking IG11 .353 B2
Dagenham RM10 ..... 354 A7
Stevanne Ct 8 CM7 .369 A1
Stevenage Rd E6 ..... 352 A6
Stevens Cl
Canvey Island SS8 ..... 364 D4
Colchester CO4 ..... 109 E3
Stevens La CM6 ..... 152 F6
Stevenson Rd IP1 ..... 17 B6
Stevens Way SS17 ..... 321 C5
Stevens Rd
Dagenham RM8 ..... 334 C1
Witham CM8 ..... 183 E1
Stevens Way IG7 ..... 311 E6
Stevens Wlk CO4 ..... 136 F7
Stewards Cl Epping CM16 .268 B4
Harlow CM17 ..... 173 E8
Stewards Elm Farm La
  SS4 ..... 326 D6
Stewards Green Rd
  CM16 ..... 268 B6
Stewards Rd CM18 ..... 223 A4
Stewards Wlk RM1 ..... 335 E6
Stewart Ave RM14 ..... 337 B1
Stewart Pl SS12 ..... 321 F5
Stewart Rainbird Ho 1
  E12 ..... 352 A7
Stewart Rd CM2 ..... 254 A6
Stewarts The CM23 ..... 145 E8
Stewarts Way CM23 ..... 92 F2
Steyning Ave SS2 ..... 348 C4
Stickland Rd DA17 ..... 369 A2
Stifford Clays Jun & Inf Schs
  RM16 ..... 373 B5

Stifford Clays Rd
Grays RM16 ..... 373 B6
Orsett RM16 ..... 373 B7
Stifford Hill RM16 ..... 372 C5
Stifford Prim Sch RM17 .372 F1
Stifford Rd Aveley RM15 .371 E5
South Ockendon RM15 .372 B6
Stile Croft CM18 ..... 224 A6
Stile La SS8 ..... 363 D2
Stilemans SS11 ..... 321 D8
Stilemans Wood CM7 .128 D1
Stiles Cl IG48 ..... 369 B1
Stiles The CM9 ..... 237 E3
Stilwells SS4 ..... 326 A2
Stirling Ave SS9 ..... 346 B2
Stirling Cl Rainham RM13 355 B2
Rayleigh SS6 ..... 323 B5
Stirling De IP9 ..... 8 E8
Stirling Pl SS13 ..... 343 B8
Stirrup Cl CM1 ..... 232 A5
Stirrup Mews CO3 ..... 134 E6
Stisted Ce Prim Sch
  CM7 ..... 129 B6
Stivvy's Rd CM9 ..... 235 C3
St. Michael's Chase CO6 133 D2
Stile Ce Prim Sch CM4 275 D3
Stock Chase CM9 ..... 237 E3
Stock Cl SS2 ..... 347 F4
Stockdale Rd RM8 ..... 334 C2
Stocker Gdns RM9 ..... 353 C5
Stockfield Ave RM11 ... 221 B8
Stockhouse Cl CM9 ..... 187 B8
Stockhouse Rd CO5 ..... 187 B7
Stock Ind Pk SS2 ..... 348 A4
Stocking La SS6 ..... 39 C1
Stock La CM4 ..... 274 D3
Stockland Rd RM7 ..... 335 D5
Stockley Cl CB9 ..... 9 F7
Stockman's La CM7 ..... 154 C8
Stockmen Field CM23 .145 C5
Stockmers End 1 CM9 ... 35 A1
Stock Park Ct SS9 ..... 346 E6
Stock Rd Billericay CM12 .297 C5
Gallywood CM2 ..... 254 B2
Southend-on-S SS2 ..... 347 F4
Stock CM4 ..... 276 B6
Stocksfield CM15 ..... 271 F2
Stocks La CM15 ..... 271 F1
Stock Terr CM9 ..... 237 B5
Stockwell 6 CO1 ..... 135 F7
Stockwood SS7 ..... 345 D7
Stokeash Cl CO15 ..... 195 A3
Stoke Ave IG6 ..... 312 A4
Stokebridge Maltings 1
  IP 17 C4
Stoke-by-Nayland Mid Sch
  CO6 ..... 56 C6
Stoke-by-Nayland Prim Sch
  CO6 ..... 56 C5
Stoke Cott CO10 ..... 11 C3
Stoke Hall Rd IP2 ..... 17 C4
Stoke Park Dr IP2 ..... 17 A1
Stoke Park Gdns IP2 .17 A1
Stoke Quay IP2 ..... 17 C4
Stoke Rd Clare CO10 ..... 12 A6
Nayland CO6 ..... 56 B2
Rainham RM13 ..... 355 D2
Stokesay Ct 1 DA2 .376 B1
Stokes Cotts IG6 ..... 311 C2
Stokes Cl SS2 ..... 348 E2
Stoke St IP2 ..... 17 C3
Stokes The CO14 ..... 171 B8
Stonard Rd RM8 ..... 353 B8
Stonards Hill
Epping CM16 ..... 268 C8
Loughton IG10 ..... 288 F4
Stondon Rd CM5 ..... 249 B1
Stonebridge Hill CO6 .104 E7
Stonebridge Rd DA11 .378 B2
Stonechat Rd
Billericay CM12 ..... 319 C8
Ipswich IP2 ..... 16 D2
Stone Cl Braintree CM7 .127 F2
Dagenham RM8 ..... 334 F2
Stone Cotts CO10 ..... 52 D2
Stonecrop CO4 ..... 109 C2
Stone Cross CM20 ..... 199 D1
Stone Crossing Halt DA9 376 F1
Stone Ct DA8 ..... 369 F1
Stonegate CM4 ..... 274 C3
Stonegrove Rd CM11 ... 381 B1
Stonehall Ave IG1 ..... 332 E5
Stonehall Dr CM13 ..... 116 D1
Stonehall La CO12 ..... 115 B1
Stoneham St CO6 ..... 130 F7
Stonehill Cl SS9 ..... 346 F4
Stonehill Ct E4 ..... 287 B2
Stonehill Rd Roxwell CM1 229 F3
Stonehill Way CO5 ..... 218 A6
Stone House Hospl DA2 376 C1
Stone La Tiptree CO5 ..... 186 A2
Wrabness CO11 ..... 88 F5
Stoneleigh CM21 ..... 171 B2
Stoneleigh Dr CM11 ... 197 B1
Stoneleigh Pk CO3 ..... 134 F4
Stoneleighs SS7 ..... 344 F6
Stone Lodge Farm Pk *
  DA3 ..... 376 C1
Stone Lodge La IP2 ..... 17 A3
Stone Lodge La W IP2 .16 F3
Stone Lodge Wlk IP2 ... 17 A3
Stone Path Dr CM3 ..... 210 B5
Stone Place Rd DA9 ..... 376 E2
Stone Rd CO7 ..... 113 B1
Stone's Green Rd CO12 .115 C2
Stone St DA11 ..... 379 B1
Stonewood Rd DA8 ..... 369 E1

Stoney Bridge Dr EN9 .266 A5
Stoney Brook CM24 ... 119 E5
Stoney Comm CM24 ... 119 E5
Stoney Common Rd
  CM24 ..... 119 E5
Stonycroft Rd IG8 ..... 310 E4
Stoneyfield Dr CM24 .119 E4
Stoney Hills
Burnham-on-C CM0 ... 306 C8
Ramsden Heath CM11 .298 B5
Stoney La CO7 ..... 193 A8
Stonham Ave CO16 ..... 195 A4
Stony La
Chipping Ongar CM5 ... 248 C8
Thaxted CM6 ..... 70 A2
Stony Path IG10 ..... 288 F8
Stonyshotts EN9 ..... 265 E5
Stony Wood CM18 ..... 223 E7
Stopford Ct 2 IP1 ..... 17 A6
Storas Ct 9 RM19 ..... 371 B1
Storelands Ho IP11 ..... 381 B6
Stores Rd CO5 ..... 186 C6
Stores The CO11 ..... 115 A8
Stormonts Way SS16 ... 341 D2
Storms Way CM2 ..... 233 B2
Stornoway Rd SS2 ..... 348 D1
Storr Gdns CM13 ..... 295 D4
Stortford Hall Ind Pk
  CM23 ..... 146 A8
Stortford Hall Pk CM23 .146 B8
Stortford Rd 3
  CM23 ..... 146 B8
Stortford Rd
Clavering CB11 ..... 65 C4
Great Dunmow CM6 .123 C1
Hatfield Heath CM22 .173 E4
Hoddesdon EN11 ..... 221 C7
Leaden Roding CM6 .204 B7
Takeley CM6 ..... 149 D7
Stort Lodge CM23 ..... 145 D8
Stort Mill CM20 ..... 200 B6
Stort Rd CM23 ..... 145 F6
Stort Valley Ind Pk
  CM23 ..... 119 B2
Stour Ave IP11 ..... 381 C3
Stour Cl Glemsford CO10 ...2 C7
Harwich CO12 ..... 90 D2
Southend-on-S SS3 ..... 368 E6
Stour Ct CM7 ..... 128 D1
Stourdale Cl CO11 ..... 86 A3
Stour Estuary Nature
  Reserve* CO12 ..... 89 C3
Stour Gdns CO10 ..... 34 B4
Stour Gn CO10 ..... 12 B6
Stour Rd Dagenham RM10 335 A2
Grays RM16 ..... 374 A1
Harwich CO12 ..... 91 D5
Stourside IP9 ..... 64 C8
Stour St Cavendish CO10 .13 C8
Manningtree CO11 ..... 86 D4
Sudbury CO10 ..... 33 E7
Stourton Rd CM8 ..... 183 E3
Stour Vale Clare CO10 ... 12 A6
Stoke by C CO10 ..... 10 D2
Stourview Ave CO11 ... 87 A4
Stourview Cl CO11 ..... 87 B4
Stour View Ct CO12 ..... 91 D5
Stour Way RM14 ..... 337 C1
Stow Cl CM3 ..... 194 C5
Stourvale Rd CO14 ..... 110 E2
Stow Ct CO4 ..... 109 F5
Stowe Ct SS0 ..... 347 E1
Stowe Pl SS2 ..... 348 C2
Stowell La CM0 ..... 263 D4
Stowe Villas CM20 ..... 199 F2
Stow Rd CM3 ..... 280 D5
Stow The CM20 ..... 199 F2
Stow Villas CM3 ..... 280 C4
Stoup Ct CM3 ..... 211 A4
Stuart Cl
Canvey Island SS8 ..... 364 B4
Great Baddow CM2 ..... 255 B6
Great Wakering SS3 ..... 349 A4
Ipswich IP4 ..... 17 F7
Pilgrims Hatch CM15 ... 294 B4
Southend-on-S SS2 ..... 348 A2
Stuart Ct E4 ..... 309 F8
Stuart Ho 1HO 265 F6
Stuart Pawsey Ct CO7 .137 C1
Stuart Rd Barking IG11 .352 F4
Gravesend DA11 ..... 379 A1
Grays RM17 ..... 373 B1
Southend-on-S SS2 ..... 348 A2
Stuarts RM11 ..... 336 C3
Stuart St SS2 ..... 348 B2
Stuart St SS2 ..... 348 A3
Stubbings Way CM7 ..... 128 A2
Stuart Way CM11 ..... 297 C1
Stubbers La RM14 ..... 356 C5
Stubbins Cl Ipswich IP3 .18 A1
Kirby Cross CO13 ..... 170 C6
Lawford CO11 ..... 86 B4
Stubbs La CO6 ..... 131 B1
Stubbs Mews RM8 ..... 353 B8
Stublands SS14 ..... 342 F6
Stuart St SS14 ..... 342 F6
Studd Ho CO4 ..... 109 D4
Studley Ave E4 ..... 309 D3
Studley Ct IG4 ..... 332 D5
Studley Dr IG4 ..... 332 D5
Studley Rd RM9 ..... 353 D6
Stump's Cross CO10 ..... 15 B3
Stump La CM1 ..... 232 D4
Stumps Cross CO9 ..... 29 A2
Sturdee Ave E17 ..... 309 B1
Sturgeon Way CM1 ..... 205 E7
Sturmer Ct 8 CO10 ..... 34 F7
Sturmer End Ind Est CB9 .9 C6
Sturmer Rd
Haverhill, Calford Green CB9 .9 F7
Haverhill CB9 ..... 9 E7
Sturrick La CO7 ..... 139 D1
Sturrocks SS16 ..... 342 E3
Sturton Ce Prim Sch IP9 .62 A2
Sturton Cl IP9 ..... 62 C1
Sturton Gn IP9 ..... 62 C1

Stutton La IP9 ..... 61 C5
Stutton Rd CO11 ..... 61 A2
Stylemans La CM22 ... 146 B5
Styles CM7 ..... 71 D2
Sub-Station Rd IP12 ... 381 B2
Subbourne Ave CO16 ... 195 F4
Subbourne Rd IP11 ..... 381 B6
Sudbrook Cl SS12 ..... 321 D6
Sudbury Cl SS5 ..... 324 F4
Sudbury Rd Barking IG11 352 F7
Bulmer CO10 ..... 32 F6
Bures CO8 ..... 55 F1
Canvey Island SS8 ..... 363 F5
Castle Hedingham CO9 ... 52 B4
Downham CM11 ..... 299 A5
Felixstowe IP11 ..... 381 A4
Gestingthorpe CO9 ..... 31 F2
Great Cornard CO10 .... 34 F7
Great Maplestead CO9 ... 53 C2
Halstead CO9 ..... 76 F3
Long Melford CO10 ..... 15 C3
Stoke-by-N CO6 ..... 56 C6
Sudbury Sta CO10 ..... 33 D6
Sudbury Upper Sch CO10 .15 F1
Sudeley Gdns SS5 ..... 324 D6
Sudicamps Ct EN9 ..... 266 A6
Sue Ryder Mus* CO10 ... 1 D1
Suffield Rd E4 ..... 309 B6
Suffolk Ave
Southend-on-S SS9 ..... 346 F3
West Mersea CO5 ..... 218 D7
Suffolk Cl
Clacton-on-S CO15 ..... 196 E7
Colchester CO4 ..... 110 B1
Harlow CM17 ..... 17 E5
Suffolk Coll (Argyll St
  Annexe) IP4 ..... 17 D6
Suffolk Cres CM9 ..... 236 E1
Suffolk Ct Ilford IG3 ..... 333 E5
Rochford SS4 ..... 325 E2
Suffolk Dr Basildon SS15 .341 B6
Chelmsford CM2 ..... 233 A4
Suffolk Ent Pk IP1 ..... 17 B5
Suffolk Ho RM7 ..... 313 A2
Suffolk Knowle CO8 ..... 55 F1
Suffolk Rd Barking IG11 .352 D5
Dagenham RM10 ..... 354 C2
Gravesend DA12 ..... 379 D1
Ilford IG3 ..... 333 E5
Ipswich IP4 ..... 17 D7
Maldon CM9 ..... 236 E1
Sudbury CO10 ..... 33 E8
Suffolk Ret Pk IP1 ..... 17 A6
Suffolk Sq Ct* IP2 ..... 37 E8
Suffolk Ski Ctr* IP2 ..... 33 E8
Suffolk St CO10 ..... 171 C8
Suffolk Way
Canvey Island SS8 ..... 363 E4
Hornchurch RM11 ..... 337 A2
Suffolk Wlk SS8 ..... 363 E4
Sugar La CO9 ..... 74 E7
Sugden Ave SS12 ..... 321 A7
Sugden Way IG11 ..... 352 F3
Sulleys Hill IP7 ..... 58 B8
Sullivan Cl CO4 ..... 136 E6
Sullivan Rd SS2 ..... 348 A1
Sullivan Way SS16 ..... 341 A5
Sultan Rd E11 ..... 332 B3
Summercourt Rd SS0 .366 E8
Summer Inf Sch
  CM23 ..... 146 C8
Summercroft Jun Sch
  CM23 ..... 146 C8
Summerdale
Althorne CM3 ..... 283 A3
Billericay CM12 ..... 297 A2
Summerfield Cl CM4 ... 18 D8
Summerfield Ct E4 ..... 18 D8
Summerfield Rd IG10 .288 D3
Summerfields
Ingatestone CM4 ..... 274 C3
Sible Hedingham CO9 ... 51 E1
Summerhill CM23 ..... 283 A3
Summer Hill Rd CM23 ... 43 D8
Summerlands SS8 ..... 363 F4
Summerleaze CM7 ..... 154 D2
Summerwood Ct SS7 .345 C2
Summit Dr IG8 ..... 310 D1
Summit The IG10 ..... 288 F8
Summers Farm CV19 223 A3
Sumpters Link SS15 .340 E6
Sumpters Way SS2 ..... 347 F5
Sunbank CM6 ..... 150 E7
Sunbeam Ave CO15 ..... 220 E6
Sunbeam Cl CO15 ..... 164 A8
Sunbury's Cl CO7 ..... 137 C1
Sunbury Way CM9 ..... 349 E2
Sunbury Wy Cres CM9 .188 E8
Sundale Cl CO15 ..... 196 F6
Sunderland Way E12 .332 D2
Sundew Ct RM17 ..... 378 D8
Sundridge Cl DA1 ..... 376 A1
Sunflower Cl 3 RM3 ... 314 A1
Sunflower Way RM3 ... 314 A1
Sun Lido Square Gdns
  SS7 ..... 127 C2
Sunnedon SS16 ..... 342 D5
Sunningdale
Bishop's Stortford CM23 .118 D3
Canvey Island SS8 ..... 364 C4
Sunningdale Ave
Barking IG11 ..... 352 D5
Felixstowe IP11 ..... 381 F6
Southend-on-S SS9 ..... 347 A1
Sunningdale Cl SS5 ..... 367 A8
Sunningdale Dr IP11 ..... 381 B4
Sunningdale Fall CM3 .211 B4
Sunningdale Rd
Althorne CM3 ..... 282 E2

Sunningdale Rd *continued*
Chelmsford CM1 231 E4
Rainham RM13 355 A5
Sunningdale Way CO13 170 E7
Sunninghill Gdns IG2 333 F6
Sunnings La RM14 356 D5
Sunnybank Cl SS9 346 F6
Sunny Croft CM18 223 F5
Sunnycroft Gdns RM14 337 F4
Sunnydene Ave E4 309 D5
Sunnydene Cl RM3 314 F3
Sunnyfield Gdns SS5 324 B6
Sunnyfields Rd CM7 102 D2
Sunnymead Flats 10
CM0 306 C4
Sunnymede IG7 312 B7
Sunnymede Cl SS7 345 A6
Sunnymede Dr IG6 333 B7
Sunnymede Inf Sch
CM11 297 D1
Sunny Mews RM5 313 C3
Sunny Point CO14 144 E3
Sunny Rd SS5 324 E5
Sunnyside Basildon SS16 340 F4
Braintree CM7 127 E3
Lower Nazeing EN9 221 F1
Stansted Mountfitchet
CM24 119 E6
Sunnyside Dr E4 287 C2
Sunnyside Gdns RM14 337 C1
Sunnyside Rd
Epping CM16 267 F7
Fordham CO6 107 D5
Ilford IG1 333 D1
Sunnyside Way CO16 168 C1
Sunny Way CM0 262 C8
Sunnyway Cotts CM3 256 E3
Sunray Ave IP11 381 F6
Sun Ray Ave CM13 295 E3
Sunray Ho SS0 366 D8
Sun Rd DA10 377 F1
Sunrise Ave
Chelmsford CM1 232 A5
Hornchurch RM12 336 C1
Sunrise Lodge RM12 336 C1
Sunset Ave Chingford E4 287 B1
Woodford IG8 309 F6
Sunset Ct 4 IG8 310 C3
Sun St Billericay CM12 297 A1
Sawbridgeworth CM21 172 F1
Waltham Abbey EN9 265 C6
Surbiton Ave SS1 367 D8
Surbiton Rd Ipswich IP1 16 F8
Southend-on-S SS2 348 D1
Surig Rd SS8 364 A4
Surman Cres CM13 295 C2
Surmans Cl RM9 353 C4
Surman Terr RM1 336 A6
Surrey Ave SS9 346 F3
Surrey Ct CO15 196 A2
Surrey Dr RM11 337 A7
Surrey Ho RM7 313 A2
Surrey La CO5 186 C4
Surrey Rd Barking IG11 352 E5
Dagenham RM10 354 B7
Felixstowe IP11 381 D4
Ipswich IP1 17 A6
Surrey Way SS15 341 B6
Surridge Cl RM13 355 C2
Susan Cl RM7 335 C8
Susan Fielder Cotts 3
SS8 364 A3
Susan Lawrence Ho 4
E12 352 A8
Sussex Ave RM3 314 F3
Sussex Cl Basildon SS15 341 B6
Boreham CM3 233 F8
Canvey Island SS8 364 A5
Hoddesdon EN11 221 A7
Redbridge IG4 332 F6
Sussex Ct CM12 297 B6
Sussex Gdns CO15 196 E6
Sussex Ho RM7 313 A2
Sussex Rd
Brentwood CM14 316 B6
Colchester CO3 135 C7
Wallend E6 352 A4
Sussex Terr 2 RM19 371 B1
Sussex Way
Billericay CM12 297 B6
Canvey Island SS8 364 A5
Sutcliffe Cl SS12 321 D6
Sutherland Bvd SS9 346 B2
Sutherland Cl DA9 376 F2
Sutherland Ho
Chelmsford CM1 232 A4
5 Redbridge IG8 311 A3
Sutherland Pl SS12 321 D5
Sutherland Rd DA17 369 A3
Sutor Cl CM8 183 E1
Sutton Acres CM22 173 D7
Sutton Cl IG10 288 E2
Sutton Court Dr SS4 347 F7
Sutton Ct SS2 348 C2
Sutton Ford Cotts SS4 348 B8
Sutton Gdns IG11 352 E3
Sutton Gn IG11 352 E4
Sutton Mead CM2 233 A4
Sutton Park Ave CO3 135 A3
Sutton Rd Barking IG11 352 E4
Rochford SS3,SS4 348 B6
Southend-on-S SS2 348 B2
Suttons Ave RM12 336 D1
Suttons Bsns Pk RM13 354 E2
Suttons Gdns RM12 336 D1
Suttons La RM12 355 D7
Suttons Prim Sch RM12 355 D8
Suttons Rd SS3 368 H8
Swains Ct CO10 32 E5
Swale Cl RM15 371 C7
Swale Rd SS7 345 B5
Swallow Cl Grays RM16 372 C2
Swallow Cl *continued*
Greenhithe DA9 376 F2
Harwich CO12 90 E1
Layer-de-l-H CO2 162 A5
Rayleigh SS6 323 B3
Swallowcliffe SS3 349 D1
Swallow Ct
6 Brentwood CM14 316 C7
Chingford IG8 309 D3
Ilford IG2 333 B6
Swallowdale
Clacton-on-S CO15 195 F6
Colchester CO2 136 C3
Swallow Dale SS16 342 C4
Swallow Dr SS7 344 C2
Swallow Field CO6 105 B6
Swallow Path CM2 254 B5
Swallow Rd Ipswich IP2 16 C3
Wickford SS11 299 C2
Swallows CM17 200 C4
Swallow's Row CO7 167 B8
Swallows Row CO7 140 B1
Swallows The CM11 319 C8
Swallowtail Cl IP8 36 E8
Swallow Wlk Halstead CO9 76 F1
5 Hornchurch RM12 355 B6
Swanage Rd Chingford E4 309 C3
Southend-on-S SS2 348 B1
Swan Ave RM14 337 F3
Swanbourne Dr RM12 355 D8
Swan Chase CO9 75 E8
Swan Cl Basildon SS15 341 E6
Colchester CO4 136 E5
Hatfield Peverel CM3 210 F4
Swan Cotts CM3 210 F4
Swan Ct
2 Bishop's Stortford CM23 145 F6
Maldon CM9 237 B4
New Mistley CO11 87 A3
Sible Hedingham CO9 75 E8
South Benfleet SS7 344 B5
Swan Dale CO15 195 F7
Swan Farm Mews IP8 16 A1
Swanfield CO10 15 C7
Swan Gr CO6 106 C5
Swan Hill IP8 16 A2
Swan La Haverhill CB9 9 A8
Kelvedon Hatch CM15 271 E2
Long Melford CO10 15 C7
Loughton IG10 288 C2
Stock CM4 275 C5
Wickford SS11 299 D1
Swan Mdw CO7 58 C1
Swan Mead SS16 342 D4
Swan Paddock 3 CM14 316 C8
Swan Pas 13 CO1 135 F7
Swan & Pike Rd EN3 265 A1
Swan Rd CO16 141 D5
Swanscombe Bsns Ctr
DA10 377 E2
Swanscombe Cross
DA10 377 D2
Swanscombe St DA10 377 F1
Swanscombe Sta DA10 377 F2
Swanscomb Rd CO6 105 F5
Swansea Ave IP2 17 B1
Swans Green Cl SS7 345 A6
Swanshope IG10 289 B7
Swan Side CM7 127 F3
Swans Pasture CM1 232 D6
Swan St Chappel CO6 106 C3
Kelvedon CO5 158 D3
Sible Hedingham CO9 51 E1
Swanstead SS16 342 E4
Swan Wlk RM1 335 E6
Swan Yd CO6 131 A2
Swatchway Cl IP3 38 B8
Swatchways SS1 367 D6
Swaynes CO7 58 C2
Sweden Cl CO12 90 F4
Swedish Est CO11 115 B5
Sweet Briar CM23 145 B6
Sweet Briar Ave SS7 344 D2
Sweet Briar Dr SS15 319 D1
Sweetbriar Lodge SS8 363 E4
Sweet Briar Rd CO3 134 C7
Sweet Mead CB10 22 E3
Sweyne Ave Hockley SS5 325 A4
Southend-on-S SS2 347 F1
Sweyne Cl SS6 323 B4
Sweyne Ct SS2 347 F1
Sweyne Park Sch The
SS6 323 C4
Sweyne Rd DA10 377 E1
Sweyns CM17 224 C6
Swift Ave
Clacton-on-S CO15 220 F6
Colchester CO3 134 C4
Swift Cl Braintree CM7 155 A7
Stanstead Abbotts SG12 197 C3
Upminster RM14 337 E3
Swift Ho 8 E18 332 B8
Swiftsure Rd RM16 372 C2
Swinborne Ct SS13 321 B2
Swinborne Rd SS13 321 C1
Swinbourne Dr CM7 127 D3
Swinburne Gdns RM18 379 B6
Swindon Cl Ilford IG3 333 E3
Romford RM3 314 F5
Swindon Gdns RM3 314 F5
Swindon La RM3 314 F5
Swingboat Terr 3 SS1 367 C7
Swinton Cl IP2 16 D1
Swiss Ave CM1 232 A4
Sworders Yd 3 CM23 145 F7
Sycamore Cl
Canvey Island SS8 363 F3
Ipswich IP8 16 C1
Loughton IG10 289 B7
Rayleigh SS6 323 B6
Takeley CM22 148 C7
Tilbury RM18 379 A5
Witham CM8 184 A5
Sycamore Ct Erith DA8 369 D1
Southend-on-S SS3 368 F7
Sycamore Ct *continued*
Wickford SS12 321 D8
Sycamore Dr CM14 294 C1
Sycamore Field CM19 223 A5
Sycamore Gr
Braintree CM7 127 E1
Southend-on-S SS2 348 B2
Sycamore Ho
4 Buckhurst Hill IG9 310 D8
Wickford SS11 321 E7
Sycamore Mews DA8 369 D1
Sycamore Pl CO7 166 E8
Sycamore Rd
Colchester CO4 136 D8
Great Cornard CO10 34 B7
Heybridge CM9 237 C6
Sycamores The
14 Basildon SS13 343 C6
Bishop's Stortford CM23 146 B6
Aveley RM15 371 D5
Sycamore Way
Brantham CO11 60 D1
Canewdon SS4 304 D1
Chelmsford CM2 254 C6
Clacton-on-S CO15 195 C3
Kirby Cross CO13 170 D6
South Ockendon RM15 357 D1
Sycamore Wlk IG6 333 C7
Sydenham Cl RM1 335 F7
Sydervelt Rd SS8 364 A4
Sydner Cl CM2 255 A5
Sydney Rd Redbridge IG6 311 C1
South Benfleet SS7 344 C4
Southend-on-S SS9 346 B2
Tilbury RM18 379 A5
Wanstead E11 332 B5
Woodford IG8 310 A6
Sydney Russell Sch The
RM9 353 D7
Sydney St
Brightlingsea CO7 192 F6
Colchester CO2 136 B1
Syers Field CM7 74 B2
Sykes Mead SS6 323 D1
Sylvan Ave
Dagenham RM6 334 F5
Hornchurch RM11 336 F5
Sylvan Cl Basildon SS15 341 B6
Canvey Island SS8 364 B2
Chelmsford CM2 254 B6
Grays RM16 372 E3
Sylvan Ct SS15 340 F7
Sylvan Mews DA9 377 B3
Sylvan Rd Ilford IG1 333 C2
Wanstead E11 332 A6
Sylvan Tryst CM12 297 B4
Sylvan Way Basildon SS15 340 F7
Chigwell IG7 312 B7
Dagenham RM8 334 B1
Southend-on-S SS9 346 A4
Sylvester Gdns IG6 312 B5
Sylvesters CM19 222 F6
Sylvia Ave CM13 317 C8
Sylvia Pankhurst Ho 10
RM10 335 A1
Symmons Cl CM77 126 F1
Symons Ave SS9 346 E7
Syracuse Ave RM13 355 E2
Syringa Ct
6 Colchester CO4 136 E7
Grays RM17 378 D8

T

Taber Pl CM8 184 B3
Tabora Ave SS8 363 F5
Tabor Ave CM7 127 E3
Tabor Cl CO7 192 F8
Tabor High Sch CM7 127 D4
Tabor Rd CO1 136 C7
Tabors Ave CM2 254 F8
Tabors Ct CM15 294 F2
Tabor's Hill CM2 254 F7
Tabrum's La SS11 301 A6
Tabrums The CM3 279 C1
Tabrums Way RM14 337 E4
Tacket St IP4 17 D5
Tacon Ct IP11 381 C1
Tacon Rd IP11 381 C1
Tadlows Cl RM14 356 B7
Tadworth Par RM12 355 B8
Taffrail Gdns CM3 301 E5
Tailors CM23 145 B5
Tailors Cl CM77 154 C8
Tailors Ct SS2 347 F5
Tait Mews CM9 237 A2
Taits SS17 360 F2
Takeley Cl Romford RM5 313 D1
Waltham Abbey EN9 265 D6
Takeley Pk CM22 148 C6
Takeley Prim Sch CM22 148 C8
Takely End SS16 342 A5
Takely Ride SS16 342 A5
Talbot Ave
Clacton-on-S CO15 220 F6
Rayleigh SS6 323 C3
Talbot Gdns IG3 334 A2
Talbot Rd Dagenham RM9 353 F5
Little Clacton CO16 168 C4
Sudbury CO10 15 F2
Wallend E6 352 A3
Talbots IP11 381 D3
Talbot St CO12 91 D5
Talbrook CM14 315 F7
Talcott Rd CO2 136 A2
Talgarth Ho 3 RM3 314 E4
Talisman Cl 2 Ilford IG3 334 B3
Tiptree CO5 186 D6
Talisman Wlk
Billericay CM11 297 D6
Tiptree CO5 186 D6
Tallis Cl SS17 360 C3
Tallis Ct RM2 336 C8
Tallis Rd SS15 341 D8
Tallis Way CM14 316 B5
Tallon Rd CM13 295 E4
Tallow Gate CM3 301 E6
Tall Trees CO4 109 E3
Tall Trees Cl RM11 336 E5
Tally Ho CO4 110 B4
Tally Ho Cnr CO7 58 D1
Tally-Ho Dr CM13 296 C1
Talmash Gdns IP2 17 A4
Talus Cl RM19 371 D2
Tama Cotts RM14 337 F2
Tamar Ave CM8 183 E2
Tamar Cl RM14 337 E5
Tamar Dr RM15 371 C7
Tamarisk SS7 344 C4
Tamarisk Rd RM15 357 C1
Tamarisk Way
Clacton-on-S CO15 220 F6
Colchester CO4 136 E8
Tamar Rise CM1 232 C6
Tamar Sq IG8 310 B4
Tambour Cl CO6 132 C8
Tamdown Way CM7 127 C4
Tamworth Ave IG8 309 E4
Tamworth Chase CO2 136 A2
Tanfield Dr CM12 297 A2
Tanfield Tye Cotts CM2 276 E7
Tangent Link RM3 314 D2
Tangent Rd RM3 314 D2
Tangerine Cl CO4 136 D6
Tangham Wlk SS14 342 C7
Tangmere Cl SS11 322 B6
Tangmere Cres RM12 355 B6
Tan House La
Navestock Heath CM14 292 F5
Navestock Side CM14 293 A6
Tankerville Dr SS9 346 D3
Tank Hill Rd RM19 371 A2
Tank La RM19 371 B2
Tan La CO16 168 F4
Tanner Cl CO16 195 B3
Tanners La IG6 333 C8
Tanners Mdw CM7 128 D2
Tanner St IG11 352 C6
Tanners View IP1 16 F7
Tanners Way
Hunsdonbury SG12 198 D8
Saffron Walden CB10 22 E1
South Woodham Ferrers
CM3 301 C8
Tannery Cl RM10 335 B1
Tanswell Ave SS13 343 B6
Tanswell Cl SS13 343 B6
Tanswell Ct SS13 343 B7
Tansy Cl RM3 314 E4
Tantelen Rd SS8 363 F5
Tantony Gr RM6 334 D8
Tanyard The CM6 70 A2
Tany's Dell CM20 200 A3
Tany's Dell Com Prim Sch
CM20 200 A3
Tapestry Ct CO6 105 B6
Tapestry Wlk CM7 128 D2
Tapley Rd CM1 231 F7
Tapsworth Cl CO16 195 D5
Tapwoods CO3 135 A7
Tara Cl CO4 110 D1
Tara Ct 9 IG9 310 C8
Taranto Rd SS8 364 D3
Tarlings CM20 199 F3
Tarnworth Rd RM3 315 A4
Tarragona Mews CO2 136 B4
Tarragon Cl CO5 186 C4
Tasker Ho IG11 352 D3
Tasker Rd RM16 374 B3
Tasman Cl SS17 360 F4
Tasman Ct CM1 231 E5
Tasmania Ho RM18 379 A6
Tasmania Rd IP4 18 D6
Tasman Rd CB9 9 C7
Tatsfield Ave EN9 243 E8
Tatsford Villas EN9 221 C1
Tattenham Rd SS15 341 B7
Tattersall Gdns SS9 346 A1
Tattersalls Chase CM0 284 E4
Tattersall Way CM1 253 E7
Tattershall Ct 19 DA2 376 B1
Tattingstone CE Prim Sch
IP9 61 D7
Taunton Cl IG6 311 F4
Taunton Dr SS0 347 B4
Taunton Ho RM3 314 F5
Taunton Rd
Chelmsford CM1 232 E5
Felixstowe IP11 381 D6
Northfleet DA11 378 A2
Romford RM3 314 C6
Taveners Green Cl SS12 321 E6
Taverners Way
Chingford E4 287 E1
Hoddesdon EN11 221 A6
Taverners Wlk CM8 183 F4
Tavern St IP1 17 C6
Tavistock Cl RM3 314 D2
Tavistock Dr CM12 296 F5
Tavistock Gdns IG3 352 E8
Tavistock Ho 1 IG8 311 A3
Tavistock Rd
Basildon SS15 341 C8
Chelmsford CM1 232 E5
Wanstead E18 332 A8
Tawell Mews CO5 186 D5
Tawney Cl IP9 35 A1
Tawney Comm CM16 269 B7
Tawney La RM4 269 D4
Tawneys Rd CM18 223 F6
Tawneys Ride CO8 80 A8
Tawny Ave RM14 356 B7
Taylifers CM19 223 A3
Taylor Ave CM1 231 E5
Taylor Cl RM5 313 A3
Taylor Ct CO1 135 F7
Taylor Dr CO11 86 C4
Taylor Gdns RM3 314 C8
Taylors Ave EN11 221 A5
Taylors End Rd CM24 120 E1
Taylor's Rd CO5 163 F8
Tayside Wlk 6 SS12 321 E5
Tayspill Ct CO2 135 B3
Tay Way RM1 313 F2
Teagles SS15 341 E6
Teak Wlk CM8 184 A4
Teal Ave CM3 283 A8
Teal Cl Colchester CO4 137 A8
Great Notley CM77 154 B5
Ipswich IP2 16 D3
Teal Ct CM3 283 A8
Teale Ho 5 EN11 221 D8
Teal Way CO5 158 D2
Teapot Cnr IP7 57 E8
Tedder Cl CO2 136 A4
Ted Hennem Ho RM10 335 B1
Tees Cl Upminster RM14 337 D5
Witham CM8 183 E2
Tees Dr RM3 314 D7
Tees Rd CM1 232 C6
Teign Dr CM8 183 D2
Teigngrace SS3 368 D8
Teignmouth Dr SS6 323 D5
Telegraph Mews
Ilford, Goodmayes IG3 334 A3
Ilford, Seven Kings IG3 333 F3
Telese Ave SS8 364 D3
Telford Ho 2 DA17 369 A3
Telford Pl CM1 232 D4
Telford Rd Braintree CM7 128 A1
Clacton-on-S CO15 196 C8
Telford Way CO4 110 D6
Telham Rd E6 352 A3
Temperance Yd CO6 105 B6
Tempest Mead CM16 247 B4
Tempest Way RM13 355 A6
Templar Ct RM7 335 B7
Templar Ho RM13 354 D3
Templar Rd CM7 128 D2
Templars Cl CM8 183 F4
Templar's Ct CB9 8 E7
Templars Jun Sch CM8 183 F5
Temple Ave RM8 335 A3
Temple Bank CM20 200 B5
Temple Cl Basildon SS15 341 C7
Billericay CM12 296 F5
Frinton-on-S CO13 171 A6
Hadleigh SS7 345 F3
Temple Ct Colchester CO4 110 D2
Southend-on-S SS2 348 C3
Temple Farm Trad Est
CM2 276 C6
Templefields Ent Ctr
CM20 200 A3
Temple Gate Cotts SS2 348 B5
Temple Gdns RM8 334 D1
Temple Hall Ct E4 309 D8
Temple Hill Prim Sch
DA1 376 A2
Temple La CM8,CM77 156 C3
Templemead CM8 183 F3
Temple Mead CM19 198 B1
Temple Pattle CO11 86 C7
Templer Ave RM16 374 A2
Temple Rd
Colchester CO2 135 A2
Ipswich IP3 18 C4
Temple Sutton Prim Sch
SS2 348 C3
Templeton Ave E4 309 B6
Temple Way CM9 236 F5
Templewood Ct SS7 345 D3
Templewood Rd
Colchester CO4 110 E1
Hadleigh SS7 345 D3
Temptin Ave SS8 364 E4
Ten Acre App CM9 236 F5
Tenby Cl RM6 334 E5
Tenby Rd Dagenham RM6 334 E5
Ipswich IP2 17 B1
Tendring Ave SS6 323 A3
Tendring Ct CM13 295 D4
Tendring Prim Sch CO16 140 F6
Tendring Rd
Harlow CM18 223 E6
Little Bentley CO7 140 A8
Tendring CO12 114 E2
Thorpe-le-S CO16 141 D4
Tendring Tech Coll
Thorpe-le-S CO16 142 A1
Walton-on-t-N CO13 171 A7
Tendring Way RM6 334 C6
Tenney Ho RM17 378 C7
Tennyson Ave
Grays RM17 373 C3
Southend-on-S SS2 348 B2
Waltham Abbey EN9 265 E5
Wanstead E11 332 A4
Tennyson Cl
Braintree CM7 154 F8
Southend-on-S SS9 346 A2
Tennyson Dr 9 SS13 343 B5
Tennyson Ho CM16 268 A8
Tennyson Rd
Brentwood CM13 295 D2
Chelmsford CM1 231 F5
Dartford DA1 376 A2
Ipswich IP4 17 F5
Maldon CM9 259 A8
Romford RM3 314 C3
Tennyson Way RM12 335 F2
Tennyson Wlk RM18 379 B5
Tenpenny Hill CO7 165 E5
Tensing Gdns CM12 297 A1
Tenter Cl CM7 127 F5
Tenterden Rd RM8 334 F2
Tenterfield CM6 150 E8
Tenter Field CO7 58 D1
Tenterfield Rd CM9 237 A2
Tenterfields
Basildon SS13 321 C1
Newport CB11 42 F1
Tenth Ave CM24 120 C2
Teramo Rd SS8 364 D3
Tercel Path IG7 312 B6
Terence Webster Rd
SS12 321 E6
Terling SS16 342 B5
Terling CE Prim Sch
CM3 182 C3
Terling Cl CO2 136 A1
Terling Hall Rd CM3 210 C7
Terling Rd
Dagenham RM8 335 A2
Hatfield Peverel CM3 210 F6
Witham CM8 183 B3
Terlings Pk CM20 199 D4
Terlings The CM14 316 A7
Terminal Cl SS3 368 F7
Terminal Rd N CM22,
CM24 121 B4
Terminal Rd S CM22,
CM24 121 B4
Terminus Dr SS16 343 B4
Terminus St CM20 199 D1
Termitts Chase CM3 211 A7
Terms Ave SS8 364 A5
Tern Cl Haverhill CB9 9 C7
Kelvedon CO5 158 D3
Mayland CM3 283 A8
Tern Ct CM14 315 F6
Terndale CO15 195 F6
Tern Gdns RM14 337 E3
Terni Rd SS8 364 D3
Tern Mews CO7 164 B8
Tern Rd IP2 16 E2
Tern Way CM14 315 E6
Terrace Hall Chase CO6 109 D6
Terrace St DA12 379 B1
Terrace The Cavendish CO10 1 D1
Chingford E4 309 E7
Felsted CM6 152 B5
2 Gravesend DA12 379 C1
Hatfield Peverel CM3 211 B5
Rayleigh SS6 323 C7
Southend-on-S,Chalkwell
SS9 365 E8
Southend-on-S SS3 368 F6
1 Woodford IG8 310 A4
Terrace Wlk RM9 353 E7
Terra Cotta Pl CO10 2 E8
Terr The SS7 363 D8
Teviot Ave RM15 371 C7
Tew Cl CO5 186 D5
Tewkesbury Cl IG10 288 E3
Tewkesbury Rd CO15 195 F4
Tewkes Rd SS8 364 D5
Tey Rd Aldham CO6 106 E1
Coggeshall CO6 131 C4
Earls Colne CO6 105 D4
Tey Road Cl CO6 105 D6
Thackeray Ave RM18 379 B6
Thackeray Cl CM7 155 A8
Thackeray Dr RM6 334 B4
Thackeray Row 1 SS12 321 C5
Thal Massing Cl CM13 317 B8
Thames Ave
Chelmsford CM1 231 D4
Dagenham RM9 354 C2
Thames Cl Braintree CM7 128 D1
Corringham SS17 361 A3
Rainham RM13 370 B7
Rayleigh SS6 323 C1
Southend-on-S SS9 346 B1
Thames Cres SS17 361 C5
Thames Ct SS8 364 B1
Thames Dr Grays RM16 374 A1
Southend-on-S SS9 346 A1
Thames Gate DA1 376 A3
Thames Gateway Pk
RM9 353 F2
Thames Haven Rd SS17 361 B3
Thameshill Ave RM5 313 C1
Thameside Cres 6 SS8 364 A3
Thameside Inf Sch
RM17 378 C8
Thameside Jun Sch
RM17 378 C8
Thames Ind Pk RM18 375 B1
Thames Rd Barking IG11 353 A2
Canvey Island SS8 363 F2
Grays RM17 378 B7
Thames View
Basildon SS16 341 C1
Grays RM16 374 A1
Greenhithe DA9 377 C2
Thamesview Ct SS7 345 F2
Thames View Inf Sch
IG11 353 A3
Thames View Jun Sch
IG11 352 F3
Thames View Lodge
IG11 352 E2
Thames Way
Burnham-on-C CM0 306 A6
Gravesend DA11 379 A1
Thamley RM19 371 A2
Thanet Grange SS0 347 C5
Thanet Rd IP4 18 B6
Thanet Wlk CO5 164 A8
Thatchers Cl IG10 289 C7
Thatchers Croft CM3 281 F6
Thatchers Dr CO7 137 F6
Thatchers The CM23 145 C5
Thatchers Way CM77 154 C8
Thatches Gr RM6 334 E7
Thaxted Bold CM13 295 D4
Thaxted Gn CM13 295 C4
Thaxted Ho RM10 354 B5
Thaxted Lodge 3 E18 332 B8
Thaxted Prim Sch CM6 70 A2
Thaxted Rd
Buckhurst Hill IG9 288 E2
Debden CB11 68 C6
Elder Street CB10 44 C4
Saffron Walden CB10 43 F8
Thaxted CB10 69 E8
Thaxted Way EN9 265 D6
Thaxted Wlk
Blackheath CO2 163 A8

Thaxted Wlk continued
  Rainham RM13 .....354 E5
Thear Cl SS0 .....242 C4
Theberton Rd IP3 .....18 B1
The Bungalows CM7 .....100 F5
Thele Ave SG12 .....197 E4
Thele Est SG12 .....197 E4
Thelma Ave SS8 .....364 A4
Thelford Wlk CO4 .....136 F7
Theobalds Ave RM17 .....373 C1
Theobalds Cl SS9 .....346 C1
Theobalds Rd SS9 .....346 C1
Thetford Ct CM1 .....231 E1
Thetford Gdns RM9 .....353 E4
Thetford Pl SS15 .....319 D1
Thetford Rd
  Dagenham RM9 .....353 D5
  8 Ipswich IP1 .....17 A7
Theydon Bois Prim Sch CM16 .....267 E3
Theydon Bois Sta CM16 .....267 F3
Theydon Bold CM16 .....295 D4
Theydon Bower CM16 .....268 A8
Theydon Cres SS14 .....320 F1
Theydon Ct EN9 .....266 A6
Theydon Gdns RM13 .....266 A6
Theydon Gr Epping CM16 .....266 A1
  Woodford IG8 .....310 C4
Theydon Park Rd CM16 .....267 F1
Theydon Pl CM16 .....267 F8
Theydon Rd CM16 .....267 D6
Thicket Gr RM9 .....353 C6
Thielen Rd SS8 .....364 A4
Thieves' Cnr CM1 .....215 C4
Third Ave Basildon SS16 .....340 E3
  Canvey Island SS8 .....363 E4
  Chelmsford CM1 .....232 B5
  Clacton-on-S CO15 .....196 C4
  Dagenham RM10 .....354 B3
  Frinton-on-S CO13 .....170 E4
  Glemsford CO10 .....2 C5
  Grays RM20 .....177 A6
  Halstead CO9 .....77 B1
  Harlow CM18,CM19 .....223 C7
  Harwich CO12 .....91 C3
  Ilford RM6 .....334 C5
  Seawick CO16 .....220 B6
  Stanford-le-H SS17 .....360 E4
  Stansted Mountfitchet CM24 .....120 B2
  Walton-on-t-N CO14 .....144 E3
  Wickford SS11 .....322 A6
Third Wlk SS8 .....363 E4
Thirlmere Cl CM77 .....154 D7
Thirlmere Rd SS7 .....344 E7
Thirslet Dr CM9 .....237 C4
Thirtieth St CM24 .....120 F3
Thirtle Cl CO16 .....195 D6
Thisselt Rd SS8 .....364 B4
Thistle Cl Basildon SS15 .....319 F1
  Ipswich IP2 .....16 E4
Thistledene Ave RM5 .....313 B5
Thistledown
  Basildon SS14 .....342 C6
  Highwoods CO4 .....110 B3
  Panfield CM7 .....127 A7
Thistledown Ct SS14 .....342 C6
Thistle Mead IG10 .....289 A6
Thistley Cl
  Goldhanger CM9 .....238 G6
Thistley Cl SS11 .....46 E1
Thistley Green Rd CM7 .....128 B7
Thoby La CM15 .....273 C1
Thomas Arnold Prim Sch CM23 .....146 A7
Thomasin Rd SS14 .....321 C1
Thomas, Lord Audley Sch CO2 .....135 F2
Thomas Bd Basildon SS13 .....343 E7
  Clacton-on-S CO15 .....195 D4
Thomas Sims Ct CM12 .....355 B7
Thomas St CO7 .....192 F6
Thomas Wakley Cl CO9 .....109 F5
Thomas Willingale Sch IG10 .....289 C6
Thomas Wlk CB11 .....20 F1
Thompson Ave
  Canvey Island SS8 .....364 F3
  Colchester CO3 .....134 F6
Thompson Cl IG1 .....333 C2
Thompson Rd
  Dagenham RM9 .....334 F1
  Ipswich IP1 .....16 F8
Thorington Ave SS7 .....345 D6
Thorington Cl CM77 .....154 C6
Thorington Rd SS6 .....324 A1
Thorin's Gate CM3 .....301 C6
Thorley High CM23 .....145 E5
Thorley Hill CM23 .....145 F5
Thorley Hill Prim Sch CM23 .....145 F4
Thorley La CM23 .....145 F3
Thorley La E CM23 .....145 D5
Thorley La W CM23 .....145 B4
Thorley Neighbourhood Ctr CM23 .....145 D4
Thorley Park Rd CM23 .....145 F4
Thorley Rd RM16 .....373 A5
Thornbera Cl CM23 .....145 F5
Thornbera Gdns CM23 .....145 F5
Thornbera Rd CM23 .....145 F4

Thornberry Ave CO16 .....140 F1
Thornborough Ave CM3 .....301 F7
Thornbridge SS7 .....344 B4
Thornbury Ave SS9 .....197 B2
Thornbury Ho 8 RM3 .....314 D5
Thornbury Rd CO15 .....195 F4
Thornbush La IP8 .....16 A8
Thorncroft
  Hornchurch RM11 .....336 B5
  Saffron Walden CB10 .....22 F2
Thorndale SS7 .....345 B7
Thorndales CM14 .....316 D6
Thorndon App CM13 .....317 D3
Thorndon Cl IG10 .....289 C6
Thorndon Ct CO16 .....195 A4
Thorndon Country Pk★ CM13 .....317 D1
Thorndon Countryside Ctr★ CM13 .....316 F3
Thorndon Ct CM13 .....316 C4
Thorndon City Pk★ CM13 .....316 F3
Thorndon Gate CM13 .....317 B4
Thorndon Park Cl SS9 .....346 C5
Thorndon Park Cres SS9 .....346 B5
Thorndon Park Dr SS9 .....346 C5
Thorne Rd CO5 .....158 B2
Thorney Bay Rd SS8 .....364 A2
Thorneycroft Dr EN3 .....265 A2
Thorney Rd IP9 .....35 A1
Thornfield Ct SS0 .....136 D2
Thornfield Rd CM21 .....145 E8
Thornford Gdns SS2 .....347 F5
Thorn Gr CM23 .....146 B4
Thorn Grove Prim Sch CM23 .....146 B6
Thornhayes Cl IP2 .....17 A3
Thornhill
  North Weald Bassett CM16 .....247 C5
  Purleigh CM3 .....258 D1
  Southend-on-S SS9 .....346 E4
Thornhill Cl CO13 .....170 F7
Thornhill Gdns IG11 .....352 C5
Thorn La RM13 .....355 D3
Thornley Dr IP4 .....18 C8
Thornridge CM14 .....294 B1
Thorns The CM5 .....293 E8
Thorns Way CO14 .....171 A8
Thornton Dr CO4 .....109 F2
Thornton Ho 8 E11 .....332 A5
Thornton Pl CM11 .....275 E2
Thornton Rd
  Belvedere DA17 .....369 B2
  Ilford IG1 .....352 B8
  Takeley CM6 .....148 F7
Thorntons CM13 .....317 D4
Thorntons Farm Ave RM7 .....335 D2
Thornton Way SS15 .....341 A6
Thorn Way IP11 .....381 C4
Thornwood CM4 .....109 F4
Thornwood Cl
  West Mersea CO5 .....218 D6
  Woodford IG8 .....310 B1
Thornwood Common SS8 .....346 D6
Thornwood Ho IG10 .....289 C6
Thornwood Rd CM16 .....246 B2
Thorogood Way RM13 .....354 E4
Thorold Rd IG1 .....333 C3
Thorolds SS16 .....342 E3
Thoroughfare 8 IP1 .....17 C6
Thoroughgood Rd CO15 .....195 F3
Thorpe Bay Gdns SS1 .....368 B6
Thorpe Bay Sch The SS1 .....348 F1
Thorpe Bay Sta SS1 .....368 B8
Thorpe Bold CM14 .....295 D4
Thorpe Cl Hockley SS5 .....324 F4
  Wickford SS12 .....321 F6
Thorpe Cress CO16 .....169 D8
Thorpedale Gdns IG1,IG6 .....333 B7
Thorpedene Ave SS0 .....301 C2
Thorpedene Gdns SS3 .....368 D6
Thorpedene Inf Sch SS3 .....368 C7
Thorpedene Jun Sch SS3 .....368 C7
Thorpe Espl SS1 .....368 B6
Thorpe Gdns SS5 .....324 F4
Thorpe Greenways Jun & Inf Sch SS1 .....367 E2
Thorpe Hall Ave SS1 .....368 A7
Thorpe Hall Cl SS1 .....368 A8
Thorpe Hall Prim Sch E17 .....309 C2
Thorpe Hall Rd E17 .....309 C2
Thorpe Hall Sch SS1 .....349 A2
Thorpe-le-Soken Sta CO16 .....168 D3
Thorpe Lodge
  Romford RM1 .....336 D5
  Southend-on-S SS1 .....349 D5
Thorpe Park La CO16 .....169 B7
Thorpe Rd Barking IG11 .....352 D5
  Beaumont CO16 .....141 B5
  Chingford E17 .....309 C1
  Clacton-on-S CO15 .....195 F2
  Hockley SS5 .....324 F3
  Hockley SS5 .....324 F4
  Kirby Cross CO13 .....170 C8
  Wanstead E7 .....332 A1
  Weeley CO16 .....141 A2
Thorpe Wlk CO4 .....136 F7
Thorpe Leas SS8 .....364 B2
Thorrington Bold CM14 .....295 D4
Thorrington Cross
  Basildon SS14 .....342 E3
  Thorrington CO7 .....165 F5
Thorrington Rd
  Great Bentley CO7 .....166 C8
  Little Clacton CO16 .....168 E5
Thorrington Tide Mill★ CO7 .....165 E3
Thors Oak SS17 .....360 E2
Thracian Cl CO2 .....135 A3

Thrapston Ho 10 RM3 .....314 E5
Threadneedle St
  2 Chelmsford CM1 .....232 B2
  Dedham CO7 .....84 F7
Three Acres CO16 .....194 A4
Three Crowns Rd CO4 .....109 E2
Three Gates Cl CO9 .....103 C8
Three Horseshoes Rd CM19 .....223 B6
Three Mile Hill CM4 .....253 C2
Thremhall Ave
  Bishop's Stortford CM23 .....146 F8
  Great Hallingbury CM22,CM24 .....147 C8
  Takeley CM22 .....121 A2
Threshelford SS16 .....341 F4
Threshelfords Bsns Pk CO5 .....158 E3
Thresher Cl CM23 .....145 C5
Thresher Rise CM77 .....154 C8
Threshers End CO3 .....134 D5
Thrift Rd CM21 .....145 D4
Thrifts Mead CM16 .....267 E2
Thrift Wood CM3 .....256 F1
Thriftwood Sch CM2 .....254 B3
Thrimley La CM23 .....118 C6
Throwley Cl SS13 .....343 C5
Thrushdale CO15 .....195 F6
Thunderer Rd RM9 .....353 C8
Thundersley Church Rd SS7 .....344 D5
Thundersley Gr SS7 .....344 D5
Thundersley Jun & Inf Schs SS7 .....344 D5
Thundersley Park Rd SS7 .....344 E3
Thurgood Rd EN11 .....221 D8
Thurlby Cl IG8 .....310 F5
Thurlby Rd IG8 .....310 F5
Thurlestone Ave IG3 .....352 F8
Thurloe Gdns RM1 .....335 F5
Thurloe Wlk RM17 .....173 A3
Thurlow Cl E17 .....309 B4
Thurlow Ct SS13 .....343 B4
Thurlow Dr SS1 .....367 F8
Thurlow Gdns IG6 .....311 D4
Thurlow Pl 10 CB9 .....9 B8
Thurlston Cl CO4 .....110 D1
Thurlstone SS7 .....345 C5
Thurrock & Basildon Coll (Nethemayne Campus) SS16 .....341 F4
Thurrock & Basildon Coll (Woodview Campus) RM16 .....373 F2
Thurrock Bsns Ctr RM20 .....177 B8
Thurrock Com Hospl RM16 .....373 C5
Thurrock Commercial Ctr RM15 .....370 F4
Thurrock Ent Ctr RM17 .....378 A8
Thurrock Local History Mus★ RM17 .....378 D4
Thurrock Park Way RM18 .....378 D7
Thurso IG4 .....315 B4
Thurstable Cl SS16 .....216 E2
Thurstable Rd CM9 .....216 C6
Thurstable Sch CM9 .....186 D6
Thurstable Way CM9 .....216 E2
Thurstans CM19 .....222 E3
Thurston Ave SS2 .....348 E1
Thurston Cl IP11 .....381 A2
Thyme Mews CM3 .....183 C5
Thyme Rd CO5 .....186 C5
Thynne Rd CM1 .....297 C2
Tiberius Cl
  Colchester CO4 .....110 B6
  Haverhill CB9 .....9 D7
Tickenhall Dr CM17 .....224 D7
Tickfield Ave SS2 .....347 F2
Tideswell Cl RM17 .....173 A3
Tideway Maldon CM9 .....259 B8
Tideway Ct SS3 .....367 D6
Tidings Hill CO9 .....103 E8
Tidworth Ave SS11 .....299 E2
Tidy's La CM6 .....246 B2
Tiffin Dr CO5 .....186 E5
Tighfield Wlk CM3 .....301 C5
Tilburg Rd SS8 .....364 A4
Tilbury Ave SS5 .....324 E3
Tilbury Manor Inf Sch RM18 .....379 B7
Tilbury Manor Jun Sch RM18 .....379 B7
Tilbury Mead CM18 .....224 A6
Tilbury Rd
  Great Yeldham CO9 .....30 A3
  West Horndon CM13 .....339 E5
Tilbury Town Sta RM18 .....378 F5
Tildesley Cl CO13 .....170 A6
Tile Barn La CO11 .....87 C1
Tilegate Rd Harlow CM18 .....223 F6
  Tilgate Green CM5 .....225 D5
Tile House Rd CO6 .....109 B8
Tillingham Bold CM3 .....295 D4
Tillingham Ct EN9 .....266 A6
Tillingham Gn SS15 .....341 A6
Tillingham Rd
  Dagenham RM8 .....284 F6
Tillingham Way CM13 .....323 A3
Tillwicks Cl IG1 .....333 A4
Tillwicks Rd CM18 .....224 A6
Tilney Ct IG9 .....310 A8
Tilney Rd
  Buckhurst Hill IG9 .....310 B8
  Dagenham RM9 .....353 F6
Tilney Turn SS16 .....342 F4

Timber Ct RM17 .....378 A8
Timberdene Ave IG6 .....311 C2
Timber Hill CO1 .....136 C6
Timberlog La SS14 .....342 E6
Timberlog La SS14,SS16 .....342 E6
Timbermans View SS16 .....342 F4
Timbers Cl CM77 .....154 C7
Timber Wharf Cotts SS11 .....300 C2
Time Sq SS14 .....342 A5
Timsons La CM2 .....232 E4
Tinabrook Cl IP2 .....16 E1
Tindal Cl RM3 .....315 C2
Tindal St CM1 .....232 B2
Tindal St 8 CM1 .....232 B2
Tindon End Rd CB10 .....46 D2
Tinker Rd CM22 .....121 F6
Tinker Ct CM7 .....73 C6
Tinker's La SS4 .....325 F1
Tinkler St CO12 .....116 D8
Tinkler Side SS14 .....342 B6
Tinnocks La CM0 .....240 B1
Tintagel Ct RM11 .....337 A3
Tintagel Way CM9 .....258 E8
Tintagel Way SS0 .....347 C2
Tintern Cl IP2 .....17 A2
Tintern Mews SS0 .....347 C1
Tiplers Bridge CM11 .....298 B5
Tippersfield SS7 .....344 D5
Tippett Cl CO4 .....136 G6
Tipps Cross CM4 .....272 B4
Tipps Cross La CM15 .....272 B4
Tipps Cross Mead CM15 .....272 B4
Tiptree Cl Chingford E4 .....309 C7
  Hornchurch RM11 .....337 A3
  Southend-on-S SS9 .....346 F4
Tiptree Cres Ilford IG5 .....333 A8
  Redbridge IG5 .....311 A1
Tiptree Ct CM13 .....295 D4
Tiptree Gr SS12 .....321 D7
Tiptree Hall La CO5 .....186 B2
Tiptree Heath Prim Sch CO5 .....186 B3
Tiptree Mus★ CO5 .....186 E4
Tiptree Rd
  Great Braxted CM8 .....185 B8
  Wickham Bishops CM8 .....212 F6
Tisdale Cl SS12 .....321 D5
Tiree Chase SS12 .....321 F5
Titania Cl CO4 .....136 F7
Titan Rd RM17 .....373 A1
Titchwell Dr IP3 .....38 D7
Tithe Barn Agricultural & Folk Mus The★ RM11 .....337 D4
Tithe Cl CM8 .....183 E3
Tithelands CM19 .....223 A5
Tithe The SS12 .....321 B6
Titley Ct E4 .....309 A5
Titus Way CO4 .....110 B6
Tiverton Ave IG5 .....333 A8
Tiverton Rd RM3 .....315 A5
Tobruk Rd
  Chelmsford CM1 .....231 F6
  Colchester CO2 .....135 D3
Toddbrook CM17 .....223 B7
Todd Cl RM13 .....355 D1
Toft Ave RM17 .....373 D2
Tofts Chase CM3 .....234 E5
Tofts Wlk 8 CM7 .....127 F3
Toga Cl CO2 .....135 A2
Tog La Great Horkesley CO6 .....82 A3
  Little Horkesley CO6 .....81 F3
Tokely Rd CO7 .....139 A3
Tokio Rd IP4 .....18 A6
Tolbut Cl 8 RM1 .....335 F5
Tolcairn Ct 10 DA17 .....369 A1
Toledo Cl SS3 .....367 D8
Toledo Rd SS1 .....367 D8
Toller Rd IP3 .....17 E3
Tollesbury Cl SS12 .....321 E6
Tollesbury Ct CM23 .....146 D6
Tollesbury Gdns IG6 .....333 D8
Tollesbury Rd CM9 .....215 F3
Tollesbury Prim Sch CM9 .....215 D4
Tolleshunt D'Arcy Prim Sch CM9 .....214 F3
  Wivenhoe CO7 .....137 B2
  Writtle CM1 .....230 D7
Tollesbury D'Arcy Prim Sch
  CM9 .....214 F3
Toll Gate Rd IP9 .....35 A1
Tollgate Rdbt CO3 .....134 B3
Tollgate W CO3 .....134 B3
Tolliday Cl CO7 .....137 A2
Tolly Cobbold Brewery Tours & Brewery★ IP3 .....17 E1
Tolworth Gdns RM6 .....334 E6
Tolworth Par RM6 .....334 E6
Tom Davies Ho 8 CM7 .....127 F2
Tomkins Cl SS17 .....360 F1
Tomkyns La
  Romford RM14 .....315 D1
  Upminster RM14 .....337 D7
Tomline Rd
  Felixstowe IP11 .....381 E4
  Ipswich IP3 .....18 A4
Tomlins Orch IG11 .....352 C4
Tomlyns Cl CM13 .....295 E3
Tom Mann Cl IG11 .....352 A3
Tom's La CM7 .....72 A4
Tomswood Ct IG6 .....333 D7
Tomswood Hill IG6 .....333 C1
Tomswood Rd IG7 .....333 A7
Tom Tit La CM9 .....257 E7
Tonbridge Rd
  Hockley SS5 .....324 F8
  Romford RM3 .....314 D3
Tongres Rd SS8 .....364 A4
Tony Webb Cl CO4 .....110 B6

Took Dr CM3 .....301 C6
Tooley's Ct (Almshouses) 8 IP4 .....17 C5
Toot Hill Rd CM5 .....247 F1
Topaz Ct 8 RM3 .....355 A1
Top House Rise E4 .....287 C2
Toplands Ave RM15 .....371 C5
Toppesfield Ave SS12 .....321 C5
Toppesfield Gr CO9 .....50 F8
Top Rd
  Tolleshunt Knights CM9 .....187 A2
  Wimbish CB10 .....45 E3
  Woodham Walter CM9 .....235 D2
Torbitt Way IG2 .....333 F6
Tor Bryan CM4 .....274 B2
Torells Rd RM16 .....373 F4
Torell 8 E18 .....309 F1
Torney Cl SS16 .....340 F4
Toronto Rd Ilford IG1 .....333 C3
  Tilbury RM18 .....379 A6
Torquay Cl SS9 .....346 E1
Torquay Dr SS9 .....346 E1
Torquay Gdns IG4 .....332 D7
Torquay Rd CM1 .....232 D5
Torrance Cl RM11 .....336 C3
Torrell's Hall Cotts CM5 .....228 E5
Torridge Rd CM12 .....375 C2
Torrington SS3 .....368 D8
Torrington Cl CM23 .....232 E5
Torrington Dr IG10 .....289 C5
Torrington Gdns IG10 .....289 C5
Torrington Rd
  Dagenham RM8 .....334 F3
  Wanstead E18 .....332 A8
Torsi Rd SS8 .....364 D3
Tortoiseshell Cl IP8 .....16 A8
Tortoiseshell Way CM7 .....127 F1
Tortosa Cl CO2 .....136 B4
Torver Cl CM77 .....154 C6
Totham Hill Gn CM9 .....213 G6
Tot La CM23,CM24 .....119 D4
Totlands Dr CO15 .....196 A7
Totman Cl SS6 .....345 D8
Totman Cres SS6 .....345 D8
Totnes Wlk CM1 .....232 E6
Totteridge Cl CO16 .....195 D5
Toucan Cl IG5 .....349 E1
Toucan Way
  Basildon SS14 .....342 A3
  Clacton-on-S CO15 .....195 E1
Toulmin Rd CM18 .....211 A4
Tovells Rd IP4 .....17 F6
Tovey Ave EN11 .....221 A8
Tovey Cl EN9 .....243 E8
Tower Ave Basildon SS14 .....342 A3
  Chelmsford CM1 .....231 F4
Tower Cl
  North Weald Bassett CM16 .....247 D7
  Redbridge IG5 .....333 A8
Tower Ct
  Brentwood CM14 .....316 C8
  Chipping Ongar CM5 .....249 A2
  4 Haverhill CB9 .....8 F7
  Southend-on-S SS0 .....366 F7
Tower Ctr CO7 .....221 A6
Tower Cut CO7 .....192 F6
Tower Cvn Pk
  Clacton-on-S CO15 .....195 E1
  Hullbridge SS5 .....301 E4
Tower Est CO16 .....168 C6
Towerfield Cl SS3 .....368 E7
Towerfield Rd SS3 .....368 E7
Tower Hill CM1 .....214 A1
Tower Hill Rd CM5 .....228 C1
Tower Ho CM13 .....295 D2
Tower Hts 10 SS13 .....221 A7
Tower Park Rd IP1 .....16 F7
Tower Ramparts IP1 .....17 C6
Tower Ramparts Ctr 8 IP1 .....17 C6
Tower Ramparts Sch IP1 .....17 C6
Town Croft CM1 .....232 A5
Towneley Cotts RM4 .....259 E1
Town End Field CM8 .....195 C2
TownFields SS2 .....348 B2
Townfield St CM1 .....232 A5
Townfield Wlk SS3 .....349 E4
Towngate Bsns Pk IG11 .....353 A2
Town Gate Ct SS15 .....340 F2
Town Mead Rd EN9 .....265 D5
Town Pier Sq DA11 .....379 B1
Town Quay IG11 .....352 A4
Town Quay Wharf IG11 .....352 B4
Townsend Cl CM2 .....206 C7
Town Sq SS14 .....342 A5
Towse Cl CO15 .....196 A2
Tracyes Rd CM18 .....224 B3
Traddles Ct CM1 .....231 F6
Trafalgar Bsns Ctr IG11 .....352 F1
Trafalgar Ho IP4 .....17 D4
Trafalgar Pl 4 IP4 .....17 C6
Trafalgar Rd
  Clacton-on-S CO15 .....195 E1

Trafalgar Rd continued
  Colchester CO3 .....134 E6
  Rainham RM13 .....354 F3
  Southend-on-S SS3 .....368 D7
Trafalgar Way
  Billericay CM12 .....297 B5
  Braintree CM7 .....128 B4
Trafford Cl IG6 .....311 F4
Trajan Cl CO4 .....110 B6
Tranquil Rise DA8 .....369 E1
Trap's Hill IG10 .....288 F5
Trasa Ct RM17 .....378 C8
Travers Way SS13 .....343 A6
Trayford Cl 8 RM19 .....371 E1
Trebble Rd DA10 .....377 E1
Tredgetts CB10 .....6 B1
Treebeard Copse CM3 .....265 C4
Treeby Ct EN3 .....265 A2
Tree Cl Abridge RM4 .....290 B6
  Clacton-on-S CO15 .....195 F7
Treecot Dr SS9 .....347 A4
Treelawn Dr SS9 .....346 F4
Treelawn Gdns SS9 .....346 F4
Tree Top Mews RM10 .....354 D6
Treetops IP11 .....381 C6
Tree Tops
  Brentwood CM15 .....294 C1
Treetops Ho IG8 .....310 A6
Treetops Ct CO4 .....109 F5
Treetops Sch RM17 .....373 B2
Treetops View IG10 .....288 D2
Trefgarne Rd RM10 .....335 A2
Trefoil Cl IP2 .....16 F4
Trefoil Ct 8 CM7 .....155 A5
Trefoil Ho RM17 .....173 B7
Tregaron Ho 8 RM3 .....314 D4
Trehearn Rd IG6 .....311 D3
Trelawn CM3 .....233 E8
Trelawney Rd IG6 .....311 D3
Trelawney Cl E4 .....334 A1
Trenchard Cres CM2 .....206 A3
Trenchard Lodge CM1 .....232 D7
Trenders Ave SS6 .....323 B7
Trenham Ave SS13 .....343 D7
Trent Ave E18 .....309 F1
Trent Cl RM14 .....337 D5
Trentbridge Cl IG6 .....311 F4
Trent Cl
  Burnham-on-C CM0 .....306 A6
  Wickford SS12 .....321 D6
Trent Ct CM11 .....332 A6
Trent Rd
  Buckhurst Hill IG9 .....288 B1
  Chelmsford CM1 .....231 D5
  Ipswich IP3 .....17 F2
  Witham CM8 .....183 G2
Tresco Gdns RM5 .....313 C5
Tresco Rd SS12 .....321 F5
Tresham Rd IG11 .....352 F5
Treswell Rd RM9 .....353 E4
Trevera Ct EN11 .....221 A7
Trevor Cl CM12 .....318 F7
Trevor Rd IG8 .....310 A4
Trevose 8 E17 .....309 D2
Trevose Rd E17 .....309 D2
Trewithen Ct SS6 .....346 A8
Trews Gdns RM5 .....158 C3
Triangle Garage CM7 .....237 B5
Triangle Sh Ctr CO14 .....170 F7
Triangle The
  Barking IG11 .....352 C6
  Basildon SS14 .....341 B4
Trianon Ct 8 SS13 .....343 C6
Trickett Cs CO7 .....137 B1
Trident Ind Est EN11 .....221 C7
Trienna Ct CM13 .....317 B7
Trilo Ct IG1 .....333 E4
Trimble Cl CM4 .....274 B4
Trimley Cl Basildon SS14 .....342 C7
  Clacton-on-S CO16 .....195 E1
Trimley Sta IP11 .....381 A7
Trimley St Mary Prim Sch IP11 .....381 A2
Trindehay SS15 .....341 E5
Trinder Way SS12 .....321 F6
Tring Cl Ilford IG2 .....333 D6
  Romford RM3 .....314 F6
Tring Gdns RM3 .....314 F6
Tring Wlk RM3 .....314 F6
Trinidad Gdns RM10 .....354 D5
Trinity Ave
  Felixstowe IP11 .....381 A4
  Southend-on-S SS0 .....366 E7
Trinity Cl Basildon SS15 .....341 C6
  Billericay CM11 .....319 C6
  Bishop's Stortford CM23 .....145 F6
  Chelmsford CM2 .....232 D3
  Mannington CO11 .....86 D3
  Rayleigh SS6 .....323 E1
  Rushmere St A IP5 .....18 F7
  West Mersea CO5 .....218 C7
  Wivenhoe CO7 .....137 C1
Trinity Ct Chingford E4 .....309 C8
  Halstead CO9 .....76 E1
Trinity Farm Ct 8 CO11 .....86 D4
Trinity Gdns IG11 .....332 B8
Trinity Lodge SS8 .....348 D1
Trinity Mews CO5 .....218 C7
Trinity RC High Sch (Lower) IG8 .....310 A6
Trinity RC High Sch (Upper) IG8 .....310 A6
Trinity Rd Billericay CM11 .....319 C6
  Chelmsford CM2 .....232 D2
  Halstead CO9 .....76 E1
  Ilford IG6 .....333 C8
  Manningtree CO11 .....86 D3
  Rayleigh SS6 .....323 E1

Trinity Rd continued
Southend-on-S SS2 ....348 D3
Trinity Road Prim Sch
CM2 ....232 D2
Trinity Sch
Belvedere DA17 ....369 E2
Dagenham RM10 ....354 A8
Trinity Sq
🔟 Colchester CO1 ....135 F7
South Woodham Ferrers
CM3 ....301 E7
Trinity St
Bishop's Stortford CM23 .145 F6
Colchester CO1 ....135 F7
Halstead CO9 ....76 D2
Ipswich IP3 ....17 E4
Trinity St Mary's CE Prim Sch
CM3 ....301 E7
Trinity Terr
Buckhurst Hill IG9 ......288 B2
🔟 Halstead CO9 ....76 D1
Trinity Way CM23 ....145 F6
Trinity Wood Rd SS5 .325 A8
Trinovantian Way CM7 .128 A2
Tripat CI SS17 ....361 D5
Tripton Rd CM18 ......223 E7
Triton Ct IG9 ....310 A8
Triton Lodge DA8 .....369 E1
Triton Way SS7 ....345 B6
Triumph Ave CO15 ....220 E7
Triumph CI
Colchester CO4 ....136 E5
Grays RM16 ....372 C2
Triumph Ho IG11 ......353 A2
Trivett CI DA9 ....377 E2
Trojan Terr CM21 .....172 E3
Trojan Way CO15 ......190 B8
Troopers Dr RM3 ......114 D6
Trotters Field CM7 ...128 B3
Trotter's Gap SG12 ...197 E4
Trotters Rd CM18 .....224 A5
Trotwood IG7 ....311 D4
Trotwood CI
Brentwood CM15 ....294 E1
Chelmsford CM1 ....231 E7
Troubridge CI CM3 ....301 F7
Trowbridge Rd RM3 ...314 E4
Troys Chase CM3 ......182 C6
Truelowes La CM4 .....254 C7
Truman CI 🔟 SS15 ....341 A6
Trumpeter Ct CM12 ...296 F3
Trunette Rd CO15 .....195 C3
Trunnions The SS4 ....325 C5
Truro Cres SS2 ....323 C5
Truro Gdns IG1 ....332 E4
Truro WIk RM3 ....324 F4
Trusses Rd
Bradwell-on-S CM0 .....242 A3
Bradwell Waterside CM0 .241 F3
Trustons Gdns RM11 ..336 A4
Trust The RM12 ....336 E7
Truswell Terr CO11 ....86 D7
Tryfan CI IG4 ....332 D6
Tryon Ct 🔟 CO9 ....76 D1
Tucker Dr CM8 ....183 F1
Tucker's Row 🔟 CM23 .145 F6
Tuck Rd RM13 ....355 A6
Tuddenham Ave IP4 ...17 E7
Tuddenham Rd IP4 .....17 E8
Tudor Ave Romford RM2 .336 A8
Stanford-le-H SS17 .....360 E4
Tudor CE Prim Sch CO10 .15 F1
Tudor CI Brentwood CM3 .295 A3
Brightlingsea CO7 ....192 D8
Chigwell IG7 ....311 A6
Hunsdonbury SG12 .....198 D8
Ingatestone CM4 ....254 C7
Jaywick CO15 ....195 A1
Rayleigh SS5 ....323 F2
Southend-on-S SS9 .....346 C7
Sudbury CO10 ....15 E1
Thundersley SS7 ....344 F5
Walton-on-t-N CO14 ....144 D2
Witham CM8 ....183 F1
Woodford IG8 ....324 F4
Tudor Court Prim Sch
RM16 ....372 F4
Tudor Cres IG6 ....311 C4
Tudor Ct Basildon SS15 .319 F2
Romford RM3 ....315 B4
Sawbridgeworth CM21 ..172 E3
West Mersea CO5 ......218 C7
Tudor Dr RM2 ....336 A7
Tudor Gdns Romford RM2 .336 A7
Ilford IG1 ....352 C7
Tudor Rd Basildon SS13 .342 F5
Canvey Island SS8 .....369 C3
Chingford E4 ....309 B4
Southend-on-S, Noblesgreen
SS9 ....346 C7
Southend-on-S SS0 .....347 E2
Sudbury CO10 ....15 E1
Tudor Rose CI CO3 ....134 C7
Tudor Way Hockley SS5 .324 F4
Sible Hedingham CO9 ...265 D6
Wickford SS12 ....321 B7
Tudor WIks SS12 ......321 A7
Tudwick Rd CM9 ......214 E6

Tufnell Way CO4 ......109 D2
Tufted CI CM7 ....127 C5
Tufter Rd IG7 ....311 F5
Tufton Rd E4 ....309 A6
Tugby PI CM1 ....231 E6
Tukes Way CB11 ......43 F7
Tulip CI Chelmsford CM2 .232 F7
Pilgrims Hatch CM15 ...294 B4
Romford RM3 ....314 D4
Tulip Gdns Chingford E4 .309 D7
St Osyth CO16 ....352 B6
Tulip Way CO16 ....195 C4
Tulip WIk CO4 ....136 D7
Tumbler Rd CM18 .....224 B7
Tumulus Way CO2 .....135 A3
Tunfield Rd Colchester CO2 .322 A7
Tunfield Rd RM11 .....337 A8
Tunnel Cotts RM20 ....377 A8
Tunnel Est RM20 ......371 F2
Tunnmeade CM20 .....200 A1
Tunstall Ave IG6 ......311 C1
Tunstall CI Basildon SS13 .343 C5
St Osyth CO16 ....194 B5
Tupman CI CM1 ....231 D6
Turin St IP2 ....17 C4
Turkentine CI CO10 ...34 C5
Turkey Cock La CO3,CO6 .133 E7
Turkey Oaks CM1 .....232 D3
Turnage Rd RM8 ......334 E3
Turner Ave CO11 .....86 E5
Turner Ct
Black Notley CM77 .....155 B4
Southend-on-S SS3 .....368 F8
Wivenhoe CO7 ....127 C1
Turner Rd Colchester CO4 .109 F3
Hornchurch RM12 ......335 F2
Ipswich IP3 ....38 A8
Turners CI CM3 ....248 F2
Turners Cres CM23 ...145 C4
Turners Rd E4 ....290 B6
Turnors CM20 ....219 D2
Turnpike CI CO7 ......110 E8
Turnpike La RM18 .....374 D1
Turnpike PI CM7 ......128 A3
Turnstone End 🔟 CO4 .136 F8
Turold Rd SS17 ....360 E4
Turp Ave RM6 ....373 C4
Turpin Ave RM5 ......313 B4
Turpin CI EN3 ....265 A2
Turpins Ave CO15 ....196 C5
Turpins CI CO15 ......196 C5
Turpins La IG8 ....310 A8
Turpins La
Kirby Cross CO13 ....170 E7
Kirby-le-S CO13 ....170 E8
Turpin's La IG8 ....310 F5
Turpins The SS14 .....342 C7
Turret Green Ct 🔟 IP1 .17 C5
Turret Ho CO15 ....196 A2
Turret La IP4 ....17 C5
Turstan Rd CM8 ......211 E8
Tusser CI CM8 ....184 B7
Tusser CI CM2 ....254 D8
Tusset Mews CO3 .....134 E7
Tutors Way CM3 ......301 E7
Tuttlebee La IG9 .....310 A8
Tuttleby Cotts RM4 ...290 E2
Twain Terr 🔟 SS2 ....321 C5
Tweed Ho RM18 ......375 C3
Tweed CI CO9 ....103 D8
Tweed Glen RM1 ......313 D3
Tweed Rd RM1 ....313 D3
Tweed Way RM1 ......313 D3
Twelve Acre Ho 🔟 E12 .333 A1
Twelve Acres CM7 ....128 D3
Twenty First St CM24 .120 F3
Twickenham CI 🔟 IG3 .310 A5
Twine CI IG11 ....353 B2
Twining Rd CO3 ....134 E4
Twin Oaks CM2 ....233 A4
Twinstead SS12 ....321 F6
Twitten La CM2 ....254 B2
Twitty Fee CM2 ....257 A8
Two Acres IP9 ....35 E7
Two Tree Island Nature
Reserve* SS9 ....365 B7
Twyford Bsns Ctr SS4 .350 A4
Twyford Bsns Ctr The
CM23 ....146 A4
Twyford Bury La CM22,
CM23 ....146 A4
Twyford CI CM23 .....146 A5
Twyford Gdns CM23 ..146 A5
Twyford Mill CM22 ...146 A3
Twyford Rd
Bishop's Stortford CM23 .146 A5
Ilford IG1 ....352 C7
Twyford Rd SS8 ......168 A5
Tyburn Hill C06 ......106 A6
Tyburns The CM13 ...317 D8
Tycehurst Hill IG10 ...288 F5
Tydeman CI CO3 ......134 C4
Tye CI CO10 ....34 B7
Tye Common Rd CM2 .318 E7
Tye Croft CO10 ....134 D6
Tyefields SS13 ....343 C7
Tye Gn CO10 ....2 B5
Tye Green Paddocks CO8 .2 B5
Tye Green Rd CM22 ..120 D6
Tye Green Village CM18 .223 F5
Tyehurst Cres CO4 ...110 C2
Tye La CO7 ....137 E3
Tyelands CM12 ....318 F8
Tye Rd CO7 ....137 E7
Tye Rd The CO7 ......167 B7
Tye The CM3 ....270 C7
Tyle Gn RM11 ....336 F7
Tylehurst Gdns IG1 ...352 C7
Tyler Ave Basildon SS15 .341 C6
Clacton-on-S CO15 .....195 B3
Tylers CB10 ....23 D3
Tylers Ave Billericay CM12 .297 C5
Tylers CI Chelmsford CM2 .254 B6
Loughton IG10 ....288 E2

Tylers Cres RM12 .....355 C7
Tylers Ct 🔟 CM14 ....316 C6
Tylers Gn IP11 ....381 A7
Tylers Rd CM19 ....222 D3
Tylers Ride CM3 ......301 E7
Tyler St Harwich CO12 .90 F5
Southend-on-S SS2 .....17 D4
Tyler Way CM4 ....294 B1
Tylewood SS7 ....345 C3
Tylney Ave SS4 ....325 E3
Tylney Croft CM19 ...223 B6
Tylneys Rd CO9 ......77 A3
Tymperley CE CO1 ....136 A6
Tymperleys Clock Mus*
CO1 ....135 F7
Tyms Way SS6 ....323 E4
Tyndale CI SS5 ....301 D3
Tyndale Dr CO15 .....195 A1
Tyndale Rd SS5 ....301 D3
Tyndales La CM3 ......257 B5
Tyne CI CM14 ....337 D5
Tynedale Ct CO4 .....110 B4
Tynedale Sq CO4 .....110 B4
Tyne Gdns RM15 .....371 C6
Tyne Way CM1 ....231 D5
Tyrel Dr SS1 ....367 B8
Tyrell Rise CM14 .....316 C5
Tyrells SS5 ....324 D5
Tyrells CI Chelmsford CM2 .232 E4
Upminster RM14 ....337 B2
Tyrells The SS17 .....361 A3
Tyrells Way CM2 .....254 F7
Tyrone CI CM11 ......319 C6
Tyrone Rd Billericay CM11 .319 C6
Southend-on-S SS1 .....368 A7
Tyrrell CI 🔟 SS13 ....343 C6
Tyrrell Rd SS7 ....344 B2
Tyrrells Hall CI RM17 .378 D8
Tyrrells Rd CM11 .....319 D6
Tyrrells Sch The CM1 .232 C5
Tysea CI CM18 ....223 F5
Tysea Hill RM4 ....291 F2
Tysea Rd CM18 ....223 F5
Tyssen Mead CM8 ....233 E8
Tyssen PI RM15 ......357 C2
Tythe Barn Way CM3 .301 C8
Tythe CI CM1 ....232 E8
Tythings The CO9 ....103 D8

U

Udall Gdns RM5 ....313 A4
Ufford PI 🔟 CB9 ......9 B8
Ullswater CI CM77 ....154 C6
Ullswater Ct 🔟 E18 ..310 A1
Ullswater Rd SS7 .....344 E7
Ullswater Way RM12 ..335 C3
Ulster Ave SS3 ....368 D6
Ulting Hall Rd CM9 ...235 E7
Ulting La CM9 ....235 E6
Ulting Rd
Hatfield Peverel CM3 ...211 C2
Ulting CM9 ....235 C8
Ulting Way SS12 .....322 A8
Ulverston Ho 🔟 RM3 .314 E4
Ulverston Rd
Chingford E17 ....309 D1
Rochford SS3 ....303 C1
Una Rd Basildon SS13 .343 F6
Harwich CO12 ....90 F5
Undercliff Rd W IP11 ..381 D3
Underhill Rd SS7 .....344 E3
Underwood Rd
Chingford E4 ....309 B5
Woodford IG8 ....310 D3
Underwood Sq SS9 ...346 C2
Unicorn WIk DA9 .....376 F2
Union La SS4 ....325 E2
Union Rd CO15 ....220 G8
Union St 🔟 IP4 ....17 D4
Unity CI CO2 ....136 B4
Unity St IP3 ....17 E4
University Way DA1 ...376 A4
Univ of East London
RM8 ....353 A8
Univ of Essex CO4 ....136 E6
Unwin PI CM1 ....275 C2
Uphall Rd IG1 ....352 B7
Uphall Sch IG1 ....352 B7
Uphavering Ho RM12 ..336 C2
Upland CI CM12 ......296 F4
Upland Court Rd RM3 .343 F6
Upland Cres CO5 .....218 C7
Upland Dr Billericay CM12 .296 F4
Colchester CO4 ....110 C2
Upland Rd Billericay CM12 .296 F4
Ipswich IP4 ....18 A8
Southend-on-S SS9 .....366 A8
Thornwood CM15 ......245 F6
West Mersea CO5 .....218 C7
Uplands CI Hockley SS5 .324 F5
South Benfleet SS7 .....344 B3
Uplands Comb Mid Sch
CO10 ....15 E1
Uplands Cres CO10 ...15 E1
Uplands Ct CO15 .....195 D1
Uplands Dr CM1 ......232 D7
Uplands Park Ct SS6 .323 E3
Uplands Park Rd SS6 .323 E3
Uplands Rd
Brentwood CM14 ....316 E6
Clacton-on-S CO15 .....191 D1
Hockley SS5 ....324 F5
Ilford RM6 ....334 D8
South Benfleet SS7 .....344 B3
Sudbury CO10 ....15 E1
Woodford IG8 ....310 D4
Uplands The IG10 ....288 F6
Upminster Bridge Sta
RM12 ....336 F2
Upminster Inf & Jun Sch
RM14 ....337 C2
Upminster Mill* RM14 .337 B2
Upminster Rd RM12 ...336 F2
Upminster Rd N RM13 .355 D2

Upminster Rd S RM13 .355 B1
Upminster Sta RM14 ..337 C2
Upminster Trad Pk
RM14 ....338 D4
Upney CI RM12 ....353 E1
Upney La IG11 ....352 F5
Upney Sta IG11 ....352 F5
Uppark Dr IG2 ....333 C5
Upper Abbey Rd DA17 .369 A2
Upper Acres SS8 .....183 F5
Upper Ave SS13 ......343 E8
Upper Barclay St 🔟 IP4 .17 D6
Upper Branston Rd
CO15 ....195 D6
Upper Brentwood Rd
RM2 ....336 C8
Upper Bridge Rd CM2 .232 A1
Upper Brook St CM .17 C5
Upper Cavendish St IP3 .18 A5
Upper Chapel St CO9 ..76 E2
Upper Chase
Althorne CM3 ....270 B8
Chelmsford CM2 ....254 A8
Upper Church Hill DA9 .377 E2
Upper Cornsland CM14 .316 D7
Upper East St CO10 ...33 F8
Upper Farm Rd CO10 ..29 D8
Upper Fenn Rd CO9 ...77 A2
Upperfield Dr SS11 ...381 F6
Upper Fourth Ave CO13 .170 F5
Upper Heath Rd CM2 ..254 B3
Upper Holly Hill Rd
DA17 ....369 B1
Upper Holt St CO6 ....105 C6
Upper Hook CM18 ....223 F6
Upper Lambricks SS6 .323 F4
Upper Market Rd SS1 ..321 C8
Upper Marsh La CM11 .224 A5
Upper Mayne SS14,SS15 .341 F7
Upper Mealines CM18 .224 A5
Upper Mill Field CM6 ..150 E7
Upper Moors CM3 ....207 F7
Upper Orwell St IP4 ..17 D5
Upper Park Rd
Belvedere DA17 ....369 B2
Brightlingsea CO7 .....192 E7
Clacton-on-S CO15 .....195 D3
Wickford SS12 ....321 D4
Upper Pk Harlow CM20 .199 B1
Loughton IG10 ....288 D4
Upper Rainham Rd
Hornchurch RM12 ......335 F2
Rainham RM12 ....354 C1
Upper Rd Basildon SS13 .320 D5
Bures CO10 ....55 E8
Upper Roman Rd CM2 .232 B1
Upper Ryle CM14 .....294 B2
Upper Second Ave CO13 .170 E5
Upper Sheridan Rd
DA17 ....369 A2
Upper Sq Stanstead CO10 .2 B8
Upper St Stanstead CO10 .2 B8
Stratford St M CO7 .....58 D1
Upper Stonyfield CM19 .223 B8
Upper Swaines CM6 ...245 F1
Upper Third Ave CO13 .170 E5
Upper Trinity Rd CO9 ..76 E1
Upsheres CB11 ....43 F8
Upshire Prim Foundation Sch
EN9 ....266 B6
Upshire Rd EN9 ......266 A6
Upton CI Ipswich IP4 ..17 E6
Stanford-le-H SS17 .....360 D2
West Bergholt CO6 .....108 D4
Upway SS6 ....323 D3
Upway The SS14 .....342 C8
Upwood Ct RM1 ......335 F7
Urban Ave RM12 .....336 C1
Urban Rd CM23 ......146 B8
Urmond Rd SS8 ....364 A4
Ursula Rd RM9 ....353 E5
Urswick Rd RM9 .....353 E5
Usk Rd RM15 ....371 D7
Usterdale Rd CM3 ....218 C2
Uttons Ave SS0 ....366 E6
Uvedale Rd RM10 ....335 A1
Uxbridge CI SS11 ....321 F6
Uxbridge IP3 ....18 C1

V

Vaagen Rd SS8 ....364 B4
Vadsoe Rd SS8 ....364 B5
Valance Ave E4 ......287 F1
Valance CI CB11 .....65 A7
Valance Way SS14 ...341 A2
Vale CI Chelmsford CM2 .232 B3
Pilgrims Hatch CM15 ...293 F4
Vale Ct CM4 ....297 D6
Vale End CM2 ....254 C3
Vale La IP9 ....61 B4
Valence Ave RM8 ....334 D2
Valence Cir RM8 .....334 D3
Valence House Mus*
RM8 ....334 E2
Valence Inf Sch RM8 .334 D3
Valence Jun Sch RM8 .334 D2
Valence Rd RM8 ......334 E1
Valenta CI CO4 ......136 C6
Valentine Ct CM7 ....127 E4
Valentines Cres CM4 ..275 F2
Valentines Dr CO4 ...136 B8
Valentines La CO4 ...110 C1
Valentines High Sch IG2 .333 A5
Valentines Rd IG1 ....332 A6
Valentines Way RM7 .352 E6
Valerie Ho SS0 ......346 F3
Valerie Way CM8 ....156 D2
Valerie Ho SS0 ....366 F3
Vale The Basildon CM14 .294 C1
Stock CM4 ....297 D7

Vale The continued
Woodford IG8 ....310 A3
Valfreda Way CO7 ....137 B2
Valiant CI RM7 ....313 B1
Valkyrie CI CM9 ......216 D2
Valkyrie Rd SS0 ......366 D8
Vallance CI SS2 ......348 E3
Valletta CI CM1 ......232 A3
Valley Bridge CM1 ...136 B5
Valleybridge Rd CO15 .196 A5
Valley CI Brantham CO11 .60 D1
Colchester CO3 ....134 E3
Loughton IG10 ....288 F3
Waltham Abbey EN9 ...265 C7
Valley Cres CO6 ......108 E3
Valley Dr
Bishop's Stortford CM23 .145 E5
Wickford SS12 ....310 B3
Valley Farm Camping Ground
CO15 ....196 B5
Valley Gdns DA9 .....377 B1
Valley La Lattingstone IP9 .36 F8
Wherstead IP9 ....37 A3
Valley Rd Billericay CM11 .297 C2
Braintree CM7 ....128 A4
Clacton-on-S CO15 .....196 A5
Colchester CO4 ....136 F4
Erith DA8 ....369 E2
Harwich CO12 ....90 D2
Ipswich IP1 ....17 B8
Sudbury CO10 ....34 F8
Wivenhoe CO7 ....164 C8
Valley Side E4 ....287 A1
Valley Side Par E4 ...309 A8
Valley View
Finchingfield CM7 ......72 D6
Greenhithe DA9 ....377 B1
Stanstead CO10 ....2 F7
West Bergholt CO6 ....108 C3
Valley View Ct CO4 ...110 A4
Valleyview Dr IP4 ....18 F4
Valley WIk
Walton-on-t-N CO14 ...171 A7
Welwyn Garden CM19 ..223 B8
Vallis Way CO5 ......163 E7
Valmar Ave SS17 ....360 B1
Valonia Dr CO7 ......164 B8
Vandenburg Circ CM7 .73 D6
Vanderbilt Ave SS6 ..323 C8
Vandervalt Ave SS8 ..364 C3
Van Diemans La CM2 .254 C8
Van Dieman's Rd CM2 .254 C8
Van Diemens Pass SS8 .364 F3
Vandyck Rd IP3 ......38 A8
Van Dyck Rd CO3 ....135 B5
Vane Ct CM8 ....184 A5
Vane La CO6 ....131 A2
Vanessa CI DA17 .....369 A1
Vanessa Dr CO7 .....137 B1
Vange Com Prim Sch
SS17 ....342 D2
Vange Corner Dr SS16 .342 B1
Vange Hill Ct SS16 ...342 E3
Vange Hill Dr SS16 ...342 E3
Vange Park Rd SS16 ..342 B1
Vange PI 🔟 SS7 ......9 B8
Vange Riverview Ctr
SS16 ....342 F4
Vanguard CI RM7 ....313 B1
Vanguards The SS3 ...368 F7
Vanguard Way
Braintree CM7 ....128 B4
Southend-on-S SS3 .....368 F7
Vanners Rd CB9 ......9 F7
Vanryne Ho IG10 .....288 E6
Vansittart St CO12 ...91 D5
Vantorts CI CM21 ....172 E2
Vantorts Rd CM21 ...172 E2
Varden CI CM1 ....231 F6
Vardon Dr SS9 ....346 B3
Vaughan Ave
Hornchurch RM12 ......355 E8
Southend-on-S SS2 .....348 E1
Vaughan CI Rayne CM7 .126 F2
Rochford SS4 ....325 E5
Vaughan Gdns Ilford IG1 .333 A4
Redbridge IG1 ....332 F4
Vaughan St 🔟 IP2 ...17 C4
Vaughan Williams Rd
SS15 ....341 C8
Vaughan Williams Way
CM14 ....316 B6
Vaulx Rd SS8 ....364 B4
Vaux Ave CO12 ......90 F1
Vauxhall Ave CO15 ...220 E6
Vauxhall Dr CM7 .....222 D2
Vega CI CO1 ....136 C6
Velizy Ave CM20 .....199 D1
Vellacotts CM1 ......232 B7
Venables CI
Canvey Island SS8 .....364 C4
Dagenham RM10 ....354 B8
Oxenette RM13 ....370 B8
Venlo Rd SS8 ....364 B5
Venmead Ct CM7 ....369 A2
Venmore Dr CM6 ....96 B8
Venta Way CM9 ......259 B8
Ventnor Dr CO15 ....196 A8
Ventnor Gdns IG1 ....352 E6
Ventnor Mans IG1 ...352 E6
Ventris CI IP2 ....16 E5
Ventura Dr CO1 ......136 C6
Veny Cres RM12 .....335 D2
Vera Rd CM11 ....299 A2
Verbena CI RM15 ....372 C7
Verderers Rd IG7 ....312 A6
Vere Rd IG10 ....289 C5
Vermeer Cres SS3 ...368 G8
Vermeer Ride CM1 ...232 F7
Vermont CI Basildon SS13 .343 C8
Clacton-on-S CO15 .....196 A4
Vermont Cres IP4 ....17 D7
Vermont Rd IP4 ......17 D7
Verney Gdns RM9 ....353 E8

Verney Rd RM9 ....353 E8
Vernon Ave Rayleigh SS6 .323 B4
Woodford IG8 ....310 B3
Vernon Cnr CM4 .....273 D2
Vernon Cres CM13 ...317 A7
Vernon Ct
Bishop's Stortford CM23 .145 E4
Southend-on-S SS9 .....346 C1
Vernon Rd Ilford IG3 ..333 F3
North Fambridge CM3 ..281 A1
Romford RM5 ....313 C5
Southend-on-S SS9 .....346 C1
Swanscombe DA10 ....377 F1
Vernon's CI CM22 ....94 F4
Vernon Rd CO6 ....106 E5
Vernon St IP2 ....17 C4
Vernons WIk 🔟 SS13 .321 C1
Vernon Way CM7 ....128 C5
Veronica CI RM3 .....314 D4
Veronica WIk CO4 ...136 E7
Veronique Gdns IG6 ..333 C6
Vert Ho RM17 ....378 C7
Vesey Gdns RM10 ...335 A1
Vesta CI CO6 ....130 F2
Vestry CI SS15 ....341 C7
Vexil CI RM19 ....371 D2
Veyses End CO7 .....58 D2
Viaduct Rd CM1 .....232 A2
Viaduct The E18 .....310 B1
Viborg Gdns CM9 ...258 E8
Vica Cotts CM3 ......234 D5
Vicarage Ave CM8 ...155 F1
Vicarage CI Basildon SS13 .343 C7
🔟 Bishop's Stortford CM23 .145 F7
Brentwood CM14 ......315 E6
Canvey Island SS8 .....363 D3
Panfield CM7 ....126 A8
Roxwell CM1 ....230 B5
Tolleshunt D'arcy CM9 .215 D4
Vicarage Cres CM3 ..211 B4
Vicarage Ct
Billericay CM12 ....297 B2
Halstead CO9 ....76 D2
Waltham Abbey EN9 ...266 A5
Woodford IG8 ....310 A3
Vicarage Dr Barking IG11 .352 C5
Northfleet DA11 ....378 C1
Vicarage Field CO10 ..34 B5
Vicarage Field Sh Ctr
IG11 ....352 C5
Vicarage Gdns CO15 .195 E2
Vicarage Hill SS7 .....344 E2
Vicarage La Berden CM23 .92 B8
Chigwell IG7 ....311 D7
Great Baddow CM2 ....254 F5
Ilford IG1 ....333 D3
London CM0 ....259 E2
North Weald Bassett CM16 .247 E7
North Weald Bassett CM16 .247 C7
Thaxted CM6 ....70 A3
Thorpe-le-S CO16 .....141 F2
Tillingham CM0 ....263 E4
Ugley CM22 ....93 E5
Wakes Colne CO6 .....79 E8
Wallend E6 ....352 A2
🔟 Walton-on-t-N CO14 .171 C8
Wherstead IP9 ....37 B4
Vicarage Mdw CM0 ..280 D3
Vicarage Mead CM6 ..70 A3
Vicarage Meadow CO9 .76 E1
Vicarage Mews CM2 ..254 F6
Vicarage Rd
Belchamp St P CO10 ...13 A8
Chelmsford CM2 ....254 A8
Coopersale CM16 .....246 C2
Dagenham RM10 ......354 B5
Felixstowe IP11 ....381 C4
Finchingfield CM7 .....72 D6
Hornchurch RM12 .....336 A3
Pleshey CM3 ....178 E2
Roxwell CM1 ....230 D5
Woodford IG8 ....310 E4
Vicarage Sq RM17 ...378 B1
Vicarage Wood CM20 .200 A1
Vicars Orch CO10 ...32 B3
Vicars WIk RM8 .....334 B1
Vicerons PI CM23 ...145 D4
Viceroy CI CO2 ......136 B3
Viceroy Ct
Horndon-on-t-H SS17 ..359 F3
Southend-on-S SS2 .....366 B7
Vickers Rd Erith DA8 .369 D1
Victor App RM12 .....336 D2
Victor Ave SS13 ......343 D6
Victor CI RM12 ....336 D3
Victor Ct
Hornchurch RM12 .....336 D3
Rainham RM13 ....354 D3
Victor Dr SS9 ....365 F8
Victor Gdns Hockley SS5 .324 F5
Hornchurch RM12 .....336 D3
Victoria Ave
Basildon SS16 ....341 C3
Grays RM16 ....373 C4
Kirby-le-S CO13 ....170 D8
Rayleigh SS6 ....323 B4
Romford RM5 ....313 B4
Saffron Walden CB11 ..22 E1
Southend-on-S SS2 .....347 C2
Wickford SS12 ....321 C7
Victoria Chase CO1 ..135 F8
Victoria CI Basildon SS15 .341 B7
Grays RM16 ....373 C4
Wivenhoe CO7 ....137 B2
Victoria Cotts
Heybridge CM9 ....237 A5
Ilford IG6 ....333 C6
Victoria Cres
Basildon SS15 ....341 C8
Chelmsford CM1 ....232 A3
Lawford CO11 ....86 C4
Wickford SS12 ....321 B7
Victoria Ct St Braintree CM7 .128 C2
Clacton-on-S CO15 .....195 D3

Victoria Ct continued
Colchester CO3 134 F7
Harwich CO12 91 C3
Romford RM1 336 A6
1 Southend-on-S SS2 347 F1
Southend-on-S,Westcliff-on-S SS0 366 E7
1 Wanstead E18 332 B8
Wickford SS11 322 A5
Victoria Dr
Great Wakering SS3 350 C2
Southend-on-S SS9 346 E1
Victoria Espl CO5 218 E5
Victoria Gdns
Colchester CO4 110 B3
Saffron Walden CB11 22 E1
Victoria Ho
Felixstowe IP11 381 E4
Ipswich IP2 17 B4
2 Romford, Ardleigh Green RM2 336 C7
1 Romford RM1 335 F5
Victoria Lanes Sh Ctr SS1 367 A7
Victoria Pl
Brightlingsea CO7 192 F6
Colchester CO1 136 B6
Victoria Plaza 4 SS1 367 A8
Victoria Plaza Sh Ctr 1 SS1 367 A8
Victoria Rd Barking IG11 352 B6
Basildon,Laindon SS15 341 A7
Basildon,Vange SS16 342 D2
Brentwood CM14 316 C6
Buckhurst Hill IG9 310 D8
Bulphan RM14 358 F8
Chelmsford CM1 232 B3
Chingford E4 287 E1
Chingford, Highams Park E17 309 C1
Clacton-on-S CO15 196 A3
Colchester CO3 135 C6
Cold Norton CM3 280 F6
Dagenham RM10 354 C7
Felixstowe IP11 381 D3
Haverhill CB9 8 D7
Horndon-on-t-H SS17 359 F3
Maldon CM9 237 A2
Rayleigh SS6 323 E3
Romford RM1 335 F6
Southend-on-S,Chalkwell SS9 365 E8
Southend-on-S SS1 367 D7
South Woodham Ferrers CM3 301 D6
Stanford-le-H SS17 360 C2
Waltham Abbey EN9 265 C5
Walton-on-t-N CO14 171 C8
Wanstead E18 332 B8
Weeley Heath CO16 168 B5
Writtle CM1 230 F1
Victoria Rd S CM1 232 B2
Victoria St Braintree CM7 128 A2
Felixstowe IP11 381 E4
Harwich CO12 91 D4
Ipswich IP1 17 A6
Victor Mew Cl SS12 321 D5
Victor Rd CO1 136 B6
Victor's Cres CM13 317 B8
Victor Wlk RM12 336 D3
Victory Cl Grays RM16 372 D2
Wickford SS11 322 A5
Victory Ct Barking IG11 353 B2
Colchester CO3 134 E6
Victory Gdns CM7 128 B4
Victory La SS4 325 D6
Victory Lodge DA8 369 E1
Victory Rd
Clacton-on-S CO15 195 D3
Ipswich IP4 18 A7
Rainham RM13 355 A3
Wanstead E11 332 B7
West Mersea CO5 218 A6
Victory Way Dartford DA2 376 C3
Romford RM7 313 B1
Vienna Cl Harwich CO12 91 A1
Woodford IG5 310 D1
View Cl IG7 311 D5
Vigerons Way RM16 374 B2
Vignoles Rd RM7 335 A4
Vi & John Rubens Ho IG2 333 A5
Viking Bsns Ctr RM7 335 C4
Viking Ct SS3 368 C7
Viking Rd CM9 236 E1
Vikings Way SS8 363 D3
Viking Way
Belvedere DA8 369 C3
Holland-on-S CO15 196 F6
Pilgrims Hatch CM15 294 B3
Rainham RM13 355 A1
Wickford SS11 299 E2
Villa Ct 4 CO1 136 C6
Village Arc The 2 E4 287 D1
Village Cl Chingford E4 309 C5
Hoddesdon EN11 221 D8
Kirby Cross CO13 170 D7
Little Clacton CO16 168 D1
Village Dr SS8 363 E3
Village Gate CM2 233 A2
Village Gn SS4 304 D1
Village Hall Cl SS8 363 D3
Village Home The IG6 333 C8
Village Hts IG8 309 F5
Village Inf Sch RM10 354 A5
Village Sq CM2 233 A3
Village Way CO13 170 D6
Villa Ho CO3 134 C6
Villa Rd Colchester CO3 134 C5
South Benfleet SS7 344 C4
Villiers Pl CM3 233 E8
Villiers-Sur-Marne Ave CM23 145 D4
Villiers Way SS7 344 F5
Vince Cl CO5 218 C6
Vincent Ave SS17 359 F3
Vincent Cl
Corringham SS17 361 B3
Ipswich IP1 16 E8
Redbridge IG6 311 C4
Southend-on-S SS3 368 E7
Vincent Ct CM14 316 B8
Vincent Lodge CM3 301 E6
Vincent Mews SS3 368 E7
Vincent Rd Chingford E4 309 D4
Dagenham RM9 353 E5
Rainham RM13 355 C1
Rochford SS4 303 B1
Vincent Way CM12 297 A5
Vine Cl SS14 342 E6
Vine Ct 10 DA11 379 B1
Vine Dr CO7 137 C3
Vine Farm Rd CO7 137 C3
Vine Gdns IG1 352 C7
Vine Gr CM20 199 E5
Vine Par CO7 137 C3
Vine Rd CO5 186 C6
Vineries Cl RM9 353 F6
Vinesse Rd CO6 81 D3
Vine St Great Bardfield CM7 72 B2
Romford RM7 335 C7
Vineway CM14 294 C1
Vineway The CO12 91 B4
Vine Wlk IP9 35 A1
Vineyard Gate 4 CO2 135 F6
Vineyard St CO2 135 F6
Vineyards The* CM7 153 D6
Great Baddow CM2 254 F7
Vinnicombe Ct 3 IP2 16 E1
Vint Cres CO3 135 C6
Vintners The SS2 347 F5
Viola Cl RM15 357 C2
Viola Wlk CO4 136 E7
Violet Cl Chelmsford CM1 232 E7
Ipswich IP2 16 F4
Violet Rd E18 310 B1
Virgil Rd CM8 183 F5
Virginia Cl Jaywick CO15 195 A1
Romford RM5 313 C3
South Benfleet SS7 344 B7
Virginia Gdns IG6 311 D1
Virley Cl CM9 237 D4
Viscount Dr CO4 110 C5
Visitor Ctr & Country Wlk* CB9 9 C6
Vista Ave CO13 143 D1
Vista Dr IG4 332 D6
Vista Rd
Clacton-on-S CO15 196 A3
Wickford SS11 321 F7
Vitlus Cl CO4 110 B6
Vivian Ct CO14 171 C8
Voluntary Pl E11 332 A5
Volwycke Ave CM9 258 F8
Voorburg Rd SS8 364 D4
Vowler Rd SS16 341 B4
Voysey Gdns SS13 321 B1

W

Waalwyk Dr SS8 364 C4
Waarden Rd SS8 364 B4
Waarem Ave SS8 364 B4
Waddesdon Rd CO12 91 D4
Wade Rd CO15 196 B8
Wade Reach CO14 171 B8
Wadeville Ave RM6 334 F4
Wadeville Cl DA17 369 A1
Wadgate Rd IP11 381 C4
Wadham Ave E17 309 B3
Wadham Cl CM4 274 B4
Wadham Park Ave SS5 302 A1
Wadham Rd E17 309 B2
Wadhurst Ct E6 352 A3
Wadhurst Rd IP3 18 D3
Wadley Cl CO5 186 E5
Wagon Mead CM22 174 A3
Wagstaff Gdns RM9 353 E4
Wagtail Dr CM9 237 C5
Wagtail Pl CO5 158 C2
Waikato Lodge IG9 288 C1
Wainfleet Ave RM5 313 C1
Wainsfield Villas CM6 70 B2
Wainwright Ave
Brentwood CM13 295 D3
Great Notley CM77 154 D8
Wainwright St CM23 145 C5
Wake Arms Rdbt IG10 266 F3
Wakefield Ave CM12 297 A2
Wakefield Cl
Colchester CO1 136 A8
Great Chesterford CB10 3 D3
Wakefield Gdns IG1 332 E5
Wakefield Rd DA9 377 C2
Wakelin Chase CM4 274 A3
Wakelin Way CM8 184 B2
Wakerfield Cl RM11 336 F6
Wakering Ave SS3 368 G7
Wakering Rd
Barking IG11 352 C5
Great Wakering SS3 350 B1
Southend-on-S SS1,SS3 349 A2
Wakerings The IG11 352 C6
Wakescolne SS11 322 A6
Wakeshall La C10 30 C8
Wakes St CO6 106 C6
Walace Ct EN3 265 A2
Walbrook 9 E18 332 A8
Waldeck Ct CB11 43 D7
Waldeck Rd DA1 376 A1
Waldegrave SS16 342 B4
Waldegrave Cl CO11 86 B3
Waldegrave Ct
11 Barking IG11 352 D4
Upminster RM14 337 B3
Waldegrave Gdns RM14 337 B2
Waldegrave Rd
Dagenham RM8 334 C2
Lawford CO11 86 C3
Waldegraves Farm Cvn Site CO5 218 G6
Waldegraves La CO5 218 G7
Waldegraves The CO8 79 F8
Waldegrave Way CO11 86 B3
Walden Ave
Elder Street CB10 44 E2
Rainham RM13 354 D3
Walden Castle* CB10 22 D2
Walden Cl CM9 213 A4
Walden Ho CO13 170 F4
Walden House Rd CM8, CM9 213 A4
Walden Pl CB10 22 D2
Walden Rd Ashdon CB10 23 E6
Great Chesterford CB10 3 E3
Hadstock CB1 5 B6
Hornchurch RM11 336 D5
Littlebury CB10 21 F4
Radwinter CB10 45 D7
Sewards End CB10 23 D1
Thaxted CM6 69 F5
Wendens Ambo CB11 42 F6
Wendens Ambo CB11 43 A6
Walden Way
Frinton-on-S CO13 171 A6
Hornchurch RM11 336 D5
Redbridge IG6 311 E3
Waldgrooms CM6 123 C1
Waldingfield Rd CO10 33 F8
Waldon RM18 375 C3
Waldringfield SS14 342 B7
Walford Cl CO6 131 A2
Walford Pl CM2 232 F2
Walfords Cl CM17 200 C3
Walford Way CO6 131 A2
Walfrey Gdns RM9 353 E5
Walker Ave CM5 227 D2
Walker Cl IP3 18 C5
Walker Dr SS9 346 A2
Walkers Cl CM1 232 D7
Walkers Sq SS17 360 D1
Walkey Way SS3 368 H7
Walk The Billericay CM12 297 A1
Eight Ash G CO6 134 A8
Felixstowe IP11 381 C5
Hornchurch RM11 336 F2
Hullbridge SS5 301 D3
10 Ipswich IP1 17 C6
Walkways SS8 363 F5
Wallace Binder Cl CM9 236 F1
Wallace Cl SS5 301 D3
Wallace Cres CM2 254 D8
Wallace Dr SS12 321 E5
Wallace Gdns DA10 377 E1
Wallace La CM3 179 B7
Wallace Rd
Colchester CO4 109 E3
Grays RM17 373 A2
Ipswich IP1 16 E8
Wallace's La CM3 209 F4
Wallace St SS3 368 F7
Wallasea Gdns CM1 232 F5
Wall Chase CM6 178 F7
Wall Ct 6 CM7 127 F1
Wall End Ct E6 352 A4
Wall End Rd E6 352 A5
Wallenger Ave RM2 336 B8
Wallers Cl Dagenham RM9 353 F4
Woodford IG8 310 F4
Waller's Gr IP2 16 F4
Waller's Hoppet IG10 288 F7
Wallers Way EN11 197 B1
Wallflower Ct 11 CM1 232 F6
Wallingford Ho 2 RM3 314 E4
Wallington Rd IG3 333 F4
Wallis Ave SS2 347 F2
Wallis Cl RM11 336 B3
Wallis Ct CO3 134 E3
Wallis Pk DA11 378 B2
Wall La CO11 88 D4
Wall Rd SS8 364 F3
Wall St CO16 219 D6
Wallis The CO11 86 E4
Walmer Cl Chingford E4 309 B8
Romford RM7 313 B1
Walnut Cl IG6 333 C7
Walnut Cotts CM21 172 E3
Walnut Ct SS5 324 E7
Walnut Dr
Bishop's Stortford CM23 145 D3
Witham CM8 184 A4
Walnut Gr Braintree CM7 127 E2
Hornchurch RM12 336 D3
Walnut Tree Ave CM21 172 E4
Walnut Tree Cl EN11 221 A6
Walnut Tree Cotts CM3 207 E5
Walnut Tree Cres CM21 172 E3
Walnuttree Hospl CO10 33 D7
Walnut Tree La
Harkstead IP9 63 B2
Sudbury CO10 33 D7
Walnut Tree Rd
Dagenham RM8 334 E2
Erith DA8 369 E1
Walnut Tree Way
Colchester CO2 135 B3
Tiptree CO5 186 C7
Walnut Way
Brightlingsea CO7 192 E7
Buckhurst Hill IG9 310 D7
Clacton-on-S CO15 195 C2
Walpole Cl RM17 373 C2
Walpole Rd E18 309 F2
Walpole Wlk SS6 324 A2
Walsham Ent Ctr RM17 373 C1
Walsingham Cl
Basildon SS15 341 C7
Great Cornard CO10 34 C5
Walsingham Ct IP2 37 A8
Walsingham Ho E4 287 D2
Walsingham Rd
Colchester CO2 135 F6
Southend-on-S SS2 348 B2
Walsingham Way CM12 297 B5
Walter Hurford Par 5 E12 352 A8
Walter Porter Ct CO4 110 D1
Walter Radcliffe Way CO7 164 C7
Walters Cl
Galleywood CM2 254 C3
Southend-on-S SS9 346 E6
Walters Yd 6 CO1 135 F7
Walter Way CM8 156 D4
Waltham Abbey* EN9 265 C6
Waltham Cl
1 Brentwood CM13 295 C3
Ipswich IP2 17 A2
Waltham Cres SS2 348 B3
Waltham Ct E17 309 C2
Waltham Forest Coll E17 309 B1
Waltham Glen CM2 254 C7
Waltham Holy Cross Jun & Inf Schs EN9 265 D6
Waltham Park Way E17 309 A3
Waltham Pk E17 309 A2
Waltham Rd
Boreham CM3 210 A3
Lower Nazeing EN9 244 A6
Rayleigh SS6 323 B3
Terling CM3 182 A2
Woodford IG8 310 E4
Walthams SS13 343 B7
Walthams Pl SS13 343 B7
Walthamstow Ave E4 309 A3
Walthamstow Ave (North Circular Rd) E4 309 A3
Walthamstow Bsns Ctr E17 309 C1
Waltham Way
Chingford E4 287 A1
Frinton-on-S CO13 171 A5
Walton Ave IP11 381 A2
Walton Ct Basildon SS15 341 C8
Colchester CO4 136 F4
Felixstowe IP11 381 D6
Hoddesdon EN11 221 C8
Walton Gdns
Brentwood CM13 295 C4
Waltham Abbey EN9 265 B6
Walton Hall Farm Mus* SS17 375 B5
Walton Hall La CM3 258 B1
Walton Ho 4 Ipswich IP1 17 A6
Walton-on-t-N CO14 171 B8
Walton Maritme Mus* CO14 144 D1
Walton-On-Naze Sta CO14 171 C7
Walton-on-the-Naze Prim Sch CO14 144 D1
Walton Rd
Clacton-on-S CO15 196 A3
Frinton-on-S CO13 170 F6
Hoddesdon EN11 221 C8
Kirby-le-S CO13 170 E8
Little Ilford E12 352 A8
Romford RM5 312 F3
Southend-on-S SS1 367 F6
Thorpe-le-S CO13, CO16 142 D2
Walton-on-t-N CO13,CO14 171 B7
Walton's Hall Rd SS17 375 B5
Wambrook SS3 349 D1
Wambrook Cl CM13 295 C1
Wamburg Rd SS8 364 E4
Wanderer Dr IG11 353 C2
Wangey Rd RM6 334 D4
Wannock Gdns IG6 311 B3
Wansfell Coll CM16 267 D4
Wansfell Gdns SS1 367 F8
Wansford Cl CM14 315 F7
Wansford Rd IG8 310 C2
Wanstead Church Sch E11 332 A6
Wanstead High Sch E11 332 C5
Wanstead Hospl E11 332 B7
Wanstead La IG1 332 E5
Wanstead Park Ave E12 332 D2
Wanstead Park Rd
Ilford IG1 333 A2
Redbridge IG1 332 E3
Wanstead Pl E11 332 A6
Wanstead Sta E11 332 B5
Wantage Ho 10 RM3 314 D4
Wantfield Cotts CM4 274 F8
Wantz Chase CM9 237 A2
Wantz Cnr CM2 276 E5
Wantz Haven CM9 237 A2
Wantz La RM13 355 B1
Wantz Rd
Dagenham RM10 354 B7
Maldon CM9 237 A2
Margaretting CM4 275 A8
Wapping La CO7 165 B2
Warboys Cres E4 309 C5
Warburton Ave CO9 75 D8
Warburtons SS17 361 A3
Warburton Terr E17 309 B1
Ward Ave RM17 373 B2
Ward Cres CM23 145 E6
Warde Chase CO14 171 B8
Warden Ave RM5 313 C5
Warder Cl CM6 123 E1
Ward Gdns RM3 314 E1
Ward Hatch CM20 200 A3
Wardle Way CM1 231 E7
Wardley Cl IP2 16 D1
Wardona Ct DA10 377 F1
Wardour Ct 9 DA2 376 B1
Ward Path CM2 233 B4
Ward Rd IP8 16 B2
Wards Croft CB11 43 D7
Wards Rd IG2 333 D4
Wareham Ave IP3 18 D3
Warehouse Rd CM6 124 F4
Warehouse Villas CM6 125 A4
Waremead Rd IG2 333 B6
Ware Rd EN11 197 A1
Warescot Cl CM15 294 B2
Warescot Rd CM15 294 B2
Wares Rd
Margaret Roding CM1 205 E5
Mashbury CM1 206 A4
Wargrave Rd CO15 195 D4
Warham Rd CO12 90 F1
Warley Ave RM8 334 F4
Warley Cl CM7 128 C3
Warley Gap CM13 316 C3
Warley Hall La RM14 338 F4
Warley Hill CM13,CM14 316 C5
Warley Hill Bsns Pk The CM13 316 C4
Warley Hospl CM14 316 B5
Warley Mount CM14 316 C6
Warley Prim Sch CM14 316 C5
Warley Rd
Great Warley CM13 316 B3
Redbridge IG5 311 A1
Romford CM13 315 E1
Woodford IG8 310 B3
Warley St CM13,RM14 338 C5
Warley Way CO13 171 B6
Warleywoods Cres CM14 316 B6
Warlow Cl EN3 265 A2
Warminster Ho RM3 314 F5
Warner Cl Billericay CM11 297 D1
Rayne CM77 126 F1
Warner Dr CM7 127 D4
Warners CM6 150 D8
Warners Bridge Chase SS4 347 F6
Warners Cl IG8 310 A5
Warners Gdns SS4 347 E6
Warner Way CO10 34 A8
Warnham Cl CO16 195 B6
Warren Chase SS7 345 A4
Warren Cl Broomfield CM1 208 B3
Rayleigh SS6 345 C8
Stanford-le-H SS17 360 D1
Takeley CM22 148 D7
Warren Ct Chigwell IG7 311 D6
12 Haverhill CB9 8 E7
Warren Dr Basildon SS14 342 E6
Hornchurch RM12 336 B1
Wickford SS11 322 A8
Warren Dr The E11 332 C4
Warren Farm Cotts RM6 334 F7
Warren Field CM16 268 A7
Warren Hastings Ct DA11 378 F1
Warren Heath Ave IP3 18 D2
Warren Heath Rd IP3 18 D2
Warren Hill IG10 288 C4
Warren Hts Grays RM16 372 E2
Loughton IG10 288 C4
Warren Jun Sch RM6 334 F6
Warren La Colchester CO3 134 C2
Doddinghurst CM15 294 A8
Grays RM16 372 D2
Warren Lingley Way CO5 186 E6
Warren Pond Rd E4 287 F2
Warren Prim Sch RM16 372 C3
Warren Rd Braintree CM7 128 C2
Chingford E4 309 C8
Halstead CO9 76 D1
Ilford IG6 333 D6
Southend-on-S SS9 346 A3
South Hanningfield CM3 299 D7
Wanstead E11 332 C4
Warren Sch The RM6 334 F6
Warrenside CM7 155 A8
Warrens The
Kirby Cross CO13 170 E6
Wickham Bishops CM8 212 F5
Warren Terr Grays RM16 372 D4
Ilford RM6 334 D7
Warren The CM12 296 E4
Warriner Ave RM12 336 D2
Warrington Gdns RM11 336 D5
Warrington Rd
Dagenham RM8 334 E2
Ipswich IP1 17 B7
Warrington Sq
Billericay CM12 296 F3
Dagenham RM8 334 D2
Warrior Ho 7 SS1 367 A8
Warrior Sq
Little Ilford E12 352 A8
Southend-on-S SS1 367 A8
Warrior Sq E SS1 367 A8
Warrior Sq N SS1 367 A8
Warrior Square Rd SS3 368 F5
Warwick Bailey Cl CO4 109 D2
Warwick Cl
Braintree CM7 128 B4
Canvey Island SS8 364 A5
Little Easton CM6 122 F5
Maldon CM9 237 A1
Rayleigh SS6 323 F1
South Benfleet SS7 344 D7
Warwick Cres
Clacton-on-S CO15 195 E3
Maldon CM9 237 A1
Warwick Ct
Brentwood CM13 317 B7
2 Haverhill CB9 8 E8
Warwick Dr Maldon CM9 237 A1
Rochford SS4 347 F7
Warwick Gdns Ilford IG1 333 B3
Rayleigh SS6 323 F1
Romford RM2 336 C8
Warwick Gn SS6 324 A1
Warwick La RM13,RM14 356 B3
Warwick Par CM3 301 D8
Warwick Pl Basildon SS16 340 F4
Northfleet DA11 378 B2
Pilgrims Hatch CM14 293 C5
Warwick Rd
Bishop's Stortford CM23 146 B6
Chingford E4 309 A5
Clacton-on-S CO15 195 E3
Ipswich IP4 17 E6
Warwick Rd continued
Rainham RM13 355 D2
Rayleigh SS6 324 A1
Southend-on-S SS1 367 F6
Takeley CM6 148 E7
Wanstead E11 332 B6
Warwick Sq CM1 231 F4
Washall Dr CM77 154 D8
Wash Cnr Aldham CO6 107 C3
Ramsey CO12 89 E1
Washford Gdns CO15 195 D2
Washington Ave SS15 341 A6
Washington Cl CM9 236 E1
Washington Ct
Colchester CO3 134 E5
Maldon CM9 236 E1
Washington Rd
Harwich CO12 91 A2
Maldon CM9 236 F1
2 Woodford E18 309 F1
Wash La
Clacton-on-S CO15 195 D1
Goldhanger CM9 238 B7
Wash Rd Basildon SS15 319 E2
Brentwood CM13 295 E4
Wasses Cnr CO16 141 D5
Watchfield La SS6 323 C1
Watch House Rd CM6 124 F5
Watchouse Rd CM2 254 C3
Waterbeach Rd RM9 353 C6
Waterdene SS8 363 F5
Waterfalls The SS16 341 B3
Waterfield Cl DA17 369 A3
Waterford Rd SS3 368 D5
Waterfront Terr CO14 144 D1
Waterfront Wlk SS14 320 B1
Waterglade Ind Pk RM20 376 F8
Waterglade Ret Pk CO15 195 E2
Waterhale SS1 349 A1
Waterhall Ave E4 309 E6
Water Hall La CM7 100 F6
Waterhouse La
Ardleigh CO7 112 B5
Chelmsford CM1 231 F1
Waterhouse Moor CM18 223 F7
Waterhouse St CM1 231 F1
Water La
Bishop's Stortford CM23 145 F8
Bures CO8 55 E1
Cavendish CO10 1 D2
Colchester CO3 135 D8
Debden CB11 44 B1
Great Easton CM6 122 C7
Harlow CM19 223 A5
Helions Bumpstead CB9 26 D7
Ilford IG3 333 F1
Little Horkesley CO6 81 F8
Newport CB11 43 A1
Pebmarsh CO9 78 A7
Purfleet RM19 371 A2
Radwinter CB10 45 E8
Roydon CM19 222 E4
Shalford CM7 100 F3
Stansted Mountfitchet CM24 119 E6
Steeple Bumpstead CB9 27 B6
Stisted CM77 129 C5
Stoke-by-N CO6 56 E8
Sturmer CB9 9 F5
Water Lane Prim Sch CM19 223 A4
Waterloo Gdns RM7 335 E5
Waterloo La CM1 232 C2
Waterloo Rd
Brentwood CM14 294 C1
Ipswich IP1 17 A7
Redbridge IG6 311 C1
Romford RM7 335 E5
Southend-on-S SS3 368 D7
Watermans RM1 335 F6
Watermans Way
Greenhithe DA9 377 B3
North Weald Bassett CM16 247 A4
Water Mdws
Basildon SS13 343 A4
Linford SS17 375 A3
Watermill Rd CO5 158 E4
Waters Edge SS0 366 D7
Waters Edge Ct DA8 369 F1
Waters Gdns RM10 354 A7
Waterside
Brightlingsea CO7 192 F5
Southend-on-S SS1 367 D6
Stansted Mountfitchet CM24 119 E6
Waterside Bsns Pk CM8 184 B4
Waterside Cl
Barking IG11 353 A8
Romford RM3 315 A3
Waterside Ind Est EN11 221 D5
Waterside Mead SS8 363 F6
Waterside Pl CM22 173 A2
Waterside Rd
Bradwell Waterside CM0 241 F3
Paglesham Eastend SS4 328 A5
Waters Mead SS1 368 A6
Watersmeet CM19 223 B4
Waterson Rd RM16 374 C2
Waterson Vale CM2 254 C8
Waters Villas CM22 175 A6
Water Tower Rd CM14 316 C5
Waterville Dr SS16 343 A4
Waterville Mews CO2 136 B3
Waterwick Hill CB11 40 B1
Waterworks Cl CO2 161 E3
Waterworks Cotts CO5 186 A6
Waterworks Dr CO16 195 B5
Waterworks La SS17 361 D6
Waterworks Rd CM9 216 D2
Waterworks St 6 IP4 17 D5
Watery La
Battlesbridge SS11 301 C1

Watery La continued
Coggeshall CO6 . . . . .130 A1
Great Dunmow CM6 . . . . . .150 A2
Manuden CM23 . . . . .92 C1
Matching Green CM17 . . . . .226 D8
Wates Way CM15 . . . . .294 D1
Watford Rd RM3 . . . . .314 F5
Watkin Mews EN3 . . . . .265 A2
Watkins Cl SS13 . . . . .321 D1
Watkins Way SS3 . . . . .349 F1
Watling La CM6 . . . . .69 F3
Watling St CM6 . . . . .70 F2
Watlington Rd
Harlow CM17 . . . . .200 D4
South Benfleet SS7 . . . . . . .344 B2
Watsham Pl CO7 . . . . .137 C2
Watson Ave E6 . . . . .352 A5
Watson Cl Grays RM20 . . . .377 A6
Southend-on-S SS3 . . . . . . .368 D7
Watson Gdns RM3 . . . . .314 E1
Watson's Cl CB10 . . . . .47 B4
Watsons Lodge ❶ RM10 . . .354 B6
Watts Cl CM6 . . . . .151 B4
Watts Cres RM19 . . . . .371 C2
Watts La CO4 . . . . .325 F1
Watts Rd CM23 . . . . .135 E2
Watts Yd CM23 . . . . .93 A2
Wat Tyler Ctry Pk*
SS16 .343 B2
Wat Tyler Wlk ❶ CO1 . . . .135 F7
Wavell Ave CO2 . . . . .135 C4
Wavell Cl CM1 . . . . .232 D8
Waveney Dr CM1 . . . . .232 C6
Waveney Rd
Felixstowe IP11 . . . . .381 C3
Ipswich IP1 . . . . .16 F4
Waverley Terr CB9 . . . . .9 A7
Waverley Bridge Ct CM9 237 B5
Waverley Cl E18 . . . . .310 C1
Waverley Cres
Romford RM3 . . . . .314 C3
Wickford SS11 . . . . .299 C3
Waverley Gdns
Barking IG11 . . . . .352 E3
Grays RM16 . . . . .373 A4
Redbridge IG6 . . . . .311 C1
Waverley Rd
Basildon SS15 . . . . .319 E1
Rainham RM13 . . . . .355 B2
South Benfleet SS7 . . . . . . .344 C6
Woodford E18 . . . . .310 C2
Wavertree Rd
South Benfleet SS7 . . . . . . .344 B4
Woodford E18 . . . . .310 A1
Waxwell Rd SS5 . . . . .301 E2
Wayback The CB10 . . . . .22 E2
Waycross Rd RM14 . . . . .337 E5
Wayfarer Gdns CM0 . . . . . .306 A5
Wayfaring Grn RM17 . . . . . .372 F1
Waylands Ct IG1 . . . . .352 D8
Waylett Basildon SS15 . . . . .341 A8
Southend-on-S SS9 . . . . . . .346 B6
Wayletts Dr CM23 . . . . .146 C2
Waymans RM15 . . . . .371 D7
Wayre St CM17 . . . . .200 C4
Wayre The CM17 . . . . .200 C4
Wayside CM3 . . . . .256 E8
Wayside Ave RM12 . . . . .336 D2
Wayside CM8 . . . . .52 D8
Wayside Commercial Est
IG11 . . . . .353 A3
Wayside Gdns RM9 . . . . . . .354 A6
Wayside Mews IG2 . . . . .333 A6
Waytemore Castle*
CM23 . . . . .146 C7
Waytemore Rd CM23 . . . . . .145 E6
Weald Bridge Rd CM16 . . .225 E2
Weald Cl CM14 . . . . .316 A7
Weald Ctry Pk* CM14 . . . .293 E2
Weald Ctry Pk Visitor Ctr*
CM14 . . . . .293 D1
Wealden Ho CM15 . . . . .114 A8
Weald Hall La CM16 . . . . . .246 E6
Weald Hall Lane Ind Est
CM16 . . . . .246 C6
Weald Park Way CM14 . .315 F7
Weald Pl CM14 . . . . .316 C8
Weald Rd
South Weald CM14 . . . . . . .293 C1
South Weald CM14 . . . . . . .293 F1
Weald The SS3 . . . . .363 E4
Weald Way RM7 . . . . .335 B8
Weale Rd E4 . . . . .309 D7
Wear Dr CM1 . . . . .232 D6
Weare Gifford SS3 . . . . .368 C8
Weathervane Cotts CM7 . .72 B1
Weaver Dr CO10 . . . . .2 B8
Weaverdale SS3 . . . . .349 B6
Weaverhead Cl CM6 . . . . . . .70 A3
Weaverhead La CM6 . . . . . . .70 A3
Weavers SS16 . . . . .343 A4
Weavers Cl
❻ Billericay CM11 . . . . .297 B2
Braintree CM7 . . . . .127 F3
Colchester CO3 . . . . .134 F5
Weavers Ct Halstead CO9 . .76 E1
❻ Sudbury CO10 . . . . .33 E7
Weavers Dr CO10 . . . . .2 B8
Weaversfield CM6 . . . . .150 A2
Weavers Gn CO6 . . . . .107 D6
Weavers Ho IG11 . . . . .332 A5
Weavers La CO10 . . . . .33 E7
Weavers Row CO9 . . . . .76 F1
Weaver St CM23 . . . . .145 C4
Weavers Terr ❻ CO10 . . . . .33 E7
Webb Cl CM2 . . . . .233 A2
Webber Ho ❻ IG11 . . . . . . .352 B5
Webb St ❸ RM10 . . . . .335 A1

Webbscroft Rd RM10 . . . . . .354 B8
Webb St IP2 . . . . .17 C3
Webley Ct EN3 . . . . .265 A2
Webster Cl
Hornchurch RM12 . . . . .336 D1
Sible Hedingham CO9 . . . . . .75 D8
Waltham Abbey EN9 . . . . . .246 A6
Webster Ct SS6 . . . . .323 D2
Webster Pl CM4 . . . . .275 E2
Webster Rd SS17 . . . . .360 E2
Websters Way SS6 . . . . .323 D2
Weddell Rd CB9 . . . . .9 C6
Wedderburn Rd IG11 . . . . . .352 E4
Wedds Way SS3 . . . . .350 B4
Wedgewood Cl CM16 . . . . .246 A1
Wedgewood Ct SS4 . . . . . . .325 D6
Wedgewood Dr
Colchester CO4 . . . . .109 E2
Harlow CM17 . . . . .224 E7
Wedgwood Way SS4 . . . . . .325 C6
Wedhey CM19 . . . . .223 C8
Wedlake CI RM11 . . . . .336 E3
Wedmore Ave SS5 . . . . .311 A2
Wednesbury Gdns RM3 . .314 F3
Wednesbury Grn RM3 . . . .314 F3
Wednesbury Rd RM3 . . . . .314 F3
Wedow Rd CM6 . . . . .70 A3
Welshwood Park Rd
CO4 . . . . .110 F2
Welton Way SS4 . . . . .326 A1
Wembley Ave CM3 . . . . .283 A8
Wendene SS16 . . . . .342 F4
Wenden Rd CB11 . . . . .43 B7
Wendon Cl SS4 . . . . .325 C4
Wendover Cl SS17 . . . . .360 D1
Wendover Gdns CM13 . . . .317 B7
Wendover Way RM12 . . . . .355 C7
Wendy Cl IP9 . . . . .63 F7
Wenham Dr SS0 . . . . .347 D2
Wenham Gdns CM13 . . . . .295 C3
Wenham La CO7 . . . . .59 D6
Wenham Rd IP6 . . . . .35 C7
Wenlock Rd CO10 . . . . .167 F6
Wenlocks La CM4 . . . . .272 E6
Wennington Rd RM13 . . . . .370 C7
Wensley Ave IG8 . . . . .310 A3
Wensley Ct RM5 . . . . .313 A5
Wensleydale Ave IG5 . . . . .310 E1
Wensley Rd SS7 . . . . .345 B5
Wentford Ct CB9 . . . . .8 C8
Wents Cl CO7 . . . . .139 E8
Wentworth CM3 . . . . .211 B4
Wentworth Cres CM7 . . . . .127 E6
Wentworth Ct ❺ E4 . . . . . .309 D5
Wentworth Dr
Bishop's Stortford CM23 . . .145 D6
Ipswich IP8 . . . . .16 F3
Wentworth Ho ❶ IG8 . . . . .311 A3
Wentworth Mdws CM7 . . .127 E6
Wentworth Pl RM16 . . . . . .373 D2
Wentworth Prim Sch
CM9 . . . . .236 F1
Wentworth Rd SS2 . . . . . . .348 B3
Clacton-on-S CO15 . . . . .195 E4
Colchester CO3 . . . . .135 E6
Ilford IG1 . . . . .333 B3
Ipswich IP4 . . . . .17 F5
Wanstead E11 . . . . .332 A6
Wentworth Terr ❺ CB9 . . . .8 E7
Wernerth Hall Rd
Ilford IG5 . . . . .333 A8
Redbridge IG5 . . . . .333 A8
Wesel Ave IP11 . . . . .381 B3
Wesley Ave CM14 . . . . .136 C8
Wesley Ct SS1 . . . . .347 B8
Wesley End Rd CO9 . . . . . . .28 D4
Wesley Gdns CM12 . . . . . . .296 F5
Wesley Rd SS1 . . . . .367 B7
Wesley Way IP1 . . . . .16 B8
Wessem Rd SS8 . . . . .364 B5
Wessex Cl IG3 . . . . .333 E5
Wessley Cl CM0 . . . . .263 E4
West Acre Ct CO3 . . . . .135 B7
Westall Rd IG10 . . . . .289 C6
West Area IP1 . . . . .16 F6
West Ave Althorne CM3 . . .282 F2
Basildon SS16 . . . . .340 E4
Chelmsford CM1 . . . . .231 F5
Clacton-on-S CO15 . . . . .195 F2
Hullbridge SS5 . . . . .301 D2
Mayland CM3 . . . . .260 E1
West Bank IG11 . . . . .352 B4
West Bank Ferry Terminal
IP2 . . . . .17 C2
West Beech Ave SS11 . . . . .322 A3
West Beech Cl SS11 . . . . . . .321 E7
West Beech Mews SS12 . . .321 D7
West Belvedere CM3 . . . . . .256 F5
Westborough Prim Sch
SS0 . . . . .347 E2
Westborough Rd SS0 . . . . .347 D2
Westbourne Cl
Hadleigh SS7 . . . . .345 D5
Hockley SS5 . . . . .325 A7
Westbourne Ct
❶ Haverhill CB9 . . . . .9 D8
Southend-on-S SS9 . . . . . . .347 B2
Westbourne Gdns CM12 . .297 B5
Westbourne Gr
Chelmsford CM2 . . . . .255 D8
Southend-on-S SS0 . . . . . . .347 B3
Westbourne Rd IP1 . . . . .16 F8
West Bowers Rd CM9 . . . . .257 C5
Westbury SS7 . . . . .324 D5
Westbury CI SS6 . . . . .133 D5
Westbury Ct
❶ Barking IG11 . . . . .352 A5
❶ Buckhurst Hill IG9 . . . . . .310 C8
Westbury Dr CM14 . . . . .316 B6
Westbury La CO15 . . . . .186 D6
Westbury Lo IG9 . . . . .310 C8
Stock CM4 . . . . .275 E1
Westbury Rd
Barking IG11 . . . . .352 A5
Brentwood CM14 . . . . .316 B6
Buckhurst Hill IG9 . . . . .310 C8
Clacton-on-S CO15 . . . . .188 C3
Ilford IG1 . . . . .333 A5
Ipswich IP4 . . . . .18 B8
Redbridge IG1 . . . . .332 F2

Wells Ct Chelmsford CM1 . .232 D5
Great Dunmow CM6 . . . . . .123 C1
❶ Romford RM1 . . . . .335 E5
Wellsfield SS6 . . . . .323 E4
Wells Gdns
❼ Basildon SS14 . . . . .342 F8
Dagenham RM13 . . . . .354 F6
Rainham RM13 . . . . .354 F6
Redbridge IG1 . . . . .332 E4
Wells Hall Com Prim Sch
CO10 . . . . .34 B4
Wells Hall Rd CO10 . . . . .34 C4
Wells Ho ❶ IG11 . . . . .353 C5
Well Side CO6 . . . . .132 E3
Wells Mead CB11 . . . . .67 D4
Wells Park Sch IG8 . . . . . . .311 F6
Wells Rd CO1 . . . . .136 B8
Well's St CM1 . . . . .232 A3
Well St CO7 . . . . .192 E7
Wellstead Gdns SS0 . . . . . .347 B3
Wellstead Rd E6 . . . . .352 A3
Wellstye Gn SS14 . . . . .342 E8
Well Terr CM9 . . . . .237 B5
Wellum Cl ❶ IP9 . . . . .62 D6
Wellwood Rd IG3 . . . . .334 A4

Westbury Rd continued
Mundon CM9 . . . . .259 E1
West Cl Hoddesdon EN11 . .221 C4
Rainham RM13 . . . . .355 B1
Westcliff Ave SS0 . . . . .366 E7
Westcliff Ct CO15 . . . . .195 E1
Westcliff Dr SS9 . . . . .346 D1
Westcliff Gdns SS8 . . . . . . .364 E2
Westcliff High Sch (Boys)
SS0 . . . . .347 A3
Westcliff High Sch (Girls)
SS0 . . . . .347 A3
Westcliff Par SS0 . . . . .366 E7
Westcliff Park Dr SS0 . . . . .347 A3
Westcliff Sta SS0 . . . . .366 D8
West Cloister CM1 . . . . .297 B2
Westcott Cl CO10 . . . . .195 D6
West Cres SS8 . . . . .363 F4
West Crescent Rd ❶
DA12 . . . . .379 C1
Westcroft CM1 . . . . .297 B1
Westcroft Ct EN10 . . . . .221 A4
West Ct CM21 . . . . .172 E3
West Dene Dr RM3 . . . . .314 D5
West Dock Rd CO2 . . . . .90 E5
West Dr CM7 . . . . .73 C3
West End La CO12 . . . . .91 B1
West End Rd Ipswich IP1 . .17 A5
Tiptree CO5 . . . . .186 A3
Westerdale CM1 . . . . .232 D7
Westerfield Ct IP4 . . . . .17 D7
Westerfield Rd IP4 . . . . .17 D8
Westergreen Meadow
CM7 . . . . .127 E1
Westerings
❸ Basildon CM13 . . . . .256 F2
Purleigh CM3 . . . . .258 D1
Westerings Prim Sch The
CM13 . . . . .324 E4
Westerings The
Great Baddow CM2 . . . . . . .254 F5
Hockley SS5 . . . . .324 E5
Westerings Way CM3 . . . . .364 D3
Westerings The CM7 . .155 E6
Western Approaches
SS2 . . . . .347 A7
Western Ave
Brentwood CM14 . . . . .294 C1
Dagenham RM10 . . . . .354 D6
Epping CM16 . . . . .267 F7
Romford RM2 . . . . .314 C1
Western Cl
Rushmere St A IP4 . . . . .18 F4
Silver End CM8 . . . . .156 E3
Western Cross Cl CO4 . . . .377 C1
Western Ct ❷ RM1 . . . . . . .335 E6
Western La CO10 . . . . .34 E3
Western Mews CM7 . . . . . .297 A2
Western Prom
Point Clear CO16 . . . . .192 D5
Point Clear B CO16 . . . . . . .192 E4
Western Rd
Billericay CM12 . . . . .297 A2
Brentwood CM14 . . . . .316 C8
Brightlingsea CO7 . . . . .192 E6
Burnham-on-C CM0 . . . . . .306 C4
Hadleigh SS7 . . . . .345 A6
Sawbridgeworth CM21 . . . .172 C3
Southend-on-S, Cambridge Town
SS3 . . . . .368 D6
South Ockendon RM15 . . . .357 B2
Stansted Mountfitchet
CM24 . . . . .119 E6
West Ridge CM10 . . . . .319 A8
Westridge Rd CO15 . . . . . . .196 A6
Westrop Ct CO10 . . . . .15 C5
Westrow Dr IG3 . . . . .333 F1
Westrow Gdns IG3 . . . . .333 F1
Westside Bsns Ctr CM19 . .222 F7
Westside Ctr CO3 . . . . .134 A5
West Sq Harlow CM20 . . . .199 C1
Maldon CM9 . . . . .236 F3
St Osyth CO16 . . . . .187 B5
Colchester CO2 . . . . .135 C6
Erith DA8 . . . . .369 E1
Gravesend DA11 . . . . .379 B1
Grays RM17 . . . . .378 A8
Harwich CO12 . . . . .91 D6
Rochford SS4 . . . . .325 E2
Rowhedge CO5 . . . . .164 F8
Southend-on-S,Chalkwell
SS9 . . . . .365 E8
Southend-on-S SS1 . . . . . . .367 B6
Tollesbury CM9 . . . . .216 C1
Wivenhoe CO7 . . . . .164 B8
West Station Ind Est
CM9 . . . . .258 E8
West Station Rd CM9 . . . . .236 E4
West Stockwell St CO1 . . .135 F7
West Thorpe SS16 . . . . .342 A3
West Thurrock Prim Sch
RM20 . . . . .377 A8
West Thurrock Way
Grays RM20 . . . . .377 C8
Purfleet RM20 . . . . .371 F2
West View Ilford RM6 . . . . .334 C6
Loughton IG10 . . . . .288 D3
Takeley CM22 . . . . .148 C8
West View Cl
Colchester CO4 . . . . .110 B3
Romford RM6 . . . . .334 C6
Westview Dr IG8 . . . . .310 D1
West View Rd SS6 . . . . .323 B1
West Ward Ho SS1 . . . . .366 F7

Westlake Ave SS13 . . . . .343 E6
Westlake Cres CO7 . . . . . . .137 A2
Westland Ave RM11 . . . . . . .336 E3
Westlands Com Prim Sch
CM1 . . . . .231 E2
Westland View RM16 . . . . .373 A5
West Lawn
Galleywood CM2 . . . . .254 C2
Ipswich IP4 . . . . .18 C8
Westleigh Ave SS9 . . . . .346 D1
Westleigh Ct
Southend-on-S SS9 . . . . . . .346 D1
❶ Wanstead E11 . . . . .332 A6
West Leigh Jun & Inf Schs
SS9 . . . . .346 D2
Westleton Way IP11 . . . . . . .381 B5
West Ley CM0 . . . . .306 C5
Westley La CB10 . . . . .22 D5
Westley Rd SS16 . . . . .341 C2
West Lodge RM17 . . . . .373 B2
West Lodge Rd CO3 . . . . . .135 D6
Westlyn Cl CM13 . . . . .355 C1
West Malling Way SS12 . .321 C7
Westmana Rd SS8 . . . . .364 E3
Westmarch CM1 . . . . .301 C6
West Mayne SS15 . . . . .340 E6
Westmayne Ind Pk SS15 . .340 D5
Westmede Basildon SS14 . .321 C1
Chigwell IG7 . . . . .311 C4
West Mill DA11 . . . . .378 F1
West Mill Gn IP9 . . . . .60 E6
Westminster Ct IP4 . . . . . . .18 B5
Westminster Ct
Clacton-on-S CO15 . . . . .196 B3
Colchester CO2 . . . . .136 C4
❶ Wanstead E11 . . . . .332 B5
Westminster Dr
Hockley SS5 . . . . .324 D6
Southend-on-S SS0 . . . . . . .347 B2
Westminster Gdns
Barking IG11 . . . . .352 E3
Braintree CM7 . . . . .128 B4
Chingford E4 . . . . .287 E1
Redbridge IG6 . . . . .311 D1
Westminster Mans SS0 .347 B2
Westmoreland Ave
RM11 . . . . .336 C6
Westmorland Cl
New Mistley CO11 . . . . .87 B3
Wanstead E12 . . . . .332 D2
Weston Ave RM20 . . . . .371 F1
Weston Cl CM13 . . . . .295 C2
Weston Gn RM9 . . . . .353 F8
Weston Rd
Colchester CO2 . . . . .136 B4
Dagenham RM9 . . . . .353 E8
Southend-on-S SS1 . . . . . . .367 A7
West Park Ave CM12 . . . . . .297 A3
West Park Cres CM12 . . . . .297 A2
West Park Dr RM6 . . . . .334 E6
West Park Hill CM14 . . . . . .316 A7
West Park Rd SS0 . . . . .347 A3
West Point Pl SS8 . . . . .363 C3
West Quay CO7 . . . . .164 B7
Westray Wlk SS12 . . . . .322 A5
West Rd
Bishop's Stortford CM23 . . .145 E6
Chingford E4 . . . . .288 D8
Dagenham RM6 . . . . .334 E5
Halstead CO9 . . . . .76 E1
Ipswich IP3 . . . . .38 E8
Romford RM3 . . . . .335 D4
Saffron Walden CB11 . . . . . .43 D8
Sawbridgeworth CM21 . . . .172 C3
Southend-on-S SS2 . . . . . . .368 B2

Westward Rd E4 . . . . .309 A5
Westwater SS7 . . . . .344 B4
Westway Chelmsford CM1 253 E8
Colchester CO1, CO3 . . . . . .135 A4
South Woodham Ferrers
CM3 . . . . .301 C7
West Way CM14 . . . . .316 A7
West Wlk CM20 . . . . .223 C8
Westwood Ave
Brentwood CM14 . . . . .316 A6
Ipswich IP1 . . . . .17 A8
West Wood Cl SS7 . . . . .345 C4
Westwood Ct IP1 . . . . .17 A7
Westwood Dr CO5 . . . . .218 E6
Westwood Gdns SS7 . . . . . .345 D5
West Wood Hill CO4 . . . . . .109 B3
Westwood Lodge SS7 . . . . .345 C5
Westwood Prim Sch
SS7 . . . . .345 D4
Westwood Rd
Canvey Island SS8 . . . . .364 B3
Ilford IG3 . . . . .334 A4
West Yd CO9 . . . . .103 E8
Wetherfield CM24 . . . . .119 D7
Wetherfield SS16 . . . . .341 F5
Wetherly Cl CM17 . . . . .200 F4
Wethersfield CE Prim Sch
CM7 . . . . .73 C3
Wethersfield Cl SS6 . . . . . . .323 A3
Wethersfield Rd
Blackheath CO2 . . . . .163 A8
Shalford CM7 . . . . .100 C8
Sible Hedingham CO9 . . . . . .51 C1
Wethersfield Way SS11 .322 B5
Wet La CO4 . . . . .82 E5
Wetzlar Ct CO2 . . . . .136 B4
Weybourne CS32 . . . . .348 B3
Weybourne Gdns SS3 . . . . .348 B3
Weybridge Wlk SS3 . . . . . . .349 C1
Weydale SS17 . . . . .361 B5
Weyland Rd RM8 . . . . .334 F1
Weymarks SS15 . . . . .341 D7
Weymouth Ct CO15 . . . . . . .220 J8
Weymouth Rd
Chelmsford CM1 . . . . .232 E6
Ipswich IP4 . . . . .17 F6
Whalebone Ave RM6 . . . . . .334 F5
Whalebone Ave RM6 . . . . . .334 F5
Whalebone Cnr CO4 . . . . . . .83 F7
Whalebone Gr RM6 . . . . . . .334 F5
Whalebone La N RM6 . . . . .334 E8
Whalebone La S RM6,
RM8 . . . . .334 E5
Whaley Rd CO4 . . . . .136 C7
Wharfe Cl CM8 . . . . .183 E2
Wharf La CO8 . . . . .79 F8
Wharf Pl CM23 . . . . .146 A6
Wharf Rd
❶ Bishop's Stortford CM23 145 F6
Brentwood CM14 . . . . .316 C7
Chelmsford CM2 . . . . .232 C2
Fobbing SS17 . . . . .361 D4
Gravesend DA12 . . . . .379 C1
Grays RM17 . . . . .377 F8
Heybridge Basin CM9 . . . . .237 F4
Hoddesdon EN10 . . . . .243 A7
Stanford-le-H SS17 . . . . .375 E7
Wharf Rd S RM17 . . . . .377 F8
Wharfside Cl DA8 . . . . .369 F1
Wharley Hook CM18 . . . . . .224 A5
Wharncliffe DA9 . . . . .377 B1
Wharton Dr CM1 . . . . .233 A7
Wheat Croft CM23 . . . . .145 E4
Wheatear Pl CM11 . . . . .297 C1
Wheatfield Ind Est CM8 . . .134 D5
Wheatfields
❸ Brentwood CM14 . . . . . . .316 C6
Harlow CM17 . . . . .200 D6
Rochford SS4 . . . . .326 D4
Wheatfield Way
Basildon SS14 . . . . .341 A4
Chelmsford CM1 . . . . .203 F3
Wheatlands Ardleigh CO7 111 C7
Elmstead CO7 . . . . .137 F6
Wheatley Ave CM7 . . . . .128 C3
Wheatley Dr
Greenhithe DA9 . . . . .377 A2
Hornchurch RM11 . . . . .336 D6
Rochford SS4 . . . . .325 D4
Wheatley Mans ❶ IG11 . .353 A5
Wheatley Rd SS17 . . . . .361 B5
Wheaton Rd CM8 . . . . .184 B2
Wheatsheaf La CO11 . . . . . . .88 D3
Wheatsheaf La CO11 . . . . . . .88 D3
Wheatsheaf Rd RM1 . . . . . .335 F5
Wheatstone Rd RM8 . . . . . .349 D1
Wheeler Cl
Colchester CO4 . . . . .136 E6
Woodford IG8 . . . . .310 F6
Wheeler's La
Clacton-on-S CO16 . . . . .203 A7
St Osyth CO16 . . . . .186 D6
Wheelers Cross ❶ IG11 . .352 D3
Wheeler's Hill CM3 . . . . . . .208 D6
Wheelers La
Fobbing SS17 . . . . .361 D5
Pilgrims Hatch CM14 . . . . . .293 B6
Wheelwrights CM23 . . . . . .145 C4
Wheelwrights The
Southend-on-S SS2 . . . . . . .348 A5
Wheelwright Ct CO7 . . . . .81 A8
Wherneside Ave SS8 . . . . . .364 C5
Wherry La ❶ IP4 . . . . .17 D5
Wherry Quay IP7 . . . . .17 C5
Whinchat Cl IP2 . . . . .16 D3